FROM IRENAEUS TO GROTIUS

A Sourcebook in Christian Political Thought

FROM IRENAEUS TO GROTIUS

A Sourcebook in Christian Political Thought
100–1625

Edited by

Oliver O'Donovan *and* Joan Lockwood O'Donovan

WILLIAM B. EERDMANS PUBLISHING COMPANY
GRAND RAPIDS, MICHIGAN / CAMBRIDGE, U.K.

© 1999 Wm. B. Eerdmans Publishing Co.
255 Jefferson Ave. S.E., Grand Rapids, Michigan 49503 /
P.O. Box 163, Cambridge CB3 9PU U.K.

Printed in the United States of America

05 04 03 02 01 00   7 6 5 4 3 2

ISBN 0-8028-3876-6 (cloth)
ISBN 0-8028-4209-7 (pbk.)

Contents

Acknowledgments   ix

Copyright Acknowledgments   x

Abbreviations   xii

General Introduction   xv

PART 1

The Patristic Age

Introduction   1

An Apologetic Miscellany   8

Irenaeus of Lyons   15

Tertullian   23

Clement of Alexandria   30

Origen   39

Lactantius   46

Eusebius of Caesarea   56

Ambrose of Milan   66

John Chrysostom   89

Augustine   104

Paulus Orosius   164

CONTENTS

PART 2

Late Antiquity and Romano-Germanic Christian Kingship

Introduction   169

Gelasius I   177

Agapetos   180

Justinian   189

Gregory I   195

Isidore of Seville   204

John of Damascus   212

Jonas of Orléans   216

Sedulius Scottus   221

The Donation of Constantine   228

PART 3

The Struggle over Empire and the Integration of Aristotle

Introduction   231

Gregory VII   240

Norman Anonymous   250

Honorius Augustodunensis   260

Bernard of Clairvaux   268

John of Salisbury   277

Rufinus the Canonist   297

Nikephoros Blemmydes   306

Bonaventure   309

Thomas Aquinas   320

Giles of Rome   362

James of Viterbo   379

Contents

PART 4

Political Community, Spiritual Church, Individual Right, and *Dominium*

Introduction	389
John of Paris	397
Dante Alighieri	413
Marsilius of Padua	423
William of Ockham	453
Nicolas Cabasilas	476
John Wyclif	482
Antonios IV	514
Jean Gerson	517
John Fortescue	530
Nicholas of Kues	541

PART 5

Renaissance, Reformation, and Radicalism: Scholastic Revival and the Consolidation of Legal Theory

Introduction	549
Thomas More	558
Desiderius Erasmus	570
Martin Luther	581
Francisco de Vitoria	609
The Schleitheim Articles	631
Hans Hergot	638
Stephen Gardiner	647
Philipp Melanchthon	650
John Calvin	662
John Knox	685
John Ponet	695
Thomas Cartwright	702

CONTENTS

Vindiciae, contra Tyrannos 711

Francisco Suárez 723

Richard Hooker 743

Johannes Althusius 757

William Perkins 771

The Convocation Book 778

Hugo Grotius 787

Subject Index 821

Scripture Index 831

Acknowledgments

On the part of the editors, production of this sourcebook has been a long and arduous road, on which we have suffered setbacks, encountered obstacles, and occasionally been forced into diversions. Only once, however, did our work grind to a halt, in the face of mounting expenses that we could not ourselves afford to carry. We are greatly indebted to Fieldstead and Company for delivering us from this impasse by undertaking to fund our project. Through their generosity in meeting all our financial needs, we were able to push on to a happy conclusion of our labours. We are also grateful to Emory University, Law and Religion Program, for associating itself with our sourcebook by appointing Joan Lockwood O'Donovan as Fellow in Law and Religion for the academic year 1996 and taking over the administration of its funding. Principal thanks for this association must go to the enthusiastic support and administrative skill of the program's director, John Witte, Jr. Closer to home, we owe thanks to Garry Williams for his brilliant technical assistance on many fronts, Raphaela Schmid for her expertise in formatting our legal references, Carole Ligat for many hours of efficient typing, and our elder son, Matthew, for keeping our work afloat by almost daily trouble-shooting in the computer department. Among our scholarly friends, colleagues, and acquaintances who have provided valuable advice and direction, we should mention with appreciation Paul Marshall, John Kilcullen, Jean-Marie Salamito, Henry Mayr-Harting, Diarmaid McCulloch, Gillian Evans, James Reimer, and Bishop Kallistos Ware. We are also, as always, indebted to the Christ Church library for graciously furnishing early editions of books. And finally, we are indebted to those public-spirited publishers who allowed us to reproduce copyrighted material at little or no cost, and to all the translators and editors who promptly and supportively responded to our requests to use their work, as well as to those who prepared new translations for the sourcebook.

Copyright Acknowledgments

We gratefully acknowledge the kind permission of the following publishers to reprint material from the works listed:

Augsburg Fortress, Minneapolis: *Luther's Works*, vol. 45, ed. Walther I. Brandt, © Muhlenberg Press, 1962

Blackwell Publishers, Oxford: *Aquinas: Selected Political Writings*, ed. A. P. D'Entrèves, tr. J. G. Dawson, © Basil Blackwell & Mott, 1959

The Boydell Press, Woodbridge, Suffolk: *Giles of Rome: On Ecclesiastical Power*, tr. with introduction by R. W. Dyson, © 1986

Burns & Oates, Tunbridge Wells: *Church and State Through the Centuries*, ed. and tr. S. Z. Ehler and J. B. Morrall, © 1954

Cambridge University Press:

John of Salisbury, *Policraticus*, ed. and tr. Cary J. Nederman, © 1990

Nicolas of Cusa, *The Catholic Concordance*, ed. and tr. Paul E. Sigmund, © 1991

Origen, *Contra Celsum*, tr. Henry Chadwick, © 1953

Thomas Aquinas, *Summa Theologiae*: vol. 28, ed. and tr. Thomas Gilby, © Blackfriars, 1966; vol. 29, ed. and tr. David Bourke and Arthur Littledale, © Blackfriars, 1969; vol. 37, ed. and tr. Thomas Gilby, 1975; vol. 38, ed. and tr. Marcus Lefébure, © Blackfriars, 1975

William of Ockham, *A Short Discourse on Tyrannical Government*, ed. Arthur Stephen McGrade and tr. John Kilcullen, © 1992

William of Ockham, *A Letter to the Friars Minor and Other Writings*, ed. Arthur Stephen McGrade and John Kilcullen, tr. John Kilcullen, © 1995

Vitoria: Political Writings, ed. Anthony Pagden and tr. Jeremy Lawrance, © 1991

The Radical Reformation, ed. and tr. Michael G. Baylor, © 1991

Catholic University Press of America, Washington D.C.: *The Fathers of the Church: A New Translation*, vol. 20, © 1953

Centre for Medieval and Early Renaissance Studies, SUNY Binghamton: *Sedulius Scottus: On Christian Rulers and The Poems*, tr. with introduction by Ed-

Abbreviations

Books of the Bible:

Gen.	Genesis
Exod.	Exodus
Lev.	Leviticus
Num.	Numbers
Deut.	Deuteronomy
Josh.	Joshua
Judges	Judges
Ruth	Ruth
1 Sam.	1 Samuel
2 Sam.	2 Samuel
1 Kings	1 Kings
2 Kings	2 Kings
1 Chron.	1 Chronicles
2 Chron.	2 Chronicles
Neh.	Nehemiah
Job	Job
Ps.	Psalms (numbers are corrected to follow the Massoretic numbering throughout)
Prov.	Proverbs
Eccl.	Ecclesiastes (Qoheleth)
Song of Sol.	Song of Solomon
Isa.	Isaiah
Jer.	Jeremiah
Ezek.	Ezekiel
Dan.	Daniel
Hos.	Hosea
Mic.	Micah

Nahum	Nahum
Hab.	Habakkuk
Zeph.	Zephaniah
Zech.	Zechariah
Mal.	Malachi
Tob.	Tobit
1 Esdr.	1 Esdras
2 Esdr.	2 Esdras
Sir.	Ben Sirach (Ecclesiasticus)
Sap.	Wisdom (Sapientia)
1 Macc.	1 Maccabees
Matt.	Matthew
Mark	Mark
Luke	Luke
John	John
Acts	Acts of the Apostles
Rom.	Romans
1 Cor.	1 Corinthians
2 Cor.	2 Corinthians
Gal.	Galatians
Eph.	Ephesians
Phil.	Philippians
Col.	Colossians
1 Thess.	1 Thessalonians
2 Thess.	2 Thessalonians
1 Tim.	1 Timothy
2 Tim.	2 Timothy
Tit.	Titus
Heb.	Hebrews
James	James
1 Pet.	1 Peter
2 Pet.	2 Peter
1 John	1 John
Jude	Jude
Rev.	Revelation (Apocalypse)

The following abbreviations apply to civil and canon law references.

The principal source for civil law texts is: *Corpus Iuris Civilis,* ed. T. Mommsen, P. Krüger, R. Schöll (Berlin, 1954).

The principal source for canon law texts is: *Corpus Iuris Canonici,* ed. A. Friedberg (Leipzig 1879).

Canon law references are given according to the form recommended in James A. Brundage, *Medieval Canon Law* (London & New York: Longman, 1996), pp. 190-205.

Cod.	Justinian's *Codex* (in *Corpus iuris civilis*)
C.	*Causa* (in pt. 2 of Gratian's *Decretum*)
c.	*capitulum* (in Gratian's *Decretum*)
D.	*Distinctio* (in pts. 1 and 3 of Gratian's *Decretum*)
d.a.c.	*dictum ante capitulum* (in Gratian's *Decretum*)
d.p.c.	*dictum post capitulum* (in Gratian's *Decretum*)
Dig.	*Digest* (in *Corpus iuris civilis*)
Glos. ord.	*Glossa ordinaria*
Gratian	Gratian's *Decretum* (in *Corpus iuris canonici*)
Inst.	Justinian's *Institutes* (in *Corpus iuris civilis*)
Nov.	Justinian's *Novellae leges* (in *Corpus iuris civilis*)
pr.	*prooemium* (in Gratian's *Decretum*)
q.	*quaestio* (in Gratian's *Decretum*)
VI	*Liber sextus* (in *Corpus iuris canonici*)
X	*Liber extra* (Gregory IX's *Decretals* in *Corpus iuris canonici*)

Other common abbreviations:

NE	Aristotle, *Nicomachean Ethics*
PL	J. P. Migne, *Patrologia Latina,* Paris 1844-55
PG	J. P. Migne, *Patrologia Graeca,* Paris 1857-66.
ST	Thomas Aquinas, *Summa Theologiae*

General Introduction

The texts in this volume have been chosen to illustrate the use of Christian theological arguments in political discussion, throughout the period in which those arguments were commonplace. For a millennium and a half, from the patristic age to the early modern period, the themes of creation, fall, Christology, the church, and eschatology, and the appeal to a wide range of Old and New Testament texts, dominated the way political discussion was conducted. This collection is intended to provide access to those strands of theopolitical argument, through primary literature, for readers who are not specialists in the various historical periods, and so to illustrate how Christian beliefs fashioned Christian political ideals and practices.

In the course of doing so, it hopes to provide a reasonably comprehensive and coherent overview of the history of Christian political thought, illuminating the continuities and discontinuities, internal diversities and lines of influence, historical interactions and divergences, and the relation of the theopolitical tradition to changing historical settings. In addition, it makes available in English translation selections from some otherwise inaccessible texts. Some of the pieces included in this volume have never been translated into English before; others are to be found only in antique, inaccurate, or unreadable versions.

The collection is offered to any reader who can enjoy getting to know these texts and can make use of them in any way. But it has especially in mind two classes of reader for whom the interaction of theology and politics is a live issue today. These are, on the one hand, theologians who concern themselves with the bearing of Christian faith on political action, but whose reflections are nourished almost exclusively from twentieth-century, perhaps only late twentieth-century, sources. The revival of political theology in our generation is a phenomenon with many hopeful aspects as well as some ambiguities. But contemporary political theology, without renouncing its concern to *be* contemporary, can proceed with much greater confidence if it is acquainted with the originating tradition from which Western politics sprang.

The second class of reader comprises political and legal thinkers who, in approaching their own intellectual concerns as Christian believers, wish to know how they were handled in the era when Christian faith provided most of the threads from which political and legal categories were woven. Their curiosity is given point by the strong inclination which our generation has evinced to question the presuppositions of modern society, and to think through our present situation afresh with a more critical perspective on "modernity."

Interest in Christian political thought has been facilitated by recent developments in the study of the history of political ideas. Although the political meaning of the sixteenth-century Reformation has always commanded attention, recent explorations have filled out the picture, giving more weight to the Catholic contribution, especially that of the Salamanca school, and to the humanists and Anabaptists. By comparison, the study of political ideas in the patristic age is undeveloped, notwithstanding the attention traditionally paid to Augustine. But the major contribution of the last generation or so has been a strong concentration upon medieval political thought. Here an undertaking such as our own has to acknowledge a major debt, while at the same time asking and answering a few questions. Light has been shed in a thousand corners previously inaccessible to the nonspecialist and, indeed, to the specialist too. The importance of liturgy to the Carolingian age, for example, and of canon law to the high medieval period, has been brilliantly illuminated. Some of the results of this endeavor have flowed into the mainstream of political history, so that a few of the leading medieval texts have become generally available through inclusion in that valuable series of translations, the Cambridge Texts in the History of Political Thought.

Yet there has been a consistent underemphasis on the contribution of theological arguments to political thought. "Theology as an elevated branch of legal studies," as Ullmann summarized it, has as often as not been the outlook, not only of the medieval canonists, but of their twentieth-century historians, too. "Whig history," though ranging more widely than it once did, has not lost its homing instincts. One has only to mention the cardinal role of classic post-Chalcedonian christological categories in the Norman Anonymous or in James of Viterbo, the emphasis on the life of Christ in the Franciscans, the central place of divine grace in Wyclif, the doctrine of Providence in Gregory the Great, the conception of the Holy Spirit in Nicholas of Kues, to appreciate how the brilliant light has thrown deep pools of shadow, often in the very places where the medieval mind was most characteristically itself. The institutional achievements of the medieval *apparatchiks* hardly afford a sufficient purchase upon medieval convictions. If anyone is inclined to doubt this claim, let us recommend a systematic study of the use of Scripture in any one of the major political texts represented here — the authors and books to which the writer chiefly attends, the peculiarities of the hermeneutic, the interpretation of the major characters of Old and New Testament history, and so on. This exercise may invite some stimulating reflection on what was *not* to be learned from the wealth of secondary literature!

On such a ground we would justify our undertaking against predictable anxieties and scruples which some historians may bring to it. To move from the eastern Mediterranean in the early second century to northern Europe in the early seventeenth is to embrace a perilous amount of historical change and a dizzying variety of social settings, and one may wonder whether it portends an exercise in "history of ideas" of the most seriously deracinated kind. Well, the shape of the inquiry is governed by a question which is, in the end, a theological one: *Is there a tradition of Christian political thought?* That question is bound to engage, at least implicitly, anybody who wants to know not only the facts about the Christian ages of Europe, but about their meaning. To ask the question is not, of course, to be oblivious to the complexities involved in answering it. Indeed, those complexities come more to light the more seriously the question is pressed. It is only by pressing it back to the level of texts, indeed, that sweeping general theories of "Christendom," whether supportive or (more commonly) deprecating, can be engaged and refined. Nor is it to forget that the tradition, if such it was, was constantly mediated through shifting social settings and reflected out of very contrasting points of view. The meaning of "tradition" in its theological context is precisely that. It is not a series of opinions that are handed on unchanged from one generation to the next, but a framework of religious and moral conviction that is capable of defining differences of opinion among those who stand within it and of orienting people in different settings to quite different tasks within a recognizable continuity.

*   *   *

In determining the contents of the book, we have had a number of decisions to make, and offer the following brief account of them.

    1. We have tried to represent the Greek-speaking world of the eastern Mediterranean alongside the Latin-speaking world of western Europe up until the fall of Byzantium, but after the age of Justinian this aspect of the story assumes a secondary place. Several lines of explanation converge to explain this. In the first place, there is the simple matter of the weight of scholarship, on which a collection like this inevitably depends. Byzantine historians have not focused on questions of political theory with the intense concentration of Western medievalists. But this, in turn, reflects something about the two civilizations themselves. The long survival of the East–Roman Empire preserved certain basic theopolitical concepts which were little challenged and little developed. When it failed, it was succeeded by Islamic cultures which did not take up these concepts in the same terms. In the West, however, where the empire failed early, the successor kingdoms were Christian, and in their protracted struggle to establish new political and ecclesiastical institutions, they relied heavily on the theological legacy of the Christian empire. This, furthermore, produced an important intellectual difference in the way the two cultures discussed politics. Byzantium was less dependent upon its theological matrix, and its literary output attests a cleavage between subjects of a dogmatic and devotional cast and public ones, which were handled in a classically Hellenistic style with little theological content. The division between sacred and secular intellectual spheres (rather than as spheres of jurisdiction), a division we associate with early modernity in the West, is already advanced in Byzantium. For our present concerns, then, a good deal of Byzantine political writing has not much to contribute.

    2. Within the terms of our enterprise, we might have included some parts of the New Testament. But it seemed sensible to draw a line in principle between Scrip-

ture and tradition, as all our sources do. If anyone has dogmatic hesitations about that division, we can fall back on dull practicalities: Who would want it, since a Bible is so easily come by? More difficult was the exclusion of non-Christian texts which were constantly in the minds of our Christian writers: Plato and Aristotle, Cicero, Plutarch, and (the hardest decision) that very theological Jew, Philo of Alexandria. At the other end of our period, we decided to exclude Renaissance writers who had already, in essence, broken with the theological tradition, among whom, no doubt, Machiavelli springs first to mind. The sixteenth-century humanist impulse is represented here through Erasmus and More, for whom the interaction with theology was still of crucial importance, though the texts we have chosen display their very indirect way of glancing off theological questions. Our last Byzantine excerpt glances northeast to the young Orthodox church in Russia, and the question naturally posed itself whether a text from that source would enrich the survey of the sixteenth century. We were deflected partly by a sense of how difficult it would be to make a fragment from that context fit coherently. The same thought deterred us from including a piece from the Syriac-speaking Christianity of an earlier period.

3. It could well be argued that we should have drawn our collection to a close at a later date, since the mid- and late seventeenth century is full of political theorists who make theological appeals, not only the conservative ones like Bossuet and Filmer, but radicals, too. As recent reappraisals have done well to emphasize, Hobbes and Locke were both explicitly theological in their arguments, more so, indeed, than Milton. We had, of course, another of those dull practical reasons for this decision: *Leviathan* and the *Two Treatises of Civil Government* are almost as easy to come by as a Bible — and just as unappetizing when served up in excerpts. Grotius, by contrast, has the attraction of being a figure of major importance, largely unknown to the general run of political historians, and allows us to take our leave without overstaying our welcome. Yet we are inclined to think that the choice of 1625 also has an intellectual fitness. There are, to be sure, no absolute caesuras in history, but there are bends in the road, some of which have the effect of occluding the traveler's view quite quickly. What makes the mid-seventeenth-century bend so fascinating is not that there were no continuities, for there were legion; but that those who came after it so quickly managed to be oblivious of them, and to conduct themselves as those who have just discovered a new continent. In this decisive moment of amnesia, theology — or the rejection of it — played a central part.

4. There are major and minor figures. Without the former, a collection would be of no importance; without the latter, of no interest. Some figures impose themselves, however well known and available their writings. Augustine, Thomas, Luther, and Calvin are examples. These we have tried to present in ways which highlight their relation to the wider development. Others, including one or two whom we regard as very major figures, are comparatively unknown. We take some satisfaction in presenting for the first time in English some passages from Wyclif's remarkable political theology, the *Summa de Dominio,* and hope that it may not be long before this initiative is overtaken. Our view of Grotius, too, may attract the interest of those who have known him hitherto only by five misleading Latin words. There have, of course, been difficult decisions, and we do not expect them all to command agree-

ment. Some figures of great historical influence, such as Hincmar of Rheims among the Carolingians, are less interesting as writers than lesser names. Texts, similarly, which have a purely historical interest, and were written without the intention of communicating a theopolitical argument, we have excluded. On this account the early martyrologies were denied a showing. We will not bore our readers by mentioning everything and everybody we might possibly have included, but will count upon their courtesy in accepting that each unpardonable omission was made only after anxious thought.

5. The material displays a considerable variety not only of viewpoint and situation but of style and genre. A letter, a sermon, a polemical tract, a philosophical treatise, an encyclopedia entry, a commentary on a law-text or on a passage of the Bible: all need to be read in different ways. The variety is such as to make a strict uniformity of presentation unattainable and undesirable, but we have attempted in each case to give the reader something more than a statement of some key idea. We have hoped to give a flavor at least of what each text is like to read. If history is, as Samuel Johnson said, "inexcusable lies, and consecrated lies," we may add, to complete the triad: "and quotations." It is one thing to produce isolated tags to illustrate a thesis, quite another to evaluate the purport of an argument within its literary context. Political theology is not a matter of postures and positions, but of trains of thought which need to be followed. This collection is meant to bring the reader to that point of sympathetic engagement which can conceive where a thought has come from and where it is going to. Thereafter, it hardly needs saying, the editors hope that the reader will leave this collection behind, get a full text from a library, and make the author's better acquaintance.

For those who are interested, we may mention that the bulk of the work on the selection and introduction of medieval and Reformation texts was undertaken by Joan Lockwood O'Donovan, the selection and introduction of patristic texts by Oliver O'Donovan, who also undertook the translations attributed to the editors. But every word has been approved, and a surprising number of them discussed at length, by both editors together, who therefore assume full joint responsibility.

General Reading: The six-volume work of the Carlyle brothers (R. W. and A. J.), *A History of Medieval Political Theory in the West* (Edinburgh: Blackwood, 1903-36), provided the foundation for a great deal of the scholarly advances of the twentieth century in the history of political thought. Though out of date on many points, their judgments are frequently as convincing, their use of texts as careful and responsible, as the best of their successors; and they pay much more attention to patristic contributions. In the subsequent generation the study of the medieval period is dominated by the name of Walter Ullmann, whose contribution is illustrated by *Principles of Government and Politics in the Middle Ages,* 4th ed. (London: Methuen, 1978); *The Growth of Papal Government in the Middle Ages,* 2nd ed. (London: Methuen, 1962); and *Law and Politics in the Middle Ages: An Introduction to the Sources of Medieval Political Ideas* (Cambridge: Cambridge University Press; Ithaca, N.Y.: Cornell University Press, 1975). An authoritative recent review of the whole period is to be found in the two volumes of *The Cambridge History of Political Thought,* ed. J. H. Burns (Cambridge: Cambridge University Press, 1988-91), which gives, however, very short weight to the patristic period. The Renaissance and Reformation period has been well served by Q. Skinner, *The Foundations of Modern Political Thought*, 2 vols. (Cambridge: Cambridge University Press, 1978). The patristic period still awaits a good comprehensive survey. Among partial steps toward this, the value of Charles Norris Cochrane, *Christianity and Classical Culture: A Study of Thought and Action from Augustus to Augustine* (Oxford: Clarendon Press, 1940), is not yet exhausted, and the last year has produced Lester L. Field, Jr., *Liberty, Dominion, and the Two Swords: The Origins of Western Political Theology (180-398)* (Notre Dame, Ind.: University of Notre Dame Press, 1998). But we still lack a treatment that does justice to both East and West over the whole period up to the collapse of the Western Empire and the reign of Justinian.

PART 1

THE PATRISTIC AGE

The age of the church fathers is the age in which the church grew to strength within the context of the politically united, but linguistically divided, Mediterranean culture of the Roman Empire. There is no self-evident termination of this period. Its thought world persisted centuries longer in the Greek-speaking East than in the Latin-speaking West of the Mediterranean. We have settled, conventionally, to mark the end of this period with the collapse of the Western empire. From the late fifth century on we confront the uneasy cohabitation of Germanic tribal kingdoms in Gaul, Spain, Italy, and North Africa with a mainly Greek-speaking empire based on Constantinople, and this situation sets the scene for the new "medieval" construction of church-state relationships.

The four-hundred-year period, which saw the church grow from its beginnings as an eschatological movement in Palestinian Judaism to a dominating position in European society, inevitably saw more change in the church's self-awareness than any other comparable period in its history. In attempting to introduce it as a whole, together with its political thought, we must begin by marking the great fault lines which divide it — though on close inspection they lose some of the appearance of finality and decisiveness that they present to the distant view.

The eye is struck first, inevitably, by a crucial chronological turning point, that of the Constantinian turn of the early fourth century, the moment at which, with dizzying suddenness, the church ceased to be the persecuted sect of the catacombs and became at first a favored, and then the established, religion of the empire. The significance of that moment continues to excite reflection and disagreement. We are familiar with talk about the church's "fall"; the word "Constantinianism" has gained new currency in recent years as a term of criticism in contemporary debates about the posture of Christian faith in society. Yet the full measure of what had occurred was not wholly apparent at the time to those who lived close to it, and the reaction of the church to its newly favored status was by no means univocal. In the selected readings below we can observe two sharply contrasted responses. Both were, to a large extent, dictated by the way in which their representatives read the history of the

1

church *before* the turn, and by their determination to be true to it. For Eusebius it had been an age of mission, in which the triumphantly expansive word of monotheistic truth had laid hold on the conscience of the world, to the point where the demons had had to yield their ground. The Constantinian moment had, as it were, always been the end the church had foreseen. To Ambrose, on the other hand, it had been an age of martyrdom, in which the purity of the gospel had thrown itself into conflict with the world, a conflict now to be continued by a firm and independent church leadership not afraid to call emperors to account. Both of these strands of thought were foundational for the social synthesis we have come to call "Christendom."

On one point, however, it is clear that continuity did not prevail in the church's thinking, and that was in its attitude to military service. Yet beyond saying that there was a change of mind, we have a complex situation to account for, which continues to excite a great deal of discussion, not because the facts as such are contested, but because they are difficult to interpret in a way that yields a coherent and consistent view. It is important enough to require a summary comment, though it surfaces only occasionally in the readings we have included, because the problem of relating life and thought is here at its most acute. A great deal of the important evidence about the early church's attitude comes from unsystematic, administrative sources, not from the *prises de position* of theologians and thinkers. Those sources are of various kinds. Apart from inscriptions which prove the presence of Christians in the army from the second century onward, there are baptismal regulations, determining the admissibility of candidates; narratives of martyrdom involving soldiers; conciliar decrees pronouncing on the ecclesiastical standing of soldiers in various situations. Each sings its own note; the different notes may form a harmony, but they are certainly not in unison.

We may sum up the situation briefly as follows:

a. Baptismal rules consistently treat the military as a problematic profession, along with many others (brothel keepers, schoolteachers because of the pagan literature, actors, gladiators, charioteers, etc.). The earliest extant example is in Hippolytus's *Apostolic Tradition,* of the early third century, which is followed by the large, late fourth-century collection of laws, the *Apostolic Constitutions.* Restrictions continue to appear in fourth- and fifth-century documents. Some make a distinction between lower and higher ranks, but all agree to refuse baptism to those who have senior responsibilities.

b. There were Christians serving in the army from the second century on, and a number of military martyrs are known. The narratives collected by Musorillo illustrate how hazardous life could be for a Christian soldier who was resolved not to act contrary to conviction; yet they also show that many sustained the difficulties for a considerable time. It is unlikely that they were all converted *after* entering upon military service, as Tertullian wished to believe. We have no way of telling how many were actually baptized, whether before or during their military service, nor whether they all drew the moral line in roughly the same place.

2

   c. The difficulty in military service was twofold: (1) the military oath, the offensiveness of which was not confined to its quasi-religious implications, symbolized in the offensive "chaplet" worn as ceremonial dress; (2) responsibility for bloodshed, which made the civil tasks of keeping the peace certainly as offensive, if not more so, than service in battle. Civil magistracy, therefore, was also problematic for the same reason. It is, however, rare to find Christians saying that judicial bloodshed is wrong *simpliciter,* as distinct from being wrong *for Christians.*

   d. The opinion of Christian teachers changed imperceptibly. There is no reason to think Tertullian idiosyncratic for the second and third centuries, Montanist though he was, except in the aggressiveness of his rhetoric. Fourth-century writers, however, found no moral difficulty with military service in war, unaware, apparently, of the gulf dividing their attitudes from earlier ones. ("Homicide in war is not reckoned by our fathers as homicide," Basil, *Ep.* 188.) This is in striking contrast to the conscientious anxiety which frequently surfaced in the fourth and fifth centuries about responsibility for capital punishment.

   e. This general unawareness of the change of attitude makes it unlikely that the modification of the church's stance was at all self-conscious. An act like that of the Council of Arles (314), discouraging Constantine's soldiers from leaving the service in peacetime, should be seen as an improvised response and an interesting measure of what some Christian opinion had come to expect by that point, but not as a decisive reversal of traditional judgments. Difficulties over the place of senior magistrates in the church continued to arise in the early Christian empire from their official duty to impose capital punishment and to take evidence under torture.

   f. The extensive practice of deferring baptism protected a situation in which the church could maintain contradictory attitudes. Here is the heart of the ambiguity, for the large numbers of unbaptized Christians in the church allowed rigorous principles of baptismal candidacy to be maintained alongside an increasing acceptance of military Christians, as of others who would not meet the baptismal criteria. In the fifth century, infant baptism became more generally insisted on; the more rigorous principles became transferred to clergy and religious. The legal exemption and exclusion of the priesthood from military service developed in the fourth century just when the presence of lay soldiers in the church was becoming unremarkable.

        *   *   *   *East/West*

But besides the chronological fault line presented by the conversion of the empire, we have to consider another, possibly more significant division. The Mediterranean world was divided into two major language groups, a Latin-speaking West and a Greek-speaking East. The empire itself, and with it Christendom, finally fell apart along this fault line. By the High Middle Ages it was accepted that the two were divided, among other things, by their doctrine of church and state: the dual-authority scheme of the West contrasting with the (hostilely named) "caesaropapist" monism

[margin note: East/West Divide]

of the East. Can we see anticipations of this in the first four hundred years? If we take Ambrose and Eusebius as typical of the two poles, it is extremely tempting to do so; and it has led some thinkers to speak of a "republican" tradition in the West as opposed to a "monarchist" tradition in the East, the one asserting the independent responsibility of church and individual, the other seeing earthly government as part of the divine economy. There is enough truth in this characterization for it to constitute a standing temptation.

Adding to the temptation, perhaps, is the sense that the bifurcation of political traditions continues to shape the sociopolitical experiences of Eastern and Western Europe. Is it an accident that sixth-century Byzantium speaks in accents reminiscent of the welfare state and socialism? (The comparison warns us, of course, against illegitimate conclusions: the fact that Eastern European Christians have in our century had larger expectations of the state's role has not meant that they have shrunk from courageous confrontations, while the fact that Western Christians have lauded individual responsibility has not proved them incapable of craven conformism.) Yet it would be wrong simply to let this fascinating parallel stand without pointing out the moments of potent influence which Byzantine models of society and government have had in the West: in Carolingian society, most notably, and again at the Reformation, while the Western Middle Ages were profoundly shaped by Justinian's East-Roman legacy of law. Whatever connections we presume to find between the ancient world and our own times, it is by no means the case that the two traditions have simply gone their own way without influencing each other.

It was certainly a significant factor that the two poles of the Mediterranean *entered* the Roman Empire with widely differing political experiences. Rome itself brought centuries of experience as a small aristocratic city-state, and naturally spoke of a political society as a *respublica*. The Greek-speaking world brought nearly as many centuries of experience of imperial rule, and naturally saw the Roman emperor (known at home as *princeps*, "first citizen," or *imperator*, "general") as the successor to Persian and Macedonian rulers whom they had called *basileis*, "kings." Intellectually, these two different experiences were mediated through different philosophical influences. The Greek-speaking intelligentsia, such as the delightful Plutarch, naturally framed political reflections within the terms left them by Plato's *Republic* and *Laws*, and reverted constantly to the ideal of the philosopher-king. The Latin-speaking world drew no less easily on Cicero's potent mixture of Stoic moral reflection and republican ideals, and thought in terms of a natural state of universality, equality, and freedom, in relation to which the goods of government could only be concessional and provisional. This contrast, repainted in biblical colors, can be seen in early Christian writers. Clement of Alexandria's Moses (like that of Philo before him) obviously accords with Plato's ideal, while Lactantius's original state is indistinguishably the Garden of Eden and the Golden Age.

But even to say this much, we must recognize that philosophical traditions attracted Christian thinkers precisely for their apparent capacity to express elements of the biblical tradition. The doctrine that political rule is not a gift of created nature but a providential preservation against evil does not depend on Stoicism alone; it is arguably implicit in the Yahwist history of Genesis itself, and may plausibly be found in the divorce pericope in St. Mark's and St. Matthew's Gospels. And there are many other elements in Jewish and Christian Scripture that are strongly in play: the narrative of Jesus' trial, for example, and especially the confrontation with Pontius Pilate in St. John's Gospel; the pericope about taxation in St. Mark and St. Matthew; St. Paul's careful statement of the service rendered by the "authorities" in the age of the church; and so on. If we want to characterize the difference of emphasis between Greek and Latin traditions in the early church, perhaps the best way is to point to the greater use made by the Greek Fathers of the Old Testament ideal of law. *Nomos,* "law," and *logos,* "word" or "reason," belonged together in a pattern of mutual association so that the figure of Moses the lawgiver became a richly fruitful one, pointing not simply to the divine source of law in itself, but to the gift of the Word made flesh in Christ. In the West the link between political imagination and Christology was formed far more by the narratives of Jesus' confrontations with the authorities and the prophecies of his future final judgment of the kings of the earth. What, then, was the cause for this Eastern interest in the *nomos-logos* link and the figure of Moses? We may certainly not omit to mention the influence of the first-century Jewish philosopher Philo, so little mentioned and so much attended to by the Christian thinkers who followed him in Alexandria.

But as well as differing emphases in reading the Bible, there were differing pastoral tasks and challenges that affected the way the early church read its texts and thought about its context. Particularly in the earliest period, *literary genre* makes a considerable difference to the church's posture vis-à-vis political society. The earliest Christian writing on political questions is apologetic; it has to defend the community against charges of antisocial and subversive behavior. This genre developed later into a tradition of antipagan polemic, of which Origen's long book *Against Celsus* is an outstanding example, and to which both Eusebius's pro-Constantinian speeches and Orosius's *Anti-Pagan History* belong. The crowning glory of this tradition was Augustine's *City of God*. Quite different, in manner and emphasis, was literature addressed to the church in response to the threat of heresy, to teach the way of faith. There were many heresies in the early church, but those that threw up interesting political questions followed a line of gnostic reflection, through Marcionism, to the Manicheism faced by the younger Augustine in his *Against Faustus,* which denied the identity of YHWH, the Creator God of Hebrew Scripture, with the God and Father of Jesus. Here it was necessary to vindicate the Old Testament conception of political life and order, wrung from experience on the underside of world politics, as the rule of a God who judged the wicked, individuals and nations alike, and established his law by the unpredictabilities of war.

It is often observed that our adversary sets the terms of a discussion, or to take a less fatalistic view, that we find the adversary who has something to say *to* us. In defending themselves against the accusations of the pagan world, Christians presented themselves as supportive of due political order. In defending themselves against sectarian, antipolitical moralism, they presented themselves as a people oppressed, awaiting the judgment of God where the judgment of man had failed. In such a rhetorician as Tertullian one can sometimes almost catch them speaking out of both sides of their mouths — what was this doughty opponent of military service doing boasting of his prayers that the emperor's armies might be brave? Yet, for the most part Christian thinkers deserve the credit for searching after an authentically theological dialectic, a way of conceiving themselves "in the world but not of it," such as is most powerfully achieved in the famous nineteenth book of Augustine's *City of God*.

But this is closely connected with the way they understood themselves *as church*. The early apologetic *Letter to Diognetus,* drawing on an important phrase in Paul's letter to the Philippians (3:12) and certain ideas in the First Letter of Peter, presented the church as a distinct *politeia* distributed throughout the various civic communities. How was this conception to be interpreted and developed? One possible model for such a thing was that of a *philosophical school*. The Greek noun *politeia* could be taken as an abstract noun, "a way of conducting oneself," and was frequently used by Hellenistic philosophers in such a sense to refer to the self-conscious lifestyles adopted by philosophers. (Diogenes' famous barrel, for example, was a *politeia!*) Alternatively it was possible to take the word concretely, to suggest a form of political community compatible with international dispersion. The *Jewish identity* was the obvious model for this, and had indeed been in the mind of the author of 1 Peter. In the West this latter idea of the church prevailed over the former one, and there arose a conception of a Christian political identity confronting the empire as a foreign power (even when the emperor was a Christian). This conception never fully appeared in the East, where conflict tended to be described in *intra*communitarian terms, as in Chrysostom's depiction of the conflict between the priest and king. Yet, once again, as soon as such a contrast is made, it dissolves itself. Chrysostom's priest-versus-king model was taken up later by Pope Gelasius I and became a commonplace in Western medieval reflection. And the East it was that first, in the fourth century, exploited the possibilities of *monastic community* as a form of concrete common life, a development that would have enormous significance for the medieval West. The two emphases diverge for a moment, but only to converge again.

*   *   *

If the strength of the *logos-nomos* orientation was its capacity to shape a conception of law at once divine and human, and so to open an avenue of law-governed political practice which had much more constructive content than anything a Western bishop might have outlined, its weakness lay in the expectation of an immediately perspicuous rational order, an idealizing approach that could not help being impatient with those who failed to appreciate the disclosure of God's truth.

Paganism had little future. The future for the Jews lay in insulated self-contained communities, unhealthily excluded from the public sphere. But heresy was the nemesis of the Christian empire. Under Constantine's own auspices the Council of Nicaea (325) inaugurated the persistent attempt to achieve a definitive standard of catholic faith that would identify and unify orthodox Christians for public purposes. The definition of the church against heresy had, of course, been a concern from the beginning, and the struggle against it had been waged with a range of churchly resources from argument to excommunication. What is different in the fourth century and after, is the

6

attempt to regulate it by ecclesiastico-political means, the "council." Was this means authentic to the church, or was it a secular device? Did the pope have to be represented at a council, and did the emperor have to allow it? By the fifth and sixth centuries the concept of a council itself had become a battleground.

It would be a mistake to be moved by the tragic aspects of the history of conflict in the church to accept an oversimple judgment on the development. The council, one might say, was one way in which the *potential for public existence* present in Christian faith could be realized, the kind of social presence which philosophical doctrines could never have. As such, it offered the civilized world something that it had been wanting, a mode of constructing social and political institutions upon a basis of truth. But in exploiting this possibility, something was compromised in the practice of faith itself, which became converted into "public doctrine" of the most illusory kind. The excitement of believing was lost in the urgency of conforming — conforming, that is, not necessarily to the empire or to political authority of any kind, but to whatever sectional identity one's security was most deeply bound up with. In Justinian's debacle at the Second Council of Constantinople (553), we meet the paradox of patristic conciliarism at its sharpest: the emperor as the champion of ecumenical unity, believing in the essential inclusiveness of catholic truth expressed in the appropriate way; the ecclesiastics on each side alienated by every attempt to reassure those on the other; finally, in desperation, the highest of high-handed measures invoked in an impotent attempt to bully Christians out of identities wholly constructed by the championing of one formula against another.

The history of ecumenism in the modern period, however, hardly entitles us to adopt superior airs.

Bibliography: C. Avila, *Ownership: Early Christian Teaching* (New York: Orbis; London: Sheed & Ward, 1983); H. Berkhof, *Kirche und Kaiser: eine Untersuchung der Entstehung der byzantinischen und der theokratischen Staatsauffassung im vierten Jahrhundert* (Zürich: Evangelischer Verlag, 1947); P. Brown, *The Rise of Western Christendom* (Oxford: Blackwell, 1996); H. Chadwick, *The Early Church* (Harmondsworth: Penguin, 1967); J. Daniélou and H. Marrou, *The Christian Centuries,* vol. 1, The First Six Hundred Years (English translation) (London and New York: Darton, Longman and Todd, 1964); F. Dvornik, *Early Christian and Byzantine Political Philosophy: Origin and Background* (Washington, D.C.: Dunbarton Oaks Centre, 1966); L. L. Field, Jr., *Liberty, Dominion, and the Two Swords: On the Origins of Western Political Theology (180-398)* (Notre Dame, Ind.: University of Notre Dame Press, 1998); J. L. González, *Faith and Wealth* (San Francisco and London: Harper & Row, 1990); A. Harnack, *Militia Christi, the Christian Religion and the Military in the First Three Centuries* (English translation) (Philadelphia: Fortress, 1981; originally published, 1905); M. Hengel, *Property and Riches in the Early Church* (English translation) (London: SCM, 1974); J.-M. Hornus, *It Is Not Lawful for Me to Fight* (English translation) (Scottdale, Pa., 1980); R. A. Markus, *The End of Ancient Christianity* (Cambridge: Cambridge University Press, 1990); F.-X. Murphy, *Politics and the Early Christian Church* (Paris: Desclée de Brouwer, 1967); H. Musurillo, *Acts of the Christian Martyrs* (Oxford: Clarendon Press, 1972); K. M. Setton, *Christian Attitudes towards the Emperor in the Fourth Century* (New York: Columbia University Press, 1941).

An Apologetic Miscellany

The earliest Christian reflection on the nature of society and its politics, after that of the New Testament itself, arose in the context of apologetics — that is, in the course of the young church's struggle for toleration by a suspicious and antagonistic pagan society. In the second century persecution was locally, not centrally, initiated and an occasional, rather than a consistent, occurrence; nevertheless, membership of the Christian church was illegal as such, and the position of Christians was precarious. The excerpts gathered here, from the second or early third century, illustrate how, in the course of refuting accusations and explaining elementary Christian religious practice in readily accessible terms, apologists found themselves accounting for their relation to society as a whole.

Justin, from modern Nablus in Palestine, who died a martyr around A.D. 165, illustrates one pole of the apologetic endeavor: Christians are described as philosophers, a category of independent-minded citizens well recognized within Hellenistic society. In the Socratic manner they bring to bear upon the conventional practices of political society the critical perspective of a search for truth. Such a conception was congenial to Justin's own intellectual and spiritual development, as he describes it in the *Dialogue with Trypho:* a disciple in turn of Stoic, Peripatetic, Pythagorean, and finally Platonic schools, he came to Christianity as the "only reliable and helpful philosophy." It was also congenial to the moment in political history at which he was writing. For the successors of Trajan attempted to consolidate the empire on the basis of a program of philosophic enlightenment. Thus, from the outset of the first of his two *Apologies,* an open letter addressed to the emperor Antoninus Pius (138-61), Justin exploits traditional themes of Platonic philosophy to challenge the official hostility directed at Christians: the Socratic opposition of truth and conventional opinion, the conviction that the only harm that can befall a rational being is incurred by flying in the face of truth, Plato's ideal of the philosopher-king. Not only are Socrates' doctrines appealed to, but his example as well, along with that of Jesus, to reinforce the perils of blind opposition to philosophy on the part of political authorities.

More distinctly Christian is Justin's demand for, and emphasis upon, "judgment" — this being a central biblical category for political rule. Distinctly Christian, too, is his discussion of the "kingdom" to which Christians are called, taking up a central theme of Jesus' own teaching recorded in the synoptic Gospels. Justin initially seems to put a great distance between God's kingdom and earthly political rule, yet the distance is not infinite. For earthly kingdoms are beholden to the kingdom of the "Logos" (i.e., "Word") — this title for Christ is highly characteristic of the apologists. Its earliest appearance in Christianity is, of course, in the prologue to St. John's Gospel, though it is uncertain whether Justin knew that text. The religious authority of the Word of God blends with the philosophical authority of the truth to provide a basis for the functioning of society and a criterion for the reasonable exercise of political authority.

The short, anonymous letter *To Diognetus* and Theophilus's *To Autolycus* are both examples of apologetic literature written in the form of letters to private individuals. Neither can be dated definitively, but both probably come from the later second century. We include the famous passage from *To Diognetus* which depicts the Christian church as a political society disseminated throughout other political societies — a conception apparently derived from the First Epistle of Peter, with its designation of Christians as "resident aliens," though the author by preference quotes St. Paul. A sharper contrast with Justin's picture of Christians as a philosophical school can hardly be imagined, and indeed this conception is unique for its period. It is complemented by another analogy with a long future, the church as the "soul" of society; but if this at first seems to point to a greater identification between church and society, we must be struck by the mainly antithetical terms in which the body-soul relation is explored. Far more prepared to identify Christians as loyal citizens of the empire is Theophilus, who was bishop of Antioch. In this short excerpt he deals directly with the chief obstacle, the emperor cult. Prayers for the emperor, he claims, typically of the apologists in general, fulfill the proper expectation of political obedience.

Further Reading: L. W. Barnard, *Justin Martyr: His Life and Thought* (Cambridge: Cambridge University Press, 1967); H. Chadwick, *Early Christian Thought and the Classical Tradition: A Study in Justin, Clement, and Origen* (Oxford: Clarendon Press, 1966); J. Danielou and H. Marrou, *The Christian Centuries*, vol. 1, The First Six Hundred Years (English translation) (London and New York: Darton, Longman and Todd, 1964); E. R. Goodenough, *The Theology of Justin Martyr* (Jena: Fromann, 1923); R. M. Grant, *Greek Apologists of the Second Century* (London: SCM, 1988); H. B. Timothy, *The Early Christian Apologists and Greek Philosophy Exemplified by Irenaeus, Tertullian, and Clement of Alexandria* (Assen: Van Gorcum, 1973).

From Justin's *First Apology*

1. To the Emperor Titus Aelius Hadrianus Antoninus Pius Augustus Caesar, and to his philosopher son Verissimus, and to Lucius the philosopher, Caesar's natural son

and Pius's adopted son, a lover of culture, and to the Sacred Senate and all the Roman people — on behalf of people of every nation who are unjustly hated and grossly abused, I, Justin, son of Priscus and grandson of Bacchius, from Flavia Neapolis in Syria-Palestine, myself being one of them, have drawn up this address and petition.

2. Reason dictates that those who are truly pious and philosophers should honour and love only the truth, declining to follow the opinions of the ancients, if they are worthless. For not only does sound reason dictate that one should not follow those who do or teach unjust things, but the lover of truth should choose by all means, and even before his own life, even though death should remove him, to speak and do righteous things. So you, then, since you are called pious and philosophers and guardians of justice and lovers of culture, listen in every way; and it will be shown if you are such. For we have come into your company not to flatter you by this writing, nor please you by our address, but to ask that you give judgment, after an exact and searching enquiry, not moved by prejudice or by a wish to please superstitious people, nor by irrational impulse or long prevalent rumours, so as to give a decision which will prove to be against yourselves. For we indeed reckon that no evil can be done to us, unless we are proved to be evildoers, or shown to be wicked. You are able to kill us, but not to hurt us. 3. But that nobody should think that this is an unreasonable and daring utterance, we ask that the charges against us be investigated, and that, if they are substantiated let us be punished as is fitting. But if nobody can prove anything against us, true reason forbids you because of an evil rumour to wrong innocent people, and indeed rather to wrong yourselves, who think fit to instigate action not by judgment but by passion. Every honourable person will recognise this as the only fair and righteous challenge, namely, that the subjects should give a straightforward account of their own life and teaching; and likewise that the rulers should give their decision as having followed not violence and tyranny but piety and philosophy. For thus both rulers and subjects would reap benefit. For even one of the ancients said somewhere: "Unless both rulers and ruled love wisdom, it is impossible to make cities prosper" (Plato, *Republic* 473e). It is then our task to offer to all an opportunity of inspecting our life and teachings, lest, on account of those who do not really know of our affairs, we should incur the penalty due to them for mental blindness. But it is for you, as reason demands, to listen to us and to be found good judges. For if, having learned the truth, you fail to do what is righteous, you have no defence before God.

4. By the mere statement of a name, nothing is decided, either good or evil, apart from the actions associated with the name; indeed, as far as the name with which we are accused goes, we are most gentle (*chrēstos*) people. But we do not think it just to ask to be acquitted on account of the name if we are convicted as evildoers; so on the other hand, if we are found to have committed no wrong either in the appellation of the name or in our citizenship, you must be exceedingly anxious against incurring righteous judgment by unjustly punishing those who are not convicted. For from a name neither approval nor punishment could fairly come, unless something excellent or evil in action could be shown about it. For you do not punish the accused among yourselves before they are convicted; but in our case you take the

name as proof against us, and this although, as far as the name goes, you ought rather to punish our accusers. For we are accused of being Christians, and to hate what is favourable *(chrēstos)* is unjust. Again, if one of the accused deny the name, saying that he is not a Christian, you acquit him, as having no proof that he is an evildoer; but if any one acknowledges that he is one, you punish him on account of this acknowledgement. You ought also to enquire into the life both of the confessor and the denier, that by his deeds it would appear what kind of person each is. For as some who have been taught by the Teacher, Christ, not to deny him encourage others when they are put to the test, so similarly do those who lead evil lives give some excuse to those who, without consideration, like to accuse all the Christians of impiety and wickedness. And this also is improper. For in philosophy, too, some assume the name and the dress who do nothing worthy of their profession; and as you are aware, those among the ancients whose opinions and teachings were quite different are yet called by the one name of philosopher. And some of these taught atheism; and those who became poets get a laugh out of the impurity of Zeus with his own children. And those who follow such teaching are unrestrained by you; but, on the contrary, you offer prizes and honours to those who euphoniously insult them. [. . .]

10. But we have received from tradition that God does not need material offerings from people, seeing that he himself is the provider of all things. And we have been taught and are persuaded and believe that he accepts only those who imitate the good things which are in him, temperance and righteousness and well-doing, and whatsoever else truly belongs to God who is called by no given name. And we have been taught that in the beginning he of his goodness, for people's sakes, formed all things out of unformed matter; and if they by their actions show themselves worthy of his design, they are accounted worthy, so we have received, of reigning with him, being delivered from corruption and suffering. For as in the beginning he created us when we were not, so we consider that those who likewise choose what is pleasing to him are, on account of their choice, counted worthy of incorruption and of fellowship with him. For the coming into being was not our choice; but in order that we may follow those things that please him, choosing them by means of the rational powers he has given us, he both persuades us and leads us to faith. And we think it for the good of all people that they are not prevented from learning these things but are even urged to consider them. For the restraint which human laws could not bring about, the Logos, being divine, would have brought about, save that the evil demons, with the help of the evil desire which is in every person and which expresses itself in various ways, had scattered abroad many false and godless accusations, none of which apply to us.

11. And when you hear that we look for a kingdom, you uncritically suppose that we speak of a human one; whereas we speak of that with God, as appears also from the confession of their faith made by those who are charged with being Christians, although they know that death is the penalty meted out to him who so confesses. For if we looked for a human kingdom, we would deny it, that we might not be slain; and we would try to escape detection, that we might obtain the things we look for. But since we do not have our hope on the present, we do not heed our executioners, since death is in any case the debt of nature.

12. And more than all other people we are your helpers and allies in the cause of peace, convinced as we are that it is alike impossible for the wicked, the covetous, the conspirator, and the virtuous to escape the notice of God, and that everyone goes to eternal punishment or salvation in accordance with the character of his acts. If all people knew this, no one would choose wickedness even for a little while, knowing that he goes to eternal punishment by fire; but would by all means restrain himself, and order his path with virtue, that he might receive the good gifts of God, and avoid the punishments. There are some people who endeavour to conceal their wrongdoing because of the laws and punishments you impose, knowing that since you are only men and women it is possible for wrongdoers to escape you; if they were to learn and were convinced that our thoughts as well as our acts cannot be hidden from God, they would by all means live decently, at least because of the impending penalties, as even you yourselves will admit. But you seem to fear lest all people become righteous, and you no longer have any to punish. This would be the concern of public executioners, not of good rulers. But, as we said before, we are convinced that these things are brought about by evil spirits, who demand sacrifices and service from people who live irrationally; but as for you, we assume that you who aim at piety and philosophy will do nothing unreasonable. But if you also, like thoughtless people, prefer the custom to truth, do what you have power to do. But just so much power have rulers who respect reputation rather than truth as brigands have in a desert. And that you will not succeed is shown by the Word, and after God who begat him we know of no ruler more kingly or more just than he. For as all people shrink from inheriting the poverty or sufferings or obscurity of their fathers, so whatever the Word forbids to be chosen, the sensible person will not choose. That all these things would come to pass, I say, our teacher foretold, who is both Son and Apostle of God the Father and Master of all, that is Jesus Christ; from whom also we have received the name of Christians. We are more assured that all the things taught by him are so, since whatever he predicted before is seen in fact coming to pass; and this is the work of God, to announce something before it happens, and as it was predicted so to show it happening.

Translation: L. W. Barnard, *Ancient Christian Writers* (New York: Paulist Press, 1997). Used with permission.

From the *Letter to Diognetus*

5. For the distinction between Christians and other men is neither in country nor language nor customs. For they do not dwell in cities in some place of their own, nor do they use any strange variety of dialect, nor practise an extraordinary kind of life. This teaching of theirs has not been discovered by the intellect or thought of busy men, nor are they the advocates of any human doctrine as some men are. Yet while living in Greek and barbarian cities, according as each obtained his lot, and following the local customs both in clothing and food and in the rest of life, they show

forth the wonderful and confessedly strange character of the constitution of their own citizenship. They dwell in their own fatherlands, but as if sojourners in them; they share all things as citizens, and suffer all things as strangers. Every foreign country is their fatherland, and every fatherland is a foreign country. They marry as all men, they bear children, but they do not expose their offspring. They offer free hospitality, but guard their purity. Their lot is cast "in the flesh," but they do not live "after the flesh" (2 Cor. 10:3). They pass their time upon the earth, but they have their citizenship in heaven (Phil. 3:20). They obey the appointed laws, and they surpass the laws in their own lives. They love all men and are persecuted by all men. They are unknown and they are condemned. They are put to death and they gain life. "They are poor and make many rich" (2 Cor. 6:10); they lack all things and have all things in abundance. They are dishonoured, and are glorified in their dishonour; they are spoken evil of and are justified. "They are abused and give blessing" (1 Cor. 4:12), they are insulted and render honour. When they do good they are buffeted as evildoers, when they are buffeted they rejoice as men who receive life. They are warred upon by the Jews as foreigners and are persecuted by the Greeks, and those who hate them cannot state the cause of their enmity.

6. To put it shortly, what the soul is in the body, that the Christians are in the world. The soul is spread through all members of the body, and Christians throughout the cities of the world. The soul dwells in the body, but is not of the body, and Christians dwell in the world, but are not of the world. The soul is invisible, and is guarded in a visible body, and Christians are recognised when they are in the world, but their religion remains invisible. The flesh hates the soul, and wages war upon it, though it has suffered no evil, because it is prevented from gratifying its pleasures, and the world hates the Christians though it has suffered no evil, because they are opposed to its pleasures. The soul loves the flesh which hates it, and the limbs, and Christians love those that hate them. The soul has been shut up in the body, but itself sustains the body; and Christians are confined in the world as in a prison, but themselves sustain the world. The soul dwells immortal in a mortal tabernacle, and Christians sojourn among corruptible things, waiting for the incorruptibility which is in heaven. The soul when evil-treated in food and drink becomes better, and Christians when buffeted day by day increase more. God has appointed them to so great a post and it is not right for them to decline it.

7. For it is not, as I said, an earthly discovery which was given to them, nor do they take such pains to guard some mortal invention, nor have they been entrusted with the dispensation of human mysteries. But in truth the almighty and all-creating and invisible God himself founded among men the truth from heaven and the holy and incomprehensible word, and established it in their hearts, not, as one might suppose, by sending some minister to men, or an angel or ruler, or one of those who direct earthly things, or one of those who are entrusted with the dispensations in heaven, but the very artificer and creator of the universe himself, by whom he made the heavens, by whom he enclosed the sea in its own bounds, whose mysteries all the elements guard faithfully; from whom the sun received the measure of the courses of the day; to whose command the moon is obedient to give light by night; whom the stars obey, following the course of the moon; by whom all things were ordered and

ordained and placed in subjection, the heavens and the things in the heavens, the earth and the things in the earth, the sea and the things in the sea, fire, air, abyss, the things in the heights, the things in the depths, the things between them — him he sent to them. Yes, but did he send him, as a man might suppose, in sovereignty *(tyrannis)* and fear and terror? Not so, but in gentleness and meekness, as a king sending a son he sent him as king, he sent him as God, he sent him as man to men; he was saving and persuading when he sent him, not compelling, for compulsion is not an attribute of God. When he sent him he was calling, not pursuing; when he sent him he was loving, not judging. For he will send him as judge, and "who shall endure his coming" (Mal. 3:2)?

Translation: Kirsopp Lake, Loeb Classical Library (London: Heinemann; Cambridge, Mass.: Harvard University Press, 1913). Used with permission.

From Theophilus of Antioch's *To Autolycus,* Book 1

11. Accordingly, I will pay honour to the emperor not by worshipping him but by praying for him. I worship the God who is the real and true God, since I know that the emperor was made by him. You will say to me, "Why do you not worship the emperor?" Because he was made not to be worshipped but to be honoured with legitimate honour. He is not God but a man appointed by God, not to be worshipped but to judge justly. For in a certain way he has been "entrusted with a stewardship" (1 Cor. 9:17) from God. He himself has subordinates whom he does not permit to be called emperors, for "emperor" is his name and it is not right for another to be given this title. Similarly worship must be given to God alone. You are entirely mistaken, O man. "Honour the emperor" (1 Pet. 2:17) by wishing him well, by obeying him, by praying for him, for by so doing you will perform "the will of God" (1 Pet. 2:15); the law of God says, "Honour, my son, God and the king, and be disobedient to neither one; for they will suddenly destroy their enemies" (Prov. 24:21f.).

Translation: Robert M. Grant (Oxford University Press, 1970). Used with permission.

Irenaeus of Lyons
(fl. ca. 180)

The major work of Irenaeus, bishop of Lugdunum (Lyons) from A.D. 178, is a polemic against Gnostic heresies, elaborated with extensive treatments of orthodox Christian teaching. Born in Asia Minor, the author wrote it in Greek, but our knowledge of it stems from a later Latin translation, which can be compared at many points against quotations from the Greek original to be found in other writers and from fragments of an Armenian translation. It is a work of a different literary *genre* from that of the apologists, and expects a different kind of readership, i.e., a Christian one. This should be borne in mind when we reflect on the very different approach to questions of political rule. Irenaeus raises the subject under the heading of Satanology; the devil and the coming Antichrist are the major elements in his treatment. A cosmic dualism which divided the universe between the powers that governed the world and the spiritual powers which guarded the steps of the soul's ascent to salvation was a major feature in the worldview of those deviant Christian groups that go by the general name of "Gnostics." Irenaeus, then, had to insist that no power was in command of civil government other than God himself.

His theology is stamped throughout by an interest in the history of God's dealings with mankind, the "economy" of salvation, in which creation, incarnation, and judgment form the key dramatic moments. This is the context for his apocalypticism. He displays a serious interest in engaging the concept, found in the apocalyptic books of the Old and New Testaments, of empire as a demonic force. The somewhat bewildering kaleidoscope of images drawn from long quotations from the book of Daniel should not conceal from us that *that* book was conceived as serious political comment on the circumstances which evoked it (the attempted suppression of Jewish culture by the Antiochene heirs of Alexander's empire in the second century B.C.), and that Irenaeus, aided by the Apocalypse of John, by and large grasps the point about empire that the book of Daniel wants to make. He is not particularly careful to avoid giving the impression that the empire in which he himself lives is a natural precursor to the final apocalyptic events. For empire is the platform on which the ultimate rebellion against God's purposes must emerge; world history is the story of the growth of empire and of its final collapse before divine judgment. Universal judgment is Irenaeus's response to the political aspects of dualism: it corresponds to the universality of God's creation and providence.

From this point of reference several ideas follow which are typical of later Western Christian political thinking. Christ's incarnate coming to the world was *already* an act of judgment; the division between good and evil lay at the center of God's redeeming purposes. Consequently, the God-given role of civil rulers is to maintain this division, which they must do "clothed in law," for only so can they be agents, rather than objects, of divine judgment. God's judgment is already exercised providentially through civil rulers, whether they are mild or harsh. Irenaeus's threefold typology of rulers allows not only for mild, educative rulers on the one hand and tyrannical, arbitrary rulers on the other, "for mockery, insolence and pride," but, in between them, for a harsh but not unjust type of rule "for the purposes of fear and punishment and rebuke." A people gets the government it deserves, he thinks; and he will not be the last to think so.

Further Reading: A. Benoît, *Saint Irénée, introduction à l'étude de sa théologie* (Paris: Presses Universitaires de France, 1960); Y. de Andia, *Homo Vivens, incorruptibilité et divinisation de l'homme selon Irénée de Lyon* (Paris, Études Augustiniennes, 1986); J. Fantino, *La Théologie d'Irénée* (Paris: Éditions du Cerf, 1994); D. Minns, *Irenaeus* (London: Geoffrey Chapman, 1994).

From *Against Heresies,* Book 5

24. As therefore the devil lied at the beginning, so did he also in the end, when he said: "All these are delivered unto me, and to whomsoever I will I give them" (Matt. 4:9). For it is not he who has distributed the kingdoms of this world, but God; for "the heart of the king is in the hand of God" (Prov. 21:1). And the Word also says by Solomon: "By me kings do reign, and princes administer justice. By me chiefs are raised up, and by me kings rule the earth" (Prov. 8:15). Paul the apostle also says to the same purpose: "Be ye subject to all the higher powers; for there is no power but of God; now those which are have been ordained of God." And again, in reference to them he says: "For he beareth not the sword in vain; for he is the minister of God, the avenger for wrath to him who does evil." Now, that he spake these words, not in regard to angelical powers, nor of invisible rulers — as some venture to expound the passage — but of actual human authorities, he shows when he says: "For this cause pay ye tribute also; for they are God's ministers attending to this very thing" (Rom. 13:1, 4, 6). This also the Lord confirmed, when he did not do what he was tempted to by the devil; but he gave directions that tribute should be paid to the tax-gatherers for himself and Peter (Matt. 17:27); because "they are the ministers of God, attending to this very thing."

For since man, by departing from God, reached such a pitch of bestiality as even to look upon his kinsman as his enemy, and engaged without fear in every kind of disordered conduct, murder and avarice, God imposed upon mankind the fear of man, as they did not acknowledge the fear of God; in order that, being subjected to the authority of men, and under the custody of their laws, they might attain to some degree of justice, and exercise mutual forbearance through dread of the sword suspended full in their view, as the apostle says: "For he beareth not the sword in vain; for he is the minister of God, the avenger for wrath upon him who does evil." And for this reason, too, magistrates themselves, having laws as a clothing of righteousness, shall not be called in question for their conduct whenever they act in a just and legitimate manner. But whatsoever they do to the subversion of justice, iniquitously, and illegally, and tyrannically, in these things shall they also perish; for the just judgment of God comes equally upon all, and in no case is defective. Earthly rule, therefore has been appointed by God for the benefit of the nations (and not by the devil, who is never at rest at all, nay, who does not love to see even nations conducting themselves after a quiet manner), so that under the fear of it men may not eat each other up like fishes; but that, by means of the establishment of laws, they may keep down the great wickedness of the nations. And in this way they are "God's ministers."

As, then, those who collect taxes from us are "ministers of God attending to this very thing" and as "the powers that be are ordained of God," it is clear that the devil lied when he said: "These are delivered unto me; and so to whomsoever I will, I give them." For he at whose command men are born is he at whose command kings are also appointed, suited to those who are at the time placed under their government. Some of these rulers are given for the correction and the benefit of their subjects, and for the preservation of justice; but others for the purposes of fear and punishment and rebuke; others, as the subjects deserve it, are for mockery, insolence and pride; while the just judgment of God, as I have observed already, passes equally upon all. The devil, however, as he is the rebellious angel, can only do as he did at the beginning, namely deceive and lead astray the mind of man into disobeying the commandments of God and gradually darken the hearts of those who would endeavour to serve him, to the forgetting of the true God but to the adoration of himself as God.

Just as if anyone, being a rebel and seizing control of a territory by an act of brigandage, should harass its inhabitants and usurp for himself the glory of a king among those ignorant of his rebellion and brigandage, so likewise also the devil, being one among those angels who are placed over the spirit of the air (as Paul has declared in the Epistle to the Ephesians [2:2]), becoming envious of man, became a rebel from the divine law; for envy is a thing foreign to God. And as his rebellion was exposed by man and man became the touchstone of his thoughts, he has set himself in opposition to man with greater and greater determination, envying him his life and wishing to involve him in his own rebellious power. The Word of God, however, the Maker of all things, conquering him by means of human nature and showing him to be a rebel, has, on the contrary, put him under the power of men. For he says, "Behold I confer on you the power of treading upon serpents and scorpions and

upon all the power of the enemy" (Luke 10:19), in order that, as he obtained dominion over men by rebellion, so again his rebellion might be deprived of power by
means of men turning back again to God.

25. And not only by the particulars already mentioned, but also by means of
the events which shall occur in the time of Antichrist is it shown that he, being a rebel and a brigand, presumes to be adored as God; and that although a mere slave, he
wishes himself to be proclaimed as king. For Antichrist, being endued with all the
power of the devil, shall come not as a just king, nor as a lawful king, i.e. one in subjection to God, but a lawless and irreligious one; as a rebel, iniquitous and murderous, as a brigand, concentrating in himself all satanic rebellion, and setting aside
idols to persuade men that he himself is God, raising up himself as the only idol,
having in himself the multifarious errors of the other idols. This he does in order
that they who do now worship the devil by means of many abominations, may serve
himself by that one idol, of whom the apostle thus speaks in the Second Epistle to
the Thessalonians: ". . . unless there shall come a falling away first, and the man of sin
shall be revealed, the son of perdition, who appeareth and exalteth himself above all
that is called God, or that is worshipped; so that he sitteth in the temple of God,
showing himself as God" (2 Thess. 2:3f.). The apostle therefore clearly points out his
rebellion and that he will be lifted up above all that is called God, or that is worshipped — that is, above every idol — for these are indeed so called by men, but are
not really gods — and that he will endeavour in a tyrannical manner to set himself
forth as God.

Moreover, the apostle has also pointed out this which I have shown in many
ways, that the temple in Jerusalem was made by the direction of the true God. For
the apostle himself, speaking in his own person, called it, quite precisely, the temple
of God. Now I have shown in the third book, that no one is termed God by the apostles when speaking for themselves, except Him who truly is God, the Father of our
Lord, by whose directions the temple which is at Jerusalem was constructed for those
purposes which I have already mentioned; in which temple the enemy shall sit,
endeavouring to show himself as Christ, as the Lord also declares: "But when ye shall
see the abomination of desolation, which has been spoken of by Daniel the Prophet,
standing in the holy place (let him that readeth understand), then let those who are
in Judaea flee into the mountains; and he who is upon the house-top, let him not
come down to take anything out of his house: for there shall then be great hardship,
such as has not been from the beginning of the world until now, nor ever shall be"
(Matt. 24:15-17, 21).

Daniel, too, looking forward to the end of the last kingdom, i.e. the ten last
kings, amongst whom shall be shared the kingdom of those upon whom the Son of
Perdition shall come, declares that ten horns shall spring from the beast, and that another little horn shall arise in the midst of them, and that three of the former shall be
rooted up before his face. He says: "And, behold, eyes were in this horn as the eyes of
a man, and a mouth speaking great things, and his look was more stout than his fellows. I was looking, and this horn made war against the saints, and prevailed against
them, until the Ancient of Days came and gave judgment to the saints of the most
high God, and the time came, and the saints obtained the kingdom" (Dan. 7:20-22).

Then, further on, in the interpretation of the vision, there was said to him: "The fourth beast shall be the fourth kingdom upon earth, which shall excel all other kingdoms, and devour the whole earth, and tread it down, and cut it in pieces. And its ten horns are ten kings which shall arise; and after them shall arise another, who shall surpass in evil deeds all that were before him, and shall overthrow three kings; and he shall speak words against the most high God, and wear out the saints of the most high God, and shall purpose to change times and the Law; and everything shall be given into his hand until a time of times and a half time" (Dan. 7:23f.), that is, for three years and six months, during which time, when he comes, he shall reign over the earth. Of whom also the Apostle Paul again, speaking in the Second Epistle to the Thessalonians, and at the same time proclaiming the cause of his advent, thus says: "And then shall the wicked one be revealed, whom the Lord Jesus shall slay with the spirit of his mouth, and destroy by the presence of his coming; the wicked one whose coming is after the working of Satan, in all power, and signs and portents of lies, and with all deceivableness of wickedness for those who perish; because they did not receive the love of the truth, that they might be saved. And therefore God will send them the working of error, that they may believe a lie; that they all may be judged who did not believe the truth, but gave consent to iniquity" (2 Thess. 2:8-12).

The Lord also spoke as follows to those who did not believe in him: "I have come in my Father's name, and ye have not received me; when another shall come in his own name, him ye will receive" (John 5:43), calling Antichrist "the other" because he is alienated from the Lord. This is also the unjust judge whom the Lord mentioned as one "who feared not God neither regarded man" to whom the widow fled in her forgetfulness of God — that is, the earthly Jerusalem — to be avenged of her adversary (Luke 18:2f.). Which also he shall do in the time of his kingdom: he shall remove his kingdom into that city, and shall sit in the temple of God, leading astray those who worship him to believe that he is the Christ. To this purpose Daniel says again: "And he shall desolate the holy place; and sin has been given for a sacrifice, and righteousness has been cast to the earth, and he has been active and gone on prosperously" (Dan. 8:12). And the angel Gabriel, when explaining the visions to him, states with regard to this person: "And towards the end of their kingdom a king of a most fierce countenance shall arise, one understanding dark questions, and exceedingly powerful; and he shall be amazingly destructive, and effective in his undertakings; he shall put strong men down, the holy people likewise; and his yoke shall hold their necks as in a collar; deceit shall be in his hand, and he shall be lifted up in his heart; he shall also ruin many by deceit and lead many to perdition, crushing them in his hand like eggs" (Dan. 8:23f.). And then he points out the time that his tyranny shall last, during which the saints shall be put to flight, they who offer a pure sacrifice unto God: "And in the midst of the week," he says, "the sacrifice and the libation shall be taken away, and the abomination of desolation shall be brought into the temple: even unto the consummation of the time shall the desolation be complete" (Dan. 9:27). Now three years and six months constitute the half-week.

From all these passages are revealed to us not merely the particulars of the rebellion and the doings of him who concentrates in himself every satanic error, but also that there is one and the same God the Father, who was declared by the prophets but made manifest by Christ. For if what Daniel prophesied concerning the end has been confirmed by the Lord when he said, "When ye shall see the abomination of desolation, which has been spoken of by Daniel the prophet" (Matt. 24:15); and if the angel Gabriel, who gave the interpretation of the visions to Daniel, is the archangel of the Creator who also proclaimed to Mary the visible coming and the incarnation of Christ; then it is manifestly clear that there is one and the same God, who sent the prophets and then sent the Son and called us into his knowledge.

26. In a still clearer light has John in the Apocalypse indicated to the Lord's disciples what shall happen in the last times and concerning the ten kings who shall then arise, among whom the empire which now rules the earth shall be partitioned. He teaches us what the ten horns shall be which were seen by Daniel, telling us that thus it had been said to him: "And the ten horns which thou sawest are ten kings, who have received no kingdom as yet, but shall receive power as if kings one hour with the beast. These have one mind, and give their strength and power to the beast. These shall make war with the Lamb, and the Lamb shall overcome them, because he is the Lord of lords and the King of kings" (Rev. 17:12-14). It is manifest, therefore, that of these potentates, he who is to come shall slay three, and subject the remainder to his power, and that he shall be himself the eighth among them. And they shall lay Babylon waste, and burn her with fire, and shall give their kingdom to the beast, and put the church to flight. After that they shall be destroyed by the coming of our Lord. For that the kingdom must be divided and thus come to ruin the Lord declares when he says: "Every kingdom divided against itself is brought to desolation, and every city or house divided against itself shall not stand" (Matt. 12:25). It must be therefore that the kingdom, the city, and the house be divided into ten; and for this reason he has already foreshadowed the partition and division which shall take place. Daniel also says particularly that the end of the fourth kingdom consists in the toes of the image seen by Nebuchadnezzar, upon which came the stone cut out without hands; and as he does himself say: "The feet were indeed the one part iron, the other part clay, until the stone was cut out without hands, and struck the image upon the iron and clay feet, and dashed them into pieces, even to the end" (Dan. 2:33f.). Then afterwards, when interpreting this, he says, "And as thou sawest the feet and the toes, partly indeed of clay and partly of iron, the kingdom shall be divided, and there shall be in it a root of iron as thou sawest iron mixed with baked clay. And the toes were indeed the one part iron, but the other part clay." The ten toes, therefore, are these ten kings, among whom the kingdom shall be partitioned, of whom some indeed shall be strong and active, or energetic; others, again, shall be sluggish and useless, and shall not agree; as also Daniel says: "Some part of the kingdom shall be strong, and part shall be broken from it. As thou sawest the iron mixed with the baked clay, there shall be minglings among the human race, but no cohesion one with the other, just as iron cannot be welded onto pottery ware." And what its end shall be he declares: "And in the days of these kings shall the God of heaven raise up a kingdom which shall never decay, and his kingdom shall not be left to another people. It shall break in pieces and shatter all kingdoms, and shall itself be exalted for ever. As thou sawest that the stone was cut without hands from the mountain, and brake in pieces the baked clay, the iron, the brass, the silver and the gold, God has pointed out to the king what shall come to pass after these things; and the dream is true and the interpretation trustworthy" (Dan. 2:41-45).

If, therefore, the great God showed future things by Daniel, and confirmed them by his Son; and if Christ is the stone which is cut out without hands, who shall destroy temporal kingdoms and introduce an eternal one, which is the resurrection of the just; as he declares, "the God of heaven shall raise up a kingdom which shall never be destroyed," let them accept their defeat and come to their senses, who reject the Creator and do not agree that the prophets were sent beforehand from the same Father from whom also the Lord came, but who assert that prophecies originated from diverse powers. For those things which have been predicted by the Creator alike through all the prophets has Christ fulfilled in the end, ministering to his Father's will and completing his dispensations with regard to the human race. Let those persons, therefore, who blaspheme the Creator, either by openly expressed words such as the disciples of Marcion, or by a perversion of the sense of Scripture as those of Valentinus and all the Gnostics falsely so called, be recognised as agents of Satan by all those who worship God; through whose agency Satan now, and not before, has been seen to speak against God, even him who has prepared eternal fire for every kind of apostasy. For he does not venture to blaspheme his Lord openly of himself; as also in the beginning he led man astray through the instrumentality of the serpent, concealing himself as it were from God. Truly has Justin remarked that before the Lord's appearance Satan never dared to blaspheme God, inasmuch as he did not yet know his own sentence, because it was contained in parables and allegories; but that after the Lord's appearance, when he had clearly ascertained from the words of Christ and his apostles that eternal fire has been prepared for him as he rebelled against God of his own free will, and likewise for all who unrepentant continue in the rebellion, he now blasphemes, by means of such men, the Lord who brings judgment upon him as being already condemned, and imputes the guilt of his rebellion to his maker, not to his own voluntary disposition. Just as it is with those who break the laws, when punishment overtakes them they throw the blame upon those who frame the laws, but not upon themselves. In like manner do those men, filled with a satanic spirit, bring innumerable accusations against our Creator, who has both given to us the spirit of life and established a law adapted for all; and they will not admit that the judgment of God is just. Wherefore also they set about imagining some other Father, who neither cares about nor exercises a providence over our affairs, nay, one who even approves of all sins.

27. For if the Father does not exercise judgment, it must be either that he has no interest in our acts or that he approves of all those actions that take place; and if he does not judge, all persons will be treated as equal and accounted in the same condition. The advent of Christ is therefore without an object, and, indeed, in contradiction to his failure to judge. For he "came to divide a man against his father, and the daughter against the mother, and the daughter-in-law against the mother-in-law" (Matt. 10:35); and when two are in one bed, to take the one and to leave the other; and of two women grinding at the mill, to take one and leave the other (Luke 17:34f.); also at the time of the end, to order the reapers to collect first the tares together, and bind them in bundles, and burn them with unquenchable fire, but to

gather up the wheat into the barn (Matt. 13:30); and to call the lambs into the kingdom prepared for them, but to send the goats into everlasting fire, which has been "prepared" by his Father "for the devil and his angels" (Matt. 25:33f., 41). And why is this? The Word has come "for the ruin and for the resurrection of many" (Luke 2:34): for the ruin of those who do not believe him, to whom also he has threatened a greater damnation in the judgment-day than that of Sodom and Gomorrah (Luke 10:12); but for the resurrection of believers, and those who do the will of his Father in heaven. If, then, the advent of the Son reaches all alike, judging and separating the believing from the unbelieving (since it is by their own choice that those who believe do his will, by their own choice the disobedient do not consent to his doctrine); it is manifest that his Father has made all in a like condition, each person having a choice of his own and free discretion; and that he has regard to all things, and exercises a providence over all, "making his sun to rise upon the evil and on the good, and sending rain upon the just and unjust" (Matt. 5:45).

And to as many as continue in their love towards God, does he grant communion with him. But communion with God is life and light, and the enjoyment of all the benefits which he has in store. But on as many as, according to their own choice, depart from God, he inflicts that separation from himself which they have chosen of their own accord. But separation from God is death, and separation from light is darkness; and separation from God consists in the loss of all the benefits which he has in store. Those therefore who cast away by rebellion these forementioned things, being in fact destitute of all good, do experience every kind of punishment. God, however, does not punish them immediately of himself, but that punishment falls upon them because they are destitute of all that is good. Now, good things are eternal and without end with God, and therefore the loss of these is also eternal and never-ending. In the same way, because light is permanent, those who have blinded themselves, or have been blinded by others, are for ever deprived of the enjoyment of light. It is not, however, that the light has inflicted upon them the penalty of blindness, but it is that the blindness itself has brought calamity upon them. And therefore the Lord declared, "He that believeth in me is not condemned," that is, not separated from God, for he is united to God through faith. On the other hand, he says, "He that believeth not is condemned already, because he has not believed in the name of the only-begotten son of God"; that is, he separated himself from God of his own accord. "For this is the condemnation, that light is come into this world, and men have loved darkness rather than light. For every one who doeth evil hateth the light, and cometh not to the light, lest his deeds should be reproved. But he that doeth truth cometh to the light, that his deeds may be made manifest, that he has wrought them in God" (John 3:18-21).

Translation: A. Roberts and J. Donaldson, Ante-Nicene Fathers, corrected to bring the text into line with that of the Sources Chrétiennes edition, ed. A. Rousseau and L. Doutrelau (Paris: du Cerf, 1969).

Tertullian

(fl. ca. 200)

Most of the traditional elements in the biography of Quintus Septimius Tertullianus having fallen victim to historical doubt — he was the son of a Roman centurion; he was born in the middle of the second century; he was a lawyer; he later became a priest — we are left with little hard biographical detail. What remains is what is evident from his writing. A resident of Carthage, a married man, he was a master of rhetorical style and intellectual debate, who, when his church was touched by a movement of charismatic rigorism — "the new prophecy" he called it, but it is known to us as Montanism — took sides with it against the predominant mood of his church, and became increasingly alienated from what he saw as the compromising and self-protective stance of the catholic majority. Despite this fact, his extensive writings, belonging to a period of less than twenty years between about A.D. 195 and 215, had an enormous effect upon subsequent Latin theology, a tribute to a literary and intellectual force which had no antecedents in the earlier decades of the church. And also to their comprehensive range, for he handled a wide variety of subjects: the doctrines of the Trinity, the incarnation, the resurrection of the dead, the inspiration of the Holy Spirit; the relation of Christians to a hostile and pagan society; Christian ethics, especially sexual ethics; the heresies of Gnosticism and Marcionism. His personality is one of the strongest in the patristic age: dialectically aggressive, mordantly witty, passionately disapproving, rigorous in his demands upon himself and others, loyally credulous of claims to visions and revelatory experiences, yet at the same time fiercely loyal to the orthodox tradition of teaching, profoundly moved by martyrdom.

For his church was a martyr church. It is important to recall as we read the brilliant pyrotechnics of the *Apology*, his first great work (A.D. 197) addressed to the provincial administration of the proconsul in Carthage, that the lives of Tertullian and his fellow Christians were in the balance as the new emperor, Septimius Severus, moved determinedly to crush opposition, real or suspected. Tertullian had made himself master of the apologetic genre. The themes that had become the traditional stuff of second-century apologetic reappear in its pages transformed by his intellectual energy and dialectical brilliance. The contrast between truth and custom, for example, has now become a contrast between truth and law. A sense of the contingency and arbitrariness of law was, paradoxically, more characteristic of the Latin culture, preeminent in jurisprudence, than of the Hellenistic (the famous saying *summum ius, summa iniuria* originates from a law-court speech of Cicero). The Christians' (nonliturgical) prayers for the emperor have become more extensive than before, and within them the shape of a pious emperor begins to emerge, a sketch, one might say, for a future Constantine who will know from where his preeminence comes. Yet the idea of the church as a political society is firmly repudiated by Tertullian, for whom world citizenship meant something more like apolitical noncitizenship.

The other two excerpts come from a decade or so later, just before Tertullian's breach with his fellow Christians over the new prophecy. The *Military Chaplet (De corona militis)* is the pre-Nicene church's fullest and strongest statement of opposition to Christians accepting military office; and for all its rhetorical severity, it betrays all the ambiguities which surround that opposition. By concentrating on the particular issue of whether a Christian should wear the military chaplet on ceremonial occasions, it manages to take for granted the more fundamental case against military service — which, no doubt, from the point of view of the average civilian Christian in Tertullian's church was perfectly reasonable, for there is no reason to think him idiosyncratic on this point. Yet what *was* the case? Was it to do with the impossibility of shedding blood, even in the service of the magistrates whom God had authorized to bear the sword? At the very moment that Tertullian seems about to tell us, he turns aside. We never actually *hear* the case Tertullian's church might have made in answer to the post-Nicene view that a Christian may shed blood in the moderate exercise of lawful authority. The truth is, the association of civil society and its institutions with idolatry was so much the fundamental reality for the pre-Nicene church, that it swallowed up all other reasons.

Tertullian's long polemic work *Against Marcion*, however, curiously prepares the way for later arguments that will be mounted to support the legitimacy of war. The second-century heretic Marcion, like the Gnostics in some respects but without their characteristic speculative and cosmological interests, held, in anticipation of some modern history of religion, that the God of the Old Testament and the God of the New Testament were two different gods, one, the Creator, a god of law and judgment, the other, the Redeemer, a god of grace and goodness. Tertullian's argument is of profound importance for the understanding of law that will prevail in the Western Church, and for rescuing the Gospel portrait of Christ as a teacher of God's law from the solvent effects of an ultra-Paulinism which made the antithesis of law and grace primary. The morality of the gospel is to be understood as a motivational deepening and fulfillment of the legal requirements, not as an abrogation of them. The legal structure of the Old Testament law, including the *lex talionis*, was to be understood as a judicial restraint on sin to prepare the way for an internalized morality of redemption. In Augustine's *Against Faustus* (see below, pp. 76-77), the same argument will include the Old Testament wars.

24

Further Reading: T. D. Barnes, *Tertullian: A Historical and Literary Study* (Oxford: Clarendon Press, 1971, 1985); E. F. Osborne, *Tertullian, First Theologian of the West* (Cambridge: Cambridge University Press, 1997); C. Rambaux, *Tertullien face aux morales des trois premières siècles* (Paris: Les Belles Lettres, 1979); D. Rankin, *Tertullian and the Church* (Cambridge: Cambridge University Press, 1995).

From *Apology*

4. Truth, which is ours, meets all the charges; and yet, in the last resort, the authority of the laws is cited against her — to the effect, either that, after the laws have spoken, there is (they say) no re-opening the matter, or that necessity of obedience, though you regret it, takes precedence of truth; in view of all which I will meet you, as guardians of the laws, on the legal issue first. To begin, then: when you harshly cut the case short by saying, "Your existence is illegal"; when you lay it down without any more humane reconsideration, your dictum means mere force, an unjust tyranny from the citadel — if you say a thing is not lawful simply because that is your will, and not because it *ought* not to be lawful. If, because a thing *ought* not to be lawful, you therefore wish it not to be lawful, all will agree that what is ill done ought not to be lawful — a principle which involves a presumption that what is a right thing to do is lawful. If I find that to be good which your law has forbidden, does not that presumption imply that the law cannot forbid me to do it, since it would only rightly forbid it if it were bad? If your law has made a mistake, well, I think, it was the creation of man; it did not come down from heaven.

Do you wonder that a man may have made a mistake in framing a law, or returned to sense in disallowing his law? Is it not the fact that the laws of Lycurgus himself were altered by the Spartans and that this caused their author such grief that he withdrew and condemned himself to starve to death? Yes, and you yourselves, as experiment every day lightens the darkness of antiquity, do *you* not lop and fell all that old and squalid jungle of laws with the new axes of imperial rescripts and edicts? Why, those absurd Papian laws which require people to have children at an earlier age than the Julian laws require them to be married — did not the valiant Emperor Severus clear them out but yesterday for all their old age and authority? Yes, and the laws had it of old that the debtor should on being sentenced be cut up by the creditors; yet by common agreement that cruelty was erased, and for the punishment of death there was substituted a mark of disgrace; the confiscation of his goods that was applied meant a preference for the blush spread rather than the blood shed.

How many of your laws lie forgotten, still to be reformed? What recommends a law is not the number of its years nor the dignity of its makers, but its equity and nothing else. So when laws are recognized to be unjust, they are deservedly condemned, even if they do condemn. But why do we say "unjust"? I will go further, and, if they punish a name, I will say "silly." If it is deeds they punish, why in our case do they punish deeds on the score of the name alone, while in the case of others they must have them proved not from a name but from an act committed? I am incestuous, say they; why do they not inquire into it? If it be murder of babies, why do they not torture the fact from me? I commit something against a god or a Caesar, why, when I am able to clear my character, am I not heard? No law forbids the investigation of the act of which it forbids the commission. The judge does not justly avenge, unless he knows that the unlawful act was committed; nor does the citizen faithfully obey the law, if he does not know what sort of act the law avenges. A law does not owe to itself alone a sure sense of its own justice; it owes it to those from whom it expects obedience. Contrariwise, a law is suspect, which is unwilling to be examined — yes, and bad, if without such examination it tyrannizes. [. . .]

30. For we, on behalf of the safety of the emperors, invoke the eternal God, the true God, the living God, whom the emperors themselves prefer to have propitious to them beyond all other gods. They know who has given them the empire; they know, as men, who has given them life; they feel that he is God alone, in whose power and no other's they are, second to whom they stand, after whom they come first, before all gods and above all gods. Why not? seeing that they are above all men, and men at any rate live and so are better than dead things. They reflect how far the strength of their empire avails, and thus they understand God; against him they cannot avail, so they know it is through him that they do avail. Let the emperor, as a last test, make war on heaven, carry heaven captive in his triumph, set a guard on heaven, lay taxes on heaven. He cannot. So he is great, because he is less than heaven. He himself belongs to him whose is heaven and all creation. Thence comes the emperor, whence came the man before he was emperor; thence his power, whence his spirit. Looking up to heaven the Christians — with hands outspread, because innocent, with head bare because we do not blush, yes! and without one to give the form of words, for we pray from the heart — we are ever making intercession for all the emperors. We pray for them long life, a secure rule, a safe home, brave armies, a faithful senate, an honest people, a quiet world — and everything for which a man and a Caesar can pray. All this I cannot ask of any other but only of him from whom I know I shall receive it, since he it is who alone gives and I am one to whom the answer to prayer is due, his servant, who alone worships him, who for his teaching am slain, who offer to him that rich and better sacrifice which he himself commanded — I mean prayer, proceeding from flesh pure, soul innocent, spirit holy. [. . .]

38. Unless I am mistaken, the reason for prohibiting associations clearly lay in forethought for public order — to save the state (civitas) from being torn into parties, a thing very likely to disturb election assemblies, public gatherings, local senates, meetings, even the public games, with the clashing and rivalry of partisans, especially since men had begun to reckon on their violence as a source of revenue, offering it for sale at a price. We, however, whom all the flames of glory and dignity leave cold, have no need to combine; nothing is more foreign to us than the state (res publica). One state we know, of which all are citizens — the universe.

Translation: T. R. Glover, Loeb Classical Library (London: Heinemann; Cambridge, Mass.: Harvard University Press, 1931). Used with permission.

From *The Military Chaplet*

11. To come now to the real question, that of the military chaplet, I think we must first ask whether military service in and of itself is compatible with Christianity. For when the thing is vitiated from the start, what sense can there be in working through the endless circumstantial questions: Can we believe we may take a human pledge (*sacramentum*) on top of a divine one? May one who owns Christ as master answer to another master, renouncing father and mother and nearest relations, whom the law bids us honor and, after God, love, to whom the Gospel, too, accords comparable honor, giving precedence to Christ alone? Shall a Christian be free to walk around in a sword, when the Lord has said that whoever takes the sword shall perish by the sword? Shall a son of peace, who would not even go to law, be embroiled in battle? Shall he administer chains and imprisonment and torture and punishment, though he will not even take vengeance for wrongs done himself? Shall he stand on watch for others than Christ — or even, on a Sunday, *instead of* Christ? Shall he mount guard over the temples he foreswore, and even take his meals there, notwithstanding the apostle's ruling? (Imagine him — protecting by night the demons he was exorcising during the day, leaning for rest on the spear which pierced Christ's side!) Shall he carry a banner in rivalry to Christ's? Shall he ask the emperor for a watchword, having received one from God? Shall he be disturbed in death's sleep by the bugler's blast, while he waits to be roused by the angel's? Shall he be consigned, as by camp custom, to the flames, when the flame of sacrifice was forbidden him, the flame of eternal punishment by Christ forgiven him? You can see at a glance how many further offenses are attributable to the one decisive step of assuming military duties. The line is crossed in transferring one's name from the camp of light to the camp of darkness.

Of course, if faith comes later, when one is already a soldier, that is another matter. This was the case with those whom John admitted to baptism, and with those centurions of outstanding faith, the one whom Christ commended and the other whom Peter instructed. In such cases, however, once faith is born and sealed in baptism, either one must leave the service at once, as many have done; or one must practice constant equivocation, also untenable in civilian life, to avoid committing some act against God; or one must suffer for God in the end, which is just what the faith of a civilian can lead to. For it is not as though military service is an excuse for one's crimes or an insurance against martyrdom. For the Christian the Gospel is everywhere one and the same: Jesus, who will deny every one who denies him, and acknowledge every one who acknowledges him; who will save every life that is lost for him, and will cause every life to be lost that is gained in denying his name. With him every faithful civilian is a soldier, every faithful soldier a civilian.

When it comes to taking a stand for the faith, there is no room for the plea of necessity. You can be under no necessity to sin if you have made up your mind that the one necessity is not to sin. True, one may be driven by necessity to offer sacrifice or deny Christ outright under threat of torture or punishment. Yet our teaching makes no concessions even to that necessity, since there is a greater necessity than avoiding suffering and discharging duties, which is to shun denial and accomplish

27

one's martyrdom. That line of pleading undermines the whole content of our pledge, even giving a loose rein to willful sins — for the will, too, can present itself as a kind of necessity, driven by its own compulsion. So I would like to make this point first, before coming to more detailed arguments about chaplets as official dress, in which the plea of necessity is continually cropping up: it is precisely to avoid occasions of sin that we should keep clear of official responsibilities; or else, accepting martyrdom, we should break with our responsibilities for ever.

Translation: Editors, from Corpus Christianorum, Series Latina, vol. 2.

From *Against Marcion,* Book 4

16. "But," he says, "to you I say who hear" (proving that this is a longstanding command of the Creator, "Speak in the ears of them that hear" [2 Esdr. 15:1]) — "Love your enemies, and bless them that hate you, and pray for them that speak evil of you" (Luke 6:27f.). All this the Creator has enclosed in one sentence by Isaiah (66:5 Septuagint), "Say to them that hate you, 'Ye are our brethren.'" For if we have to address as brethren those who are our enemies, who hate us and curse us and speak evil of us, evidently he who gave instructions for them to be reckoned as brethren is the one who has given the command to bless those that hate us and pray for those who speak evil of us. Admittedly Christ teaches a new degree of forbearance, when he puts restraint on that retaliation for injury which the Creator permitted by demanding an eye for an eye and a tooth for a tooth: for he on the contrary orders us rather to offer the other cheek, and in addition to the coat to let go of the cloak also. Evidently Christ will have added this as supplementary, yet in agreement with the Creator's rules. So we need an immediate decision on this question, whether the rule of forbearance is contained in the Creator's teaching. When by Zechariah he gives the instruction, "Let not any one of you remember his brother's malice," that includes his neighbour. For again he says, "Let not any one of you think over his neighbour's malice" (Zech. 7:10, 8:17). He who has charged them to forget the injury has even more than given them charge to bear with it. But again when he says, "Vengeance is mine and I will avenge" (Deut. 32:35f. but quoted as in Rom. 12:19, Heb. 10:30), he inculcates forbearance, as that which stands in expectation of vengeance. So then, in so far as it is quite incredible that the demand of tooth for tooth and eye for eye in return for an injury should proceed from the same one who forbids not only retaliation, not only vengeance, but even the remembrance and recollection of injury, to that extent it becomes clear to us in what sense he decreed an eye for an eye and a tooth for a tooth — not so as to permit a second injury of retaliation, seeing he had forbidden this by prohibiting vengeance, but so as to set restraint upon the first. This he had forbidden by the interposition of retaliation, so that every man, having regard to that permission for a second injury, might abstain from committing the first. For he is aware that violence is more readily restrained by the immediate application of retaliation than by the promise of future revenge. Both of these had to be provided for, to meet human nature and men's faith, so that the man who believed God might expect God to exact vengeance, while the man who was deficient in faith should have respect for the laws of retaliation. This was the intention of that law, but it was in difficulties through lack of understanding, until Christ, as Lord both of the sabbath and of the law and of all his Father's ordinances, both revealed its purpose and made it capable of comprehension when he commanded the offering even of the other cheek: for by so doing he put an end to those reprisals for injury which the law had intended to check by retaliation, reprisals which beyond doubt the prophecy had manifestly brought under restraint when it forbade the remembrance of injury and referred vengeance back to God. Consequently, whatever addition Christ made, he caused no destruction of the Creator's rules: for the command he gave was not in opposition but in furtherance of them. So then if I look for his actual reason for enjoining forbearance, forbearance so full and complete, it can only be convincing if it appertains to that Creator who promises vengeance and presents himself as judge. Otherwise if such a burden of forbearance, in not only not striking back but even of presenting the other cheek, in not only not returning insults but even of kindly speaking, in not only not holding on to one's coat but even of letting go of one's cloak also, is imposed upon me by one who is not going to be my defender, in vain does he enjoin forbearance: for he sets before me no reward for following his injunction, I mean, no fruit of my endurance: and this is the revenge which he ought to have left in my discretion if he himself does not provide it, or else, if he was not leaving it to me, he ought to provide it for me: because it is in the interest of good conduct, that injury should be avenged. For it is by fear of vengeance that all iniquity is kept in check. But for that, if indiscriminate liberty is accorded, iniquity will get the mastery, so as to pluck out both eyes and knock out all the teeth, because it is convinced of impunity.

Translation: Ernest Evans (Oxford: Clarendon Press, 1972). Used with permission.

if you don't have faith in God, the law keeps you in check w/ fear of retaliation

1. the law checks ~~retaliation~~ injury to others w/ the idea of retaliation

2. prophecy restrains retaliation by deferring vengeance to God

3. Christ adds "turn the other cheek", complete forebearance, b/c he is our defense

Tertullian

29

Clement of Alexandria

(ob. ca. 215)

Founder of the Christian catechetical school in Alexandria, Clement, who flourished at the turn of the third century, contemporary with Tertullian in Carthage, is an unusual figure among the intellectual leaders of the patristic church. A layman, philosopher, and litterateur, his concern was the cultivation of an intellectually serious Christianity that could justify its claims to be a "wisdom" in apologetic engagement with the various strands of classical philosophy. His philosophical credentials certainly do not rest in tight and rigorously ordered argument. His style is rambling and discursive, full of quotation in which classical authors jostle with the Bible, and can often seem frankly ill focused. His enthusiasm for making classical sources interact with Christian theology can border on the preposterous, as, perhaps, in the passage below where Herodotus, Xenophon, an oracle, and three tragedians are brought in to show that the Greeks had read the narrative of Exodus about the journey through the wilderness. Yet he must not be underestimated as a pioneer of serious Christian thought. He communicates, however unsystematically, a coherent and consistent conception, dependent on the blend of Platonic metaphysics and Stoic ethics current in his day, and deeply engaged in the reading and exposition of Scripture.

For the most part Clement's reflections on practical questions would be classed as ethics rather than politics; yet this excerpt from his major work, the *Strōmateis* (Miscellanies), illustrates a point of entry into political reflection that was to be of great importance for the Eastern Christian tradition: the relation between *nomos* (law) and *logos* (word — as we have translated it, though the reader should not forget that for the Greeks "word" is "reason") and especially the divine *Logos*, the Word of God who was incarnate in Jesus Christ. The presentation of the Word as law is a demonstration of Christ's "kingship" *(basileia)*. What Clement's account provides, then, is an overarching theory of authority, including both intellectual and political authority, which derives it from the sovereignty of divine rationality. This approach has a natural sympathy for Plato's political doctrines, with their understanding of justice as an analogical disposition: within the individual, a disposition of the parts of the soul; within the city, a disposition of the corresponding elements of society; in both cases to be ruled by reason. This is the archetypal conception of "idealist" political theory. Proceeding on the assumption, shared among many Christian apologists of this period, that Plato borrowed from Moses, Clement is free to make the fullest use of Plato (of whom he knew a great deal more than the customary compulsory reference to philosopher-kings) without compromising his polemical distance on pagan culture. But he organizes his Platonic material in a way more reminiscent, perhaps, of Aristotle: politics, with its various subdivisions, is treated as a science, and organized into an ambitious and complex scheme that maps out all the sciences and their specialities under the broad headings of natural, physical, and theoretical science.

There is a major difference of orientation between Plato's political thought and Clement's use of it. Where Plato's political agenda is always implicitly constructive, Clement is concerned to speak of philosophical kingship as something already present, because God has undertaken it and manifested it in his Son. (It would be a mistake to overlook the central place accorded to Saint Paul — however deaf Clement seems to the apostle's antithesis between law and gospel — and especially the weight given to the text Philippians 2:10f.: "At the name of Jesus. . . .") The discussion of human kingship is for him a critical, rather than a constructive, discussion. In distinguishing four types of kingship, which follow the standard Platonic analysis of the three parts of the soul — the reason, the "active part" *(thumos* or *thumoeides),* and the passions — Clement shows how political order as we experience it in history falls short of the sovereign rule of the divine Word. The two lower forms, the autonomous rule of the active part and the rule of the passions, are clearly perversions. The second highest (that of the active part guided by reason) is political order as we normally experience it. But can human rule (apart from that of Moses himself) aspire to share the highest form, the rule of reason unaided by force? Could there be a philosophically governed society apart from the kingdom of heaven? This, perhaps, is one of the most important recurrent questions in Christian political thought; and Clement will not give us a direct answer to it. Yet, because kingship is so wide-ranging a notion, any Christian "gnostic" who masters his own passions and acquires the wisdom that is the central focus of Clement's program, is already "ruling" in precisely that way, over however limited a sphere. For if one side of the idealist approach is that society is the individual writ large, the other side is that the individual is society writ small, and every true philosopher is a king.

In making a conjunction between biblical religion and the Hellenistic understanding of kingship, Clement is following another source, closer to him in time and place than Plato. Philo of Alexandria, the great first-century Jewish thinker, wrote commentaries on themes in the Pentateuch from within a very similar "Middle Platonist" philosophical framework. His *Life of Moses (V.M.)* is the general inspiration for this passage, and a particular source for the claim that Moses was "king, legislator, priest and prophet" (*V.M.* 2.1.3). It shares with Clement a fondness for the saying (originally Plato's, but a commonplace in Hellenistic Platonism) that the king was a "living law" (*nomos empsychos, V.M.* 1.28.162; 2.1.4). That phrase has a long

31

future ahead of it, and will often make Christian thinkers uncomfortable because of what it seems to imply about the relation of monarchs to the law. For Clement, however, the phrase is innocuous, since it applies only to the ideal king, that is, to Moses and to Christ whom he foreshadows, and who already speaks through him.

Does the religious turn given to political philosophy deprive it of all real political meaning? That would be too hasty a judgment. Clement's ethics actually contain a great deal about society. Within this excerpt the emphasis on the socially educative function of law is dominant; when Paul calls the law a *paidagōgos* (Gal. 3:24), Clement understands that quite seriously to mean "a teacher." (It was a favorite self-designation; one of his major writings was called *Paidagōgos*.) Elsewhere we find Clement insistent in his concern for the handling of property and wealth. (Besides many discussions in his major works, a minor work was devoted to this topic, *Who Is the Rich Man That Is Saved?*) He did not deny the principle of private ownership as Chrysostom would do later (though the difference on this point sometimes appears more rhetorical than substantial), for how could one give away one's wealth if one never owned it in the first place? But Clement insists upon the criterion of *use* as opposed to *enjoyment,* and of *common use* as opposed to *private use.* Sufficiency and simplicity are the appropriate measures for personal consumption; and the best goods to acquire are the cheapest, most easily got hold of, and quickest got rid of. An economical efficiency which maximizes care for others is how the kingship of the divine Word expresses itself in the management of earthly goods.

Further Reading: H. Chadwick, *Early Christian Thought and the Classical Tradition: Studies in Justin, Clement, and Origen* (Oxford: Clarendon Press, 1966); J. Daniélou, *Gospel Message and Hellenistic Culture* (English translation) (London and Philadelphia: Darton, Longman and Todd, 1973); S. R. C. Lilla, *Clement of Alexandria: A Study in Christian Platonism and Gnosticism* (Oxford: Clarendon Press, 1971).

From *Strōmateis,* Book 1

24. Moses, we may say then, is a prophet, legislator, controller and commander, politician and philosopher. In what sense he was a *prophet* we shall explain shortly when we come to treat of prophecy. "Control" *(taktikon)* is an aspect of "command" *(stratēgikon),* and command is an aspect of kingship. "Legislation," again, is one of the functions of kingship, as is also judicial activity.

We can divide kingship as follows: — One kind is divine; that is the rule of God and of his holy Son, by whom the earthly and external goods are supplied as well as perfect happiness. "Seek what is great," as Scripture says, "and little things will be added to you" (probably a reminiscence of Matt. 6:33). The second kind, inferior to the purely rational *(logikon)* divine administration, brings to the task of kingly rule only the active part of the soul *(thumoeides);* which is how Heracles ruled the Argives and Alexander the Macedonians. The third kind aims at only one thing, to conquer and overthrow. Turning conquest to good or bad effect is not within the purview of this

[margin note: 4 kinds of kingship]

[margin note: Control & command]

kind of kingship; the Persians in their campaign against Greece are an example. For the active part of the soul may engender mere competition, the struggle for power for its own sake; alternatively, when the soul directs its active part to noble ends, it may engender constructive action. The fourth kind of kingship, and the worst, is that which operates at the promptings of passion; Sardanapalus is an example, and there are others who have made their aim complete gratification of the passions.

The instrument of kingship — i.e., of the first two kinds, the one achieved by virtue the other by force — is *control*. How control is exercised varies with what exercises it and on what material. In controlling weapons and battle animals, our inanimate or animate instruments, the controlling agent is the soul, exercising *skill*. In controlling the soul's passions which are mastered by virtue, the controlling agent is *the reason;* this seals the soul with continence and sanctified restraint and with knowledge of the truth, leading it on to godly religion as its goal. In the same way the controlling agent over mature and virtuous human beings is *reflection*. We call it "wisdom" when it has to do with the divine, "politics" when it has to do with the human; and the overall category is "kingship." He is a king, then, who governs by laws and knows how to rule voluntary agents. Such is the Lord, who draws to himself all who believe on him and through him. For God has delivered and subjected all things to Christ our king, "that at the name of Jesus every knee should bow, of things in heaven and things in earth and things under the earth, and every tongue confess that Jesus Christ is Lord, to the glory of God the Father" (Phil. 2:10f.). Now, *command* involves three ideas: caution, risk taking, and the union of the two. And each of these comprises three kinds of activity: words, deeds, and the two combined, which will achieve their result either by persuasion or by offensive or retaliatory force; these, in turn, may be acts of justice, or they may be true or false acts of speech, or any of these in combination.

The Greeks were indebted to Moses for instruction about all these, and about the use to which each might be put. For illustration I shall cite one or two instances of command. Moses, on leading the people out, suspecting that the Egyptians would pursue them, left the short and direct route and turned to the desert, marching mostly by night. This was a different kind of disposition, by which the Hebrews were kept in the great wilderness for a long time, to be schooled in self-control and endurance, and taught to believe in the existence of one God alone. The strategy of Moses shows the necessity of discerning what will be of use before danger approaches, and so to encounter it prepared. It turned out precisely as he anticipated, for the Egyptians pursued with horse-drawn forces, but were quickly destroyed by the sea breaking over them and submerging them together with their horses and chariots, so that not a remnant was left. After this the pillar of fire which accompanied them, going before them as a guide, conducted the Hebrews by night through a pathless region, training them as they went by toils and wanderings to courage and endurance, so that having experienced what seemed formidable difficulties, the benefits of the land to which the path through the desert was leading them might be apparent. Moreover, such was the quality of his command that he routed and slew the occupants of the land, falling on the enemy from a desert and rugged march. Taking the enemy territory was a task for experience and skilled command.

Miltiades, the Athenian general who conquered the Persians at the battle of Marathon, took note of this and modeled his tactics on it. Leading his Athenian forces on a night march across pathless terrain, he outwitted the barbarian watch. For Hippias, the Athenian defector, had conducted the barbarian forces into Attica, and, knowing the country, seized and held the points of vantage. The task, then, was to elude him, which Miltiades, by shrewd use of the night march through the desert, did successfully, attacked the Persians under Datis and with his followers got the better of the contest. Thrasyboulos, too, at the head of the exiles from Phyla, wishing to escape observation, followed a pillar that guided him across the desert — a pillar of fire in a moonless, storm-swept sky, which appeared to lead them on until it brought them safely to Mounychia and left them where the altar of Phosphoros stands now. Such instances should give credence with the Greeks to our own narratives; it was possible for the omnipotent God to send a fiery pillar before the Hebrews by night and guide them in their way. The oracle which says "A pillar to the Thebans is joy-inspiring Dionysos" is also dependent upon Jewish history. So is the line of Euripides's *Antiopē:* "Within the herdsmen's chambers the pillar of the Evoaean god is decked with ivy."

The pillar represents the imagelessness of God. When illuminated, it also represents the stability and permanence of God and his unchangeable and inexpressible light. Before the art of statuary was perfected, the ancients erected columns and worshiped them as symbols of the deity. The author of *Phorōnis* writes: "Callithoē, keybearer of the Olympian queen, Hera of Argos, who first adorned the queen's tall column with fillets and fringes." Again, the author of *Eurōpia* [Eumelos] says that the Delphian statue of Apollo was a pillar: "That to the god we may hang tithes and first fruits from the sacred pillars and the high column." But Apollo, a name symbolically interpreted as "absence of many," means the one God. Well, then, the fire in the form of a pillar going through the desert is a symbol of the all-penetrating holy light, that reaches from earth back up to heaven through the cross, the light by which intellectual sight is bestowed on us.

25. Plato, the philosopher, whose understanding of legislation was influenced by that of Moses, criticized the political institutions of Minos and Lykourgos because they thought no further than developing military virtues. His ideal of a serious polity was one which expressed a unified principle and followed it consistently. Philosophy, he tells us, should be determined, serious, and intellectually focused. With the verdict of heaven in view, it should apply, without vacillation, like judgments to like cases. (Is this not another way of saying what we find in the law, that we should acknowledge one God and do justice?)

Politics (*politikon*) he divides into two spheres: law and politics proper. Paradoxically he calls the creator the Supreme Politician (in the book of that name, *Politikos*); and those who acknowledge him, living active and just lives with an element of contemplation, he also calls "political." The sphere of politics proper (i.e., parallel to law) he divides into two, the universal and the private; the virtue of the one is "scope of vision," and the virtue of the other, "good order" (otherwise, "orderliness," "harmony," "good sense"). On the one hand, rulers accommodate themselves to their subjects; on the other, subjects defer to their rulers, something emphasized by Moses's way of handling things. Again, when he says that law is based on birth, politics on association and consent, it is another of Plato's debts. In the *Epinomis* he associates with laws the philosopher who knows about the planetary influence on generation; but he introduces another philosopher, Timaios, an astronomer and student of the courses, attractions, and conjunctions of the stars, to be associated with the political realm.

The goal of all politics, I believe, as of all law-governed life, is contemplation. A well-conducted polity is a necessity of life; but philosophy is the best and highest aim. Anyone with intelligence will apply his powers to knowledge, will direct his course of life to worthwhile undertakings (and reject the opposite kind), and will pursue the studies which contribute to the truth. Law is not merely what is customarily observed, any more than vision is what is customarily seen. Nor is it judgment of any kind, for there is bad judgment as well as good. It is sound judgment; but that means true judgment, which is to say, judgment which finds out the reality and holds to it. "I AM has sent me," Moses says (Exod. 3:14). Some have called law "the right word, which enjoins what is to be done and forbids what is not to be done" (Chrysippus); and that definition, certainly, is in keeping with sound judgment.

26. The law, then, was rightly said to have been "given by Moses" as a rule of right and wrong. And in the strictest sense we could call the law given by God through Moses a "sacred ordinance," since it constitutes our way of approach to the divine. Paul says: "The law was instituted because of transgressions, till the offspring should come to whom the promise had been made" (Gal. 3:19). Then he adds, to explain this idea: "Before faith came, we were confined under the law" — by fear, that is, because of our sins — "kept under restraint until faith should be revealed. So that the law was our tutor *(paidagōgos)* until Christ came, that we might be justified by faith" (3:23f.). The legislator is one who appoints what is appropriate to each part of the soul and its functions; Moses, in a pregnant phrase, was a "living law," directed by the good word. His political arrangements, at any rate, were good, a fine "social education of mankind." For one thing, he handled the science of judgment, which is the science of the corrective response to offenses required by justice. Closely akin to this is penal science, which deals with the measure of punishments — just punishment is the correction of the soul. Moses, one might say, propounds a complete system for training those who are in the way to becoming responsible, and for attracting others like them, all of which belongs to "command." And the wisdom most useful and appropriate to those who have been attracted by the word is "legislation." Its distinguishing feature, highly characteristic of kingly rule, is getting hold of things and making use of them. The philosophers, at any rate, say that only a wise man can be king, legislator, commander, just and holy, loved by God. If we discover that all these things are true of Moses, as the Scriptures make it clear they were, then we can confidently declare Moses to be truly wise.

We describe the shepherd's art as "providing for livestock" — "the good shepherd lays down his life for his sheep." Similarly we may describe the art of legislation, which cultivates human virtue and fans the good in man as far as may be into flame, as "presiding and caring for the human flock." The Lord's "flock," within the terms of the metaphor, is the flock of mankind; he himself is the Good Shepherd and Law-

[margin note: law? → king God, Jesus]

giver of the one flock, that is, those sheep who hear his voice. He is the one Carer, who seeks what is lost and finds it by law and word. For the law is spiritual, leading to happiness, since it is given by the Holy Spirit. And he is the true Lawgiver, who not only promises the best, but understands it. His law, embodying this understanding, is the saving precept; or, better, law is the *precept of knowledge,* for "God's Word is power and wisdom." And he, through whom the law was given, is at the same time the exponent of laws, the first exponent of divine precepts who expounds "the bosom of the Father," that is, the Only-begotten Son.

It follows that those who obey the law have some knowledge of him, and cannot be thought disobedient or ignorant of truth; it is those who disobey the law and prove unwilling to undertake its works who, more than any, should be judged ignorant of truth. What, then, is the disobedience with which we charge the Greeks? It is that they are wholly unwilling to obey the truth which tells them that the law was given through Moses, even while they respect things in Greek authors which show Moses' influence. They tell us that Minos went to Zeus's cave and received the laws from Zeus over nine years; that Lykourgos was taught legislation on his frequent visits to Apollo at Delphi (Plato and Aristotle and Ephoros record this); that Zaleukos the Lokrian received the laws from Athene (Chamaileōn of Herakleia in his *Drunkenness,* and Aristotle in *The Lokrian Constitution).* But attributing the credit of Greek jurisprudence to a divine source, as Moses' prophecy did, they ungratefully refuse to admit the same source for the true original [i.e., Moses' legislation], from which the tales they tell about themselves derive.

[margin note: greeks deny moses]

27. Let no one, then, run down the law, as if it were ignoble because it imposed penalties. If one who expels disease from the body is thought a benefactor, should not one who keeps wickedness from the soul be counted more so, as the soul is more precious than the body? Again, we undergo surgery and cautery and drugs for the sake of physical health; and one who administers the treatment we call "savior" and "healer." No one would suggest the healer's art was badly motivated by malice or hostility to the patient; amputation is undertaken, as the principles of the art prescribe, to prevent the infection of healthy flesh. Similarly, then, for the soul's sake, should we not undergo exile, fine, or imprisonment, if only to attain righteousness instead of unrighteousness? The law in its care for the obedient educates them in piety, prescribing what is to be done while restraining them from misdeeds by imposing penalties on such offenses as can be contained. But when it sees anyone running to extremes of wickedness and to all appearances beyond cure, then in its care that others should not be corrupted, it takes the course most conducive to health and puts him to death, like an amputation performed upon the body politic. "When we are judged by the Lord," the apostle says, "we are chastened so that we may not be condemned along with the world" (1 Cor. 11:32). And earlier the prophet had said: "The Lord has chastened me sorely, but he has not given me over to death" (Ps. 118:18). "It was to teach you righteousness that he chastened you," it says elsewhere, "and tested you and let you hunger and thirst in the wilderness, that all his commandments and judgments might be known to your heart which I command you this day, and that you might know in your heart that as a man disciplines his son, the Lord our God disciplines you" (Deut. 8:2f., 5, 11 [loosely adapted]). And again, to

[margin note: discipline?]

36

prove that example makes us sensible, he says: "The clever man seeing the wicked punished, is himself forcefully instructed," since "the beginning of wisdom is the fear of the Lord" (Prov. 22:3f. Septuagint).

The greatest and most perfect good that one can do is to lead someone back from wicked courses to a virtuous and constructive life; which is precisely what the law does. But even when one has fallen victim to incurable vice, the prey of wickedness and greed, the law acts beneficially in putting one to death. For the benefits the law can do may be seen in both forms: those whom it can, it changes from unrighteous into righteous, those, that is, who will heed it; those whom it cannot, it delivers from a life enslaved to evils. Its promise to those who choose to live sensibly and righteously is immortality. "The knowledge of the law is characteristic of good reflection" (Prov. 9:10 Septuagint). And again: "Evil men do not understand the law; but those who seek the Lord have understanding in all that is good" (Prov. 28:5 Septuagint).

The providence that orders all things cannot but be sovereign and good; and it lies within the power both of sovereignty and of goodness to afford salvation. Sovereign, it operates through punishment to impose good sense; graciously disposed, it shows us mercy and kindness. It is up to us not to be "children of disobedience," but "to turn from darkness to life." Lending an ear to wisdom, one may be, at first, the lawful slave of God; then a dutiful servant in awe of his sovereign authority; finally, as one progresses to be numbered among his children, when "love covers a multitude of sins" [i.e., in baptism], one may receive the consummation of the blessed hope through growth in love, and be inscribed in the select company of children dear to God, singing the hymn, "May the Lord be my God!" St. Paul is unambiguous about the blessings of the law under the dispensation of Jewish circumcision, writing: "If you call yourself a Jew and rely upon the law and boast of your relation to God and know his will and approve what is excellent, because you are instructed in the law, and if you are sure that you are a guide to the blind, a light to those who are in darkness, a corrector of the foolish, a teacher of children, having in the law the embodiment of knowledge and truth . . ." (Rom. 2:17-20). There is no doubt, you see, that the law is capable of all this, even if there are those whose manner of life does not conform to the law they make a show of living by. "Happy is the man who finds wisdom, and the man who gets understanding. . . . From her mouth" — Wisdom's, that is — "comes righteousness; law and mercy are on her tongue" (Prov. 3:13, 16a Septuagint, not in English Bible). The law and the Gospel are together the working of the one Lord, who is the "power and wisdom of God." The terror which the law begets is merciful in its effects and leads to salvation. "Let not mercy and faithfulness and truth forsake you; bind them about your neck" (Prov. 3:3 Septuagint). The prophets and Paul are at one in reproaching the people who did not understand the law: "'In their paths are ruin and misery, and the way of peace they do not know.' 'There is no fear of God before their eyes'" (Rom. 3:16-18, quoting Isa. 59:7f., Ps. 36:1). "Claiming to be wise, they became fools" (Rom. 1:22). "We know that the law is good, if any one uses it lawfully . . ." although, the apostle tells us, there are those who "desire to be teachers of the law, without understanding either what they are saying or the things about which they make assertions." But "the aim of the

37

commandment is love that issues from a pure heart and a good conscience and sincere faith" (1 Tim. 1:8, 7, 5).

28. Moses' philosophy, then, has four broad divisions: history, legislation (in the proper sense), priestly ordinances, and theology. The first two belong to the study of ethics, the third to physical science [i.e., the study of how natural objects are to be handled]. The fourth and crowning science is that "vision" which Plato says is the essential character of the Great Mysteries, and which Aristotle calls "metaphysics."

Translation: Editors, from Griechischen Christlichen Schriftstellen (Leipzig: Hinrichs, 1906).

Origen

(ca. 185–ca. 254)

Origen's standing as one of the major thinkers of the patristic church is firmly established in contemporary judgments, despite the intense controversy which surrounded aspects of his doctrinal legacy from the fourth century onward. This resulted in a very damaged manuscript tradition, so that many works are known to us only in fragments, in alternative versions, or in carefully vetted Latin translations. But Origen accomplished major innovations on three fronts: in establishing a critical text of the Bible (the *Hexapla*); in laying the foundations for later mystical theology, by his instructions on prayer, ascetic discipline, contemplation, and martyrdom; and in the first major attempt to systematize Christian doctrine philosophically, *On First Principles (Peri Archōn)*. He also wrote extensive exegetical works, and the crown of the apologetic tradition of the pre-Nicene church, the long *Against Celsus (Contra Celsum)*, written in response to an anti-Christian writer of half a century before. At this time Origen was over sixty years old, having been the leading intellectual figure in the Eastern Church for a generation. According to Eusebius of Caesarea's *Ecclesiastical History*, he established his reputation as a layman in his native Alexandria, where he was in charge of Clement's catechetical school; subsequently he left after a dispute with the bishop and settled in Caesarea, where he was ordained a priest. He died in the wake of the persecutions of 250, which broke his health.

The Platonic cast of his teaching stands in contrast to Irenaeus's supposedly more "Western" sense of historical drama. Cosmology is the character he gives to Christian doctrine, the graduated orders of being, spiritual and material, forming the frame against which God's grace and the soul's redemption are thought out. He offers little reflection on society or its structures. The question of civic responsibility emerges only in this short exchange from the closing pages of *Against Celsus*, which follows broadly conventional lines.

Celsus sees Christians as an antipolitical force, denying the prerogatives of government and promoting the disintegration of the Roman Empire. Origen replies that they believe the emperor to have been raised to his responsibilities by God, and that Christian faith is a force for moral and social cohesion. He explains the pacifist practice of Christians in a way characteristic of the elusive logic of the pre-Nicene church on the subject: without saying that fighting in war is simply wrong, he claims for the church a priestly role that entitles it to exemption, set apart from bloodshed to offer the sacrifice of prayer. Here we may detect an echo of the idea we encountered in the *Epistle to Diognetus*, of the church as the soul of society. An even stronger echo is heard in the argument that Christians cannot take office because they belong to a distinct "country" within each city. Since we first met that idea, however, the church has come to be more sharply defined organizationally, governed by those whose moral qualifications and faith equip them for the task of leadership.

The debate takes a distinctive turn when Celsus suggests that a converted Roman Empire would be a prey to invading forces, and mischievously suggests that it might be overwhelmed time and again, as often as the church managed to convert it! Origen is irritated, but what alternative does he have? He offers an expansive political eschatology, in which the conversion of the empire accompanies its extension to the whole world with a single language and the dawning of a universal rule of reason. The natural affinity between a philosophical stress on the rule of Logos and the idea of world empire was already apparent to non-Christian Hellenistic thinkers. Plutarch, for example, wrote in the first century, of Alexander of Macedon, that he "desired to bring all on earth into subjection to one Logos and one government (*politeia*), revealing that all men are one people (*dēmos*)." Had he not died, "one law (*nomos*) would govern all mankind and they would look to one source of justice as they look to one common source of light" (*Moralia* 330). On this account Rome's destiny was to complete the striving of history toward universal empire, a tendency which Christians could readily affirm conditionally upon the conversion of its peoples. (Here is the opposite to the treatment of empire as the Antichrist which we find in Irenaeus.) That this must presuppose, in Origen's opinion, a deliverance from the body does not make it any less a hope for world history. It is easy to see how such an outlook, buoyed up by a grand missionary confidence, was ready, when the moment came, to embrace Constantine in such terms as Eusebius of Caesarea used.

Further Reading: C. Andresen, *Logos und Nomos* (Berlin: Walter de Gruyter, 1955); H. Chadwick, *Early Christian Thought and the Classical Tradition: A Study in Justin, Clement, and Origen* (Oxford: Clarendon Press, 1966); H. Crouzel, *Origen* (English translation) (Edinburgh: T. & T. Clark, 1989); J. Daniélou, *Origen* (English translation) (New York: Sheed & Ward, 1955); P. Nautin, *Origène, sa vie et son oeuvre* (Paris: Éditions Beauchesne, 1977); J. Trigg, *Origen: The Bible and Philosophy in the Third Century Church* (Atlanta: John Knox, 1983).

From *Against Celsus,* Book 8   Origen

68. Then Celsus next says that "we ought not to disbelieve the ancient man who long ago declared,

> Let there be one king, him to whom the son of crafty Kronos gave the power."

And he continues: "For, if you overthrow this doctrine, it is probable that the emperor will punish you. If everyone were to do the same as you, there would be nothing to prevent him from being abandoned, alone and deserted, while earthly things would come into the power of the most lawless and savage barbarians, and nothing more would be heard among men either of your worship or of the true wisdom."

"Let there be one ruler, one king," I agree, yet not "him to whom the son of crafty Kronos gave the power," but the one whose power was given by him who "appoints and changes kings and from time to time raises up a useful man on the earth" (Dan. 2:21, Sir. 10:4). Kings are not appointed by the son of Kronos who drove his father from his rule, and, as the Greek myths say, cast him down to Tartarus, not even if anyone were to interpret the story allegorically; but by God who governs all things and knows what he is doing in the matter of the appointment of kings.

Accordingly we do "overthrow the doctrine" of the words "to whom the son of crafty Kronos gave the power," because we are convinced that a God or the Father of a God would have no crafty or crooked designs. But we do not overthrow the doctrine of providence, and of the things which are produced by it, either as those which are primarily intended or as those which are the product of certain consequences. Moreover, it is not "probable" that an emperor would punish us for asserting that the son of crafty Kronos did not give him the power to reign, but that it was he who "changes and appoints kings." Let "all men do just the same as I." Let them deny the Homeric doctrine, while keeping the doctrine of the divine right of the king and observing the command "Honour the king" (1 Pet. 2:17). Yet on such a basis as this neither would the emperor be left alone, nor would he be deserted, nor would earthly things be in the power of the most lawless and savage barbarians. For if, as Celsus has it, every one were to do the same as I, obviously the barbarians would also be converted to the word of God and would be most law-abiding and mild. And all other worship would be done away and only that of the Christians would prevail. One day it will be the only one to prevail, since the word is continually gaining possession of more souls.

69. Then as if Celsus did not understand himself, his remarks are inconsistent with his words "For if every one were to do the same as you," when he says: "You will surely not say that if the Romans were convinced by you and were to neglect their customary honours to both gods and men and were to call upon your Most High, or whatever name you prefer, he would come down and fight on their side, and they would have no need for any other defence. In earlier times also the same God made these promises and some far greater than these, so you say, to those who pay regard to him. But see how much help he has been to both them and you. Instead of being masters of the whole world, they have been left no land or home of any kind. While in your case, if anyone does still wander about in secret, yet he is sought out and condemned to death."

He raises the question of what would happen if the Romans were to become convinced by the doctrine of the Christians, and neglect the honours paid to the supposed gods and the old customs observed among men, and were to worship the Most High. Let him hear, then, what our opinion is on these matters. We believe that if two of us agree on earth as touching any thing, if they pray for it, it shall be given to them by the heavenly Father of the righteous (Matt. 18:19). For God rejoices when the rational beings agree and turns away when they disagree. What must we think if it is not only, as now, just a few who agree but all the Roman Empire? For they will be praying to the Logos who "in earlier times" said to the Hebrews when they were being pursued by the Egyptians: "The Lord will fight for you, and you shall keep silence" (Exod. 14:14). And if they pray with complete agreement they will be able to subdue many more pursuing enemies than those that were destroyed by the prayer of Moses when he cried to God and by the prayer of his companions. If God's promises to those who keep the law have not come to pass, this is not because God tells lies, but because the promises are made on condition that the law is kept and that men live in accordance with it. If the Jews, who received the promises upon these conditions, have neither land nor home left, the reason for that is to be found in all their transgressions of the law and especially in their crime against Jesus.

70. However, if as Celsus suggests, all the Romans were convinced and prayed, they would be superior to their enemies, or would not even fight wars at all, since they would be protected by divine power which is reported to have preserved five entire cities for the sake of fifty righteous men. For the men of God are the salt of the world, preserving the permanence of things on earth, and earthly things hold together so long as the salt does not turn bad. For if the salt has lost its savour, it is of no further use either for the earth or for the dunghill, but is cast out and trodden under foot by men (Matt. 5:13). Let him who has ears to hear, understand what this means. We, moreover, are only persecuted when God allows the tempter and gives him authority to persecute us. And when it is not God's will that we should suffer this, even in the midst of the world that hated us by a miracle we live at peace, and are encouraged by him who said: "Be of good cheer, I have overcome the world" (John 16:33). And he really has overcome the world, so that the world prevails only in so far as he who overcame it wills, for he received from his Father the victory over the world. And by his victory we are encouraged.

If it is his will that we should again wrestle and strive for our religion, let antagonists come forward. To them we will say: "I can do all things by Christ Jesus our Lord who strengthens me" (Phil. 4:13). For, though sparrows are sold, as the Bible has it, at two for a farthing, "one does not fall into a snare against the will of the Father in heaven." And to such an extent has divine providence included everything that not even the hairs of our head have escaped being numbered by him (Matt. 10:29-30).

71. Then again, as usual with Celsus, he gets muddled, and in his next remarks says things which none of us has written. This is what he says: "It is quite intolerable of you to say that if those who now reign over us were persuaded by you and were taken

42

debunked Celsus

prisoner, you would persuade those who reign after them, and then others, if they too are taken prisoner. There will be a ruler who, being a sensible man and foreseeing what is happening, will utterly destroy you all before you destroy him first." Reason does not require us to speak about these remarks; for none of us says of those who now reign that if they are persuaded and taken prisoner, we will then persuade their successors, and if they are taken prisoner we will in turn persuade those who follow them. And how did he come to remark that if the last in the succession are persuaded by us and are taken prisoner because they fail to defend themselves against their enemies, there will be a ruler who, being a sensible man and foreseeing what is happening, will utterly destroy us? In these words he seems to be putting together nonsensical statements and to have shrieked out stuff he invented out of his own head.

72. After this he utters a sort of wish: "Would that it were possible to unite under one law the inhabitants of Asia, Europe, and Libya, both Greeks and barbarians even at the furthest limits." As if he thought this impossible he continues that "he who thinks this knows nothing." If I must say something about this subject which needs much study and argument, I will say a little in order to make it clear that his remark about uniting every rational being under one law is not only possible but even true. The Stoics say that when the element which, as they think, is stronger than the others becomes dominant, the conflagration will take place and all things change into fire. But we believe that at some time the Logos will have overcome the entire rational nature, and will have remodelled every soul to his own perfection, when each individual simply by the exercise of his freedom will choose what the Logos wills and will be in that state which he has chosen. And we hold that just as it is unlikely that some of the consequences of physical diseases and wounds would be too hard for any medical art, so also it is unlikely in the case of souls that any of the consequences of evil would be incapable of being cured by the rational and supreme God. For since the Logos and the healing power within him are more powerful than any evils in the soul, he applies this power to each individual according to God's will, and the end of the treatment is the abolition of evil. But to teach whether or not the consequence is that it can under no circumstances be allowed any further existence, is not relevant to the present discussion.

The prophecies say much in obscure terms about the total abolition of evils and the correction of every soul. But it is enough now to quote the passage from Zephaniah which reads as follows: "Get ready and wake up early; all their small grapes are destroyed. On this account wait patiently for me, saith the Lord, in the day when I rise up for a witness; for my decision is to assemble the peoples to receive the kings, to pour out upon them all the anger of my wrath. For in the fire of my zeal all the earth shall be consumed. Then I will turn to the peoples a language for its generation, that they may all call upon the name of the Lord and serve him under one yoke. From the furthest rivers of Ethiopia they shall offer sacrifices to me, in that day thou shalt not be ashamed of all thy habits which thou hast impiously practised against me. Then I will take away from thee the contempt of thy pride, and thou shalt no longer continue to boast upon my holy mountain. And I will leave in you a people meek and humble, and the remnants of Israel shall fear the name of the Lord, and they shall not do wickedness nor say foolish things, and a crafty tongue shall not be found in their mouth. Wherefore they themselves shall feed and lie down and there shall be none to make them afraid" (3:7-13). Anyone who has the ability to enter into the meaning of the Scripture and has understood all these statements may show the explanation of the prophecy, and, in particular, may study what is the meaning of the words that when all the earth is consumed there will be turned to the people "a language for its generation," which corresponds to the state of affairs before the Confusion. And let him understand what is the meaning of the words "That all men may call upon the name of the Lord and may serve him under one yoke," so that "the contempt of their pride" is taken away and there is no more wickedness nor foolish words nor crafty tongue.

I have thought it right to quote this passage, with an ordinary interpretation and without a careful discussion, because of the remark of Celsus who thinks that it is impossible for the inhabitants of Asia, Europe, and Libya, both Greeks and barbarians, to be agreed. And it is probably true that such a condition is impossible for those who are still in the body; but it is certainly not impossible after they have been delivered from it.

73. Then Celsus next exhorts us to "help the emperor with all our power, and cooperate with him in what is right, and fight for him, and be fellow-soldiers if he presses for this, and fellow-generals with him." We may reply to this that at appropriate times we render to the emperors divine help, if I may say so, by taking up even the whole armour of God. And this we do in obedience to the apostolic utterance which says: "I exhort you, therefore, first to make prayers, supplications, intercessions, and thanksgivings for all men, for emperors, and all that are in authority" (1 Tim. 2:1-2). Indeed, the more pious a man is, the more effective he is in helping the emperors — more so than the soldiers who go out into the lines and kill all the enemy troops that they can.

We would also say this to those who are alien to our faith and ask us to fight for the community and to kill men: that it is also your opinion that the priests of certain images and wardens of the temples of the gods, as you think them to be, should keep their right hand undefiled for the sake of the sacrifices, that they may offer the customary sacrifices to those who you say are gods with hands unstained by blood and pure from murders. And in fact when war comes you do not enlist the priests. If, then, this is reasonable, how much more reasonable is it that, while others fight, Christians also should be fighting as priests and worshippers of God, keeping their right hands pure and by their prayers to God striving for those who fight in a righteous cause and for the emperor who reigns righteously, in order that everything which is opposed and hostile to those who act righteously may be destroyed? Moreover, we who by our prayers destroy all daemons which stir up wars, violate oaths, and disturb the peace, are of more help to the emperors than those who seem to be doing the fighting. We who offer prayers with righteousness, together with ascetic practices and exercises which teach us to despise pleasures and not to be led by them, are cooperating in the tasks of the community. Even more do we fight on behalf of the emperor. And though we do not become fellow-soldiers with him, even if he presses for this, yet we are fighting for him and composing a special army of piety through our intercessions to God.

74. If Celsus wishes us to be generals for our country, let him realize that we do this; but we do not do so with a view to being seen by men and to being proud about it. Our prayers are made in secret in the mind itself and are sent up as from priests on behalf of the people in our country. Christians do more good to their countries than the rest of mankind, since they educate the citizens and teach them to be devoted to God, the guardian of their city; and they take those who have lived good lives in the most insignificant cities up to a divine and heavenly city. To them it could be said: You were faithful in a very insignificant city; come also to the great city where "God stands in the congregation of the gods and judges between gods in the midst," and numbers you even with them, if you no longer "die like a man" and do not "fall like one of the princes" (Ps. 82:1, 7).

75. Celsus exhorts us also to "accept public office in our country if it is necessary to do this for the sake of the preservation of the laws and of piety." But we know of the existence in each city of another sort of country, created by the Logos of God. And we call upon those who are competent to take office, who are sound in doctrine and life, to rule over the churches. We do not accept those who love power. But we put pressure on those who on account of their great humility are reluctant hastily to take upon themselves the common responsibility of the church of God. And those who rule us well are those who have had to be forced to take office, being constrained by the great King who, we are convinced, is the Son of God, the divine Logos. Even if it is power over God's country (I mean the Church) which is exercised by those who "hold office" well in the Church, we say that their rule is in accordance with God's prior authority, and they do not thereby "defile" the appointed "laws."

If Christians do avoid these responsibilities, it is not with the motive of shirking the public services of life. But they keep themselves for a more divine and necessary service in the church of God for the sake of the salvation of men. Here it is both necessary and right for them to be leaders and to be concerned about all men, both those who are within the Church, that they may live better every day, and those who appear to be outside it, that they may become familiar with the sacred words and acts of worship; and that, offering a true worship to God in this way and instructing as many as possible, they may become absorbed in the word of God and the divine law, and so be united to the supreme God through the Son of God, the Logos, Wisdom, Truth, Righteousness, who unites to Him every one who has been persuaded to live according to God's will in all things.

Translation: Henry Chadwick (Cambridge University Press, 1979). Used with permission.

Lactantius

(saec. 3-4)

L. Caecilius Firmianus Lactantius, who wrote in the latter half of the third century and lived through Diocletian's persecution to see the Constantinian revolution, stands in an interesting relation to those great events, having risen under Diocletian to a prominent teaching position in Nicomedia, from which he was driven out into obscurity. Surviving the next decades with difficulty, he rose again to a distinguished educational appointment at the Western court of Constantine. His major work, the *Divine Institutes,* written in the earlier part of his life, can be seen as the crown of the apologetic tradition, now gone onto the offensive: an extensive and detailed demolition of the classical culture, with Christianity presented as the only solution to the intolerable internal moral and social contradictions. So popular did its confident rhetoric and schoolroom learning become that they demanded a new edition after the church's change in fortunes, with dedications added to Constantine himself.

Almost equally striking are the classicism of Lactantius and the high moral pretensions of his account of Christianity. The history that carries weight with him is that of the classical poets and philosophers, not of the Old Testament. The presence on his pages of Saturn and Jupiter where we might expect Adam and Eve — and treated literally as historical figures, human beings later misconstrued as gods — is disconcerting. His Christianity, on the other hand, has made no moral concessions to classical civilization. It sets itself in the sharpest contrast to a demoralized culture, as the justice of the Golden Age returned to earth, without violence, coercion, or inequality. (Not without private property, however; though this wholly serves the charitable concern of sharing goods.) The emphasis on revelation *in history* is a central element in Lactantius's apologetic thrust. Like all the apologists, he sees the revelation in Christ as inaugurating a new civilization which is spearheaded within the church.

His special interest to us is as the first Christian thinker to subject the idea of *justice* to serious analysis. The English reader has to be aware that the Latin *iustitia*, like the Greek *dikaiosunē* has a wider range of meaning than our word "justice." At one end it refers to the equitable organization of the community, the justice of fair distribution and reward. It refers, also, to the temper of mind which produces such a social order, the "fairness" of individuals who participate in society. And thirdly, it serves as a general term for the totality of individual goodness, for that "righteousness" which makes a person acceptable with God. In Lactantius it is clear that the first, and to a lesser extent the second, of these ideas is the prevailing concern. Classical civilization had a serious problem with justice in society. Skepticism, as represented by the figure of Carneades in the famous debate in Cicero's *Republic,* doubts that justice refers to anything other than the interest of the stronger party and the folly of the weaker: it is, as we would say, an ideology designed to shore up given distributions of power. But without it society lacks a rationale and a coherence. For Lactantius this is proof that classical civilization, though possessed of an idea of justice, did not know in what it consisted. Above all, it did not know that justice required true religion (a theme in which he anticipates Augustine's *City of God*), and that all relations between human beings are corrupted when the proper relation with God is lacking.

The analysis of justice formally follows the lines of Christ's two commands, love of God and neighbor. But the content is distinctive. The second of the two commands is presented as *equality* and *humanity,* and the interaction of these two ideas is important to observe. Starting from the classical definition of justice as equality, he attempts to demonstrate that this notion can only be rendered concretely in terms of community. The abstract notion of equality as equal access to goods without defining structures of ownership, he dismisses by way of a broad polemic against a famously controversial passage of Plato's *Republic.* The connection he insists on between "owning" property and "owning" intimate relations is not, perhaps, the equivocation that it may appear at first glance. (A very similar move occurs in the opening paragraphs of Leo XIII's *Rerum Novarum*!) To his Christian eyes the meaning of property is given precisely by the structures of community relations in which material goods are communicated. Correspondingly, the meaning of equality is given precisely by the activity of mutual assistance and sharing goods which binds the members of a community. In this way "equality" turns easily into "humanity," which means, for Lactantius, the practical recognition of the fundamental sociality and interdependence of human existence. Everything has to do with sharing in community. In the light of the controversies of the modern period, his rejection of ancient versions of the "social contract" acquires a particular fascination. It is an idea, he tells us, that springs from pagan polygenist myth. Only Christianity, with its knowledge of the origin of all human beings in *one* ancestor, can lay secure foundations for the sociality of human existence. In the end, then, Adam turns out to be important.

Further Reading: J. Fontaine and M. Perrin, eds., *Lactance et son temps* (Paris: Éditions Beauchesne, 1978); P. Monat, *Lactance et la Bible* (Paris: Études Augustiniennes, 1982); M. Perrin, *L'homme antique et chrétien* (Paris: Éditions Beauchesne, 1981).

From *Divine Institutes,* Book 3

21. Let us see, however, what he learned from Socrates, who, after rejecting the whole sphere of natural philosophy, turned to the investigation of virtue and duty, and so, doubtless, instructed his hearers in the principles of justice. Under Socrates' tuition it did not escape Plato's notice that the force of justice consists in equality, since all are born in an equal condition. "Therefore," he says, "they must have nothing private or their own; but that they may be equal, as the method of justice requires, they must possess all things in common" (Plato, *Republic* 416d). This can perhaps be supported so long as it appears to refer only to money — though actually I could show in many ways that even so it is both impossible and unjust. Let us, at any rate, admit the possibility: everyone shall be wise enough to despise money! To what conclusion did his principle of the community of goods lead him? "Marriages, too," he says, "ought to be in common" (457c); so that the males may crowd together like dogs to the same female, and whoever turns out strongest may have her; or, if they are patient like philosophers, they may take their turn, as in a brothel! An impressive idea of equality! But where is the virtue of chastity? Or of conjugal fidelity? Yet if you abolish these, justice, taken as a whole, is subverted. (The same philosopher said that "states would be prosperous if either philosophers were kings or kings philosophers" [473d]. But would you entrust a kingdom to this champion of equal justice, who would take this man's property and give it to that man, and who would prostitute the chastity of women, going further than any king, any tyrant indeed, has ever gone?)

What reason did he offer, then, for this degrading policy? "The state will be harmonious and bound together with bonds of mutual love, if everyone is everyone else's husband, father, wife, child ..." (463c). What sort of a turmoil in human relationships is that! How can we preserve the loyalties of love *(caritas)* when our emotional attachments *(quod ametur)* are so insecure? How will a man ever care for *(diliget)* a woman, or a woman for a man, if they have not lived together and created an inseparable bond of loyalty by devoted attention and sustained faithfulness to one another? That kind of virtue has no place in such a scene of promiscuous satisfactions. Then, if everyone were everyone else's *children,* how could one love any children as one's own, when one could not know with certainty that any children *were* one's own? How could one honor someone *as* one's father, when one could frame no idea of one's origins? The corollary of looking on the stranger as a parent must be to look on the parent as a stranger. Not to mention that, though a wife can be held in common, a child cannot, since he can only have one biological father in fact. In this one instance the community of goods cannot obtain; nature itself has entered a protest. A final consideration: it was solely for the sake of concord that he proposed community of wives, yet there is no fiercer source of discord than the jealous rivalry of many men for one woman. If Plato could not find that out a priori, he had plenty of empirical evidence, both from dumb animals, whose competition on this account can rise to a pitch of fury, and from mankind, whose most impassioned conflicts have always arisen from this cause.

22. The conclusion is that "community of goods" means no more than adultery and indulgence, the very things that virtue is especially needed to eradicate root and branch. Plato did not find the concord that he looked for, because he did not see *what is equality?* [handwritten]

AMEN! [handwritten, left margin]

where it springs from. For justice is not expressed in outward conditions, not even in the conditions of the human body, but operates wholly upon the human mind. So making men equal is not a matter of abolishing marriage and private property, but of abolishing ambition, pride, and self-importance, of making those self-confident wielders of power realize that they are the equals of beggars. Take from the rich their insolence and injustice, and the difference between the rich and poor will cease to matter, since they will think of themselves as equal; and that is something only religion can achieve. Plato, then, thought he had found justice, when in fact he was undermining it, since community cannot be a matter of destructible possessions but of minds. If justice is the mother of all virtues, when you remove individual virtues you subvert justice. But think of the virtues Plato did away with: frugality first of all, which is exercised on one's own property; abstinence, which is exercised on other people's; self-control and chastity, the greatest virtues in either sex; self-respect, shame, and sexual modesty, which disappear when what is thought base and depraved comes to be seen as normal and acceptable. See how his program for universal virtue destroyed virtue universally! For the ownership of property is the material of virtue and vice, while community of goods is merely a license for vice. Men who keep a crowd of mistresses deserve to be called nothing but self-indulgent narcissists; women who have a queue of lovers are not adulteresses (for marriage is not in question) but prostitutes and whores.

From Book 5

5. Now I must present the discussion of justice which was promised.

Justice is either the *supreme virtue,* or it is the *source of virtue.* It is treated not only in philosophical discussion, but in poetry, which long predated philosophy in the strict sense as a source of wisdom. The poets clearly understood that justice was absent from human affairs. The explanation they devised was that it took offense at the viciousness of human life and withdrew to the heavens. To instruct us, then, in what living justly means — for poets customarily adopt indirect means of pedagogy — they give illustrations from the age of Saturn, the Golden Age, and describe the condition of human society while justice still had dealings on the earth. This should not be taken for poetic fiction, but as simple truth.

During the reign of Saturn the cults of the gods were not established, for his descendants had not yet been elevated to the status of divinity. It was God that was worshiped. Correspondingly, there were no disputes, no hostilities or wars.

> Nor yet had madd'ning fever bared the sword,
> Nor strife divided kin of the one blood.
>
> (Germanicus Caesar, after Aratus)

Nor of different blood, for that matter, since there were as yet no swords to bare! With justice present and prevailing, why would anyone worry about defending himself, there being no one to fear? or about harming someone else, there being nothing to gain? It is a feature reminiscent of our own religion that

> they lived content upon a modest plot
>
> (Cicero, after Aratus)

nor was it

> ... lawful even to divide the plain with landmarks and boundaries:
> All produce went to a common pool,
>
> (Virgil, *Georgics* 1.126)

the reason being that God gave the earth to all in common, that they might live a common life, without insatiable and obsessive greed laying claim to everything, and that no one should go short of what nature produced for all. We should not understand this line, though, to mean that there was no private property; it is a poetic way of saying that people were too generous to enclose the crops that nature gave them or to store them away to keep for themselves, rather than allow the poor a share in what their labor had produced.

> The rivers ran with milk and nectar,
>
> (Ovid, *Metamorphoses* 1.111)

which is not surprising, since the storehouses of the just were laid generously open to all comers, with no greed to block the stream of God's blessings and spread hunger and thirst everywhere. On the contrary, the haves bestowed their goods so plentifully upon the have-nots that all were equally well off.

> But after Saturn's banishment to Latium,
> an exile deprived of his kingdom, fleeing the power of Jove,
>
> (Virgil, *Aeneid* 8.320)

the people, whether induced by fear of the new king or degenerating of their own momentum, began to look on their king as a god; and since he, being more or less a parricide, served as an example to others to violate their sacred obligations,

> the virgin Justice straightway fled the earth,
>
> (Germanicus)

though not, as Cicero maintains, "to settle in Jove's heavenly realm." How could she settle or make her home in the realm of one who had usurped his father's kingdom, driven him out by war and expelled him from the known world?

> Jove put the wicked poison in the black serpent's tooth,
> Jove told the wolf to ravin.
>
> (Virgil, *Georgics* 1.129)

That is to say, he introduced hatred, suspicion, and deceit to mankind, who thus became as poisonous as serpents and as ravenous as wolves. That indeed is the conduct of those who persecute the just and God's faithful, and confer on their judges the power of tormenting the innocent. Perhaps we can attribute something of this kind to Jove in his eradication and extirpation of justice, which gained him the reputation of making the serpents dangerous and the wolves savage. Then followed

> an age . . .
> of mad aggression and the lust for gain,
>
> (Virgil, Aeneid 8.327)

which is hardly surprising. For with the disappearance of the worship of God, the knowledge of good and evil was lost to them. So the common life died out among men, and the bonds of human society were torn apart. So began conflict and treachery and pride in the shedding of human blood.

6. Acquisitiveness was the source of all these evils, acquisitiveness which sprang out of the contempt of true majesty. It was not simply that those who had plenty of something would not share it with others, but they actually got hold of others' goods and turned them all to their private profit; so that, whereas previously property had been a matter of one person contributing his labor for the use of all, now it was the concentration of goods in a few wealthy households. First they began to accumulate and monopolize the necessaries of life and keep them inaccessible, to bring others under their power as slaves. The gifts of heaven they made out to be their own — not for humanity's sake, for they had none of that, but to sweep up every means that could serve their acquisitive greed. They had laws passed which represented as "justice" the grossest inequities and injustices, to protect their rapacious practice and purpose against mass resistance. So they laid claim to authority to sanction what force, resources, and sheer unscrupulousness had achieved for them. And since there was actually no trace of justice in them — which would have been expressed in humanity, equality, and compassion — they began to find satisfaction in arrogant and inegalitarian self-promotion, which put them on a higher rank than others, with retinues of staff, armed guards, and distinguishing dress. This is the origin of honors, marks of nobility, official status: relying on the terror of the axe and sword, they were to rule a cowed and craven people with the "right of masters." Such was the condition of human life introduced by the king who, after driving his father out by war, established not a kingdom but an unprincipled tyranny by force of arms, destroying that "golden age" of justice and forcing men to be harsh and conscienceless — all by the singular means of diverting worship from God to himself, a demand enforced by terror of his pitiless power. [. . .]

7. But God, the all-pardoning father, sent an emissary as the last days approached to restore the primitive age and its long-banished justice, sparing the human race the turmoil of its egregious and unyielding errors. The form of that Golden Age returned. Justice, which is simply the devout and single-minded worship of the one God, was restored to earth — but entrusted to a few. [. . .]

14. But first I would like to propose a concise and economical definition of

justice, which will explain why the philosophers knew next to nothing of it, and so were incapable of defending what they hardly knew about. Although justice as an inclusive term encompasses all the other virtues, there are two virtues in particular which are inseparably bound up with it: *piety* and *equality*. Faith, temperance, honesty, incorruptibility, integrity, and so on can be found, whether by nature or education, in people who have no idea of justice. And this has always been the case. For the ancient Romans, who used to boast of their justice, were in fact boasting of virtues which derive from justice and may be sustained independently of it. But piety and equality are, as it were, its veins. Justice as a whole comprises these two constituents; but its originating impulse is to be found in the first of them, while in the second are all its energy and method.

But as we said above [in bk. 2, not included here], *piety*, which Hermes Trismegistus defined perfectly correctly, is simply "the knowledge of God." But if this is so, and knowing God is essentially worshiping him, no one who does not maintain reverence for God knows anything of justice. How could one know the thing itself without knowing what gave rise to it? Plato had much to say about one God, who he said created the world, but nothing about religion. He had dreamed of God, not known him. If he, or anyone else, had really wished to make a full defense of justice, he should have begun by refuting the polytheistic cults, which are the antithesis of piety. It was for trying to do this that Socrates was thrown in jail, a premonitory indication of what would happen to those who undertook the defense of true justice and the service of one God.

The second constituent part of justice is *equality*. I mean this not in the sense of "equity," the virtue of giving judgment, praiseworthy as this is in a just man, but in the sense of treating others as one's equals — what Cicero calls "equability." For God who gives being and life to men wished us all to be equal, that is, alike. He laid down the same terms of life for us all, making us capable of wisdom and promising us immortality, excluding nobody from the benefits of heaven. And so, as he gives us all a place in the daylight, waters the earth for us all, provides nourishment and precious, relaxing sleep, no less does he endow us all with moral equality. With him there is no slave or master. Since we all have the same father, so we are all alike his freeborn children. No one is poor in his eyes, except for want of justice; no one is rich except in moral qualities. No one is prominent, except in being incorruptible; no one is famous, except for works of mercy performed on a grand scale; no one has the title "Excellency" without accomplishing all the stages of moral growth. And that is why neither the Romans nor the Greeks could sustain justice, since they had so many levels of disparity in their societies, separating poorest from richest, powerless from powerful, the obscure from the most elevated dignities of royal state. Where all are not alike, there is no equality; and inequality is enough to rule out justice, the very point of which is to afford like treatment to those who have entered this life on like terms.

15. With these two sources of justice compromised, virtue and truth as a whole are subverted, and justice itself removes to heaven. That is why that true good was not identified by the philosophers, who were unaware both of its source and its effect — something disclosed to none but our community.

God desires equality

But someone will say, "Don't you have poor and rich, slaves and masters, in your community? Aren't there distinctions between one member and another?" Not at all! That is precisely the reason that we address one another as "Brother," since we believe we are one another's equals. Since human worth is measured in spiritual not in physical terms, we ignore our various physical situations; slaves are not slaves to us, but we treat them and address them as brothers in the spirit, fellow slaves in devotion to God. Wealth, too, is no ground of distinction, except insofar as it provides the opportunity for preeminence in good works. To be rich is not a matter of *having*, but of *using* riches for the tasks of justice; and those whom one would suppose poor are actually no less rich, in that they are short of nothing and hanker after nothing. Yet although our attitude of humility makes us one another's equals, free and slave, rich and poor, there are, in fact, distinctions which God makes, distinctions in virtue, that is: the juster, the higher. For if justice means behaving as the equal of inferiors, then, although it is *equality* that one excels in, yet by conducting oneself not merely as the equal of one's inferiors but as their subordinate, one will attain a far *higher* rank of dignity in God's sight. It is true, the brevity and fragility of everything in this transitory life makes men compete with one another for status — a most repellent, most self-assertive style of behavior, and entirely irrelevant to mature rationality, since this whole realm of earthly preoccupation runs counter to the values of heaven. For as "the wisdom of men is utter folly with God" (1 Cor. 3:19) and "folly," as I have argued, is the highest wisdom, so it follows that one who achieves earthly prominence is insignificant and contemptible to God. Leaving aside all the highly regarded goods of this world that militate against virtue and weaken our mental resources, what security is there in rank, wealth, or power, when God can bring even kings lower than the low? And so among the commands which God took care to give us, he included this in particular: "Whoever exalts himself will be humbled, and whoever humbles himself will be exalted" (Matt. 23:12). We learn from this wholesome prescription that whoever adopts a modest, unassuming style in the sight of men, stands out with distinction in the sight of God. There is truth in the quotation from Euripides, which goes:

What are taken here for evils may be known in heaven for goods.

(fragment 1100)

From Book 6

10. I have described our duties to God, and will now describe what is due to man — though the due we render man is in fact rendered to God, since man is the image of God. Nevertheless, we distinguish fellowship with God, as the primary duty of justice, from fellowship with man as the secondary duty, and use different names: for the primary duty, *religion*, for the secondary, *mercy* or *humanity*. The reason that humanity is the proper concern of justice and the service of God, is that it includes the whole principle of life in community. For God, in denying them wisdom, equipped

other animals with better natural defenses against attack and danger; human beings he created naked and vulnerable that he might teach them wisdom instead; and gave them, beside all else, this deep sense of obligation to protect, love, and cherish one another, to proffer and accept assistance against every danger. The chief tie, then, binding human beings to each other is humanity; to violate it is to be held outcast and parricide. If we are all sprung from one man whom God made, we are certainly connected by blood, and so it must count as a hideous crime to hate a human being, even a criminal. That is why God commanded us not to prosecute hostilities but to overcome them, mollifying those who are hostile to us by reminding them of our relationship. Again, if we are all given a life of soul and spirit by one God, what are we but brothers — closer, indeed, as soul brothers than as physical brothers? Lucretius has it right, when he says:

> Sprung from the heavenly seed are we,
> Children of one father.

(The Nature of the Universe 2.991f.)

It is bestial savagery, then, to hurt, despoil, torture, kill, eliminate a human being, contrary to the law of humanity and every religious principle.

For the sake of this familial relationship God teaches us never to do evil, always good. And his own command makes it clear what doing good means: providing help to the oppressed and struggling, food to those who need it. For God, a god of loyalty, willed that we should be a social species of animal; which is why we should always see ourselves in others. We deserve no rescuing from danger if we will not go to the rescue, no assistance if we render none. The philosophers have no guidance to offer on this point, since they were taken in by a false ideal of virtue and, corrupting what they proposed to remedy, removed compassion from the qualities of human nature. To be sure, they concede for the most part that participation in human society must be maintained; yet the austerity of their inhuman ideal of virtue sets them apart from it. Here too, then, we must take issue with the mistaken view that there is no place for sharing things with others.

Of the origin and cause of civil society there is no single philosophical account. One theory conjectures that those who first sprang from the earth, living nomadically in forests and on the plains without social ties of language or law, using shoots and grasses to lie on and the caves and hollows for shelter, were the prey of beasts and of the stronger animal species; until some, made aware of their danger by escaping after a mauling themselves or by seeing their family mauled, sought out other humans to beg for assistance, making their meaning clear by gestures at first and then venturing on the rudiments of speech, so that bit by bit, giving names to particular things, they mastered the art of language. But since the gathered company itself needed protecting from beasts, they began to build stockaded communities, to ensure safety in sleep at night, or to defeat the beasts' raids by barricades without the need to fight them off. To compose such superficialities in the first place is hardly worth the employment of a human talent; but one can only feel embarrassment for those who have unhappily committed their jejune speculations to writing and repetition. They could see that dumb animals have instinctive ideas of combining, herding, escaping danger, watching for threats, constructing coverts and lairs; but human beings, they supposed, could never have learned to fear this, look out for that, do the other, without object lessons to warn them; would never have associated together or discovered the art of speech without being eaten first by beasts! Another theory, dismissing this as it deserves, claims that the ground of association was not the maulings of beasts but humanity itself; they formed groups because human nature abhors isolation and looks for ways of sharing in society. Actually, there is no great difference between them, since the concept of association is the same, whatever different reasons they assign to it. They could both be true, since they are not mutually contradictory. But in fact, neither is true. There never were dispersed originals of the human race in every land, sprung from the earth as though sown from some dragon's teeth, as in poets' tales. There was one man made by God and from that one man the whole world was filled with the human race, just as happened again later, after the flood — which they cannot deny. There never was, then, an original association of this kind. Nor were there ever human beings on the earth who lacked the powers of speech, apart from infancy, as anyone who has a mind can understand.

Suppose, though, for the sake of argument, these jejune old folks' tales are true, and see where they lead on their own terms. If it was for mutual assistance in the face of weakness that the primitive association of men took place, then we ought to offer assistance to any man who needs it. For since protection was the purpose of mankind's entering and binding himself to society, and this covenant has been observed ever since it first arose, it is outrageous to violate it or to fail to respect it. One who opts out of giving help opts out of accepting it, since in refusing aid to another he thinks he needs no other's aid. His life, then, set apart from the body of human society, must be lived like an animal, not a man. If this is impracticable, then we need to maintain the bond of human society in every way, since one man simply cannot live without another. Maintaining society, though, is a matter of community: that is, proffering assistance in order to accept it. If, as the other school maintains, the cause of association is humanity, then human beings must respect each other. If those primitive and wild men did so even before they had mastered the art of speaking, what should we expect of civilized man, connected by language and every kind of exchange, and so accustomed to others' company that he would find isolation intolerable?

Translation: Editors, from Corpus Scriptorum Ecclesiasticorum Latinorum, vol. 19. Quotations from Virgil in the version by C. Day Lewis (Oxford University Press, 1966).

Eusebius of Caesarea

(ca. 260–ca. 340)

That Eusebius's portrait of Constantine was an idealization goes without saying. The literary energies of this first systematic church historian, devoted to recovering and preserving sources and information on the church's first three hundred years, were overtaken first by the great persecution of Diocletian and then by the dizzying reversal of the church's fortunes under Constantine. The historian found himself living out the climax of his own history, and the impact on his imagination (which must have been typical of his generation) was extraordinarily profound. "It is, as it were, an event of yesterday. . . ." The account of Constantine is at the service of another, more existential task: that of bearing witness to the meaning of the era in which he lived, in which the hand of God had been at work breathtakingly. The interesting question is what kind of ideal for the emperor's role this rather representative Christian promoted. We learn a lot about what the generation that survived the persecution hoped for, from what they declared they had found. Constantine himself, of course, was alive to their expectations and went out to meet them in his self-presentation. The "ideology" of the new Christian regime — here, certainly, that rather overused word is in place — is the product of collaboration between theologically driven expectation and politically driven promotion.

The two speeches from which these excerpts come date from the end of Constantine's reign. In 335 the dedication of the Church of the Holy Sepulchre in Jerusalem afforded an occasion for a paean on the events which led up to it. The next year Eusebius delivered a celebratory panegyric in the emperor's presence to celebrate the thirtieth anniversary of his accession. They were both florid exercises in the fashionable style of Greek rhetoric, but nonetheless sincerely meant. They were preserved as an appendix to the author's *Life of Constantine*, undertaken at the emperor's death in 337. The historian, now an old man, had been bishop of Caesarea for nearly as long as the emperor had reigned. The interacting of their lives had had its climax at the Council of Nicaea (325), where Eusebius, under suspicion for sympathies with the heretic Arius, had been allowed to prove his orthodoxy and had signed, not without hesitations, the creed which the emperor had vigorously promoted. Now his last fulsome testimony to what God had done in his days through Constantine was to be, suitably, his last literary task. Together with a speech by Constantine himself, these two speeches were tacked on to the *Life*, apparently in the wrong order, and they came down to us in the manuscripts as one work, often referred to as the *Praise of Constantine*.

The themes running through the speeches are familiar from earlier political theology in the Greek Christian tradition. As in Clement of Alexandria, the concept of "kingdom" (*basileia* — in this translation also rendered "royalty," "sovereignty," and "empire") provides a unifying category for the work of man and God. The Word of God, the second person of the Trinity, mediates the kingship of God to facilitate the exercise of kingship by mankind, the "kingly species"; so that the emperor, ruling first over himself and then over his empire, embodies at once God's kingship, as its "image," and man's. He is at once law-governed (*ennomos*) and absolute (*autokratorikē*). Again, since the unity of God is the presupposition of kingship, monotheism is the presupposition of its true exercise. Into this constellation of ideas Eusebius draws Origen's conception of the providential role of the Roman Empire as a unifying force provided to facilitate the spread of the gospel. But now the moment long awaited has come, and the empire has embraced the monotheism which it presupposes. Yet, despite this theory of the empire, Eusebius is clear that the legitimation of Constantine owed nothing to the institutional succession of the imperial throne, but was given directly by the activity of God's Word. Though Constantine's accession was a fit reward for a godly father, the history of the imperial court as such had been one of bloodshed and polytheism, and Constantine had been brought up in it like Moses in the household of Pharaoh (*Life of Constantine* 1.12). His sons, on the other hand, owe everything to him. Here, then, is a new departure in the government of the world, and a decisive proof of the living power of Christ's resurrection.

And the fate of early Christian pacifism? It has been a popular theme among idealists of our own century that the Constantinian turn marked the "Fall" of the church and the abandonment of its pacifist ideals. The one side of Eusebius's ideal construction, the pre-Nicene church of saints and martyrs, has facilitated the deconstruction of the other side. Yet it is clear that the Christian emphasis on peace actually plays a major role in fashioning this celebration of Constantine's achievements. Among those achievements likely to appeal to a civilian population all too used to being held ransom to the demands of armies, that of teaching soldiers religious and moral disciplines was not the least hopeful. Whether fairly or not, Christian apologetics was able to draw on a mood of revulsion and suspicion which thought of pagan cults in terms of bloody altars, and credited them with the spilling of too much human blood in intercommunal strife. This complex of associations invited the assertion of a determinedly rational religion, which could take great satisfaction in the thought of all those statues melted down and put to useful purposes, while at the same time encouraging a sumptuous style of church-building to celebrate the public triumph of enlightenment. The victories of Constantine, then, are, to hopeful Christian eyes, as much victories *against* war as *in* war. Eusebius is certainly not the last thinker coming from a pacifist tradition to rest gratefully in the promise of a war that will end all wars.

Further Reading: T. D. Barnes, *Constantine and Eusebius* (Cambridge, Mass.: Harvard University Press, 1981); R. M. Grant, *Eusebius as Church Historian* (Oxford: Clarendon Press, 1980); R. MacMullen, *Constantine* (London: Weidenfeld and Nicolson, 1970); D. S. Wallace-Hadrill, *Eusebius of Caesarea* (London: Mowbray, 1960).

From a Speech on the Dedication of the Holy Sepulchre Church

16. Of old the nations of the earth, the entire human race, were variously distributed into provincial, national, and local governments, subject to kingdoms and principalities of many kinds. The consequences of this variety were war and strife, depopulation and captivity, which raged in country and city with unceasing fury. Hence, too, the countless subjects of history, adulteries and rapes of women; hence the woes of Troy and the ancient tragedies so known among all peoples. The origin of these may justly be ascribed to the delusion of polytheistic error. But when that instrument of our redemption, the thrice-holy body of Christ, which proved itself superior to all Satanic fraud and free from evil both in word and deed, was raised, at once for the abolition of ancient evils and in token of his victory over the powers of darkness; the energy of these evil spirits was at once destroyed. The manifold forms of government, the tyrannies and republics, the siege of cities and devastation of countries caused thereby, were now no more, and one God was proclaimed to all mankind. At the same time one universal power, the Roman empire, arose and flourished, while the enduring and implacable hatred of nation against nation was now removed; and as the knowledge of one God and one way of religion and salvation, even the doctrine of Christ, was made known to all mankind; so at the self-same period the entire dominion of the Roman empire being vested in a single sovereign, profound peace reigned throughout the world. And thus by the express appointment of the same God, two roots of blessing, the Roman empire and the doctrine of Christian piety, sprang up together for the benefit of men. For before this time the various countries of the world, as Syria, Asia, Macedonia, Egypt and Arabia, had been severally subject to different rulers. The Jewish people, again, had established their dominion in the land of Palestine. And these nations, in every village, city and district, actuated by some insane spirit, were engaged in incessant and murderous war and conflict. But two mighty powers starting from the same point, the Roman empire which henceforth was swayed by a single sovereign and the Christian religion, subdued and reconciled these contending elements. Our Saviour's mighty power destroyed at once the many governments and the many gods of the powers of darkness, and proclaimed to all men, both rude and civilized, to the extremities of the earth, the sole sovereignty of God himself. Meantime the Roman empire, the causes of multiplied governments being thus removed, effected an easy conquest of those which yet remained, its object being to unite all nations in one harmonious whole, an object in great measure already secured and destined to be still more perfectly attained, even to the final conquest of the ends of the habitable world, by means of the salutary doctrine and through the aid of that divine power which facilitates and smoothes its way.

And surely this must appear a wondrous fact to those who will examine the question in the love of truth and desire not to cavil at these blessings. The falsehood of demon superstition was convicted; the inveterate strife and mutual hatred of the nations was removed; at the same time one God and the knowledge of that God were proclaimed to all; one universal empire prevailed; and the whole human race, subdued by the controlling power of peace and concord, received one another as brethren and responded to the feelings of their common nature. Hence as children of one God and Father, and owning true religion as their common mother, they saluted and welcomed each other with words of peace. Thus the whole world appeared like one well-ordered and united family; each one might journey unhindered as far as and withersoever he pleased; men might securely travel from West to East and from East to West, as to their own native country; in short, the ancient oracles and predictions of the prophets were fulfilled, more numerous than we can at present cite, and those especially which speak as follows concerning the saving Word: "He shall have dominion from sea to sea and from the river to the ends of the earth" (Ps. 72:8). And again: "In his days shall righteousness flourish, and abundance of peace" (Ps. 72:7). "And they shall beat their swords into ploughshares, and their spears into pruninghooks; nation shall not lift up sword against nation, neither shall they learn war any more" (Isa. 2:4). [. . .]

Who else but our Saviour has taught his followers to offer those bloodless and reasonable sacrifices which are performed by prayer and the secret worship of God? Hence is it that throughout the habitable world altars are erected and churches dedicated wherein these spiritual and rational sacrifices are offered as a sacred service by every nation to the one supreme God. Once more, who but he, with invisible and secret power, has suppressed and utterly abolished those bloody sacrifices which were offered with fire and smoke as well as the cruel and senseless immolation of human victims; a fact which is attested by the heathen historians themselves? For it was not till after the publication of the Saviour's divine doctrine, about the time of Hadrian's reign, that the practice of human sacrifice was universally abandoned. Such and so manifest are the proofs of our Saviour's power and energy after death. Who, then, can be found of spirit so obdurate as to withhold his assent to the truth, and refuse to acknowledge his life to be divine? Such deeds as I have described are done by the living, not the dead, and visible acts are to us as evidence of those which we cannot see. It is as it were an event of yesterday that an impious and godless race disturbed and confounded the peace of human society, and possessed mighty power. But these, as soon as life departed, lay prostrate on the earth, worthless as dung, breathless, motionless, bereft of speech, and have left neither fame nor memorial behind.

emperor or God

From a Speech for the Thirtieth Anniversary
of Constantine's Accession

1. Today is the festival of our great emperor *(basileus)*; and we his children rejoice therein, feeling the inspiration of our sacred theme. He who presides over our solemnity is the Great Sovereign *(basileus)* himself; he, I mean, who is truly great; of whom I affirm (nor will the sovereign who hears me be offended, but will rather approve of this ascription of praise to God) that he is above and beyond all created things, the highest, the greatest, the most mighty one; whose throne is the arch of heaven and the earth the footstool of his feet. His being none can worthily comprehend; and the ineffable splendour of the glory which surrounds him repels the gaze of every eye from his divine majesty. His ministers are the heavenly hosts; his armies the supernal powers, who own allegiance to him as their master, lord and king. The countless multitudes of angels, the companies of archangels, the chorus of holy spirits, draw from and reflect his radiance as from the fountains of everlasting light. Yea, every light and specially those divine and incorporeal intelligences whose place is beyond the heavenly sphere, celebrate this august sovereign with lofty and sacred strains of praise. [. . .]

Lastly, he who is in all, before and after all, his only begotten preexistent Word, the great high priest of the mighty God, elder than all time and every age, devoted to his Father's glory, first and alone makes intercession with him for the salvation of mankind. Supreme and pre-eminent ruler of the universe, he shares the glory of his Father's kingdom; for he is that light which, transcendent above the universe, encircles the Father's person, interposing and dividing between the eternal and uncreated essence and all derived existence; that light which, streaming from on high, proceeds from that deity who knows not origin or end, and illumines the supercelestial regions and all that heaven itself contains with the radiance of wisdom bright beyond the splendour of the sun. This is he who holds a supreme dominion over this whole world, who is over and in all things and pervades all things visible and invisible, the Word of God. From whom and by whom our divinely favoured emperor, receiving as it were a transcript of the divine sovereignty, directs in imitation of God himself the administration of this world's affairs. [. . .]

3. Lastly, invested as he is with a semblance *(eikōn)* of heavenly sovereignty *(basileia)*, he directs his gaze above, and frames his earthly government according to the pattern of that divine original, feeling strength in its conformity to the monarchy of God. And this conformity is granted by the universal sovereign to man alone of the creatures of this earth; for he only is the author of sovereign power who decrees that all should be subject to the rule of one. And surely monarchy far transcends every other constitution and form of government; for that democratic equality of power, which is its opposite, may rather be described as anarchy and disorder. Hence there is one God, and not two, or three, or more; for to assert a plurality of gods is plainly to deny the being of God at all. There is one Sovereign, and his sovereign Word and Law is one; not uttered in syllables and words, not written or engraved on tablets and therefore subject to the ravages of time, but the living and self-subsisting divine Word, who administers his Father's kingdom on behalf of all who are after

60

him and subject to his power. His attendants are the heavenly hos
God's angelic ministers, the super-terrestrial armies of unnumbere
those unseen spirits within heaven itself, whose agency is employed
order of this world. Ruler and chief of all these is the sovereign W
gent of the supreme Sovereign. To him the names of Captain and C
Prophet of the Father, Angel of Mighty Counsel, Brightness of the ratner's Light,
Only begotten Son, with a thousand other titles, are ascribed in the oracles of the sacred writers. And the Father, having constituted him the living Word, and Law, and Wisdom, the fullness of all blessing, has presented this best and greatest gift to all who are the subjects of his sovereignty. And he himself, who pervades all things and is everywhere present, unfolding his Father's bounties to all with unsparing hand, has accorded a specimen of his sovereign power even to his rational creatures of this earth, in that he has provided the mind of man, who is formed after his own image, with divine faculties, whence it is capable of other virtues also which flow from the same heavenly source. For he only is wise, who is the only God. He only is essentially good, he only is of mighty power, the parent of justice, the father of reason and wisdom, the fountain of light and life, the dispenser of truth and virtue, in a word, the author of empire *(basileia)* itself and of all dominion *(archē)* and power *(exousia)*.

4. But whence has man this knowledge, and who has ministered these truths to mortal ears? Or whence has a tongue of flesh the power to speak of things so utterly distinct from fleshly or material substance? Who has gazed on the invisible king and beheld these perfections in him? The bodily sense may comprehend elements and their combinations of a nature kindred to its own; but no one yet has boasted to have scanned with corporeal eye that unseen kingdom which governs all things, nor has mortal nature yet discerned the beauty of perfect wisdom. Who has beheld the face of righteousness through the medium of flesh? And whence came the idea of lawful government *(ennomos archē)* and imperial power to man? Whence the thought of absolute dominion *(autokratorikē dynamis)* to a being composed of flesh and blood? Who declared those ideas which are invisible and undefined and that incorporeal essence which has no external form to the mortals of this earth? Surely there was but one interpreter of these things, the all-pervading Word of God. For he is the author of that rational and intelligent being which exists in man; and being himself one with his Father's divine nature, he sheds upon his offspring the outflowings of his Father's bounty. Hence the natural and untaught powers of thought which all men, Greeks or barbarians, alike possess; hence the perception of reason and wisdom, the seeds of integrity and righteousness, the understanding of the arts of life, the knowledge of virtue, the precious name of wisdom, and the noble love of philosophic learning. Hence the knowledge of all that is great and good; hence apprehension of God himself, and a life worthy of his worship; hence the royal authority of man, and his invincible lordship over the creatures of this world. And when that Word, who is the parent of rational beings, had impressed a character on the mind of man according to the image and likeness of God, and had made him a royal creature *(basilikon zōon)*, in that he gave him alone of all earthly creatures capacity to rule and to obey (as well as forethought and foreknowledge even here concerning the promised hope of his heavenly kingdom; because of which he himself

came and as the parent of his children disdained not to hold converse with mortal men); he continued to cherish the seeds which himself had sown, and renewed his gracious favours from above, holding forth to all the promise of sharing his heavenly kingdom. Accordingly he called men and exhorted them to be ready for their heavenward journey, and to provide themselves with the garment which became their calling. And by an indescribable power he filled the world in every part with his doctrine, expressing by the similitude of an earthly kingdom that heavenly one to which he earnestly invites all mankind, and presents it to them as a worthy object of their hope.

5. And in this hope our divinely favoured emperor partakes even in this present life, gifted as he is by God with native virtues and having received into his soul the outflowings of his favour. His reason he derives from the great source of all reason, he is wise, and good, and just as having fellowship with perfect wisdom, goodness and righteousness, virtuous as following the pattern of perfect virtue, valiant as partaking of heavenly strength. And truly may he deserve the imperial title who has formed his soul to royal virtues according to the standard of that celestial kingdom. But he who is a stranger to these blessings, who denies the sovereign of the universe and owns no allegiance to the heavenly Father of spirits, who invests not himself with the virtues which become an emperor but overlays his soul with moral deformity and baseness, who for royal clemency substitutes the fury of a savage beast, for a generous temper the incurable venom of malicious wickedness, for prudence folly, for reason and wisdom that recklessness which is the most odious of all vices (for from it, as from a spring of bitterness, proceed the most pernicious fruits, such as inveterate profligacy of life, covetousness, murder, impiety and defiance of God), surely one abandoned to such vices as these, however he may be deemed powerful through despotic violence (*tyrannikē bia*), has no true title to the name of emperor. For how should he whose soul is impressed with a thousand absurd images of false deities, be able to exhibit a counterpart of the true and heavenly sovereignty? Or how can he be absolute lord of others, who has subjected himself to the dominion of a thousand cruel masters, a slave of low delights and ungoverned lust, a slave of wrongfully extorted wealth, of rage and passion as well as of cowardice and terror, a slave of ruthless demons and soul-destroying spirits?

Let, then, our emperor, on the testimony of truth itself, be declared alone worthy of the title; who is dear to the supreme Sovereign himself, who alone is free, nay, who is truly lord, above the thirst of wealth, superior to sexual desire, victorious even over natural pleasures, controlling, not controlled by, anger and passion. He is indeed an emperor and bears a title corresponding to his deeds, a Victor in truth, who has gained the victory over those passions which overmaster the rest of men, whose character is formed after the divine original of the supreme sovereign and whose mind reflects as in a mirror the radiance of his virtues. Hence is our emperor perfect in discretion, in goodness, in justice, in courage, in piety, in devotion to God; he truly and only is a philosopher, since he knows himself, and is fully aware that supplies of every blessing are showered on him from a source quite external to himself, even from heaven itself. [. . .]

9. And now we may well compare the present with former things, and review

these happy changes in contrast with the evils that are past, and mark the elaborate care with which in ancient times porches and sacred precincts, groves and temples were prepared in every city for these false deities, and how their shrines were enriched with abundant offerings. The sovereign rulers of those days had indeed a high regard for the worship of the gods. The nations also and people subject to their power honoured them with images both in the country and in every city, nay, even in their houses and secret chambers, according to the religious practice of their fathers. The fruit, however, of this devotion, far different from the peaceful concord which now meets our view, appeared in war, in battles, and seditions, which harassed them throughout their lives and deluged their countries with blood and civil slaughter. Again, the objects of their worship could hold out to these sovereigns with artful flattery the promise of prophecies and oracles and the knowledge of futurity; yet could they not predict their own destruction, nor forewarn themselves of the coming ruin, and surely this was the greatest and most convincing proof of their imposture. Not one of those whose words once were heard with awe and wonder had announced the glorious advent of the Saviour of mankind or that new revelation of divine knowledge which he came to give. Not Pythian Apollo himself nor any of those mighty gods could apprehend the prospect of their approaching desolation, nor could their oracles point at him who was to be their conqueror and destroyer. What prophet or diviner could foretell that their rites would vanish at the presence of a new deity in the world, and that the knowledge and worship of the almighty Sovereign should be freely given to all mankind? Which of them foreknew the august and pious reign of our victorious emperor, or his triumphant conquests everywhere over the false demons, or the overthrow of their high places? Which of the heroes has announced the melting down and conversion of the lifeless statues from their useless forms to the necessary uses of men? Which of the gods have yet had power to speak of their own images thus melted and contemptuously reduced to fragments? Where were the protecting powers, that they should not interpose to save their sacred memorials thus destroyed by man? Where, I ask, are those who once maintained the strife of war, yet now behold their conquerors abiding securely in the profoundest peace? And where are they who upheld themselves in a blind and foolish confidence, and trusted in these vanities as gods; but who, in the very height of their superstitious error, and while maintaining an implacable war with the champions of the truth, perished by a fate proportioned to their crimes? Where is the giant race, whose arms were turned against heaven itself, the hissings of those serpents whose tongues were pointed with impious words against the almighty King?

These adversaries of the Lord of all, confident in the aid of a multitude of gods, advanced to the attack with a powerful array of military force, preceded by certain images of the dead and lifeless statues as their defence. On the other side our emperor, secure in the armour of godliness, opposed to the numbers of the enemy the salutary and life-giving sign [i.e., the cross] as at the same time a terror to the foe and a protection against every harm, and returned victorious at once over the enemy and the demons whom they served. And then with thanksgiving and praise, the tokens of a grateful spirit, to the author of his victory, he proclaimed this triumphant sign by monuments as well as words to all mankind, erecting it as a mighty trophy against every enemy in the midst of the imperial city and expressly enjoining on all to acknowledge this imperishable symbol of salvation as the safeguard of the power of Rome and of the empire of the world. Such were the instructions which he gave to his subjects generally; but especially to his soldiers, whom he admonished to repose their confidence not in their weapons or armour or bodily strength but to acknowledge the Supreme God as the giver of every good and of victory itself. Thus did the emperor himself, strange and incredible as the fact may seem, become the instructor of his army in their religious exercises and teach them to offer pious prayers in accordance with the divine ordinances, uplifting their hands towards heaven and raising their mental vision higher still to the king of heaven on whom they should call as the author of victory, their preserver, guardian and helper. He commanded, too, that one day should be regarded as a special occasion for religious worship; I mean that which is truly the first and chief of all, the day of our Lord and Saviour; that day the name of which is connected with light and life and immortality and every good. Prescribing the same pious conduct to himself, he honoured his Saviour in the chambers of his palace, performing his devotions according to the divine commands and storing his mind with instruction through the hearing of the sacred word. The entire care of his household was entrusted to ministers devoted to the service of God and distinguished by gravity of life and every other virtue; while his trusty bodyguards, strong in affection and fidelity to his person, found in their emperor an instructor in the practice of a godly life.

Again, the honour with which he regards the victorious sign is founded on his actual experience of its divine efficacy. Before this the hosts of his enemies have disappeared; by this the powers of the unseen spirits have been turned to flight; through this the proud boastings of God's adversaries have come to nought and the tongues of the profane and blasphemous been put to silence. By this sign the barbarian tribes were vanquished; through this the rites of superstitious fraud received a just rebuke; by this our emperor, discharging as it were a sacred debt, has performed the crowning good of all by erecting triumphant memorials of its value in all parts of the world, raising temples and churches on a scale of royal costliness and commanding all to unite in constructing the sacred houses of prayer. Accordingly these signal proofs of our emperor's magnificence forthwith appeared in the provinces and cities of the empire, and soon shone conspicuously in every country, convincing memorials of the rebuke and overthrow of those impious tyrants who but a little while before had madly dared to fight against God and, raging like savage dogs, had ventured on unconscious buildings that fury which they were unable to level against him, had thrown to the ground and upturned the very foundations of the houses of prayer, causing them to present the appearance of a city captured and abandoned to the enemy. Such was the exhibition of that wicked spirit whereby they sought as it were to assail God himself, but soon experienced the result of their own madness and folly. But a little time elapsed, when a single blast of the storm of heaven's displeasure swept them utterly away, leaving neither kindred nor offspring nor memorial of their existence among men; for all, numerous as they were, disappeared as in a moment beneath the stroke of divine vengeance.

Such, then, was the fate which awaited these furious adversaries of God; but he who, armed with the standard of salvation, had alone opposed them (rather, not alone, but aided by the presence and the power of him who is the only Sovereign) has replaced the ruined edifices on a greater scale and made the second far superior to the first. For example, besides erecting various churches to the honour of God in the city which bears his name [Constantinople] and adorning the Bithynian capital [Nicomedia] with another on the greatest and most splendid scale, he has distinguished the principal cities of the other provinces by structures of a similar kind. Above all, he has selected two divisions of the eastern empire, the one that of the Palestinian race (since from thence the life-giving stream has flowed as from a fountain for the blessing of all nations), the other of that metropolis of the East which derives its name from Antiochus [Antioch]. In this, as head of that portion of the empire, he has consecrated to the service of God a church of unparalleled size and beauty: the entire building is encompassed by an enclosure of great extent, within which the church itself rises to a vast elevation, of an octagonal form surrounded by many chambers and courts on every side and decorated with ornaments of the richest kind. Such was his work here, while in the province of Palestine, in that city which was once the seat of Hebrew sovereignty [Jerusalem], on the very site of the Lord's sepulchre, he has raised a church of noble dimensions and adorned a temple sacred to the saving cross with rich and lavish magnificence, honoring that everlasting monument and the trophies of the Saviour's victory over the power of death with a splendour which no language can describe.

Translation: E. C. Richardson, Nicene and Post-Nicene Fathers, adapted.

Ambrose of Milan

(339-97)

In a characteristically waspish remark, Jerome refused to offer an assessment of Ambrose's literary importance, "lest I should be criticised on one side for flattering him, or on the other for telling the truth." Recent scholarship, faced with the choice between *adulatio* and *veritas*, has preferred the latter; there has been a fashion for stripping Ambrose of venerable and saintly qualities. We are invited to see him in the new light shed by valuable historical research into the later Arian controversy and late fourth-century imperial politics: instead of the serene, authoritative doctor who brought emperors to his feet and made heresy turn tail, we are shown an adroit, risk-taking court politician, often hard-pressed but adept at saving a difficult situation with a flamboyant *coup de théâtre*. It certainly presents a vital figure, this new portrait of Ambrose, though perhaps not quite so free of idealizing traits as it pretends to be, even if traits modern scholars idealize are different from those their predecessors admired. Such a great deal is now attributed to the capacity for improvised theater — the reshaping of Western theological history, for instance — that one might think the old-style *adulatio* required less belief in miracles! But when all is said and done, the Ambrose we now see is not really new. The portrait has been cleaned up to let the colors stand out, and is hung in a brighter light. But he is as we knew him: not an original thinker like Augustine, not a great individualist like Jerome, but a supremely representative voice, a reverberant spokesman for the instincts of the Western Church in a formative generation, the first generation to have been born and grown up in a Christian Roman Empire. His capacity to maneuver, though agile, does not explain his achievement. It was his capacity to place himself precisely in line with the evolving self-understanding of the church that made him effective at the time and interesting now.

It was, of course, not surprising that the bishop of Milan should have become a significant figure in the imperial court after the Western emperor, Gratian, relocated it there in 378; nor that he should have had the struggles that every church leader experienced in that time of passionate religious controversy. What does deserve notice is that he could rally his church to a vision of church-world relations that has nothing in common with the Eusebian emperor-theology, and is heavy with echoes of the pre-Constantinian conflict, above all in the importance assigned to the memory of the martyrs. That church was coming to see its relation to the authorities in confrontational terms, as though nothing had changed. What was the source of its sense of alienation?

Immediately, it lay in the doctrinal conflicts of the fourth century and the attempts of successive Christian emperors to establish their position by suppressing them. The so-called Arian controversy, over the relation of the Father and the Son within the Godhead, was, by Ambrose's heyday, sixty years old and had passed through many phases. Decisive for the virulence of the struggle in the latter half of the century had been the ill-judged attempt of Constantius II to impose a "Homoian" resolution: the Son is simply "like" the Father, with no mention of "substance," whether "like substance" or "same substance." The comparative ease with which the emperor mastered the Councils of Ariminum and Constantinople (359-60) had badly frightened those who were most determined to resist the subordinationism which lay at the heart of the doctrinal stance which went by Arius's name; it produced a sharp backlash which resulted in the formation of a common front taking as its standard the earlier Creed of Nicaea (325) and its affirmation of "same substance." By Ambrose's day there were, in effect, two parties: a strengthening Nicene party to which he belonged, and a weakening Ariminian party to which his predecessor as bishop had belonged. Between them successive Western emperors tried, with only moderate success, to hold a neutral posture; but granted the principle of imperial arbitration in controversies of Christian doctrine, neutrality was the hardest of all positions to maintain in the proximity of the court. Before Gratian's arrival in Milan, Ambrose had managed, with apparent success, to lead a church which contained adherents of both parties among the clergy. Once in the imperial limelight, he found himself under attack, summoned to answer accusations of heresy made against him from the Homoian quarter.

The *Sermon against Auxentius* comes from a phase in the struggle that arose some years later, in 386. The emperor in Italy — the empire is currently divided three ways — is a child, Valentinian II, and his court is leaning ominously in the Homoian direction. Ambrose has been asked to make one of the city churches available to the Homoian bishop, Auxentius, to celebrate Easter there with his congregation. He is uncomfortably aware that he has accommodated Milan's separatist Homoians before, to oblige Gratian, but in 386 the request seems fraught with dangers. In the first place, it appears that the emperor himself intends to worship with the Homoians. Furthermore, Auxentius regards him, Ambrose, as a heretic, and seems intent on challenging him for his position. The story of how Ambrose's congregation (which included Augustine's mother, Monnica) staged a sit-in in the church from Palm Sunday to Maundy Thursday while surrounded by the soldiers sent to expropriate it, and of how their hymn singing (an innovation Ambrose is credited with having introduced) infuriated the opposition, and of how the court's nerve collapsed when the soldiers began to defect to Ambrose's congregation quickly became legendary. The setting for the speech is, apparently, the next phase in the confrontation. The emperor has summoned Auxentius and Ambrose to a hearing in his consistory. Each of them is required to appoint judges to advise the emperor, and Auxentius has readily complied, naming, as Ambrose contemptuously observes, some non-Christians. If Ambrose does not comply, he is told, he may simply quit Milan, accompanied by as many of his congregation as care to leave with him. The bishop's icy letter of defiance challenged the competence of the emperor's court with a sweeping claim to the sovereignty of episcopal jurisdiction in the church. It was impossible, he argued, for any hearing to take place while the issue was effectively prejudged by a decree promulgated earlier in the year to strengthen the emperor's hand. The emperor was attempting to subordinate God's law to his own, but that could only extort conformity by fear, not inspire faith. Finally, with a veiled warning of unrest, "the bishops and people" refused to let Ambrose attend the consistory, insisting that "a matter of faith must be dealt with in the church before the people." The church, for Ambrose, was the only true public space: "I neither know nor care to know the secrets of the palace!" (*Ep.* 75). This message then formed the heart of the sermon from which our excerpt comes, exploiting the echoes of the church's martyr history: *vasa tradere*, "surrender the vessels," was a phrase that evoked the memory of the worst crises of the third century. Exactly how the moment of confrontation passed, we do not know. But Ambrose did not lose ground as a result: later in the year his discovery of the remains of two martyrs, and their reburial at the dedication of his new church, was seen by contemporaries to seal his triumph.

We can only be struck by Ambrose's sharp sense of the opposed roles: Christian or not, Valentinian is an "emperor of this age," and "I am ready to bear the usual fate of a bishop, if he follows the usual practice of kings." A former governor, Ambrose had operated on both sides of the church-world divide. He understood, and profoundly shared, the sense of irreconcilable tension between Christian profession and the exigencies of a brutal style of justice. The story was told that in an attempt to avoid election as bishop in 374, he had ostentatiously ordered the interrogation of suspects under torture, a routine judicial procedure which should have had the effect of making him ineligible for ordination. In this context the little letter on capital punishment is of especial interest (*Ep.* 50). It speaks of the practical dilemmas of magistrates over this penal practice, as well as of the profound dislike the church felt for it. Was "justice," then, as he once wrote to the emperor Theodosius, bound to "yield to religion"? The discussion of justice in *The Duties of Clergy* (*De officiis ministrorum*) is in search of a different resolution to the tension: a new, Christianized concept of justice which will transfigure its savage outlines into an evangelical shape, renouncing retaliation and private property. Like much of Ambrose's writing — it was one of the things that so disgusted Jerome — this book self-consciously uses material from a classical model, in this case Cicero's *De officiis.* The dependence on the model, however, should not conceal the Christian reworking of the content.

One way in which the church of the late fourth century defined itself against the world was in its hostility to private wealth. This aligned it with the ascetic movement, which was seen as carrying the torch for an authentic Christianity in the midst of a compromised wider church. Ambrose, like John Chrysostom a few years later, taught the original community of goods and denounced private property as an extortion. Neither of them thought this incompatible with extensive proprietorship on the part of the church as a corporation, which was used to support a growing network of organized charity, occasional and institutionalized: the redemption of prisoners, hospitals, monasteries, schools, and so on. (Not until the Middle Ages do we find corporate ownership falling under suspicion. For Ambrose it was as though the church possessed goods in trust for mankind, and especially for those who most needed them.) He was always a sharp observer of social and economic matters, who could produce a clearly focused description of (for example) price-fixing. His meditation on the story of Naboth's vineyard links the two themes of poverty and of the church-world tension; Naboth's struggle with Ahab had been a model in the crisis over the basilica. Similarly, his praise of Joseph in the discussion of liberality in *The Duties of Clergy* presents his ideal for charitable organization. Joseph was a true "lord" of earthly goods, because he knew how to put them to use for the relief of the needy. He could really "use" them; and that was the work of intelligence, in which alone true command resides. Ambrose's angry outburst (2.15) against those who tried to reenslave prisoners bought out of captivity by the church is typical of his social alertness. The details of this scenario have to be reconstructed hypothetically, but it may concern rich landowners who sought to take advantage of a flood of recently repatriated and penniless prisoners of war by settling them with serf status on their estates. (We are indebted to Dr. J.-M. Salamito for this suggestion in private correspondence.)

The alternative to lordship was servitude, and that thought is carried forward in the discussion of slavery in *Epistle 7*, an illuminating instance both of how the church thought of slavery and of how Ambrose acquired and developed his ideas. Modern readers, who approach it with the distinct idea of slavery as an "institution" that one has to be either for or against, find the early church's attitude especially difficult to understand. It saw the dependence and subjection of a slave as simply an aspect of the wider range of dependent and subject relations: the dependence of women, children, or subjects of a tyrannical regime, for example. All of these reflected what it took to be the core reality of dependence and subjection: the moral and psychological impotence of sin. Its talk about slavery, therefore, is wide-ranging and fluid, shifting constantly from one manifestation of dependence to another. The vocabulary often fails to make a clear distinction between "servitude" and "service." Where we may be frustrated with the evasion of what seems to us the "real" point, i.e., the point as it became sharpened in the battles against eighteenth-century colonial slavery, the patristic church insists on weaving its discussion of slavery into a broad context of social and moral experience.

But once we appreciate that, we see that the theoretical statement "every wise man is free, every fool is a slave" is not intended as a mere metaphor. It is meant, rather, to strike below the socio-legal appearances to get at the realities. It invites us to consider the legal and economic forms of slavery as an unreal fiction, which has no purchase except on the mind enslaved to fear. In taking this line Ambrose, like other Christians of his age, follows a path that the Stoics had beaten before him. He has, once again, a literary model with which to work, Philo of Alexandria's early Stoic essay *Every Good Man Is Free*. To Philo's satirical and literary illustrations of the theme Ambrose has not only added a few biblical ones — Joseph makes another appearance — but has articulated a christological thesis: the Christian is free, because the Christian has been purchased by Christ; and in Christ the truest expression of freedom has been shown us, the service of others. The reader may feel that the Stoic conception of freedom as the exercise of unimpaired good will (remarkably like the idea that Kant would bring back into currency many centuries later) and the Christian conception of freedom as service do not always live very comfortably together.

Further Reading: G. Madec, *Saint Ambroise et la philosophie* (Paris: Études Augustiniennes, 1974); N. B. McLynn, *Ambrose of Milan: Church and Court in a Christian Capital* (Berkeley: University of California Press, 1994); B. Ramsey, *Ambrose* (London: Routledge, 1997); H. Savon, *Saint Ambroise devant l'exégèse de Philon le Juif* (Paris: Études Augustiniennes, 1977); D. H. Williams, *Ambrose of Milan and the End of the Nicene-Arian Conflict* (Oxford: Oxford University Press, 1995).

From the *Sermon against Auxentius* (Epistle 75a)

1. I notice that you are more troubled than usual, and watchful of me. I am amazed at this; but perhaps some of you have seen me with soldiers, and others have heard of an imperial order: that I should leave and go where I choose, and that those who wish may go with me. Were you afraid that I would abandon the church and leave you, because I feared for my own safety? You might have paid attention to what I told you: — I could not find it in me to abandon the church, since I fear the Lord of the world more than the emperor of this age. Were some force to tear me from the cathedral, only my body could be moved, not my mind. And I am ready to bear the usual fate of a bishop, if he follows the usual practice of kings.

2. So why are you troubled? I will never willingly leave you, and I do not know how to retaliate against force. I shall be able to grieve, to weep, to sigh; against the weaponry and the Gothic troops my tears, too, are weapons; for such are the defenses of a bishop! I should not and cannot fight in any other manner. But flight, and abandoning the church, are not my way. I would not like anyone to think I was afraid of some worse punishment. You know yourselves that my way is to defer, but not to yield, to emperors, to expose myself freely to their punishments, without fear of their purposes.

3. If only I could be sure that the church would not be handed to the heretics! I would gladly go to the emperor's palace, were it consistent with the duties of a bishop to fight his battles in the palace rather than in church. But in the council chamber Christ is properly the judge, not the defendant. Who can deny that a question of faith should be heard in church? Let anyone with faith come here! Let him

not expect any softening of the emperor's decision, published with the full authority of law and hostile to our faith; nor let him wait for negotiators to come round with new offers. I am not engaged in this battle so that anyone may auction off the right to affront Christ!

4. Soldiers swarming everywhere, the clash of arms surrounding the cathedral, do not shake my faith; but they greatly disturb my mind, in case, while you look on me as a troublemaker, something may come in the way of your salvation. I have learned by now not to be afraid; but I begin to be the more afraid for you. Please, let your bishop speak; we have an enemy who is attacking us, for, as the apostle says, our enemy "the devil prowls about like a roaring lion, looking for whomsoever he can devour" (1 Pet. 5:8). He has been given — there is no mistake, we have been warned — he has certainly been given the power to tempt us in this way, to see if bodily wounds can shake me from the conviction of my faith. You, too, have read how the devil tempted holy Job with many such trials as these, and finally asked for and was given the power to afflict his body, which he covered with sores.

5. When it was proposed that we should surrender the church's vessels, I sent back this reply: were he to demand something from my own possessions, be it land, property, gold, or silver, I would gladly offer anything at my disposal; but from the temple of God I can sequestrate nothing, nor can I hand over what I was given for safe keeping, not to dispose of. In sum, I act out of concern for the emperor's welfare; for it would neither be good for me to hand them over, nor for him to receive them. Let him hear the words of an intractable bishop: if he wants me to be concerned for him, he should desist from affronting Christ.

6. These words were full of humility, and full, I think, of the care which a bishop owes an emperor. But because "our struggle is not only against flesh and blood but" — more seriously — "against the spirits of wickedness in high places" (Eph. 6:12), that fiend and tempter steps up the contest through his minions, and determines to put it to the test by wounding my body. Brothers, I know that these wounds received for Christ's sake are no wounds. They do not take our life away, but regenerate it. Permit the contest, please, to take place! You may be spectators. Consider! If a city has an athlete or an expert in some other noble art, it chooses him to enter for a contest. Why depart, in a matter of some seriousness, from your normal practice in more humdrum affairs? He fears no arms, no savages, who fears not death. No impulse of the flesh impedes him.

7. If the Lord has appointed us to this contest, at any rate, it is to no effect that you organize your watch around the clock for so many days and nights. Christ's will must be fulfilled. Our Lord Jesus is omnipotent (so we confess our faith). What he commands to be, shall be fulfilled, and it ill becomes you to stand in the way of God's decision.

8. You heard today's lesson: the Savior ordered the foal of an ass to be brought by the apostles, and anyone who objected to be told: "the Lord has need of it" (Luke 19:31). What if he has ordered that foal of an ass to be brought to him now — that animal used to carrying a heavy load, like our human state, to which he said: "Come to me, all you who labor and are burdened, and I will refresh you; take my yoke upon you, because it is light" (Matt. 11:28-30)? What, I say, if he has ordered that foal to be brought to him now, sending out his apostles who, rid of the body, bear an angelic form inaccessible to our eyes? Will they not say to any who oppose them: "The Lord has need of it" (Luke 19:31)? If our craving for this life should resist? If flesh and blood should resist? If our human connections should resist (since there are those who are fond of us)? But whoever loves us in this world, loves us far more if he allows us to become Christ's sacrificial victim, since "it is better by far to depart and to be with Christ, though to remain in the body is more necessary for you" (Phil. 1:23-24). Therefore, my dear brothers, there is nothing to fear. I know that whatever I suffer, I shall suffer for Christ. I have read that I should not fear those who can destroy the body; and I have heard him say, "Whoever loses his life for my sake, will gain it" (Matt. 10:39). [. . .]

24. So, does this man steeped in blood and gore [Auxentius] dare even to mention "discussion"? He thinks that whoever he cannot beguile with his speech must be cut down with the sword. His lips dictate, and his hand inscribes, laws of blood, for he thinks that law can impose faith. He did not hear today's lesson: since "a man is not justified by the works of the law . . . ," Paul says, "through the law I died to the law, that I might live to God" (Gal. 2:16, 19); which is to say that through the spiritual law he is dead to the material interpretation of the law. Let us, too, by the law of our Lord Jesus Christ die to this law which gives authority to treacherous decrees! Faith in Christ, not law, founded the church. Law is not "by faith"; but "the righteous man lives by faith" (Gal. 3:11). Faith, then, not law, makes one righteous, for righteousness is not by law but by faith in Christ. Anyone, then, who disclaims faith and relies upon legal prescriptions proves himself unrighteous, for "the righteous man lives by faith" (Gal. 3:11).

25. Can anyone, therefore, follow that law which ratified the Council of Ariminum, where it was said that Christ was a creature? They say, "God sent his son, made of a woman, made under the law" (Gal. 4:4), and interpret "made" (factus) to mean "created." Don't they see the implication of the text they quote, that when Christ is called "made" it is "of a woman," i.e., by virtue of his birth of the virgin; in respect of generation from God he was "born" (natus)? And they have read today's lection, which says that "Christ has freed us from the curse of the law, having been made a curse for our sake" (Gal. 3:13). It is not in his divinity that Christ is "a curse"! But the apostle tells you why the word "curse" is used: "Because it is written: every man who has hung on the tree is cursed" (Gal. 3:13; Deut. 21:23), which means that he who bore our flesh in his flesh, our weaknesses in his body, bore, too, our curses, to crucify them. He was not cursed himself, but cursed for you. And elsewhere it says: "He who did not know sin, was made sin for our sakes" (2 Cor. 5:21), because he took our sins on himself to destroy them by the mystery of his passion.

26. I would have debated these matters among you at greater length, my brothers, in Auxentius' presence, but he, knowing that you are well versed in faith, shrank from your scrutiny and chose about four or five pagans (if he actually *chose* them) to be his adjudicators: I would like them to be present among you all, not to pronounce judgment on Christ but to hear of Christ's majesty. They, however, have given their verdict on Auxentius — by refusing to believe him when he was preaching day by day! What greater condemnation for him than to be defeated before judges of his

own choosing, and with no adversary! We, then, agree with their decision against Auxentius!

27. He deserves to be condemned, too, for choosing pagans, since he ignored apostolic instructions. The apostle says: "Does any one of you, who has a dispute against another, dare to be judged before the unjust and not before the saints? Do you not know that it is the saints who will judge this world?" (1 Cor. 6:1-2). And later on he says, "Is it the case that there is not a single wise man among you who is able to judge between his fellow believers, but that one believer goes to law with his fellow, and before the heathen at that?" (1 Cor. 6:5). You see how his proposal runs counter to Paul's teaching. You must choose whether we ought to take Auxentius, or Paul, as our teacher.

28. But why should I speak of Paul, when the Lord himself proclaims through the prophet: "Hear me, my people, you who know judgment, you who have my law in your heart" (Isa. 51:7). God says, "Hear me, my people, you who know judgment," but Auxentius says "You do not know judgment." Do you see how the man who rejects the verdict of the heavenly oracle scorns even God in your midst? The Lord says "Hear me, my people"; he does not say "hear me, pagans," or "Hear me, Jews." For the Jewish people that used to be God's people is so no longer, but has become a people of error; while what used to be the people of error has come to be the people of God, since it has believed in Christ. That people, then, is the judge; it has divine law, not human, in its heart, the law "written not with ink but with the spirit of the living God" (2 Cor. 3:3), not scratched upon paper but inscribed on the heart, the law of grace and not of blood. So who is it who wrongs you, he who rejects your judgment, or who chooses it?

29. Hemmed in from all sides, he has resorted to the guile of his ancestors. He wishes to start a controversy about the emperor, saying that this youth, a catechumen ignorant of Holy Scripture, ought to give judgment, and give it in the council chamber, too! Is he suggesting that last year, when I was summoned to the palace for a debate in council before senior ministers over the emperor's wish to confiscate a church, I was so distracted by the sight of the royal apartment that I let go my resolution as a bishop, and left with my authority diminished? My opponents surely remember that when the people learned I had gone to the palace, they rushed there in an irresistible mêlée, all of them offering themselves to death for faith in Christ to the captain who had gone out with an armed band to disperse the crowd. Wasn't I then asked to pacify the crowd with a long address, and to promise them solemnly that no one would invade a church building? My services were requested as a favor, yet it was held against me that the people had thronged to the palace. Into this atmosphere of animosity, then, they now wish me to return. **30.** I quieted the people, but did not escape ill will; but I think that this ill will should be confronted and quelled, not feared. For what should we fear in the name of Christ? Do you think I should be cowed when they say: "Should the emperor, then, not have a single church for his own attendance? Does Ambrose intend to control the emperor, and deny the emperor the freedom to go out?" With such words they are eager to catch me in my speech, like the Jews who tempted Christ with a wily interrogation: "Teacher, is it lawful to pay tax to Caesar or not?" (Matt. 22:17). Is malice against the servants of

God forever aroused in Caesar's name? Has impiety acquired this excuse of the emperor's name as a tool for its false accusations? And can those who have learned such a lesson from such a source, disclaim all part in their teachers' sacrilege?

31. But see how the Arians are worse than the Jews. The Jews asked whether Christ thought that Caesar ought to be allowed the right of taxation, but the Arians would give the emperor the right of the church. But as the heretics follow their teacher, so let us answer as our Lord and teacher taught us. Jesus sized up the Jews' stratagem, and said: "Why try to catch me out? Show me a denarius!" (Matt. 22:18-19). And when they gave it him, he said: "Whose likeness and inscription does it bear?" (Matt. 22:20). They replied: "Caesar's" (Matt. 22:21). And Jesus said to them: "Pay to Caesar what belongs to Caesar, and to God what belongs to God" (Matt. 22:21). So I, too, say to those who oppose me: "Show me the denarius!" Jesus saw the imperial denarius and said: "Pay to Caesar what belongs to Caesar, and to God what belongs to God." But when it comes to seizing churches, have they an imperial denarius to produce?

32. In the church I know only one image, and that is the image of the invisible God. Of this God said: "Let us make man in our image and after our likeness" (Gen. 1:26), that same image of which it is written that Christ is "the radiance of his glory and the image of God's being" (Heb. 1:3). I perceive the Father in that image, as the Lord Christ himself said: "Whoever sees me, sees the Father too" (John 14:9). For this image is not separate from the Father; and it taught me the unity of the Trinity, when it said, "The Father and I are one" (John 10:30), and later, "All that the Father has is mine" (John 16:15). It taught me, too, of the Holy Spirit, that it is the Spirit of Christ, and has taken what is Christ's. For Scripture says: "He will take what is mine and will declare it to you" (John 16:14).

33. How, then, was our reply not humble? If the emperor wants tax, we do not refuse. The church's estates are taxed. If the emperor needs estates, he has the power to appropriate them, and not one of us stands in his way. The congregation's donations are more than enough for the poor; there is no reason for resentment about our estates. Let them sequestrate them, if the emperor pleases; I am not offering, but I do not refuse them. They ask for gold, and I can say "I seek neither silver nor gold"; yet they harbor resentment because gold is disbursed. I do not tremble at this resentment. I have my treasurers; my treasurers are Christ's poor; and this is the treasure I have learned to amass. I would be glad if the charge against me was always this: disbursing money to the poor! If they complain that I shall ask for the support of the poor, I do not deny it. I actively seek their support. Yes, I have my support, but it lies in the prayers of the poor. The blind and the crippled, the powerless and the aged, are stronger than mighty warriors. In short, gifts to the poor put God under an obligation, for Scripture says: "He who is generous to the poor lends to the Lord" (Prov. 19:17). Squads of soldiers often fail to earn God's favor.

34. They allege, too, that the people are beguiled by the "magic spells" of my hymns, and I certainly do not deny this either. It is a mighty spell, none more powerful! For what has greater might than a confession of faith in the Trinity, repeated every day on the lips of all the congregation? They all compete in their eagerness to profess their faith; and they know how to proclaim Father, Son, and Holy Spirit in

their hymns. In this way everybody has become a teacher, who before was scarcely fit to be a pupil.

35. So what can be more obedient than to follow the example of Christ, who, "being found in appearance as a man, humbled himself and became obedient even to death" (Phil. 2:8)? He freed us all by his obedience: "For as through the disobedience of one man many were made sinners, so through the obedience of one man many will be made righteous" (Rom. 5:19). If he, then, was obedient, let them learn from that example of obedience to which we hold when we say to those who incite ill will against us before the emperor: "We pay to Caesar the things which are Caesar's and to God the things which are God's." Taxation is a matter for Caesar, that is beyond question; but the church is God's, and so it ought not to be given over to Caesar, because Caesar's sway cannot extend over the temple of God.

36. No one may gainsay anything said to the emperor's honor. And what could do him greater honor than to be called a "son of the church"? This phrase is without offense and in good part. The emperor is within the church, not above it; the good emperor asks for the church's help, he does not refuse it. We say these things with deference, but we insist on them invariably. Our enemies threaten fire, execution, exile. We servants of Christ have learned not to fear, and those who do not fear have nothing to dread. It is written: "Their blows have become like children's arrows" (Ps. 63:8 Vulg.).

37. I think that their points have been answered sufficiently. Now I put to them the question that the Savior put: "Was the baptism of John from God or from men?" (Luke 20:4). The Jews could not answer him; and if Jews could not invalidate the baptism of John, can Auxentius invalidate the baptism of Christ? That baptism comes not from men but from God, brought down to us by the angel of the great counsel [i.e., Christ], we may be justified for God. So why does Auxentius hold that believing communities, baptized in the name of the Trinity, must be rebaptized, though the apostle says: "one faith, one baptism" (Eph. 4:5)? How can Auxentius say that it is men, not Christ, that he opposes, while he ignores God's counsel and rejects the baptism which Christ bestowed to redeem us from our sins?

Translation: Paul Arnold and editors, from Corpus Scriptorum Ecclesiasticorum Latinorum, vol. 82.

From *The Story of Naboth*

1. The story of Naboth is an ancient one, but an everyday experience. What rich man does not daily set his heart on other people's goods? What millionaire is not engaged in tearing the poor man from his tiny holding and driving him empty-handed from the borders of his family allotment? Who is satisfied with what he has? What rich man's heart is not fired by the prospect of acquiring his neighbor's property? There was more than one Ahab born. An Ahab is born every day, alas! and Ahab will never die in this age. When one falls, countless others arise; there are more robbers than robbed. There was more than one poor Naboth slain. A Naboth is cut down every day; every day a poor man is killed. Driven by such fears, the human race is in flight from the land. You see the poor migrant with his youngsters; all that he can count his own upon his back; his wife behind, weeping as though she were escorting her husband to his grave. But she would have less to weep about if she were mourning her family's dead: if she had lost her husband's protection, she would have his grave at least; if she no longer had her sons, she would not be grieving for them in exile, or lamenting something worse than the death of her young: I mean, their starvation.

2. How far can you take this mad acquisitiveness, you rich? Will you make yourselves the only inhabitants of the earth? Why grasp at nature's possessions, and keep nature's companions at bay? The earth was created for all in common, rich and poor alike. Why arrogate to yourselves a sole and exclusive right? Nature knows no rich men, she makes us all poor at birth. We are born without clothing, given life without gold and silver. We are brought forth naked to the light, in need of food, clothing, and drink. And naked as it produced us the earth receives us back, and can accommodate no broad landholdings in the grave. The narrow covering of turf is room enough for poor and rich alike; clay, which had no hold on the rich man's affections while he lived, holds the whole of him at the last. Nature makes no distinctions, either when we are born or when we die. It creates us all equals; as equals it enfolds us all in the grave's embrace. Who can tell the classes of dead men apart? Open up the earth and find the rich man if you can. Clear up the graves a little after burial, and if you identify the subject as a poor man, prove it. Perhaps you can prove it by this one fact, that there is more junk rotting beside a rich man. 3. Silk garments and gold-threaded covers that wrap the rich man's body are an expense to the living, but no resource to the dead. You are anointed, rich man, but you stink all the same; you are a charge on somebody's good offices, but dispose of none yourself. You leave behind you heirs who squabble in the courts. What you bequeath them is more a responsibility than a free gift, they are so afraid to deplete or damage what they have been left. If they are thrifty, they care for their patrimony; but if they are extravagant, they drain it dry. You sentence your heirs, if they are honest, to perpetual anxiety; or you leave bad heirs, who undo your achievements.

4. But why suppose that while you live you have everything? You who call yourself rich, do you not realize how poor you are, how impoverished your appearance — even to yourself? The more you possess, the more you demand, and however much you acquire you go on needing more. Greed is inflamed, not assuaged, by gain. Acquisitiveness has its ladder of ascent: the more steps one climbs, the more one hurries on up, to where a fall will be a serious matter when one slips. That man was more tolerable when he had less; with a sober estimation of his worth, he made reasonable demands; but since he came into his inheritance, he has come into a higher band of acquisitiveness. He does not wish to have aspirations that are beneath him, or to be parsimonious in his ambitions. And so he combines two intolerable things at the same time: the expansive breadth of a rich man's grasp, and an unyielding sense of deprivation.

To come to the point: Scripture teaches us how piteously lacking the rich man is, and how contemptible his poverty is. 5. Ahab was king of Israel and Naboth was a poor man. The former possessed the riches of his kingdom in abundance, the latter owned a strip of thin earth. The poor man coveted none of the rich man's possessions, but the king thought himself hard done by because his poverty-stricken neighbor owned a vineyard. So which of the two do you think looks poor? The one who is happy with what he has, or the one who covets what someone else owns? The one is poor in monetary terms, the other is poor in feeling. To be rich in feeling is to have no want; to have full coffers is to know no satisfaction for the yearnings of the breast. That is why the rich man is so greedy: he combines the possessiveness of wealth and the complaints of poverty. [. . .]

11. And Ahab said: "I shall have a vegetable garden" (1 Kings 21:2). This, then, was the sum of his madness, the whole matter of his outrage! He wanted room for some cheap vegetables! Your desires have no pretext of utility; you simply want to drive other people off! You are more interested in despoiling the poor than in enriching yourselves. You consider it an affront if a poor man owns anything worth a rich man's getting hold of. A credit on another's balance you count as a loss on your own.

What is the attraction nature's bounty has for you? The world was created for all; but you, the few rich men, try to keep it for yourselves. Not only land, but the very sky, air, and sea are appropriated for the use of the rich minority. How many communities can this air support, which you enclose in your extensive holdings? Do angels divide the sky into lots, as you portion out the earth with your boundary fences? 12. The prophet Isaiah cries, "Woe to those who join house to house and estate to estate" (Isa. 5:8), and he accuses them of useless avarice. For they shrink from living with their fellow men and drive their neighbors away; but they cannot avoid them, because when they have expelled one lot, they find others, and when they have driven those out, too, they find themselves in the neighborhood of others again. They cannot possibly live alone on the earth. Birds unite with other birds, until the sky is more or less blotted out with the huge flock in flight; cattle gather with other cattle, fish with other fish. They reckon it no hardship, but simply the business of life, when they make up a large company and gain reinforcement with the security of a closer grouping. It is only you, mankind, who drive your fellow man out, and welcome the wild beasts in, who build shelters for your livestock and demolish human habitations, who channel water onto your estates to support the game, and extend your fences so as to have nobody nearby. [. . .]

36. The rich man says [to his soul], "you have ample goods" (Luke 12:19). The greedy man has no idea of "goods," except investments. I agree with him: financial assets may be called "goods." So why make evils out of goods, when you ought to make goods out of evils? Scripture says: "make friends for yourselves by means of dishonest wealth" (Luke 16:9). Riches are goods for whoever knows how to use them properly, but evils for whoever does not. "He has distributed freely, he has given to the poor, his righteousness will endure for ever" (Ps. 112:9). What could be better? They are goods if you give them to the poor; by doing this you make God your debtor by a kind of pious loan. They are goods if you open up the storehouses of your righteousness, to be bread to the poor, life to the destitute, sight to the blind, a father to orphans.

37. Let me put it to you as you might to yourself: — You have the means to act, so what are you afraid of? You have ample goods laid up for many years. You can provide enough for yourself and others. You are a man of substance in the public eye. Why pull down your storehouses? Let me show you where you can keep your produce better, where you can lock it up securely, so that thieves cannot steal it from you (Matt. 6:20). Store it in the hearts of the poor, where the weevil cannot consume it and it cannot decay with age. The hearts of the needy, the homes of widows, the mouths of children are your repositories, so that they may say to you: "Out of the mouths of babes and sucklings thou hast perfected praise" (Ps. 8:2). These are the storehouses which will stand for ever, the granaries which future prosperity will not tear down. (For what will you do next, if there is an even larger yield next year? Will you pull down these barns which you are now building, and build others yet bigger?) God gives you prosperity, either to overcome or to condemn your greed, so that you may have no excuse. But you keep for yourself the yield that was meant, by your means, to do for many — or rather, you *steal* it, for you would *keep* it better if you shared it with others! The rewards of good offices return to those who grant them, and the good will expressed in generosity comes back to its source. To sum it up, Scripture says: "sow for yourselves righteousness" (Hos. 10:12). Be a spiritual farmer! sow what brings in a yield! There is good tillage in the hearts of widows. If the earth gives more fruit back than you put in, how many more times over will the interest on compassion return your capital! [. . .]

52. You are slaves, you rich men, and what a pitiful form of slavery it is, enslaved to delusion, to grasping desire, to insatiable greed! As a raging torrent gains force, it sweeps things along in its flood, discolored with mud like an overflowing well, gnawing away its earthen banks to no purpose. Or perhaps this illustration will be a serviceable warning: — If you draw no water, a well readily becomes fetid with disuse and stagnation, but when kept working it gleams to the sight and is sweet to drink. Similarly a dusty heap of riches looks attractive when used, but useless when idle. Draw something off from this well. "As water extinguishes a blazing fire, so almsgiving atones for sin" (Sir. 3:30). But stagnant water quickly breeds grubs. Don't let your treasure stand idle, nor your fire smoulder. It will smoulder within you, unless you get rid of it with charitable works. Think, rich man, of the fires you are in! Yours is the voice that cries: "Father Abraham, tell Lazarus to dip the tip of his finger in the water and cool my tongue!" (Luke 16:24).

53. Whatever you give to a poor man is for your good; whatever you lay out makes an increase for you. The food you give the poor man feeds yourself, since he who pities the poor is fed; and there is a harvest in such deeds. Compassion is sown in the earth, and buds in heaven; it is planted in the poor man, and blossoms before the face of God. "Do not say," God says, "'I will give tomorrow'" (Prov. 3:28). Will he who forbids you to say, "I will give tomorrow," allow you to say, "I will not give at all"? It is not from your own store that you give to the poor; it comes from his, and you simply return it. You take for yourself what is common, what is given for everyone's use. The earth is for all, not only for the rich; but the rich are the few who make no use of their wealth, as opposed to the many who do. So you are paying what you owe, not making a gratuitous donation. Which is why Scripture says to you: "turn your heart to the poor man and pay your debt, and answer him politely and courteously" (Sir. 4:8 Vulg.). [. . .]

63. The psalmist showed who they are [the "unwise of heart" in the text] by describing them precisely as "all men of riches" (Ps. 76:5 Vulg.). He said "all," making no exception. And he used the appropriate phrase, "men of riches," as opposed to "riches of men," showing that they were not the masters of their riches, but mastered by them. A possession should belong to its owner, not the other way round. So whoever does not employ his wealth as though he owned it, whoever has never learned to give to the poor and distribute alms, is the slave, not the master, of his resources. He is like a steward looking after someone else's, not a master making use of his own. Of such a state of mind we say that the man belongs to the riches, not the riches to the man. "A good understanding have all those who use it" (Ps. 111:10); but those who do not understand can claim no credit for understanding, and are fallen asleep in a drunken stupor. Men of this kind "sleep their own sleep" (Ps. 76:5); it is *their own* sleep they sleep, not Christ's. And those who do not sleep Christ's sleep, do not have Christ's peace, and do not rise with Christ's resurrection. The psalmist says: "I lay down and I rested, and I woke up, because the Lord will sustain me" (Ps. 3:5).

Translation: Paul Arnold and editors, from Corpus Scriptorum Ecclesiasticorum Latinorum, vol. 32.

From *Letter 7*

[Ambrose's correspondent, Simplicianus, would appreciate a discussion of St. Paul, either of his "counsels" (i.e., his mystical and spiritual theology) or his "judgments" (his moral teaching). Ambrose would prefer to leave the more exacting of these two tasks for when Simplicianus is to hand.]

4. Since you are away from home, I shall write about the judgments by which the apostle Paul summons us from slavery to freedom, saying: "You were bought for a price; do not become the slaves of men" (1 Cor. 7:23), showing that our freedom is in Christ and in the knowledge of wisdom. This doctrine is commonly tossed back and forth and bandied about in debate by philosophers, who say that "every wise man is a free man; every foolish man is a slave."

5. But Solomon said it long before this: "The foolish man changes like the moon" (Sir. 27:11 [Ben Sirach, not Solomon!]). The wise man is not broken by fear, nor affected by power, nor puffed up by success, nor overwhelmed by sorrows. For where there is wisdom, there is strength of spirit, resolution, and endurance. So the wise man has a constant mind, neither diminished nor inflated by fluctuating circumstances: he is not like the child whose mind wavers and is blown about "by every wind of doctrine" (Eph. 4:14), but he remains perfect in Christ, "grounded in love" and "rooted" in faith (Eph. 3:17). So the wise man takes no notice when his situation is unfavorable, and knows no inconsistency in spirit, but "will shine like the sun" (i.e., of righteousness), which shines "in his father's kingdom" (Matt. 13:43; Mal. 4:2).

6. But let us examine the sources in the moral and practical wisdom of our ancestors from which philosophy has imbibed this doctrine more extensively. Was not Noah the first, when, observing how his son Ham foolishly mocked his father's nakedness, he cursed him, saying: "Cursed be Ham, who shall be the household slave of his brothers" (Gen. 9:25)? He made his brothers his masters since they had wisely considered the respect due to their father's old age. 7. Did not Jacob, the source of all learning, deservedly promoted above his elder brother for his wisdom, instill the rich nourishment of this theme into all men's hearts? His virtuous father Isaac divided his fatherly affection equally between his two sons, but judged them differently, for affection grows out of a connection, whereas a judgment is formed by deserts. He showed favor to one, compassion to the other, favor to the wise one, compassion to the foolish; and since Esau could not attain to virtue by his own abilities nor take a step on his own account, Jacob blessed him by making him serve his brother as his slave, so demonstrating that foolishness is worse than slavery, and slavery is its remedy; for a foolish man cannot govern himself, and without a master is driven by his own volitions. 8. Esau's father, then, who loved him and cared for him, made him his brother's slave, to be guided by his good sense. Similarly, in public assemblies it is the wise who are put in command, to control the wayward populace with their special capacity and establish control with a show of their power. So by dint of their authority the wise compel people to obey, even reluctantly, those who know better and to comply with the laws. This was why Isaac laid the yoke on the fool as on an untamed animal, and in predicting that he must "live by his sword," denied him his freedom (Gen. 27:40). To protect him from heedlessly ruining himself, he was put in his brother's charge, under whose guiding authority he might progress to conversion. And because servitude has different levels — compulsory servitude is worse, voluntary better, as any good thing is finer when chosen rather than imposed — he imposed the yoke of obligation upon Esau first, and afterwards gave him the blessing of voluntary submission.

9. It is not nature, then, that makes a man a slave, but folly; and it is not emancipation which makes him free, but learning. Esau, after all, was born a free man and made a slave. Joseph was sold into slavery and was appointed to a position of power, ruler of those who had purchased him. Yet he did not scorn the duty of hard work, but retained the highest measure of virtue, preserving the freedom of innocence and the authority that probity commands. So the psalmist aptly says: "Joseph was sold into slavery, they bruised his feet in shackles" (Ps. 105:17-18). He says "he was sold into slavery," not "he became a slave"; and "they bruised his feet," not his spirit. 10. For how could his spirit be subdued, when, as the psalmist says: "His soul passed through iron" (Ps. 105:18)? For where others' souls are penetrated by sin (for "iron" stands for a sin which is capable of penetrating the soul), the "soul" of holy Joseph was so closed to sin that it penetrated the sin instead. Nor was he deflected by the allure of his mistress's seduction. Indeed, it was hardly surprising that he did not feel the flames of lust, for he burned more strongly with passion for God's favor. So it is aptly said of him that "the word of the Lord inflamed him" (Ps. 105:19), by which

means he "quenched the flaming arrows of the devil" (cf. Eph. 6:16). **11.** How could this man be a slave, who instructed the princes of the people in the administration of the grain supply, to give thought to the impending famine and to take steps against it? How could he be a slave, who "bought the whole land" and "reduced to servitude" the entire "population" of Egypt (Gen. 47:20-21), not to inflict a state of dishonorable slavery on them, but to establish a tax — "excepting the holdings of the priests" (Gen. 47:22), which he exempted from tax that the priesthood might be sacrosanct among the Egyptians too? **12.** His being sold did not make him a slave. He had, of course, been sold to traders; but if you were to make a sale-price your criterion, you would find many men who have bought young girls of quite attractive appearance, but captivated by love for them have surrendered themselves to degrading slavery. Apame, the concubine of Darius the king, was seen "sitting at his right hand, lifting off the crown from his head and placing it on her own, repeatedly striking his face with the palm of her left hand; and yet the king gazed open-mouthed at her, laughing whenever the woman smiled at him; but if she were resentful, he thought himself pitiable and ruined, so that he laid aside his power and wove a web of flattery, imploring her to be reconciled towards him" (1 Esdr. 4:29-31).

13. But what do we learn from this long digression? Do we not often see parents who have fallen into the hands of pirates or of brutal barbarians ransomed by their children? Is it possible that the laws of commerce are more powerful than the laws of nature? Is it possible that filial respect is prejudiced in the state of slavery? Many who buy lions do not master the lions, but are mastered; so that if they see them restlessly "shaking the collars from their neck" they run and hide. Therefore money makes no difference, for money generally buys masters for itself; and the same goes for sale lists at auctions, on which the buyer himself may often be advertised and sold up. A contract does not change a man's species, nor reduce the freedom bestowed by wisdom. In short, as it is written, "many sons serve a wise servant" (cf. Prov. 17:2), and it is the intelligent slave who rules foolish masters.

14. So then, which do you consider the more free? Only wisdom is truly free, which has set poor men over rich, and which makes "slaves lend at interest to their own masters" (cf. Prov. 22:7) — lend, that is, their intelligence, not money, but that "talent" which they have from the Lord's eternal treasure, which is never tarnished and commands a high rate of interest. Wisdom makes them lend the intellectual coin of heavenly oracles, about which the law states: "You will lend to the nations, but you shall not borrow" (Deut. 15:6). What a Hebrew lent to the nations, was not some learning acquired from popular culture. To him the Lord had opened his treasure, and he passed it on, that he might refresh the nations with the rain of his discourse, and become a prince of the nations, while himself having no prince over him.

15. The free man, therefore, is the wise man, "bought with a price," i.e., of heavenly oracles, with the "gold" and "silver" of God's discourse, "redeemed by the precious blood" (1 Pet. 1:18f.) — for it is important to recognize our Purchaser — "bought with the coin" of grace, the man who has heard and understood Isaiah's words: "Everyone who is thirsty, come to the water, and whoever does not have money, come and buy, drink and eat" (Isa. 55:1). **16.** The free man is the man who, if on going into battle he sees a beautiful woman, and in plundering the wealth of his enemies he finds her and desires her there (Deut. 21:10-14), when she has removed what is superfluous and put off her captive's garb, makes her his wife, treating her not as a slave but as a free woman; for he understands that wisdom and learning cannot support a servile status. And so the law states: "she must not be sold for money" (Deut. 21:14); for her worth cannot be matched by any precious thing. Job says, "draw wisdom deep within yourself, for the topaz of Ethiopia cannot be compared with it" (Job 28:18f. Old Latin Version), because it is considered more valuable than gold and silver.

17. Yes, he is free who has not suffered the highest bidder as his master, nor seen the finger raised to bid at auction; but freer still is he who is free within himself, free by the laws of nature. He knows that the rule of nature governs morals, not status, and that the measure of what a man contributes does not correspond to human *fiat* but to natural principles. Is it enough, do you think, to say this man is free, or should we think of him as a kind of judge, a supervisor of morality? So Scripture rightly says that "the poor will be commanders of the rich" (Prov. 22:7), that is to say, private citizens of those who run affairs.

18. Or is he free, do you think, who buys votes and cares more for popular acclaim than for the prudent judgment of the wise? Is he free, who is swayed by the winds of popular opinion, who dreads the whispers of the masses? It is not freedom which the slave receives on manumission, and acquires from the hand of the magistrate. For freedom consists, I believe, in virtue — not the virtue of expansive liberality, but a virtue which is demanded and possessed by a sense of own proper pride, unswayed by others' opinions. For the wise man is always a free man, always highly regarded, always presiding over the laws. "The law," after all, "has not been ordained for the just man, but for the unjust" (1 Tim. 1:9). The just man "is the law to himself." He has no further need to call the image of virtue to mind, since he carries it locked within his heart, "having the work of the law written on the tablets of his heart" (cf. Rom. 2:14f.). To him it could be said: "drink water from your own cisterns and from the springs of your own wells" (Prov. 5:15). For what is as near to us as the word of God? This is the "word which is in our hearts and on our lips" (cf. Rom. 10:8; Deut. 30:14), which we can neither perceive nor grasp.

19. The wise man, then, is free, since whoever does what he wills is free; but not every volition is good, and it is the sign of the wise man that he wills whatever is good; he hates evil, because he has chosen the good. So if he has chosen what is good, in determining his own choice and making choice of his own activity, he is free. He does what he wills; it follows that the wise man is free.

Translation: Paul Arnold and editors, from Corpus Scriptorum Ecclesiasticorum Latinorum, vol. 82.

Letter 50

To Studius:

I am grateful for your kindly and well-motivated feelings toward me, for your commitment to the faith and for the fear in which you hold our Lord Jesus Christ. On such a matter even I would hesitate to give an answer, confined as I am on the one hand by the commission you hold to enforce the law, and on the other by the demands of mercy and benevolence. Yet on precisely this point you have the apostle's authority: the judge "bears not the sword in vain . . . for he is the avenger of God" against wrongdoers (Rom. 13:4).

Though you know this well enough, you have thought it worth pursuing the question further. For some believers — not, however, in fellowship with the church — refuse to admit to communion in the sacraments of heaven those who have been party to death sentences. And there are magistrates who, refraining of their own accord from such a measure, are admired for it. We cannot refuse them praise, though accepting the apostle's authority, we cannot refuse the others communion either.

Authority, you see, has its rights; but compassion has its policy. You will be excused if you do it; but you will be admired if you refrain when you might have done it. And, as a priest, I have no more enthusiasm for leaving people to rot in noisome dungeons without trial, only to set them free later. It might transpire, after all, that once the case had been tried, the convicted person could sue successfully for pardon or, at any rate, better conditions in which to "live out his days in jail" (a quotation, I can't think from whom). Yet I know that pagan governors have sometimes made a boast of returning from their tour of duty without a drop of blood on their blade. If pagans can do as much, what should Christians be doing?

Here is the reply our Savior gives to all such questions. When the Jews caught the adulteress, they brought her under guard to the Savior, to see if he would let her go, and so abolish the law of which he said "I have not come to abolish the law, but to fulfill it" (Matt. 5:17), or if he would condemn her and so run up against a limit to his purpose of redemption. Anticipating it all, the Lord Jesus stooped down and "wrote upon the ground." As for what he wrote, the text from the prophet Jeremiah about King Jeconiah tells us: "Earth, earth . . . write these men down as forsaken!" (Jer. 22:29f.). The names of Jewish accusers are written on the ground; the names of believing Christians are written in heaven. On the ground are the names of those forsaken by their true father, who have tempted him and brought reproach against the author of salvation. Faced with Jewish accusers, Jesus lowers his head, and then, since he "has nowhere to lay his head," raises it again as though to pronounce judgment, saying: "'Let him who is without sin be the first to throw a stone!' Again he lowered his head and wrote on the ground. Hearing this, they began to leave, one by one, beginning with the eldest" (John 8:7-9). Perhaps they had more on their consciences, having lived longer; or perhaps they had acquired more discretion and saw the force of his judgment more quickly. Anyway, having first come to accuse someone else's fault, now they began to experience compunction at their own.

When they left, Jesus remained alone. Raising his head, he addressed the woman: "Where are your accusers? Has nobody thrown a stone?" And she replied,

"No one." "Neither shall I condemn you," he said. "Go, and take care to sin no more" (John 8:9-11). He does not condemn, for he is the Redemption. He corrects faults, for he is the Life. He washes sins away, for he is the Source. When he stoops, it is to lift up those who are down; and that is why his voice is the voice of forgiveness: "Neither shall I condemn you."

There is your model. It may be that this criminal has the potential to be reformed. If he is unbaptized, it may be that he will come to accept the forgiveness of sins; if he is baptized, he may do penance and offer his body for Christ. There are many routes to salvation! But the reason our predecessors preferred to err on the side of permissiveness to judges, is that their sword should command terror, so that criminal madness should be suppressed, not encouraged. If they were refused communion, it would look as though punishing criminals were itself to be punished. They came to the view that it should lie with the magistrate's free exercise of restraint, not be a matter of legal requirement.

Farewell. Think of us with the affection with which we think of you.

Translation: Editors, from Corpus Scriptorum Ecclesiasticorum Latinorum, vol. 82.

From *The Duties of Clergy,* Book 1

28. Justice, then, enables the association of the human race and its community. For the social principle can be analyzed under two heads, *justice* and *goodwill* (also called "liberality" and "kindness"). Justice seems to me to be the higher, liberality the more attractive. The one has to do with criticism, the other with generosity.

But we dismiss what philosophers take to be the fundamental exercise of justice: for they present it as the primary criterion of justice that we do no harm except in return for harm done. This is refuted by the authority of the gospel, for Scripture would have us indwelt by the Spirit of the Son of Man, who came to bring grace, not to inflict harm. The secondary criterion of justice they identify is to treat common or public property as public, private as private. But this is not even natural. Nature's bounty is universal, for the common use of all. God has so ordained the law of universal generation that there is common food for all and that the earth is a kind of common possession. Nature, therefore, is the source of *common* right; it was greed that created *private* right.

In this connection we are told that the Stoics taught that everything produced from the earth was created for the use of men, but that men come forth for men's sake, to be of help to one another. But where have they got such doctrines, if not from our Scriptures? Moses wrote that God said, "Let us make man in our image, after our likeness; and let them have dominion over the fish of the sea, and over the birds of the air, and over the cattle, and over every creeping thing that creeps upon the earth" (Gen. 1:26). And David said, "Thou hast put all things under his feet, all sheep and oxen, and also the beasts of the field, the birds of the air, and the fish of the sea" (Ps. 8:6f.). So these philosophers have learned from our teachers that all things are subject to man, and that is why they think they were produced for man's sake. That man was made for the sake of man we also find in the books of Moses, where the Lord says, "It is not good that the man should be alone; let us make him a helper fit for him" (Gen. 2:18). So the woman was given to the man to help him, to bear him children, and in that way men began to be of help to one another. Again, before the woman was formed it was said of Adam, "There was not found an helper fit for him" (Gen. 2:20). For only a human being could be of help to another. Among all the living creatures, then, none was found like him, or to put it plainly, to be his helper. The female sex was what was looked for as a help.

So in keeping with the will of God (or, to put it another way, with the natural law of association) we ought to be of help to one another and to vie with each other in rendering services; we ought to put all our advantages in the common pool, as it were, and be a "helper" (as Scripture says) by sympathetic interest, by discharging responsibilities, by giving money, by performing tasks, or however; so that the attractiveness of human fellowship may be seen among us to the best advantage. Nor should we ever be deterred from our responsibilities by anxiety about the risks, but treat adversity as something in which we have as much a common stake as we do in prosperity. Saintly Moses, after all, did not shrink from undertaking terrible wars for his people's sake; he was not afraid when the mightiest king offered battle, nor was he frightened at savage barbarian cruelty. He set aside his own safety to give his people freedom.

Justice, then, is a resplendent quality. By serving the good of others rather than self, it makes community and association possible. It holds the highest place, has everything subject to its judgment, offers help, supplies resources, does not refuse responsibility but accepts the risks that others bring. Here, surely, is a veritable fortress of virtue, which any strategist would be glad to hold — but for that elemental greed which can weaken and drain the resistance even of a virtue so well defended? For while our policy is to expand our capital, accumulate resources, include new territories in our acquisitions, achieve a commanding financial standing, we have stripped away the formal condition of justice by letting go the practice of mutual assistance. How can anyone be just whose goal is to get something for himself which someone else has? Hunger for power, too, gives a womanly weakness to the masculine contours of justice. How can one take the part of others, when one's purpose is to make them subject to oneself? How can one aid the weak against the strong, when one's aim is power to subvert their liberty?

29. The scope of justice is apparent. There is no place, no person, no time to which it is irrelevant. Even our enemies benefit from it. If, for instance, a site or a day is agreed on with them for a battle, it would be considered unjust to preempt the place or time; for it makes a difference whether one is taken in a battle where the forces have been seriously engaged or merely as the result of some chance advantage or hazard. The more savage and perfidious our enemies' behavior, the greater the harm they do, the more savage the retaliation. We can see this in the case of the Midianites, who used their women to entice many of the Jewish men to sin, which resulted in the wrath of God being poured out on the people of that generation; which is why Moses, when victory was won, allowed none of them to live (Num.

31:17). The Gibeonites, on the other hand, who had used fraud rather than warfare to entrap the people, were not exterminated but subjected to slavery (Josh. 9:21). But the Syrians, escorted into the city they were besieging when they had been struck with sudden blindness and could not tell where they were going, Elisha would not agree to slay. He said to the king of Israel who proposed it, "You shall not slay those whom you have not taken captive with your spear and with your sword. Set bread and water before them, that they may eat and drink and go back to their home." They would make known to the world their appreciation for the generous gesture; and we read, "the Syrians came no more on raids into the land of Israel" (2 Kings 6:22f.).

If, then, justice is binding even in war, all the more should it be observed in peace. This same gesture of kindness was the prophet's response to those who had come to arrest him. The narrative tells how the king of Syria had sent his army to kidnap him, knowing that it was Elisha who frustrated all his plans and deliberations. Gehazi the prophet's servant, seeing the army, became afraid for his safety; but the prophet said: "Fear not, for those who are with us are more than those who are with them." And in response to the prophet's prayer, the servant's eyes were opened, and Gehazi saw the whole mountain covered with horses and chariots protecting Elisha. As they closed in Elisha cried: "Strike, O God, the army of Syria with blindness!" His prayer granted, he said to the Syrians: "Follow me, and I will bring you to the man whom you seek." Then they saw Elisha, whom they were intending to arrest, yet though they saw him they could not lay their hands on him (2 Kings 6:15-19). The moral is that good faith and justice should be observed even in war; and that there can be no honor in a war where faith is violated.

The ancients used to call their enemies "strangers," a less harsh name; it was ancient custom that foes should be referred to in this way. This too we can say they adopted from our writings; for the Hebrews used to call their foes *allophylloi*, that is, "of another race." For so we read in the first book of Kings [i.e., 1 Sam.]: "It came to pass in those days that they of another race put themselves in array against Israel" (1 Sam. 4:1 Septuagint).

The foundation, then, of justice is faith, for the hearts of the just are preoccupied with faith; and the person who justly accuses himself constructs his justice upon good faith, for his justice is apparent when he confesses the truth. So the Lord says through Isaiah (28:16): "Behold I am laying in Zion for a foundation a stone." This refers to Christ as the foundation of the church. For the faith of all believers is simply Christ; and the Church is, as it were, the form that justice takes, the common right of all. Her prayer is the prayer of the community; her works are the works of the community; her trials are the trials of the community. A just man, in sum, worthy of Christ, is someone who accepts that he is not his own. And that is why Paul insisted that Christ must be the foundation; because faith is the foundation of our works of justice, it is on him that they should be constructed. Iniquity is what characterizes our evil works, justice our good works.

From Book 2

15. There are many ways for liberality to be expressed. There is the daily dole for those who need a square meal to keep body and soul together. Then whatever is left over from this may be used to help and support those too embarrassed to show their need publicly in the dole queue. (Here, of course, I am speaking of what may be done by someone in a position of responsibility, such as a priest or an almoner. He should report names to the bishop — all the names of those whom he knows to be in want, whether their condition has always been so or whether they have been reduced to want from wealth, especially if it is not a case of youthful irresponsibility but of invasion or loss to an estate, bringing them to a pass where they cannot find the next meal.)

An outstanding act of liberality is to redeem prisoners from enemy captivity, rescuing men from slaughter, women from violation, reuniting children with parents and parents with children, repatriating citizens to their homeland. These activities were sadly much in evidence during the invasions of Illyricum and Thrace. What a glut of prisoners there was on the world's slave markets — yet the total number of those exported for sale elsewhere did not amount to the number on sale in that one province! (But there was actually a move to reenslave those whom the church had bought out — a nastier business than slavery itself, working in opposition to other people's deeds of mercy! Had those responsible been taken prisoner themselves, *they* would have had to serve as slaves, however free their legal status! Had they themselves been sold at market, *they* would have had to accept the purchaser's claims on their service! How, then, did they pretend to set aside others' free status, when in such circumstances they could not have set their own servile condition aside — unless the purchaser was willing to accept his money back, which would not be setting aside but buying out?) So it is an especially fine act of liberality to redeem prisoners, particularly from uncivilized enemies, who will show no more common humanity in pitying their prisoners than is prompted by their greed at the thought of the redemption price.

Other examples of liberality are: to assume debts, which the debtor cannot discharge when he is pressed to do so, being without resources to meet a lawful claim; to undertake the education of children; to act as guardian to orphans. Others arrange marriages for young women who have lost their parents, in a way that will not offend decency, putting not only their good offices at their disposal but a dowry, too. And there is that other form of liberality of which the Apostle instructs us: "If any believer has relatives who are widows let him assist them; let the Church not be burdened, so that it may assist those who are real widows" (1 Tim. 5:16).

Liberality of this description, then, is valuable; but it is not for all to exercise it. For there are many good men of limited means, who are content with the little they need for their own use and are not equipped to give aid to relieve others' poverty. But they can show kindness in another way and be of assistance to those less well-off. For liberality is of two kinds: one to give material support, that is, putting out money; the other to engage in practical assistance, which is often much finer and nobler. For Abraham to rescue his son-in-law from captivity by a victory in arms was so much more impressive than to buy him back! Saintly Joseph was of so much greater use to king Pharaoh with his planning for the future than he would have been had he brought him money! Money would not have bought back the fruitfulness of a single city; his policies kept the famine at bay for five years from the whole of Egypt.

Money is easily spent; practical wisdom can never be exhausted, but grows more resourceful as it is used. Financial reserves are reduced, and quickly run out, so that charitable projects, too, find themselves short. The more cases one wants to help, the fewer one can actually help. You often end up short of something that you had planned to give to others. But advice and active help replenish their own source. They are no less available for being shared. The rich capital of prudence regenerates itself; the more it is put out, the more active what is left becomes.

16. It is clear, then, that there should be method in liberality, that our generosity may not be wasted. A judicious attitude must be preserved, especially by priests, whose giving should not be for show but for justice. The greed of beggars today is quite without precedent. They come in the pink of health, for no reason but their vagrancy. They are perfectly prepared to drain the resources and dry up the support of the poor. They are never satisfied with little, always asking for more. By parading the state of their clothing they elicit a favorable first reaction, and then they make up a story about their origins to get the most out of it. If one were too trustful, one would quickly exhaust the funds meant for the relief of the poor. We need to be methodical, so that beggars may not depart empty-handed, but neither will the paupers' fund be signed away as rich pickings for extortioners. We must act with a sense of proportion, not suppressing humane sympathy, not leaving true need without a recourse.

Translation: Editors, from *PL,* vol. 16.

John Chrysostom

(ca. 349-407)

It is inviting to make a comparison between John Chrysostom and Ambrose, as Eastern and Western versions of the church's champion in an imperial capital, wrestling not only with secular but with rival ecclesiastical forces, prepared to be boldly confrontational but by no means above the obsequiousness endemic to court life. Both mobilized their forces from the pulpit of their churches as great rhetoricians. ("Chrysostom" means, of course, "Golden-mouth." John's extensive literary corpus consists almost entirely of sermons transcribed by copyists, sometimes apparently unrevised.) Neither was a thinker of great intellectual individuality, though both had a cultivated intelligence and spoke to, and on behalf of, the reflective Christian conscience of their age. Both had strong social agendas, promoted the ascetic movement, and were the two most prominent fourth-century critics of private wealth and advocates of church-organized welfare provision. John is a demonstration that the Latin-speaking West had no monopoly on conflict between ecclesiastical and secular government in the new Christian empire.

The comparison once established, the differences are as instructive as the similarities. Some are simply personal and historical. Ambrose was already entrenched in his see when the court arrived; John was imported to Constantinople by a government eager to reinforce the standing of its capital city with a reputation already established at Antioch. In confrontation, John failed where Ambrose succeeded. Banished in 404 by an imperially stage-managed council of ecclesiastical opponents, he spent his last three years in unhappy exile in Anatolia, driven finally to death from exhaustion by an unforgiving government that could not feel safe while there remained the possibility of his return. Temperamentally, John was the less secure: there was a rigidity in his dealings with his church and an instability in his reactions to the fluctuations of his protracted quarrel with the empress Eudoxia. And there were intellectual differences, too.

Many of John's sermons are in exegetical series, and it is in this mode of preaching that he displays his intelligence to the best advantage. Through the flamboyant discursiveness of his moral exhortation we can discern one of the most careful readers of the biblical text that the patristic church produced. The exposition of Romans, from the Antioch years, is a fine example. His insistence that Paul thought God appointed government as such, not each and every government, illustrates his care with important nuances of meaning, and is almost certainly right. His analysis of Paul's argument into two parallel trains of thought, one presenting government as a deterrent to crime, the other as a beneficial support for virtue, though probably not right as it stands, is a thoughtful reading worthy of serious engagement. Yet both interpretative moves accord well with the Greek-Christian predisposition to find in government a direct mediation of God's beneficial providence. Social subordination of one being to another is simply a reflection of that subordination we come to expect from the natural order, a Platonizing conception of society which contrasts sharply with the assumption of original equality that we find in Western Christians such as Irenaeus or Lactantius.

With this accords also a rather different model for understanding church-state conflict, not as a conflict of *societies* but as a conflict of *ruling offices*. In the fourth of the disjointed series of sermons on Isaiah's vision in the temple ("I saw the Lord," Isa. 6:1), the relation of priest and king in ancient Israel provides the pattern by which sacred and secular are to be distinguished. This passage probably does not come directly from Chrysostom's hand, but it is certainly based wholly upon his material. Uzziah's presumptuous sin, as recounted in 2 Chronicles, is used to emphasize the higher dignity of the priestly role and the need for each role to know the limits of its sphere of authority. The limits of the priestly role, however, were to be widely drawn. The passage from the Eleventh Homily on Acts (dating from 400, when John had been in Constantinople for three years) illustrates the grandiose scale of his ambitions for a city-wide welfare system which would be centralized in the hands of the church authorities and would serve to promote the missionary absorption of the pagan population into the church.

Some of John's most interesting views on the relation of the spheres of priesthood and secular rule were evoked by an incident early in his career, in 387, when, newly ordained as a priest at Antioch under the elderly bishop Flavian, he was forced to adapt his series of Lenten sermons to respond to a crisis precipitated by a riot in the city, in which statues of the emperor Theodosius and his family were desecrated. Prompt action by the authorities resulted in the suppression of the rioters; but then the horror began. An assault on the emperor's statues was an affront to his person and high treason. Theodosius, a military man, was capable of extremes both of piety and violence; a few years later an outrage in Thessalonica would provoke a retaliatory massacre, for which he would do penance before Ambrose. A two-man commission was sent to investigate and try the city councillors. Their sentence included the political degrading of the city, the replacement of civic by military rule, the closing of city amenities and the banishment or execution of various councillors. Before the death penalties were carried out, however, the commissioners were persuaded to refer them to the emperor for ratification. And Flavian, who had set out for Constantinople as soon as the incident occurred, was ready to see what he could do in the capital.

This drama affords us a close view of the church's practice, which had grown up in the fourth century, of intercession in capital charges. Chrysostom's accounts of the intercession of local monks with the commissioners and of Bishop Flavian with the emperor are highly idealized, but they show us clearly what fourth-century Christians thought this practice was about. We may detect in them what may be called an *aesthetic* of Christian government: the drama of overcoming wrath with mercy, subduing political and military power with spiritual, is reenacted in a crisis to provide a kind of ritual legitimation of the governing authorities in a Christian society. The role of the ascetics is of great significance in this imaginative construct, since they represent an authority from beyond the social structure, divine messengers who intervene in the hard logic of crime and punishment. But how much subversion can this logic tolerate? Such a dramatic incident occurs, we may suspect, only at the *limit* of governmental power. Precisely because it is not a routine case, but involves such extraordinary considerations as a personal insult to the emperor and a whole city's liability, the incident at Antioch provides the opportunity for church and state to play out their roles of reconciler and reconciled. It is the way in which Christian emperor and Christian citizens pledge their mutual understanding that *these* great gestures of injured wrath are unfitting for those forgiven by Christ's blood. The failure of this understanding at Thessalonica five years later was to be a shock, one which required a very formal and public gesture to make good.

The rhetorical argument against wealth, typical of many, taken from the Homilies on 1 Timothy (probably from the Constantinople period), centers on his objection to *private* property. It would be a misunderstanding to read it as an attack on material goods as such, nor do we ever find in John the suspicion that ownership by communities could be as greedy as ownership by individuals. Separating resources from the common stock and keeping them in private hands is the root offense; anything that perpetuates the result of that offense perpetuates its guilt. The moral worth of charitable giving is to reverse it; in passing to others the resources that they need, the giver reasserts the original community of goods. John therefore sets a high moral premium on the *mobility* of wealth, while opposing the acquisitive instinct which in some modern theories is thought to serve it, as well as opposing the conservative desire to perpetuate inherited estates. A curious feature is his preference for animate forms of wealth, such as livestock and slaves; the reason presumably is that possession in these cases implies an element of beneficent care. Of interest, too, is his appeal not only to the necessary community in natural goods (sun, air, water, etc.), a venerable Stoic argument, but also to a necessary community in certain political goods. This yields an unusual argument for aristocratic and monarchical organization: that they sustain at different levels the equal community of goods which any form of individualism destroys. And here we find that John has his own idea of equality as *unhindered access* to the benefits of common property. The significance of the natural orders of society is that they define the communities within which equal access is safeguarded.

Further Reading: G. Dagron, *Naissance d'une capitale, Constantinople et ses institutions de 330 à 451* (Paris: Presses Universitaires de France, 1974); A.-J. Festugière, *Antioche paienne et chrétienne: Libanius, Chrysostome et les moines de Syrie* (Paris: Éditions de Boccard, 1959); J. N. D. Kelly, *Golden Mouth: The Story of John Chrysostom, Ascetic, Preacher, Bishop* (London: Duckworth, 1995); A. M. Ritter, *Charisma im Verständis des Johannes Chrysostomos und seiner Zeit* (Göttingen: Vandenhoeck & Ruprecht, 1972).

From the Twenty-Fourth Homily on Romans

"Let every person be subject to the governing authorities" (Rom. 13:1). This is a theme he develops at length in other epistles, too; and the subjection he expects of household servants to their masters is extended here to subjects and their rulers. This is to show that it was not to overthrow the shared political arrangements *(politeia)* that Christ promulgated his laws, but to reform them and to teach us not to be accepting of needless and purposeless wars. We encounter quite enough hostility from antagonism to the truth, without needless and purposeless things to endure in addition!

Note how appropriate the occasion for embarking on this subject. He has demanded of us great wisdom that can put us at the service of friend and foe alike, and can make us useful equally to those in prosperity and adversity, to the needy and, in short, to all. He has planted a society fit for angels, leaving the spirit of resistance without an object, subjecting disorder to restraint, and establishing a calm perspective on every front. And at that point he introduces advice in this sphere. For if we are bound to repay those who injure us with treatment of the opposite kind, we are bound *à fortiori* to obey our benefactors. But he places this argument at the climax of his exhortation, and at this juncture does not develop the line of thought I indicate, but sticks to the argument that performance is demanded as a matter of obligation.

At the outset he is clear that the requirement applies to everyone, priests and monks included, not to those in secular occupations alone, saying, "Let every person be subject to the governing authorities," — whether you are an apostle, an evangelist, a prophet, or whatever, since this "subjection" does not subvert religion. "Be subject," he says, not simply "obey." And the first claim which such an enactment has on us, a reason persuasive to believers, is that this is an ordinance of God: "For there is no authority except from God."

"What?" you ask Paul. "Is every ruler appointed by God?" "That is not my meaning," he replies. "I am not talking about each ruler individually, but about the institution of government. That there should be structures of government, that some should govern and others be governed, that things should not drift haphazard and at random, with whole populations tossed like waves to and fro: this, I say, is the achievement of God's wisdom." That is why the text does not say, "there is no ruler except from God," but, speaking of the institution: "there is no authority except from God, and those that exist have been instituted by God." In the same way, when the wise man says, "By the Lord is a woman joined to a man" (Prov. 19:14 Septuagint), he means that God instituted marriage, not that he joins each couple individually.

For we see many badly mismatched couples joined in lawful matrimony, and we would never attribute this state of things to God. But the point the wise man was making is precisely what Christ said: "He who made them from the beginning made them male and female, and said, 'For this reason a man shall leave his father and mother and be joined to his wife, and the two shall become one flesh'" (Matt. 19:4f.).

Equality of rank often breeds strife, and that is why God made many forms of rule and subordination: man and wife, child and parent, elder and younger, slave and free, ruler and ruled, teacher and student. It is hardly surprising that he should have made the same principle operate in society as in our physical constitution. For the parts of the body are not all equal, but some smaller, some greater, some control operations and some are subject to control. And you will see the same principle at work in irrational creatures: in bees, for example, or cranes, or herds of wild grazing animals. Neither is the sea devoid of this social organization; but many marine species marshal themselves behind a leading fish and so make long expeditions in formation. In every context anarchy is an evil, a source of disturbance.

Having indicated the source of government, he adds: "Therefore he who resists authority, resists what God has appointed." You see the principle to which he refers, the sanction to which he appeals, the source of obligation to which he points! In case believers should object: "Here we are destined to enjoy the Kingdom of Heaven, yet you so belittle and demean us as to demand subjection to rulers!" his argument makes it clear it is not rulers but God, once again, to whom we are subject. To be subject to government is to obey God. But that is not how he puts it, "to be subject to rulers is to obey God"; but the other way round, as a warning, sharpening the issue: "to ignore the demand is to rebel against God whose institution it is." What he is determined to make clear from every point of view is that we do not obey them as a favor, but as a duty.

This way he was more likely to attract unbelieving rulers to faith, as well as believers to obedience. For there was at that time a fair amount of slander directed at the apostles, accusing them of civil disturbance and revolution, and of acting and preaching for the overthrow of the community's laws. When you show that the master we acknowledge gives this charge to his people, you silence the slander of those who describe us as agitators and you give eloquent testimony to the true teaching. Don't be ashamed, then, he tells us, of this subordination. God has instituted it, and will penalize disregard of his provisions effectively. The punishment for recalcitrance is not routine, but grave, and there is no plea for exemption. You will be subject to the most severe of human penalties, with no one to defend you, and you will provoke God horribly. All of which is allusively implied in the words, "those who resist will incur judgment."

Turning then to complement the warnings with the positive aspects of the institution, Paul argues in its support: "For rulers are not a terror to good conduct, but to bad." He has struck a hard blow, and floored them; now, like a good doctor applying soothing ointment, he sets them on their feet again with some encouragement: "Why be afraid? Why nervous? Do those that do well incur censure? Do those who practice virtue have anything to fear?" So he goes on: "Would you have no fear of authority? Then do what is good, and you will receive its approval." You see how he reconciles the reader to the ruler, representing him as a judge who awards him approval. You see how he leaves the spirit of resistance without an object! "For he is God's servant for your good." He is the very opposite of terror, Paul declares: he gives approval! The very opposite of prohibition, he offers assistance! If you find he approves and assists you, why would you not be subject to him? Besides, he makes virtue easier for you by meting out punishment to the wicked, rewards and honor to the good, and cooperating with God's will; which is why Paul calls him God's "minister." Consider: I give you advice about responsible behavior, and he supports that advice through laws. I urge that it is wrong to cheat and steal, and he holds assizes to deal with just those activities. So he is a collaborator and assistant to us, sent by God for this purpose. There are two points there that demand respect: that he is sent by God, and that it is for this purpose.

"But if you do wrong, be afraid" — (it is not the ruler, then, who makes us afraid, but our own wrongdoing) — "for he does not bear the sword in vain;" — you see how he has put him on armed guard like a soldier to frighten off malefactors — "he is the servant of God to execute his wrath on the wrongdoer." Punishment, vengeance, and sword again! And to stop you darting off with fright at the sound of it, he repeats that government fulfills God's law. Without being conscious of doing so, perhaps, but what of that? God has impressed its character on it. If, then, this role of punishing and honoring, vindicating virtue and expelling vice, is a service to God that he has willed, why react against an agency of so much good, which facilitates your own good, too? Many have begun to take trouble with the right course of life because of government, and have subsequently attached themselves to it from the fear of God. There are morally insensitive people who are not so moved by the future as they are by the present. An agency, then, which deploys fear and honor to prepare the mind of the majority and make it more ready for the word of instruction, is quite reasonably described as the servant of God.

"Therefore one must be subject, not only to avoid wrath but also for the sake of conscience." What does "not only to avoid wrath" mean? He means, not only that insubordination opposes God and brings great evils on one's head, both at God's hands and the government's, but that government is highly beneficial, ensuring peace and good administration of society. Innumerable benefits accrue to cities from their governments, and if you removed them everything would disappear: neither city nor region nor houses nor market nor anything else would remain in place, but everything would be topsy-turvy while the strong swallowed up the weak. So quite apart from sanctions attached to disobedience, we should accept our subjection simply so as not to appear unconscious of our obligations and unaware of who has protected our interests.

"For the same reason you also pay taxes, for the authorities are ministers of God, attending to this very thing." Without going into detail about the benefits accruing to cities from their governments, such as civil order, peace, public services, including those responsible for military and economic arrangements, he makes his case entirely from this one observation. By contributing tax, you acknowledge that you receive benefits. See the wisdom and wit of blessed Paul! The thing that seems

94

most onerous and oppressive, the system of exactions, he takes as proof that government provides for us! Why give tax to the king? he asks. Is the payment not a recognition of his care in providing and protecting? Yet we would never have paid had we not known from the first that such a sovereignty was profitable. This has always been the reason for the community's decision to support their rulers: they neglect their own private business to look after the public business, and by spending all their time on it protect our interests.

Having spoken, then, about the extrinsic advantages, he returns to his previous argument, as more effective to carry the believer with him. He points out once again that it is God's decree, and focuses his discussion upon this point, "they are God's ministers." To this he then adds mention of the trouble and effort they expend: "attending to this very thing." This is their life, this is their concern, that you may enjoy peace. So in another letter Paul instructs us not only to be subject but to pray for them, and there again points to the common interest, adding, "that we may live a quiet and peaceable life" in all things (1 Tim. 2:2). For it is no minor contribution to the conditions of our present life that they make, providing defenses, keeping enemies at bay, suppressing disruptive forces in political communities, affording a final resolution of all disputes. Don't raise objections about one or another abuse of government, but look at the appropriateness of the institution as such, and you will discern the great wisdom of him who ordained it from the beginning.

Translation: Editors, from F. Field, ed., *Iohannis Chrysostomi interpretatio omnium epistularum Paulinarum* (Oxford, 1845-62).

From the Seventeenth Homily *On the Statues*

1. When the emperor's commissaries sent to inquire into the incident constructed that alarming platform for their hearings, and summoned everyone to answer for the outrages, so that the universal expectation was a capital sentence of one or another order, then it was that the monks who inhabited the mountain slopes displayed their philosophy. After so many years' seclusion in their cells, when they saw the dark cloud hanging over the city, at nobody's request and nobody's prompting, they left their shacks and caves and came flooding down from all directions, like so many angels from heaven. At that moment, as those saints appeared on every side, the city was like heaven to look at; the very sight inspirited the woebegone citizens, and helped them shrug their calamity off. To see them was enough to make one laugh at death and care little for one's life. But that was not the only remarkable thing. They approached the judges directly, and spoke up boldly on behalf of the arraigned. They were all prepared to shed their own blood and to lay their own heads on the block to save the prisoners from the terrible fate that awaited them, and refused to leave until the judges would either declare immunity for the city's population, or remand them with the arraigned to appear before the emperor. "He is a devout man," they said, "who rules over our region of the world. He is a believer, a man

of religious life, so we shall certainly win him round. But we will not agree to blood-letting and executions; we will not tolerate them. If you refuse to exercise restraint, we shall certainly die at their side. The outrage was deplorable, we grant you; but the lawlessness of those events is not too much for the emperor's clemency." Another observation full of profundity is attributed to one: "Statues were knocked down and set up again; their proper appearance was restored, and the mischief soon put right. But if you slay God's image, how will you ever recover the damage? How can you res-urrect the slain, or restore souls to their bodies?" And they had much to say to them on the subject of judgment. . . .

2. More striking even than the impotence of the rich and powerful, was the helplessness of those who had been empowered to judge, holders of the highest of-fices. When urged by these same monks to give a decision for mercy, they said they had no control over the outcome. It was a risky and perilous business, not only to in-sult the emperor, but to let those who had been convicted of insulting him go scot-free. Yet our monks prevailed over them all. Self-confident, persistent, and importu-nate, they cajoled them into exercising a power which lay outside their imperial terms of reference: they were able to persuade the judges, after those responsible had been convicted, not to vote on sentence but to refer the last stage to the discretion of the emperor, assuring them that they would certainly persuade him to show clem-ency to those who had sinned against him. And they began preparations for the journey; but the judges, put to shame by their philosophy and impressed by their proud resolution, declared that they would not agree to send them on so long a jour-ney; but if they were simply to take a deposition of their views, they could go them-selves and induce the emperor to make an end of his wrath — as, indeed, we expect him to do. And so, when proceedings reached the phase of giving judgment, the monks trooped in and made statements of philosophical gravity; they pleaded with the emperor through their depositions, reminded him of the Judgment, and de-clared that they would sacrifice their own heads if their plea were not granted. And the judges took these statements down in writing, and departed — an achievement that will bring our city a credit more dazzling than any victor's garland.

From the Twenty-First Homily *On the Statues*

[It was not the monks but the elderly bishop, Flavian, who had left Antioch on his mission to Constantinople as soon as the outrage occurred, to whom the credit finally accrued of persuading Theodosius to forgive the city.]

3. "Consider how great a thing it is for succeeding generations to be told that when so great a city was liable to retribution and punishment, and the terror was so gen-eral that army commanders, local authorities, and judges were all too frightened to speak up for the unhappy populace, one old man, entrusted with the priesthood of God, changed the ruler's mind by sheer personal presence and conversation; and that he, from reverence for God's laws, granted one old man what he had granted

none of his subjects. Indeed, the city paid you another significant compliment, emperor, in choosing me for this mission. For it was a supreme vote of confidence in you, that you consider God's priests, however insignificant, of more importance than all the officers under your command.

"But it is not *from* them alone that I come, but *for* them, sent from the common Lord of Angels with this message for you, a message for one of gentle and civilized disposition: 'If you forgive men their debts, your Father in heaven will forgive you your trespasses' (Matt. 6:14). Remember, then, that day on which we shall all give account for what we have done, and reflect that if indeed some wrong has been done you, you can, by your decision on this verdict, wipe out all your misdeeds without labor or exertion. Other petitioners bring gold, silver, and other such presents; I come before your throne with the sacred laws, which I offer you in preference to any other gift, exhorting you to imitate your Master, who, though encountering our affronts daily, never ceases to extend his gifts to all. Do not disappoint our hopes, or prove our promises vain. For I wish you to understand this besides: if you should agree to reconciliation, and extend to the city the same good will you used to entertain for it, making an end of your just anger, then I should leave here with full confidence. If, on the other hand, you were to exclude the city from your regard, not only would I not set foot or eye upon its soil again; I would deny all knowledge of it ever hereafter and inscribe my name on some other city's roll. For I would never be prepared to acknowledge as my abode a city with which you, the most merciful and civilized of men, would not choose to be indulgent and restore harmonious relations."

4. With these and other such words he so affected the emperor that a scene ensued like the one in the story of Joseph, when Joseph desired to weep at the sight of his brothers, but concealed his emotion for the sake of his disguise. The emperor, too, moved inwardly to tears, suppressed them since he was in public audience; but unable finally to conceal his feelings, let them be seen despite himself. After such an address there was no need for the emperor to make another speech; but he uttered just one remark, which brought him infinitely more credit than his diadem. This is what he said: "It is no great matter for wonder if we forgo our anger at those who abused us, we who are men as they are, seeing that the Master of the world came to earth for us as a servant, was crucified by those he came to help, and prayed for those who crucified him, 'Father, forgive them, for they know not what they do' (Luke 23:34). Is it remarkable, then, that we should forgive our fellow servants?" The outcome proved his words were no shallow gesture; but there was one particularly striking thing, which I shall now mention. Though it had been the priest's intention to celebrate this festival with the royal court, the emperor insisted on his hastening away at once to show his face to the city without delay. "I know," he said, "that they are shaken, and that the incident has left a serious aftermath. Go and encourage them. If they see the helmsman, they will not think of the storm that is past, but will wipe their sorrows wholly from their memory." And when the priest pleaded with him to send his son, the emperor, intending to give a clear indication that he had wholly abandoned his wrath, replied, "Pray that these hindrances may be removed and these wars ended, and then I will come myself." What could be gentler than such a disposition? Now let the Gentiles be put to shame! — no, not put to shame, but

taught to renounce their error and come back to the power of Christianity! Let them learn of our philosophy from the emperor and the priest!

Translation: Editors, from *PG,* vol. 49.

From the Fourth Homily on the Text *"I Saw the Lord. . . ."*

4. Now it happened that this Uzziah, king and crowned head as he was, conceived a high opinion of his own justice, and driven by self-esteem to overreach his station, went into the temple. I will tell you how it happened: he went, we are told, into the Holy of Holies and said, "I propose to offer incense." He laid claim to the priest's prerogative, though he was king! "I propose to offer incense," he said, "since I am a just king." Ah, but king! stay within the bounds of your own authority! The king's authority is bounded in one way, the priest's in another. (Yet the latter is superior to the former, for the king is not publicly legitimated by what public observation sees about him. It is not the golden cloak he wears, nor the jewels pinned to it, that qualify him to be thought a king.) The king is assigned the management of earthly business; the sphere of the priest's authority is located in heaven, for "whatever you bind on earth shall be bound in heaven" (Matt. 16:19). The king is charged with what must be done here; and I — when I say "I," I mean, of course, "the priest" — I am charged with what must be done in heaven.

If you see an unworthy priest, do not criticize the priesthood. It is not the good office that merits censure, but its bad occupant. Judas himself may have been a traitor, but that is no fault of the apostolic role, only of his bad disposition; just so, it is not the priesthood, but the bad disposition, that should be denounced. **5.** You, too, then, do not blame the priesthood! Blame the priest who lets his important office down! When someone in a conversation says to you, "Did you see that Christian, who did so and so?," you should reply, "I won't discuss personalities with you, only cases." How many doctors have been killers, handing out fatal prescriptions for their medicines? — but it is not the art of medicine I blame, but bad practitioners. How many navigators have sunk their ships? — that is not navigation, but bad judgment. Yes, a Christian may be a bad man, but you should not blame the faith or the priesthood, only the person who has slackened off and been a failure. Better, do not blame anyone at all. Pray with tears for his amendment.

The king, then, is entrusted with the care of our bodies, the priest with our souls. The king may remit our financial debts, the priest remits our moral debts. The one uses coercion, the other persuasion. The one bears weapons that may be seen and felt, the other bears weapons of the spirit. The one goes to war against foreign hordes, whereas *my* war is waged against demons! Yes, the priest's office is higher, which is why the king submits to the priest's hands laid upon his head, and throughout the Old Testament priests anointed kings.

Yet *this* king went beyond his mark, overriding the limits of the royal office, and sought to acquire new powers; he marched high-handedly into the temple proposing to offer incense. And what did the priest say? "It is not for you, Uzziah, to burn incense!" (2 Chron. 26:18). What outspokenness! No slavish temperament there! His tongue in tune with heaven, his freedom unabashed, he had an angel's viewpoint in a mortal's frame! He bestrode the earth, a citizen of heaven! He saw the king, but did not see the purple. He saw the king, but did not see the crown. Don't talk to me of sovereignty where there is unlawfulness! "Not for you, king, to burn incense in the Holy of Holies!" You overstep the mark. You want what was not given you, and so will lose even what you were given. "Not for you to burn incense, but for the priests," not your prerogative but mine. Did I take your imperial purple? Then don't you take my priesthood!

"It is not for you to burn incense, but for the priests, the sons of Aaron." Why did he not simply say "the priests"? What was the point of mentioning the founder of the priestly dynasty? Because back then something similar had happened, when Dathan, Abiram, and Korah rebelled against Aaron. The earth opened and swallowed them up; fire came from heaven and consumed them (Num. 16:31-35). Alluding to that story of how the priesthood was affronted but not overcome, of how the people rose up and God punished them, he said, "It is not for you to burn incense, but for the priests, the sons of Aaron." Without warning him explicitly to think of what befell those who so acted then, and of how the rebels were consumed by fire, he simply mentioned Aaron, whose position was upheld, and reminded him of the story. It was as good as saying, "Don't repeat Dathan's folly, and end up as they did back in Aaron's time."

But King Uzziah brooked no warning, but bursting with his lunatic idea, pushed on into the temple and drew open the veil of the Holy of Holies, meaning to offer incense. What did God do? Since the priest was subjected to indignity and his priestly warning disregarded, there was nothing left for him to do; for a priest has no more at his command than outspoken rebuke; he cannot resort to arms, seize hold of a shield, brandish a spear, draw a bow, let fly a missile — only, as I say, rebuke outspokenly. Since, then, the priest had uttered his rebuke and the king was unmoved, but resorted to arms, shields, and spears, and deployed his superior strength, the priest, declaring his innocence before God, said, "What lies with me, I have done, and there is no more that I can do. Come thyself to aid thy downtrodden priesthood, when laws are flouted and sacred ordinances set at nought!" What, then, did the God of mercy do? He punished the offender, so that "leprosy broke out on his forehead" (2 Chron. 26:19). For arrogance will always meet its recompense.

But you see how merciful God's recompense was! He sent no thunderbolt, no earthquake, no storm in the heavens. "Leprosy broke out," and on his forehead rather than on any other site, so that he might bear the trophy of his punishment like an inscription on a monument. This was not for his own sake, but for those who would follow him. God could have imposed a punishment of matching gravity, but did not do so; instead, like a statute published in a prominent place, he declared, "Do not imitate the crime, or you will suffer a like punishment!" Out he went, that "living law," the message on his face sounding clearer than a trumpet blast. Inscribed there was a record never to be obliterated, written not in ink, which fades, but in nature's lettering, corrupting him to make others uncorrupt. And as those sentenced to the noose are led out with the noose tied round their mouth, so he was led out with the leprous skin for his noose. And all because he insulted the priesthood. I say this not to criticize royalty as such, only those infatuated with lunatic obsessions; and that you may learn how much higher the priesthood is than kingship.

Translation: Editors, from Sources Chrétiennes edition, ed. Jean Dumortier (Paris, 1981).

From the Eleventh Homily on the Acts of the Apostles

3. "Grace was upon them all" (Acts 4:33). The reason follows: "There was not a needy person among them." That is to say, they contributed with such enthusiasm that nobody was left in need. They did not give a part of what they had, and save the rest. Nor did they give it, even all of it, as *private* charity. They ironed out the unevenness from the center, and lived altogether free of odious comparisons, so treating one another with great respect. They would never place a gift directly into someone's hand or make a ceremonious presentation, but they "laid it at the apostles' feet," leaving them to dispose of it at their discretion, so that it came from the common fund and not from private donation. This was their safeguard against pride. If it happened that way now, we would manage relations between rich and poor more satisfactorily — and the rich would find it no less satisfactory than the poor. Let us take such satisfaction as we may, at any rate, from description, since you are in no mind to try it in practice! It is perfectly plain from the way things turned out that by selling their possessions they did not end up in want, but simply enriched the poor.

For now, at any rate, let us attempt a description. Suppose, then we all sell all we possess and put it in the common store. (A description, mind! Don't get worked up, rich or poor, whichever you are!) How much gold do you think would be collected? It is impossible to be precise, but I would guess that if all of us, men and women, were to dispossess ourselves of everything, selling our lands, movables, and houses — slaves I do not include, for they did not figure then, but were given their freedom — probably we would gather a million pounds' weight of gold. No, twice or three times that amount! Tell me, how many acres is our city assessed at? How many Christians do you think it contains? Say a hundred thousand, the rest being pagans and Jews. How many thousands of pounds, then, would be collected? And what is the number of the poor? No greater, I should think, than fifty thousand. There would be more than enough to feed that number daily. Indeed, it would require no great outlay if the food were provided in bulk and they ate together.

So what happens when the money runs out? Do you think it *could* run out? Would God's grace not prove infinitely greater? Would God's grace not be poured out abundantly? Would we not make a heaven on earth? If their achievement was so spectacular with numbers of three and five thousand that nobody complained of want, how much more could we achieve with such a population as we have! You would find even the non-Christians adding their contributions! But to prove the point that it is separate provision that is wasteful and creates poverty, take a household with ten children, housewife, and husband, in which she spins and he earns an income: Is it more costly for them to eat together and live under one roof, or to live separately? Separate accommodation is clearly more costly, for if each of the ten children lived alone they would need ten apartments, ten kitchens, ten housekeepers, ten times every other provision. It is precisely for this reason that in households with large staffs of servants they all eat at a common table, to save expense. Division diminishes; harmonious community augments. In the monasteries today monks still live as all the believers did then. Which of them ever died of hunger? Which of them was not provided with plenty of everything? But people are more afraid of it these days than of falling into the infinite expanses of the sea! If we had any experience of this, we would then be prepared to venture on the early church's system. How wide, do you think, is the expanse of God's grace? If this was the effect of the venture when there were no more than three or five thousand believers, the whole world hostile and no support to be looked for from any quarter, how much more so when by God's grace there are believers in all the world! Who would be a pagan after that? Nobody, I should think. We would draw them all in and attach them to ourselves. Yes, if we really get going, I trust to God that this will happen! Just do as I say, and we will get things right stage by stage. And if God gives us life, I am confident we shall bring ourselves before long to such a level of social order *(politeia)*.

Translation: Editors, from *PG*, vol. 60.

From the Twelfth Homily on 1 Timothy

"But do you not see," says one, "those who have the luck to acquire vast goods with little exertion?" What goods are these? Money, houses, so many acres of land, crowds of slaves, loads of silver and gold? Do you call these goods? Are you not ashamed to show your face? A human being who professes heavenly wisdom, and gawking at worldly things, calling things "goods" which are of no account! If these things are goods, it follows that those who possess them must be called good. For is not someone good who possesses what is good? But, tell me, when possessors of these things are greedy and rapacious, are we still to call them good? If wealth is a good to be accumulated by greed, the more it increases, the more it entitles its possessor to be counted good. Is the greedy man good, then? But if wealth is good and increased by greed, the greedier the better. You see the contradiction? "But suppose he is not greedy," you say. And how is that possible, since the passion is so all-consuming? "Well, it *is* possible," you say. No it is not! it is not! Christ proved it himself, when he said: "Make friends for yourselves by means of *unrighteous* mammon" (Luke 16:9).

"But what if he inherited from his father?" Then he inherited what had been unjustly accumulated. It does not go back to Adam that his ancestors were rich; but one of the many that came before him must probably have taken and enjoyed the goods of others unjustly. "What, then!" you say, "did Abraham hold unrighteous wealth? and Job, that blameless, righteous, and faithful man, who 'feared God and eschewed evil'?" (Job 1:1). But their wealth did not consist of gold and silver, nor even of buildings, but of livestock. And Job was enriched by God. It is apparent that his wealth was in livestock, since the author of the book, in telling of that blessed man's calamities, mentions the loss of camels, mares, and asses, but does not speak of treasures of gold and silver being carried off. Besides this, Abraham was rich in domestics. "Aha! Did he not buy them?" Certainly not! That is why Scripture says that the three hundred and eighteen were "born in his house" (Gen. 14:14). He had sheep and oxen too. "And where did he get the gold he sent Rebekah?" From gifts brought back from Egypt, acquired without violence or wrong.

Tell me, please, what is the source of your wealth? From whom did you get it? You, sir! — "From my grandfather." — And you, sir, where does yours come from? — "From my father." But can you, tracing it back through many generations, show that the title was just? You could not avoid discovering the original source in someone's injustice. Why? Because at the beginning God did not make one man rich and another poor. Nor did *he* introduce the distinction, offering vaults of gold to one and refusing another the right to acquire it. He left the earth free for all alike. But if it is common, why have you so many acres of land, and your neighbor not so much as a spoonful? "It was bequeathed me by my father." And by whom to him? "His forefathers." But always go back and find the source of the title! Jacob had wealth, but in his case the source was his earnings from labor.

But I will not press this point too closely. Suppose wealth in itself is just, free from the imputation of piracy. You are not responsible, after all, for the greed of your father. Your wealth may derive from plunder, but you did not plunder it. Or grant that he did not plunder it either, but his gold was washed up somewhere out of the soil. What follows? On that reckoning, is wealth good? "Perhaps not; but neither is it bad," someone says. If the owner is not greedy, it is not bad — *if,* that is, he distributes to the poor. But if he does not, it is bad, because treacherous. "But as long as he does no wrong, it is not bad, even if he does no good either." Maybe; but is it not wrong to have solitary dominion and solitary enjoyment of common property? "The earth is the Lord's and the fullness thereof" (Ps. 24:1) — is it not? If our possessions belong to our common Lord, they belong to our fellow servants too. For all that the Lord owns is common. We see this arrangement in great houses: provisions are given equally to all, drawn from the lord's stores; and the lord's house is open to all. The kings' possessions, too, are all common: cities, for instance, marketplaces and public walks. We all have an equal share in them.

Take note, then, of God's dispensation! To humble mankind, in the first place, he has made some things common: the sun, the air, the earth and the water, the heaven, the sea, the light and the stars, are available equally to all as brothers. He fashioned us all with the same eyes, the same body, the same soul, the same structure in all respects, all our members from the earth, all from one man, and all in the same habitation. But none of these things were enough to convict us. So he made other things common, such as baths, cities, marketplaces, covered walks. And see how there is no strife over common goods, but all is peaceable! But once someone tries to alienate something to make it his own, contention is introduced; as though nature itself were outraged, that when God would rally us from every quarter, we compete to split off and separate by appropriating things and calling them "mine" and "thine." That is when there is strife and unpleasantness. Where this does not happen, no strife or competition is generated. This state, not that, is what was intended for us, and is in keeping with nature. Why is there never a legal suit about a marketplace? Because it is common to all. But about a house, about money, we see the whole world goes to law. We find our necessities provided for us in common; yet even in the smallest things we fail to preserve the principle of commonality. The reason God left those things free for us all, in fact, was to teach us to hold these things in common as well. Yet for all that we are taught nothing.

But, as I said, how can anyone who has wealth be good? It is simply not possible. He is good when he distributes his wealth. So when he no longer has it, he is good; when he gives it to others, he is good; but while he still has it, he cannot be good. If it is characteristic of the wicked to keep something, and of the good to get rid of it, is that thing a good? Having property, we conclude, is not a good; doing without it is an indication that someone is good. Wealth is not a good, while someone, again, who has a chance to get it and lets it go, is good. If we are good, then, when we give wealth we have to others and do not accept wealth we are offered, and if we are not good when we accept wealth or acquire it, how can wealth be good? So do not call it a good. Actually, you do not *possess* it, precisely because in thinking it a good you become *obsessed* by it. Clarify your thinking, and sharpen your critical powers; then you will be good. Learn what true goods are. What are they? Moral excellence and benevolence, these are goods. The rich man is not good. By this criterion you are good, and are counted as such, in proportion to your charitable giving, while if you are rich, you are good no longer. Let us be good in such a way as to *be* good and to *acquire* the goods of the age to come, in Jesus Christ our Lord, with whom to the Father and the Holy Spirit be glory, might, honor, now and always for ever and ever. Amen.

Translation: Editors, from F. Field, ed., *Iohannis Chrysostomi interpretatio omnium epistularum Paulinarum* (Oxford, 1845-62).

Augustine of Hippo

(356-430)

Like a mountain that assumes different shapes when seen from different angles yet always dominates the landscape, Augustine towers over the development of Christian political thought in the West, as he towers over so much else. Only Aquinas and Luther can claim anything like comparable influence, and theirs, though profound, has weighed mainly upon schools of thought derived from them, while Augustine's has been much more widely diffused. To the medieval scholastics he was an authority one could not afford to be in open conflict with, an ever present thesis to which the revival of Aristotle was the antithesis. Most confident of his support were those who proclaimed papal preeminence over secular authority. In the Reformation, however, it was not the papalists who seized on Augustine as their own, but the Reformers, who welcomed the privileging of love over law, motive over form, divine inscrutability over human custom, very much in support of secular, innovative, and authoritarian political trends. Yet in the twentieth century, again, it has been "liberals" and "realists," those who repudiate the illusions of idealism in politics, who have seen in Augustine a natural master of suspicion, stripping away the finery with which the crude struggle for power tends to disguise itself. And these very different appeals to his authority have all, in a measure, been right. Diverse as their interests were, we can trace a common thread which held the different "political Augustinianisms" together: a disinterest, we may say, in the worldly political surface, in autonomous constitutional proprieties; an eye for God's intervening direction and judgment of secular events; a due respect for agents who respond immediately to the divine command.

It is sometimes doubted that Augustine meant to write or think about politics at all. And that doubt, too, is right — if by "politics" we mean, quite strictly, the self-justifying debates about forms, procedures, and constitutions, insulated against first and last things. Yet such a definitional defense against Augustine is surely self-defeating. It would be a starved, statistical science that ruled inadmissible these probings of society and justice, on purely procedural grounds! Augustine began as a Christian Platonist, the intellectual tradition into which he was converted during his years as a young orator in Milan. The Platonism of his day was both introspective and pan-cosmic; it moved ambitiously and confidently between the soul and the universe, following an absorbing and demanding discipline of psychological self-interrogation and metaphysical philosophy. But it bypassed society, which lay "outside" — outside the self, that is, but also outside the real universe; it was a shimmering, illusory realm of self-deception, characterized by passionate violence practiced upon and within the soul. There is no reason why Augustine should not have fulfilled his role as a theologian wholly within the terms of this satisfying and absorbing tradition, as some of his greatest contemporaries did. His genius as a political theologian was to pour into this unpromising matrix a dense weave of social observation and awareness which he garnered from his role as a bishop in North Africa, so creating a Christian social theory out of the theology and self-understanding of the church.

The greatest work of his maturity, the massive *City of God: Against the Pagans (De civitate Dei)*, represents the peak of this achievement, offering a panoptic view of history, society, and cultural conflict that has scarcely an equivalent in literature. Inevitably it is here that one looks for Augustine's most developed political ideas; and every collector of excerpts has to wrestle with how much of this work cannot on any account be omitted. There is no escape from reproducing certain much-overexcerpted pages — though we have tried to turn this situation to advantage by correcting some stubborn errors ingrained in the translation tradition. But when one goes beyond the *City of God,* one can no longer escape noticing some complex crosscurrents in his thought which are, actually, also to be found in the large work. Interpreters usually remark upon the "tensions," of which the most striking for modern readers is between the "value-neutral" political order seemingly encountered in *City of God* 19 and the theocratic logic apparently deployed in defense of the coercion of Donatist heretics (in *Epistle* 93 and elsewhere). To come to grips with Augustine's thought requires us to take the measure of these tensions and explore their resolution.

"Development" has been a key to much Augustine interpretation of the past century. Those who have written on his political thought have been slower than others to take it up, but we can be grateful to the few, most notably R. A. Markus, who have shown us how illuminating it can be. It is essential to read Augustine with a sense of the chronology of his writing, even though chronology alone is not a sufficient guide to his developing ideas. But context is required, too, since, like most of us, he thought freshly in response to fresh challenges, conventionally in response to familiar ones. Yet Augustine's development is something very much more than simple change of mind. There is, as it were, a slow accretion of new layers to his thought. At points of new departure he will reorganize the way he approaches a question, while still carrying forward the observations and conclusions that he has made at earlier stages. We do not find constant innovation; it is something more like regeneration, as the familiar keeps coming back to make new and unfamiliar effects.

So one could say that the earliest of the excerpts here, the brief section from

On Free Will (*De libero arbitrio* [388]), contains the seed-thought that will flower most impressively in the *City of God:* political order is a necessary *moral mediation* between the virtue of those whose hearts are fixed on the highest and eternal good and the "lust" (i.e., disordered ambition) of those who surround them. The only order that matters ultimately is that of the divine law, claiming our love exclusively for goods which cannot in any circumstances be lost. Yet the mediation is a good thing, though the lust which makes it necessary is not. The example: it is right for the law to permit forcible self-defense, though it is not right to practice it. This prepares the way for a theory of just war which will altogether do without an appeal to "legitimate defense."

The next stage sees this straightforward Platonic distinction between divine law and the "law of the city" refracted through the prism of the church's controversy with the Manichean heresy. This we view through excerpts from the long polemical work *Against Faustus* (*Contra Faustum* [397]). The issue was the status of the Old Testament, and it turned especially on the Manicheans' objections to the unsatisfactory moral character of Old Testament law compared with Christ's teaching. Augustine had to articulate an account of Old Testament law which admitted the differences while refusing the inference that the law had simply been discarded. He did this by turning the Platonic distinction on its side, so to speak, into an account of the phases of salvation history. Removing from discussion, first of all, the purely cultural and ritual features of Old Testament law by means of an older distinction between "moral" law and "typical sacraments" performing a symbolic role now superseded, he focuses on the *different moral functions* of the old and the new laws, as follows: the one set minimal restraints, the other carried forward the moral pedagogy to its maximal expression, the law of love. They serve the same moral end in different ways.

Does this formulation admit of moral progress from the old Mosaic order to the new Christian one? The extent, and perhaps ambivalence, of Augustine's doctrine of progress is one of the most fascinating and difficult questions that we can put to him. At this point in his development there is at least a *pedagogical* progress: the age of Christlike perfection is now possible because the Mosaic order succeeded in curbing the worst bestialities of human appetite. Yet does that mean that things formerly conceded are not now conceded? If God could ordain war in the era of Joshua, does it not follow that in the era of perfection, when Christ's teaching was exemplified in the sacrifices of the Christian martyrs, God would no longer do so? No, it does not follow. There is a change in what is allowed, certainly, but it is purely attitudinal. The law of Christ can be obeyed in the practice of war if the right attitude to it is sustained. Obedient and responsible war, conducted with just cause, remains an open possibility within the sphere of political order, as is demonstrated by the "splendid victories over ungodly enemies" with which God has crowned Christian emperors. The question whether a change of method or style is required by Christian war-making has not yet been raised, but it will follow. The emperors, then, are to sustain a Mosaic discipline in a way compatible with the Christian era, themselves winning victories of one kind, while the martyrs win victories of another, superior kind. (Augustine thought the possibility of martyrdom was always present even in the Christian empire: "Nobody should say — it would be a great self-deception — nobody should say that the church does not suffer persecution now that the emperors are catholic, take decisions for the church and watch over its growth, knowing they must give account to God. Nobody should say that the church does not suffer persecution. The lion may be harmless, but the dragon is unsleeping!" [*Sermon* M5, from the newly discovered Mainz manuscript published by Dolbeau].)

We are now in a position to view Augustine's mature treatment of the responsibilities of political office in the Christian era, which we do mainly through a text which comes from the second decade of the fifth century (414). It is a letter to the provincial governor of Africa, Macedonius (*Letter* 153), in response to a courteous but menacing challenge to the bishops' traditional practice of interceding for condemned prisoners. Augustine's letter paints with the richest palette the argument for a distinctively Christian manner of conducting civil justice in dialogue with the pastoral authorities of the church. The secular magistrate is drawn wholly into the church's discourse on divine mercy and forgiveness of sins. For Augustine (in contrast to what we shall find in some later Augustinians, notably Luther) there is no other context within which his task can be described. The pursuit of penitence is the church's sole authentic weapon against human sin, and it must use that weapon with a patience that emulates the patience of God. Divine patience exceeds, Augustine admits, even the traditional practice of the church that allowed just one opportunity for a formal act of penance after grave sin. There is a second motive at work besides the imitation of God: those who deal with the sins of others must know they are sinners themselves, wholly dependent on God's mercy. Augustine touches on the story of the woman taken in adultery (John 8:2-11), in which, he claims, Jesus himself took on the role of intercessor before the judges. A good judge must heed such a plea, because — and here Luther is not far distant — he knows he himself is at one and the same time good (with Christ's goodness) and evil, daily asking for his sins to be forgiven. The tendency of the story in Augustine's hands is to subvert the distinction between good and evil people, leveling them through their uniform need of forgiveness. This is the period at which the polemic against Pelagian perfectionism is in his mind, and he cannot resist the deep theological themes of grace and merit.

What, then, does the civil magistrate contribute? He contributes "terror," ensuring a social stability within which "the good can live more peaceably amidst the evil." The magistrate performs the same role for the church as Old Testament law does for the gospel. Not every way of sparing sinners is true mercy; without the terror of the law the pastoral force of mercy is lost sight of; the whole exercise loses its redemptive energy. Civil justice, then, prepares the way for penitence; but for that very reason it should not go to the extreme of taking life. Augustine all but makes the abolition of the death penalty an absolute demand, but does not feel he has sufficiently firm ground beneath his feet to do so. He is convinced, however, that any measure, severe or lenient, must be susceptible of justification within the terms of Christ's law of love.

Might the wholesome dialectic of terror and mercy simply collapse if pastoral authorities were too insistent and magistrates too obliging? Might the essential function of deterrence be left with too little support in actual practice? Underestimating, perhaps, the logic of Macedonius's difficulty, Augustine does not face these questions, which will continue to accompany the search for a "merciful justice" through the centuries. His letter turns to the duty of reparation as a measure of true penitence, not missing the occasion for some sharp thrusts at the venality of lawyers, and to a statement of his distinctive view of property, pregnant with future development in the Middle Ages: ideally only the righteous have true title of possession (see pp. 368-70, 387, and 488-98 below). It concludes with his recurrent motif that civil justice is a state of toleration, merely securing the minimal conditions for society until the true justice of heaven is attained.

Reflecting on the doctrine of civil punishment which we meet here, we can only be struck by the all-importance of the pedagogical motif. Altogether lacking, it appears, is any sense of equivalence or consistency. Civil punishment, when subject to the pastoral discernment of the church authorities, displays a humane face, yet a disturbingly arbitrary one. It is absolutely just that we who sin should suffer punishment. But it is quite indefinite how much. If sin is, in principle, infinite, just punishment may be anything at all; and if, as Augustine believes, the most painful punishment short of the pains of hell is that to which the offender freely submits by searching his or her own conscience, how can we measure the fitness of any other penal action, save by its likelihood of evoking that one?

To this context belongs the policy toward heretics. Every aspect of Augustine's doctrine of punishment seems, indeed, to have been shaped by his long struggle with the Donatists, the civil authorities, and indeed his own conscience over the official response to this assertive and independent Christian movement. Undoubtedly his determined dislike of the death penalty, though generally shared in the church of his day, was sharpened by the sense that something essential to the church's integrity would be lost if the truth of the gospel were upheld against heretics by bloodshed; the violent suppression of paganism did not touch him so nearly. This scruple survived, strengthened, after the change of mind described in *Letter* 93, written in 408 to one Vincentius, bishop of a dissenting Donatist subgroup. He had abandoned the view that only unaided argument and pleading were serviceable to the conversion of sinners, and now defended the church's reliance on civil power, on the grounds that the Christian emperors should assist the church's task of reclaiming the wandering. The whole case could have been argued quite plausibly as a question of civil disorder, which was clearly within the competence of the secular authority to suppress, but Augustine does not take this route. Here, too, in defense of the confiscations with which the authorities pursued the heretics, we see something of his doctrine of property, not the idealist side that was in evidence before but the positivist side: if in ultimate terms all wealth belongs by right to the righteous, in the provisional order property right is determined solely by civil government.

Augustine's brief but widely influential observations on just war come directly out of the same context. The letter to Count Boniface (*Letter* 189, from 418), though theoretically undeveloped, brings together the same elements: war is justified solely on the basis of the love we owe our neighbors; it is a form of service secondary to prayer; it is made necessary by the persistence of discord and diabolical deceit until the end of history. Augustine has not ceased to think of this age as one that demands "tolerance" of evil; here, however, the inference is not, as one might anticipate, opposition to military undertakings, but a warning against an idealistic spirit of withdrawal, too weary or impatient of the burdens of maintaining order. Finally, as in the practice of civil justice, love and the desire for peace imprint the policies of the Christian war-maker with a distinctive restraint and mercy.

One further sphere of interaction between church and civil authority invites our notice: slavery, to which two of the letters recently discovered by J. Divjak are devoted, though in practical rather than theoretical terms. In one of them, not reproduced here, Augustine pleads with some urgency for forceful civil action to suppress a sudden burgeoning of the international slave trade fed by indiscriminate kidnapping. Even in this extreme case, though, he is wary of too heavy-handed a response. His church is deeply involved in the expensive business of buying back the victims of this cruel enterprise, and if the kidnappers end up being flogged to death by the authorities, the church, he thinks, will lose its zest for this charitable work. *Letter* 24* (for which no date has been proposed) shows the bishop in his role as judge, and offers a fascinating view of how Roman civil law entered Christian practice. Augustine seeks counsel's opinion on some points of law concerning slavery. The matter before him is the status of the children of someone who occupied a managerial position confined in law to slaves, though he was not himself a slave. The bishop is obliged to conform to "earthly laws" in determining such questions; yet, like many who take counsel's advice, he makes it clear what advice he hopes to receive. It does not lie within his province to release slaves, but neither is he prepared to acquiesce in any extension of the reach of slavery.

Here, then, is the working doctrine of civil authority which Augustine propounded and by which he governed his practice. Nothing suggests that he felt any discontent with it. Yet it is clear that a new paradigm comes into play with the writing of the *City of God* in the years between 411 and 426. What is new is a concern to look behind the tasks of *authority* to the *society* which gives authority its rationale. The cozy collaboration of Christian governor and Christian bishop, which was Augustine's practical ideal, suddenly turns out to span a huge gulf between two societies which, though they exist together in the same space, intermingle and interact, are constituted on radically contradictory principles, the love of God and the love of self. Always, of course, the law of the city had presupposed the divine law, which was summed up in the love of God. Now, however, there is an alternative to the love of God, a rival center to the affections. It is not real or enduring, but is able to conjure up an astounding appearance of reality: it is expressed in a history of world empire. Opposed to it, the city of God has its own history, a history of prophecy, of Christ, and of martyrdom. But not, we notice, a history of bishops. Augustine was far from taking the step which Gelasius I would take (see p. 179 below), of positing the pope as the emperor's opposite number.

His inspiration for this move was the need to mount an apologetic of a very different kind from that to which he was accustomed: not against another heretical splinter group, but against an embittered, cultured, and anti-Christian pagan revival which had exported itself from its native Italy among refugees who fled before Alaric's conquest of Rome in 410. This forced Augustine to turn his gaze on the cultural and social reality of the history of Rome. The first five books of the *City of God*, the emotional heart of the work, are devoted to the deconstruction, at once loving and despairing, of the great Roman myth. Here he confronts a long-sustained political society, militant, acquisitive, and culturally expansive. What is he to make of it? What he actually makes of it has inebriated some readers and shocked others. It had no *real* civil order at all; it was a kind of pretense, a consumer society existing by consensus at the lowest, most self-indulgent level, compensating for its lack of true authority by the sheer exercise of power and arbitrary will (2.20ff.). He can claim support from enemy witnesses: Cicero and Sallust, in the last generation of the republic, had deplored the disintegration that they saw around them. What they failed to see was that Rome had always been like that. The ideal of a Rome grown great by virtue, held together by law, was never real. There had never been a Roman "commonwealth" *(respublica)* — not in the sense that that word *ought* to bear. There never were Roman virtues, only "good disciplines" *(boni mores)* devoted to self-serving ends. There never was Roman law, since legal "right flows from the source of rightness" (19.21). To those who charge him with engaging in mere wordplay, Augustine can reply with some justice that he is simply taking the Roman self-image seriously. That image can be worn only by a society which finds its common good in God — that is, by the church; not by the Christian Roman Empire, for Rome's continuity counts for more than its conversion, and Rome, now as formerly, embodies the earthly city. If civil authority derives its rationale from the restraint of evil, it belongs to the world where evil belongs. So Constantine, Gratian, and Theodosius, about whose Christian characters some fine, even cloying things are said, still take their places as Romans in book 5. Augustine has come a long way round to end up with a view of the Christian emperors not far removed from that of Ambrose.

On the one hand those features which give social order a reality are found in the city of God alone. On the other, actual political societies belong to the earthly city. "Cain founded a city, not Abel." (Notice how Augustine deals with the political society of ancient Israel in 15.2. David himself enters the history of the city of God as a prophet, not as a king; cf. 17.1.) Has the ideal-real split apart from the actual? No: they are held together by analogy, which allows Augustine to acknowledge derivative, shadowy reflections of true order in the actual political societies of history. Of course Rome was a "commonwealth" — in the more common and less idealized sense! And so, too, was the rebel slave-kingdom of Spartacus (4.5)? If Rome is invited to see its reflection in this spontaneous association of the violent and underprivileged, can such associations see their reflection in Rome? This hint is developed in the long twelfth chapter of book 19, where Augustine explores the multiple and analogous forms of peace, and the political payoff is seen in chapter 24, where he triumphantly returns to the paradox left hanging in book 2 and propounds his new definition of a commonwealth, avoiding the term "right" *(ius)*. This is one source of that interpretation of Augustine's aims which sees him as propounding a "value-neutral" state. But, of course, this alternative conception is not value-neutral in any sense that late-modern liberalism could acknowledge. The "things they love" which form the focus of the commonwealth are, in the end, themselves. It is a despite of God, devilish and destructive. The shadowy, doubtful reality of earthly political order matches the shadowy, doubtful reality of the evil will itself: immensely strong on the stage of history, generating vast cultural achievements at the price of yet vaster miseries, but when set in the light of the first and last things, null and empty.

The excerpts we have included from the *City of God,* inevitably fragmentary given the huge scale of the work, fall into three groups. From books 2, 4, and 5 come illustrations of the critique of Rome and the praise of Christian emperors; from 15 (with a useful summary from the end of book 14) comes an outline of the theory of the two cities and their histories; finally, the extended central section and the concluding section of book 19 are in many ways the true climax of the great work.

This book introduces the last four (bks. 19-22), devoted to the last things: judgment, hell, and heaven. It treats of the "ultimate states" of the two cities, i.e., their "goals" or "destinies" — the word *finis* contains the idea of purpose and fulfillment. The topic *de finibus* was an accepted one in classical literature for basic moral theory, which allows Augustine to begin with a review, not included here, of pagan moral theories, treating a pedantic textbook presentation from a now lost text of Varro (saec. A.D. 1) with a mixture of irreverence and respect. Varro had posed the alternatives in terms of how "the wise man" should seek to be "happy," and Augustine's strategy is to accept these terms for the discussion, building a bridge from the moral goal to the eschatological, and from the individual quest for happiness to the social; to show, in other words, that there can be no intelligible human action save as participation in a society which has set its heart on eternal goods not realized within this "wretched" mortal existence.

For Varro the question of social context was a secondary one. But Augustine seizes on it, devoting the greater part of the book (chs. 5-17) to it. He constantly reverts to the impossibility of any individual "wise man" resolving the problems of society by withdrawing into solitary pursuit of his own happiness. Certainly Christians understand the good as social! But everything depends on whether one's hopes are pinned on society as we experience it or on the real society promised us at the end of history. There follows a series of vignettes of social life at different levels, full of interest in themselves: household, city, world — and universe, for spiritual communications with angels and demons are as fully determinative of a society as any other (chs. 5-9). The observations on the dilemmas of a judge and on the difficulties of maintaining friendships at a distance are especially memorable. They are all handled in a pessimistic tone — here is the "realist" Augustine with a vengeance! — but only to prepare the way for the affirmation of a real "peace" which has the essential element of being eternal (ch. 11).

This point achieved, Augustine can look back upon actual political phenomena with a more hopeful eye, using the analogy of peace to interpret even the most unpromising — wars, robber bands, even solitary predators — as instances of a general law that everything seeks a stable peace. He does not select these in order to decry more substantial cultural achievements; rather, he wants to look at the achievements together with the underside of our social experience, and to find one and the same law of equilibrium operating at every degree of sociality, great or small. He is now ready to embark upon the densest and most fascinating section of the book, the description of how the city of God exists on pilgrimage, seeking its own peace

the form of the city of God within the earthly city

amidst the peace of the earthly city (chs. 13-17). A pyramidal reconstruction, level by level, of the peace in which human beings as such participate culminates in a society where each member cares before all else for the others' love of God (ch. 14). How does this idea operate at the first level of society, the household? The answer is unexpected: it transforms the command-obedience structure so as to restore the primitive equality in which mankind was created. Here he embarks on his deepest exploration of slavery: its presence in the world is a response to sin; it is not a natural feature; it exists in many forms, of which Augustine, like Ambrose (cf. pp. 79-82), thinks moral impotence is by far the most terrible. Within the righteous household, which values eternal goods over temporal goods, the operation of neighbor-love subverts distinctions with the equalizing force of the phrase *sicut teipsum,* "as yourself." The slave by his freely given loyalty and the master by his untiring care can establish a pattern of relations that cuts across the grain of the apparent structure of domination and subjection. The outward form of the household is the same; the underlying reality is changed (chs. 15, 16).

But the household is a paradigm for the larger unit, the city (ch. 17). The heavenly city, making use of the same material resources, makes use also of the same social laws and structures that protect them; yet the transcendent end it serves means that their purport is quite different. This celebrated passage has sometimes been taken as a charter for an instrumental, value-free public space. But for Augustine the earthly city is never value-free. It is materialist and idolatrous in a decisive sense, so that the two cities are religiously incompatible, the threat of conflict never absent. (Some excerpters dare to omit this decisive paragraph!) Yet — and here is Augustine's last word on how a Christian can be a public servant — the church supports even this earthly peace, not in its idolatrous and materialist aspects, but simply *as* a peace which will assist the heavenly city in the course of its journey home.

City of God leaves us with questions on two fronts: about how this broad perspective, at once determinist and relativist, marries with the more practical political one of his other writings; and about the character of the undertaking as a whole. Has Augustine any place for a correction and transformation of the laws and conventions of the earthly city under the impact of Christian love for God and neighbor? From elsewhere we know that he has, but from this work one would hardly know it. Has he a doctrine of civilizational progress? In the *City of God* progress is swallowed up into pilgrimage; elsewhere, again, we have found indications of one. What, then, is the point of this great step backward from the arts of practical and political faith, setting the tasks of political service to one side and contemplating ultimate social goals and destinies? Is it to reassert, as one recent commentator has suggested, that Christian faith is, after all, "transpolitical"? Yes, certainly; but it is only transpolitical *as it is social.* It is the deep groundswell of social cohesion, the corporately felt commitments and unarticulated common impulses that really determine the character of communities. These make the rational plans and conscientious judgments of their leaders look like waves on the surface of the ocean. Augustine's last and greatest word is a warning not to ignore the currents of the depths. Needless to say, *sociology* for him could only be *theology.* If we once dare to ask what lies *behind* politics and its justice, we must find ourselves face-to-face with heaven and hell.

Further Reading: P. R. L. Brown, *Augustine of Hippo* (London: Faber, 1967); P. R. L. Brown, *Religion and Society in the Age of St. Augustine* (London: Faber, 1972); H. Chadwick, *Augustine* (Oxford: Oxford University Press, 1986); G. Combès, *La doctrine politique de S. Augustin* (Paris: Plon, 1927); J. B. Elshtain, *Augustine and the Limits of Politics* (Notre Dame, Ind.: University of Notre Dame Press, 1997); J. N. Figgis, *The Political Aspects of St. Augustine's "City of God"* (London: Longmans, 1921); E. Fortin, *Political Idealism and Christianity in the Thought of St. Augustine* (Villanova: Villanova University Press, 1942); G. Madec, *La patrie et la voie* (Paris: Desclée, 1989); F. G. Maier, *Augustin und das Antike Rom* (Stuttgart: Kohlhammer, 1955); R. A. Markus, *Saeculum: Religion and Society in the Theology of St. Augustine* (Cambridge: Cambridge University Press, 1970); R. A. Markus, *Sacred and Secular* (London: Variorum, 1994); R. A. Markus, ed., *Augustine: A Collection of Critical Essays* (New York: Doubleday, 1972); H. I. Marrou, *L'Ambivalence du Temps de l'histoire chez S. Augustin* (Montréal: Institut d'études médiévales, 1950); J. Rist, *Augustine: Ancient Thought Baptised* (Cambridge: Cambridge University Press, 1994); M. Ruokanen, *Theology and Social Life in Augustine's "De Civitate Dei"* (Göttingen: Vandenhoeck & Ruprecht, 1993); J. Van Oort, *Jerusalem and Babylon: A Study of Augustine's "City of God" and the Sources of His Doctrine of the Two Cities* (Leiden: Brill, 1991).

From *On Free Choice of the Will*, Book 1

5. *Augustine:* First we ought to discuss, I think, whether there is any lust in the case where an attacking enemy or an assassin in ambush is killed for the sake of life, liberty, or chastity.

Evodius: How can I think that men lack lust who fight for the things that they can lose against their will? Or, if they cannot lose these things, what need is there to go as far as murdering a man for them?

A: Therefore the law is not just which grants a traveller the power to kill a highway robber so that he himself may not be killed; or which grants a man or woman the right to slay, if they can, an assailant before he can do violence. Indeed, the law even commands a soldier to kill the enemy, and if the soldier refrains from the slaughter, he is punished by his commander. We shall not, shall we, dare say that these laws are unjust — or rather, are not laws at all, for I think that a law that is not just is not a law.

E: Surely, I think that a law is quite safe from this accusation if it permits the people it rules to do lesser evils so as to avoid greater ones. It is much better that the man who plots against another's life be killed than the man who is defending his life. It is also much worse for an innocent person to be violated than for the assailant to be killed by the person whom he tried to attack. Indeed, in killing the enemy, the soldier is the agent of the law. Thus he merely fulfils his duty without any trace of lust. Furthermore, the law which has been passed to protect the people cannot itself be accused of lust. Surely the man who passed it — if he did so at God's command, that is, if the law is what eternal justice commands — can do so without any lust whatsoever. And even if he did make the law out of some kind of lust, it does not follow from this that one's obedience to the law is tainted with lust, since a good law can be made by an evil man.

If a man seizes tyrannical power, for example, and accepts a bribe from some interested person to pass a law that no one may take a woman by force, even for marriage, this law will not be evil, though the man who made it was unjust and corrupt. Therefore it is possible to obey without lust the law ordering that an enemy's violence be repulsed with equal violence for the protection of the citizens. The same thing can be said in regard to all the officials who, for the sake of law and order, are subject to any authority. But even though the law is blameless, I do not understand how these men can be, when the law does not force them to kill, but leaves it to their power. They are free not to kill anyone for those things which they can lose against their will, and which they ought not therefore to love.

Concerning life, perhaps there is some question whether or not it can be taken in any way from the soul when the body is slain. But if life can be taken away, then it is to be despised. If life cannot be taken away, then there is nothing to fear.

As to chastity, who indeed would doubt that it is fixed in the spirit itself, since it is a virtue? Hence, not even chastity can be taken away by a violent assailant. Therefore, whatever he who is killed was about to take away is not at all in our power; so that I do not understand how it can be called our own. Thus I do not blame the law which permits such aggressors to be slain; yet I do not know how I would defend the man who kills.

A: Much less can I discover why you should seek to defend men whom no law holds to be guilty.

E: No public, man-made law, perhaps; still, I do not know whether they are not held guilty by some stronger, very secret law, if all things are governed by divine providence. How then, before divine providence, are these men free of sin when they are stained by human blood for the sake of things they ought to despise? I think, therefore, that the law that is written to rule the people is right to permit these acts, while divine providence punishes them. The law of the people deals with acts it must punish in order to keep peace among ignorant men, insofar as deeds can be governed by man; these other sins have other suitable punishments, from which, I think, only wisdom can free us.

A: I praise and approve this distinction that you have made. It is incomplete and imperfect; nevertheless it is full of faith, and aims at the sublime. The law which is made to govern states seems to you to make many concessions and to leave unpunished things which are avenged nonetheless by divine providence — and rightly so. But because it does not do all things, it does not thereby follow that what it does do is to be condemned.

Translation: Anna S. Benjamin and L. H. Hackstaff (Indianapolis: Bobbs-Merrill, 1964). Used with permission.

From *Against Faustus,* Book 19

18. The Manichaeans, therefore, have no ground for saying, in disparagement of the law and the prophets, that Christ came to abolish rather than to fulfil them (*cf.* Matt. 5:17), because Christians do not observe what is there enjoined; for the only things which they do not observe are those that prefigured Christ, and these are not observed because their fulfilment is in Christ and what is fulfilled is no longer prefigured, the typical observances having properly come to a close in the time of those who, after being trained in such things, had come to believe in Christ as their fulfilment. Do not Christians observe the precept of Scripture, "Hear, O Israel, the Lord thy God is one God" (Deut. 6:4), "Thou shalt not make unto thee an image," and so on? Do Christians not observe the precept, "Thou shalt not take the name of the Lord thy God in vain"? Do Christians not observe the Sabbath, which belongs to the comprehension of the true rest? Do Christians not honour their parents, according to the commandment? Do Christians not abstain from fornication and murder and theft and false witness, from coveting their neighbour's wife and from coveting his property — all of which things are written in the law (Exod. 20:1-17)? These moral precepts are distinct from typical sacraments; the former are fulfilled by the aid of divine grace, the latter by the accomplishment of what they promise. Both are fulfilled in Christ, who has ever been the bestower of this grace which is also now revealed in him, and who now makes manifest the accomplishment of what he in former times promised; for "the law was given by Moses, but grace and truth came by Jesus Christ" (John 1:17). Again, these things which concern the keeping of a good conscience are fulfilled in the faith which worketh by love; while types of the future pass away when they are accomplished. But even the types are not abolished, but fulfilled; for Christ, in bringing to light what the types signified, does not prove them vain or illusory. 19. Faustus, therefore, is wrong in supposing that the Lord Jesus fulfilled some precepts of righteous men who lived before the law of Moses, such as "Thou shalt not kill," which Christ did not oppose but rather confirmed by his prohibition of anger and abuse, and that he abolished some things apparently peculiar to the Hebrew law, such as "An eye for an eye and a tooth for a tooth," which Christ seems rather to abrogate than to confirm when he says, "But I say unto you that ye resist not evil; but if any one smite thee on the right cheek turn to him the other also," and so on (Matt. 5:38f.). But we say that even these things which Faustus thinks Christ abolished by enjoining the opposite were suitable to the times of the Old Testament, and were not destroyed but fulfilled by Christ. [. . .]

    25. Nor, again, is there any opposition between that which was said by them of old time, "An eye for an eye, a tooth for a tooth," and what the Lord says: "But I say unto you, that ye resist not evil; but if any one smiteth thee on thy right cheek, turn to him the other also," and so on (Matt. 5:39). The old precept as well as the new is intended to check the vehemence of hatred, and to curb the impetuosity of angry passion. For who will of his own accord be satisfied with a vengeance equal to the injury? Do we not see men, only slightly hurt, eager for slaughter, thirsting for blood, as if they could never make their enemy suffer enough? If a man receives a blow, does he not summon his assailant, that he may be condemned in the court of law? Or if he

prefers to return the blow, does he not fall upon the man with hand and heel, or perhaps with a weapon, if he can get hold of one? To put a restraint upon a revenge so
unjust from its excess, the law established the principle of compensation, that the
penalty should correspond to the injury inflicted. So the precept, "an eye for an eye,
a tooth for a tooth," instead of being a brand to kindle a fire that was quenched, was
rather a covering to prevent the fire already kindled from spreading. For there is a
just vengeance due to the injured person from his assailant, so that when we pardon,
we give up what we might justly claim. Thus, in the Lord's prayer, we are taught to
forgive others their debts that God may forgive us our debts. There is no injustice in
asking back a debt, though there is a kindness in forgiving it. But as in swearing the
one who swears, however truly, is in danger of perjury, of which one who never
swears is in no danger; and as, while swearing truly is not a sin, we are further from
sin by not swearing, so that the command not to swear is a guard against perjury; in
the same way, since it is sinful to wish to be avenged with an unjust excess, though
there is no sin in wishing for vengeance within the limits of justice, the man who
wishes for no vengeance at all is further from the sin of an unjust vengeance. It is a
sin to demand more than is due, though it is no sin to demand a debt. And the best
security against the sin of an unjust demand is to demand nothing, especially considering that we might be compelled to pay our debt to him who is indebted to none.

So I could echo Faustus' words, and say: "'It has been said by them of old time,
Thou shalt not take unjust revenge; but I say, Take no revenge at all.' *That* is fulfilment!" It is thus that Faustus, after quoting, "It has been said, Thou shalt not swear
falsely; but I say unto you, swear not at all," adds: "*That* is fulfilment!" (I could have
used the same expression, that is, if I thought that by the addition of these words
Christ *supplied a defect* in the law, rather than that the law's *intention* to prevent unjust revenge is *best* secured by not taking revenge at all, as the intention to prevent
perjury is best secured by not swearing at all.) For if "an eye for an eye" is opposed to
"If any one smite thee on the cheek, turn to him the other also," is there not as much
opposition between "Thou shalt perform unto the Lord thine oath" and "Swear not
at all"? If Faustus thinks that it is not abolition but fulfilment in the one case, he
ought to think the same in the other. For if "Swear not" is the fulfilment of "Swear
truly," why should not "Take no revenge" be the fulfilment of "Take revenge justly"?
So, according to my interpretation, there is in both cases a guard against sin, whether
of false swearing or of unjust revenge; though, as regards giving up the right to vengeance, there is the additional consideration that, by forgiving such debts, we shall
obtain the forgiveness of our debts. The old precept was required in the case of a
self-willed people, to teach them not to be extravagant in their demands. Thus when
rage, eager for unrestrained vengeance, was subdued, there would be leisure for any
one so disposed to consider how desirable it would be to have his own debt cancelled
by the Lord, and so to be led by this consideration to forgive the debt of his fellow-
servant. [. . .]

26. But, to return to the point in hand: — If Christ, in adding the words "But I
say unto you" to his quotation of ancient sayings, neither fulfilled the law of primitive times *by addition* nor abolished the law given by Moses with *opposing* precepts,
but rather paid such deference to the Hebrew law in all his quotations as to make his

own remarks either an explanation of what the law had stated less distinctly, or a means of securing the design intended by the law, (27) you see how differently we should understand the words, "I came not to abolish the law, but to fulfil it": not as though a half-adequate law was supplemented by these precepts; but that what the literal command failed in doing from the pride and disobedience of men, is accomplished by grace in those who are brought to repentance and humility. The fulfilment is not in additional words, but in acts of obedience. So the apostle says, "Faith worketh by love," and again, "He that loveth another hath fulfilled the law" (Gal. 5:6; Rom. 13:8). This love, by which alone the righteousness of the law can be fulfilled, was publicly bestowed at Christ's coming through the Spirit sent according to his promise; and that is why he said: "I came not to abolish the law, but to fulfil it." This is the New Testament in which it is promised that this love will inherit the Kingdom of Heaven, a promise veiled in the Old Testament, suitably to the times of that dispensation, in symbols. So Christ says again, "A new commandment I give unto you, that ye love one another" (John 13:34).

From Book 22 on military service

74. What is the moral evil in war? Is it the death of some who will soon die in any case, that others may be subdued to a peaceful state in which life may flourish? This is mere cowardly dislike, not any religious feeling. The real evils in war are love of violence, revengeful cruelty, fierce and implacable enmity, wild resistance, and the lust of power, and such like; and it is generally to impose just punishment on them that, in obedience to God or some lawful authority, good men undertake wars against violent resistance, when they find themselves set in positions of responsibility which require them to command or execute actions of this kind. Otherwise John, when the soldiers who came to be baptized asked, "What shall we do?" would have replied: "Throw away your arms; give up the service; never strike, or wound, or disable any one." But knowing that such actions in battle were not murderous but authorised by law, and that the soldiers did not thus avenge themselves but defend the public safety, he replied: "Do violence to no man, accuse no man falsely, and be content with your wages" (Luke 3:14). But as the Manichaeans are in the habit of speaking evil of John, let them hear the Lord Jesus Christ himself ordering this money to be given to Caesar, which John tells the soldiers to be content with. "Give," he says, "to Caesar the things that are Caesar's" (Matt. 22:21). For tribute-money is given on purpose to pay the soldiers for war. Again, in the case of the centurion who said, "I am a man under authority, and have soldiers under me; and I say to one, Go, and he goeth; and to another, Come, and he cometh; and to my servant, Do this, and he doeth it." Christ gave due praise to his faith; he did not tell him to leave the service (Matt. 8:9f.). But there is no need here to enter on the long discussion of just and unjust wars.

75. A great deal depends on the causes for which men undertake wars, and on the authority they have for doing so; for the natural order which seeks the peace of

mankind ordains that the prince should have the power of undertaking war if he thinks it advisable, and that the soldiers should perform their military duties in behalf of the peace and safety of the community. When war is undertaken in obedience to God, who would rebuke, or humble, or crush the pride of man, it must be allowed to be a righteous war; for even the wars which arise from human passion cannot harm the eternal well-being of God, nor even hurt his saints; for in the trial of their patience and the chastening of their spirit and in bearing fatherly correction they are rather benefited than injured. No one can have any power against them but what is given him from above. For there is no power but of God, who either orders or permits. Since therefore a righteous man, serving it may be under an ungodly king, may preserve the order required by civil peace in fighting at the due order of his sovereign — for in some cases it is plainly the will of God that he should fight, and in others, where this is not so plain, though it may be an unrighteous command on the part of the king, the soldier is innocent because his position makes obedience a duty — how much more must the man be blameless who carries on war on the authority of God, of whom every one who serves him knows that he can never require what is wrong?

76. If it is supposed that God could not enjoin warfare because in after times it was said by the Lord Jesus Christ, "I say unto you, that ye resist not evil; but if any one strike thee on the right cheek, turn to him the left also" (Matt. 5:39), the answer is, that what is here required is not a bodily action, but an inward disposition. The sacred seat of virtue is the heart, and such were the hearts of our fathers, the righteous men of old. But order required such a regulation of events and such a distinction of times as to show first of all that even earthly blessings (for so temporal kingdoms and victory over enemies are considered to be, and these are the things which the community of the ungodly all over the world are continually begging from idols and devils) are entirely under the control and at the disposal of the one true God. Thus under the Old Testament the secret of the kingdom of heaven, which was to be disclosed in due time, was veiled, and so far obscured, in the disguise of earthly promises. But when the fullness of time came for the revelation of the New Testament, which was hidden under the types of the Old, clear testimony was to be borne to the truth, that there is another life for which this life ought to be disregarded, and another kingdom for which the opposition of all earthly kingdoms should be patiently borne. Thus the name martyrs, which means witnesses, was given to those who by the will of God bore this testimony by their confessions, their sufferings and their death. The number of such witnesses is so great that if it pleased Christ — who called Saul by a voice from heaven and, having changed him from a wolf to a sheep, sent him into the midst of wolves — to unite them all in one army and to give them success in battle as he gave to the Hebrews, what nation could withstand them? What kingdom would remain unsubdued? But as the doctrine of the New Testament is that we must serve God not for temporal happiness in this life but for eternal felicity hereafter, this truth was most strikingly confirmed by the patient endurance of what is commonly called adversity for the sake of that felicity. So "when the time had fully come," the Son of God, "born of woman, born under the law, to redeem those who were under the law" (Gal. 4:4f.), "descended from David according to the flesh"

(Rom. 1:3), sends his disciples as sheep into the midst of wolves and bids them not fear those that can kill the body but cannot kill the soul, and promises that even the body will be entirely restored so that not a hair shall be lost (Matt. 10:16, 28, 30). Peter's sword he orders back into its sheath, restoring as it was before the ear of his enemy that had been cut off. He says that he could obtain legions of angels to destroy his enemies, but that he must drink the cup which his Father's will had given him (Matt. 26:52f.; Luke 22:51). He sets the example of drinking this cup, then hands it to his followers, manifesting thus, both in word and deed, the grace of patience. Therefore God raised him from the dead, and "bestowed on him the name which is above every name, that at the name of Jesus every knee should bow, in heaven and on earth and under the earth, and every tongue confess that Jesus is Lord, to the glory of God the Father" (Phil. 2:9-11).

The patriarchs and prophets, then, have a kingdom in this world, to show that these kingdoms, too, are given and taken away by God; the apostles and martyrs had no kingdom here, to show the superior desirableness of the Kingdom of Heaven. The prophets, however, could even in those times die for the truth, (as the Lord himself says, "From the blood of Abel to the blood of Zechariah" [Matt. 23:35]); and in these days, since the commencement of the fulfillment of what is prophesied in the psalm of Christ (under the figure of Solomon, which means "the peacemaker" as Christ is our peace), "All kings of the earth shall bow to him, all nations shall serve him" (Ps. 72:11), we have seen Christian emperors, who have put all their confidence in Christ, gaining splendid victories over ungodly enemies whose hope was in the rites of idolatry and devil-worship. There are public and undeniable proofs of the fact that on one side the prognostications of devils were found to be fallacious, and on the other the predictions of saints were a means of support; and we have now writings in which those facts are recorded.

Translation: R. Stothert and A. Newman, Nicene and Post-Nicene Fathers, adapted.

Letter 153 *on the intercession for condemned persons*

Augustine, bishop, servant of Christ and of his household, gives greeting in the Lord to his beloved son, Macedonius.

1. When a man is as much burdened with public duties and as devoted to the interest of others and to the public welfare rather than his own, as you are — and I congratulate you — it is not right for us to deprive you of our conversation nor to delay you with a foreword. Here, then, is what you wanted to learn from me, or to discover whether I knew the answer. If you judged that it was a trifling or superfluous matter, you would see that there was no place for it among such great and such exigent cares. You ask me why we say that it is part of our priestly duty to intercede for condemned persons, and to be displeased if we do not succeed, as if we were failing to carry out that part of our duty. You then say that you have a serious doubt about this, whether it is part of religion. Thereupon, you add your reason for being

disturbed and you say: "If sin is so strictly forbidden by the Lord that no opportunity of repentance is granted after the first, how can we argue that any crime of whatever sort should be forgiven?" You press the point still more closely and you say that we approve an act by wishing it to go unpunished, and, if it is a fact that the one who approves of a sin is involved in all the circumstances of it no less than the one who commits it, it is clear that we are implicated in a share of the guilt as often as we wish the one who is subject to the penalty to go unpunished.

2. Anyone who did not know your gentleness and kindness would be affronted by these words. But we who know that you wrote this in order to raise the question, not to give an opinion, have no hesitation in answering these words at once by other words of yours. As if you did not wish us to delay on this question, you either forestalled what we were going to say, or you advised us what we ought to say, and you said: "Besides, here is another point, which is even more serious. All sins seem to deserve forgiveness when the guilty person promises amendment!" Before I discuss that more serious point which follows in your letter, I shall take up this concession which you have made and use it to remove that obstacle which makes it seem possible for our intercession to be curtailed. So, then, as far as opportunity is granted, we intercede for all sins because "all sins seem to deserve forgiveness when the guilty person promises amendment." This is your sentiment and it is also ours.

3. We do not in any way approve the faults which we wish to see corrected, nor do we wish wrong-doing to go unpunished because we take pleasure in it; we pity the man while detesting the deed or crime, and the more the vice displeases us, the less do we want the culprit to die unrepentant. It is easy and simple to hate evil men because they are evil, but uncommon and dutiful to love them because they are men; thus, in one and the same person you disapprove the guilt and approve the nature, and you thereby hate the guilt with a more just reason because by it the nature which you love is defiled. Therefore, he who makes war on the crime in order to free the man is not involved in a share of the wrong-doing, but, rather, of human feeling. Moreover, there is no other place but this life for correcting morals; whatever anyone has sought out for himself in this life, the same will he have after it. Consequently, we are forced by our love for humankind to intercede for the guilty lest they end this life by punishment, only to find that punishment does not end with this life.

4. Do not doubt that this duty of ours is a part of religion because God, "with whom there is no iniquity," whose power is supreme, who not only sees what each one is but also foresees what he will be, who alone cannot err in his judgment because he cannot be deceived in his knowledge, nevertheless acts as the Gospel expresses it: "He maketh his sun to rise upon the good and bad, and raineth upon the just and the unjust." The Lord Christ, exhorting us to imitate his wonderful goodness, says: "Love your enemies, do good to them that persecute you, that you may be the children of your Father who is in heaven, who maketh his sun to rise upon the good and bad and raineth upon the just and the unjust" (Matt. 5:44f.). Is there anyone who does not know that many abuse this divine clemency and kindness to their own destruction? The Apostle upbraids these and reproves them gravely, saying: "And thinkest thou, O man, that judgest them that do such things, and dost the same, that thou shalt escape the judgment of God? Or despiseth thou the riches of his goodness and patience and

longsuffering? Knowest thou not that the benignity of God leadeth thee to penance? But according to thy hardness and impenitent heart thou treasurest up to thyself wrath against the day of wrath and revelation of the just judgment of God, who will render to every man according to his works" (Rom. 2:3-6). Is the fact that some persist in their wickedness any proof that God does not persist in his patience, punishing very few sins in this world lest we fail to believe in his divine providence, and saving many for the last judgment to justify his future decree?"

5. No, I do not think that heavenly Master commands us to love wickedness when he commands us to love our enemies, to do good to those who hate us and pray for those who persecute us, although, without doubt, if we worship God devoutly, we can have no enemies and persecutors roused to bitter hatred against us except the wicked. Are we, then, to love the wicked? Just so. He who commands this is God, yet he does not for this include us in the ranks of the wicked, nor does he himself join their ranks by sparing them and granting them life and health. His intention, as far as it is given to the good man to know it, is expressed by the Apostle when he says "Knowest thou not that the benignity of God leadeth thee to penance?" We wish to add that we do not spare or favour the sins of those for whom we intercede.

6. In the case of some whose sins are public, after they have been released from your severe sentence, we keep them from participation in the Sacrament of the altar so that, by repentance and by punishing themselves, they may be able to make atonement to him whom they have flouted by their sin. The one who repents sincerely effects nothing less than this: he does not allow his wrong-doing to remain unpunished. Thus God spares the one who does not spare himself, but no one who despises his high and holy judgement escapes it. But, if he shows such patience by sparing the wicked and abandoned, and by granting them life and health, although he knows that many of them will not do penance, how much more, in the case of those who promise amendment, even though we are not sure whether they will do what they promise, should we be merciful to the extent of bending your inflexible decision by interceding for them! Without presumption, because he commands it, we pray for them to God from whom none of their future conduct is hidden.

7. Vice, however, sometimes makes such inroads among men that, even after they have done penance and have been readmitted to the Sacrament of the altar, they commit the same or more grievous sins, yet God makes his sun to rise even on such men and gives his gifts of life and health as lavishly as he did before their fall. And, although that same opportunity of penance is not again granted them in the Church, God does not forget to exercise his patience toward them. Suppose one of these were to say to us: "Either give me the same chance of doing penance again or pronounce me hopeless and let me do whatever I please as far as my resources allow and human laws do not forbid, indulging in illicit love and every kind of riotous living, condemned, indeed, by God but praised by most men; or, if you withdraw me from this baseness, tell me whether it will do me any good for the next life to despise in this life all the enticements of the most seductive pleasure, to curb the impulses of my passions, to chastise my body by withholding from it many lawful and allowable pleasures, to punish myself by penance more severe than the former, to groan more sorrowfully, to weep more freely, to live better, to give more lavish alms to the poor,

to burn more ardently with that charity which 'covereth a multitude of sins'" (1 Pet. 4:8), would anyone of us be so far gone in folly as to say to this man: "None of those acts will do you any good for the life to come; go and enjoy the sweetness of this life at least"? May God keep this monstrous and sacrilegious madness far from us! It may, therefore, be a careful and useful enactment that the opportunity of that very humble penance be granted only once in the Church, lest that remedy, by becoming common, be less helpful to sick souls, for it is now more effective by being more respected. Yet, who would dare say to God: "Why do you pardon this man a second time when he has been caught again in the snare of sin after his first penance?" Who would dare to say that such are not included in the saying of the Apostle: "Knowest thou not that the patience of God leadeth thee to penance?" (cf. Rom. 2:4) or that this other saying is limited so as to exclude them: "Blessed are all they that trust in him" (Ps. 2:12), or that the following does not apply to them: "Do ye manfully and let your heart be strengthened, all ye that hope in the Lord" (Ps. 30:25)?

8. Since, therefore, God shows such great patience and mercy toward sinners that they are not damned forever if they amend their conduct in this life, and since he looks to no one to show him mercy, because no one is happier than he, no one more powerful, no one more just, it follows that we men ought to be such toward other men, for, whatever praise we heap up on this life of ours, we never say that it is without sin, because, if we did, "We deceive ourselves," as it is written, "and the truth is not in us" (1 John 1:8). Consequently, although the prosecutor and the defender are two different persons, and the role of intercessor is not the same as that of judge — it would take too long, and is not necessary in this speech to discourse on these various duties — the very avengers of crime, who are not to be influenced by their personal anger but are to act as agents of the law, and those who enforce the law against proved injuries done to others, not to themselves, as judges should do, all these quail before the divine judgement, recalling that they have need of the mercy of God for their own sins, and they do not think they do an injury to their office if they show mercy to those over whom they have the lawful power of life and death.

9. When the Jews brought the woman taken in adultery to the Lord Christ they tempted him by saying that the Law commanded such a person to be stoned, and when they asked what he would command for her he answered: "He that is without sin among you, let him first cast a stone at her" (John 8:3-7). Thus, he did not reject the Law which commanded the stoning of a woman guilty of this sin, and at the same time, by rousing fear in those whose verdict could have put her to death, he recalled them to thoughts of mercy. I think that upon hearing this verdict of the Lord, her husband himself, if he was there and demanding satisfaction for this breach of marital fidelity, was thoroughly frightened into changing his mind from his desire for revenge into a sentiment of pardon. See how the accuser is warned not to seek vengeance for his personal injuries, when even judges are thus forbidden to avenge themselves in punishing an adulteress, and are obliged to enforce the Law, not to indulge their private feeling! Thus, when Joseph, to whom the Virgin Mary, Mother of the Lord, was espoused, discovered that she was with child and knew that it was not his child, he could only believe that she was an adulteress, yet he was unwilling to punish her, although he was not thereby accessory to the sin. This good intention

was credited to him as virtue; therefore this is written of him: "And being a just man, and not willing publicly to expose her, he was minded to put her away privately. But when he thought on these things, the Angel appeared to him" (Matt. 1:19-20) and revealed to him that what he had thought was the result of sin was the act of God.

10. If, then, the hurt feeling of the accuser and the rigour of the judge are tempered by the knowledge of our common human weakness, what do you think the defender or the intercessor ought to do for the accused, when even you good men who are now judges, after having gained much experience by pleading men's cases in the law courts, know how much more willingly you usually undertake a defence than a prosecution? Yet there is a great difference between the defender and the intercessor, for the former expends his effort chiefly in diminishing or covering up the charge of guilt, while the intercessor works for the removal or reduction of the penalty, even when there is evidence of guilt. The just who are with God perform this service for sinners; sinners themselves are exhorted to do the same for themselves, for it is written: "Confess your sins one to another and pray one for another" (James 5:16). Every man claims for himself from every other man, where possible, this human consideration, for what each one would punish if it occurred in his own house he wishes to leave unpunished in another's house. For, if he is summoned to a friend's house and if the friend is angry in his presence at someone on whom he has the power to avenge himself, or if he suddenly comes upon an angry man, he is considered, not a man of great uprightness, but a most inhumane one, if he does not intervene. I know that you yourself with some of your friends in the church at Carthage interceded for a cleric whose bishop was deservedly angry with him and certainly there was no fear there of a physical punishment, but of a disciplinary measure short of bloodshed — yet, when you wished something to go unpunished which even you disapproved of, we did not estimate you as favourers of guilt; we listened to you as most considerate intercessors. So, if it is right for you to moderate an ecclesiastical sanction by intercession, how much more ought a bishop to intercede against your sword, since the sanction is invoked that the one against whom it is directed may lead a good life, but the sword is drawn that he may not live at all!

11. Finally, the Lord himself intervened among men that the adulteress might not be stoned, and thus he commended to us the duty of intercession, except that he achieved by fear what we gain by prayer. He is the Lord, we are the servants; he used fear in such a way that we ought to be afraid, for who of us is without sin? When he said to those who offered the sinful woman to him for punishment, that he who knew himself to be without sin should first cast a stone at her, their savagery died as their conscience trembled, for then they slipped away from that gathering and left the poor woman alone with the merciful Lord. Let the piety of Christians yield to this sentence as the impiety of the Jews yielded to it; let the humility of adorers yield as the pride of persecutors has yielded; let the submission of the faithful yield as the lying pretence of the temper yielded. Pardon the wicked, good Sir; be more perfect as you are more merciful, humble yourself more profoundly as you rise higher by your power.

12. Looking upon your conduct, I have called you a good man, but do you look upon the words of Christ and say to yourself: "None is good but God alone"

(Mark 10:18; Luke 18:19). Although this is true — and Truth has said it — it ought not to be imagined that I said that through a deceitful flattery, or that I set myself up as if in contradiction to the Lord's words, calling you a good man, whereas he says: "None is good but God alone," for the Lord did not contradict himself when he said: "A good man out of the good treasure of his heart bringeth forth good things" (Matt. 12:35; Luke 6:45). God, therefore, is uniquely good, and this he cannot lose. He is good; he is not good by sharing in any other good, because the good by which he is good is himself. But when a man is good, his good is from God, because he cannot be his own good. All who become good do so through his Spirit; our nature has been created to attain to him through acts of its own will. If we are to become good, it is important for us to receive and hold what he gives, who is good in himself; whoever neglects this is evil in himself. Therefore, in so far as a man acts uprightly, that is, performs his good works intelligently, lovingly, and devoutly, in so far he is good; whereas, in so far as he sins, that is, turns away from truth and love and piety, in so far he is evil. But, who is without some sin in this life? We say a man is good whose good deeds predominate, and a man is perfect whose sin is very slight.

13. For this reason, those whom the Lord himself calls good because they receive a share of divine grace he also calls evil because they have the defects of human weakness, until the whole of which we are composed is healed of all evil tendency and crosses over into that life where there will be no more sin forever. Certainly it was the good, not the wicked, whom he taught to pray when he instructed them to say: "Our Father who art in heaven" (Matt. 6:9). These then become sons of God, not by natural generation, but by grace; to them, as to those who receive him, "He gave the power to be made the sons of God" (John 1:12). In the fashion of the Scriptures this spiritual generation is called adoption, to distinguish it from the generation of God from God, of the Co-eternal from the Eternal; hence it is written: "Who shall declare his generation?" (Isa. 53:8). He showed then that those are good who by his will say truthfully to God: "Our Father who art in heaven," but in the same prayer he taught them to say, among other things: "Forgive us our debts as we also forgive our debtors" (Matt. 6:12). Although it is evident that these debts are sins, he afterward expressed this more definitely when he said: "For if you will forgive men their offences, your Father will forgive you also your offences" (Matt. 6:14). The baptised recite this prayer, and thenceforth none of their past sins remain, for Holy Church grants the baptised forgiveness of all. But, as they live afterward in a state of mortal frailty, they necessarily contract other guilt which requires forgiveness; otherwise they could not truthfully say: "Forgive us our debts." They are good, then, in virtue of being sons of God, but, in so far as they sin, as they admit by their own truthful confession, they are evil.

14. Possibly, someone may say that here is a difference between the sins of the good and the sins of the bad, which is not improbably said on frequent occasions. Nevertheless, the Lord Jesus spoke without any ambiguity when he said that God was the Father of those whom he called evil. In the same sermon in which he taught that prayer, he said in another place exhorting them to pray to God: "Ask and you shall receive, seek and you shall find, knock and it shall be opened to you. For everyone that asketh receiveth and he that seeketh findeth and to him that knocketh it

shall be opened"; and a little further on: "If you then being evil know how to give good gifts to your children, how much more will your Father who is in heaven give good things to them that ask him?" (Matt. 7:7, 8, 11; Luke 11:9, 10, 13). Is God, then, the Father of evil men? Perish the thought! How, then, does he say "Your Father who is in heaven" to those whom he addresses as "You, being evil," except that Truth shows both what we are by God's goodness and what we are by human defect, praising the one, correcting the other? Well was it said by Seneca, a contemporary of the Apostles, several of whose letters to the Apostle Paul are extant: "He who hates bad men hates all men." Yet, bad men are to be loved, so that they may not continue to be bad, just as sick men are to be loved so that they may not remain sick, but may be cured.

15. Whatever sin we commit during our sojourn in this life, after that remission of sin which is effected by baptism, even if such sin is not of a kind to entail segregation from the divine altar, is not expiated by unprofitable regret, but by the sacrifices of mercy. Therefore, what we accomplish in making you act on our intercession you know that you offer to God for yourselves, for you need the mercy which you grant to others. Notice who said: "Forgive and you shall be forgiven, give and it shall be given to you" (Luke 6:37, 38). Yet even if our life were such that there would be no reason for us to say: "Forgive us our debts" (Matt 6:12; Luke 11:4), our soul ought to be more full of mercy the more it is free from evil, so that, if we are not pierced through by the words of the Lord: "He that is without sin among you, let him first cast a stone at her," we may at least follow the example of him who was certainly without sin, and who said to the woman, deserted by her terrified captors: "Neither will I condemn thee, go now and sin no more" (John 8:7-11). The sinful woman could have feared, after the departure of those who had recognised their own sins as a prelude to forgiving another's, that he who was without sin might have condemned her with perfect justice. But, when she answered that no man had condemned her, he, untroubled in conscience and overflowing with mercy, said: "If wickedness could pardon thee, why dost thou fear innocence?" And lest he should seem to approve rather than to forgive her evil deeds, he said: "Go now and sin no more," to show that he pardoned the person but did not condone the guilt of the person. You see, then, that it is a matter of religion and does not involve us in a share of the evil-doing when we intercede, if not as criminals for criminals, at least as sinners for sinners, and, I think, with sinners — please take this as spoken sincerely, and without offence.

16. Surely it is not without purpose that we have the institution of the power of kings, the death penalty of the judge, the barbed hooks of the executioner, the weapons of the soldier, the right of punishment of the overlord, even the severity of the good father. All those things have their methods, their causes, their reasons, their practical benefits. While these are feared, the wicked are kept within bounds and the good live more peacefully among the wicked. However, men are not to be called good because they refrain from wrong-doing through their fear of such things — no one is good through dread of punishment but through love of righteousness — even so, it is not without advantage that human recklessness should be confined by fear of the law so that innocence may be safe among evil-doers, and the evil-doers them-

selves may be cured by calling on God when their freedom of action is held in check by fear of punishment. However, the intercession of bishops is not a violation of this arrangement of human affairs; on the contrary, there would be neither motive nor opportunity for intervention if it were not for this. The more the penalty of the offender is deserved, the more gratefully the bounty of the intercessor and of the one who pardons is received. It is for this reason, as I see it, that a more unyielding justice shines forth in the Old Testament in the time of the ancient Prophets, to show that penalties were levied against the wicked for a good purpose; but in the New Testament we are urged to pardon offenders with mercy, either as a saving remedy by which our own sins may be pardoned, or as a means of commending gentleness, so that truth, when preached by those who pardon, may not be so much feared as loved.

17. It is a matter of great importance what intention a man has in showing leniency. Just as it is sometimes mercy to punish, so it may be cruelty to pardon. For, to use a well-worn case as an example, who would not truthfully say that a person is cruel who would allow a child to play with snakes because he was obstinately set on so doing? Who would not call another kind-hearted who would restrain the child even to the extent of beating him if words had no effect? For this reason, restraint should not go so far as death, because there must be someone to whom restraint is beneficial. Yet it makes a great difference when one man is killed by another, whether it happened through a desire of injuring him, or of carrying off something dishonestly, as it might be done by an enemy, a thief; or whether it happened in the course of inflicting punishment or carrying out an order, as by a judge, an executioner; or through self-defence or the rescue of another, as a thief is killed by a traveller or an enemy by a soldier. And sometimes the one who was the cause of death is more at fault than the killer, as would be the case if a man were to default on the one who stood bail for him, and the latter should pay the required penalty instead of the other. Nevertheless, not everyone who causes another's death is guilty. What if a man were to seek to ravish someone and should kill himself because he did not get his wish? Or if a son, fearing the blows which he deserved from his father, should kill himself by falling? Or if someone should commit suicide because one man had been set free or to prevent another from being freed? Because these circumstances have been the cause of another's death, are we to consent to sin? are we to deprive a father of the authority to inflict punishment for wrongdoing — which is done through a desire of correcting, not of injuring — or are we to forego the works of mercy? When these things happen, we owe them human regret, but we have no right for that reason to put restraint on the will of the doers to prevent them from happening again.

18. In the same way, when we intercede for an offender who deserves condemnation, there sometimes are consequences which we do not intend, either in the person who is set free through our intercession, so that he goes rioting about more extravagantly, because his unchecked boldness goes to greater lengths of passion, being ungrateful for the leniency shown; and his single escape from death may be the cause of many other deaths. Or it may be that the object of our kindness changes for the better and mends his morals, but he may be the cause of another's perishing as a result of an evil life, because the latter, seeing that the former has escaped punishment,

commits the same crimes or even worse ones. Yet, I think, these evil consequences are not to be laid to our charge when we intercede with you, but, rather, the good aims which we have in view and which we intend when we act thus, that is, to commend mildness so as to win men's love for the word of truth, and to ensure that those who are freed from temporal death may so live as not to fall into eternal death from which they can never be freed.

19. There is good, then, in your severity which works to secure our tranquillity, and there is good in our intercession which works to restrain your severity. Do not be displeased at being petitioned by the good, because the good are not displeased that you are feared by the wicked. Even the Apostle Paul used fear to check the evil deeds of men, fear not only of the judgment to come but even of your present instruments of torture, asserting that they form part of the plan of divine providence, when he said: "Let every soul be subject to higher powers, for there is no power but from God; and those that are ordained of God. Therefore he that resisteth the power, resisteth the ordinance of God, and they that resist, purchase to themselves damnation: for princes are not a terror to the good work but to the evil. Wilt thou then not be afraid of the power? Do that which is good and thou shalt have praise for the same; for he is God's minister to thee for good. But if thou do that which is evil, fear, for he beareth not the sword in vain: for he is God's minister, an avenger to execute wrath upon him that doth evil. Wherefore be subject of necessity, not only for wrath but also for conscience sake. For therefore also you pay tribute, for they are the ministers of God, serving unto this purpose. Render therefore to all men their dues, tribute to whom tribute is due, custom to whom custom, fear to whom fear, honour to whom honour. Owe no man anything but to love one another" (Rom. 13:1-8). These words of the Apostle show the usefulness of your severity. Thus, as those who fear are ordered to render love to those who cause them fear, so those who cause fear are ordered to render love to those who fear. Let nothing be done through desire of hurting, but all through love of helping, and nothing will be done cruelly, inhumanly. Thus, the sentence of the judge will be feared, but not so as to cause the religious motive of the intercessor to be scorned, because it is only by yielding and pardoning that the good effect of amending a man's life is produced. But, if perversity and impiety are so great that neither punishment nor pardon can avail to correct them, it is still true that, whether severity or leniency is shown, the obligation of charity is fulfilled by the good through their intention and upright conscience which God beholds.

20. In the following part of your letter where you say: "But now human behaviour has come to this pass that men wish to have the punishment of their crime remitted and at the same time to keep the profit which they gained by their evil deeds," you are speaking of the lowest kind of men, who are absolutely unable to be helped by the remedy of repentance. If the offence committed has involved theft, and restitution is not made, although it is possible to make it, there is no repentance but only pretence. If, however, there is true repentance, the sin will not be forgiven unless there is restitution of stolen goods, but, as I said, where restitution is possible. Often, however, the thief dissipates the goods either by connivance with other offenders or by living an evil life himself, and has nothing left with which to make restitution. To

127

him we certainly cannot say, "Pay back what you took," unless we believe that he has it and denied it. But in the case where he suffers some physical punishment at the hands of the offended party, because it is believed that he has the means of paying back what he took, he pays the penalty of the sin by which he wrongfully stole through the corporal pains applied to make him pay back. It is not an uncivilised thing to intercede for such persons, as one does for those convicted of crimes, since it is not done to save them entirely from making restitution, but so that man may not show cruelty to man, especially the one who has already been given satisfaction for the guilty act, but still wants his money and fears to be cheated of it, without seeking to be avenged. Finally, in such cases, if we can convince the injured party that those for whom we intercede do not possess what is demanded, there is a cessation of their importunity on us. Sometimes, indeed, merciful men, in a state of real doubt, are not willing to inflict certain punishment for the sake of uncertain money. This is the mercy which it befits us to challenge and exhort them to show, for it is better for you to lose the money if he has it than to torture or kill him if he does not have it. In this case it is more effective to intercede with creditors than with judges, because the judge who has the power to enforce restitution and does not do it might seem to be a party to the theft, although in using force he must display a regard for honesty without losing human feeling.

21. This, indeed, I would say with complete assurance: that the one who intercedes for a man to save him from restoring his ill-gotten goods and who fails, when someone has fled to him for refuge, to force him to make restitution as far as he honestly can, is a party to the theft and the guilt. It would be more merciful for us to withhold our succour from such men than to offer it to them, for he does not succour who helps someone to sin when he should hinder him and turn him away from it. But can we or ought we for that reason either to extort the money from them or hand them over to another's extortion? We act within the limits of our episcopal jurisdiction, threatening them sometimes with human, but especially and always with divine, judgment. In the case of those who refuse to make restitution, of whom we know that they have stolen and have the means to pay, we rebuke and reproach them, showing our detestation of them, some in private, some publicly, according as the diversity of characters shows the possibility of reforming them. Yet, in this we avoid rousing them to greater madness, sometimes, if an aggravation of the fault to be cured is not feared, we even cut them off from communion at the holy altar.

22. Indeed, it often happens that they deceive us either by saying that they have not stolen or by insisting that they have no means of making restitution, but often, too, you are deceived by thinking either that we do not make them pay back or that they have the means of paying back. All or almost all of us men love to call or consider our suspicions knowledge, since we are influenced by the credible evidence of circumstances; yet some credible things are false, just as some incredible ones are true. Therefore, mentioning some who "wish to have the punishment of their crime remitted and at the same time to keep the profit which they gained by their evil deeds," you added something else when you said: "Your priestly office thinks that intercession should be made for these, also." It is possible that you might know something I do not know and that I might think I ought to intercede for someone in a

case where I could be deceived, but you could not, because I believed that a man did not possess what you knew that he did possess. Thus it could be that we might not have the same idea of a man's guilt, but neither of us would approve a failure to make restitution. As men we have different ideas about a man, but in the concept of justice we are one. In the same way it is also possible for me to know that someone has nothing, while you are not too sure that he has, but you have good grounds for suspecting him and in this way it seems to you that I intercede for a man "who wished to have the punishment of his crime remitted and to keep the profit which he gained by his evil deed." To sum up, then, neither to you, nor to men such as we rejoice to find you — if any others can be found — nor to those who with great eagerness pursue interests foreign to them, utterly unprofitable and even extremely dangerous and deadly, nor to my own heart would I dare to say, as I would not think or decide, that intercession should be made for anyone to enable him to possess unpunished what he has wrongfully taken, when his offence has been pardoned, always supposing that he still has either what he took or some other means of making restitution. *on legal fees*

23. It is not true, however, that everything which is taken from an unwilling donor is wrongfully taken. Most people do not want to give due credit to their doctor, or to pay a workman his hire, yet when these receive their due from unwilling debtors they do not acquire anything unlawfully; on the contrary, it would be wrong to deprive them of it. But there is no reason for a judge to take money for a just judgment or a witness for true testimony, because the advocate is paid for legal protection and the lawyer for truthful advice; the two former have to make an inquiry into both sides, the latter stand on one side. But when verdicts and testimony are sold, they are unfair and untrue, because just and true ones are not to be sold, and it is much more infamous for money to be taken when it is infamously even if willingly paid. The one who pays for a just verdict usually demands his money back on the ground that it was wrongfully taken from him, since justice ought not to be for sale; while the one who pays for an unjust verdict would like to demand his money back, if he were not afraid or ashamed of having paid it.

24. There are other personages of lower rank who not uncommonly take pay from both sides, such as a court attendant by whom a service is performed or on whom it devolves. What is extorted by these with excessive dishonesty is usually demanded back, but if paid according to accepted custom it is not asked back, and those who do demand it contrary to custom we disapprove of more vigorously than those who accept it according to custom, since many officials, necessary to human affairs, are influenced or attracted by gains of this kind. If these latter change their way of life and attain to a higher degree of virtuous living, they are more ready to distribute to the poor, as if it were their own, what they have acquired in this way than they are to pay it back to those from whom they have received it, as a form of restitution of what is not their own. However, we think that those who have done an injury to human society by theft, rapine, calumny, oppression, housebreaking ought to pay what they owe rather than give it away, following the example of the tax collector, Zacchaeus, in the Gospel, who received the Lord into his house, was suddenly

converted to a holy life, and said: "The half of my goods I give to the poor, and if I have wronged any man of anything I restore him fourfold" (Luke 19:8).

25. If there is to be a more sincere regard for justice it would be more honest to say to the advocate: "Pay back what you received when you stood against truth, supported evil-doing, deceived the judge, won your case by lying, as you see that many of the most honourable and eloquent men seem to allow themselves to do, not only with safety, but even with renown," rather than to say to any minor official struggling to perform some duty: "Pay back what you received when at the judge's order you held a man who was needed for some case, when you tied him so that he could not resist, shut him up so that he could not run away, and finally produced him while the trial was going on, or dismissed him when it was finished." It is easy to see why no one says this to an advocate, because a man naturally does not wish to ask back what he gave a patron to win a bad case, just as he does not wish to pay back what he received from his opponent when he won his case dishonestly. Finally, how hard it is to find an advocate or a truly good man who has become an advocate, who would say to his client: "Take back what you paid me for representing you so dishonestly, and give back to your opponent what you took from him as a result of my dishonest pleading." Yet, anyone who thoroughly repents of his dishonest former life ought to do even this, so that, if the dishonest litigant is not willing to make amends for his injustice after this warning, he at least will take no pay for the injustice. Otherwise, it might happen that there is an obligation to pay back what is secretly taken from another by theft, but none to pay back what is gotten by deceiving the judge and evading the law in the very court of law where offences are punished. And what about lending money at interest, which the very laws and judges require to be paid back? Who is more cruel: the one who steals from or cheats a rich man or the one who destroys a poor man by usury? What is acquired this way is certainly ill-gotten gain, and I would wish restitution to be made of it, but it is not possible to sue for it in court.

26. And now, if we look carefully at what is written: "The whole world is the wealth of the faithful man, but the unfaithful one has not a penny" (Prov. 17:6 Septuagint), do we not prove that those who seem to rejoice in lawfully acquired gains, and do not know how to use them, are really in possession of other men's property? Certainly, what is lawfully possessed is not another's property, but "lawfully" means justly and justly means rightly. He who uses his wealth badly possesses it wrongfully, and wrongful possession means that it is another's property. You see, then, how many there are who ought to make restitution of another's goods, although those to whom restitution is due may be a few; wherever they are, their claim to just possession is in proportion to their indifference to wealth. Obviously, no one possesses justice unlawfully: whoever does not love it does not have it; but money is wrongly possessed by bad men while good men who love it least have the best right to it. In this life the wrong of evil possessors is endured and among them certain laws are established which are called civil laws, not because they bring men to make a good use of their wealth, but because those who make bad use of it become thereby less injurious. This comes about either because some of them become faithful and fervent — and these have a right to all things — or because those who live among them are not

hampered by their evil deeds, but are tested until they come to that City where they are heirs to eternity, where the just alone have a place, the wise alone leadership, and those who are there possess what is truly their own. Yet, even here, we do not intercede to prevent restitution from being made, according to earthly customs and laws, although we should like you to be indulgent to evil-doers, not to make them take pleasure or persist in their evil, but because, whenever any of them become good, God is appeased by a sacrifice of mercy, and if evil-doers did not find him merciful there would be no good men.

For a long time I seem to have been putting a burden on a busy man by my talk, whereas it would have been possible to explain quickly what was asked by a man as clear-sighted and experienced as you are. I ought to have made an end of this long since, and I would have if I had thought you would be the only one to read what you urged me to write. May you enjoy a happy life in Christ, my dearest son.

Translation: Sister W. Parsons, S.N.D., Fathers of the Church (New York, 1953). Used with permission.

From *Letter 93*

3. You say that no example is found in the writings of evangelists and apostles, of any petition presented on behalf of the church to the kings of the earth against her enemies. Who denies this? None such is found. But at that time the prophecy, "Be wise now, therefore, O ye kings; be instructed ye judges of the earth; serve the Lord with fear" (Ps. 2:10f.), was not yet fulfilled. Up to that time the words which we find at the beginning of the same Psalm were receiving their fulfilment, "Why do the heathen rage, and the people imagine a vain thing? The kings of the earth set themselves, and the rulers take counsel together against the Lord and against his anointed" (Ps. 2:1f.). Truly, if past events recorded in the prophetic books were figures of the future, there was given under King Nebuchadnezzar a figure both of the time of the church under the apostles, and of her present time. In the age of the apostles and martyrs that was fulfilled which was prefigured when the aforesaid king compelled pious and just men to bow down to his image and cast into the flames all who refused. Now, however, is fulfilled that which was prefigured soon after in the same king, when, being converted to the worship of the true God, he made a decree throughout his empire that whosoever should speak against the God of Shadrach, Meshach and Abednego, should suffer the penalty which their crime deserved (Dan. 3:29). The earlier time of that king represented the former age of emperors who did not believe in Christ, at whose hands the Christians suffered because of the wicked; but the later time represented the age of the successors to the imperial throne, now believing in Christ, at whose hands the wicked suffer because of the Christians.

It is manifest, however, that towards those who, under the Christian name, have been led astray by perverse men, a moderate severity, or rather clemency, is carefully observed, lest Christ's sheep be among the wandering who by such measures must be brought back to the flock; so that by punishments such as exile and fines they are admonished to consider what they suffer and why, and are taught to prefer the Scriptures which they read to human legends and calumnies. For which of us, yea, which of you, does not speak well of the laws issued by the emperors against heathen sacrifices? In these, assuredly, a penalty much more severe has been appointed, for the punishment of that impiety is death. But in repressing and restraining you the thing aimed at has been rather that you should be admonished to depart from evil, than that you should be punished for a crime. [. . .]

5. You see, therefore, I suppose, that the thing to be considered when anyone is coerced is not the mere fact of the coercion but the nature of that to which he is coerced, whether it be good or bad; not that any one can be good in spite of his own will, but that, through fear of suffering what he does not desire, he either renounces his hostile prejudices or is compelled to examine the truth of which he had been contentedly ignorant; and under the influence of this fear he repudiates the error which he was wont to defend, or seeks the truth of which he formerly knew nothing, and now willingly holds what he formerly rejected. Perhaps it would be utterly useless to assert this in words if it were not demonstrated by so many examples. We see not a few men here and there, but many cities, once Donatist now Catholic, vehemently detesting the diabolical schism and ardently loving the unity of the church; and these became Catholic under the influence of that fear which so offends you, by the laws of emperors from Constantine, before whom your party of its own accord impeached Caecilianus, down to the emperors of our own time, who most justly decree that the decision of the judge whom your own party chose and whom they preferred to a tribunal of bishops should be maintained in force against you.

I have therefore yielded to the evidence afforded by these instances which my colleagues have laid before me. For originally my opinion was that no one should be coerced into the unity of Christ, that we must act only by words, fight only by arguments and prevail by force of reason, lest we should have those whom we knew as avowed heretics feigning themselves to be Catholics. But this opinion of mine was overcome not by the words of those who controverted it, but by the conclusive instances to which they could point. For in the first place there was set over against my opinion my own town, which, although it was once wholly on the side of Donatus, was brought over to the Catholic unity by fear of the imperial edicts, and which we now see filled with such detestation of your ruinous perversity that it would scarcely be believed that it had ever been involved in your error. There were so many others which were mentioned to me by name, that from facts themselves I was made to own that to this matter the word of Scripture might be understood as applying: "Give opportunity to a wise man, and he will be yet wiser" (Prov. 9:9). For how many were already, as we assuredly know, willing to be Catholics, being moved by the indisputable plainness of truth, but daily putting off their avowal of this through fear of offending their own party! How many were bound, not by truth — for you never pretended to that as yours — but by the heavy chains of inveterate custom, so that in them was fulfilled the divine saying: "By mere words a servant who is hardened will not be disciplined; for though he understand, he will not give heed" (Prov. 29:19). How many supposed the sect of Donatus to be the true church merely because ease

132

had made them too listless, or conceited, or sluggish to take pains to examine Catholic truth! How many would have entered earlier had not the calumnies of slanderers, who declared that we offered something else than we do upon the altar of God, shut them out! How many, believing that it mattered not to which party a Christian might belong, remained in the schism of Donatus only because they had been born in it, and no one was compelling them to forsake it and pass over into the Catholic church! [. . .]

12. We disapprove of every one who, taking advantage of this imperial edict, persecutes you, not with loving concern for your correction, but with the malice of an enemy. Moreover, although, since every earthly possession can be rightly retained only on the ground either of divine right, according to which all things belong to the righteous, or of human right, which is in the jurisdiction of the kings of the earth, you are mistaken in calling those things yours which you do not possess as righteous persons and which you have forfeited by the laws of earthly sovereigns, and plead in vain, "We have laboured to gather them," seeing that you may read what is written, "The wealth of the sinner is laid up for the just" (Prov. 13:22); nevertheless we disapprove of any one who, availing himself of this law which the kings of the earth, doing homage to Christ, have published in order to correct your impiety, covetously seeks to possess himself of your property. Also we disapprove of any one who, on the ground not of justice but of avarice, seizes and retains the provision pertaining to the poor, or the chapels in which you meet for worship, which you once occupied in the name of the church, and which are by all means the rightful property only of that church which is the true church of Christ. We disapprove of any one who receives a person that has been expelled by you for some disgraceful action or crime on the same terms on which those are received who have lived among you chargeable with no other crime beyond the error through which you are separated from us. But these are things which you cannot easily prove; and although you can prove them, we bear with some whom we are unable to correct or even to punish; and we do not quit the Lord's threshing-floor because of the chaff which is there, nor break the Lord's net because of the bad fishes enclosed therein, nor desert the Lord's flock because of goats which are to be in the end separated from it, nor go forth from the Lord's house because in it there are vessels destined to dishonour.

Letter 189

To Boniface, my noble lord and justly distinguished and honourable son, Augustine sends greetings in the Lord:

I had already written a reply to Your Charity, but while I was waiting for an opportunity of forwarding the letter, my beloved son Faustus arrived here on his way to Your Excellency. After he had received the letter which I had intended to be carried by him to Your Benevolence, he stated to me that you were very desirous that I should write you something which might build you up unto the eternal salvation of which you have hope in Christ Jesus our Lord. And, although I was busily occupied at the time, he insisted, with an earnestness corresponding to the love which, as you know, he bears to you, that I should do this without delay. To meet his convenience, therefore, as he was in haste to depart, I thought it better to write, though necessarily without much time for reflection, rather than put off the gratification of your pious desire, my noble lord and justly distinguished and honourable son.

All is contained in these brief sentences: "Love the Lord thy God with all thy heart and with all thy soul and with all thy strength, and love thy neighbour as thyself"; for these are the words in which the Lord, when on earth, gave an epitome of religion, saying in the gospel, "On these two commandments hang all the law and the prophets" (Matt. 22:37-40). Daily advance, then, in this love, both by praying and by well-doing, that through the help of him who enjoined it on you and whose gift it is it may be nourished and increased until, being perfected, it render you perfect. "For this is the love which," as the apostle says, "is shed abroad in our hearts by the Holy Ghost which is given unto us" (Rom. 5:5). This is the "fulfilling of the law" (Rom. 13:10); this is the same love by which faith works, of which he says again: "Neither circumcision availeth anything nor uncircumcision, but faith which worketh by love" (Gal. 5:6).

In this love, then, all our holy fathers, patriarchs, prophets and apostles pleased God. In this all true martyrs contended against the devil even to the shedding of blood, and because in them it neither waxed cold nor failed, they became conquerors. In this all true believers daily make progress, seeking to acquire not an earthly kingdom but the kingdom of heaven, not a temporal but an eternal inheritance, not gold and silver but the uncorruptible riches of the angels, not the good things of this life, which are enjoyed with trembling and which no one can take with him when he dies, but the vision of God, whose grace and power of imparting felicity transcend all beauty of form in bodies not only on earth but also in heaven, transcend all spiritual loveliness in men, however just and holy, transcend all the glory of the angels and powers of the world above, transcend not only all that language can express but all that thought can imagine concerning him. And let us not despair of the fulfilment of such a great promise because it is exceeding great, but rather believe that we shall receive it because he who has promised it is exceeding great, as the blessed apostle John says, "Now are we the sons of God; and it doth not yet appear what we shall be; but we know that, when he shall appear, we shall be like him, for we shall see him as he is" (1 John 3:2).

Do not think that it is impossible for any one to please God while engaged in active military service. Among such persons was the holy David, to whom God gave so great a testimony; among them also were many righteous men of that time; among them was also that centurion who said to the Lord: "I am not worthy that thou shouldest come under my roof, but speak the word only, and my servant shall be healed; for I am a man under authority, having soldiers under me, and I say to this man, Go, and he goeth, and to another, Come, and he cometh, and to my servant, Do this, and he doeth it"; and concerning whom the Lord said: "Verily, I say unto you, I have not found so great faith, no, not in Israel" (Matt. 8:8-10). Among them was that Cornelius to whom an angel said: "Cornelius, thine alms are accepted, and thy prayers are heard," when he directed him to send to the blessed apostle Peter and to hear from him what he ought to do, to which apostle he sent a devout soldier, requesting him to come to him (Acts 10:4). Among them were also the soldiers who, when they had come to be baptised by John — the sacred forerunner of the Lord, and the "friend of the bridegroom" of whom the Lord says: "Among them that are born of women there hath not arisen a greater than John the Baptist" (Matt. 11:11) — and had inquired of him what they should do, received the answer, "Do violence to no man, neither accuse any falsely, and be content with your wages" (Luke 3:14). Certainly he did not prohibit them to serve as soldiers when he commanded them to be content with their pay for the service.

They occupy, indeed, a higher place before God who, abandoning all these secular employments, serve him with the strictest chastity; but "every one," as the apostle says, "hath his proper gift of God, one after this manner and another after that" (1 Cor. 7:7). Some, then, in praying for you, fight against your invisible enemies; you, in fighting for them, contend against the barbarians, their visible enemies. Would that one faith existed in all, for then there would be less weary struggling, and the devil with his angels would be more easily conquered! But since it is necessary in this life that the citizens of the kingdom of heaven should be subjected to temptations among erring and impious men, that they may be exercised and "tried as gold in the furnace" (Sap. 3:6), we ought not before the appointed time to desire to live with those alone who are holy and righteous, so that by patience we may deserve to receive this blessedness in its proper time.

Think, then, of this first of all, when you are arming for the battle, that even your bodily strength is a gift of God; for considering this, you will not employ the gift of God against God. For when faith is pledged it is to be kept, even with the enemy against whom the war is waged. How much more with the friend for whom the battle is fought! Peace should be the object of your desire; war should be waged only as a necessity, and waged only that God may by it deliver men from the necessity and preserve them in peace. For peace is not sought in order to kindle war, but war is waged in order that peace may be obtained. Therefore even in waging war cherish the spirit of a peacemaker, that by conquering those whom you attack you may lead them back to the advantages of peace; for our Lord says: "Blessed are the peacemakers, for they shall be called the children of God" (Matt. 5:9). If, however, peace among men be so sweet as procuring temporal safety, how much sweeter is that peace with God which procures for men the eternal felicity of the angels! Let necessity, therefore, and not your will slay the enemy who fights against you. As violence is used towards him who rebels and resists, so mercy is due to the vanquished or the captive, especially in the case in which future troubling of the peace is not to be feared.

Let the manner of your life be adorned by chastity, sobriety and moderation; for it is exceedingly disgraceful that lust should subdue him whom man finds invincible, and that wine should overpower him whom the sword assails in vain. As to worldly riches, if you do not possess them, let them not be sought after on earth by doing evil; and if you possess them, let them by good works be laid up in heaven. The manly and Christian spirit ought neither to be elated by the accession, nor crushed by the loss of this world's treasures. Let us rather think of what the Lord says:

"Where your treasure is, there will your heart be also" (Matt. 6:21); and certainly when we hear the exhortation to lift up our hearts, it is our duty to give unfeignedly the response which you know that we are accustomed to give.

In these things, indeed, I know that you are very careful, and the good report which I hear of you fills me with great delight, and moves me to congratulate you on account of it in the Lord. This letter, therefore, may serve rather as a mirror in which you may see what you are than as a directory from which to learn what you ought to be; nevertheless, whatever you may discover either from this letter or from the Holy Scriptures to be still wanting to you in regard to a holy life, persevere in urgently seeking it both by effort and by prayer; and for the things which you have, give thanks to God as the fountain of goodness whence you have received them; in every good action let the glory be given to God and humility be exercised by you, for, as it is written: "Every good gift and every perfect gift is from above, and cometh down from the father of lights" (James 1:17). But however much you may advance in the love of God and of your neighbour and in true piety, do not imagine as long as you are in this life that you are without sin, for concerning this we read in Holy Scripture: "Is not the life of man upon earth a life of temptation?" (Job 7:1 Septuagint). Wherefore, since always as long as you are in this body it is necessary for you to say in prayer, as the Lord taught us, "Forgive us our debts, as we forgive our debtors" (Matt. 6:12), remember quickly to forgive if any one shall do you wrong and shall ask pardon from you, that you may be able to pray sincerely and may prevail in seeking pardon for your own sins.

These things, my beloved friend, I have written to you in haste, as the anxiety of the bearer to depart urged me not to detain him; but I thank God that I have in some measure complied with your pious wish. May the mercy of God ever protect you, my noble lord and justly distinguished son.

Translation: J. G. Cunningham, Nicene and Post-Nicene Fathers, ser. 1, vol. 1, adapted.

From *Letter 24** on slavery

To Eustochius, my distinguished lord and justly honourable and greatly longed for son, from Augustine: greetings in the Lord.

Since to all who seek your counsel you owe in good faith a truthful response, how much more to us ministers of Christ, by faith in whom you are one of the faithful in the hope of receiving that inheritance whose testament, my distinguished lord and justly honourable and greatly longed for son, is the Gospel. Because the apostle has laid down that legal actions between Christians over earthly concerns should take place not in court but in church, we accordingly have to cope with the kind of arguments from complainants that require from us judgments even in terms of secular law, especially concerning the temporal status of people — for we can enjoin slaves, in keeping with the apostolic discipline, to be subject to their masters, but we cannot inflict the yoke of slavery on free persons. I therefore request your most genuine charity kindly to instruct me in the procedure to be followed with individuals born to a free mother and a slave father. I am already aware that the offspring of a slave woman and a free man are slaves by birth.

How does it stand also with those whose fathers sell their labour for a fixed number of years? I ask particularly whether, once their fathers who sold them are deceased, they are compelled to complete the same number of years or instead are released by the death of those who sold them — or rather hired them out a certain way — since they now begin to be, as is said, legally independent. I also ask whether free fathers can sell their sons into permanent slavery, and whether mothers can sell even their sons' labour. Again I ask whether, if a tenant farmworker (*colonus*) sells his son, as a father is permitted to do, the purchaser has a superior right over the one sold than the master of the estate where the tenant originally belongs. And is it lawful for such a proprietor to turn his tenants or their sons into slaves?

Furthermore, what has been clearly determined by the jurists or the laws concerning managers (*actores*)? It seems to me very harsh that a person's freeborn status should be prejudiced by his own advantage. Free men are often invited to become managers and imagine that they advantage themselves in doing as requested — and in reality they do, to the extent of gaining the gratitude of the person inviting them if he succeeds in obtaining their compliance. If as a result of benefitting himself in this way a free man is made a slave, nobody knowing this would on any account accept — nor would anyone have the audacity to ask someone who knew. Nevertheless I am disturbed by certain constitutions drawn to my notice when just such a case was referred to us concerning the sons of a man who perhaps will be proved to have been a manager. But I do not want to require the claimant to prove it without first knowing what course to pursue if he succeeds in proving it. I have accordingly sent these same constitutions for Your Excellency's evaluation. Two of them, I judge, speak to this very issue, but the rest either I do not understand or else they are entirely irrelevant to the question in dispute. I beg you to assist me despite my absence, just as you are accustomed to do when I am present.

Translation: David F. Wright, from *Lettres 1*-29**, ed. Johannes Divjak, Oeuvres de Saint Augustin, vol. 46b (Paris: Études Augustiniennes, 1987).

From *City of God,* Book 2

20. Yet the worshipers and devotees of those divinities, who take satisfaction, too, in being their imitators when it comes to criminal adventures, are unconcerned that the commonwealth degenerates into an abyss of crime. "So long as it survives," they say, "so long as it prospers, rich in resources, self-confident in victory, or, better still, secure in peace, what difference does it make to us? What matters is that there is money to be made to support our lavish style of life, and to give the stronger their hold over the weaker; that the poor treat the wealthy with compliance, to ensure their daily bread — the poor depending on the patronage of the wealthy for a quiet

life, the wealthy calling on the poor for support to boost their public standing. Popularity should accrue not to those whose policies promote public welfare, but to the big providers of public entertainment. Law should not be rigorous; low indulgences should not be proscribed. Rulers should not bother themselves with getting virtuous subjects, simply quiescent ones. Territories should view their rulers not in the light of moral educators, merely as economic managers and purveyors of satisfactions. It does not matter if they do not seriously respect them, so long as they treat them with a calculating and subservient fear. Law should prohibit economic harm to our neighbors, not moral harm to ourselves. No one should be liable to court proceedings if he has not infringed on or done harm to the property, real estate, or physical safety of another person without consent; but everyone should be free to do with himself, his dependents, and consenting associates exactly what he likes. Sexual satisfactions should be freely available on the open market for those who want them, especially those who cannot afford to maintain facilities privately. Domestic architecture should be expansive and ornate, to accommodate large and lavish parties where anyone may game and drink all day and night, if he pleases, till he brings it up or sweats it out. The sound of dancing should be heard in every neighborhood, and theaters should be humming with excitement at their coarse amusements and their various brash and bloodthirsty entertainments. Should someone disapprove of this perfect contentment, he must expect to meet public hostility; and should someone attempt to reform or abolish it, the spirit of popular freedom must know what to do with him: shut him up, pack him up, beat him up! Religion ought to make a case for itself by guaranteeing and perpetuating these conditions of life for the greatest number of people. Let the gods have all the worship they want, and all the games that they want, to enjoy them with (and at the expense of) their worshipers, just so long as they ensure this satisfactory state of affairs against threat from enemy, plague, or disaster."

Translation: Editors, from Bibliothèque Augustinienne.

From *City of God,* Book 4

3. Is it reasonable, is it sensible, to boast of the extent and grandeur of empire, when you cannot show that men lived in happiness, as they passed their lives amid the horrors of war, amid the shedding of men's blood — whether the blood of enemies or fellow citizens — under the shadow of fear and amid the terror of ruthless ambition? The only joy to be attained had the fragile brilliance of glass, a joy outweighed by the fear that it may be shattered in a moment.

To help us form our judgment let us refuse to be fooled by empty bombast, to let the edge of our critical faculties be blunted by high-sounding words like "peoples," "realms," "provinces." Let us set before our mind's eye two men; for the individual man is, like a single letter in a statement, an element, as it were, out of which a community or a realm is built up, however vast its territorial possessions. Let us imagine one of the two to be poor, or, better, in a middle station of life, while the other is excessively rich. But the rich man is tortured by fears, worn out with sadness, burnt up with ambition, never knowing serenity of repose, always panting and sweating in his struggles with opponents. It may be true that he enormously swells his patrimony, but at the cost of those discontents, while by this increase he heaps up a load of further anxiety and bitterness. The other man, the ordinary citizen, is content with his strictly limited resources. He is loved by family and friends; he enjoys the blessing of peace with his relations, neighbours and friends; he is loyal, compassionate, and kind, healthy in body, temperate in habits, of unblemished character, and enjoys the serenity of a good conscience. I do not think anyone would be fool enough to hesitate about which he would prefer.

It is the same with two families, two peoples, or two realms. The same canon of judgment applies as in the case of the two men. If we apply the canon scrupulously, without allowing our judgment to be warped, we shall not have slightest difficulty in seeing where true happiness lies, and where an empty show. And therefore it is beneficial that the good should extend their dominion far and wide, and that their reign should endure, with the worship of the true God by genuine sacrifices and upright lives. This is for the benefit of all, of the subjects even more than the rulers. For the rulers, their piety and integrity — great gifts of God — suffice for true happiness, for a good life on earth, and for eternal life hereafter. And in this world the reign of the good is a blessing for themselves, and even more for the whole of human society. In contrast, the reign of the wicked is more harmful to those who wield the power, who bring destruction on their own souls through the greater scope thus given for their misdeeds, whereas those who are enslaved beneath them are harmed only by their own wickedness. For the evils inflicted on the righteous by their wicked masters are not punishments for crime but tests of virtue. The good man, though a slave, is free; the wicked, though he reigns, is a slave, and not the slave of a single man, but — what is far worse — the slave of as many masters as he has vices. It is in reference to vices that the scripture says: "When a man is vanquished he becomes the bond-slave of his conqueror" (2 Pet. 2:19).

4. Remove justice, and what are kingdoms but gangs of criminals on a large scale? What are criminal gangs but petty kingdoms? A gang is a group of men under the command of a leader, bound by a compact of association, in which the plunder is divided according to an agreed convention.

If this villainy wins so many recruits from the ranks of the demoralized that it acquires territory, establishes a base, captures cities and subdues peoples, it then openly arrogates to itself the title of kingdom, which is conferred on it in the eyes of the world not by the renouncing of aggression but by the attainment of impunity.

For it was a witty and a truthful rejoinder which was given by a captured pirate to Alexander the Great. The king asked the fellow, "What is your idea, in infesting the sea?" And the pirate answered, with uninhibited insolence, "The same as yours, in infesting the earth! But because I do it with a tiny craft, I'm called a pirate; because you have a mighty navy, you're called an emperor."

5. I shall not discuss the question of what kind of people Romulus collected; it is known that he took measures to ensure that when they were granted a share in the

community after abandoning their former way of life, they should no longer have to think about the punishment to which they were liable, the fear of which had impelled them to greater crimes, so that in the future they should be less aggressive in their attitude to society.

What I want to say is that when the Roman Empire was already great, when she had subjugated many nations and was feared by all the rest, this great empire was bitterly distressed and deeply alarmed, and had the utmost difficulty in extricating herself from the threat of overwhelming disaster, when a tiny handful of gladiators in Campania escaped from the training-school and collected a large army. Under three commanders [Spartacus, Oenomaus, Crixus] they wrought cruel havoc over a wide area of Italy. Would our opponents tell us the name of the god who assisted them, so that from a small and contemptible gang of thugs they developed into a "kingdom" inspiring fear in the Romans, for all Rome's great resources and all her strongholds? Are they going to say they did not receive divine help because they did not last long [73-71 B.C.]? Come now, no man's life is very long! On this argument the gods never help any man to a throne, since individuals soon die; and one should not count something a benefit which vanishes like smoke in the case of each man — and so, to be sure, in all, as one individual succeeds another. What does it matter to those who worshipped the gods under Romulus, and died so long ago, that after their death the Roman Empire grew to such greatness, since they have to plead their cause in the world below? Whether their cause be good or bad is not relevant to our argument. The same consideration applies to all those who in the few days of the rapid course of their lives have wielded temporary power in the Roman Empire. However long the extension of that empire's duration, as the generations succeed one another in their rise and fall, those individuals have passed on, taking with them the bundle of their deeds.

Now if even the benefits of the briefest space of time are to be attributed to the help of the gods, those gladiators received no inconsiderable assistance. They broke the chains of their servile condition; they escaped; they got clean away; they collected a large and formidable army; and in obedience to the plans and orders of their "kings" they became an object of dread to the soaring might of Rome. They were more than a match for many Roman generals; they captured much booty; they gained many victories; they indulged themselves at will, following the prompting of every desire; in fact, they lived in all the grandeur of kings, until their eventual defeat, which was only achieved with the greatest difficulty.

Translation: Henry Bettenson (Harmondsworth: Penguin Books, 1972). Used with permission.

From *City of God,* Book 5

24. When we describe certain Christian emperors as "happy," it is not because they enjoyed long reigns, or because they died a peaceful death, leaving the throne to

their sons; nor is it because they subdued their country's enemies, or had the power to forestall insurrections by enemies in their own land and to suppress such insurrections if they arose. All these and other similar rewards or consolations in this life of trouble were granted to some of the worshippers of demons, as their due; and yet those pagan rulers have no connection with the Kingdom of God, to which those Christian rulers belong. Their good fortune was due to the mercy of God; for it was God's intention that those who believe in him should not demand such blessings from him as if they represented the highest good.

We Christians call rulers happy if they rule with justice; if amid the voices of exalted praise and the reverent salutations of excessive humility, they are not inflated with pride, but remember that they are but men; if they put their power at the service of God's majesty, to extend his worship far and wide; if they fear God, love him and worship him; if, more than their earthly kingdom, they love that realm where they do not fear to share the kingship; if they are slow to punish, but ready to pardon; if they take vengeance on wrong because of the necessity to direct and protect the state and not to satisfy their personal animosity; if they grant pardon not to allow impunity to wrong-doing but in hope of amendment of the wrong-doer; if, when they are obliged to take severe decisions, as must often happen, they compensate this with the gentleness of their mercy and the generosity of their benefits; if they restrain their self-indulgent appetites all the more because they are more free to gratify them, and prefer to have command over their lower desires than over any number of subject peoples; and if they do all this not for a burning desire for empty glory, but for the love of eternal blessedness; and if they do not fail to offer to their true God, as a sacrifice for their sins, the oblation of humility, compassion and prayer.

It is Christian emperors of this kind whom we call happy; happy in hope, during this present life, and to be happy in reality hereafter, when what we wait for will have come to pass.

25. God, in his goodness, did not wish that those who believed he was to be worshipped for the sake of life eternal, should suppose that no one could attain to the highest stations and the kingdoms of this world unless he made his supplications to demons, on the ground that those evil spirits have great power in this sphere. And for that reason he heaped worldly gifts such as no one would have dared to hope for, on Constantine, who made no supplication to demons, but worshipped only the true God. And God even granted him the honour of founding a city, associated with the Roman Empire, the daughter, one might say, of Rome herself, but a city which contained not a single temple or image of any demon. Constantine had a long reign [306-37], and as the sole Augustus he ruled and defended the whole Roman world; he was victorious above all others in the wars which he directed and conducted; fortune favoured his efforts in the repression of usurpers; and he died of sickness and old age after a long life, leaving the throne to his sons.

On the other hand, so that no emperor should become a Christian in order to earn the good fortune of Constantine (whereas it is only with a view to life eternal that anyone should be a Christian), God removed Jovian [363-64] more quickly than Julian [the Apostate, 361-63]; he allowed Gratian [367-83] to be slain by the

141

usurper's sword — but in far less painful circumstances than attended the murder of the great Pompey, who worshipped the pretended gods of Rome. For Pompey could not be avenged by Cato, whom he had, as it were, made his heir to the Civil War; while Gratian was avenged by Theodosius [379-95] — although pious souls do not look for such consolation — whom Gratian had taken as a partner in his rule, although he had a young brother. Gratian was more concerned to have a trustworthy associate than to enjoy excessive power.

26. [. . .] Men like Cinna, Marius and Sulla wished the civil strife to continue when the wars were ended. Very different was Theodosius; far from wanting any harm to come to anyone after the end of civil war, he was deeply grieved that such conflicts should ever break out. Among all these anxieties Theodosius, from the beginning of his reign, never relaxed his endeavours to help the church against the ungodly by just and compassionate legislation; and the church at that time was in difficulties, for the heretic Valens [364-78] had dealt her heavy blows in his support of the Arians. Theodosius was more glad to be a member of that church than to be ruler of the world. He ordered the demolition of pagan images, knowing that even this world's prizes are not in the gift of demons, but in the power of the true God.

But nothing could be more wonderful than the religious humility he showed after the grievous crime committed by the people of Thessalonica [390: the mob murdered the governor, Botheric, and other officials after the imprisonment of a popular charioteer]. On the intercession of the bishops he had promised a pardon; but then the clamour of certain of his close supporters drove him to avenge the crime [in a massacre]. But he was constrained by the discipline of the church to do penance in such a fashion that the people of Thessalonica, as they prayed for him, wept at seeing the imperial highness thus prostrate, with an emotion stronger than their fears of the emperor's wrath at their offence. These and other good works of like nature, which it would take too long to recount, Theodosius took with him when he left the loftiest summit of power — which is nothing but a passing mist. The reward of those works is eternal happiness; God is the giver; and the only recipients are the truly devout. But all the rest that this world offers, whether the peaks of power or the bare necessities of life, God dispenses freely to good and evil alike — just as he gives to all alike the world, the light, the air, earth and water and the fruits of earth, and man's soul, body, senses, intelligence, and life. Among those gifts is dominion, of whatever extent; and this God bestows in accordance with his government of temporal affairs.

Translation: Henry Bettenson (Harmondsworth: Penguin Books, 1972). Used with permission.

From *City of God,* Book 14

28. We see then that the two cities were <u>created by two kinds of love</u>: the earthly city was created by self-love reaching the point of contempt for God, the heavenly city by

the love of God carried as far as contempt of self. In fact, the earthly city glories in itself, the heavenly City glories in the Lord. The former looks for glory from men, the latter finds its highest glory in God, the witness of a good conscience. The earthly lifts up its head in its own glory, the heavenly city says to its God: "My glory; you lift up my head" (Ps. 3:3). In the former, the lust for domination lords it over its princes as over the nations it subjugates; in the other both those put in authority and those subject to them serve one another in love, the rulers by their counsel, the subjects by obedience. The one city loves its own strength shown in its powerful leaders; the other says to its God, "I will love you, my Lord, my strength" (Ps. 18:1).

Consequently, in the earthly city its wise men who live by men's standards have pursued the goods of the body or of their own mind, or of both. Or those of them who were able to know God "did not honour him as God, nor did they give thanks to him, but they dwindled into futility in their thoughts, and their senseless heart was darkened; in asserting their wisdom" — that is, exalting themselves in their wisdom, under the domination of pride — "they became foolish, and changed the glory of the imperishable God into an image representing a perishable man, or birds or beasts or reptiles" — for in the adoration of idols of this kind they were either leaders or followers of the general public — "and they worshipped and served created things instead of the Creator, who is blessed for ever" (Rom. 1:21-25). In the Heavenly City, on the other hand, man's only wisdom is the devotion which rightly worships the true God, and looks for its reward in the fellowship of the saints, not only holy men but also holy angels, "so that God may be all in all" (1 Cor. 15:28).

From *City of God*, Book 15

1. [. . .] I classify the human race into two branches: the one consists of those who live by human standards, the other of those who live according to God's will. I also call these two classes the two cities, speaking allegorically. By two cities *(civitates)* I mean two societies *(societates)* of human beings, one of which is predestined to reign with God for all eternity, the other doomed to undergo eternal punishment with the Devil. But this is their final destiny, and I shall have to speak of that later on. At present, since I have said enough about the origins of these societies, whether in the angels, whose number is unknown to us, or in the two first human beings, it seems to me that I should undertake to describe their development from the time when that first pair began to produce offspring up to the time when mankind will cease to reproduce itself. For the development of these two societies which form my subject lasts throughout this whole stretch of time, or era, in which the dying yield place to the newly-born who succeed them.

Now Cain was the first son born to those two parents of mankind, and he belonged to the city of man; the later son, Abel, belonged to the City of God. It is our own experience that in the individual man, to use the words of the Apostle, "it is not the spiritual element which comes first, but the animal; and afterwards comes the spiritual" (1 Cor. 15:46), and so it is that everyone, since he takes his origin from a condemned stock is inevitably evil and carnal to begin with, by derivation from Adam; but if he is reborn into Christ, and makes progress, he will afterwards be good and spiritual. The same holds true of the whole human race. When those two cities started on their course through the succession of birth and death, the first to be born was a citizen of this world, and later appeared one who was a pilgrim and stranger in the world, belonging as he did to the City of God. He was predestined by grace, and chosen by grace, by grace a pilgrim below, and by grace a citizen above. As far as he himself is concerned he has his origin from the same lump which was condemned, as a whole lump, at the beginning. But God like a potter (the analogy introduced by the Apostle is not impertinent but very pertinent) made "out of the same lump one vessel destined for honour, and another for dishonour" (Rom. 9:21). But the first one made was the vessel for dishonour, and afterwards came the vessel for honour. For in the individual man, as I have said, the base condition comes first, and we have to start with that; but we are not bound to stop at that, and later comes the noble state towards which we may make progress, and in which we may abide, when we have arrived at it. Hence it is not the case that every bad man will become good, but no one will be good who was not bad originally. Yet the sooner a man changes for the better the more quickly will he secure for himself the title belonging to his attainment and will hide his earlier appellation under the later name.

Scripture tells us that Cain founded a city (Gen. 4:17), whereas Abel, as a pilgrim, did not found one. For the city of the saints is up above, although it produces citizens here below, and in their persons the city is on pilgrimage until the time of its kingdom comes. At that time it will assemble all those citizens as they rise again in their bodies; and then they will be given the promised kingdom, where with their Prince, "the king of ages" (1 Tim. 1:17), they will reign world without end.

2. There was certainly a kind of shadow and prophetic image of this city which served rather to point towards it than to reproduce it on earth at the time when it was due to be displayed. This image was also called the holy city, in virtue of its pointing to that other city, not as being the express likeness of the reality which is yet to be. Concerning this image, in its status as a servant, and that free city to which it points, the Apostle says, when writing to the Galatians (4:21–5:1):

> Now tell me, you who want to be under law; have you not listened to what the Law says? We are told in Scripture that Abraham had two sons, one by a slave-woman, one by his free-born wife. The slave-woman's son was born in the course of nature, the free woman's as a result of a promise. These facts are allegorical. For the two women stand for two covenants. The one bearing children for slavery is the covenant from Mount Sinai; this is Hagar. Now Sinai is a mountain in Arabia and it stands for the present Jerusalem; for she is in slavery with her children. But the Jerusalem above is free; and she is our mother. For Scripture says: "Rejoice, you barren woman who bear no child: break into a cry of joy, you who are not in labour; for the deserted woman has many sons, more than the woman who has a husband" (Isa. 54:1). Now we, my brothers, are sons of the promise, as Isaac was. But just as at that time the son who was born in the course of nature persecuted the son who was spiritually born, so it is now. But what does Scripture say? "Send away the slave

woman and her son; for the son of the slave shall not be joint-heir with the son of the free woman" (Gen. 21:10). Thus you see, brothers, that we are not the sons of a slave-woman, but of the free woman, by reason of the freedom brought us by Christ's liberation.

This manner of interpretation, which comes down to us with apostolic authority, reveals to us how we are to understand the Scriptures of the two covenants, the old and the new. One part of the earthly city has been made into an image of the heavenly city, by symbolizing something other than itself, namely that other city; and for that reason it is a servant. For it was established not for its own sake but in order to symbolize another city; and since it was signified by an antecedent symbol, the foreshadowing symbol was itself foreshadowed. Hagar, the servant of Sarah, represented, with her son, the image of this image. But the shadows were to pass away with the coming of the light, and Sarah, the free woman, stood for the free city which the shadow, Hagar, for her part served to point to in another way. And that is why Sarah said, "Send away the slave-woman and her son; for the son of the slave shall not be joint-heir with my son Isaac," or as the Apostle puts it, "with the son of the free woman."

Thus we find in the earthly city a double significance; in one respect it displays its own presence, and in the other it serves by its presence to signify the heavenly city. But the citizens of the earthly city are produced by a nature which is vitiated by sin, while the citizens of the heavenly city are brought forth by grace, which sets nature free from sin. That is why the former are called "vessels of wrath," the latter "vessels of mercy" (Rom. 9:22-23). This difference is also symbolized in Abraham's two sons: the one, Ishmael, son of the slave named Hagar, was born in the course of nature, whereas the other, Isaac, son of Sarah, the free woman, was born in fulfilment of a promise. Both sons, it is true, were born of Abraham's seed; but one was begotten by the normal procedure, a demonstration of nature's way, while the other was given by a promise, a symbol of God's grace. In one case we are shown man's customary behaviour, in the other we are given a revelation of the goodness of God. 3. [. . .] Isaac therefore, who was born as a result of a promise, is rightly interpreted as symbolizing the children of grace, the citizens of the free city, the sharers in eternal peace, who form a community where there is no love of a will that is personal and, as we may say, private, but a love that rejoices in a good that is at once shared by all and unchanging — a love that makes "one heart" out of many (Acts 4:32); a love that is the whole-hearted and harmonious obedience of mutual affection.

4. The earthly city will not be everlasting; for when it is condemned to the final punishment it will no longer be a city. It has its good in this world, and rejoices to participate in it with such gladness as can be derived from things of such a kind. And since this is not the kind of good that causes no frustrations to those enamoured of it, the earthly city is generally divided against itself by litigation, by wars, by battles, by the pursuit of victories that bring death with them or at best are doomed to death. For if any section of that city has risen up in war against another part, it seeks to be victorious over other nations, though it is itself the slave of base passions; and if, when victorious, it is exalted in its arrogance, that victory brings death in its train.

Whereas if it considers the human condition and the changes and chances common to mankind, and is more tormented by possible misfortunes than puffed up by its present success, then its victory is only doomed to death. For it will not be able to lord it permanently over those whom it has been able to subdue victoriously.

However, it would be incorrect to say that the goods which this city desires are not goods, since even that city is better, in its own human way, by their possession. For example, that city desires an earthly peace, for the sake of the lowest goods; and it is that peace which it longs to attain by making war. For if it wins the war and no one survives to resist, then there will be peace, which the warring sections did not enjoy when they contended in their unhappy poverty for the things which they could not both possess at the same time. This peace is the aim of wars, with all their hardships; it is this peace that glorious victory (so called) achieves.

Now when the victory goes to those who were fighting for the juster cause, can anyone doubt that the victory is a matter for rejoicing and the resulting peace is something to be desired? Those things are goods and undoubtedly they are gifts of God. But if the higher goods are neglected, which belong to the city on high, where victory will be serene in the enjoyment of eternal and perfect peace — if these goods are neglected and those other goods are so desired as to be considered the only goods, or are loved more than the goods which are believed to be higher, the inevitable consequence is fresh misery, and an increase of the wretchedness already there.

5. The first founder of the earthly city was, as we have seen, a fratricide; for, overcome by envy, he slew his own brother, a citizen of the eternal city, on pilgrimage in this world. Hence it is no wonder that long afterwards this first precedent — what the Greeks call an *archetype* — was answered by a kind of reflection, by an event of the same kind at the founding of the city which was to be the capital of the earthly city of which we are speaking, and was to rule over so many peoples. For there also, as one of their poets says when he mentions the crime,

> Those walls were dripping with a brother's blood.
>
> Lucan, *Pharsalia* 1.95

For this is how Rome was founded, when Remus, as Roman history witnesses, was slain by his brother Romulus. The difference from the primal crime was that both brothers were citizens of the earthly city. Both sought the glory of establishing the Roman state, but a joint foundation would not bring to each the glory that a single founder would enjoy. Anyone whose aim was to glory in the exercise of power would obviously enjoy less power if his sovereignty was diminished by a living partner. Therefore, in order that the sole power should be wielded by one person, the partner was eliminated; and what would have been kept smaller and better by innocence grew through crime into something bigger and worse.

In contrast, the earlier brothers, Cain and Abel, did not both entertain the same ambition for earthly gains; and the one who slew his brother was not jealous of him because his power would be more restricted if both wielded the sovereignty; for Abel did not aim at power in the city which his brother was founding.

146

But Cain's was the diabolical envy that the wicked feel for the good simply because they are good, while they themselves are evil. A man's possession of goodness is in no way diminished by the arrival, or the continuance, of a sharer in it; indeed, goodness is a possession enjoyed more widely by the united affection of partners in that possession in proportion to the harmony that exists among them. In fact, anyone who refuses to enjoy this possession in partnership will not enjoy it at all; and he will find that he possesses it in ampler measure in proportion to his ability to love his partner in it.

Thus the quarrel that arose between Remus and Romulus demonstrated the division of the earthly city against itself; while the conflict between Cain and Abel displayed the hostility between the two cities themselves, the City of God and the city of men. Thus the wicked fight among themselves; and likewise the wicked fight against the good and the good against the wicked. But the good, if they have reached perfect goodness, cannot fight among themselves. However, while they are on their way towards the perfection they have not yet attained, there may be fighting among them insasmuch as any good man may fight against another as a result of that part of him which makes him also fight against himself. And in the individual it is true that "the flesh has desires which resist the spirit, and the spirit has desires which resist the flesh" (Gal. 5:17). Accordingly, spiritual desire can fight against the carnal desire of another person, or carnal desire against another's spiritual desire, just as the good and the wicked fight against one another. Or even the carnal desires of two good men (who have obviously not yet attained perfection) may fight, just as the wicked fight among themselves, until those who are on the way to recovery are finally brought to triumphant health.

Translation: Henry Bettenson (Harmondsworth: Penguin Books, 1972). Used with permission.

From *City of God,* Book 19

[Augustine has reviewed the survey of different schools of philosophy and their views on the supreme good presented by the first-century Roman author Varro, and has taken as the agenda for his discussion the five variables which Varro identifies: *(a)* what the supreme good is held to be; *(b)* how virtue is related to the natural goods within it; *(c)* whether it is social; *(d)* whether it is held as a dogmatic certainty or as a hypothesis; *(e)* whether the school that maintains it is distinguished by idiosyncratic dress or customs. In chapter 4 he has announced the Christian answer to the first two of these questions: the supreme good, Christians believe, is eternal life; it cannot be enjoyed by pure virtue within the evil conditions of this world, but supposes a state of circumstantial blessedness and immortality as well as virtue. He now turns to a lengthy discussion of the third question: whether the supreme good can be achieved by solitary individuals or must be social.]

5. Now we turn to the view that "the wise man's life is social," which we can support
— and much more strongly than they do! Here we are with the nineteenth book of
the *City of God* in our hands, and how could that city ever set out, advance or reach
its appointed end if the life of the saints were not social? But within the care-laden
conditions of this mortal life human society brims over with evils too numerous, too
extensive to be told.

Consider this line from a pagan comedy — it is a commonplace which is
grasped instinctively:

> Married a wife. That was a curse.
> Then came the kids. They made it worse.
>
> (*The Brothers* 5.4.13)

And the same comedian, Terence, has an observation on the wretched course of love:

> Cheating, rows and fights, and then
> Half an hour of peace again.
>
> (*The Eunuch* 1.1.14)

Isn't this the tale of human experience? Doesn't it happen in the best and most affec-
tionate relationships? Don't we find "cheating, rows and fights," in fact, entirely predictable in every sphere of human life? Peace, on the other hand, is quite unpredict-
able, since we do not know the hearts of those with whom we wish to be at peace;
and if we knew them today, we would certainly not know how they would stand tomorrow. Where, then, might we reasonably expect to find true affection, if not
among members of a single *household?* Yet who can feel secure from unpleasant sur-
prises, all too frequently sprung on us from that quarter? And these are the harder to
bear when we have valued our domestic peace so highly as to place confidence in
what turns out to be no more than a carefully manicured appearance! Cicero's words
strike a chord, and always elicit a murmur of sympathy: "No trap is harder to detect
than that which lies concealed behind apparent loyalty or family connection. The
open enemy, with care, can be avoided. But the threat from within the walls, the hidden threat from the domestic hearth, is upon us and overpowers us before we see it
coming and take its measure" (*Verrine Orations* 2.1.13). So, too, the text of Holy
Scripture, "A man's foes shall be those of his own household" (Matt. 10:36), has a de-
pressing ring. One may be strong enough to face without illusion the machinations
of those who assume a pose of friendship, alert enough to keep one's guard against
them; yet for a good man to discover malice in that quarter, whether it was always
there disguised or whether it grew up where there was once good will, is inevitably
an immensely painful thing.

If the household, our common refuge from the ills of humankind, offers no
safety, what can we say of the *city?* Its larger scale affords a larger scope for disputes
in criminal and civil courts, to say nothing of civil discords — civil bloodshed and
civil war, as they too frequently become — which may lie quiet for a spell but are always menacing possibilities. 6. And what of the courts themselves, never absent from

the city's life, however peaceful? What idea can we form of the pitiable predicament of men who sit in judgment on other men without being able to read their consciences? They are often forced to interrogate the innocent under torture: witnesses not party to the case, or a defendant pleading innocence, making him pay for an unproven crime an all too proven penalty, not because he has been shown to have done the deed, but because he has not been shown not to have! It is the innocent for whom the judge's ignorance spells disaster. And there is worse to come, enough to drive one nearer to distraction, if that were possible, enough to make one dissolve into tears. To establish the defense, the judge may commit the defendant to be tortured, meaning to avoid the mistake of killing an innocent man; yet the outcome of his wretched blunder may be that he kills him, innocent *and* tortured! For his victim may prefer, in keeping with Stoic philosophy, to leave this life than to put up with the torture any longer, and so may confess to a crime he has not committed. Sentence pronounced, execution carried out, the judge is as ignorant as ever whether the man he killed was innocent or guilty, though he tortured him precisely to avoid the miscarriage of killing an innocent man. To ensure his innocence, he had him tortured; then had him put to death because he wasn't sure!

With life in society cloaked in this kind of obscurity, will the philosophers' "wise man" take the responsibility of being a judge, or will he shy off? Clearly, he will take the responsibility. For the ties of human society constrain him; they compel him to accept this duty, which he would think it wicked to neglect. It is not *wicked*, from his point of view, that innocent witnesses suffer torture in others' cases; that accused persons driven by despair make false confessions and, having been tortured for what they have not done, may finally be punished for it too; that those not subject to the death penalty may yet die under torture; that the very advocates, who have acted public-spiritedly to ensure the punishment of crime, may fail to prove their accusations in the face of lying witnesses and the stubborn denials of the accused even under torture, and so end up themselves condemned by the bamboozled judge. These many appalling miscarriages of justice are not *sins*. The wise man acting as a judge does not perpetrate them out of malice. Mistakes are unavoidable, but so is the duty of judgment, too, since human society demands it of us. Yet here, after all, is the human wretchedness we speak of, even if there is no malpractice on the bench. Or do you think that when he tortures and punishes the innocent, unable to avoid either the mistakes or the duties of a judge, he will think us mealymouthed if we merely say he is not to blame? Will he insist we call him happy, too? It would be more thoughtful, more worthy of the name of man, to recognize the wretchedness of necessary evils such as these and to hate them; and, if his wisdom extends to piety, to cry to God: "Deliver me from my necessities!" (Ps. 25:17).

7. After the city, or political community, comes the *world*, following the convention that treats the household, city, and world as three successive levels of human society. Here, as in the ocean, the vast scale implies an immense expanse of dangers. In the first place differences of language alienate us from our kind. Imagine two people with no common language whose paths have crossed and who for some reason cannot go their separate ways but have to stay together: they will have greater difficulty getting on as fellow humans than dumb beasts would, even of different species.

For when we cannot communicate, our common human nature, important as it is, will not suffice; difference of language is enough to inhibit society, so that a man would rather have the company of his dog than that of a foreigner.

I shall be told that the imperial city was at pains to impose its language, not its yoke only, on the conquered races that it pacified, with the result that there was no lack of interpreters, but an abundance of them rather. True enough; but at what cost was this achieved, in constant wars of such a scale, in slaughter and the shedding of human blood! And with pacification these miseries were not over. For though foreign enemies emerged in plenty, as they still do, against whom wars continued to be waged, as they still are, a worse kind of war was engendered by the actual expansion of the empire: social and civil war, I mean, which distresses the human race much more, not only while it is raging and we wait for it to flicker out at last, but while we live in anxiety that it will blaze up again. If I were to try to pen an adequate description of the incessant and innumerable devastations, the unrelenting and unrelieved horrors of such events, I should in any case fail, and there would be no end to my discussion. But the wise man, they say, will undertake *just* wars. As though just wars will not cause him all the more grief, if he is mindful of his own humanity! If they were not just, the wise man would not have to wage them; and then he would have no wars at all. It is the wrong done by the other side that drives the wise man to just war. And even should no need for war arise, the wrong alone, since it is man's wrong, ought to inspire grief in a man's heart. Whoever, then, experiences grief as he reflects upon these vast, abominable, and cruel evils, had better acknowledge his wretchedness. Whoever experiences no grief, when they occur or when he simply contemplates them, is without doubt much more wretched; he thinks himself happy solely for want of all human sensibility!

8. There is, of course, one source of consolation in the illusions and anxieties of human society (though one not immune from that all-too-frequent delusion which cannot tell who is a friend and who is not): I mean the sincere faith and mutual affection of true and honorable friends. But what if these are dispersed in different corners of the world? The wide reach of our sympathies exposes us to fears about the vast accumulation of disasters that can befall them in this age. It is not only famines, wars, disasters, captivity, or the unimaginable horrors of slavery that may concern us. It is the gnawing fear that they may prove untrue, turn enemies, or become morally degenerate. And when we learn that this has happened, as it must sometimes do if we have many friends, the affliction of heart is something no one who has not experienced it can tell. We would prefer to hear that they were dead. To be sure, that would cause us grief enough, for how could we not mourn the death of those whose life had afforded us the solace of friendship? Disapprove of that, if you can, and you will disapprove of friendly intercourse itself; you will forbid or suppress all its affection, you will callously break off all ties of human relations or decree they must be so conducted as to empty them of their soul-penetrating sweetness! But since this cannot be, how shall we have the sweet taste of their lives without the sharp taste of their deaths? Mourning is like a wound or ulcer on the feeling heart, in need of treatment with the customary consolatory applications. That the healthy mind recovers with reasonable speed and ease, does not mean there was nothing to

recover from. Anyway, though the death of loved ones, especially those on whose services we most depend for society, brings us affliction light or grave, we would rather hear of their deaths, or see them, than of the deaths of their souls, their fall from faith or virtue. But of this extensive category of ills the earth is full, as Scripture says: "Is not man's life on the earth a temptation?" (Job 7:1), and the Lord himself: "Woe to the world for temptations to sin!" (Matt. 18:7), and again: "Because wickedness is multiplied, most men's love will grow cold" (Matt. 24:12). And so we are glad for our good friends when they die. Though the death may distress us, it also affords sure consolation; for they have been spared those evils by which even the good are exhausted in this life, or subverted, or exposed to the risk of both.

9. Moving from the world to *the universe,* including heaven, we find a fourth level of society admitted by philosophers who maintain that there is friendship between men and divine beings: that of the holy angels. These we have no cause to fear will ever hurt us by their deaths or moral decay. But they do not fraternize with us like human beings (a point itself to be mentioned among the cares of this life); while Satan, we read, may transform himself into an angel of light to tempt us, as an instruction for our good or a deception we have earned. Only the great mercy of God protects us, when we think we have the angels as our friends, from the false friendship of demons, who are dangerous, alert and deceptive enemies. Another indication of the misery of our condition, so impenetrably ignorant and susceptible to their illusions, that we should stand so wholly in need of the divine mercy! Certainly the philosophers of that ungodly city who claim divine beings as their friends have fallen into the clutches of malignant demons, by which the city is subverted as a whole and with which it will suffer everlasting punishment. What the objects of their worship are, is made plain enough by the very beings who have initiated and insisted on such vile obscenities; they have made it plain through the consecrating — or desecrating! — rites which are supposed to worship them, by the lewd games honoring their crimes which are supposed to guarantee their favor. **10.** But neither are worshipers of the one true sovereign God, though holy and faithful, immune from their illusions or from any other kind of temptation.

For even this source of disquietude serves a useful purpose for our condition of weakness in these evil days. It strengthens the determination of our quest for that security where full and certain peace is to be found. There all the attributes of our nature, the gifts, that is, that God, the creator of every natural species has endowed us with, will be not merely good but enduring, not only in the soul healed by wisdom but in the body renewed in resurrection. There our virtues will not contend against vices or evils of other kinds, but will enjoy the reward of victory, eternal peace which no enemy can destroy. There is our "final" blessedness, the end (i.e., perfection) which has no end (i.e., expiry). Yes, we are said to be happy in this life when we have some kind of peace, such as the good life may come to enjoy; but this happiness, compared with that final happiness, looks like mere wretchedness. The benefits of this peace — peace available here to mortals, if we live well, in our mortal condition — can be put to right use; the evils to which our human condition is liable when we do not have this peace can also be put to good use. It is virtuous to make use of them; but the only real virtue is that which relates everything — the benefits it uses, the deeds it accomplishes while it makes good use of good and evil; yes, which relates even itself — to the end of that peace which could never be bettered or outdone.

11. We could say, then, that *peace* is the true "final good," as we have already said eternal life is [ch. 4, not included in this selection]. It is the city of God, the subject of our laborious exposition, which is addressed in the sacred psalm (147:12-14):

> Praise the Lord, O Jerusalem!
>   Praise your God, O Zion!
> For he strengthens the bars of your gates;
>   he blesses your sons within you.
> He makes peace in your borders.

When the bars of her gates are strengthened, no one will enter or leave. And so the "peace" which he makes in her borders is that final peace which is the goal of our argument. For the symbolic name of that city, Jerusalem, means "city of peace," as we have said before. But since the word "peace" is constantly used in connection with human affairs that offer anything but eternal life, we have preferred until now to speak of "eternal life" rather than of "peace" as the end, as the apostle does: "But now that you have been set free from sin and have become slaves of God, the return you get is sanctification and its end, eternal life" (Rom. 6:22). But, of course, the term "eternal life" is also susceptible of misunderstanding by those who are not familiar with sacred Scripture; it could be taken to mean the life of the wicked, either (as in some philosophical schools) by virtue of the immortality of the soul, or (as we believe) by virtue of the endless punishment of the wicked, who could hardly suffer torment for eternity if they were not alive for eternity. The best description, then, to avoid misunderstanding, of the end of this city in which she will possess the highest good, is either *peace in eternal life* or *eternal life in peace.*

¶

Peace is so great a good, that even in ephemeral earthly politics there is no more persuasive appeal, no more popular policy, no more valued achievement. I do not think my readers will find a short digression on the subject unwelcome; it will clarify the theme of our discussion, the end of the heavenly city, and is in any case an inviting and comforting theme in its own right.

12. I can count on the agreement of any observer, however casual, of human affairs and human nature, when I say that as there is no one who does not desire happiness, so there is no one who does not desire peace. Even those who stir up wars have victory in view; so what they hope to achieve is a peace to satisfy their vanity. Victory is simply the opponents' defeat, and when one has that, one has peace. Peace, after all, is what they have in mind, even those whose business is to master the art of war in command and engagement. It is commonly said that peace is the "choiceworthy end" of war: one makes war to secure peace, not peace to secure war. Those who wish to overthrow the peace that now obtains, do not hate peace, but want to change it to their liking. It is not peace as such that they reject, simply an-

other peace that they prefer. Even though they foment revolution against the rest of society, there is formal peace of a kind maintained among their conspirators and adherents; otherwise nothing of what they purpose would be accomplished.

Yes, even brigands need peace among associates, simply to give effect and security to their assaults on the peace of others. But imagine there were one so much stronger than the rest, so canny in his dealings with those who knew about him, as to have no need to commit himself to an associate, but could set about his depredations alone and supreme, despoiling all whom he could cow or eliminate. Even so he would need to establish a shadowy kind of peace with those whom he could not kill and from whom he kept his activities a secret. At home with his wife and children and whoever else there was he would certainly want to live in peace. When they ran at his beck and call, that would be how he liked it; when they didn't, he would be outraged, protest, inflict punishments; by all necessary means, even savagery, he would restore the peace of his household, which depended, in his view, on there being one sovereign principle, himself in his own home, to which all other functions of that household must be subordinate. Well, then, imagine he had the chance of a greater number of people to do his bidding as he liked it done at home, a whole city, say, or a nation. In that case he would not skulk in a cave as a brigand, but would mount the public stage as a king; yet his greed and wickedness would be just the same. So, then, everyone wants peace with his own, wants them, in fact, to conduct their lives as he chooses. When he makes war, it is to make his enemies his own if he can, and to impose the terms of his own peace upon them.

But let us extend our thought experiment to such a creature as we meet in poetry and myth: the "half-man" (*semihomo*) as they prefer to call him, probably because of his antisocial ferocity. His kingdom is a solitary cave in the wilderness; his malice so extraordinary that it gives him his name, Cacus (from the Greek *kakos*, "evil"); he has no wife to exchange soft sentiments with, no children to play with when they are small and instruct as they are growing up; he has no friendly conversation, not even with his father Vulcan, whose condition is so much more enviable than his own (except in the one point that *he* has not fathered such a monster!); he gives to nobody, but takes what he wants from whom he can, makes away with whom he wants when he can. Yet in his lonely cave (the floor, so we read, always warm with fresh blood!) he wants nothing more than peace: no one to trouble him, no force or threat of force to be raised against his placid existence. In sum, he wants to be at peace with his body; and the more he is so, the better he finds it. When his limbs obey his orders, when he seizes, kills, and devours his prey, appeasing urgently the revolt of his needy mortal frame, the agitation of a hunger that would sunder and expel the soul from the body; then, ferocious wild man though he is, it is peace, his own life and security, that so wildly and ferociously concerns him. We may conclude that if he would only extend to others the pursuit of peace that he maintains within his cave and in himself, no one would call him "evil," "monster," or "half-man."

(Or perhaps his savagery was imposed on him, not by desire for harm but by the need to live, his appearance and his belching of sooty flames proving too great a disincentive to association? Or perhaps he never existed, or was different from the

way artistic license has depicted him? — not improbably, since a heroic Hercules requires a demonic Cacus! Better believe that such a man ["half-man," I beg your pardon!] never existed, like so many products of poetic imagination.) The wildest
beasts — as "half-beast," too, he shares *their* behavior — protect their species in a
kind of peace by mating, breeding, giving birth, rearing and feeding the young; I
don't mean only sheep, deer, doves, starlings, bees, and such like, but even the most
unsociable and solitary, like lions, wolves, foxes, eagles, and owls. The tigress purrs
affectionately over her young, laying her savagery aside in fondling them. The kite,
solitary enough as he hovers above his prey, mates with his partner, builds his nest,
sits on the eggs, feeds the chicks, and in partnership with the mother of his family,
does his best to keep the little community in peace. The human being, even more, is
induced (so to speak) by the laws of his nature to engage in society and maintain
peace with all men, so far as lies with him. Even the wicked make war for the peace of
those who belong to them. They would like it if they could have everyone belong to
them, so that then just one man would be in command of every person and thing;
but how could this be except by consent, willing or reluctant, to peace — peace, that
is, on *his* terms?

⟨In this way pride is a perverted imitation of God. It cannot tolerate association
on equal terms of those who are subject to him, but must imprint the association
with its own control, in place of him.⟩It cannot tolerate the just peace of God, but
prefers the unequal peace of its own devising. Yet it cannot do without loving peace
of some sort. Nobody is so vicious as to take leave of nature entirely, destroying its
last traces. For this reason, knowing the difference between upright and twisted,
well-ordered and perverted, we do not *call* the peace which the wicked impose
"peace," when we compare it with the peace of the righteous. Yet even something
perverted must be at peace, subsisting in some aspect, deriving from some aspect, relating to some aspect of reality in which or from which it subsists; otherwise it could
not exist at all.

To illustrate: hang a man upside down, and you have, I suppose, the body and
its parts in a perverted posture. What nature wants on top is underneath, what she
wants underneath is on top. So the peace of the body is disturbed, with harmful consequences. Even so, the soul is at peace with its body while it struggles to preserve it;
for that is precisely the meaning of pain. If, then, the soul leaves the body under the
force of this assault, there yet remains a certain peace among the bodily parts for as
long as the frame retains its integrity; there is still "somebody" hanging there. And
the fact that the body's mass is pulled toward the ground while held up by the rope
on which it hangs, shows that it conforms to the order of its own material peace; its
weight "demands" (one might say) a point of repose. Even as a lifeless, senseless object it adheres, in equilibrium or motion, to the ordered peace that is natural to it. If
embalming chemicals are applied to prevent dissolution, there is a peace which
holds the members together and contains the mass within appropriate spatial
bounds. If this is not done, but things are left to the course of nature, it becomes unstable, emits volatile, and to our senses most unpleasant, vapors which we recognize
as putrefaction, until finally it is reduced to its material elements and dispersed,
slowly and bit by bit, into the peace which befits them. At no point in the process

does anything diverge from the laws of the sovereign Creator and Ordainer, by which the peace of the whole is determined. Even when grubs appear in the carcass of a larger animal, the same law takes effect: each tiny body obeys its tiny soul in the peace of its own health. And when carrion is devoured by other living things, wherever it is taken to, whatever it is joined to, whatever it is transformed and transmuted into, it finds the same laws diffused throughout the universe, making peace between matching elements to effect the welfare of each mortal species.

§ PEACE

13. What, then, is peace? The peace of any and every thing is the tranquillity of order: —

The peace of the body is the ordered functioning of its organs.

The peace of the irrational soul is the ordered satisfaction of its appetites.

The peace of the rational soul is the ordered coherence of thought and action.

The peace of the body-soul union is the ordered life and health of animal existence.

The peace of man and God is the ordered obedience of faith governed by the eternal law.

And the peace of a human community? That is *cooperative order:* —

Domestic peace is the cooperative order for giving and accepting commands among members of a household.

Civic peace is the cooperative order for giving and accepting commands among fellow citizens.

The peace of the heavenly city is the supremely cooperative, supremely ordered association of those who enjoy God and one another in God.

And what is order? It is *the disposition of all things, equal and unequal, in their appropriate positions.*

Consider the case of those who are wretched. To the extent of their wretchedness they are, of course, not at peace; they lack the tranquillity of order which nothing can disturb. But to the extent that their wretchedness is deserved, neither is it exempt from order. They are not in the same state as those who are happy; yet it is the principle of order that determines their difference of state. When they are not actually distressed, they come to terms, to a degree, with their condition, and so possess a measure of tranquillity and peace. They are still wretched, whatever their freedom from care and pain, since they are not in the position where they ought to be free of care and pain; yet they could be more wretched still if they were not at peace with the law that governs the order of nature. When, on the other hand, they undergo suffering, their peace is disturbed by suffering, yet still subsists to the extent that their suffering is not all-engulfing, and their bodily constitution is not torn apart by it. There can be life without pain, but no pain without life of a kind; peace without war, but no war without peace of a kind — not *as* war, but as waged between living beings which could not be living beings were they not constituted as such by a kind of peace.

The principle is, there are beings free of evil, free even of the possibility of evil; but a being free of good there cannot be. Not even the devil is a being evil as such; his corruption has made him evil. That is why, though he "did not stand firm in the truth" (John 8:44), he did not escape the judgment of the truth. Though he did not remain in tranquillity of order, he did not evade the power of the Ordainer. The goodness that God gave him with his being he cannot steal away from God's righteousness which imposes order in punishing him. It is not that God assaults the good that he himself made, but the evil which the devil has done. Nor does he withdraw the good of being entirely; he withdraws a part, but leaves a part to be the seat of suffering for what has been withdrawn. Suffering itself attests that good has been withdrawn and not withdrawn. What is not withdrawn is needed for the suffering of what has been withdrawn. The sinner is in a worse state if he actually takes pleasure in the loss of his justice; to endure torment, though it acquires no good, is at least to suffer over lost salvation. And since justice and salvation are both goods, and the loss of good should be deplored rather than made a source of pleasure (assuming that there is no higher good to compensate, as justice in the soul might compensate for loss of bodily health), the offender's suffering punishment is clearly an improvement on the pleasure he first took in his offense. Pleasure in sinning, when one forsakes the good, proves that one's will is evil; suffering when good is taken away as punishment proves that one's being is good. To suffer pain at the lost peace of one's being presupposes residual elements of peace that make one's being precious to one.

So it is right that in final punishment the unrighteous and ungodly in their torments lament the loss of the goods natural to them. It is the supreme justice of God that they now experience when he takes these goods away; when he lavished them upon them, they despised his supreme generosity. God, supremely wise Creator, supremely just Ordainer of all beings, founded the race of perishable mankind, the highest of all the splendors of this earth. He gave men goods which befitted this life: temporal peace within the limits of this temporal existence, which includes health, welfare, and human society; and with it all the means necessary to safeguard and restore that peace, means appropriate and accessible to the senses, for example, such as light, sound, air to breathe, water to drink, bodily nourishment, clothing, medication, and adornment. The condition was very fair: good use of perishable goods fit for the peace of this perishable race would earn more and higher goods, imperishable peace with the glory and honor that belong to it, a life eternally devoted to enjoying God and one's neighbor in God; wrong use, on the other hand, would preclude those future blessings and entail the loss of the present ones.

14. In the earthly city, then, all use of temporal goods is related to the enjoyment of earthly peace. In the heavenly city, on the other hand, it is related to the enjoyment of eternal peace. To develop this: —

If we were irrational animals, we would seek nothing but the ordered functioning of our bodily organs and the satisfaction of our appetites; nothing, that is, but physical ease and a wealth of pleasures, so that the body's peace ensured the peace of the soul. (The irrational soul cannot enjoy peace without the body's doing so, since it is denied the satisfaction of the appetites.) These two in conjunction constitute a peace common to body and soul, the peace of ordered life and health. Animate beings show their love for the body's peace when they avoid pain; they show their love for the soul's peace when they seek pleasure in satisfying the demands of the appetites; and they show their love for the common peace of body and soul when they shun death. But human beings have a rational soul, and all their animal behavior is subordinated to holding an object before the mind and fashioning action in accord with it. "Ordered coherence of thought and action" is how we described the peace of the rational soul. The purpose, then, for which we humans avoid the attacks of pain, the agitations of passion, and the dissolution of death, should be to acquire useful knowledge and shape our lives and habits accordingly. But this demands divine instruction and help. If through the weakness of our human minds we are not to fall victim, precisely in our search for truth, to a dangerous error, we need something to grasp with confidence and follow with freedom. Since we are "away from the Lord" in this mortal body, we walk by faith, not by sight. That is why we relate every form of peace — body's peace, soul's peace, peace of the body and soul together — to the peace uniting mortal man to immortal God: an ordered obedience of faith governed by the eternal law.

Divine instruction, furthermore, teaches us two commands above all, the love of God and neighbor. In these there are three objects for our love, God, neighbor, and self; but the only safe way of loving self is loving God. From which it follows that we must take care for our neighbor's love of God, in that he or she (wife, children, domestic servants, anyone else) is to be loved as we love ourselves; and, of course, that we desire our neighbor to take care for us, if we need it, in just the same way. By this means we shall live in peace with all men, as far as lies with us; this is a human peace, a cooperative order of which the principle is that we harm no one and do good to whomever we can. Our first responsibility is to our family; for we have the opportunity and the access for our care provided by the arrangements of nature and society itself. So the apostle says: "If any one does not provide for his own relations, and especially for his own family, he has disowned the faith and is worse than an unbeliever" (1 Tim. 5:8). At this point, then, we encounter domestic peace, that is to say: "the cooperative order for giving and accepting commands among members of a household." Commands are the business of those who take care: husband for wife, parents for children, masters for servants. Obedience is the responsibility of those who receive care: wives to husbands, children to parents, servants to masters.

But in the household of the just man who lives by faith, those who command really serve. Though they appear to command, their commands do not issue from a craving to dominate, but from a readiness to take care, not from a pride which asserts mastery, but from a compassionate acceptance of responsibility. 15. This, of course, is what the arrangements of nature require; it is how God created mankind. "Let him have dominion over the fish of the sea, and over the birds of the air . . . , and over every creeping thing that creeps upon the earth" (Gen. 1:26). The rational creature made in God's image was given dominion over irrational creatures, no more: not man over man, but man over beast.

That is why God made the first righteous men shepherds of flocks, not rulers of men: to point out the difference between the system of created beings and the requirements of sin. For the state of servitude is rightly understood as a measure imposed on sinners; accordingly, we read of no servant in Holy Scripture before righteous Noah uses the word in punishing his son's sin. It was a term required by the fact of guilt, not by nature. The Latin word is supposed to have originated in warfare, when victors spared those whom they might lawfully have killed and made slaves of them: *servus* from *servare,* to save. And that in itself implies sin and its deserts; even in just war we suffer *for* sin when we contend *against* sin; even an undeserved victory is God's judgment to humble the defeated, to correct, or perhaps to punish, their sins. Daniel, that man of God, confirms this, by confessing in captivity his own and his people's sins, admitting with contrite sorrow that they were the cause of their captivity. Sin, then, is the first cause of servitude, which binds one man in subjection to another, something arising only from God's judgment, with whom there is no unrighteousness and who knows how to assign differing punishments according to the offenders' deserts.

However, as the Lord on high says, "Everyone who commits sin is a slave to sin" (John 8:34). This is why we often see godly servants with unjust masters. For the masters are not truly free: "Whatever overcomes a man, to that is he enslaved" (2 Pet. 2:19). It is better, surely, to serve a man than a lust! Domination exercised upon the hearts of mortals by — to name but one — the lust for domination itself, is destructive. Within the terms of that true peace which consists in being subject to each other, it is a positive advantage to the servant to have a lowly status, just as it positively harms the dominating master to be proud. In nature, though, that is, as God made humankind at first, no one is servant either to man or sin. Penal servitude arises from the law which requires nature's arrangements to be protected from disturbance. Were there no offenses against that law, there would be no call for the sanction of penal servitude. This is the reason the apostle tells slaves to be subject to their masters, and to serve them with sincere goodwill. If their masters do not free them, they can make their servitude a form of freedom on their own, by serving with loyalty and love, rather than craven fear, till injustice pass away and every human principality and power be brought to nothing, so that God shall be all in all.

16. The righteous patriarchs, then, who had slaves, and in the management of their domestic economy made a distinction with regard to temporal goods between the situation of their children and their slaves, made no distinction at all when it came to worshiping God, where permanent goods are looked for; rather, they cared for every member of their household with an equal love. This practice conforms so well to the arrangements of nature that the title "father of the family," *paterfamilias,* arose from it and gained such popularity that even those who oppress their households like to be known by it. True fathers of families care for everyone in their household as regards the worship and service of God precisely as they care for their children. Their desire and wish is that they should come to the heavenly household, where there is no need for someone to give orders as there is with mortals, since in that immortal state where all are happy there will be no need for someone to take care of others. In the meantime heads of household should have more to put up with in their task than their servants have in theirs. But if any member of the household disobediently disrupts the domestic peace, he is punished — by word, or blow, or whatever form of just and fitting punishment society accepts; and this is for his own welfare, to reintegrate him into the peace that he has fallen out with. It is not kindness to cooperate in the loss of greater good, not blameless to acquiesce and to per-

mit a slide into greater evil. The part of the blameless man is not to do no harm simply, but to restrain from sin or punish it: either the one punished will learn from his experience, or others will learn from the example.

Now, the household must be the beginning, or the cell, of the city; and every beginning relates to some end of its own kind, every part to its corresponding whole. It follows clearly enough that domestic peace relates to the peace of the city; which is to say, the cooperative order for giving and accepting commands among members of a household relates to the cooperative order for giving and accepting commands among fellow citizens. It is from the city's laws, then, that the head of the household should derive rules to govern the household in accord with the peace of the city. 17. But a household of those who do not live by faith pursues an earthly peace based on resources and benefits of this temporal life; whereas a household of those who do live by faith looks forward to the eternal blessings promised for the future. Earthly, temporal resources it makes use of like a traveler, not held up and diverted from its journey toward God, but sustained, to support and control the burden of disintegration by which the body saps the soul. Both groups of men, then, and both types of household make use in common of the necessaries of this mortal life; but each has its own very different end in using them.

So it is that the earthly city, too, which does not live by faith, aims at an earthly peace, and determines the cooperation of its citizens in giving and accepting commands so as to ensure some community of interest in the resources for this mortal life. The heavenly city, on the other hand, or rather that part of it which is journeying through mortality and lives by faith, needs to make use of that peace, too, until mortality, which requires that peace, is past. And so, while it leads a kind of captive existence on its journey through this earthly city, with the promise of redemption and the gift of the Spirit as its pledge, it has no scruples in conforming to the laws of the earthly city which regulate things designed for the support of mortal life. Since mortality itself is common to both, it is fitting to preserve cooperation between the two cities in mortal affairs. *heavenly citizens w/in the earthly city*

But since the earthly city produced its own savants, rejected by divine teaching, who, through speculation or deceit of demons, reached the conclusion that there are many gods to be won round to support our human enterprises, each as it were with its own sphere of interest and its own function — one for the body, one for the mind; within the body one for the head, one for the neck, etc.; within the mind one for intelligence, one for learning, one for anger, one for desire; among the concerns of life one for livestock, one for grain, one for wine, one for oil, one for woodland, one for money, one for shipping, one for war and victory, one for marriage, one for childbirth and fertility, and so on and so on — and since the heavenly city knew that there was only one God to serve, and decreed, in faithful devotion, that he should be the sole object of religious service (in Greek, *latreia*) which is due to God alone; so it came about that the heavenly city could not have common religious laws with the earthly city. On this count dissension was inevitable. And that meant antagonizing those who thought differently, confronting all their resentment and anger, enduring wave after wave of persecution, except sometimes when their animosity was driven back by alarm at the city's numbers and at the help which God continually gave it.

This heavenly city, then, while on its pilgrimage on earth, calls out its citizens from every nation, and gathers a society of travelers in every linguistic community. It is not concerned what differences there may be in those morals, laws, or institutions by which earthly peace is achieved and preserved. These do not have to be abolished or destroyed; no, though different traditions prevail in different peoples, they may be protected and observed insofar as they serve the one end of earthly peace, provided they do not impede the religion which teaches the worship of the one supreme and true God. So the heavenly city makes use of the earthly peace on its pilgrimage here; as far as true religion and piety allow, it supports and encourages the community of interest in resources for human mortal existence. It relates this earthly peace to that heavenly peace which, for rational beings at least, is the only peace worthy the name, the most perfect arrangement for the most perfectly cooperative association of those who enjoy God and one another in God. When we arrive at that point, life will be "mortal" life no more, but simply and plainly *life;* the body will be animal no more, sapping the animation of the soul as it disintegrates, but spiritual, without needs, wholly at the disposal of the will. *This* peace, meanwhile, it experiences on its pilgrimage in faith; and it lives justly by its faith when it relates to *that* peace whatever good works it performs toward God and neighbor.

Yes, the life of the city is undeniably a social life!

[. . .]

[Augustine then disposes briefly of the fourth and fifth questions. In the discussion that now follows a great deal is made of the terms *ius* and *iustitia*. *Ius* means "legal right," in the sense of the French *droit* or the German *Recht*. *Iustitia* means "justice" in a social context, "righteousness" in an individual one. So important is it, however, to retain the sense of a cognate relationship between the two, that in the following translation we have used "justice" only occasionally, to help out, and have rendered *iustitia* mainly by expressions which preserve the connection with "right."]

20. To conclude: — The supreme good of the city of God is perfect and eternal peace, not that peace through which mortals pass as they are born and die, but the peace in which those who will not die remain, without any obstacle to overcome. Who, then, can deny that that life is the most happy? or that this life which we live here, full as it may be of good things of body, soul, or circumstance, is by comparison the most unhappy? All the same, those who make use of this life to relate it to that other life as their end, those who love that life passionately and hope for it with unflinching confidence, can be said, not inappropriately, to be happy now — happy not in their present life, but in the hope they have of the future one. This life without that hope offers nothing but a pretense of happiness, which is great unhappiness. It cannot dispose of the real goods of the mind; for the so-called wisdom that is intent on this life's business, managing it prudently, coping with it resolutely, exercising temperate restraint, making just distributions, all without directing it to that end where God is all in all, where eternity is certain and peace entire, that is not real wisdom at all.

§

21. This brings me to the point at which I must explain as briefly and as clearly as I can what I said, and promised to prove, in Book Two (2.21): that by the definitions proposed by Scipio in Cicero's *Republic* there never was a Roman commonwealth *(res publica)*. His briefest definition of a "commonwealth" is "a people's wealth" *(res populi)*. But if that definition is sound, there never was a Roman commonwealth because there never was a people's wealth to constitute it. For a "people" he defines as "a gathered multitude united by consent to right *(ius)* and common interest." What he means by "consent to right" he explains in the course of the discussion where he argues that a commonwealth cannot be conducted without right-dealing *(iustitia)*. For where no true right-dealing obtains, there is no true right. What is done "of right" is done rightly; what is not done rightly cannot be done of right. For the term "rights" cannot be applied to the inequitable constitutions of men. They themselves have a saying that "right flows from the source of rightness"; which rejects the slogan bandied about by corrupt intellectuals, that right is what serves the interest of the most powerful.

So, then, where there is no true right-dealing, there may be no gathering united by consent to right, and so no people and no people's wealth, merely an indeterminate multitude unworthy of the name of "people." The argument, then, runs as follows: a commonwealth is a people's wealth, and there exists no right where there is no rightness, so the conclusion is irresistible that without right-dealing there is no commonwealth. But right-dealing, or justice, is the virtue of giving each his own. What "human rightness" can there be in taking man himself away from God and subjecting him to unclean demons? Is that giving each his own? To take an estate from its purchaser and to give it to someone with no title to it, is not right. Is it right to take ourselves back from our owner, God who made us, and to serve evil spirits?

To be sure, the same work, *The Republic,* contains a powerful and effective argument supporting a policy of doing right against a policy of wrongdoing. Earlier in that work the case was put by an advocate of wrong against right, that without wrongdoing the commonwealth cannot be maintained or governed. This argument took it as axiomatic that it was not right for one man to serve another; but the imperial city, the seat of the greatest commonwealth, so the argument went, had to make a policy of such wrongdoing in order to rule her provinces. In support of right the reply was made that such subjection is beneficial to such subjects, and, when imposed properly, is imposed for their benefit; that is, to deny occasions of wrongdoing to those who are minded to take them and to make subject populations better off than they were before. Reinforcing the argument with an impressive illustration from nature, he adds: "Why, then, does God command men, the soul the body, the intellect the appetite and other tendencies to vice within the soul?" Clearly the illustration shows that there are cases where subjection is beneficial, and that to serve God is beneficial to all. But it is only the soul *that serves God* that can rightly command the body; and within the soul it is the intellect *subject to the Lord God* which can command the appetite and other vices. Where man does not serve God, what rightness is there in such dispositions? One who refuses God service cannot command the body (as soul) or the vices (as intellect) rightly. And if there is no rightness in such a one, it can scarcely be doubted that a gathering of men which is composed of such lacks rightness as well. Here there is none of that consent to right which will make a multitude a people, and so a commonwealth. There is no need to discuss the common interest, the other bond of unity which is supposed, according to the definition, to make a multitude a people. One could, of course, point out that on close inspection there can be no "interest" to be shared in impious lives devoted to the service not of God but of demons yet more impious, who demand in their obscenity the sacrificial worship due to gods. But what I have said about consent to right will be sufficient to show that by this definition there is no people, and so no commonwealth either, without rightness. [. . .]

24. But let us try a different definition. A people, we may say, is a gathered multitude of rational beings united by agreeing to share the things they love. Then you have a differentiated notion of a people. There can be as many different kinds of people as there are different things for them to love. Whatever those things may be, there is no absurdity in calling it a people if it is a gathered multitude, not of beasts but of rational creatures, united by agreeing to share what they love. The better the things, the better the people; the worse the things, the worse their agreement to share them. By *this* definition the Roman people is unquestionably a people and its "people's wealth" unquestionably a commonwealth. What it loved, in its early days and through succeeding generations; how it conducted itself; how it ended in bloody sedition, social and civil war, and finally the breach and dissolution of the agreement which is the basis, in one sense, of a people's continuing existence; all this is history, and we have written much about it in the preceding books. But I would not conclude from this that Rome was not a people, nor that its people's wealth was not a commonwealth; not, at any rate, while there remains some kind of gathered multitude of rational beings united by agreeing to share what they love. And what holds true for Rome and its commonwealth holds true for Athens, for any of the Greek city-states, for Egypt, for that earlier Babylon in Assyria, for every commonwealth, in fact, that held imperial sway, whether small or great; indeed, it holds true for any commonwealth of any race.

Of course, any city of pagan people, speaking generally, must lack true rightness; not obedient to God's command to refrain from sacrifice except to him, it lacks the conditions for a command of body by soul or of vice by intellect. 25. For however impressive the appearance may be of soul commanding body or intellect vice, if soul and intellect do not serve God as he commanded, the body, or vice, is not under the command that it requires. What sort of body, what sort of vice is governed by a mind ignorant of the true God and resistant to his dominion, exposed instead to the vicious and corrupting influence of demons? If the virtues which it thinks it displays in commanding body or vice are related to the acquisition or retention of any object other than God himself, they are more properly vices than virtues. Some, it is true, think that they are true and honest virtues when they are practiced for their own sake and not for something else. But in that case they are puffed up, proud virtues, and so not properly considered virtues at all, but vices. The life of the body derives not from the body itself but from something above it; similarly, the life of man derives not from man but from above man; and that is true not only of man himself but of every power he displays, every heavenly virtue. 26. The life of the body is the soul, and the life of man — the happy life, that is — is God, as the sacred Hebrew Scriptures say: "Happy the people whose God is the Lord" (Ps. 144:15). It follows that a people alienated from that God is wretched.

Nevertheless, even such a people loves its own peace — something not to be despised, though it will not possess it at the end because it has not used it well before the end. That it should have this peace in this life in the meantime, is a matter that concerns us as well; for while the two cities are mingled together, we, too, make use of the peace of Babylon. By faith the people of God is freed from it, yet pursuing a traveler's existence in its sphere in the meantime. That is why the apostle counseled the church to pray for its kings and authorities, adding explicitly, "that we may live a quiet and peaceable life with all godliness and love" (1 Tim. 2:2). The prophet Jeremiah, too, in telling God's ancient people of their captivity and commanding them in God's name to go obediently to Babylonia and serve their God there precisely by their patience, instructed them to pray for it: "because in its peace is your peace" (Jer. 29:7). He meant, of course, the temporal peace of the meantime which is shared by good and wicked alike; (27) though our own proper peace, peace with God, is experienced here by faith, too, and not only by sight in eternity.

Yet here there is no peace, neither that shared peace nor our own proper peace, which is more than a solace to unhappiness. There is yet no delighting in happiness. Our righteousness, too, "truly right" as it may be by virtue of the truly good end to which it relates, is in this life no more than forgiven sin. There is yet no perfection of virtue. The proof of this lies in that prayer which the whole of God's city makes use of while it journeys on earth, crying out through every member to God, "Forgive us our trespasses, as we forgive those who trespass against us" (Matt. 6:12). This prayer is not for those whose faith is without works and so dead; it is for those whose faith works through love. For since even the intellect subject to God does not command vice perfectly, since in this mortal state the soul is oppressed by the corruptible body, even the righteous stand in need of such a prayer.

Translation: Editors, from Bibliothèque Augustinienne.

Paulus Orosius

(fl. 420)

Orosius laid the responsibility for his seven books of *Anti-Pagan History (Historiae adversus paganos)* on Augustine, who, having just completed ten books of the *City of God*, encouraged him to reinforce the argument with an extended refutation of the claim that Rome had known more prosperity in pagan times. Remembering, perhaps, his master's preferences as to company (*City of God* 19.7; see p. 150 above), Orosius presents himself self-deprecatingly as Augustine's dog, ready to come and go obediently at a whistle. What he brought back, tail wagging, has caused some surprise: it is a view of the course of world history in sharp contrast, with its frankly progressivist optimism, to the subtlety and ambiguity of Augustine's own.

He began, he tells us, with the common assumption that the period of history through which he lived was exceptionally troubled. Rome was taken by the Goths in 410; invading Vandals drove Orosius himself from his home (in modern Portugal) two or three years later. But he came to realize how much more full of bloodshed and disaster pagan times had been (clothed now, in the imagination of conservatives, with a romantic aura) the further removed they were from the revelation of true religion. As true religion had gained ground, so the rule of death had shrunk before it. Soon it must pass entirely away, except, of course, for the appearing of Antichrist and the final tribulation, an element of scriptural anticipation which he is somewhat embarrassed to accommodate.

The argument, expounded from the fall of Adam to the year 417, was that sinful human nature needed the providential discipline of "alternating good and evil." All history's woes were either "manifest sins" or "hidden punishments of sin." Divine government was seen, in part, in the rise of empires, of which (following Dan. 7) there had been four: Babylon, Macedon, Carthage, and Rome, one in each quarter of the known world. Like Augustine, Orosius reduces the four to two significant ones, the Eastern and the Western. Here, however, their interpretations divide sharply. Augustine has the Roman ascendancy follow directly on the fall of Babylon (*City of God* 18.2); it is seen in the lust for power and the continual ambition for conquest that marked the republican period. For Orosius the empire was a phenomenon quite distinct from the wars of republican Rome; founded in the principate of Augustus, it is linked in chronology and divine purpose with the birth of Christ. The very year in which Augustus closed for the third time the doors of the Temple of Janus, signifying peace, and refused the acclamation *"dominus,"* the true Lord of the world was born, a Roman citizen and beneficiary of the Pax Romana (*Hist.* 6.22).

Orosius's enthusiasm for the benefits of empire displays the ebullient gratitude of a refugee, the zest of someone who has acquired a taste for travel (having spent time in Palestine as well as in North Africa) and a simple monotheistic ideology which united pagans and Christians of that era: one God, one human race, one church, one seat of earthly power. What Augustine thought of it we may infer from the later books of the *City of God*. In 18.52 he rejects the theory that there can be no more persecutions before the final tribulation, pointedly criticizing a proof which Orosius advanced, based on the number of plagues in Egypt (*Hist.* 7.27). In 19.7 (above, p. 150), in one of his most somber passages, he dismisses the claims made for the imperial Pax Romana by turning against it precisely the argument that Orosius deploys (below) against the heroic victories of the republic.

Further Reading: H. W. Goets, *Die Geschichtstheologie des Orosius* (Darmstadt: Wissenschaftliche Buchgesellschaft, 1980); T. E. Mommsen, *Medieval and Renaissance Studies* (Ithaca, N.Y.: Cornell University Press, 1966).

From *Anti-Pagan History,* Book 5

1. In the light of the events directly following those I have just related, I realise that some people may be influenced by the fact that Roman victories continued to grow more numerous as the result of the overthrow of many peoples and cities. If they weigh the evidence carefully, however, they will find that more harm than good resulted. For none of these wars against slaves, allies, citizens or fugitives should be dismissed lightly since they certainly brought no benefits, but only great disasters. Nevertheless, I shall ignore this fact in order to treat the situation in the light in which these people saw it. I think that they would say: Has there ever been an age happier than this with its continuous triumphs, famous victories, rich prizes of war, imposing processions, and with kings and conquered peoples marching in a long line before the triumphal chariot? I shall answer them briefly and point out that they are pleading for, and that we are talking about, times and events which must be considered not merely from the point of view of one city but by taking the whole world into consideration. It will then appear that whenever Rome conquers and is happy the rest of the world is unhappy and conquered. Should we therefore attach too much importance to this small measure of happiness when it has been obtained at so enormous an expenditure of effort? Granted that these times did bring about some happiness to a particular city, did they not also weigh down the rest of the world with misery and accomplish its ruin? If these times are to be considered happy

because the wealth of a single city was increased, why should they not rather be judged as most unhappy in view of the wretched destruction and downfall of mighty realms, of numerous and civilized peoples?

Did Carthage perhaps not view the situation differently at that time? Over a period of one hundred years the city alternately dreaded the disasters of war and the terms of peace. At one time deciding to renew war and at another to sue humbly for peace, Carthage was continually exchanging peace for war and war for peace. In the end her wretched citizens throughout the city were driven to desperation and threw themselves into the flames. The whole city became one funeral pyre. The city is now small in size and destitute of walls, and it is part of her unhappy lot to hear of her glorious past.

Let Spain present her opinion. For two hundred years Spanish fields were drenched with her own blood. The country was unable either to drive back or to withstand a troublesome enemy that was persistently attacking on every frontier. Towns and country districts everywhere were in ruins. The inhabitants were crushed by the carnage of battle and exhausted by the famines accompanying sieges. Men killed their wives and children, and to end their own sufferings ran at one another, cut one another's throats, and suffered wretched deaths. What was Spain, then, to think about her own condition?

And now let Italy speak. Why should Italy have oppressed, resisted, and placed all sorts of obstacles in the way of her own Romans over a period of four hundred years? She certainly could not have acted in this way had the happiness of the Romans not spelled her own disaster and had she not felt that she was promoting the welfare of all by preventing the Romans from becoming masters of the entire world.

I am not now raising the question concerning innumerable peoples of various countries, who, after enjoying long periods of freedom, had been defeated in war, forcibly carried away from their native lands, sold into slavery, and dispersed far and wide. I do not ask what they would have preferred for themselves, what they thought of the Romans, and how they judged the times. I am not mentioning one word about kings of vast wealth, great power, and widespread renown, who, after enjoying a long supremacy, were later captured, chained like slaves, sent under the yoke, led before the triumphal chariot, and slaughtered in prison. To inquire their opinion is as foolish as it is difficult not to pity their misery.

Let us question ourselves then, I say, about the way of life which we have chosen and which we are accustomed to live. Our forefathers waged wars, sought peace, and offered tribute; for tribute is the price of peace. We ourselves pay tribute to avoid war and by this means have come to anchor and are remaining in the harbor in which our ancestors finally took refuge in order to escape the storm of evils. Therefore I should like to know whether our times are not happy. Certainly we, who continuously possess what our forefathers finally chose, consider our days happier than those earlier days; for the tumult of wars that exhausted them is unknown to us. We ourselves are also born and raised in a state of peace that they enjoyed only for a brief time after the rule of Caesar and the birth of Christ. The payment which subjection compelled them to make we contribute freely for the common defense. How great is the difference between the present and the past can best be judged by the fact that what Rome once extorted from our people by the sword merely to satisfy her thirst for luxury, she now contributes with us for the maintenance of government. And if anyone asserts that the Romans at that time were much more tolerable enemies to our forefathers than the Goths are now to us, his knowledge and understanding of conditions are quite at variance with the facts.

In former days the entire world was ablaze with wars, and each province was governed by its own king, laws and customs. A feeling of common fellowship was also lacking when different powers were disagreeing with one another. What was it then that could finally draw into one bond of fellowship barbarian tribes which were scattered far and wide and, moreover, separated by differences in religion and ritual? Suppose that in those days a person was driven by the bitterness of his misfortune to utter desperation and that he decided to abandon his own country and to leave in company with the enemy. What strange country would he, a stranger, approach? What people, usually enemies, would he, an enemy, supplicate? In what man, at first meeting, would he place his confidence? He would not be invited because he belonged to the same race, he would not be induced to come because he obeyed the same law, and he would not be made to feel secure because he believed in the same religion. We have plenty of examples to illustrate what happened. Did not Busiris most brutally offer as sacrifices all strangers who had the misfortune to cross his path? Did not the people on the shores of Taurian Diana act most cruelly toward visitors and perform sacred rites that were crueler still? Did not Thrace and its own Polymestor treat guests, who were at the same time their relatives, in a most criminal fashion? Without dallying too long on events of antiquity, I shall merely cite the testimony of Rome with regard to the murder of Pompey and the testimony of Egypt with regard to Ptolemy, his murderer.

2. At the present, however, I feel no apprehension over the outbreak of any disturbance, since I can take refuge anywhere. No matter where I flee, I find my native land, my law, and my religion. Just now Africa has welcomed me with a warmth of spirit that matched the confidence I felt when I came here. At the present time, I say, this Africa has welcomed me to her state of absolute peace, to her own bosom, and to her common law — Africa, concerning whom it was once said, and truly said:

> "We are debarred the welcome of the beach,
> They stir up wars and forbid us to set foot even on the land's edge."
> (Virgil, *Aeneid* 1.540f.)

Africa of her own free will now opens wide her kindly bosom to receive friends of her own religion and peace, and of her own accord invites those weary ones whom she cherishes.

The width of the East, the vastness of the North, the great stretches of the South, and the largest and most secure settlements on great islands, all have the same law and nationality as I, since I come there as a Roman and Christian to Christians and Romans. I do not fear the gods of my host. Neither do I fear that his religion will bring death to me. Nor am I afraid of any place where a native may do whatever he wishes and a stranger may not do whatever is lawful, where my host's law will not be my own. One God, who established the unity of this realm in the days when he willed himself to become known, is loved and feared by all. The same laws, which are subject to this one God, hold sway everywhere. Wheresoever I go, stranger though I be, I need harbor no fear of sudden assault as would a man without protection. Among Romans, as I have said, I am a Roman; among Christians, a Christian; among men, a man. The state comes to my aid through its laws, religion through its appeal to the conscience, and nature through its claim of universality.

For a time I enjoy any country as if it were my own, because that native land, which is my real home and the one which I love, is not wholly on this earth. I have lost nothing where I have loved nothing. I have everything when I have with me him whom I love; especially since he is the same among all. He made me not only known to all but also very near to all. Neither does he forsake me when I am in need, because the earth is his and its fullness, whereof he has ordered all things to be common to all men. The blessings of our age, which our ancestors never had in their entirety, are these: the tranquillity of the present, hope for the future, and possession of a common place of refuge. Our ancestors had to wage incessant wars, because, not feeling free to move as a body and to change their abodes, they continued to remain at home where they had the misfortune to be slaughtered or to be basely enslaved. This will appear clearer and more evident when the actual deeds of our ancestors are unrolled in due order.

Translation: I. W. Raymond (New York: Columbia University Press, 1936). Used with permission.

PART 2

LATE ANTIQUITY AND ROMANO-GERMANIC CHRISTIAN KINGSHIP

The gradual decline of the Roman Empire over several centuries or more of barbarian invasion and occupation of Roman territory circumscribes the period known as "late antiquity." On the broadest historical canvas, this period presents the emergence of separate political and ecclesiastical destinies in the eastern and western Mediterranean basins, the north-south division crossing the mouth of the Adriatic Sea. The West's political identity was bound up with the collapse of the imperial administration and rise of the Germanic kingdoms, with their distinctive blendings of imperial, Christian, and indigenous traditions; its ecclesiastical identity, with the dialectic of dependence and independence characterizing the relationship of Germanic churches to Rome. The East's political identity reflected the determination of emperors to augment the imperial glory of Constantinople and its sphere of influence in the face of the rival empire of Persia; its ecclesiastical identity, the preoccupation of emperor and Constantinopolitan patriarch with overcoming theological divisions, schisms, and heresies.

The failure of the emperor Justinian's vision of restoring the old empire through territorial reconquest, promulgation of a codified imperial law, and establishing theological consensus is generally regarded as the decisive anticlimax of late antiquity. By the end of the sixth century the Mediterranean had entered a period of political, economic, and cultural disintegration that warrants the epithet "dark age," but in which was laid the soil of a later renaissance. In the West the non-Roman powers — Frankish, Visigothic, Vandal, Celtic, and Lombard — were consolidating their political domains and their churches, while in the East the Constantinopolitan imperial administration was reorganizing along military lines to cope with ongoing territorial losses, threats of invasion, and shrinking economies. The political and ecclesiastical divisions of East and West were exacerbated by the advance of Islamic Arabia to the eastern and southern shores of the Mediterranean. Throughout the Christian world churchmen were in the strongest position to shape ecclesiastical and political culture, but especially in the rapidly evolving barbarian kingdoms where classical learning was most fragmentary and secular aristocratic patronage a vanishing asset. From Western bishops, and especially from the chief bishop of Rome, issued the models of civil and ecclesiological society and government that informed the Carolingian *renovatio imperii*.

I. *Late Antiquity*. Like the Germanic kingdoms themselves, the theory of Christian kingship that came to characterize the converted kingdoms in the West arose, Phoenix-like, from the ashes of the Christianized Roman Empire. It exhibited an enduring attachment to biblically centered, patristic political thought and an adaptation of Latin and Greek imperial traditions to the new circumstances. Throughout the invasions, the imperial authorities signed treaties with the victorious intruders, acceding to their occupation of Roman territory as allies and granting to their commanders the status of "military commander," *magister militum*, within the empire. The status was frequently cemented by marital alliances into the Roman aristocracy and the education of sons at the imperial court. During the fifth and sixth centuries a succession of Romano-Christian aristocrats with close connections to Frankish and Gothic warrior-rulers furnished a royal alternative to the divinizing oriental emperor cult: a portrait of kingship that drew on Ciceronian and senatorial conceptions of Roman rule and the theological inheritance of Jerome, Ambrose, and Augustine.

The Gallic imperial official and later bishop, Sidonius Apollinarius (ca. 430–ca. 486), contrasted the corrupt, inefficient, dynastic empire with a republican model of "citizen-emperor" — humane, ascetically disciplined, public spirited, respectful of the Senate — and well advisedly cast the Visigoth king Theodoric II in this image. Subsequently, Cassiodorus (ca. 490–ca. 580), a Roman official in northern Italy and later a monk, portrayed the Ostrogoth king Theodoric as the incarnation of the imperial *civilitas* type of law-abiding monarch reigning over free subjects. While Gregory of Tours (538/39–94), in celebrating the legacy of Clovis's conversion of Gaul to Catholic orthodoxy, struck a somewhat more Constantinian note by stressing the Frankish king's role in the evangelization and salvation of his people, he, too, laid weight on the royal virtue of humility, manifested especially in the veneration of bishops (Reydellet 1981, 368; Burns 1988, 134-35).

These royal portraits comported well not only with the inherent feudal restraints of Germanic kingship but with the growing Western conception of ecclesiastical authority as a *separate and superior jurisdiction* to secular rule. By the end of the fifth century, four ecumenical church councils had established the universal jurisdiction of the episcopacy over the church to define doctrinal orthodoxy, to condemn heresy, and to enforce uniformity on key points of church practice. From the late fourth century, a succession of Roman pontiffs had bid quite successfully to anchor episcopal and conciliar jurisdiction in the "apostolic" primacy of the Roman bishop: in the unique power bestowed by Christ on St. Peter and his papal successors to "bind and loose" on earth and in heaven (Matt. 16:18-19). Pope Gelasius I's exposition of the separate and reciprocal functioning of the priestly and imperial jurisdictions, together with his statement of priestly "spiritual" superiority and Roman primacy, became a touchstone in the medieval controversies of church and empire.

Although the predominant Arianism of the Germanic tribes (originally converted by Arian Gothic missionaries) raised a barrier between them and Roman orthodoxy, they increasingly aligned themselves with the papal defense of the Nicaean and Chalcedonian formulas against imperial attempts to effect reconciliation on an Eastern quasi-Monophysite basis, with or without the backing of an ecumenical church council. Not only was there a gradual conversion of the Arian tribes to Catholicism, but through Rome's tireless expansion of missionary activity, a steady stream of new Germanic converts to a thoroughly Roman church.

It was partly their exposure to collections of canons emanating from councils and bishops that prompted barbarian kings and their nobles to promulgate law codes, with the object of teaching as well as implementing divine and human law. The most famous new codes of *Roman* law, the *Lex Romana Visigothorum* (506) and the *Lex Romana Burgundionum* (517), applicable only to Romanized subjects in the respective kingdoms, were largely unreflective reproductions of fragments of imperial texts. But among the codes of *barbarian* law (Visigothic, Frankish, Ostrogothic, Burgundian, Lombard, and Saxon), a distinctly biblical motif appeared: that of Moses, the first civil legislator, establishing Israelite identity as a chosen race by promulgating a particular collection of divinely revealed laws (Burns 1988, 139). Not only the identification of Germanic kings with Israelite royalty, but the identification of Germanic peoples with the Israelite nation, had a distinguished history before it.

The monumental codification of law in late antiquity emanated, however, not from the barbarian kingdoms but from the imperial court of Justinian between 529 and 534, and consisted in the *Digest* (or *Pandects*), the *Institutes*, and the *Codex*, to which were later added the *Novels*. Spanning four centuries of imperial statutes and edicts, juristic judgments, opinions, and maxims, the *Corpus iuris civilis*, as it came to be known, comprised the textual foundation of the medieval science of civil law in the West. Although largely an assemblage of concrete, practical legal casuistry, displaying few abstract principles and no overall theoretical systematization, Justinian's codification was transformed by successive "schools" of legal commentators, from the twelfth century onward, into a system of universal political-legal principles, regarded increasingly as coterminous with legal rationality itself (Berman 1983, 127-43). Its meager theoretical elements, located mainly in the *Digest* and *Institutes*, became the controversial reference points for medieval legal culture, chiefly among civilian lawyers, but also among canonists, philosophers, and theologians. These included: the discriminations of *ius civile*, *ius gentium*, and *ius naturale*, of written and unwritten law; the relating of law to the work of justice in assigning to each his right *(ius suum cuique)*; propositions concerning imperial authority, e.g., that the emperor is above the law *(legibus solutus)*, that his decision has the force of law *(quod principi placuit)* because the people have conferred on him all their power of rule *(lex regia, lex de imperio)*, that he should profess himself bound by the laws, as his authority rests on their authority *(digna vox)* (Burns 1988, 37-47; Carlyle, I, 1962, 32-79).

Justinian's own legislative contributions to the *Codex* conveyed the traditional Hellenic cast of his imperial self-understanding, his devotion (undiminished by the reduced circumstances of his Western Empire) to restoring Roman splendor in its political, cultural, and above all, religious aspects. His *imperium* made no apparent concession to the Gelasian dualism of powers, in that it encompassed the authority to impose practice of the orthodox faith on all peoples subject to him: to establish sound doctrine, to root out heresies with punitive economic and social measures, to purify education of pagan remnants, and to regulate the selection of ecclesiastics to ensure their integrity (preamble to *Novel* 6). The portrait of emperorship informing his ambitions was concisely sketched in the apothegms of praise and advice composed by Agapetos, which extol the emperor as the Socratic philosopher-king who, in imitating divine rule, is an image of God to his subjects, being humanly equal to them but raised above them by the majesty of his state and his sublime equipment.

II. The Post-Justinianic "Dark Age." Justinian's grandiose schemes of Western reconquest and of doctrinal unification of Christendom had the bitterly ironic results of disrupting the cultural Romanization of the Germanic tribes and their conversion to Catholic orthodoxy. Constantinople's supplanting of barbarian rule aroused hostility throughout the Germanic kingdoms, while the devastations of war and the policies of Byzantine administrations in the reclaimed territories generated anti-imperial sentiments among their barbarian and Roman populations alike. At the same time Arians and many orthodox in the West looked upon Justinian as a persecuting, heretical tyrant.

The towering Christian political thinkers of the late sixth and early seventh centuries, Pope Gregory I and his disciple, Archbishop Isidore of Seville, both labored in the shadow of Justinian's negative legacy, but in contrasting circumstances. Gregory ruled in a Rome depleted by war and imperial neglect, decimated by famine and pestilence, almost without aristocratic presence, and cut off from the essentially military imperial administration of northern Italy at Ravenna (the de facto capital city) by a corridor of Arian Lombards who constantly threatened its security. In addition to the burdens of Rome's spiritual primacy in East and West (which he self-consciously assumed), of zealous missionary enterprises and local episcopal administration, Gregory bore a host of civil and social responsibilities, owing to the city's exposed and isolated situation. By contrast, Isidore ruled in a metropolitan city of the rising Visigothic kingdom in Spain, patronized by a succession of orthodox Christian kings that would, within his reign, unite the entire peninsula (including a small Byzantine province) under a single monarchy. His politically stable and supportive environment enabled him to devote his energies to building up an orthodox, yet independently minded, Visigothic church and to salvaging classical learning and law. Both men looked on their own time as the world's end; but Gregory was inspired by the cataclysmic manifestations of God's judgment and by a sense of missionary urgency, whereas Isidore was inspired by the Christian achievement in Spain, the jewel of Christ's earthly kingdoms.

Isidore's different circumstances in their own way reinforced his adoption of Gregory's ecclesiological conception of kingship, nurtured on biblical, patristic, and Merovingian writers. He concurred in Gregory's move to make the episcopate the model of rule within Christian society, so that temporal rulers would *imitate* as well as *reverence* their spiritual counterparts. In Isidore's case, as in Gregory's, the episcopate's paradigmatic political role expressed not only the interpenetration of civil and ecclesiastical government within the Byzantine ethos, but also the pervasive authority of Christian teaching in the cultural vacuum created by the loss of empire.

The controlling theme of this theology of rule was that oversight and administration within the body of Christ was a definable ministry or service to it, so that public authority was ministerial in character. This meant not only that authority was conformable to the specific requirements of the ministry performed, but, more significantly, that both ministry and authority were conformable to the pattern of Christ as elaborated for the early church by the apostolic writers. Thus political authority and office, whether episcopal or regal, were simultaneously shaped by directive and judicial purposes of ordering and disciplining the church, and infused with christological virtues of humility, obedience, self-sacrificial care of others, patience with human moral frailty, and compassion for the poor and defenseless. The rule of the Christian "ruler" (*rector,* Gregory the Great's generic term for all in authority) emulated the rule of the heavenly king who, as Sulpicius Severus (363-420) had earlier observed, manifests himself not in the "purple robe and glittering diadem" of imperial conceit, but "in the garments and lineaments of his passion . . . bearing upon him the wounds of the cross" (*Vita Martini* 24). Christian rule was a form of discipleship of the divine servant who, unlike "the princes of the Gentiles," came "not to be ministered to, but to minister" (Matt. 20:28). Through Gregorian theology King David attained enduring popularity as an embodiment of royal humility: divinely exalted from humble origin, submissive to priestly correction, inspired by the "fear of the Lord" to meditate continually on his law. His royal wisdom, shared by Solomon, was the fruit of his receptivity to God's admonition in Scripture, from which issued both private rectitude and the public administration of justice.

III. The Carolingian Empire. It is generally accepted that Pope Stephen II (752-57) launched Western Christendom on a novel course (though not without anticipations) when, in the wake of Ravenna's fall to the Lombards, he appealed to King Pippin of the Franks to reconquer papal territory and restore it to the Roman Church, bestowing on him the title of *patricius Romanorum.* Stephen's epoch-making desertion of Byzantine protection for Frankish was justified, to later ages at least, by a document possibly forged in his or his successor's reign, known as the *Donation of Constantine* (see pp. 228-30 below), in which Emperor Constantine I, prior to moving his court to Constantinople in the fourth century, transfers his imperial authority and privileges in the West to Pope Sylvester. Several centuries after Stephen, Pope Gregory VII would read this forgery as establishing the Roman bishop's universal temporal sovereignty over Christendom, by virtue of which he "translated" the empire in the eighth century from the Greeks to the Franks; but its author's intention (assuming that it was not a mere *jeu d'esprit*) was undoubtably more modest, probably that of shoring up Rome's claim to her recovered Italian territories at the expense of Ravenna, having in view Constantinople's recent adoption of "schismatic" iconoclasm. However, Pope Leo III's crowning of Pippin's son Charlemagne in St. Peter's in Rome in 800, to the popular acclamation of "Emperor of the Romans," suggested a more grandiose papal plan of substituting a Western for an

Eastern emperor. There was an inevitable uncertainty as to how "Frankish," or indeed how "Byzantine," the new imperial protector of the Roman Church would prove to be.

Assuredly, a potent idea of Carolingian political theology was *renovatio imperii Romani,* the rebirth of Christian empire in the West. The extent of Charlemagne's dominion gave him a claim, unprecedented in the Germanic kingdoms, to be called "the new Constantine." Implied in this epithet was a renaissance of Byzantine emperor-ideology, absorbed in part though a Latin translation of Eusebius of Caesarea. The theocratic king-priest *(rex et sacerdos),* endowed with episcopal powers, was responsible for the temporal and eternal welfare of his subjects. Regenerated by baptism, supernaturally equipped by royal anointing, the new Moses (or David, or Solomon, or Melchizedek), vicar of God or of Christ, superintended his imperial church, mediating the divine will by teaching and enforcing Christian doctrine and morality. His ecclesiastical administration and jurisdiction was Byzantine in scope, including nomination of bishops, convening of church councils and promulgating of canons, creation and regulation of external church organization, oversight of clerical training and discipline, and maintenance of doctrinal orthodoxy. In his measures to promote biblical scholarship and exegesis, the circulation of Bibles, popular catechesis, and a better-educated clergy, Charlemagne displayed an episcopal self-consciousness not unlike that of King Henry VIII of England at his exceptional best, and not least because it was a self-consciousness infused with Gregorian ideals of royal humility and service.

It was universally professed by Charlemagne's subjects, clerical and lay, that strict obedience was owed to the commands of their monarch, who ruled not only "by God's grace" *(gratia Dei),* as had Byzantine emperors, Merovingian kings, and Frankish bishops, but "in God's place" *(pro vice Dei),* provided that his commands did not flagrantly violate divine law and justice. Rebellion or conspiracy against "the Lord's anointed," entrusted with the protection of the Lord's people, was an affront to God himself that merited the anathema of the church. As the progress of Carolingian kingship reveals, the implication of the king's immediate divine appointment and vicarate was to lessen the role of mundane factors in his title such as heredity and election, while increasing the role of the episcopate in his institution and the possibility of episcopal intervention in his reign.

Nevertheless, for some time after the division of the empire, West-Frankish rule continued to be, on the one hand, dynastic and patrimonial, and on the other, dependent on the formal election (or at least consent) and informal support of the lay magnates. Indeed, surviving documentation of royal pledges at elections and consecrations, and "compacts" *(pacta)* entered into by hard-pressed kings with their leading subjects, indicate the enlarged extent of popular reciprocity in Carolingian rule (Carlyle 1903, 240-50). But the bishops, who largely framed the Carolingian political legacy, constantly promoted their collective role in establishing and, to some extent, overseeing monarchs. Their intellectual mentor, Hincmar of Rheims, led the campaign to attach constitutive significance to the episcopal acts of anointing, crowning, and acclaiming the king. Hincmar and his colleagues took the occasion of the coronation of Charles the Bald as king of the annexed kingdom of Lorraine

(869) to pronounce that the bishops' endorsement of his title and administration of unction were the sure sign of God's election and equipment, leaving the nonepiscopal participants merely to recognize God's manifest choice. This interpretation of royal institution was transmitted through the adoption of the "structure, doxology and liturgy" of Charles the Bald's coronation by subsequent coronation rites (Ullmann 1969, 95).

Although inspired by papal anointings and crownings of Frankish royalty, the Carolingian prelates did not view their authority in these proceedings as depending on the pope's. The church in which they and their kings were to minister as Christ's vicegerents was less the universal Roman imperial church than the West-Frankish *populus Dei*. Nevertheless, they were ever mindful that the orthodox faith the emperor was elevated to protect was preeminently that of the Church of Rome. And, moreover, the Roman Church seized upon the political-liturgical innovations of the Frankish bishops with alacrity, as popes in the final quarter of the ninth century tried with little success to bind the empire to the Lombard kingdom and the emperors to the protection of papal interests. It was only with the penetration of the Ottonian emperors into Italy a century later that the identification of the East-Frankish church with the papacy became vigorous again, though on imperial rather than papal terms.

It seemed desirable to these ninth-century West-Frankish bishops to place kingship on a solid Gregorian-Isidorian footing at the expense of Constantinian strains. They propounded the complementary royal and episcopal governments within the church rather than royal headship, emphasizing the paternal authority of spiritual over temporal rulers, not without a judicial edge (as evidenced by the part played by episcopal assemblies in the forced abdication and eventual restoration of Charlemagne's son, the "pious" Louis I). The synodists at the Council of Paris (829) led by Bishop Jonas of Orléans set the tone for their contemporaries by solemnly proclaiming the authority of bishops to pronounce on matters of the Christian religion, indeed, to interpret God's law, for the whole Frankish people. The episcopal commission extended, it would seem, to reminding temporal rulers of their obligation to uphold *just* human laws and constitutions: preeminently ecclesiastical laws, jurisdiction, and "privileges" (or immunities), but also the secular legal inheritance of tribal customs, imperial collections, and the capitularies of Christian predecessors. Anticipating Hildebrandine principles, Hincmar defended episcopal independence in administering the church's temporalities and the canonical procedure for episcopal election without lay interference. In short, the Carolingian clergy and laity insisted that only a properly instructed monarch, respectful of divine and human law, could fulfill his office of vindicating right and punishing wrongdoing; protecting Christian belief, morality, and social order; and (in the words of the civic poet Sedulius Scottus) "decid[ing] what is just for every person" (*On Christian Rulers* 19).

Bibliography: H.-X. Arquillière, *L'Augustinisme Politique: Essai sur la Formation des Théories Politiques du Moyen-Age,* 2nd ed., Librarie Philosophique (Paris: J. Vrin, 1955); E. Barker, *Social and Political Thought in Byzantium from Justinian I to the Last*

Palaeologus (Oxford: Clarendon Press, 1957); H. J. Berman, *Law and Revolution: The Formation of the Western Legal Tradition* (Cambridge, Mass.: Harvard University Press, 1983); P. R. L. Brown, *Society and the Holy in Late Antiquity* (London: Faber, 1982); F. Dvornik, *Early Christian and Byzantine Political Philosophy: Origin and Background*, 2 vols. (Washington, D.C.: Dumbarton Oaks Centre, 1966); R. Folz, *The Concept of Empire in Western Europe from the Fifth to the Fourteenth Century* (English translation) (London: Edward Arnold, 1969); J. Herrin, *The Formation of Christendom* (Oxford: Blackwell, 1987); J. M. Hussey, *The Orthodox Church in the Byzantine Empire* (Oxford: Oxford University Press, 1986); F. Kern, *Kingship and Law in the Middle Ages* (English translation) (Oxford: Basil Blackwell, 1939); P. D. King, *Law and Society in the Visigothic Kingdom* (Cambridge: Cambridge University Press, 1972); R. A. Markus, *From Augustine to Gregory the Great* (London: Variorum, 1983); K. F. Morrison, *The Two Kingdoms: Ecclesiology in Carolingian Political Thought* (Princeton: Princeton University Press, 1964); J. L. Nelson, *Politics and Ritual in Early Medieval Europe* (London: Hambledon Press, 1986); M. Reydellet, *La Royauté dans la Littérature Latine de Sidoine Apollinaire à Isidore de Séville* (Paris and Rome: École Française de Rome, 1981); J. Richard, *The Popes and the Papacy in the Early Middle Ages, 476-752* (London: Routledge, 1979); S. Runciman, *The Byzantine Theocracy* (Cambridge: Cambridge University Press, 1977); W. Suerbaum, *Vom antiken zum frümittelalterlichen Staatsbegriff: über Verwendung und Bedeutung von Res Publica, Regnum, Imperium und Status von Cicero bis Jordanis*, 3rd ed. (Münster: Aschendorff, 1977); W. Ullmann, *Principles of Government and Politics in the Middle Ages* (London: Methuen, 1961); W. Ullmann, *The Carolingian Renaissance and the Idea of Kingship* (London: Methuen, 1969).

Gelasius I

(Pope 492-496)

Gelasius inherited the first formal schism between the Eastern and Western Churches. It was provoked by the attempts of the emperor Zeno (474-91) to mend the rift in the Eastern Church between the Chalcedonian ("one person in two natures") and Monophysite ("one nature" or "one person out of two natures") confessions of the person of Christ, a matter of great importance to a ruler who had to keep Egypt and Syria within the same empire as Greece and Constantinople. His "union formula" *(henōtikon)* of 482 had had some success with the Eastern churches whose ills it was intended to heal, but had fallen foul of a Roman synod convened by Pope Felix III in 484, so that communion was broken between the pope and the patriarch of Constantinople, Acacius. Some of the offense caused to the Western Church in the new formula lay in its implied downgrading of Pope Leo I's *Tome*, which the Council of Chalcedon had treated as a doctrinal authority; and so the Western Church took its stand on the issue of the primacy of the Roman see. Now, with the principals dead, the "Acacian schism" was in its second generation. A new pope, confronting a new patriarch, Euphemius, and a new emperor, stood firmly on the ground occupied by his predecessor. But an additional factor gave the schism new urgency: the emperor Anastasius (491-518), though at the head of a church supporting Chalcedonian orthodoxy, leaned toward Monophysitism — an alarming indication, in Roman eyes, of where the *henōtikon* would lead. This created the conditions for a new kind of confrontation between ecclesiastical and secular authority, one elevated to a universal level. The patriarch of Constantinople was of no significance; it was for a universal pope to confront a universal emperor. And in this context the pope defined the relation of ecclesiastical and secular authority in a form which would prove decisive within the Western Church for subsequent centuries.

In articulating the confrontation, Gelasius drew upon the implications of a century or more of Roman practice by which the popes had carefully modeled their office upon that of the emperors. The verbal contrast between the "authority" of one and the "power" of the other is not of great moment: the pontiff had his "judgment" as the emperor had his "sentence," and the pope was happy to describe the priestly office as a "power" otherwise. Balance, rather than differentiation, was the primary concern. The distinction lay in the respective spheres of responsibility. Yet, if this took Gelasius some way toward assimilating the dual responsibility to the universal distinction of the sacred and profane, his sense of salvation history imposed a restraint. What is distinctive about the Christian era is that the sacred and the political *must* be separated, for Christ, combining in himself the two roles of priest and king, has made it impossible for anyone else to combine them. As the Epistle to the Hebrews thought of Christ, the great High Priest, as the last high priest, so Gelasius, with a similar reference to Melchizedek, thought of him as the last priest-king. Only the devil could now propose an emperor who was also an object of a religious cult. The distribution of functions in Christendom is an eschatological sign, ensuring that everyone is humble, acknowledging that the priestly-royal character of the church is not for one individual alone to reflect but depends on mutual service. But was the emperor's rule exercised *over* the church? In the Carolingian age Gelasius was sometimes understood (e.g., by Jonas of Orléans; see pp. 217-18 below) to speak of two by which the *church* was ruled. It was a hairsbreadth change, but it made all the difference.

Further Reading: W. Ullmann, *The Growth of Papal Government in the Middle Ages,* 3rd ed. (London: Methuen, 1970); W. Ullmann, *A Short History of the Papacy in the Middle Ages* (London: Methuen, 1972); W. Ullmann, *Gelasius I. Das Papsttum an der Wende des Spätantike zum Mittelalter* (Stuttgart: Hiersemann, 1981).

From *The Bond of Anathema*

[. . .] If they shrink from extending themselves so far [as to lay claim to God's grace by their own efforts], knowing that their sphere of competence, granted the jurisdiction only of human affairs, does not include the charge of divine affairs as well, why are they so presumptuous as to deliver judgment on the ministers of divine service? Before Christ's Advent, it may be, there were those who combined the role of kings with that of priests — as a prophetic sign, to be sure, yet in actual practice; the sacred history tells us that holy Melchizedek was such a one (Gen. 14:18). (This was the pattern which the devil imitated, usurping tyrannously, as always, what belongs to the worship of God, when pagan emperors used to bear the title *pontifex maximus*.) But once the true priest-king entered on the stage of history, there was no ruler who assumed the name of priest, nor any priest who laid claim to the royal scepter. For though the members of Christ, the true priest-king, partake of his nature, and so are said all-encompassingly to have assumed the two aspects of it — generically within the holy people, the "royal priesthood" (1 Pet. 2:9) — he has mediated this privilege by an all-encompassing manner of distributing it. Mindful of human weakness, as befits his care for his own, he has made a distinction between the two roles, assigning each its sphere of operation and its due respect. In this way he planned that the medicine of humility should keep his people free from further infection by human pride. Christian emperors were to depend on priests for their eternal life, priests were to profit from imperial government for their historical existence. Spiritual activity must have a distance from routine interruptions; so God's soldier does not involve himself in secular affairs (2 Tim. 2:4), while those involved in secular affairs are seen to have no charge of divine affairs. That way is safeguarded, on the one hand, the modesty of each order, avoiding the pride to which the double responsibility might give rise; on the other, each sphere has a specially qualified and trained profession. Put all that together, and it is clear that the secular power cannot "bind and loose" a pontiff.

From *Letter to Emperor Anastasius*

Two there are, august Emperor, by which this world is ruled: the consecrated authority of priests and the royal power. Of these the priests have the greater responsibility, in that they will have to give account before God's judgment seat for those who have been kings of men. You know, most clement son, that though first of the human race in dignity, you submit devoutly to those who are preeminent in God's work, and inquire of them the causes of your salvation, so learning, as concerns the reception and due administration of the sacraments, to be subordinate in religious matters. You know, therefore, that you should depend upon their judgment in such questions, not attempt to bring them to your will. Even the masters of religion, conscious that divine providence has conferred the empire upon you, obey your laws as public discipline requires, lest they should seem to obstruct the judgment you pronounce even in trivialities. How resolutely, then, do you think, should you obey those who were appointed to promulgate the venerable mysteries? As it is a serious matter, indeed, for bishops to remain silent on a question of proper observance in worship, so there would be grave danger if (perish the thought!) those who should obey them were to disregard them. And if the faithful ought in general to submit to the priesthood as a whole when it handles divine mysteries rightly, how much more should deference be shown to the occupant of the highest see, chosen by divine sovereignty to be first among priests and held in religious honor by the whole church ever since? Your Piety can plainly see that by no human counsel whatever can one raise himself to the prerogative or status of one whom Christ's own words set over all, whom the venerable church has always acknowledged and devoutly accepted as its Primate. Things fixed by divine judgment may by human presumption be assailed; overwhelmed by anybody's power they cannot be.

Translation: Editors, from E. Schwartz, *Publizistische Sammlungen zum Acacianischen Schisma* (Munich: Verlag der Bayerischen Akademie, 1934).

Agapetos
(fl. 530)

From a literary point of view, here is a formal exercise: seventy-two apothegms on political governance, the initial letters of which form an acrostic, "Agapetus the least of deacons to our divine and most religious emperor Justinian." Crammed with elegant *bons mots* and drawing heavily on literary and rhetorical commonplaces from pagan as well as Christian Hellenistic sources, it was curiously conceived and executed as a grammatical textbook, with interlinear notes parsing and commenting on the more difficult Greek words. Original and creative thought is hardly to be looked for from this author, of whom, apart from his status as a deacon of Hagia Sophia in Constantinople, nothing is known. That he shared a name with the contemporary pope who intervened to restrain one of Justinian's periodic attempts to reconcile the Monophysites, is apparently a simple coincidence.

Yet his work found a considerable public and was much imitated. The genre of advice offered to rulers (the "mirror of princes") seems to have its source in a speech addressed by the Athenian orator Isokrates to the king of Cyprus, Nikokles, in the late 370s B.C. This work seems to have inspired Agapetos directly, but there are echoes of other Hellenistic sources (note the recurrence of Plato's "philosopher king" motif, 17), pagan, Christian, and Jewish — Philo of Alexandria can be detected. The genre became popular in Byzantium and beyond. The occasion for this offering is almost certainly Justinian's enthronement as co-emperor with his uncle Justin in 527. Having played an influential role in formulating policy throughout his uncle's reign, the new emperor was no unknown figure, but, as Agapetos delicately points out (52), brought to the imperial office a track record for energy, orthodox Christianity, and public benevolence which he could now be expected to live up to.

The interest of Agapetos's work is greater than the sum of the interest of its seventy-two parts. It presents us with a full and rounded view of the reflective but not profound, religious but not theological, ideology which sustained the character of the Eastern Roman Empire for centuries after. The emperor (or "king," *basileus*, as he continued to be known in the East) is "God's own representation of religion." Christology has shaped this picture of his role: like the god-man Christ, he mediates between God and men. The paradox of an elevation above his subjects which is compatible with equality with them is constantly exploited; the two corresponding emphases meet in a presentation of the emperor as a representative man-before-God. Yet, christological as the conception is, Christology itself is completely absent from Agapetos, as, indeed, is every trace of salvation history. The emperor, one might say, has replaced Christ. The universe is purely cosmic, ahistorical. It is a paradox of Byzantinism that, while the empire was racked politically by christological controversy — the rise of the emperor's family to power was directly due to the political crisis let loose by Anastasius's Monophysitism — it thought of itself as though it belonged to a deist universe.

Law, which was to be the field of Justinian's greatest accomplishment, is more in Agapetos's thoughts than Christology, though hardly prominent. It is constantly subsumed under the more general conception of justice, itself subsumed under reason. The association of power and right is the rational balance which justifies the kingdom: an apparently unlimited power to do good matched by an apparently unlimited obligation. True to the Hellenistic tradition, this objective cosmic rationality is traced back to a subjective root: "religious reason" *(eusebēs logismos)*, the psychological disposition of the emperor, wherein the battles he fights against temptation and vice are as significant as, or more significant than, the battles he fights in the external field.

The preoccupation with the question of wealth, characteristic of the Eastern tradition, is here developed in terms which, without challenging the existence or propriety of private wealth, lay weight consistently upon the emperor's undertaking on behalf of the needy. (Mazdakite influence from Persia has been suggested to explain this emphasis, but the explanation is superfluous in the city of John Chrysostom.) Here is the welfare state, indeed. Society is held together by a distinctive religious bond linking the head of government with the poor. The recurrent term *eleos*, "mercy" or "compassion," means, in practice, something very much like the term "aid," as we have come to use it in reference to the relief of poverty in the developing world. As with our term, it must be seen as embracing a wide range of types of expenditure susceptible of moral justification. By sustaining this bond, the emperor contributes to the realm a moral stability that curbs the unstable and fluid phenomena of property.

Further Reading: P. Henry, "A Mirror for Justinian: The *Ekthesis* of Agapetus Diaconus," *Greek, Roman and Byzantine Studies* 8 (1967): 281-308; I. Ševcenko, "Agapetus East and West," in *Ideology, Letters, and Culture in the Byzantine World* (London: Variorum, 1982).

Heads of Advice

1. Since your position is the most honorable of all, O king, render honor above all to God, who gave you your position, granting you the scepter of earthly government in

imitation of his own heavenly rule; that you should instruct men how to preserve justice, and should repress the rabid yelping of its opponents, yourself ruled by his laws and ruling your subjects lawfully.

2. The steersman is always watchful, and so is the king's all-seeing intelligence, keeping a firm hold of the helm of lawful government, and charting a resolute course against the currents of lawlessness, that the ship of the universal State may not run into the waves of injustice.

3. The first lesson which God teaches men is: Know yourself! To know oneself is to know God; to know God is to be like God; to be like God is to be worthy of God; to be worthy of God is to do nothing unworthy of him, but to think what is divine, to speak as one thinks, and to act as one speaks.

4. No one should be vain about noble ancestry; for all of us have clay for our ancestor: those who flaunt themselves in purple and linen and those who waste away in poverty and disease, those who adorn themselves with coronets and those who abase themselves with petitions. Let us not be proud of descent from clay, then, but find a ground of self-respect in good behavior.

5. Be aware (for you are God's own representation of religion) that the greater the gifts God has seen fit to grant you, the greater the return which you owe him. Pay your benefactor, then, the debt of gratitude, for he treats your debt as a favor (charis), and gives freely, his favors for yours. For he is the author of all favors, repaying them as if they were debts of his own. From us he asks gratitude, rendered not in fine words but in religious deeds.

6. What earns a man respect is to have the power to do what he wills, and what he wills and does to be always benevolent. But God has bestowed on you the power which your good will stood in need of for our sakes. Will, then, and do whatever pleases the giver.

7. Unstable material wealth flows like a river. For a while it flows toward you, and you think you possess it. But it soon flows past you to others. Only the treasury of good deeds remains with those who acquire it. For the kindnesses (charites) done in good works flow back upon those who initiate them.

8. Remote from ordinary men you may be through the relative eminence of kingship here below; yet through the influence of authority above you are accessible to those who need you: to those beset with want you open your ears, that you may find God's ear open to you. As we show ourselves to our fellow servants, so God shows himself to us.

9. The king's soul, clouded with cares, must be wiped like a mirror that it may always sparkle with God's light. So he will learn to exercise judgment in affairs, for nothing makes one clear-sighted about one's obligations as a soul continually kept clean.

10. On a voyage a sailor's mistake does little harm to the passengers, but when the steersman makes a mistake he can wreck the whole ship. And so it is in politics: when a subject does wrong, it is not the community so much as himself that he injures; but when the ruler does wrong, he harms the whole state. Both his speech and his action must be scrupulously careful, for he will bear such great responsibility if he neglects any aspect of his duty.

11. There is a wheel of human fortunes which revolves, carrying them this way, that way, and now back again. They have no equilibrium; nothing remains the same. You then, most excellent king, in the midst of so much volatile change must keep to a stable religious reason.

12. Ignore the deceptive words of flatterers. They are like scavenger crows, which pluck out the eyes from the body; but they attack the soul, disabling its power of reason, so that one cannot see the truth of anything. Sometimes they admire discreditable courses; often they decry praiseworthy ones. One way or the other they go wrong, admiring evil or despising good.

13. The king's purpose must maintain an equilibrium; constant fluctuation with the changes of events argues instability of disposition. To be firmly attached to good policies, as is your own most religious regime, and to be inclined neither to overconfidence nor to panic, is the way of those who walk securely and whose soul is imperturbable.

14. Who keeps his mind unclouded by the illusions of humanity, remembers the worthlessness of his own nature, the brevity and transience of life on earth, and the indecencies associated with the flesh, comes not upon the precipice of vanity, however high his position.

15. Above all the regalia of kingship, the crown of religion is the king's greatest ornament. Wealth vanishes, glory perishes. But the renown of a godly course of life extends for endless ages, and those who gain it are set beyond reach of oblivion.

16. It is a great paradox, it seems to me, that the rich and the poor suffer like harm from unlike causes. The rich burst with overindulgence, the poor are brought to nothing by hunger; the rich occupy the ends of the earth, the poor have nowhere to set the soles of their feet. That both may recover health, they must undergo the cure by subtraction and addition, and inequality must be replaced by equality.

17. In our own times that age of well-being has been disclosed which one of the ancients prophesied would come to pass when philosophers would be kings or kings philosophers. Pursuing the study of philosophy, you were appointed to kingly rule; and on taking up the kingship, you did not give up philosophy. For if the love of wisdom is what makes philosophy, and if the beginning of wisdom is the fear of God, whom you always hold first in your heart, it is clear that what I say is true.

18. I count you a king indeed because you exercise your power in royal mastery of personal comfort. Temperance is the crown you wear, justice the purple you put on. Other authority is overtaken by death; but a kingdom of this order perpetuates itself forever. Other authority is dissolved with this age, but this is delivered from agelong punishment.

19. If you wish to reap the respect of all, be the common benefactor of all. For there is nothing to induce good will like practical favor conferred on those who need it. For the deference induced by fear is nothing but an assumed unctuousness, a pretended respect which cheats those who place their reliance on it.

20. Your kingdom earns respect for demonstrating authority over foes and treating its subjects with humanity (*philanthrōpia*). Externally victorious in arms, internally it is overwhelmed by the unarmed forces of its supporters. Its manner in dealing with the two is as different as that of the wolf and the lamb.

21. In the substance of his body the king is the equal of all men; in the authority of his position he is like God over all; for he has no superior on earth. As befits God, then, he must not be angry; as befits mortality he must not be proud. Privileged as he is to bear the image of divinity, he is also bound up with the image of dust, which teaches him equality with all.

22. Keep good advisers by you, not those who always want to flatter; those who have a comprehensive and realistic view of policy, not those who limit their view to the current reigning doctrines in circles of power, and, like shadows clinging to their bodies, want to be heard agreeing with them.

23. Treat your staff as you pray that God may treat you. As we listen, we shall be listened to; as we observe, so we shall be observed by the all-seeing eye of God. Let us, then, take the initiative in giving aid, that we may receive like in our turn.

24. Like a precision-made mirror that reflects the exact cast of the face, whether radiant or sullen, so God's just judgment matches our deeds. Like the deeds we have done, so is the fate with which it visits us.

25. Prolonged deliberation, energetic performance. It is risky to embark on ill-considered measures. As one appreciates the blessing of health after being sick, so anyone who has acted imprudently will know the value of prudence well enough. You, then, most prudent king, should redouble the penetrating counsel and earnest prayer which go to frame your detailed policies for the whole world's benefit.

26. You will administer your good kingdom to the best advantage if you take pains to pay attention to everything and let nothing slip. Something may seem comparatively trivial; yet it is not so when it comes from you. The bare word of the king can have great effects for everyone else.

27. Compel yourself to keep the laws, since no one on earth has power to compel you. In this way you will demonstrate the majesty of the law, by being yourself the first to respect it; and so, too, it will be clear to your subjects that breaking the law has its perils.

28. Failure to prevent crime must be reckoned no better than crime itself. For however law-abiding someone's conduct is, if he tolerates unlawful behavior in others, in God's view he is an accomplice. Your own reputation will be doubly secure if you promote the most deserving and censure the most discreditable.

29. It is highly beneficial, I judge, to avoid evil company. Someone who mingles constantly with dishonest people is bound to be the victim, or the apprentice, of dishonesty. In good company, however, one acquires good practices, or one's faults are reduced by good training.

30. Entrusted by God with earthly kingship, do not employ bad characters in managing affairs; for God will set the wrong they do to the account of whoever gave them the power. So appointments to positions of authority should only be made after careful investigation.

31. It is equally wrong to be incensed at the machinations of one's enemies and to be charmed by the flattery of one's friends. Both temptations should be resolutely resisted, and the right course maintained, returning neither the unreasoning hatred from the one quarter nor the affected friendship from the other.

32. Count as your truest friends not those who applaud every word you speak,

but those who always take the trouble to exercise discriminating judgment, congratulating you on your better suggestions and wrinkling their brows at your worse. These are the ones who really give proof of unaffected friendship.

33. The pretensions of this earthly state must not affect your high purpose; but remembering how vulnerable your rule may be, keep a stable mind in unstable conditions, not elated by encouragements nor disheartened by disappointments.

34. Gold is worked by the craftsman this way and that and fashioned into various types of ornament, yet retains its identity unaltered. So it is with you, most illustrious king: though your responsibilities have changed with the various positions of authority you have filled, until now you have reached the highest position of all, you have remained unvaryingly attentive to your duty, always the same.

35. Count your kingdom safe when you rule with consent. An oppressed people rises up at the first opportunity, but one that is tied to its rulers by good will can be relied on to comply with government.

36. To make your regime renowned, you must treat your own misdeeds with no less indignation than the offenses of your subjects. As there is no one in a position to correct someone placed in such authority, your own reflection on your misdeed must do it.

37. Someone who has acquired great authority should imitate as far as possible the source of that authority. And if he bears the image of the universal God through whom he exercises universal rule, he will most reflect God in making mercy his chief policy.

38. Better than gold or gem, we should accumulate the treasure of benevolence, which rejoices us here with hope of satisfaction to come, and delights us there with the substance of bliss hoped for. The world about us means nothing to us and should have no attraction for us.

39. Take care to give the most glittering rewards to those who do your bidding cheerfully; for that way you will encourage the virtuous and teach the wicked to acquire better ways. It is exceedingly wrong that those who have deserved differently should be treated identically.

40. Kingship is the most honored of all states, yet especially when he who wears it shows no tendency to inflexibility, but looks for what is reasonable (*epieikeia*). Avoid the inhumanity of beasts; display the humanity (*philanthrōpon*) of God.

41. You must give judgment equally to friend and foe alike, not moved by loyalty to favor those who are loyal to you, nor by dislike to take sides against those who show you ill will. It is equally improper to justify the unjust party, however good a friend, and to wrong the just party, however great an enemy. The evil is the same in either case, contrasted as the two occasions may be.

42. Those who judge causes must listen intently. For justice is an elusive prey, easily escaping the half-attentive. But if we set aside the facility of the pleaders and leave behind the speciousness of the arguments, we may get to the bottom of the principles involved and draw up what we want in our bucket. So we shall avoid the double mistake: betraying the right cause, and letting others do so.

43. You may count to your reckoning as many good deeds as the stars, but you

will never exceed the goodness of God. Whatever we offer God from our store, it is his own that we bring him. We will as soon leap over our own shadow in the sunlight, which is always ahead however hard we hurry, as outdo with our poor human benevolence the inexhaustible kindness of God.

44. The treasury of benevolence is never spent. In giving, we receive; in distributing we gather. With this treasure in your soul, most generous king, give freely to all who ask you. You will receive your return many times over on that day when men are rewarded for their deeds.

45. By God's decree you have received the kingdom; so imitate him in good works. You were born among those who have power to do good, not among those who stand in need of others' goodness. A ready supply of material wealth is no bar to benevolence to the needy.

46. As the eye is set in the body, so is the king in the world: he is God's provision for coordinating what is beneficial. So he should look out for his fellow men, like the limbs of his own body, that they may move forward in good, not bad ways.

47. Your best protection is to do no wrong to any of your citizens. One who wrongs no one need suspect no one's intentions. And if doing no wrong makes for safety, kindness does so all the more. Kindness makes safe and betrays no friends.

48. To your subjects, most religious king, you should be both an object of fear by virtue of your preeminent authority, and an object of affection by virtue of your good deeds. Do not underestimate the role of fear in comparison with affection, nor overlook the importance of affection in comparison with fear. Your gentleness should not be taken for weakness; and if you are taken for weak, you should not be gentle.

49. Your laws convey in words what your actions have already exemplified; so that the words by which you prevail upon your subjects are supported by your noble conduct. This is how you will demonstrate the credit of your regime: by words that act, and by actions that speak.

50. Think more highly of those who seek your favors, mildest of kings, than of those who vie to bring you gifts. To the latter you put yourself in debt; the former put God in your debt, who takes what is done for them as done for himself, and requites with generous rewards your aim of loving God and man.

51. The sun's task is to illuminate creation with its beams; the prince's distinction is to aid the needy. So the religious king shines brighter than the sun; for the one makes way for night in its turn, but the other gives no way to the encroachments of mischief-makers; rather, he exposes secret injustice with the ray of truth.

52. Previous kings have drawn their splendor from their position; you, Excellency, have made your position more attractive by tempering the weight of its authority with a gentle manner and overcoming the fears of suppliants by your kindness. Those in search of aid who have brought their ship to your harbor, and have made calm water from the high seas of their need, are loud in singing their gratitude to you.

53. Your political position is preeminent; take pains that your achievement be preeminent as well. You will find it expected of you that the measure of your power should be reflected in your positive accomplishments. If God is to proclaim you with the crown of imperial victory, you must also win the garland of kindness to the needy.

54. Consider before commanding at your pleasure, that you may order what is right. The tongue is a slippery organ, a source of peril for the careless. But if you prescribe religious reason as its music, its song will be the sweet strain of virtue.

55. Severity befits a prince, especially when sitting as a judge in scandalous cases; but he should not be quick to display anger. Yet total imperturbability breeds disrespect; so his manner should alternate moderate anger with restraint: the first is needed to put down mischievous enterprises, the second to allow worthy initiatives to come to view.

56. Within the scrupulous council-chamber of your heart, examine the manners of your associates carefully, distinguishing attentively the loyal servants from dissembling flatterers. There are plenty who make themselves out to be well disposed, but do great harm in a position of trust.

57. Information of potential value should be listened to, but then taken up into practical considerations. It brings distinction to the imperial power to have a comprehensive surveillance of its own, or alternatively to draw upon others', unashamedly acquiring knowledge and putting it to service promptly.

58. The impregnably walled citadel can laugh at the enemy in siege around it. But the walls of the religious kingdom are of almsgiving, its towers of prayer. Unscathed by enemy missiles, it may raise famous monuments of victory against them.

59. Make proper use of your earthly kingdom, and treat it as a ladder to heavenly renown; for the good administration of the one is an equipment for the other. It is good administration to show a father's concern for subjects, earning in return a prince's respect, and, while using threats to nip mischief in the bud, not actually taking vengeance.

60. The cloak of kindness is a robe that does not wear; care for the needy is a garment never in rags. These are the garments to dress the soul of one who would be a religious king. Love of the needy is the purple which fits him for the heavenly kingdom.

61. From God you received the scepter of the kingdom. Seek to please him who gave it. As he has conferred on you the highest dignity, so be the first on earth to pay him honor. And what is the honor that he esteems most? To look on those he has made as on himself, and to complete your acts of benevolence like the payments of a debt.

62. Every one who desires salvation must have recourse to supernatural support; the king more than any, for he bears responsibility for the whole. Under God's protection he defeats his foes triumphantly, secures his friends effectively.

63. God stands in need of nothing, and the king in need of God alone. Make God's abundance, then, your model, and lavish aid on those who ask. Do not keep close accounts with your staff, but supply all their requirements for subsistence. It is better that the undeserving be aided with the deserving, than that the deserving be denied with the undeserving.

64. As you ask for your sins to be forgiven, so you should forgive those who offend you. For pardon requites pardon, and conciliation with our fellow servants is the way to friendship and alliance with God.

65. One who would put his reign beyond criticism should not only guard against others' bad opinions, but cultivate a sense of shame within himself; external constraints will keep him from public misconduct, and internal from private misdemeanor. For if a sense of shame befits his subjects, it befits the king far more.

66. I call a citizen bad when he commits offenses meriting punishment; but I call a ruler wicked simply by default of positive and salutary measures. There is no negative approval for a governor who avoids mischief, only a positive approval for one who effects good. His policy, then, should not be to avoid wrong, but to pursue justice energetically.

67. Death is not put out of countenance by glittering honors, but his ravening teeth make prey of all. Before his coming, then, which may not be denied, we should transfer our abundance of wealth to Heaven. For no one, when he journeys thither, takes with him what he amassed on earth; but, leaving all behind, is summoned naked to account for his life.

68. The king is sovereign of all, but fellow servant of all in the service of God. Sovereign he may indeed be called, when he is master of himself and slave to no unseemly indulgence; when, with religious reason as his ally, indefeasible master of unreasoning passions, he subdues the yearnings that cannot be repressed with the weaponry of self-control.

69. As shadows follow the bodies that cast them, so misdeeds cling to our souls. They are the vivid representations of our active powers, which is why there is no denying them at the judgment; for each man's deeds will bear witness against him, not in articulate speech, but by faithfully appearing exactly as they were performed.

70. The brief course of our present life is like the passage of a seagoing vessel, which makes headway by degrees too small to be perceptible to us who sail on it, but brings us each at last to his appointed end. Since this is so, let us allow the business of this world to slip abaft, setting our course for that which is everlasting.

71. The swaggering proud man, let him not rear like a tossing bull, but bethink the condition of his flesh and repress the vainglory of his heart. If he rules *(archōn)* upon earth, let him not forget that he is subject *(huparchōn)* of the earth, rising from dust to throne, and shortly descending there again.

72. Sustain your exertions continually, unconquered king! As one who mounts a ladder never ceases climbing till he reaches the highest rungs, so in your moral ascent you must press upward, to attain the joy of the kingdom on high. May Christ, king of kings and king of kings' subjects, grant you that goal, together with your consort, for ever. Amen.

Translation: Editors, from *PG*, vol. 86.

Justinian

(482-565)

The task of reducing the corpus of Roman law to a systematic and authoritative form was undertaken at the beginning of (Petrus Sabbatius) Justinian's long reign (527-65), and is characteristic of that emperor's imagination and energy. He worked through commissions: the first produced in 529 the *Codex*, a collation of imperial constitutions based on earlier collections, and including many enacted by Justinian — a revised edition appeared in 534; the second produced in 533 the *Digest* (in Greek, *Pandects*), an arrangement of extracts from the writings of the classical Roman jurists, particularly of Ulpian and Paul; the third produced the *Institutes*, an official textbook of Roman law, based on the earlier manual of Gaius. It is from this tripartite source, known collectively as the *Corpus Iuris Civilis*, that three of our four excerpts come, chosen to convey the temper of Justinian's program on political-theological questions. The fourth comes from the *Novellae*, the later legislation of Justinian, put into collections after his reign and eventually regarded as part of the *Corpus*.

Justinian's corpus shows us how an unusually clear-sighted, ambitious, and theologically self-conscious Christian emperor saw his task of government. Not only the new law, but the enterprise of collection itself, reflected a distinctive vision of Christian society. The appearance of traditionalism was made to serve the purposes of reconstruction; in Evans's phrase, it was "innovation disguised as conservatism." The laws do not, of course, tell us how the empire was actually governed. In some parts of the empire it appears that Roman law was not greatly used; the emperor's goal was to establish a normative form for the courts of the major cities and the law schools of Constantinople and Beirut. In terms of its effective influence, then, the significance of the Eastern emperor's work lay primarily in the West; six centuries later the law school of Bologna created "civil law," as the Middle Ages came to understand it, taking Justinian's *Corpus* as its definitive text.

The struggle against heresy and schism was a major theme of Justinian's work:

in 518, at the very beginning of the reign of his uncle, Justin I, we find the future emperor busy on his behalf mending the Acacian schism (see above, p. 177). That was achieved on the basis of a more or less complete reaction against Anastasius's Monophysitism and capitulation to the papal demands. From this point on, however, until the days before his death at the age of eighty-three, Justinian continued to search for a doctrinal formula that would reconcile the Chalcedonian and Monophysite parties; his own agile theological mind and his empress Theodora's avowed Monophysite sympathies produced an extraordinary sequence of ecumenical initiatives, some of them very alarming to Western and Chalcedonian opinion, over which one can only pronounce a verdict of magnificent disaster. One of the few of his age sophisticated enough to understand the deceptiveness of formulaic divisions, theologically agile enough to conceive of ways to overcome them, and convinced that a common faith in the incarnation underlay the verbal differences, he succeeded only in leaving the Christian world more divided than he found it. For this the growing separation and mutual incomprehension of the various regions of the Mediterranean world were in part to blame, as were the characteristic independence of monastic communities and the impatience and overconfidence of the emperor himself.

Little of Justinian's capacity for sympathetic engagement, however, is evident in this sample of his early laws depriving heretics and pagans of civil rights, except, perhaps, in the fact that the major deviant Christian traditions represented in his empire, Arianism and Monophysitism, are not mentioned. Anti-Arian legislation there was; yet in dealing with Arians in the territories of Italy and Africa recaptured for the empire, he was prepared to be flexible, though he never regarded Arian claims, as he regarded Monophysite ones, as genuinely open for discussion. Against the dwindling power of late paganism he was uncompromising. It was in his day that the Academy in Athens, the last center of pagan philosophical independence, was shut down. The other major deviant tradition was the Jews, and here the verdict on Justinian's reign is ambiguous. An initial legislative flourish attempted to include the Jews with heretics and pagans, ignoring their traditional status, still recognized by previous Christian emperors, as a *religio licita*. Subsequently he followed a more adapting line, and Jewish communities flourished, relatively speaking, though nothing could prevent the increasing isolation which resulted from the decay of the urban culture of the ancient world and the growth of a more rural, monastically dominated, and intolerant pattern of Christian society.

The organization of the political community makes no concessions to Gelasius's doctrine of the two rules. The emperor provides for every advantage of his subjects, and chiefly for the salvation of their souls. Under him the secular and spiritual officials of the empire watch over each other and supervise each other's business; the care of prisoners is an episcopal concern, while the selection and ordination of priests is an imperial concern. Yet this potentially dangerous conflation of authorities is kept in balance by the crucial reciprocity of "priesthood" and "kingship" itself, with its recognition that the task of civil authority in church affairs is to sustain an apostolic tradition that exists prior to it and independently of it. The emperor has jurisdiction over ecclesiastical estates, one may say, but not unfettered discretion.

Further Reading: R. Browning, *Justinian and Theodora* (London and New York: Thames & Hudson, 1987); J. A. S. Evans, *The Age of Justinian: The Circumstances of Imperial Power* (London: Routledge, 1996); H. F. Joolwicz and B. Nicholson, *Historical Introduction to the Study of Roman Law*, 3rd ed. (Cambridge: Cambridge University Press, 1972); J. Moorhead, *Justinian* (London: Longman, 1994); B. Nicholas, *Introduction to Roman Law* (Oxford: Clarendon Press, 1962); P. Stein, *Regulae Iuris: From Juristic Rules to Legal Maxims* (Edinburgh: Edinburgh University Press, 1968).

Codex I.5.18

In providing for our subjects' every advantage, we have made it the chief and first object of our most urgent consideration how their souls may be saved; how all persons may revere the orthodox faith with sincere intention, worshiping and glorifying the Holy and Consubstantial Trinity and acknowledging and venerating the Holy, Glorious, and Ever-Virgin Mary, the Mother of God. And finding many astray in various heresies, we have taken vigorous measures, using devotional exhortations and religious edicts to change their minds for the better, and using laws to correct the wrong decisions which have affected their judgments, preparing them to recognize and revere the faith of Christians, which alone can bring salvation.

This general policy toward heresy has been applied especially in the scandalous case of Manicheism (as instanced in our decrees about the Borboritans). And our legislative provisions in the case of the Samaritans we command to be extended to the Montanists, (or Tascodrugitae) and Ophites, i.e., that they may not summon a public assembly for irreligious and contemptible discourse or practice; and that they may not lawfully be able to transfer property either by bequest or by trust through legal testament or intestate succession, whether to kin or stranger, save that the person so designated as successor or named in writing as heir or appointed trustee shall embrace the orthodox faith. In the case of other heresies (to wit, any doctrine or practice departing from the catholic apostolic church and orthodox faith) we wish the law established by ourself and our father of divine appointment [i.e., the emperor Justin, his uncle] to hold sway, in which appropriate provisions are made not only about these heretics but about Samaritans and pagans: to wit, that those infected shall neither serve in the army nor hold any public rank; nor by adopting the style of a teacher in some supposed branch of education shall they pervert more impressionable minds to their own error and disaffect them toward the true and pure faith of the orthodox; but only those who are of the orthodox faith shall teach and draw public salaries.

And if someone shall simulate acceptance of the true and orthodox faith for the sake of holding a commission or legation or rank or public office, and after gaining promotion by this pretense shall be found to have a wife or children who cling to the condemned heresy without leading them to the knowledge of the truth, we command him to be ejected from his legation, commission, rank, or public office. But if he escape detection, he shall not be empowered to transfer any of his possessions, whether by deed of gift, last will, or any other contract, to a heretical person; but whatever shall be bequeathed to heretical persons or whatever portion of his property shall be conveyed to a heretic, shall be forfeit to the public treasury. For we prohibit absolutely anyone to benefit from such portions of property as may devolve upon a heretic from inheritance, gift, or any other source; but if anyone shall be found to benefit in such a way, the property so gifted or bequeathed shall be forfeit to the public treasury, there being no bar, however, to prevent truly orthodox Christians receiving the property either by gift during the lifetime of the grantor or by bequest after his death. In general we order that those appointed to or occupying ranks, commissions, or legations, or who profit from any form of public credit or support, shall have as heirs only orthodox Christians, whether they be children, kin, or strangers designated for the purpose.

If a man who is a heretic shall be married to an orthodox wife, or *vice versa*, we order that the children shall be in all respects orthodox; and if it happen that some of these same children are orthodox while others for any reason cling to the same or any other heresy, only the orthodox children shall inherit from their father and mother, and those who remain heterodox shall have no claim on the parental estate. And if all the children in the household cling to the same heresy, then they shall be excluded from the couple's inheritance; and if a relative of any degree to the household shall present himself who is of the orthodox faith, he shall be designated heir to the couple's estate. And if no orthodox Christian shall appear, our most sacred treasury shall receive the property, His Magnificence the Count of the Privy Estates for the time being and his Department carefully investigating the provisions made by us and expropriating such property as following upon a transgression of these foregoing shall accord with them. [. . .]

Codex I.4.22

To Menas, Praetorian Prefect. It is our will that no one be committed to prison without a warrant from Their Excellencies, or Their Honors, or Their Worships the Governors of this Blessed City [Constantinople] or of any Province, or from the Public Advocates of cities. With respect to those who have been imprisoned or are in process of imprisonment, the Right Reverend the Bishops in each place shall have authority to inspect the prisoners on one day of each week, either Wednesday or Friday, inquiring carefully into the causes of their detention, ascertaining their status, whether servile or free, and whether they have been imprisoned for debt, on complaint of another kind, or for violent affray. Their Excellencies, Their Honors, and Their Worships the Governors of this Blessed City and the Provinces should make arrangements for prisoners in accord with the specific requirements of our Sacred Constitution on this subject issued to Their Excellencies the Prefects. The Right Reverend the Bishops in office at the time should report any negligence they observe on the part of Their Excellencies, Their Honors, and Their Worships the Governors in office at the time, or on the part of their staffs, in order that appropriate disciplinary steps may be taken against those guilty of negligence. 18th January, Constantinople, Decius consul [529].

Codex III.1.14

To Julian, Praetorian Prefect. The matter we address is neither new nor uncommon, but has been the subject of legislation from of old; neglect of it, however, has significantly harmful consequences for the courts. It is well known that ancient jurists did not regard the judges' vote as valid unless preceded by an oath that they would give judgment wholly in accordance with the truth and the law. Since, then, we have found that we must take a well-trodden road, and since our previously promulgated laws about oaths have given decisive proof of their value to litigants and earned a general approbation, we have reached the point of sanctioning this law, which is to have perpetual validity: that all judges, superior or inferior, both those who have appointment to administrative office either in this royal city or in the world subject to our government, and those who have been granted powers of holding hearings by us, *either* by delegation from superior judges *or* by virtue of powers implied in their jurisdiction, *or* from assuming the resolution of disputes by engagement (i.e., on judicially binding undertaking of the parties), *or* chosen by the parties to make morally binding arbitrations; and, universally, all judges whatsoever who administer Roman law; shall not permit the hearing of a process to begin unless there is a copy of the Holy Scriptures placed before the judicial bench. And this shall be in place not only for the inauguration of the process but throughout the proceedings until they have been terminated by the definitive pronouncement of the judgment. Attending in this way to the Holy Scriptures and consecrated by the presence of God, they will have greater assistance in their decisions from the knowledge that they are as much judged as judging, and that judgment is more terrible for them than for the parties, since the weighing of a litigant's cause is matter for man's supervision, the weighing of a judge's cause is reserved for God's. This judicial oath shall be known to all and shall be added by us as a valuable addition to the laws of Rome and observed by all judges; evasion shall be accompanied by grave danger to those who disregard it.

Counsel who appear in support of either party in a court of any kind, a superior or inferior court or a court of arbiters, whether they are constituted on binding undertaking, or otherwise constituted, or chosen by the parties, shall, after the introduction of the case, the presentation of the allegations and their rebuttal, give an oath on the Gospels that they shall deploy all their skill and render all their service to enter on their clients' behalf what they think to be right and true, omitting no possible effort; but, if they learn that the case that they have undertaken is dishonest or hopeless or composed of lying allegations, that they shall not represent it in court knowingly and in conscious bad faith; and that if in the course of the contest any such thing become known to them, they shall withdraw and dissociate themselves entirely from involvement in such a case. When this occurs, no permission shall be granted to the litigant rejected by his counsel to transfer his case to another representative, lest he should resort to the most unscrupulous advocacy available. If, however, the party has retained more than one counsel, all of whom have taken the oath, and, as the case unfolds, some of these believe that they should represent the client, others decline to do so, then those who decline may retire from the case and those who are willing remain. The outcome of the case will show whether those who withdrew were too cautious or those who proceeded were lacking in discretion. Permission shall not be granted to the litigants to replace the counsel who decline to proceed. March 29th, Lampadius and Orestes consuls [530].

Novella 6

[The following constitutes the preamble to a series of regulations entitled "On the Selection of Bishops, Presbyters, and Male and Female Deacons, and the Penalties for Departing from the Procedure Herein Prescribed."]

The greatest of God's gifts among men, bestowed by that outflowing love of humankind *(philanthrōpia, clementia)*, are priesthood and empire *(basileia, imperium)*, the one in service of the things of God, the other providing government and care for the concerns of men, the two proceeding from one and the same source and together providing the organizing principles of human life. Nothing, then, can so require the emperors' attention as the integrity of priests, not least since it is on the emperors' own behalf that the priests perpetually intercede with God. If the priesthood is above reproach from any quarter and stands before God with confidence, and if the imperial authority organizes the commonwealth committed to it rightly and fittingly, there will be a balanced harmony to ensure whatever may be of value to the human race. We therefore exercise the greatest care over the true doctrines of God and the integrity of priests; and we are confident that if they maintain their integrity, great favors will be granted us by God, so that what we now have we shall keep securely, and what as yet we have not shall be added to us. But good and seemly administration in this sphere demands a foundation fitting and pleasing to God. This, we believe, will be assured if we safeguard the observance of the sacred canons handed down to us by the apostles, whom we do right to celebrate and revere, the eyewitnesses and servants of the word of God; those canons which the holy fathers have preserved and expounded.

Translation: Editors, from *Corpus iuris civilis,* ed. P. Krüger, R. Schöll, and G. Kroll (Berlin: Weidmann, 1877, 1904).

Gregory I
(ca. 540-604)

Of distinguished Roman family and educated for public life, holder of civic office before entering monastic orders and subsequently papal representative at the imperial court of Constantinople, Gregory the Great brought to the papacy in 590 a mixture of Roman civic and Christian ascetical culture. He was heir to the Ciceronian revival of the fourth century which celebrated the *civilitas* of the imperial prince, the freedom of his subjects, and the rule of law. He was heir also to the biblical and patristic association of royalty with spiritual and moral self-discipline, anchored in the conception of the communion of saints, the community of participation in Christ's spiritual perfection, as a "royal priesthood" (1 Pet. 2:9) (Reydellet 1981, 42).

Reputed to be the theoretical founder, along with Cassiodorus and Isidore, of Christian "Romano-Germanic" kingship, Gregory's signal achievement in this regard was to construct on a biblical and Augustinian basis a general account of government, temporal and ecclesiastical, equally applicable to kings and emperors, abbots and bishops. He sketched this account in broad theoretical strokes in his *Magna moralia (Moral Exposition of the Book of Job)*, which originated in talks to his monastic companions at Constantinople. He elaborated it in practical detail with reference to the episcopal office in his *Pastoral Rule (Regula pastoralis)*, issued at the beginning of his reign. To be sure, his uniform conception of rule reflected the interpenetration of secular and ecclesiastical responsibilities in the royal and episcopal offices of his day — as pope, he was involved in imperial diplomacy with the Germanic kingdoms, the defense of Rome against Lombard invasion, and the administration of far-flung estates, as well as episcopal oversight of the church within and beyond the empire. But it also expressed his personal experience of the necessity of contemplative retreat as well as pastoral outgoing in the life of the Christian *rector* — especially the *rector* who governs amidst the turbulence of the last days, conscious of the nearness of God's final judgment.

According to Gregory, following Romans 13:1-7, political power or authority is a divinely appointed office (station) whose function is juridical or disciplinary. The power holder, owing to his superior moral merit, is placed by God above his fellows to correct their faults and suppress their evildoing through judgment and punishment (*Rule* 2.6). His exterior social exaltedness is both required and limited by the end of disciplinary effectiveness: only manifest power and awesome authority can subdue the bestiality of sin, but this only should they subdue — never the fellow human being. All the ruler's nondisciplinary relations to others should be structured by "a communion of equality" in which he is a "helper" alongside of them (*Rule* 2.6; *Moralia* 25.45). Even when outwardly restraining others, the Christian "rector" is inwardly restrained by humility — by that continuous assent to the equality of human beings by nature (*Rule* 2.6; *Moralia* 21.15; 26.46) which issues in continuous self-judgment, self-correction, and regard for the merits and wisdom of others. In seeking the righteousness of his subjects, the earthly ruler gains the heavenly reward of an eternal royal soul, a share in the divine kingship (*Moralia* 26.28); but in seeking to dominate them out of a lust for power or to indulge them out of "false affection," the earthly ruler reaps a heavenly judgment more severe than falls on them (*Rule* 2.6).

Confident that all political authority belongs to God's providential ordering of the world, even in its "old age," Gregory views wicked rulers as God's just punishment of communal sinfulness. He conceives a real, almost symbiotic, affinity between royal tyranny and popular corruption: the reprobate hypocrite on the throne satanically seduces his people to sin, enslaving them inwardly to the Antichrist and outwardly by unjust oppression, while the good ruler degenerates in response to his subjects' perversity, thus rendering to them their divinely ordained deserts. He concludes, therefore, that it pertains to the proper humility of subjects not to condemn irreverently the reprehensible conduct of wayward rulers, but rather to be mindful of their own moral frailty and of the divine wisdom of imposing the "worldly cares" of rule on "hard and laborious hearts," sparing "the tender minds of spiritual men" (*Moralia* 25.34-38). Throughout the medieval Latin West, Gregory was probably the most widely invoked patristic authority for the injunction of popular nonresistance to tyrants.

Further Reading: C. Dagens, *Saint Grégoire le Grand: culture et expérience chrétiennes* (Paris: Études Augustiniennes, 1977); R. A. Markus, *From Augustine to Gregory the Great* (London: Variorum, 1983); R. A. Markus, *Gregory the Great and His World* (Cambridge: Cambridge University Press, 1997); P. Meyvaert, *Gregory, Bede, and Others* (London: Variorum, 1977); J. Richards, *Consul of God* (London and Boston: Routledge and Kegan Paul, 1980); C. Straw, *Gregory the Great: Perfection in Imperfection* (Berkeley: University of California Press, 1988).

From *Pastoral Rule,* Part 2

6. The ruler should be, through humility, a companion of good livers, and, through the zeal of righteousness, rigid against the vices of evil-doers; so that in nothing he prefer himself to the good, and yet, when the fault of the bad requires it, he be at once conscious of the power of his priority; to the end that, while among his subordinates who live well he waives his rank and accounts them as his equals, he may not fear to execute the laws of rectitude towards the perverse. For, as I remember to have said in my book on morals (*Moralia* 21.10), it is clear that nature produced all men equal; but, through variation in the order of their merits, guilt puts some below others. But the very diversity which has accrued from vice is ordered by divine judgment, so that, since all men cannot stand on an equal footing, one should be ruled by another. Hence all who are over others ought to consider in themselves not the authority of their rank, but the equality of their condition, and rejoice not to be over men, but to do them good. For indeed our ancient fathers are said to have been not kings of men, but shepherds of flocks. And when the Lord said to Noah and his children: "Increase and multiply, and replenish the earth" (Gen. 9:1), he at once added, "And let the fear of you and the dread of you be upon all the beasts of the earth." Thus it appears that, whereas it is ordered that the fear and the dread should be upon the beasts of the earth, it is forbidden that it should be upon men. For man is by nature preferred to the brute beasts, but not to other men: and therefore it is said to him that he should be feared by the beasts, but not by men; since to wish to be feared by one's equal is to be proud against nature. And yet it is necessary that rulers should be feared by their subjects, when they find that God is not feared by them; so that those who have no dread of divine judgments may at any rate, through human dread, be afraid to sin. For superiors by no means shew themselves proud in seeking to inspire this fear, in which they seek not their own glory but the righteousness of their subordinates. For in exacting fear of themselves from such as live perversely, they lord it, as it were, not over men, but over beasts, inasmuch as, so far as their subordinates are bestial, they ought also to lie subdued to dread.

But commonly a ruler, from the very fact of his being pre-eminent over others, is puffed up with elation of thought; and, while all things serve his need, while his commands are quickly executed after his desire, while all his subjects extol with praises what he has done well, but have no authority to speak against what he has done amiss, and while they commonly praise even what they ought to have reproved, his mind, seduced by what is offered in abundance from below, is lifted up above itself; and, while outwardly surrounded by unbounded favour, he loses his inward sense of truth; and, forgetful of himself, he scatters himself on the voices of other men, and believes himself to be such as outwardly he hears himself called rather than such as he ought inwardly to have judged himself to be. He looks down on those who are under him, nor does he acknowledge them as in the order of nature his equals; and those whom he has surpassed in the accident of power he believes himself to have transcended also in the merits of his life; he esteems himself wiser than all whom he sees himself to excel in power. For indeed he establishes himself in his own mind on a certain lofty eminence, and, though bound together in the same condition of nature with others, he disdains to regard others from the same level; and so he comes to be even like him of whom it is written: "He beholdeth all high things: he is a king over all the children of pride" (Job 41:34). Nay, aspiring to a singular eminence and despising the social life of the angels, he says: "I will place my seat in the north, and I will be like unto the Most High" (Isa. 14:13). Wherefore through a marvellous judgment he finds a pit of downfall within himself, while outwardly he exalts himself on the summit of power. For he is indeed made like the apostate angel, when, being a man, he disdains to be like men. Thus Saul, after merit of humility, became swollen with pride when in the height of power: for his humility he was preferred, for his pride rejected; as the Lord attests, who says: "When thou wast little in thine own sight, did I not make thee the head of the tribes of Israel?" (1 Sam. 15:17). He had before seen himself little in his own eyes, but when propped up by temporal power, he no longer saw himself little. For preferring himself in comparison with others because he had more power than all, he esteemed himself great above all. Yet in a wonderful way, when he was little with himself, he was great with God; but when he appeared great with himself, he was little with God. Thus commonly, while the mind is inflated from an affluence of subordinates, it becomes corrupted to a flux of pride, the very summit of power being pander to desire. And in truth he orders this power well who knows how both to maintain it and to combat it. He orders it well who knows how through it to tower above delinquencies, and knows how with it to match himself with others in equality. For the human mind commonly is exalted even when supported by no authority: how much more does it lift itself on high when authority lends itself to its support! Nevertheless he dispenses this authority aright, who knows how, with anxious care, both to take of it what is helpful, and also to reject what tempts, and with it to perceive himself to be on a par with others, and yet to put himself above those that sin, in his avenging zeal.

But we shall more fully understand this distinction if we look at the examples given by the first pastor. For Peter, who had received from God the principality of Holy Church, refused to accept from Cornelius, acting well and prostrating himself humbly before him, immoderate veneration, saying: "Stand up; do it not; I myself also am a man" (Acts 10:26). But when he discovers the guilt of Ananias and Sapphira, he soon shews with how great power he had been made eminent above all others (Acts 5:1-11). For by his word he smote life of them whom he detected by the penetration of his spirit; and he recollected himself as the chief agent against sins within the church, though he did not acknowledge this before his brethren who acted well, when honour was eagerly paid him. In one case holiness of conduct merited the communion of equality; in the other avenging zeal brought out to view the just claims of authority. Paul, too, knew that he was not preferred above his brethren who acted well, when he said: "Not for that we have dominion over your faith, but are helpers of your joy" (2 Cor. 1:24). And he straightway added, "For by faith ye stand," as if to explain his declaration by saying, "For this cause we have not dominion over your faith, because by faith ye stand; for we are your equals in that wherein we know you to stand." He knew that he was not preferred above his brethren, when he said: "We became babes in the midst of you" (1 Thess. 2:7); and again, "But ourselves your servants through Christ" (2 Cor. 4:5). But when he found a fault that required to be corrected, straightway he recollected himself as a master, saying, "What will ye? Shall I come unto you with a rod?" (1 Cor. 4:21).

Supreme rule, then, is ordered well, when he who presides lords it over vices, rather than over his brethren. But when superiors correct their delinquent subordinates, it remains for them anxiously to take heed how far, while in right of their authority they smite faults with due discipline, they still, through custody of humility, acknowledge themselves to be on a par with the very brethren who are corrected; although for the most part it is becoming that in our silent thought we even prefer the brethren whom we correct to ourselves. For their vices are through us smitten with the vigour of discipline; but in those which we ourselves commit we are lacerated by not even a word of upbraiding. Wherefore we are by so much the more bounden before the Lord as among men we sin unpunished: but our discipline renders our subordinates by so much the freer from divine judgment, as it leaves not their faults without retribution here. Therefore, in the heart humility should be maintained, and in action discipline. And all the time there is need of sagacious insight, lest, through excessive custody of the virtue of humility, the just claims of government be relaxed, and lest, while any superior lowers himself more than is fit, he be unable to restrain the lives of his subordinates under the bond of discipline. Let rulers, then, maintain outwardly what they undertake for the benefit of others: let them retain inwardly what makes them fearful in their estimate of themselves. But still let even their subjects perceive, by certain signs becomingly displayed, that in themselves they are humble; so as both to see something to be afraid of in their authority, and to acknowledge something to imitate in their humility.

Therefore let those who preside study without intermission, that in proportion as their power is seen to be great externally, it be kept down internally, that it vanquish not their thought; that the heart be not carried away to delight in it, lest the mind become unable to control that which in lust of domination it submits itself to. For, lest the heart of a ruler should be betrayed into elation by delight in personal power, it is rightly said by a certain wise man: "They have made thee a leader: lift not up thyself, but be among them as one of them" (Sir. 32:1). Hence also Peter says: "Not as being lords over God's heritage, but being made examples to the flock" (1 Pet. 5:3). Hence the Truth in person, provoking us to higher virtuous desert, says: "Ye know that the princes of the Gentiles exercise dominion over them, and they that are greater exercise authority upon them. It shall not be so among you, but whosoever will be greater among you, let him be your minister; and whosoever will be chief among you, let him be your servant; even as the Son of Man came not to be ministered to, but to minister" (Matt. 20:28). Hence also he indicates what punishments are in store for the servant who has been elated by his assumption of government, saying: "But and if that evil servant shall say in his heart, My lord delayeth his coming, and shall begin to smite his fellow-servants, and to eat and drink with the drunken, the lord of that servant shall come in a day when he looketh not for him, and in an hour that he is not aware of, and shall cut him asunder, and appoint him his portion with the hypocrites" (Matt. 24:48-51). For he is rightly numbered among the hypocrites, who under pretence of discipline turns the ministry of government to the purpose of domination. And yet sometimes there is more grievous delinquency, if among perverse persons equality is kept up more than discipline. For Eli, because, overcome by false affection, he would not punish his delinquent sons, smote himself along with his sons before the strict judge with a cruel doom (1 Sam. 4:17f.). For on this account it is said to him by the divine voice: "Thou hast honoured thy sons more than Me" (1 Sam. 2:29).

Hence, too, he upbraids the shepherds through the prophet, saying: "That which was broken ye have not bound up, and that which was cast away ye have not brought back" (Ezek. 34:4). For one who had been cast away is brought back when anyone who has fallen into sin is recalled to a state of righteousness by the vigour of pastoral solicitude. For ligature binds a fracture when discipline subdues a sin, lest the wound should bleed mortally for want of being compressed by the severity of constraint. But often a fracture is made worse when it is bound together unwarily, so that the cut is more severely felt from being immoderately constrained by ligaments. Hence it is needful that when a wound of sin in subordinates is repressed by correction, even constraint should moderate itself with great carefulness, to the end that it may so exercise the rights of discipline against delinquents as to retain the bowels of loving-kindness. For care should be taken that a ruler shew himself to his subjects as a mother in loving-kindness, and as a father in discipline. And all the time it should be seen to with anxious circumspection, that neither discipline be rigid nor loving-kindness lax. For, as we have before now said in our book on Morals (*Moralia* 20.5.14), there is much wanting both to discipline and to compassion, if one be had without the other. But there ought to be in rulers towards their subjects both compassion justly considerate, and discipline affectionately severe. For hence it is that, as the Truth teaches (Luke 10:34), by the care of the Samaritan the man is brought half dead into the inn, and both wine and oil are applied to his wounds: the wine to make them smart, the oil to soothe them. For whosoever superintends the healing of wounds must administer in wine the smart of pain, and in oil the softness of loving-kindness, to the end that through wine what is festering may be purged, and through oil what is curable may be soothed. Gentleness, then, is to be mingled with severity; a sort of compound is to be made of both; so that subjects be neither exulcerated by too much asperity, nor relaxed by too great kindness. Which thing, according to the words of Paul (Heb. 9:4), is well signified by that ark of the tabernacle in which, together with the tables, there is a rod and manna; because, if with knowledge of Sacred Scripture in the good ruler's breast there is the rod of constraint, there should be also the manna of sweetness. Hence David says: "Thy rod and thy staff have comforted me" (Ps. 23:4). For with a rod we are smitten, with a staff we are supported. If, then, there is the constraint of the rod for striking, there should be also the comfort of the staff for supporting. Wherefore let there be love, but not enervating; let there be vigour, but not exasperating; let there be zeal, but not immoderately burning; let there be pity, but not sparing more than is expedient; that, while justice and mercy blend themselves together in supreme rule, he who is at the head may both soothe the hearts of his subjects in making them afraid, and yet in soothing them constrain them to reverential awe.

Translation: James Barmby, Nicene and Post-Nicene Fathers, adapted.

From *Moralia*, Book 25

16. [34] In the words, "Who makes a hypocrite reign for the sins of the people" (Job 34:30 Vulgate), he tells us what Jewry really deserves. For Jewry was unwilling to accept the reign of its true king [God], and so, in keeping with its deserts, received a hypocrite as king. As the Truth himself says in the Gospel: "I have come in my Father's name, and you do not receive me; if another comes in his own name, him you will receive" (John 5:43). And as Paul says: "They refused to love the truth and so be saved. Therefore God sends upon them a strong delusion, to make them believe what is false" (2 Thess. 2:10f.).

In the words, "Who makes a hypocrite reign for the sins of the people," there may be intended Antichrist, the captain of all hypocrites. For that arch-deceiver, when he appears, will make a pretense of sanctity to draw people into wrongdoing. For the sins of the people, however, he is permitted to reign; for then it is that those who, from before all ages, have been foreknown as fit subjects for his control, are predestined to fall under his rule; their sins, which follow later, require that God's judgment, which comes earlier, should make them subservient to him. It is no injustice, therefore, on the judge's part that Antichrist comes at that time to rule the ungodly; it is the fault of those who fall subject to him — and that despite the fact that most of them are enslaved to his ascendancy without observing it, simply by virtue of their sins; not noticing in any way the control he exercises over them, they reverence it, we may be sure, by the perversity of their lives. But those who attempt to maintain an unreal appearance with a show of assumed holiness — are they not the members of Antichrist? He himself is the prince of hypocrites, making himself out to be God when he is no more than a condemned man and an evil spirit (2 Thess. 2:4). But it is certainly from his body that there emerge in our time some who veil their misdeeds with a cloak of consecrated dignity, hoping to sustain a profession that their actual practice refuses to support. For since Scripture says that "whoever commits sin is the servant of sin" (John 8:34), the unbridled scope of their willful perversity in this age binds them inexorably to Antichrist's service.

Yet those who suffer under such a ruler cannot put the blame on him, since it is certainly their own fault that they are subject to the dictates of a corrupt ruler. They should blame their own conduct, not their government's wrongdoing. Scripture says: "I will give you kings in my anger" (Hos. 13:11). Why, then, ignore the meaning of their coming to power, i.e., that through the Lord's anger we have brought their regimes upon ourselves? If, then, the wrath of God assigns us rulers to fit our deserts, we may infer from their performance how to weigh our own worth. To be sure, it often happens that the elect are subject to government by the wicked. David had to endure Saul for a long time; but his subsequent sin of adultery (2 Sam. 11:2ff.) makes it plain that his exposure to this oppressive treatment from his lord was not undeserved.

[35] The qualities of rulers, then, are assigned as their subjects deserve, which frequently operates to produce a transformation in those who look promising, as soon as they have acquired power. Saul, again, is blamed in Holy Scripture for a change of heart that went with his change of status. It says: "When you were little in your own eyes, I made you head of the tribes of Israel" (1 Sam. 15:17). So dependent is the policy of rulers upon the character of their subjects, that even the conduct of a fundamentally good shepherd may be corrupted by an evil flock. David himself, a prophet commended by God and acquainted with heavenly mysteries, driven by a

sudden gust of arrogance, sinned in conducting a census of the people (2 Sam. 24:1-17). Though it was David that sinned, the people suffered the punishment. Why was this? It was, I suppose, because the hearts of rulers are disposed according to their people's deserts. The just judge dealt with the sinner's offense by punishing those who had provoked the offense; but since David was not free of blame but responsible for his own pride, he, too, had to accept punishment for what he had done. The blazing wrath which inflicted physical ills upon the people laid their ruler prostrate in brokenhearted grief. What is certain, however, is that the moral worth of rulers and of people are so intimately connected that the people's conduct is often corrupted by blameworthy pastors, the pastors' conduct often affected by the moral worth of the people.

[36] But since rulers have their own judge, subjects must be very careful not to judge the conduct of their rulers precipitately. It was not to no point that the Lord scattered the money of the changers and overturned the seats of those who sold doves (Matt. 21:12) — indicating clearly that he judges the conduct of the people through the agency of their masters (*magistros*), but investigates the performance of the masters in his own person. (Even subjects' sins, however, which masters omit, or are unable to judge, are certainly reserved for his judgment.) Provided that it is in good faith, then, it is a mark of virtue to put up with superiors' faults. One should, nevertheless, if there is any prospect that the offending trait could be emended, make a humble suggestion to that effect. Yet one should take great care, when defending justice, not to go too far and cross the threshold of arrogance; not, in an ill-judged love of right, to forfeit humility, the mistress of right; not to forget that the person of whose action one happens to be critical is in fact one's senior. Subjects will discipline their minds to guard humility and avoid the swelling of pride, if they keep an incessant watch upon their own weaknesses. For we neglect to examine our own strength honestly; and because we believe ourselves stronger than we really are, we judge our superiors severely. The less we know of ourselves, the more our field of vision is occupied by those whom we aspire to criticize.

These wrongs take on specific forms: there are those commonly committed by subjects against their rulers, and those commonly committed by rulers against their subjects. People in positions of leadership imagine all their subordinates to be less intelligent than themselves; while subjects criticize the conduct of their rulers, and think they could do better if they were in control. It often transpires that rulers have the less judicious view of what is to be done, their perspective distorted by their self-importance; while a subject, once raised to a high position, not infrequently does the very thing of which he used to complain; and in acting as he has judged others for acting, he is ashamed of ever having judged them. Superiors must take care that their position does not give them an exalted estimate of their exceptional wisdom, and subjects should beware of finding fault with their rulers' policies.

[37] But even when the conduct of rulers may be justly criticized, it is the duty of subjects to respect them, though they may not admire them. But you should take special care not to aspire to imitate someone simply because you owe him respect, and not to think it beneath you to pay respect to someone whom you would never wish to imitate. One must hold to the narrow path of probity and humility: in criti-

cizing his masters' deeds, the subject's attitude should show no lack of respect for the masters' position. The drunkenness of Noah illustrates this well: his good sons averted their gaze as they approached to cover his exposed private parts (Gen. 9:23). We are said to be "averse" to whatever we disapprove of. What is meant by his sons' averted gaze, as they approached their father to cover his shame with a cloak thrown across their shoulders, is that good subjects, while offended at their superiors' misdeeds, conceal them from others. They avert their eyes and cover them up. Critical of the deeds but respecting the office, they have no desire to see whatever it is that they are hiding.

[38] But some who have made a small beginning in the spiritual life, seeing their rulers engaged with worldly business and material projects, quickly become discontented with the arrangements of providence, and think it pointless to expect senior officials to rule well, since their life is a model of trivial involvement. These people, from failing altogether to moderate their criticism of rulers when improprieties demand it, have gone so far as to criticize the Creator. If they were humble, they would find his provisions perspicuously right, and for the same reason that they find them wrong because they are proud. For since the exercise of governing authority requires attention to worldly responsibilities, Almighty God, in a marvelously caring provision to liberate sensitive and spiritual minds from material cares, often imposes the burden on insensitive and preoccupied hearts. So the one group is better protected from this world, while the others exert themselves enthusiastically over material supplies. To discharge this burden, assumed for their subjects' welfare and not only their own, is a mundane drudgery, hard going indeed!

Translation: Editors, from Corpus Christianorum, Series Latina, vol. 143.

Isidore of Seville

(ca. 560-636)

Isidore, who occupied the metropolitan see of Seville from circa 600, is a figure whose historical importance is disproportionate to his intellectual achievement. A thinker of no great originality or profundity, he was, nevertheless, the vehicle of an authoritative transmission and adaptation of patristic and Roman imperial learning to the western barbarian kingdoms, and over several centuries, to medieval Christendom. Out of his encyclopedic erudition came collections and manuals that traversed theology, philosophy, medicine, law, the classical liberal arts, and diverse sciences. The most widely read and influential of these were his *Etymologies* (*Etymologiae*), an encyclopedia in twenty books commissioned by King Sisebut, and his *Sentences* (*Sententiae*), a manual in Christian doctrine and pastoral practice, both of which became models for later generations.

His episcopal career, like that of his brother, Leander, whom he succeeded in Seville, was devoted to uniting the Visigoth kingdom in one orthodox Catholic Church, with a uniform creed and liturgy in the Roman tradition, and fed by all available patristic theological resources. He labored in concert with a succession of Visigoth kings, enthusiastically endorsing their reconquest of imperial Spain and strengthening that integration of church and kingdom which their predecessor, Reccared, had accomplished, largely through his official conversion of the realm from Arianism to orthodoxy. Not surprisingly, Isidore's contribution to political theory, contained in the *Sentences* and *Etymologies*, has the two foci of kingship and law.

Regarding kingship, his ideas lie in the patristic mainstream mediated by Gregory the Great. "Kings" *(reges)*, he says famously, "are so called from ruling *(regendo)* . . . he who does not correct does not rule. Accordingly, the name of king is retained by acting rightly *(recte agendo)*, but is lost by sinning" (*Etym.* 9.3; cf. *Sent.* 3.48). From Gregory he adopts both the teleological and characterological determinants of kingship: appointed by God to suppress vice and to discipline the wicked, the ruler himself manifests self-discipline, rectitude, and respect for divine and human law, all his virtues being grounded in humility, in his orientation to heavenly rather than earthly glory. Underlying the ministerial character of royal power for Isidore is the equality of all members of Christ's mystical body incorporated through baptism into the priesthood and kingship of their divine head — this equality, rather than, as for Gregory, the equality of created human nature, though Isidore recognizes that as well (Reydellet 1981, 565). Not only baptized individuals but also converted nations or peoples are members of Christ, entrusted by God into the protection of kings for their temporal and spiritual benefit (*Sent.* 3.49.3). Whereas Gregory, the imperial citizen, viewed the Germanic kingdoms as providentially given instruments of evangelization and de facto elements of ecclesiastical order, Isidore viewed them as defining the perfected form of the church in the last historical age of Christ's reign.

Besides bequeathing, with Gregory I, a definitive conceptual shape to Christian kingship, Isidore bequeathed a definitive theory of law. It was broadly Roman, its definitions and concepts approximating formulations contained in the *Digest* and *Institutes* of Justinian's legal corpus, while showing evidence of some independent source(s). Its key elements dominated the medieval discussion in theological and canonist circles through their incorporation in Gratian's *Decretum* (1140), via the influential canonical collections of the preceding century (e.g., of Burchard of Worms, Cardinal Deusdeit, and Ivo of Chartres). As Gratian's work of systematizing and rationalizing the canonical inheritance formed the basis of all future canonist scholarship, Isidore's account exercised disproportionate clout, in view of the theoretical resources contained in Justinian's corpus of Roman civil law. Its key elements include: the twofold definition of law as divine and human; the tripartite classification of law as *ius naturale, ius gentium,* and *ius civile;* the normative characteristics of law; its coercive purpose; and the superiority of canon, statute, and reason over unwritten custom.

The following points were decisive for future legal thought. (1) Isidore's twofold identification of divine with natural law, human with customary law, implies the rationality and permanence of natural law and its superior dignity over variable and transient human law: nature remains the transcendent norm for positive communal laws. Natural law is instinctively adhered to, not, however, by irrational instinct common to men and animals, but by universal human instinct *(commune omnium nationum)* (5.2, 4). (2) Isidore's inclusion among natural law principles of "communis omnium possessio et omnium una libertas," regularly interpreted by canonists to mean communal possession of all things and equal liberty for all men, perpetuated the patristic (Stoic) association of natural law with the prelapsarian Adamic state, devoid of private property, slavery, and political rule. However, other natural law principles such as the restitution of deposits and loans and the repulsion of force by force link it with private possession and the condition of human sinfulness. (3) Under the *ius gentium* Isidore subsumes such institutions of war as slaves and captives, considered by the church fathers and some contemporary Roman jurists to be against nature or less than nature in the fullest sense. Noteworthy in view of future developments is the dual aspect of Isidore's law of nations: that it comprises the common customs of peoples and that these largely pertain to relations among nations, to international order. (4) Isidore's proposal of Moses as the first civil legislator (found elsewhere in Germanic law collections) asserts an important parallel between the biblical record and later Greek and oriental traditions of political foundations.

Further Reading: P. Cazier, *Isidore de Séville et la naissance de l'Espagne Catholique* (Paris: Beauchesne, 1994); J. Fountaine, *Isidore de Séville et la Culture Classique dans l'Espagne Wisigothique,* 2 vols. (Paris: Études Augustiniennes, 1959; suppl., 1983); J. Herrin, *The Formation of Christendom* (Oxford: Blackwell, 1987); M. Reydellet, *La Royauté dans la Littérature Latine de Sidoine Apollinaire à Isidore de Séville* (Paris and Rome: École Française de Rome, 1981).

From *Sentences,* Book 3

47. *Subordinates.* Servitude was imposed upon the human race by divine decree as a punishment for the sin of the first man: those whom God sees to be unfit for freedom are appointed to servitude — a more merciful provision for them. Though Original Sin has been canceled for all believers through the grace of baptism, nevertheless God has decided in his equity upon men's station in life, making some slaves, others masters, so that the masters' power may restrict opportunities for the slaves to do wrong. For if there were no deterrent, who would be able to prevent another from doing wrong? And that is why nations have princes and appoint kings: to restrain their peoples from wrong by inspiring fear, and to subject them to laws that foster upright lives.

As for the reason in any particular case, "there is no respect of persons with God" (Col. 3:25). "He chose what is low and despised in the world, even things that are not, to bring to nothing things which are, so that no human being (i.e., no fleshly power) might boast in the presence of God" (1 Cor. 1:28f.). For the one Lord takes counsel equally for masters and slaves.

Servitude that is beneath itself is better than freedom that is above itself. One may find many who serve God freely under wicked masters. Though in bodily submission to them, they are their superiors in mind.

48. *Superiors.* A just man either strips himself entirely of secular power or, if vested with power of some kind, does not let it bow him down but subordinates it to himself, not puffed up with pride but standing out the more for his humility. This is shown by the apostle's example: granted authority, he did not use it even for fitting purposes, but refused what he could properly have used, adopting the bearing of a child with those whom he led (cf. 1 Thess. 2:6, 7).

He who labors and sweats continually for the honors of the age or the riches of the world, ends up with no place of rest either here or in the world to come. Traveling far from the land of good works, he is encumbered with the baggage of his sins.

The more exalted one's status in terms of secular honor, the more weighed down with a load of cares, the inferior in mind and intellect of those who yield precedence in rank. One of the Fathers has said: "The eminent are more affected by their miseries than delighted by their honors" (Gregory the Great, *Moralia* 33.19).

The more one is engaged with the wider responsibilities of the world, the more easily one falls victim to one's faults. If a quiet mind can scarcely escape sin, how shall one overwhelmed by worldly business?

No badge of power is useful in itself, but only if it is borne well. That means serving the welfare of the subjects who pay it honor in the earthly sphere. Power is good when it is given by God to deter wrong, not to perpetrate it with a high hand. Nothing is worse than power which provides an occasion for crime; nothing is more unlucky than the opportunity for malpractice.

He who exercises a temporal command well in this age, reigns forever without end. From the glory of this age he passes to eternal glory. But those who exercise their rule destructively, when they put aside the glittering robe and resplendent gems, go down naked and wretched into Hell to their torment.

"Kings" *(reges)* are so called from "acting rightly" *(recte agendo);* the title of king, then, is retained by doing right, forfeited by doing wrong. Holy men, we find, are called "kings" in sacred literature because they do right and govern their own senses well, subduing their recalcitrant impulses by rational judgment. The title "king" is well deserved by those who have learned to direct themselves as well as their subjects by ruling well. [. . .]

49. *The Justice of Princes.* He who uses royal power rightly should have a kind of distinction in which the eminence of his position is matched by his humility of mind. David's humility will serve him as an example: not puffed up because of his achievements but abasing himself humbly, he said: "My gait shall be lowly, and my appearance even lowlier before God who chose me" (2 Sam. 6:22 Vulgate).

He who uses royal power rightly makes justice take shape more in deeds than words. He is neither excited by prosperity nor troubled by adversity; he does not rely on his own strength, nor does his heart turn from the Lord. He exercises the power of rule over himself, keeping his mind lowly. Injustice does not attract him; acquisitiveness does not excite him; he can enrich a poor man without defrauding any; and what he might extract from the people with a justified exertion of his power, he will often forgo with a compassionate exercise of his mercy.

God gave precedence to princes for the government of peoples, that those who rule and those who are ruled should both alike be subject to birth and death. Princely rule, then, should benefit, not harm, the nations; it is not to dominate and oppress, but to condescend and be concerned. Then the badge of power will be a mark of service, and the gift of God will be employed to protect the members of Christ. For members of Christ they are, these Christian nations; and when they are well ruled by a power which they accept, a good return is made to God for his generosity.

It is easier for a good king to correct a mistake than to abandon a just course; which is how we know that the one is a lapse, the other an intention. He should have a fixed intention never to depart from the truth but, should he happen to stumble by a momentary lapse, to rise up again directly. [. . .]

51. *Princes are bound by laws.* It is right that a prince should comply with his own laws. Let him maintain that his laws should be kept by everyone when he reveres them himself.

Princes are bound by their own laws, and may not disallow in their own case laws which they uphold for their subjects. Justly does their voice command authority when they grant no license to themselves which they refuse to their people.

Secular powers are subject to the discipline of religion. Though invested with the highest sovereignty, they are bound by the chains of faith, to proclaim the Christian faith by their laws and to protect its proclamation by good conduct.

Secular princes often hold the highest position of power within the church, that they may use that power to reinforce church discipline. There would, however, be no need for any exercise of power within the church, were it not that the power may command with the terror of discipline what the priest is unable to accomplish by spoken instruction.

Often the heavenly kingdom profits through the earthly. Members of the church who flout the church's faith and discipline are kept in order by the severity of princes. And that discipline which the church is too humble to exert, is imposed upon the necks of the proud by princely power, ensuring by virtue of power that it has the respect it deserves.

Secular princes should know that they owe God a reckoning for the church, which they have as a charge from Christ. For he who entrusted the church to their power will demand a reckoning, whether its peace and its discipline have been enhanced by Christian princes or destroyed.

52. *Judges.* It is a failure on the princes' part when corrupt judges are appointed in defiance of God's will in Christian nations. As it is the people's fault when the princes are bad, so it is the prince's responsibility when the judges are unjust.

A good judge is incapable of hurting citizens and should be of service to them all. To some he shows the severe aspect of justice, to others the kindly. Impartiality in court depends on there being not a flicker of personal interest to undermine justice, no ambition to take from someone else something that he would like himself.

Good judges administer justice with no aim other than eternal salvation, and they do not grant it in return for payments. By seeking no temporal gain from just judgment, they enrich themselves with an eternal reward.

One who judges rightly holds the scales in his hand, with justice and mercy in the two pans. Justice is for the verdict on the crime; mercy for the sentence on the criminal. It is a nice balance between what to put right, what to overlook, between equity and pity.

He who keeps God's judgments before his eyes looks to his every undertaking with fear and trembling, lest he wander from the path of justice and fall, receiving greater condemnation where he fails of justice.

Neither a stupid nor a dishonest man should be appointed judge. The stupid man is ignorant of justice; the dishonest man distorts with avarice even the truth he knows.

The poor are more hurt by corrupt judges than by bloodthirsty enemies. No raider is as greedy for foreigners' goods than an unjust judge for his own people's. . . .

54. *Payments.* One who judges rightly and then expects a reward for it, cheats God, for he sells justice, which ought to be dispensed free of charge, for a price.

To give just judgment for material gain is to make bad use of a good thing. What draws you to the truth is not the defense of justice but the hope of a return. Take away the monetary expectation and you quickly pull back from defending justice.

Payments compromise the truth. So the just man is said to "shake every payment from his hands . . . and to dwell on the heights" (Isa. 33:15f.).

The rich man quickly corrupts the judge with payments. The poor man, having nothing to offer, is not only slighted of a hearing but ill-treated even in defiance of a true verdict.

Justice is quickly violated by gold, and a defendant troubles little about his guilt when he thinks that money can buy the verdict. For love of money has a stronger hold than equity of judgment on the mind of an assessor.

There are three types of payment for which men in their vanity resist justice: friendship, admiration, and material payment. But material payment corrupts the soul more easily than goodwill or appreciation.

There are four things that pervert the judgment of men: fear, cupidity, hatred, and love. Fear, when afraid of some power we dare not tell the truth. Cupidity, when some payment in return corrupts us. Hatred, when we devise means to oppose someone. Love, when we engage for friend or family. By these four equity is often violated and innocence harmed. [. . .]

56. *Litigants.* Those who prosecute cases in the courts should give up their secular interests for the sake of neighbor-love; or if they pursue them, they should do so only within the limits of charity. But since it is so rare that charity survives between warring parties, they should put their legal action second to the survival of love.

The ancients used to call legal rhetoric "dogs' eloquence," since, to say nothing of the claims they pursue, litigants battling over a case tear each other apart like dogs, and do themselves nothing but harm by their legal struggle.

Translation: Editors, from *PL,* vol. 83.

From *Etymologies,* Book 5

1. *Lawgivers.* Moses of the Hebrew race was the first to publish divine laws in sacred writings. King Phoroneus was the first to give laws and judgments to the Greeks; Mercury Trismegistus was the first to give laws to the Egyptians. Solon was the first legislator among the Athenians. Lycurgus was the first to give the Lacedaemonians statutes on the authority of Apollo. Numa Pompilius, the successor of Romulus as king, was the first to publish laws for the Romans. Then, when the people could not tolerate the antisocial magistracies, it set up Decemvirs to transcribe the laws, and these translated laws from the books of Solon into Latin and published them in the Twelve Tables. The Decemvirs were: Appius Claudius, Genucius, Veterius, Iulius,

Manlius, Sulpicius, Sextius, Curatius, Romilius, Postumius. These were chosen as Decemvirs for the writing of the laws. Pompey as consul was the first to resolve upon having the laws edited in books, but he did not persist with the idea for fear of opposition. Then Caesar began the work, but was assassinated before he could complete it. One by one the ancient laws have fallen out of use through obsolescence and neglect, laws which it is necessary to know, even if there is now no use for them. New laws began with Constantine Caesar and his successors, but they were varied and in no particular order. Later the Emperor Theodosius II organized a codex, like the Gregorian and Hermogenian codices, of constitutions dating from the time of Constantine, each arranged under the name of the Emperor who promulgated it. He gave it his name, the "Theodosian Code."

2. *Divine and Human Laws.* All laws are either divine or human. Divine laws are established by nature, human by custom. Human laws, then, are not consistent, since different races acknowledge different laws. *Fas* is the name we give to divine law, *ius* (Right) to human. To go across another person's property is *fas* but not *ius*.

3. *The difference between Right, law, and morality.* Right is the general term, law is a species of Right. Right *(ius)* is so called because it is just *(iustum)*. The whole sphere of Right is constituted by law and morality *(mores)*. A law is a written constitution. A moral practice *(mos)* is a custom proved by long survival, or an unwritten law. The word "law" comes from *legere,* to read, because law is written. A moral practice is a long-established custom, supported always by appeal to morality. A custom is a kind of Right based on morality, which is taken for law where no law exists. It makes no difference whether something is written down or based on reason, since law is supported by reason, too. If, then, law is based on reason, "law" may be considered as everything that is based on reason, provided it is compatible with religion, appropriate to discipline, beneficial for welfare. The term *consuetudo* (custom) arises from *communis usus* (common use).

4. *Natural Right.* Right is either Natural, Civil, or International. Natural Right is common to all nations, and consists of what is universally held by natural instinct, not by constitution, *e.g.,* the mating of male and female, the succession and education of children, universal common possession, universal liberty, the right to acquire by hunting whatever may be caught in the sky, on land, and at sea. Again: the restoration of a deposit or of money lent; the offering of forcible resistance to violence. All this (and anything like it) is never unjust, but is held to be natural and equable.

5. *Civil Right.* Civil Right is what each people or civil community has established for itself in matters human and divine.

6. *The Right of Nations.* The Right of Nations *(ius gentium)* is: the occupation of sites, the construction of buildings, armament, war, captivity, enslavement, the right of return to one's home, peace treaties, truces, the sacrosanct inviolability of ambassadors, the prohibition of mixed-race marriages. It is called the Right of Nations since all nations, more or less, observe it.

7. *Military Right.* Military Right is: the formal procedure for declaring war, the binding forms for making a truce, the signals accompanying the beginning of an armed expedition or contest; the cancellation of a signal given; the discipline for military offense, *e.g.,* the desertion of one's post; military stipends, the grades of mil-

itary rank, military rewards and honors, such as the conferral of the chaplet or necklace; the determination of booty, and its just distribution in relation to rank and service; the prince's portion.

8. *Public Right.* Public Right governs sacred and priestly offices and magistracies. [. . .]

10. *Law.* A law is a popular constitution in which the elders, together with the commons, have sanctioned something. [. . .]

13. *Constitution or Edict.* A constitution or edict is something that a king or emperor has constituted or published.

19. *The power of law.* All law either permits something — *e.g.,* a strong man may seek the prize — or forbids something — *e.g.,* no one may seek to marry a holy virgin — or punishes something — *e.g.,* he who kills another must pay with his head. For human life is regulated by reward and punishment.

20. *The purposes of law.* Laws are made to restrain the audacity of men by fear, to preserve innocence safe among dishonest men, and by fear of punishment to restrain the freedom of impious men to do harm.

21. *The proper character of law.* A law will be honest; just; practicable; natural; in keeping with the custom of the country; appropriate to the time and place; necessary; useful; well-publicized, so that it contains nothing obscure which may entrap someone; it will serve no private interest but the common welfare of the citizens.

Translation: Editors, from Oxford Classical Text, ed. W. M. Lindsay (1911).

John of Damascus
(ca. 670–ca. 750)

The iconoclastic controversy, which broke out with the edicts of Emperor Leo III the Isaurian, ordering the destruction of sacred images and icons (726), was to last a century or more, and to be tossed between major councils: a council at Hieria in 754 was repudiated by the Second Council of Nicaea (787), which failed, however, to curb repeated iconoclastic initiatives by ninth-century emperors. The West, too, became involved: Nicaea II was strongly supported by the papacy, but viewed with suspicion by churches under Frankish influence. The deeper sources of iconoclasm are much debated: Manicheism and Monophysitism have been blamed, as well as Islam. Leo's edict, however, was explained in terms of the need to convert Jews and Muslims, and was contemporary with Muslim attempts to eradicate Christian icons. It was met with widespread resistance, led by the patriarch of Constantinople, Germanus, who was deposed in 730, and followed by an extensive persecution.

John of Damascus's three speeches, written in the immediate wake of Leo's edicts, were the work which brought their author, the most creative and influential theologian of a century not overrich in such, to prominence. His native city of Damascus lay under the rule of a Muslim caliph, in whose service John gained a career as an administrator. In middle life he left to become a monk and priest under the patriarch of Jerusalem, the occasion of his theological flowering. His work had a doctrinal and synthetic bent, and his *Fount of Knowledge*, treating of philosophy, heresies, and the orthodox faith, may be reckoned among the first attempts at a systematic theology.

John's invective against an emperor's ambitions to interfere in questions of Christian doctrine and practice immediately invites comparison with Gelasius's resistance to Anastasius (see pp. 177-79 above). In this case, too, the emperor was regarded as a heretic, and his opponent situated outside the reach of the empire. Each takes his stand upon a necessary duality of role between the clerical and the political authorities. Yet once those points are granted, the two approach their task very differently. John's case is not juridical. He has no idea of an equal and opposite sovereign power, vested in a supreme bishop, such as we find Gelasius advancing. It is an argument that turns substantially on the theological claim that the incarnation has hallowed and sanctified matter, making material representations an appropriate trophy of the victory of Christ, and so reversing the Old Testament prohibition of images, which was fit for a humanity too ashamed to show its face. Formally, his argument rests on the authority of tradition. Here he turns to good effect the charge quite reasonably brought against his opponents by the emperor, that they denied him the right to theological initiatives that had traditionally been allowed the emperor in the East. But the question is, which is the authentic tradition of the church? Boldly John asserts a continuity of practice, more extensive than the scriptural witness, which must be supposed to spring from the apostles. This it is that has shaped the laws of the church over the generations, and on which priests and bishops rely for their authority.

Further Reading: A. Bryer and J. Herrin, *Iconoclasm* (Birmingham: Centre for Byzantine Studies, 1977); J. M. Hussey, *The Orthodox Church in the Byzantine Empire* (Oxford: Oxford University Press, 1986); J. Nasrallah, *Saint Jean de Damas* (Harissa, Lebanon: Saint Paul, 1950).

From *Second Speech against Those Who Reject Images*

11. [. . .] In the Old Testament Israel had no temples dedicated to saints, no feasts commemorating men. That is because human nature was still under a curse, and death was the judgment under which it labored. A dead body was reckoned a defilement, and to defile anyone who touched it. But since the divinity was mingled with our nature like life-giving and healing medicine, our nature was clothed in glory and transformed into immortality. So now we celebrate the death of saints, dedicate temples to them, and paint their images. Everyone should understand that to destroy an image made, with zeal and devotion, to celebrate Christ or his holy mother the Theotokos or any of the saints, and to celebrate the defeat and disgrace of the devil and his angels; to refuse it reverence, honor, and devotion (but as a precious icon, not as God), is to be an enemy of Christ and the holy Theotokos and the saints, and an emissary of the devil and his angels. It is a practical expression of resentment that God and his saints enjoy honor and praise, while the devil incurs contempt. The icon is a kind of victory procession, a publication or memorial of the victory of heroes and champions, as well as of the humiliation of the defeated and banished demons.

    12. Kings have no right to make laws for the church. As the apostle says, "God has appointed in the church first apostles, second prophets, third pastors and teachers" (1 Cor. 12:28) "for the equipment" of the church (Eph. 4:12). No mention of kings! Again: "Obey your leaders and submit to them, for they are keeping watch over your souls and will give an account" (Heb. 13:17). Again: "Remember your

leaders, those who spoke the word of God to you; consider the outcome of their way of life and imitate their faith" (Heb. 13:7). It was not kings that spoke the word of God to us, but apostles and prophets, pastors and teachers. When God instructed David to build his house, he added: "You shall not build a house for me, for you are a man of blood" (1 Chron. 22:8). And the Apostle Paul declares: "Pay to all what is due to them, honor to whom honor is due, respect to whom respect is due, tax to whom tax is due, revenue to whom revenue is due" (Rom. 13:7).

Kings have responsibility for political welfare, pastors and teachers for the state of the church. And this, brothers, is a raid. Saul tore the cloak of Samuel, and what became of him? God tore the kingdom from him, and gave it to David, a man of self-restraint. Jezebel pursued Elijah, and the swine and dogs licked up her blood, and the prostitutes washed in it (1 Kings 22:38 [misremembered]). Herod destroyed John, and was eaten by worms and perished. Now the blessed Germanus, a shining example in life and word, is beaten up and exiled, together with many other bishops and fathers, whose names are unknown to us. Is not this an act of brigands?

When the scribes and Pharisees came to the Lord to try him, to entrap him in his words, and asked, "Is it lawful to give tax to Caesar?" he answered them, "Show me a coin"; and when they did so, he said, "Whose image is this?" and when they answered "Caesar's," he said, "Give to Caesar what is Caesar's, and to God what is God's" (Matt. 22:15-21). We defer to you, O king, in the affairs of life, in tax and revenue and privileges, and in all of our affairs that are your responsibility. In the management of the church we have pastors who have spoken the word of God to us, and have given form to the law of the church. We do not move the ancient landmarks that our ancestors set up (Prov. 22:28) but retain the traditions as we have received them. If even in small ways we begin to pull down the building of the church, by degrees the whole will be demolished. [. . .]

15. We depict Christ as king and Lord, without stripping him of his array. The Lord's array is his saints. Let the earthly king strip himself of his own array before he strips his own king and lord. Let him lay aside his purple robe and his diadem, and robe himself in the regard of those who have struggled against tyranny and made themselves kings over their passions. For if they are "heirs of God and fellow heirs of Christ" (Rom. 8:17), and if they shall share in the glory and kingdom of God, why should the friends of Christ not have a share in earthly glory? "I do not call you servants," says God, "you are my friends" (John 15:14f.). Shall we deny them the honor which the church has conferred on them? What a rash undertaking! What an overweening purpose, opposing God and resisting his commands! If you do not reverence the image, do not pretend to reverence the Son of God, the living image and unchanging imprint of the invisible God! The temple which Solomon built was consecrated by the blood of irrational beasts and decorated with images of irrational things — lions, oxen, palms, and pomegranates. But the church has been consecrated by the blood of Christ and of his saints, and it is decorated by the image of Christ and of his saints. Either abolish the worship of the image in its entirety, or leave it alone. "And do not move the ancient boundaries which your fathers set" — and I do not mean only those from before Christ's incarnation, but those from after his earthly life. For God speaks critically of the traditions of the Old Testament, in saying, "I gave them statutes that were not good" (Ezek. 20:25), statutes, that is, designed for their hardness of heart. With the change of priestly order, a change in the law was required, too.

16. The "eyewitnesses and servants of the word" (Luke 1:2) transmitted the law of the church not in writing only, but by unwritten traditions. How do we know the location of the holy place of Calvary, and of the sepulchre of resurrection? There was no written record, but sons learned it from their fathers. Scripture tells us that the crucifixion took place on Calvary and that the Lord was buried in the tomb which Joseph had hewn in the rock; but that these are the places which we now treat as holy is known by unwritten tradition; and there are many other similar cases. From where do we derive the practice of triple baptism (i.e., with three immersions)? Or of turning to the east to pray? Or of reverencing the cross? From unwritten tradition again. The divine apostle, Paul says: "Stand firm, then, brethren, and hold fast to the traditions that you were taught by us, either by word of mouth or by letter" (2 Thess. 2:15). Since, then, there are many unwritten traditions in the church that are maintained to this day, why do you disparage images? The Manicheans wrote a "Gospel according to Thomas." You might as well write the "Gospel according to Leo"! I do not accept that an emperor should tyrannously take over the priestly role. The emperor has no power to bind and loose.

Translation: Editors, from *PG*, vol. 94.

Jonas of Orléans

(ca. 780-842/43)

A leading Frankish bishop from 818, Jonas of Orléans made a key contribution to the episcopal formulation of Carolingian political ecclesiology, chiefly through his intellectual leadership of the Synod of Paris of 829 and his subsequent composition for King Pepin of Aquitaine of a tract on kingship (831 or 834), incorporating synodal material. *The Institution of the King (De institutione regia)* deftly fashions Pope Gelasius's dualism of priestly authority and regal power into a framework for incorporating the civil ruler firmly within the church and subjecting his piety, morality, and public administration of justice to the paternal oversight of the episcopacy. With his contemporaries, Jonas affirms that the monarch receives his kingdom directly from God and not from man, but for specific divinely ordained purposes, the chief of which is to defend the church (4). His detailed list of the duties entailed in governing "the people of God," reproduced from the bishops' synodal address to Louis the Pious, reflects the prophetic injunctions to the Israelite kings, the royal psalms, and other Old Testament kingship literature. The Frankish monarch, though divinely endowed, is less the emperor who, incarnating wisdom, holds all laws in his breast than King David meditating on God's written laws night and day. From God's immediate appointment of the king Jonas draws two conclusions which stand in permanent tension: that all subjects are equally bound to obey the ruler's divinely exalted will (8), and that all natural hereditary and communal claims to the throne are superseded by divine choice (7). While the first conclusion raises the king above all social estates, extricating him from the mesh of feudal and customary obligations, the second reinforces his ecclesial status, his role within the church, opening the royal office to priestly influence.

Further Reading: E. Delaruelle, "Jonas d'Orléans et le moralisme carolingien," *Bulletin de la littérature ecclésiastique* 55 (1955): 129ff., 221ff.; J. Reviron, introduction to *Jonas of Orléans: "De Institutione Regia"* (Paris: J. Vrin, 1930).

From *The Institution of the King*

1. Every believer must know that the universal church is the body of Christ; that its head is Christ; and that within it there are two persons that stand out preeminently, the person of the priest and the person of the king, of which the priest is the superior inasmuch as he will account to God even for kings. Gelasius, the venerable pontiff of the Roman church, wrote to the emperor Anastasius, "There are two principles, august emperor, by which this world is ruled: the consecrated authority of priests and the royal power. Of these the priests have greater responsibility, in that they will have to give account before God's judgment seat for those who have been kings of men" [cf. p. 179 above]. Fulgentius, in *The Truth about Predestination and Grace* (2.22), wrote, "As regards the life of this age, no one is more powerful in the church than the bishop, no one more eminent in the Christian world than the emperor." Since, then, the priesthood is a ministry of such authority — such critical authority, indeed, that it will give account to God for the king, it is very necessary that we should have a perpetual concern for your salvation, admonishing you vigilantly not to stray from his will (God forbid!) in the service he has entrusted to you. And should you (God forbid!) deviate in any measure from it, we must admonish you with a humble pastoral devotion, taking constructive measures to hold a timely consultation in the interest of your welfare, so as not to be condemned for our uncommunicative silence, but to earn Christ's reward for our solicitous attention and constructive advice. [. . .]

3. [Jonas here introduces an extended quotation from a work called *On the Twelve Abuses of the Age*, which he believes to come from the pen of St. Cyprian of Carthage, though in fact it is an Irish composition of the seventh century. It was an influential piece, which we take the occasion of including.] "The ninth stage of abuse is a wicked king. For a king should not be wicked, but a corrector of the wicked, and the dignity of the title in itself should keep him such. For the title 'king' *(rex)* implies the idea that he has the responsibility of correction *(rectoris)* of all his subjects. But how shall he be able to correct others, if he does not correct the wickedness of his own behavior? For the justice of a king exalts his throne, and the government of peoples is secured by truth. But 'the justice of a king' means: to oppress no one unjustly with his power; to judge between a man and his neighbor without regard for persons; to be the defender of strangers, orphans, and widows; to repress crimes against property and to punish crimes against chastity; to deny promotion to the wicked; to provide no support for pornographers and stage players; to weed out the irreligious from the land; not to permit parricides and perjurers to live; to defend the churches, to support the poor with charitable gifts; to set the righteous over the affairs of the kingdom; to have old, wise, and sober counselors; to give no ear to the superstitions of magicians, soothsayers, and diviners; to defend the nation bravely and justly against its enemies; to live in all respects in God; not to be elated by times of prosperity, but to bear every adversity with patience; to hold the catholic faith in God; to prevent his sons adopting irreligious ways; to insist on prayers at set hours of the day; not to dine earlier than the appropriate hour. 'Woe betide the land when a child becomes its king, and its princes begin feasting in the morning' (Eccles. 10:16). These are the things that make a kingdom prosper now, and bring a king to a better

kingdom in heaven. But whoever does not manage his kingdom by this law incurs a multitude of perils to the realm. This is why the peace of nations is often disturbed, and from within the realm, too, difficulties arise: the fruits of the earth are diminished and the labor of the peoples comes to nothing. Many catastrophes afflict the prosperity of the realm: deaths of loved ones and children bring sorrow; invasions of enemies devastate provinces on every side; wild beasts ravage stables and herds; spring and winter storms prevent the harvest of the land and the employment of the sea; and sometimes bolts of lightning scorch the standing corn, the blossom on the trees, and the foliage on the vine. Above all a king's injustice not only darkens the countenance of the present reign, but casts a shadow over sons and descendants whose tenure of the realm is threatened. For Solomon's sin the Lord took the kingdom of the house of Israel from the hands of his sons, and for King David's merit he left a lamp from his seed forever in Jerusalem. See, it is clear to those who look how much difference the justice of the king effects in this world: it is the peace of peoples, the security of the nation, the protection of the common folk, the defense of families, the remedy of weaknesses, the joy of men, the temperateness of the climate, the calmness of the sea, the fruitfulness of the earth, the consolation of the poor, the heredity of sons, and for himself the hope of future blessedness. Yet he should know that as he is placed first among men on the throne, so in the punishment too he will have first place, if he has not wrought justice. While he rides above all sinners in the present life, he will sink beneath them in that future punishment."

4. The specific service of royalty is to govern the people of God and to rule it with equity and justice, devising policies for its peace and concord. The king himself should be before all else the defender of the churches and of the servants of God. It is the duty of kings, too, to provide conscientiously for the welfare of the priests and the continuance of their ministry. Under the protection of their arms the church of Christ should be secure, and the vulnerability of widows, orphans, and other destitute persons, of all, indeed, who are in any kind of want, should find protection. It is his authority and initiative which ensures, as far as possible, that there shall be no injustice perpetrated in the first place; then, if it does occur, that it shall certainly not be allowed to continue; that no person shall be left with any hope of criminal gain or confidence in wrongful undertakings; everyone shall understand that any wrong they have done that shall come to his notice will not pass without punishment or reprisal, but that the punishment will be justly proportioned to the nature of the deed. The reason he has been placed on the throne of the realm for the proper conduct of justice, is that he may personally take responsibility for ensuring that no court shall lapse from truth and equity. He should realize that the cause for which he discharges his responsibilities is not man's cause but God's. In the dread day of judgment he will give account of how he has served it. It is appropriate, then, that one who sits in judgment on judges should hear the suit of the poor himself, and should carefully investigate whether those whom he has appointed to public functions in his place unjustly or negligently permit practices which oppress the poor. [. . .]

7. A king should not suppose he has received the realm from his ancestors, but truly and humbly believe that God has given it him. "From me come counsel and equity," he says; "understanding and power are mine. Through me kings hold sway,

and governors enact just laws. Through me princes wield authority, and rulers decree justice" (Prov. 8:14-16). The prophet Daniel (4:17) declares that God, and not men, confers earthly kingdom, saying: "The issue has been determined by the watchers and the sentence pronounced by the holy ones. Thereby the living will know that the Most High is sovereign in the kingdom of men; he gives the kingdom to whom he wills, and may appoint over it the lowliest of mankind." Again, the same prophet says to Belshazzar, speaking of Nebuchadrezzar: "until he came to acknowledge that the Most High God is sovereign over the realm of men and appoints over it whom he will" (5:21). And Jeremiah (27:4f.): "These are the words of the Lord of Hosts the God of Israel: Say to your masters: It was I who by my great power and outstretched arm made the earth, along with mankind and the animals all over the earth, and I give it to whom I see fit." Those who imagine that they have inherited their earthly kingdoms rather than received them as God's gift, earn the repudiation which we find in prophecy: "They became kings, but not on my authority; they became princes, but without my knowledge" (Hos. 8:4). When God is said "not to know" something, it means, clearly enough, that he will have nothing to do with it.

Someone who holds sway over other mortals for a time, then, should realize that God, not men, has given him the kingdom. There are those who rule by divine gift, and others who rule by divine permission. Those whose reign is religious, just, and merciful, evidently rule "by God." Where it is otherwise, they rule not by his gift but solely by his permission. And of these the Lord says in the prophecy, "I shall give you a king in my anger" (Hos. 13:11); and Job (34:30) says: "He makes a hypocrite king for the sins of the people." As Isidore puts it: "By God's wrath the peoples receive the ruler their sins have deserved." It is clear, then, that no human cunning, no human pleading, no human might confers a kingdom on earth, but virtue — or rather, the hidden decision of divine providence; and for that reason anyone to whom God grants a kingdom should arrange for its management and government in keeping with his will, inasmuch as he hopes to reign in perpetuity together with him from whom he received it; for it does him no good to be head of a kingdom on earth if he ends up (God forbid!) in eternal banishment. [. . .]

11. There is something else that must astonish us about Christendom (*Christiana religio*). Human laws, which for the most part merely deter the potential offender rather than instilling Christ's precepts, have more force, to all appearance, than divine, though obedience to the former can only avert a temporal punishment, obedience to the latter an eternal one. When some sovereign of royal or imperial dignity who holds temporal power over other mortals, issues an edict for his subjects to heed and to carry out dutifully and perceptively, which of his subjects would not pay attention and take trouble to conform to his requirements? Who would risk the effrontery of a violation? Who would venture to incur the peril of ignoring them? Which is why it is continually astonishing that men are so blinded as to put their Creator's law so blatantly in second place. Men make laws, and they are observed by their subjects. God, the creator of all, who rules from eternity, and who increases not at all as we grow stronger and diminishes not at all as we grow weaker, in whose hand we are like clay in the hand of a potter, has given us a law to secure the welfare of our souls. And we take no trouble to listen; or if we listen with the outward ear,

with the ear of the heart we are inattentive; or if we attend with the ear of the heart, we do not act on what we hear. What excuse will Christians have to offer their Lord, for accepting the regime of this world's laws for fear of this world's sanctions, yet refusing to bow their necks to the yoke of Christ, which is easy and light and leads to eternal life? The Lord says, "Come to me all who are weary and whose load is heavy, and I will give you rest. Take my yoke upon you, and learn from me, for I am gentle and humble-hearted, and you will find rest for your souls. For my yoke is easy, my load is light" (Matt. 11:28-30). Yet we refuse to come to him — to *him* — when he calls, to learn lowliness and gentleness from him, and to take his yoke upon us! What is this, if not to default on our own salvation — a thing too wretched and dreadful to describe! It is clear to see, at any rate, that in very many cases in modern times the Christian profession is taken nothing like so seriously and earnestly as it was by the early Christians.

Translation: Editors, from *Les idées politico-réligieuses d'un éveque du ix siècle: Jonas d'Orléans et son "De institutione regia"* (Paris, 1930).

Sedulius Scottus

(fl. 840-860)

An émigré Irish scholar, probably driven from his homeland by the Viking invasions, Sedulius Scottus established himself as the foremost civic poet of the Frankish city of Liège in the second half of the ninth century. His diverse writings demonstrate his skill as a Latin grammarian with a passable knowledge of Greek and an unusually wide-ranging familiarity with classical Latin texts. *On Christian Rulers (De rectoribus Christianis)*, written between 855 and 859 to instruct Lothar II, Emperor Lothar I's son and king of Lotharingia, in his royal duties, is an early and influential example of the "mirror of princes" genre that gained popularity in the Carolingian period. Composed "in Boethian style" (Doyle 1983, 18), each section of prose is recapitulated in verse.

With Jonas, Sedulius stresses the priority of orthodox piety in the king's spiritual equipment and promotion of the church's welfare in his practical responsibilities. At the same time he is clear that the ruler ministers by *governing:* divinely appointed as "God's vicar in the government of his church," he exercises "authority" and "direction" over "both orders" (clerical and lay), determining "what is just for every person," ensuring proper discipline, providing suitable clergy, and convening annual "synodal assemblies" to discuss "ecclesiastical laws and affairs" (19). While always humbly and prudently seeking episcopal counsel, lest he rashly "[prefer] his own judgments to better ones" (especially on dogmatic matters), the ruler alone, having "perspicaciously attend[ed] to what is just and lawful according to the canonical decrees," confers on "those which are true and upright the consent and support of authority" (11). He cultivates obedience to the "beneficial admonitions and reproofs of priests" (12), but as one whose royal soul is imbued with divine wisdom and understanding (4), and who cherishes the "divine counsels" contained in Holy Scriptures over merely human ones (6).

Further Reading: R. Düchting, *Sedulius Scottus* (Munich: Wilhelm Fink Verlag, 1968); K. Hughes, *The Church in Early Irish Society* (Ithaca, N.Y.: Cornell University Press,

1966); F. J. E. Raby, *A History of Christian Latin Poetry* (London: Clarendon Press, 1927); H. Waddell, *The Wandering Scholars* (Boston: Houghton Mifflin, 1927).

From *On Christian Rulers*

1. As soon as a Christian ruler has received the royal sceptre and the government of the kingdom, it is fitting that he first return acts of thanksgiving and suitable honors to God and to Holy Church. In fact, from the very beginning the state is most gloriously consecrated when royal solicitude and sacred devotion are aroused with both holy fear and love of the Heavenly King and when care is taken for the glorious benefit of the Church by prudent counsel, so that he whom royal purple and other symbols of royal authority adorn externally will also be adorned internally by praiseworthy vows to God and to His Holy Church. For indeed, a king is notably raised to the summit of temporal rule when he devotes himself with pious zeal to the Almighty King's glory and honor. And so, let the pious ruler fervently strive to obey the will and holy commands of the Supreme Master of all things by whose divine will and ordination he does not doubt himself to have risen to the summit of authority. This is affirmed by the apostle who says: "There is no authority unless it be from God; moreover, all the authorities which exist have been established by God" (Rom. 13:1). Therefore, so much as an upright ruler acknowledges that he has been called by God, to the same degree he is vigilant with dutiful care that he regularly determines and examines all things before God and men according to the scales of justice. For, what are the rulers of the Christian people unless ministers of the Almighty? Moreover, he is a faithful and proper servant who has done with sincere devotion whatever his lord and master has commanded to him. Accordingly, the most upright and glorious princes rejoice more that they are appointed to be ministers and servants of the Most High than lords or kings of men. For this reason blessed David, an illustrious king and prophet, often called himself the servant of the Lord. Also, renowned Solomon, David's son, calling upon the Almighty, said, among other things: "Consider your servant's prayer and his entreaties, O Lord, my God; hear the hymn and prayer which your servant utters before you this day, so that your eyes both day and night may watch over this temple about which you said: 'There will be my name!'" (1 Kings 8:28-29). The emperor Constantine the Great of celebrated memory, who believed and fulfilled the mystery of the saving cross and the Catholic faith, did not claim credit for himself when by his joyous rule religion vigorously flourished. Rather, he gave thanks that the Almighty God had deigned to make him the useful servant of his will. Lo, that most distinguished emperor rejoiced more to have been a servant of God than to have possessed an earthly empire. Thus Constantine, because he had been the servant of divine will, extended a peaceful reign from the sea of Britain to the lands of the East. And because Constantine had subjected himself to the Almighty, with power and faith he won all the hostile wars which were waged under him. He constructed and enriched Christ's churches with splendid treasures. As a result, divine favor granted him triumphant victories, for, without doubt, the more pious rulers subject themselves humbly to the King of Kings, the more they ascend on high to the summit of glorious distinction. [...]

2. He who has ascended to the summit of royal dignity by the grace of God should remember that he whom divine will has ordained to rule others should first rule himself. *Rex* is from the verb *regere,* to rule. A man may know that he is rightly addressed by the title of king if he does not fail to rule himself with reason [cf. Isidore, *Sententiae* 3.48, p. 207 above]. Hence, let an orthodox king strive with utmost effort so that he who desires to command his subjects well and determines to correct others' errors may not himself commit the evils he strictly reproves in others and may endeavor to practice before all the virtues which he enjoins upon them. Moreover, a just ruler commendably rules himself in six ways: first of all, when he restrains with severity the illicit designs of the will; second, when he considers useful counsels pertaining both to his own benefit and to that of his people; third, when he avoids issuing idle, useless or noxious trifles of inane speech; fourth, when he savors with his mind's palate, more than honey and the honeycomb, both the prudence and words of glorious princes as well as the words of divine Scripture; fifth, when he is fearful of committing any dishonor or a pernicious deed; and sixth, when he notably performs lofty deeds whether praiseworthy or of glorious spirit so that he who shines inwardly before the Lord with a devout will may also shine publicly before the people in word and action.

4. All royal power, which has been divinely established for the benefit of the state, should be embellished not so much with vain powers and earthly might as with wisdom and the veneration of God. For, if the eminence of the king is adorned by religion and wisdom, then, without doubt, the people will be governed by the art of prudent counsel, enemies will be cast down by a merciful Lord and both the provinces and the kingdom will be preserved. Indeed, God intended this to be the nature of man, that he should desire and seek after two things, namely religion and wisdom. Moreover, devout wisdom is the most salutary virtue, the light of pious souls, a heavenly gift and a joy which will last forever. Whoever, therefore, wants to rule gloriously, to govern the people wisely, and to be mighty in counsels should seek wisdom from the Lord who gives abundantly and ungrudgingly to all. And let him strive for such wisdom with zealous effort and love so that this saying: "Blessed the man who finds wisdom, and who abounds in understanding" (Prov. 3:13), as well as other things which are enumerated among the praises of wisdom, may distinguish him. For that blessed ruler truly merits praise who is illumined with the splendor of wisdom which is the source of counsels, the font of sacred religion, the crown of princes and the mother of virtues, and compared to it all the glitter of precious gems is deemed worthless. Wisdom is most prudent in counsels, remarkable in eloquence, magnificent in deeds, strong in adversity, moderate in prosperity, and perspicacious in judgments. It adorns those who love it with heavenly grace and makes them shine like the heavenly firmament, as it is written: "Just men will shine like the stars, and wise men like the heavenly firmament" (Sap. 3:7; Dan. 12:3).

Wisdom exalted Solomon above all the kings of the earth, for he cherished it from his youth and became a lover of its beauty. Hence, as it is written in the Book of Kings, the Lord appeared to Solomon one night and said: "Ask something of me and I will give it to you" (1 Kings 3:5). When Solomon, though just a boy, requested a discerning heart that he might judge the Lord's people and distinguish between good and evil, he received this promise from God: "Since you have asked for the word, and since you have not asked for a long life for yourself or riches or the lives of your enemies but for the wisdom for a discerning judgment, here and now I have done what you asked. I have given you a heart so wise and shrewd that there has never been anyone like you up till now, and after you there will come no one to equal you. I have also granted you what you did not ask for, namely wealth and glory, so that not one of all the kings of former days can compare with you. And I will give you long life, if you follow my ways and keep my laws and commandments, just as your father, David, followed them" (1 Kings 3:10-14). O how ineffable is the bountifulness of divine grace! For, if divine grace is sought with a just heart and a pious intention, it gives more than what is asked. Lo, King Solomon asked for neither gold, nor silver, nor any other earthly treasures but rather for the riches of wisdom; moreover, he who had rightly requested a single gift received double, for he was not only enriched with wisdom, but was exalted by the illustrious glory of kingship. Hence, an excellent example is given to the kings of the earth: if they wish to reign long and prosperously in this world, let them ask with a pious heart for spiritual rather than carnal gifts. It befits a prince worthy of God's love, therefore, to have the will to learn and the desire of heavenly things; thus he truly sets his heart in God's hand and will peacefully rule his kingdom by God's grace throughout a multitude of years.

6. In human affairs no art, as they say, is more difficult than to rule well amidst the stormy tempests of this turbulent world and to govern the state wisely. And this art attains its highest degree of perfection when the state itself has prudent and superlative counselors. Three rules, however, ought to be observed in deliberations. The first is that divine counsels should be preferred over human ones, since it is more important to heed God than men. If anyone, therefore, intends and desires to guide the ship of state successfully as a just ruler, let him not fail to observe the excellent counsels of the Lord which have been set forth in Holy Scriptures. The second rule is that a wise ruler should rely not so much on his own counsel as upon that of his most prudent counselors. Whence, the excellent maxim of the emperor Antoninus in deliberations was always: "It is better that I follow the counsel of so many excellent friends than that so many such friends should follow my will alone" (in *Scriptores Historiae Augustae*, 22:4). Solomon also confirms this, saying "Plans come to naught where there is no counsel; where there are many counselors they succeed" (Prov. 15:22), and "There will be security where there are many counsels" (Prov. 11:14). For a prudent man summons other prudent men into counsel and does nothing without their advice; but a foolish man deliberates by himself and does whatever he hastily desires without the counsel of others. Finally, the third rule in counsels to be observed is that a just ruler should not have deceitful and pernicious counselors. Who, indeed, should trust in the counsels of the wicked? For, just as holes in the midst of fields, and pitfalls in open thoroughfares, and unexpected snares impede the feet of travelers, so do the counsels of the wicked mixed with villainous poisons evilly hinder the just and holy in their paths. And just as good counselors raise the state upwards, so evil ones press it downwards in ruinous calamity. Such wicked counselors, therefore, should be in every way repudiated and detested, since those who scorn God's commandments by living evilly will never be devoted to an earthly prince. Indeed, for whom can those who are evil to themselves be of any benefit?

10. In considering these things it should also be understood, as wise men hold, that there are eight pillars which strongly support the kingdom of a just king. The

first pillar is truth in all royal affairs; the second pillar is patience in every matter; the third, generosity in gifts; the fourth, persuasiveness or affability in speech; the fifth, the correction or suppression of evil men; the sixth, the friendship and exaltation of good men; the seventh, the lightness of tribute imposed upon the people; and the eighth, the equality of justice between the rich and the poor. And so, there are eight pillars which both uphold the kingdom of a just king in this world and guide him to the immutability of eternal glory.

11. Since the summit of royal power is sustained by these eight pillars, it behooves a ruler worthy of God's love to subordinate his personal interests to what will benefit the church so that in so far as he is mindful of God's blessings which divine favor has bestowed upon him, to such a degree he may honor the giver of such blessings. A just prince is then known to honor the Most High when he shows himself the helper and protector of those who labor in the Lord's field, as it were, the stewards of the Great King. For, it is certain that the Almighty in his kindness will graciously dispose the affairs of an earthly prince to the degree He sees that prince solicitous with regard to His affairs, namely, those of Holy Church. Hence, a prudent ruler should strive to accomplish those things which are pleasing to God, if he desires that God may bring about those things which are prosperous and glorious to him. Moreover, such a ruler, with diligent care, should wisely plan to convene synodal assemblies two or three times every year, in order that what is known to pertain to the true worship of God, to the reverence of his churches, and to the honor of his priests, or what may have been committed against the Lord's commandments, in such a holy and harmonious assembly may be discussed. As a result, what has been done well may be corroborated, and, if wicked deeds have been committed, they may be corrected for the better. And, in that assembly, it is proper that the prefects themselves of the churches be examined as to how they perform their ministries, or how they both instruct the people entrusted to them with divine doctrine as well as inspire them with the example of holy behavior. If all these matters are subtly handled with harmonious peace and canonical justice, there arises a fruitful benefit to Holy Church, and for the venerable ruler, by whose benevolent deliberation and authority such matters are resolved, a garden of great merit is generated.

Indeed, a sacred council of bishops is the precious crown of a religious prince. In such a council the most famous emperor Constantine the Great, exulting in the Lord, gloried, for he assembled the holiest men from nearly all the nations under heaven and in which Christ's gospel is proclaimed, that is, more than three hundred bishops, radiant both in doctrine and miracles, to discuss the Catholic faith in one body, the Council of Nicaea. And so, the Christian practice has grown to such an extent that among all orthodox princes of the churches synods are convened to discuss the necessary services of Holy Church which should only be examined by synodal councils and determined by canonical decrees. It is essential, therefore, that a king be prudent, humble, and exceedingly careful lest he presume to judge anything with respect to ecclesiastical affairs before he examines synodal decrees. For ecclesiastical judgments are especially perilous before God unless they are administered with utmost justice, and particularly so, if the innocent are tried in their absence by false accusers and lying witnesses, since that is inconsistent with Christianity. Wherefore, we read in the Gospel: "Since when does our law judge a man without first hearing from him and knowing what he is about?" (John 7:51). Above all, therefore, a pious ruler, like a luminous eye, should perspicaciously attend to what is just and lawful according to the canonical decrees of holy bishops, and should apply to those which are true and upright the consent and support of authority. By no means should he pass judgment by himself in such matters, lest, perhaps, by erring he may incur some detestable offense in the sight of the Lord.

For this reason, the emperor Valentinian of blessed memory, when asked by the bishops to what extent he deigned to participate in the emendation of sacred dogma, said: "Since I am the least of the people, it is not right for me to examine such matters, but rather, priests, to whom this responsibility belongs, should be assembled among themselves in a place that they have chosen" (Cassiodorus, *Historia Tripartita* 7:12). Moreover, the emperor, both endowed with the virtue of humility and fortified with the fear of God, said these things, lest he might, perhaps, offend the Most High by preferring his own judgments to better ones. As I mentioned earlier, the magnificent and most wise emperor Constantine did this very thing by not trusting in himself, but rather in the prudence and wisdom of holy bishops. The blessed Jovianus, a prince worthy of God's love, observed this with resolute faith; for, when he was an enemy of the Arian heresy and a follower of the decrees of the Nicaean council, he procured for himself from the momentary height of an earthly kingdom the glory of an eternal one. What can I report about the two most blessed emperors, Theodosius I and Theodosius II, and the manifestation of divine favor? They pleased God so much that with the Lord's inspiration, they subjected royal dignities, their authority, and the summit of imperial honor to divine precepts and canonical regulations and always maintained pious zeal towards the churches of God with indefatigable charity. Thus, the Lord of the universe exalted them in this world, and after the glory of their earthly happiness, blesses them forever in heaven as his beloved ministers. If anyone, however, would emulate the fame of such princes, if any Christian ruler wishes to reign prosperously in this world and to attain the palm of eternal happiness, let him imitate the always faithful devotion of those emperors towards the worship of God; and let him show himself to be benevolent, merciful, strict in judgments, gentle in humility of heart, compassionate with heartfelt mercy, bounteous in liberality, and sparkling with a zeal for God's church in accord with His will, if he looks to reign perpetually with holy and just rulers among the citizens of heaven.

12. A virtuous ruler must become endowed with the weight of humility and with the virtue of obedience that he might perceive in himself the virtues, namely humility and obedience, which he esteems in his subjects. And, thus, if it happens that he is censured by prudent men, let him bitterly lament that he, himself, is reprehensible and make haste to fly immediately to the remedies of penance; besides, he who has willingly sinned should freely and gladly accept the rod of correction, and before the Creator stirs his hand to strike, he should be extremely diligent in correcting the crime committed lest, afterwards, the severe judge strike that much more sharply in proportion to how much longer and mercifully he waits. If any ruler of a kingdom has sinned in private or in public, let him hasten to go before the face of the Lord in confession (Ps. 95:2 Vulgate), even as it is read concerning the holy king and prophet David. When David was censured by the prophet Nathan after his violation of Bathsheba and the murder of Uriah the Hittite, he was not angry at his ac-

cuser, but rather, acknowledging his sin, he immediately became furious at himself. And he who grew merry after the crime was committed now bewailed himself with bitter penance. After that, by his tears, he who had perpetrated such grave crimes before the Lord obtained mercy and from the fountain of tears attained to abundant joy, just as he says elsewhere: "Those who sow in tears reap in exultation" (Ps. 126:5).

19. [. . .] Just and prudent kings, however, because they themselves live rightly, with pious zeal refute and reform transgressors in an instructive manner. Hence they acquire for themselves a double token of reward from the Lord inasmuch as they strive to refute evils in their subjects and to incite them to good by words and examples. Indeed, it behooves a ruler beloved by God, whom the divine order has appointed God's vicar in the government of his church and to whom it has granted authority over both orders (of prelates and subjects), that he decide what is just for every person; that under his direction the first order (of prelates) should preside over teaching and ministering properly; and that the order of subjects be faithfully and devoutly obedient. Thus, there should be a praiseworthy intention on a just ruler's part to see to it with appropriate zeal that the stewards of God's churches may lawfully maintain their office. Moreover, royal generosity should impart assistance to them in order that they may fully carry out their office according to God's commandments and the regulations of sacred canons. The secular authorities should not become a hindrance to the stewards of God, but rather should promote the preservation of God's faith and the cultivation of justice. Thus, as we have said previously, it is necessary that each year synodal assemblies be convened in which ecclesiastical laws and affairs may be justly and lawfully discussed. Therefore, let the just and pious ruler diligently see that the sanctity of the Lord's name, which abides in places consecrated to God, is maintained, insofar as it is possible, with no fault whatsoever. Let him provide that such rectors and stewards are appointed in them who conduct divine affairs without insatiable greed and luxury, who grant sufficient food and clothing to God's servants and handmaids, and who, above all, in accordance with the canons, dispense suitable provisioning to widows, orphans, and paupers. And likewise, let those stewards show service appropriate for an orthodox ruler from the resources which are left over, so that in first place should come what pertains to the divine, and in second place what pertains to human service. For, if with prudent skill stewardship should be shown towards soldiers of the flesh so that they are paid all necessary salaries and if those who labor more in war's tumults and become ever more devoted, steadfast and useful to the success of the state receive more of reward and honor, how much ought provision to be made for Christ's spiritual soldiers by whose sacred labors and prayers the state itself is preserved whole and unimpaired; enemies, too, both visible and invisible are overcome; an abundance of temporal benefits is increased by the event of prosperity; blessed angels are summoned to the people's assistance; the serenity of peace is restored; the dominion expanded; and finally, royal dignity and honor are extended long and happily with the Lord's protection and the sons of sons are rendered famous upon the summit of sovereignty.

Translation: E. G. Doyle, Center for Medieval and Early Renaissance Studies (1983). Used with permission.

The Donation of Constantine

The *Constitutum Constantini* is thought to have been forged by a Roman cleric circa 755/60. Drawing on a legend about the miraculous cure of Emperor Constantine's leprosy by baptism at the hands of Pope Sylvester, the document purports in Constantine's name to confer on his benefactor jurisdictional primacy over all other churches and to convey the imperial insignia, privileges, palaces, and territories of "Rome and Italy and of the regions of the West" prior to the emperor's translation of his court to Constantinople. The purpose, scope, and seriousness of the forgery's pretensions are much debated by scholars. However, it remains plausible that the *Donation* was contrived to counter Byzantine claims on the papal patrimony in Italy, recently recovered for the Roman Church out of Lombard hands by the military interventions of the Frankish king Pippin, father of Charlemagne. The document found its way to Rome in the eleventh century by its incorporation into the ninth-century Pseudo-Isidorian canonical collection "as a proof-text for the inviolability of ecclesiastical property against lay encroachment" (Burns, ed., 1988, 231). It is this ninth-century provenance that our placement of this document reflects.

Whatever the *Donation*'s original pretensions, they were used to great effect several centuries later by reforming popes and their bishops, from Leo IX onward (see Gregory VII, p. 241 below), to defend the universality and supremacy of Roman jurisdiction over lay rulers and their subjects in Western Christendom. Canonist reserve about the imperial donation of papal privileges was largely overcome by Innocent IV's official reinterpretation of the "donation" as a "restitution" to Christ's earthly vicar of the Petrine endowment (see p. 265 below). However, civilian doubts lingered over the illegality of such an alienation of imperial rights. Not until the fifteenth century was the document's inauthenticity demonstrated by Nicholas of Kues and, more sensationally, by the Italian humanist Lorenzo Valla.

Further Reading: H. Fuhrmann, "Konstantinische Schenkung und obendländisches Kaisertum," *Deutsches Archiv* 22 (1966): 63-178; H. Fuhrmann, *Einfluss und Verbrietung der pseudoisidorischen Fälschungen,* 3 vols. (Stuttgart: Hiersemann, 1972-74); H. Fuhrmann, "Konstantinische Schenkung," *Lexikon des Mittelalters,* 5 (1991), 1385-87; N. Huyghebaert, "Une légende de fondation: le *Constitutum Constantini,*" *Moyen Age* 85 (1979): 177-209; T. F. X. Noble, *The Republic of St. Peter: The Birth of the Papal State, 680-825* (Philadelphia: University of Pennsylvania Press, 1984); W. Ullmann, *The Growth of Papal Government in the Middle Ages,* 2nd ed. (London: Methuen, 1962).

From *The Donation of Constantine*

And so the first day after my reception of the mystery of Holy Baptism and the cure of my body from the filthiness of leprosy I understood that there is no other God than the Father, the Son and the Holy Spirit, whom most blessed Silvester, the Pope, preaches, a Trinity in unity and Unity in trinity. For all the gods of the nations, whom I have hitherto worshipped, are shown to be demons, the works of men's hands. And the same venerable father told us clearly how great power in heaven and earth our Saviour gave to his Apostle, blessed Peter, when in answer to questioning He found him faithful and said: "Thou art Peter, and upon this rock I will build My church; and the gates of hell shall not prevail against it" (Matt 16:18). Attend, ye mighty, and incline the ear of your heart to what the good Lord and master gave in addition to His disciple when He said: "I will give unto thee the keys of the kingdom of heaven, and whatsoever thou shalt bind on earth shall be bound in heaven, and whatsoever thou shalt loose on earth shall be loosed in heaven" (Matt 16:19). And when I learned these things at the mouth of the blessed Silvester, and found that I was wholly restored to health by the beneficence of blessed Peter himself, we — together with all our satraps and the whole senate, and the magnates and all the Roman people, which is subject to the glory of our rule — considered that, since he is seen to have been set up as the vicar of God's Son on earth, the pontiffs who act on behalf of that prince of the apostles should receive from us and our empire a greater power of government than the earthly clemency of our imperial serenity is seen to have conceded to them; for we choose the same prince of the apostles and his vicars to be our constant witnesses before God. And inasmuch as our imperial power is earthly, we have decreed that it shall venerate and honour his most holy Roman Church and that the sacred see of blessed Peter shall be gloriously exalted above our empire and earthly throne. We attribute to him the power and glorious dignity and strength and honour of the Empire, and we ordain and decree that he shall have rule as well over the four principal sees, Antioch, Alexandria, Constantinople, and Jerusalem, as also over all the churches of God in all the world. And the pontiff who for the time being presides over that most holy Roman Church shall be the highest and chief of all priests in the whole world, and according to his decision shall all matters be settled which shall be taken in hand for the service of God and for the confirmation of the faith of Christians. For it is right that the sacred law should have the centre of its power there where the Founder of the sacred laws, our Saviour, commanded blessed Peter to have the chair of his apostolate, and where, bearing the suffering of the cross, he accepted the cup of a blessed death and showed himself an imitator of his Lord and Master; and that there the nations should bow their necks in confession of Christ's name, where their teacher, blessed Paul, the apostle, offered his neck for Christ and was crowned with martyrdom. There forever let them seek a teacher, where lies the holy body of that teacher; and there, prone in humility, let them perform the service of the heavenly King, God, our Saviour, Jesus Christ, where proudly they used to serve the empire of an earthly king. [. . .]

To the holy apostles, my lords the most blessed Peter and Paul, and through them also to blessed Silvester, our father, supreme pontiff and universal pope of the city of Rome, and to the pontiffs, his successors, who to the end of the world shall sit in the seat of blessed Peter, we grant and by this present we convey our imperial Lateran palace, which is superior to and excels all palaces in the whole world; and further the diadem, which is the crown of our head; and the mitre; as also the super-humeral, that is, the stole which usually surrounds our imperial neck; and the purple cloak and the scarlet tunic and all the imperial robes; also the rank of commanders of the imperial cavalry. [. . .]

And we decree that those most reverend men, the clergy of various orders serving the same most holy Roman Church, shall have that eminence, distinction, power and precedence, with which our illustrious senate is gloriously adorned; that is, they shall be made patricians and consuls. And we ordain that they shall also be adorned with other imperial dignities. Also we decree that the clergy of the sacred Roman Church shall be adorned as are the imperial officers. [. . .]

Wherefore that the pontifical crown should not be made of less repute, but rather that the dignity of a more than earthly office and the might of its glory should be yet further adorned — lo, we convey to the oft-mentioned and most blessed Silvester, universal pope, both our palace, as preferment, and likewise all provinces, palaces and districts of the city of Rome and Italy and of the regions of the West; and, bequeathing them to the power and sway of him and the pontiffs, his successors, we do (by means of fixed imperial decision through this our divine, sacred and authoritative sanction) determine and decree that the same be placed at his disposal, and do lawfully grant it as a permanent possession to the holy Roman Church.

Wherefore we have perceived that our empire and the power of our government should be transferred and removed to the regions of the East and that a city should be built in our name in the best place in the province of Byzantium and our empire there established; for it is not right that an earthly emperor should have authority there, where the rule of priests and the head of the Christian religion have been established by the Emperor of heaven. [. . .]

Given at Rome, March 30th, when our lord Flavius Constantinus Augustus, for the fourth time, and Galliganus, most illustrious of men, were consuls.

Translation: E. Bettenson (Oxford University Press, 1947). Used with permission.

PART 3

THE STRUGGLE OVER EMPIRE AND
THE INTEGRATION OF ARISTOTLE

Between the eleventh and fourteenth centuries the Roman Church and the Roman Empire became locked in a rivalry of imperial projects. Both sides continued to invoke Pope Gelasius's formulation of the *dual rulership* of priestly authority and royal power (see p. 179 above), but they did so anachronistically; for, while the formulation had never excluded ambiguities and tensions arising from intersecting spheres of responsibility, it had excluded the routine combining of the two in a single person. It was just this combining of secular and sacred offices in the late Roman, Merovingian, Carolingian, and Ottonian regimes that abetted a theoretical tendency to harmonize the orders hierarchically, incorporating the one within the other — a development that presupposed the coextensiveness of church and empire brought about by successive imperial measures to impose orthodoxy. The civil administration and jurisdiction awarded to Frankish bishops, the Frankish emperor's authorization of church legislation, control of appointments to the episcopate (and occasionally the papacy), convening of synods and oversight of church policy, the pope's temporal rule in central Italy and involvement in imperial coronations and politics — all these interpenetrations of "ministries" fueled the impulse for a theoretical fusion of ecclesiastical and civil orders. A fateful consensus reigned among rulers in both orders that they were set over the "people of God" by divine ordination to protect the faith of Christ and to promulgate his laws.

I. Roman Hierocratic Imperialism. Against this background it is scarcely surprising that the eleventh-century papacy, whose towering figure was Gregory VII, should conceive a vast ecclesiastical reformation in the light of a "renovation of the Roman Empire," fulfilling Rome's universal mission of Christianizing conquest and rule, which was the meaning of the fourth and last monarchy prophesied by Daniel. Arguably, such an imperialist program of reform was not required by, was even repugnant to, its substance; namely, the purification of clerical life from the corrupt worldliness and venality into which it had sunk largely as a result of its secular en-

slavements, i.e., to feudal tenure, to marital responsibilities and concubinage, to simoniacal practices. Would not a purely ecclesiastical program of "spiritualizing the
priesthood" have been better suited to achieve the separation of the two spheres? But
clerical reform appeared to necessitate a conquest of lay power.

Even before Gregory's reign the Roman reform movement, steered by Cardinal
Humbert of Silva Candida, had focused its attack on the practice of "lay investiture"
as the root of clerical corruption and ecclesiastical bondage. Humbert waged a campaign to abolish the royal and imperial prerogative of elevating clergy to bishoprics
by ceremonially investing them with the pastoral staff and ring, on the grounds that
the ceremonial investiture constituted a usurpation by the lay ruler of episcopal sacramental and jurisdictional authority, in that it entailed his conferring of both a
spiritual office and its temporal endowments, and as well, his effective appointment
of bishops. He resisted even the counterarguments from episcopal colleagues anxious to defend the feudal rights of kingship, being firmly convinced that the issue at
stake was nothing less than the divinely ordained structure of the *ecclesia:* the subjection of lay to priestly orders as of body to soul. To his mind, the Byzantine aspirations alarmingly manifested by the Ottonian and Salian monarchs persistently
threatened the integrity not only of the clerical hierarchy, but of the whole *societas
Christianorum,* and no amount of royal and imperial benefaction and support for
clerical reform measures could remove this threat to the church's welfare.

Gregory VII shared Humbert's conception of the battle lines and magnified
the Roman victory to be pursued. He ascended the throne of St. Peter believing that
subjection of the lower ranks of the church, both clerical and lay, to papal authority
was inescapably political and legal as well as spiritual, required by the justice
(iustitia) and the law *(ius)* of Christ. His belief was reinforced by the fierce opposition of the French and German kings and of the German episcopate to his legislation
for the canonical election of bishops and their investiture by metropolitans. In their
resistance Gregory discerned the satanic pride of worldly rulers who put their inflated wills above the manifest will of God. His subsequent dealings with lesser authorities consistently aimed at enlarging Rome's jurisdictional and political control
at their expense. The primary theological mechanism of Rome's aggrandizement
under Hildebrand and his successors was a juristic elaboration of St. Peter's vicariate, of the structure and unity of the *corpus Christianum* and, in increasingly explicit
detail, of Christ's earthly kingship, the foundation of the edifice. This elaboration
drew heavily on three sources, the Vulgate Bible, Roman legal theory, and earlier canonical collections, and was largely the work of canon lawyers, instigated and over-
seen by canonist popes.

1. *St. Peter's Vicariate and Christ's Earthly Kingship.* From the eighth century
onward the "care" of the church entrusted by Christ to St. Peter (Matt. 16:18-19;
John 21:15-17), in which the primacy of the Roman see resided, was construed
(though by no means universally) as a sovereign jurisdiction from which authority
descended to the subordinate jurisdictions. This juristic construction of the Petrine
primacy came to depend in the eleventh century on an extension of the "power of
the keys," i.e., the power of "binding" and "loosing," beyond the realms of purgatory
and penance, to the external government of the church. Indeed, as St. Peter's juris-

diction over purgatory reached new heights at the century's close with the granting of the first "plenary indulgence" for those joining the First Crusade, so his earthly jurisdiction had assumed a temporal unlimitedness (Berman 1983, 171). The "power of the keys," which in earlier times had designated the general clerical authority of convicting sinners and declaring absolution, or at most the apostolic authority of the whole episcopate, was now to be reserved for the sovereign rule of St. Peter's vicar over the Christian world in its directive, moral, legislative, and judicial dimensions.

From the *Corpus Iuris Civilis* of Justinian, adorned by the flourishing commentaries of the glossators, and from the Roman-leaning Pseudo-Isidorian *(False) Decretals,* canonists over two centuries garnered the images, allegories, principles, and concepts for explicating papal supremacy. Roman law doctrines of imperial sovereignty, that what the emperor wills has the force of law (Dig. 1.4.1; cf. Inst. 1.2.6), that the emperor is unbounded by laws (*legibus solutus,* Dig. 1.3.31), and that he is the sole legislator (Cod. I.14.12, 3 and 4), were taken over for the pope. Their application was reinforced by a spate of papal legislation and new canonical collections whose traditional content was authenticated by Roman approval, as well as by increasingly frequent papal dispensations from established church law. Pressed into service were assertions contained in Pseudo-Isidore concerning the freedom of legal appeal to Rome, the pope's exclusive authority to judge bishops, and the immunity of the Roman see from judgment (Burns 1988, 286-87). A declaration of Rome's original possession of the norm of the apostolic faith became a touchstone of the doctrine of papal inerrancy. Finally, a Pseudo-Isidorian construction from a letter of Pope Leo I (440-61) provided the concept of papal monarchy that would receive the most extensive theoretical development of all medieval papalist ideas, that of *plenitudo potestatis.* Pope Leo had told a papal legate that he was called to a share of ecclesiastical responsibilities *(in partem sollicitudinis)* but not to the "fullness of power" (*Ep.* 14.1); in the *False Decretals* Leo's phrases were applied to the distinction of episcopal and papal authority (Ps.-Vigilius, *Ep.* 7).

The concept of *plenitudo potestatis* acted as a catalyst for the combination of metaphysical, cosmological, political, and doctrinal themes that characterized the fullest flowering of papalist political theology in the late thirteenth and early fourteenth centuries. Its key theopolitical element, however, was influentially explicated a century earlier by three contemporary figures, Honorius Augustodunensis, Hugh of St. Victor, and Bernard of Clairvaux. Together they furnished the definitive formulation of the idea that the papal dignity embraced both spiritual and temporal authorities. Honorius approached papal authority by way of the startling proposition that, from the creation, God ordained the priesthood to rule always and everywhere on account of its superior dignity; from which he concluded that royal rule is divinely authorized only as subject to priestly rule, either joined to it in a single priestly ruler or chosen and instituted by it and obedient to it. The Roman bishop's possession of universal empire flowed from Christ's commission to St. Peter rather than from Constantine's donation to Pope Sylvester (see p. 265 below). Constantine's bestowal of the imperial crown on the "prince of priests" was merely his public surrender of what was rightfully St. Peter's, in return for which he was instated in his

Christian ministry of defending the church. When, a century after Honorius, Pope Innocent IV repeated this reading of the donation in an encyclical defending his deposition of Emperor Frederick II, he took care to contrast the "inordinate tyranny" of Constantine's pagan rule with the "ordered power" of his Christian office (Tierney 1964, 148).

Hugh supplied the classic metaphysical statement of the superior dignity of the spiritual over the temporal order by comparing the former to the soul deriving life from God and the latter to the body deriving life from the soul. From this he drew the jurisdictional implication that spiritual power was responsible both for establishing the temporal power and for judging it (*De sacramentis* 2.2.2-4). While the political relationship between the powers remained tantalizingly undeveloped, it is certain from his Gelasian emphasis on duality that Hugh never envisaged the priesthood's ongoing oversight of and interference with lay rule.

Bernard expressed the spiritual-temporal duality of the papal *plenitudo* by elaborating the allegory of the "two swords" drawn from Christ's exchanges with his disciples during his arrest (Luke 22:38, 49-51; John 18:10-11). According to Bernard, both swords, of spiritual and temporal judgment, belong to the church, but the latter belongs to her only in the sense of being at her disposal to command, rather than for her direct use; thus Peter is instructed to sheathe the sword with which he cut off the ear of the slave of the high priest. While Bernard's primary intention was to dissuade Pope Eugenius III from dealing with Roman civil revolt by force of arms, readers of his *On Consideration* (see pp. 269-76 below), and particularly the Decretists and Decretalists who glossed and disputed the "two swords" doctrine, were occupied with resolving conflicting accounts of imperial and papal authority on terms generally satisfactory to Rome.

The fierce battles that broke out over the rival ambitions of the papacy and the Hohenstaufen emperors in the late twelfth and thirteenth centuries generated a more detailed practical and legal elaboration of the powers inherent in papal plenitude and a more extravagant theological presentation of them. From the "two swords" doctrine Decretalists extrapolated that the pope was the emperor's judge because he confirmed, consecrated, crowned, and could depose him. Pope Innocent III's intrepid declarations that as mediator between God and man, he exercised certain judgments not human but divine authority prompted a further canonical distinction (with obvious theological overtones) between the pope's "ordinary power" (*potesta ordinata*) and the extraordinary power (*potesta absoluta*) that he exercised as Christ's vicar. Although papal action, especially in the temporal sphere, was frequently accorded more modest rationales, these elaborations reflected dimensions of Rome's real political and spiritual hegemony: the legal and administrative centralization of the church, the feudal subordination of various royal kingdoms (including England and Ireland), its unparalleled diplomatic influence and formidable interventions in imperial affairs.

The mature refinement of the theory of papal plenitude supplied by the literary supporters of Pope Boniface VIII in his quarrels with Philip IV of France testifies to the threat to Roman wealth and jurisdiction posed by the emergence of strong national monarchs ruling kingdoms with relatively centralized financial, judicial, and legislative structures, and armed with the new Aristotelian political naturalism.

Faced with royal encroachments on the property and privileges of the French church as well as on papal jurisdictional rights, and confronting novel arguments for the moral, legal, and political self-sufficiency of the civil polity, the papal publicists, who included Ptolemy of Lucca, Giles of Rome, James of Viterbo, and Augustinus Triumphus, undertook to define carefully the modes of papal jurisdiction over *things* as well as persons, and to demonstrate the universality of papal plenitude and its exclusive derivation from Christ's earthly plenitude. By explicating Christ's un- limited earthly lordship *(dominium)* in its proprietary as well as jurisdictional as- pects, Giles of Rome and James of Viterbo led the counterassault on naturalistic jus- tifications of both property right and political authority. While Giles derived just or licit rule and ownership from the universal agency of the pope as Christ's vicar, con- demning as unjust all *dominium* without obedience to Rome, James admitted a licit natural jurisdiction apart from the church, which, nevertheless, was required to be completed or *in-formed* by the church's confirmation and institution. In the spirit of the Gregorian tradition, both theologians responded to secularizing pressures by producing positivist ecclesiological versions of Augustine's thought on just rule and just possession.

2. Corporational Ecclesiology. Papalist ecclesiology construed the universal so- ciety of which the pope was earthly head simultaneously as a mystical body *(corpus mysticum)* and a political body *(corpus politicum),* a spiritual unity after the pattern of its heavenly head and a political-legal corporation *(universitas)* with the full range of proprietary and political rights established for corporations in Roman civil law. The role of its clerical government was to translate the church's divine essence through the agency of law into visible institutional structures: liturgical, disciplin- ary, administrative, proprietary, and economic. Three centuries of Gregorian reform produced an ecclesiastical "corporation of corporations," a hierarchy of relatively self-governing, property-owning corporational units formed at various administra- tive levels (congregational, parochial, diocesan, archdiocesan, etc.) and including a variety of establishments (e.g., monastic houses, confraternities, universities, and hospitals). While each lesser corporation was the legal owner of property held for the fulfillment of specific religious and charitable purposes (e.g., administering the sacraments, preaching, teaching, and alms-giving), its particular head occupying the office of property administrator, the whole church had assumed the universal own- ership *(dominium)* of ecclesiastical property, with the pope occupying the office of universal administrator *(universalis dispensator),* and eventually universal owner *(dominus),* of corporate assets. In that many lesser ecclesiastical corporations also corresponded to civil units, the church's corporational structure effectively assisted the absorption of civil into ecclesiastical polity, and the papal claims of plenary juris- diction over both orders.

Two biblical models for the church's corporate property were frequently applied. One was the common possession and distribution of material goods in the postresurrection Jerusalem community (Acts 2:44-45), which was regulative for cenobitical monasticism. A second, the "purse" or "money bag" carried by Christ (or his disciple) to provide for himself and his disciples and for the poor (cf. John 12:6), was applied to church property more generally, for the church's "fisc," like Christ's "purse," comprehended the offerings of the faithful held in common by Christ's ministers to meet their own and others' needs (Dawson 1983, 317-19). In the second half of the thirteenth century, these biblical rationales for property-amassing church corporations were challenged by the Franciscan theology of absolute poverty, which proposed communal and individual *nonownership* and *deprivation* of earthly goods as the highest form of discipleship on the model of the apostolic missionary journeys commissioned by Christ. St. Bonaventure's authoritative *Defence of the Mendicants (Apologia pauperum)* laid out a theology of Christ's obedient suffering, powerlessness, and dereliction that sat ill with Rome's imperial Christology, and would in the future be pitted against it, despite his own and other Franciscan attempts at reconciling them.

II. From Christ-Centered to Law-Centered Kingship. In their repudiation of the lay monarch's vicarship of Christ, the Gregorians prosecuted a largely successful campaign to de-sacerdotalize secular royal authority. Under pressure from papal imperialism, neither King Henry IV nor his Hohenstaufen successors attempted seriously to revive the episcopal pretensions of their Ottonian predecessors. They consistently presented themselves as championing the Gelasian separation of spiritual and temporal authorities, "the two swords" principle, against systematic papal violations of it. Not that they surrendered their claim to a divine vicariate. No European royal dynasty, whether the German Hohenstaufen or English Angevin or French Capetian, would countenance the resumption of political jurisdiction into spiritual authority that hierocratic papalism was advocating. But they set it firmly on a nonsacerdotal footing, principally that of lawgiving and legal judgment. Imperial and royal resistance claimed at least an independent divine commission for secular jurisdiction and, less modestly, a divine commission for secular jurisdiction alone. Although the more extreme claim surfaced most blatantly in the quarrels of Philip IV of France with Rome, it had never entirely lacked exponents who claimed to find *the temporality of jurisdiction as such* given in Scripture and Roman law.

A late expression of the "West-Byzantine" phase of christocentric royalism from about 1100 demonstrates the continuity between the different phases of royalist theory. While conceding that both king and priest carry the "image" of Christ, the "Norman Anonymous" reserved to the king alone the image of Christ's divine, uncreated, and eternal rulership, allocating to the priest the contrasting image of his suffering, self-sacrificing humanity. The outcome of this division of the image of Christ was a royal monopoly of divine jurisdiction in its creative, legislative, administrative, and judicial aspects, over both civil and ecclesiastical orders. In the thirteenth century the English monarch, if he did not bluntly arrogate to himself a jurisdictional monopoly, still operated as much as possible on the principle that the church held her jurisdiction on royal sufferance and the Crown determined the precise demarcation of spiritual and temporal powers in ambiguous cases. So much was still clearly Byzantine in spirit. But the christological basis of the thought had dwindled by the thirteenth century, and nowhere more clearly than in Byzantium itself, as evidenced by an account of kingship, rationalist in spirit and only superficially theological, offered to a Lascarid emperor by the high-standing monk Nikephoros Blemmydes.

The ascendancy of the "law-centered" or "juristical" kingship ideal, associated especially with the German emperor Frederick II's revival of Roman imperial law in the early to mid–thirteenth century, tended to reinforce this jurisdictional monopoly. The legal theory of Frederick's *Liber augustalis* (his collection of Sicilian Constitutions) cast the monarch as the origin and the protector, the lord and the servant, "the father and the son of justice," while the civilian Glossators cast the Roman emperor as the mediator of justice, standing above positive human law but under the divine laws of nature and reason. In the spirit of Israelite kingship refracted through Justinian's legal theology, Frederick II assumed the role of the law's high priest who, as the "living law" *(lex animata)*, offered the true "sacrifice of justice," the judges and lawyers of his court performing the solemn, mystical function of priests (Kantorowicz 1957, 97-101, 107-10). The replacement in civilian thought of the royal titles "vicar of Christ" and "image of Christ" by "vicar of God" and "God on earth" suggested the independent nonecclesiastical origin of his *imperium*.

The king's servitude to justice and law affirmed by imperial theology was most effectually elaborated by Henry Bracton (or the author of the work commonly attributed to him), within the English feudal tradition, though under civilian influence, and by the theologian John of Salisbury, writer of the first sustained political treatise. Both theorists construed the monarch's supreme lawmaking power as rational, disciplined, bounded by customary human as well as divine legal constraints, and dependent on his voluntary imitation of Christ's royal submission to his Father's law. Both venerated positive law (in which the intention of justice and equity is made manifest) as the unifying form of the body politic, embodying both the natural and supernatural ends of the *respublica*. Indeed, John of Salisbury's celebrated justification of tyrannicide focused precisely on the tyrant's treason against the "public power" in which the legal unity of the kingdom is anchored.

III. The Integration of Aristotle. The absorption of Aristotle's writings in the Latin West from the early twelfth to the late thirteenth centuries created an intellectual watershed that left no theoretical inquiry unaffected. Thinkers of the twelfth century were chiefly influenced by his logic and natural philosophy, frequently mediated through Latin translations of Arabic texts. The logical refinements of scholastic method contributed greatly to the rapid advances in legal science, leading to Gratian's unprecedented synthesis of canonist material in the *Decretum* (1140), while the philosophy of natural organisms inspired John of Salisbury's extended organic analysis of political society in the *Policraticus*. But it was only after 1260, in the wake of Grosseteste's and Moerbeke's translations from the Greek of the complete *Nichomachean Ethics* and the *Politics* respectively, that the full impact of Aristotle's naturalism was felt in ethics, law, and politics. The next century saw the rise of a natural law theology of quite a different stripe from the patristic theology that had held sway until then.

In the earlier Western tradition, authoritatively but somewhat ambiguously transmitted by Isidore of Seville and more coherently explicated by Rufinus in his commentary on Gratian's *Decretum*, the substance of "natural justice" or "natural law" *(ius naturale, lex naturae)* was internally differentiated according to four somewhat discontinuous communal modes, those of created, fallen, redeemed, and perfected human nature. Each mode had its distinct ethical, legal, and institutional determinations: Created community was constituted by the natural laws of sexual union, the begetting and parenting of children, the common possession of material goods, and the equality and unrestrained freedom of persons. Fallen community, by contrast, was constituted by the *ius gentium* (law of nations) and the *ius civile* (civil law) which, as secondary refractions of the natural law, established private property, inequality of master and slave, ruler and ruled, and the positive legal curtailment of individual freedom. Redeemed community was constituted by Christ's gospel law of faith, hope, and love; and this was raised to a higher level of earthly perfection in the ascending clerical, monastic, and mendicant disciplines of the imitation of Christ. Temporal jurisdiction was understood to be closely aligned, but not coterminous, with the institutions and laws of fallen human nature. It had to do with the distribution and protection of private property and privilege, and with the safeguarding of human life and its necessities. Spiritual jurisdiction, on the other hand, extended to those institutions and communities constituted by the laws of created, redeemed, and sanctified human nature: marriage and family, monastic community and religious confraternity, churches, charitable and educational institutions.

The reception of Aristotle provided a theoretical rationale for blurring these communal-legal discontinuities, as the thought of Thomas Aquinas demonstrates. By adopting Aristotle's organic construction of the self-sufficient political society from lesser, insufficient communities, and by endorsing the natural moral dignity and rationality of the encompassing civil "perfect community," Thomas minimized the spiritual distance between "prelapsarian" and "postlapsarian" communities and institutions, so weaving social life into a unified moral and legal texture. Sinful society retained the inherent harmony of a hierarchy of natural ends and functions, each part having its place within the whole, its political and nonpolitical elements suffering no disjunctive division, but together constituting a social totality, a common will directed toward a common good. Far from rendering the ruler a passive caretaker, Thomas's integration of society enlarged his role to that of defining through legislation the order of public and private benefits constituting common utility, and organizing the populace to pursue them. Moreover, Thomas accorded to the common welfare a broader, less narrowly juridical, scope than the Augustinian tradition had allowed, comprehending within it not only temporal safety and material sufficiency, but virtuous conduct and mutual fellowship.

Thomas's moderate political Aristotelianism paved the way for less moderate political postures. His positions were overtaken by: (1) the more complete assimilation of the ethics of created and redeemed human nature to the universal status quo of the *ius gentium,* as evidenced in the high papalist theory of Christ's universal political and proprietary *dominium;* (2) the more thorough and radical elaboration of the powers of political corporations, precociously provided by John of Paris; and (3) the more extreme separation of the foundations and goals of universal secular empire and universal church proposed with a highly original twist by Dante.

Bibliography: H. J. Berman, *Law and Revolution: The Formation of the Western Legal Tradition* (Cambridge, Mass.: Harvard University Press, 1983); D. Burr, *Poverty in the Middle Ages* (Werl, Westfalen: Coelde Verlag, 1975); J. D. Dawson, "Richard FitzRalph and the Fourteenth-Century Poverty Controversies," *Journal of Ecclesiastical History* 34 (1983): 315-44; T. Gilby, *Principality and Polity: Aquinas and the Rise of State Theory in the West* (London and New York: Longmans, 1958); E. H. Kantorowicz, *The King's Two Bodies: A Study in Medieval Political Theology* (Princeton: Princeton University Press, 1957); G. Leff, *Heresy in the Later Middle Ages: The Relation of Heterodoxy to Dissent, c. 1250-1450*, 2 vols. (Manchester: Manchester University Press, 1967); E. Lewis, *Medieval Political Ideas*, 2nd ed., 2 vols. (London: Routledge and Kegan Paul, 1974); C. Morris, *The Papal Monarchy: The Western Church from 1050 to 1250* (Oxford: Clarendon Press, 1989); G. Post, *Studies in Medieval Legal Thought* (Princeton: Princeton University Press, 1964); B. Smalley, ed., *Trends in Medieval Political Thought* (Oxford: Blackwell, 1965); B. Tierney, *The Crisis of Church and State, 1050-1300* (Englewood Cliffs, N.J.: Prentice-Hall, 1964); W. Ullmann, *Medieval Papalism: The Political Theories of the Medieval Canonists* (London: Methuen, 1949); W. Ullmann, *The Growth of Papal Government in the Middle Ages* (London: Methuen, 1955); W. Ullmann, *A Short History of the Papacy in the Middle Ages* (London: Methuen, 1972); M. Wilks, *The Problem of Sovereignty in the Later Middle Ages* (Cambridge: Cambridge University Press, 1963).

Gregory VII

(ca. 1030-85)

His papacy was only of moderate length, his theological reflections scattered and repetitive, his legislation not voluminous by later standards; nevertheless, Gregory VII (Hildebrand) is a churchman of legendary historical proportions. He is credited with fathering an ecclesiastical revolution which revolutionized Western political society in its wake, and with being the architect of the papal church (Berman 1983). Hildebrand has become synonymous with medieval triumphalist, imperialist, and juridical ecclesiology. An astonishingly few documents in his official *Register* appear to contain all the foundational elements of the Roman system.

There has been much scholarly discussion about exactly how innovative and programmatic Gregory's reforming thought and action were. On the one hand, he stood in a succession of reforming popes (Leo IX, Nicholas II, and Alexander II) who had sought to purify and spiritualize clerical and monastic orders by legislating against the root causes of ecclesiastical immorality and worldliness, diagnosed to be the practices of simony (the purchase of holy orders or offices), clerical marriage and concubinage, and lay investiture (the real and ceremonial granting of ecclesiastical offices by lay patrons). Admitting Gregory's association with all three reforming papacies and his increasing influence over papal policy from 1059 onward, decisive contributions to the Roman reform movement were made by other ecclesiastics as well. The cardinals Humbert of Silva Candida and Peter Damian, for example, crystallized a broad clerical consensus by their passionate cries against the enslavement of holy orders and offices to feudal proprietorship, their exalting of the priest's apostolic authority above lay jurisdiction, their anchoring of the church's apostolicity in the divinely founded jurisdiction of Rome, and infusion of her renovation with the urgency of apocalyptic warfare. In short, many of the future pope's aspirations, and his devices for effecting and authenticating them, had considerable coinage among his contemporaries.

On the other hand, Gregory VII gave a sharpness of focus to these aspirations and wedded them to the defeat of both lay and episcopal recalcitrance through unrelenting assertion of Rome's unrivaled authority. With novel bravado he commanded obedience to his decrees from the kings of France and Germany (Philip I and Henry IV) and their bishops, threatening them with excommunication (even deposition) and their realms with general interdiction were they obdurately to violate ecclesiastical law, and carrying out the threats with equal bravado when he judged it necessary. As unprecedented was his arrogation to himself of the Roman imperial right of universal jurisdiction, setting himself up as supreme judge and arbiter, especially of disputes involving princes, and even of a disputed election to the German throne.

While Gregory's more radical pronouncements were undoubtedly responses to dire provocations, the programmatic bent of his mind and totalitarian bent of his will are also evident. Although the *Dictatus Papae* (1075) is a simple list of papal prerogatives drawn, with one exception, from previous (true and false) decretals, the very fact of its compilation exhibits the unity in Gregory's mind of supreme spiritual and temporal government of the church. It combines a virtually unlimited Roman jurisdiction (legislative, administrative, fiscal, doctrinal, and judicial) over the visible church, at grave episcopal expense, with assertions of papal imperial sovereignty. These assertions probably allude to the *Donation of Constantine* (see pp. 229-30 above), a mid-eighth-century forgery, in which Emperor Constantine I, prior to moving his court from Rome to Constantinople, transfers to the contemporary pope his imperial insignia, privileges, palaces, and territories of "Rome and Italy and of the regions of the West."

For Hildebrand, as H.-X. Arquillière perceives (1934, 135), the unity of papal powers resides in the exclusive Petrine responsibility of executing divine justice *omnibus modis*. Time and again, he reminds us, Gregory VII's writings appeal to the "power of the keys" bestowed on Peter by Christ (Matt. 16:18-19) — the power of rendering binding justice in heaven as on earth — as proof of the pope's universal juridical authority, extending beyond the judgment of human sin, the imposing and remitting of purgatorial and earthly punishments, to the judgment of all human causes insofar as they bear on the spiritual welfare of Christian communities and individuals. Hildebrand's conception of justice as a seamless web of divine judgment penetrating all spheres of human action depends for its full theological intelligibility on the Augustinian dualism expounded in his famous letter of 15 March 1081 to Bishop Hermann of Metz defending his excommunication and deposition of Henry IV. For Hildebrand the warring kingdoms of Christ and the devil, of obedient love of God and tyrannous self-love, are coterminous with the church militant that is obedient to Petrine authority and the community of ignorance and refusal of papal sovereignty, in bondage to humanly invented substitutes. Temporal potentates situate themselves in either kingdom by their acts of humble service to or rapacious domination over the Roman pontiff and his clergy.

Further Reading: H.-X. Arquillière, *Saint Grégoire VII, essai sur sa conception du pouvoir pontifical* (Paris: Vrin, 1934); H. J. Berman, *Law and Revolution: The Formation of the Western Legal Tradition* (Cambridge, Mass.: Harvard University Press, 1983); L. F. J.

Meulenberg, *Der Primat der römischen Kirche im Denken und Handeln Gregors VII* (The Hague, 1965); A. Murray, "Pope Gregory VII and His Letters," *Traditio* 22 (1966): 149-201; C. Schneider, *Prophetisches Sacerdotium und Heilsgeschichtliches Regnum im Dialog 1073-1077: zur Geschichte Gregors VII und Heinrich IV* (Munich: Fink, 1972).

Dictatus Papae

1. That the Roman Church was founded by God alone.
2. That the Roman Pontiff alone is rightly to be called universal.
3. That he alone can depose or reinstate bishops.
4. That his legate, even if of lower grade, takes precedence, in a council, of all bishops and may render a sentence of deposition against them.
5. That the Pope may depose the absent.
6. That, among other things, we also ought not to stay in the same house with those excommunicated by him.
7. That for him alone it is lawful to enact new laws according to the needs of the time, to assemble together new congregations, to make an abbey of a canonry; and, on the other hand, to divide a rich bishopric and unite the poor ones.
8. That he alone may use the imperial insignia.
9. That the Pope is the only one whose feet are to be kissed by all princes.
10. That his name alone is to be recited in churches.
11. That his title is unique in the world.
12. That he may depose Emperors.
13. That he may transfer bishops, if necessary, from one See to another.
14. That he has power to ordain a cleric of any church he may wish.
15. That he who has been ordained by him may rule over another church, but not be under the command of others; and that such a one may not receive a higher grade from any bishop.
16. That no synod may be called a general one without his order.
17. That no chapter or book may be regarded as canonical without his authority.
18. That no sentence of his may be retracted by any one; and that he, alone of all, can retract it.
19. That he himself may be judged by no one.
20. That no one shall dare to condemn a person who appeals to the Apostolic See.
21. That to this See the more important cases of every church should be submitted.
22. That the Roman Church has never erred, nor ever, by the witness of Scripture, shall err to all eternity.
23. That the Roman Pontiff, if canonically ordained, is undoubtedly sanctified by the merits of St. Peter; of this St. Ennodius, Bishop of Pavia, is witness, many Holy Fathers are agreeable and it is contained in the decrees of Pope Symmachus the Saint.

24. That, by his order and with his permission, subordinate persons may bring accusations.
25. That without convening a synod he can depose and reinstate bishops.
26. That he should not be considered as Catholic who is not in conformity with the Roman Church.
27. That the Pope may absolve subjects of unjust men from their fealty.

Translation: S. Z. Ehler and J. B. Morrall (Burns & Oates, 1954). Used with permission.

Letter 8.21

Gregory . . . to his beloved brother in Christ, Hermann, bishop of Metz, greeting. . . .

We know you to be ever ready to bear labour and peril in defense of the truth, and doubt not that this is a gift from God. It is a part of his unspeakable grace and his marvellous mercy that he never permits his chosen ones to wander far or to be completely cast down; but rather, after a time of persecution and wholesome probation, makes them stronger than they were before. On the other hand, just as among cowards one who is worse than the rest is broken down by fear, so among the brave, one who acts more bravely than the rest is stirred thereby to new activity. We remind you of this by way of exhortation that you may stand more joyfully in the front ranks of the Christian host, the more confident you are that they are the nearest to God the conqueror.

You ask us to fortify you against the madness of those who babble with accursed tongues about the authority of the Holy Apostolic See not being able to excommunicate King Henry as one who despises the law of Christ, a destroyer of churches and of the empire, a promoter and partner of heresies, nor to release anyone from his oath of fidelity to him; but it has not seemed necessary to reply to this request, seeing that so many and such convincing proofs are to be found in Holy Scripture. Nor do we believe that those who abuse and contradict the truth to their utter damnation do this as much from ignorance as from wretched and desperate folly. And no wonder! It is ever the way of the wicked to protect their own iniquities by calling upon others like themselves; for they think it of no account to incur the penalty of falsehood.

To cite but a few out of the multitude of proofs: Who does not remember the words of our Lord and Saviour Jesus Christ: "Thou art Peter and upon this rock I will build my Church, and the gates of hell shall not prevail against it. And I will give thee the keys of the kingdom of heaven and whatsoever thou shalt bind on earth shall be bound in heaven and whatsoever thou shalt loose on earth shall be loosed in heaven" (Matt. 16:18f.). Are kings excepted here? Or are they not of the sheep which the Son of God committed to St. Peter? Who, I ask, thinks himself excluded from this universal grant of the power of binding and loosing to St. Peter unless, perchance, that unhappy man who, being unwilling to bear the yoke of the Lord, subjects himself to the burden of the Devil and refuses to be numbered in the flock of Christ? His wretched liberty shall profit him nothing; for if he shakes off from his proud neck the power divinely granted to Peter, so much the heavier shall it be for him in the day of judgment.

This institution of the divine will, this foundation of the rule of the Church, this privilege granted and sealed especially by a heavenly decree to St. Peter, chief of the Apostles, has been accepted and maintained with great reverence by the holy fathers, and they have given to the Holy Roman Church, as well in general councils as in their other acts and writings, the name of "universal mother." They have not only accepted her expositions of doctrine and her instructions in (our) holy religion, but they have also recognised her judicial decisions. They have agreed as with one spirit and one voice that all major cases, all especially important affairs and the judgments of all churches ought to be referred to her as to their head and mother, that from her there shall be no appeal, that her judgments may not and cannot be reviewed or reversed by anyone.

Thus Pope Gelasius, writing to the emperor Anastasius, gave him these instructions as to the right theory of the principate of the Holy and Apostolic See, based upon divine authority: — "Although it is fitting that all the faithful should submit themselves to all priests who perform their sacred functions properly, how much the more should they accept the judgment of that prelate who has been appointed by the supreme divine ruler to be superior to all priests and whom the loyalty of the whole later church has recognised as such. Your Wisdom sees plainly that no human capacity whatsoever can equal that of him whom the word of Christ raised above all others and whom the reverend Church has always confessed and still devotedly holds as its Head" [cf. p. 179 above].

So also Pope Julius, writing to the eastern bishops in regard to the powers of the same Holy and Apostolic See, says:

> You ought, my brethren, to have spoken carefully and not ironically of the Holy Roman and Apostolic Church, seeing that our Lord Jesus Christ addressed her respectfully, saying, "Thou art Peter and upon this rock I will build my church, and the gates of hell shall not prevail against it; and I will give thee the keys of the kingdom of heaven." For it has the power, granted by a unique privilege, of opening and shutting the gates of the celestial kingdom to whom it will.

To whom then, the power of opening and closing Heaven is given, shall he not be able to judge the earth? God forbid! Do you remember what the most blessed Apostle Paul says: "Know ye not that we shall judge angels? How much more things that pertain to this life?" (1 Cor. 6:3).

So Pope Gregory declared that kings who dared to disobey the orders of the Apostolic See should forfeit their office. He wrote to a certain senator and abbot in these words:

> If any king, priest, judge or secular person shall disregard this decree of ours and act contrary to it, he shall be deprived of his power and his office and shall learn that he stands condemned at the bar of God for the wrong that he has done. And

244

unless he shall restore what he has wrongfully taken and shall have done fitting penance for his unlawful acts he shall be excluded from the sacred body and blood of our Lord and Saviour Jesus Christ and at the last judgement shall receive condign punishment.

Now then, if the blessed Gregory, most gentle of doctors, decreed that kings who should disobey his orders about a hospital for strangers should be not only deposed but excommunicated and condemned in the last judgment, how can anyone blame us for deposing and excommunicating Henry, who not only disregards apostolic judgments, but so far as in him lies tramples upon his mother the Church, basely plunders the whole kingdom and destroys its churches — unless indeed it were one who is a man of his own kind?

As we know also through the teaching of St. Peter in his letter touching the ordination of Clement (Pseudo-Clement, *Letter to James* 18), where he says, "If any one were friend to those with whom he (Clement) is not on speaking terms, that man is among those who would like to destroy the Church of God and, while he seems to be with us in the body, he is against us in mind and heart, and he is a far worse enemy than those who are without and are openly hostile. For he, under the forms of friendship, acts as an enemy and scatters and lays waste the Church." Consider then, my best beloved, if he passes so severe a judgment upon him who associates himself with those whom the pope opposes on account of their actions, with what severity he condemns the man himself to whom the pope is thus opposed.

But now, to return to our point: Is not a sovereignty invented by men of this world who were ignorant of God subject to that which the providence of Almighty God established for his own glory and graciously bestowed upon the world? The Son of God we believe to be God and man, sitting at the right hand of the Father as High Priest, head of all priests and ever making intercession for us. He despised the kingdom of this world wherein the sons of this world puff themselves up and offered himself as a sacrifice upon the cross.

Who does not know that kings and princes derive their origin from men ignorant of God who raised themselves above their fellows by pride, plunder, treachery, murder — in short, by every kind of crime — at the instigation of the Devil, the prince of this world, men blind with greed and intolerable in their audacity? If, then, they strive to bend the priests of God to their will, to whom may they more properly be compared than to him who is chief over all the sons of pride? For he, tempting our High Priest, head of all priests, son of the Most High, offering him all the kingdoms of this world, said: "All these will I give thee if thou wilt fall down and worship me" (Matt. 4:9).

Does anyone doubt that the priests of Christ are to be considered as fathers and masters of kings and princes and of all believers? Would it not be regarded as pitiable madness if a son should try to rule his father or a pupil his master and to bind with unjust obligations the one through whom he expects to be bound or loosed, not only on earth but also in heaven? Evidently recognising this, the emperor Constantine the Great, lord over all kings and princes throughout almost the entire earth, as St. Gregory relates in his letter to the emperor Maurice, at the holy synod of

Nicaea took his place below all the bishops and did not venture to pass any judgment upon them but, even as addressing them as gods, felt that they ought not to be subject to his judgment but that he ought to be bound by their decisions.

Pope Gelasius, urging upon the emperor Anastasius not to feel himself wronged by the truth that was called to his attention said: "There are two powers, O august Emperor, by which the world is governed, the sacred authority of the priesthood and the power of kings. Of these the priestly is by so much the greater as they will have to answer for kings themselves in the day of divine judgment"; and, a little further: "Know that you are subject to their judgments, not that they are to be subjected to your will" [cf. p. 179 above].

In reliance upon such declarations and such authorities, many prelates have excommunicated kings or emperors. If you ask for illustrations: Pope Innocent excommunicated the emperor Arcadius because he consented to the expulsion of St. John Chrysostom from his office. Another Roman pontiff [Pope Zachary] deposed a king of the Franks [Childeric III], not so much on account of his evil deeds as because he was not equal to so great an office, and set in his place Pippin, father of the emperor Charles the Great, releasing all the Franks from the oath of fealty which they had sworn to him. And this is often done by Holy Church when it absolves fighting men from their oaths to bishops who have been deposed by apostolic authority. So St. Ambrose, a holy man but not bishop of the whole Church, excommunicated the emperor Theodosius the Great for a fault which did not seem to other prelates so very grave and excluded him from the Church. He also shows in his writings that the priestly office is as much superior to royal power as gold is more precious than lead. He says: "The honour and dignity of bishops admit of no comparison. If you liken them to the splendour of kings and the diadem of princes, these are as lead compared to the glitter of gold. You see the necks of kings and princes bowed to the knees of priests, and by the kissing of hands they believe that they share the benefit of their prayers." And again: "Know that we have said all this in order to show that there is nothing in this world more excellent than a priest or more lofty than a bishop."

Your Fraternity should remember also that greater power is granted to an exorcist when he is made a spiritual Emperor for the casting out of devils, than can be conferred upon any layman for the purpose of earthly dominion. All kings and princes of this earth who live not piously and in their deeds show not a becoming fear of God are ruled by demons and are sunk in miserable slavery. Such men desire to rule, not guided by the love of God, as priests are, for the glory of God and the profit of human souls, but to display their intolerable pride and to satisfy the lusts of their mind. Of these St. Augustine says in the first book of his Christian doctrine: "He who tries to rule over men — who are by nature equal to him — acts with intolerable pride." Now if exorcists have power over demons, as we have said, how much more over those who are subject to demons and are limbs of demons! And if exorcists are superior to these, how much more are priests superior to them!

Furthermore, every Christian king when he approaches his end asks the aid of a priest as a miserable suppliant that he may escape the prison of hell, may pass from darkness into light and may appear at the judgment seat of God freed from the bonds of sin. But who, layman or priest, in his last moments has ever asked the help of any earthly king for the safety of his soul? And what king or emperor has power through his office to snatch any Christian from the might of the Devil by the sacred rite of baptism, to confirm him among the sons of God and to fortify him by the holy chrism? Or — and this is the greatest thing in the Christian religion — who among them is able by his own word to create the body and blood of the Lord? Or to whom among them is given the power to bind and loose in Heaven and upon earth? From this it is apparent how greatly superior in power is the priestly dignity.

Or who of them is able to ordain any clergyman in the Holy Church — much less to depose him for any fault? For bishops, while they may ordain other bishops, may in no wise depose them except by authority of the Apostolic See. How, then, can even the most slightly informed person doubt that priests are higher than kings? But if kings are to be judged by priests for their sins, by whom can they more properly be judged than by the Roman pontiff?

In short, all good Christians, whosoever they may be, are more properly to be called kings than are evil princes; for the former, seeking the glory of God, rule themselves rigorously; but the latter, seeking their own rather than the things that are of God, being enemies to themselves, oppress others tyrannically. The former are the body of the true Christ; the latter, the body of the Devil. The former rule themselves that they may reign forever with the supreme ruler. The power of the latter brings it to pass that they perish in eternal damnation with the prince of darkness who is king over all the sons of pride.

It is no great wonder that evil priests take the part of a king whom they love and fear on account of honours received from him. By ordaining any person whomsoever, they are selling their God at a bargain price. For as the elect are inseparably united to their Head, so the wicked are firmly bound to him who is head of all evil — especially against the good. But against these it is of no use to argue, but rather to pray God with tears and groans that he may deliver them from the snares of Satan, in which they are caught, and after trial may lead them at last into knowledge of the truth.

So much for kings and emperors who, swollen with the pride of this world, rule not for God but for themselves. But since it is our duty to exhort everyone according to his station, it is our care with God's help to furnish emperors, kings and other princes with the weapons of humility that thus they may be strong to keep down the floods and waves of pride. We know that earthly glory and the cares of this world are wont especially to cause rulers to be exalted, to forget humility and, seeking their own glory, strive to excel their fellows. It seems therefore especially useful for emperors and kings, while their hearts are lifted up in the strife for glory, to learn how to humble themselves and to know fear rather than joy. Let them therefore consider carefully how dangerous, even awesome is the office of emperor or king, how very few find salvation therein, and how those who are saved through God's mercy have become far less famous in the Church by divine judgment than many humble persons. From the beginning of the world to the present day we do not find in all authentic records (seven) emperors or kings whose lives were as distinguished for virtue and piety as were those of a countless multitude of men who despised the world — although we believe that many of them were saved by the mercy of God. Not to speak of Apostles and Martyrs, who among emperors and kings was famed for his miracles as were St. Martin, St. Antony and St. Benedict? What emperor or king ever raised the dead, cleansed lepers or opened the eyes of the blind? True, Holy Church praises and honours the emperor Constantine, of pious memory, Theodosius and Honorius, Charles and Louis, as lovers of justice, champions of the Christian faith and protectors of churches, but she does not claim that they were illustrious for the splendour of their wonderful works. Or to how many names of kings or emperors has Holy Church ordered churches or altars to be dedicated or masses to be celebrated?

Let kings and princes fear lest the higher they are raised above their fellows in this life, the deeper they may be plunged in everlasting fire. Wherefore it is written: "The mighty shall suffer mighty torments" (Sap. 6:6). They shall render unto God an account for all men subject to their rule. But if it is no small labour for the pious individual to guard his own soul, what a task is laid upon princes in the care of so many thousands of souls! And if Holy Church imposes a heavy penalty upon him who takes a single human life, what shall be done to those who send many thousands to death for the glory of this world? These, although they say with their lips, *mea culpa*, for the slaughter of many, yet in their hearts they rejoice at the increase of their glory and neither repent of what they have done nor regret that they have sent their brothers into the world below. So that, since they do not repent with all their hearts and will not restore what they have gained by human bloodshed, their penitence before God remains without the fruits of a true repentance.

Wherefore they ought greatly to fear, and they should frequently be reminded that, as we have said, since the beginning of the world and throughout the kingdoms of the earth very few kings of saintly life can be found out of an innumerable multitude, whereas in one single chair of successive bishops — the Roman — from the time of the blessed Apostle Peter nearly a hundred are counted among the holiest of men. How can this be, except because the kings and princes of the earth, seduced by empty glory, prefer their own interests to the things of the Spirit, whereas pious pontiffs, despising vainglory, set the things of God above the things of the flesh. The former readily punish offenses against themselves but are not troubled by offenses against God; the latter quickly forgive those who sin against them but do not easily pardon offenders against God. The former, far too much given to worldly affairs, think little of spiritual things; the latter, dwelling eagerly upon heavenly subjects, despise the things of this world.

All Christians, therefore, who desire to reign with Christ are to be warned not to reign through ambition for worldly power. They are to keep in mind the admonition of that most holy pope Gregory in his book on the pastoral office: "Of all these things what is to be followed, what held fast, except that the man strong in virtue shall come to his office under compulsion? Let him who is without virtue not come to it even though he be urged thereto." If, then, men who fear God come under compulsion with fear and trembling to the Apostolic See where those who are properly ordained become stronger through the merits of the blessed Apostle Peter, with what awe and hesitation should men ascend the throne of a king where even good and humble men like Saul and David become worse! What we have said above is thus stated in the decrees of the blessed pope Symmachus — though we have learned it by experience: "He, that is St. Peter, transmitted to his successors an unfailing endowment of merit together with an inheritance of innocence"; and again: "For who can doubt that he is holy who is raised to the height of such an office, in which if he is lacking in virtue acquired by his own merits, that which is handed down from his predecessor is sufficient. For either he (Peter) raises men of distinction to bear this burden or he glorifies them after they are raised up."

Wherefore let those whom Holy Church, of its own will and with deliberate judgment, not for fleeting glory but for the welfare of multitudes, has called to royal or imperial rule — let them be obedient and ever mindful of the blessed Gregory's declaration in that same pastoral treatise: "When a man disdains to be the equal of his fellow men, he becomes like an apostate angel. Thus Saul, after his period of humility, swollen with pride, ran into excess of power. He was raised in humility, but rejected in his pride, as God bore witness, saying: 'Though thou wast little in thine own sight, wast thou not made the head of the tribes of Israel?'" (1 Sam. 15:17) and again: "I marvel how, when he was little to himself he was great before God." Let them watch and remember what God says in the Gospel: "I seek not my own glory" (John 8:50), and "He who would be first among you, let him be the servant of all" (Mark 10:44). Let them ever place the honour of God above their own; let them embrace justice and maintain it by preserving to everyone his right; let them not enter into the counsels of the ungodly, but cling to those of religion with all their hearts. Let them not seek to make Holy Church their maidservant or their subject, but recognising priests, the eyes of God, as their masters and fathers, strive to do them becoming honour.

If we are commanded to honour our fathers and mothers in the flesh, how much more our spiritual parents! If he that curseth his father or his mother shall be put to death, what does he deserve who curses his spiritual father or mother? Let not princes, led astray by carnal affection, set their own sons over that flock for whom Christ shed his blood if a better and more suitable man can be found. By thus loving their own son more than God they bring the greatest evils upon the Church. For it is evident that he who fails to provide to the best of his ability so great and necessary an advantage for our holy mother, the Church, does not love God and his neighbour as befits a Christian man. If this one virtue of charity be wanting, then whatever of good the man may do will lack all saving grace.

But if they do these things in humility, keeping their love for God and their neighbour as they ought, they may count upon the mercy of him who said: "Learn of me, for I am meek and lowly of heart" (Matt. 11:29). If they humbly imitate him, they shall pass from their servile and transient reign into the kingdom of eternal liberty.

Translation: Ephraim Emerton (Columbia University Press, 1932). Used with permission.

Norman Anonymous

(fl. ca. 1100)

The title "Norman Anonymous" refers to the supposed author of a collection of thirty-four tracts that appear to belong to the antipapal polemics of the early twelfth century, composed in the shadow of Gregory VII. Traversing a spectrum of political and ecclesiological issues, some of which are connected with the churches of York and Rouen, the tracts have been variously attributed to Archbishop Gerard of York — hence the name "York Tracts" *(Tractatus Eboracenses)* — and, more recently, to an anonymous Norman canon of Rouen. One tract in particular (24a) has attracted the interest of political historians such as A. J. Carlyle and E. H. Kantorowicz on account of its exceptional theological defense of the supremacy of royal over episcopal authority and its demolition of the Roman primacy. Authorship of this tract by an English cleric would link it to the investiture controversy in England, and so distinguish it from other radical repudiations of papal hierocracy emanating from imperial circles (e.g., those of Peter Crassus and Bishop Benzo of Alba). Although textual evidence for a Rouen author comes from the orders for royal coronation and episcopal consecration incorporated into this tract, which appear to be the versions in the current Rouen liturgy (see Nineham 1963, 31-45), this solution has not yet accounted satisfactorily for the enduring influence of the tract in English political thought, as is witnessed by Wyclif's repetition of its central theological argument (see below, p. 509), although the key may lie in the channels of Continental influence on the Anglo-Norman church in the early twelfth century (Barker 1991, 30-33).

The core of the royalist argument, extracted from the episcopal and coronation orders, is a twofold christological theory of kingship and priesthood, undoubtedly intended as the theological answer to the pope's Petrine commission and the "power of the keys." According to this theory, both king and priest at their consecration receive the sacramental image of Christ, the "god-man," which is the Spirit of sanctification, so that they become two persons, one by nature and another by grace. The king, however, receives the image of Christ's eternal and uncreated kingship in which he is equal to and one with the Father, whereas the priest receives the image of Christ's assumed human priesthood, in which he is separated from and inferior to the Father. Moreover, the royal office reflects Christ's divine kingly functions of creating, governing, disposing, and saving, whereas the priestly office reflects his human sacerdotal function of redeeming humanity through the sacrifice of himself to suffering and death. Thus the relationship of the earthly offices mirrors the christological offices, in which kingship is ontologically prior to priesthood and the latter is teleologically subordinate to the former — a reversal of the papalist conception. Only as eternal ruler does Christ assume human priesthood in order that mankind may be made partaker of his divine kingdom and power.

This means that earthly kings (for whom the Israelite kings are paradigmatic) rule over the entire body of Christians in their kingdoms, laity and clergy, ensuring the unity, outward order, spiritual and corporeal welfare of the "temple of God." Of their creative power they institute bishops, endowing them not only with temporal possessions but with the spiritual sword of ecclesiastical jurisdiction. Kings administer divine justice, punish violations of God's law, protect the church against enemies from within and without, and call councils to legislate and judge for the "people of God." And in that the royal unction (anointing) alone imitates the Father's eternal anointing of the Son, the royal power excels and includes the sacerdotal, even to the point of remitting sins and offering the bread and wine in the eucharistic sacrifice. Here is the sacral kingship of the later Ottonians and Salians taken to its theoretical limit.

Further Reading: L. K. Barker, "Ivo of Chartres and the Anglo-Norman Cultural Tradition," *Anglo-Norman Studies* 13 (1991): 15-33; N. F. Cantor, *Church, Kingship, and Lay Investiture in England, 1089-1135* (Princeton: Princeton University Press, 1958); E. H. Kantorowicz, *The King's Two Bodies: A Study in Medieval Political Theology* (Princeton: Princeton University Press, 1957); R. Nineham, "The So-called Anonymous of York," *Journal of Ecclesiastical History* 14 (1963): 31-45; K. Pellens, "The Tracts of the Norman Anonymous: CCCC 415," *Transactions of the Cambridge Bibliographical Society* 4:2 (1965): 155-65; G. H. Williams, *The Norman Anonymous of 1100 A.D.: Toward the Identification and Evaluation of the So-called Anonymous of York* (Cambridge, Mass.: Harvard University Press, 1951); K. M. Woody, "Marginalia on the Norman Anonymous," *Harvard Theological Review* 66 (1973).

From *The Consecration of Bishops and Kings*

Holy Church is the Bride of Christ, who is true King and Priest; but it is not as priest that he is said to make her his bride, but as king. That is why she is called "queen," as Scripture says: "At your right hand stands the queen in golden clothes and robed in many colors" (Ps. 45:9). St. Augustine, in a sermon beginning *They rightly celebrate the church's festival* [not identified], unambiguously gives the church the title of queen. The prophets, too, in predicting that Christ would come to his Holy Church, foretold the advent of a king, not a priest. Think of what the prophets Isaiah and Zedekiah said: "Shout aloud O daughters of Zion. . . . Lo, your king comes to you, a righteous Saviour" (Zech. 9:9; cf. Isa. 40:9). And Jeremiah: "Behold the days are coming, says the Lord, when I will raise up for David a righteous branch, and he shall reign as king . . . and Israel will dwell securely" (Jer. 23:5f.). And you will find it similarly foretold throughout Scripture that a king would come for the marriage of Holy Church, not a priest. Which is why it is called a *royal* wedding, as we sing at the Epiphany: "Today the heavenly bride is joined to the Church . . ." and so on as far as ". . . royal wedding." A royal wedding, not a priestly one; and to a queenly bride, not a priestess. The sacramental sign *(sacramentum)* of this wedding, then [i.e., the ceremony of a coronation], is connected with royal, not priestly dignity, and kings in the image of Christ the King are more fit for this wedding, since it is they who have represented it sacramentally. Christ was told, "You are a priest for eternity," and the words go on, "after the order of Melchizedek" (Ps. 110:4 = Heb. 7:17), i.e., "king of righteousness." ("Melchizedek" means "king of righteousness.") The priesthood conferred on him was not from the Levitical order but from that of the king of righteousness. Christ's priesthood, then, is clearly modeled on the order of the king of righteousness, since Christ himself is king of righteousness who reigns *from* eternity and shall reign *for* eternity *and aye*. He is said to be a priest "for eternity," but not "and aye." For priesthood will not be needed *in* eternity nor *for aye*.

By divine authority and the institution of the holy fathers kings in God's church are ordained and consecrated at the sacred altar with holy unction and benediction, that they may have authority to rule a Christian people, the Lord's people, "a chosen race . . . a holy nation, a people of his possession" (1 Pet. 2:9), i.e., God's Holy Church. For God's Church is quite simply a congregation of faithful Christians united in faith, hope, and love and occupying the house of God together. When kings are consecrated, they receive the power to rule this body: to rule it, to confirm it in judgment and justice, and to organize it according to the system of Christian law. That is what it is to "reign" in the church, which is God's realm: i.e., to reign jointly with Christ, i.e., to rule, protect, and defend the church. To reign means to rule one's subjects well and to serve God in fear.

But this is the very purpose for which the order of bishops is instituted and consecrated by sacred unction and benediction, too; it, too, is to rule Holy Church by the pattern of teaching transmitted from God. So the blessed Pope Gelasius says, "There are two principals, august emperor, by which this world is ruled: the consecrated authority of priests and the royal power" [see p. 179 above]. By "this world" he means Holy Church, which is on pilgrimage through the world. In this world, then, the principal rule is shared by priestly authority, governing in holy things, and kingly power. There is a popular opinion that the principal position is divided between the two so that the priest is principal in ruling souls, the king in ruling bodies — as though souls could be ruled without bodies and bodies without souls! But this could in no way be so. What counts as good rule of bodies is necessarily good rule of souls, too, and vice versa, since the rule of both is intended to ensure the salvation of both together at the resurrection of the dead. However, if it were the case that the king was principal only in the rule of Christians' bodies, would that not make him

252

the principal in ruling the temple of God, which is holy? For the apostle says: "Do you not know that your bodies are the temple of the Holy Spirit?" (1 Cor. 6:19). And again: "You are the temple of the living God, which is holy" (2 Cor. 6:16); and, "Now you are no longer strangers and sojourners. . . . you are built into a dwelling place of God in the Holy Spirit" (Eph. 2:19-22). St. Ambrose says: "The bodies of Christians are sanctified in baptism and consecrated by sacred anointing, after which they are clothed with a mystical robe, that they may acquire both royal and priestly dignity" [quotation not identified]. This being so, the king is clearly principal in ruling those who have priestly dignity. The king must not, then, be barred from governing Holy Church, that is, the Christian people, since this would divide the Church's kingdom and waste it. "Every kingdom divided against itself shall be laid waste," says the Lord (Luke 11:17). It is not good that Holy Church's kingdom be laid waste, since the church itself would quickly be laid waste without a kingdom. But it will be without a kingdom if kings are barred from superintending and protecting it.

Even the bodies of Christians, in fact, would hardly be ruled at all if royal power were cut off from the church. The holy fathers and apostolic bishops understood this when, by divine providence, they consecrated kings to protect Holy Church and defend the Catholic faith; for were there no royal power to control pagans and heretics, they would have brought the church, the catholic faith, and the Christian religion to frustration and confusion. But Christian kings repulsed the pagan assaults upon the church and condemned the heretics, eliminating corrupt doctrines from deep in the church's heart. They reigned together with Christ — in fact, they administered Christian laws within Christ's kingdom. This could not be done by priestly authority alone; that is why royal power was indispensable to priestly authority, to guard it and defend it and preserve the peace and security of the church inviolate. So these two persons, priest and king, represent Christ and reflect him.

As St. Augustine claims (*De consensu evangelistarum* I.3.5): "Our Lord Jesus Christ, one and the same true king and true priest to rule us and to cleanse us, identified these two persons, which were borne by separate people in earlier times, as enacting his own role (*figura*)." In the Old Testament we read that these two persons were consecrated by the unction of holy oil and sanctified by divine benediction, that in ruling the people they might occupy the figure and function (*vices*) of the Lord's Christ, bearing his image sacramentally. The Spirit of the Lord and the divine power came upon them by this same unction and divine benediction, so that they took on the role and image of Christ and were "turned into another man" (cf. 1 Sam. 10:6). Accordingly, they were, in each case, one man in their own persons, another man in Spirit and power. Aaron, the first anointed pontiff, and Saul, the first anointed king, for instance — each became one man in his own person and another in spirit and power. In their own persons Aaron and Saul were different persons, but not in Spirit and power, for then they were the Lord's Christ. In each was understood to subsist a double person: one by nature, the other by grace, one in human personal distinctiveness, the other in Spirit and power; one like other men through natural conditions, the other surpassing all others through the transcendence of the divine and the effect of the sacrament. That is to say, one person was the natural individual human being, the other, by grace, was Christ the God-man, the one distinctive to each, the other common to them; for it is something common to king and priest that they should be the Lord's Christ, though in Holy Scripture you will more commonly find the term "Christ" applied specifically to the king, rather than to the bishop. [. . .]

[665] Common to king and priest are the anointing with holy oil and the spirit of sanctification and power of benediction; common, too, is the name of God and Christ, and the reality to which the name belongs. If the reality were not there, the name would be misleading. But they have the reality in fact, and the name applies to them, too, though by grace and not by nature. Only Christ, the Son of God and Son of man, has that name both by grace and nature. By nature he is God, not made god by someone else. By nature he is holy, not made holy by someone else. Yet, as I said, he is so by grace, too, since in his humanity he was made god and made holy by the Father. But the king and priest who are the image and figure of this Christ, the God-man, are both of them wholly man, and so entirely *made* god and made holy by the grace of unction and the consecrating benediction. To employ a Greek etymology: "consecration" is *apotheosis*, which means "deification." If, then, the priest and king are, through grace, each of them God and the Lord's Christ, whatever each undertakes and performs in this grace is undertaken and performed not by man but by God and the Lord's Christ. And whatever is done to him in this grace, is done not to a man but to God and to the Lord's Christ. And whatever he approves or bestows, whether as king he grants a bishopric or as bishop he grants a kingdom, it is not a man who approves or bestows but God and the Lord's Christ.

And to tell the truth, as the Lord's Christ, the king may properly be called a priest and the priest a king. For it is a priestly function to rule the people in the Spirit of Christ, and a royal function to offer sacrifice and burnt offerings in the Spirit. It is his function, indeed, to present himself "a living sacrifice, holy and acceptable to God" (Rom. 12:1) and to offer God a sacrifice of praise, which is the sacrifice of righteousness, the sacrifice of a contrite spirit, all of which is signified by the sacrifice of flesh which the priest would offer in the visible ritual of the sacrament. If anyone wishes to pursue the question why the visible sacrifice was performed by a priest and not by the king, it was to demonstrate the very considerable difference between them deriving from their contrasting sacramental meanings. For the royal sacrament was in considerable measure different from the priestly: that is, the priest prefigured one of Christ's natures, the human nature; the king prefigured the other nature, the divine. The king stood for the higher nature in which Christ was equal to God the Father, the priest for the lower nature in which he was subordinate to the Father. The priest foretold that Christ would, for a while, be subject to death and "give himself up . . . a fragrant offering and sacrifice to God the Father" (Eph. 5:2). The king foretold that Christ would reign for ever and be seated on the throne in heavenly places "far above all rule and authority and power and dominion" (Eph. 1:21), to be crowned with glory and honor and set over every work of God, till all be subject to him (cf. Heb. 2:7ff.). Saul and David are said to have been chosen by God and anointed over God's possession, Israel; and they sat on the throne of the kingdom in Jerusalem. But the throne on which Christ will sit for eternity is higher than this, as both prophetic and angelic words declare. For Isaiah says (9:7): "Of the increase of his government and of peace there will be no end, above the throne of David and over his kingdom, to establish it and to uphold it with justice and with righteousness from this time forth and for evermore." And the angel to Mary (Luke 1:32): "The Lord will give to him the throne of his father David . . . ," etc. Not, "he will give him the throne of his father Aaron," nor "he will sit above the throne of Aaron and over his kingdom, to establish it." He says, the Lord will give him the throne of David and he will sit over the throne and kingdom of David. These words prove that there is one throne and one seat and one kingdom, which belongs to Christ and David. Christ and David are one in spirit, and have one power, one glory, and one dignity. So David's seat and throne and kingdom, his power and glory and dignity, are over all, greater than all, and holier than all. We conclude that the Lord gave him authority and rule even over the Lord's own priests. *The Lord* gave him, I say — the Lord who does nothing wrong but all things right. It was right, then, that the king should have authority and rule over priests. [. . .]

[667] Now let us come to the New Testament. Here, too, priests and kings are sanctified by holy oil and consecrated by chrism and divine benediction. In my judgment, what has been said so far about kings and priests in the Old Testament carries even greater truth and conviction here, since it is even more certain and true that they are partakers in divine grace and the divine nature. They are one with God and his Christ; they are Gods and Christs through the spirit of adoption. Through them Christ and the Holy Spirit speak; in them Christ has his representatives, and does his work; in them he sacrifices, reigns, and governs his people. Each of them, therefore, is Christ and God in the Spirit; each, in fulfilling his office, has the role and image of Christ and God, the priest Christ's priestly role and image, the king Christ's kingly role and image; the priest Christ's lower, human office and nature, the king Christ's higher, divine office and nature. For Christ the God-man is truly and supremely king and priest. He is king by virtue of his eternal divinity: not made, not created, not inferior to or separate from the Father, but equal to and one with the Father. He is priest by virtue of his assumption of humanity, made so according to the order of Melchizedek, created, and so subordinate to the Father. As king he created all things, rules all things, governing and preserving men and angels alike. As priest he has redeemed mankind alone, that they may reign with him.

There was one all-inclusive reason for his becoming a priest and offering himself in sacrifice: that mankind might be his partner in his kingdom and royal power. The Kingdom of Heaven is promised to believers throughout Scripture, but we are never promised the Priesthood of Heaven. The conclusion is plain: Christ's royalty is superior and of greater moment than his priestly power, just as his divinity is superior and of greater moment than his humanity. This explains the view held by some that in human affairs, too, kingly power is superior and of greater moment than priestly power, and the king of greater moment than the priest, since it reflects that nature of Christ, and imitates that power, which is superior and of greater moment. It is not contrary to divine justice, they maintain, that priestly appointments are instituted by royalty, or even subject to it, since in Christ the priestly office was instituted by his own royal power and was as such subordinate to the Father, to whom he is equal in royalty. If someone claims that a priest, too, is a king — for anyone who exercises rule may properly be called a king — that argument seems to lend support to the conclusion: a king may be instituted by a king, a lesser king, that is, by a greater. And they can reply that in the text of the holy benediction [i.e., in the coronation] the king is called "first prince."

However that may be, king and priest have some privileges in common and the same grace; but they have also some peculiar privileges and differing offices. For though in exercising rule they apparently have grace in common, there are matters in which priests must proceed in one way, kings in another, so that the grace conferred for the fulfilling of their responsibilities is different. But when a priest is instituted by a king, it is not by human power that he is instituted, but divine. For the king's power is God's power — God's by nature, the king's by grace. So the king *is* God in Christ — but by grace; and whatever the king does is done not by a mere man, but by one who by grace has *become* God and his Christ. One might even say that it is God-in-Christ by nature who acts — through the agent whom he has entrusted to represent him.

But let us see what the king confers upon a candidate for bishop when he presents him with the pastoral staff. It is not the episcopal order as such, nor his priestly right that the king confers on him, but what belongs to his own right and to the sphere of earthly rule, i.e., dominion over real property, the responsibility for care of the church, and the authority to rule God's people, which is the temple of the living God and the bride of our Lord Christ, Holy Church. Augustine (*On the Gospel of John* 6.25f.) testifies that it is by the right of kings that a bishop controls earthly property, i.e., possesses estates: "There are estates. By what right do you defend your estates? Divine or human? Suppose they answer, 'Both divine and human — the first in the Scriptures, the second in royal laws.' The implication is that it is by *human* right that anyone holds possessions. For by divine right 'the earth is the Lord's and the fulness thereof' (Ps. 24:1). God has made poor and rich from the one and the same clay; poor and rich are supported on one and the same earth. It is by human right that we say, 'My estate, my house, my servant.' By human right, which means the right of emperors. Why so? Because human rights, too, are distributed among the human race by God through emperors and temporal kings." [. . .]

[669] If we take note only of their respective methods of consecration, it will appear that the anointing, consecration, and authorization of king and priest is one and the same. But if we take note of the models of the divine reason which determines the method of their anointing and consecration, then the anointing, consecration, and authorization of the king is superior to that of the priest. The oil of consecration and the visible sacramental sign may be the same in the anointing and consecration of king and priest, yet in terms of the interior grace and invisible meaning of the spiritual anointing, and most of all in terms of the representation of God's son for which it is instituted, it is apparent that the unction, consecration, and authorization of the king are better and holier than that of the priest. For priestly anointing and sanctification were constructed on the model of Aaron, whom Moses anointed and sanctified — and, more importantly, on the model of the apostles, whom God the Father anointed with spiritual unction and the grace of the Holy

Spirit. But the anointing of the king was constructed on the model of him whom God the Father "anointed" from the beginning "beyond all his fellows" (Heb. 1:9), namely Jesus Christ our Lord. Now, the "fellows" of kings in their anointing are the bishops, presbyters, and all Christians. But God "anointed" him "with the oil of gladness," i.e., the grace of the Holy Spirit *"beyond"* all these (Ps. 45:7).

As has been said, he anointed priests, as he did apostles, with a spiritual anointing, but the king he anointed as he did his firstborn Son, begotten beyond all his fellows before the ages. We have this on the authority of the text of the sacred liturgies of consecration, through which heaven bestows on them whatever sanctification, grace, and power they have. As the Son of God is superior to his apostles, as his anointing is holier than theirs, as his power surpasses their power, so it would seem, the king is superior to priests, his anointing is holier than their anointing, his power surpasses theirs. In the same way, as the throne of God's Son has precedence of the apostles' thrones, so the king's throne has precedence of the priest's, and the scepter of his kingdom of the staff of their pastoral office, since the scepter and throne of the king is a sacrament of the scepter and throne of Christ. The text of the two benedictions is further proof of this fact. The king is blessed with the words, "that in all things you may be worthy to follow him, to whom it is said: 'Your throne, O God, is for ever and ever, your righteous scepter is the scepter of your kingdom'" [Coronation liturgy, quoting Ps. 45:6]. Not: "worthy to follow Peter or Paul or the other apostles," as bishops do in keeping with their order; but, "in all things you may be worthy . . . ," etc. It is the king who, before anyone else, *follows* Christ, i.e., by representing him and imitating him. Bishops may follow Christ, but they do so only through the mediation of the apostles who represent him and imitate him. So we can see that the king's authority and ordination is superior to that of the bishops, or, if not superior, at least it is obviously not inferior. [. . .]

[672] This, then, is the way in which the power of the king is Christ, as "the Lord is the strength of his people" (Ps. 28:8). The king has no power without Christ, but it is Christ who exerts both strength in the people and power in the king. "Thine, O Lord, is the power . . . thine is the kingdom, O Lord" (1 Chron. 29:11). It is he who reigns in kings and has dominion over peoples. And this is the mighty grace bestowed upon Christ: he wills that men may participate in his power and name, to the extent that they may rule a people and be called "anointed" *(christi)*. For bishops are anointed with chrism, and kings receive the keys of the kingdom of heaven, which are more appropriate to royal than to priestly power. For we say "the keys of the kingdom of heaven," not "of the priesthood of heaven," which indicates that priests are destined to become kings. These keys are properly the king's, insofar as a kingdom is the honor that belongs to a king. And through the sacrament of blessing he is shown to be the Lord's anointed, since "he who is united to the Lord becomes one spirit with him" (1 Cor. 6:17). So it is that he himself, in the spirit of Christ, becomes "the key of David" and the scepter of the house of Israel, "who opens and no one shall shut, who shuts and no one opens" (Isa. 22:22; Rev. 3:7). He "brings out the prisoner from the dungeon" (Isa. 42:7), "him who sits in darkness and in the shadow of death" (Luke 1:79), for this is the grace he has been given, to be in every respect like him whose nature it is to be all these things. By grace, therefore, where appropri-

ate, he opens the kingdom of heaven, that no one shall close, and leads the prisoner from the dungeon (i.e., delivers him from sin) and him who sits in darkness and in the shadow of death (i.e., brings him into the kingdom of life and light). Such a key is rightly called "the key of the kingdom of heaven" (Matt. 16:19).

This grace, of course, is common to kings and priests, insofar as priests, too, are kings. It should puzzle no one that I say "insofar as they, too, are kings," for the keys of the kingdom — that is, the power and rule of the kingdom and the kingdom itself — are an honor that belongs to kings, *not* to the priesthood *as such*. Peter and the other apostles received the keys of the kingdom from Christ *before* they entered the priestly office but when they were already partners in Christ's rule of his disciples, which shows that these keys belong properly not to priests but to kings.

We should note, however, that the keys are sometimes spoken of in the plural as the "keys of the kingdom of heaven," sometimes in the singular, as the "key of David." But the plural is a figure of speech, the singular is literal. There is only one key, which is at the same time the key of the kingdom of heaven and the key of David, i.e., the king of heaven. Similarly, there is only one power, virtue, and wisdom of God, by which kings reign, priests consecrate, and both kings and priests exercise judgment. God's power, wisdom, and virtue is not divided into two; and kings and priests can have no other power, wisdom, and virtue than that which is in God, because apart from God no power can be discerned, conceived, or constituted. Whether, then, the king institutes the priest or the priest institutes the king, it is not one man who institutes another, but the sacred power, the sacred virtue, and the sacred wisdom of God which institutes both the one and the other, each by the other's agency. [. . .]

[676] So runs the text of the preface [to the coronation rite], from which you may judge how far the emperor takes precedence of pontiffs and is exalted by God's providence to heaven, "that he should summon the pontiffs of the world to council and, the grace of our Lord Jesus Christ working with him, remove the pestilence of falsehood from the flock of Christ, and restore it with the pastures of truth." For it says, "At the motion of supernal grace" and so on. A high and sacred power, indeed, is the emperor's: working together with the grace of God to feed his flock on the pastures of his truth, and granted to rule all men, to convene the pontiffs of the world in council, to treat of the sacraments of the catholic faith and of heavenly matters, and, through the grace of God working with him, even to command the pontiffs that they treat of them. So he is said to be exalted to heaven by the Lord Jesus Christ. To heaven, I say — but not that corporeal heaven which we see, but the incorporeal heaven which we do not see, that is, the invisible God. To God he is exalted, for he is conjoined to him in power, so that no power is nearer God or more exalted than the emperor's, but every other power lies beneath him. The supreme heavenly emperor and the earthly emperor next in rank have but one and the same power, belonging first to the heavenly emperor, second to the earthly. [. . .]

[677] "Together with God's blessing he receives the sword, with which through the Holy Spirit's power to drive out all his enemies and every adversary of Holy Church, to safeguard the realm committed to him and to protect the camps of God, that his enemies' every resolve may be shattered by the valor of the spiritual sword." This is a double sword — one aspect is material, the other sacramental. In its

material aspect it is physical, but in its power it is spiritual, and has the effect of ex-communication. Which explains the words, "Look, here are two swords!" to which the reply was, "It is enough" (Luke 22:38).

He also receives the crown "of glory and justice, which is the honor and the work of fortitude" and sign of the heavenly crown, of which the prayer says to God: "you have placed it on his head" — the king's — that is, the crown of the Lord's anointed, a crown "of precious stones." With this, moreover, he receives the function of blessing, "so that wheresoever he shall call upon God's help for any, God shall speedily be at hand to protect and defend them."

He receives, too, "the scepter, the emblem of royal power, the upright staff of kingly rule, the staff of virtue, with which he may rightly govern himself, with valor defend the Holy Church which God has committed to him against the wicked, cor-rect the depraved, bring peace to the upright, and, that they may keep to the path of righteousness, direct them by his own (*sc.* divine) assistance, until he pass from the temporal to the eternal kingdom." Evidently it is this scepter that is called, in the spirit and symbolically, "the key of David and the scepter of the house of Israel," that is, Christ the right hand of God, "who opens and no one shall shut, who shuts and no one opens" (Isa. 22:22; Rev. 3:7). Accordingly, he carries it in his right hand, since symbolically he is the right hand of God, i.e., Christ, "'who brings out the prisoner from the dungeon' (Isa. 42:7), 'him who sits in darkness and in the shadow of death' (Luke 1:79), so that in all things he may be worthy to follow and imitate him to whom is said: 'Your throne, O God, endures for ever and ever, your scepter, the scep-ter of your kingdom, is upright. You have loved justice and hated iniquity, wherefore God, your God, has anointed you with the oil of gladness above your fellows' (Ps. 45:6f.). In whose pattern," therefore, he is anointed and deified, and is able to follow him in everything. He can therefore remit sins, and can offer bread and wine in sac-rifice, which, indeed, he does on the day of his coronation, a day of extraordinary so-lemnity. [. . .]

[679] No one is blessed in more expansive and generous terms, no one conse-crated and divinized by more numerous and imposing rites, no one, in fact, may take precedence of him on whom these blessings and rites are bestowed. No one, indeed, has blessings and rites of comparable weight, who could be thought his equal. That is why he should not be called a "layman," for he is the Lord's anointed, by grace a god, supreme ruler, senior pastor, teacher, defender and instructor of Holy Church, lord of his brothers, to be reverenced by all, chief and supreme protector. It should not be thought that since the pontiff consecrates him he is below the pontiff, for it is common enough for the lesser to consecrate the greater, the inferior the superior, as cardinals do the pope and suffragan bishops their metropolitan. They are not au-thors of the consecration but administrators of it. God effects the sacrament; they simply render ministry. The greater sacraments God grants to whom he will, to whom he will the lesser. In this that we have said about the king, my Lord the Pope has no ground of offense, since his own supreme pontificate also is a form of king-ship.

Translation: Editors, from *Libelli de Lite*, vol. 3, ed. H. Boehmer.

Honorius Augustodunensis

(ca. 1080/90–ca. 1156)

A "prolific and popular" theological writer (Southern 1990, 376), Honorius Augustodunensis ("of Autun," though no connection with that place is to be traced) appears to have been an itinerant scholar-monk who spent considerable time in Canterbury in the first decade of the twelfth century and settled at Regensburg from 1120 onward, probably in an Irish monastic community. While his early writings exhibit the influence of St. Anselm of Canterbury, his style of Christian Platonism also has affinities with the schools of Chartres, Laon, and St. Victor. His apology for priestly as against royal rule, entitled *Summa gloria,* provides a measure of the impact of christocentric kingship theory in certain circles before 1150. For it appears devoted to reversing the ontological and historical status comparatively assigned to the royal and sacerdotal offices by such royal polemicists as the Norman Anonymous.

Honorius's central argument is that the higher dignity of the priesthood, and its inherently superior jurisdictional authority, is not only finally established by Christ, but divinely revealed throughout human history. Surveying the progeny of Adam and Noah, he divides them into the two types of "spiritual" priesthood and "carnal" kingship, after the prototypes of Abel and Cain: the shepherd of sheep whose sacrifice was acceptable to God and the vengeful murderer who founds and rules a city. Among the posterity of Abraham, the types are continued by Isaac and Ishmael, Jacob and Esau — divinely elevated to lordship and divinely cast down to servitude, until God's institution of priestly rule over the Israelite nation through the agency of Moses. According to Honorius, Israelite monarchy was a further phase of priestly supremacy: elected and anointed by priests or prophets, kings were divinely sustained in their authority over temporals only as they obeyed their spiritual masters; royal disobedience and rebellion brought dispersion, captivity, and reversion to the government of priests.

Similarly, Petrine rule over the church was not altered by the pagan emperor's conversion, for Constantine conceded the imperial crown to Pope Sylvester, who, holding the highest spiritual and temporal dominions, invested the erstwhile emperor with the sword of temporal judgment for the punishment of incorrigible malefactors. Honorius's rendering of the *Donation of Constantine*, the most innovative feature of his treatise, changes the original eighth-century document in two respects: the scope of the "donation" is no longer confined to the Western Empire only, but extends to *empire as such;* and the character of the "donation" is less a gift than a restitution, a restitution to the priesthood of its perpetual, divinely bestowed authority. These novelties, left undeveloped, will undergo significant elaboration in future papalist literature. Nevertheless, one political consequence is spelled out: the Roman emperor should be elected by the pope and the "spiritual (i.e., episcopal) princes" of the empire.

Honorius's hierocratic radicalism is softened by his recollection (5, 6) of an earlier Gelasian and Gregorian (Gregory I) theological appraisal of kingship which, for example, requires subjects of a "tyrant" (i.e., a heretic, schismatic, apostate, or rebel against the Roman see) to endure his waywardness patiently, while at the same time declining communion with him.

Further Reading: W. Beinert, *Die Kirche, Gottes Heil in der Welt. Die Lehr von der Kirche nach den Schriften des Rupert von Deutz, Honorius Augustodunensis and Gerhoch von Reichersberg: ein Beitrag zur Ekklesiologie des 12. Jahrhunderts* (Münster: Aschendorff, 1973); V. I. J. Flint, *Honorius Augustodunensis of Regensburg* (Aldershot: Variorum, 1995); H.-W. Goetz, "Die '*Summa Gloria*'. Ein Beitrag zu den politischen Vorstellungen des Honorius Augustodunensis," *Zeitschrift für Kirchengeschichte* 89 (1978): 307ff.; R. W. Southern, *Saint Anselm: A Portrait in a Landscape* (Cambridge: Cambridge University Press, 1990).

From *Summa Gloria*

1. The whole community of the faithful is divided into clergy and people; for we ascribe to the clergy a life of contemplation, but to the people one of business. (The first is often called "spiritual" and the latter "secular"; the former is ruled by the priestly, the latter by the royal rod.) The question is therefore commonly asked: should priestly rule rightly be judged superior to royal in privilege (*dignitas*), or royal rule to priestly? Certainly I could reply to this briefly that, just as the spiritual is placed before the secular, or just as the clergy surpass the people in order of eminence, so priestly rule transcends royal rule in privilege. But nothing seems valid to the ignorant, greatly blinded by worldly wisdom, unless it is strengthened by a large number of testimonies from Scripture. So in order that this question may be more clearly analysed, let us inspect the root of the solution to the problem more diligently, from the origin of the world.

The first Adam was created from pure earth, but he who should take flesh from a pure Virgin bore the form of a second, heavenly Adam. Adam begot two sons from his wife, as Christ ordained that clergy and people should take their origin from his spouse the church. Now each son represented one of the two orders in the work that he did. For Abel, who was a shepherd of sheep, represented priestly rule, that with pastoral care keeps watch to guard the sheep of Christ against the rabid wolves of heretical depravity; and he sacrificed a lamb that represented the Lamb who bears the sins of the world, the Word of God. We read that his sacrifice was acceptable to God, because the priestly rule placed upon him was entrusted to him by the Father. Also, it is not written that he begot children, since the priestly rule of the Church is kept separate from carnal union; he was killed by his brother since priestly rule is often oppressed by royal rule. On the other hand, Cain, who cultivated the land and founded a state in which he was also king, showed forth the type of royal rule. We do not read that the Lord was mindful of this man's gifts, because tradition says he usurped his brother's office for himself. Therefore the Lord declares most clearly the greatness of the excellence with which priestly rule towers over royal: he praised the priest Abel highly and approved his sacrifice, but he censured Cain the king and rejected his gifts. Do not be swayed by the fact that it is written that Cain was the elder by birth, for what is meant is that the carnal precedes the spiritual, since here in our experience, too, one is weighed down by the concerns of the flesh while one lives in the flesh, later to be clothed with appropriate glory in the state of spiritual rest. [. . .]

Now, Holy Scripture declares in the following places the privileges with which priestly rule shines forth before royal rule. It says: "The sons of God went in to the daughters of men" (Gen. 6:4). Behold, the descendants of Seth, who succeeded Abel as priest, were named "sons of God"; the descendants of Cain, who succeeded to his kingdom, were called "sons of men." [. . .]

2. But it must be marked that these men also, who were called "sons of God," were drowned in the flood, since certainly priesthood does not save those who are condemned by a life worthy of reproach. Noah, who directed the Ark over the waves, full of various sorts of creatures, bore the type of Christ who directs the church, full of various kinds of humanity, over the waves of this age. His two sons, Shem and Japhet, most clearly bear the images of priestly and kingly rule, and represent the clergy and people. For from Shem is said, by very learned men, to have descended Melchizedek, who (it is written) was the priest of the Most High. We also read that Melchizedek was king of Salem, because the ruler *(rector)* of any state used then to be called "king" *(rex)*. It is also written that he was the first-born, because true priestly rule is said to have started from him. Now, we find that the Roman empire proceeded from Japhet. Furthermore, the third son [Ham], who was bound in slavery to his two brothers, is generally accepted to represent the people subject both to priestly and to royal rule, and we see that the Jewish people served under both. He, though his father's son, laughed at things which should have been reverenced, as the Jewish people harassed Christ in his humanity, or as the crowd harasses the prelates in their vulnerability. Hence, the divine voice makes clear through Noah how great is the dignity which differentiates priestly from royal rule. It says, "God will extend Japhet; he will dwell in the tents of Shem" (Gen. 9:27). Indeed, although the Roman empire (which descends from Japhet) has been extended over all the globe, yet He lives in

the tents of Shem, that is in the churches of the priests. Canaan was their servant, as the Jewish people, now deprived of priestly and royal rule, have been made Christian subjects, whether they like it or no.

We should not pass over in silence the fact that Nimrod the giant descended from the seed of Ham — Nimrod, who built the tower of Babel against God, by which he became the first to acquire a worldwide tyranny. He was the first to teach the worship of idols. From this root came forth Ninus [founder of Nineveh], who first usurped the sceptre of monarchy for himself, and by his strength subdued the families of the other brothers, that is of Shem and Japhet. Tyrants imitate him even now, who seize improper control of the laws of the kingdom and cruelly oppress the clergy and people. Since the princely rule of this Ninus and his successors was not supported by divine authority, it is called not "royal rule," but "tyranny." For this reason also Abraham and his family did not submit to him, but rather, following a divine command, fled his dominion. As a priest he instructed the chosen people of God to live in the land which was to be given to their descendants, where, too, it is written, they did not serve kings; more often, rather, kings bowed down before them.

Since the royal and priestly rule of the faithful people had its beginning in this man, he had two sons as types: of these, Isaac represented priestly rule, since he blessed his son like a pontiff; but Ishmael, who spent his time in the pursuit of hunting, manifested royal rule. The difference, then, between Isaac, who (it is written) was his father's heir, and Ishmael, who (we read) was expelled, is the same as the distance between priestly and royal rule which we know of by divine authority. So it is that, just as Ishmael used to persecute Isaac, even now royalty persecutes the priesthood.

Now Isaac, offered as a sacrifice by his father, bears the form of Christ who was crucified by his father for us. Isaac's two sons not only represent priestly and royal rule as types, but exercise them in their deeds. For since Jacob offered his sacrifice over a stone, he very clearly represents priestly rule; Esau, however, manifests royal rule, since he brought forth twelve rulers from his own stock. But the divine voice declares in the blessing of their father how far Jacob's office excels Esau's: their father said to Jacob "The peoples will serve you and the tribes will adore you; be your brothers' master, and the sons of your mother will bend low before you" (Gen. 27:29). He also said to Esau: "I have made him your master and I have subjugated all his brothers to this man's service; you will live by the sword and you will serve your brother." (27:37). And when they were still growing in their mother's womb, it was said by the Lord: "The elder shall serve the younger" (25:23).

What more do we seek? What could be said more clearly? Who would be so mad as to go against divine authority? Behold how loudly the voice makes it clear to the numerous laity that they should serve the devoted clergy. Therefore if a peasant will rightly serve a deacon, then so will a soldier a priest; and if a soldier will rightly serve a priest, then so will a prince a bishop; and if a prince will rightly serve a bishop, then a king, who is certainly one of the laity, will most rightly be subject to the apostolic see. But perhaps talkative people, swelling with pride, argue that a king is not one of the laity because he has been anointed with the oil of the priests. An obvious argument makes these irrational men a laughing-stock, and well-known truth will silence the ignorance of all impudent men; for is the king a lay-person or a cleric? If he is a cleric, then he is either a door-keeper, a reader, an exorcist, an acolyte, a sub-deacon, a deacon, a priest, or a bishop. If he is not a member of these orders, then he is not a cleric. Furthermore, if he is neither a lay-person nor a cleric, then he is a monk; but his wife and his sword deny that he is a monk: "For he does not bear the sword in vain, for he is the avenger of God's wrath, established for this very purpose" (Rom. 13:4). Neither a monk nor even a cleric is allowed to carry weapons. Therefore, since on this clear evidence the king is a lay-person, and since a priest through his office has been set over all laity, the king must be wholly subject in matters of divinity to the highest priest, inasmuch as he is subject to the head of the Church. On the other hand, the highest priest, along with all the clergy, is subject to this same king, as to a superior, in secular affairs. So it is that these two princes of the people come before each other in turn; and both, firmly adhering to Christ the King and Priest, shall reign eternally with him.

3. But now let Moses come to centre-stage with the light of the law, and let him shake out the darkness of ignorance from deep within our minds. He led the people of God out of Egypt and established their laws. He set up not a king but a priest to govern them. It is also from his brother Aaron that legal constitutions for the priesthood take their origin.

Thus it was that from the time of Moses right up to the time of Samuel the people of God were governed not by kings but by priests, and the judges, who seemed to have command of the people in secular matters, were controlled in everything by the decrees of the priests. However, when the people had refused to be governed by the gentle rule of priests, and decreed that they would experience the greatness of a king, Samuel, the prophet and priest, anointed a king for them by divine command, and soon wrote down the law of royal rule. This king used to obey Samuel in everything — that is, in such matters as lay within the sphere of divine law; in the same way Samuel also used to obey the king in all that lies in the provenance of royal law. Indeed, prophets were regarded as priests, as they are often said to have made sacrifices. When this same king, however, appropriated the office of priest for himself by making sacrifices, divine judgment forthwith banished him from exercise of his royal power.

Now good King David and the whole line of kings over Judah or Israel who succeeded him were chosen for the royal power by prophets (or priests, which was almost the same thing), and anointed by them. This did not prevent the kings being subject to the prophets (priests) in divine matters, as is recorded of almost all of them, while the prophets (priests) in turn paid them the homage due from subjects in secular matters. Above all, King David obeyed the counsel of Nathan and the prophets, and attended humbly when they reproached him. Solomon, the wisest of prophets and most powerful of kings, treated the priesthood with remarkable distinction and gave it a remarkable prominence, according it the highest respect and enriching it with splendid endowments. Other kings are also found to have been devoted to the prophets and priests of the Lord, and to have been subject to them in spiritual matters, as Hezekiah was devoted to Isaiah, and Ahab, that wicked idolater, held Elijah in great honour, though heavily rebuked by him. Joash is said to have been subject to Elisha, and Josiah to Jeremiah. And as long as the kings honoured the priests who consecrated them, and listened to the prophets as their teachers, their own preeminence was stable. However, when they spurned the priests and killed the prophets they were soon driven from their kingdom and scattered to the nations in dishonour. So from the time of the Babylonian exile, the priests alone ruled the people of God, since royal rule had been lost completely; until he should come, from the tribe of Judah in the flesh, to whom royal sceptre and priestly rule were both entrusted. Therefore, while the kingship was subject to frequent change, the priesthood always remained secure, though sometimes troubled.

But why relate how Jewish kings have respected their priests, when Holy Scripture tells us that even the gentiles were exceedingly devoted to their priests. For as Moses attests, when the Egyptians were compelled by famine to sell their land, and were reduced to servitude under Joseph, the priests alone were not compelled to sell their land, since a public stipend was supplied them from the king's granary. But all the histories of the gentiles, too, tell of kings who have honoured their own priesthoods, so that even certain consuls and emperors are said to have undertaken the office. But enough about the ancients; now let us consider the period of the Christian religion.

4. Our Lord Jesus Christ, true King and Priest after the order of Melchizedek, set up laws and constitutions for his Bride, and for her governance ordained not royal rule but priestly. He made the apostle Peter the leader in this, and said to him, "You are Peter [the Rock], and on this rock I will build my church," and so on up to "shall be loosed in heaven" (Matt. 16:18f.). Peter received this power of priestly rule from the Lord, and himself left it to his successors. Therefore, just as priests led the people of God from the time of Moses until Samuel, so from the time of Christ until Sylvester priests alone ruled the Church of God. They gave it excellent direction, with excellent customs and laws, and perfectly prepared it for its eternal home; yet it was attacked on all sides by kings, who strove by every means to turn it — no, drive it — away from true worship to the worship of demon spirits. But after that stone, cut out by no human hand from the mountain, rejected by the builders of the wall of iniquity, but chosen of God and raised to be head of the corner, became a great mountain and filled the whole earth with its greatness, the times were changed and kingdoms removed; and the loftiness of royal rule began to bow itself beneath Christ's feet, and the height of empire to be humbled within the congregation of the church [cf. Dan. 2:21, 34f.; Ps. 118:22; 1 Pet. 2:4]. Surely God, the priest of peace, changed the time of persecution into a time of great peace; the great King above all gods transferred the rebellious empire of the pagans into a kingdom of Christians.

Thus Constantine, prince of royal princes, was turned to the faith of Christ through the mediation of Sylvester, prince of the Church's priests, and the whole world was clothed in the new rite of the Christian religion. This Constantine laid the royal crown upon the Roman pontiff, and decreed with imperial authority that none thereafter should succeed to the Roman empire without the approval of the apostolic see. Sylvester received this privilege from Constantine, and left it to his successors. When all the care of priestly and royal rule hung on the judgment of Sylvester, a man full of divine inspiration, he realised that he could not constrain those who rejected the priests with the sword of God's word, but only with a material sword, and so took this same Constantine as his helper in working God's fields and as defender of the Church against pagans, Jews and heretics. To him he conceded a sword to punish the wicked; and laid on him the crown of royal rule, to praise the good.

Thenceforth the tradition began for the Church of having kings or judges for secular jurisdictions. They are vigorously to drive out pagans who harass the Church or any other enemies who assail her, and within the Church to subdue through fear of punishment those who rebel against the divine laws. Secular judgments alone, therefore, are the provenance of kings; which is why, when certain bishops sued their fellow bishops before the Emperor Constantine, he, knowing that it was no part of his jurisdiction, replied: "Go, since you are anointed, and consider this matter amongst yourselves: I will not be your judge."

Therefore just as the soul is of higher dignity than the body to which it gives life, and the spiritual than the secular to which it gives life, so is the priesthood of higher dignity than the kingship to which it appoints and gives order. The next question is: by whom should these persons be chosen or appointed? [...]

The Roman emperor ought to be selected by the apostolic see in agreement with the princes and by the acclamation of the people, and ought to be set at the head of the populace, consecrated and crowned by the Pope. It lies within his governance, according to civil justice or the laws of the land, to dispose of prefectures, advocacies, governorships, dukedoms and countships: to institute for the people taxes, law-courts, and laws, according to the nature of the times. By him are kings and judges of provinces and regions to be appointed, and princes to be set over states.

But here, perhaps, argumentative men, unskilled in speech and knowledge, will break in and claim that the emperor must not be chosen by the apostolic see, but by princes. I ask them whether a king should be appointed by subordinates or by dignitaries *(praelati)*? By dignitaries, they say. By which dignitaries? By dukes and counts. But dukes and counts are subject to lords — to bishops indeed, since they hold benefices and church estates from them. Therefore a king should be appointed by the priests of Christ, who are the true princes of the Church, although the agreement of the laity is required. Therefore, since priestly rule appoints to royal rule rightfully, royal rule is rightfully subject to priestly rule. [...]

6. But it may be asked whether one ought to obey in everything, or may sometimes resist? This is my answer. As long as the demands clearly lie within the competence of the law of the kingdom, they certainly must be obeyed. If, however, kings command things contrary to the Christian religion, they must be opposed. Indeed, we read that at one time Christian soldiers fought under pagan kings against enemies of the kingdom, and yet did not desert the worship of Christ; but if they were required to renounce Christian worship, they would soon bear witness even by their very deaths that God is to be obeyed rather than men. For John and Paul, on the orders of the most Christian emperor Constantine, took part in the expedition of the patrician Gallicanus, still a pagan, against enemies of the Roman empire. But they completely separated themselves from the court of Julian the Apostate. Therefore, if the king, supported by the Roman Church, the head and mother of all the churches, behaves obediently as a son crowned by her, a minister of God and an avenger of

God's wrath; if he constrains the Christian populace to keep all the divine laws, and defends it against pagans, Jews and heretics, he should be obeyed by everyone in everything. But if he turns rebel against the Roman and apostolic see, which the King of Kings and Lord of Lords appointed head of the Church and placed at the very head of the nations; or if he distresses the Church by falling into some heresy, like Constantius [II, emperor 337-61] and Valens [364-78, both tainted in the eyes of later Catholicism with sympathy for Arianism], or like Julian [the Apostate, emperor 361-63] persecutes it by forswearing the faith, or divides it into parts through schism like Philippicus [Bardanes, Byzantine emperor 711-13]; such a man as this, I say, should be borne patiently but wholly refused communion, since he is not an emperor but a tyrant. This is the kind of empire that Martin [of Tours] rejected when he said "I am a soldier of Christ: I may not fight."

But there are some who say that they are wise, but in truth have become foolish, who dare to affirm that kings may give bishoprics or abbacies or other preferments. For they say: the king is anointed with holy oil, he is set over clergy and people; therefore it is shown conclusively that he gives preferment of both kinds rightfully. The falsity of this affirmation is demonstrated by the truth of its denial; and that denial is supported by true affirmation. So, I inquire of them whether the aforementioned bishoprics and abbacies are spiritual preferments or secular? They will reply, unless they are mad, "spiritual." But I shall say "Is the king a spiritual or secular person?" "Secular," they say. But spiritual dignity does not belong to a secular person. To prove this point I demand that they tell me whether a king may celebrate mass or not. "Certainly not," they say. "Why?" "Because he is not a priest," they say. But I reply, "Then if he is not allowed to celebrate the mass because he is not a priest, neither can he award a church in which mass is celebrated, since he is of the laity." Therefore, since the king is lay and secular; since he both carries the sword of vengeance on evil-doers and has been appointed through the priestly office as the avenger of the wrath of God; since he is leader of the people only in secular matters, he neither ought nor can award bishoprics or abbacies or the things mentioned above, which are spiritual honours; all reason is against it. However, he both can and ought to award honours which are truly secular, such as dukedoms, governorships, earldoms; but the Church alone ought to bestow spiritual posts on spiritual persons. Hence sacred canons are laid down to the effect that if anyone comes into the dignity of a canonry through secular power, he may be deposed. Indeed, we read that Jehoiadah the priest set up Joash as king (2 Kings 11:17); but a king is never found to have created a priest. [. . .]

Translation: Katie Gilchrist, from *PL*, vol. 172.

Bernard of Clairvaux

(1090-1153)

Contemplative, speculative theologian, abbot, ecclesiastical statesman, adviser to popes, Bernard of Clairvaux was one of the more spectacular figures of the monastic reform movement, reminiscent of the most formidable monk-popes. His rise to ecclesiastical prominence from his position as founding abbot of Clairvaux, the most successful Cistercian house in Europe, coincided with the waxing of the pope's political influence and jurisdiction outside of Italy — in Germany, France, England, and Spain — and his struggle for political survival in central Italy. Owing to the need of politically unstable monarchs for reliable episcopal support and papal endorsement, Rome was interfering to an unprecedented degree with diocesan elections, administration, and courts, exempting monasteries from episcopal control and running the most popular appellate court in the West. The time was ripe for a "mirror of princes" for the papal "prince of princes."

Bernard's *On Consideration (De consideratione ad Eugenium papam)*, written between 1148 and 1153, is such a "mirror" of the papal office, but it is more theologically speculative and spiritually interior than is typical of the secular genre. For Bernard situates the self-examination which he prescribes for his spiritual son, Eugenius III (a former monk at Clairvaux), within a more comprehensive theopolitical order of "considerations": of the ecclesiastical hierarchy, of the pope's immediate entourage and flock, and of the angelic order of offices and dignities ascending to the divine Unity in Trinity.

Respecting papal government of the whole church, Bernard emphasizes the universality and supremacy of Roman rule, contrasting it with the territorial and canonical limitations of episcopal jurisdiction (2.15-16). At the same time he declares its fiduciary, ministerial character, bounded by faith, righteousness, and good order in the church (2.9-10, 12b-14; 3.1, 14-15). To Bernard's mind, the greatest subversion of the church's (and the world's) good comes from papal collusion with the worldly greed and ambition of Christians, especially prelates, through the ecclesiastical appeals system (1.13-14; 3.6-12). To stem the tide of abuses, Eugenius is advised to hear only cases of manifest injustice, and to punish false or frivolous appellants (3.7). Another impediment to the church's welfare is the "dismemberment" of subordinate jurisdictions by irresponsible papal granting of exemptions, which, while lawful, does not edify (3.14).

Respecting papal government of Rome, Bernard exhorts Eugenius to confront the city's persistent rebellion with a display of apostolic rather than imperial power, unsheathing the spiritual sword of God's Word rather than the material sword of royal conquest. However, his confident assertion that the material sword, too, belongs by right to the pope, "to be drawn [. . .] at your command, although not by your hand," proved the most memorable phrase of his admonition for all future papalists (4.7).

Further Reading: G. R. Evans, *The Mind of St. Bernard of Clairvaux* (Oxford: Oxford University Press, 1983); E. Gilson, *The Mystical Theology of Saint Bernard* (English translation) (London: Sheed & Ward, 1940); B. Jacqueline, *Papauté et Épiscopat selon Saint Bernard* (Paris: Éditions du Centurion, 1963); E. Kennan, "The *De Consideratione* of St. Bernard of Clairvaux and the Papacy in the Mid-Twelfth Century: A Review of Scholarship," *Tradition* 23 (1967): 73-115.

From *On Consideration,* Book 1

4. Do not reply now with the words of the Apostle: "Although I was free from all men, I made myself a slave to all" (1 Cor. 9:19). This is hardly your situation. Did Paul in his slavery aid men in the acquisition of mere financial gain? Were the ambitious, the avaricious, the simoniacal, the sacrilegious, the fornicating, the incestuous and every other kind of monstrous person crowding around him from every corner of the earth to obtain or retain ecclesiastical honors by his apostolic authority? Truly, this man for whom life was Christ and death gain, made himself a slave to win more for Christ, not to increase the profits of avarice. You should not, therefore, claim a precedent for your life or servitude in Paul's productive labor and in his charity, so free and unrestrained. It would be much more worthy of your apostolic office, much more beneficial to your conscience, and much more fruitful for the Church of God, if you would listen instead to another of his statements: "You were bought for a price, do not become slaves of men" (1 Cor. 7:23). What is more servile and more unworthy, especially for the Supreme Pontiff, than every day, or rather every hour, to sweat over such affairs for the likes of these? Tell me this, when are we to pray or to teach the people? When are we to build up the Church or meditate on the law? Oh yes, every day laws resound through the palace, but these are the laws of Justinian, not of the Lord. Is this just? Consider for a moment. Surely, the Law of the Lord is perfect, converting souls. But these are not so much laws as wrangling and sophistry, subverting judgment. Tell me, therefore, how can you, as bishop and shepherd of souls, allow the Law to stand silent before you while these others rattle on? I am at a loss if this perversity does not cause you anxiety. I think that sometimes this should cause you to cry with the Prophet to the Lord: "Evil people have told me tales, but they are not like your Law" (Ps. 119:85). Go ahead, dare to claim that you are free even while burdened by this impropriety which you should not endure. For if you can be free but will not, you are a slave even more of your own wicked will. Is he not a slave whom wickedness governs? Indeed he is. But perhaps you think it more degrading for a man to dominate you than for a vice to do so. What difference does it make whether you serve willingly or unwillingly? Although enforced servitude is more wretched, still, voluntary servitude is more to be deplored. "And what do you want me to do?" (Acts 9:6) you ask. Spare yourself these demands upon you. You may say this is impossible, that it would be easier to bid farewell to the papal throne. You would be correct if I were urging you to break with them rather than to interrupt them. [. . .]

6. But listen to what the Apostle thinks about this: "Is there no wise man among you who can judge between brothers?" (1 Cor. 6:5). And he adds, "I say this to shame you; set them to judge who are most despised in the Church" (1 Cor. 6:5, 4). According to the Apostle, you, as a successor of the Apostles, are usurping a lowly, contemptible office, which is unbecoming of you. This is why a bishop instructing a bishop said: "No one who fights for God entangles himself in secular affairs" (2 Tim. 2:4). However, I spare you, for I speak not of the heroic, but the possible. Do you think these times would permit it if you were to answer in the Lord's words those men who sue for earthly inheritance and press you for judgment: "Men, who set me as judge over you?" (Luke 12:4). What kind of judgment would they soon pass on you? "What is he saying, this ignorant, unskilled man who is unaware of his primacy, who dishonors his supreme and lofty throne, who detracts from the apostolic dignity?" And yet I am sure that those who would say this could not show where any of the Apostles at any time sat to judge men, to survey boundaries, or to distribute lands. I read that the Apostles stood to be judged, not that they sat in judgment. This will happen in the future; it has not happened yet. Therefore, does it diminish the dignity of a servant if he does not wish to be greater than his master, or a disciple if he does not choose to be more than the one who sent him, or a son, if he does not transgress the boundaries which his parents set for him? (Prov. 22:28). "Who appointed me judge?" says our Lord and Master. Will it be wrong for his servant and disciple not to judge everything? It seems to me that a person is not a very shrewd observer if he thinks it is shameful for Apostles or apostolic men *not* to judge such things since judgment has been given to them in greater matters. Why should those who are to pass judgment in heaven even on the angels not scorn to judge the paltry worldly possessions of men? Clearly your power is over sin and not property, since it is because of sin that you have received the keys of the heavenly kingdom, to exclude sinners not possessors. The Lord confirms this when he says: "That you may know that the Son of Man has power on earth to forgive sins" (Matt. 9:6). Tell me, which seems to you the greater honor and greater power: to forgive sins or to divide estates? But there is no comparison. These base worldly concerns have their own judges, the kings and princes of the world. Why do you invade someone else's territory? Why do you put your sickle to someone else's harvest? Not because you are unworthy, but because it is unworthy for you to be involved in such affairs since you are occupied by

more important matters. On the other hand, where necessity demands it, listen not to me but to the Apostle: "If this world will be judged by you, are you unworthy to judge the smallest matters?" (1 Cor. 6:2). [. . .]

10. But let that be; a different custom has developed. The times and the habits of men are different now. Dangers are no longer imminent, they are present. Fraud, deceit and violence run rampant in our land. False accusers are many; a defender is rare. Everywhere the powerful oppress the poor. We cannot abandon the downtrodden; we cannot refuse judgment to those who suffer injustice. If cases are not tried and litigants heard, how can judgment be passed?

Let cases be tried, but in a suitable manner. The way which is frequently followed now is completely detestable. It would hardly suit civil courts, let alone ecclesiastical. I am astonished that you, a man of piety, can bear to listen to lawyers dispute and argue in a way which tends more to subvert the truth than to reveal it. Reform this corrupt tradition; cut off their lying tongues and shut their deceitful mouths. These men have taught their tongues to speak lies. They are fluent against justice. They are schooled in falsehood. They are wise in order to do evil; they are eloquent to assail truth. These it is who instruct those by whom they should have been taught, who introduce not facts but their own fabrications, who heap up calumny of their own invention against innocent people, who destroy the simplicity of truth, who obstruct the ways of justice. Nothing reveals the truth so readily as a simple straightforward presentation. Therefore, let it be your custom to become involved in only those cases where it is absolutely necessary (and this will not be every case) and decide them carefully but briefly, and to avoid frustrating and contrived delay. The case of a widow requires your attention, likewise the case of a poor man and of one who has no means to pay. You can distribute many cases to others for judgment and many you can judge unworthy of a hearing. What need is there to hear those whose sins are manifest before the trial?

From Book 2

6. We cannot ignore the fact that you have been elected to the supreme position, but, indeed, it must earnestly be asked, "for what purpose?" Not, in my opinion, to rule. For the Prophet, when he was raised to a similar position, heard, "So that you can root up and destroy, plunder and put to flight, build and plant" (Jer. 1:10). Which of these rings of arrogance? Spiritual labor is better expressed by the metaphor of a sweating peasant. And, therefore, we will understand ourselves better if we realize that a ministry has been imposed upon us rather than a dominion bestowed. [. . .] Learn by the example of the Prophet to preside not so much in order to command as to do what the time requires. Learn that you need a hoe, not a sceptre, to do the work of the Prophet. Indeed, he did not rise up to reign, but to root out. Do you think that you also can find work to be done in the field of your Lord? Much indeed. Certainly the Prophets could not correct everything. They left something for their sons, the Apostles, to do; and they, your parents, have left something for you. But you cannot

do everything. For you will leave something to your successor, and he to others, and they to others until the end of time. Still around the eleventh hour the workers are scolded for their idleness and sent into the vineyard. Your predecessors, the Apostles, heard that "The harvest indeed is great, but the laborers are few" (Matt. 9:37). Claim your inheritance from your fathers. For, "if a son, then you are also an heir" (Gal. 4:7). To prove you are an heir, be watchful in your responsibilities; do not become sluggish and idle lest it also be said to you, "Why do you stand here the whole day idle?" (Matt. 20:6).

It is hardly fitting for you to be found relaxing in luxury or wallowing in pomp. Your inheritance does not include any of these things. But what does it include? If you were content with its meaning you would realize that you are to inherit responsibility and labor rather than glory and wealth. Does the throne flatter you? It is a watchtower; from it you oversee everything, exercising not dominion, but ministry through the office of your episcopacy. Why should you not be placed on high where you can see everything, you who have been appointed watchman over all? In fact, this prospect calls forth not leisure but readiness for war. And when is it suitable to boast, where it is not even possible to relax? There is no place for leisure where responsibility for all the churches unremittingly presses upon you. But what else did the holy Apostle leave to you? He says, "What I have I give to you" (Acts 3:6). What is that? I am sure of one thing: it is neither gold nor silver; for he himself says, "I do not have silver and gold" (Acts 3:6). If you happen to have these, use them not for your own pleasure, but to meet the needs of the time. Thus you will be using them as if you were not using them. These things are neither good nor bad when you consider the good of the soul, but the use of them is good, the abuse bad, solicitude for them is worse, and using them for profit is shameful. You may claim these things on some other ground but not by apostolic right. For the Apostle could not give you what he did not have. What he had he gave: responsibility for the churches, as I have said. Did he give dominion? Listen to him: "Not lording it over your charge but making yourself a pattern for the flock" (1 Pet. 5:3). You should not think he was prompted to say this only by humility and not by truth, for the Lord says in the Gospel: "The kings of the nations lord it over them and those who have power over them are called benefactors" (Luke 22:25). And he adds: "But you are not like this" (Luke 22:26). It is clear: dominion is forbidden for Apostles. [. . .]

Go out into the field of your Lord and consider how even today it abounds in thorns and thistles in fulfilment of the ancient curse. Go out, I say, into the world, for the field is the world and it is entrusted to you. Go out into it not as a lord, but as a steward, to oversee and to manage that for which you must render an account. [. . .]

One time the patriarch Isaac went out into this field, when Rebecca first met him, and, as Scripture has it, he went out to meditate; you must go forth to root out. You should have meditated already; the time for action is at hand. If you start to hesitate now, it will surely be too late. According to the Savior's counsel, you should have sat down beforehand to make an estimate of the task, to measure your strength, to ponder your wisdom, to reflect on the rewards of virtue, and to determine their cost. Come, therefore, see that this is the time for pruning, but only if you have already had time for meditation. If you have moved your heart, now move your tongue, and also your hand. Put on your sword, the sword of the spirit which is the word of God. Glorify your hand and your right arm, and deal out vengeance on the nations and punishment on the peoples; bind their kings in chains and their nobles in fetters of iron. Do this and you will honor your ministry and it will honor you. This is no ordinary sovereignty: you must expel evil beasts from your boundaries so your flocks may be led to pasture in safety. Vanquish the wolves, but do not lord it over the sheep. [. . .]

8. Come, let us investigate even more diligently who you are; that is, what part you play in the Church of God at this time. Who are you? The high priest, the Supreme Pontiff. You are the prince of the bishops, you are the heir of the Apostles; in primacy you are Abel, in governing you are Noah, in patriarchate you are Abraham, in orders you are Melchizedek, in dignity you are Aaron, in authority you are Moses, in judgment you are Samuel, in power you are Peter, by anointing you are Christ. You are the one to whom the keys have been given, to whom the sheep have been entrusted. It is true that there are other doorkeepers of heaven and shepherds of flocks; but you are more glorious than all of these, to the degree that you have inherited a name more excellent than theirs. They have flocks assigned to them, one flock to each; to you all are assigned, a single flock to a single shepherd. You are the one shepherd not only of all the sheep, but of all the shepherds. Do you ask how I can prove this? From the word of the Lord. For, to whom, and I include not only bishops but also Apostles, were all the sheep entrusted so absolutely and completely? "If you love me, Peter, feed my sheep" (John 21:17). What sheep? The people of this or that city or region, or even of this or that kingdom? "My sheep," he said. To whom is it not clear that he did not exclude any, but assigned them to all? There is no exception where there is no distinction. And perhaps the rest of the disciples were present when the Lord, entrusting all to one man, commended unity to all in one flock with one shepherd according to the statement, "One is my dove, my beauty, my perfect one" (Song of Sol. 6:9). Where unity is, there is perfection. [. . .]

Therefore, according to your own canons, others are called to share part of the responsibility for souls; you are called to the fullness of power. The power of the others is bound by definite limits; yours extends even over those who have received power over others. If cause exists, can you not close heaven to a bishop, depose him from the episcopacy, and even give him over to Satan? Your privilege is affirmed, therefore, both in the keys given to you and in the sheep entrusted to you.

From Book 3

1. [. . .] It seems to me that you have been entrusted with stewardship over the world, not given possession of it. If you proceed to usurp possession of it, he contradicts you who says, "The world and its fullness are mine" (Ps. 50:12). You are not that one about whom the Prophet says: "And all the earth shall be his possession" (Num. 24:18 in a variant form). That is Christ, who claims this possession for himself by right of creation, by merit of redemption, and by gift from the Father. To what other person has it

been said: "Ask of me and I will give you the nations as your inheritance and the ends of the earth as your possession" (Ps. 2:8)? Leave possession and rule to him; you take care of it. This is your portion; beyond it do not stretch your hand.

"What?" you say, "You do not deny that I preside, yet you forbid me to rule?" This is exactly my point. It is as if he cannot preside well who presides with care. Is not an estate made subject to a steward and a young lord to a teacher? Nevertheless, the steward is not lord of the estate nor is the teacher lord of his lord. So also, you should preside in order to provide, to counsel, to administer, and to serve. Preside so as to be useful; preside so as to be the faithful and prudent servant whom the Lord set up over his family. For what purpose? So you may give them food in due season; that is, so you may administer, not rule. Do this and as a man yourself do not strive to rule over men, so that no iniquity may rule over you. [. . .]

It is important, therefore, for you to do what you can so that unbelievers may be converted to the faith, that converts may not turn away, that those who have turned away may return; moreover, that the perverse may be directed toward righteousness, the corrupted called back to the truth, and the corrupters refuted by invincible arguments so that they either correct their error, if that is possible, or, if it is not, that they lose their authority and the means of corrupting others. And you must not completely neglect the worst kind of fools; by this I mean heretics and schismatics, for these are the corrupted and the corrupters. Like dogs they tear apart; like foxes they deceive. You should make the greatest effort either to correct such men lest they perish, or to restrain them lest they destroy others. Granted, time excuses you from dealing with the Jews: they have their boundary which cannot be passed. The full number of the Gentiles must come in first. But what do you say about these Gentiles? Rather, what does your consideration respond to you when you ask such questions as the following? Why did it seem good to the Fathers to set limits for the Gospel and to suspend the word of faith while unbelief was obdurate? Why do we suppose the word which runs swiftly stopped short? Who first checked this way of salvation? Perhaps the Fathers had a reason which we do not know, or perhaps necessity could have hindered them.

What is the reason for our dissembling? With what feeling of assurance, with what kind of conscience do we fail to offer Christ to those who do not possess him? Or do we restrain the truth of God in our injustice? Indeed, at some time it is necessary for the full number of the Gentiles to come in. Are we waiting for faith to fall upon them? To whom has belief come by chance? How shall they believe without preaching? Peter was sent to Cornelius and Philip to the Eunuch; and if we ask for a more recent example, Augustine, commissioned by blessed Gregory, brought the teachings of the faith to the English. And you should follow their examples.

2. [. . .] I think he ought to undergo the same treatment who has appealed without cause. This formula of justice has been set before you both by the unchanging order of divine equity and, unless I am mistaken, by the law of appeals itself, so that an appeal which has been illegally made may neither benefit the appellant nor harm the defendant. Why should a man be harassed for no reason? How perfectly just that a man injure himself when he wants to injure his neighbor! To have appealed iniquitously is evil; for iniquitous appeals to be made with impunity is an in-

centive for their continuance. Moreover, every appeal is iniquitous which is not the result of a lack of justice.

Appeal is permitted not when you want to injure others, but when you are injured. Appeal must be made from a court decision, unless it is a clear case of injury. Thus, anyone who appeals but who is not injured, clearly intends to cause injury or to gain time. Appeal is not, however, a subterfuge but a refuge. How many men do we know who, when they are accused, appealed in order that, pending a decision, they might be free to do whatever is permitted! Indeed, we know that some people, through their decision to appeal, have been permitted to commit crimes all their lives, such as incest and adultery. How is it that the very thing which ought to be feared especially by the depraved is protecting depravity? How long will you ignore or turn away from the complaints of the whole world? How long will you sleep? How long will your consideration fail to keep watch over the confusion and abuse of appeals? Appeals are made beyond what is just and right, contrary to custom and order. No account is taken of place, means, time, cause or person. Everywhere appeals are undertaken lightly, and for the most part with evil intent. [. . .]

4. [. . .] I speak of murmuring complaint of the churches. They cry out that they are being mutilated and dismembered. There are none, or only a few, who do not suffer the pain of this affliction, or live in fear of it. Do you ask what affliction this is? Abbots are freed from the jurisdiction of bishops, bishops from that of archbishops, archbishops from that of patriarchs or primates. Does this seem good? I wonder whether this practice can even be excused. In doing this you demonstrate that you have the fulness of power, but perhaps not of justice. You do this because you have the power; but the question is whether you ought to do it. You have been appointed, not to deny, but to preserve the degrees of honor and of dignities and the ranks proper to each, as one of your predecessors says, "Render honor to whom honor is due" (Rom. 13:7).

The spiritual man is one who judges all things so that he is judged by no one. He will precede every undertaking with a three-fold consideration: first, whether it is lawful; second, whether it is suitable; last, whether it is also advantageous. Even if it can be established, in Christian philosophy at least, that nothing is suitable unless it is lawful, and that nothing is advantageous unless it is suitable and lawful, nevertheless, it does not necessarily follow that all that is lawful will be suitable or advantageous. [. . .]

I do not want you to offer me the result of these exemptions as an excuse; indeed, the only result is that the bishops become more insolent and monks even more dissolute. And what about the fact that they even become poorer? Look carefully at the property and the lives of those who have been liberated all around to see whether the poverty of the former and the worldliness of the latter are not totally shameful. These are the twin progeny of a pernicious mother, liberty! Why should a wandering and wrongly liberated throng not sin more freely, since there is no one to censure it? Also, why should an unarmed monastery not be more freely plundered and pillaged, since there is no one to defend it? Where, indeed, is their refuge? Is it with the bishops, grieving over their injury? Indeed, they look on with eyes of ridicule whether the monks commit evils or suffer them. What profit at all is there in that blood? I fear that which God threatened in the Prophet, saying, "He shall die in his iniquity;

but I will demand his blood from your hand" (Ezek. 3:18). How is he innocent who grants the exemption, if the one who is exempted is haughty and the one from whom he is exempted is enraged?

From Book 4

3. [...] I know where you dwell; unbelievers and subversive men are with you. They are wolves, not sheep; but still you are the shepherd of such men. It is useful for you to consider how you might find a way — if this is possible — to convert them, so they do not subvert you. Why do we doubt that they can be changed back into the sheep from which they were turned into wolves? Here, indeed, I do not spare you, in order that God may spare you. Either deny openly that you are the shepherd of these people or show it by your actions. You will not deny it unless you deny that you are the heir of him whose throne you hold. This is Peter, who is known never to have gone in procession adorned either with jewels or silks, covered with gold, carried on a white horse, attended by a knight or surrounded by clamoring servants. But without these trappings, he believed it was enough to be able to fulfil the Lord's command, "If you love me, feed my sheep" (John 21:15). In this finery, you are the successor not of Peter, but of Constantine. I suggest that these things must be allowed for the time being, but are not to be assumed as a right. Rather, I urge you on to those things to which I know you have an obligation. You are the heir of the Shepherd and even if you are arrayed in purple and gold, there is no reason for you to abhor your pastoral responsibilities: there is no reason for you to be ashamed of the Gospel. If you but preach the Gospel willingly you will have glory even among the Apostles. To preach the Gospel is to feed. Do the work of an evangelist and you have fulfilled the office of shepherd.

"You instruct me to feed dragons and scorpions, not sheep," you reply. Therefore, I say, attack them all the more, but with the word, not the sword. Why should you try to usurp the sword anew which you were once commanded to sheathe? Nevertheless, the person who denies that the sword is yours seems to me not to listen to the Lord when he says, "Sheathe your sword" (John 18:11). Therefore, this sword also is yours and is to be drawn from its sheath at your command, although not by your hand. Otherwise, if that sword in no way belonged to you, the Lord would not have answered, "That is enough" (Luke 22:38), but "That is too much," when the Apostles said, "Behold here are two swords." Both swords, that is, the spiritual and the material, belong to the Church; however, the latter is to be drawn for the Church and the former by the Church. The spiritual sword should be drawn by the hand of the priest; the material sword by the hand of the knight, but clearly at the bidding of the priest and at the command of the emperor. But more of this elsewhere. Now, take the sword which has been entrusted to you to strike with, and for their salvation wound, if not everyone, if not even many, at least whomever you can.

Translation: John D. Anderson and Elizabeth T. Kennan (Kalamazoo, Mich., 1976). Used by permission.

John of Salisbury
(1115/20–1180)

Like his elder contemporary, Bernard of Clairvaux, John of Salisbury was an ecclesiastical bureaucrat of high political standing and formidable learning. He had been taught by many of the intellectual lights of the day (including Peter Abelard, Robert of Melun, Thierry of Chartres, and Gilbert of Poitiers) and was on intimate terms with some of the period's most prominent personages, e.g., the young Henry II; Pope Adrian IV; Archbishop Theobald of Canterbury, whose secretary he became in 1147; and Thomas Becket, a fellow member of the archiepiscopal household. As Canterbury bureaucrat and envoy, John of Salisbury was a constant participant in and observer of court life, royal and papal.

His best-known writing, *Policraticus: Of the Frivolities of Courtiers and the Footprints of Philosophers,* composed between 1156 and 1159, is widely reputed by scholars to be the first treatise of political theory; however, it is an eclectic and composite piece, being "equally a work of moral theology, satire, speculative philosophy, legal procedure, self-consolation, biblical commentary and deeply personal meditation" (Nederman 1990, xv). Along with his *Entheticus Maior* and *Metalogicon,* it has secured John's place in the twelfth-century renaissance of classical letters, philosophy, and science. Begun during a period of banishment from Henry II's court (that preceded a more protracted exile for his opposition, in league with Becket, to royal infringement of the church's liberties), the treatise is described by the author as primarily critical and controversial, an exposé of "the frivolities of courtiers" (prologue, 5), an investigation into the nature, causes, and consequences of their vices. But this diagnosis of political vice is balanced by a constructive analysis of the best polity, of "the universal and public welfare" (3.1) in its theological, moral, and legal constitution.

The constructive analysis as well as the critical diagnosis are Augustinian in theological inspiration, frequently mediated by papal ecclesiology. According to John of Salisbury, the "universal and public welfare" is securely realized where God's Spirit of truth and goodness occupies the soul of every member of the commonwealth, bestowing knowledge through "the exercise of reason" and "the revelation of grace" and increasing "the love of honour and the cultivation of virtue" (3.1). Thus the animating soul of this republic is the priesthood, which possesses by divine and natural right directive rule over "the whole body," including its royal head (4.3; 5.2). The prince receives from the church the sword of "bodily coercion" for "the punishment of wrongdoers" and "enforcement of devoted service to the laws" (4.1). His exercise of "power over all his subjects" is ordered by his law-abiding will that invariably seeks justice, equity, "the utility of the republic," and "the advantage of others" over his own (4.1-2). His power is by delegation from God, as from a liege-lord who never parts with it, but uses princely authority as "a substitute for His hand, making all things learn His justice and mercy" (4.1). In stark theological opposition to the godly republic stands "the republic of the impious," whose tyrannical head is an image not of divinity but of "the strength . . . and depravity of Lucifer," and the soul "is formed of heretical, schismatic and sacrilegious priests . . . assailing the laws of the Lord" (8.17).

At points the Augustinian orientation of the *Policraticus* is overshadowed by competing influences from civil and canon law, and also by classical political and ethical ideas undergoing a renaissance. John's classicizing tendencies are most pronounced in his theory of law, which reflects his acquaintance with the lawbooks of Justinian, possibly with Gratian's *Decretum* (1140), and Ciceronian and Stoic principles, though these are filtered, for the most part, through patristic sources and his assiduous reading of the Old Testament. "The law," he says in a highly synthetic passage, "is a gift of God, the likeness of equity, the norm of justice, the image of the divine will, the custodian of security, the unity and confirmation of a people, the standard of duties, the excluder and exterminator of vices" (8.17). The divine law is equity, "according to which reason equalises the whole and seeks just equality in matters of inequality," granting "to each person that which is his own"; and human law "interprets" or "makes known the will of equity and justice" (4.2). It is the fabric of law, before all else, that unifies a people, creating and sustaining the Christian body politic by embodying its natural and supernatural ends. For this reason the princely "head," though "an absolutely binding law unto himself," is still "the servant of law," seeking its guidance, conforming his will to its intention, and drawing his authority from legal right (4.1, 2). John makes a comparison later to be enshrined in English legal literature by Henry Bracton when he likens the royal head to "the King of Kings — created from woman, created under the law [who] carried out the whole justice of law, to which He was subject not by necessity, but by will because his will is law, and He meditated day and night on the Law of God" (4.6).

In the tradition of Aristotle, Cicero, and many civilians, political society was a natural, organic, harmoniously ordered whole. John's signal contribution to this tradition is his detailed elaboration of the organic political metaphor. (His claim to derive this metaphor from an otherwise unknown work by Plutarch is possibly a literary device for introducing his own innovations.) The organic analogy facilitates his diagnosis of dysfunctional political practices and vices, as well as his formulation of healthy civic order and virtues (bks. 5, 6), and reinforces his habit of translating particular features of the Roman legal-political constitution into universally applicable concepts and principles. Thus, he employs the Latin term *princeps*, conventionally reserved for the Roman emperor or the imperial office, to refer to any political ruler, and the term *res publica* to refer to the commonality or polity formed by any set of subjects. He expresses the essential moral-legal bond between ruler and ruled by designating the prince as "the public power" in whom "the public persona is borne" (4.1, 2). Completing the ruler-ruled relationship is the principle of moderation, "the golden mean," borrowed from Aristotle's *Organon*, which defines the structural limitation not only of virtue as such but of just and equitable government (3.3; 4.8, 9).

The interconnection of legality, equity, and moderation in John's thought generates, by negation, his celebrated discussion of tyranny. The tyrant flouts and suppresses the law by his passionate excesses, and violates his subjects' freedoms by the domination of his private will (3.15; 4.1; 7.17; 8.17, 18). His oppressed subjects respond not with law-abidingness — the free and true conformity of their wills to the will of the laws — but with deceitful flattery — the unfree and pretended conformity of their wills to their master's intemperate lawlessness (3.10) — so that the tyrant is thrice guilty of "high treason": against the public power received from God, against the commanding laws, and against the whole body of justice (3.15). Here follows the astonishing political axiom that "him whom it is permitted to flatter, it is permitted to slay," and "not only permitted," but "also equitable and just to slay" (3.15). However, he qualifies the justice of tyrannicide by several considerations: (1) of the difference between tolerable royal "vices" and intolerable "crimes" (6.26); (2) of God's ordination of tyrants to punish the evil and discipline the good (8.18); and (3) of the binding obligation "of fealty or a sacred oath" and (4) the biblical illegality of the method of poisoning (8.20). In addition, he invests the concept of tyrant with a broader social/psychological content, applying it, beyond secular and ecclesiastical rulers, to anyone "who abuses any power over those subject to him . . . conceded from above" (8.18), or fails to restrain his aggressive self-assertion (7.17).

Further Reading: M. Kerner, *Johannes von Salisbury und die logische Struktur seines "Policraticus"* (Wiesbaden: Franz Steiner Verlag, 1977); H. Liebeschütz, *Medieval Humanism in the Life and Writings of John of Salisbury* (London: Warburg Institute, University of London, 1950); Kraus (reprint, 1968); M. Wilks, ed., *The World of John of Salisbury* (Oxford: Basil Blackwell, 1984).

From *Policraticus*, Book 3

1. [*Universal and Public Welfare*]. The public welfare is therefore that which fosters a secure life universally and in each particular person. There is nothing worthwhile in human life which is not advantageous for a secure life. The ancient philosophers have defined human life as consisting of a rational soul and corruptible flesh. Yet flesh takes its life from the soul, since the body otherwise cannot be alive, inasmuch as that which is always inert will remain inactive unless it is moved with the aid of some spiritualised nature. This latter also has a life of its own. For God is the life of the soul, a thought which is profoundly and truly embraced by one of the moderns,

although in light verse: "God is the life of the soul, the soul the life of the body; the one dissolves when the other flees, lost when it is undermined by God" (Augustine, *De libero arbitrio*, 2.16.41 and *De civitate Dei*, 13.24.6). [. . .]

God occupies totally the soul that lives perfectly; he possesses it totally; He rules and vitalises it in total. No corner of it is excepted. But why say "corner" or "part" regarding the soul? It is devoid of parts, uncompounded in nature and utterly unacquainted with duplication. Were such parts possible, they could be claimed only from the distributor of all that is good. It may be asked, what parts could be claimed? At minimum these would be the virtues through which the soul grows strong, functions and gives itself tests. If, therefore, it does not develop through the manipulation of its parts and quantitative extension, still it is enlarged in its reason and understanding by an appetite for the good and an aversion for the bad while retaining its uncompounded nature. When spirit fills these parts (for God is spirit), the life of the soul is completed and perfected. For when God, who is the greatest good, is understood — the sight of him apprehended as clearly as is possible and permitted — and when the good which one sees is sought by an incorruptible will, and when reason reveals the way so that no one who is attracted by a sober impulse towards the good will stray to the right or the left, then the soul attains to a measure of the glory of immortality. [. . .]

10. [*Roman Vanity and Flattery*]. [. . .] Romulus consecrated to his gods the city of Rome upon the auguries of sacrilegious fratricide and the shedding of a brother's blood, after which, being harassed by ghosts, he endeavoured to redeem the slaughter of his brother by the empty horror of pretending to share supreme power. The emperors, whom the Roman people by their custom faithfully murdered, were also deified with still greater faithfulness, the Romans disguising their manifest treachery with empty solace, just as if they were handing out a small curative to him whom they had slain; they pretended that the late emperors had been transformed into the status of divinities, as though the hand of the Omnipotent did not suffice to rule His heaven and His earth except with the approval of tyrants. Thus are made indigenous divinities or (as others prefer to say) heroes, to whom the faithless Romans did not even ascribe the dignity of human status. An appellation was thereby introduced according to which princes, conspicuously adorned with noticeable virtue and true faith, dared — not to mention rejoiced — to pronounce themselves divine; for longstanding and vicious habits endure in opposition to the universal faith. If it comes to words, the Romans take precedence in such matters over the Greek infidels, since it is the former who were taught the use of flattering allurements to the extent that they readily were transformed into a race of teachers themselves. This nation invented the speech by which we deceive superiors, in so far as we confer distinction on a single person by honouring him in the plural, and by the authority of their name the Romans have transmitted this technique to their neighbours and to posterity.

If you inquire into those times, direct yourself to that period when Julius Caesar's dictatorial powers were either uncovered or perfected (I know not which); just as he was made all things, so he took possession of all things. My image of those times frequently presents itself in connection with the disposition of all subjects according to the pleasure of the ruling powers, and although in their souls they may have struggled against domination, they were prepared to prescribe the sentence of exile or death upon themselves. Hence arises a truly dreadful power; hence the torment of pain and the inflammation of the mind arouse a fearfulness of heart and they claim for themselves the principal authority over all matters. This is so to such a degree that, for example, priests disguise the precepts of divine law, elders are ignorant of wisdom, the judge is ignorant of justice, the prelate knows no authority, the subject knows no discipline, the freeborn disdains liberty; in sum, the whole populace despises calm and peace. For so long as all are led by a single preeminent will, they are deprived of their own free will, universally and individually. Was this not the situation during the period when

> the patricians were prepared to sit and vote,
> if he demanded a kingdom, a temple, the slaying of the Senate,
> the unspeakable prostitution of a young woman?

And so it is only fortunate, with regard to the acts of citizens, that "there was more that Caesar was ashamed to command than that Rome was ashamed to permit" (Lucan, *Pharsalia*, 3.109-112). Were not the opinions of the tyrant transmitted to his successors in tyranny, inasmuch as it might be suspected that he preferred the law to be taken into his own hands rather than to be respected by humbler people? In this way, the semblance of liberty is retained, if everyone pretends to will that which has been directed — making, or by all means appearing to make, a virtue of necessity, in so far as necessity is joined to consent — and embraces gratefully that which is pressed upon one. There are no elements of true and natural liberty, however, where flattery claims everything for itself, where vanity claims everything, leaving behind nothing of either truth or virtue. [. . .]

15. [*Permitted Flattery, Permitted Slaying*]. Still, to whom is owed that sinner's oil of which he who walks before faithful kings disapproves and for the acquisition of which the words of the Gospel sent the foolish virgins who shut themselves out? It is owed to he who is involved in vile affairs and who, by the judgment of the just God, becomes more vile yet, and who aspires to glitter in the preference of popular opinion rather than to glare in the blaze of his charitable works. In the secular literature there is even caution because one is to live one way with a friend and another way with a tyrant. It is not permitted to flatter a friend, but it is permitted to delight the ears of a tyrant. For in fact him whom it is permitted to flatter, it is permitted to slay. Furthermore, it is not only permitted, but it is also equitable and just to slay tyrants. For he who receives the sword deserves to perish by the sword.

But "receives" is to be understood to pertain to he who has rashly usurped that which is not his, not to he who receives what he uses from the power of God. He who receives power from God serves the laws and is the slave of justice and right. He who usurps power suppresses justice and places the laws beneath his will. Therefore, justice is deservedly armed against those who disarm the laws, and the public power treats harshly those who endeavour to put aside the public hand. And, although there are many forms of high treason, none of them is so serious as that which is executed against the body of justice itself. Tyranny is, therefore, not a public crime, but, if this can happen, it is more than public. For if all prosecutors may be allowed in the case of high treason, how much more are they allowed when there is oppression of laws which should themselves command emperors? Surely no one will avenge a public enemy, and whoever does not prosecute him transgresses against himself and against the whole body of the earthly republic.

From Book 4

1. [*The Prince and the Tyrant*]. There is wholly or mainly this difference between the tyrant and the prince: that the latter is obedient to law, and rules his people by a will that places itself at their service, and administers rewards and burdens within the republic under guidance of law in a way favourable to the vindication of his eminent post, so that he proceeds before others to the extent that, while individuals merely look after individual affairs, princes are concerned with the burdens of the entire community. Hence, there is deservedly conferred on him power over all his subjects, in order that he may be sufficient in himself to seek out and bring about the utility of each and all, and that he may arrange the optimal condition of the human republic, so that everyone is a member of the others. In this, nature, that best guide to living, is followed, since it is nature which has lodged all of the senses in the head as a microcosm, that is, a little world, of man, and has subjected to it the totality of the members in order that all of them may move correctly provided that the will of a sound head is followed. The prince is raised to the apex and becomes illustrious, therefore, as a result of his many and great privileges which are as numerous and extensive as are thought to be necessary for him. Certainly this is proper because nothing is useful to the people except that which fulfils the needs of the prince, since his will should never be found opposed to justice.

Therefore, according to the general definition, the prince is the public power and a certain image on earth of the divine majesty. Beyond doubt the greatest part of the divine virtue is revealed to belong to the prince, in so far as at his nod men bow their heads and generally offer their necks to the axe in sacrifice, and by divine impulse everyone fears him who is fear itself. I do not believe that this could have happened unless it happened at the divine command. For all power is from the Lord God, and is with him always, and is his forever. Whatever the prince can do, therefore, is from God, so that power does not depart from God, but it is used as a substitute for his hand, making all things learn from his justice and mercy. "Whoever therefore resists power, resists what is ordained by God," in whose power is the conferral of authority and at whose will it may be removed from them or limited. For it is not even the ruler's own power when his will is harsh to his subjects, but a divine dispensation at His good will to punish or train subjects. From this we see that during the persecution by the Huns, Attila was questioned by the holy bishop of a certain city about who he was, to which he responded: "I am Attila, scourge of God"; the bishop venerated him (it is written) as a divine majesty. He said: "The minister of God is well honoured"; and also, "Blessed is he who comes in the name of God." The gates of the church were mournfully unbarred to admit the persecutor through whose hand martyrdom was attained. For he had not the audacity to exclude the scourge of God because he knew that His cherished son had been scourged and that there was no power to scourge him except from the Lord.

If, consequently, power is regarded as venerable by those who are good, even to the degree that it is a plague upon the elect, who ought not to venerate what is instituted by God for the punishment of wrongdoers, for the approval of the truly good, and for the enforcement of devoted service to the laws? "It is indeed an adage worthy," as the Emperor has it, "of the majesty of kings that the prince professes an obligation to his own laws. Because the authority of the prince is determined by the authority of right, and truly submission to the laws of princes is greater than the imperial title" (Cod. 1.14.4), so it is the case that the prince ought to imagine himself permitted to do nothing which is inconsistent with the equity of justice.

2. [*The Law and the Prince*]. Princes should not suppose that they are disparaged by the belief that the justice of God, whose justice is eternal justice and whose law is equity, is preferable to the justice of their own statutes. Furthermore, equity (as the experts in law assert) is a matter of what is appropriate, according to which reason equalises the whole and seeks equality in matters of inequality; what is equitable to all is what grants to each person that which is his own. Its interpreter is law, inasmuch as law makes known the will of equity and justice. And thus, Chrysippus asserted that law has power over all divine and human affairs, for which reason it presides over all good and evil and is ruler and guide of things as well as of men. Papinian, a man of the greatest experience in matters of jurisprudence, and Demosthenes, the influential orator, would seem to support this and to subject all men to its obedience because all law is a sort of discovery and gift from God, the teaching of the wise, the corrective to excesses of wilfulness, the harmony of the city, and the banishment of all crime. It is proper for all who dwell in the community of political affairs to live according to it. All are, for this reason, obligated to be restrained by the necessity of observing the laws, unless perhaps someone imagines that he is granted the licence of iniquity.

Still the prince is said to be an absolutely binding law unto himself, not because he is licensed to be iniquitous, but only because he should be someone who does not fear the penalties of law but someone who loves justice, cherishes equity, procures the utility of the republic, and in all matters prefers the advantage of others to his private will. But who in public affairs may even speak of the will of the prince, since in such matters he is not permitted his own will unless it is prompted by law or equity, or brings about judgments for the common utility? For in fact his will in these matters should have the force of judgment; and that which most rightfully pleases him in all matters has the force of law because his determination may not be inconsistent with the design of equity. "From your visage," it is said, "my judgment proceeds, your eyes must look at equity" (Ps. 17:2), for indeed the uncorrupted judge is one whose determination is on the basis of the assiduous contemplation of the image of equity. The prince is therefore the minister of the public utility and the servant of equity, and in him the public persona is borne since he punishes all injuries and wrongs, and also all crimes, with moderate equity. In addition, his rod and staff, exercised with the moderation of wisdom, return all deviations and errors to the way of equity, so that the Holy Spirit may meritoriously congratulate the prince, saying: "Your rod and your staff, they are comforts to me" (Ps. 23:4). While his shield is also strong, still it is a shield for the feeble and one which deflects the darts of malignance from the innocent. Those who are advanced most by his duties of office are those who can do least for themselves, and those who most desire to do harm are those who draw the greatest hostility.

That sword with which blood is shed innocently is therefore not borne without cause, so that one may frequently kill and still not be a man of blood nor incur the accusation of murder or crime. For if one may believe the great Augustine, David is called a man of blood not as the result of war, but as a result of Uriah. And Samuel is nowhere indicted as a man of blood or a murderer, although he killed Agag, the obese king of Amalek. This is indeed the sword of the dove, which quarrels without bitterness, which slaughters without wrathfulness and which, when fighting, entertains no resentment whatsoever. For since law will prosecute the blameworthy without personal animosity, the prince most properly punishes transgressors not according to some wrathful motive, but by the peaceful will of law. For although it may be seen that the prince has his own public executioners, we ought to think of him as the sole or primary executioner to whom it is permitted to allow a substitute hand. And we may agree with the Stoics, who have diligently investigated the reasons for names, when they say that "public executioner" (lictor) is derived from "stick of the law" (legis ictor) because it is the aim of his duties to strike down whoever the law adjudges must be struck down. And, for this reason, those officials of antiquity by whose hand the judge punished the guilty would be told, "Comply with the will of the law" or "Satisfy the law," when they hung the sword over the criminal, so that the grief of the situation might be mitigated by the mercifulness of these words.

3. [The Prince as Minister of the Church]. This sword is therefore accepted by the prince from the hand of the Church, although it still does not itself possess the bloody sword entirely. For while it has this sword, yet it is used by the hand of the prince, upon whom is conferred the power of bodily coercion, reserving spiritual authority for the papacy. The prince is therefore a sort of minister of the priests and one who exercises those features of the sacred duties that seem an indignity in the hands of priests. For all duties of sacred law are in fact the affairs of the religious and the pious, yet that duty is inferior which executes the punishment of crime and which seems to be represented by images of executioners. And for this reason, Constantine, the most faithful emperor of the Romans, when he had convened the Nicean Council of priests, neither ventured to take the foremost position nor allowed himself to mingle with the presbyters, but occupied the hindmost seat. The decisions which were heard to be approved by them were venerated by him, just as if he supposed them to emanate from the court of the divine majesty. And when written accusations involving the crimes of priests were presented in their turn to the emperor, he accepted them and placed them unopened in the fold of his toga. After he called them back to charity and concord, he himself said that inasmuch as he was a human who was subject to the verdict of the priests, it was not allowed for him to

284

examine divine cases which none except God alone could adjudicate. Those rolls which he had accepted he consigned to the flames uninspected, fearful to publicise the crimes or abuses of the Fathers and to incur the same curse as Ham, the reprobate son, who did not share in the reverence of his forefathers. And thus, in the writings of Nicholas, the Roman Pontiff, it is narrated that the same Constantine had said: "Truly if my own eyes had seen a priest of God or any of those who wrap themselves in the robes of the monastery sinning, my cloak would have been stretched out and would have covered him up, so that no other would see him."

The great Emperor Theodosius was suspended by the priest of Milan from the use of regalia and imperial insignia because he deserved punishment (although not on account of a serious error), and the emperor patiently and solemnly did the penitence for homicide imposed upon him. Indeed, according to the useful testimony of the Teacher of the gentiles, he who blesses is greater than he who is blessed, and he who is in the possession of the authority of conferring a dignity takes precedence over him who is himself conferred with a dignity. Furthermore, by the law of reason, whoever wills is he who nullifies, and he who can confer rights is he who can withdraw them. Did Samuel not impose a sentence of deposition upon Saul by reason of disobedience, and substitute for him the humble son of Jesse atop the kingdom? If the properly constituted prince administers faithfully the office undertaken, such honour and such reverence are exhibited for him as to match that superiority which the head has over the other members of the body. In addition, he administers his office faithfully when, mindful of his special situation, he remembers to cherish the unique character of the community subject to him, and when he is cognizant that he does not owe his life to himself but to others, and when he allots things to them according to the order of charity. Therefore, he owes the whole of himself to God, most to his country, much to his parents and relatives, and less (although still a little) to foreigners. He is thus duty bound "to the wise and to the foolish, to the insignificant and to the great" (Rom. 1:14).

Inspection of such persons is common to all prelates, both those who administer care in spiritual matters and those who exercise temporal jurisdiction. Consequently, we have Melchizedek, the first whom Scripture introduces as king and priest (making no mention at present of the mystery by which he prefigures Christ, who was born in heaven without a mother and on earth without a father). It may be read of him, I say, that he had neither father nor mother, not that he was deprived of either one, but because according to reason, kingship and priesthood are not generated of flesh and blood, since in founding either one, respect for lineage should not prevail apart from respect for the merits of the virtues, but the desire for the benefit of faithful subjects should be prevalent. And when someone ascends to the summit atop either mountain, he must be oblivious to carnal desires and must do only what is demanded for the welfare of those subject to him. Accordingly, he is father and mother to his subjects or, if he knows of a more gentle form of affection, he should use that; he desires love more than fear, and reveals himself to his subjects as someone whose life they would out of devotion prefer to their own, so that they count his safety as equivalent to the life of the people; and then all affairs will proceed properly for him, and a small body of obedient guards will prevail (if necessary) over innumerable adversaries. For love is stronger than death; and the military formation that is tied together by the bonds of love will not break easily. [. . .]

6. [*The Ruler and God's Law*]. "When he sits upon the throne of his kingdom, he will write for himself a copy of this law of Deuteronomy in a book" (Deut. 17:18). See that the prince must not be ignorant of law and, although he takes pleasure in many privileges, he is not permitted to be ignorant of the laws of God on the pretext of the martial spirit. The law of Deuteronomy, that is, the second law, is therefore to be written in the book of his heart so that the first law, which is impressed upon the page, corresponds to the second, which is recognised by the mystical intellect. The first could be written on stone tablets; but the second was not imprinted, except upon the purer intelligence of mind. And the prince properly writes Deuteronomy in a book because he may thus reflect upon the law in his reason without the letter disappearing from before his eyes. And hence, the letter of the law is followed in such a fashion that there is no divergence from the purity of its spirit. For in fact the letter destroys, while the spirit confers life, and with the ruler rests the moderate interpretation of human law and equity in accordance with necessity and general circumstance.

"Taken," it is said, "from the exemplar of the priests of the tribe of Levi" (Deut. 17:18). Surely this is fitting. All censures of law are void if they do not bear the image of the divine law; and the ordinance *(constitutio)* of the prince is useless if it does not conform to ecclesiastical discipline. Nor did this escape the notice of the most Christian prince, who proclaimed that his laws were not to disdain imitation of the sacred canons. And not only should one aspire to be ruled by the examples of priests, but the prince is despatched to the tribe of Levi in order to obtain its benefits. For the legitimate priests are thus to be heeded, so that the just man shall shut off his hearing to all reprobates and those who thrive at the expense of their opponents. But who are the priests of the tribe of Levi? They are those without an avaricious motive, without an ambitious impulse, without a disposition towards flesh and blood — those whom law has introduced into the Church. This refers not to the letter of the law, which mortifies, but to its spirit, which stimulates the qualities of sanctity of mind, cleanliness of body, sincerity of faith and charitableness of works. For just as the law of the shadow both regulated all affairs figuratively and expressed to the priests its preference for a single line of flesh and blood, so after the cessation of the shadow, when truth was disclosed and justice from heaven was seen, those who were commended by their meritorious lives and the scent of good opinion, and who were set apart for the work of ministry by the agreement of the faithful or the diligent prudence of prelates, were attached by the Spirit to the tribe of Levi and were consecrated as legitimate priests.

It is added: "And it will be with him and he shall read it all the days of his life" (17:19). Note how diligent in guarding the law of God should be the prince, who is commanded to hold it, to read it and to reflect upon it always, just as the King of Kings — created from woman, created under law — carried out the whole justice of law, to which He was subject not by necessity, but by will because His will is law, and He meditated day and night on the Law of God. But perhaps someone will suppose that we ought not to imitate Him who embraced the faith of the poor rather than the

[handwritten: kings must follow the example of JX.]

glory of kings and who, assuming the form of a servant, did not seek a place on earth to lay His head and who confessed under interrogation by a magistrate that His kingdom is not of this world. To such an argument, we may respond with the examples of illustrious kings who are remembered in our blessings. From the strongholds of Israel proceed, therefore, David, Hezekiah and Josiah and others who believed the glory of their kingship to consist in this: that they and their subjects were to be fastened by the bonds of divine law if they were to seek God's glory. And lest these examples appear to be remote, and less follow from them because we seem to depart appreciably from their laws and tradition of conduct and religious worship and profession of faith (although their faith and ours are the same, with the exception that what they had expected in the future, we for the most part rejoice in and venerate in completed form, since the figures of the shadow have been tossed aside by that truth which arose from the earth and is revealed in the sight of the gentiles) — lest, I say, their examples be disparaged as somewhat foreign or profane, Christian princes can be instructed by our Constantine, Theodosius, Justinian and Leo and other most Christian princes. For in fact they gave particular effort in order that the most sacred laws, which bind the lives of all, should be known and upheld by all, and that no one was to be ignorant of them, except if either the cost of their error is compensated by some utility to the public or the legitimate sting of harshness is avoided by reason of pity for the aged or the infirmities of gender. Accordingly, their deeds are incitements to virtue; their words are so many lessons in moral matters. Ultimately their lives, in which vice was subdued and captured, have been constructed like triumphal arches consecrated to posterity: arches which list their magnificent virtues, proclaiming in everything the faithful acknowledgement that all these excellent acts were done not by our hands, but by the Lord's. [. . .]

As for the rest, when I reflect upon the words of the previously set out law, each seems full of meaning to me and they are presented to the mind as though fertilised by the spirit of intelligence. "He will therefore," it is stated, "have the law with him," making provision lest, when it is necessary to have it, it be held against him towards his own damnation. For in fact "the powerful will suffer powerful torments" (Sap. 6:6). And it is added: "He must read it." It indeed seems too little to have the law in one's purse, unless it is also faithfully protected in one's soul. It is to be read, therefore, all the days of his life. As a result of this, it is clearly accepted that it is necessary for princes, who are commanded to reflect daily upon the text of the divine law, to be proficient in letters. And perhaps you do not commonly find that priests are commanded to read the law daily. Yet the prince is to read it each and every day of his life because the day that the law is not read is not a day of his life, but the day of his death. Of course, an illiterate would not be able to do this without difficulty. And thus, in a letter which I recall that the King of Romans transmitted to the King of Franks, who was exhorted to procure for his offspring instruction in the liberal disciplines, it was added elegantly to the rest that an illiterate king was like a crowned ass.

Yet if, by reason of a dispensation on account of the merit of preeminent virtue, a prince happens to be illiterate, then it is necessary that he receive the counsel of those who are literate, in order that his affairs proceed properly. Let him, therefore, stand beside the prophet Nathan and the priest Zadok and the faithful sons of the prophets who will not permit him to be diverted from the law of God, and when what is before his eyes is not manifested in his soul, the men of letters are to introduce it through speech into the opening of his ears. Accordingly, the mind of the prince is to be read through the tongue of the priests, and anything illustrious he observes in their moral conduct he is to venerate as the law of God. For the life and speech of the priesthood is like a book set before the sight of the people. Perhaps this is what was in mind when it was commanded to receive the example of law from the priests of the tribe of Levi, since their proclamations should moderate the governmental power of the commissioned magistrates. [. . .]

8. [*Merciful Justice*]. What obtains for the prince ought to obtain for everyone: no one is to prefer his own affairs to the affairs of others. Yet truly the amount of that affection, with which subjects are to be embraced like brothers in the arms of charity, must be confined to the limits of moderation. And thus, for him to love his brothers, he must correct their errors in medical fashion; he must acknowledge the flesh and blood in them so that he may subject them to the words of the Spirit. It is above all the habit of physicians that when they are not able to cure an affliction with palliatives and gentle medicines, they employ harsher cures, as for example fire or iron. They would never use the harsher ones except when they have despaired in their desire to promote health gently. And thus, when mild power does not suffice for the ruler to cure the vices of inferiors, he properly administers intensely painful blows of punishment; pious cruelty rages against the evil, while the good are looked after in safety.

But who is so strong as to amputate a part of his body without pain? He grieves, therefore, when he is asked for the required punishment of the guilty, yet he executes it with a reluctant right hand. For indeed the prince has no left hand and in tormenting the parts of the body of which he is the head, he serves the law mournfully and with groans. [. . .]

12. [*The Cause of Transferring Kingdoms*]. It is well known from Wisdom that "kingdoms will be transferred from dynasty to dynasty on account of injustice and injury and abusiveness and diverse forms of deceit" (Sir. 10:8). [. . .]

Injustice is (as the Stoics agree) a mental disposition (*mentis habitus*) which removes equity from the realm of morals. For indeed the soul is proclaimed to be deprived of justice by reason of the private suffix. Moreover, justice consists chiefly in this: do not do harm and prevent the doing of harm out of a duty to humanity. When you do harm you assent to injury. When you do not impede the doing of harm, you are a servant of injustice. Furthermore, abusiveness is when mental passion is accompanied by actions which result in manifest harm to others. And it serves iniquity because it insolently rises up against one to whom reverence is owed by reason of status, office or natural bond. Finally, deceit is (as Aquilius defines it) when one thing is done and another is pretended; whenever it is performed with the intention of doing harm it is always bad. Deceit differs in many ways from abusiveness, which is haughty and palpable, whereas deceit does harm fraudulently and virtually by means of a trap.

These vices are the ones which, when they occur, subvert all power everywhere because the glory of princes is perpetuated by their contraries. For indeed deceit encompasses the mark of weakness represented by timidity, and is most opposed to courage. Prudence curbs abusiveness, repeating constantly: "Why are dust and ashes arrogant towards dust and ashes?" Temperance does not admit of injury, refusing to submit others to that which it would itself refuse to suffer at the hands of another. And justice excludes injustice, at all times doing to others those acts which it wishes done by others to itself. These are the four virtues which the philosophers have called "cardinal" because they are believed to flow like the main channels from the primary fount of honour and to propagate from themselves all the streams of goodness. Perhaps these are the four rivers which depart from God's paradise of delights, so that they irrigate all the earth, which in its own time will bear desirable fruits. . . . I believe that neither leaders nor powerful men are excepted from this because the glory of kings is to be transferred if they are found to be unjust, injurious, abusive or deceitful, since "the mouth of the Lord has spoken it" (Isa. 1:20). [. . .]

From Book 5

2. [*The Republic according to Plutarch*]. The parts of this political constitution follow thereafter in a pamphlet entitled "The Instruction of Trajan," which I have sought to incorporate partially into the present treatise, yet in such a way as to reproduce the outlines of its meanings rather than its actual words. It is first of all required that the prince evaluate himself entirely and direct himself diligently to the whole body of the republic, whose condition he enjoys. For a republic is, just as Plutarch declares, a sort of body which is animated by the grant of divine reward and which is driven by the command of the highest equity and ruled by a sort of rational management. By all means, that which institutes and moulds the practice of religion in us and which transmits the worship of God (not the "gods" of which Plutarch speaks) acquires the position of the soul in the body of the republic. Indeed, those who direct the practice of religion ought to be esteemed and venerated like the soul in the body. For who disputes that the sanctified ministers of God are his vicars? Besides, just as the soul has rulership of the whole body so those who are called prefects of religion direct the whole body. Augustus Caesar himself was constantly subject to the sacred pontiffs until the time when he created himself a Vestal pontiff and shortly thereafter was transformed into a living god, in order that he would be subject to no one.

The position of the head in the republic is occupied, however, by a prince subject only to God and to those who act in his place on earth, inasmuch as in the human body the head is stimulated and ruled by the soul. The place of the heart is occupied by the senate, from which proceeds the beginning of good and bad works. The duties of the ears, eyes and mouth are claimed by the judges and governors of provinces. The hands coincide with officials and soldiers. Those who always assist the prince are comparable to the flanks. Treasurers and record keepers (I speak not of those who supervise prisoners, but of the counts of the Exchequer) resemble the shape of the stomach and intestines; these, if they accumulate with great avidity and

289

tenaciously preserve their accumulation, engender innumerable and incurable diseases so that their infection threatens to ruin the whole body. Furthermore, the feet coincide with peasants perpetually bound to the soil, for whom it is all the more necessary that the head take precautions, in that they more often meet with accidents while they walk on the earth in bodily subservience; and those who erect, sustain and move forward the mass of the whole body are justly owed shelter and support. Remove from the fittest body the aid of the feet; it does not proceed under its own power, but either crawls shamefully, uselessly and offensively on its hands or else is moved with the assistance of brute animals. [. . .]

6. [*The Election, Privileges, and Rewards of the Prince*]. It follows that in imitation of Plutarch's path, we must scrutinise the members of the republic. It is said that the prince occupies the place of the head, and is regulated solely by the judgment of his own mind. And so, as was said already, divine disposition places him on top of the republic and prefers him over others, at one time on the basis of the mystery of His secret providence, at another time just as His priests have determined, while at still another time he is put in charge when the wishes of the whole people concur. And for this reason, it may be read in the Old Testament how Moses, when ordaining him who should preside over the people, had assembled the whole synagogue in order that the ruler might be selected while standing before the people, so that there would remain neither grounds for later retraction nor any lingering doubts. It may be read in the Book of Kings how the future king, Saul, appearing in front of the people, had been lifted up over the community of the people upon their shoulders. For what reason, I ask, unless because he who ought to preside over others must extend his heart and head almost as if he were able to embrace the whole breadth of the people in the arms of good works and to protect them — indeed, just as if he were more learned, more holy, more circumspect, and more distinguished in all the virtues? For the Lord said to Moses: "Take Joshua, son of Nun, a man who has the spirit of God in him, and lay your hands on him, and set him before Eleazar the priest, and give him commandments in the presence of the whole synagogue, and give instructions about him publicly, and you will set your distinction upon him in order that the children of Israel will listen to him" (Num. 27:18-20). Evidently, we are listening to the ordination of a prince of the people, so clearly described that it almost does not need exposition. Yet if you question its clarity, I will explain it to you on the authority of the Lord, adding the significance of the vestments and some aspects of the sacraments, when enjoined at the proper place and time. Yet plainly there was never popular acclamation here, never the rationale of blood ties, never was there contemplation of nearby relatives. Upon the death of Zelophehad, his children claimed their paternal inheritance before Moses. God himself testifies that their petition was just; for in fact relatives are to be left the hereditary lands and estates and as many public functions as possible. Still, governance of the people is handed over to him whom God has elected, namely, such a man who has in him the Spirit of God and in whose sight are the commandments of God, one who is well known to and familiar with Moses, that is, in whom there is the distinction and knowledge of the law, in order that the children of Israel might listen to him.

Nevertheless, it is not permitted to withdraw in preference to new men from the bloodline of princes who by divine promise and genealogical right are owed the privilege of the succession of their offspring, if (as was previously written) they have walked in the justice of the Lord. Moreover, if they have for a short time deserted the path, they should not immediately be cast entirely aside, but should be admonished patiently about injustice, until finally it becomes conspicuous that they are firm in their evil. For Rehoboam was not immediately removed from his father's throne for the reason that, disregarding the counsel of older and better men, he departed from the path of Solomon, seeking to impose an insupportable burden upon the shoulders of the children of Israel. But his kingdom was split with the departure of the ten tribes behind Jeroboam, the servant of Solomon, and the kingdom was divided in so far as Judah and Israel each had a kingdom. He therefore felt the punishment for his obstinacy, as well as the mercy of the grace of God and the privilege of blood, inasmuch as he at least remained king but the greater part of the kingdom was cut off. For what reason did this happen to him? Because he adhered to the counsel of the young, disregarding the ways and precepts of prudence. For it is impossible that he should dispose rulership advantageously who does not act upon the counsel of the wise. [. . .]

From Book 6

1. [*The Armed and the Unarmed Hand of the Republic*]. And so the hand of the republic is either armed or unarmed. The armed hand is of course that which is occupied with marching and the blood-letting of warfare; the unarmed hand is that which expedites justice and attends to the warfare of legal right, distanced from arms. For the soldiers of the republic are not only those who, protected by helmets and breastplates, turn loose their swords or spears or whatever other weapons against the enemy, but also advocates of cases who invigorate the weary and, relying upon the fortification of an illustrious voice, lift up the fallen; and no less do they provide for mankind than if, working with the armour of life, hope and posterity, they provided protection from the enemy. Even tax collectors and public servants and all officials of courts of law are soldiers. For just as some are offices of peace and others are offices of war, so likewise it is necessary for some to arrange the first sort of task, others the second.

And so the armed hand is exercised strictly against enemies, but the unarmed is extended also against the citizen. In addition, discipline is necessary for both because both are notoriously accustomed to being wicked. The use of the hand testifies to the qualities of the head itself because, as Wisdom asserts, the iniquitous king has entirely impious ministers; "and of whatever kind is a city's leader, of the same kind also are its inhabitants" (Sir. 10:2). Censuring his colleague Sophocles, Pericles said that it is necessary that not only the hands but also the eyes of the governor have continence. For the continence of governors is laudable when they restrain their hands and hold back the hands of others from exactions and injuries. [. . .]

26. [*Endurance and Removal of Vices*]. [. . .] In the satire *Manipean*, which is

about the duties of the institution of matrimony, Varro asserts: "The vices of a spouse are to be either removed or endured. He who removes the vices is a preferable spouse; he who tolerates them makes himself a better person" (Aulus Gellius, *Noctes Atticae*, 1.7.4). Thus, the vices of princes and subjects are to be either endured or removed; for in fact their confederation either equals or surpasses conjugal affection. But even the words "to endure" and "to remove" are themselves cleverly adapted by Varro. It appears that "removing" is meant in the sense of correction. It is beyond doubt that his actual judgment was that what cannot be removed is to be endured. Yet a faithful interpretation of this adds that what is understood by "vice" is what honour and religion can securely endure. For vices are more insignificant than flagrant crimes; and there are a number of acts which one is not permitted to endure or which cannot faithfully be endured. A spouse may legally be separated from a spouse by reason of fornication, and he is very often a patron of turpitude who conceals the crime of his wife. Perhaps for that reason it is said: "He who cherishes an adulteress is both silly and impious." Moreover, this obtains equally of any sort of physical and spiritual adultery, even though the spiritual form is the worse and is to be more carefully avoided.

Similarly, even in the connection between the members, Varro's rule about enduring and removing is to be admitted. For in fact no one questions that members ought to be cured, whether the cure for their wound proceeds from the palliative of oils or from the austere wine which the Samaritan administered. That the members are likewise to be removed is clear from that which is written: "If your eye or your foot offend you, root it out and cast it away from you" (Matt. 18:9). I think that this is to be observed by the prince in regard to all of the members to the extent that not only are they to be rooted out, broken off and thrown far away, if they give offence to the faith or public security, but they are to be destroyed utterly so that the security of the corporate community may be procured by the extermination of the one member. Who will be spared, I say, by him who is commanded to do violence against even his own eyes? Indeed, neither the ears nor the tongue nor whatever else subsists within the body of the republic is safe if it revolts against the soul for whose sake the eyes themselves are gouged out. When God is offended by abuses of criminals or the Church is spurned, the well-being of the entire soul is in jeopardy. This is so foreign to the office of the prince that, whenever these things occur in the republic, it is to be believed that the prince either is entirely unaware or is asleep or is on a journey. [...]

From Book 8

17. [*How the Tyrant Differs from the Prince*]. [...] As the image of the deity, the prince is to be loved, venerated and respected; the tyrant, as the image of depravity, is for the most part even to be killed. The origin of tyranny is iniquity and it sprouts forth from the poisonous and pernicious root of evil and its tree is to be cut down by an axe anywhere it grows. For unless iniquity and injustice had advanced tyranny through the extermination of charity, secure peace and perpetual calm would have

dwelled among the people throughout eternity, and no one would think of advancing his borders. As the great father Augustine has testified, kingdoms would be as calm and friendly in their enjoyment of peace as are different families in orderly cities or different persons in the same family. Or perhaps it is more believable that there would be absolutely no kingdoms, for as is evident from the ancient historians, these were iniquitous in themselves; they either encroached upon or were extorted from God. And of course not only kings practise tyranny; many private men are tyrants, in so far as the powers which they possess promote prohibited goals. One is not to be troubled that I am appearing to have associated kings with tyranny, since, although it is said that "king" *(rex)* is derived from the "right" *(recte)* which is fitting for princes, still this name incorrectly refers to tyrants. [. . .]

And so the king is sometimes called by the name of tyrant and conversely the tyrant is sometimes called by the name of prince, according to the maxim: "Your princes are faithless, associates of thieves" (Isa. 1:23). And elsewhere: "The princes of the priesthood made counsel so that they might detain Jesus by deceit and kill Him" (Matt. 26:4), who by the just judgment of the law ought to be freed. For even among the priesthood many may be found who are driven by all their ambition and all their talents so that they can be tyrants under the pretext of exercising their duties. For the republic of the impious has both its head and members, and it endeavours to be fashioned like the civil institutions of the legitimate republic. Its tyrannical head, therefore, is the image of the devil; its soul is formed of heretical, schismatic and sacrilegious priests and, to use the words of Plutarch, prefects of religion, assailing the laws of the Lord; the heart of impious counsellors is like a senate of iniquity; its eyes, ears, tongue and unarmed hand are unjust officials, judges and laws; its armed hand is violent soldiers, whom Cicero labels mercenaries; its feet are those among the more humble occupations who oppose the precepts of the Lord and legitimate institutions. Of course all of these can be readily controlled by their superiors. [. . .]

A thief is someone who is to be restrained in a twofold respect. For he who ascends from earthly habitation by means of pride up the ladder of ambition and through the levels of the vices supported by contempt for the sheep of Christ — that is, neglecting the right path, he tunnels straight under the twisting curves in the road to the entrance or he breaks through the joinery of the walls or he enters through the tiles on the roof — is a thief or a robber. Yet also he who walks through the door opened by Christ, that is, one who is called to the church, and who thereafter is made into a persecutor under the pretext of a shepherd, that is, plunders, destroys, kills and corrupts, is indubitably a thief (cf. John 10:1f.). You must consider into which category would seem to be placed those for whom the licence of divine right to shear and devour the flock does not suffice but who also appeal to the aid of secular laws and who, making themselves officials of princes, are not afraid to commit deeds which would readily embarrass any other tax collector. Meanwhile, they serve their own pleasures or avarice, and they pillage and oppress those who selected or admitted them into custody over themselves, and they desire the death of those whom they ought to have supported in flesh and spirit. Surely they recall the statement of the prophet: "Behold I have empowered you over peoples and kingdoms so that you may eradicate and destroy and disperse and build and plant" (Jer. 1:10). Therefore, what they have found planted they strive to pull up, so that they may build the house of the Lord themselves by means of the presents offered from the hand or the tongue or obedience; or they substitute the uprooted plants for those which they select out of carnal affection, that is, either their offspring or the offspring of the flesh of someone other than themselves. [. . .]

18. [*Tyrants as God's Ministers*]. Yet I do not deny that tyrants are ministers of God, who by his just judgment has willed them to be pre-eminent over both soul and body. By means of tyrants, the evil are punished and the good are corrected and trained. For both the sins of the people cause hypocrites to reign and, as the history of kings witnesses, the defects of priests introduced tyrants into the people of God. The first fathers and the patriarchs were in obedience to nature, the best guide to living. They were succeeded by leaders following the laws of Moses and by judges who ruled the people according to the authority of the law; and we read that these were priests. Finally, against the wrath of God, they were given kings, some good, yet others bad. For Samuel had become old and, when his sons did not walk in his path but pursued avarice and impurity, the people, who perhaps had deserved that such priests should preside over them, had extorted a king for themselves from God, whose will was disregarded. Therefore, Saul was selected according to the aforementioned rights of the king, that is, one who would take away their sons in order that they might be made into charioteers, and their daughters in order that they might become bakers and cooks, and their lands and estates in order that they might be distributed to his servants according to his will, and who would oppress all people with the yoke of servitude. Yet the same man was called the anointed of the Lord and, exercising tyranny, he did not lose the honour of kingship. For God had aroused fear in everyone, so that they venerated Saul like a minister of God, whose image he would in a certain measure display.

I might also add more: even the tyrants of the gentiles, condemned to death from eternity, are the ministers of God and are called the anointed of the Lord. For this reason the prophet says: "Leaders will enter the gates" of Babylon, namely, Cyrus and Darius; "for I have commanded my sanctified and summoned my strong in my anger and those exultant in my glory" (Isa. 13:2-3). Behold that He called the Medes and the Persians "sanctified," not because they were holy men but because they carried out the will of the Lord against Babylon. Elsewhere it is also said: "Behold that I will bring to you Nebuchadnezzar my servant and because he has served me well at Tyre, I shall give him Egypt" (Ezek. 29:18-19). All power is good since it exists only from him from whom everything good and only good exists. Yet occasionally power is not good, but bad, for the person who uses it or suffers under it, although it is good in general, created by him who uses our wickedness for goodness. For just as in a painting a dark or blackened or some other colour is considered unattractive in itself and yet is appropriate within the whole painting, so certain things are viewed as shameful or evil in themselves, yet they appear excellent and good when related to the broader perspective, since all things are adapted by him whose works are absolutely good. Therefore, even the power of tyrants is in a certain sense good, yet nothing is worse than tyranny. For tyranny is an abuse of power conceded to man by God. Yet this evil is used for many and great goods. It is therefore evident that tyranny exists not among princes alone, but that everyone is a tyrant who abuses any power over those subject to him which has been conceded from above. Furthermore, if power is assumed by the wise man, who knows and has experience of all things, it is agreeable to all good men and to the utility of all. Yet if power falls to the foolish man, even though it cannot be an evil for the good man, to whom everything works jointly for the good, still it is injurious for a short period of time. It is clear that power falls to the lot of both sorts, although (driven by the wickedness of our contemporaries who have constantly roused the anger of God against us) it is more frequently conceded to bad, that is, foolish, men.

20. [*Lawful Tyrannicide*]. [...] There is a famous history in the Books of Kings and Chronicles in which, on the authority of Jerome, it is taught that Israel had laboured under tyrants from the beginning and it is demonstrated that all the kings of Judah are to be considered damned except for David, Josiah and Hezekiah. Yet I would readily believe that Solomon and perhaps some others in Judah would have flourished once the Lord summoned them back. And I will be easily persuaded that tyrants instead of princes would have been deserved by a people of stiff neck and wild heart and a people who always resisted the Holy Spirit and who had provoked not only Moses, the servant of the law, but God Himself, the Lord of the law, to anger by their gentile abominations. For penitence annihilates, drives out and kills those tyrants whom sins obtain, introduce and encourage. And even before the time of their kings, just as the history of Judges narrates, the children of Israel were repeatedly enslaved under tyrants. They were afflicted at many and various times according to divine dispensation, and they were often freed by crying out to the Lord. And after the termination of the period of divine supervision, the death of their tyrants permitted them to remove the yokes from their necks. Not a single one of those by whose virtues a penitent and humble people was liberated is to be censured, but the memory of posterity is to recall them favourably as ministers of God.... [...]

The histories teach that we are to take care, lest anyone cause the death of a tyrant who is bound to him by the obligation of fealty or a sacred oath. For it is read that even Zedekiah was taken captive as a result of his neglect of sacred fealty; and, in another instance, a king of Judah (I do not recall who) had his eyes plucked out because, lapsing into unfaithfulness, he did not keep his promise before the sight of God, to whom he swore an oath, since even the tyrant is justly to be given surety in lawsuits (2 Kings 25:6f.). And I do not read that poison was licensed by the indulgence of any legal right at any time, although I have read that it was sometimes made use of by infidels. Not that I do not believe that tyrants are to be removed from the community, but they are to be removed without loss to religion and honour. For even David, the best of the kings about whom I have read and one who (except for his plot against Uriah the Hittite) advanced blamelessly in all his affairs, endured the most grievous of tyrants. Although he enjoyed frequent opportunities to destroy the tyrant, David preferred to spare him, trusting in the compassion of God who could free him without sin. He therefore decided to wait patiently to the end that the tyrant might be visited by God with a return to chastity or might fall in battle or might otherwise be extinguished by the just judgment of God. For indeed his patience can be distinguished in the fact that, at the time when David had cut off his cloak in the cave and on the other occasion when, entering into camp by night, he found fault with the negligence of the guards, the king himself was compelled to admit that David acted upon the more just cause. And this method of eradicating tyrants is the most useful and the safest: those who are oppressed should humbly resort to the protection of God's clemency and, raising up pure hands to the Lord in devoted prayer, the scourge with which they are afflicted will be removed. For in fact the sins of transgressors are the strength of tyrants. [. . .]

Translation: Cary J. Nederman (Cambridge, 1990). Used with permission.

better to
pray than
kill the
tyrant

Rufinus the Canonist

(fl. 1150–ca. 1191)

Rufinus was an Italian canonist who taught canon law at Bologna probably from about 1150, was elevated to the episcopal see of Assisi before 1179 and to the archiepiscopal see of Sorrento before 1186. His lasting accomplishment was to produce (possibly between 1157 and 1159) the *Summa Decretorum,* reputed to be the first comprehensive and detailed commentary on Gratian's *Decretum,* the textbook of ecclesiastical law published circa 1140 that revolutionized medieval canonist study. To read the *Summa* properly and understand its achievement requires some knowledge of the format, content, and method of this monumental work of Gratian, who may well have taught Rufinus at Bologna.

In his *Harmony of Discordant Canons,* commonly referred to as the *Decreta* or *Decretum,* Gratian set out not only to amass the accumulated law of the church but, as his title suggests, to systematize and rationalize it, so as to facilitate its study and use. The sources and content of church law were vast and multifarious, and included legal, historical, and theological material from the Bible and the church fathers, enactments of church councils and synods, papal letters and decretals (both authentic and spurious), and borrowings from Roman civil law. Gratian worked with a modest number of fairly recent canonical collections, applying discernible principles of selection, and techniques of organization and analysis developed by the Bologna civilians in their work of reducing Justinian's corpus to rational order (see p. 189 above). The result, as we have it from the late twelfth century, with substantial alterations and additions, was a textbook divided into three sections. The first consists of 101 "distinctions" (abbrev. D.), each comprising a group of texts (*capitula,* abbrev. c.) arranged around a particular point. Distinctions 1-20 form an influential "treatise" on law and authority. The second section consists of thirty-six "fictional cases" (*causae,* abbrev. C.), each of which poses "an interlocking set of questions about a given legal situation," the questions being treated in sets of *capitula.* The third, known as *De poenitentia,* consists of five distinctions concerned with worship and the sacraments.

Interestingly, Gratian himself incorporated no Roman law texts (although about two hundred were subsequently inserted), suggesting an intention to keep church law free of secular sources (Christensen 1993, xii-xiv). His great innovation was to introduce his own commentary (referred to as *dicta*, abbreviated d.) after his presentation of sources, in which he attempted to resolve discrepancies and contradictions among them. Although never officially adopted by the church, his work became part of what would much later be called the *Corpus iuris canonici*, in which it stood alongside subsequent collections of papal decretals (the *Liber extra, Liber sextus, Extravagantes,* and *Clementinae*).

Rufinus never envisaged his commentary as a mere sequence of marginal glosses on Gratian's text, but rather as a work of serious exegesis, critical analysis, and theoretical development. He brought to his labor theological training and the most recent literature, including Peter Lombard's *Sentences*. The scope and originality of his enterprise may be gauged from his discussion of the divisions of laws set out by Gratian in his first distinction (D. 1): into divine-natural ordinances and human usages (c. 1) and into natural law, civil law, and the law of nations (cc. 6-9). Already in his preface, having situated the main types of law within the theological schema of creation/fall/restoration, he can now expand on the relationships between the natural law, divinely revealed law, the law of nations and human civil codes, resolving difficulties in the tradition that Gratian had not wholly surmounted. One key difficulty inherited by Gratian from Isidore concerned the apparent contravention of the natural-law stipulations of "common possession of goods" and "one freedom for all" by the historical institutions of property and slavery. Rufinus resolves the dilemma by distinguishing within natural law the three aspects of commandments, prohibitions, and indications, and subsuming common possession and a single freedom under those things indicated by nature to be good or convenient but neither prescribed nor prohibited. In the spirit of the Latin Fathers, particularly Augustine, he attempts to show that slavery and property, while derogating from the *form* of the natural law, nevertheless fulfill its *intention* under the conditions of human sinfulness. His resolution was taken up by later canonists and theologians, most notably by Aquinas, who, however, sheds the master's association of property with man's postlapsarian state.

A second difficulty arose from the discrepancy in Roman juristic opinion as to whether the "forcible repulsion of violence" belongs to the natural law or to the *ius gentium*. Realizing that the discrepancy was rooted in the different understandings of natural law entertained by the jurists of the *Digest*, Rufinus sets out the *normative canonist understanding* of it — as identical with the moral law of mankind — and, by means of a further *moral* distinction (between self-defense and vengeance), shows how the forcible repulsion of violence belongs to the natural law.

His other discussions included in our excerpts elaborate principles and distinctions of importance for the developing legal-political tradition of the West: e.g., between "pure" and "mixed" canon law, between canons that can or cannot be dispensed from or abrogated, the conditions of legitimate political authority, and those of just war. His further distinction (not included below) between the episcopal powers of "administration" and "authority" (later known as the powers of "jurisdiction" and "order"), deriving, respectively, from episcopal election ("from below") and from consecration ("from above"), became a linchpin of papalist ecclesiology and theory of church-empire relations (Benson 1968, ch. 3).

Further Reading: R. L. Benson, *The Bishop-Elect: A Study in Medieval Ecclesiastical Office* (Princeton: Princeton University Press, 1968); S. Chodorow, *Christian Political Theory and Church Politics in the Mid Twelfth Century: The Ecclesiology of Gratian's "Decretum"* (Los Angeles: University of California Press, 1972); K. Christensen, introduction to *Gratian, The Treatise on Laws with the Ordinary Gloss*, trans. J. Gordley (Washington, D.C.: Catholic University of America Press, 1993); Y. M.-J. Congar, "Maître Rufin et son *De bono pacis*," *Revue des sciences philosophiques et théologiques* 41 (1957): 428-44; S. Kuttner, *Gratian and the Schools of Law, 1140-1234* (Aldershot: Variorum, 1983); H. Singer, ed., *Die Summa Decretorum des Magister Rufinus* (Paderborn: Schöningh, 1902).

From *Summa Decretorum*, Preface

[. . .] Before the Fall the human creature enjoyed an exalted dignity, upheld, as it were, on two strings, the rectitude of justice and the lucidity of knowledge. The one served to protect his engagements with human beings, the other gave him access to heavenly mysteries. But, through the mounting envy of the Devil, the rectitude of his justice was dragged down by the oppressive weight of vice, and the light of knowledge darkened by the fog of error. And since with every wrong step he became the more blinded by ignorance, it needed the practice of justice in keeping with the demand of natural order, to restore him to the proper state of knowledge. Accordingly, since man's natural capacities were not completely extinguished, he began to pay special attention to the differences between himself and the brute animals, that is, to the privilege of knowledge and, in consequence, to a law-governed conduct of life. And so, when he decided to come together with his fellows to consult on matters of mutual interest, the sparks of justice which smouldered, as it were, among the dead ashes, all at once quickened the principles of modesty and restraint, which in turn taught him to change the customs of an uncultivated and wild humanity into decent and respectable ones, to submit to peaceable constraints and to enter upon enduring treaties. These are called the "law of nations" *(ius gentium)* because they are used by almost all peoples, in that there are sales, contracts of letting and hiring, exchanges, and other such things.

But since these measures were by no means sufficient to restore our weak condition entirely to virtuous conduct, the merciful God, reinforcing that law of life which he had written in the heart of men from eternity, spelled out in words Ten Commandments, received and given by Moses, which we call the Old Law or the "law of the synagogue." Yet since the law did not achieve perfection, as the Apostle testifies, in the fullness of time God sent his Son, through whom he instituted for us a law of life, a spotless law converting souls (Ps. 19:7), which, in a happy expression, we call the Gospel. And when, thanks to God, the church grew and was equipped with different ranks and orders, the Gospel was clearly not enough to define the distinctions among these, let alone to settle disputes arising among the clergy. Many things were then added by the apostles, their representatives, and other ministers of the church, which, though they have various special names, are generally called by the one term, "canons." All of these Gratian includes as the subject matter of this book. His intention is to arrange canons which are scattered all over the place into an orderly structure and to resolve their contradictions by inserting distinctions. [. . .]

From Part 1

[Small capitals indicate the text of Gratian's *Decretum.*]

Distinction 1. (*On Gratian's Introduction to* D. 1 c. 1): Before treating of canon law, Gratian, as though to cast his net wider, adopts a wide perspective for his work and begins with natural law, which is older and of greater dignity. The legal tradition defines this law very broadly: Natural law is what nature teaches all living beings. For our purposes, however, which are not concerned with the general notion that includes all living beings, we may briefly examine that natural law that is peculiar to humankind, analyzing what it is, of what it consists, how it came to be, and to what degree it has been reduced or expanded. Natural law is a kind of natural propulsion, implanted by nature in each human being, to do good and to avoid evil. Furthermore, it has three constituents: commandments, prohibitions, and indications. It *commands* what is beneficial, as in "Love the Lord your God"; it *prohibits* what does harm, as in, "Do not kill"; and it *indicates* what is convenient, as in "Let them have all things in common" or "Let there be one freedom for all," etc. This natural law, though, was surrounded by such confusion as a result of original sin that people eventually considered nothing illicit, so that the Apostle says: "Sin is not imputed when there is no law" (Rom. 5:13).

Later natural law was reestablished through the Ten Commandments written on two tables, yet it was not restored completely; for while evil deeds were strictly condemned, of course, the intention to do evil was not completely covered by its condemnations. To remedy this, the Gospel was substituted, in which natural law was restored entirely, and so, perfected.

Since, however, natural law has to do with the essential nature of things, and shows no more than that one thing is essentially just and another essentially unjust, it was necessary for its adaptation and elaboration that a moral code be developed, through which a suitable order and decorum might be preserved. For example: the uniting of man and woman is a matter of natural law; but in order that human beings should not make use of this good indiscriminately and precipitously like animals, this natural right was modified through a discreet and honorable code of practice, so that only certain kinds of persons with a certain degree of ceremony could be joined together in matrimony. Here it becomes clear what has been added to natural law from outside it, namely a systematic code of behavior *(modus et ordo morum)*. There has been derogation from natural law, but not in any case from the commandments or prohibitions, which cannot be repealed, but only from the indications *(demonstrationes)* which nature does not prohibit or prescribe but simply shows to be good.

And there has been derogation especially from the principle that in everything there should be one freedom and common possession; for in civil law, this is "my" servant and that is "your" territory. Yet all these things which seem opposed to natural law, ultimately refer back to it. For example, because some people began to live without restraint and, like the Acephali, without a ruler, committing every conceivable crime without punishment, it was established that obstinate rebels against rightful authority should, when subjugated and captured in war, be enslaved perpetually. What was the purpose of this, but that those whose moral indiscipline made them savage, arrogant, and destructive, should become tame, humble, and innocuous through the discipline imposed on slaves? No one doubts that in accordance with natural law arrogance and malice are abhorrent, innocence and humility to be preferred. By this channel, then, the streams of human decency flow back to the sea of natural law, which, when almost lost in the first man, was revealed in the Mosaic law, perfected in the Gospel, and elaborated by the moral code. Of course, those norms of behavior are partly written down and called "statute law" *(ius constitutionum)*; in part they are unwritten and are left to the discretion of those who observe them: and this is called simply, "custom" *(consuetudo)*.

Every law that goes beyond natural law is either civil law or the law of nations. What civil law and the law of nations are is made clear by Isidore's authority.

(On D. 1 c. 2 quoting Isidore, *Etymologies* 5 [cf. p. 210 above]): "Ius is the general term" for divine and human ordinances *(constitutiones)*. "Lex is a species of ius" — that is, a part, for in one system of law *(ius)* many laws *(leges)* are contained. [. . .]

So I will not assemble a lot of human ordinances in this present work, both because I am not knowledgeable about such things, and also because it would be a waste for theologians to encumber this lengthy volume with such matter, except when occasional problems require it, one of which, however, arises in this text (D. 1 c. 7 and Isidore, ibid.): that "forcibly to repel violence" is a matter belonging to natural law. For the first title of the *Digest* maintains that overcoming violence and injustice is a matter for the law of nations; but if it belongs to the law of nations, it does not belong to natural law, as the law of nations is one thing, natural law another. However, the legislators [pre-Justinianic Roman jurists] themselves make a distinction between merely repelling *violence* and overcoming *injustice*. The first, they state, is a matter of natural law, because it is what nature teaches all living beings — for even wild animals repel violence — but the second is a matter of the law of nations because only humans, not animals, are said to suffer and commit injustice. In this text, however, we believe that both the repulsion of violence and the overcoming of injustice are in question. It has been pointed out above that the legislators understand natural law differently from ourselves: their conception takes it to involve all living beings, but we define it more specifically, attributing it to human beings only. And since they know that overcoming violence in this way is not something we share with wild animals, they assign it not to natural law but to the law of nations.

Similarly, the formula, "it is fair to repel violence with force," agrees sufficiently with laws embodying the tradition that all laws *(leges)* and systems of law *(iura)* permit force to be met with force. It seems contradictory to this, however, when it is maintained elsewhere that those who exact vengeance for injuries are not to be made clerics (see below, D. 46 c. 8). Yet it is one thing to defend oneself in the course of a struggle, quite another to come back to the fight with renewed zest, and take vengeance for past injustice without appeal to a judge. The former is permitted in the one text, the latter forbidden in the other. This becomes clear through the similarity of what is said below (C. 3 q. 1 c. 6). [. . .]

"CIVIL LAW," etc. Civil law is what is established through the community or what is constitutive of community itself. Indeed, it is designated by the addition of a proper name, such as "Athenian civil law"; but when it is called "civil law" absolutely, what is meant is Roman law, which is civil law *par excellence.*

"THE LAW OF NATIONS *(ius gentium)* IS" what "ALMOST ALL NATIONS" establish, such as the law of the "OCCUPATION OF POSITIONS," that is, of the enemy's privileges. For having defeated the enemy, a victor occupies the place of their king or other authority and the privileges thereof; and by the law of nations his tenure is secure.

The term *captivitates* is used to mean the practice of taking captives; *servitutes* to mean the enslavement of captives by their captors. *Postliminia* (reinstatement) means that those who return home from captivity regain all their former rights. The expression *postliminium* comes from *limen* (threshold) and *post* (beyond), so that we refer to *postliminium* in the case of one who, after capture by the enemy, comes home later. Thresholds mark, as it were, the domestic boundaries; and so the ancients conceived the boundary of the empire as a threshold. The term *postliminium* thus came to be applied when someone returned across the boundary with which he had lost connection, and took up all his former rights.

"AN AMBASSADOR IS NOT TO BE KEPT BY FORCE": that is, when enemies exchange messengers, they are not to be seized or forcibly held captive, but are to be allowed to return safely and unharmed. Which is why the Roman legates in ancient times carried *sagmina*, some herbs attached to their banner, so that no one would attack them. From *sagmina* we call inviolable objects *sancta*, or "holy."

"MIXED MARRIAGES ARE FORBIDDEN," in that people with different rites are not to be joined together in matrimony, such as a gentile to a Jew or a Christian to a pagan.

Distinction 8. (*On Gratian's Introduction to* D. 8 c. 1): "NATURAL LAW DIFFERS . . .," etc. There are three aspects in which natural law *(ius naturale)* differs most from customary law *(ius consuetudinis)* and statute law *(ius constitutionis):* in its origin, its extent, and its dignity. How it differs in *origin* has already been stated above. How it differs in *dignity* has been treated, but Gratian now repeats with more latitude how natural law has a dignity distinct from that of all other law; anything in custom or statute that is contrary to natural law, i.e., to its commandments and prohibitions, is declared void and of no effect. That is why the Lord says, "I am the truth," not: "I am the custom" or "I am the statute." Natural law also differs from other law in *extent*, because by natural law all things are held in common, whereas by customary or statute law, this thing is mine, while that is yours.

The objection is raised: — If by statute this is my house and that yours, and statute really is law, it follows that this house is mine and that one yours *lawfully;* and if lawfully, not unjustly. What can it mean, then, when we read elsewhere: "*by injustice* one person claimed this thing for himself, another that" (C. 12 q. 1 c. 2)? This point should be understood similarly to the exaction of obedience and oppressive dominion, which Nimrod initiated of old by injustice (as remarked above . . .), but which, since it has been extended over time, now has the force of customary law. In the same way, private property was first brought about through some people's burning avarice; later, however, given long-standing use and legalization, it was judged irreproachable. [. . .]

Distinction 10. (*On Gratian's Introduction to* D. 10 c. 1): If, therefore, the laws of worldly leaders in any matter are opposed to ecclesiastical constitutions, they are to be suspended altogether. But where they have proven not to oppose the decrees of the Gospel and the canons, they are to be cherished with all respect and invoked in support of the church. What is said in the ensuing text, that "THE LAW OF THE WORLDLY RULERS CANNOT ANNUL ECCLESIASTICAL RIGHTS" (D. 10 c. 1: *Letter* of Nicholas I), should not be let pass entirely without explanation. It should be understood that the law of the church (*ius ecclesiasticum*) strictly speaking, derived from divine constitution or that of the holy fathers (e.g., the right of tithes, of dioceses, and so on), is one thing. Quite another is the "joined" or "mixed" law that depends on human statutory provision, such as the right of prescription and other similar rights. *Purely* ecclesiastical rights, therefore, can by no means be annulled by the laws of the secular rulers, neither wholly nor in part. Of those ecclesiastical rights, though, which depend on the ordinances of the secular rulers, there are some, such as the aforementioned right of prescription, which we believe could be done away with by the law of secular rulers wholly or in part, as they were certainly established more to obstruct some opponent than for the general benefit of the church. This ecclesiastical right is partially suspended every day, whenever any one church obtains a privilege from the secular ruler that prohibits another church from exercising its right of prescription against it. We think that this right could be wholly abolished; for if the secular ruler were to introduce a statute saying that all prescription against all parties, for however long a period, was henceforth to cease, from that point forward, the church could not exercise a right of prescription in any way.

From Part 2

Case 1 q. 7: One should know, however, that of the statutes of the canons, some are indispensable, some may be dispensed from, and some may even be set aside. Of these, some are set aside because they are contrary to statute, others because they are contrary to custom. Indispensable statutes are those which derive their mandates or prohibitions mainly from moral law or from evangelical and apostolic institution. For example: someone who has freely made a promise should keep it; a man, as long as his wife is alive, may not marry another; no one not in holy orders may ordain anyone else to ecclesiastical office or celebrate mass; no benefits of the church may be bought; and other things that easily occur to anyone who thinks carefully. In no case can there be a breach of these rules without sin, unless invincible or unavoidable ignorance provides an excuse, whether in response to the demands of the times or of the circumstances. And why is that so? Because all these statutes form part of natural law, against which no dispensation is admitted, as is said above on Distinction 13 (D. 13 d.a.c. 1). Those that *can* be dispensed with are other statutes of the canons which were promulgated and confirmed solely on the authority of the saints and later fathers, such as: monks should not celebrate mass publicly; those who do public penance or who have been married twice are not to be promoted into the clergy; and similar things. All these, in fact, are occasionally disregarded in response to the demands of circumstances or times or for reasons of utility, except where the prominence of the matter or person involved prevents it. [. . .]

Case 23 q. 1: [. . .] Now, the existence of corrupt authority is permitted by God, and on that account is said to be from God, but with no implication that he permits *sin*, or, in consequence, that sin might be from God. One should understand corrupt authority to stem from God's permission in this light: although God is the creator of something, he is not responsible for its misuse. Sin, however, may not be thought of in that way.

And because the subject of the discourse here is secular authority in particular, it must be understood that good authority rests on two pillars, without which no authority is legitimate: lawful institution and temperate exercise of justice. To elaborate this: — (i) *lawful institution* depends on three things: the institutor, the one instituted, and those subject to the authority. *(a)* With respect to the *institutor,* anyone who institutes something has to have the public authority to do so, such as an emperor or prefect and similar others. *(b)* With respect to *the one instituted,* anyone to be girt with the sword of secular authority has to be a fit person, not a cleric bound by religious vows, for instance, but a competent layman. *(c)* With respect to *those subject to the authority,* secular authority should rule the laity and have no validity over the body of clergy.

(ii) *Temperate exercise of justice* is set out in five articles, according to person, matter, manner, place, and time. *(a)* Something may or may not be permitted to the secular power according to *person,* e.g., when a layman has sinned, it may release him, but not a cleric. *(b)* Justice varies according to *matter,* in that secular matters are examined by the worldly power, but not spiritual ones. *(c)* Justice is given according to *degree* or *manner,* whenever any guilt has the appropriate punishment meted out to it, without personal hatred adding to penalty of sufficient gravity, and without personal favor detracting from the required severity. *(d)* Justice is done according to *place* when a trial is held in the proper place, with due respect to sacred sites: for example, no guilty person is to be punished in a church, and no fugitive dragged from one to be handed over for corporal punishment. *(e)* And it is done according to *time,* in that reverence is shown to holy and feast days by sparing those who were due to be punished for their offenses.

q. 2: "THE QUESTION, WHAT IS JUST WAR," etc. A war is considered just in respect of who declares it, who fights it, and against whom hostilities are directed. *(a)* In respect of *who declares it:* anyone who actually initiates hostilities or permits them must have the proper authority to do so. *(b)* In respect of *who fights it:* anyone who wages war should do so with good intention, and hold a social position in which fighting is no disgrace. *(c)* In respect of *who is to be subdued by the hostilities:* he should deserve to have war waged against him or, if he does not actually deserve it, he should be believed on reasonable grounds to have deserved it. Where any of these three proves to have been lacking, the war cannot, strictly speaking, be just.

Translation: Raphaela Schmid and Editors, from H. Singer, ed., *Die Summa Decretorum des Magister Rufinus* (Paderborn: Schöningh, 1902).

Nikephoros Blemmydes

(1197-1272)

After the capture of Constantinople by the Crusaders in 1204, the capital of the Eastern Empire was relocated at Nicaea. Nikephoros Blemmydes, who is remarkable in having left two autobiographies, began his career in court circles, initially under the emperor's patronage, then, after his ordination, at the patriarch's court. As a monk he became a highly influential man of letters, not without political influence, too. His irascible temper, a source of moody satisfaction to himself as well as of frequent conflict, prompted him to refuse an offer of the patriarchate from the dedicatee of this work and a former pupil, the emperor Theodoros Laskaris II.

The *Andrias Basilikos*, or "King's Statue," his essay in the "mirror of princes" genre, has not been much admired. It contains a great deal more recital of traditional moral narratives from Greek historical and biblical sources than of political observation. Yet, though it presents an idealized abstraction, and tells us nothing about the operations of those who actually sat on the throne, such idealizations can tell us a great deal about what those who lived in the shadow of the throne hoped for, and how they justified to themselves the form of government to which they were bound. It would be difficult to find a more focused presentation of the distinctly Byzantine conception of the emperor ("king," *basileus,* as always in Greek writing) as the universal and representative person, the embodiment of the state, than in these opening pages of the treatise. If Eastern Christendom at any point gave voice to ideas that had no currency in the West, it was in thinking of its ruler as the *basis,* "foundation" of society, and of political prudence as economic *pronoia,* "provisions." The implication of this for taxation in general, and for the role of the philosopher as the highest form of taxpayer, is sketched in decisive strokes. The Platonic conception of philosophical "transcendence" has here been wholly integrated into a functional sociology — the kind of transformation that has exposed philosophy in modern times to sociological critique.

The following excerpt is translated from Nikephoros's original version of the treatise, not from the rhetorically more elaborate adaptation in which the treatise gained popularity later in the thirteenth century.

Further Reading: M. Angold, *Church and Society in Byzantium under the Commeni, 1081-1261* (Cambridge: Cambridge University Press, 1995); E. Barker, *Social and Political Thought in Byzantium* (Oxford: Oxford University Press, 1957).

From *The King's Statue*

1. There is an ancient law associated with public affairs, that subjects should make contributions to the king. This is most convenient for themselves, since there is no other way in which the essentials would be secured, a universal authority by means of which universal provisions are made. Having no property of his own, and standing apart from private proprietors, the king must draw on common property for the sake of the community, bringing the resources of the whole into harmony with the interests of the whole. In this way proprietors ensure the security of their possessions by supporting one another with their contributions, and the distinctive endowment of each contributory source is maintained within a whole without splitting the community. It is how a living body resists destruction, every limb and organ performing its own function with integrity. The king, as head or mind of his subjects, is perfectly within his rights in expecting appropriate supplies from every quarter for the preservation of the body politic as a whole. Those whose business lies with material production naturally contribute the usual proportion of their produce (or commute it in accordance with the judgment of the authorities). But those whose studies lie with speech and truth, should produce truthful speech; one could pay no more valuable form of tribute than this, since those studies are, without qualification, the most important. If, then, the king transcends all men, and philosophy transcends all science and art, what could be more fitting for the king than a philosophical gift? Superior gifts for our superiors, first things for our first men. Kingship is the image of the power of God, and philosophy is the image of God's wisdom and providence. But power without wisdom and prudence is remote from God, so that philosophical reflections and undertakings are always especially appropriate for the king.

2. First, then, since a term is a concise definition, it is reasonable to expand it, and so clarify just what a king is. *A king is the foundation of a people.* Security is not achieved in the usual manner by increment and adaptation. The foundation is itself the securest point in relation to what rests upon it, carrying no suggestion of ambiguity or contradiction. How could someone tossed around by inappropriate desires or unreasonable passions ever be the foundation of a people? That would be confusion and chaos. And since he would be an object of aspiration, a bad example to those who happened to be ruled by him and strove to imitate him, the king must first rule what is in himself, and only then rule the external things that surround him. One who cannot rule a single private household can hardly in all seriousness be proclaimed the ruler of many cities. The abject and gluttonous character of the bas-

est pleasures can only appear contemptible and incompatible with such commanding might and exalted dignity. Who would not be appalled at the very thought of the king's sacred majesty declining into such depravity? Among the victims of such a fate should be mentioned those who were deprived of their reason by Circe, turned from men into swine and dogs, a most humiliating affliction; — "swine" meaning that they rolled around in the mud of self-indulgence, "dogs" that they went mad with desire (cf. Homer, *Odyssey* 10). But it is the role of the king to apply the moly [a mythological healing plant] of Hermes, the medicine of rationality, an antidote to the spells of pleasure. And a two-edged sword as well, the sharp blade of discernment, which can distinguish at a glance the better from the worse, showing favor and support for the one and reproving the other. With such defenses, the story is told, the son of Laertes [Odysseus] not only protected himself against Circe's tricks, but rescued his comrades who had been taken by them. The king, similarly, should not only guard himself from captivity to self-indulgences, but should liberate those taken captive both by word and example, and should constantly be hearing solemn hymns in his own praise. "Thou art gone up on high" (i.e., in wisdom) "and hast led captivity captive" (i.e., to the good) (Ps. 68:18).

Translation: Editors, from *Scriptorum Veterum Nova Collectio*, ed. A. Mai (Rome, 1827).

Bonaventure

(1217-74)

Pledged to St. Francis from an early age, educated in the Augustinian tradition by his illustrious Parisian master, Alexander of Hales (d. 1245), Bonaventure (Giovanni di Fidanza) remained throughout his life devoted to St. Francis and St. Augustine, his spirituality and thought being of an ascetical, mystical, universalist, and above all, christocentric cast.

Although his election in 1257 as minister general of the Franciscans (or "Friors Minor") terminated his academic career and reoriented his intellectual acumen toward immediate pastoral and apologetic needs, it did not diminish his passion for the more speculative and scholarly theological enterprise, especially the defense of a christocentric theological science against the advance of philosophical naturalism (whether Averroist or merely Aristotelian) in the Paris schools. Bonaventure perceived an underlying unity behind the assaults of naturalist philosophy on traditional theology and those of the secular masters on the mendicant way of life. The former asserted the self-sufficiency of reason apart from faith, the latter the holiness of worldly benefits apart from suffering and ascetic deprivation.

When Bonaventure assumed the Franciscan headship, hostility from outside the order was deepening an internal rift that had come about through the progressive relaxation of the "Rule" of St. Francis. The order had abandoned its original conditions of itinerant poverty in favor of a more settled communal organization and longer-term provision of the necessities for life and ministry. The central stratagem of this papally legislated relaxation was a definition of Franciscan poverty in legal rather than purely practical terms; i.e., the friars renounced, individually and in common, all ownership of property, so that they had *mere use*, not *legal possession*, of temporal goods. Ownership of their movable goods was vested in the pope; ownership of immovables remained with the donors. This emphasis on legal poverty failed to satisfy the rigorists who saw material want and begging as the heart of the friars' apostolic mission. The involvement of the rigorist cause in "Joachite" theological heterodoxy (from Joachim of Fiore, the twelfth-century mystic) made it an easy target for the secular masters in the University of Paris. From the start Bonaventure was engaged on a number of fronts simultaneously: pacifying the disputing Minorite parties, preserving the order's relationship with the papacy, and fighting off its critics. His engagement produced two "official" *Lives* of St. Francis and a succession of expositions and defenses of the Rule and of the friars' privileges and ministries, the fullest and most influential of which was his *Defence of the Mendicants* (*Apologia pauperum*, ca. 1269).

In this skillfully constructed treatise, Bonaventure provided a *theological* and *legal* clarification of the practice of absolute poverty, demonstrating its centrality to life in conformity with Christ's teaching and example. He situated the practice within the "way" of "evangelical perfection" which seeks to accomplish Christ's work of love by fulfilling not only God's commandments, but the Savior's "spiritual counsels" delivered in the Sermon on the Mount and elsewhere: counsels to surrender material goods (to practice poverty, Matt. 19:21), to deny self-will (to practice obedience, Matt. 16:24), and to refrain from sexual activity (to practice chastity, Matt. 19:12). Of these three forms of self-sacrifice, the practice of poverty was foundational because it overcomes the radical spiritual evil of covetousness (1 Tim. 6:10) by removing temptations and strengthening the habit of resistance. Like Augustine, Bonaventure discerned the intimate relationship between covetousness and pride in disordered human love: that the soul's excessive love of other beings and things, its consuming passion to possess them, is always for the sake of aggrandizing its *own powers;* these powers it seeks to *possess privately,* i.e., to hold them as belonging to itself rather than to God as their source and owner. The remedy for sinful self-possession and self-aggrandizement lay in embracing the extreme poverty freely adopted by Christ and enjoined on his disciples during their missionary journeys. Through the discipline of seeking and using only the barest necessities and giving away all superfluous goods, of working manually without demanding remuneration, of depending chiefly on alms for daily sustenance, and of renouncing altogether the legal ownership of the goods that they used, the "apostolic men" attained the fullest participation in the "nakedness" of Christ's "naked cross" by which he proved himself obedient to his Father's will.

Renunciation of the legal right of possession was for the Minorites inseparable from the Son of Man's perfect destitution, because the claim created by legal property right *for oneself* and *against another* involved the right-bearing will in a degree of self-possession, separation from other wills and self-referential attachment to the material good, which approximated to selfishness and covetousness. The renunciation of property right as well as transient wealth was an efficacious sign that the apostolic wayfarer was not a self-possessor, not a proprietor of his physical powers, but was possessed by Christ, from whom he received all the good that he was, had, and did. Moreover, by maximizing the disciple's dependence on other creatures and minimizing his control over them, the discipline trained his spirit to receive the truth, beauty, and goodness of the world as the gift of divine generosity.

Mindful of the persistent efforts of secular critics to set the Franciscan Rule at loggerheads with the rest of the church, Bonaventure repeatedly situated it positively in relation to the other ecclesiastical "estates" and "grades of perfection," emphasizing the plurality of ways of Christian discipleship. In giving legal as well as spiritual determination to the different parts of the church, he distinguished four types of "community of temporal goods" *(temporalium rerum communitas)* or forms of common possession, in accordance with four "rights," or laws. These were:

1. in accordance with the *natural right* of using necessary things universally available in creation, the *community of earthly goods indispensable to sustenance;*
2. in accordance with the *divine right* by which all things belong to the just, the *community* of righteous possession *of the whole earth and of the Lord who made it;*
3. in accordance with *civil right,* the *community of private ownership* of temporal things;
4. in accordance with the *right of ecclesiastical dotation,* the *community of holding goods dedicated to God* and conferred upon the churches.

Bonaventure construed the Franciscans' nonproprietary or "simple" use *(simplex usus)* of goods owned and conceded by others as identical with the first two forms of common use and possession of things by natural and divine right, apart from the *civil dominion* entailed in the third and fourth forms enjoyed by the lay and nonmendicant clerical estates respectively. Thus he portrayed the Minorite "way" as a recovery of the original and just use of the earth's bounty belonging to Adamic community — not, however, a direct return to prelapsarian nature but a restoration mediated by participation in the Cross of Christ.

Bonaventure's impressive theoretical undertaking, to reconcile Franciscan poverty with a proprietary and relatively wealthy ecclesiastical community, did not forestall for long the increasingly virulent attacks on the clerical establishment by Minorite rigorists such as Peter John Olivi, which effectively brought about the deep rift between the friars and the papacy for which critics of the order had labored. Fortunately, the christological and ecclesiological insights of Bonaventure's theology of poverty provided a continuing impetus for the ethical and political reflection of future generations, including the novel and profoundly influential formulations of William of Ockham, Marsilius of Padua, Richard FitzRalph, and John Wyclif.

Further Reading: E. Gilson, *The Philosophy of Saint Bonaventure* (English translation) (London: Sheed & Ward, 1938); J. F. Quinn, *The Historical Constitution of St. Bonaventure's Philosophy* (Toronto: Pontifical Institute of Mediaeval Studies, 1973); J. Ratzinger, *The Theology of History in St. Bonaventure* (English translation) (Chicago: Franciscan Herald Press, 1971).

From *A Defence of the Mendicants*

7. [. . .] Jesus Christ, the source of all good things, at once the foundation stone and founder of the city, the New Jerusalem, "appeared for the very purpose of undoing the devil's work" (1 John 3:8). So he was bound to embrace wholeheartedly, in act and precept, example and word, the very opposite of this covetousness. The fault of covetousness, its disorderedness, is rooted in the affections of the mind. Yet because it is also occasioned and fueled by external possessions, uprooting it completely must proceed on both fronts, spiritual and material; the corroding affection of covetousness and the seductive possession of earthly wealth must both be given up. "Peter said in reply, 'Lo, we have left everything'" (Matt. 19:27); a text on which Bernard comments: "Well done! You weren't stupid! For 'the world passes away, and the lust of it' (1 John 2:17); and it is better to abandon it than to find oneself abandoned. And the chief reason to shun riches is that one can almost never possess them without loving them" (*Declamationes ex sancti Bernardi sermonibus* II.2 [actually by Goffridus]).

This double renunciation of the world and its lusts, also called "poverty of spirit," is the means by which the root of all evil is decisively cut off, the foundation of Babylon overthrown. And so by consistent analogy with what we have said so far, we may safely conclude that poverty of spirit, too, is a "root" and a "foundation" — *viz.* of that evangelical perfection by which we are conformed to Christ, implanted with him, and are made his dwelling. Which is why Christ himself, in his teaching of perfection to his disciples on the Mount — laying "the foundations . . . on the holy mountains" (Ps. 87[86]:1) of "the new Jerusalem descending from heaven" (Rev. 21:2), — the foundations, of course, are the several lights of evangelical perfection, and the holy mountains are the minds of the apostles — began his encomium of all the virtues with the preeminent one, holy poverty: "Blessed are the poor in spirit; the kingdom of heaven is theirs" (Matt. 5:3). On a later occasion, giving counsel on how to achieve perfection, he summoned someone to poverty first, pointing to his own example: "If you wish to be perfect, go, sell your possessions, and give to the poor . . . then come and follow me" (Matt. 19:21). Jerome, in his letter to Demetrias (*Ep.* 130.14), remarks on this text: "Such is the climax of complete and apostolic virtue, to sell all that one has to distribute to the poor, and thus freed from all earthly encumbrance, to fly up to the heavenly realms with Christ!" But in the possession of temporal goods there are two things to be considered: ownership *(dominium)* and use *(usus)*. Since the use of temporal goods is a necessary feature of this present life, the abandonment of earthly possessions in which evangelical poverty consists has to do with ownership and property *(proprietas)*. We cannot entirely dispense with use, but we can contain it, following the Apostle's advice to Timothy (1 Tim. 6:8), "If we have food and clothing, let us rest content."

From this may be inferred the definition of evangelical perfection. It is the virtue which renounces temporal goods, so that someone who has no property of his own is maintained on what is not his own. There are two ways of renouncing the ownership of temporal goods, and so two ways of being maintained on what is not one's own — two ways, in fact, of practicing evangelical poverty, and two ways of being perfect. For there are two kinds of ownership, private and common. The one is held by a particular person, the other by a particular community of people (*collegium*). Either the first can be renounced but not the second, or the first and second can be renounced together. Correspondingly, there are two ways in which the perfection of poverty can be professed. In the first way someone renounces the private or personal ownership of all temporal goods, and is maintained on what is *1* not his own, i.e., not his property but a *shared possession* held in a common association with others. In the second way someone renounces all ownership of goods, whether private or common, and is maintained on what is not his own, i.e., not his *2* property but *someone else's*, charitably and lawfully supplied by that person for his support.

The first kind of poverty was developed among the mass of believers of which *communal poverty* it is said in Acts (4:32): "The whole company of believers was united in heart and soul. Not one of them claimed any of his possessions as his own; everything was held in common." Jerome comments on that text in his letter to Demetrias: "We read in the Acts of the Apostles how, while the blood of the Lord was still warm and believers were in the fervor of their first faith, they all sold their possessions and laid the price of them at the apostles' feet (to show that money ought to be trampled underfoot), and 'distribution was made unto every man according as he had need.'" This was the source of the monastic or cenobitic life, as Bede (quoted in the *Gloss*) says on the same passage: "Those whose plan of life is to share everything in the Lord are called 'coenobites'. It is a happy way of life since it anticipates the life of the age to come, when everything will be held in common" (*Glossa ordinaria*, quoting Bede, *Liber retractionis in Act. Ap.*).

But the model of the second kind of poverty was developed among the apos- *mendicant poverty* tles. Christ, the teacher of perfection, prescribed it for them when he sent them out to preach, as we read in Matthew (10:9f.): "Keep no gold, nor silver, nor copper in your belts, no bag for your journey, nor two tunics, nor sandals, nor a staff; for the laborer deserves his food." The *Gloss* comments: "He all but denies them the necessities of life, so that those who teach that everything is ruled by God should not think about tomorrow. They are to carry no necessities with them, and no supplies; their clothing, and nothing else besides" (*Glossa Interlinearis* [weaving together quotations of Jerome and Augustine]). In these words the Lord imposes on his apostles and the preachers of the Truth the observance of a pattern of extreme and rigorous poverty. It extends not only to the absence of possessions, but even of money and other disposables by which the life of a community is generally maintained and provided for. They are to be like real paupers in a position of utter want: with no money, carrying no supplies, content with simple clothing, traveling unshod, their poverty in act and habit carried on high before them as a kind of banner of perfection.

This was the standard of poverty which Christ observed in his own life, prescribed for the observance of the apostles, and counseled to whoever may desire to follow in his steps, as a special grace of perfection. To show that Christ himself observed it, Chrysostom argues as follows (*Hom. in Matt.* 22.4): "'Keep no gold, nor silver . . . no bag for your journey.' Having displayed this by his practice, he later imposes it with stronger sanction as a law based on his teaching. But only after the

degrees of perfection

teaching has first been made accessible by practical demonstration. Where, then, did he give the practical demonstration? Listen to his words: 'The Son of Man has nowhere to lay his head' (Matt. 8:20). But that is not enough: his disciples, too, are assigned the task of demonstrating it." [. . .]

It should be carefully noted that the apostles were, on the one hand, *founding figures of Christianity*, and on the other, *professors of the way of highest perfection*. And they filled this latter role in two senses: as *individual persons* and as *models*. The Lord's words, then [sc. Matt. 10:9f. and parallels], can be understood: — (i) to be addressed to them as the founding figures of Christianity, and as such to include all Christians. But not all Christians are constrained to conform to this rule of life, contrary to the false doctrine of the Manicheans; and so Augustine, that hammer of the heretics, argues against them that if these words are to be understood as universally applicable commands, they must be interpreted spiritually. They can also be understood (ii)*(a)* to be addressed to the apostles as models of perfection. In this sense they are understood as *counsels,* which of themselves impose no obligation on those who have not freely professed this pattern of life and taken vows. And they can be understood (ii)*(b)* to be addressed to the apostles as particular persons, the first preachers of the Gospel Law. There are two things mentioned in the text which, when it is read in this sense, should be treated differently: renouncing temporal goods and accepting remuneration. The first of these must be taken as a *command* — as the text itself says, as well as the *Gloss*. Bede, *On Luke's Gospel* (bk. 6), writes: "When he sent the disciples to preach, 'he commanded them to take nothing on the way'" (Mark 6:8). But the second must be taken not as a command but as a *concession* or *permission*. So the *Gloss* (Glos. ord., quoting Gregory the Great) on Luke 10:7: "He forbade a purse and a bag, but permitted support from preaching." Also Rabanus Maurus, *Commentary on Matthew* (bk. 3, quoting Augustine): "It is clear that the Lord did not command that evangelists gain their living only from the offerings of those to whom they preach; otherwise the apostle would have broken the command when he supported himself by the work of his own hands. But the Lord gave them the authority to know what was their due. But authority implies the discretion not to exert it, and, so to speak, to forgo one's right." The conclusion of these reflections is evident: the Lord's words can be understood either (i) spiritually or (ii) literally; and literally as *(a)* counsels, *(b)* either commands or permissions. By grasping the multiple application of the text we may dispose of the unwarranted charge of internal contradiction.

This interpretation is presented with no difficulty by the observation of Jerome (*Letter* 52.5) about "living on tithes and sustained by the offerings of the altar . . . a naked follower of the naked cross," which suggests that the highest achievement of perfect poverty is to live off tithes and offerings like priests and clergy. But there are different levels of nakedness. There is, in the first place, the distinction between *nakedness of heart* and *nakedness of heart and body*. Nakedness of heart is achieved by stripping the spirit of every corrupt impulse of greed and covetousness; of which Gregory (the Great) says: "We must wrestle naked with our naked adversary. If one tries to wrestle with a naked opponent fully clothed, one is quickly thrown to the ground — held fast by what one has on" (*Homily on the Gospels*

Nakedness of the heart
vs
Nakedness of heart & body

2.32.2). This is meant to apply to all Christians universally. Nakedness of heart and body, on the other hand, itself has three levels. First there is *the great nakedness,* which is found in ridding oneself of superfluous consumption and of one's property-holdings. (It is not indispensable for the clergy, but it is certainly fitting.) This is the subject of Jerome's remark to Nepotianus: "If I am the Lord's portion and the line of his inheritance, and receive no portion among the remaining tribes but am like the priest and the Levite, living on tithes and maintained by the offerings of the altar I serve, then having food and clothing I shall rest content, a naked follower of the naked cross." In the second place there is *the greater nakedness,* which consists, over and above this, in renouncing the right to possess property and surrendering one's will. This is appropriate to the regular cenobitic orders, as Jerome says to Heliodorus (*Letter* 14.1): "Do not call to mind old ties; the desert is for the naked." "Naked," that is, not only stripped of resources of one's own, but stripped of one's own will, as Bernard says in the "Colloquy of Simon and Jesus" (*Declamations* 3.3): "Come, then, you who plan to leave all, and remember to include yourself in what you leave. Indeed, it is yourself you must deny first and foremost, if you intend to follow him who 'emptied himself' for your sake." The third nakedness adds, in addition to these, the renunciation of every transitory resource, i.e., penury and the lack of day-to-day supplies. This level is for the apostles and for men who live like the apostles. Of this we read in St. Matthew (10:42): "Anyone who gives so much as a cup of cold water to one of these little ones because he is a disciple of mine, will certainly not go unrewarded." On which the *Gloss* (Glos. ord.) says, "The 'little ones' are those who have absolutely nothing in this world." Such were the apostles; hence Jerome remarks to Exsuperantius (*Letter* 145): "Never were any men poorer than the apostles; never did any leave more for the Lord than they. The poor widow in the gospel who cast but two mites into the treasury was set before all the men of wealth because she gave all that she had." If the widow, then, as the Lord tells us, gave all that she had and kept nothing back, she adopted the posture of *utter nakedness.* [. . .]

Although we read in Acts that "the whole company of believers . . . held everything in common," and that they laid the price of the property they sold at the feet of the apostles, it is certainly not right to interpret this as meaning that the apostles themselves had property, not even property in common. The reference to common ownership is not to the apostles but to the mass of believers, as the *Gloss* (Glos. ord.) on the passage indicates: "There is a distinction here between teachers and hearers. The 'company of believers', dispossessing themselves of property, were held together by the bond of charity; the apostles, on the other hand, excelling in miraculous power, demonstrated the mysteries of Christ." On the basis of the text itself the *Glossa* attributes common ownership to the mass and the power of miracles to the apostles. [. . .]

8. The practice of the Law [sc. of the Old Testament] is not inconsistent with the perfection of utter poverty. Neither is the manner of the apostles' life; neither is the purse of Christ; neither, as we have shown, is the promise of the hundredfold reward (Mark 10:30); neither, above all, are the plentiful resources of the church — a subject in which the Enemy of the Poor [i.e. Gerard of Abbeville] encases himself as he proceeds like a suit of mail, but not to defend the fortress of ecclesiastical dignity

so much as to overthrow the tower of evangelical poverty! If he had defended the church's possessions as permissible, convenient, and compatible with a state of perfection, both on the part of the communities which own them and the administrators who put them to holy use, he would be following the lead of theologians and canons in rejecting the heretical assertion that the church, in accepting possessions, has fallen from its state of righteousness and perfection. A doctrine of this kind poses no threat to holy poverty, since, as we have shown at the beginning of our reply, there are differing modes of perfection within it. As it is, however, in attempting to persuade us that ecclesiastical possessions contribute to the state of perfection, so that it is actually *more* perfect to enjoy plenty in Christ than to suffer want for Christ's sake, not only does he set the glory of poverty at nought, but he undermines the foundations of the church itself. That, at any rate, is the effect of his attempt to show that Christ and the Apostles set an example of perfection by possessing temporal goods.

Christ said of himself that he had nowhere to lay his head; but he confidently asserts the contrary, that Christ "had a house, because we read, 'My house shall be a house of prayer'" (Matt. 21:13), and adds: "In right of property Christ had nowhere to lay his head *as man,* but *as very God* all the goods of the Levites were his possession." These words betray an astonishing lack of theological intelligence in failing to attribute correctly what belongs to Christ's divinity and his humanity. When we say "Christ was poor," it refers to the humanity he assumed in the Incarnation, a humanity which gave us the pattern of perfect life. It has no bearing at all on his divine power, through which it is not only the Temple and the goods of the Levites that fall under his ownership, but "heaven and earth and all that is contained in the circle of heaven." The prophet says: "The earth is the Lord's and all that is in it" (Ps. 24:1). [. . .]

[Bonaventure has quoted Jerome, *Letter* 125.20, on the strenuous efforts of Exsuperius, bishop of Toulouse, in distributing food to the hungry.] In this passage Saint Jerome, separating the precious from the base, shows there is a difference between the perfection of a senior churchman *(praelatus),* who is a representative of the community *(persona communis),* and the perfection of a private person. Any member of a religious order may be appointed to a rank in the church in which, rather than living in a state of poverty, he administers temporal goods; yet it would be improper to draw the wrong conclusion from this. Pastoral responsibility may make it appropriate for prelates to be engaged in worldly business without prejudice to their state of perfection. Yet we cannot infer that in their private capacities it is a matter of indifference whether they have worldly tasks that make them "troubled about many things" like Martha, or, like Mary, sit quietly at the Lord's feet, heart ablaze with inward ecstasies of joy (cf. Luke 10:38-42). Similarly in the matter we are discussing. The highest ranks of priests and bishops, with responsibility for the weak and inadequate as well as for the perfect and the strong, must give pastoral care by example, teaching and, as place and time require, by material assistance, too; and in this they may handle possessions for the support of the poor and of the church's ministry without prejudice to their perfection. That does not mean, however, that we can or may affirm of any and every private person in any and every rank in the

[margin, handwritten: Ok to distribute goods to the poor]

church, that it is a matter of indifference to his perfection whether he has ample possessions or practices poverty to the highest degree. [. . .]

10. The sacred canons assert *(a)* that what is offered to the churches is offered to the Lord; *(b)* that ministers may not claim dominion of them on the basis of "accursed property"; *(c)* that goods of this kind are more properly heavenly than earthly, more common than they are private. In the light of which, to remove any shadow of contradiction or uncertainty, we must be quite clear that there are four kinds of "community of goods," corresponding to four different sources of right.

The first kind of community is derived from the right of *natural necessity:* anything capable of sustaining natural existence, though it be somebody's private property, may belong to someone who is in the most urgent need of it. This kind of community of goods *cannot be renounced.* It derives from the right that naturally belongs to man as God's image and noblest creature, on whose behalf all other things on earth were made.

The second kind of community is derived from the right of *brotherly love:* everything belongs to the righteous, and the private property of individuals is common to all by virtue of the sharing which is natural to love, as the apostle says (1 Cor. 3:22), "All things are yours." On this basis Augustine (*Tractates on John* 6.26) argues against the Donatist heretics: "Let them come to the catholic church, and share with us not the earth alone, but him who made the heaven and the earth." This kind of community of goods *absolutely may not be renounced.* It derives from a right poured into us by God, the right by which "the dove" (i.e., the universal church) is assured its unity, a unity of sharing, from which no one can depart without defiance of the law of God which enfolds all things in love.

The third kind of community is derived from the right of *worldly civil society:* there is a common political identity within a single empire, kingdom, or city-state; there is a common profit and loss within a single association, e.g., of merchants or wrestlers; there is a common inheritance within a single family that has not split up. This kind of community of goods *must be renounced to attain evangelical perfection,* because this kind of community implies individual property. It is derived from a humanly instituted right which contains provisions that may incidentally prove an obstacle to good or an encouragement to evil, and is therefore incompatible with evangelical perfection. So the holy soul is urged to renounce this kind of right, as we find in Psalm 45:10: "Hear, O daughter, consider and incline your ear; forget your people and your father's house."

The fourth kind of community is derived from the right of *ecclesiastical endowment:* All goods bestowed upon the churches are dedicated to the Lord to provide for the ministry and for the poor. This kind of community of goods, which is found in all collegial churches with possessions, *need not be renounced to attain perfection* since it can be maintained without prejudice to perfection, as is clear in the case of bishops and religious who are holy and perfect. Such a community is derived from a right instituted by God, that "he who serves the altar may live from the altar" (1 Cor. 9:13); and its members have everything common because there is one heart and mind among them, one spiritual father and one pattern of life. Yet this kind of community *may be renounced without prejudice to perfection* — in pursuit of it, rather — since it springs not only from divine right but from human, it is not only spiritual but temporal, too; and since, though it excludes *individual* property, *collegial* property is allowed, and the share of every member of the college must be understood not merely as *use* but as *ownership,* since every member has in law an action to recover the property of his church and an exception to defend it; the clear implication of which is that the subject of the action or exception is in some way co-owner of the goods in question.

It is profoundly difficult to renounce all that one has and take delight in poverty alone; as it is, indeed, to renounce individual property and rest content with the church's community of goods. Both forms of perfection, then, were instituted not by human tradition, as the Enemy of the Poor maintains, but by divine right; and this is manifestly so when poverty is accompanied by a vow of chastity and the renunciation of the will. But it demeans the perfection of the church considerably to declare, as our Slanderer of the Poor so confidently does, that clergy may attain perfection merely by renouncing secular estates and retaining any amount of ecclesiastical revenues; and that the only inadequate and compromised clergy are those who live, even very meagerly, on family income. The most simpleminded will detect the absurdity in saying that a clergyman with hardly enough to feed and clothe himself is, when supported by a family income, worldly and compromised, while one with unlimited ecclesiastical revenues, is, on the basis of renouncing family wealth, upright and perfect. Even the most covetous, the most worldly, the most intellectually incompetent of men would eagerly exchange the one state for the other! Is *this* the perfection of the Gospel truth which Christ commends and proclaims as a high and hard path — this state of life on which every soul-sick, inadequate, compromised, covetous, vainglorious, and worldly cleric sets his ambitions on?

11. [. . .] To silence these and similar unfriendly evasions and devices, we must have it understood quite clearly that there are four possible relations to temporal goods: property, possession, usufruct, and simple use. The life of mortals may be sustained without the first three, but the last is a necessity. There can, then, be no profession of renunciation of temporal things which extends to their use. But it is appropriate that a profession which freely vows to follow Christ in utter poverty should renounce the *ownership* of things, and should be content with the mere use of things which other people own and make available. As it is put in the *Rule* of the Friars Minor: "Brethren shall own nothing, neither house, nor place nor any other thing."

In case anyone should think that these words forbid only individual, not corporate property, here is Gregory IX's reply to the Friars' consultation: "Our judgment is that they should have neither common nor private property; the Order should have the use of the utensils, books, and all permitted objects; and it should be at the discretion of the General or Provincial Ministers of the Order to assign the use to brethren in particular. Movables should not be sold or alienated from the Order without authority or agreement to that effect given to the General or Provincial Ministers by the Cardinal of the Roman church who shall be the Governor of the Order." These are the terms of the papal rescript in which a perceptive and sensitive authority made the distinction between property and use. Property was reserved for

318

the Pope and the church; use was conceded to the needs of the Friars in a form compatible with holiness — a perceptive and sensitive provision. For if, as is clear from our third reply (ch. 8), bishops suffer no loss of perfection when they possess and administer temporal goods on others' behalf, even when they receive emoluments and expenses, there will be even less prejudice to the perfection of the Pontiff from a purely supervisory relation where no temporal advantage could be looked for. Indeed, he will acquire merit from it in the sight of God.

To the objection that there is legal provision against the perpetual separation of use from ownership, we reply that that part of civil law has no relevance here. The purpose of the provision in civil law was to prevent ownership from seeming useless and unworthy of the name. But to retain the ownership of goods in this way, while conceding the use of them to the poor, is by no means unprofitable. The Father of the Poor gains merit by it; his children, the servants of Christ, gain the convenience it affords to their profession. Nor can an effective objection be sustained that property is inseparable from use in the case of goods which are consumed as they are used. There is a counter-example in the allowance received by a son in a family: the son has use of it, but property at no point resides in him. And this is how we must understand the relation of such an Order of Paupers to the Roman church. All Christ's faithful are sons of the supreme Pontiff by common right, but by a particular right the Friars are his obedient subjects and committed to his care. Others are like adult sons, to whom is granted the legal authority to manage their churches' goods so long as they do not depreciate them; but they are like infant children of the household, wholly subject to his government.

Translation: Editors, from *Opera Omnia*, vol. 8, Quaracchi (St. Bonaventure's College, 1898).

Thomas Aquinas

(ca. 1225-74)

In the history of Christian political thought, the legacy of St. Thomas is the only close rival to that of St. Augustine. Together they ensured the classical cast of the Western political inheritance, its continuing conversations with Greek and Roman sources into the present. The unsurpassed influence of both thinkers across the terrains of theology and philosophy springs in part from the synthetic and architectonic character of their voluminous literary output. While Thomas's political ideas are not governed by a single overarching schema such as the two cities, they are unified by a consistent (but not slavish) Aristotelian inspiration and by his treatment of law.

Thomas's teaching and writing career falls into three periods. The first covers his initial seven years of theological study and teaching in Paris, where he arrived in 1252 from four years of enriching his knowledge of Aristotle's works under the tutelage of Albert the Great in Cologne. To this period belongs his *Commentary on the Sentences* (1254-56), in which his political discussion, predating his acquaintance with Aristotle's *Politics,* has been described as "mingling apostolic counsels and Stoic sentiments in the style of his theological predecessors," notwithstanding his liberal use of the *Nichomachean Ethics* (Gilby 1958, 96). From this source comes the passage below on Christian obedience to secular rulers and its limits (44.2.2).

His second period covers his sojourn of nine years in Italy (1259-68) spent teaching and writing, in frequent attendance at the papal court. This period saw the completion, among other works, of his major treatise of Aristotelian philosophical and theological apologetics, the *Summa contra Gentiles,* and the first part of his great *Summa Theologiae (ST).* Conceived as the initial portion of a massive encyclopedic textbook for theological novices, traversing subjects in natural and revealed theology, metaphysics, cosmology, and anthropology, the *Prima pars* of the *Summa Theologiae* contains no developed political theory but has some revealing Aristotelian moments. The most striking are his arguments for the naturalness of political

320

rule that invoke ideas of original inequalities and the need for wise direction of the multitude, flowing from the difference between the common good and private goods (1a.92.1; 96.3, 4).

Together with other Aristotelian political themes, these arguments are more fully elaborated in *On Kingship: To the King of Cyprus (De regno)*, which, if written by Thomas, is his only full-fledged political treatise, thought to be begun before his departure from Italy. The apparent unsubtlety of its synthesis of Aristotelian and Neoplatonic ideas, and its disjointed and fragmentary character, have undoubtably caused some among Thomas's admirers to feel relief at the long-standing suspicions surrounding its authenticity. These have not been assuaged by the modern disentanglement of an original, incomplete base from its continuation in the work *On Princely Government (De regimine principum)*, widely attributed to his disciple Ptolemy of Lucca. While many contemporary scholars and interpreters of Thomas continue to regard the text of *De regno* as substantially authentic up to 2.4, a significant number have denied the authenticity of the entire work (see Blythe 1997). Theoretically considered, the initial portion contains comparatively unnuanced statements of the ethical subordination of the individual to the community as part to whole, the natural self-sufficiency of political society, and the unification of the corporate body by the will of its royal head — while, nevertheless, upholding the spiritual subjection of regal to priestly (especially papal) government. Whatever the significance of its dedication, the text has features of the "mirror of kings" genre, including the retailing of classical political commonplaces in a digestible form.

Thomas's third period covers his second Paris professorship (1268-72) and subsequent time in Naples (1272-73) organizing a Dominican house of theological studies. Back in his former university chair, he was occupied with defending the mendicant orders against renewed attacks from hostile fellow masters, and charting a moderate Christian Aristotelianism capable of standing up to both the Averroist extreme attracting ecclesiastical condemnation and the Augustinian opposition to all Aristotelian theological reconstruction. (Unlike Bonaventure, Thomas never saw an intimate connection between the arrival of Aristotelian naturalism and the persecution of the friars.) His longer-term strategy for carving out a Christian Aristotelian middle way took the form of a succession of detailed commentaries written between 1269 and 1273 on Aristotle's major works in psychology, physics, logic, ethics, metaphysics, and politics on the basis of William of Moerbeke's recent Latin translations. His most celebrated achievement of this period was the second part of his *Summa Theologiae* (subdivided in printed editions into the *Prima Secundae* and the *Secunda Secundae*), which laid out his ethical theory with unprecedented fullness, being generously indebted in arrangement and substance to the *Nichomachean Ethics*.

From his opening Aristotelian identification of human happiness with activity in accordance with virtue, Thomas proceeds in the *Prima Secundae* to comprehensive analyses of human action, the generic principles of morality, the emotions and psychological dispositions, and the particular disposition of virtue — its moral and intellectual, natural and supernatural, modes, and earthly perfection in Christlike action and contemplation. Then, after examining sin and its effects, he embarks on his politically crucial treatment of law — its nature, types, human sources, communal functioning, and Old and New Testament revelations — to conclude with justification of the sinner. The *Secunda Secundae* contains his in-depth consideration of the separate virtues and their opposing vices, passing from the theological to the cardinal virtues, and finally to a comparison of the active and contemplative lives that opens onto the church's pastoral and monastic orders. From the wealth of politically relevant material embedded in these discussions we have selected elements of Thomas's treatments of: the ethical conditions of waging war (40.1); justice, comprehending right and natural right (57.1, 3) and the commutative and distributive types (61.3); the relationship between temporal and spiritual authorities (60.6 ad 3); property right and theft (66.1, 2, 3, 7, 8); just price in buying and selling (77.1); and the practice of usury (78.1). Constraints of space have forced us to choose between the above and inclusions from Thomas's commentary on Aristotle's *Politics*, unfinished at his death.

The historical influence of Thomas's political thought, as of his thought generally, has been incalculably far-reaching and diverse. By the turn of the fourteenth century, despite condemnations of some propositions at Paris and Oxford (1277), his political conceptualizations had entered the theoretical artilleries of both papalist and imperialist publicists, and were subsequently absorbed by a plethora of theoretical movements: conciliarism, Gersonian scholasticism, and English legal theory in the fourteenth and fifteenth centuries; Protestant and Catholic resistance theories, Spanish neo-scholasticism, "natural law" jurisprudence, and systems of international law and federalism in the sixteenth and seventeenth centuries. In more recent times, since the pontificate of Leo XIII, St. Thomas's theology and social philosophy have acquired an official standing in the Roman Catholic Church, unprecedented in the theological tradition and only approached by St. Augustine's magisterial authority in the medieval papal church and the Lutheran Reformation.

Although the close interweaving of the various concepts and principles makes topical division a somewhat strained exercise, an organization under the headings of political rule, law, and justice is a convenient expository device that matches quite well the chronological sequence of Thomas's thought.

1. *Political Rule, Civil Community, and the Common Good.* The starting point for conveying Thomas's theoretical debt to Aristotle as well as his participation in the emerging civil awareness of his century is his proposal that political rule is *natural to human community*. His supporting arguments in *Summa Theologiae* 1a.96.3, elaborated more fully in *De regno* 1.1, vividly demonstrate the impact of the *Politics*, contrasting with his earlier, more traditional association of political authority with servility and property in the *Commentary on the Sentences* (44.q.2.a.2). Comparison of parallel passages from *Summa Theologiae* and *De regno* reveals a noteworthy difference: whereas in *Summa Theologiae* Thomas argues for the necessity of free political rule (as opposed to servitude) in humankind's state of created innocence, in *De regno* he argues for its indispensability to human society *as such*, ignoring the distinction between pre- and postlapsarian community. His argument in *De regno* that only wise guidance will orient persons of disparate interests and capabilities to the common good conveys an understanding of natural society as less participatory and

communicative on the spiritual plane than the patristic understanding of Adamic society.

Thomas's cosmological models of rule, in confirming the paradigmatic position of monarchy, reveal another facet of its naturalness, its mirroring of every other fundamental ordered relationship involving control (*De regno* 1.1). Particularly germane to royal rule are the two models of sovereign control offered by God's governance over his created universe and reason's governance over the lesser powers of soul and body (2.1), both of which disclose the work of rule as having a *creative* and a *directive* aspect. As God first acts to create the world and the soul to inform the body, so the king's first act may be to found a city or kingdom. Although the king "cannot create out of nothing" the constituent elements of political society, he can bring them into being by organizing and distributing the resources that "nature has already provided" (2.2). Even kings who do not found kingdoms must grasp the rudiments of this art if they are to master the art of directing the social totality, i.e., of preserving and enhancing the arrangement and integrated functioning of its parts in accordance with the organic hierarchy of communal ends (2.2).

The controlling idea of the art of ruling for Thomas is the "common good" that embraces the mesh of communal ends — religious, moral, legal, political, and economic. In places he defines the civil *bonum commune* in terms of a single (albeit complex) concept such as peace (*ST* 1a2ae.72.4; 2a2ae.96.6 ad 2; 97.1) or justice (2a2ae.58.5, 6; 59.1), sometimes to draw out its more narrowly political or legal character. In *De regno* he takes the alternative route of elaborating three components of the "good life" of the community, which the ruler has the task of establishing, preserving, and extending: the continuation of peaceful unity, the orientation to well-doing, and a sufficiency of the material goods indispensable to virtuous action (2.4). He assigns to the civil jurisdiction pursuit only of the *natural perfections* of the social totality (as of individuals), reserving the "final blessedness" of individual and communal life, unattainable by natural virtue, to the government of Jesus Christ entrusted to the priesthood (2.3).

In his moderately Hildebrandine view of the relation of spiritual to temporal authorities, the universal subjection of Christian kings to the Roman pope as Christ's vicar is balanced by a conception of papal direction as preeminently theological and moral (2.4; *ST* 2a2ae.60.6 ad 3). He concurs with the opinion that the church may punish the apostasy of kings with excommunication, thereby releasing subjects from their oaths of fealty. He does not, however, allow the teleological subjection of temporal to spiritual rule to undercut the former's independent foundation in the *ius gentium* left intact by the "law of grace" (2a2ae.10.10; 12.2). His conclusion, long-standing in imperialist polemics and of historical consequence, is that the rule of infidels (even over the faithful) is not *of itself* invalid, and *as such* liable to ecclesiastical abrogation. While always entitled to prevent the constitution of infidel rule, the church may abrogate an established jurisdiction only if the ruler's conduct jeopardizes his subjects' spiritual welfare (2a2ae.10.10; 12). The use made of this argument by sixteenth-century Thomists is most powerfully illustrated in Vitoria's work on the American Indians (see pp. 613-14 below).

Apart from crimes against the faith, the injustice of tyrannical rulers typically has nonecclesiastical remedies. In his *Commentary on the Sentences,* Thomas distinguishes between the tyrant who usurps political authority, lacking legitimate title, and the tyrant who abuses in practice legitimately held authority (44.2.2). As both tyrannies represent the failure of political authority "to derive from God," they properly elicit resistance from the ruled, which may range from "rejection" of the usurper to (mere) disobedience to the abuser. *De regno* proposes that the remedy for gross and endemic abuse of legitimate authority lies either with the *electing* community or with the appointing superior (1.6). Thomas offsets the precedents for *unofficial tyrannicide* in the Old Testament with its counterwitness to God's sovereign intervention to convert or destroy tyrants without human aid, and reinforces its witness with the apostolic counsel of patient suffering and the warnings of universal political prudence (1.6). With the Hebrew prophets and Latin Church Fathers he invokes collective repentance and reformation as the most fitting response of the multitude to this kind of divine chastisement (1.6).

(2) *Law.* Thomas's treatment of law in the *Prima Secundae,* Questions 90-97, offers an unprecedented integration of juristic, theological, and philosophical contributions that transcends his debts to Aristotle, Augustine, his immediate Franciscan and Dominican predecessors, and to the Roman legal scholarship in full flowering at both the papal and imperial courts. Readers continue to find breathtaking his opening presentation of law in Question 90 as the rational measure of human action, as binding obligation and enforceable command, as moral stimulus and political artifact, as communal in origin and end, involving representation and participation.

The analogical structure of Thomas's concept of law is apparent in its fivefold classification into eternal, natural, human and divine law, and the law of sin (91). The aspects of law take on different complexions depending on whether it is promulgated by the divine or the human legislator; is enforced externally as well as internally; belongs to the working of created nature, sinful disposition, or justifying and sanctifying grace. For instance, in that God's *eternal law* includes his foreknowledge and preordination of created beings and their contingent motions and actions, it remains inscrutable to human understanding. But as the divine exemplar governing all ordered movement of creatures toward their proper ends, the eternal law is dimly intelligible to unassisted human reason, and more fully available to humankind in God's revealed Word (91.1; 93). The *natural law,* being the appropriation by rational creatures of the divine exemplar, is an inner apprehension of right, an inborn habit of judgment and persistent impulse to specific conduct — called by Aristotle *synderesis* (*ST* 2a2ae.94.1; Gilby 1958, 137). Truly law, as divine command, it nevertheless comprehends the manifold, permanent inclinations of human being as biologically, socially, and rationally constituted (so Thomas synthesizes Isidorean and Roman juristic conceptions; see p. 210 above) (94.2). By contrast, *human law,* being constructed from natural law by reasoned deliberation under particular historical conditions, is marked by externality, a degree of arbitrariness, coercion, variability, and transience. Thomas's preferred nomenclature of "positive law," in contemporary legal vogue, conveys the crucial dependence of human law on the ruler's legislative will (95.2). While *divine law* retains an element of externality, in the sense that God's revelation in Scripture confronts the human creature from beyond its natural and sinful capacities for knowledge and obedience, it nevertheless summons the total conformity of intellect and will (94.4, 5). The New Law of Christ embodies the development of the Old Law toward a "spiritual and heavenly" common good: a fuller, inward and outward, realization of justice, and the reign of divine love as the spring of action in the soul (91.5, 106). Unlike every other category, the *law of sin* lacks all the immanent qualities of law, being irrational, nonobligatory, and directed "toward private satisfaction," retaining only the extrinsic lawfulness of belonging to the order of divine penal justice (91.6).

We comment in turn on the relationship of human law to *(a)* natural law, *(b)* political authority, *(c)* virtue, and *(d)* the Old Law.

a. Thomas endorses the juristic commonplace that all positive law, to the extent that it is just or rational, derives from the natural law. He views this derivation as taking the mode either of conclusions from principles or of determinations of common directives, to render laws of increasing specificity and concreteness (95.2). Determinations or specifications of the natural law are more inventive than demonstrable conclusions, owing to the many circumstantial factors that enter into their formulation: compare a law specifying the penalty for murder to a law prohibiting murder (95.2). Hence Thomas's voluntarist proposal that positive legal determinations have their binding force in conscience only from the fact of their enactment (95.2) — by which, however, he does not imply that they may display capriciousness, excessive arbitrariness, or opaqueness (95.3).

Mindful of Isidore, Thomas typically views the *ius gentium* as comprised of conclusions from natural law premises, and so, substantively, as an extension of the natural law, or as secondary natural law. Its "positive" character remains somewhat ambiguous, in view of his denial in 57.3 (contradicted elsewhere), of its origin in the deliberate agreement or enaction of nations. Reminiscent of Rufinus's division of the natural law into commands, prohibitions, and demonstrations (see p. 300 above), he also proposes that the universally recognized institutions of property and slavery accord with natural right in the sense that they do not run contrary to nature's commands, being additions to, and not contraventions of, the natural condition of mankind (94.5).

b. Both positive law and rulership embody the political authority of the community subject to them, while the community, its laws, and its ruler stand equally under the higher authority of God and nature. Thomas develops a dialectic of political authority in which: the sovereign is subject to the *"directive"* but not the *"coercive"* power of just communal laws (96.5); he authoritatively interprets the intention of the laws in the light of the requirements of the common good (96.6), being both bound by established (rational) custom and entitled to abrogate it for compelling (moral and political) reasons (97.2); and the community exercises its power of altering and abrogating existing laws through repeated observance or nonobservance of them (97.3).

c. His discussion of the power of positive law to produce virtuous subjects exhibits a studied complexity, if not ambiguity, expressing, perhaps, the tension between Augustinian and Aristotelian orientations. With Aristotle, Thomas proposes that the extent and quality of the virtue produced in subjects is commensurable with the quality of the common good intended by the lawmakers, whether it be narrow and partial or true and complete (92.1). Elsewhere, however, Thomas presents the purposes of law and the character of political obedience in such a way as to cast doubt on the law's efficacy to produce the fulness of virtue, even in the best polity; e.g., his portrayals of law as the pedagogical discipline needed by less amenable youths (95.1) and as the necessary restraint on only the grave and dangerously anti-social vices in the majority (96.2), or conversely, as promoting public rather than private virtues (96.3).

(d. He describes the Old Law as intending the "special sanctification" of the Jewish people, comparing its obligations to the observances binding on clerics and monastics (98.5). Like other civil laws, the Old Law binds a whole political commu-nity, but unlike them, its content is a divinely revealed rather than humanly con-structed application of the natural law (99.4), and as such, manifests the outworking of the natural law in the history of God's judgment and salvation of sinful humanity (100.8). Although its judicial (as opposed to ceremonial) precepts are available to other political communities only as human and not divine law (104.3), they none-theless offer significant political benefits, being eminently just provisions for a model polity (105).

3. *Justice and Right.* On the human plane, justice and injustice comprise for Thomas that adjustment and maladjustment of persons to one another made possi-ble by language (*In lib. pol. Aris.* I.1 ad 1253a7). He makes two sets of distinctions, neither unproblematic: he first distinguishes the "general" and "particular" aspects of justice — the former aspect concerns, subjectively, the moral virtue of rendering to others their due (*ST* 2a2ae.57.1), and objectively, the common welfare, while the latter concerns the relations of fairness among persons as individuals — and then proceeds to distinguish, within the particular aspect, commutative and distributive justice. The unsatisfactory nature of these distinctions is indicated by the seemingly anomalous character of public punishment, which, in spite of his efforts, defies both the commutative logic of arithmetic proportionality and the distributive logic of geometric proportionality, and impinges on both relations of fairness and the public utility.

Construing right *(ius)* as the objectivity of justice, Thomas distinguishes natu-ral right *(ius naturale)* from the right of nations *(ius gentium)* as the self-standing and self-evident principle from its concrete consequences or implications (*S.T.* 2a2ae.57.4), and includes within the latter not only property right (and derivative rights of exchange) and slavery, but also the waging of war. He views private prop-erty as the concrete elaboration of man's natural dominion over material things in respect of his "title to care for and distribute" them (66.1, conclusion). Ownership is a legal positivizing of the natural right of dominion that serves its primary purpose, the use of the earth's resources for the benefit of all, when its moral limits are ob-served. These limits are the claims of human need on abundance, which require charitable relief of the destitute, and may on occasion justify theft (66.7). Notewor-thy is his move away from the Augustinian perspective on property which elevates communicating use over distribution, and attributes private acquisition to the con-dition of sin.

His arguments regarding usury and the just price in trading transactions flow from the interaction of the principles of commutative justice and property, and an infusion of additional Aristotelian ideas, such as the sterility (nonproductivity) of money (*ST* 2a2ae.77.1; 78.1). Together they present fairly stringent moral constraints on profit-making from trade and commercial investment. Along with the principles of just war (40.1), taken over from canonist sources, they have exercised a decisive and salutary influence on later developments in both Protestant and Catholic political, legal, and economic theory.

Further Reading: J. M. Blythe, *Ptolemy of Lucca, "On the Government of Rulers"* (Philadephia: University of Pennsylvania Press, 1997); Y. M.-J. Congar, *Thomas d'Aquin: sa vision de théologie et de l'Église* (Aldershot: Variorum, 1983); M. Crofts, *Property and Poverty: A Treatise on Private Ownership according to Thomas Aquinas* (Dublin: Irish Rosary Office, 1948); B. Davis, *The Thought of Thomas Aquinas* (Oxford: Clarendon Press, 1992); J. Dunn and I. Harris, *Aquinas* (Cheltenham: Edward Elgar, 1997); J. Finnis, *Aquinas: Social, Legal, and Political Theory* (Oxford: Oxford University Press, 1997); T. Gilby, *Principality and Polity: Aquinas and the Rise of State Theory in the West* (London: Longmans, 1958); L. Lachance, *L'humanisme politique de St. Thomas d'Aquin* (Paris and Montréal: Éditions Sirey & du Lévrier, 1965); J.-P. Torrell, *Saint Thomas Aquinas* (English translation), 2 vols. (Washington, D.C.: Catholic University of America Press, 1996).

From *Summa Theologiae* 1a.90-102 (On the First Making of Man)

96, 3 *Reply:* We must admit that there had to be some disparity among men, even before the fall, at least with respect to the sexes. For without the sexes there could have been no procreation. Similarly with regard to age; as children were born of one generation and they, marrying, produced further children. There would have been a difference of spiritual capacities also, with respect both to justice and to knowledge. For man would not have acted from blind necessity, but from free choice, being thus able to apply his powers to a greater or less degree in acting, willing and knowing. Thus some would have made greater progress in righteousness and in knowledge than others. Equally, there would have been a certain difference of bodily powers; for the human body was not altogether exempt from the laws of nature, but was capable of receiving greater or less assistance from natural agencies. Even in the state of innocence food was necessary for the sustenance of the human frame. So we may well say that according to the different states of the ether, and of different portions of the stars, some would have been born with more powerful bodies, some taller, or more beautiful and better favoured. This, however, would not constitute any defect or shortcoming in those less favoured, either in body or in soul.

    96, 4 *Reply:* Dominion is to be understood in two senses. In the first it is contrasted with servitude. So a master is one to whom another is subject as a slave. In the second sense it is to be understood in opposition to any form of subjection. In this sense one whose office it is to govern and control free men may also be called a

[handwritten: pre-Fall no slavery - but there was dominion in the sense of governing free people = common good]

lord. The first sort of dominion which is servitude did not exist between man and man in the state of innocence. Understood in the second way, however, even in the state of innocence, some men would have exercised control over others. The reason for this is that a slave differs from a free man in that the latter is "a free agent of his own actions" as is said in the *Metaphysics* (982b26). A slave, however, is completely under the control of another. Thus a person rules another as a slave when the latter is ordered about solely for the benefit of the ruler. But since it is natural for every one to find pleasure in their own satisfaction, such satisfaction cannot be surrendered to another without suffering loss. Such dominion, then, cannot occur without the accompanying penalties of subjection; and for this reason could not have existed between man and man in the state of innocence.

The control of one over another who remains free, can take place when the former directs the latter to his own good or to the common good. And such dominion would have been found between man and man in the state of innocence for two reasons. First, because man is naturally a social animal; and in consequence men would have lived in society, even in the state of innocence. Now there could be no social life for many persons living together unless one of their number were set in authority to care for the common good. Many individuals are, as individuals, interested in a variety of ends. One person is interested in one end. So the Philosopher says (*Politics* 1254a28ff.): "Whenever a plurality is directed to one object there is always to be found one in authority, giving direction." Secondly, if there were one man more wise and righteous than the rest, it would have been wrong if such gifts were not exercised on behalf of the rest; as is said in 1 Pet. 4:10: "Every one using the grace he has received for the benefit of his fellows." So Augustine says (*City of God* 19.14f. [see pp. 156-57 above]) "The just rule not through desire of domination, but because it is their duty to give counsel"; and "This is ordained by the natural order, for thus did God create man."

[handwritten left margin: 1. = political authority is natural & necessary (even pre-Fall)]
[handwritten left margin: 2]

Translation: J. G. Dawson (Oxford, 1959). Used with permission.

From *Commentary on the Sentences of Peter Lombard*, Book 2

44, 2 *Reply:* We must observe that, as has been stated already, in the observance of a certain precept, obedience is connected with the obligation to such observance. But such obligation derives from the order of authority which carries with it the power to constrain, not only from the temporal, but also from the spiritual point of view, and in conscience; as the Apostle says (Rom. 13:5), and this because the order of authority derives from God, as the Apostle says in the same passage. For this reason the duty of obedience is, for the Christian, a consequence of this derivation of authority from God, and ceases when that ceases. But, as we have already said, authority may fail to derive from God for two reasons: either because of the way in which authority has been obtained, or in consequence of the use which is made of it. There are two ways in which the first case may occur. Either because of a defect in the person, if he

[handwritten bottom: Obedience to authority from God / 2 criteria for when it's NOT from God]

is unworthy; or because of some defect in the way itself by which power was acquired, if, for example, through violence, or simony or some other illegal method.
The first defect is not such as to impede the acquisition of legitimate authority; and
since authority derives always, from a formal point of view, from God (and it is this
which produces the duty of obedience), their subjects are always obliged to obey
such superiors, however unworthy they may be. But the second defect prevents the
establishment of any just authority: for whoever possesses himself of power by violence does not truly become lord or master. Therefore it is permissible, when occasion offers, for a person to reject such authority; except in the case that it subsequently became legitimate, either through public consent or through the
intervention of higher authority. With regard to abuse of authority, this also may
come about in two ways. First, when what is ordered by an authority is opposed to
the object for which that authority was constituted (if, for example, some sinful action is commanded or one which is contrary to virtue, when it is precisely for the
protection and fostering of virtue that authority is instituted). In such a case, not
only is there no obligation to obey the authority, but one is obliged to disobey it, as
did the holy martyrs who suffered death rather than obey the impious commands of
tyrants. Secondly, when those who bear authority command things which exceed the
competence of such authority; as, for example, when a master demands payment
from a servant which the latter is not bound to make, and other similar cases. In this
instance the subject is free to obey or to disobey.

Answers to the Objections: So, to the first objection we may reply that authority
which is instituted in the interests of those subject to it, is not contrary to their liberty; so there is no objection to those who are transformed into sons of God by the
grace of the Holy Spirit, being subject to it. Or again we can say that Christ speaks of
Himself and of His disciples, who were neither of servile condition nor had they any
temporal possessions for which to pay tribute to temporal lords. So it does not follow that all Christians should enjoy such liberty, but only those who follow the apostolic way of life, without possessions and free from servile condition.

With regard to the second objection we must note that baptism does not take
away all the penalties which derive from the sin of our first parents, as for instance
the inevitability of death, blindness, and other such evils. But it regenerates in the
living hope of that life in which we shall be free from such penalties. Therefore, from
the fact that a man is baptized it does not necessarily follow that he should be freed
from servile condition, even though this is a consequence of sin.

To the third objection we reply that the greater bond does not absolve from the
lesser, unless the two be incompatible, since error and truth cannot be found together; therefore with the coming of the truth of the Gospel the darkness of the Old
Law passed away. But the bond with which one is bound in baptism is compatible
with the bond of servitude, and does not in consequence absolve from it.

To the fourth objection we reply that those who attain power by violence are
not truly rulers; therefore their subjects are not bound to obey them except in the
cases already noted.

With regard to the fifth objection it must be noted that Cicero (*De officiis* 1.26
[justifying the assassination of Julius Caesar]) was speaking of a case where a person

had possessed himself of power through violence, either against the will of his subjects or by compelling their consent, and where there was no possibility of appeal to a higher authority who could pass judgement on such action. In such a case, one who liberates his country by killing a tyrant is to be praised and rewarded.

Translation: J. G. Dawson (Oxford, 1959). Used with permission.

From *On Kingship,* Book 1

1. *What is meant by the word "king."* The first step in our undertaking must be to set forth what is to be understood by the term *king.*

In all things which are ordered towards an end, wherein this or that course may be adopted, some directive principle is needed through which the due end may be reached by the most direct route. A ship, for example, which moves in different directions according to the impulse of the changing winds, would never reach its destination were it not brought to port by the skill of the pilot. Now, man has an end to which his whole life and all his actions are ordered; for man is an intelligent agent, and it is clearly the part of an intelligent agent to act in view of an end. Men also adopt different methods in proceeding towards their proposed end, as the diversity of men's pursuits and actions clearly indicates. Consequently man needs some directive principle to guide him towards his end.

To be sure, the light of reason is placed by nature in every man, to guide him in his acts towards his end. Wherefore, if man were intended to live alone, as many animals do, he would require no other guide to his end. Each man would be a king unto himself, under God, the highest King, inasmuch as he would direct himself in his acts by the light of reason given him from on high. Yet it is natural for man, more than for any other animal, to be a social and political animal, to live in a group.

This is clearly a necessity of man's nature. For all other animals, nature has prepared food, hair as a covering, teeth, horns, claws as means of defence or at least speed in flight, while man alone was made without any natural provisions for these things. Instead of all these, man was endowed with reason, by the use of which he could procure all these things for himself by the work of his hands. Now, one man alone is not able to procure them all for himself, for one man could not sufficiently provide for life, unassisted. It is therefore natural that man should live in the society of many.

Moreover, all other animals are able to discern, by inborn skill, what is useful and what is injurious, even as the sheep naturally regards the wolf as his enemy. Some animals also recognize by natural skill certain medicinal herbs and other things necessary for their life. Man, on the contrary, has a natural knowledge of the things which are essential for his life only in a general fashion, inasmuch as he is able to attain knowledge of the particular things necessary for human life by reasoning from natural principles. But it is not possible for one man to arrive at a knowledge of all these things by his own individual reason. It is therefore necessary for man to live in a multitude so that each one may assist his fellows, and different men may be occupied in seeking, by their reason, to make different discoveries — one, for example, in medicine, one in this and another in that.

This point is further and most plainly evidenced by the fact that the use of speech is a prerogative proper to man. By this means, one man is able fully to express his conceptions to others. Other animals, it is true, express their feelings to one another in a general way, as a dog may express anger by barking and other animals give vent to other feelings in various fashions. But man communicates with his kind more completely than any other animal known to be gregarious, such as the crane, the ant or the bee. With this in mind, Solomon says: "It is better that there be two than one; for they have the advantage of their company" (Eccles. 4:9).

If, then, it is natural for man to live in the society of many, it is necessary that there exist among men some means by which the group may be governed. For where there are many men together and each one is looking after his own interest, the multitude would be broken up and scattered unless there were also an agency to take care of what appertains to the commonweal. In like manner, the body of a man or any other animal would disintegrate unless there were a general ruling force within the body which watches over the common good of all members. With this in mind, Solomon says: "Where there is no governor, the people shall fall" (Prov. 11:14).

Indeed it is reasonable that this should happen, for what is proper and what is common are not identical. Things differ by what is proper to each: they are united by what they have in common. But diversity of effects is due to diversity of causes. Consequently, there must exist something which impels towards the common good of the many, over and above that which impels towards the particular good of each individual. Wherefore also in all things that are ordained towards one end, one thing is found to rule the rest. Thus in the corporeal universe, by the first body, *i.e.* the celestial body, the other bodies are regulated according to the order of Divine Providence; and all bodies are ruled by a rational creature. So, too, in the individual man, the soul rules the body; and among the parts of the soul, the irascible and the concupiscible parts are ruled by reason. Likewise, among the members of a body, one, such as the heart or the head, is the principal and moves all the others. Therefore in every multitude there must be some governing power.

Now it happens in certain things which are ordained towards an end that one may proceed in a right way and also in a wrong way. So, too, in the government of a multitude there is a distinction between right and wrong. A thing is rightly directed when it is led towards a befitting end; wrongly when it is led towards an unbefitting end. Now the end which befits a multitude of free men is different from that which befits a multitude of slaves, for the free man is one who exists for his own sake, while the slave, as such, exists for the sake of another. If, therefore, a multitude of free men is ordered by the ruler towards the common good of the multitude, that rulership will be right and just, as is suitable to free men. If, on the other hand, a rulership aims, not at the common good of the multitude, but at the private good of the ruler, it will be an unjust and perverted rulership. The Lord, therefore, threatens such rulers, saying by the mouth of Ezekiel (34:2): "Woe to the shepherds that feed themselves (seeking, that is, their own interest): should not the flocks be fed by the shepherd?" Shepherds indeed should seek the good of their flocks, and every ruler, the good of the multitude subject to him.

If an unjust government is carried on by one man alone, who seeks his own benefit from his rule and not the good of the multitude subject to him, such a ruler is called a *tyrant* — a word derived from *strength* — because he oppresses by might instead of ruling by justice. Thus among the ancients all powerful men were called tyrants. If an unjust government is carried on, not by one but by several, and if they be few, it is called an *oligarchy,* that is, the rule of a few. This occurs when a few, who differ from the tyrant only by the fact that they are more than one, oppress the people by means of their wealth. If, finally, the bad government is carried on by the multitude, it is called a *democracy, i.e.* control by the populace, which comes about when the plebeian people by force of numbers oppress the rich. In this way the whole people will be as one tyrant.

In like manner we must divide just governments. If the government is administered by many, it is given the name common to all forms of government, viz. *polity,* as for instance when a group of warriors exercise dominion over a city or province. If it is administered by a few men of virtue, this kind of government is called an *aristocracy, i.e.* noble governance, or governance by noble men, who for this reason are called *optimates.* And if a just government is in the hands of one man alone, he is properly called a *king.* Wherefore the Lord says by the mouth of Ezekiel (37:24): "My servant, David, shall be king over them and all of them shall have one shepherd."

From this it is clearly shown that the idea of king implies that he be one man who is chief and that he be a shepherd seeking the common good of the multitude and not his own.

Now since man must live in a group, because he is not sufficient unto himself to procure the necessities of life were he to remain solitary, it follows that a society will be the more perfect the more it is sufficient unto itself to procure the necessities of life. There is, to some extent, sufficiency for life in one *family of one household,* namely, insofar as pertains to the natural acts of nourishment and the begetting of offspring and other things of this kind. Self-sufficiency exists, furthermore, in one *street* with regard to those things which belong to the trade of one guild. In a *city,* which is the perfect community, it exists with regard to all the necessities of life. Still more self-sufficiency is found in a *province* because of the need of fighting together and of mutual help against enemies. Hence the man ruling a perfect community, *i.e.* a city or a province, is antonomastically called *the* king. [Antonomasia is the figure of speech by which a generic predicate is used to designate an individual to which the predicate belongs in an eminent degree, as when Rome is designated "the city."] The ruler of a household is called father, not king, although he bears a certain resemblance to the king, for which reason kings are sometimes called the fathers of their peoples.

It is plain, therefore, from what has been said, that a king is one who rules the people of one city or province, and rules them for the common good. Wherefore Solomon says (Eccles. 5:9 Vulgate): "The king ruleth over all the land subject to him." [. . .]

6. *How provision might be made that the king may not fall into tyranny.* Therefore, since the rule of one man, which is the best, is to be preferred, and since it may happen that it be changed into a tyranny, which is the worst (all this is clear from

332

what has been said), a scheme should be carefully worked out which would prevent the multitude ruled by a king from falling into the hands of a tyrant.

First, it is necessary that the man who is raised up to be king by those whom it concerns should be of such condition that it is improbable that he should become a tyrant. Wherefore Samuel, commending the providence of God with respect to the institution of the king says: "The Lord hath sought him a man according to his own heart, and the Lord hath appointed him to be prince over his people" (1 Sam. 13:14). Then, once the king is established, the government of the kingdom must be so arranged that opportunity to tyrannize is removed. At the same time his power should be so tempered that he cannot easily fall into tyranny. How these things may be done we must consider in what follows.

Finally, provision must be made for facing the situation should the king stray into tyranny.

Indeed, if there be not an excess of tyranny it is more expedient to tolerate the milder tyranny for a while than, by acting against the tyrant, to become involved in many perils more grievous than the tyranny itself. For it may happen that those who act against the tyrant are unable to prevail and the tyrant then will rage the more. But should one be able to prevail against the tyrant, from this fact itself very grave dissensions among the people frequently ensue: the multitude may be broken up into factions either during their revolt against the tyrant, or in process of the organization of the government, after the tyrant has been overthrown. Moreover, it sometimes happens that while the multitude is driving out the tyrant by the help of some man, the latter, having received the power, thereupon seizes the tyranny. Then, fearing to suffer from another what he did to his predecessor, he oppresses his subjects with an even more grievous slavery. This is wont to happen in tyranny, namely that the second becomes more grievous than the one preceding, inasmuch as, without abandoning the previous oppressions, he himself thinks up fresh ones from the malice of his heart. Whence in Syracuse, at a time when everyone desired the death of Dionysius, a certain old woman kept constantly praying that he might be unharmed and that he might survive her. When the tyrant learned this he asked why she did it. Then she said: "When I was a girl we had a harsh tyrant and I wished for his death; when he was killed, there succeeded him one who was a little harsher. I was very eager to see the end of his dominion also, and we began to have a third ruler still more harsh — that was you. So if you should be taken away, a worse would succeed in your place" (Valerius Maximus, *Memorabilia* 6.2.2).

If the excess of tyranny is unbearable, some have been of the opinion that it would be an act of virtue for strong men to slay the tyrant and to expose themselves to the danger of death in order to set the multitude free (cf. John of Salisbury, *Policraticus* 8.18-20 [cf. above, p. 295]). An example of this occurs even in the Old Testament, for a certain Ehud slew Eglon, King of Moab, who was oppressing the people of God under harsh slavery, thrusting a dagger into his thigh; and he was made a judge of the people (Judges 3:14ff.).

But this opinion is not in accord with apostolic teaching. For Peter admonishes us to be reverently subject to our masters, not only to the good and gentle but also the froward: "For if one who suffers unjustly bear his trouble for conscience'

333

sake, this is grace" (1 Pet. 2:18f.). Wherefore, when many emperors of the Romans tyrannically persecuted the faith of Christ, a great number both of the nobility and the common people were converted to the faith and were praised for patiently bearing death for Christ. They did not resist although they were armed, and this is plainly manifested in the case of the holy Theban legion. Ehud, then, must be considered rather as having slain a foe than assassinated a ruler, however tyrannical, of the people. Hence in the Old Testament we also read that they who killed Joash, the king of Judah, who had fallen away from the worship of God, were slain and their children spared according to the precept of the law (2 Kings 14:5f.).

Should private persons attempt on their own private presumption to kill the rulers, even though tyrants, this would be dangerous for the multitude as well as for their rulers. This is because the wicked usually expose themselves to dangers of this kind more than the good, for the rule of a king, no less than that of a tyrant, is burdensome to them since, according to the words of Solomon (Prov. 20:26): "A wise king scattereth the wicked." Consequently, by presumption of this kind, danger to the people from the loss of a good king would be more probable than relief through the removal of a tyrant.

Furthermore, it seems that to proceed against the cruelty of tyrants is an action to be undertaken, not through the private presumption of a few, but rather by public authority.

If to provide itself with a king belongs to the right of a given multitude, it is not unjust that the king be deposed or have his power restricted by that same multitude if, becoming a tyrant, he abuses the royal power. It must not be thought that such a multitude is acting unfaithfully in deposing the tyrant, even though it had previously subjected itself to him in perpetuity, because he himself has deserved that the covenant with his subjects should not be kept, since, in ruling the multitude, he did not act faithfully as the office of a king demands. Thus did the Romans, who had accepted Tarquin the Proud as their king, cast him out from the kingship on account of his tyranny and the tyranny of his sons; and they set up in their place a lesser power, namely, the consular power. Similarly Domitian, who had succeeded those most moderate emperors, Vespasian, his father, and Titus, his brother, was slain by the Roman senate when he exercised tyranny, and all his wicked deeds were justly and profitably declared null and void by a decree of the senate. Thus it came about that Blessed John the Evangelist, the beloved disciple of God, who had been exiled to the island of Patmos by that very Domitian, was sent back to Ephesus by a decree of the senate.

If, on the other hand, it pertains to the right of a higher authority to provide a king for a certain multitude, a remedy against the wickedness of a tyrant is to be looked for from him. Thus when Archelaus, who had already begun to reign in Judaea in the place of Herod his father, was imitating his father's wickedness, a complaint against him having been laid before Caesar Augustus by the Jews, his power was at first diminished by depriving him of his title of king and by dividing one-half of his kingdom between his two brothers. Later, since he was not restrained from tyranny even by this means, Tiberius Caesar sent him into exile to Lugdunum, a city in Gaul. [Actually Augustus sent him to Vienne (Josephus, *De bello Iudaico* 2, 111).]

Should no human aid whatsoever against a tyrant be forthcoming, recourse

334

must be had to God, the King of all, who is a helper in due time in tribulation (Ps. 9:9). For it lies in his power to turn the cruel heart of the tyrant to mildness. According to Solomon (Prov. 21:1): "The heart of the king is in the hand of the Lord, withersoever He will He shall turn it." [. . .]

10. *What advantages which are rendered to kings are lost by the tyrant?* [. . .] First of all, among all worldly things there is nothing which seems worthy to be preferred to friendship. Friendship unites good men and preserves and promotes virtue. Friendship is needed by all men in whatsoever occupations they engage. In prosperity it does not thrust itself unwanted upon us, nor does it desert us in adversity. It is what brings with it the greatest delight, to such an extent that all that pleases is changed to weariness when friends are absent, and all difficult things are made easy and as nothing by love. There is no tyrant so cruel that friendship does not bring him pleasure. When Dionysius, sometime tyrant of Syracuse, wanted to kill one of two friends, Damon and Pythias, the one who was to be killed asked leave to go home and set his affairs in order, and the other friend surrendered himself to the tyrant as security for his return. When the appointed day was approaching and he had not yet returned, everyone said that his hostage was a fool, but he declared he had no fear whatever regarding his friend's loyalty. The very hour when he was to be put to death, his friend returned. Admiring the courage of both, the tyrant remitted the sentence on account of the loyalty of their friendship, and asked in addition that they should receive him as a third member in their bond of friendship.

Yet, although tyrants desire this very benefit of friendship, they cannot obtain it, for when they seek their own good instead of the common good there is little or no communion between them and their subjects. Now all friendship is concluded upon the basis of something common among those who are to be friends, for we see that those are united in friendship who have in common either their natural origin, or some similarity in habits of life, or any kind of social interests. Consequently there can be little or no friendship between tyrants and their subjects. When the latter are oppressed by tyrannical injustice and feel they are not loved but despised, they certainly do not conceive any love, for it is too great a virtue for the common man to love his enemies and to do good to his persecutors. Nor have tyrants any reason to complain of their subjects if they are not loved by them, since they do not act towards them in such a way that they ought to be loved by them. Good kings, on the contrary, are loved by many when they show that they love their subjects and are studiously intent on the common welfare, and when their subjects can see that they derive many benefits from this zealous care. For to hate their friends and return evil for good to their benefactors — this, surely, would be too great a malice to ascribe fittingly to the generality of men.

From Book 2

1 (1.12). *On the duties of a king.* The next point to be considered is what the kingly office is and what qualities the king should have. Since things which are in accor-

king's duties

rule w/ reason

dance with art are an imitation of the things which are in accordance with nature (from which we accept the rules to act according to reason), it seems best that we learn about the kingly office from the pattern of the regime of nature.

In things of nature there is both a universal and a particular government. The former is God's government whose rule embraces all things and whose providence governs them all. The latter is found in man and it is much like the divine government. Hence man is called a *microcosmos* (cf. Aristotle, *Physics*: 252b26f.). Indeed there is a similitude between both governments in regard to their form; for just as the universe of corporeal creatures and all spiritual powers come under the divine government, in like manner the members of the human body and all the powers of the soul are governed by reason. Thus, in a proportionate manner, reason is to man what God is to the world. Since, however, man is by nature a social animal living in a multitude, as we have pointed out above, the analogy with the divine government is found in him not only in this way that one man governs himself by reason, but also in that the multitude of men is governed by the reason of one man. This is what first of all constitutes the office of a king. True, among certain animals that live socially there is a likeness to the king's rulership; so we say that there are kings among bees. Yet animals exercise rulership not through reason but through their natural instinct which is implanted in them by the great ruler, the author of nature.

Therefore let the king recognize that such is the office which he undertakes, namely, that he is to be in the kingdom what the soul is in the body, and what God is in the world. If he reflect seriously upon this, a zeal for justice will be enkindled in him when he contemplates that he has been appointed to this position in place of God, to exercise judgment in his kingdom; further, he will acquire the gentleness of clemency and mildness when he considers as his own members those individuals who are subject to his rule.

2 (1.13). *What it is incumbent upon a king to do and how he should go about doing it.* Let us then examine what God does in the world, for in this way we shall be able to see what it is incumbent upon a king to do.

Looking at the world as a whole, there are two works of God to be considered: the first is creation; the second, God's government of the things created. These two works are, in like manner, performed by the soul in the body since, first, by the virtue of the soul the body is formed, and then the latter is governed and moved by the soul.

govern the kingdom

Of these works, the second more properly pertains to the office of kingship. Therefore government belongs to all kings (the very name *rex* is derived from the fact that they direct the government), while the first work does not fall to all kings, for not all kings establish the kingdom or city in which they rule but bestow their regal care upon a kingdom or city already established. We must remember, however, that if there were no one to establish the city or kingdom, there would be no question of governing the kingdom. The very notion of kingly office, then, comprises the establishment of a city and kingdom, and some kings have indeed established cities in which to rule: for example, Ninus founded Nineveh, and Romulus, Rome. It per-

preserve it

tains also to the governing office to preserve the things governed, and to use them for the purpose for which they were established. If, therefore, one does not know how a kingdom is established, one cannot fully understand the task of its government.

Now, from the example of the creation of the world one may learn how a kingdom is established. In creation we may consider, first, the production of things; secondly, the orderly distinction of the parts of the world. Further, we observe that different species of things are distributed in different parts of the world: stars in the heavens, fowls in the air, fishes in the water, and animals on land. We notice further that, for each species, the things it needs are abundantly provided by the divine power. Moses has minutely and carefully set forth this plan of how the world was made (Gen. 1:1-31). First of all, he sets forth the production of things in these words: "In the beginning God created the heavens and the earth." Next, he declares that all things were distinguished from one another by God according to a suitable order: day from night, higher things from lower, the sea from the dry land. He next relates that the sky was adorned with luminaries, the air with birds, the sea with fishes, the earth with animals; finally, dominion over earth and animals was given to men. He further states that, by divine providence, plants were made for the use of men and the other animals.

Of course the founder of a city and kingdom cannot produce anew men, places in which to dwell, and the other necessities of life. He has to make use of those which already exist in nature, just as the other arts derive the material for their work from nature; as, for example, the smith takes iron, the builder wood and stone, to use in their respective arts. Therefore the founder of a city and kingdom must first choose a suitable place which will preserve the inhabitants by its healthfulness, provide the necessities of life by its fruitfulness, please them with its beauty, and render them safe from their enemies by its natural protection. If any of these advantages be lacking, the place will be more or less convenient in proportion as it offers more or less of the said advantages, or the more essential of them. Next, the founder of a city and kingdom must mark out the chosen place according to the exigencies of things necessary for the perfection of the city and kingdom. For example, when a kingdom is to be founded, he will have to determine which place is suitable for establishing cities, and which is best for villages and hamlets, where to locate the places of learning, the military training camps, the markets — and so on with other things which the perfection of the kingdom requires. And if it is a question of founding a city, he will have to determine what site is to be assigned to the churches, the law courts, and the various trades. Furthermore, he will have to gather together the men, who must be apportioned suitable locations according to their respective occupations. Finally, he must provide for each one what is necessary for his particular condition and state in life; otherwise, the kingdom or city could never endure.

These are, briefly, the duties that pertain to the office of king in founding a city and kingdom, as derived from a comparison with the creation of the world.

3 (1.14). *That the office of governing the kingdom should be learned from the divine government.* Just as the founding of a city or kingdom may suitably be learned from the way in which the world was created, so too the way to govern may be learned from the divine government of the world.

Before going into that, however, we should consider that to govern is to lead the thing governed in a suitable way towards its proper end. Thus a ship is said to be governed when, through the skill of the pilot, it is brought unharmed and by a direct route to harbour. Consequently, if a thing be directed to an end outside itself (as a ship to the harbour), it is the governor's duty, not only to preserve the thing un-harmed, but further to guide it towards this end. If, on the contrary, there be a thing whose end is not outside itself, then the governor's endeavours will merely tend to preserve the thing undamaged in its proper perfection.

Nothing of this kind is to be found in reality, except God himself, who is the end of all. However, as concerns the thing which is directed to an end outside itself, care is exercised by different providers in different ways. One might have the task of preserving a thing in its being, another of bringing it to a further perfection. Such is clearly the case in the example of the ship; (the first meaning of the word *gubernator* is *pilot*). It is the carpenter's business to repair anything which might be broken, while the pilot bears the responsibility of bringing the ship to port. It is the same with man. The doctor sees to it that a man's life is preserved; the tradesman supplies the necessities of life; the teacher takes care that man may learn the truth; and the tutor sees that he lives according to reason.

Now if man were not ordained to another end outside himself, the above-mentioned cares would be sufficient for him. But as long as man's mortal life endures there is an extrinsic good for him, namely, final beatitude which is looked for after death in the enjoyment of God, for as the Apostle says: "As long as we are in the body we are far from the Lord" (2 Cor. 5:6). Consequently the Christian man, for whom that beatitude has been purchased by the blood of Christ, and who, in order to attain it, has received the earnest of the Holy Ghost, needs another and spiritual care to direct him to the harbour of eternal salvation, and this care is provided for the faithful by the ministers of the church of Christ.

Now the same judgment is to be formed about the end of society as a whole as about the end of one. If, therefore, the ultimate end of man were some good that existed in himself, then the ultimate end of the multitude to be governed would likewise be for the multitude to acquire such good, and persevere in its possession. If such an ultimate end either of an individual man or a multitude were a corporeal one, namely, life and health of body, to govern would then be a physician's charge. If that ultimate end were an abundance of wealth, then knowledge of economics would have the last word in the community's government. If the good of the knowledge of truth were of such a kind that the multitude might attain to it, the king would have to be a teacher. It is, however, clear that the end of a multitude gathered together is to live virtuously. For men form a group for the purpose of *living well* together, a thing which the individual man living alone could not attain, and *good life* is virtuous life (Aristotle, *Politics* 1252b30; 1280b33). Therefore, virtuous life is the end for which men gather together. The evidence for this lies in the fact that only those who render mutual assistance to one another in living well form a genuine part of an assembled multitude. If men assembled merely to live, then animals and slaves would form a part of the civil community. Or, if men assembled only to accrue wealth, then all those who traded together would belong to one city. Yet we see that only such are regarded as forming one multitude as are directed by the same laws and the same government to live well.

Yet through virtuous living man is further ordained to a higher end, which consists in the enjoyment of God, as we have said above. Consequently, since society must have the same end as the individual man, it is not the ultimate end of an assem-

bled multitude to live virtuously, but through virtuous living to attain to the posses- *[handwritten: ✗]*
sion of God. *[handwritten: the end of society]*

If this end could be attained by the power of human nature, then the duty of a *[handwritten: can a]*
king would have to include the direction of men to it. We are supposing, of course, *[handwritten: king do this?]*
that he is called king to whom the supreme power of governing in human affairs is
entrusted. Now the higher the end to which a government is ordained, the loftier
that government is. Indeed, we always find that the one to whom it pertains to
achieve the final end commands those who execute the things that are ordained to
that end. For example, the captain, whose business it is to regulate navigation, tells
the shipbuilder what kind of ship he must construct to be suitable for navigation;
and the ruler of a city, who makes use of arms, tells the blacksmith what kind of
arms to make. But because a man does not attain his end, which is the possession of
God, by human power but by divine — according to the words of the Apostle (Rom.
6:23): "By the grace of God life everlasting" — therefore the task of leading him to
that last end does not pertain to human but to divine government.

Consequently, government of this kind pertains to that king who is not only a
man, but also God, namely, our Lord Jesus Christ, who by making men sons of God
brought them to the glory of Heaven. This then is the government which has been
delivered to him and which "shall not be destroyed" (Dan. 7:14), on account of
which he is called, in Holy Writ, not priest only, but king. As Jeremiah says: "The
king shall reign and he shall be wise" (23:5). Hence a royal priesthood is derived
from him, and what is more, all those who believe in Christ, in so far as they are his *[handwritten: distinction: spir/earthly]*
members, are called kings and priests (Rev. 1:6, 5:10, 20:6).

Thus, in order that spiritual things might be distinguished from earthly things,
the ministry of this kingdom has been entrusted not to earthly kings but to priests,
and most of all to the chief priest, the successor of St. Peter, the Vicar of Christ, the *[handwritten: PRIESTLY TASK]*
Roman pontiff. To him all the kings of the Christian People are to be subject as to
our Lord Jesus Christ himself. For those to whom pertains the care of intermediate *[handwritten: — kings are subject]*
ends should be subject to him to whom pertains the care of the ultimate end, and be
directed by his rule.

Because the priesthood of the gentiles and the whole worship of their gods existed merely for the acquisition of temporal goods (which were all ordained to the
common good of the multitude, whose care devolved upon the king), the priests of
the gentiles were very properly subject to the kings. Similarly, since in the old law
earthly goods were promised to the religious people, not indeed by demons but by
the true God, the priests of the old law, we read, were also subject to the kings. But in
the new law there is a higher priesthood by which men are guided to heavenly goods.
Consequently, in the law of Christ, kings must be subject to priests.

It was therefore also a marvellous disposition of divine providence that, in the
city of Rome, which God had foreseen would be the principal seat of the Christian
priesthood, the custom was gradually established that the rulers of the city should be
subject to the priests, for as Valerius Maximus (*Memorabilia* 1.1.9) relates: "Our city
has always considered that everything should yield precedence to religion, even
those things in which it aimed to display the splendour of supreme majesty. We
therefore unhesitatingly made the imperial dignity minister to religion, considering

that the empire would thus hold control of human affairs if faithfully and constantly it were submissive to the divine power."

And because it was to come to pass that the religion of the Christian priesthood should especially thrive in France, God provided that among the Gauls too their tribal priests, called Druids, should lay down the law of all Gaul, as Julius Caesar relates in the book which he wrote about the Gallic war (*De bello Gallico* 6.13.5).

4 (1.15). *That regal government should be ordained principally to eternal beatitude.* As the life by which men live well here on earth is ordained, as to its end, to that blessed life which we hope for in heaven, so too whatever particular goods are procured by man's agency — whether wealth, profits, health, eloquence, or learning — are ordained to the good life of the multitude. If, then, as we have said, the person who is charged with the care of our ultimate end ought to be over those who have charge of things ordained to that end, and to direct them by his rule, it clearly follows that, just as the king ought to be subject to the divine government administered by the office of priesthood, so he ought to preside over all human offices, and regulate them by the rule of his government.

Now anyone on whom it devolves to do something which is ordained to another thing as to its end is bound to see that his work is suitable to that end; thus, for example, the armourer so fashions the sword that it is suitable for fighting, and the builder should so lay out the house that it is suitable for habitation. Therefore, since the beatitude of heaven is the end of that virtuous life which we live at present, it pertains to the king's office to promote the good life of the multitude in such a way as to make it suitable for the attainment of heavenly happiness; that is to say, he should command those things which lead to the happiness of Heaven and, as far as possible, forbid the contrary.

What conduces to true beatitude and what hinders it are learned from the law of God, the teaching of which belongs to the office of the priest, according to the words of Malachi (2:7): "The lips of the priest shall guard knowledge and they shall seek the law from his mouth." Wherefore the Lord prescribes in the Book of Deuteronomy (17:18f.) that "after he is raised to the throne of his kingdom, the king shall copy out to himself the Deuteronomy [so Vulgate, followed by Thomas; understand, "a copy"] of this law in a volume, taking the copy of the priest of the Levitical tribe; he shall have it with him and shall read it all the days of his life, that he may learn to fear the Lord his God, and keep his words and ceremonies which are commanded in the law." Thus the king, taught the law of God, should have for his principal concern the means by which the multitude subject to him may live well.

This concern is threefold: first of all, to establish a virtuous life in the multitude subject to him; second, to preserve it once established; and third, having preserved it, to promote its greater perfection.

For an individual man to lead a good life two things are required. The first and most important is to act in a virtuous manner, for virtue is that by which one lives well; the second, which is secondary and instrumental, is a sufficiency of those bodily goods whose use is necessary for virtuous life. Yet the unity of man is brought about by nature, while the unity of multitude, which we call peace, must be procured through the efforts of the ruler. Therefore, to establish virtuous living in a multitude three things are necessary. First of all, that the multitude be established in the unity of peace. Second, that the multitude thus united in the bond of peace, be directed to [*peace & unity necessary*] acting well. For just as a man can do nothing well unless unity within his members be presupposed, so a multitude of men lacking the unity of peace will be hindered from virtuous action by the fact that it is fighting against itself. In the third place, it is necessary that there be at hand a sufficient supply of the things required for proper living, procured by the ruler's efforts.

When virtuous living is set up in the multitude by the efforts of the king, it then remains for him to look to its conservation. Now there are three things which prevent the permanence of the public good. One of these arises from nature. The good of the multitude should not be established for one time only; it should be in a sense perpetual. Men, on the other hand, cannot abide forever, because they are mortal. Even while they are alive they do not always preserve the same vigour, for the life of man is subject to many changes, and thus a man is not equally suited to the performance of the same duties throughout the whole span of his life. A second impediment to the preservation of the public good, which comes from within, consists in the perversity of the wills of men, inasmuch as they are either too lazy to perform what the commonweal demands, or, still further, they are harmful to the peace of the multitude because, by transgressing justice, they disturb the peace of others. The third hindrance to the preservation of the commonweal comes from without, namely, when peace is destroyed through the attacks of enemies and, as it sometimes happens, the kingdom or city is completely blotted out.

In regard to these three dangers, a triple charge is laid upon the king. First of all, he must take care of the appointment of men to succeed or replace others in charge of the various offices. Just as in regard to corruptible things (which cannot [*appointment*] remain the same forever) the government of God made provision that through generation one would take the place of another in order that, in this way, the integrity of the universe might be maintained, so too the good of the multitude subject to the king will be preserved through his care when he sets himself to attend to the appointment of new men to fill the place of those who drop out. In the second place, by his laws and orders, punishments and rewards, he should restrain the men subject [*laws*] to him from wickedness and induce them to virtuous deeds, following the example of God, who gave his law to man and requites those who observe it with rewards, and those who transgress it with punishments. The king's third charge is to keep the [*protection*] multitude entrusted to him safe from the enemy, for it would be useless to prevent internal dangers if the multitude could not be defended against external dangers.

Finally, for the proper direction of the multitude there remains the third duty of the kingly office, namely, that he be solicitous for its improvement. He performs this duty when, in each of the things we have mentioned, he corrects what is out of [*correction*] order and supplies what is lacking, and if any of them can be done better he tries to do so. This is why the Apostle exhorts the faithful to be "zealous for the better gifts" (1 Cor. 12:31).

These then are the duties of the kingly office, each of which must now be treated in greater detail.

Translation: G. B. Phelan and I. T. Eschmann (Toronto, 1949). Used with permission.

From *Summa Theologiae* 1a2ae.90-108 (On Law)

90, 2 *Reply:* To be a principle of human acts, as we have said [90.1], is part of the nature of law, since it is for them a rule and measure. As their beginning lies in the reason, so also one phase of its activity is the start of what follows; this first and foremost is where law comes in. Now the deeds we perform, these being the concern of the practical reason, all originate from our last end. We have shown that the last end of human living is happiness or well-being. Consequently law is engaged above all with the plan of things for human happiness.

Again, since the subordination of part to whole is that of incomplete to rounded-off reality, and since a human individual man is part of the full life of the community, it must needs be that law properly speaking deals with this subordination to a common happiness. Thus Aristotle, having explained what he means by "legal," mentions the happiness of the body politic when he says in the *Ethics* (1129b17) that "we call those acts legally just that tend to produce and preserve happiness and its components for the political community," the perfect community, according to the *Politics* (1252a5), being the state.

When we speak of "a-most-of-all" in any class of things then it is the principle and centre of reference for them all, as fire, for instance, which is the hottest thing of all, is the cause of heat in bodies mixed with other elements, and they are called hot in so far as they share its nature. And since we speak of law most of all in terms of the common good, it follows that any other precept about more particular business will not have the nature of law except in so far as it enters into this plan for the common good. Therefore every law is shaped to the common good.

90, 3 *Reply:* The chief and main concern of law properly so called is the plan for the common good. The planning is the business of the whole people or of their vicegerent. Therefore to make law is the office of the entire people or of the public personage who has care of them. For, as elsewhere, to plan for an end belongs to the power matching that end.

91, 2 *Reply:* Law is a rule and measure, as we have said [90.1 ad 1], and therefore can exist in two manners, first as in the thing which is the rule and measure, second as in the thing that is ruled and measured, and the closer the second to the first the more regular and measured it will be. Since all things are regulated and measured by Eternal Law, as we have seen [91.1], it is evident that all somehow share in it, in that their tendencies to their own proper acts and ends are from its impression.

Among them intelligent creatures are ranked under divine Providence the more nobly because they take part in Providence by their own providing for themselves and others. Thus they join in and make their own the Eternal Reason through which they have their natural aptitudes for their due activity and purpose. Now this sharing in the Eternal Law by intelligent creatures is what we call "natural law."

That is why the Psalmist after bidding us, "Offer the sacrifice of justice," and, as though anticipating those who ask what are the works of justice, and adding, "There be many who say, Who will show us any good?" makes reply, "The light of thy countenance, O Lord, is signed upon us" (Ps. 4:5f.), implying that the light of natural reason by which we discern what is good and what evil, is nothing but the impression of divine light on us.

Accordingly it is clear that natural law is nothing other than the sharing in the Eternal Law by intelligent creatures. (reason)

91, 3 *Reply:* As we have seen [90.1 ad 2], law is a kind of dictate of the practical reason. Now the processes of the theoretic and practical reasons are parallel; both, we have held, start from certain principles and come to certain conclusions. Accordingly we say this, that just as from indemonstrable principles that are instinctively recognized the theoretic reason draws the conclusions of the various sciences not imparted by nature but discovered by reasoned effort, so also from natural law precepts as from common and indemonstrable principles the human reason comes down to making more specific arrangements.

Now these particular arrangements human reason arrives at are called "human laws," provided they fulfil the essential conditions of law already indicated. Hence Cicero says that "justice took its start from nature, and then certain things became custom by reason of their usefulness; thereafter the things put forward by nature and approved by custom were sanctioned by fear and reverence for the law" (*De inventione* 2.53).

91, 4 *Reply:* The guidance of human conduct required a divine law besides natural law and human law. And for four reasons.

First, because law directs men to the actions matching what they are made for. Were they destined only to an end not beyond their natural abilities they would need no directive of reason over and above natural law and human law built on it. Yet they are set towards an eternal happiness out of proportion to their natural resources, as we have shown, and therefore must needs be directed by a divinely given law above natural and human law.

Second, because of the untrustworthiness of human judgment, notably on contingent and particular issues, different people come to differing decisions about human conduct, with the result that diverse and conflicting laws are passed. That men may know without any doubt what should or should not be done there was required a divinely given law carrying the assurance that it cannot be mistaken.

Third, men can make laws on matters on which they are competent to judge. They cannot pronounce on inward motions which are hidden, but only on outward and observable behaviour. Nevertheless full virtue means that a man is right in both. Since human law is not enough, the complement of divine law is needed to check and guide what goes on within us.

Fourth, Augustine remarks that human law cannot forbid or punish all wrongdoing, for were it to try to do away with all evils it would also take away much that was good, and so hinder what the common good requires in civilized intercourse. Hence the need of a divine law which misses nothing and leaves no evil unforbidden or unpunished.

These four reasons are touched on in the Psalm (19:7) which declares, "The law of the Lord is unspotted," that is allowing no filth of sin, "converting hearts," that is, directing us within and without, "the testimony of the Lord is sure," that is, reliably truthful and right, "giving wisdom to little ones," that is, lifting humanity to a divine and supernatural end.

Old vs. New Law

91, 5 *Reply:* We saw in the *Prima Pars* [30.3] that distinction is the cause of number. Now things may be distinct in two manners. First, as being quite different in kind, for instance a horse and an ox. Second, as being fully developed or undeveloped things of the same kind, for instance a grown-up and a child. It is in this second manner that the divine law is divided into the Old Law and the New Law. Accordingly St. Paul in Galatians compares the Old Law to the condition of a schoolboy under a tutor and the New Law to the condition of an adult who is no longer subject to one.

Their differences of development appear according to three elements in law already observed.

First, we have stated [90.2] that the purpose of law is to be ordained to the common good, and this can be twofold. The one is material and earthly benefit; this was directly envisaged by the Old Law, which from the start invited the chosen people to the promised land of Canaan. The other is spiritual and heavenly good; to this *Earthly vs spiritual benefit* we are directed by the New Law. At the opening of his ministry our Lord invited us to the kingdom of heaven: "Repent, for the kingdom of heaven is at hand" (Matt. 4:17). Accordingly Augustine (*Contra Faustum* 4.2) says that the Old Testament contains the promise of temporal things, which is why it is called "old," whereas the New Testament offers the promise of eternal life.

Second, it is the rôle of law to guide human acts according to the plan of justice, and here also the New Law is much fuller than the Old Law by governing also *New exceeds the Old (fuller)* the inner acts of heart and soul; "Unless your righteousness shall exceed that of the Scribes and Pharisees you shall in no case enter the kingdom of heaven" (Matt. 5:20). Hence the saying that the Old Law restrains the hand, but the New Law the spirit (Lombard, *Sentences* 3.40.1).

Third, it is the office of law to lead men into keeping its commandments. This *motivation: fear vs. love* the Old Law did through fear of penalty, but the New Law through love shed in our hearts by the grace of Christ. This is imparted by the New Law, but only prefigured in the Old. So Augustine remarks, "fear and love — the difference in brief between the Law and the Gospel" (*Contra Adimantum* 17).

92, 1 *Reply* [. . .] Every law aims at this, to be obeyed by its subjects. It is plain, therefore, that leading its subjects into the virtue appropriate to their condition is a proper function of law. Now since virtue is that which makes its possessor good, the consequence is that the proper effect of law on those to whom it is given is to make them good, either good simply speaking or good in a certain respect.

If the lawmaker's intention bears on true good, namely the common good regulated by divine justice, the consequence will be for men through the law to become quite simply good. If, however, the intention is not for good without reservation, but something that serves his own profit or pleasure, or against divine justice, then keeping the law will make men good, not simply, but relatively, namely amenable to the régime. This manner of being good can be found even in things bad in themselves as when we speak of a good thief when referring to his skill and success.

Answer to Objections: 3. You assess the goodness of any part in relationship to its whole; so Augustine notes that "any part which does not fit in with the whole is ugly" (*Confessions* 3.8). Since every person is part of a political community he cannot be good unless he be well-adjusted to the common good, nor can the community be sound unless its parts are in keeping. Hence the political commonwealth cannot flourish unless its citizens are virtuous, at least those in leading positions: it is enough for the good of the community if others are so far virtuous that they obey the commands of the ruling authorities. That is why Aristotle remarks (*Politics* 1277a20) that "the virtue of a good ruler is the same as that of a good man, but that the virtue of the good citizen and of the good man are not quite the same."

4. A tyrannical law is not according to reason, and therefore is not straightforwardly a law, but rather a sort of crooked law. All the same it possesses some quality of law in wanting the citizens to be good. This it does as being the decree of a presiding authority set on rendering its subjects amenable, which is for them to be good from the point of view of the government, not thoroughly good in themselves.

bad laws

94, 2 *Reply:* [. . .] Now we discover that the things which enter into our apprehension are ranged in a certain order. That which first appears is *the real*, and some insight into this is included in whatsoever is apprehended. This first indemonstrable principle, "There is no affirming and denying the same simultaneously," is based on the very nature of the real and the non-real: on this principle, as Aristotle notes, all other propositions are based.

To apply the analogy: as to be *real* first enters into human apprehending as such, so to be *good* first enters the practical reason's apprehending when it is bent on doing something. For every agent acts on account of an end, and to be an end carries the meaning of to be good. Consequently the first principle for the practical reason is based on the meaning of good, namely that it is what all things seek after. And so this is the first command of law, "that good is to be sought and done, evil to be avoided"; all other commands of natural law are based on this. Accordingly, then, natural-law commands extend to all doing or avoiding of things recognized by the practical reason of itself as being human goods.

Now since being good has the meaning of being an end, while being evil has the contrary meaning, it follows that reason of its nature apprehends the things towards which man has a natural tendency as good objectives, and therefore to be actively pursued, whereas it apprehends their contraries as bad, and therefore to be shunned.

Let us continue. The order in which commands of the law of nature are ranged corresponds to that of our natural tendencies. Here there are three stages. There is in man, first, a tendency towards the good of the nature he has in common with all substances; each has an appetite to preserve its own natural being. Natural law here plays a corresponding part, and is engaged at this stage to maintain and defend the elementary requirements of human life.

Stages of good

1.

Secondly, there is in man a bent towards things which accord with his nature considered more specifically, that is in terms of what he has in common with other animals; correspondingly those matters are said to be of natural law which nature teaches all animals, for instance the coupling of male and female, the bringing up of the young, and so forth.

2.

Thirdly, there is in man an appetite for the good of his nature as rational, and this is proper to him, for instance, that he should know truths about God and about living in society. Correspondingly whatever this involves is a matter of natural law,

3.

for instance, that a man should shun ignorance, not offend others with whom he ought to live in civility, and other such related requirements.

94, 5 *Reply:* A change can be understood to mean either addition or subtraction. As for the first, there is nothing against natural law being changed, for many things over and above natural law have been added, by divine law as well as by human laws, which are beneficial to social life.

As for change by subtraction, meaning that something that once was of natural law later ceases to be so, here there is room for a distinction. The first principles of natural law are altogether unalterable. But its secondary precepts, which we have described as being like particular conclusions close to first principles, though not alterable in the majority of cases where they are right as they stand, can nevertheless be changed on some particular and rare occasions, as we have mentioned in the preceding article, because of some special cause preventing their unqualified observance.

Answers to Objections: 3. You speak of something being according to natural right in two ways. The first is because nature is set that way; thus the command that no harm should be done to another. The second is because nature does not bid the contrary; thus we might say that it is of natural law for man to be naked, for nature does not give him clothes; these he has to make by art. In this way common ownership and universal liberty are said to be of natural law, because private property and slavery exist by human contrivance for the convenience of social life, and not by natural law. This does not change the law of nature except by addition.

Aug.

95, 2 *Reply:* Augustine observes that "there never seems to have been a law that was not just" (*On Free Choice of the Will* 1.5): hence a command has the force of law to the extent that it is just. In human matters we call something "just" from its being right according to the rule of reason. The first rule of reason is natural law, as appears from what has been stated. Hence in so far as it derives from this, every law laid down by men has the force of law in that it flows from natural law. If on any head it is at variance with natural law, it will not be law, but spoilt law.

human law is rel. to natural law

Reflect on this, however, that commands can be traced to natural law in two ways; one, drawn deductively like conclusions from premises (*sicut conclusiones ex principiis:* ["deductively" is superfluous to the translation and potentially misleading]); two, grounded on it like constructional implementations of general directives (*sicut determinationes quaedum aliquorum communium*). The first process is like that of the sciences where inferences are demonstratively drawn from principles. The second process is like that of the arts where a special shape is given to a general idea, as when an architect determines that a house should be in this or that style.

To apply: some commands are drawn like conclusions from natural law, for instance, "You must not commit murder" can be inferred from "You must do harm to nobody." Others, however, are based like constructions (*per modum determinationis*) on natural law, which, for instance, pronounces that crime has to be punished without deciding whether this or that should be the penalty; the punishment settled is like a determinate form given to natural law.

Both processes are at work in human positive law. Commands, however, that issue according to the first have part of their force from natural law, and not only from the fact of their enactment. Whereas commands that issue according to the second have their force only by human law.

95, 4 *Reply:* [. . .] Now there are several elements that belong to the essence of human law, and according to each it can be properly and essentially divided.

First of all, to depend on natural law is of the essence of human law, as has appeared; on this head positive law and justice is divided into the *jus gentium* and the civil law, and according to the two processes of derivation from natural law explained in the same place. Those precepts belong to the *ius gentium* which are drawn like conclusions from the premises of natural law, such as those requiring justice in buying and selling and so forth, without which men cannot live sociably together; this last is a condition of natural law, since, as is shown in the *Politics* (1253a2), man is by nature a sociable animal. Constructions, however, put upon natural law are proper to civil law, and here each political community decides for itself what is fitting.

Secondly, it is of the essence of human law to be ordered to the benefit of the commonwealth; on this head it can be divided according to the diversity of those whose special business it is to work for the common good; for instance, priests who pray to God for the people, rulers who govern them, soldiers who fight for their welfare. Correspondingly these men enjoy special rights (*iura* [i.e., legal provisions]) adapted to such duties.

Thirdly, it is of the essence of law to be instituted by the governor of the political community, as we have shown already; on this count law can be divided according to the type of the régime. One is kingship or royalty where, says Aristotle (*Politics* 1279a32), the State is governed by a monarch, and corresponding to this you have princely ordinances; another is aristocracy, or the rule of the best or politically best, and corresponding to this you have the advice of learned counsel and senatorial resolutions; another is oligarchy, where a few rich or powerful men are in control, and from this you get prætorian law, also called honorary law; another is popular rule, called democracy, and from this come decrees of the commonalty. Another régime is tyranny, which is so thoroughly corrupt that it affords no law. There is another type of régime blended of the others, and this is the best, and provides law as Isidore understood it, namely that "which men of birth together with the common people have sanctioned" (*Etymologies* 5.10 [cf. p. 211 above]).

Fourthly, it is of the essence of law to be the directive of human acts; matching the various subject matters of legislation there are several laws which are entitled from their authors, thus the *Lex Julia* about adultery, the *Lex Cornelia* about assassination, and so forth, which are differentiated by the things to which they refer, not by their authors.

96, 2 *Reply:* As we have seen, law is established as a kind of rule or measure for human acts. Now, as noted in the *Metaphysics* (1053a24), a measure ought to be of the same kind as the thing it measures; different things have different standards. Hence laws should be appointed to men according to their condition; Isidore remarks how law should "be possible both according to nature and the custom of the country" (*Etymologies* 5.21 [cf. p. 211 above]).

The ability of and resource for acting in a certain way spring from an interior disposition or habit; the same course of action is not possible for a man who has a habit of virtue and for a man who lacks it, nor for a grown-up and a child: this is why the same laws do not apply, for many things are allowed in the young for which older people are punished, or at least blamed. Likewise many things may be let pass in people of mediocre morals which cannot be countenanced in their betters.

Law is laid down for a great number of people, of which the majority have no high standard of morality. Therefore it does not forbid all the vices, from which upright men can keep away, but only those grave ones which the average man can avoid, and chiefly those which do harm to others and have to be stopped if human society is to be maintained, such as murder and theft and so forth.

96, 3 *Reply:* Virtues are specifically differentiated according to their objectives, as we have seen. All these objectives involve the private good of the individual person or the common good of the people; thus deeds of courage may defend the rights of a friend or of the state.

Now we have seen that law is ordained to the common good, and consequently there is no virtue of which some activity cannot be enjoined by law. Nevertheless human law does not enjoin every act of every virtue, but those acts only which serve the common good, either immediately, as when the social order is directly involved from the nature of things, or mediately, as when measures of good discipline are passed by the legislator to train citizens to maintain justice and peace in the community.

Hence: Neither are all acts of virtue commanded nor all acts of vice forbidden by an obligation set up by a human law. Nevertheless some acts of each virtue come under its precept just as some acts of each vice come under its ban.

96, 4 *Reply:* Human positive laws are either just or unjust. If they are just, they have binding force in the court of conscience from the Eternal Law from which they derive, according to Proverbs (8:15): "Through me kings reign, and the lawmakers decree just things."

Now laws are said to be just on three counts: from their end, when they are ordered to the common good, from their authority, when what is enacted does not exceed the lawgiver's power, and from their form, when for the good of the whole they place burdens in equitable proportion on subjects. Since an individual is part of a group, each in all that he is and has belongs to the community, as also is any part what it is because of the whole: nature itself offers hurt upon a part for the health of the whole. Accordingly laws which apportion in due measure the burdens of responsibility are just, legitimate, and oblige at the bar of conscience.

Laws are unjust in two ways. They are contrary to human good on the three counts made above; from their end, when the ruler taxes his subjects rather for his own greed or vanity than the common benefit; from their author, when he enacts a law beyond the power committed to him; and from their form, when, although meant for the common good, laws are inequitably dispensed. These are outrages rather than laws; Augustine remarks: "There never seems to have been a law where justice was not present" (*On Free Choice of the Will* 1.5). Such commands do not oblige in the court of conscience, unless perhaps to avoid scandal or riot; on this account a man may be called to yield his rights, according to the text of Matthew (5:40f.): "If any one forces you to go one mile, go with him two miles, and if any one would sue you and take your coat, let him have your cloak as well."

348

Laws can be unjust because they are contrary to God's rights *(ad bonum divinum)*; such are the laws of tyrants which promote idolatry or whatsoever is against divine law. To observe them is in no wise permissible, for as is said in the Acts (5:29), "We must obey God rather than men."

96, 5 *Answers to Objections:* 3. A sovereign is described as being exempt from law with respect to its coercive power, for, to be precise, nobody is compelled by himself, and law has its restraining force only from the sovereign's power. That is why he is referred to as being exempt from the law, since no one can pass sentence condemning him if he breaks it. Accordingly on the words of the Psalm (51:4), "Against thee, thee only, have I sinned," a gloss says: "The king has no man to pronounce judgment on his deeds" (*Glossa Lombardi,* quoting Cassiodorus).

Yet of his own will a sovereign is subject to the directive power of the law, according to the *Decretals* (X 1.2.6): "Whoever establishes a law for another, the very same he should practise himself." And a wise authority says: "Be open yourself to the law you produce" (Ps.-Ausonius, *VII Sapientium Sententiae* 2.5). Our Lord reproaches those who do not practise what they preach, and who "lay heavy burdens on men's shoulders, but they themselves will not stir a little finger to move them" (Matt. 23:4).

Before God's judgment, then, the sovereign is not exempt from the law's directive power, and he ought to fulfil the law, freely not forcedly. Yet he is above the law in that he can change it if expedient, and grant dispensations from it adapted to place and season.

96, 6 *Reply:* As already stated, every law is ordained for the common well-being, and to that extent gets the force and quality of law; in so far as it falls short here it has no binding force. Hence the Jurist says, "No reason in law nor goodwill in equity brooks that we should put harsh interpretations on healthy measures brought in for men's welfare, and take them to a grimness that conflicts with the benefits they bring" (Dig. 1.3.25).

Now it often happens that it is advantageous to the common welfare for a measure to be observed in the majority of cases, while in some cases this is highly harmful.

Since he cannot envisage every individual case, the legislator frames a law to fit the majority of cases, his purpose being to serve the common welfare. So that if a case crops up where its observance would be damaging to that common interest, then it is not to be observed. Suppose a siege, then a decree that the city gates are to be kept closed is a useful general measure for the public safety. Yet say some citizens among the defenders are being pursued by the enemy, the cost would be heavy were the gates not to be opened to them. So opened they are to be, against the letter of the decree, in order to defend that very common safety the ruling authority had in view.

All the same notice this: if observing the letter of the law does not involve a sudden risk calling for instant decision and to be dealt with at once, it is not for anybody to construe the law and decide what is or what is not of service to the city. This is only for the governing authorities who, because of exceptional cases, have the power to grant dispensations from the laws. If, however, the danger is urgent, and admits of no delay, or time for recourse to higher authority, the very necessity carries a dispensation with it, for necessity knows no law.

Situations where judgment is needed re: application of laws

Answers to Objections: 1. He who acts counter to the letter of the law in case of need is not questioning the law itself, but judging the particular issue confronting him, where he sees that the letter of the law is not to be applied.

2. A man who follows the lawmaker's intention is not interpreting the law, simply speaking, as it stands, but setting it in its real situation; there, from the prospect of the damage that would follow, it is evident that the lawmaker would have him act otherwise. If he is in doubt then he should follow the letter and consult his superior.

3. Nobody is so wise as to be able to forecast every individual case, and accordingly he cannot put into words all the factors that fit the end he has in view. Even were the legislator able to take every event into consideration, he still should not set them all down in detail, for this would lead to muddle; but he should frame a law according to the usual run of things.

97, 2 *Reply:* The preceding discussion has shown that human law is rightly altered so far as this will provide for the common benefit. Now a change in the law, looked at merely as a change, inflicts a kind of loss on the common well-being, because custom avails much for the observance of law, so much so that breaches of common custom seem so much the graver on that account, though they be light matters otherwise. That is why when law is altered the restraining power of law is weakened in so far as custom is done away with. Hence a human law should never be altered, unless the gain to the common well-being on one head makes up for what has been lost on another.

Such compensation comes either from some highly important and evident gain produced by the new statute; or from the urgent necessity for change, either because of the manifest wrong the old customary law contained or because its observance was highly harmful. So it is said by the Jurist Ulpian, "In establishing new laws the benefit to be gained by departing from what for ages has been looked upon as equitable should be evident" (Dig. 1.4.2).

97, 3 *Reply:* All law proceeds from the reason and will of the lawgiver; divine and natural law from the intelligent will of God, human law from the will of man regulated by reason. Man's reason and will in matters of practice are manifested by what he says, and by what he does as well; each carries into execution what he has chosen because to him it seems good.

As manifesting interior concepts and motions of the human mind it is clear that words serve to alter a law as well as express its meaning. So also by repeated deeds, which set up a custom, a law can be changed and explained, and also a principle can be established which acquires the force of law, and this because what we inwardly mean and want is most effectively declared by what outwardly and repeatedly we do. When anything is done again and again it is assumed that it comes from the deliberate judgment of reason.

On these grounds custom has the force of law, and abolishes a law, and is the interpreter of laws.

Answers to Objections: 1. Divine and natural law proceed from the divine will, as we have said, and hence cannot be altered by custom proceeding from the will of man; change can come only by divine authority. Accordingly no custom can acquire

350

[handwritten: use or custom]

the force of law against divine or natural law. Isidore says, "Let usage bow to author-ity, and reason and law prevail over vicious habits" (*Synonyma* 2.80).

2. As we have observed, in some cases human laws do not meet a situation. Sometimes therefore it is possible to act beside the law, namely when the law fails to meet the case, and then the act will not be wrong. When such cases are multiplied because of changed human conditions, then custom is an index that a law is no lon-ger serviceable, as would be shown by the verbal promulgation of a law that super-seded it. If, however, the reason still holds good which made the law advantageous in the first place, then law prevails over custom, not custom over law. An exception would be a law that is useless because "not possible according to the customs of the country," which is one of the essential conditions of human law (Isidore, *Etymologies* 5.21 [cf. above, p. 211]). To set aside the customs of a whole people is impracticable.

3. A human group with its own customs can be in one of two conditions, self-governing or not. If it is a free country, where people are able to make their own laws, their common consensus about a particular observance, expressed in custom, is more important than the authority of the ruler, who has the power of making law only in so far as he represents the people; a whole people can make law, not a single individual. If, however, people are not free to make their own laws, or to put aside a law laid down for them by superior authority, then all the same a prevailing custom among them obtains the force of law when it is allowed by those whose office it is to make laws for them; by this very fact authority seems to approve what has been brought in by custom.

[handwritten margin: Consent implied by custom — laws conform to our way of life]

98, 5 *Reply:* The Old Law clearly set forth the obligations of the natural law, and over and above these added certain precepts of its own. It follows that, as far as the obligations of the natural law contained in the Old Law were concerned, all were bound to observe the Old Law. But this was not because these obligations came un-der the Old Law, but because they came under the natural law. But as far as the fur-ther clauses added on by the Old Law were concerned, no one was bound to observe the Old Law except the Jewish people alone.

[handwritten margin: cf. Old Law / natural law.]

The reason for this is that, as has been said, the Old Law was given to the Jew-ish people in order that they might attain to a certain pre-eminence in sanctity, and this was from the reverence due to Christ, who was to be descended from that peo-ple. Now statutes of any kind which are designed for the special sanctification of cer-tain people are binding upon those people alone. Thus, for instance, certain obser-vances are obligatory for clergy inasmuch as these are committed to the sacred ministry, which are not obligatory for laymen. Similarly certain works conducive to perfection are obligatory for religious in virtue of their vows, yet these are not oblig-atory for non-religious. And it is in the same way that certain special obligations were imposed on that people, which were not imposed upon other peoples. This is why we find it said, "You shall be perfect and without spot before the Lord your God." For the same reason also they used some form of public declaration, thus, "I profess before the Lord your God . . ." etc. (Deut. 18:13, 26:3).

99, 4 *Reply:* As has been said above [90.2-3], it is the function of divine law to regulate relationships between men, and the relationship of men to God. Now as a matter of general principle both of these relationships are subject to the dictates of natural law, to which the moral precepts relate. But both of them require to be applied in the concrete by a further law, either divine or human. The reason for this is that both in the speculative and practical spheres those principles which we are led to recognize by our very nature are universal. We have seen that the concrete application of the universal precept concerning divine worship is made by means of the ceremonial precepts. In the same way, therefore, the concrete application of the universal principle that justice must be observed among men is made by means of judicial precepts.

On this showing it is necessary to divide the precepts of the Old Law into three classes: the moral precepts, arising from the dictates of natural law, the ceremonial precepts, which are concrete applications of the principle of divine worship, and judicial precepts, which are concrete applications of the principle that justice has to be observed among men. This is why when St. Paul has said that "the law is holy" he goes on to say that "the commandment is just, and holy and good" (Rom. 7:12): just in the judicial precepts which it contains, holy in the ceremonial ones (for that which is consecrated to God is said to be holy), good, that is conducive to virtue, in its moral precepts.

100, 8 *Answers to Objections:* 3. The decalogue forbids the taking of human life in so far as it is undue; in this the precept embodies the very nature of justice. Nor can human law permit that a man be lawfully killed when he does not deserve it. But it is no infringement of justice to put to death criminals or the state's enemies. This does not contravene the commandment; nor is it the homicide which is forbidden, as Augustine says. Likewise, when someone is deprived of what belongs to him, if he deserves to lose it, this is not the theft or robbery which is forbidden by the commandment.

Therefore when the children of Israel, by God's command, took the spoils of the Egyptians, it was not theft, because these were due to them by the sentence of God. Likewise Abraham, in consenting to kill his son, did not consent to homicide, since it was right that his son should be put to death by the command of God, the Lord of life and death. For it is God who inflicts the punishment of death on all men, just as well as unjust, on account of the sin of our first parent; and if man carries out this sentence on the authority of God, he is no murderer any more than God is. In the same way, Hosea, in taking to wife a harlot or adulteress, was not guilty of adultery or fornication, since she was his by the command of God, the author of the institution of marriage.

Accordingly, the precepts of the decalogue are immutable in so far as they embody justice in its essence; but as applied to particular acts — as, for example, whether they constitute homicide, theft or adultery or not — they admit of change. Such change may be effected by divine authority alone, when it concerns what God alone has instituted, as marriage and the like, or else by human authority as to what has been entrusted to human jurisdiction. In these matters, though not in all, men act in the place of God.

104, 3 *Reply:* The judicial precepts were not binding for ever, but were made void by the coming of Christ, though not in the same way as the ceremonial precepts. These became not only *dead*, but also *deadly* to those who should keep them after Christ had come, and particularly after the promulgation of the Gospel. The judicial precepts, on the other hand, are dead, since they have no binding force, but not deadly. For should any ruler order their observance in his territory, he would not be committing a sin, unless they were observed, or ordered to be observed, as binding through enactment in the Old Law. To keep them on that ground would be mortally sinful.

The reason for this difference can be inferred from what has been said [104.2], namely that the ceremonial precepts were figurative primarily and in themselves, being instituted principally as figuring the mysteries of Christ yet to come. Consequently, their observance would militate against the truth of faith, in which we profess that those mysteries are now fulfilled. But the judicial precepts were not instituted as figuring, but as ordering the state of that people, which was directed to Christ. Therefore, with the coming of Christ and the change in their state, the judicial precepts lost their force; for the Law was a *pedagogue* leading men to Christ. Since, however, the judicial precepts were ordained not to prefigure, but to bring about certain things, their observance in itself does not militate against the truth of faith; but the intention to keep them as binding by the Law would be contrary to the truth of faith, since it would imply that the former state still existed and that Christ had not yet come.

105, 1 *Reply:* There are two things to be observed concerning the right ordering of rulers in a state or people. One is that all should have some share in government; this makes for peace among the people, and commends itself to all, and they uphold it, as Aristotle says. The other regards the kind of government, or how the rulers are instituted. There are various kinds of regimen, as he also points out, but the principal ones are monarchy, in which one man rules as specially qualified, and aristocracy, that is the rule of the best, in which a few rule as specially qualified. Hence the best system in any state or kingdom is one in which one man, as specially qualified, rules over all, and under him are others governing as having special endowments, yet all have a share inasmuch as those are elected from all, and also are elected by all. This is the best form of constitution, a mixture of monarchy, in that one man is at the head, of aristocracy, in that many rule as specially qualified, and democracy, in that the rulers can be chosen from the people and by them.

This was the form established by divine law. Moses and his successors governed the people as one man over all, which was a kind of monarchy. Seventy-two elders were chosen for their fitness; for we read, "I took out of your tribes men wise and honourable, and appointed them rulers" (Deut. 1:15) — an element of aristocracy; and it was democratic in that they were chosen from all the people, since we read, "Provide out of all the people wise men," etc. (Exod. 18:21), and also because the people chose them, as we read, "Let me have from among you wise men" (Deut. 1:13). Thus it is clear that the Law established the best system of government.

Answers to Objections: 2. Monarchy is the best form of government, provided it has not become corrupted; but with so much power in the hands of a king it easily degenerates into tyranny, unless he be a man of solid virtue, for, as Aristotle says, only the virtuous can behave aright in prosperity (*NE* 1124a30). Real virtue, however, is to be found in few men; and the Jews were particularly liable to avarice, which is the most potent inducement to tyranny. For this reason the Lord did not at first give them a king with full power, but judges and protectors. Only later, on their petition, did he allow them a king, somewhat angrily, as is clear from what he said to Samuel: "They have not rejected thee, but me, that I should not reign over them" (1 Sam. 8:7).

He did, however, from the very beginning, make certain provisions regarding the king, and, in the first place, the mode of election. As to this, he made two conditions: that they should wait for the Lord's judgment, and that they should not make king someone of another people, since such kings have usually little liking for the people over whom they are placed, and so are unconcerned for their welfare. In the second place, he prescribed for the kings their mode of life: they were not to have a number of chariots and horses, or wives, or immense wealth, since the desire for these leads rulers to become tyrants and abandon justice. He also prescribed their conduct towards God: they should continually read and meditate on the law of God, and ever fear and obey him. He laid down, in addition, how they should behave to their subjects, not despising them out of pride, or oppressing them, or departing from justice.

Translations: Thomas Gilby, O.P. (London, 1966), 90-97; David Bourke and Arthur Littledale (London, 1969), 98-105. Used with permission.

From *Summa Theologiae* 2a2ae.23-46 (On Charity)

40, 1 *Reply:* For a war to be just three conditions are necessary. First, the authority of the ruler within whose competence it lies to declare war. A private individual may not declare war; for he can have recourse to the judgement of a superior to safeguard his rights. Nor has he the right to mobilize the people, which is necessary in war. But since responsibility for public affairs is entrusted to the rulers, it is they who are charged with the defence of the city, realm, or province, subject to them. And just as in the punishment of criminals they rightly defend the state against all internal disturbance with the civil arm; as the Apostle says (Rom. 13:4): "He beareth not the sword in vain. For he is God's minister: an avenger to execute wrath upon him that doth evil." So also they have the duty of defending the state with the weapons of war against external enemies. For this reason rulers are told in Psalm 82:4 to "Rescue the poor; and deliver the needy out of the hand of the sinner." And St. Augustine says in his book, *Contra Faustum* (23.73): "The natural order of men, to be peacefully disposed, requires that the power and decision to declare war should lie with the rulers."

Secondly, there is required a just cause: that is that those who are attacked for some offence merit such treatment. St. Augustine says (*Quaestiones in Heptateuch* 6.10): "Those wars are generally defined as just which avenge some wrong, when a nation or a state is to be punished for having failed to make amends for the wrong done, or to restore what has been taken unjustly."

Thirdly, there is required a right intention on the part of the belligerents: either of some achieving some good object or of avoiding some evil. So St. Augustine says in the book *De verbis Domini* [wrongly attributed; the text known from Gratian, D. 2.23.1]: "For the true followers of God even wars are peaceful, not being made for greed or out of cruelty, but from desire of peace, to restrain the evil and assist the good." So it can happen that even when war is declared by legitimate authority and there is just cause, it is, nevertheless, made unjust through evil intention. St. Augustine says in *Contra Faustum* (22.74): "The desire to hurt, the cruelty of vendetta, the stern and implacable spirit, arrogance in victory, the thirst for power, and all that is similar, all these are justly condemned in war."

Translation: J. G. Dawson (Oxford, 1959). Used with permission.

From *Summa Theologiae* 2a2ae.57-122 (On Justice)

57, 1 *Reply:* The proper characteristic of justice, as compared with the other moral virtues, is to govern a man in his dealings towards others. It implies a certain balance of equality, as its very name shows, for in common speech things are said to be adjusted when they match evenly. Equality is relative to another. The other moral virtues, however, compose a man for activities which befit him considered in himself. So then that which is correct in their working and which is the proper object of their bent is not thought of save in relation to the doer. Whereas with justice, in addition to this, that which is correct is constituted by a relation to another, for a work of ours is said to be just when it meets another on the level, as with the payment of a fair wage for a service rendered.

So then something is said to be just because it has the rightness of justice; it is this that engages the activity of justice, even abstracting from the temper in which it is done; by contrast, the rightness of the other moral virtues is not determined apart from the frame of mind of the person acting. This is why for justice especially, in comparison with other virtues, an impersonal objective interest is fixed. We call it *the just thing,* and this indeed is a right. Clearly, then, right is the objective interest of justice.

57, 3 *Question:* Is the *ius gentium* the same as natural right?

1. So it would seem. For all men do not agree save in that which is natural to them. Now all agree on the *ius gentium,* for a jurist observes that it is adopted by all nations (Dig. 1.1.1). Therefore it is natural right.

2. Further, among men servitude is natural; according to Aristotle some are congenital slaves (*Politics* 1254a15). But servitude is part of the *jus gentium,* as Isidore notes (*Etymologies* 5.6 [cf. above, p. 210]). Therefore it is natural right.

3. Moreover, we have agreed on the division between natural and positive right [57.2]. Now the *jus gentium* is not positive right, for the nations have never come together to lay down anything by common agreement. So then the *jus gentium* is natural right.

On the other hand, there is the teaching of Isidore, "Right is either natural or civil or the *ius gentium*" (*ibid.*)

Reply: We have said that natural right or the naturally just is that which of it-self is adequate to and commensurate with another [57.2]. There are two ways of arriving at this. First, by looking at it purely and simply in itself, thus it is of the bi-ology of male to mate with female in order to generate from her and of parents to respond to their young in order to rear them. Second, by looking at the natural matching of one with another, not absolutely or in the abstract, but as involving a consequence. Take the ownership of property; considered in itself there is no rea-son why this field should belong to this man rather than to that man, but when you take into account its being put under cultivation and farmed without strife, then, as Aristotle makes clear (*Politics* 1263a21), it tallies with being owned by this not that individual.

Now to perceive a fact simply as such and apart from its implications is not only for men but for other animals as well. And so the right which is called natural in the first sense is common to us and to other animals. The *ius gentium*, says a jurisconsult, departs from such natural right, "in which all animals share, for only men share in it among themselves" (Dig. 1.1.1). Yet to consider something by con-necting it with its consequences is proper to reason. Hence to prescribe something accordingly is natural to man by his native reason. Accordingly the jurisconsult Ga-ius says, That which natural reason constitutes between all men and is observed by all people is called the *ius gentium (ibid.)*. Hence:

Answers to the Objections: 1. The reply to the first objection is clear.

2. From the bare nature of the case there is no reason for this man rather than that man being a slave. It is only when it is looked at pragmatically in its results that, as Aristotle says, it is expedient for him to be ruled by a wiser whom he serves. Servi-tude, which is part of the *ius gentium*, is natural then in the second sense of our ex-planation, not the first.

3. Matters of the *ius gentium* are dictated by natural reason as being closely bound up with equity. And so they call for no special enactment, for, according to the authority cited, natural reason provides them.

61, 3 *Reply:* We have said that justice is engaged with certain external activities concerning distributions and exchanges [58.8, 10]. These consist in the application or use of what is outside us, whether things or persons or works we do. Things, as when we take from or restore to another his property; persons, as when we strike or insult another or, alternatively, treat him with respect; works, as when we justly claim an-other's labour or do a job for him. Now if we take as subject-matter what each kind of justice employs, then there is no difference between them, for things of the same sort can be apportioned out of the common stock and be also exchanged between individ-uals, and likewise hard work can be a matter both of allotment by the community and also of repayment according to private contract. If, however, in the subject-matter of the two kinds of justice we stress the dominant for each in dealing with persons, using things, and performing works, then there is a difference on either side. For distributive justice governs the apportioning of community goods, whereas commutative governs the exchanging that may take place between two persons.

Of these exchanges some are involuntary, some voluntary. They are involun-tary when somebody employs another's thing, person, or work without his consent.

This may be done secretly by deceit or openly by violence. In either way injury may be committed against another's property or person or against the person of one close to him. Against his property: if taken secretly it is called theft, if openly it is called robbery. Against his person, if his life and health be attacked, and also his good-name and dignity: the first may be done secretly, as when he is treacherously slain, struck, or poisoned, or openly, as when he is publicly executed, struck, maimed, or sent to prison. His dignity is injured secretly by false witness, detraction, and the like, whereby he is robbed of his good name; it is done openly by accusation in a court of law or public insult. Against the person of a connection of his, as when he is injured by adultery with his wife, which is usually secret, or by the enticement of a servant; it can also be done openly. Whatever injury may be done to the principal victim under the headings outlined above may also be done to persons connected with him. Yet adultery and enticement are injuries properly against him, and the latter, since a servant in a sense is his belonging, comes back to theft.

Exchanges are called voluntary when a person willingly transfers something he owns to another. If he simply passes it to another in such wise that the recipient incurs no strict debt, as when he makes a gift, this is an act of liberality, not of justice. A voluntary transfer comes under justice in so far as it involves the notion of something due. This can enter in several ways. First, when somebody simply transfers what is his in payment for something else, as happens in buying and selling. Second, when somebody transfers a thing he owns that another may have the use of it with the obligation of returning it later: if the use is granted without charge, then for things that bear fruit it is called usufruct, and for things that do not, such as cash, crockery, and so forth, it is called borrowing or lending. If there is a charge on the use, it is called renting or hiring. Third, when somebody hands over his property for safekeeping, not for use, and means to recover it, as with a deposit, or because of an obligation, as when he pledges a piece of property or stands surety for another.

In all dealings of this sort, whether involuntary or voluntary, the just mean is taken in the same sense according to a balance or equality in requital. Accordingly they all come under the same species of justice, namely commutative justice.

Hence: The reply to the objections is clear.

61, 4 *Reply:* The term *contrapassum* [from Aristotle, *NE* 1132b23, *to antipeponthos*] literally "counter-suffered," spells an exact concordance of a reaction with the antecedent action. Such a tit-for-tat most properly applies when injury is undergone caused by a man harming the person of his neighbour: for instance if he strike him let him be struck in return. The Old Law determines such a just requital: "if any harm follows, you shall give life for life, eye for eye, tooth for tooth" (Exod. 21:23), and so forth. In the second place, because to take from another his property is a thing unjust, the notion of retaliation also applies there, so that one who inflicts loss on another should also suffer loss in his belongings. This, too, is contained in the Old Law (Exod. 22:1): "if a man steals an ox or a sheep, and kills it or sells it, he shall pay five oxen for an ox, and four sheep for a sheep." Finally, the notion is extended to voluntary exchanges, where there is something done and undergone on either side. Remember, however, that the passive character of undergoing something is lessened by its voluntariness. In all such cases the nature of commutative justice demands that equivalent recompense be made, namely that the reaction as repayment matches the action.

This would not always be the case were the doer to undergo the same in kind to that which he caused. Take the case, to begin with, of a subordinate who injures his superior; his action is more serious than a like action done on him in return. And so he who strikes a ruler is not only struck back, but also much more severely punished. Then take the case of one who unjustly takes another's property without the owner's consent; his action would exceed his undergoing the consequences, were only that property to be taken away from him, for he who inflicted loss on another would suffer no loss of property in return. In consequence he is punished by a fine heavier than the simple disgorgement of his gain, for he did an injury, not only to a private person, but also to the commonwealth by breaking the security which is in its charge. So too neither in voluntary exchanges is requital always the give and return of things of the same sort, for sometimes they are unequal. Consequently, in exchanges the equalization of what is done and what is undergone in return requires a certain proportionate standard of measurement: for this purpose was money invented. It is in this sense that a *quid pro quo* is what is right and just for commutative justice.

Note, however, that in distributive justice such reciprocity has no place, for the equalization is not taken there according to the proportion of thing to thing, or of doing an action to undergoing the reaction (whence the term *contrapassum*), but according to the proportionality of things to persons, as already explained.

66, 2 Reply: Man has a twofold competence in relation to material things. The first is the title to care for and distribute the earth's resources. Understood in this way, it is not merely legitimate for a man to possess things as his own, it is even necessary for human life, and this for three reasons. First, because each person takes more trouble to care for something that is his sole responsibility than what is held in common or by many — for in such a case each individual shirks the work and leaves the responsibility to somebody else, which is what happens when too many officials are involved. Second, because human affairs are more efficiently organized if each person has his own responsibility to discharge; there would be chaos if everybody cared for everything. Third, because men live together in greater peace where everyone is content with his task. We do, in fact, notice that quarrels often break out amongst men who hold things in common without distinction.

Man's other competence is to use and manage the world's resources. Now in regard to this, no man is entitled to manage things merely for himself, he must do so in the interests of all, so that he is ready to share them with others in case of necessity. This is why Paul writes to Timothy (1 Tim. 6:17f.): "As for the rich of this world, charge them to be liberal and generous."

Answers to Objections 1. Community of goods is said to be part of the natural law not because it requires everything to be held in common and nothing to be appropriated to individual possession, but because the distribution of property is a matter not for natural law but, rather, human agreement, which is what positive law is about, as we saw above. The individual holding of possessions is not, therefore, contrary to the natural law; it is what rational beings conclude as an addition to the natural law.

66, 7 *Reply:* The dictates of human law cannot derogate from natural or divine law. The natural order established by God in his providence is, however, such that lower things are meant to enable man to supply his needs. A man's needs must therefore still be met out of the world's goods even though a certain division and apportionment of them is determined by law. And this is why according to natural law goods that are held in superabundance by some people should be used for the maintenance of the poor. This is the principle enunciated by Ambrose [actually Basil of Caesarea] and repeated in the *Decretum* (D. 1.47.8 [where it is misattributed to Ambrose]): "It is the bread of the poor which you are holding back; it is the clothes of the naked which you are hoarding; it is the relief and liberation of the wretched which you are thwarting by burying your money away." At the same time those who suffer want are so numerous and they cannot all be supplied out of one stock, and this is why it is left to each individual to decide how to manage his property in such a way as to supply the wants of the suffering. If, however, there is so urgent and blatant a necessity that the immediate needs must be met out of whatever is available, as when a person is in imminent danger and he cannot be helped in any other way, then a person may legitimately supply his own needs out of another's property, whether he does so secretly or flagrantly. And in such a case there is strictly speaking no theft or robbery.

charity derived fr. natural law

77, 1 *Reply:* To practise fraud so as to sell something for more than its just price is an outright sin in so far as one is deceiving one's neighbour to his detriment. This is why Cicero declares (*De officiis* 3.15): "Contracts are to be free of lies: the seller is not to plant a sham-bidder or the buyer somebody who undercuts the sale price."

Granted, however, that there is no fraud, there are two ways of looking at a contract of sale. If we look at it first of all as it is in itself, we can say that such a transaction was introduced for the common benefit of both parties, in so far as each one needs something which the other has, as Aristotle explains (*Politics* 1257a6). But what is equally useful to both should not involve more of a burden for one than for the other and any contract between two parties should, therefore, be based on an equality of material exchange. But the value of consumer products is measured by the price given, which as Aristotle pointed out (*NE* 1133a19), is what coinage was invented for. It follows that the balance of justice is upset if either the price exceeds the value of the goods in question or the thing exceeds the price. To sell for more or to buy for less than a thing is worth is, therefore, unjust and illicit in itself.

The other way in which we can look at a contract of sale is in so far as it happens to bring benefit to one party at the expense of the other, as in the case where one badly needs to get hold of something and the other is put out by not having it. In such a case the estimation of the just price will have to take into account not merely the commodity to be sold but also the loss which the seller incurs in selling it. The commodity can here be sold for more than it is worth in itself, though not for more than it is worth to the possessor.

If, on the other hand, a buyer derives great benefit from a transaction without the seller suffering any loss as a result of relinquishing his property, then the latter is not entitled to charge more. This is because the surplus value that accrues to the other is due not to the seller but to the buyer's situation: nobody is entitled to sell another what is not his own though he is justified in charging for any loss he may suffer. All of this is not, of course, to deny that somebody who has benefited greatly from a transaction might spontaneously offer more than the due price; this is a matter of his honourable feeling.

divine vs-
human
law

Answers to Objections: 1. Human law, as we have already seen [1a2ae.90.2; 96.1-3], is made for the people as a whole, which includes many who fall short of being virtuous, and not merely for the virtuous. Human law cannot, therefore, prohibit whatever is contrary to virtue; it is enough for it to prohibit whatever destroys social intercourse, allowing everything else to be permissible, not in the sense of approving it, but of not attaching a penalty to it. It is in this sense, i.e. of withholding punishment, that the law holds it to be permissible for a seller to over-charge and for a buyer to under-pay, unless there is either fraud or a gross disparity; in such a case even human law compels restitution, as, for instance, in the case where somebody is tricked into paying or losing more than fifty percent of the just price. Divine law, on the other hand, leaves nothing contrary to virtue unpunished, so that any failure to keep a due balance in contracts of sale is counted to be contrary to divine law. He who profits is, therefore, bound to make restitution to the party who loses out, provided the loss is an important one. And I use this latter term advisedly, because we cannot always fix the just price precisely; we sometimes have to make the best estimate we can, with the result that giving or taking a little here or there does not upset the balance of justice.

77, 4 *Reply:* What men are in business for is the making of exchanges. But, as Aristotle points out (*Politics* 1253b13, 1256b40), there are two sorts of exchange. The first sort is as it were natural and necessary, and consists in the exchange of commodity for commodity or of commodity for money, for the maintenance of life. And such exchanges are the affair, not strictly of businessmen, but of heads of families or governments, who have to provide the necessities of life for their households or peoples. The other sort of exchange is of money for money, or even of any commodity for money, though now for the sake of making a profit, and this is the sort of exchange that belongs to business men in the strict sense. According to Aristotle (*Politics* 1258a38), the former sort of exchange is praiseworthy because it supplies natural needs, whereas the second sort is rightly open to criticism since, just in itself, it feeds the acquisitive urge which knows no limit but tends to increase to infinity. It follows that commerce as such, considered in itself, has something shameful about it in so far as it is not intrinsically calculated to fulfil right or necessary requirements.

Nevertheless, profit, which is the point of commerce, while it may not carry the notion of anything right or necessary, does not carry the notion of anything vicious or contrary to virtue either. There is, therefore, nothing to stop profit being subordinated to an activity that is necessary, or even right. And this is the way in which commerce can become justifiable. This is exemplified by the man who uses moderate business profits to provide for his household, or to help the poor; or even by the man who conducts his business for the public good in order to ensure that the country does not run short of essential supplies, and who makes a profit, as it were, to compensate for his work and not for its own sake.

usury

78, 1 *Reply:* Making a charge for lending money is ~~unjust~~ in itself, for one party sells the other something non-existent, and this obviously sets up an inequality which is contrary to justice. To understand this, one has to realize that there are some things the use of which consists in their being consumed, in the way in which we consume wine by using it for drinking and consume corn by using it for eating. We should not, therefore, reckon the use of such things apart from the things themselves. For, instead, when we grant to someone the use, by that very fact we grant also the thing, and for this reason to lend things of this kind is to transfer the ownership, so that somebody who wanted to sell wine and the use of wine separately would be selling the same thing twice over or be selling something non-existent. And this would obviously be to commit the sin of injustice. By the same token, however, somebody commits an injustice if he lends corn or wine and asks for a twofold recompense — not merely the restoration of some equivalent but also a charge for its use, which is what usury strictly is.

rent

There are, however, other things the use of which does not consist in their being consumed, so that, for instance, the use of a house is its being lived in, not its being used up. It follows that in such cases the two aspects can be dealt with separately, as in the case where somebody transfers the ownership of a house to another whilst reserving the use of it to himself for a stated time, or where, on the contrary, somebody allows another to use the house but retains the ownership for himself. And this is the reason why one is fully entitled to make a charge for the use of a house and then to ask for its return in due course, as in the case of renting and letting.

Now money, however, according to Aristotle (*NE* 1133a20, *Politics* 1257a35), was invented chiefly for exchanges to be made, so that the prime and proper use of money is its use and disbursement in the way of ordinary transactions. It follows that it is in principle wrong to make a charge for money lent, which is what usury consists in. Similarly a man is just as much bound to restore money earned in this way as he is to make restitution for any other ill-gotten gains.

Translation: Thomas Gilby, O.P. (London, 1975), 57-62; Maurice Lefébure, O.P. (London, 1975), 63-79. Used with permission.

Giles of Rome
(ca. 1243-1316)

Giles, or Aegidius, of Rome, traditionally thought to belong to the powerful Colonna family, enjoyed a "lengthy, distinguished and colourful career . . . as theologian, diplomat, confidant of popes and kings, as well as head of his religious order and prelate" (Monahan 1990, x). Educated in philosophy and theology at the University of Paris, he became its first Augustinian master of theology in 1285, vicar-general of his order in 1292, and archbishop of Bourges in 1295.

After gaining renown for an Aristotelian treatise on princely rule, *De regimine principum* (1285), dedicated to the young Philip IV, Giles turned to a career as frontline papal apologist, publishing in 1292 a defense of Pope Celestine V's resignation intended to vindicate the election of his successor, Boniface VIII *(De renunciatione papali)*. Almost a decade later came *On Ecclesiastical Power (De ecclesiastica potestate)*, his apology for extreme papal hierocracy, to arm Boniface in his quarrels with the French king.

When surveyed together, John of Paris's *On Royal and Papal Power* and Giles's *On Ecclesiastical Power* appear to be mutual refutations. Although the issue of literary dependence is not yet resolved, it is probable that the treatises were written concurrently in 1301. While both are impressive compendiums of current arguments for their rival viewpoints, Giles's work has the more oppressive spiritual and intellectual feel, owing partly to its inordinate repetition and partly to its lack of the arresting tensions and complexities characteristic of imperialist theory. It exhibits no tension between concepts of power "from above" and "from below," power exercised publicly in "jurisdiction" and privately in "ownership," or between the overlapping claims and concerns of spiritual and temporal authorities undergirded by the diverse requirements of divine and human laws. By means of a synthesis of Neoplatonic realism and political Christocentrism, Giles portrays the *corpus Christianum* as a seamless spiritual and temporal garment: at once a universal, indivisible, mystical communion and an earthly hierarchy of law and power. The divine-human person of Christ is its essence, the celestial head which imparts to the body its unity of being, order, and action, while the pope terrestrially mediates the christological emanation of power and structure to all lesser ranks of agents and authorities. Like the cosmos, Christendom admits no rivalry of parallel orders and powers, but only strict subordination and superordination.

At the heart of Giles's political cosmology is "the two swords" hierarchy. All his arguments and proofs from nature, Scripture, canon law, and universal history aim to demonstrate the pope's supreme jurisdiction *(plenitudo potestatis)* over persons and material things, and conversely, the subjection of temporal rule in origin, purpose, and practice. This twofold demonstration of papal plenitude and royal subjection was a counterattack on the French king for his assault on papal jurisdiction and on ecclesiastical privileges and property in his kingdom. Both attack and counterattack appropriated the tradition of Roman *imperium*. On the one hand, Philip the Fair and his more extreme apologists tried to prove the civil law dictum that "the king is emperor in his own kingdom," demonstrating his sole and supreme possession of coercive legal jurisdiction, and deriving the royal plenitude directly from God and the people. On the other hand, the papalists defended their master's overlordship of the *imperium Christi*, of which the *imperium Romanorum* was the temporal face, asserting his jurisdictional supremacy over rulers as well as their subjects. While the history of the fourteenth century shows Boniface VIII and his publicists to be clear losers in the ideological and political struggles, the papalist literature remains of abiding interest as the fullest elaboration of Roman hierocratic theory.

Although haphazardly organized, *On Ecclesiastical Power* is loosely divided into three parts: (1) a general explication of papal supremacy that comes to focus on the "two swords" paradigm; (2) an argument wedding papal jurisdictional supremacy to universal proprietorship of temporal goods; and (3) a more detailed elaboration of the nature and occasions for papal exercise of *dominium* over temporalities.

Illustrative of Giles's method is his juxtaposition in 1.4 of a biblical, historical, and cosmological proof of supreme papal monarchy. He begins with the well-worn papalist interpretation of Jeremiah 1:10 ("Behold I have constituted thee . . .") as a prophecy of the church's power to establish, judge, remove, and transfer political rule. As an historical confirmation, he invokes the papal transfer of the empire from the East to the West (the coronation of Charlemagne in 800). He subsequently appeals to the Pseudo-Dionysian cosmological principle that "the order of the universe . . . requires the lowest things to be brought to the highest through an intermediary," which, transposed to the political order, requires the earthly spiritual authority to mediate between the inferior temporal and the divine authorities.

In the style of Honorius Augustodunensis, Giles mines the Old Testament for proofs of his contention that all divinely sanctioned kingship is either attached to or established by and subject to the priesthood. He argues that its historical record shows either the temporal rule of priests themselves — including Adam, Abel, Noah, Melchizedek, and Moses, who offered sacrifices (1.5) — or the temporal rule of judges and kings established and superintended by the priesthood, including, e.g., the judges of Deuteronomy 17:9, who resolved difficult cases by appeal to the Levitical priests, and the king of Deuteronomy 17:15-19, established on his throne by receiving from the priesthood a copy of the divine law, implying that royal commands follow priestly advice and the laws of the church (1.8).

In part 2 his wedding of the pope's jurisdictional supremacy with universal proprietorship brings to the fore metaphysical-cosmological reflections on the relationship between universal and particular causality. A universal cause, he explains, acts both *efficiently* in controlling lesser agencies to produce particular effects, and *teleologically* as the end served by more particular causal action. Accordingly, the church, as the agency of universal spiritual salvation, establishes and regulates the temporal exercise of justice, the end of which — the peaceable "sufficiency of corporeal life" — serves the work of salvation by assisting "the faithful in peace of conscience and . . . tranquillity of mind" (2.6). Likewise the church, as the agency of Christ's universal possession of earthly goods, establishes and regulates the exercise of hereditary dominion over property, assisting the title afforded by birth with the title afforded by rebirth, so that the just possession of property serves the salvation of the soul (2.7). In regard to both temporal jurisdiction and proprietorship, the church's universal agency is indispensable to particular agency, such that without it only factual (de facto) but no true or right (de jure) jurisdiction or possession is possible (2.8, 10). The implication is that "nonbelievers" or "infidels" hold usurped, unjust, and unlawful dominion (2.10; 3.2).

The church's universal agency resides supremely in her earthly head, the vicar of Christ, who is the vehicle of divine judgments about the worthiness or unworthiness of individuals for dominion. Indeed, even judgments about justice rendered by temporal magistrates are authorized by papal authority, just as all temporal laws "take their force" from papal law (2.10). In part 3 Giles portrays the papal plenitude as resembling God's government of his creation: "God's vicar governs, waters and suffuses the whole Church according to a common law" (3.2), conducting himself toward temporalities as God does toward "the world of visible natural things," by "allowing material things to follow their own courses and material swords to exercise their own judgments" without ordinary intervention. However, as God is always approachable in "spiritual matters," hearing and responding to the appeals of the faithful, so the pope is "the ordinary judge" to whom every Christian may legally appeal (3.3).

Although, like God, the pope chooses for the most part to exercise lawful jurisdiction over temporalities, permitting lesser powers to function, he nevertheless, like God, possesses "absolute power" over them, and may on occasion exercise "immediate and executive" jurisdiction himself (3.7), doing without the secondary causes (3.9). In regard, for instance, to episcopal election, besides establishing the procedure to be followed by the electing canons and confirming their choice, he may also "for a reasonable cause" dispense with the secondary agent, making provision for the diocese himself (3.9). In regard to temporalities, the pope regularly intervenes in certain matters, e.g., tithes, marital dowries, and inheritances, by virtue of his "higher and primary jurisdiction," and their "spiritual" character or relationships. Occasionally he assumes "direct and executive" jurisdiction over issues "involving an accusation of crime" or "mortal sin" (3.5), including disputes among rulers that threaten to disrupt, or have disrupted, peace within Christendom, especially peace secured by treaties (3.6). Finally, the pope's legal hegemony renders him the appeal judge in all cases that prove difficult of settlement (3.8).

Further Reading: R. Kuiters, "Aegidius Romanus and the Authorship of *In Utramque Partem* and *De Ecclesiastica Potestate*," *Augustiniana* 8 (1958): 267-80; A. P. Monahan, *Aegidius of Rome, "On Ecclesiastical Power"* (Lampeter: Edwin Mellen Press, 1990); E. A. Moody, "Ockham and Aegidius of Rome," *Franciscan Studies* 9 (1949): 417-42; W. Ullmann, "Boniface VIII and His Contemporary Scholarship," *Journal of Theological Studies* 27 (1976): 58-87; M. Wilks, *The Problem of Sovereignty in the Later Middle Ages: The Papal Monarchy with Augustinus Triumphus and the Publicists* (Cambridge: Cambridge University Press, 1963).

From *On Ecclesiastical Power,* Part 1

4. Hugh of Saint Victor, in the Second Book of the *De sacramentis fidei christianae* (2.2.4) says that the spiritual power must both institute the earthly power and judge it if it is not good. Thus, that prophecy of Jeremiah is shown to be true of the Church and of ecclesiastical power: "Behold, I have today placed you above nations and kingdoms, to uproot and destroy and disperse and scatter, to build and to plant" (Jer. 1:10). That prophecy was brought to fulfilment in Jeremiah himself whenever he prophesied the destruction and building-up of any kingdoms. For, through the spirit of prophecy, he was placed above kingdoms: to build, as regards the kingdoms for which he prophesied building; and to destroy, as regards the kingdoms for which he prophesied destruction. Today, however, that prophecy is fulfilled in the Church herself, as though the Lord had said to the Church: "Behold, today," that is, from the day upon which you were made, "I have placed you above nations and kingdoms, to destroy and uproot by transferring them from their place, and to build and to plant by building and planting those same kingdoms in another place." For this has indeed already been accomplished; for the Supreme Pontiff has transferred the Empire from the East to the West, as is recorded in the wisdom of the law (X.1.6.34).

The established facts, then, agree with the authority of learned men. For, as Hugh has made clear, the spiritual power must institute the earthly power and must judge whether it be good, which would not be so unless it could plant and uproot it. It can indeed plant it, inasmuch as it institutes it, and it certainly uproots inasmuch as it judges whether it be good. [. . .]

5. There can be no doubt amongst wise men that priestly power precedes royal and earthly power in dignity and nobility. We can show this in four ways: first, from the payment of tithes; second, from blessing and sanctification; third, from the inception of power itself; fourth, from the government of things themselves.

The first way proceeds as follows. By divine law and by divine institution, we are all bound to pay tithes; and so every earthly power, since it is earthly and temporal, is bound to pay tithes to the spiritual power. And such tithes are paid in recognition of due servitude, as each man acknowledges himself to be the servant of God.

Therefore, just as inferiors are tributaries to their superiors, so that they may acknowledge themselves to hold and possess what they have from their superiors, so also have we received from God what we hold and possess, according to 1 Corinthians (4:7): "What have you that you have not received?" It is fitting, therefore, that we be tributaries to God himself for all our possessions. For, as is written elsewhere, God himself is rich in himself, but others are rich from loans; for God has lent us whatever we have. And so it is neither strange nor beyond reason if on this account we should be taxpayers and tributaries to God himself.

Earthly and temporal power, then, inasmuch as it is earthly (that is, inasmuch as it receives the fruits of the earth), and inasmuch as it is temporal (that is, inasmuch as it possesses temporal goods) is a tributary and taxpayer to the ecclesiastical power, to which, acknowledging that it stands in the place of God, it is bound to pay tithes in recognition of its own servitude. Every earthly power, therefore, is under the ecclesiastical power, and especially under the supreme pontiff, who in the ecclesiastical hierarchy has attained to the summit of the church, and under whom all men — kings, as excelling, and all others — must be subject.

The second way towards the same conclusion is derived from blessing and sanctification; and this is Hugh's way in the *De sacramentis,* where he says that, in the church of God, the priestly dignity consecrates and blesses royal power. "Therefore, if 'he who blesses is the greater and he who is blessed is the less,'" as the Apostle says in Hebrews (7:7), "then it is established beyond all doubt that the earthly power, which receives blessing from the spiritual, is rightly deemed inferior."

The third way is derived from the institution of power itself. And in the same book and in the same part Hugh touches upon this way also, saying: "Moreover, that the spiritual power is greater in dignity and sight than the earthly is manifestly shown amongst that ancient people of the Old Testament, where first the priesthood was instituted by God and, subsequently, royal power was ordained through the priesthood at the command of God." Royal power, therefore, must acknowledge the priestly dignity as superior: as that through which it was instituted at the command of God. And if it be said that not all royal power was instituted through the priesthood, we shall reply that any royal power not instituted through the priesthood was either not rightful, in that it was more robbery than power; or was united with the priesthood; or was the successor of that which had been instituted through the priesthood. For where, under the law of nature, there were kingdoms of the gentiles, almost all such kingdoms came into being through invasion and usurpation. Thus Nimrod, of whom we read that he was the first king, whose reign began in Babylon (as can be gathered from Genesis 10:8-12), made himself a king by invasion and usurpation; and so it is said of him in the same place that he began to be mighty on earth: he acquired his kingdom through civil might and not through justice. But according to Augustine in the *De civitate Dei* (4.4 [see p. 139 above]), kingdoms without justice are great bands of robbers. And although such men are called kings, they are not kings, but thieves and robbers.

Kingship not instituted through the priesthood, therefore, was either not kingship, but robbery, or was united with the priesthood. For even before Saul was instituted and appointed as king through Samuel as through a priest of God, Melchizedek was king of Salem (Gen. 14:18). But this Melchizedek, besides being a king, was also a priest. And so, in the same place, it is said that he was a priest of the most high God. In this case, therefore, kingship did not exist without priesthood, but was united with priesthood, so that priesthood might here be superior to (mere) kingship. But the kingships of our own day are the successors of kingships instituted through the priesthood; for the kingship was instituted through the priesthood [i.e., Saul by Samuel] before such kingships were in being. And since former things are the patterns and a mirror of later, all later kingships must be referred back to the first, which was instituted through the priesthood at the command of God. When we speak of kingship, then, we are speaking of rightful kingship, and of that which is distinct from priesthood.

[...] Therefore, let kings acknowledge themselves to be instituted through the priesthood. For if we give diligent attention to whence royal power has come and whence it has been instituted, it follows that, since it has been instituted through the priesthood, royal power must be subject to priestly power, and especially to the power of the Supreme Priest.

The fourth way is derived from the government of things themselves. Therefore, if we wish to see which power stands under which power, we must pay attention to the government of the whole fabric of the world. And we see in the government of the universe that the whole of corporeal substance is governed through the spiritual. Inferior bodies are indeed ruled through superior, and the more gross through the more subtle and the less potent through the more potent; but the whole of corporeal substance is nonetheless ruled through the spiritual, and the whole of spiritual substance by the Supreme Spirit: that is, by God. Thus Augustine in *De Trinitate* (3.4.9) says that "certain more gross and inferior bodies are ruled in a certain order through the more subtle and the more potent; but all bodies through spirit, and the whole of creation by its Creator." And what we see in the order and in the government of the universe we must picture to ourselves in the government of the entire Christian people. For that same God who is the universal director of the whole fabric of the world is the special governor of his church and of his faithful people.

From Part 2

6. Now the ecclesiastical power is more universal than the earthly because the church herself is said to be catholic, that is, universal, as Isidore says in the final chapter of *Etymologies* 7 (14. 4); for he asserts that "catholic" is to be translated as "universal" or "general," and adds that "catholic" is the Greek word for "universal." Therefore, if it is an article of faith that we must believe in the Holy Catholic Church, he is not truly a faithful man who does not believe the church to be catholic, that is, universal, and holy, that is, established and made firm because she is founded upon a firm rock (Matt. 16:18); or holy, that is, pure and spotless, according to what is said in Ephesians (5:27): "That Christ might present it to himself as a glorious church, having no spot or blemish." The church, therefore, is holy and catholic, that is, universal; but she would not be truly universal if she did not rule universally over all things.

But the remaining ruling powers are particular, for none of them is a power without which a man cannot obtain salvation. And this is especially so if we speak of secular rulers and earthly powers, for he who withdraws himself from these comes nearer to salvation. For the clergy, who are not under the earthly power, are in a more perfect state than are the laity, who are placed under the earthly power. Thus, the earthly power is not universal in such a way that no one can obtain salvation unless he is under it. On the contrary, as we have said, the clergy, who are not under the earthly power, are in a more perfect state than the laity.

For ecclesiastical lordship imitates the forces of heaven, whose task it is to exert influence over all things; but earthly lordship imitates those inferior (natural) forces whose task it is to bring about particular effects. Thus, fire heats in such a way that it cannot of itself be said to cool; and water cools in such a way that it cannot of itself be said to heat. But the force of heaven accomplishes both: for it assists water to cool since, according to the order which we see, water could not cool if the force of heaven were withdrawn. And, in the same way, it assists fire to heat. For all these inferior forces, as servants of heaven, effect whatever they accomplish through the power of heaven. And so earthly lords, as the Church's servants in all their actions and in everything that belongs to them, must acknowledge that the Church is catholic and universal — that is, universal in lordship. Thus, the earthly power will be under the ecclesiastical as the particular is under the universal, which form of subjection is displayed by the inferior (natural) forces relative to the heavenly.

Second, the earthly power will be under the ecclesiastical as the art which prepares material is under that for which it prepares it. For it pertains to the earthly power to receive the material sword through the church and under the church, and to exercise lordship over material things and temporal affairs, and — so far as lay persons and the property over which they have received power are concerned — over human bodies also. Therefore, it will be the duty of the earthly power to do justice in these respects, so that no one may injure another in his own body or in his own property, but every citizen and every faithful man may enjoy his goods. Therefore, it is the duty of the earthly power to prepare material so that the ruler of the church may not be impeded in spiritual tasks. For the body was made to serve the soul and temporal goods to serve the body. The body is therefore well-disposed when it serves the soul well, and temporal goods are well-disposed and ordered when they are subordinated to the requirements of bodily life and the needs of human bodies. Therefore, the whole duty of the earthly power is to govern and rule these external and material goods in such a way that the faithful are not impeded in the peace of conscience and in peace of soul and in tranquillity of mind. For, in this way, not only have justice and peace kissed in those things which pertain to God — since unless we live justly with God we shall not have peace with Him — but also justice amongst these external goods conduces greatly to tranquillity of soul and to peace of mind. [. . .]

7. Now in the present chapter we wish to show that there is no lordship with justice, be it a lordship over temporal things or (and here there is more possibility that doubt may arise) over lay persons, except under the church and as instituted through the church. For we shall prove by arguments and authorities that for a

man to be carnally begotten does not suffice to enable him to be lord of anything or to possess anything with justice unless he is spiritually regenerated through the church; so that the man who is begotten of a carnal father cannot with justice succeed to a paternal inheritance, and cannot with justice acquire lordship of the paternal estate, unless he is regenerated through the church. Thus, if his possession of the paternal inheritance and his succession to the lordship of the paternal inheritance has its origin in the fact that he has been carnally begotten of a father, such lordship is nonetheless completed and his succession made perfect by the fact that he is regenerated through the church. And so, if a father holds the lordship of an inheritance (jointly) with his son, yet has a superior lordship to that which his son has, the church has lordship over every inheritance and over all things, and has such lordship in a superior and more excellent manner than do the faithful people. And since, as we have noted, to succeed to a paternal inheritance because begotten of a father is the beginning of justice, but to succeed to such an inheritance because regenerated through the church is justice perfected and consummated, then that justice which we say is thus perfected and consummated is so much more fruitful and universal than the former that, if it is lacking, the former is annulled. For, as will become clear, if a man were carnally begotten of a father but not also spiritually regenerated through the church, he could not with justice possess lordship over the paternal inheritance.

8. [. . .] For the time being, it may be said that he who is not subject to God worthily loses and unjustly possesses all that he holds from God. For the difference between the Eternal King and a temporal king is so great that, if he who is not subject to a temporal king is justly liable to lose all that he holds from that king, it is manifestly clear that he who is not subject to God is still more liable to lose, and more unjust in possessing, that which he holds from God. For if the crime of treason *(lese maiestatis)* renders you worthy of death and unworthy of life and of all your property, then, since majesty *(maiestas)* is an attribute reposed pre-eminently in God, he who is not subject to God is unworthy of himself and of all his possession. And since through original sin we are born not subject to God, and through actual sin we are not subject to Him, then through both kinds of sin we are worthy to lose and unworthily possess all that we hold from God. [. . .]

Therefore, through the sacrament of baptism, which is the direct remedy against original sin, and through the sacrament of penance, which is the remedy against actual sin, you will be made a worthy lord and a worthy prince and possessor of things. And since these sacraments are not conferred except *in* the church and *through* the church, no one is made a worthy lord or a worthy prince or possessor of things except under the church and through the church. For no one can receive baptism unless he desires to subject himself to the church and to be a son of the church, for the church is catholic, that is, universal, and there can be no salvation outside her; and no one may receive the sacrament of penance except under the church and through the church, for the Lord said to Peter: "Whatever you shall bind," and so on (Matt. 16:19).

10. [. . .] In this chapter we intend to make two matters clear concerning temporal things: first, the nature of the church's lordship with respect to these temporal

things, for this is universal; and, second, the nature of the lordship of the faithful themselves, for, as of right and with justice, this is particular. And we say "as of right and with justice" because, in point of fact, an earthly power might usurp to itself a universal temporal lordship: not by divine command, but only by permission. But if this were done, such lordship would not be held as of right and with justice; rather, it would be held only in point of fact and with injustice. And, third, we must discuss the nature of the lordship of unbelievers; for such lordship cannot be held truly and with justice in both respects. We say indeed "with justice in both respects," for there is no power except of God (Rom. 13:1): thus, even that power which unbelievers have over temporal things is of God. There are, therefore, two aspects to consider in relation to such power: namely, God's having justly permitted it, and the unjust use made of such power by the unfaithful men to whom it is permitted. And this was made clear by Augustine, who says in *De Trinitate* (3.8.13) that with this — that is, by means of this, or by means of the power permitted them — wicked men can commit no injustice except insofar as God justly permits. Therefore, such power is not just in every respect; for, although it is just in respect of God's permitting it, it is not just in respect of his (the wicked man's) using and abusing it. We intend, then, to make these three matters (i.e. the lordship of the church, of the faithful, and of unbelievers) clear in turn. [. . .]

Thus, it will not rest with the bodily physician, but with the spiritual, to judge whether things are possessed justly. Indeed, if due consideration is given to what has been said, (it will be seen that) the earthly power, being royal or imperial power, will have no capacity to judge what is just or unjust except insofar as it does this by virtue of (a delegated) spiritual power. For if justice is a spiritual property and a perfection of soul and not of body, then it will rest with the spiritual power to judge concerning such justice; and earthly and bodily power will have no capacity to judge concerning it unless it does so by virtue of (a delegated) spiritual power. And so all imperial laws and those of the earthly power must be subordinated to the canons of the church, so that they may derive strength and also firmness from them. Again, all such laws enacted by the earthly power must not contradict the ecclesiastical laws, but must rather be confirmed by the spiritual and ecclesiastical power, so that they may have strength and firmness. For justice is a spiritual property, since it is a kind of rectitude perceptible only to the mind. For we can judge by means of sense what is done or what is not done; but it is with the intellect that we shall judge what is just and what is not just.

If, therefore, the church is catholic and universal because her lordship is universal, then the faithful are catholic, that is, universal, because they must be universally subject and subservient to the church. The faithful, then, if they are truly catholic, must be truly subject to the church universally, so that their manner of possessing themselves and whatever they have is such that they are faithful subjects of the church in themselves and in all that is theirs. Therefore, from the manner in which things are possessed — since men must hold their possessions as the church's subjects — (it follows that) the church will have a universal and total lordship over the possessions of the faithful, but that the lordship which the faithful themselves have will be able to be called (only) particular and partial.

From Part 3

2. [. . .] Just as there is one fount in the government of the whole world — there is one God, in whom there is every power, from whom all other powers are derived, and to whom all powers are reduced — so also in the government of men and in the whole church militant, it must be that there is one fount, that there is one head in which is fulness of power: in which there is almost every power as over the mystical body or over the church herself, and in which there are both swords, for, otherwise, all power would not be in it. From this fount all other powers are derived, and to this fount all other powers are reduced. [. . .]

But although, according to the common law, this fount stands in the same relation to all things because it preserves them all in their order and protects them all in their condition, things nonetheless do not all stand in the same relation to it; for some contain more of its influence and of its power, and others less. Thus, there are some greater and some lesser ruling powers, whether these ruling powers be ecclesiastical or earthly; for all ruling powers, whether ecclesiastical or earthly, are derived from this fount and must acknowledge that their power comes through the influence of this fount. Therefore, that which must be considered true of God insofar as he governs the whole world according to a common law, must also be considered true of the Vicar of God insofar as he governs and waters and irrigates the whole church according to a common law. For, according to this argument, he can be likened to a kind of sea or to a kind of fount, from which come all other streams and all other powers, to each of which it offers the whole of itself, but none of which contains the whole of it. This sea or this fount stands in the same relation to all things insofar as it governs the church according to a common law; but things do not all stand in the same relation to it.

But kings or princes are said, or can be said, to be made or to be such through the church when, of herself or by her authority, the church deposes this one or appoints that: just as the church has transferred even the empire from the East to the West, or just as she deposes other princes, or has by her authority caused them to be deposed and by the same authority has caused others to be instituted. Thus, those who have been so instituted must be said to be kings or to be princes through the church; for they were not such, nor could they be such, before, and have been made such after, the church's exercise of authority. Nor, if ruling power comes to him by inheritance, does it matter whether it is the king himself or his parent or grandparent or ancestor who has been made such through the church. For if consideration be given to the fact that his root and first parent was made a king through the church, then it follows that he who has acquired ruling power by right of inheritance has also himself been made such through the church. Therefore, many have been made princes through the church; but if not all of them have been made princes or kings (immediately) through the church, all have nonetheless been made truly and worthily such through the church. . . . And because every man is by nature born a child of wrath, and every man is made a child of wrath by each mortal sin, no prince will be a true and worthy prince unless he is spiritually regenerated through the church, and if he falls into mortal sin, unless he is sacramentally absolved through the church.

Third, kings and princes are said to be such through the church absolutely and without diminution if they are blessed or anointed by the church. For, in the case of anointed kings and princes who succeed to a kingdom or to a principality by right of inheritance, the law of inheritance accomplishes in them, or seems to accomplish, what the law of election accomplishes in the case of the prelates of the church. And because those who are elected as prelates of the church are said to be not absolutely such until confirmed by a superior prelate, so also, to kings and princes who are anointed by a prelate of the church, this blessing and this anointing is as it were a kind of ecclesiastical approval. For by such anointing, he (the king or prince) is as though consecrated to God, and so thenceforth should be entirely given to God and should place himself entirely at the church's disposal, so that from then on he may be a king absolutely and without diminution, and should be called a king.

In three ways, therefore, are kings said to be made through the church: either because they are instituted through the church, or because they are regenerated and absolved through her, or, third, because they are anointed and blessed by the church. It must be noted, however, that if not all kings and princes are or have been made such through the church in all three of these ways, nonetheless, as regards the second way — that is, inasmuch as a man is made a true and worthy king by regeneration and sacramental absolution through the church — there is at all events no one who ought not to acknowledge that he receives his kingdom from the church, through whom he reigns justly and without whom he could not reign justly. [. . .]

3. And just as, so far as those natural things which we see are concerned, God continuously governs the world in such a way that, in most cases, he deals with them according to a common law in order not to impede them in their activities; yet, albeit rarely, when certain special circumstances are present, he does not allow these natural agents to pursue their own courses: so also the supreme pontiff should conduct himself according to the common law in relation to temporal affairs and in relation to material things, so that he may allow them to pursue their own courses, and so that material swords may execute their own judgments — unless there are perhaps some special circumstances present which must be taken into account, by reason of which he may intervene in temporal disputes. And in the same temporal disputes, by reason of such special circumstances, it will also be possible to appeal from civil judges and earthly powers to the pope.

In spiritual matters, therefore, whenever we turn to God and petition him while we are in this life, where a time of penance is given to us, God always hears our petition and always receives our appeal. Thus, the supreme priest, the Vicar of God, must always have the special care of spiritual things, so that all cases involving such things are specially reserved to him, and he is everywhere the ordinary judge in such cases. But so far as temporal cases are concerned, he should not receive an appeal or intervene in them save in some special circumstances. Rather, such cases should be relinquished to the earthly powers and to the civil judges.

5. [. . .] Therefore, when it is asked what are those special circumstances and what are those cases in which the spiritual power concerns itself with temporal affairs, we shall reply that the spiritual power will exercise its jurisdiction in temporal matters in all the ways in which temporal things can be called spiritual.

It must be noted, therefore, that temporal things can themselves be considered in three ways: first, with reference to the things themselves; second, in relation to the temporal power under which they are; and, third, in relation to the power of the supreme pontiff. In all these ways, temporal things can be called spiritual; and so, considered in all these ways, it will be possible for temporal things to be placed under the jurisdiction of the spiritual power. [. . .]

It must be known, therefore, that the jurisdiction of the spiritual power extends itself to temporal matters by reason of things themselves in all those cases in which temporal things can be called spiritual; of which, for our present purpose, there are three: first, if they are commanded by the supreme Spirit; second, if they are annexed to spiritual things; and, third, if spiritual things are annexed to them. For whether spiritual things are annexed to temporal things or the converse, it will always be possible for temporal things to be called spiritual: for spiritual things are greater than temporal, and so the spiritual things, as greater, define the temporal whether they are annexed to the temporal things or the converse. . . .

Thus, even temporal things can be called spiritual if they are commanded by the supreme Spirit. In this sense, tithes are numbered amongst spiritual things; for they were instituted, not by man, but by God, who is the supreme Spirit (John 4:24). Therefore, tithes can be said to be debts owed to churches, to be the consecrated property of churches; and so they can be called spiritual things, for the sake of which all the laws [which would apply to them if they were not given as tithes] can be modified. And this is clear from the *Liber extra* under the title *De decimis* [where the canon law relating to tithes abrogates the civil laws ordinarily applying to the inheritance and transmission of property]: the laity are indeed forbidden to possess tithes by right of inheritance, for they are the consecrated property of God; and the laity are forbidden to distribute tithes (X. 3.30.15, 17, 31). This, therefore, will be one case derived from things themselves: the church will concern herself with temporal things if temporal possessions become spiritual and pertain to tithes.

But there is another case derived from a consideration of things themselves: if temporal things are spiritual because they are annexed to spiritual things, as dowries are annexed to matrimony and succession to an inheritance is annexed to the legitimation of sons; for, as the Apostle says in Romans (8:17): "If sons, heirs also." [. . .]

Third, a temporal thing is said to be spiritual not only if it is annexed to spiritual things, but also if spiritual things are annexed to it. And since, in a sense, all crimes and all mortal sins can be called spiritual in that they slay our spirit and our soul, it follows that the spiritual power will be able to intervene in disputes involving any temporal question whatsoever if those disputes are brought forward together with an allegation of crime; for it rests with the spiritual power to judge every mortal sin and to rebuke every Christian for it. Otherwise God would not have said in St. Matthew's Gospel (18:15-17): "And if your brother should sin against you, go and rebuke him between yourself and him; and if he will not hear you, take one or two persons with you; and if he will not hear them, tell the church." He would not have said this if it did not rest with the church to rebuke every Christian for every mortal sin. [. . .]

6. Therefore, just as amongst natural phenomena, it rests with the general heavenly power to attract things in order to prevent discontinuities, so in the government of men it will especially rest with the heavenly and ecclesiastical power, which is catholic and universal, to draw factions and their disputes together, lest wars arise, and lest peace, which is the bond of love which unites the faithful, be destroyed, so that the ecclesiastical prince may fully govern and rule them.

For we shall say that a corporeal vacuum is a kind of discontinuity of bodies, on account of which the heaven itself may neither continue to exert influence nor influence all bodies. So too in the matter before us: war is as it were a kind of spiritual vacuum, for it is a kind of discontinuity of souls. Thus, the church desires to remove this spiritual vacuum from all the faithful as far as possible, and it pertains especially to her to do so: to remove such war and to make peace amongst all the faithful so that she may exercise her government and rule over all faithful men.

What is said in the decretal *Novit,* therefore, was well said: that even though the Supreme Pontiff can rebuke every Christian for every mortal sin — so that if any dispute concerning any temporal matter whatsoever is brought forward together with an allegation of crime, the Church will be able to intervene in this dispute by reason of criminal sin — she must nonetheless do this especially when that criminal sin militates against the peace and can stir up wars amongst the peoples (X. 2.1.13). And this is made clear by an example drawn from natural phenomena: that, although the heaven co-operates in the production of every effect, it is nonetheless given especially to the force of heaven to ensure that the concord and unity and conjunction of inferior things be not impeded. Thus, even though the ecclesiastical power could — that is, could fittingly — intervene in any temporal dispute whatsoever by reason of an allegation of criminal sin, the church must nonetheless do this especially when the crime is detrimental to the peace by which the faithful are bound to one another and united and conjoined.

Having seen how the church must concern herself particularly with temporal affairs in order that she may be able to restore treaties of peace between her sons, it remains, finally, to see how she must do this when such treaties are confirmed by oath. For we shall say that the breaking of an oath is called an ecclesiastical crime because it rests with the ecclesiastical judge to judge cases of perjury or oath-breaking. Therefore, when the supreme pontiff was willing to intervene in the dispute between the King of France and the King of England over a certain fief, he did so not because of the fief as such, but for three other causes. The first cause was that the question at issue was alleged to involve a criminal sin. The second cause was that it was alleged to involve a criminal sin which was detrimental to peace, with which, as is now clear, the church must especially concern herself. And the third and last cause was that the peace was confirmed by oath; and, by reason of this third cause, because oath-breaking is an ecclesiastical crime, it therefore pertained especially to the church to concern herself with the question at issue.

7. For the sake of a greater understanding of what has been said and of what must still be said, however, we shall make a twofold distinction as to the power of the Supreme Pontiff and his jurisdiction in temporal matters and say that it is in one sense absolute and in another is governed by rules. For as those learned in philosophy have taught, he who establishes the law should observe the law. Therefore, if the supreme pontiff is in other respects without bridle and without halter by reason of his absolute

power, he must nonetheless impose bridle and halter upon himself by observing the statutes and laws in his own actions. For although, speaking of positive laws, he himself is above the laws, nonetheless, in order that he may give stability to his laws and statutes, it is fitting that he govern the church entrusted to him according to statutes and laws. Moreover, just as we have distinguished a twofold power in the supreme pontiff, so can we make a twofold distinction as to his jurisdiction in temporal cases. In one sense, it is direct and regular; and this, as we have said, is the superior and primary jurisdiction which he has in all cases, over earthly powers and temporal goods alike, by reason of which he can chastise earthly powers for their fault or for some other good cause. But the supreme pontiff has another kind of jurisdiction over temporal matters, which is not direct and regular, but which comes into play only on the examination of certain causes, and occasionally. This jurisdiction is not only superior and primary, but is also immediate and executory.

But because such jurisdiction is thus occasional, it is to be attributed, not to his power considered as absolute, but to his power insofar as it is governed by certain rules. In this way we can say that it is not according to the strictness of the law that appeal may be made from a civil judge to the pope because, to the extent that the power of the supreme pontiff is governed by rules, this is not a regular but an occasional practice. That occasional jurisdiction which applies in certain cases and on the examination of certain causes indeed overrides and outweighs that regular jurisdiction which the secular lord has; but it must nonetheless be known that our works, and especially the works of the ecclesiastical judge, should conform to the nature of things: that the ecclesiastical judge should not concern himself with temporal matters which are subject to secular lords in the normal course of events and indiscriminately, but only occasionally — only in cases where he sees this to be expedient to the church and to the public good. In the normal course of events and ordinarily, however, regularly and according to the common law, he must so conduct himself in spiritual matters that he permits the earthly powers to exercise their office in temporal, taking his example from God himself whose vicar he is: who, as we have said, governs things in such a way that he allows them to pursue their own courses.

8. First, there are the unusual and particular cases which can as it were be said to fall outside the laws, by reason of which the church intervenes in temporal affairs for certain causes and occasionally. Second, she does this in difficult cases; third, in doubtful cases. And all these cases are derived from that fulness of power which resides in the church, by reason of which fulness of power the church stands in a threefold relation to the statutes and to the laws: first, because it is her task to establish laws; second, because it rests with her to promulgate these established laws to the faithful peoples; and, third, because it pertains to her to expound and interpret the laws which she has first established and then promulgated to the nations. And so it is said in Deuteronomy: "When you shall see the words of the judges to be at variance, arise and go to the place which the Lord your God shall choose," and so on (Deut. 17:8). For it is there intimated that when the words of the judges are at variance and, consequently, when a judgment is divided because one judge judges in one way and another judges in another, we should then go to the place which the Lord has chosen, and we should have recourse to the supreme priest.

But we can say that there are three reasons why the words of the judges are wont to vary, or why the judgments of the judges are apt to differ. The first is when certain cases arise which are as it were outside the laws. For, since the laws are certain rules governing what can be done, according to which rules we must measure and dispose other things, when certain cases arise which are outside the laws or which are not contained under the laws, the judgment of those judges may then be divided, and different judges will judge in different ways. The judgments of those judges may be at variance, therefore, when certain cases arise which are outside the laws.

Second, they may be at variance when certain cases arise in which it is difficult to observe the laws. For it is sometimes possible for certain cases to arise which, even though they are not outside the laws, but are contained within the laws, perhaps touch great kings and great princes. And so it is difficult to observe the laws in these cases, for every man is afraid to say anything against the kings and princes because of the civil might which they possess. In such cases, therefore — even if not by reason of ignorance, nonetheless by reason of fear, because of which it is then difficult to observe the laws — the judgment of the judges will be at variance and, by reason of fear, different judges will judge differently.

Third, the judgments of the judges are wont to vary by reason of doubtfulness, as when certain cases arise which, although they are not outside the laws, and although it is not difficult to observe the laws in them, are nonetheless perhaps such that the laws speak ambiguously concerning them.

9. Because we have spoken in many chapters of fulness of power, we therefore wish in the present chapter to show what fulness of power is. Also, we shall show that there is such fulness in the supreme pontiff, by reason of which his power is without limit of number, weight and measure. [. . .]

Many illustrations might be adduced to show what fulness of power is. For our present purposes, however, it may suffice to show only this: that fulness of power resides in some agent when that agent can do without a secondary cause whatever it can do with a secondary cause. For if an agent does not have such power, it follows that it does not have a full power because it does not have a power in which all power is contained. Thus, inasmuch as the Supreme Pontiff possesses a power in which all power is contained, we say that he has a full power. And, so that we may pass to the government of men by way of those natural phenomena which we see in the government of the world, we shall say that fulness of power does not reside in the heaven or in any secondary agent whatsoever; for the heaven cannot do without a secondary cause what it can do with a secondary cause. For example, although the heaven and a lion bring about the generation of a lion, the heaven could not produce a lion without a lion, nor could it produce a horse without a horse. In God himself, however, there is fulness of power, for whatever he can do with a secondary cause he can do without a secondary cause. And so the power of all agents is contained within the primary agent, that is, in God; for, in bringing forth the world, he brought forth a man without a pre-existing man and a horse without a pre-existing horse. [. . .]

And, although he can do all things, he nonetheless directs things in such a way that he allows them to pursue their own courses. Sometimes, however, God performs a miracle, or even miracles, so that he may act beyond the ordinary course of nature and not according to the established common laws of nature.

So also, to such extent as there is power within the church, the supreme pontiff has fulness of power, and he can do without a secondary cause whatever he can do with a secondary cause. For example, the election of a bishop depends upon the ordinance of the supreme pontiff as to how the election of prelates is to be conducted and as to what manner of men the electors should be in respect of zeal and merit and number, so that there should be such a number of electors, and electors of such a kind, as to ensure that he who is elected is properly chosen. Thus, such election depends upon the establishing and ordaining of the mode of election by the supreme pontiff, just as the production of natural things depends upon God as a primary cause, who establishes his laws for natural things which regulate how they act and how they produce their effects. And the election of a prelate depends also upon the assent of the canons and upon their choice as upon a secondary cause, just as the production of natural things depends upon natural things themselves, which are under one primary agent: that is, under God.

Truly, therefore, to such extent as there is power within the church, fulness of power resides in the supreme pontiff; for he can do without a secondary cause whatever he can do with a secondary cause. For he could make provision [of a bishop] for any church without election by the chapter, and, by so doing, he would not act according to the established common laws, but according to his fulness of power. For, as we have said, the election of a prelate is brought about as by a primary cause — by the supreme pontiff establishing how the election is to be conducted — and by a secondary cause, namely, by the choice of the electors according to the form given to them. But the supreme pontiff could provide a prelate for any church without this secondary cause, that is, without the choice of the electors. And what has been said of the election of a prelate is true of the other things which are done within the church: the supreme pontiff, having fulness of power, in whom all the power of the church is acknowledged to reside, can act without other agents.

The supreme pontiff should note, however, that God, who has all power — not only conditionally (that is, in relation to this or in relation to that), but absolutely — nonetheless almost always acts according to the laws which he has established for things, lest the works of his wisdom should be in vain; and he almost always observes the laws (of nature) in order to accomplish the effects of secondary agents by means of secondary agents. [. . .]

11. Therefore, Caesar has some right — indeed, a great right — in temporal things, and more of a right of use than the church has, even though he does not have so great a right of lordship as the church has. Moreover, Caesar has not only a right of use, but also a right of power and lordship in temporal things: in cities, castles and lands. For he has a right and lordship of use in them inasmuch as he receives gains and profits from them; and he has a lordship of power inasmuch as he executes justice and the judgment of blood in them. But that lordship which Caesar and the temporal lord has, whether it be a lordship of use or of power, does not take away the lordship of the church, which is superior and primary. And because of the superior and primary lordship which the church has over temporal things, all who possess

temporal goods are the tributaries of the church, owing to her the tithes which are gathered from their temporal possessions. And that lordship of the church is more a lordship of ownership, and is more elevated over temporal things, than is the lordship which Caesar or any temporal lord has. [. . .]

But Caesar, or the earthly power, whose task it is to bear the material sword, has a right of power in temporal things — for example, in cities, castles or farms and vineyards, and in all other lands — because he judges and punishes offenders. Therefore, the lordship of power which the church has is far more excellent than that of Caesar or the earthly power, because the earthly power can chastise only members of the laity, but the church all men. For she can chastise even the earthly power, however exalted, for fault or other good cause, and deprive it of its temporal goods; and this would not be so if temporal goods and the possessors of temporal goods were not under the church.

Translation: R. W. Dyson (Woodbridge, Suffolk, 1986). Used with permission.

James of Viterbo

(d. 1308)

A member of the Augustinian Order of Hermits from his youth (ca. 1270), Jacopo Capocci of Viterbo studied philosophy and theology at Paris and replaced Giles of Rome as the order's regent-master at the university in 1293. In 1300 he returned to Italy to oversee a fledgling *studium generale* in Naples, was elevated to the archbishopric of Benevento in September 1302, and translated to the archbishopric of Naples three months later.

During the bitter dispute between Philip the Fair of France and Pope Boniface VIII, he produced the treatise *On Christian Government (De regimine christiano)*, probably in the first half of 1302. It did not propound the dominant royalist line of his former Parisian colleagues, but generally aligned itself with the papalist apologetics of his fellow Augustinians, Giles of Rome and Augustinus Triumphus. The warmth of the pope's reception of his literary effort may perhaps be gauged by his rapid promotions. However that may be, his contribution is distinguished by his relatively original theological approach and subtle combination of Aristotelian and Augustinian ideas, the balance and moderation of which give his thought an enduring intellectual appeal.

H.-X. Arquillière's boast that this is the first treatise in ecclesiology ("le plus ancien traité de l'Église") is of more hermeneutical than historical value. It focuses attention on the striking decision to approach the papal *principatus* discussed in part 2 through a general analysis of the church as a universal political society in part 1. (This reflects, or is perhaps reflected by, Boniface's *Unam Sanctam* of 1302, which opens with the article on the church from the Nicene Creed.) The obvious biblical and doctrinal starting points for conceiving the church as a kingdom do not deter James from approaching the ecclesiological use of the term from its secular political features. He argues that, of the three natural societies posited by Augustine (*City of God* 19) and Isidore (*Etymologies* 15), household, city, and kingdom, it is the most perfect of them, the kingdom, that the church best resembles. Its defining criteria of inclusive universality, self-sufficiency in satisfying human needs, and political hierarchy are fulfilled by the church, which encompasses peoples and nations throughout the world, contains what is sufficient for human salvation, and is a hierarchy of jurisdictional units (1.1). Moreover, the church is properly called "a glorious kingdom," fulfilling ten requisite natural conditions (further specifying the original three), reducible to the four "marks," affirmed in the Nicene Creed, of unity, holiness, catholicity, and apostolicity — "et in unam, sanctam, catholicam et apostolicam ecclesiam" (1.2). His exposition of these marks constantly shows the influence of Augustinian ecclesiological and political concepts: peace dependent upon order; justice wedded to divine love; temporal, spatial, and ontological universality; the commonwealth *(respublica)*. Nevertheless, he takes issue with Augustine's dismissal of the natural virtues and just laws of pagan Rome, insisting that there can be genuinely "praiseworthy disciplines" *(laudabiles mores)* without faith (1.2).

James's concern to affirm the workings of nature as well as grace carries over into the discussion of priesthood and kingship in part 2. Here he draws parallel distinctions between "natural" and "spiritual" priesthood and kingship. Both natural priesthood and natural kingship are human institutions, products of instinctive morality realizing virtues through the mediation of natural law, and coterminous with human community (2.3). Spiritual priesthood and spiritual kingship are divine institutions, powers transmitted to men *immediately* from Christ as communicable properties of his human nature, so as to make them cooperative instruments of his primary agency (2.2, 4). The powers are, nevertheless, distinct: the priestly office is concerned with sanctification and reconciliation with God, the royal with regulating external conduct toward God and neighbor (2.2). Whereas natural priesthood and kingship are typically exercised by different people on account of their disparate action, their spiritual equivalents are always exercised together by the apostolic representatives of Christ, a personal unity foreshadowed by the Aaronic priesthood's imperfect exercise of both offices under the Mosaic Law (2.3). Thus the christological priesthood, with its sacramental power of order and Petrine power of jurisdiction, is a more excellent *royal* as well as priestly government. James dismisses the royalist claim that jurisdiction held by priests is conceded to them by temporal rulers; moreover, Christ's sole earthly vicar exercises a plenitude of "spiritual" priestly and royal power by divine rather than imperial law (2.3, 4).

His un-Thomistic exposition of the relation between natural and spiritual powers, utilizing categories of matter and form suggested by Hugh of St. Victor, leads to mainstream papalist conclusions. The unformed incompleteness of natural powers requires their in-forming completion, or completing formation, by the spiritual powers. This means that temporal kingship is to be instituted, directed, and judged by the papal church, a summation of the tradition of Honorius Augustodunensis, Hugh of St. Victor, and Bernard of Clairvaux (2.7). With Giles of Rome, James speaks of a twofold formation of temporal power by natural and divine agency and law, which renders it wholly valid. With Giles, he extends the hegemony of spiritual jurisdiction over things as well as persons, so that valid ownership of property depends on the owner's submission to spiritual authority (2.7).

It is difficult to surmise what, if any, practical implications flow from his affirmations of natural law and natural institutions. Perhaps he gives an ambivalent recognition to heathen rule and religion, absent in Giles, and shows more respect for the integrity of the civil law than Giles demonstrates. He gives little sign, however, of regarding infidel ownership as other than abusive and unjust.

Further Reading: H.-X. Arquillière, *Le plus ancien traité de l'Église. Jacques de Viterbe, De regimine christiano (1301-1302). Étude des sources et édition critique* (Paris: Beauchesne, 1926); R. W. Dyson, *James of Viterbo, "On Christian Government"* (Woodbridge, Suffolk: Boydell Press, 1995); M. Wilks, *The Problem of Sovereignty in the Later Middle Ages: The Papal Monarchy with Augustinus Triumphus and the Publicists* (Cambridge: Cambridge University Press, 1963).

From *On Christian Government,* Part 1

ch. 1. *The church is properly called a kingdom.* [94] However, that the Church is called a kingdom appears in the Apostle Paul, 1 Cor. (15:24) where, speaking of Christ, he says: "Then comes the end, when he shall have delivered up the Kingdom to God, even the Father." About these words the Gloss (Glos. ord.) says: "Surely his faithful whom he redeemed by his blood are called here his kingdom, whose kingdom is also all creation." In one way the kingdom of Christ is said to be all creation, in another way the church: for the kingdom of Christ is said to be all creation according to divine power, whereas the church is truly said to be the kingdom of Christ in a special sense, by virtue of the faith which comes from him and through which he reigns in the faithful themselves. And although the church is rightly called by these three names which designate community (i.e., "household," "city," and "kingdom"), it is called a kingdom by far the most appropriately, since it: (1) includes a great multitude gathered from different peoples and nations, and scattered and spread out through the whole world; (2) contains all things sufficient to the salvation and the spiritual life of men; (3) was instituted for the common good of all men; and (4) comprehends many congregations ordered to each other and increasing in size, as provinces, dioceses, parishes, and colleges. [. . .]

From Part 2

ch. 2. *Christ's power communicated to men.* [163] First it must be made plain that the power of Christ was for communication to men, and which power, and in what manner. On this point it must be understood that the power of creating which is proper to Christ only in so far as he is God is in no way communicable. For if it was not communicated nor communicable to his humanity which was united in person to his divinity, how much less can it be communicated to other men — not through an inadequacy of God, as if he could not communicate it, but through a fault of the

381

creature which is fitted in the least degree for so great a power. [. . .] The priestly power which is proper to Christ in so far as he is man, and the power of working miracles and the royal power which are proper to him both as God and as man, are communicable and are communicated to men. For all of these powers belong to the power of governing, which is transmissible. [. . .]

This power of governing of Christ's is threefold, as has been said above: first priestly, second royal, and third to effect miraculous changes. Moreover, Christ communicated all of these to men, since each was of use to the church. For by the working of miracles the doctrine of faith is confirmed and man is roused to praise God's power; through the priestly office man is sanctified and reconciled to God; and through royal actions he is directed in his dealings with others and governed in what is owed to God and neighbor. [. . .]

Indeed both those who have the priestly and those who have the royal power are called Christ's Vicars, Christ's minister's and Christ's fellow laborers. For Christ conveys his power to others in such a way that he does not deprive himself of it but retains it himself, and according to it works as first cause (*principaliter*) in all who share in it and work by his virtue, and so are called his fellow laborers. The power of working miracles has also been, and is even yet, conveyed to men by Christ: not however in the same manner as Christ has it, since in both sacraments and miracles Christ has the power of authority as God and the instrumental power of a certain primacy (*principalitatis*) and preeminence as man; for he cannot only work miracles, but pour out this power and grace on others, as is said in Luke (9:1): "He gave the apostles power over all devils, and to cure diseases." Others, therefore, have from Christ a secondary and instrumental power. For in every power that he communicates to men, Christ has the primacy and preeminence, and man a secondary ministry and cooperation.

ch. 3. *To whom royal and priestly powers have been communicated.* [172] It seems to some, however, that this twofold power (priestly and royal) is not to be communicated, nor has it been communicated, to the same person; but that since the powers are distinct, they are to be conveyed to different and distinct persons (cf. D. 96.10), as is apparent in the dispensation of the Old Testament where the kingly and priestly dignities were assigned to different persons, and similarly in the New Testament. For the priestly power belongs to those in the church called priests and pontiffs, who preside spiritually. Royal power, however, belongs to earthly princes and temporal lords, also called kings, under whom there exist powers of various degrees. Accordingly, it is apparently necessary to say that although Christ was king and priest, his vicars (that is, the apostles and their successors) are not priests and kings, but rather that the priestly or pontifical power alone belongs to them by Christ's concession. If kingly power belongs to some of them, it is only by the concession of earthly princes: as the Roman pontiff holds imperial power by the concession of (the Emperor) Constantine. Although this might seem on first sight to be a reasonable and probable conclusion, it is proper for those who wish to ponder the truth more deeply to say more, and to propose a different conclusion.

First, therefore, we must draw a distinction bearing on priesthood and kingship, or royal power. We should, it seems, distinguish between them as between varieties of knowledge. For some knowledge, as that of natural science, is humanly discovered, while other knowledge, as that of Holy Scripture, is divinely revealed: both are from God who is the lord of knowledge and the primary authority, and from whom is all wisdom; yet they are from God in different ways. The first kind of knowledge is from God by the natural mediation of the human intellect through which it is discovered, and by the mediation of the objects which are its cause; and since both the human intellect *in* which there is knowledge and the things *of* which there is knowledge are God's work, this knowledge is said to be from him, as a work of nature is his work. Whence also God himself is said to be the primary teacher of men, as Augustine shows in *De magistro* (11.38ff.). The second kind of knowledge is from God without the mediation of discovery by the human intellect: it is from him in a special way, by revelation and by the inspiration of those men through whom it has been passed to us. For the holy men of God — the prophets, apostles, and other sacred writers — have spoken by the inspiration of the Holy Spirit.

A similar distinction should be made concerning the priesthood. For there was one priesthood by human institution, that was in the law of nature before the time of written law, and even after the law was given, among those who lived by the natural law alone. Then either the firstborn were instituted as priests, or others, offering themselves of their own accord, used to fulfill the priestly office, albeit they might not perhaps be called priests. There was, however, another priesthood by divine institution, which began with Aaron (for the former priesthood began with the very origin of the human race). In his book *De ecclesiasticis officiis* (2.5) Isidore writes: "Aaron was the beginning of the priesthood, even though Melchizedek had offered the sacrifice first, and after him Abraham, Isaac, and Jacob, inasmuch as these latter offered it by their own free will and not by priestly authority. Aaron was first in the law to receive the name of priest, and to offer victims, dressed in the pontifical robe, as the Lord ordered, speaking to Moses, 'Take Aaron and his sons etc.,'" as Exodus has it where it deals with the ritual of priestly ornaments, anointing, and consecration (Exod. 28:1f.). Such ritual was no part of priesthood in the law of nature, although some then might have had an interior anointing, as can be inferred from the Gloss [Glos. ord.] on the Letter to the Hebrews (8:1), which says of Melchizedek that "he was not of the Jewish people and served in the priesthood before the circumcision, so that the nations did not receive the priesthood from the Jews, but the Jews from the nations; and that he was not anointed with the visible oil instituted by Moses, but with the oil of exultation and with purity of faith; nor did he sacrifice animals, but dedicated the priesthood with the bread and wine of Christ."

Thus there is a twofold priesthood, and both types are from God, but in different ways. The first is from him by the mediation of nature, since the natural law prescribes that God is to be worshiped, and sacrifices and offering made to him, and to offer and to sacrifice belongs to priests. So men have exercised the priestly office from the dictates of natural law, either of their own accord or by human institution. Hence the prophets posit among the virtues that have their aptitude from nature and their completion from human application a certain virtue called "religion" (*religio*), to which pertains showing proper worship to God, and they designate it a type of justice. Thus this priesthood is said to come from God because it arises out of a natural inclination placed in men by the author of nature. The other priesthood, to which we now address ourselves, is from God by his spiritual institution and mediation. Indeed it began with Aaron, but was transferred to Christ, whom God established as a priest after the order of Melchizedek. It is Christ's priesthood, which is superior to and more complete than the priesthood of the law (the Aaronic priesthood), that the church has received from him.

And so it is possible to distinguish a threefold priesthood: (1) a priesthood of human institution, dictated by natural reason, incomplete and as if formless; (2) the priesthood of the law instituted by God through Moses, the lawmaker, also incomplete and figurative; (3) the divinely instituted priesthood bestowed on the man Christ, not by any human ministry nor according to any rite of visible anointing, but by anointing with the fullness of invisible grace. This is the true and perfect priesthood of the Gospel and of grace, by participation in which there have been and are those called priests in the church, to whom is administered, as in the priesthood of the law, a visible anointing as a sign of invisible grace. Hence the natural priesthood is not destroyed through the Gospel, but perfected and given form, since grace does not destroy nature but perfects it and gives it form. The priesthood of the law has indeed ceased, because it was a figure, and figures cease at the arrival of the truth. The priesthood of the Gospel, however, continues, being true and perfect, and containing the priesthood of nature, while fulfilling the priesthood of the law transferred to it.

Another distinction may be drawn between the "individual" *(proprium)* and "public" *(commune)* modes of priesthood. The priesthood is individual in the sense that each of the faithful is said to be a priest, when he offers to God for himself a spiritual sacrifice, whether of a contrite heart or of mortification of the flesh or of any good work. This is the priesthood about which St. John in the Apocalypse speaks when he says of Christ: "he made us a kingdom and priests unto God and his Father" (Rev. 1:6); and about which the Gloss [not traced] says: "I have made you priests, that we who hitherto sacrificed to demons, should henceforth sacrifice to God; and who hitherto offered the sacrifice of sins to the devil, should henceforth offer the sacrifices of good works." The public priesthood (with which we are here concerned), is that which is granted to someone for the salvation of many, as certain priests are ordained in the church to sacrifice to God for the salvation of the people and to offer up to him its desires and prayers. (There is, however, yet another priesthood which is neither natural nor of the law, nor of the Gospel, but rather of the devil, being contrary to nature and the law and the Gospel. To this belongs the priesthood of abominable idols and false gods, which ought not to be called priesthood so much as the perversion of priesthood.)

The threefold distinction must now be applied to kingship or regal power. There is a kingship instituted by the natural inclination of men. As government of sorts is found among brute beasts who belong to flocks and are by instinct social, how much greater in men is the instinct to establish government (for whom living in society is natural) than in any other animal. This kind of government is said to be from human law because it arises in nature. Some regal power, however, is divinely instituted, or from divine law proceeding from grace. Both types of kingly power are from God, but in different ways. For the first is from God by the mediation both of natural human inclination and of human institution that completes the inclination, and so is called human and natural; but the second is from God in the special manner of being instituted and handed down by him, and so is called divine and supernatural. The first kind of power, pertaining to the government *(regimen)* of temporal and earthly things, is designated "temporal" or "secular," while the second, pertaining to the government of spiritual and heavenly things, is designated (and actually is, as will be explained below) "spiritual" and "heavenly." [. . .]

Both kinds of regal power are distinct from priesthood, as will be shown by the diversity of the offices and acts. The first kind, on the one hand, is distinct from priesthood in being bestowed on different persons; lest the two powers, on account of their diverse actions, impede each other's operation. Nevertheless, at any time in the past they could be found combined in some manner in a single person, as, e.g., in the time of the law of nature Melchizedek was both king and priest, and similarly Job was both (since he offered burnt sacrifices). . . . On the other hand, the second kind is distinct from priesthood in such a way that both powers are found in one and the same person. All bishops have both, in that their distinct episcopal powers of order and jurisdiction are priestly and royal respectively.

Moreover, in the Old Testament the spiritual kind of regal power was conveyed in some manner and in some part to priests, to whose office belonged judging in certain spiritual matters, e.g., between leprosy and leprosy, clean and unclean, and other such things (cf. Lev. 13:1-59). In the New Testament, the power was communicated and handed down by Christ to the apostles and their successors, at least in his saying: "whatsoever you will bind on earth will also be bound in heaven," etc. (Matt. 18:18). For although the power of binding and loosing is a judicial power that undoubtably belongs to kings, it was, nevertheless, given particularly and primarily to the blessed Peter, and in him to each of his successors, or rather to the whole church, when Christ said: "to you I will give the keys of the kingdom of heaven" (Matt. 16:19), the assumption here being that the key carries the spiritual power of bringing into the kingdom of heaven or of excluding from it. And because judging properly pertains to the royal office, this priestly judicial power is royal. Indeed, those with this power in the church are called kings not less truly and properly but more so than those with temporal jurisdiction, as much as government in spiritual things is more lofty and worthy than government in temporal things. Thus, they who are truly and properly called judges are truly and properly called kings. Moreover, on this account they are called pastors, since feeding *(pascere)* is properly a kingly power, for which kings used once to be called pastors. Thus Christ's words to Peter, "Feed my sheep," through which he gave him the government *(regimen)* of the church, and made him king and prelate of it.

ch. 7. *The relationship between the spiritual and temporal powers.* [231] The spiritual power is as a primary cause of temporal power in three ways — first, by way of instituting it, as Hugh of St. Victor said *(De sacramentis* 2.2.4); although there appear to be contrary opinions on the institution of temporal rule. For some say that it is from God alone, and in no way depends on the spiritual power for its institution. Others, by contrast, propose that the temporal power, if it is to be legitimate and just, must either be joined to the spiritual in the same person, or be instituted by the spiritual: otherwise it is unjust and illegitimate. It is possible, however, to take a *via media* between these opposed opinions, which appears more reasonable. This proposes that temporal power is instituted materially and incompletely from men's natural inclinations (and so also from God working in nature), but completely and *in form* from the spiritual power derived in a special way from God. For, far from destroying nature, grace bestows it perfecting form. Thus the spiritual power, reflecting grace, does not exclude the temporal, reflecting nature, but in-forms and perfects it. Indeed, all human power needs to be in-formed and perfected by the spiritual. And this formation consists in approval and confirmation. Thus power among infidels, although it may spring from natural inclination and so be legitimate, is nonetheless without form, as it lacks the approval and confirmation of spiritual authority. Likewise temporal power among the faithful is incomplete and unformed until approved and confirmed by spiritual authority. Thus we should understand that *human or temporal power as such* requires a twofold formation to be complete according to the principle *(ratio)* of power. It needs a formation by faith, because, just as there is no true virtue without faith — as Augustine said: "Where knowledge of the highest and unchangeable truth is lacking false virtue is found even in the best morals" (Prosper of Aquitaine, *Sententiae ex Augustino delibatae* 106), so there is no true power without faith. Not that mere human power is nothing and absolutely illegitimate, but it is not true or perfect; as the marriage of infidels is not perfect and entirely valid, although it is in some way true and legitimate.

Besides faith temporal power needs the confirmation and approval of the spiritual power in order to be formed and complete, and cannot be formed and complete without spiritual establishment. Hence kings are anointed not only as a requisite sign of holiness, but also as a sign of their approval and formation by the spiritual power, which is why they are anointed by bishops. Thus the spiritual power may be called the form of the temporal in the same manner as light may be called the form of color. For color has in it something of the form of light, but only weakly; so that, without the presence of a brighter light "forming" it, color cannot move sight by its own capacity *(inherenter)*, but virtually *(virtualiter)*. Similarly, the temporal power has something of true power, being from human law, but requires formation by the spiritual for its perfecting, and so is said to be "instituted" by it.

Thus Hugh of St. Victor said (*De sacramentis* 2.2.4) that in the church the priestly dignity hallows and makes holy the royal dignity by blessing, and gives it form by institution. He explains himself further as follows. The elevation of one man over another is of human law, being achieved by nature, whereas the elevation of a man of faith over his fellow men of faith is of divine law, arising as it does from grace. For grace and not nature makes men faithful; and as the divine law is *with* Christ's vicar, to him belongs the institution of faithful kings, and temporal power over the faithful, in so far as they are faithful. Thus the temporal princes in the church have power over men from human law, but over the faithful from divine law. Since, therefore, faith forms nature, the temporal power is instituted by being formed, and conversely, formed by being instituted (that is, approved and confirmed) by the spiritual power. So is it plain how the spiritual power has the nature of primary cause *(rationem agentis cause)* in respect of the constitution of the temporal.

Moreover, according to Hugh, the spiritual power has judgment of the temporal, since it can and ought to direct, correct, and punish it for its crimes and faults not only with spiritual but also with temporal penalties, even to the extent of proceeding to depose it, should the gravity of the fault necessitate it. The deposition is not of the power itself, which would destroy the order of powers, but of the individual who is abusing the power granted to him. Thus, the "power" said to be deposed means the one who has power. As is indicated by the Gloss (Glos. ord.) on the passage of Romans (13:1), "Let every soul be subject to the higher powers": "Sometimes 'power' refers to the power itself that someone has from God, at other times it refers to the man who has the power." The power that is good and ordained for the good is not to be deposed or condemned, but rather the person who uses it unduly. For just as temporal power over the faithful is conferred by the spiritual, so it can be removed by the same. No prince is altogether excepted from the judgment that reinforces the elevation of spiritual over temporal power, since the latter is everywhere subject to spiritual judgment, and especially that of the Roman pontiff who has full temporal power. For although other pontiffs can judge the temporal power, (a bishop can excommunicate a king at the diocesan level), the highest pontiff has full judgment over all princes, according to the type of judgment conveyed to the spiritual power.

In that the spiritual power can exclude from the community of the faithful, and in that temporal possession, property, and action are founded on being part of the community, the spiritual power extends into temporal things. According to divine law no one can justly and legitimately possess any temporal thing if he does not submit himself willingly to the divine lordship *(dominio)* from which he holds it, and if he does not use it rightly. Therefore, infidels and sinners who remove themselves from God's lordship and use temporal things perversely, possess those things unworthily and unjustly according to divine law, whatever the position of human law. This bears out Augustine's saying that "by divine law all things belong to the just" (cf. *Ep.* 153.26 [pp. 130-31 above]). Moreover, he who is not subject to ecclesiastical power has not submitted to God. The right use of temporal things is ordered use: use ordered to the end at which the spiritual power aims and to which it directs. Wherefore no one possesses any temporal thing justly unless, in possessing it, he submits himself to the spiritual power — which would not be the case unless the spiritual power extended to those temporalities.

Translation: Editors, from H.-X. Arquillière, *Le plus ancien traité de l'Église: Jacques de Viterbe, De regimine christiano (1301-1302)* (Paris: Gabriel Beauchesne, 1926).

PART 4

POLITICAL COMMUNITY, SPIRITUAL CHURCH, INDIVIDUAL RIGHT, AND *DOMINIUM*

The humiliation of Pope Boniface VIII by King Philip IV of France, with which the fourteenth century opened, had a symbolic importance greater than its practical effects. Of more moment than the royal curtailment of both curial finances and the administrative and juridical independence of the French church was the defeat of papalist corporational ecclesiology. This construed the church as a hierarchy of corporations, whose spiritual and temporal unity, authority, and right finally resided in the papal head. Against it the French government and its more radical publicists set the conception of a national church, whose temporal unity, authority, and right finally resided in king and realm. Twenty-five years later Marsilius of Padua gave a radical twist to the state-church idea by amalgamating it with the contention that the clerical estate should be *without jurisdiction as such* and, borrowing from the Franciscan Spirituals, without property. This French royalist ecclesiology was a milestone on the way to the spiritualized church.

The royalist ecclesiology also advanced the concept of *political community*, a defining idea of the fourteenth and fifteenth centuries, drawing on the notion of *corpus mysticum*, "the mystical body." The history of the concept is telling (Kantorowicz 1957, especially ch. 5). Inspired by St. Paul's idea of the church as the body of Christ, the phrase was first applied to the consecrated eucharistic host (cf. 1 Cor. 10:17), but within canonist circles from the mid–twelfth century onward was steadily transferred to the church's institutional hierarchy and the complex apparatus wielded by it. The consequent politicizing of the church's spiritual communion was at the same time a spiritualizing of her political order, which held attraction for other polities. Although further civilian application of the term to all kinds of secular corporations involved in many cases the loss of its spiritual overtones (*corpus mysticum* becoming synonymous with the *corpus fictum* of corporational law), its application to inclusive political communities tended to retain them. The regular employment of the term by French legists and theorists from the thirteenth century lent an exalted moral and religious aura to the national realm, which abetted Philip the Fair and his successors in their Gallicanizing of the church. Of comparable effect (especially in connection with war levies) was use of the term *patria* (fatherland) with its evocation of eternal Rome, seat of empire, Augustine's heavenly city, the church militant on earth, and even the Holy Land, for which the crusader martyrs died. (Later, however, the mystique of *patria* would undergo a sharp detachment from its ecclesiological associations in the civic patriotism of Renaissance humanists such as Petrarch, Boccaccio, Salutati, and Bruni.)

The defeat of papalist theory entailed more than the simple translation of an ecclesiological motif into the secular medium. It entailed a theoretical transformation in which jurisdictional plenitude was redistributed, so as to be situated in the body politic as well as in the head. Not that theocratic kingship was a wasting political asset in the consolidating European kingdoms, least of all in France; rather, it was reminted as a stronger currency by merging with the transcendent power of the political community. Philip the Fair convoked an unprecedented assembly of prelates and barons in the wake of Boniface VIII's bull *Unam Sanctam,* to throw the weight of the realm behind the demand that the pope be tried before a general church council, so testifying to the authority of both "mystical bodies," that of the state and that of Christ. The greatest theological apologist of the French church and realm, John of Paris, defined the intrinsic political powers and principles of secular communities as well as ecclesiastical, making a two-pronged contribution to constitutional theory that was to be repeated in the next century by the equally powerful Parisian theologian Jean Gerson.

Indeed, the interdependence of political theory and ecclesiology was as striking in the fourteenth and fifteenth centuries as it had been in earlier exchanges between empire and papacy. Many of the ablest political thinkers of these centuries, whom contemporary scholarship has rediscovered as important proto-modern theorists, developed their political conceptuality systematically in relation to both church and commonwealth. While Christian political thought had always had this dual focus, these thinkers were distinguished by their self-conscious and systematic comparisons of the two institutions. Three features marked their style of political argument: the formulation of general concepts and principles equally applicable to civil and ecclesiastical polities, the investigation of differences between the two polities, and the articulation of divine and human components in political action.

No doubt many factors accounted for this novel orientation. In some instances the comparisons were motivated by interlocking crises within the secular and ecclesiastical realms. John of Paris, Marsilius, and Ockham were closely associated with monarchs struggling to consolidate their power, and with popes under attack for spiritual as well as civil offenses. A more general factor was the differentiation and complexification in every sphere of life. Political forms proliferated to include commune and city-state as well as manor, dukedom, principality, kingdom, and empire, not to speak of the vast variety of ecclesiastical corporations; legal forms proliferated to include structures of mercantile and urban law, as well as feudal, manorial, royal, imperial, and canon laws (Berman 1983; see p. 238). In the intellectual sphere, the absorption of Aristotle's political writings accustomed thinkers to the comparative evaluation of different types of regime.

Linked to the motifs of *political community* and *spiritual church* was that of *individual power*. In this, too, political theory and ecclesiology interacted, and many of the contributory factors were the same. The multiplication of religious and secular orders, guilds, confraternities, and societies enabled an increasing number of individuals to participate actively in voluntary associations on the basis of explicit commitments, oaths, or vows. Many religious orders and confraternities were concerned with cultivating personal piety and striving for spiritual perfection, while the escalation of economic societies was tied up with the capitalist expansion of trade and the resulting rise in social mobility. Spiritual and economic purposes were regularly combined in vocational, mercantile, and urban communes, many of the latter being founded by charters establishing the "liberties" of citizens and their equal rights and role in self-government.

A key strand in the growth of individualism was the crystallization of the concept of subjective (as distinct from objective) rights. To this Ockham, Marsilius, and Gerson were crucial contributors, drawing on Franciscan theological developments, nominalist and Aristotelian philosophical concerns, and new formulations in feudal, civil, and canon law (Tierney 1997). While John Wyclif's theory of "evangelical dominion" situated the concept of subjective right within an Augustinian-Platonist and christological framework that emptied it of much of its proto-modern content, he nevertheless reinforced the rivalry between an *epistemic* authority inalienable from individuals and a *coercive* authority residing in institutions, a Socratic tension that Ockham had already revived in his groundbreaking discussion of infallibility within the church.

I. Political Community. The idea of a political community was that of an original moral totality with intrinsic rights or powers. For fourteenth-century thinkers the Aristotelian notion of a self-sufficient polity revitalized the old Roman-law idea that the people *(populus, universitas)* were the source of political authority and law, so that the attributes of a legal corporation came to be applied to the people as a whole. While earlier civilians, and even more, feudal jurists such as Glanvill and Bracton, had upheld the authority of the community in customary and statute law, only now were its full implications systematically explored.

In a first wave of theorizing John of Paris, followed by Marsilius of Padua and William of Ockham, elaborated the powers of a political community: making and approving law; electing, advising, and correcting its rulers; even removing rulers, should they present an extreme threat to corporate existence and well-being. All three explored these powers while repudiating the papal claim to exercise a "plenitude of power" in temporal as well as spiritual government, finding in the people a restraint upon the divinely constituted monarch. In their arguments, the *universitas* might sometimes be the whole church (or empire), sometimes a corporate part of it, e.g., the French community of the realm. But in either case, rulers other than the pope, whether kings, bishops, or emperors, were understood to derive their authority from the community they represented and from God — but not from his earthly vicar!

In assigning such powers to civil and ecclesiastical polities, these thinkers argued from both natural and divine law, thereby exhibiting a convergence of reason and revelation in establishing political principles. Of the three, Marsilius went furthest in separating the two sets of arguments, giving theoretical priority to those from natural law interpreted in the light of Aristotelian political philosophy. By contrast, John of Paris and Ockham combined the arguments, while giving priority to divine law and scriptural revelation. Marsilius, too, offered the most voluntarist and rationalist account of the body politic as sovereign: the communal will is the perpetual "legislator," the "primary efficient cause" of governing acts and of law, in relation to which the elected ruler is only the "secondary efficient cause" (i.e., instrumental, or executive), accountable to the "legislator." The whole people (or its "weightier part") is the most virtuous, prudent, and observant judge of what action and law is required by the common good. Ockham, on the other hand, stood furthest removed from any theory of popular sovereignty, emphasizing both the direct divine source of the ruler's authority and the fallibility of a council representing the whole, even of a general council of the church. Marsilius, finally, came closest to conflating commonwealth and church in a single corporation, whose political powers would ideally be exercised by laity alone.

For these thinkers, however, the parallel principles of secular and ecclesiastical order did not eclipse the divergences between the two spheres. They all recognized that clerical government (or authority), regulated by the law of salvation, rested on a different foundation and conformed to a different pattern from secular government. It was ministerial rather than dominative, pedagogical rather than juristic, and less dependent on (or independent of) coercive measures and wealth for its effectiveness. John of Paris carefully separated the relations of ecclesiastical and civil governments to proprietorship, emphasizing the priority of private ownership in the civil order as opposed to common ownership in the ecclesiastical order. With even more theoretical subtlety, Ockham distinguished the ways in which papal and imperial power could be said "to depend on God alone," attributing a constitutive function to the community in the case of imperial power, and a merely instrumental agency in the case of papal power.

A second wave of theorizing came with the conciliarist movement that arose out of the Great Schism (1378-1417), in which, as the result of a disputed papal election, rival claimants established separate obediences from Rome and Avignon. The first objective of conciliarist writers was to justify the resolution of the schism by a general council convoked without the papal consent required in law; so the early tracts, emanating largely from Paris masters, stressed the supreme right of the ecclesial community to take whatever measures were necessary to preserve its unity. Drawing on Marsilius and Ockham, they invoked the principles of equity (*epieikeia*) and the natural right of communal self-preservation as supplementary to the controlling scriptural theme of the presence of Christ through the Holy Spirit to a gathering of the whole church (cf. 1 Cor. 12:12-27; Eph. 4:11-16).

By the time of the Council of Constance (1414), which had to judge not two but three papal claimants, the conviction was widespread that the council's work should go beyond uniting the church to restore sound ecclesiastical government by reinforcing episcopal rights and curtailing papal and curial powers. Thus the decree *Haec sancta synodus* (1415) invested the general council with supreme authority, held "immediately from Christ," to reunite and reform the church; and *Frequens* (1417), in calling for the regular convocation of general councils, affirmed the active, continual (as opposed to occasional) character of conciliar power. Nevertheless, the leading theologians of Constance, Pierre d'Ailly and Jean Gerson, resisted pressures for conciliar sovereignty. Rather, they argued that the plenitude of church power resided simultaneously in Christ's vicar as the highest authority and in the general council as comprehending the whole hierarchy, a formulation similar to that proposed fifty years later by English jurist John Fortescue for civil government. Indeed, d'Ailly and Gerson regarded church and kingdom as two species of "perfect political community," and the mixed constitution as the best for both; in the church, however, the mixed regime was prescribed by divine law, while in the commonwealth it was only recommended by political prudence.

The Council of Basel (1431-49) did, however, tend toward ecclesiastical corporatism, rendering the pope a minister of conciliar policy with inferior jurisdiction to the council's, liable to correction, suspension, and deposition. The major contributors propounded the infallible and divine grace of Christ's mystical body to an extent that left the pope's infallibility and representative status severely undermined. Typically, they combined theological conceptions of the church's supernatural communion with natural corporational principles, such as that the head is sovereign over the members separately but subject to them collectively. Basel was also distinguished by its incorporation of laity and ordinary clergy as equal voting members together with the bishops.

The dominating intellectual figure at Basel was the mystical theologian and philosopher Nicholas of Kues, whose conciliar treatise *The Catholic Concordance* was easily the most original and commanding political work of the first half of the fifteenth century. Drawing on Neoplatonic ideas of harmony, hierarchy, equality, and the coincidence of opposites, he forged an unparalleled account of the interlocking principles of representation and consent. Of particular interest were the place of symbolism and delegation in his representational theory, and the coincidence of divine with human law, intention, and action, in his examples of consent and consensus: e.g., the election of rulers and the making and ratification of laws. Rationalism and mysticism blend in a holistic political theory that, with historical hindsight, appears distinctively Germanic.

II. Spiritual Church. At the opposite end of the ecclesiological spectrum from Constance and Basel, which focused attention on jurisdictional issues, was the articulation in the fourteenth century of a nonjurisdictional ecclesiology, the architect of which was Marsilius of Padua, and its theological interpreter, John Wyclif. While the two thinkers wrote in different political cultures and were subject to different influences, they displayed a striking concurrence on the need for a unified civil jurisdiction with hegemony over external church order, and on the "spiritual" character of clerical authority, undermined by the pernicious papal usurpation of lay power. For Marsilius, as for his fellow countryman Dante, in an Italy desolated by factional strife and war between and within its city-states, in which the papacy was implicated directly and indirectly, a united jurisdiction was merely a hope — a hope pinned to the success of imperial expeditions. For Wyclif, unified civil polity was an English political reality, but one under strain from the financial losses of the Hundred Years' War and the excessive exactions and interference of the papal court. As with other impulses for church reform in the fourteenth century, theirs was fed by repugnance at the venality, bureaucracy, and decadence of the Avignonese papacy.

For their model of a dispossessed and powerless church, both Marsilius and Wyclif drew inspiration from the Franciscan discipline of poverty, purportedly founded on the practice of Christ and the postresurrection church in Jerusalem. For their conception of the church's mission as proclamatory and pedagogical, they drew inspiration from the primacy of preaching and teaching among the friars. They were significantly divided, however, on their theology of the church's ministry. Marsilius followed Dante down the Averroist path of positing a sharp disjunction between natural and supernatural, this-worldly and otherworldly goals, construing clerical ministry and authority almost entirely in terms of otherworldly ends. The clergy teach and administer Christ's law of salvation with a view to the future life, declaring his judgment on sin committed in this world and warning of punishment in the next. Their juridical role is confined to the sacrament of penance, which applies to the "internal forum" of the conscience; while the "external forum" is controlled by the "faithful human legislator," that is, by the consensus of the whole "body of the faithful" articulated by its "weightier part" and acted on by the ruler.

Wyclif, in contrast, stayed close to the christological idealism of the Bonaventuran tradition, construing the proper "lordship" *(dominium)* of the clergy as contemplative and communicative participation in the love and truth of Christ in the world, with no otherworldly or juridical focus. In Wyclif's "evangelical lordship," which is both nonproprietary and nonjurisdictional, the perfection of created and sanctified humanity is a present power, acting alongside civil power in a sinful human polity and exercising spiritual influence over it, though subject to its political dispositions in church affairs. Unlike Marsilius, Wyclif set up no popular will as an independent political locus, but only the saving rule of Christ through the gospel law of love. He conceived civil government as merely a more remote participation in Christ's lordship tailored to the needs of sinful humanity, a view echoed by Fortescue a century later, perhaps suggesting an exceptionally close continuity of English political theology with the christocentric kingship of the Carolingian tradition. Wyclif's dialectic of evangelical and civil lordship, gospel law and human law, appears to have a dynamic subtlety and fruitfulness that is lacking in the more static, juristic dualism of Marsilius and Dante; yet it failed to offer a defense against the secularizing bent of the Marsilian program. Fortescue executed a naturalistic turn within English juristic theology (wedded, in his case, to Thomistic legal humanism) in an appealing but all too facile identification of the mixed rule in the English commonwealth with the communion of saints in the kingdom of Christ.

III. Individual Power. The exploration of individual power in the fourteenth and fifteenth centuries was intimately linked with the articulation of the spiritual church and, less obviously, with the articulation of political society. Regard for the individual was by no means a cultural novelty, having emerged as one strand of the twelfth-century renaissance, clearly perceptible in canonist developments, and again as an element in the spirituality of the new disciplines of the thirteenth century. Yet in the late medieval period it underwent a fuller theoretical development.

Ockham's contribution has long been recognized, more in lamentation than approval, by scholars inclined to see it as part and parcel of the disintegrative effects of a nominalist metaphysic and voluntarist theology. Recently, however, a more sympathetic reading of his political writings, with closer attention to his sources (especially canonist and Franciscan), has discerned a more balanced interest in the spiritual good of individuals and in communal welfare. It is not incidental that his most precise formulation of individual natural right appeared in his defense of the Franciscan use of temporal goods without positive legal right, i.e., without ownership. For the Franciscan wedding of spiritual perfection to a renunciation of property had focused attention not only on the venial sins to which proprietors were prone, but also on the place of ownership within the condition of fallen humanity. Ownership belonged to humanity's second nature, i.e., to the universal rational arrangements comprehended by the *ius gentium,* the law of nations (which, for much civilian thought, was identical with the law of nature). Thus, Ockham's association of the individual right to the material necessities of life with the state of man's created perfection was neither daring nor original, though none the less influential. He thematized "right" as a dimension of the original moral standing of human individuals. Moreover, in repudiating the doctrine of papal plenitude, he wrote of liberties as well as rights, "granted to mortals by God and nature," and, most importantly, incorporated these liberties into his concept of Christian freedom, understood not only as emancipation from the burdens of the Mosaic Law and from sin, but also as original individual powers of action.

Marsilius, too, formulated a concept of individual natural right in defense of the Franciscans' nonproprietary use of goods owned by others. His discussion achieved a startlingly clear distinction between objective right and subjective right, and, with the same crystal clarity, construed human freedom as the individual's ownership of his acts.

It was Wyclif's genius to derail (though not for long) the course of individual natural right with his much misunderstood theory of "lordship of grace" *(dominium ex gratia).* This completely inverted the notion of *dominium,* which previously had denoted unrestricted civil jurisdiction or ownership, and so emphasized the transcendent, communal, and contemplative aspects of redeemed human agency as to set *dominium* at loggerheads with a natural-law-based individualism. At the same time, it expressed the epistemological authority of the Christ-centered believer to judge the failures of political authorities in church and commonwealth.

Jean Gerson, in the footsteps of d'Ailly, was largely responsible for recasting *dominium* in the natural law mold, and advancing the development of subjective rights theory. Reversing Wyclif, he asserted a self-standing "natural dominion" distinct from evangelical lordship and independent of regenerating grace, identical with the natural right of individuals to appropriate and use the necessities of life. As with Ockham's natural rights and liberties, this *dominium* could not be alienated or forfeited, even by sinful humanity, and so persisted among infidels. As a conciliarist,

Gerson was chiefly preoccupied with the rights of the church as a corporation; but individual natural right had a place, it would seem, as a speculative extension of the corporational rights of individual officeholders, an extension motivated by his concern for Christian liberty.

Bibliography: G. de Lagarde, *La naissance de l'esprit laïque au déclin du moyen âge,* 2nd ed., 5 vols. (Paris: Éditions Nauwelaerts, 1956-70); E. Kantorowicz, *The King's Two Bodies: A Study in Medieval Political Theology* (Princeton: Princeton University Press, 1957); G. Leff, *Heresy in the Later Middle Ages: The Relation of Heterodoxy to Dissent, c. 1250-1450,* 2 vols. (Manchester: Manchester University Press, 1967); J. Muldoon, *Popes, Lawyers, and Infidels: The Church and the Non-Christian World* (Liverpool: Liverpool University Press, 1979); F. Oakley, *Natural Law, Conciliarism, and Consent in the Late Middle Ages* (London: Variorum, 1961); B. Smalley, ed., *Trends in Medieval Political Thought* (Oxford: Blackwell, 1965); Q. Skinner, *The Foundations of Modern Political Thought,* vol. 1 (Cambridge: Cambridge University Press, 1978); B. Tierney, *Foundations of the Conciliar Theory: The Contribution of the Medieval Canonists from Gratian to the Great Schism* (Cambridge: Cambridge University Press, 1955); B. Tierney, *The Idea of Natural Rights: Studies on Natural Rights, Natural Law, and Church Law, 1150-1625* (Atlanta: Scholars Press, 1997); C. E. Trinkaus, *"In Our Image and Likeness": Humanity and Divinity in Italian Humanist Thought,* 2 vols. (London: Constable, 1970); R. Tuck, *Natural Rights Theories, Their Origin and Development* (Cambridge: Cambridge University Press, 1979); M. Villey, *La formation de la pensée juridique moderne* (Paris: Montchrétien, 1968; 4th ed., Paris, 1975); D. Weinstein, *Savonarola and Florence: Prophecy and Patriotism in the Renaissance* (Princeton: Princeton University Press, 1970).

John of Paris

(ca. 1250-1306)

Jean Quidort (John of Paris) appears in retrospect to be a thinker wholly in sympathy with his time and place, a product of the spirit of his age, at the leading edge of its intellectual movements. Trained at the University of Paris in the 1270s in a theological environment dominated by the debate about alleged Aristotelian novelties, he sided with his fellow Dominican Thomas Aquinas, defending his work against Franciscan charges of infidelity to the teachings of Scripture and the Fathers.

In his relatively brief life his political writings made a late appearance during the protracted quarrel of King Philip IV of France and Pope Boniface VIII (1296-1303) over jurisdiction in the French kingdom. The inciting issue in the dispute was Philip's exaction of a war levy from the French clergy without the papal consent established in church law; to which, in Boniface's judgment, he added further infringements of the church and the pope's juridical, economic, and administrative rights. Boniface's initial response (*Clericis laicos* [1296]) was simply an uncompromising prohibition of such taxation, but his later, more far-ranging censure of Philip (*Asculta fili* [1301]) asserted the pope's divinely granted jurisdictional supremacy over secular rulers, his right to judge universally in temporal matters "on account of sin" *(ratione peccati)*, in proof of which he summoned the senior clergy of France to a consultation over reform of kingdom and church. The bull and summons caused the French laity and clergy to rally behind their monarch's temporal sovereignty. Among the royalist contributions from clerical masters at the University of Paris appeared Jean Quidort's treatise *On Royal and Papal Power (De potestate regia et papali)*, probably just prior to Boniface's most celebrated bull, *Unam Sanctam*, toward the end of 1302. This apogee of hierocratic imperialism, which derived secular rule from, and subjected it to, papal lordship, hardened the resolve of the French government to prosecute the pope before a general council, and precipitated his arrest. With other Dominican colleagues John pledged to cooperate in the council's convocation and may also have collaborated in another antipapal treatise (*Rex pacificus* [ca. 1303]; see Saenger 1981).

Although neither highly original nor particularly radical as compared with other specimens of royalist polemics from the dispute, *On Royal and Papal Power* was the most learned and able theoretical response to Rome from the French camp. (A recent attempt to situate its argments within earlier Dominican/Franciscan disputes, while overstating the case, reveals some interesting continuities of theological controversy; Coleman 1991, 187-224.) Its importance for future developments, difficult to overestimate, lay in the so-called proto-modern conceptual strands embedded in its exposition of antipapal arguments. These included ideas of communal representation and election, political office as public stewardship, the conformity of political acts to law and the common utility. Taken chiefly from Scripture and Roman law, they were drawn together within a Thomistic-Aristotelian conception of political society that enhanced their usefulness for future generations.

At the same time the treatise contained an important counterfoil to political naturalism in its christocentric ecclesiology. To undermine the papal claim of imperial "plenitude of power" *(plenitudo potestatis)*, i.e., universal and unbounded jurisdiction over men and their possessions, John argued that Christ had endowed the apostolic ministry with *exclusively spiritual powers* of sacramental administration, teaching, and correction. This spiritualizing of clerical power implied an extension of lay authority over the church's temporal possessions and external administration, and a reduction of clerical authority over lay property and civil administration.

These moves did not, however, prevent him from subjecting ecclesiastical and civil polities to *the same normative principles*. He foreshadows conciliarist thought not only in applying the same corporational principles to both governments, but also in explicating certain of them in terms of a conjunction of divine and human action.

Let us note the following details:

1. John radically qualifies his conventional presentation of the subordination of temporal to spiritual ends (ch. 5) by arguing that there may be "true and complete justice necessary to the government of a kingdom without Christ's rulership," on account of the completeness of "acquired moral virtues" without the "theological virtues" (ch. 18.27). The independent integrity of natural justice and virtue reinforces his view of secular rule as neither derived from nor answering to spiritual rule.

2. Of the six spiritual powers conferred by Christ on his apostles and disciples (and their clerical successors), John regards as the most contentious the power of ecclesiastical jurisdiction, i.e., coercive judgment in the church's "external forum" (ch. 12). His chief concern is to reduce the opportunity for clerical infringement of secular authority. Accordingly, he confines regular ecclesiastical cognizance to "spiritual cases" (i.e., crimes against the church), and occasional cognizance of temporal cases to those which involve "sin of belief or error" (e.g., "if a man thinks that usury is no mortal sin"), repudiating the papal claim to universal "cognizance of sin" (ch. 13). Ecclesiastical censure he confines to the *spiritual* punishments of "excommunication, suspension and interdict," allowing beyond this only sanctions undertaken "indirectly and incidentally" and voluntary temporal penances (ch. 13).

In appearing to grant the unique papal power of "establishing ecclesiastical jurisdiction," he does not concede an original or ongoing dependence of episcopal upon papal authority. Rather, he affirms that all clerical authority at the episcopal level and below derives directly from God and from popular election and consent (ch. 10), a central thesis of future Gallican and conciliarist ecclesiology.

By recognizing a power of receiving remuneration for ministry, on the other hand, John invests the priesthood with a subjective right to something not yet possessed, and so extends the concept of right beyond property ownership to subjective entitlement, undoubtedly under the influence of civilian and canonist thought.

3. On the relationship of government to ownership, he achieves some important clarifications. Regarding the church's temporalities, he distinguishes the "proprietary right" belonging to individual congregations (corporations), the "right of usage" enjoyed by the clergy, and the "general administration and dispensation" exercised by the episcopacy. Moreover, he assigns the "general" *proprietorship* of ecclesiastical temporalities to the universal church (the community of communities), and the "general" *stewardship* of them to her papal head, in opposition to the doctrine of Rome's universal *proprietorship*. The civil community, by contrast, he presents as organized around the private ownership of property acquired by individuals (in Lockean fashion!), over which rulers hold *neither proprietary nor administrative, but juridical, authority,* ordered to the temporal and the spiritual common goods (ch. 7). Both his concept of acquisition and his sharp distinction between ownership (*dominium*) and jurisdiction *(iurisdictio)* may well be adventurous theoretical responses to the transition of late medieval society from feudal to commercial relationships (Coleman 1983; 1985).

4. Secular and spiritual authorities have parallel and separate foundations in two earthly communal wills, and concurrently in the divine will. Thus royal power comes "from God and the people who choose a king, either as an individual or as a member of a dynasty" (ch. 10), while papal power comes from God and the whole church, who choose a pope through the representative college of cardinals. The primary right of correction and deposition of either authority rests with the electing communities (chs. 5, 13). A secondary right, however, rests with the rival authority (king or pope), whose juridical interference may be regular or "incidental" depending on the sphere in which the occasioning offense has occurred — a theory adroitly developed by Ockham. In line with these principles, the author dismantles the papalist theories of the "donation of Constantine" (see pp. 228-30 above) and the "translation of the Roman Empire" (ch. 21).

Further Reading: J. Coleman, "Medieval Discussions of Property: *Ratio* and *Dominium* according to John of Paris and Marsilius of Padua," *History of Political Thought* 4 (1983): 209-28; J. Coleman, "*Dominium* in Thirteenth and Fourteenth-Century Political Thought and Its Seventeenth-Century Heirs: John of Paris and Locke," *Political Studies* 33 (1985): 73-100; J. Coleman, "The Dominican Political Theory of John of Paris in Context," in *The Church and Sovereignty c. 590-1918,* ed. D. Wood (Oxford: Basil Blackwell, 1991); J. Leclercq, *Jean de Paris et l'Ecclésiologie du XIII siècle* (Paris: Vrin, 1942); J. A. Watt, *The Theory of Papal Monarchy in the Thirteenth Century: The Contribution of the Canonists* (London: Burns & Oates, 1965); C. T. Wood, ed., *Philip the Fair and Boniface VIII* (New York and London: Holt, Rinehart & Winston, 1967).

From *On Royal and Papal Power*

Proemium: It is in similar fashion that the truth about sacerdotal power can be found in the middle position between two erroneous opinions. On the one hand, the Waldensians have erred with their assertion that the successors of the Apostles, namely the pope and ecclesiastical hierarchy, were denied any power in temporal affairs and that it was unlawful for them to possess temporal wealth. They go on to argue that the true church of God with genuine apostolic succession in its prelates endured only until Pope Sylvester's time. For when the church accepted Constantine's donation it became Roman and no longer the true church of God. In their view the true church has been eclipsed except in so far as it is preserved and restored by themselves. [. . .]

On the other hand, standing opposed to the Waldensian error is the position of Herod who on learning of the birth of a king called Christ believed that his kingship was of the human kind. Certain moderns seem to have taken their views from this source. For they have moved so far from the first error as to assert that the pope, in so far as he stands in Christ's place on earth, has a power over the properties of princes and barons as well as cognizance and jurisdiction of them. They say that the pope has power in temporalities in a more excellent way than the prince because he has primary authority, derived directly from God, whereas the prince has his power mediately from God through the pope. They go on to argue that the pope only exercises this power in certain determined cases, as the decretal *Per venerabilem* (X 4.17.13) states. It is the prince who has the immediate executive power. Anyone who has spoken differently has in their view taken the part of the princes. If the pope sometimes says that he has no temporal jurisdiction, this must be understood as referring to regular and immediate exercise of jurisdiction, or because he wants to maintain peace between church and princes or to ensure that prelates are not overprone to become preoccupied with temporal matters and secular business. They argue further that the relationship of the pope to temporalities is different in kind from that of princes and prelates. For he is sole true lord in that he can at will absolve a usurer from the debt he owes through his crime, take from another as he wishes what otherwise belongs to him, and that should he do such an act it is valid, even though he commits sin in doing it, though he should only do it for such reasonable cause as defence of the church or the like. Other prelates and princes, by contrast, are not lords but guardians, agents, stewards. [. . .]

As between these antithetical views (everyone would agree that the first is false) truth *lies* midway. Against the first opinion, it must be believed that it is not wrong for prelates to have lordship and jurisdiction in temporalities. But this power is not theirs because of what they are or because they are vicars of Christ and successors of the Apostles. It can be quite appropriate for them to have such in virtue of the concession and permission of rulers if they are so endowed through the piety of rulers or receive them from some other source. [. . .]

ch. 5. *The precedence in dignity of kingship or priesthood.* The arguments presented in the last chapter make it easy to see which comes first in dignity, kingship or priesthood, for what is later in time is generally higher in dignity, as is the perfect in respect of the imperfect and as is end to means. We say therefore that sacerdotal power is greater than the royal and excels it in dignity, because we always find this:

what is concerned with the final end is more complete and more worthy and gives direction to what is concerned with an inferior end. Now kingship is ordained to the end that the community may live according to virtue, as has been said already, and it is further ordered, under the care and direction of Christ, whose ministers and representatives are the priests, to a higher end, namely the enjoyment of God. [. . .]

Yet though it be said that in principle the priestly is a more dignified function than the royal, it does not follow that it is superior in every respect. For the lesser power, the secular, does not stand related to the greater, the spiritual, as to its origin and derivation in the way that, for example, the power of a pro-consul is related to the emperor who is his superior in all ways since his power derives from the imperial power. The relationship is much more comparable to that between a head of household and a military commander, for the power of neither of these derives from the other but rather both from some superior power. So therefore in temporal matters the temporal power is greater than the spiritual, and in these matters is in no way subject to the spiritual since it is not derived from it. Both take their origin immediately from one supreme power, namely, God. Hence the inferior is not subject to the superior in all things but only in those matters in which the supreme power has subordinated the inferior to the superior. [. . .]

ch. 6. *The way in which the pope has lordship of ecclesiastical property.* There are some who wish to elevate the pre-eminence of the priesthood over the royal dignity to the degree where the priesthood is not merely superior in dignity, as discussed earlier, but even superior in the order of causality. They claim that the secular power is contained within the spiritual power and is established by it. It now remains, therefore, to discuss in what way the pope who has the chief place among Christ's priests has or has not got secular power. The method of argument will be to examine firstly, papal lordship of property and then, secondly, it being established that he is not the true lord but the administrator in both principle and practice, whether he has at least the original and primary authority, as superior and as one who exercises jurisdiction.

On the first point what has to be examined to start with is the form of power he has over the property of ecclesiastics in so far as they are ecclesiastics. Here it must be appreciated that ecclesiastical property, as ecclesiastical property, has been given to communities, not to individual persons. So therefore, no one person has proprietary right and lordship over ecclesiastical property. It is the community concerned which itself has these, as in the case, for example, of the church of Chartres or some similar church, where it is the community which has right of lordship over its property. An individual person may have a right of usage for his maintenance judged according to his needs and considering what is appropriate for his rank. He has this not as an individual in his own right but purely as part and member of the community. Difference of rank is relevant here for there is a difference between an ordinary canon, who has no right other than the one just mentioned, and the member who is the principal and head of the community, the bishop. The congregation would not be an ordered unity unless it had one head and chief member, and he has not only the right of use of the goods of the community according to the needs of his position in the manner already mentioned, but has, in addition, general administration and dispensation of all the property of the community, allocating here to someone his just due, dispensing there in good faith as seems to him expedient for the good of the whole. This is the position of any bishop in any cathedral church.

It is not only the particular community of ecclesiastics which is joined in unity of the spirit. There is a certain general unity among all ecclesiastical communities since all together make up the one church united with one principal member, the lord pope, on whom falls the charge of the church as a whole. He therefore as head and supreme member of the universal church is general steward of all ecclesiastical goods, whether spiritual or temporal. He is not indeed lord of them, for only the community of the universal church is mistress and proprietress of all goods generally, and individual communities and churches have lordship in the property allocated to them. In like manner also, individual persons, whoever they may be, do not enjoy lordship; principal members have stewardship only, except in so far as they draw recompense for their service, according to the need of the person and position, with perhaps something in addition granted by the general steward, with good faith the determining factor. [...]

From all this, it appears that they speak ill who say that no individual other than the pope, nor any corporate body or community has right and lordship in ecclesiastical property. They say that the pope is not only general administrator and steward but that he alone is true lord and proprietor of ecclesiastical property. They argue that he can make decisions about it and alienate it as he wishes and that what he decides has legal validity, though it is granted that he commits sin if he acts without reasonable cause. They urge further that other prelates or even princes or communities do not hold true lordship but are only the guardians, protectors and stewards of such properties. This is false as has been shown, for the pope is no more universal lord of all ecclesiastical property than are lesser prelates lords of the property of their chapters. The pope is in fact manager and steward of ecclesiastical property; further, he takes for himself a greater share of the common store according to the demands of his position, which is that of the holder of fulness of power, than other prelates who are called only to a part of the pastoral charge. [...]

Further, it cannot be argued that the pope has right and lordship of such property not in his private capacity but in his public office, in that he acts as general vicar of Jesus Christ, who is principal lord of all property. Such a proposition carries no force because it is as God that Christ is lord of all property, ecclesiastical and non-ecclesiastical. As man, he does not have communication or contact with those who are in the church; those who have given property to the church did not intend to transfer proprietary right and lordship to Christ either as God, because everything already is his, or as man, because he now has no use for such authority. What they intended was to transfer proprietary right to Christ's ministers. Hence such property belongs to the church as proprietor, to the prelates as stewards, as has been said.

It follows from this that the pope has no authority to take away ecclesiastical property at will, claiming that whatever he commands has legal validity. This would be true were he lord of all ecclesiastical property; since, however, he is but steward for the community, he must keep good faith with it and he has no power therefore over this property, except such as the common necessity and welfare of the church requires. Thus it is written in 2 Corinthians (10:8, 13:10) that God has given power to prelates for building up, not for destruction. Hence if the pope deprives anyone arbitrarily, not in good faith, what he does is illegal. This means that not only is he obliged to do penance for his sin as if guilty of misusing his own property, but also, as betrayer of a trust, he is bound to make restitution either from his patrimony, should he have one, or from what he has acquired, since he has cheated in what is not his.

A monastic community can act to depose its abbot and a church might do the same to its bishop, if it has been established that he has squandered the property of the monastery or church and that he has broken faith in taking for his private gain what was for the common good. In the same way, should a pope betray his trust in taking the property of churches for reasons other than the common good, which as chief bishop is his especial charge, he can be deposed should he not, on admonition, make amends. This argument is based on D. 40 c. 6, where it is said: "those who can judge all cannot be judged by anyone, except if detected in error of faith" on which the *Gloss* comments: "Should he be detected in any other fault and having been admonished does not amend and is giving scandal to the church, the same shall be done," though others say, arguing from D. 21 c. 7, that this should only be done by a general council.

If the pope knows that there are persons, whether ecclesiastics or laymen, who are laying complaint against him on the score of unjust stewardship as they are permitted and indeed under obligation to do, he can in no manner legally remove them or depose them from what is theirs; he has no authority from God to do this. They set their mouths against heaven (cf. Ps. 72:9) and do injury to our most holy father the pope, who preach that his will is absolute in this way when it ought rather to be supposed that his will is not contrary to law and that he would not wish to deprive anyone of what is his without reasonable cause, since to do so is illegal. . . . So therefore, since it is the trust of stewardship which God has given to Peter and the pope, the pope may not go against the express will of God to take away arbitrarily from anyone any right of administration which has been received justly and properly, if he has not manifestly been at fault. This then is the power that the pope has over ecclesiastical property.

ch. 7. *The power of the pope over lay property.* What has been said already makes clear what the true relationship of the pope to lay property is. He is even less the lord of it, nor is he its steward, unless perhaps in some extreme need of the Church. In such a case of necessity he would be acting as one who declares what the law is, not as steward. In order to prove this principle, it must be remembered that lay property is not granted to the community as a whole as is ecclesiastical property, but is acquired by individual people through their own skill, labour and diligence, and individuals, as individuals, have right and power over it and valid lordship; each person may order his own and dispose, administer, hold or alienate it as he wishes, so long as he causes no injury to anyone else since he is lord. Such properties therefore are not mutually interordered or interconnected nor do they have any common head who might dispose of and administer them, since each person may arrange for his own what he will. Thus neither prince nor pope has lordship or administration of such properties. For the reason that sometimes the peace of everybody is disturbed because of these possessions, when someone takes what belongs to another and also because at times some men, through excessive love of their own, do not place it at the service of the common need and welfare of the country, a ruler has been established by the people to take charge of such situations, a judge between the just and the unjust, a punisher of injustices, a measurer of the just proportion owed by each to the common need and welfare. The pope is in a similar position by virtue of that supreme headship which he holds not merely over the clergy but generally over all believers, in so far as they are the faithful. In any major necessity of faith and morals all the possessions of the faithful are common property and must be shared, even the chalices of churches. The pope, as general teacher of faith and morals, has the power to manage the goods of the faithful and to decide what should be expended on the common defence of the faith, which might otherwise be destroyed by pagan invasion or some such disaster, and so great and obvious might this need be that he could demand tithes and fixed contributions from individual members of the faithful, though these should be according to their means, since some people for no reasonable cause might otherwise be burdened more than others in giving aid for defence of the faith, a matter which concerns everybody. Such a disposition by the pope is no more than a declaration of law. He would have the power to coerce by ecclesiastical censure those who disobeyed or spoke against his measures. [. . .]

ch. 10. *Granted that Christ had jurisdiction over lay property, still he did not hand it on to Peter.* [. . .] Some people think they can escape from some of the foregoing arguments by making a pithy distinction. They argue that secular power belongs to the pope immediately and as the prime source of authority, that he does not have immediate executive power but grants it to the secular ruler, so that while it can be acknowledged that the power itself is from the pope, the exercise of it is the secular ruler's. These are the words of those who attempt to refute some of the arguments advanced above. There are too some other writers who say that God has given the pope the primary authority of temporal jurisdiction, but not its exercise. The emperor has the executive power from God, not from the pope. This argument is intended to refute some of what has been said above.

That sort of evasion, however, is completely absurd and it is inconsistent with their own arguments. For if the Church acknowledged the executive power to be the secular ruler's, then the secular prince might judge such exercise of it as fell to the pope and take it away from him. But they do not allow this since they assert that the pope cannot be judged by anyone. If God gave the pope the primary authority of secular power, but not its exercise because this would be inappropriate, how can he accept from a prince what God has judged he cannot or ought not to have? And how does he give him what he gets back from him? Again, if the pope has secular power directly from God and the secular ruler its exercise directly from the pope, then the secular ruler is the minister of the pope, just as the pope is the minister of Christ. But this seems to go against the canon of Scripture. For the Apostle says of the king and prince in Romans 13:4-6: "If thou do that which is evil, fear; for he beareth not the sword in vain. For he is God's minister: an avenger to execute wrath etc." and again, later: "Therefore also you pay tribute." He is the minister of God, then; the Apostle does not say, minister of the pope, but minister of God: "For in this do they serve him" and the *Gloss* (Glos. ord.): "Serve God." Again, royal power existed in its own right in both principle and practice before papal power and there were kings before there were any Christians in France. Therefore in neither principle nor practice does the royal power there come from the pope but from God and the people who choose a king either as an individual or as a member of a dynasty, as was in fact done formerly. To say that royal power came first directly from God and afterwards from the pope is quite ludicrous. For this cannot be unless Christ gave to Peter the power of conferring the royal office. But as has been shown, this comes indisputably from God. [. . .]

Further, the argument for the proposition that the pope is the intermediary of the power of lesser bishops and priests would seem to be stronger than any argument that he is the mediate agent of the power of kings. For the prelates of the church are more immediately dependent on him than are secular rulers. Nevertheless the power of prelates does not come to them from God indirectly through any papal mediation, but directly and also from the people who elect them or consent to their election. For it was not Peter, of whom the pope is successor, who sent forth the other Apostles whose successors are the bishops, or the seventy-two disciples whose successors are priests with pastoral responsibility, but Christ who sent them himself and not through any intermediary, as is found in Matthew 10:5 and Luke 10:1. Neither was it Peter who breathed on the other Apostles, giving them the Holy Spirit and the power of forgiving sins, but Christ himself, as is written in John 20:22. D. 21 c. 2 tells how all received similar and equal power from Christ at the same time. Paul declares that he did not receive his apostolate from Peter but from Christ, that is from God without intermediary: "Paul, an apostle not of men, neither by man, but by Jesus Christ and God the Father" and later, "For neither did I receive it of man nor did I learn it," and further on still, he says that he had not seen Peter until he went to Jerusalem in order to see him, three years after his call to preach the Gospel. Therefore the argument that royal power is derived from the pope in any way whatsoever is correspondingly less tenable.

ch. 12. *The powers given by Christ to Peter and the Apostles.* For a clear solution of these problems [concerning the pope's temporal authority], one must decide first what kind of power the Apostles and disciples of the Lord, and through them the bishops and priests, received from Christ. For the *Gloss* on Luke 10 says, just as the Apostles provide a model for the episcopate, so the seventy-two disciples provide a model for the priesthood of second rank, and all sacerdotal power is concentrated in these two ranks. [. . .]

According to the Gospel, six powers were granted to the Apostles and disciples of the Lord and so therefore, to their successors, the ministers of the Church. One is that power of consecration, sometimes called the character or power of order, which the Lord gave to his disciples at the Last Supper when, in giving them his body in the form of bread, he bade them: "Do this in remembrance of me" (Luke 22:19). Another is the power of administering the sacraments and especially the sacrament of penance, which is the power of the keys or of spiritual jurisdiction in the sphere of conscience, consisting in the authority of judging between leprosy and non-leprosy (cf. Lev. 13:1-59), in the power of absolving from guilt and changing the condition of the guilty from deserving the punishment of eternal damnation to being punishable by temporal punishment. This power in the spiritual forum was promised to Peter as Matthew says, "I will give you the keys etc. . . ." (16:19), and in Matthew 18:18 where it was promised to all: "Truly, I say to you, whatever you bind on earth etc. . . ." It was actually given to them when it was said to them in John 20:21-23: "'As the Father has sent me, even so I send you.' And when he had said this, he breathed on them and said to them, 'Receive the Holy Spirit. If you forgive the sins of any, they are forgiven etc.'" In some people's opinion, this power of administering the sacraments is the same in essence as the power of consecration, though differing according to the different ways it is used in respect of the body of Christ, true or mystical, and this is the completion of the sacerdotal power. Hence in the ordination of mere priests and also of bishops, who are high priests, the same words are pronounced, namely, those already mentioned above: "Receive the Holy Spirit. If you forgive etc."

The third power is the authority of the apostolate or of preaching which the Lord gave them, as is recounted in Matthew (10:7) when he said, "And preach as you go, saying 'the kingdom of heaven is at hand,'" and in the last chapter of Matthew (28:19): "Go therefore and make disciples of all nations."

The fourth power is judicial, that power to coerce in the external forum by which sins are corrected through fear of punishment, especially sins in scandal of the church. The concession of this power is in Matthew 18:15-18: "If thy brother shall offend against thee etc. . . . . If he will not hear them, tell the church; and if he will not hear the church let him be to thee as the heathen and publican." [. . .] It is especially to be reflected upon that in these three acts, illumination through doctrine, purification through correction, perfection through the sacraments, priests have the full power of priestly rule over the community of the faithful.

The fifth is the power, according to the opinion of some, of distributing ministers by establishing ecclesiastical jurisdictions, so that confusion be avoided. This power was granted to Peter and his successors in virtue of what was said to him: "Feed my sheep" (John 21:17). For the power of the keys and the power of jurisdiction were given to all equally without establishing boundaries and each could use it effectively on any sinner at all, since the sinner is the proper subject on which the action of the jurisdiction, the absolution, falls, in the same way as wheaten bread, without qualification, is the matter on which falls the exercise of the power of order. Thus it was that St. Paul exercised his priestly rule over the people uncircumscribed by any boundaries, as is obvious to anyone who examines his letters. Because, as has been said already, confusion could have arisen from this state of affairs, the Lord in his foresight granted to Peter and his successors the authority to distribute ministers of the church and determine their jurisdictional boundaries, when he said: "Feed my sheep," implying that there was a general administration of sheep and sheepfold. This command was not given to any other apostle.

The sixth power would seem to spring logically from all the foregoing. It is the power to receive what is necessary to maintain a suitable standard of living from those to whom they minister spiritually. This power was given to Peter and the Apostles and declared obligatory when, in Matthew (10:8-10), after Christ had bade them go out and preach, he added instruction as to how they should conduct themselves towards temporal possessions: "You received without pay, give without pay" and the *Gloss (Glossa interlinearis):* "Just as I give you such power without pay, do you also give freely lest the grace of the gospel be corrupted"; and again the text: "Take no gold, nor silver, nor copper in your belts," *Gloss:* "You who exhort others to despise riches"; and again in the text, "No bag for your journey, nor two tunics, nor sandals, nor a staff," *Gloss:* "He deprives them of the near necessity of the help of a stick lest they who teach that all things are ruled by God should take heed for the morrow." The text goes on about their power to accept: "For the labourer deserves his food," *Gloss:* "See here why he ordered them to carry nothing, since all is their due," and elsewhere in the *Gloss* (Glos. ord. on Matt. 5): "Receive necessities only in so far as they satisfy need and then, untroubled in mind, you will be the freer for what is eternal." More is said concerning this power to accept what is necessary for livelihood in the last chapter of St. Matthew and in Luke 10.

These six then, are the powers which the Apostles received from Christ. They received no other except that of working miracles to confirm faith. There is no necessity for bishops and priests to follow them here, for the confirmation of our faith is so manifest as no longer to need confirmation by miracles.

ch. 13. *Prelates of the Church have neither lordship nor jurisdiction in temporal affairs.* [. . .] The second power is that of the keys in the sphere of conscience. This too is wholly spiritual: Chrysostom commenting on John 20:22, "Receive the Holy Spirit etc." says, "The spiritual power was granted to them only for the forgiveness of sins" (cf. *Hom. in Ioh.* 86.3). The pope gets no authority in temporal affairs from this power except when, in the sphere of conscience, he persuades the penitent to make satisfaction, imposing this as he imposes other penances, even corporal ones. Yet no one becomes hereby subject to him in any unqualified sense, but under conditions, namely if he sins and wishes to do penance. If a person should not wish to do penance, then the pope cannot compel him because of the power of the keys as a secular prince can compel a culprit by fine or other correction imposed and enforced even on one unwilling to accept punishment. [. . .]

The nub of the difficulty lies in the fourth power, that of judgment in the external forum. It must be appreciated that there are two facets of this power. The first is that authority to judge and settle cases which is indicated in the text: "Tell the church" (Matt. 18:17). The other is the power to coerce, spoken of in the text: "Let him be to thee as a heathen etc." These are the two keys of the external forum. About the first of them it must be understood that the ecclesiastical judge, in so far as he is an ecclesiastic, has no regular cognizance of anything in the external forum except for spiritual cases which are called ecclesiastical, and none at all in temporal cases, save for reason of sin. If, however, the nature of the sin is well understood, it is not proper to make an exception even of this case, since the Church does not have cognizance of sin except in so far as it is brought into the spiritual and ecclesiastical sphere. Sin can be committed in temporal matters in two ways. One way is by sin of belief or error; for example, if a man thinks that usury is no mortal sin or when in property matters there is a doubt as to the legality in God's eyes of the titles by which he holds or sells. Since it is the divine law which rules on such questions and it is by this law that the ecclesiastical judge must frame his judgments, there can be no doubt that legal process concerning them is for the ecclesiastical judge only. The other way of committing sin in relation to temporal property is in aiming to secure another's property for oneself or making threats to do so. Cognizance of such matters belongs to the civil judge only and he judges according to those human civil laws which regulate the buying and selling of property in order to ensure that property is put to those proper human uses which would be neglected if everyone held everything in common. For if things were held unreservedly in common, it would not be easy to keep the peace among men. It was for this reason that private possession of property was introduced by the emperors, as Augustine says in his commentary on St. John's Gospel reproduced in D. 8 c. 1: "Take away the laws of emperors and you are not then able to say, this thing is mine." [. . .]

In the matter of the power of correction or ecclesiastical censure, it should be appreciated that its relevance is purely spiritual, for it can impose no penalty in the external forum save only a spiritual one, except it be conditionally and incidentally. It is for the ecclesiastical judge to lead men back to God, preventing them from sinning and correcting them; this function is exercised in the way God had laid down, which is that of excluding sinners from the sacraments and from the community of the faithful and the other penalties appropriate to ecclesiastical coercion. In saying that temporal punishments might only be imposed "conditionally," I mean on the condition that the sinner wishes to repent and to accept money penance. For an ecclesiastical judge cannot, for reason of sin, impose a corporal or money penalty as can a secular judge, except on the condition that the guilty party is willing to accept it. Should he not be willing to accept it, then the ecclesiastical judge coerces him by excommunication or other spiritual penalty, which is the very most he can inflict; he can impose nothing beyond that. I also said "incidentally," because if a ruler were an incorrigible heretic and despises ecclesiastical sanctions, the pope might take such action with the people as would lead them to deprive him of office and to depose him. The pope might do this in a case of ecclesiastical crime of which the cognizance is his, by excommunicating all who continued to obey him as their ruler. Thus it would be the people who actually deposed him, with the pope acting "incidentally." Conversely, if the pope were an incorrigible criminal, a cause of scandal to the church, a secular ruler might indirectly bring about his excommunication and deposition, by warning him, personally or through the cardinals. Should the pope refuse to submit, the ruler might take such action with the people as would force the pope to resign or be deposed by the people. For the emperor could prevent each and everyone from obeying such a pope or serving him as such, by taking securities or imposing corporal penalties. Thus each can take action against the other, for both the pope and emperor have universal jurisdiction, though the one has spiritual jurisdiction and the other temporal.

A distinction must be made here. Where a king offends in spiritual matters like faith and marriage and the other categories of offences which fall to the ecclesiastical jurisdiction, the pope's first action should be to admonish him. If the offender persists in his conduct and proves incorrigible, he should then be excommunicated. But the pope may inflict no further penalties, as was said, except incidentally by acting with the people after the guilty party has despised ecclesiastical correction. Where, however, the king offends in those temporal matters of which cognizance is not ecclesiastical, then the initiative in starting the corrective process is not the pope's but belongs to the barons and peers of the kingdom. If they cannot act, or dare not, they can ask for the help of the church and the church, on this request from the peers to uphold the law, can admonish the prince and proceed against him according to the procedure already described.

A similar principle applies should a pope commit a temporal offence, cognizance of which belongs to the secular ruler, as for example, if he lend at usury or protect usurers and especially if he does what the civil law forbids. In such a case it would fall to the emperor, if there were one, as having primary right, to correct by admonition and punishment, for it is to the prince that belongs primary right of correcting all evil-doers: "For he beareth not the sword in vain" (Rom. 13:4). [...]

If, however, a pope were delinquent in spiritual matters, for example, in conferring benefices simoniacally or squandering church property or depriving churchmen and chapters of their rights or by false profession or teaching in matters touching faith and morals, then he ought first to be warned by the cardinals who stand in the place of the whole clergy. Should he prove incorrigible and the cardinals cannot on their own remove this scandal from the church, then they may have recourse to the secular arm to support the rule of law. Then the emperor, as a member of the church, at the request of the cardinals, should proceed against him to accomplish his deposition. For this is the manner that the church holds the secular sword, not indeed to wield of itself or at its command but at its signal and entreaty, as Bernard told Eugenius. For this is the way the two swords are bound to lend help to each other in that common charity which unite[s] the members of the church.

ch. 18. *Replies to papalist arguments.* (27) *Society cannot be ruled without justice.* It must be said that acquired moral virtues can be complete without theological virtues; they are not completed by them, except by a certain incidental completion, as Augustine suggested in the book of his opinions compiled by Prosper [reference not found in Prosper of Aquitaine's *Sententiae*]. Thus there is that true and complete justice necessary to the government of a kingdom without Christ's rulership, since a kingdom is ordered to life according to acquired moral virtue. This may be completed incidentally by virtues of other sorts. Or it can be put this way: Augustine's argument was that there is no true justice where Christ is not ruler, not because it could not exist at all, but because there was not even acquired virtue in a society whose members were in slavery to demons and idols and yet believed they served justice. It was these people whom Augustine denounced as not preserving true justice. It can be said that the commonwealth of the Christian people is not rightly ruled unless its leader is the pope who is the vicar of Christ in spiritual things, nor can justice be preserved otherwise than by obedience to him, as is just in spiritual matters.

ch. 21. *The Donation of Constantine.* It has been seen what the ministers of the Church can do by virtue of their position as vicars of Christ. It remains now to examine what popes can do by virtue of the gift of Emperor Constantine the Great. For it is claimed that he gave the western empire to Silvester and his successors and the imperial emblems such as his palace, crown and the like. Some people propose therefore that by reason of this gift, the pope is emperor and lord of the world and that he can appoint kings and get rid of them like an emperor, especially during a vacancy of empire, and that he can be appealed to, just like an emperor. But to make matters clearer, there must be set out the relevant facts concerning this donation and translation of the empire, as they are recorded in the chronicles and ancient histories. It will then be possible to form a better appreciation of what authority the pope may have by virtue of the donation, particularly over the king of France.

It must be understood then of the above said donation that on the evidence of Hugh of Fleury's *Chronicle*, of the *Cosmography*, of Constantine's *Letter to the bishops*, and of *The Testament of Constantine*, Constantine only donated one province, namely Italy, along with certain other territories, not including France, and translated the empire to the Greeks, where he built a New Rome. About the alleged translation of the empire from Greeks to Germans, made by the Romans and the pope, in the person of Charlemagne, it must be understood that these same chronicles make it clear that the translation was of such a nature that the substance of the empire remained Greek, whilst its title became western. Another way of looking at it is: a division was made whereby two emperors were named, one at Rome, the other at Constantinople. The Romans, it may be read, seceded from the Greeks for three reasons: for the defence of the republic they had accepted from Charlemagne when the emperor Constantine was negligent; because they were provoked to hatred of Empress Irene who blinded her son Constantine and her grandsons in order to secure the empire for herself alone; because they were angered and chagrined at Constantine's transference of the empire from themselves to the Greeks. Hence they chanted the imperial praises for the victorious Charles. These considerations make it clear that the donation and translation confer no power on the pope over the king of France. There are four reasons to be considered.

[. . .] Thirdly, even granting the validity of the donation and its general applicability to the empire as a whole, it is clear that it gives the pope no power over the king of France. For although it can be discovered of the Gauls that they are subject in certain respects to the Romans at the time of Emperor Octavian, the Franks never were subject. [. . .]

Fourthly, granting again that the donation was valid and was made of the whole empire and granting, in addition, that the Franks were then subject to the empire (which we do not admit), nevertheless it gives no power over the kingdom of France to the pope. For he is not the emperor. But granting that he were the emperor, the Franks were exempt by prescription from imperial jurisdiction down to the time in question. [. . .]

ch. 22. *Whether it is lawful to debate and make judgment about these issues concerning the pope.* [. . .] Thus, in my view, when a pope palpably does wrong, for example, by depriving churches of their rights, by dispersing the Lord's flock, by scandalizing the church through some act of his, he can be judged, prevailed upon and censured by anyone at all, not in virtue of his office but in ardour of charity, and not with imposition of punishment but with reverend exhortation. For the love which every person is owed, is not less owed by reason of the greater position to which he has been raised. Thus the pope is not less owed the compassion of charity because of his position, but while heedful of authority, according to Augustine, everyone is bound under the obligation of charity to fraternal correction of one who does wrong; the obligation to show the compassion of charity is not the less for its recipient being the pope, though it must be shown with humility and reverence. Hence when Peter had come to Antioch, Paul withstood him to his face because he was blameworthy (Gal. 2:11). It cannot be said then that to speak out in this context is to "touch the sacred mountain" or "set the mouth against heaven," because when a pope manifestly offends, that is not heaven, nor when he is corrected can it be said that the mouth is being set against him; rather is it for him. No one should fear that on this account scandal would touch the pope, for general scandal does not bother grown men, only children. Hence to fear scandal about the pope in this respect is to hold the pope to be childish, less mature than someone whom others dare to correct when he does wrong. Therefore in truth, it is these people who "set their mouths against heaven," in saying about the most holy father such things as that he is revengeful and acts harshly towards anyone who judges anything of what he does. This view certainly should not be held, since he is not a man of petty spirit but is righteous, and more righteous than others.

What if the pope were to announce that he considered any man a heretic who maintained a certain opinion about which the learned differ and were to make this pronouncement without a general council? For example, if he were to say that he considers every person who denies the temporal subjection of the king of France and similar dignitaries to himself as a heretic? I reply that words spoken by a pope without precision should, as far as possible, always be given a reasonable meaning. Thus the pronouncement should not be interpreted as meaning that appeal can be made to him in temporal matters or that he has lordship in temporal property or that he can intervene to decide disputes of property possession. This interpretation would be obviously contrary to Scripture and commonly accepted doctrine and would constitute a novelty of a kind which the pope should only put forward after deep deliberation, the holding of a general council and discussion by the learned everywhere. Therefore, having regard to how he has disclosed his mind on the matter, the pronouncement ought to be interpreted in this reasonable sense: the subjection referred to is subjection by reason of crime, that is, in an issue concerning sin, or further, it should be understood with reference to the forum of conscience, as was said earlier. Should he finally disclose, however, that he intended a novel and injurious meaning (perish the thought), he must be endured in patience, as far as this is possible without endangering justice and truth, in the spirit of Matthew 5:41: "And whosoever will force thee one mile, go with him the other two." Recourse must be had to God who, having in his hand the heart of the pope, just as he has the heart of a king, can bring about change of heart in him. So too can he remove a pope, just as he can remove a king from his throne. If, however, there lies danger to society in delay, because the people are being led into evil opinion and there is danger of rebellion, and if the pope should disturb the people unduly by abuse of the spiritual sword, if there is not hope that he will otherwise desist, then I consider that the Church ought to move into action against him. The prince acting with moderation may resist the violence of the papal sword with his own sword. In this he does not act against the pope as pope but against an enemy of himself and of society, just as Aod [Ehud] the Israelite who slew Eglon king of Moab with the dagger he had tucked away against his thigh because he oppressed God's people in harsh servitude (Judges 3:16-22), was not considered to have killed a ruler but a wicked man who was an enemy. This was not action against the church, but for it. So the people, fired by the ardour of faith, commendably deposed Pope Constantine, a source of scandal to the church, and put out his eyes. So too the emperor Henry [III] going to Rome, deposed by imperial and canonical sanction Benedict IX and two others whose contentions for the papacy scandalized the Church, and made Clement II pope of the Roman church, as may be read in the *Chronicles of the Romans.*

Translation: J. A. Watt (Toronto, 1971). Used with permission.

Dante Alighieri

(1265-1321)

Dante was born into a tumultuous and futile period of Italian political life, dominated by power struggles among and within the Italian states. He was himself a victim of the factional strife ruining Florence, exiled as a "White Guelf" in 1301 (never to return) when the "Black Guelfs," supported by Pope Boniface VIII, took control of his native city, so terminating his youthful participation in its public affairs. It is hardly surprising that Dante would see political peace and well-being as lying beyond the aggressive independence of small communities in some more comprehensive political unity, or indeed, that he should appeal to the Roman Empire as the political panacea, despite his earlier repudiation of "Ghibelline" imperial loyalties. What is surprising is that the author of *The Divine Comedy* should produce such a naturalistic apology for the Roman Empire as *Monarchia:* a mixture of Aristotelian, Averroist, and Neoplatonic philosophical conceptions, combined with the romanticism of Roman historians and poets, Virgil above all.

His apology, dated either between 1310 and 1312 or as late as 1317 (Shaw 1995), consists of three distinct arguments. The first is that universal monarchy alone brings the uninterrupted and all-encompassing peace that enables mankind to fulfill its divinely willed, natural task of actualizing the "possible intellect" in its multifarious potentialities. This conception of a single work for the human race as an organized totality is Dante's original contribution, a bold translation of the Averroist idea of a unified intellectual substance in which all humans participate into a dynamic principle of civilizational perfection. For only as universal humanity attains the form of political community can it actualize its full theoretical, moral, and artistic potentialities. The excerpts below are chosen to represent the development of this argument.

Dante's second argument is that the Roman people acquired universal empire by divine and natural right. God justly rewarded the natural virtue of the Roman people with the right to rule (2.3), manifesting their providential mission by many miraculous interventions (as attested by pagan authors!) (2.4), but chiefly by willing his Son to be born, registered, judged, and punished under Roman law promulgated by Roman juridical authority (2.11, 12). According to Dante, the effectualness of Christ's atonement for human sin depended on the universality of Roman law and judicial process, embracing all mankind (2.12). Moreover, the Roman people have vindicated their right to world rule by pious and public-spirited action to establish the universal common good, which is peace with liberty (2.5).

The concluding argument is that, since the goals and foundations of empire and church are so disparate, their earthly heads must be independently constituted and must act independently. In defending the full scope of the emperor's temporal jurisdiction, he undermines the papal claim of "plenitude of power" by explicating the logic of political delegation (3.7). He leaves us with such an extreme disjunction between earthly bliss and heavenly bliss, between the perfection of natural powers under the tutelage of the emperor's reason and the perfection of the theological virtues under the tutelage of the Holy Spirit, that we despair of the church making any contribution to the political common good (3.16).

Further Reading: C. T. Davis, *Dante and the Idea of Rome* (Oxford: Clarendon Press, 1957); A. P. D'Entrèves, *Dante as a Political Thinker* (Oxford: Clarendon Press, 1952); K. Foster, *The Two Dantes and Other Studies* (London: Darton, Longman & Todd, 1977); G. Holmes, *Dante* (Oxford: Oxford University Press, 1980); U. Limentani, ed., *The Mind of Dante* (Cambridge: Cambridge University Press, 1965); P. Shaw, ed., *Dante, "Monarchia"* (Cambridge: Cambridge University Press, 1995).

From *Monarchia,* Book 1

3. Therefore let us see what is the ultimate end of human society as a whole; once that is grasped our task is more than half accomplished, as the Philosopher says in the *Nichomachean Ethics* (1098b6-7).

In order to clarify the issue it may be noted that nature forms the thumb for one end and the whole hand for another, and the arm for yet another, whilst each of these ends is different from that to which the whole man is destined. Similarly the end towards which the individual's life is directed is different from that of the family community; the village has one end, the city another and the kingdom yet another; and last of all there is the end that the eternal God has established for the whole human race by means of nature, which is the mode of his art. It is this last-mentioned end that we are looking for and that will be the guiding principle in our inquiry.

The first point to realize is that "God and nature never do anything in vain," for whatever is brought into existence has some purpose to serve. Yet it is not the being of any creature but its proper function that is the ultimate end of the Creator in creating, and so the proper function is not instituted for the sake of the creature but the latter is created to serve its proper function. From this it follows that there must be some particular function proper to the human species as a whole and for which the whole species in its multitudinous variety was created; this function is beyond the capacity of any one man or household or village, or even of any one city or kingdom. What this function is will become clear once the specific capacity of mankind as a whole is evident.

I say therefore that no property that is common to beings of different species represents the specific capacity of any one of them; because, since its ultimate capacity is what constitutes each species, it would follow that one being would be specifically constituted by several specifying factors — which is impossible. And so the specific capacity of man does not consist simply in *being*, since the very elements also share in being; nor does it consist in *compound being*, which the plants also enjoy; nor in the capacity to apprehend things, for this is shared by brute animals; but it consists in the capacity to apprehend by means of the *possible intellect*, and it is this that sets man apart both from inferior and from superior beings. For although there are other beings endowed with intellect, their intellect is not *possible* like that of man, since such beings are completely intellectual; in them intellect and being coincide, and their very *raison d'être* is to perform intellectual operations without pause, otherwise they would not be eternal. From which it is evident that the specific capacity of mankind is an intellectual capacity or potentiality. And because the potentiality cannot wholly and at once be translated into action by one man, or by any one of the particular communities listed above, mankind has to be composed of a multitude through which this entire potentiality can be actualized. Similarly there needs to be a multitude of things which can be generated from prime matter if the entire potency of that matter is to be brought into action all the time. The alternative is for potentiality to exist separately; this is impossible. Averroes agrees with this opinion in his commentary on the *De anima*.

This intellectual power of which I am speaking not only deals with universal forms or species but also extends to particulars. Hence it is commonly said that the speculative intellect becomes practical by extension, and is thereby directed towards action and making things. I am referring to action as governed by the virtue of political prudence, and to the making of things as governed by art. But both are subordinate to speculation as the highest function for the sake of which the supreme goodness brought mankind into being.

From all this one begins to appreciate what is meant in the *Politics* by the sentence: "Men of superior intellect naturally rule over others" (1252a31).

4. Thus it is quite clear that the task proper to mankind considered as a whole is to fulfil the total capacity of the possible intellect all the time, primarily by speculation and secondarily, as a function and extension of speculation, by action. Now since what applies to the part applies also to the whole, and since the individual man becomes perfect in wisdom and prudence through sitting in quietude, so it is in the quietude or tranquillity of peace that mankind finds the best conditions for fulfilling its proper task (almost a divine task, as we learn from the statement: "Thou hast made him a little lower than the angels" [Heb. 2:7]). Hence it is clear that universal peace is the most excellent means of securing our happiness. This is why the message from on high to the shepherds announced neither wealth, nor pleasure, nor honour, nor long life, nor health, nor strength, nor beauty, but peace. The heavenly host, in-

deed, proclaims: "Glory to God on high, and on earth peace to men of good will" (Luke 2:14). "Peace be with you" was also the salutation given by the Saviour of men (Matt. 10:12; John 20:21), because it was fitting that the supreme Saviour should utter the supreme salutation — a custom which, as everyone knows, his disciples and Paul sought to preserve in their own greetings.

This argument shows us what is the better, indeed the very best means available to mankind for fulfilling its proper role; and also what is the most direct means of reaching that goal to which all our doings are directed — universal peace. This will serve as the basis for our subsequent argument. Such is the common ground which we declared to be essential so as to have something axiomatic to which all our proofs and demonstrations can refer.

5. Let us now return to what was said at the beginning; that there are three main problems to be solved concerning temporal monarchy, or, as it is more commonly called, the empire. As we promised, we intend to investigate them in the order signified and on the basis of the axiom that we have established.

Thus the first question is whether temporal monarchy is necessary for the well-being of the world. Now no substantial objection either from reason or authority can be urged against it, and its truth can be demonstrated by the clearest and most cogent arguments, the first of which is derived from the authority of the Philosopher in his *Politics* (1254a28). There the acknowledged authority states that when several things are directed towards a single end it is necessary for one of them to act as director or ruler and for the others to be directed or ruled. This statement is supported not only by the glorious renown of its author but also by inductive reason. Again, if we consider an individual man we see the same principle verified: since all his faculties are directed towards happiness, his intellectual faculty is the director and ruler of all the others — otherwise he cannot attain happiness. If we consider a home, the purpose of which is to train its members to live well, we see that there has to be one member who directs and rules, either the *"paterfamilias"* or the person occupying his position, for, as the Philosopher says, "every home is ruled by the eldest." And his function, as Homer says (*Odyssey,* IX. 114 quoted in Aristotle, *Politics* 1252b20), is to rule the others and lay down laws for them; hence the proverbial curse, "May you have an equal in your home." If we consider a village, whose purpose is mutual help in questions of persons and goods, it is essential for one person to be supreme over all others, whether he is appointed from outside or raised to office by the consent of the others; otherwise, not only would the community fail to provide mutual sustenance, but in some cases the community itself would be utterly destroyed through some members' scheming to take control. Similarly if we examine a city, whose purpose is to be sufficient unto itself in everything needed for the good life, we see that there must be one governing authority — and this applies not only to just but even to degenerate forms of government. If this were not so, the purpose of civil life would be frustrated and the city, as such, would cease to exist. Lastly, every kingdom (and the end of a kingdom is the same as that of a city but with a stronger bond of peace) needs to have a king to rule over and govern it; otherwise its inhabitants will not only fail to achieve their end as citizens but the kingdom itself will crumble, as is affirmed by the infallible Word: "Every kingdom divided against itself shall be laid waste" (Matt. 12:25).

If this is true of all communities and individuals who have a goal towards which they are directed, then our previous supposition is also valid. For, if it is agreed that mankind as a whole has a goal (and this we have shown to be so), then it needs one person to govern or rule over it, and the title appropriate to this person is Monarch, or Emperor.

Thus it has been demonstrated that a Monarch or Emperor is necessary for the well-being of the world. [. . .]

10. And wherever there is a possibility of dispute there has to be a judgment to settle it; otherwise there would be imperfection without a remedy to heal it, which is impossible, since God and nature never fail in essentials.

It is clear that a dispute may arise between two princes, neither of whom is subject to the other, and that this may be their fault or their subjects'; therefore a judgment between them is indispensable. However, since neither can take cognizance over the other (neither being subject to the other — and equals do not rule over equals), there needs to be a third person enjoying wider jurisdiction who by right rules over both of them. This person must be either the monarch (in which case our argument is complete) or not the monarch (in which case he himself will have an equal outside his own jurisdiction, and it will again be necessary to have recourse to a third person). Either this process will go on to infinity (which is impossible) or eventually it will lead us back to a first and supreme judge whose judgment will either directly or indirectly solve all disputes: he will be the Monarch, or Emperor.

Therefore monarchy is necessary to the world. And the Philosopher appreciated this truth when he wrote: "Things resent being badly ordered; but 'to have different rulers is bad; therefore one Prince'" (*Metaphysics* 1076a4 quoting Homer, *Iliad* 2.204).

11. Besides, the world is best ordered when justice is at its strongest. Hence Virgil, wishing to praise the new order that seemed to be emerging in his day, sang: "Now the Virgin is again returning; and the Saturnian reign begins once more" (*Eclogue* 4.6). By "Virgin" he meant Justice, which is also called Astrea; by "Saturn's rule" he referred to the finest ages, which are also described as "golden." Justice is at its strongest only under a Monarch; therefore monarchy or empire is essential if the world is to attain a perfect order.

If we are to understand the minor premise fully, it is essential to appreciate that justice, in itself and strictly considered, is rectitude, a rule permitting no deviation; consequently it is not subject to shades of more or less, any more, for instance, than *whiteness* considered in the abstract. For such forms, though realised in particular circumstances, are simple and unchangeable in essence, as the Master of the Six Principles (*De sex principiis,* wrongly attributed to Gilbert de la Porrée) rightly says. In actuality, however, these qualities vary in intensity according to the degree in which the subjects of them are subject also to their contraries. But where the contrary of justice is at its faintest (whether actively or potentially), there justice is at its strongest; and then one may truly say — as, indeed, the Philosopher does — "Neither Lucifer nor Hesperus is so wonderful" (Euripides, fr. 490, quoted by Aristotle, *N.E.* 1129b28-9). For then she is like Phoebe in the rosy serenity of the dawn gazing across at her brother on the opposite horizon.

Considered in its potentiality the contrary of justice sometimes lies in the will; for even when justice is present, if the will is not entirely purified of all cupidity, justice is not present in all the splendour of its purity; because such a subject offers a certain resistance to it, however slight; hence those who try to arouse a judge's passions deserve to be censured. In regard to acts, the contrary of justice is to be found in limitations on power; for since justice is a virtue governing relations between people, how can it operate in practice without the power of rendering to each his due? Hence the stronger the just man is in practice, the greater will be his justice.

On the basis of this exposition we reason as follows: justice is most powerful in the world when located in a subject with a perfect will and most power; such is the Monarch alone; therefore justice is at its most potent in this world when located in the Monarch alone.

This preparatory syllogism is of the second figure, with intrinsic negation, and takes the following form: all B is A; only C is A; therefore only C is B. That is: all B is A; nothing except C is B. The first proposition clearly holds, for the reasons already given; the other follows by reference first to the will and then to power.

To see the first clearly we must recognize, as Aristotle affirms in the fifth book of his *Nichomachean Ethics* (1129a32ff.), that the greatest obstacle to justice is cupidity. When cupidity is entirely eliminated there remains nothing opposed to justice: hence the Philosopher's maxim that nothing which can be judged by the law should ever be left to the judge's discretion (*Rhetoric* 1354a31); and he gave this salutary warning because he feared that cupidity which all too easily distorts men's minds. But when there is nothing to be desired there can be no cupidity, because the passions cannot remain when their objects have been eliminated. But the Monarch has nothing to desire, since the ocean alone is the limit of his jurisdiction — unlike other princes, such as the Kings of Castile and Aragon, whose jurisdictions are limited by one another's frontiers. It follows that of all mortals the Monarch can be the purest incarnation of justice. Moreover, just as cupidity invariably clouds the vision of justice no matter how slightly, so charity, or rightly ordered love, illuminates and sharpens it. Therefore justice finds its strongest bastion in the place where rightly ordered love is the most intense. Such is the Monarch; and so justice is at its most powerful, or at least can be, when there is a Monarch. That rightly ordered love does have this effect can be shown as follows: cupidity, scorning man's intrinsic nature, aims at other things; but charity scorns those other things, is directed towards God and man, and so towards the good of man. And since to live in peace, as we previously demonstrated, is the chief of human blessings, and since justice is the most powerful means towards it, charity gives force to justice, so that the more powerful it is the more force justice will have. That rightly ordered love should be found most of all in the Monarch is shown thus: an object is the more loved the nearer it is to the lover; but men are nearer to the Monarch than to other princes; therefore they are more greatly loved by him, or ought to be.

The first proposition becomes evident if we consider the general nature of agents and patients; the second is demonstrated by the fact that it is only as belonging to different parts that men are drawn to other princes, whereas it is through belonging to the whole that they are related to the Monarch. Again, they are brought into contact with other princes through the Monarch, and not vice versa. So prior and immediate tutelage over them all belongs to the Monarch, and to other princes through the Monarch, which means that their tutelage is derived from his. Again, the more universal a cause is, the more perfect a cause it is, because the subordinate cause is only such in virtue of the superior, as is shown in the (Ps-Aristotle) *De causis;* and the more perfect the cause, the more it loves its proper effect, because this love is a function of the cause as such. Since, therefore, the Monarch is of all mortals the most universal cause of human well-being (because other princes, as we have seen, are only effective in virtue of him), it follows that the good of man is most keenly desired by him.

And who but a person ignorant of the world's meaning would doubt that justice is most powerfully served by the Monarch? For if there is a Monarch, then he cannot have any enemies.

The minor premise having been proved, the conclusion is certain: that monarchy is necessary for perfect world-order.

12. And the human race is at its best when most free.

This statement will become clear if we explain the principle of freedom, for then it will be seen that the fundamental principle of our freedom is free choice; and though many pay service to this truth with their lips, few do with their understanding. They do indeed go so far as to say that free choice is a free judgment exercised upon the will; and they speak the truth — but are far from understanding the meaning of the words. They are like our logicians who produce certain propositions mechanically, as examples in logic, such as "A triangle has three angles equal to two right angles." Therefore I say that a judgment is the middle term connecting apprehension and appetite. First of all, something is apprehended; then it is judged to be either good or bad; and finally the person judging either seeks or rejects it. If the judgment completely directs the appetite and is in no way deflected by it, then it is free; but if the judgment is in any way deflected or influenced by the appetite it cannot be free, because it is not independent but is dragged along captive in the wake of another. And this is why the brute beasts cannot enjoy free judgment; because their judgments always follow their appetites. It also explains how intellectual substances (i.e. angels) whose wills are immutable, and disembodied souls who depart this life in a state of grace, do not lose their free choice on account of their wills being immutable, but rather enjoy it in its highest perfection.

Once this is realized, it becomes equally clear that this liberty, or this principle of all our liberty, is God's most precious gift to human nature, for by it we are made happy here as men, and happy as gods in the beyond. In which case who would not agree that mankind is at its best when it is able to make fullest use of this principle? But this plenitude of freedom it enjoys only under a monarchy.

Hence it must be recognized that to be free means "self-dependence, and not dependence on another," as the Philosopher maintains in the *Metaphysics* (982b25). For whatever is dependent on another is conditioned by it even as the means is conditioned by the end it serves. But only under a monarchy is mankind self-dependent and not dependent on another; then only are perverted forms of government rectified, such as democracies, oligarchies and tyrannies (which force mankind into slavery, as is obvious to anyone who considers the matter); their government is conducted by kings, aristocrats (known as *optimates*) and zealots for the people's freedom, because, as we have already shown, the Monarch in his supreme love for men wishes all of them to be good. This is impossible for the perverted forms of government. Hence the Philosopher says that "in the perverted forms a good man is a bad citizen, whereas in the true forms to be a good citizen is the same as being a good man" (*Politics* 1276b15ff.). And these true forms of government aim at liberty; they intend men to go on living for their own sakes. Here the citizens do not exist for the sake of the consuls, nor the people for the sake of the king; on the contrary, the king is for the sake of the people, and the consuls for the citizen. Because just as the laws are made for the sake of the body politic rather than the body politic for the laws, likewise those living under the law do not exist for the sake of the legislator, but he for them (as the Philosopher asserts in the writings which he has left to us on this issue [*Politics* 1289a13]). From which it is evident that although the consul or the king are lords over others in regard to means, they are themselves ministers toward others in regard to ends. And this is particularly true of the Monarch, who is to be considered the minister of everyone. Thus one can already recognize how the very purpose of law-making postulates the necessity of monarchy.

Therefore mankind is in its best condition under a Monarch; from which it follows that monarchy is necessary for the well-being of the world. [. . .]

14. And it is better, wherever possible, for something to be performed by one single means rather than by several.

This is demonstrated as follows. Let A be the means by which a certain thing can be accomplished, and let A and B be several means by which the same thing can be accomplished. But if A alone is adequate for doing what A and B together can do, the introduction of B is unnecessary; because no consequence follows from making the assumption B, for the consequence desired has already been achieved by A alone. And since all similar assumptions are idle or superfluous, and superfluity is displeasing both to God and nature, and everything displeasing to God and nature is evil (as is self-evident), then not only is it better for something that can be accomplished by a single means to be done by that single means rather than by several, it is good in itself to use the single means and plain evil to employ several. Moreover, a thing is considered better the nearer it is to the best; and the best is found in the end envisaged; but to use a single means is to shorten the distance towards the end: therefore it is the better. That it is nearer is obvious: let C be the end; let it be reached by a single means A; let it be reached by several, A and B; clearly the distance from A through B to C is greater than from A straight to C.

But mankind is capable of being governed by a single supreme prince, who is the Monarch.

Of course, when we say "mankind can be governed by one supreme prince" we do not mean to say that minute decisions concerning every township can proceed directly from him (though even municipal laws sometimes prove wanting and need supplementing from outside, as we see from the Philosopher's remarks in the fifth book of the *Ethics* [*NE* 1137a31ff.], where he commends the principle of equity). For nations, kingdoms and cities have different characteristics which demand different laws for their government, law being intended as a concrete rule of life. The Scythians, for instance, live outside the seventh circle, experience extreme inequalities of day and night and endure an almost intolerably piercing frost; they require a different rule from the Garamantes who live in the equinoctial zone, where the days and nights are of equal duration and where the excessive heat makes it unbearable to wear clothes. But our meaning is that mankind should be ruled by one supreme prince and directed towards peace by a common law issuing from him and applied to those characteristics which are common to all men. This common rule, or law, should be accepted from him by particular princes, in the same way as the practical reason preparing for action accepts its major proposition from the speculative intellect and then derives from it the minor proposition appropriate to the particular case, and finally proceeds to action. It is not only possible for one movement to issue from a single source, it is necessary for it to do so in order to eliminate confusion about universal principles. Indeed this was precisely what Moses says he did in writing the Law; having called together the chiefs of the tribes of Israel he left minor judgments to them whilst reserving to himself the major decisions that affected everyone; these were then applied by the chiefs of the tribes according to the particular needs of each tribe.

Therefore it is better for mankind to be ruled by one person than by several (that is, by the Monarch who is the sole prince) and if better, then more acceptable to God; for God always wills the better. And since when only two things are being compared the better is the same as the best, then not only is rule by "one" more acceptable to God than rule by "several," it is the *most* acceptable. It follows that mankind is at its best when under a single ruler; and so monarchy is essential to the well-being of the world.

15. Again, I say that priority is attributed to "being," "unity" and "goodness," in that order, according to the fifth sense of the word "priority." For being naturally comes before unity, and unity before goodness: the perfect being is perfect unity and the perfect unity is perfect goodness, and the further anything is removed from perfect being the further it is from being one and being good. Therefore within each kind of being the best is that which is most one, as the Philosopher maintains in the *Metaphysics* (1053b20ff.). Hence unity seems to be the ground of goodness and multiplicity the ground of evil; for this reason Pythagoras in his Correlations places unity on the side of goodness and multiplicity on the side of evil, as we are told in the first book of the *Metaphysics* (986a15ff.). Hence we can see that to sin is to despise and abandon unity for the sake of multiplicity. The Psalmist perceived this when he said: "They are multiplied in the fruit of corn and wine and oil" (Ps. 4:8).

It is clear, then, that every good thing is good in virtue of being one. And since concord, as such, is a good, it is obviously rooted in unity. The root of concord is discovered if we examine its definition and nature. Concord is a harmonious movement of several wills. This definition shows that the unity of wills connoted by "harmonious movement" is the root of concord or is itself concord. For just as we should describe several clods which all fell towards the same centre as concordant and say that several flames shooting out towards the same circumference were concordant (if they did so voluntarily), similarly we describe several men as being in concord when their wills are simultaneously directed towards the same formal object (which is present in their wills as the quality of gravity is present in the clods and levity in the flames). But the capacity for willing represents a potentiality and the good it apprehends its form. This form, though one in itself, like other forms, becomes multiplied through the multiplicity of the matter on which it impressed — just like soul and number, and other composite forms.

These premisses having been stated we can now develop the argument for the proposition we wish to maintain: all concord depends upon the unity of wills; mankind is at its best in a state of concord; for as a man is at his best in body and soul when he is in a state of concord, the same is true of a house, a city and a kingdom, and of mankind as a whole. Therefore mankind at its best depends upon unity in the wills of its members. But this is impossible unless there is one will which dominates all others and holds them in unity, for the wills of mortals, influenced by their adolescent and seductive delights, are in need of a director, as the Philosopher teaches at the end of the *Nichomachean Ethics* (1179b32f.). Nor can there be such a single will unless there is a prince over all, whose will guides and rules those of all others.

Now if the preceding conclusions are all true — as they are — then monarchy is necessary for the perfect order of mankind in this world. Consequently a Monarch is essential to the well-being of the world.

16. The preceding arguments are confirmed by a noteworthy historical fact, that is, by the state of humanity which the Son of God either awaited or himself brought about when He was to become man for the salvation of men. For if we survey the ages and condition of men since the fall of our first parents (the false step from which all our errors have proceeded), at no time do we see universal peace throughout the world except during the perfect monarchy of the immortal Augustus. The fact that mankind at that time was resting happily in universal peace is attested by all the historians and the illustrious poets. Even the recorder of Christ's gentleness has deigned to bear witness to it (Luke 2:1). Finally Paul, also described that blissful state as "the fulness of time" (Gal. 4:4). The times are indeed full, and temporal desires fulfilled because nothing that ministers to our happiness was without its minister. But what state the world has been in since that seamless garment was rent on the nail of cupidity (John 19:23) we may easily read — would that we could not behold it!

O humanity, in how many storms must you be tossed, how many shipwrecks must you endure, so long as you turn yourself into a many-headed beast lusting after a multiplicity of things! You are ailing in both your intellectual powers, as well as in heart: you pay no heed to the unshakeable principles of your higher (speculative) intellect, nor illumine your lower (practical) intellect with experience, nor tune your heart to the sweetness of divine counsel when it is breathed into you through the trumpet of the Holy Spirit: "Behold how good and pleasant it is for brethren to dwell together in unity" (Ps. 132:1).

Translation: D. Nicholl and C. Hardie (London, 1954). Used with permission.

Marsilius of Padua

(1275/80–1342/43)

The literary fame of Marsiglio dei Mainardini (of the prominent Paduan Mainardini family) issues from a single political work, the publication of which in 1324 altered the course of his life. So hostile was the reception given to *Defender of the Peace* (*Defensor pacis*) in ecclesiastical circles that its author, on discovery of his identity in 1326, was forced to flee the University of Paris for the safety of Ludwig of Bavaria's court at Nürnberg, along with his colleague, John of Jandun. There he became embroiled in the war with Pope John XXII over Ludwig's claim to the German and imperial throne, accompanying his protector on an expedition into Italy in 1327 and participating in his short-lived rule over Rome and the papal patrimony. Along with William of Ockham and the Franciscan minister general, Michael of Cesena, two other refugees from papal censure, he endorsed Ludwig's deposition of John for heresy and installation of a Spiritual Franciscan as antipope. With them he shared in Ludwig's humiliating defeat by John two years later, which made permanent his sojourn at the Bavarian court in Munich, where he summarized and extended his larger treatise in the short *Defensor minor*.

Anathematized by John in 1327 and placed on the Index in 1559, *Defensor pacis* deserves such flamboyant epithets as "radical," "pivotal," and "revolutionary," for it marks a momentous turn in the imperialist tradition to present the novel face of secular political monism, the counterface of the dominant hierocratic monism of the papalists.

The genius of *Defensor pacis* lies in its reorientation of widely established or long-established medieval traditions, opening them to new uses. For instance, by applying an Aristotelian hermeneutic to the ancient theory of the constitution of the Roman Empire through *lex regia*, the law by which the Roman people conferred on the *princeps* all their "*imperium* and power" (Dig. 1.4.1), Marsilius converts it into a general foundation of popular sovereignty. On the theological side, he converts the Franciscan theory of the supreme poverty of Christ and his apostles into a paradigm for the entire church, setting it within the Averroist polarity of "this-worldly" and "otherworldly" states of existence. Running through the distinct strands of Marsilius's revision is his method of separating arguments from reason and arguments from faith — hence the two "Discourses" comprising the work — subordinating the latter to the former, to produce a political theory dominated by rational constructions, to which theological doctrine is apparently marginal.

If we compare *Defensor pacis* with Dante's *Monarchia*, it is the latter which strikes us as the more perfect early flowering of the southern Renaissance spirit, in which the concept of universal human society comes into its own. Without denying universal human nature, the prevailing political tradition had conceived the church, whose saving essence is both divine and human, as the universal commonwealth; but the *Monarchia* invests with axiological completeness a universal secular body politic, whose essence is the natural human inclination toward civil peace, order, theoretical and practical self-fulfillment. *Defensor pacis* projects a closer relationship between the *societas humana* and the *societas fidelium*, between aspirations for this-worldly and for otherworldly happiness; yet at the same time it accords civil life a high degree of self-sufficiency and autonomous intelligibility. Compared with the earlier Thomistic absorption of Aristotle, in which the end of human society, friendship rooted in natural virtue, opened beyond itself to the higher end of communion in divine grace, civil society cast in the Averro-Aristotelian mold of Marsilius, as well as of Dante, is a closed system, the analysis and evaluation of which need not move beyond autonomous self-referential political concepts.

The political conceptuality of Marsilius combines naturalist and rationalist, voluntarist and corporatist themes in such a way as to carry classical political order toward modern positivism and statism. Controlling this theoretical dynamic is his polemical purpose of exposing the temporal jurisdictional pretensions of the papacy as the single most potent and universal cause of disruption (both overt and insidious) to civil polities (1.1.7), whether cities, kingdoms, or the Empire. To achieve this, he must conceive the goal and function of civil polities so as to render papal authority irrelevant. Accordingly, his conception has three strategic strands: Averroist, Augustinian, and Aristotelian.

The Averroist strand places the maximum distance between acts designed to achieve "living well" in this world and acts ordered to "living well" in the next world (1.4.3; 1.5.2; cf. Aristotle, *Politics* 1252b29f.). The former are deliberate ("controlled"), either "immanent" or "transient," governed by reason and art, and, if "transient," sometimes coercively regulated by positive statutes and customs (1.5.2-4; 1.10.2-4; also 2.8.3-5). The latter, although similarly "controlled" and either "immanent" or "transient," are governed by faith and the "evangelic law" of Christ, and coercively regulated, but only by rewards and punishments in eternity (1.5.10; 1.6.8, 10; also 2.8.5). The dominant relationship admitted by Marsilius between these different kinds of human action inverts the traditional ordering of natural to supernatural virtue; it is the contribution of religious belief, rite, and morality to civic virtue and order that interests him. This contribution, he suggests with Machiavellian evasiveness, is indifferent to the religious truth or falsity of the beliefs and practices in question, depending only on their ethical efficacy (1.5.11, 14).

The Augustinian strand assigns temporal government the primarily judicial role of determining and punishing wrongdoing, or as Marsilius says, of "correcting" (i.e., "reducing to equality or due proportion") the "excesses" of transient acts that cause this-worldly "harm or injury" (1.5.7). By commanding justice, prohibiting injustice, and bestowing rewards and punishments, the ruler conserves the peace or "tranquillity" of the civil community, defined, however, in an Aristotelian manner as the "perfect action and intercommunication" of its parts, in which each and all harmoniously perform their proper and common functions (1.2.3; 1.5.1; 1.15.11; 1.19.2). Marsilius proceeds along Aristotelian lines to invest the civil ruler with responsibility and authority unapproachable by the other parts of the state, because it pertains to *establishing* as well as preserving political tranquility. The government not only corrects but prevents harmful excesses by rationally proportioning the other parts of the state, determining their "quality" and "quantity," the "number" and "ability" of their personnel (1.15.6-10). Even the priesthood as a civic office is subject to the ruler in respect of selection, training, and all institutional aspects of its employment (1.15.8, 10).

In a further secularizing move, he appropriates coercive judgment exclusively to civil rule. He distinguishes the temporal ruler from other judges not by his authority to discriminate what is "just and beneficial in accordance with the laws or customs," but by his authority to "command and execute through coercive force the sentences made by him" (2.2.8). Admittedly, the civil power shares coercive judgment with Christ himself, but with the crucial difference that Christ's coercive judgments have effect in his future kingdom alone, never in this world (2.4.7). Marsilius regards the monopoly of coercive judgment by a single agency as essential to the operation of political jurisdiction (1.17). At the same time he secularizes and voluntarizes lawmaking: he politicizes and positivizes the very concept of law so that its "most proper sense" is that of "a command coercive through [this-worldly] punishment or reward" (1.10.4; 1.11.1). Thus he renders the natural, rational, and divine substance of law inessential to its definition (1.10.5). Divine law parallels divine judgment in meeting the full definitional requirements only in reference to the future world. In this world divine "laws" are mere admonitions.

Finally, Marsilius follows the route of voluntarist corporatism in his rational construction of the state, setting up the common will of "the people" as the original and perpetual source of political authority and law. It is not, however, an irrational source, in that the people establish the best laws, being the best judge of the common good (1.12.5). In all his political acts the ruler is the secondary, not the primary, efficient cause (1.15.4); he acts as "instrumental or executive cause" by virtue of authority granted by the primary "legislator," which is "the whole body of the citizens" (1.15.3, 4). Marsilius favors political institutions that render transparent the ruler's instrumentality and continuing dependence on the corporate body politic: institutions of corporate election, of the ruler's correction, of corporate consent to laws (1.11-13, 15, 16, 18). The elements of transcendent right in the ruler's action, whether rational or divine, are always bound to the immanent political right bestowed by the popular will. In anticipation of later theories of representation — conciliarist and parliamentarian — he identifies the unified will of the community with the consensus of its "weightier part" wherein wise judgment about the common benefit resides (1.12.13).

In the second "Discourse" Marsilius purports to offer confirmation from reve-lation of his prior arguments from reason, his primary objective being to disprove papalist jurisdictional ecclesiology and to prove his alternative nonjurisdictional ecclesiology on the testimony of Scripture supported by theological and canonical authorities. This twofold exercise produces a number of startling anticipations of Reformation ideas.

The central proto-Protestant idea that bridges the two discourses is his "apos-tolic" definition of the church as "the whole body of the faithful who believe in and invoke the name of Christ, and all the parts of this whole body in any community, even the household" (2.2.3; cf. 1 Cor. 1:2; Acts 20:28). To be sure, this nonclerical definition of the church had appeared in French royalist polemics at the turn of the century; nevertheless, Marsilius followed through its "Erastian" implications with unprecedented thoroughness. The foremost of these was the authority of the ruler, as representing the body politic, to decide and impose all the external, institutional features of Christian belief and practice.

No more than Luther does Marsilius deny independent authority to the priest-hood, but this authority has an immediate divine cause and an inward, otherworldly import. In so far as priestly action (e.g., in the sacrament of penance) conveys divine judgment on the status of persons, it merely "declares" and does not execute this judgment, which in any case takes effect in the future, and not in the present life (2.6). In so far as priestly action conveys God's law, it is pedagogical and not jurisdic-tional, teaching "doctrine" rather than issuing "commands" (2.9). Like John of Paris and the Norman Anonymous before him, Marsilius appeals to the earthly authority exercised by Jesus Christ *as man*, and not *as God* (2.4), which, the Gospels show, ex-cluded not only jurisdiction over men but jurisdiction over things, being nonpropri-etary as well as nonjuridical. He joins forces with Ockham and Michael of Cesena in defending the Franciscan doctrine of the perfect poverty of Christ and his apostles, i.e., of their double renunciation of "all acquired legal ownership" of temporal goods, whether in private or in common, and all "holding" or "use" of goods beyond the requirements of "present subsistence" (2.13.22). But he departs from his con-temporaries in the Franciscan mainstream by committing the entire priesthood, and not only the friars, to the state of supreme poverty. All clergy, he argues, have the simple use of things (including consumables) according to divine and natural right, without positive legal ownership or right of use (2.13), the proprietorship of ecclesi-astical and clerical possessions resting with the lay donors and patrons, on the men-dicant model (2.14.8). Significantly, Marsilius not only offers an unequivocal expo-sition of subjective right (2.12.7-10), but allows that the concept of "ownership" may be applied to "the human will or freedom in itself" with reference to acts controlled naturally by it (2.12.16).

As well as being the greatest proprietor of church goods, the "human legisla-tor," i.e., the entire civil/ecclesial community (2.14.8), exercises a host of other eccle-siastical powers — over clerical appointment, discipline, deposition, external church organization and administration, largely through the agency of the secular ruler. Moreover, through the instrumentality of the general church council assembled by "the ruler who knows no superior," it exercises further powers of doctrinal definition and scriptural interpretation (2.19, 20), of excommunication and imposition of an interdict (2.21), and regulation of papal appointment or election (2.21.5). Marsilius's vision of a representative church council whose divinely inspired judgments both uphold scriptural authority and are upheld by scriptural testimony foreshadows the most "Protestant" theme of the conciliar movement, while his vision of a spiritualized communion of faith and sacrament embodied in a civil institution foreshadows the secularist and statist leaning of Luther's mature ecclesiology. Reining in these "Protestant" anticipations, however, and threatening to obstruct the spiritualizing and secularizing movements of his ecclesiology, is the author's residual penitentialism, his recognition of the priestly "power" of commuting purgatorial punishment into "this-worldly satisfaction" (2.6.8).

Further Reading: A. Gewirth, trans., *Marsilius of Padua, "Defensor Pacis"* (New York: Columbia University Press, 1956); G. de Lagarde, *La naissance de l'esprit laïque au déclin du moyen-âge,* vol. 3 (Louvain: Éditions Nauwelaerts, 1970); M. Löffelberger, *Marsilius von Padua: das Verhältnis zwischen Kirche und Staat im "Defensor pacis"* (Berlin: Duncker & Humblot, 1992); C. J. Nederman, *Community and Consent: The Secular Political Theory of Marsiglio of Padua's "Defensor Pacis"* (Lanham, Md.: Rowman & Littlefield, 1995); J. Quillet, *La philosophie politique de Marsile de Padoue* (Paris: Vrin, 1970); J. Quillet, "Nouvelles études marsiliennes," *History of Political Thought* 1 (1980): 391-409; D. Sternberger, *Die Stadt und das Reich in der Verfassungslehre des Marsilius von Padua* (Wiesbaden: Steiner, 1981).

From *Defensor Pacis,* Discourse 1

ch. 5. *On the differentiation of the parts of the state.* [1] [. . .] Let us say, then, that the parts or offices of the state are of six kinds, as Aristotle said in the *Politics* (1328b 2ff.): the agricultural, the artisan, the military, the financial, the priestly, and the judicial or deliberative.

[2] Although the necessity of these parts has been indicated in the preceding chapter, we wish to indicate it again more distinctly, assuming this proposition as having been previously demonstrated from what is self-evident, namely, that the state is a community established for the sake of the living and living well of the men in it. Of this "living" we have previously distinguished two kinds: one, the life or living of this world, that is earthly; the other, the life or living of the other or future world. From these kinds of living, desired by man as ends, we shall indicate the necessity for the differentiation of the parts of the civil community. [. . .]

[3] Hence, we must note that if man is to live and to live well, it is necessary that his actions be done and be done well; and not only his actions but also his passions. By "well" I mean in proper proportion. And since we do not receive entirely perfect from nature the means whereby these proportions are fulfilled, it was necessary for man to go beyond natural causes to form through reason some means whereby to effect and preserve his actions and passions in body and soul. And these

means are the various kinds of functions and products deriving from the virtues and arts, both practical and theoretic.

[4] Of human actions and passions, some come from natural causes apart from knowledge. Such are those which are effected by the contrariety of the elements composing our bodies, through their intermixture. In this class can properly be placed the actions of the nutritive faculty. Under this head also come actions effected by the elements surrounding our body through the alteration of their qualities; of this kind also are the alterations effected by things entering human bodies, such as food, drink, medicines, poisons, and other similar things. But there are other actions or passions which are performed by us or occur in us through our cognitive and appetitive powers. Of these some are called "immanent" because they do not cross over *(non transeunt)* into a subject other than the doer, nor are they exercised through any external organs or locomotive members; of this kind are the thoughts and desires or affections of men. But there are other actions and passions which are called "transient" because they are opposed in either or in both respects to the kind which we have just described.

[7] In order to moderate the excesses of the acts deriving from the locomotive powers through knowledge and desire, which we have called transient acts and which can be done for the benefit or for the harm or injury of someone other than the doer for the status of the present world, there was necessarily established in the state a part or office by which the excesses of such acts are corrected and reduced to equality or due proportion. For without such correction the excesses of these acts would cause fighting and hence the separation of the citizens, and finally the destruction of the state and loss of the sufficient life. This part of the state, together with its subsidiaries, is called by Aristotle the "judicial" or "ruling" and "deliberative" part, and its function is to regulate matters of justice and the common benefit.

[8] In addition, since the sufficient life cannot be led by citizens who are oppressed or cast into slavery by external oppressors, and also since the sentences of the judges against injurious and rebellious men within the state must be executed by coercive force, it was necessary to set up in the state a military or warrior part, which many of the mechanics also subserve. For the state was established for the sake of living and living well . . . ; but this is impossible for citizens cast into slavery. For Aristotle the pre-eminent said that slavery is contrary to the nature of the state. Hence, indicating the necessity for this part, he said in the *Politics* (1291a6): "There is a fifth class, that of the warriors, which is not less necessary than the others, if the citizens are not to be slaves of invaders. For nothing is more truly impossible than for that which is by nature slavish to be worthy of the name 'state'; for a state is self-sufficient, but a slave is not self-sufficient." [. . .]

[10] It remains for us to discuss the necessity of the priestly part. All men have not thought so harmoniously about this as they have about the necessity of the other parts of the state. The cause of this difference was that the true and primary necessity of this part could not be comprehended through demonstration, nor was it self-evident. All nations, however, agreed that it was appropriate to establish the priesthood for the worship and honoring of God, and for the benefit resulting therefrom for the status of the present or the future world. For most laws or religions promise

that in the future world God will distribute rewards to those who do good and punishment to doers of evil.

[11] However, besides these causes of the laying down of religious laws, causes which are believed without demonstration, the philosophers, including Hesiod, Pythagoras, and several others of the ancients, noted appropriately a quite different cause or purpose for the setting forth of divine laws or religions — a purpose which was in some sense necessary for the status of this world. This was to ensure the goodness of human acts both individual and civil, on which depend almost completely the quiet or tranquillity of communities and finally the sufficient life in the present world. For although some of the philosophers who founded such laws or religions did not accept or believe in human resurrection and that life which is called eternal, they nevertheless feigned and persuaded others that it exists and that in it pleasures and pains are in accordance with the qualities of human deeds in this mortal life, in order that they might thereby induce in men reverence and fear of God, and a desire to flee the vices and to cultivate the virtues. For there are certain acts which the legislator cannot regulate by human law, that is, those acts which cannot be proved to be present or absent to anyone, but which nevertheless cannot be concealed from God, whom these philosophers feigned to be the maker of such laws and the commander of their observance, under the threat or promise of eternal reward for doers of good and punishment for doers of evil. [. . .] From fear of these, men eschewed wrongdoing, were instigated to perform virtuous works of piety and mercy, and were well disposed both in themselves and toward others. As a consequence, many disputes and injuries ceased in communities. Hence too the peace or tranquillity of states and the sufficient life of men for the status of the present world were preserved with less difficulty; which was the end intended by these wise men in laying down such laws or religions.

[12] Such, then, were the precepts handed down by the Gentile priests; and for the teaching of them they established in their communities temples in which their gods were worshipped. They also appointed teachers of these laws or doctrines, whom they called priests *(sacerdotes)*, because they handled the sacred objects of the temples, like the books, vases, and other such things subserving divine worship.

[14] Now correct views concerning God were not held by the Gentile laws or religions and by all the other religions which are or were outside the catholic Christian faith or outside the Mosaic law which preceded it or the beliefs of the holy fathers which in turn preceded this — and, in general, by all those doctrines which are outside the tradition of what is contained in the sacred canon called the Bible. For they followed the human mind or false prophets or teachers of errors. Hence too they did not have a correct view about the future life and its happiness or misery, nor about the true priesthood established for its sake. We have, nevertheless, spoken of their rites in order to make more manifest their difference from the true priesthood, that of the Christians, and the necessity for the priestly part in communities.

ch. 6. *Final cause of the priesthood.* [4] It was such [eternal] happiness, however, to which merciful God had ordered the human race and which he wished to restore to it after leading it back from the fall, following the appropriate order. Hence, most recently of all, through his son Jesus Christ, true God and true man in unity of person, he handed down the evangelical law, containing commands and counsels of what must be believed, done, and avoided. By observance of these, not only are men preserved from sensory punishment, as they had been by observance of the prior commands, but also through God's gracious ordainment they merit, by a certain congruity, eternal happiness. And for this reason the evangelical law is called the law of grace, both because through the passion and death of Christ the human race was redeemed from its guilt and from the penalty of losing eternal beatitude which it had incurred as a result of the fall or sin of its first parents; and also because, by observing this law and receiving the sacraments established with it and in it, we are given divine grace; after it is given it is strengthened in us, and when we lose it, it is restored to us. Through this grace, by the ordainment of God and the passion of Christ, our works come by a certain congruity (as we have said) to merit eternal happiness.

[7] As teachers of this law, and as ministers of its sacraments, certain men in the communities were chosen, called priests and deacons or Levites. It is their office to teach the commands and counsels of the Christian evangelical law, as to what must be believed, done, and spurned, to the end that a blessed status be attained in the future world, and the opposite avoided.

[8] The end of the priesthood, therefore, is to teach and educate men in those things which, according to the evangelical law, it is necessary to believe, do, and omit in order to attain eternal salvation and avoid misery.

[9] To this office appropriately pertain all the disciplines, theoretic and practical, discovered by the human mind, which moderate human acts, both immanent and transient, arising from desire and knowledge, and which make man well disposed in soul for the status of both the present and the future world. [...]

ch. 10. *Meanings of the term "law."* [1] [...] Now a government has to regulate civil human acts . . . and according to a standard *(regulam)* which is and ought to be the form of the ruler, as such. We must, consequently, inquire into this standard, as to whether it exists, what it is, and why. For the efficient cause of this standard is perhaps the same as that of the ruler.

[2] The existence of this standard, which is called a "statute" or "custom" and by the common term "law," we assume as almost self-evident by induction in all perfect communities. We shall show first, then, what law is; next we shall indicate its final cause or necessity; and finally we shall demonstrate by what person or persons and by what kind of action the law should be established; which will be to inquire into its legislator or efficient cause, to whom we think it also pertains to elect the government. [...]

[3] Following this procedure, then, we must first distinguish the meanings or intentions of this term "law," in order that its many senses may not lead to confusion. For in one sense it means a natural sensitive inclination towards some action or passion. This is the way the Apostle used it when he said in Romans 7:23: "I see another law in my members, fighting against the law of my mind." In another sense this term "law" means any productive habit and in general every form, existing in the mind, of a producible thing, from which as from an exemplar or measure there emerge the forms of things made by art. This is the way in which the term was used

430

in Ezekiel 43:12-13: "This is the law of the house. . . . And these are the measurements of the altar." In a third sense "law" means the standard containing admonitions for voluntary human acts according as these are ordered toward glory or punishment in the future world. In this sense the Mosaic law was in part called a law, just as the evangelical law in its entirety is called a law. Hence the Apostle said of these in his epistle to the Hebrews (7:12): "Since the priesthood has been changed, it is necessary that there be a change of the law also." In this sense "law" was also used for the evangelic discipline in James 1:25: "He who has looked into the perfect law of liberty, and has continued therein . . . this man shall be blessed in his deeds." In this sense of the term "law" all religions, such as that of Mohammed or of the Persians, are called laws in whole or in part, although among these only the Mosaic and the evangelic, that is, the Christian, contain the truth. So too Aristotle called religions "laws" when he said, in the second book of his Philosophy: "The laws show how great is the power of custom" (*Metaphysics* 995a 4); and also in the twelfth book of the same work: "The other doctrines were added as myths to persuade men to obey the laws, and for the sake of expediency" (*Metaphysics* 1074b3). In its fourth and most familiar sense, this term "law" means the science or doctrine or universal judgment of matters of civil justice and benefit, and of their opposites.

[4] Taken in this last sense, law may be considered in two ways. In one way it may be considered in itself, as it only shows what is just or unjust, beneficial or harmful; and as such it is called the science or doctrine of right *(iuris)*. In another way it may be considered according as with regard to its observance there is given a command coercive through punishment or reward to be distributed in the present world, or according as it is handed down by way of such a command; and considered in this way it most properly is called, and is, a law. It was in this sense that Aristotle also defined it in the last book of the *Ethics* (*NE* 1180a 21) when he said: "Law has coercive force, for it is discourse emerging from prudence and understanding." Law, then, is a "discourse" or statement "emerging from prudence and" political "understanding"; that is, it is an ordinance made by political prudence, concerning matters of justice and benefit and their opposites, and having "coercive force," that is, concerning whose observance there is given a command which one is compelled to observe, or which is made by way of such a command.

[5] Hence not all true cognitions of matters of civil justice and benefit are laws unless a coercive command has been given concerning their observance, or they have been made by way of a command, although such true cognition is necessarily required for a perfect law. Indeed, sometimes false cognitions of the just and the beneficial become laws, when there is given a command to observe them, or they are made by way of a command. An example of this is found in the regions of certain barbarians, who cause it to be observed as just that a murderer be absolved of civil guilt and punishment on payment of a fine. This, however, is absolutely unjust, and consequently the laws of such barbarians are not absolutely perfect. For although they have the proper form, that is, a coercive command of observance, they lack a proper condition, that is, the proper and true ordering of justice.

ch. 12. *The efficient cause of human laws.* [1] We must next discuss that efficient cause of the laws which is capable of demonstration. For I do not intend to deal here with that method of establishing laws which can be effected by the immediate act or oracle of God apart from the human will, or which has been so effected in the past. It was by this latter method, as we have said, that the Mosaic law was established; but I shall not deal with it here even insofar as it contains commands with regard to civil acts for the status of the present world. I shall discuss the establishment of only those laws and governments which emerge immediately from the decision of the human mind.

[3] Let us say, then, in accordance with the truth and the counsel of Aristotle in the *Politics* (1281a39ff.) that the legislator, or the primary and proper efficient cause of the law, is the people or the whole body of citizens, or the weightier part thereof, through its election or will expressed by words in the general assembly of the citizens, commanding or determining that something be done or omitted with regard to human civil acts, under a temporal pain or punishment. By the "weightier part" I mean to take into consideration the quantity and the quality of the persons in that community over which the law is made. The aforesaid whole body of citizens or the weightier part thereof is the legislator regardless of whether it makes the law directly by itself or entrusts the making of it to some person or persons, who are not and cannot be the legislator in the absolute sense, but only in a relative sense and for a particular time and in accordance with the authority of the primary legislator. And I say further that the laws and anything else established through election must receive their necessary approval by that same authority and no other, whatever be the case with regard to certain ceremonies or solemnities, which are required not for the being of the matters elected but for their well-being, since the election would be no less valid even if these ceremonies were not performed. Moreover, by the same authority must the laws and other things established through election undergo addition, subtraction, complete change, interpretation or suspension, insofar as the exigencies of time or place or other circumstances make any such action opportune for the common benefit. And by the same authority, also must the laws be promulgated or proclaimed after their enactment, so that no citizen or alien who is delinquent in observing them may be excused because of ignorance.

[5] [...] The absolutely primary human authority to make or establish human laws belongs only to those men from whom alone the best laws can emerge. But these are the whole body of the citizens, or the weightier part thereof, which represents that whole body; since it is difficult or impossible for all persons to agree upon one decision, because some men have a deformed nature, disagreeing with the common decision through singular malice or ignorance. The common benefit should not, however, be impeded or neglected because of the unreasonable protest or opposition of these men. The authority to make or establish laws, therefore, belongs only to the whole body of citizens or to the weightier part thereof.

[...] That the best law is made only through the hearing and command of the entire multitude, I prove by assuming with Aristotle in the *Politics* that the best law is that which is made for the common benefit of the citizens. As Aristotle said: "That is presumably right," that is, in the laws, "which is for the common benefit of the state and the citizens" (1283b40). But that this is best achieved only by the whole body of the citizens or by the weightier part thereof, which is assumed to be the same thing, I show as follows: That at which the entire body of the citizens aims intellectually and emotionally is more certainly judged as to its truth and more diligently noted as to its common utility. For a defect in some proposed law can be better noted by the greater number than by any part thereof, since every whole, or at least every corporeal whole, is greater in mass and in virtue than any part of it taken separately. Moreover, the common utility of a law is better noted by the entire multitude, because no one knowingly harms himself. Anyone can look to see whether a proposed law leans toward the benefit of one or a few persons more than of the others or of the community, and can protest against it. Such, however, would not be the case were the law made by one or a few persons, considering their own private benefit rather than that of the community. [. . .]

[6] [Moreover] the authority to make the law belongs only to those men whose making of it will cause the law to be better observed or observed at all. Only the whole body of the citizens are such men. To them, therefore, belongs the authority to make the law. The first proposition of this demonstration is very close to self-evident, for a law would be useless unless it were observed. Hence Aristotle said in the *Politics* (1294a3): "Laws are not well ordered when they are well made but not obeyed." He also said (1322a5): "Nothing is accomplished by forming opinions about justice and not carrying them out." The second proposition I prove as follows. That law is better observed by every citizen which each one seems to have imposed upon himself. But such is the law which is made through the hearing and command of the entire multitude of the citizens. [. . .]

ch. 13. *Objections to statements in the preceding chapter and their refutation.* [3] Now that we have laid down these obvious truths, it is easy to refute the objections whereby one might try to prove that the making of the law does not pertain to the whole body of the citizens or the weightier multitude thereof but rather to a certain few. As for the first objection, that the authority to make laws does not belong to those who in most cases are vicious and undiscerning, this is granted. But when it is added that the whole body of citizens is such, this must be denied. For most of the citizens are neither vicious nor undiscerning most of the time; all or most of them are of sound mind and reason and have a right desire for the polity and for the things necessary for it to endure, like laws and other statutes or customs, as was shown above. For although not every citizen nor the greater number of the citizens be discoverers of the laws, yet every citizen can judge of what has been discovered and proposed to him by someone else, and can discern what must be added, subtracted, or changed. Hence in the major premise's reference to the "undiscerning," if what is meant is that because most of the citizens cannot discover the law by themselves, therefore they ought not to establish the law, this must be denied as manifestly false, as is borne out by sense induction and by Aristotle in the *Politics*, bk. 3, ch. 6. By induction we can see that many men judge rightly about the quality of a picture, a house, a ship, and other works of art, even though they would have been unable to discover or produce them. Aristotle also attests this in the place just cited, answering the proposed objection with these words: "About some things the man who made them is not the best judge" (*Politics* 1282a17). He proves this in many species of arts, and indicates that the same is true for all the others.

[4] [. . .] Moreover, even if we assume what is indeed true, that some of the less learned do not judge about a proposed law or some other practical matter equally as well as do the same number of the learned, still the number of the less learned could be increased to such an extent that they would judge about these matters equally as well as, or even better than, the few who are more learned. Aristotle stated this clearly [. . .] when he undertook to confirm this view: "If the multitude be not too vile, each member of it will indeed be a worse judge than those who have knowledge; but taken all together they will be better judges, or at least not worse" (*Politics* 1282a 15ff.).

ch. 15. *On the efficient cause of the best method of establishing the government.* [1] It now remains to show the efficient cause of the ruler, that is, the cause by which there is given to one or more persons the authority of rulership which is established through election. For it is by this authority that a person becomes a ruler in actuality, and not by his knowledge of the laws, his prudence, or moral virtue, although these are qualities of the perfect ruler. For it happens that many men have these qualities, but nevertheless, lacking this authority, they are not rulers, unless perhaps in proximate potentiality.

[2] Taking up the question, then, let us say, in accordance with the truth and the doctrine of Aristotle in the *Politics* (1281b31ff.) that the efficient power to establish or elect the ruler belongs to the legislator or the whole body of the citizens, just as does the power to make the laws [. . .]. And to the legislator similarly belongs the power to make any correction of the ruler and even to depose him, if this be expedient for the common benefit. For this is one of the more important matters in the polity; and such matters pertain to the entire multitude of the citizens [. . .]. For "the multitude is dominant in the more important matters," as was said there (*Politics* 1282a 38) by Aristotle. The method of coming together to effect the aforesaid establishment or election of the ruler may perhaps vary according to the variety of provinces. But in whatever ways it may differ, this must be observed in each case, that such election or establishment is always to be made by the authority of the legislator, who, as we have very frequently said, is the whole body of the citizens, or the weightier part thereof. [. . .]

[3] [. . .] Since, therefore, it pertains to the whole body of the citizens to generate the form, that is, the law, according to which all civil acts must be regulated, it will be seen that it pertains to the same whole body to determine this form's matter, that is, the ruler, whose function it is to order, according to this form, the civil acts of men. And since this is the best of the forms of the civil community, there ought to be determined for it the subject with the best qualities [. . .]. Hence it seems that it can appropriately be inferred that the ruler who is elected without hereditary succession is put at the head of the polity by a method which is absolutely superior to that which operates in the case of non-elected rulers, or of rulers named with hereditary succession ensuing.

[4] Having shown the efficient cause of this part of the state, we must now discuss, in accordance with our frequently announced plan, the efficient cause which establishes and determines the other parts or offices of the state. Now the primary efficient cause we say is the legislator; the secondary, as it were the instrumental or

executive cause, we say is the ruler through the authority granted to him for this purpose by the legislator, in accordance with the form which the legislator has given to him. This form is the law, in accordance with which the ruler must always, so far as possible, perform and regulate civil acts, as was shown in the preceding chapter. For although the legislator, as the primary and proper cause, must determine which persons must exercise what offices in the state, the execution of such matters, as also of all other legal provisions, is commanded, or as the case may be, prohibited, by the ruling part of the state. For the execution of the legal provisions is effected more conveniently by the ruler than by the entire multitude of the citizens, since in this function one or a few rulers suffice, whereas the entire community would needlessly be occupied therein, and would be distracted from the other necessary functions. For when the rulers do this, the entire community does it, since the rulers do it in accordance with the legal determination of the community, and, being few or only one in number, they can execute the legal provisions more easily.

ch. 18. *On the correction of the ruler.* [1] We have previously stated that it pertains to the legislator to correct governments or to change them completely, just as to establish them. In this connection, someone may well wonder whether it is expedient that rulers be corrected by coercive judgment and force; and if it is expedient, whether they should be corrected for every kind of excess, or only for some and not for others; also who should make such judgments against the rulers, and execute them by coercive force — for it was said above that it pertains to the rulers alone to issue civil sentences and to punish transgressors of the laws by coercive force.

[2] Let us say that the ruler through his action in accordance with the law and the authority given to him is the standard and measure of every civil act, like the heart in an animal, as was sufficiently shown in ch. 15. Now if the ruler received no other form beside the law and the authority and the desire to act in accordance with it, he would never perform any action which was wrong or corrigible or measurable by someone else. And therefore he and his action would be the measure of every civil act of men other than himself, in such manner that he would never be measured by others, like the well-formed heart in an animal. For since the heart receives no form that inclines it to an action contrary to the action which has to emerge from its natural virtue and heat, it always does naturally the appropriate action and never the contrary. Hence it regulates and measures, through its influence or action, the other parts of the animal, in such a manner that it is not regulated by them nor does it receive any influence from them.

[3] But since the ruler is a human being, he has understanding and appetite, which can receive other forms, like false opinion or perverted desire or both, as a result of which he comes to do the contraries of the things determined by the law. Because of these actions, the ruler is rendered measurable by someone else who has the authority to measure or regulate him, or his unlawful actions, in accordance with the law. For otherwise every government would become despotic, and the life of the citizens slavish and insufficient. [. . .]

Now the judgment, command, and execution of any correction of the ruler, in accordance with his demerit or transgression, must be done by the legislator, or by a person or persons appointed for this purpose by the authority of the legislator [. . .].

And it is well to suspend for some time the office of the ruler who is to be corrected, especially in relation to the person or persons who must judge of his transgression, because otherwise there would then be a plurality of governments in the community, from which would result schism, agitation, and fighting; and also because he is corrected not as a ruler but as a subject who has transgressed the law.

    ch. 19. *On the efficient causes of the tranquillity and intranquillity of the city or state.* [12] This wrong opinion of certain Roman bishops, and also perhaps their perverted desire for rulership, which they assert is owed to them because of the plenitude of power given to them, as they say, by Christ — this is that singular cause which we have said produces the intranquillity or discord of the city or state. For it is prone to creep up on all states [. . .] and by its hateful action it has for a long time distressed the Italian state, and has kept and still keeps it from tranquillity or peace, by preventing with all its force the appointment or institution of the ruler, the Roman emperor, and his functioning in the said empire. From lack of this function, which is the just regulation of civil acts, there readily emerge injuries and contentions, and these, if not measured by a standard of justice or law because of the absence of the measurer, cause fights, whence there have resulted the separation of the citizens and finally the destruction of the Italian polities or cities, as we have said. With this opinion, therefore, and perhaps also with that we have called a desire for ruling, the Roman bishop strives to make the Roman ruler subject to him in coercive or temporal jurisdiction, whereas that ruler neither rightly ought to be, as we shall clearly show below, nor wishes to be subject to him in such judgment. From this there has arisen so much strife and discord that it cannot be extinguished without great effort of souls and bodies and expenditure of wealth.

From *Defensor Pacis,* Discourse 2

ch 4. *Against the coercive jurisdiction of bishops.* [1] We now wish from the opposite side to adduce the truths of the holy Scripture in both its literal and its mystical sense, in accordance with the interpretations of the saints and the expositions of other approved doctors of the Christian faith, which explicitly command or counsel that neither the Roman bishop called pope, nor any other bishop or priest, or deacon, has or ought to have any rulership or coercive judgment or jurisdiction over any priest or non-priest, ruler, community, group, or individual of whatever condition. [. . .]

    [2] The more clearly to carry out this aim, we must not overlook that in this inquiry it is not asked what power and authority is or was had in this world by Christ, who was true God and true man, nor what or how much of this power he was able to bestow on St. Peter and the other apostles and their successors, the bishops or priests; for Christian believers have no doubts on these points. But we wish to and ought to inquire what power and authority, to be exercised in this world, Christ wanted to bestow and in fact *(de facto)* did bestow on them, and from what he excluded and prohibited them by counsel or command. For we are bound to believe

that they had from Christ only such power and authority as we can prove to have been given to them through the words of Scripture, no other. [. . .]

[3] Therefore for the present purpose it suffices to show [. . .] that Christ himself came into the world not to dominate men, nor to judge them by judgment in the third sense, nor to wield temporal rule, but rather to be subject as regards the status of the present life; and moreover, that he wanted to and did exclude himself, his apostles and disciples, and their successors, the bishops or priests, from all such coercive authority or worldly rule, both by his example and by his words of counsel or command. I shall also show that the leading apostles, as Christ's true imitators, did this same thing and taught their successors to do likewise; and moreover, that both Christ and the apostles wanted to be and were continuously subject in property and in person to the coercive jurisdiction of secular rulers, and that they taught and commanded all others, to whom they preached or wrote the law of truth, to do likewise, under pain of eternal damnation. [. . .]

[4] [. . .] This is first shown clearly beyond any doubt by the passage in the Gospel of John 18:36. For when Christ was brought before Pontius Pilate, vicar of the Roman ruler in Judaea, and accused of having called himself king of the Jews, Pontius asked him whether he had said this, or whether he did call himself a king, and Christ's reply included these words, among others: "My kingdom is not of this world," that is, I have not come to reign by temporal rule or dominion, in the way in which worldly kings reign. And proof of this was given by Christ himself through an evident sign when he said: "If my kingdom were of this world, my servants would certainly fight, that I should not be delivered to the Jews," as if to argue as follows: If I had come into this world to reign by worldly coercive rule, I would have ministers for this rule, namely, men to fight and to coerce transgressors, as the other kings have; but I do not have such ministers, as you can clearly see. [. . .]

[8] Moreover, the same is shown very evidently by Christ's words and example in the following passage of Luke 12 (13-14): "And one of the multitude said to him, Master speak to my brother, that he divide the inheritance with me. But he," that is Christ, "said to him, Man who hath appointed me judge or divider over you?" As if to say: I did not come to exercise this office, nor was I sent for this, that is, to settle civil disputes through judgment; but this, however, is undoubtedly the most proper function of secular rulers or judges. Now this passage from the gospel contains and demonstrates our proposition much more clearly than do the glosses of the saints, because the latter assume that the literal meaning, such as we have said, is manifest, and have devoted themselves more to the allegorical or mystical meaning. Nevertheless, we shall now quote from the glosses for a stronger confirmation of our proposition, and so that we may not be accused of expounding Scripture rashly. These words of Christ, then, are expounded by St. Ambrose as follows: "Well does he who descended for the sake of the divine avoid the earthly, and does not deign to be judge over disputes and appraiser of wealth, being the judge of the living and the dead and the appraiser of merits" (*Tract. in Ev. Luc.* 7.122, quoted from Aquinas, *Catena aurea* 12.145). [. . .]

[9] It now remains to show that not only did Christ himself refuse rulership or coercive judgment in this world, whereby he furnished an example for his apostles

and disciples and their successors to do likewise, but also he taught by words and showed by example that all men, both priests and non-priests, should be subject in property and in person to the coercive judgment of the rulers of this world. By his word and example, then, Christ showed this first with respect to property, by what is written in Matthew 22. For when the Jews asked him: "Tell us therefore, what dost thou think? Is it lawful to give tribute to Caesar, or not?" Christ, after looking at the coin and its inscription, replied: "Render therefore to Caesar the things that are Caesar's, and to God the things that are God's" (Matt. 22:17, 20-21). Whereon the interlinear gloss says: "that is, tribute and money" (Glossa interlinearis, ad loc). [. . .] Note, therefore, what it was that Christ came into the world to demand. Furthermore, Chrysostom writes as follows: "When you hear: 'Render to Caesar the things that are Caesar's,' know that he means only those things which are not harmful to piety, for if they were, the tribute would be not to Caesar but to the devil" (Hom. in Matt. 70.2, quoted from Aquinas, Catena aurea 11, 253). So, then, we ought to be subject to Caesar in all things, so long only as they are not contrary to piety, that is, to divine worship or commandment. [. . .]

ch. 9. *On the relation of human acts to divine law and judgment.* [1] According to this reasoning, therefore, there is also a certain judge who has coercive authority over transgressors of divine law, which we have called the coercive standard of some human acts both immanent and transient. But this judge is one alone, Christ, and no one else. Whence in James 4:12: "There is one lawmaker and judge, that is able to destroy and to deliver." But this judge's coercive power is not exercised over anyone in this world, to punish or reward transgressors or observers of the law made immediately by him, which we have often called the evangelic law. For in his mercy Christ wished to give every person the opportunity to become deserving up to the very end of his life and to repent of sins committed against Christ's law, as will be shown below by the authorities of Holy Scripture.

[2] But there is also another judge according to the evangelic Scripture [. . .]. This other judge is the priest, who is the teacher in this world of divine law and of its commands concerning what must be done or shunned in order to attain eternal life and to avoid punishment. However, he has no coercive power in this world to compel anyone to observe these commands. For it would be useless for him to coerce anyone to observe them, since the person who observed them under coercion would be helped not at all toward eternal salvation [. . .]. Hence this judge is properly likened to the physician, who is given the authority to teach, command, and predict or judge about the things which it is useful to do or omit in order to attain bodily health and avoid illness or death. It was for this reason, too, that Christ called himself a physician in and for the status of the present life, and not a ruler or a judge. Hence in Luke 5:31 Christ spoke of himself to the Pharisees as follows: "They that are well do not need a physician, but they that are sick." For Christ did not ordain that anyone should be forced to observe in this world the law made by him, and for this reason he did not appoint in this world a judge having coercive power over transgressors of this law.

[3] Hence it must be noted that the evangelic law can stand in a twofold relation to men, over whom it was made by Christ. In one way, it can be related to them

in and for the status of the present life; and in this way it has in its various parts the nature more of a doctrine, theoretic or practical or both, than of a law taken in its last and proper sense [. . .] as a coercive standard, that is, a standard in accordance with which its transgressor is punished by the coercive force which is given to the man who must judge in accordance with it. But now the evangelic doctrine, or the maker of that law, does not command that anyone be compelled in this world to observe the things which it commands men to do or omit in this world. Consequently, in its relation to man's status in and for this world, it ought to be called a doctrine, not a law, except in the way we have said. This was also the view of the Apostle in 2 Timothy 3:16, when he said: "All Scripture divinely inspired is useful for teaching, for reproof, for correction, for instruction in righteousness." But never did the Apostle say: for coercion or punishment in this world. Hence in 2 Corinthians 1:23: "Not because we exercise dominion over your faith, but we are the helpers of your joy; for by faith ye stand." Whereon Ambrose wrote [. . .]: "And lest they," that is, the Corinthians, "resent what might appear almost as dominion, in that he," the Apostle, "had said 'to spare you I did not come' (1.23), he," the Apostle, "adds: But I do not say 'to spare you' 'because we exercise dominion over your faith,' that is, because your faith undergoes dominion and coercion, for faith is of the will, not of necessity; but I say it rather 'because we are the helpers,' if you wish to cooperate." Note then, they are helpers, that is, by teaching, and "if you wish to cooperate." "For 'by faith,' which works through choice, 'ye stand,' not by dominion" [Marsilius derives the quotation immediately from Peter Lombard, *Collectanea in Ep. Pauli*, but its source is untraced].

But the evangelic Scripture or law can also stand in another relation to men, for their status in the other world, in which alone, and not in this one, those men will be punished who have transgressed this law in the present life. And viewed in this other relation it is most properly given the name of law, and he who will then judge in accordance with it is most properly called a judge, in the third sense as having great coercive power. But inasmuch as the priest or bishop, whoever he be, guides and regulates men in accordance with this law in the status of the present life alone, although with reference to the future life, and since the immediate maker of that law, Christ, has not granted to the priest the authority to coerce anyone in accordance with it in this world, it follows that the priest is not properly called a judge, in the third sense as having coercive power, and he neither can nor should coerce anyone in this world by such judgment through punishment in property or in person. [. . .]

ch. 12. *Terms concerning supreme poverty.* [6] [. . .] Thus, then, in one sense right is the same as law, divine or human, or what is commanded or prohibited or permitted according to these laws.

[7] There is also another division of right, and properly of human right, into natural and civil. Natural right *(ius naturale),* according to Aristotle in the *Ethics* (*NE* 1134b19), the treatise on justice, is that statute of the legislator with respect to which almost all men agree that it is honourable and should be observed. Examples are that God must be worshipped, parents must be honoured, children must be reared by their parents up to a certain age, no one should be injured, injuries must be lawfully repulsed, and the like. Although these depend upon human enactment,

they are metaphorically called "natural" rights because in all regions they are in the same way believed to be lawful and their opposites unlawful, just as the acts of natural things which are devoid of will are everywhere uniform, like fire, which "burns here just as it does in Persia" (1134b25).

[8] However, there are some men who define natural right as the dictate of right reason in practical matters, which they place under divine right; and consequently everything done in accordance with divine law and in accordance with the counsel of right reason is lawful in an absolute sense; but not everything done in accordance with human laws, since in some things the latter fall away from right reason. But the word "natural" is used equivocally here and above. For there are many things which are in accordance with the dictate of right reason, but which are not agreed upon as honourable by all nations, namely, those things which are not self-evident to all, and consequently not acknowledged by all. So too there are some commands, prohibitions, or permissions in accordance with divine law which do not agree in this respect with human law; but since many cases of this are well known, I have omitted to cite examples for the sake of brevity.

[9] And hence too, some things are lawful according to human law which are not lawful according to divine law, and conversely. However, what is lawful and what unlawful in an absolute sense must be viewed according to divine law rather than human law, when these disagree in their commands, prohibitions, or permissions.

[10] "Right" is used in a second sense to refer to every controlled human act, power, or acquired habit, internal or external, both immanent and transient or crossing over into some external thing or something pertaining thereto, like its use or usufruct, acquisition, holding, saving, or exchanging, and so on, whenever these are in conformity with right taken in its first sense. What the use or usufruct of a thing is, together with the other lawful or rightful ways of handling things, we shall assume for the present from the science of civil acts.

It is in this sense that we usually say: "This is someone's right," when he wishes or handles some thing in a manner which is in conformity with right taken in the first sense. Hence, such wish or handling is called right because it conforms to the command, prohibition, or permission of right; just as a column is called right (*dextra*) or left because it is situated nearer to the right or the left side of an animal. Right, then, taken in this second sense, is none other than what is willed by the active command, prohibition, or permission of the legislator, and this is what we called above the passive meaning of these three words. And this too is what we previously called lawful.

[11] In another sense this term "right" means the sentence or judgments made by judges in accordance with the law or with right taken in its first sense. It is in this sense that men usually say: "The judge or ruler has done or rendered right to someone," when he has convicted or acquitted someone by a legal sentence.

[12] "Right" is also used to refer to an act or habit of particular justice; in this sense we say that he wishes right or justice who wishes what is equal or proportional in exchanges or distributions.

[13] Next we must distinguish the meanings or senses of "ownership" or "lordship" (*dominium*). In its strict sense, this term means the principal power to lay

claim to something rightfully acquired in accordance with right taken in its first sense; that is, the power of a person who knows about this and does not dissent therefrom, and who wants to allow no one else to handle that thing without his, the owner's express consent, while he owns it. This power is none other than the actual or habitual will thus to have the rightfully acquired thing, as we have said. [. . .]

[14] Again, this term is more commonly used for the aforesaid power, whether it be only over a thing, or only over the use or the usufruct of the thing, or over all of these at once.

[15] The same term is also used for the aforesaid power, but as belonging to a person who does not know of it or consent to it but who yet does not explicitly dissent therefrom or renounce it. In this sense, an infant or person who is absent or generally unaware thereof, but yet capable, can acquire, by himself or through another, a thing or something pertaining thereto together with the ownership of it, or the power to claim it before a coercive judge from any person who steals or wants to steal it. And we have said that this power belongs to a person who does not explicitly dissent; for one who does explicitly dissent, or who renounces a thing or something pertaining thereto, does not acquire such things, or ownership of them, or the power to lay claim to them. For anyone can lawfully renounce a right which is offered to him in accordance with human laws, nor is anyone compelled by any law to accept, against his will, the benefit of a right. But the aforementioned kinds of ownership are legal, for they are acquired or may be acquired by ordainment of the law or of its legislator, and by men's choice.

[16] Again, this term, "ownership," is used to refer to the human will or freedom in itself with its organic executive or motive power unimpeded. For it is through these that we are capable of certain acts and their opposites. It is for this reason too that man alone among the animals is said to have ownership or control of his acts; this control belongs to him by nature, it is not acquired through an act of will or choice.

[17] Next we must distinguish the meanings of "possession." Taken broadly, it signifies in one sense the same as ownership in either of its first three senses, or some temporal thing in relation to a person who has and wishes to have it in the manner defined in the first two senses of ownership. Whence in Genesis (13:2): "He was very rich in possession of gold and silver"; and in the same book (17:8): "And I will give unto thee, and thy seed after thee, all the land of Canaan, for an everlasting possession."

[18] In another sense, and more strictly, "possession" means the aforementioned ownership together with the actual corporeal handling of the thing or of its use or usufruct in the present or in the future; it is in this sense that this word is most often used in the science of civil acts.

[19] Again, this term means the lawful corporeal handling of a thing whether it belongs to oneself or even to someone else; as in Acts (4:32): "Neither said any of them that aught of the things which he possessed was his own; but they had all things in common."

[20] "Possession" is also used, although improperly, to refer to the unlawful corporeal holding of a thing by oneself or through someone else, in the present or in the future.

[21] And now we have to distinguish the meanings of the terms "private" or "proper" *(proprium)* and "common" *(commune)*. In one sense, "proper" or "property" is used to refer to ownership taken in its first meaning; it is in this sense that the term is used in the science of civil acts.

[22] Again, more broadly, it is used for ownership taken in both its first and its second senses; this is the sense in which it is used by theologians, and also in much of the holy Scripture.

[23] These words "private" or "proper" and "property" are further used among theologians to refer to the individuality of a person or thing or something pertaining thereto, when it belongs to one person alone, not with any other person. For it is in this sense that theologians take "private," contrasting it with "common," when they ask whether it is more perfect, or more deserving of eternal life, to have temporal things as private property, that is, individually, or to have such things in common with another person or persons.

ch. 13. *The status of supreme poverty held by Christ and his disciples.* [1] Having thus distinguished the senses and meanings of the terms given above, we shall now infer some conclusions. The first of these is that no one can lawfully handle, individually or in common with others, some temporal thing, whether his own or someone else's, or something pertaining thereto, like the use or the usufruct, without right or without having a right to the thing or to something pertaining thereto — taking "right" in its first and second senses. For every deed which is not commanded or permitted to be done by right is not lawful, as everyone can clearly see from the definition of "lawful" [. . .].

[2] The second conclusion which we can infer from what we have said is that one can handle a thing, or something pertaining thereto, lawfully according to one law, such as the divine, and unlawfully according to another, such as the human; and likewise conversely; and again, one can do the same thing lawfully or unlawfully according to each law. This is not difficult to see, since the commands, prohibitions, and permissions in these laws sometimes differ and disagree with one another and sometimes agree. [. . .] It is, however, certain that many things are permitted by human law, like fornication, drunkenness, and other sins, which are prohibited by divine law.

[3] And now I wish to show that even apart from having any ownership, in the first three senses, of any temporal thing or of anything pertaining thereto, a person may lawfully handle it in private (in the third sense of "private") or even possess it in common with someone else (understanding the third sense of "possession"), and also lawfully destroy it. This is so, I maintain, regardless of whether that thing, or something pertaining thereto, be consumable in some one use or not; whether it be private to him (in the third sense of "private") or be common to him with another person or persons; whether it be his own, that is, rightfully acquired by him, or belong to someone else who, having rightfully (in the first sense) acquired it, consents to his handling it.

I demonstrate this proposition as follows. That temporal thing, (or something pertaining thereto) which a person handles or holds apart from having ownership of it (in the first three senses of ownership), in accordance with divine law or human law or both, he can handle and destroy lawfully, apart from having ownership of it (in the above senses) whether in private or in common with others. But, regardless of whether a thing (or something pertaining thereto) be his own or belong to someone else who consents to his handling it, a person can, in accordance with these laws, handle the thing, as has been said, apart from having the aforementioned ownership of it. Therefore he can lawfully handle the thing without having ownership of it.

The first proposition of this deduction is self-evident from the definition of "lawful." The second I prove by an argument taken from induction, first with regard to a thing which belongs to a person privately or in common with someone else, or which he has rightfully acquired through his own act or someone else's, as by gift or legacy, by hunting, or fishing, or by some other lawful labour or deed of his. For suppose that a person has thus acquired a thing. It is then certain that he can use and handle it in accordance with the laws, since acquisition of a thing in the aforesaid ways is in accordance with the law, as is plain from induction. Also it is clear that anyone who has the capacity can lawfully renounce a right introduced on his behalf, since, according to human and divine law, a benefit is not bestowed on an unwilling person. Therefore, a person who can by his own or by another's deed acquire ownership of a thing, or of its use, will be able to renounce such ownership. Since, therefore, the same person, if he wants to, acquires both the power lawfully to use a thing and the power to claim it and to prohibit another person from it, he can lawfully renounce the power of laying claim to the thing (or something pertaining thereto) or of prohibiting another therefrom (which power is none other than ownership taken in its first three legal senses), without renouncing the power of using the thing (or something pertaining thereto). This latter power falls under right taken in its second sense, and is by some men called "simple use of a thing" (*simplex facti usus*) without the right of using (*ius utendi*), by "right of using" meaning "ownership" in any of its three senses given above.

[4] Moreover, a thing which belongs to no one (*in nullius bonis est*) a person can lawfully use in accordance with the laws; but when someone has renounced the power to lay claim to a thing and to prohibit another person therefrom, that thing can then belong to no one; therefore a person can lawfully use it. Since, therefore, a person who renounces the aforesaid power does not have the aforesaid ownership of the thing, it is apparent that one can lawfully handle and use a thing apart from having any of the aforesaid legal ownership.

[5] Again, those things are separate from each other, of which one can for any time be given up by lawful vow, and the other not. But the aforesaid ownership of a thing, or the power to lay claim to and prohibit from a temporal thing or something pertaining thereto, can be given up for any time by lawful vow; while the lawful having or simple use of a thing cannot by lawful vow be given up for any time. Therefore these two cases are properly separate from each other. The first proposition of this deduction is self-evident from the definition of "lawful"; for the same thing cannot at once be lawful and unlawful according to the same law. The second proposition I shall prove with respect to each part. And first, that to give up for any time the aforesaid ownership by vow is lawful: for that vow is lawful which can be derived from the

counsel of Christ. But such giving up is what Christ counselled, when in Matthew 19:29 he said: "And every one that hath forsaken house or lands . . . for my name's sake, shall receive an hundredfold, and shall inherit everlasting life." The same counsel is to be found in Matthew 5:40 and Luke 6:29, when Christ said: "And him that taketh away thy cloak, forbid not to take thy coat also." "And if any man will sue thee at the law, and take away thy coat, let him have thy cloak also." Whereon Augustine: "If he gives this command with regard to necessary things," that is, he counsels that one should not sue at law, "how much more so with regard to superfluities?" (*De sermone Domini in monte* 1.19.59). And in accordance with this teaching of Christ, the Apostle said in 1 Corinthians 6:7: "Now therefore there is utterly a fault among you, because ye go to law one with another. Why do ye not rather take wrong? Why do ye not rather suffer yourselves to be defrauded?" [. . .]

And as for the other part of the second proposition, that the lawful having of a thing or of its use, or the simple use of a thing, cannot be given up for any time — this is clear enough: for nothing which is prohibited by divine law can lawfully fall under a vow. But such giving up is prohibited by divine law, because it is a species of homicide. For he who observed such a vow would knowingly kill himself from hunger or cold or thirst; which is explicitly prohibited by divine law, as in Matthew 19:18, Mark 10:19 and Luke 18:20, where Christ, confirming some commands of the old law, says: "Thou shalt not kill," etc. Therefore, the simple use of a thing, or the lawful having of it, is separate from all the aforementioned kinds of ownership, or the power of laying claim to and prohibiting from the thing or something pertaining thereto.

[6] From this too clearly it follows of necessity that it is insane heresy to assert that a thing or its use cannot be had apart from the aforesaid ownership [as Pope John XXII had asserted in his bull, *Ad conditorem canonum*, published 8 December 1322]. For he who says this thinks nothing other than that Christ's counsel cannot be fulfilled; which is an open lie and, as we have said, must be shunned as vicious and heretical.

[8] Next I show that apart from having any ownership (in the senses given above), a person can have lawful use of something which belongs to another man, even to the extent of consuming the thing itself, if he exercises this use with the consent of the owner. For since the thing is assumed to be entirely in the ownership (or power to claim) of another person, it is certain that such ownership is not transferred to anyone else except by the deed and the express consent of the owner, and with no dissent on the part of the person to whom such ownership (or power to claim) of such a thing or of its use is to be transferred. Suppose, therefore, that the owner does not wish to transfer such ownership of a thing or of its use to some other person. Suppose, too, that this other person dissents from receiving such ownership, as for instance, because he has given up the ownership of all temporal things by an explicit vow, as befits those who are perfect. Suppose, further, that an owner consents to have some perfect person use some thing of his, even to the extent of consuming the thing, and that the perfect person, who has given up ownership of every thing, wishes to use such thing with the owner's consent. I say, then, that the person who thus uses the thing, uses it lawfully, and that he nevertheless has no ownership whatsoever (in the senses given above) of the thing or of its use. That he has no own-

444

ership of the thing, or of its use, is apparent from the assumed conditions with regard both to the will of the owner and to the condition of the person who is to receive the use of the thing, who has completely given up such ownership. That he uses the thing lawfully is apparent from the definition of "lawful," since everyone is permitted by law to use a thing belonging to someone else even to the extent of consuming it, if there intervenes the express consent of the owner of the thing.

[9] Now if we take ownership or control in its last sense, as meaning the human will or freedom, with that natural motive power which is not acquired but innate in us, then I say that neither lawfully nor unlawfully can we freely handle a thing, or something pertaining thereto, without having such ownership or control, nor can we give up such ownership or control. And for the sake of brevity, I pass over this without proof, since it is almost self-evident, inasmuch as without these powers no one can continue to exist.

[14] [. . .] There is no doubt, according to the views of the saints, that if poverty is deserving of the kingdom of the heavens, as Christ says, it must not be primarily the external lack of temporal goods, but an internal habit of the mind, whereby one freely wishes to be lacking in such goods for the sake of Christ. Whence on the words in Luke (6:20): "Blessed are the poor," etc., Basil writes: "Not everyone who is oppressed by poverty is blessed. For there are many persons who are poor in means, but more avaricious in desire, and these are not saved by their poverty, but damned by their desire. For nothing which is involuntary can be blessed, since every virtue is marked by free will" (in Aquinas, *Catena aurea* 12.70). Poverty, then, is a meritorious virtue, and consequently voluntary. But external lack is not in itself a virtue, inasmuch as it does not lead to salvation without the proper desire; for a person might be lacking in temporal goods under coercion and against his will, and yet he would be condemned because of his inordinate desire for these goods. This was also the view of the Apostle on this subject, when in 2 Corinthians 8:12 he said: "For if there be first a willing mind, it is accepted according to that a man hath" — "accepted," that is, meritorious.

[15] Moreover, if this choice to be lacking in temporal goods is to be meritorious, it must be made for the sake of Christ. Hence the Truth says in Matthew 19:29: "And everyone that hath forsaken houses . . . for my name's sake." [. . .]

[17] From these considerations, therefore, it can be seen that meritorious poverty is the virtue whereby a person wishes for the sake of Christ to be deprived of and to lack all the temporal goods, usually called riches, which are over and above what is necessary for his subsistence.

[22] Moreover, I say that the highest mode or species of this virtue is the explicit vow of the wayfarer, whereby for the sake of Christ he renounces and wishes to be deprived of and to lack all acquired legal ownership, both in private and in common, or the power to claim and to prohibit another from temporal things (called "riches") before a coercive judge. And by this vow, also, the wayfarer wishes, for the sake of Christ, to be deprived of and to lack, both in private and in common, all power, holding, handling, or use of temporal things over and above what is necessary quantitatively and qualitatively for his present subsistence. Nor does he wish at one time to have such goods, however lawfully they may come to him, in an amount sufficient to supply several of the future needs or necessities either of himself alone

or of himself together with a determinate other person or persons in common. Rather, he wishes to have at one time only what is necessary for a single need, as the immediately actual and present need of food and shelter; but with this sole exception, that the person who takes this vow should be in such a place, time, and personal circumstance that he can acquire for himself, on each successive day, a quantity of temporal things sufficient to supply his aforesaid individual need, but only one at a time, not more. This mode or species of meritorious poverty is the status which is considered to be necessary for evangelical perfection. [. . .]

[23] That this mode of meritorious poverty is the supreme one can be shown from this, that through it all the other meritorious counsels of Christ are observed. For in the first place, men give up by a vow all the temporal things which it is possible for a wayfarer to give up; secondly, most of the impediments to divine charity are removed for those who take this vow; thirdly, they are put in condition to endure many secular passions, humiliations, and hardships, and are willingly deprived of many secular pleasures and vanities; and in a word, they are put in the best condition to observe all the commands and counsels of Christ. [. . .]

[28] Now when we said that the perfect person is not allowed to provide for himself for the morrow, we did not mean that if anything remained from his lawful daily acquisitions, he ought to throw it away and in no manner save it, but that he ought to save it only with the firm intention of properly distributing it to any poor person or persons he met who were more needy than he. Whence in Luke 3:11: "He that hath two coats, let him impart to him that hath none: and he that hath meat, let him do likewise"; understanding by "two coats" and "meat" that which remains over and above one's own present needs.

We said that the surplus must be given to *any* poor person; for a community of men who save or have goods for certain definite persons only, such as the community of monks, canons, and the like, is not a perfect community; for the perfect community, like that of Christ and his apostles, extends to all the faithful, as is clear from Acts 4. And if it chanced to extend to infidels also, it would perhaps be still more meritorious, according to Luke 6:27: "Do good to them which hate you."

[32] Nor should we pay attention to the argument that perfect men may lawfully save real estate in order to distribute the annual income thereof to the poor. For it is more meritorious because of love of Christ and pity for one's neighbour to distribute at once to the poor both the real estate and the income thereof, rather than the latter alone; and besides, it is more meritorious to give away the real estate alone rather than its income alone. For in this way help can be given to many poor and needy persons at once, who might perhaps through want become ill or die before the income became available, or commit an act of violence, theft, or some other evil. Again, a person who kept the real estate might die before the time when the income was distributed, and thus he would never have the merit therefrom that he could have had.

Entirely the same view must be held with respect to any kind of chattels, which similarly, when thus kept, naturally affect to an inordinate degree the desire of the person who holds them. [. . .]

[34] And now I wish to show that while Christ observed supreme poverty, he did have some possessions both as private property and in common. That he had

private property (in the third sense) is shown by the passage in Mark 2:15-16: "For there were many, and they followed him. And the scribes and sinners saw him eat with publicans and sinners." Now it is certain that he lawfully had as private or individual property that which he put to his mouth and ate. Moreover, his clothes were his private or individual property, as is sufficiently clear from Matthew 27:31 [. . .]: "They took the robe off from him, and put his own raiment on him."

[35] Christ also lawfully had some things in common while observing supreme poverty. Whence in John 12:6: "This Judas said, not that he cared for the poor; but because he was a thief and had the bags," that is, the common belongings of Christ and the apostles and the other poor persons. That these were held in common is apparent from the fact that Christ ordered some of them to be distributed to the hungry crowds of the poor, as is sufficiently clear from Matthew 14:16. The "bags" were the repositories wherein was kept the alms money which had been given to them. This is again shown by the fourteenth chapter of the same book [actually, John 13:29]: "For some of them thought that Judas had the bag." [. . .] Thus too the apostles, while observing supreme poverty, had belongings in common among themselves and with other poor persons, after the resurrection of Christ. Whence in Acts 4:32: "But they had all things in common." And similarly they had some things as private property, namely, their own food and clothing, which they applied for their private use, just as did Christ.

ch. 15. *Differentiation of priestly office.* [1] But these conclusions of ours raise a difficult question which is very necessary to consider. For in chapter 15 of Discourse 1 we made a statement which we repeated at the end of chapter 8 of this discourse: that the human legislator, by itself or through the ruler, is the efficient cause of the establishment of all the offices or parts of the state. But we also recall having said, in the last chapter of Discourse 1, that the priesthood or the priestly office of the New Law was first established by Christ alone, who, however, renounced all secular rulership and temporal lordship [. . .] and who was not the human legislator [. . .]. Hence we seem to have said that that which establishes every office of the state is not the same as the human legislator or ruler. Hence it may well be wondered to whom belongs the authority to establish the priesthood, especially in communities of believers, since the above statements seem to contradict one another on this point.

[2] Attempting to resolve this apparent contradiction, we shall first repeat what we said in chapters 6 and 7 of Discourse 1: that each office of the state has one cause according as the office means a habit of the soul, and another cause according as the office is part of the state established for the sake of the benefits to be derived therefrom; and this is to be noted with respect to the priesthood as well as with respect to the other offices of the state. For according as the priesthood means a certain habit of the soul, which the teachers of the holy Scripture call a "character," its immediate and essential efficient cause, or essential maker, is God imprinting this quality upon the mind, although by means of a certain human ministry which prepares the way, as it were. This ministry, in the New Law, drew its origin from Christ. For as a human priest, Christ, who was true God and true man, performed the ministry which succeeding priests have since performed; and as God he imprinted the character upon the souls of those whom he appointed as priests; in this way he ap-

pointed first the apostles, as his immediate successors, and then later all the other priests, but through the ministry of the apostles and of his other successors in this office. For when the apostles or the other priests lay their hands on others and utter the proper words or prayers, Christ, as God, imprints this priestly habit or character on those who are worthy and willing to receive it.

And a similar view must be taken with regard to the bestowal of the other orders whereby a certain character is imprinted on the soul of the recipient. This "priestly character," whether one or many, is the power whereby the priest can consecrate from bread and water the blessed body and blood of Christ by uttering certain words, and can minister the other ecclesiastical sacraments; and by this character also the priest can bind and loose men from sin.

[4] Now with respect to this priestly character, whether one or many, which we have said to be the power of performing the sacrament of the Eucharist or of consecrating Christ's body and blood, and the power of binding and loosing men from sins, which character we shall henceforth call the "essential" or "inseparable authority" of the priest insofar as he is a priest, to me it seems likely that this character is the same in kind among all priests, and that the Roman or any other bishop has no more of it than has any simple priest. For with respect to this authority, regardless of whether it be one or many, the bishop does not differ from the priest; this is asserted not only by Jerome, but also by the Apostle, who openly holds this view, as will be seen below. For on the words in Matthew 16:19: "Whatsoever ye shall bind on earth," etc., Jerome writes: "The same judiciary power" (sc. as Peter had) "is had by the other apostles, to whom he," Christ, "said after his resurrection: 'Receive ye the Holy Ghost. Whosoever's sins ye remit, they are remitted unto them,' etc. Every church has this power through its priests and bishops" [quoted from Glos. ord., but source untraced]. [. . .]

[6] But because the number of priests had markedly increased after the days of the apostles, the priests, in order to avoid scandal and schism, elected one of their number to guide and direct the others in the exercise of the ecclesiastic office and service, in the distribution of offerings, and in the proper arrangement of other matters, lest the household and service of the temples be disturbed because of conflicting desires, by each man's acting according to his own pleasure, and sometimes wrongly. Through later custom this priest, who was elected to regulate the other priests, retained for himself alone the name of "bishop," as being an overseer, because he supervised not only the faithful people (for which reason all priests were in the primitive church called bishops), but also his fellow priests; and hence, antonomastically, the overseer later kept for himself alone the name "bishop," while the others retained the simple name "priest."

[7] But the aforesaid election or appointment made by man does not give to the person thus elected any greater essential merit or priestly authority or power, but only a certain power with regard to the ordering of the household in God's house or temple: namely, the power to direct and regulate the other priests, deacons, and officials, in the same way that the prior is today given power over monks. This power is not coercive unless the authority for such coercion shall have been granted by the human legislator to the person thus elected, as was demonstrated in chapters 4 and 8 of this discourse. [. . .]

448

[9] But there are certain other, non-essential appointments to priestly offices. Such is the election we mentioned above, whereby one of the priests is named to regulate or guide the others in matters pertaining to divine worship. Such too is the election and appointment of other priests to teach and minister the sacraments of the New Law to a specified people in a designated place of greater or lesser size, and to distribute both among themselves and among other poor persons the temporal things which have been set apart by the legislator or by individuals for the support of poor preachers in a certain province or community, and also for the support of other poor persons unable to provide for themselves on account of their age, weakness, or other misfortune (but this latter bounty must come out of what remains over and above the needs of the preachers). These temporal things, thus set apart, are now called "ecclesiastic benefices" [. . .]. For they are entrusted to ministers of temples to be distributed for the aforesaid purposes; the ministers have for these tasks been elected and appointed to a certain province, since the essential authority whereby they are successors of the apostles does not assign them to teach and minister the sacraments of the New Law to the people of one place rather than to the people of another, just as the apostles were given no definite territorial assignment. For Christ said to them, in Matthew 28:19: "Go ye therefore and teach all nations"; he did not assign the apostles to definite places, but they later apportioned among themselves the peoples to whom and the provinces in which they were to preach the word of God or the evangelical law; and sometimes, also, they learned of their mission through divine revelation. Whence in Galatians 2:9: "They," James, Cephas, and John, "gave to me and Barnabas the right hand of fellowship; that we should go unto the heathen, and they unto the circumcision."

[10] Thus, then, it is clear from the above what is the efficient cause of the appointment of the priesthood, according as it signifies a habit or character of the soul, and of the other orders which are called holy; for this cause is God or Christ, without mediation, although first there occurs a certain human, as it were preparatory, ministry, like the laying on of hands and the uttering of words, which perhaps effect nothing to this end but which thus precede by virtue of a certain pact or divine ordinance. And from what we have said it is also apparent that the above appointment is different from the human appointment whereby one priest is put at the head of the others and whereby too the priests are assigned to teach and instruct the peoples of particular provinces in the divine law, to minister the sacraments to them, and to distribute the temporal things which we have called ecclesiastic benefices.

ch. 20. *The authority to interpret Holy Scripture.* [1] [. . .] We wish to show that it is expedient and necessary to determine doubtful meanings or sentences of the holy Scripture, both those whose doubtfulness has already come to notice and those which will in the future, especially with regard to articles of the faith, commands and prohibitions. For that is expedient or rather necessary, without which the unity of the faith would not be maintained, and lack of which would lead to error and schism with regard to the faith among Christian believers. But such a necessity is the determination of the doubtful and sometimes contrary views of learned men with regard to divine law. [. . .]

[2] And now I am going to show that the principal authority, direct or indi-

rect, for such determination of doubtful questions belongs only to a general council composed of all Christians or of the weightier part of them, or to those persons who have been granted such authority by the whole body of Christian believers. The procedure is as follows: let all the notable provinces or communities of the world, in accordance with the determination of their human legislators, whether one or many, and according to their proportion in quantity and quality of persons, elect faithful men, first priests and then non-priests, suitable persons of the most blameless lives and the greatest experience in divine law. These men are to act as judges in the first sense of the word, representing the whole body of the faithful by virtue of the authority which these whole bodies have granted to them, and they are to assemble at a place which is most convenient according to the decision of the majority of them, where they are to settle those matters pertaining to divine law which have appeared doubtful, and which it seems useful, expedient, and necessary to define. [. . .]

ch. 22. *The headship of the Roman bishop.* [1] [. . .] We wish to show that it is expedient and very useful to appoint a single bishop and a single church or priestly college as the head or leader of the others. But first we must differentiate the ways or senses in which one church or bishop can be understood to be the head of all the others, so that we may separate the proper way from the ways which are improper and inexpedient. For one bishop and church to be the head of all the others can in one sense be understood to mean that all churches and individuals in the world are obliged to believe in their definitions or interpretations of doubtful senses of Scripture (especially with regard to what it is necessary to believe and observe for salvation), and to perform the church ritual or divine worship in accordance with their decrees. But in this sense no one bishop or church of any province, as such, nor any college of priests, is the head of the others, according to divine law, nor does the example of the primitive church show that it is expedient to have a head church of such a kind, nor, similarly, is such headship authorized by any decree of the faithful human legislator. For if there were such a head, one of the many evils that would follow therefrom would be this: that it would be necessary for salvation that all rulers, communities, and peoples believe, in accordance with the definition or decree of Boniface VIII, that they were all subject in coercive jurisdiction to the Roman pope, and believe further, in accordance with the ordinances of a certain so-called Roman pope, that Christ did not counsel that the possession (in private or in common) of temporal goods in excess of present needs be spurned or renounced, and likewise the ownership of such goods, that is, the power lawfully to sue for them or to lay claim to them before a coercive judge. The first of these assertions is the most horrible falsehood; and the second must be denied as heretical, as has been clearly shown above in chapters 13, 14, 16, 20, and 21 of this discourse.

[2] Another sense in which one bishop and church or college can be regarded as the head or leader of all the rest is this: that all the clergymen or clerical colleges in the world are subject to their coercive jurisdiction. But this kind of headship belongs to no bishop or church according to divine law, but is rather forbidden by counsel or command, as has been adequately shown in chapters 4, 5, 8, 9, and 11 of this discourse.

[3] This priority can be understood in still another sense: that to one bishop or

church or college pertains the appointment of all church officials and the distribution, deposit, and withdrawal of temporal goods or benefices. But that some one bishop or church is in this sense prior to the others cannot be proved by divine law, but rather the opposite. And in a word, by virtue of the words of Scripture it cannot be proved that some one bishop or church is the head or leader of the others with respect to any authority or power, as has been shown in chapters 15, 16, 17, 20, and 21 of this discourse.

[4] Consequently, one bishop can no more excommunicate another than the other can excommunicate him; nor can one bishop interdict the reception of divine sacraments or services by the people or province entrusted to the care of another bishop, any more than the other bishop can do so to the former's people or province; nor, with regard to any other authority, does one bishop have more of it over another bishop, or over this other bishop's province, than the latter has over the former bishop or over his province, unless such authority or power shall have been granted by the general council or the faithful human legislator. For all bishops are of equal merit and authority insofar as they are bishops. [. . .]

[5] By virtue of the words of Scripture, therefore, no bishop or church is the head or leader of the rest, as such. For the only absolute head of the church and foundation of the faith, by immediate ordainment of God, according to the Scripture or truth, is Christ himself, and not any apostle, bishop, or priest, as the Apostle very clearly says in Ephesians 4:11-16; 5:23-24, in Colossians 1:18, and in 1 Corinthians 10:4. And hence he says that all the apostles, prophets, teachers, and other believers constitute the "body of Christ," which is the church as meaning the other members; but no one is the "head" except Christ alone. [. . .]

[6] There is another, and proper, sense in which a bishop or church can be understood to be or to have been made the head and leader of the other bishops and churches. This proper headship is derived from the authority of the general council or the faithful legislator, and is of the following kind: It is the duty of the head bishop, although together with his college of priests (whom the faithful human legislator or the general council has willed to associate with him for this purpose), to notify the faithful legislator lacking a superior if any emergency of the faith, or clear need of the believers, is brought to his attention which, after due deliberation, seems absolutely to require the calling of a general council. The general council must then be assembled by the coercive command of the legislator, in the way we have said. It is also the head bishop's duty to hold the leading seat or position among all the bishops and clergymen at the general council, to propose questions for deliberation, to review the discussions in the presence of the whole council, to have the proceedings recorded in writing under authentic seals and notarial stamps, to communicate and publish these proceedings to all churches which so request, to know and teach these results and answer questions about them; and also, if any persons transgress the council's decisions with regard both to the faith and to church ritual or divine worship, as well as the other ordinances for the peace and unity of the believers, the head bishop has to punish such transgressors by some ecclesiastic censure, like excommunication or interdict or other similar penalty, but in accordance with the determination of the council and by its authority, and not by any coercive power inflicting

punishment in person or in property in and for the status of the present world. It is also the duty of the head bishop, acting together with the weightier part or majority of the college which has been assigned to him by the legislator, to sit in judgment over bishops and churches (not subordinated to one another) with respect to spiritual controversies properly so called [. . .], in which class fall the ordinances concerning church ritual which the council has made and ordered to be observed. However, if the other churches with comparative unanimity clearly feel that it is likely that this duty is being abused or neglected by the head church's bishop or college, then these other churches may lawfully appeal to the faithful human legislator, if the legislator, or the ruler by its authority, can conveniently correct such abuse or neglect; or else the other churches may request a general council, if, in the eyes of a majority of the other churches and in the judgment of the legislator, the case requires the calling of such a council. [. . .]

[8] We now come to the questions of what bishop and church it is most proper to choose as head of the others, and from which province or diocese this head ought to be chosen. Discussing first the qualities of the head bishop, let us say, in accordance with the truth, that he ought to be the one who excels all others in the goodness of his life and in sacred doctrine, although the former qualification should be given more weight. As to which place or province should have its church put over the others, it must be said that the headship should be given to that church whose college of priests or clergymen includes the most men who are most honorable in their lives and most pure in their sacred doctrine. But other things being equal, or not much different, it seems that the bishop and church of Rome (so long as that place remains habitable) deserves such headship for several reasons: first, because of the surpassing faith, love, and renown of the first bishop of Rome, who was St. Peter or St. Paul or both, and the great reverence paid to them by the other apostles; also, because of the venerable tradition of the city of Rome, its long leadership over the other cities, the great number of illustrious men, saints, and teachers of the Christian faith who lived at Rome in most periods from the very beginning of the established church, and the diligent care and assiduous labour which they exerted on behalf of the other churches to spread the faith and to preserve its unity; and again, because of the general monarchy and coercive authority which the people and ruler of Rome once exercised over all the rulers and peoples in the world, so that they alone had the power to make coercive commands binding on all men with respect to the observance of the faith and of the decisions of general councils, and to punish transgressors of these commands wherever they might be; and besides this, they greatly increased the size of the church, even though later on some of the Romans sometimes persecuted the Christians because of the malice of certain priests. And a final reason why it is appropriate that the bishop and church of Rome have the leadership is custom, inasmuch as all the believers have learned, or have become accustomed, to honor the bishop and church of Rome above all the rest, and to be stirred to virtuous living and the worship of God by their exhortations and admonitions, and to be recalled from vices and crimes by their reproofs, censures, and threats of eternal damnation.

Translation: Alan Gewirth (New York, 1956). Used with permission.

William of Ockham

(1285?-1347)

Of the three political thinkers that tower above the intellectual landscape in the first half of the fourteenth century — John of Paris, Marsilius of Padua, and William of Ockham — Ockham has until recently received the least scholarly recognition, at least in the English-speaking world. His strictly philosophical writings, of course, have attracted incomparably more attention than the combined literary output of the other two, on account of his seminal contribution to late medieval "nominalism" (i.e., the theory that only particulars can be said to exist, and not the "universals" of Platonic and Aristotelian metaphysics). Although his political reflection is more developed than that of John of Paris, and as far-ranging and sophisticated as that of Marsilius, it has suffered by comparison from being dispersed over a number of writings; and the moderation and subtlety of his positions have rendered their influence less obvious than that of the Paduan's more programmatic gestures. Nevertheless, recent political historians continue to discover Ockham's imprint on several centuries of political thought, largely through the Sorbonist legacy of Pierre d'Ailly and Jean Gerson.

Although all of Ockham's political writings were *pièces d'occasion,* bearing on papal dealings with the Friars Minor or with the German king, they were, nonetheless, full-blown political and ecclesiological treatises. As scholars point out, his career divides neatly into two periods, nonpolitical and political: that of the Oxford philosopher-theologian and that of the Munich refugee. The turning point was his involvement in the dispute between Pope John XXII and his own Franciscan order over evangelical poverty, into which he was drawn while at the papal court in Avignon in the mid-1320s, having been summoned, or at least detained, there to answer charges of heresy against opinions associated with his earlier writings. Enlisted to defend the Minorite discipline of supreme "legal" poverty against the pope's direct attacks (probably by the Franciscan minister general, Michael of Cesena), Ockham came to regard John's views as heretical, and so joined the Minorite voices calling for action against him. After fleeing in 1328 in Michael's company to the protection of the imperial court in Bavaria, he continued to write against papal heresy, turning to an attack on papal "tyranny" in the late 1330s, directed against John's successor, Benedict XII. Although not practically implicated, as was Marsilius, in the German king's bid to establish imperial rule over Rome, Ockham made the cause of the excommunicated Ludwig a matter of theoretical reflection in his writings of the 1340s on imperial and papal monarchy. He died excommunicated and unreconciled to John XXII and his successors, apparently the "first major western theologian to enter into protracted dispute with the papacy on matters of Christian doctrine" (McGrade and Kilcullen 1995, xiv).

The first of Ockham's major controversial writings is the *Work of Ninety Days* (*Opus nonaginta dierum*), a fairly massive treatise completed, remarkably, in just three months sometime between 1332 and 1334. With unconvincing scholastic neutrality, he expounds the dispute between Pope John XXII and the Minorites over supreme poverty. His convoluted format is to alternate quotations from John's bull, *Quia vir reprobus*, repudiating Michael of Cesena's arguments against his earlier anti-Franciscan bulls, with counterarguments of Michael's supporters. In presenting the Michelist defense of Franciscan poverty, i.e., of "mere use" of earthly goods owned and conceded by others (cf. Bonaventure and Marsilius, pp. 317-19, 442-46 above), Ockham provides: *(a)* a sophisticated typology of legal rights of ownership and use, and *(b)* the concept of an original, "natural" right of use belonging to man from creation, before the advent of positive human law.

The principal theological contribution here is to distinguish Adamic lordship (*dominium*) as a divinely ordained, common use of the earth's bounty (chs. 26-28) from legal lordship (i.e., proprietary right) as a humanly ordained curtailment of Adamic lordship necessitated by our first parents' fall into sin (chs. 65, 88). That is, Ockham refuses to identify the common human right of using temporal goods with positive property right. Also importantly, he refuses to identify property right with regal or imperial law, arguing that in human history property was established by agreement before it was established by royal ordinance. Finally, he defends the Bonaventuran thesis that the total, voluntary renunciation of property conforms not only to natural law, but to the spiritual perfection lived and commanded by Christ. In so doing, he brings gospel law and natural rationality into a dialectical unity that he will subsequently develop.

Ockham's attention had become fixed on the phenomenon of papal heresy by the time of his next major publication: part 1 of *A Dialogue on Papal and Royal Dignity (Dialogus)*, completed by late 1334. Originally projected in three parts, the second of which never materialized, this gigantic work contains many of his seminal ecclesiological ideas. Part 1 takes a novel look at the relationship between epistemological and political authority in the church, over which the Michelists' break with Pope John had cast a long shadow. The argument is deployed in three directions: *(a)* separating the two kinds of authority and assigning them different ecclesiastical loci; *(b)* elevating epistemological over political authority; and *(c)* defining both authorities, but especially epistemological, in a nonabsolute and less institutional way.

First he proposes (bk. 4, ch. 3) that "legitimate correction" of "erring" believers *necessarily* involves a clear demonstration to them of their errors: bare condemnation of imputed errors by a superior authority is insufficient. Next he proposes that theologians are better qualified than prelates (even the supreme prelate) to undertake the work of correction, on account of their superior understanding of Scripture, which is the supreme (but not exclusive) standard of doctrinal orthodoxy (ch. 14). Significantly, theological authority is exercised by demonstrably trustworthy individuals rather than an official ecclesiastical class. Thirdly, he proposes that erring believers are obliged to surrender their opinions upon a clear demonstration of their errors, regardless of whether they are corrected by an ecclesiastical superior, a peer, or even an inferior (ch. 21). As A. S. McGrade has astutely observed, in these three steps Ockham supplanted the traditional distinction "between authoritative and fraternal correction" by the more institutionally fluid concept of a "cognitively legitimate correction" (1974, 57).

The way was prepared for two more dramatic theoretical advances. In one of these Ockham universalizes epistemological authority throughout the church, cautiously reintegrating it with political authority. That is, he attributes "to all parts and grades, clerical and lay, the privilege and duty" of "interrogating, correcting and, if necessary, bringing to punishment, holders and propagators of heretical doctrine," while at the same time respecting "an institutional order of precedence for initiating public action against the offenders" (Lockwood O'Donovan 1991, 16; see p. 557 below). The Michelist rebels are, therefore, justified in opposing the pope's heretical constitutions. In the other, corresponding advance, he denies that the inerrancy promised by Christ to "the whole church" can be ascribed to any institutional part, whether the Roman Church, the episcopate, the theologians, or a general council. For "the whole church" resides on earth in the company of true believers, confirmed in faith by the Holy Spirit, a communion of indeterminately large or small number scattered throughout the institutional church (bk. 5, chs. 3, 7, 24). In these two moves Ockham detached the epistemic authority of faith from the sacramental and jurisdictional powers of the clerical hierarchy, and so opened the door to simple believers *(simplices)* to intervene unofficially in a matter of heresy, wherever it might arise.

In the first of the two surviving treatises from part 3 of the *Dialogue,* written some years later, Ockham further explains why the pronouncements of a general council are not infallible, arguing that its common wisdom is not necessarily the work of extraordinary divine inspiration or revelation (like the writing of Scripture), but of human reflection and meditation on revelation, aided by the Holy Spirit (bk. 3, chs. 8, 9). In this treatise, devoted largely to demonstrating the limitations of papal monarchy, he also elaborates the shift of authority from the visible head to the spiritual body of the church. The most startling aspect of this is his attribution to the community of the power, in exceptional circumstances, to replace papal rule temporarily with a more beneficial form of government, thereby qualifying his otherwise unambiguous affirmation of God's direct institution of the papal office. However, he sets down no procedure for such a momentous change, in keeping with the institutional fluidity of action to defend the church's common good.

The second treatise of the *Dialogue,* part 3, also incomplete, undertakes a similarly comprehensive analysis of imperial government, its basis, purpose, limitations, and personal requirements. Equally striking here are the application of identical political principles to civil and ecclesiastical spheres, and the demonstration of the differences between them. The principles are broadly Aristotelian: the natural powers of community, the common good, common necessity and equity, arguments for the best regime. These stand in a delicate balance with the differences: between the juridical character of imperial rule and the pastoral cast of ecclesiastical rule; between the prudential rationality and external virtues required of the emperor and the spirituality and supernatural virtues required of the pope. In no way can Ockham's investigations be construed as an unnuanced vindication of the rights of the Roman emperor against all challenges. Indeed, his two treatises present a recognizably Gelasian dualism of authorities, in stark contrast with the imperial hegemony advocated by Marsilius.

Another important balance struck in this treatise and in Ockham's remaining political works is between divine and human right. Here the balance is struck in an argument (bk. 3, ch. 5) that the Roman Christians have an original right to elect their bishop, the pope, by divine and natural law. While divine law requires that the pope's electors be Christian and Catholic, natural law (understood in a particular sense presupposing the institution of political rule by the law of nations) invests the right to elect in the Roman people, whose ruler the pope will be. Ockham, however, reminds us that natural law in all its senses — even as contingent on the law of nations — is also divine law, having its source in God the Creator and being contained (explicitly or implicitly) in the scriptural revelation.

The same complex interweaving of divine and human right is found in *Eight Questions on Papal Power (Octo quaestiones de potestate papae)*, in his discussion of the three ways in which jurisdiction and property may be considered to be held by someone "immediately from God" (q. 2, chs. 3-6). The first way involves a direct divine grant, with no human (third party) mediation; the second, a direct divine grant, with human mediation that is merely instrumental; the third involves a constitutive human grant, concession, or transfer; but, once granted, the jurisdiction or ownership depends on divine authority alone. Interestingly, Ockham follows a Hildebrandine tradition in proposing that papal power is held in the second way and imperial power in the third. At the same time, he is concerned to demonstrate the compatibility of this tradition with the "natural law" requirement of papal election. He completes his Gelasian political vision by distinguishing (q. 2, ch. 8) between the pope and emperor's "regular" jurisdiction in the spiritual and temporal spheres respectively and their "casual" authority to interfere in the other's sphere, when such interference is required by necessity and solicited (or agreed to) by the community.

In *A Short Discourse on the Tyrannical Ascendancy of the Pope (Breviloquium de principatu tyrannico . . .)*, composed in the early 1340s against papal tyranny, Ockham elaborates his characteristic political themes in a rounded, compelling, and accessible manner. As part of a sustained assault on the papal claim of *plenitudo potestatis*, i.e., of supreme jurisdiction and universal lordship of worldly goods, he returns to the rights and freedoms of humankind by natural and divine law, the common, nonproprietary lordship *(dominium)* of Adamic community, and the power of the fallen human race to establish property distributions and governments. On these grounds he argues explicitly for the rights of unbelievers, not subject to papal rule, to exercise jurisdiction and ownership (bk. 3, chs. 3-11). Once again (as in the *Dialogue,* part 3, treatise 1), he extols the gospel law as the law of freedom (James 1:25): not only from slavery to sin and from the ritual exactions of the Mosaic Law, but from every external servitude lacking rational justification — freedom, that is, from the arbitrary, excessive, and harsh commands of tyrants, whether popes or emperors (bk. 2, chs. 3-6, 18-19). Once again, Christ and natural reason speak with one voice in the political arena.

Further Reading: L. Baudry, *Guillaume d'Ockham: sa vie, ses oeuvres, ses idées sociales et politiques* (Paris: Vrin, 1949); A. Hudson and M. Wilks, eds., *From Ockham to Wyclif* (Oxford: Blackwell, 1987); G. de Lagarde, *La naissance de l'esprit laïque au déclin du moyen âge,* vols. 4, 5 (Paris: Éditions Nauwelaerts, 1956-70); G. Leff, *William of Ockham: The Metamorphosis of Scholastic Discourse* (Manchester: Manchester University Press, 1975); A. S. McGrade, *The Political Thought of William of Ockham: Personal and Institutional Principles* (Cambridge: Cambridge University Press, 1974); A. S. McGrade, ed., J. Kilcullen, trans., *William of Ockham, "A Short Discourse on Tyrannical Government"* (Cambridge: Cambridge University Press, 1992); A. S. McGrade, ed., J. Kilcullen, trans., *William of Ockham, "A Letter to the Friars Minor and Other Writings"* (Cambridge: Cambridge University Press, 1995); J. Miethke, *Ockhams Weg zur Sozialphilosophie* (Berlin: De Gruyter, 1969); J. J. Ryan, *The Nature, Structure, and Function of the Church in William of Ockham* (Missoula, Mont.: Scholars Press, 1979); B. Tierney, *The Idea of Natural Rights: Studies on Natural Rights, Natural Law, and Church Law, 1150-1625* (Atlanta: Scholars Press, 1997); M. Villey, *La formation de la pensée juridique moderne,* 4th ed. (Paris: Montchrestien, 1975).

From *A Dialogue on Papal and Royal Dignity,* Part 1

bk. 4 ch. 13. *Master:* One is guilty of *pertinacity* if after lawful correction he fails to reform or amend, i.e., by renouncing his heresy. . . .

Student: There are two points here on which I would like an explanation: first, *to whom* does it belong to correct the mistaken person? second, what are the *criteria* for lawful and sufficient correction?

Master: We must look first at the correction itself before we look at the person who administers it.

Student: Follow whatever order you please.

Master: The correction, then: — It may be understood that no correction can count as sufficient, and so be considered lawful, which does not present the mistaken person with appropriate proof that his opinion contradicts catholic truth. In the judgment of intelligent people, he should be left without any means of evading the admission that sufficient and appropriate proof has been given him of the inconsistency of his error with catholic truth. Imagine, for example, that someone ignorant of the Gospel text were to say (as a preacher in Avignon is said to have done) that the soldiers broke the legs of Christ; and someone were to demonstrate the contrary by showing him the text of John 19:32f., where it says, "So the soldiers came and broke the legs of the first, and of the other who had been crucified with him; but when they came to Jesus and saw that he was already dead, they did not break his legs"; that would be a sufficient correction, since in the judgment of any intelligent person he would be left without any means of evading the admission that he had been appropriately shown that his claim contradicted the truth of the Gospel. And if someone were in ignorance to hold that there were two persons and two substances in Christ, and it were shown him from the text of the Council of Ephesus that this was Nestorius's heresy which that Council condemned, he would be left without any means of evading the admission that appropriate proof had been given him that his claim was a condemned heresy and at odds with catholic truth.

As to the person who administers it, we must make a distinction. There are those who administer correction in a castigatory manner, inflicting punishment as due; and there are those who administer it as loving admonition, simply pointing out the mistake. The first is the prerogative of bishops and those with jurisdictional responsibility, the second may be undertaken by any Christian.

ch. 14. *Student:* That makes the generally accepted definition of sufficient and lawful correction clear enough, and I take the point of the distinction over who administers it. But, I wonder, are all educated people agreed that when someone is corrected for error by his bishop or ecclesiastical superior, he is bound to renounce his error even if it has *not* been clearly shown him by the authority that his error contradicts catholic truth? To put it another way, should he renounce his error solely on the basis of his bishop's warning or punishment?

Master: There is a division of opinion among the theologians. Quite a few hold that he is not obliged to renounce his error when he is corrected by the bishop who has jurisdiction until it has been shown him clearly in the way we have described that his error is incompatible with the truth. The first argument for this is as follows: — Those who have authority in expounding Holy Scripture, and therefore also in explaining matters of orthodox faith, greater than that of bishops and ecclesiastical superiors, are not required or bound, should they make an ignorant mistake, to renounce their opinions as heretical without being clearly shown that their opinions are inconsistent with orthodox truth, punished though they may be by their bishops or others. For someone who has greater authority *in some sphere* is not subject to someone of lesser authority in that sphere. Those, then, who have a greater authority than bishops in expounding Holy Scripture are not subject to them in that [Major premise]. But theologians *(doctores)* and expositors of Holy Scripture are superior to bishops and dignitaries in expounding Holy Scripture and in explaining matters of orthodox faith [Minor premise]. Theologians, then, are not bound to renounce their opinions when corrected by their bishops, mistaken though they be, unless it is unambiguously shown them that their opinions are inconsistent with the truth. The Major premise is certain. The Minor premise is proved by the authority of Gratian (D. 20 pr.), who says: "It is one thing to bring business *(causae)* to a conclusion, another to expound Holy Scripture carefully." It follows "that expositors of Holy Scripture whose scholarship exceeds that of the bishops, though their rank is inferior, have more authority in expounding Holy Scripture. In concluding business, though, they take a second and subordinate place." The conclusion is clear: that theologians are to be preferred to bishops in expounding

Scripture. This becomes apparent, too, in the argument which Gratian subsequently employs: the more anyone appeals to reason, the more authority his words command. But most expositors can be shown to have stuck more closely to rational argument, since they are more full of the Holy Spirit's grace and outclass others by the extent of their learning. So the words of Augustine, Jerome, and other expositors carry more authority than the constitutions of a great number of bishops. These are the arguments by which they demonstrate that in matters of faith theologians are to be preferred to bishops, so that without lawful correction of the type we have described they are not bound to renounce their mistaken views.

Student: I find this argument unconvincing in two respects. First, Gratian was speaking of theologians approved by the church such as Augustine, Jerome, and others like them, not those of recent times. It is very well to say that *their* judgment is better than that of bishops in expounding Scripture; but modern theologians should not be preferred to bishops and inquisitors into heresy. Secondly, it is a *non sequitur* to argue that because *theologians* are not bound to renounce their opinions on correction by their superiors without lawful correction in the prescribed form, *other ordinary Christians* are not therefore bound to renounce their errors without the same form of lawful correction that has been so constantly referred to.

Master: Those counterarguments are easy to rebut on the basis so far established. The reply is: (1) Gratian was not speaking solely about theologians approved by the church, but about others, too, just as he spoke about other bishops than those contemporary with the doctors now approved by the church. He made a generic comparison between the status of theologian and the status of bishop and so, in suggesting that theologians are preferred to bishops for explaining matters of faith, it is indifferent whether we speak of antiquity or the present day, so long as theologians are appointed to their teaching office for their eminent scholarship and worthy life, not on account of bribes and pressing petitions or human favors. To make the matter quite clear: Gratian did not speak about "theologians" *(doctores)* in the sense that that word is used today; he spoke about *intelligent expositors of Holy Scripture,* whether we call them "masters" or "students." For there are many with the title "student" who expound Holy Scripture better than the masters, and who are more worth hearing on such matters even than bishops. So Gratian's argument has the same implication for learned men of our own day as for ancient expositors of Scripture, since in our own day, too, learned men have acquired superior scholarship, and are more to be heeded on such matters than illiterate bishops and inquisitors or than ordinary Christians. (2) The same principle that applies to experts, who are not bound, when corrected by bishops or superiors, to renounce their opinions without lawful correction in the manner stipulated, also applies to ordinary Christians guided by the experts, who are not bound to renounce the opinions they have learned from the experts without lawful correction. From which it follows that other ordinary people, too, are not bound without lawful correction to renounce their mistaken views, since all ordinary people should, it seems, be treated alike. [. . .]

ch. 20. *Student:* What if someone were to defend before the pope a heresy that he claimed to think consistent with the orthodox faith?

Master: In their view he could defend his heresy a thousand times over, provided he did not know it was a heresy and provided that he stipulated, expressly or by implication, that he was ready to accept correction, should he discover his opinions to be inconsistent with the catholic faith. Not even before the pope should he be judged a heretic without being proved heretical by further lawful evidence. If it was permissible the first time round for him to offer a defense for his unwittingly mistaken view, it would be permissible the second and third times, and so on, until it was unambiguously proved to him that his opinion was to be classed as heresy.

Student: But suppose that even after his opinion were proved heretical, a defendant were to claim that he had not been shown the inconsistency of his opinion with orthodox faith, so that he could never be found guilty?

Master: It is not enough for *him* to say that his opinion has not been proved heretical. He must stand by the judgment of experts. If *they* think it has been satisfactorily shown to be heretical, he is bound to renounce it, on pain of being judged a pertinacious heretic.

Student: And what if the experts, masters of theology, and the pope are all mistaken?

Master: If they condemn an innocent man, the laws allow him the remedy of appeal to take his case higher. If a lawful appeal is refused, his only recourse is to commend himself to God's grace and to face his removal by unjust judgment from the society of men without fear, since he has no injustice in his conscience to remove him from the Book of Life.

Translation: Editors, from *Monarchia,* vol. 2, ed. M. Goldast (Frankfurt, 1614).

From *Dialogue on Papal and Royal Dignity,* Part 3, Treatise 1

bk. 2 ch. 20. *Student:* It could be said that the rulership by which the highest priest rules all the faithful is not human but divine, because it was established by God alone; therefore it is not decent, and consequently not beneficial, that the church should have power over the papal rulership.

Master: This answer is attacked. Although papal rule is divine in that Christ decided that it should exist in the church, in many respects it seems to be human. For it is for men to decide who should be appointed to it, and who should elect, and who should correct the one appointed if he needs correction, and the like. Therefore, similarly, it will be human in this respect, that it should be decided by men whether one only, or, when beneficial, many, should be appointed to such rulership.

Further, in respect of everything necessary for the things that are special to Christians, provision has been made for the community of the faithful in the best way, and not less well than for any other community or nation, so that in all such matters it has power in respect of all things that are beneficial and as they are beneficial. But if the church had power to change a regime that began to be less beneficial into another, more beneficial, regime, it would be better provided for than if it did not have such power; therefore, since in such matters it has been provided for in the best way, it has power to change rule by one into rule by many, if it notices that it is more beneficial to be ruled by many in an aristocratic regime than by one alone.

Again, it is not less beneficial for the community of the faithful to have power to abolish regimes that begin to be burdensome or less useful than to have power to abolish burdensome customs, since nothing can do more harm to the church than a burdensome and useless regime, according to the opinion of Augustine. As we read in D. 81 c. 2 he says: "No one indeed does more harm in the church than he who, though acting perversely, has the name or order of holiness and priesthood." From this we gather that nothing does more harm to the church than a perverse ruler and a perverse regime. Therefore, if the church notices that the church is ruled perversely or less usefully because of the fact that one by himself rules over all, it is beneficial for it to have power to change such a regime into another that will be more useful for the time.

Besides, it is not beneficial for the church to be tied to a regime that can be changed into the worst regime; but the regime in which one rules by himself can be changed into the worst regime, as royal government, even though it is the best, can, so far as it depends on the nature of the rulership, be changed into tyranny, which is the worst regime, as Aristotle in the *Ethics* and the *Politics* asserts and plainly proves. Therefore it is not beneficial for the church for it to be so restricted to the regime in which one rules by himself that it cannot change it into another regime, namely, aristocracy, more useful for the time.

Moreover, as the civil law also testifies, "In new matters for decision, to depart from a law that has seemed fair for a long time, the advantage ought to be evident." We gather from this that innovation should be made for the sake of evident advantage, even so as to depart from a law that has seemed fair for a long time. But a law should not be departed from more than a form of government, because in every community nothing can be more necessary to observe than law; for what is incongruous with the law should in no way be observed. Therefore, for the sake of evident advantage, innovation should be made, so as to depart from a form of government that has seemed reasonable and fair for a long time. Therefore, if it appears evident to the church that for some particular time a greater advantage will come to the church from an aristocratic regime in which many rule the community of the faithful together than from the rule of one, such innovation should be made, so as to depart from the rule of one which has seemed fair and useful for a long time. [. . .]

Further, in all churches what the greater part judges should be observed ought to be observed: (X 3.2.1; D. 65 c. 1, 2; X 1.6.6). Therefore, if the greater part of the faithful think that an aristocratic regime should be established over the whole community of the faithful, such a regime ought to be established. From this it follows that the church or community of the faithful has power to establish such a regime. [. . .]

Master: To some it seems that, even if Christ had ordained that one highest pontiff should rule over all the faithful, the church could, for the common utility, establish another regime. This is proved as follows. Necessity and utility are of equal force, as Alexander III seems to suggest (X 1.14.6). But for the sake of necessity it is permissible to act against a divine commandment, even one that is explicit, in things

461

not evil in themselves but evil only because they are prohibited. Therefore, also, for the sake of the common utility it is permissible to act against a commandment of God and an ordinance of Christ. Therefore, even if Christ had ordained that one highest pontiff should be set over all the faithful, it would be permissible for the faithful, for the sake of common utility, to establish some other regime, at least for the time. The major premise seems to have been proved manifestly, and it is also proved from the premise that necessity and piety have equal force, as Gregory IX suggests (X 2.9.5); but piety includes usefulness; therefore, necessity and utility have equal force, and consequently whatever necessity makes permissible utility also makes permissible.

bk. 3 ch. 8. *Master:* To the first argument, when it suggests that we should piously hold that the interpretations of a general council have been revealed to us by the same spirit as revealed the divine Scriptures, it is answered that it is not necessary, nor must all Christians always believe this. A general council often relies, or can rely, on human wisdom, which can deviate from what is true. Therefore it is not obligatory, of necessity for salvation, to believe that whatever a general council defines as necessary to hold concerning the faith it defines as having been revealed to it by God, and that it is then relying on a spiritual revelation.

This seems provable in many ways. (1) For when it is hoped that something will be revealed by God, it is necessary to apply oneself, not to study and human thought, but only to prayer or other good works or at least it is less necessary to apply oneself to study than to other good works. Thus when Daniel was hoping that Nebuchadnezzar's dream and its interpretation would be revealed to him by God, he exhorted his companions to seek such a great mystery, not through study, though they were learned men, but through prayer and supplication from God. Afterwards Daniel asserted that he had obtained it through prayer, when he says: "To thee, O God of my fathers, I give thanks, and I praise you, because you have given wisdom and strength; and now you have shown me what we asked of you, for you have made known to us the king's discourse" (Dan. 2:23). Thus also, because Christ promised his apostles that he would reveal to them what they ought to say when they were led before kings and governors, he forbade them to occupy themselves then in study. He said to them, as we read in Matthew 10:19: "And when they deliver you up, think not how or what to speak, for what to speak will be given to you in that hour; for it is not you that speak, but the Spirit of my Father who speaks in you." When, therefore, something is to be hoped for only through revelation, one must not devote oneself to study and human thought, but to prayer. But when there is a question of faith to be decided in a general council, effort is given to meditation on the Scriptures. It is therefore not necessarily through revelation that a question of faith should be decided in a general council, but such a question can be decided by a wisdom that is had, and can be had, through study and human meditation; although God can by a special grace reveal it, it must not be held as certain that it is had through revelation, unless God reveals this miraculously and openly.

(2) Further, when it should be held as certain that something is to be had through revelation, recourse must reasonably be had, in order to obtain it, not to those who are wiser, but to those who are better — whether they are learned or un-

learned, clergy or laity, men or women — or to prophets, because commonly God reveals his secrets not to the wiser but to the better. Truth himself seems to testify to this, when he says in Matthew 11:25: "I give thanks to you, O Father, Lord of heaven and earth, because you have hidden these things from the wise and prudent and revealed them to little ones." Thus, as we read in 2 Kings 22:14, when that holy king Josiah wished to know through revelation God's will concerning the words of the book found in the temple, he sent even the priests and experts in the divine law themselves to Hulda the prophetess, the wife of Shallum; he did not seek the truth from those priests and experts in the law, even though it is said, in Malachi 2:7: "The lips of the priest keep knowledge, and they seek the law at his mouth." For in respect of things in the law that can be had through effort and thought, the law of God must be sought from the mouth of the priest, who is obliged to know the science and law of God explicitly, but in respect of things that must be had through revelation, recourse must be had chiefly to those who have the spirit of prophecy, if there are any, and to those who are more holy, whose prayers are more accepted by God. In respect of such things, the law is not necessarily to be sought from the mouth of a priest and the highest pontiff more than from the mouth of a widow or of a layman ignorant of letters. But for deciding a question of faith in a general council, recourse is had, even according to the common opinion of men, to the wiser and more learned, whether they are better or not. Therefore it should not be held necessarily that a question of faith is always settled by divine revelation.

From these (arguments) we gather that it is not necessary to hold that a question of faith is always settled in a general council by revelation, but it must be held, unless the opposite is revealed miraculously by God, that God permits those assembled in a general council, in defining a question of faith and in other matters, to proceed according to their own intelligence, assisted by the general divine influence. It is therefore conceded that it is not impossible for a general council to err.

[. . .] We know that general councils so far have done this, because they have decided questions of faith arising out of the Scriptures by means of the sacred Scriptures. Therefore, those present in a general council who wish to decide a question of faith do not commit the whole to God and ask him through prayer alone for the definition of the question of faith, but instead they rely on human wisdom and virtue, because they rely on the expertise concerning the Scriptures that they have and can have by careful thought. But error can be found in all things that rely on human wisdom and virtue; therefore members of a general council can err in deciding a question of faith.

ch. 9. *Student:* Point out how the above opinion tries to answer other arguments brought forward above in chapter 1 of this third book.

Master: To that which is based on Christ's promise in the last chapter of Matthew, it is answered that Christ is going to be with the universal Church until the end of the world, and therefore (as Rabanus says . . .): "Until the end of the world there will not be lacking in the world some who are worthy of the divine presence and indwelling." From these words of Rabanus we gather that that promise of Christ should not be understood of a general council: First, because he says "there will not be lacking in the world," and does not say that there will not be lacking in a general council; also, because seldom is there a general council in the world, but the universal church will always be in the world until the end of the world. Therefore, according to Rabanus, that promise of Christ should not be understood of a general council but of the universal church, so that it should be held piously and without doubt that the Holy Spirit is always present to the universal church. Thus also Jerome refers to the universal church when he says that Christ "will never depart from believers," because until the end of the world there will always be some who believe in Christ, whether a general council is taking place or not. [. . .]

In the same way answer is made to a great many texts that assert in substance that whatever the holy fathers assembled in general councils defined, enacted, and did, they did under the inspiration of the Holy Spirit, and consequently that the interpretations they made to decide doubtful points of faith were revealed to them. For they are not said to have been inspired by the Holy Spirit because the Holy Spirit breathed something to them at that time in some special and unaccustomed way, beyond the influence of the Holy Spirit required for every work pleasing to God, but because the Holy Spirit moved them to make a right definition of the faith just as he moves everyone to the performance of all meritorious works whatever. Therefore, according to the opinion of the holy fathers, general councils that were held rightly, justly, in a holy way, canonically, and in a Catholic way, must be most devoutly received, embraced, and venerated by all Catholics. If, however, they had not been held in a Catholic way, even if all the bishops of the world had been present, they should be, not received, but absolutely rejected by the faithful. If it is asked who is to judge whether they were held in a Catholic way, it is answered that because they did not define anything except what can be drawn out from the divine Scriptures, therefore it is for experts in the Scriptures, and those having sufficient understanding of the other written sources, to judge in the manner of firm assertion that the things defined by them are defined in a Catholic way. If the highest pontiffs were not present, but the councils were held only by their authority with their legates present, it is for them to judge authoritatively that they were held in a Catholic way; but if the highest pontiff was present, it is enough that he should authenticate them.

From Part 3, Treatise 2

bk. 1 ch. 11. [replies to arguments advanced in chapter 2 against the subjection of the totality of mortals to a single secular ruler] *Master:* The third argument — which is founded on the premise that that form of government is better which is more like the form of government that would have existed if men had remained in the state of innocence, who would never have had one emperor of all — is excluded by this: because of the difference between the state of innocence and the state of fallen nature, the form of government more like the form of government that would have existed in the state of innocence is not always better in the state of fallen nature just as the form of government more like the form of government that will exist in the state of glory is also not better in the state of fallen nature, because then it would be better for each to rule himself and no one to have rule or prelacy over others (because in the state of glory rule or prelacy will not exist).

The fourth argument — which is based on the premise that for one emperor to be lord over all mortals is against the law of nations, which is the natural law, and is consequently never beneficial or permissible — it seems possible to refute by the things said in the preceding chapter. Although what is against the law of nations is sometimes wicked, it is not always wicked: sometimes, indeed, it is equitable as a rule and wicked on occasion. For (at least in respect of many things) the law of nations is not the absolute natural law without any condition, qualification, determination, or specification, but is the natural law conditioned, qualified, or with some specification or determination. For as we read in the *Decreta* (D. 1 c. 9): "To the law of nations belong wars, captivities, enslavements"; these, however, do not exist by natural law absolutely, without any condition, qualification, specification, or determination, because then the opposites would never be permissible, because what is against the absolute natural law is never permissible but always impermissible and beyond dispensation, X 1.4.11 and X 1.4.9 [actually X 1.4.5]. Therefore, even if one emperor is lord over all, wars, captivities, and intermarriages between foreigners may sometimes be in accordance with the law of nations and can therefore pertain to the natural law that is conditioned or qualified or with some specification or determination. However, they are not always wicked [*iniqua;* but the argument seems to require *aequa*, "right"], because they do not belong to the absolute natural law that does not vary but remains unchangeable and immovable, D. 5 pr. and D. 6 d.p.c. 3.

The fifth argument — which is founded on the premise that some mortals are believers and some unbelievers, who should not bear the same yoke or have community or peaceful society with one another or have recourse to the same judge to receive judgment and consequently should not be under one emperor — it seems can be broken in many ways. First, because even if it were true that believers should not bear the yoke of unbelievers with unbelievers and should not have community or peaceful society with unbelievers when the unbelievers attack believers or do anything in contempt of the creator or try to draw believers to mortal sin, and that believers should not have recourse to an unbelieving judge to receive judgment, it would, nevertheless, be permissible for believers to bear the yoke of believers with unbelievers and to have community and peaceful fellowship with them if they attempt nothing bad, and to have recourse with them to a believing judge to receive judgment; and therefore, even if it were not permissible for believers to be under one unbelieving emperor of all mortals, it would, nevertheless, be permissible for both unbelievers and believers to be under one believing emperor. Second, because even if believers should not bear the same spiritual yoke with unbelievers, they can licitly bear with unbelievers the same temporal yoke. And thus there were many believers in both the New and Old Testaments who bore the same temporal yoke with unbelievers, as many saints did have, though not in sin and against God's honour. It is permissible also on occasion for believers to have recourse to an unbelieving judge to undergo judgment, on the example of many saints who did this. And thus it could on occasion be beneficial that even an unbelieving emperor should preside over all mortals. Third, because it is accidental that some are believers and some unbelievers, for all mortals were believers once, and it could happen still.

Translation: John Kilcullen (Cambridge University Press, 1995). Used with permission.

From *Eight Questions on Papal Power,* Question 2

ch. 3. There are three ways in which a property or power can be understood to be "immediately from God": (1) It is given by God alone without any joint jurisdiction or ministry of a created being. In this sense Moses received his leadership "immediately from God"; so did the Children of Israel receive their ownership of the promised land, Peter the chief priesthood, and the Twelve their apostolic calling. (2) Something may be "immediately from God" when given by God alone but not without the ministry of a created being. In this sense every pope after Peter receives his power and priesthood "immediately from God"; no one has that power without human election, yet the electors do not confer his power upon him, but God alone. In the same way a candidate for baptism receives grace from God alone, but not without the ministry of the officiant. Grace is conferred only on the baptized, yet the officiant is not the source of that grace. A parish priest has his church from the bishop alone, yet not without presentation by a patron. (3) Someone may be understood to have a power or property from God alone, although at first he had it by another's bestowal, grant, or bequest, since subsequently it derives from God alone and God is his sole superior as regards that power or property. In this sense, some say, the pope has lordship or ownership "immediately from God alone" over temporal estates made over to the Bishop of Rome by Christian donors. Although he received them in the first place from the generosity of Christian people, there is subsequently no one else with any right in them but God alone. In this sense his estates and cities and other property given by Christian people are held not from man but from God alone, and he acknowledges no superior other than God for this class of temporality. In this sense, too, when Noah was left alone with his sons and their wives, he held property from God alone, without hereditary title, title of purchase, grant, or anything else, and had no superior for these holdings; though before the flood he had had superiors, i.e., the king and any other lord whose subject he may have been. [...]

    ch. 5 [Ockham has proceeded to ask whether the emperor receives a property that belongs to his position immediately from God, and has identified two views.] The two opinions agree that the supreme lay power has "property proper to it" in the second of the senses specified, i.e., that certain temporalities belong to the supreme lay power and are no concern of anyone else's property or domain. But they do not agree on how it holds this proprietorial power "immediately from God." One party maintains that although the emperor does not hold his power "immediately from God" in the first sense (i.e., as no pope after Saint Peter received the papal power immediately from God, since none received the appointment without legitimate election by whichever person or persons had the duty of electing the supreme pontiff), nevertheless, as the supreme lay power, he holds the property belonging to him "immediately from God" in the second sense (i.e., as a pope has his proper authority immediately from God). When a pope is elected, the electors confer no power upon him; but when the election is made and the chosen candidate consents, God himself confers on him all the power that he possesses. Similarly with the election of an emperor: in making the election the electors confer no power upon him, but when he consents, God confers on him every power which is proper to the imperial status. This appears to be the opinion of the glossator on dist. 96 commenting on the word "by God" (Ordinary gloss to D. 96 c. 11, divinitus): "The imperial office is not conferred by the pope, but by God alone" (cf. C. 23 q. 4. c. 45). "For the power of the sword derives from heavenly sovereignty" (Cod. 1.17.1).

This opinion can be supported as follows: it is not from men that the emperor receives the property proper to the supreme lay power; so it must be from God alone. The consequent is clear; the antecedent is proved as follows: — If it were from men, it would be either through his election, through his coronation, or through his confirmation. But it is not through his election; for electors, generally and as such, do not confer the dignity they elect someone to. What they confer is *either,* where the election needs some independent human confirmation, the right to supplicate to have the dignity conferred, i.e., by someone else, *or* the immediate power or capacity to receive the dignity from God, as in the case of the supreme pontiff, whose election needs no human confirmation, yet confers not the papal power as such but only the immediate capacity of receiving it from God, because by God's ordinance he is not already capable of such a dignity in and of himself. In the same way the emperor does not receive his property or position from the electors. But neither does he receive it from the one who crowns him, since crowning someone — when it is not combined with confirming him — confers no temporal property, just as consecrating someone confers no spiritual property or administrative power. So the emperor receives no property from whoever crowns him, because that person does not also confirm his election. But then again, neither does he receive it from someone who confirms his election, since his election, as they suppose, requires no confirmation.

ch. 6. The other opinion is that which maintains that neither in the first nor in the second sense does the supreme lay power hold the power proper to it "immediately from God," but only in the third sense, since it is by gift of the people and not by God's gift alone. For the people did not merely decide that there should be one supreme lay power to constitute an empire; nor did it "merely choose" an emperor as the cardinals "merely choose" a pope, i.e., without conferring any of the temporal goods proper to him. They ordained and decreed a supreme lay power *over temporal goods,* and also gave him, i.e., the position not the person, what was proper to him. So the emperor cannot, except in special cases, alienate those goods; but he is bound to restore anything that he has alienated, and a successor may and should demand them back from whomever they may have been given to.

There are, then, two elements in this assertion. First: that it is *not* in the first or second sense of the phrase that the supreme lay power has the property proper to him "immediately from God." This element can be argued as follows: — Only an indubitable divine revelation could establish that any position or person had property proper to it "immediately from God" in the first or second sense. Natural reason or experience could not support such a claim. But since divine revelation actually shows (Gen. 1:20) that God gave the human race a *common* ownership of temporal goods, and since there is no need to suppose that private property must be established in the particular case by God alone, i.e., apart from the consent or will of those given common ownership of it, it follows that *only* divine revelation can establish any private property as conferred by God alone, i.e., apart from the will of those given common ownership of it. By revelation it is established that God deprived the Canaanites of the promised land and specifically conferred it upon the children of Israel. By revelation we know that God specifically gave certain territories to the children of Esau and Ammon and Moab (Deut. 2:29, 37). But no divine revelation establishes that God assigned any particular temporalities to the empire or supreme lay power as its property, nor that he gave specific orders to that effect. In sum, there is no ground in revelation for thinking that the empire has its property from God alone in any other way than other kingdoms which existed before the empire, for we have nothing about it in Holy Scripture, which is where divine revelation is recorded. So it cannot be maintained that the empire has property "immediately from God" in the first or second senses.

It may be argued that the Gospel affords a proof that the empire has its property immediately from God in this sense, where Christ says, "Render to Caesar the things that are Caesar's" (Matt. 22:21). These words are taken to imply that Christ, as true God, commanded specifically that certain things should be granted to Caesar, so that Caesar held them immediately from God, i.e., from Christ. The answer is that these words of Christ made no specific grant to Caesar, but merely ordered that what was already granted Caesar by human ordinance should be given him. So he did not say, "This I have given to Caesar," but "Give him what is his own," i.e., by human grant. Those who made him or his predecessor emperor, ordered in general or specific terms what he should be entitled to by virtue of his supreme lay power. Christ gave his approval to this; but to approve is not to institute something new, any more than to confirm is to grant something new (X 2.22.6; X 2.30.4).

The second element in this opinion is that the supreme lay power *does* have the property proper to it "immediately from God" in the third sense. At the institution of the supreme lay power God did not immediately, whether by himself or by special command miraculously made known to special agents, give it certain determinate temporal goods to support the exercise of its duties. He did so only through the agency of men, who followed the leading of natural justice and considered that the interest of the state required there to be one prince richer than all the others in temporalities, so that it was not from God alone but from men, too, that he received his property initially. Subsequently, however, it was from God alone that he held them, i.e., after the initial conferral or donation, and it was God alone that he had to acknowledge as his superior in respect of them. For in assigning their property, they made over, according to rule, every right which they held in it to that supreme power which God instituted by their agency.

The argument to be made for this opinion runs as follows: — If the supreme lay power were not immediately from God in this sense, it would have some man or community as its superior in temporalities; it would hold its temporal property from that man or community, and would be obliged to recognize him or it as its superior in temporalities. But the supreme lay power does not hold temporalities from any man or community. [Reasons why not from any *man* omitted.] Not from any *community,* as is shown by the following argument: no community could appear to be in such a position other than the Romans; but it cannot be the case in fact that he holds property from this community, since the same person cannot be both vassal and lord of another person, especially in respect of the same thing; in Rome, however, they are the emperor's subordinates and vassals, and he is their lord. So, then, he cannot hold temporalities from them immediately, and must hold the property proper to the supreme lay power "from God" in the third sense. [. . .]

ch. 8. Someone may object: the pope is the supreme judge of all Christians, and so of the emperor too, if the emperor is a Christian. There are many answers. One is that the pope is the judge of all Christians only in spiritual matters which belong to his sphere of power. If the pope, apart from a situation of necessity or of such utility that would amount to necessity, should use his papal authority to pronounce on a matter of temporalities or on a particular temporal property, such a judgment would be legally null and void, as "by the wrong judge." He is not a judge in such affairs, nor have such affairs anything to do with his office, so that what he does in them is legally null and void by the rule, "Whatever a judge does beyond the scope of his office, is devoid of validity" (VI *reg. iuris* 26). The supreme judge in these matters is not the pope but the emperor, and judge not only of all Christians but of all mortals everywhere. In these matters, indeed, he is the pope's judge, since the Christian religion deprives no one of his right, as Ambrose says [untraced], based on the apostle's saying in 1 Corinthians: "In whatever state each was called, there let him remain. . . . Were you a slave when called? Never mind!" (7:24, 21). Which implies that the Christian religion does not free unbelievers' slaves from their slave-status, "so that the name of the Lord and the teaching may not be defamed" (1 Tim. 6:1). *A fortiori* the Christian religion does not free someone who is raised to the papacy from obedience to a Christian lord, since, as the apostle says, "Those who have believing masters must not be disrespectful on the ground that they are brethren; rather they must serve all the better since they too are disciples" (1 Tim. 6:2). So the emperor is still the pope's judge as he was before he became pope. Neither the pope nor the other clergy are exempt from the emperor's jurisdiction by divine right. As far as divine right goes, they remain as before, subject to the emperor in anything that offers no hindrance to observing the Christian religion and discharging the responsibilities to which they are appointed.

Translation: Editors, from Ockham, *Opera Politica,* vol. 1, ed. H. S. Offler (Manchester University Press, 1974).

From *A Short Discourse on the Tyrannical Ascendancy of the Pope*, Book 2

ch. 3. [Against the assertion that the pope, by virtue of his plenitude of power, can do by right all things not against natural or divine law]: In my opinion that assertion is not only false, and dangerous to the whole community of the faithful, but even heretical. Hence I will show first that it is heretical because it plainly conflicts with divine Scripture. For compared with the law of Moses the gospel law involves, not more servitude, but less, and hence it is called by blessed James a law of perfect freedom (James 1:25). According to blessed Peter (Acts 15:10), because the servitude of the Mosaic law was unbearable it was not to be imposed on believers. Speaking of the yoke of the Mosaic law he says: "Why do you tempt God by imposing on the necks of the disciples a yoke which neither our fathers nor we have been able to bear?" From these words we gather clearly that a yoke as heavy and as servile as the Mosaic law was has not been imposed upon Christians. Hence blessed Augustine regards as blameworthy those who wish to weigh down Christians, contrary to gospel freedom, with burdens greater than those of the Old Law. Speaking of such people he says: "That religion which God's mercy wanted to be free, with the fewest sacraments, and the clearest in performance, they weigh down with servile burdens, to such an extent that the condition of the Jews is more bearable. They have not recognized the time of liberation, but at least they are subjected to legal sacraments, and not to human presumptions" (*Epistle* 55.19.35, quoted in D. 12 c. 12).

But if the pope had by Christ's precept and ordinance such fullness of power that in temporal and spiritual matters he could by right do without exception anything not against divine or natural law, then Christ's law would involve a most horrendous servitude, incomparably greater than that of the Old Law. For all Christians — emperors and kings, and absolutely all their subjects — would be in the strictest sense of the term the pope's slaves, because there never was nor will be by right anyone with more power over any man whatever than power over him in respect of all things not against natural or divine law. The pope could therefore by right deprive the king of France and every other king of his kingdom without fault or reason, just as without fault or reason a lord can take from his slave a thing he has let him have. This is absurd. Also, if he had such fullness of power in matters both temporal and spiritual, the pope could impose on Christians many more and heavier external ceremonies than those of the Old Law, and the gospel law would be in no way a law of freedom, but a law of unbearable servitude.

ch. 5. Further, that the pope does not have such fullness of power is clearly shown from the Apostle's words. Speaking for himself and for all rulers of the church, he says: "I write these things while absent so that when I am there I will not act too harshly, according to the power which the Lord gave for your building up, not for your destruction" (2 Cor. 13:10). By these words we are given to understand that the apostolic power was set up by Christ chiefly for the advantage of its subjects. For in entrusting his sheep to Peter, Christ did not chiefly intend to provide for the honour, profit, ease, or advantage of Peter; he wished chiefly to provide for the advantage of the sheep. This is why he did not say to Peter: "Lord it over my sheep," or

"Do with my sheep what you will, whatever is for your profit or honour," but rather, "Feed my sheep" — as if to say: "Do what is for their advantage and need, and know that you are not set over them for your sake, but for theirs": and no wonder, for the common good is to be preferred to a private good. In setting blessed Peter over his sheep Christ therefore meant chiefly to provide, not for blessed Peter, but for the sheep. But if Peter had received from Christ such fullness of power, provision would have been made chiefly, not for the sheep, but for Peter himself and for his honour. It follows, therefore, that Christ did not give such fullness of power to Peter or to his successors. [. . .]

Again, Augustine says: "In the active life we should not love honour in this world or power, since all things under the sun are vanity. We should rather love the work done through that honour and power, if it is done rightly and usefully — that is, so that it avails to the subjects' salvation according to God. So when the Apostle says: 'He who desires a bishopric desires a good work,' he means to explain what a bishopric is: that it is the title of a work, not of an honour. The word is Greek, and is used because he who is set over others watches over them, that is, takes care of them. '*Scopos*' is 'intendance'; if we wish, for '*episcopein*' we can say 'superintend', to let him understand that he is no bishop if he loves to preside, and not to be useful" (*City of God* 19.19). These words plainly imply that if the Roman bishop wishes to be regarded as first among bishops, his aim should not be his own honour, so as to say that he has such fullness of power over all the faithful, but the advantage of others, so as to attribute to himself only the power that must be thought necessary and useful to the faithful: as such fullness of power is not. For of what use is it to the faithful — especially the weak and imperfect, prone to impatience and anger, when heavy and unbearable, or hardly bearable, burdens are imposed on them — to have over them a lord — perhaps stupid, rash, malicious, and wicked, as a pope may be — who can by right put upon their shoulders such unbearable burdens?

But perhaps someone will say that for the pope to have such fullness of power over them is for his subjects' good, because then his subjects are obliged to the most perfect obedience, which is known to be for their perfection and good. The answer to this is that, although by such fullness of power they might be obliged to the most perfect obedience, and although such perfect obedience might pertain to perfection, nevertheless it would not be useful, but dangerous to the whole community of the faithful, if they were all obliged to such obedience — that is, were bound to obey the supreme pontiff in everything not against natural or divine law. For many in the community of the faithful are weak and imperfect. To be obliged to so great an obedience will not benefit them, because they are ill suited to endure the burdens which the pope could by right impose if they were bound to such perfect obedience. And therefore, just as those too weak to bear the death penalty should not voluntarily offer themselves for martyrdom (as Bede, commenting on the text [Matt. 26:56], "All the disciples left him and ran away," says: "The disciples who ran away before they could be arrested teach the precaution of running away to those who know themselves to be ill suited to suffering, for whom it is safer to hide than to expose themselves to the test" [*In Matt. Exp.* 4 ad loc.]), so it is useful for the weak not to be bound to the most perfect obedience, since they are not disposed to perfection with all their strength and are not suited to endure the many heavy burdens which, if he had such fullness of power, the pope could by right impose upon them. It is safer for them to be bound to a lesser obedience than to be crushed by so heavy a yoke. It is therefore not beneficial to the whole congregation of the faithful that all kings, princes, and the rest of the faithful should be bound to obey the pope if he ordered them to abandon all their goods and rights to others, because very many are ill suited actually to fulfil such an order; similarly, it is not good for the whole congregation of the faithful to be obliged of necessity for salvation to obey the pope if he ordered every Christian to fast every day on bread and water, however much such a fast would not be against natural or divine law, because many are not suited to endure such a heavy fast; and a similar judgment is to be made in similar cases.

ch. 17. Not only must the rights of emperors, kings, and others be excepted from the power granted to Peter and his successors by Christ's words, "Whatever you bind" etc., but also the liberties granted to mortals by God and nature: so that the pope may not impose anything burdensome, especially anything notably burdensome, without reason and without fault, on anyone who does not in some special way subject himself to him. For this is the liberty of the gospel law, that nothing, especially nothing heavy, that is supererogatory, or not required by natural law or explicit divine law, can be imposed by virtue of the gospel law upon its observers against their will without some fault of theirs, except in a case of urgent necessity and clear utility. Just as the high priest of the Old Law could not introduce or establish new traditions, especially any that were notably burdensome to the people, beyond the ceremonial, sacramental, and judicial precepts explicit in the Old Law, so the high priest under the gospel law cannot introduce any novelties, especially novelties heavy and burdensome to Catholics, beyond the things explicit in the New Testament, without some fault on the part of those subject to him and without urgent necessity or clear utility, in order that the New Law should not involve a greater servitude than the Old.

For if the pope could impose on the Christian people against their will burdens beyond those expressed in the New Testament without urgent necessity or a clear utility comparable with necessity, he could most of all impose those things which are supererogatory and known to relate to perfection. Since such things are expedient and useful, and since he rules others for their benefit, the pope could claim utility in imposing such things especially. Nevertheless, since they are not necessary, not of necessity for salvation and not explicitly in the New Law, he can by no means put them upon the shoulders of the faithful. For he cannot command such things of the faithful, as blessed Ambrose testifies. Speaking of virginity, which must be regarded as one of these things, he says: "Virginity can only be recommended, it cannot be commanded; it is more a matter of vow than of precept" (C. 32 q. 1 c. 13). [. . .]

Hence, although a bishop of Rome (Telesforus and also Gregory, as we read in D. 4 c. 4, 5 and 6) enacted that all the clergy should in Lent adopt the purpose of fasting, and abstain from meat, "nevertheless," (as Gratian says in the same distinction, D. 4 d.p.c. 4) "because these things were not approved by common use, they did not prove those who did not observe them guilty of transgression." This plainly shows that the Roman pontiffs were not able to impose such fast and abstinence against their will on clergy who did not voluntarily subject themselves in such matters to the Roman pontiffs. For in a matter in which a superior has power to make law without his subjects' consent, their being obliged does not require their assent. Neither is a law of this sort confirmed by the custom of its users nor abrogated by custom to the contrary, since all are obliged to observe such a law because it has been publicly promulgated and published: a ruler's law of this sort binds everyone from two months after its publication (Auth. 48 coll. 5.16 = Nov. 66.1), it need not be brought to the ears of each person individually (X 1.5.1), and therefore much less does it need to be confirmed or approved by the custom of users. When, therefore, Gratian says that "laws are established when they are promulgated and confirmed when they are approved by custom," and that "some laws have been abrogated by the contrary custom of users" (D. 4 d.p.c. 3), he should be understood to refer to those laws which do not bind without the consent of those to whom they relate. The laws about fasting made by popes Telesforus and Gregory were of this kind. For since the Roman bishops can recommend to the faithful particular fasts and abstinences, but cannot regularly command them, their laws in these and like matters do not bind without their subjects' consent, and are therefore abrogated by the contrary custom of users even against the pope's will.

The pope therefore cannot regularly by way of precept impose on Christians anything supererogatory, nor make obligatory laws on such matters against his subjects' will. For if the pope had power in such matters to make obligatory laws against the will of Christians, he could compel any Christian against his will to enter any religious order, impose on whomever he pleased an unbroken fast of bread and water (unbroken, at least, apart from extreme necessity) and command anyone, as he chose, to renounce ownership of all things. He could therefore by right oppress Christians with greater burdens than ever oppressed the Jews, which clearly goes against the freedom of the gospel law. [. . .]

From Book 3

ch. 6. [on the lordship of temporal things and jurisdiction belonging to unbelievers]
Unbelievers, therefore — whom the divine kindness never ceases to pursue with constant benefits, giving them life and spirit, feeding and nourishing them with its good things, protecting them from demons: without whose mercy they would go down in the twinkling of an eye to punishment below — just as they are capable, while their unbelief remains, of receiving bodily sustenance, courage, beauty, and other gifts gratuitously bestowed, gifts both bodily and spiritual, are likewise capable, while their unbelief remains, of receiving lordship of temporal things, temporal jurisdiction, and other worldly rights and honours. And no wonder; such lordships and worldly rights count among the least of good things, they can be used badly, and one can live well without them. If, therefore, God has given unbelievers the blessing of bodily health, the best of all blessings, and reason, knowledge of various things,

wife, children, and countless other good things, it must not be said that God has deprived them of all lordship of temporal things and temporal jurisdiction and every other right.

ch. 7. After the foregoing we must see by what law lordship of temporal things and temporal jurisdiction were introduced. For the better understanding of this we must distinguish kinds of lordship. Of lordships over temporal things one is divine, with which we are not at present concerned, and another is human; and that is twofold: common to the whole human race, and exclusive. Lordship common to the whole human race is that which God gave Adam and his wife for themselves and all their posterity, power to manage and use temporal things to their own advantage. That power would have existed in the state of innocence without power to appropriate any temporal thing to any one person or to any particular collectivity or to certain persons, but after the fall it exists together with such a power of appropriating temporal things. The other kind is exclusive lordship (dominium proprium), called "ownership" in the legal sciences and in writings which imitate their terminology. This lordship is a principal power of managing temporal things, appropriated to one person or to certain persons or to some particular collectivity. Such power varies, as it can be greater or less.

The first kind, namely lordship common to the whole human race, existed in the state of innocence, and would have continued if man had not sinned, but without power to appropriate anything to anyone except by use, as has been said. For since there would have been among them no avarice or desire to possess or use any temporal thing against right reason, there would then have been no necessity or advantage in having ownership of any temporal thing. But after sin, because among men there grew up avarice and the desire to possess and use temporal things wrongly, it was useful and expedient that temporal things should be appropriated and not all be common, to restrain the immoderate appetite of the wicked for possessing temporal things and to drive out neglect of the proper management and administration of temporal things, since common affairs are commonly neglected by bad men. And therefore, together with (1) the lordship that existed in the state of innocence, after the fall there was (2) a power of thus appropriating temporal things. [...]

ch. 8. This twofold power, to appropriate temporal things and to establish rulers with jurisdiction, God gave without intermediary not only to believers but also to unbelievers, in such a way that it falls under precept [i.e., is commanded] and is reckoned among purely moral matters. It therefore obliges everyone, believer and unbeliever alike. And therefore, just as unbelievers are bound by God's precept and by natural law to honour father and mother and to do other things necessary to their neighbours, so, on occasion, they are bound to make such appropriation and to set up secular powers over themselves. For since these things come under a positive precept, which obliges always, though not for always [i.e., only as the occasion requires], unbelievers, just like believers, are therefore bound to these things, not for every time, but only in a situation of necessity. Hence it is that both believers and unbelievers can renounce the above-mentioned twofold power except in a situation of necessity or of a utility comparable with necessity. For this reason also, some, believers and unbelievers, can be deprived of such power for some fault or reason, so that they cannot (except in a situation of necessity) rightly exercise it, and so that if in fact they try to exercise it their act is null by the law itself.

Since, therefore, we do not read in the divine Scriptures that God deprived unbelievers of this twofold power which he gave to our first parents for themselves and for their posterity, or that he revoked this kind of affirmative precept so far as it applies to unbelievers, it follows that unbelievers, even while their unbelief continues, unless they are deprived judicially by someone with legitimate power, can rightly use this twofold power even apart from a situation of necessity; and in a situation of necessity they are obliged to use it, since necessity cannot fall under human law or precept.

ch. 14. It remains now to see how unreasonably, erroneously, and heretically John XXII has spoken of the introduction of lordship or ownership of temporal things. To understand this it must first be known that the power of making human laws and rights was first and principally in the people; and hence the people transferred the power of making laws to the emperor. Thus, also, the people, that is both the Romans and others, transferred the power of making laws to others, sometimes to kings and sometimes to others of lesser and inferior dignity and power. These things could be shown not only from histories and chronicles but also in part from divine Scripture, but for the sake of brevity I pass on.

Now from this we gather evidently that human laws have included not only the laws of emperors and kings but also the laws of peoples, and of others who got the power of making and establishing laws from peoples, and also laudable and useful customs introduced by peoples. And therefore, because the power of appropriating temporal things was given by God to the human race, temporal things possessed by human law could be possessed not only by the laws of emperors and kings but also by laudable and reasonable customs, and by human laws and ordinances brought in by peoples and by others who had power and authority from peoples; and, in fact, before there were emperors and kings many exclusive lordships were possessed by such human laws. Augustine's statement that "We have human law in the laws of kings" should therefore be understood of his time and the regions in which he and the heretics he wished to refute were living. It should not be understood of the human law which preceded the laws of emperors and kings, which by Augustine's time had been abrogated or changed, at least in great part.

Translation: John Kilcullen (Cambridge University Press, 1992). Used with permission.

Nicolas Cabasilas

(ca. 1322–ca. 1392)

Nicolas Cabasilas, valued chiefly as a spiritual writer and sympathizer of the Hesychast movement associated with Gregory Palamas, pursued an active political career in his youth, which coincided with a civil war in the Byzantine Empire. Coming from a prominent family in Thessalonike, where his uncle was later archbishop, Cabasilas played a part in securing that city's support for the pretender to the imperial throne, John Cantacuzenos, afterwards Emperor John VI, and came to be treated by the new emperor as an intimate. After Catancuzenos's abdication in 1354 to become a monk, restoring the throne to John V Palaiologos, whom he had displaced, Nicolas, too, retired into obscurity, though the question whether he took religious vows is an open one. His major works, *The Life in Christ* and the *Interpretation of the Liturgy*, which date from his retirement, are very remote from the legal and political world inhabited by the speech on *Rulers' Illegal Outrages* (usually known as the *Discourse*), which may be presumed to come from the early years.

It used to be held that the speech was directed against the activities of revolutionary "Zealots" who took control in Thessalonike in the 1340s, but this theory has been badly shaken by the observation that everything which Cabasilas charges his opponents with can be demonstrated to be a constant feature of imperial and patriarchal policy in preceding and subsequent generations, when plentiful monastic lands were increasingly relied on to support and reward an army urgently needed for defense against the Turks (Ševcenko 1957). Cabasilas divides his attack upon expropriation and taxation of monastic lands between lay and clerical offenders, neither of whom he identifies in anything but the vaguest terms. It is attractive to see the speech as a barely veiled attack on the policies of the government loyal to the infant John V.

This interpretation highlights the work's tendentious character. The question of civil taxation of church wealth was, of course, a thorny issue in the West, too, during the thirteenth and fourteenth centuries, but it was framed mainly in terms of the mutual rights and responsibilities of the dual jurisdictions of church and state. In the East, where no such dual conceptuality prevailed, Cabasilas's reaction against expropriation took a dramatic form. He explored the potential of Roman law to elevate the rights of property to a central place in freedom under law, and, like his Western contemporary Ockham, insisted on freedom as a distinct political good alongside justice. The "common good" becomes in his eyes a secondary, and highly suspect, notion.

What relation did Byzantine disputes over the dispossession of monasteries have to Western disputes about evangelical poverty? Perhaps none, if the "illegal outrages" Cabasilas complained of were in truth both traditional and legal. Attempts to find an alignment between support for these dispossessions and the Hesychast movement, giving the latter a quasi-Franciscan cast, stumble over the fact that Cabasilas himself was a friend and sympathizer of Palamas. Yet half a century later Metropolitan Cyprian of Kiev introduced just such a form of Hesychasm, dispossessionist in principle, into the Russian church.

Further Reading: S. Runciman, *The Last Byzantine Renaissance* (Cambridge: Cambridge University Press, 1970); I. Ševčenko, "Nicolas Cabasilas' 'Anti-Zealot Discourse,'" *Dunbarton Oaks Papers* 9 (1957): 81-171.

From *Rulers' Illegal Outrages against Sacred Property*

4. Monasteries possess landed property, dwellings, villages, estates, and similar sources of revenue. These should be left for the use of the monks to whom the original owners donated it; but these persons take it from the monks, partly for their own use and partly for that of others, principally by diverting revenue and crops (wheat, barley, wine) and other produce, but sometimes even alienating the peasants, the villages, and the estates themselves. Yet the donors, as lords of their property, were entitled to make a gift, and from them the recipients' claim to lordship is derived, whether they made over the property in their lifetimes or bequeathed it in their wills. It makes no difference how they had acquired it in the first place, for purchase and gift are equally valid titles of lordship. Nor does it matter whether the gift was made in the donor's life or at his death, for testamentary bequest is in no way an inferior title for an acquisition. The law protects it, and to violate the dispositions of a testament amounts to a legal offense. [. . .]

6. Criticized for these and other such abuses, they defend themselves as follows: — Those responsible for the common good must consider what benefits the community. They must act like guardians who administer the property of juveniles not as the young people think best but as they know will benefit them most. Such is the analogy they propose between the ruler in a community and the subject in his own household. Subjects may not lack years, like children, but they lack sense, and they use their property irresponsibly. The laws demand that, to have gained some sense, someone must have come of age; those who have not achieved that age they

entrust to the care of guardians — the implication being that, were children to have a full measure of adult intelligence, they would have no need of guides. But once allow that there are any, besides children, who need to be taught their own advantage, it would seem probable that there are many such; and so we need common guardians (which is how we are bound to think of rulers) to supervise them like children and to make the best use of their property, whether they like it or not, even if they react against it or resent it. Since this is the general model for political government, then, there is no harm in confiscating a portion of the vast monastic properties if it is used to feed the poor, to support priests, and to decorate churches. It will do no harm to the monks, since what is left will be sufficient for their needs, and it is not inconsistent with the intention of the original founders, who intended simply to honor God and support the poor, which is precisely what is being done. Furthermore, if these revenues are used to equip soldiers who will die in defense of holy places, laws, and civil defenses, is it not preferable to allowing those same revenues to be squandered by monks and priests, whose needs of sustenance and of other essentials are slight, who stay at home and live a sheltered life, and who offer no protection against danger to anybody? Yet this way of spending the money is the most advantageous for them, too. They need nothing so much as the security of civil defenses and laws, which soldiers above all can ensure. We do them no wrong if we require them to support those who defend their freedom, just as they would repair the roof, rebuild a dilapidated building, or manage their farms and estates. May they not draw on their sacred revenue to maintain a domestic steward, an agricultural laborer, a cook, or a builder? Then why not soldiers, too? [. . .]

9. This, then, is their defense, based on three arguments: (1) the prerogative of political rule, which allows them, they say, to manage the property of subjects as they judge best; (2) the expedient use they make of confiscated property, which is free from taint of injustice even though taken compulsorily; (3) tradition, i.e., their claim to legality by virtue of the force which law allows to tradition. We shall consider each point in turn, showing that none of them excuse these confiscations, but actually confirm their appearance of inequity.

First, then, the matter of political rule. 10. I would agree that rulers have a right to manage subjects' property, but this does not extend to private, only to common property. Everyone is in charge of his own household, and may use his property as he sees fit. Neither rulers of communities nor judges, nor even emperors with universal rule, may demand an account of what the proprietor does with it, even should he waste it, throw it away, or spend it on inappropriate objects. When emperors wish to make any activity subject to the sanctions of the courts, they pass laws to prohibit it. But on this matter the laws contain no directives; it is not a valid charge, which a judge might register or a prosecutor lodge, that such and such a one misspent his property, laid it out on the wrong things, purchased goods that were no use, named unsuitable people instead of wise and upright people as his heirs. Legislators do not penalize such conduct. They demand restraint from us all only where others can be harmed; in private affairs not only do they allow autonomy, but they enforce the observance of the owner's dispositions. Gifts, sales, and covenants are held inviolable. Owners' decisions about property have the force of law, whether or not they bring them profit, or even harm. Clearly, then, those who take this power from them and claim the right to manage their property for them, break the law.

11. "But," you may object, "it is not the owners themselves that we extrude from possession, for they are dead long ago." But it is; for you overturn their dispositions of their property. This injures both parties at once, donors and recipients. The donors are deprived of the autonomy which law assigns to all proprietors, living and dead. The recipients, for no crime of their own, are denied security of possession. Are you suggesting that this form of acquisition is not enough to establish a secure title? If somebody were to produce a deed of this kind in court, you would abide by its terms, and confirm possession; on the basis of the donation you would treat the beneficiary as you would a purchaser on the basis of the purchase, or a party to an exchange on the basis of the deed of exchange. On what ground could you treat his claims as less binding? Only that since the gift was ancient and the donors lived long ago, it had a weaker standing than more recent ones; that a right grows old, like a living body worn out by time. But since this is a silly argument, you are depriving those with proven titles without charges being laid against them. What standing have you, then, to prosecute petty thieves? You are as guilty of misappropriation as they are. Prove the difference — if you can!

12. But how, it is asked, can the beneficiaries be called lords when they are not at liberty to dispose of their property or give it away — neither land nor buildings nor anything else pertaining to the ecclesiastical estates? If the point is to establish that they are lords of their estates and buildings and other possessions, we need look no further. For it hardly needs to be proved that the profits and revenues are put entirely at their disposal by the provisions of the original owners, whether for their own use or the community's. From this it follows that the law requires us to uphold their right to them, levying no tax in money or kind.

13. But, it is said, they mismanage the property, using it contrary to the intentions of the donors. Very well, examine both sides of the case! Consult the text of the donors' stipulations, and conduct a precise inquiry into how they have been carried out! If you find misappropriation, exercise your judicial functions. And what are they? Not to enrich yourself from others' peculations, but simply to restore what was improperly taken — that, and no more! If it is your business to uphold the founders' statutes by negotiation or enforcement, you should come out of it not a penny the richer. Does your self-enrichment enhance justice in any way? On the contrary, it is incompatible with the role of a judge, whose hands should be clean from bribes. And that is not the worst of the matter. You fall foul of your own judgment and collude in the very crime for which you prosecute the defendants. Just as they are said to do, you appropriate what you were never given by those who had the right of gift at their disposal, and so you disregard their deeds of bequest. In placing obstacles in the way of others' fraudulence while advancing your own, you give the impression not of opposing corruption and punishing it, but of liking it so much that you want to keep it to yourself and acquire a private monopoly of fraud!

14. "But it is not the same," they reply. "For others it is a crime to do such things, but not for us. Even beneficiaries cannot innocently dispose of ecclesiastical possessions, but political authorities can. For they are permitted to dispose of prop-

erty with the permission of the authorities, while without that permission the transaction is invalid and they are subject to legal penalties. This clearly illustrates two points: *(a)* that the legal obligations resting on the political authorities are not in every case the same as those resting on private agents; *(b)* that political authorities have sole discretion to make the most profitable deployment of all property that falls within their jurisdiction." But, as I have argued already, you have the responsibility for *common* property, while *private* property is the owner's exclusive responsibility. The property in question is not common to the state, but belongs to particular owners and specifically to those to whom it was bequeathed. If you infer from your judicial role in confirming deeds that require some disposition to be made that you actually have a claim upon the property, why not include all buildings of every kind, levying taxes on them and enforcing these new imposts? For your jurisdiction extends to all parties alike, and enforces the laws that apply in every case. But in civil associations your role in confirming contracts extends only to certifying that they give rise to no wrong, and so are not unlawful. What further rights can you claim over monasteries and ecclesiastical property?

24. [Cabasilas proceeds to dismiss the argument that the expropriated property is put to good use in military supplies.] [...] Supplies, ships, and troops are not to be thought the ruler's supreme object, to which all his other obligations are subordinate. How would he then be different from a tyrant for whom armed force is the most important thing, who sacrifices laws, rights, sacred objects, and all else to expand his military might? Good rulers, on the contrary, rulers worthy of the name, seek power in order to preserve the laws and to secure for their subjects that freedom that is due to man. 25. This, indeed, is how tyranny falls short of the best political constitutions. Rulers of one type maintain armed force in order to defend the laws and freedom against contempt. Rulers of another type arm themselves by unlawfully enslaving their subjects. This kind takes no account of subjects' welfare, but thinks of them only as means to their advantage, making use of them and of their goods to acquire security for themselves and for their entertainments. The other kind exert themselves to ensure their subjects' welfare; they endure trouble and hardship with infinite patience to achieve whatever may benefit them, knowing that rights and laws take highest precedence. The one sort despises the lawmakers as stupid; the other is committed to upholding them, since only by proceeding in this way can government be stable and their subjects secure. By this means above all they may realize their true capacity as men, instead of being reduced to the life of cattle; they may enjoy the privilege of speech and the freedom of decision, which are what make man what he is. In that kind of life no one harms his neighbor, no one is led by wrongful passion to commit crime; but one is restrained by the laws, which is what it means to live reasonably. Conversely, no one suffers wrong or violence, which is what it means to be free.

26. How could there ever be a stable form of government which made it impossible to live in freedom? Freedom has no equivalent, no exchange value in the life of men, whether in currency, lands, or honor. Someone who seizes the reins of such a government must either keep all his subjects penned up, laying siege to them like enemies, or letting up a little, lose all his power in a rush as they bid to throw aside their

bondage. If they stay penned up, what use will they be to themselves, to one another or to the common good? For if no one is master of his own possessions but rulers may make what use they will of them, then at the very mention of the word "community," everyone will have to fall a-trembling in fear for their possessions. Who, then, — what craftsman, farmer, merchant — will take the trouble to make money, knowing that everything he earns will go to other people? How can anyone sustain the pursuit of wisdom when struggling against poverty? Or study military tactics, become a learned jurist, master the principles of military command? Where will the community's revenues come from, with every section of society in the grip of poverty? That is why perceptive rulers have always grasped the need to protect their subjects' freedoms as well as maintain justice; that is why, to secure their cities against derogation of freedom from internal sources or foreign intervention, they have always prepared for two eventualities, war and peace, constructing walls and armaments against foreign enemies, judges and laws against domestic foes. What could be more contradictory and foolish, than that those with whom the duty lay to be armed and otherwise prepared against lawless violence, should arm themselves by means of lawless violence against their subjects?

27. Besides, let it be granted as a relevant consideration that God is powerful. Not everything depends upon our human wisdom; political communities depend upon his providence, too. His favor ensures stability and welfare, his enmity destruction. If you believe this, how do you think you help political communities by injustice and sacrilege and, as the prophet says, "conceiving iniquity" (Ps. 50:21)?

Translation: Editors, from I. Ševcenko, "Nicolas Cabasilas' 'Anti-Zealot Discourse,'" *Dunbarton Oaks Papers* 9 (1957): 81-171.

John Wyclif
(ca. 1330-84)

Although probably the most brilliant political thinker of the second half of the fourteenth century, John Wyclif has never enjoyed a reputation commensurate with his achievement. Despite the dedicated labors of the nineteenth-century editors of his voluminous works, his political ideas have languished in comparative obscurity, outside the mainstream of historical scholarship.

Among theologians Wyclif's legendary standing as a precursor of the Reformation has overshadowed the political interest of his work. But a more potent reason for its neglect is its apparent remoteness from the political course of modernity. Whereas Marsilius, Ockham, and Gerson have credentials as proto-modern theorists, Wyclif seems to look back to the two medieval developments of Augustinian Neoplatonism that appear most outlandish to contemporary eyes, namely, papalist theocracy and Franciscan community. These leanings in his thought, combined with his polemical preoccupations with the church and the Bible, have hitherto made him an unpromising focus of interest for political historians. But with political reflection now casting around for alternative points of purchase which will allow a critical perspective on modernity, Wyclif's radical Augustinianism may come into its own. Nevertheless, his writings also contain anticipations of later developments as dramatic as anything in his century, or indeed, in the Reformation itself.

The predominance of political themes in the last decade of Wyclif's life, when the course of his scholarly career led him to teach theology, was related generally to the national financial crisis occasioned by the Hundred Years' War, which prompted secular magnates to look covetously and critically on the English church's wealth, and in particular to the ambitions and policies of his powerful royal patron, John of Gaunt. However, the definite *Sitz im Leben* and pervasive polemicism of Wyclif's political ideas do not make them merely occasionalist forays without a coherent theoretical framework. Their agenda comes from the Augustinian tradition of christocentric idealism that permeated all his thought, from his early philosophical speculations to his late theological "heresies."

The nonpolitical phase of Wyclif's glittering academic career, pursued uninterruptedly in Oxford for twenty years from the mid-1350s, culminated in a philosophical *magnum opus*, the *Summa de Ente (On Reality)*, completed in 1372. Its primary interest for us is its vindication of the real being of universals independent of human thought and language: their divine being as Ideas in the mind of God and their created being as transcendent forms, in which particular members of a kind participate, but which are prior and superior to particulars. Moreover, Wyclif attributed several modes of being to individual creatures: every creature has intelligible being *(esse intelligibile)* as God's eternal Idea; potential being *(esse possibile)* in its secondary causes, universal and particular; and actual being in time or existence *(esse existere)* (Leff 1967, 502; Kenny 1985, 18-22). Both the preeminent being of universals and the manifold being of individuals were to prove of critical importance for his ethic of community and his scriptural epistemology.

By the time he embarked on his twelve-book theological *Summa de dominio (On Lordship)* in 1373, a burning dispute was raging between the English crown and the papal court over rights of church taxation and provision to benefices. Wyclif's conception was monumental: a complete "political theology" (as we would say) based on the idea of "lordship." (Our preferred translation allows the same perspicuous correspondence between "lordship" and "lord" as between the Latin *dominium* and *dominus*.) After the prefatory *Divine Lordship (De dominio divino)*, which explored God's lordship over all creation and mankind's vocation of derivative lordship, it opened formally with the book *Commands (De mandatis)*, containing the theory of Right and Justice, and proceeded, by way of a discussion of Adamic lordship in *The State of Innocence*, to three lengthy books titled *Civil Lordship (De civili dominio)*. There followed two books laying out the principles of Christian society, *The Truth of Holy Scripture* and *The Church*, two books titled *The King's Office* and *Papal Power*, and finally, three polemical books: *Simony, Apostasy,* and *Blasphemy*.

The first books already give indications of Wyclif's polemical thrust, censuring irresponsible papal provisions and temporal claims, clerical financial extortions, and unbiblical canon laws on the one hand, and on the other, upholding the evangelical standard of clerical poverty, preaching, and holiness. These occupy the foreground of *Civil Lordship*, which constructs a full-blown theory of civil and ecclesiastical polity: their purposes, forms of authority, laws, actions, and modes of material possession. While his proposals here undoubtedly endorsed the Commons' petitions against ecclesiastical abuses in the 1376 Parliament, they were incomparably more radical in spirit and content. From a fund of Augustinian doctrines mediated by his Oxford predecessors, Robert Grosseteste, John Duns Scotus, William of Ockham, Thomas Bradwardine, and Richard FitzRalph, Wyclif developed positions unrivaled in sheer boldness and clarity of stroke.

In book 1 he portrays the church as the totality of the predestinate (past, present, and future), and the clergy as the preaching estate bound by divine law to absolute poverty. Inasmuch as the de facto ecclesiastical authorities, enjoying both civil wealth and jurisdiction, live in manifest contravention of God's will, it belongs to the righteous king, ruling by grace, to promulgate and enforce God's law by depriving corrupt and avaricious clergy of their property and forcing the whole estate to live on freely donated tithes or alms. Books 2 and 3, though intended to answer condemnations of book 1, set forth even more immoderately, with additional arguments, the case for secular authorities to wrest jurisdiction from the clergy and to sequestrate and redistribute church property. Predictably, the publication of *Civil Lordship* brought condemnation from English bishops and from Rome. Fortunately for Wyclif, neither the King's Council nor the university were prepared to act.

His voluminous writings toward the end of the decade reflect the deepening of his theological opposition to the papal office and its occupants occasioned by the Great Schism, that unseemly contest between rival popes in Rome and Avignon which, in all probability, spared him further papal persecution. The later books of his *Summa* were dedicated to setting ecclesiastical authority on an alternative christological and scriptural footing to canonist tradition. The linchpin of this enterprise was the doctrine and hermeneutic of Scripture laid out in *The Truth of Holy Scripture* (1378). This argued for the Bible's divine inspiration, inerrancy, and sufficiency as the repository of all truth, right, and law, and moreover, for the direct accessibility of its truth to the laity and the necessity of its translation into the vernacular. As with Marsilius and the later Luther, Wyclif curtailed the individualist tendency of his proposals by exalting the public doctrinal authority of the Christian magistrate, and of church councils convened by him. In forced retirement from 1380 at his Lutterworth living, on account of his attack on the doctrine of eucharistic transubstantiation, he completed his life's work with further diatribes against the ecclesiastical establishment, bequeathing a legacy of Bible translation, English Lollardy, and the revolutionary Hussite movement in Bohemia.

The themes of Wyclif's *Summa de dominio* are so interwoven, and so comparatively little known, that we have departed from our usual practice and have arranged the readings in six thematic groupings, concerned with (*a*) evangelical lordship, (*b*) civil lordship, (*c*) gospel law and human law, (*d*) the disendowment of the church, (*e*) political authority, and (*f*) servitude.

a. The Augustinian shape of Wyclif's theory of lordship accords the controlling place to *evangelical lordship,* a notion which combines two long-associated Augustinian titles of possession: the natural, nonproprietary use of necessary things universally open to human beings, and the belonging of all things to "the just" by a communion of divine grace and charity. Richard FitzRalph had synthesized these titles into the structure of righteous possession, arguing that Adam's natural lordship, which presupposed God's justifying grace, was only *curtailed in its exercise* by positive property right which continued to rest on the original title without bestowing a new one. Perceiving the threat posed by FitzRalph's synthesis to the theory of universal papal proprietorship, Wyclif determined to complete his predecessor's work, detaching righteous lordship from the condition of obedience to the Roman see. He therefore undercut the church's role in mediating property right by repudiating her involvement in it, insisting that the whole apostolate, and not only the Friars Minor, was obliged to practice the nonproprietary use of goods practiced by Adam, Christ, and the apostolic church, which was not only a community of belief and proclamation but also a community of goods, shared equally according to need, and without civil ownership (*Civil Lordship* 3.7).

Wyclif's theory of evangelical lordship furnishes a coherent communal ethic that is Augustinian, Christ centered, and idealist. Its central thesis is that just lordship of earthly goods involves a rightly ordered love toward them, which in turn depends on a true knowledge of them available only in Christ. For in Christ is contained the intelligible being, and therefore the potential and the actual being, of every creature (*Civil Lordship* 1.7; *Divine Lordship* 1.9; 3.3). All justified believers who "coexist" in Christ's love fully possess themselves, one another, and the nonhuman creation in knowledge and in love. From this possession flow the manifold uses to which their possession may be put, in contemplative enjoyment, aesthetic appreciation, and the fulfillment of material needs (*Civil Lordship* 1.8; 3.8, 10; *Divine Lordship* 3.2).

Moreover, God's original grant of lordship to Adam, renewed in Christ, is chiefly his gift of himself as truth and love; it is his trinitarian communication of himself and his lordship over creation without alteration or diminution. So, too, Adam's lordship is a communicating and communicable possession and use of created goods according to rational necessity (*Divine Dominion* 3.1). It is universal, inclusive, and inalienable except by sin; consequently, it is free from worldly anxiety and temptation, wholly in the service of God and the neighbor (*Civil Lordship* 3.8; also 1.11, 18f.). Wyclif's thought traces the parallel between the act of communicating *spiritual* dominion, i.e., drawing others into the revelation of God's love and grace by preaching, and the act of communicating *physical* dominion, i.e., drawing others into the rational use of the same material goods (*Civil Lordship* 3.1). In both cases the human act is merely instrumental to God's own action (*Divine Lordship* 1.10; 3.1). Here, we may profitably observe, he parts company with Thomas Aquinas, for his portrayal of Adam's relationship to the nonhuman world as primarily contemplative enjoyment rather than work, and of Adamic community as a real unity of spiritual participation, mediating each individual's use of earthly goods (*Civil Lordship* 1.14; 3.4f.), renders superfluous both the private "directive" dominion over things and the public "directive" dominion over men which Thomas regarded as necessary to human community *by nature*.

b. Unlike evangelical lordship, the meaning of *civil lordship* for Wyclif is highly equivocal. On the one hand it is a sinful necessity — humanly instituted, severely limited in distribution, alienable at will, insecure of tenure, loaded with anxiety and temptation, and chiefly serviceable to private interests (*Civil Lordship* 1.11, 18, 19). On the other hand, it is divinely authorized and structured. It rests on God's sovereign approbation bestowed only on the righteous, which no human grant, testimony, or recognition can either magnify or diminish, but merely declare (1.4). Only the inscrutability of God's judgments and of the conditions of human hearts lends an interim validity to positive legal titles (2.16; also 1.3, 6). Moreover, civil lordship is constitutive of the lay estate in the historical church militant, which achieves its proper conformity to Christ's law of love when it serves evangelical lordship, chiefly by making property available for the use of the clergy and the poor, but also in every *just* use of property that conforms to Christ's law under the conditions of human sin (1.19).

c. The relationship between evangelical and civil lordships typifies that between *gospel law and positive human law:* as the gospel law is the perfect and sufficient regime of Christian community and needs no supplement from human laws, so the latter (whether civil or canon) either interprets and applies the commandments of Christ or opposes them with contrary and irrelevant demands (*Civil Lordship* 1.17; *The King's Office* 7). Consistent with Wyclif's stress on the unity and universality of the gospel law is the movement (completed by Erasmus and Luther) to reduce the significance of the distinction between Christ's counsels and commands, which traditionally undergirded the division of the church into lay, clerical, monastic, and mendicant orders (*Civil Lordship* 2.13).

d. For the clergy, however, Christ's injunction to supreme poverty remains a strictly commanded vocational necessity, since the ministry of preaching, teaching, prayer, and sacramental administration requires their release from the worldly cares and venial sins of civil proprietorship and jurisdiction. The higher ecclesiastics in the first place, but ultimately the civil authorities, are bound (by the law of fraternal correction) to enforce clerical obedience and punish intransigent disobedience (*Civil Lordship* 1.3, 10). Authorization for *lay disendowment* and dispossession of avaricious clergy issues jointly from divine law and from the ancient charters of the English realm that prescribe "free alms" as the form of ecclesiastical dotation and reserve civil ownership and right of recovery to lay donors (*The Truth of Sacred Scripture* 25; also 18, 19, 21), leaving no room for compulsory tithes and exactions, simony, or the machinery of clerical litigation (*Civil Lordship* 2.12; also 1.41; 3.16).

e. The chief agent of Wyclif's reform is the monarch, who is not only the liege-lord of all the temporalities in his domain but also its supreme legislator and magistrate, holding a plenitude of jurisdiction by divine mandate. In the royal office civil and evangelical laws find their palpable unity (*Civil Lordship* 1.26). Wyclif expresses the unsurpassable dignity owing to Christ's temporal vicar with the memorable formula of the Norman Anonymous (see p. 254 above), that the king bears the image of Christ's Godhead and the priest, of his manhood (*The King's Office* 1.13). Echoing Gregory I, he argues that even the vicious ruler who has forfeited his *lordship* may retain a divinely bestowed *power (potestas)* to benefit the church, as long as his wrongdoings are not injurious to the cause of God (*The King's Office* 1.5-9, 16-17). From the principle that all lordship (political and proprietary) is evangelical in essence and depends on divine grace, Wyclif radically qualifies the traditional titles to rule: inheritance by primogeniture, election, and conquest, subjecting each to the higher demands of justice and charity (*Civil Lordship* 1.21, 30). His logic throughout is Augustinian, but without the papalist ecclesiological positivism that characterized the mainstream of medieval Augustinianism.

f. From the same principle he reconstructs the institution of *slavery*, rendering it analogous to political subjection. Its moral and spiritual purposes (e.g., to provide the slave with opportunities for repentance and good works) determine eligibility for the roles of master and slave (*Civil Lordship* 1.32). The evangelical structure of the master's rule and the primary importance of the slave's welfare discredit the prevailing assumptions of hereditary and commercial slavery, that the child may inherit parental sin, guilt, and punishment, and that the parent has civil property in his off-spring or, indeed, in his own body (*Civil Lordship* 1.34). Significantly, Wyclif affirms the inestimable worth of the person for whom Christ died and the nonproprietary character of moral-spiritual self-possession (1.34).

Further Reading: L. J. Daly, *The Political Theory of John Wycliff* (Chicago: Loyola University Press, 1962); W. Farr, *John Wycliff as Legal Reformer* (Leiden: Brill, 1974); A. Hudson, M. Wilks, eds., *From Ockham to Wyclif* (Oxford: Basil Blackwell, 1987); A. Kenny, *Wyclif* (Oxford: Oxford University Press, 1985); G. Leff, *Heresy in the Later Middle Ages: The Relation of Heterodoxy to Dissent, c. 1250-1450,* vol. 2 (Manchester: Manchester University Press, 1967).

(A) EVANGELICAL LORDSHIP

From *Divine Lordship*

bk. 3 ch. 1. [70c] It is plain to those philosophers not blinded by restricting their view to earthly lordship, that "communication" or "sharing" *(communicacio)* is not inconsistent with true lordship *(dominium);* neither does lordship necessarily imply property *(proprietas).* On the contrary, property was a device to deal with sin, the sin of lords, perhaps, or at least of those who would not communicate their goods. See how lordship works, and you will also see that the position of being in charge is pleasanter when shared with a subordinate, since it is more stable and of more use to the community, as, with God's help, I shall show hereafter. The alternative betrays its moral inadequacy in that contention over property right can arise only about goods of fortune, the least significant of the five kinds of good. Moreover, our Savior and the apostles did not desire to have a proprietorial lordship, but a communicative one, befitting the condition of pilgrims on the way to acquiring an eternal lordship. Spiritual gifts, too, and those which lie closer to divine lordship have the opposite character: God communicates them to mankind with no alienation or impoverishment to himself the giver, as is clear in the case of the Kingdom of Heaven, which is all the more pleasant to possess for being shared with the many others who inherit it. The same is clearly true of other spiritual riches, and of man's natural lordship as well. The seed of merit scattered wide and thick along the pilgrim's way yields the more prolific harvest from the multitude who share its benefits, and brings its lord the greater profit, as we see in the case of knowledge and instruction.

bk. 3 ch. 4. [78a] On this basis it is clear that lending *(prestacio)* is, to the fullest extent and in the strictest sense, God's own characteristic activity. We may argue this *first,* because, in a truer sense than any other, he is lord of what he lends, and so more fully at liberty to lend it to whichever of his dependents he pleases. *Secondly,* because in communicating the good that is his own entirely freely and with no expectation of return, he really and actually makes it over. *Thirdly*, because this act of communication is all-inclusive, comprising the duration of the loan, the use of the loan, and every other condition of the loan, excluding only its abuse. *Fourthly*, because he necessarily reserves the lordship to himself, though in a multitude of ways assisting the borrower to make use of the loan. *Fifthly*, on the other hand — and here his lending differs from and surpasses all our creaturely lending — he does not deny himself the use of the loan for the duration; but, on the contrary, lays unyielding claim upon every use of that of which he is lord, not thereby interfering with or detracting from the borrower's advantage, but multiplying the value derived from it so as to ensure that the use is profitable. The argument for this is that God is the lord of every created thing; but the use of the loan is itself a created thing, so that the rest follows. Again, everyone who borrows from God is God's bondservant; simply as his lord, then, God may lay claim upon every use he makes of the loan as service due to him. (This is supported in bk. 1 ch. 5 of this work, where it is shown that God makes use of the essential attributes of his creation.) Again, if in this case the lord were to forgo the use of his loan, it would no longer be use but abuse, since it would be undertaken apart from the service of God's glory; and that is a contradictory conclusion. It demonstrates, in fact, that God could not renounce the use of his loan without turning the borrower into a second god.

From *Civil Lordship*

bk. 1 ch. 7. [15d] In the light of what has been said our next task is to show that any and every righteous man is lord of the whole sense-perceptible world. *First*, because three conditions are sufficient for true natural lordship: the coexistence of extremes [the *dominativum* and *dominabile*, the subject and object of lordship]; the preeminence naturally conferred by the power of lordship; and, in the same subject, love. But these are present in each and every just man in his relation to the whole sense-perceptible world; therefore he has true lordship over it. And so the Truth says (after referring to natural anxiety about temporal matters): "Seek first God's kingdom and his righteousness, and all these things shall be yours as well" (Matt. 6:33). By which he means that of the five goods listed above [goods of glory, grace, reputation, nature, and fortune] the first must be sought preeminently, and this by way of the mediating good of righteousness; and then, if the whole realm of lower goods is possessed too, it is as a consequence of these. And the righteous man need not be concerned that he has no *civil* lordship in these goods, since in fact that would bring him no advantage, only harm.

[16c]: *Fourthly*, again, God gives only in the best way of which the recipient is capable (see ch. 6 above); but every righteous man is capable of the best gift in general; so God bestows only in that way, for as long as one is righteous. [. . .] [16d] And so God cannot give a creature any created good without first giving uncreated good. The proof runs as follows: — God can give nothing to a creature without giving grace (see ch. 2 above), and cannot give grace without giving the Holy Spirit (as has

just been shown). The conclusion is: man cannot be the recipient of that gift (*sc.* the created good) without thereby having the whole world with it. For since wisdom overcomes wickedness (see *Divine Commands* ch. 5), it is clear that, from whatever quarter wickedness may spring, the whole will withstand it, even its sinful deeds. So Romans 8:31, speaking of God's gift of the Spirit to his adopted sons and of his mercy in bringing things beautifully together to their conclusions, adds, "If God be for us, who can be against us?" Obviously, one could receive no better terms for the use of his domain than God's own assistance, both against enemies who seek the destruction of soul and body, and in pursuit of beatitude. And since material nature as a whole is at the service of every one who is predestined in grace, it follows that every such person has the most productive terms imaginable for the use of his domain.

Fifthly, in giving the principal, whatever is necessarily consequent upon it is included in the gift. But God gives no gifts to man without giving himself as the principal gift (Rom. 8:32, and see my discussion in *Divine Dominion* bk. 3 ch. 2). So God gives every accessory that necessarily goes with his gift of himself. The major premise is clear: it would be laughable to make a present of a horse or of some other subject-of-attributes, and leave some part of the horse or some attribute that went with it out of the present! Once the consequent of this syllogism is in place, a second follows obviously enough: — The intelligible-essence of every distinct creature is necessarily immanent in God. But God is given to men; and so, therefore, is the intelligible-essence of every creature. And since the intelligible-essence is the highest essence of any creature, there is given together with the intelligible-essence, in consequence and *a fortiori*, the actual essence of every creature, which is even more closely tied to the intelligible-essence, if possible, than an attribute to its subject. This argument will be completely convincing to those instructed in the doctrine of the Ideas, and is equally supported by the apostle in Romans 8:32: God "did not spare his own son, but gave him up for us all; how can he fail to lavish every other gift upon us?" It is clear that if one receives the uncreated wisdom as a gift, one's gift must include the intellectual quality of every intelligible being, and so also the intelligibility of every intelligible being, and consequently the existence of the intelligible being, which is accessory to it. This is the sense in which we should understand Wisdom 7:7f.: "I called for help, and there came to me a spirit of wisdom. I valued her above scepter and throne, and reckoned riches as nothing beside her . . . ," which goes on: "So all good things together came to me with her."

The Truth undeniably supports the conclusion, that anyone who forsakes the whole realm of temporal goods to give Christ due preeminence in his affections has all those goods added later, and better than he could have had them by loving in the wrong order. So we read in Mark 10:29f.: "Truly I tell you: there is no one who has given up home, brothers or sisters, mother, father or children, or land, for my sake and for the gospel, who will not receive in this age a hundred times as much — houses, brothers and sisters, mothers, and children, and land — and persecutions besides; and in the age to come eternal life." [. . .]

[17b] So any secular person who uses God's goods badly is laying false and pretended claim to a right to all or some of these goods. But any one who for love of Christ and of the evangelical right renounces that title in favor of the title of grace, which is

conferred directly by the principal lord, God himself, will receive a hundred times the goods, even in this life. (By "a hundred times" understand totality — since a hundred is ten squared.) The proof runs: If anyone has a title of grace or evangelical right to something, he has the whole world besides and all its goods, since God cannot confer the part without conferring the whole. (Possession by human title, on the other hand, is narrowly defined.) A second proof turns on the value of the transaction in exchanging human title to lordship: in Luke 18:30 it is said that no one makes this exchange "who will not be repaid many times over in this age, and" besides, "in the age to come have eternal life," as the two other evangelists agree. It is clear that the text in Mark should be understood spiritually, since no one would suggest that a man of the Gospel, in following Christ, would gain from the exchange a hundred times as many biological brothers, sisters, mothers, and children. But the universal church as a whole will be his brother, supporting him more than a biological one; in its earthly form [i.e., as the church militant] it will be his sister; by giving him birth as a son of the church, it will be his mother; and through the assistance that he gives in turn, that Christ may be formed in them, he will gain adopted sons in all its members. And this is the interpretation the Truth teaches us when he says "Whoever does the will of my Father in heaven is my brother and sister and mother" (Matt. 12:50). As for the goods of fortune with all their purtenances, it is clear that as far as evangelical lordship goes, they are consequences *(consequuntur)* too. Which is why I take the view that the expression in St. Mark, "with persecutions besides," does not mean that they encompass *tribulation,* but *the perfect sequence* of such real property as is grounded in the goods one seeks to possess evangelically. [Wyclif's wild interpretative conjecture turns on a philological analysis of the Latin word *persecutio* as *per-* (perfect), *-sequ-* (sequence).] Yet if all these goods belong to the righteous, it does not imply that the faults inherent in them belong to the righteous too, since there is no "perfect sequence" of sin on man's part. And so the truth of every detail in Christ's saying is clear. In the predestined, without doubt, the goods of grace and glory come first; it follows, then, that the whole realm of goods is acquired by every righteous man.

bk. 3 ch. 4. [20d] On this assumption it is clear that Christ was, in the true sense, poor, as was prophesied of him in the Old Testament. For Christ came into the world to destroy sin, and especially the worldly social customs of the nobility remote from the state of innocence, which he could never have done, had he not observed in his own person the opposite condition of poverty. Therefore he observed it perfectly. "To their own destruction they sought after wealth, to minister to their pleasures; he, on the other hand, chose poverty" (Augustine, *De vera religione* 16.31). "Poverty" in this connection does not mean only "poverty in spirit," which is the absence of lay or proprietorial passion for earthly goods. For in his divinity he is supremely rich, as, indeed, he is in his humanity by the title of original righteousness. To speak of that kind of poverty looks, I suppose, to the future. But at the time when he used the word "poverty" in teaching, there was in him no "mixture of Yes and No," as the Apostle says (2 Cor. 1:19); but he undertook both to do it and to teach it, because he held to it in his life.

ch. 5. [29c] Besides, it would have been inappropriate for Christ to assume a state of life which it is impossible to sustain without sin, even if only venial. Civil lordship is such a state; it was, therefore, inappropriate to Christ. The syllogism is supported as follows: — It would be impossible for God to arrange something even slightly unsuitable. All the more then, since venial sin is incompatible with any state of pure innocence, is it incompatible with Christ's state, which is the state of highest innocence, necessary to the perfection of mankind. The minor premise is proved as follows: — An act of civil lordship, involving the active rule of material goods, implies a care for material goods which is distracting from contemplation, and consequently from the love which man would have had in the state of innocence. But the slightest slackening of the love of God which belongs to the state of innocence is venial sin; and so . . . etc., etc. That is why Augustine states, in keeping with the Scriptures, that we are necessarily involved in venial sins continually, as I have explained in chapter 10. It is not sufficient that Christ as God supremely loved his Father. As man he was required, both with the higher and the lower parts of his mind, to be wholly attentive to his Father's business. And the confirmation of this comes from the word of the Truth, "If you wish to be perfect, go, sell your possessions, and give to the poor, and . . . come and follow me" (Matt. 19:21). It would not have been appropriate, even were it possible, that one who was rich in worldly terms should be the most perfect moral being, striving with every power of soul after heavenly goods. We may accept, therefore, that an act of civil lordship, as furthest removed from the state of innocence, was not appropriate for Christ, however meritorious it might be, just as the act of marital intercourse was not, though much closer to the state of innocence. It would have been even less fitting, then, for Christ to sue for his goods as disputant in a court of human law, or to engage in armed conflict and all the activities that go with secular lordship, than it would have been for him to procreate physically the whole of the human race beside himself, as some of the more fantastic speculations on the absolute power of God make out to have been within his power. Such was the state of life which Mahomet maintained, to his shame, and which Antichrist, with utter shamefulness, will prolong; and to get things ready for *him* there is a host of pseudo-ministers about today, who all busy themselves with the suppression of evangelical poverty.

ch. 13. [93d] All men apart from Christ, when they coexist in love, communicate in whatever domain they possess, without one holding this or that domain as a fief *from* the rest, since every member of the church holds that domain immediately from Christ, the principal lord. And that is what I call "natural lordship," "evangelical lordship," "original lordship," or "lordship of grace," depending on which of the four different grounds for it is appropriate. Now, that kind of lordship is presupposed as the basis for the possibility of civil lordship, being the natural and original way for man to have lordship by the primary title of divine grace. After the Fall it was restored by the Gospel, which is why any further form of lordship would be an irrelevance to the clergy. And that is what Augustine teaches in his Letter (243) to Laetus, i.e., that we ought to put more weight upon those relations we have in common. The fact that this woman is your biological mother is unique to you. The fact that she is a sister is common to all the predestined, because she is begotten of the marriage of Christ and his church. That is a more serious consideration than the biological one, and it teaches a theologian to recognize the community of lordship of which we speak.

(B) CIVIL LORDSHIP

From *Civil Lordship*

bk. 1 ch. 1. [2c] The first title of justice in a civil lordship must be from God.

A Catholic could hardly doubt this, since God, by virtue of his omnipotence and the efficacy of his will, is the great Lord who has within his kingdom whatever he wills and does not have whatever he does not will. It is evident that any occupation in civil law requires this Lord's authorization, ratification, and confirmation as a condition of its rightness, since nothing can be right that he does not approve. We need not labor this point since John 1:3, Colossians 1:16, and James 1:17, in harmony with philosophical teachings, declare that "through him all things exist." So if there is any creaturely lordship, it is through God's originally giving approval to it. (From this primary rule of the law of nature there derives the right of earthly monarchy forbidding an inferior lord to alienate immovable property without permission of the principal lord, especially to *mortmain* [ownership by a corporation]. This is because in all these goods he has a just interest, of which it is not right that he should be deprived. By whatever means the lord's goods are exchanged, whether by purchase, sale, donation, adjudication, it is not right unless it has his consent.)

Granted this, the next step is to show that God does not approve the lordship of any unrighteous person. Consider what this would mean in relation to an unrighteous man whom we shall call Peter, and you will see why it cannot be so. For if God approved Peter's lordship, he would approve by implication the use that Peter made of his lordship and all the property belonging to it; and since people like Peter misuse their lordly possessions (as the second argument made clear), it would follow that God approved this misuse. Since, indeed, anything done by such an unrighteous man would be sin, it would follow that God assisted and approved his sin, not merely contingently but as such; for if God willed that this man should be a lord, and he exercised his lordship solely in a tyrannical manner, it would follow that God willed that he should be tyrannical, and so sin in this way — a blasphemous conclusion! This is supported from Scripture; for in Hosea 8:4 God says of tyrants through the prophet, "They have become kings, but not through me." Tyranny is the name given to pretended kingdoms, kingdoms equivocally so called (see ch. 3 of *Divine Commands*, on simple and pretended right). It is clear, then, since the unrighteous do not exercise lordship from God, that an unrighteous person exercises no *simple* right of lordship at all. [. . .]

ch. 3. [6a] [Wyclif distinguishes natural, civil, and evangelical ways of "having."] It is clear from this that unrighteousness *(iniustitia)* can be predicated of a creature only as an attribute *(per accidens)*. So behind any unrighteousness or sin there must be a being *(essentia)*, the being of which is right and well-pleasing to God. On this basis I grant that as far as their essential being and nature go, the righteous and the unrighteous are equally human beings and so equally right. As every natural being that is evil is good, (cf. Augustine, *Enchiridion* 12), so is every natural being that is unrighteous; for something *not right* in the sphere of action is *right* in the sphere of passive experience, since it is the work of the First Rightness. In this way we concede that the righteous and unrighteous alike "have" body, soul, and every other natural endowment in the same sense, according to the first existence of a creature. Yet since the unrighteous lack the second perfection of these things, we can only say that the righteous and the unrighteous "have" them in different senses. According to the argument so far, the unrighteous man has lost all these goods, in their second perfection, and so is without that most perfect way of "having," the evangelical way that springs from love. Just as a righteous man who has civil right in some instrument or other good of fortune, but cannot make use of it, lacks it; so an unrighteous man lacks whatever he may have had, since he does not make use of his possessions, whatever they may be, but abuses them. Jerome's observation is apposite and philosophically precise: "A miser lacks what he has as much as what he has not" (*Epistle* 53.11). In the objector's argument at the beginning, the fact that the unrighteous has natural goods in the same sense as the righteous, clearly does not license the conclusion that the unrighteous is a lord in the same sense as the righteous is. The term "lordship" refers quite precisely to the second perfection founded in grace. The unrighteous man lacks that perfection, and so lacks true lordship. Whenever such a one is said to have lordship, or kingship, over some good outside himself, what is meant is that he improperly lays false and pretended claim to such a lordship.

ch. 4. [7d] Not many of those worldly compromisers who are happy to accept human right as commonly recognized agree with this; so we must prove that neither the testimony of witnesses, nor the decision of a judge, nor actual possession, nor hereditary descent, nor exchange, nor donation, nor all of them together, can confer on someone without grace either lordship or right in respect of any thing.

As to the first of these, the implication is that the duty of witnesses is to attest a true right that is not apparent. If there is no such true right, the witnesses' testimony will certainly be false, and since the false cannot prove the true, and the nonexistent cannot bring anything to existence, the plain conclusion is that witnesses' testimony confers no right, but only, supposing it is true, brings to light the right that was already there. [. . .]

Confirmation: God cannot be neutral in respect of such a testimony or judgment; for he anticipates every creature in every creaturely act, so that whenever a witness or a judge testifies or pronounces, God testifies and pronounces on that same point first. If testimony or judgment is the ground of a right, the testimony and pronouncement of the Creator is much more so. Since, then, the right is conferred first in God, and we cannot imagine that the full right is in any need of human supplement, it is clear that prior to any right a human court may award, the beneficiary of that award has full right in respect of God. In judicial processes where right is done, the earthly judges are evidently mere instruments to promulgate God's decision; and their pronouncement adds to and subtracts nothing from the litigant's right. Since, then, God could not testify or pronounce in favor of someone's right unless it were right he should have it, it is evident that a man acquires no right from testimony of witnesses unless he is *in* the right. The structure of the argument is this: human investigation confers nothing apart from God who confers the right. But

God confers no right on the unrighteous; so no creature can give judgment for the unrighteous rightly.

ch. 6. [14c] We confront the objection that in fact God has done so [entrusted his goods to unworthy stewards], since tyrants abound in riches, as Job 12:6 says, "The tents of the robbers abound," and Jeremiah 12:1: "Righteous art thou, O Lord, when I complain to thee; yet I would plead my case before thee. Why does the way of the wicked prosper? Why do all who are treacherous and behave unjustly thrive?" The answer is apparent from what we have said: God permits the unrighteous to abound in riches, which they "have" in a qualified sense, not for their benefit but for their damnation. Secondly, it is clear that two false suppositions lie behind Jeremiah's question. In the first place, Hosea 8:4 says: "They have become kings, but not through me." Which means, tyrants have only a defective use of their goods; their abusive treatment of them is unauthorized. In the second place, God grants the righteous the goods which he permits the unrighteous to give up to abuse, as in the text quoted above, Matthew 25:28: "Take the talent from him, and give it to him who has the ten talents. For to everyone who has will more be given, and he will have abundance." To resolve the question we should note that every righteous person "predestined" to endure to the end has these temporal goods in a higher way than the unrighteous who is merely "foreknown." The latter has them only in a qualified sense, making bad use of them to his own harm. Even if no sensual appetite is engaged, there is a growing and unassuageable anxiety about them until at the moment of death, with great sorrow, he is deprived of them, thenceforth to be forever tormented for his misuse and deceptive pleasure. [. . .]

[15b] It is objected: it would be better for God simply to remove a sinner's goods physically, just as, supposing that one lends a sword to someone of sound mind who then falls into a frenzy and misuses the sword, one should recover it if possible. It is obvious that it would be inappropriate to attribute such a response to God. In the first place, God would thereby compel a man to virtuous conduct, instead of leaving him free. In the second place, as soon as anyone committed a sin of thought, he would be deprived unceremoniously of every good of sense, and consequently exposed to everyone he met, which would be savage cruelty on God's part. Indeed, on reflection, his annihilation must ensue; so the removal of his goods in punishment would be of no help to him. For since the first purchase of sin is upon the power of will, it would clearly be appropriate, following that principle, to remove the power of will first, whatever else was removed; and if that were left in place, the liability to sin would remain, and when God reacted cruelly there would be occasion for blasphemy; since it would neither be reasonable nor inconsequential in God to remove a power that had less to do with sinful action and preserve one which had more. So, since the accidental cannot exist without the essential, it is clear that on that principle all unrighteousness must lead to annihilation. In the third place, it would not be appropriate because God, as provident ruler of his universe, must, from his intrinsic character, take pity upon sinners: depriving them of right and lordship, but preserving their natural being and permitting such abuse as may escape notice and cause no perceptible offense to the neighbor. So we, who have no direct experience of it from creation, may know his almighty power and infinite good-

ness most chiefly by his showing mercy and pity. For were he not of infinite goodness and power, he could not *both* preserve the natural constitution of sinners *and,* by means of fitting punishment to which that nature is subject, preserve the law condemning sin which estranges it so far from virtue. His infinite goodness and power allow him to take occasion of sin to perfect his world. It affords us an example, thirdly, of how we in our turn should have compassion on our enemies, not causing scandal by a disruptive struggle, but laying our cause, as befits brotherly love, in the Judge's hand (cf. *Divine Commands* 2). And so it is evident that the law and God's mode of giving remain unimpeachable from all sides.

ch. 18. [40c] On this basis we reach a clear distinction between natural, or evangelical, lordship and civil lordship. Natural lordship is instituted by God and rests on the primary ground of justice. It allows for any number of people to share wealth on equal terms, but not for lordship to be alienated without injustice. Civil lordship is occasioned by sin and of human institution. It is not capable of being shared or communicated, either with one other person or with more than one on equal terms, but it may without injustice be alienated. [After discussing the first of this pair of definitions, Wyclif addresses the second.]

Lordship, as such, implies the claim to property in a possession, and property, as such, implies the claim to lordship without communication on equal terms. So Augustine (*Epistle* 185.9.35) makes the distinction between divine and civil lordship on this basis: the one is communicable, the other incommunicable. God's lordship, as an aspect of its perfection, has the property of communicability. He then adds, of human (i.e., civil) lordship: "What miser wants someone to share his wealth? What power-hungry aspirant or power-crazed potentate looks around for a partner?" I have added the words "on equal terms" to explain this, since we all know that in natural and civil lordship alike you may have a principal lord with many subordinate lords, as when a king and a prince, a baron and a knight are all lords of the same estate, but at different levels. The last part of the definition is also notorious. It is accepted as a regular thing in public life that a civil lord may rid himself of civil lordship by donation, sale, or transferal of other kinds; and such a thing is not *ipso facto* unjust. So much for the proofs of the two definitions.

But this could be taken to support the view that civil lordship, as such, is tainted with wickedness, especially as Augustine, in the quotation above, associates greed and arrogance with civil lordship, and says elsewhere (*Epistle* 153.26 [see above, p. 130]) that civil law does not make us use goods well, but limits the damage when we use them badly. Obviously, if the civil law is unjust, so are the powers that it assigns to lords. On this point I have frequently wondered whether Aristotle's tenth predicate, which he calls "having," is solely of human construction or whether, like the other types, it is a permanent feature of the order of nature. I have concluded that, as the other predicates are given in nature independently of human art, so is the tenth. Neither logicians nor metaphysicians need to go begging first principles from human art! So "having," the tenth type of predicate, is grounded in natural dominion; and we must conclude from this that the justice of civil laws depends on their identifying true rights or laws. Aristotle, of course, failed to take the state of innocence and the Fall into consideration. Introduce the Fall of the human race and its

blind proclivity to rely on sensory goods, and there was need for human laws and ordinances to ensure that fallen men should not appropriate whatever quantity of the
goods of fortune to which the inclination of their wills, heedless of obligation,
should prompt them.

To be sure, if the whole human race observed the rule of charity entirely, there
would be no need to rely on such laws. The further the human race is distanced from
the law of nature or the Gospel law, the more scrupulously it is driven to rely upon
these others. So much so that it can even happen that a people, fed upon poison, as it
were, comes to accept as canons of justice those human traditions alone, renouncing
the laws of nature and the Gospel as unnecessary. What, then, is civil or human law
in its aspect as a form of justice? It is the law which contains the appropriate orders
to secure temporal resources for the welfare of the state, to restrain willful attempts
to overthrow it, and to administer them farsightedly in times of scarcity.

To achieve these three ends a civil lord must have from the community a property to care for; but if a number of persons are joined together in this responsibility,
then it is the community of those people as a whole, not any part of that community,
which is proprietary lord of the goods belonging to it, as happens with colleges. Laymen can say what civil lords can truly say, "This is my own"; but collegial lords can say
only "This is ours," or "this is mine in common." What, then, do purely natural or
evangelical lords, who follow the path of perfection, say? More truly and more scripturally than either of the others: "All this world's goods belong to every member of our
order; yet we have no civil property, whether as our own or in common." This is how I
understand the claims of the Venerable Order of Friars Minor, who, in respect of civil
responsibilities, are "as having nothing, and yet possessing everything" (2 Cor. 6:10).

This provides the proof of the assertion above, that since civil life is nothing
but an onerous duty, it can be discharged without prejudice to charity. As Augustine
says (*Sermo de disciplina Christiana* 8): "What else does it mean to say, 'I am rich' or
'I am poor', but 'I am weighed down' and 'I am unburdened'?" If I am not mistaken,
the layman has no civil right over his temporalities beyond the limits of the three
functions of reasonable security, defense, and distribution. Civil security would not
be possible without proprietory right; and this is the ground for the civil lord's
power to transfer his property by donating it in the Lord's name, selling it, lending it,
bequeathing it, and by other such reasonable means. He may also expend his goods
on his own uses without consulting his earthly lord, and may deny another, within
the bounds of reason, any use that is a hindrance to his own use. This, of course, is a
cloak of justice under which have lurked worldly arrogance, hunger for power, and
numerous tyrannical exactions. And this is Augustine's understanding of civil laws,
that, for the most part, they are shot through with wickedness.

For it does not follow that because the whole people wants Peter to have civil
lordship, his lordship must be just. Indeed, the popular consent to someone's having
civil lordship, though it may have made his tenure less sinful, could never have been
just in the first place unless this one condition had been met: that the person who
was to be lord was accepted for that duty by God. By the same token, of the principles of civil law on hereditary succession and mutual exchange of worldly goods,
only those that were elements of natural law could be either just or true.

bk. 2 ch. 15. [219d] The protests which my view has excited are directed, for the greater part, at my treatment of those who have material wealth. My view implies, it is said, that they are mere trustees, and so abolishes all notions of property, hereditary succession, and civil lordship, as suggested by Luke 14 [probably 14:12f., 26]. Indeed, the senior clergy of the church would be deprived of their powers of legislation and jurisdiction — a seemingly irrational conclusion, which would leave the leaders of the church living in tribulation and wretchedness.

To the first point I reply: — The Kingdom of Christ and the law of Christ is no impediment to civil lordship, in its perfected form, nor to any good law (on which see below). But it reorientates the conduct of civil lordship, so that those who exercise it serve God and the church in love. Yes, we should agree, I think, that all those who are wealthy (in the true sense) in this world are God's financial agents and trustees of their mother, the church. This designation, which is not dishonorable, belongs to those who are active in the administration and distribution of the church's wealth. They must have a higher regard for their mother, the church, than for their physical offspring or for themselves (cf. bk. 1 ch. 23).

And so they may have *civil property,* though (1) not "property" in the sense that excludes the obligation to communicate with any brother who may be in need, which would be inconsistent with charity. Nor (2) may their civil property stand in the way of a willingness to abandon temporal occupations if they were not required by the evil times and compelled by obedience to the head of the church. So (3) civil lords in the true sense would not take on unnecessary burdens with legal responsibilities. That would be a different style of wealth from what is usual now! There would be no attempt to impose exactions on a part of the church, no acquisition of wealth for themselves or their families, unless they believed in conscience that this could benefit the church blamelessly.

It is clear that *hereditary succession* is compatible with the law of Christ, but one who acquires it must put on with it the vesture of charity. The heir who had reason to believe that someone else would do more good to the church than he by occupying his estate, would arrange this, or at least gladly allow it. Otherwise, by loving his possessions more than Christ, who is one with the church, he would unfit himself to have Christ as his savior. "Whoever loves son or daughter more than me, is not worthy of me" (Matt. 10:37).

In this modified understanding *civil lordship* is clearly compatible with the evangelical law, which reorients it and reorients the civil law with it. In the common and more notorious usage, however, the term means, in effect or simply, lust for lordship or an inordinate situation of lordship. And so Christ says (Matt. 19:23, 26), "With men . . . it is impossible for a rich man to enter the kingdom of heaven." In this sense all civil dominion is tainted with greed. I have elsewhere, however, defined civil lordship simply as the "proprietorship held over goods of fortune wholly under human laws by a pilgrim leading the active life, which arises when the acquisition, defense, and exchange of goods is unambiguously within the terms of human right, and so carries the sanction of personal constraint."

ch. 16. [231a] So the second reply to our position is this: secular laws and courts are justified in reaching verdicts on the basis of the appearances established by the legal trial. One must presume parties innocent *(iustos),* since innocent is what they ought to be, and the contrary has not been proven. Otherwise courts could not proceed, since to know who is worthy absolutely is the prerogative of him who "tries the reins and the heart" (Jer. 11:20). This seems to be the conclusion, so far as the law is concerned, of the Lord Bishop of Armagh (Richard FitzRalph, *De pauperie salvatoris* 4.6) who also asserts (4.7) that invincible ignorance excuses a judge. But I argue against this: it is impossible for two contradictory judgments both to be right, yet this would be possible in principle if invincible ignorance excused a secular judge. So the reply is undermined. [. . .] Nor will it do to say that even though the verdict is wrong, the *judge's act of giving judgment* is right, so that a righteous man does right in performing a generically bad action, and an unrighteous man does wrong. That resolution seems to be false; for the verdict must be precisely as lawful and right as the act of judgment is. When the judgment is unjust, it should not be given; for in matters so ambiguous nobody should rush in, contrary to Christ's counsel and his own refusal to judge, and expose himself to judgment where he ought probably to hold back, in case he should wrong both parties.

(C) GOSPEL LAW AND HUMAN LAW

From *Civil Lordship*

bk. 1 ch. 17. [38c] To explain this matter further, there are three points of uncertainty which need a more extensive treatment. *First,* it would appear that since all goods should be common, all human legal constitutions *(iura)* are unnecessary. *Second,* it would seem that civil possession is ruled out by the evangelical law; or alternatively, if it is allowed, it is forbidden to engage in lawsuits or battle for the goods of nature or fortune, and consequently for any reason at all. *Thirdly,* it would seem that there exists, as a measure against offense of every kind within the church militant, an office holding final power of compulsion over those who reject God's laws.

To resolve the first point I make two assumptions: — *(a)* There is one law instituted by Christ to rule the church, that of the Old and New Testaments. (This is a matter of faith, and has been argued for in the introductory treatise [of the *Summa = Divine Commands*] ch. 7.) *(b)* Everything ought to be in common. (This was assumed in the first syllogism, and is proved by what was said in ch. 14 above.) From these two assumptions the following syllogism proceeds: — Someone who is all-powerful, all-knowing, and all-benevolent orders nothing imperfectly. (The work of redemption is no less perfect than the work of creation, see ch. 10 above.) But Christ undertook to establish the law anew (from *a*). It follows, then, that he perfected it. The conclusion is confirmed by the Savior's own words: "I have not come to abolish the law but to complete it" (Matt. 5:17, expounded in *Divine Commands* 6). If, then, that is what he came to do, that is certainly what he did.

Again, Christ is the supreme doctor of the human soul (a matter of faith); but he would not treat the soul, his beloved bride, quite rightly, if he left her on earth and liable to moral sickness without leaving behind one law sufficient to ensure her health; therefore he must have left such a law. But with the perfect direction of the soul, the body, too, and all the goods of fortune befalling it are accounted for. So he left a law sufficient for the regulation of both body and soul and of whatever goods of fortune might befall. The minor premise is proved: government of the body and the goods belonging to it follows consequentially on government of the soul, just as lordship of the goods of nature and fortune follows consequentially on lordship of the goods of grace. [. . .]

[38d] Again, if a human being can improve upon Christ's law by adding to it, since such addition would have the character of a formal complement, it would follow that the most perfect promulgation of Christ's law could be achieved by papal ordinances. But that conclusion is impossible, since it is more possible for heaven and earth to pass away than for one iota or one dot to be removed from the law of Christ (see *Divine Commands* 6, discussing Matt. 5:18). The following argument confirms this: Any law added to the Gospel law is either implied by it, unrelated to it, or contradictory to it. If it is implied by it, then it is not a new law that one declares; it is simple exposition, like that of the glossators. If the added law is contradictory to it, then beyond question it is "unjust," the term used in Isaiah 10:1, "Woe betide those who enact unjust laws!" If it is unrelated, it is added to supplement a Gospel law that is simply incomplete; and since moderns are, as they say, "valued when they don't go wrong," the value we must set on *that* law makes it seem that human beings, in finishing off Christ's law, are actually promulgating a more perfect law than Christ's. To avoid misunderstanding that could arise from the wide reference of the term "law," I should say that I understand by "Gospel law" the law expounded by Christ in the course of his pilgrimage on earth to meet the need of the church militant for government. On this basis it seems simple blasphemy to say that that law of Christ is not enough for us, but needs new additions from human sources.

ch. 44. [142a] Let us hear no more of the objection that "human laws are more effective in maintaining the peace of the church since they order the death of whoever disturbs the state, which the law of Christ by itself would not do." What we have said is enough to show that any *just* laws ordering death are the *Gospel* law. So in Matthew 18:6 Christ agreed, "it would be better for (one who causes scandal) to have a millstone hung round his neck and be drowned in the depths of the sea" — which demonstrates that Christ allows capital punishment for the sin of scandal, though administered with mildness. But let us not make it a cause of reproach against our Lawgiver, that he does not burden his disciples with the obligations of an executioner but, much more agreeably, with the duty of loving correction, indicating that that other responsibility rests upon secular rulers at the church's behest. Fraternal correction is honest, it is just, and it is carried out universally, easily, and by proper authority.

bk. 2 ch. 13. [Wyclif has argued that the law of Christ is the standard of government in the church, and that the law of charity rules all relations between men;

he now confronts objections.] [208b] The second deceitful opinion claims that it is no more than a counsel that we should endure injustice in this way, and is binding only upon moral heroes such as the saints who have been canonized by the church. It is enough to preserve common charity — and safer, indeed, than to attempt the higher reaches of morality — and so such counsels have no binding force upon ordinary men and women. Here is a "little fox" (cf. Cant. 2:15) that would soon put an end to Christ's religion! All the counsels would be obliterated, since anyone who did not want to obey them could say he was one of the weaker brethren to whom they did not apply. If Christ gives counsel to a Christian in any matter, he cannot be an unwise, unhelpful, or deceptive counselor, as is shown from Isaiah 9:6 where the "Counselor" is the "Mighty God." It is clear, then, that whoever receives his counsel, considering no less the reverence due to the counselor than the value of the counsel, must not dismiss it lightly but take care to perform it. It follows that each one of Christ's counsels binds each person addressed by it, since he must accept it and, accepting it, take care to perform it with all diligence. Otherwise, by setting the counsel of God at nought, he would incur the indignation of the Counselor and the punishment of condemnation which attaches to a failure in performance. Alternatively, he could be seen as a case of indolent negligence, receiving the grace of God in vain and resisting the Holy Spirit, like those in Acts 7:51.

Again, every Christian on his pilgrimage ought to be serving God more completely and more perfectly than in fact he does, since no one serves God in every last detail, as he ought. As it says in 1 John 1:8, "If we say that we have no sin, we deceive ourselves, and the truth is not in us"; and in James 3:2, "All of us go wrong again and again." But the counselor of whom we speak cannot make the mistake of counseling us to render God some greater and more perfect service than is actually our duty; what he counsels, then, can only be a service which it would be at least a venial fault to omit. For if his counsel were sheerly impossible, it would be pointless; and if his counsel were to render service that lay beyond our duty but was not impossible, it would be unreasonable to perform it, and so his counsel, too, would be unreasonable, implying that God was greedy in demanding what was due to him. It is clearly impossible, then, for God to counsel a greater service than we owe him, since it is our duty "to love God with all your heart and with all your mind and with all your strength" for the much greater benefits we have already received. Since, therefore, any service that God counsels is owed him, and more, it is clear that he cannot counsel us to do anything without its being our duty to obey. [. . .]

We must observe, then, what the difference is between a precept and an evangelical counsel, in so far as they are opposed to each other. A precept is a *general* teaching given by God which binds every one all the time under pain of *mortal* sin in respect of each and every fall from it. The blessed who offend temporarily in the course of their pilgrimage are mortal sinners for that space of time; while the damned, for their everlasting offense, are everlastingly sinners in hell. A counsel is a *particular* teaching of God, binding solely under pain of *venial* sin and for the period of the pilgrimage. Which is why the theologians say that a precept is for the immature, imposing duties upon them like slaves; a counsel, however, is for the perfect, which confers no further duty (sc. of a general and lasting kind) on pain of mortal sin, but counsels them as friends to avoid the occasion of sin. So if a saint falls into mortal sin for want of gratitude to God when he is offered counsel, the sin lies in the offense against the first commandment, not in the failure to observe God's counsel.

From *The King's Office*

ch. 7. [40b] Blessed Augustine says that a writing which falls short of truth in the slightest regard is suspect throughout (*Letter* 40.3). So it makes no difference that the civil law may contain a great deal of catholic teaching, even teaching on the Trinity and the catholic faith; for the devil himself sows truths among his lies. Augustine has said that whatever truth there is, is in Holy Scripture (*De doctrina Christiana* 2.42.63); one would suppose, then, that water drawn from that source would taste more wholesome. Which of these two, I ask you, makes the better argument? "Caesar said it, so it is true" or, "The Lord said it, so it is true"? How would it not strengthen the Faith to have the whole responsibility for investigating and pronouncing on the purity of Catholic truth located in the theological faculty? Again, it is a serious offense knowingly not to remove errors when one could do so. It is also an offense not to choose the easier and safer way. But the civil law contains many errors, e.g., permitting usury and prostitution in cities, failing to maintain evangelical standards of righteousness in property-acquisitions, lawsuits, and civic relationships. What need is there, then, for the practice of civil law in the papal dominions, when the other law is quite sufficient and the pope is quite as capable of banning civil law from other kingdoms as from the French?

Since, then, Christ's own law is the easier, more sufficient, and safer way, a Christian would seem to be obliged to attend to it alone, and to have nothing to do with canon law either. For when you take away the theological material from canon law, what you have left is simply civil law. Papal Letters or Decretals hardly provide an adequate foundation for such an extraordinary faculty, of which the chief element, the penitential canons which priests are required to know, has been suspended. Nor was it ever valid to base a general law upon a series of particular judgments of this kind, however just those judgments were. Most canon lawyers fail to see the weakness in argument by analogy.

To sum up my opinions on this discussion: — *First*, the clergy should respectfully accept the civil laws of secular princes to the extent that they are consonant with Holy Scripture; where they are not consonant with God's law, they should take discreet steps to abolish them. (See *Decretum* D. 9, and Daniel ch. 3, dealing with Nebuchadnezzar's law.) *Second*, if the pope's law sounds contradictory to God's law, or to the just laws of secular princes, the remainder of the church should take steps to abolish it. For error entrenched in papal law presents the greater danger, leading the church's own legislators into blasphemy and harm to the church, and so requires all the more attention to its eradication. There are some who are mad enough to claim that the pope may provide legitimate dispensation from the authority of the apostles and the Gospels, and so even from God's authority; *a fortiori*, then, from that of secular princes. This lunacy I have rebutted elsewhere. It is refuted from the decretal of Pope Fabian (*Decretum* C. xi.3.95), in which, fearing God Almighty, he refuses to do anything at all against the apostles, the prophets, or the institutions of the Holy Fathers. We need theologians, then, who will interpret these things sensibly. *Third,* if there is anywhere in the world in which civil law, canon law, or ritual law of any kind provides a distraction, or even a mere impediment, to the knowledge of theology, the two arms of the church (lay and clerical) should combine to repeal them. One should note, however, that, just as contemplation, prayer, and any other good work may from time to time assist our theological learning, so, too, the study and practice of the civil law may assist and encourage it; otherwise, indeed, it would be altogether disallowed. So that if a student is convinced that the study or practice of civil law, in Paris or elsewhere, affords an opportunity to strengthen his understanding of theology, he ought in that case to bear the abuse that they call "excommunication" with untroubled mind.

(D) DISENDOWMENT OF THE CHURCH

From *Civil Lordship*

bk. 2 ch. 3. [Wyclif addresses objections by a Benedictine monk in Oxford.] [161c] We are commanded, the Brother tells us, in the New as well as in the Old Testament: "You shall not covet your neighbor's property, or his manservant, or his maidservant, or anything that is his" (Exod. 20:17, Deut. 5:21; cf. Rom. 7:7, 13:9). If the temporal lords were to confiscate the temporal goods of religious, not only (1) would they offend against the command not to covet their neighbor's property, but (2) they would actually commit theft and sacrilege. Here, too, the argument is too insubstantial even to attract the unlettered and uninstructed. The command in the Decalogue about not coveting the neighbor's property must be taken to mean *wrongful* desire for his goods. I may, and indeed should, desire that all my brother's goods be held in common between the two of us, as they are, indeed, to the extent that we live together in mutual love. On this understanding, then, secular lords must not covet the goods of the clergy wrongfully; but in the case we have so often described where it would be right for the lords to confiscate them, the charge fails on both counts. (1) In despoiling those who have broken the law of Christ — the monks, that is, who abuse their temporal goods, the temporal lords are bound to act in a state of grace and with the charity of fraternal correction, not in a ferment of greed. That is to say, they should distribute the goods to the poor, who have been ill-treated for too long by the greedy. Since all the goods of the world belong to the just, it is clear that the temporal lords would do right in distributing these goods once they have expropriated them. Any sinner forfeits body and soul, and consequently the lordship of all temporal goods; so if monks who are hardened in greed are despoiled of their tem-

502

poral goods, it is obviously only a matter of confiscating what they have taken wrongfully from others, however much it may appear in the eyes of the church that they are the true owners. (2) From this perspective it is clear, too, that no theft, sacrilege, or rapine is in question, as the very terms themselves demonstrate. The Brother should consider Exodus 12:35f., where the Lord instructed the people to "ask of the Egyptians vessels of silver and of gold, and much clothing." It goes on: "And the Lord had given the people favor *(gratia)* in the sight of the Egyptians, so that they let them have what they asked. Thus they despoiled the Egyptians." Are we to think that *this* "despoiling," with the approval of *this* Lord, is theft, or some kind of misappropriation? Augustine proves that it was not so: in the first place, the people were in a state of grace *(gratia)* when they despoiled the Egyptians, and so deserved to enjoy the Lord's goods; in the second place the people of Egypt were in unjust possession of those goods. [. . .]

ch. 10. [193a] What circumstances, then, would justify temporal lords in confiscating the movable and immovable property of a delinquent churchman? I reply: only when the abuse is habitual, for then it necessarily devolves into heresy. Suppose, for example, that he persistently makes the defense, in word or deed, that the church's prosperity consists primarily in accumulated goods of fortune — a doctrine contrary to Holy Scripture. Or suppose that he maintains in word or deed that a churchman's primary responsibility is to worldly society — something which is also contrary to Holy Scripture, since it implies a denial that God is to be the chief object of our love. Or suppose in the third place, less specifically, that by omission or commission he habitually corrupts the rest of Christ's church. In these instances it is simply heresy which makes the churchman liable to be deprived by the coercive power. [. . .]

Our opponent should consider the situation of the clergy in the light of what we have said about heresy in chapter 7, and take note of the opinions and conduct that prevail among the clergy today. He will conclude, if I am not mistaken, that the greater part of our clergy are worse than the holy apostles were on Holy Saturday, when they lost their faith [i.e., the day between the crucifixion and the resurrection of Christ]. It seems likely to me that Peter, John, and the other apostles had loved Christ more, had exposed themselves to greater danger for the sake of his law, and that the discredit they brought upon the Christian faith on that day was no worse than that incurred by us clergy in these days. Since it is generally accepted by theologians that the apostles were unfaithful on that day, and that the whole faith of the church subsisted in the Blessed Virgin, it is perfectly clear that the freeholding clergy may, as a whole, fall into infidelity and heresy together, and could in consequence be legitimately deprived of their temporal goods, as it would have been reasonable to deprive the apostles, had they had comparable endowments and been comparably entrenched in their infidelity or heresy. Heresy alone, then, is the ground on which the clergy may be deprived.

ch. 13. [204c] To reinforce the steps we have advanced so far and have yet to advance, one further inquiry is needed, whether a clergyman may sue for his goods in a court of law or engage in battle for temporalities. The argument against the first of these runs as follows: — Any churchman, but more especially those who are in the higher ranks of the church, ought to have done with every worldly anxiety; but to sue in this way for one's temporal goods is an extreme instance of secular anxiety; therefore high-ranking churchmen should have done with it. The major premise rests on Christ's teaching (Matt. 6:26), where, just before declaring that we cannot "serve God and Mammon," he forbids anxious care about food and clothing as an unnecessary distraction from the service of God. For God cannot consistently abandon his servant. The argument runs: — God does not abandon the birds or the terrestrial creatures, nor could he do so; how much less, then, could he abandon a rational creature who serves him as is due? That would imply that he was unappreciative; or at best that he was incapable or unaware. Nor can it be said that the management of the body is not a matter for divine providence, but is solely a human concern. No one can add one cubit to his stature; and stature must certainly be taken to include quantity, form, and other natural accidents which nature, and by implication God, has constituted. It is evidently blasphemous to say that God abandons his servant by being unaware or inattentive; in that case he would not be the infinite God, the Trinity. So Matthew 6:31 concludes, "Do not be anxious, saying 'What shall we eat?' or 'What shall we drink?' or 'What shall we wear?'" If, then, these larger concerns should cause us no anxiety, neither should modest ones that are less essential to us, such as prestigious freeholds.

From *The Truth of Holy Scripture*

ch. 25. All the evidence, then, leaves us with the supposition that the whole endowment of the church came from the alms of civil lords. The documentary records of our English kingdom preserve the memory of how the king and other founders gave the church such estates in pure and perpetual alms. From which we may infer that all clergy are beggars — not merely in relation to God like other men, but in relation to men, too. They would not be so quick to demand the alms of the poor if they were not in need of them! Nor should we blush at this or be proud beggars, when Christ — in his human nature — for our sake became a beggar (cf. 2 Cor. 8:9), i.e., devoting his poverty to the end that he might be relieved by the rich. Augustine speaks in this way in *De Trinitate* 15.11 (see my discussion of the three texts in *Civil Dominion* 3.8).

It is supposed, in the second place, that all lawful benefactors of the church endowed it for the lawful cause that clergy might perform the duty of priesthood with more freedom, competence, and effectiveness. Otherwise the endowment would not have been lawful nor charitable, but hurtful; and in consequence of the damage suffered by the church, the whole endowment would have been illicit and unjust. Which is why the saints and laws agree that the church was endowed that its priests might pray with more devotion, preach with more boldness, administer the goods of the poor with more justice, and celebrate the sacraments of the church, while retaining their primitive poverty. In these tasks they must surpass lay Christians, as is apparent from the *Decretum*. This is accepted by the Archdeacon (Gratian) as well known, as is evident in the argument that follows: "The clergy should surpass the laity in knowing how to teach, preach, perform ecclesiastical duties, and interpret the articles of faith with discernment" (D. 8.1.15); because, as the *Decretum* says, "It does serious damage to the church of Christ when the laity are worthier than the clergy" (C. 8.1.21). For then the clergy, who should be a model to the laity, put a brake upon the ministry of Christ.

From this there is a third conclusion to be reached: that secular lords who endow a church retain the civil lordship of their alms. [. . .]

On these three suppositions, it is easy to demonstrate the conclusion, which applies from the most insignificant bishop to the Roman pontiff. All goods with which the church is endowed are the charitable gifts of secular lords (1), which are given to clergy for the purpose of protecting primitive religion (2). Since, then, they retain the principal lordship of these gifts (3), it follows that when the purpose for which the secular endowments were made is essentially unrealizable, they should be reassigned to their private estates.

(E) POLITICAL AUTHORITY

From *Civil Lordship*

bk. 1 ch. 21. [Wyclif has listed three false principles alleged by certain teachers of divine law on the basis of human law: *(a)* one may do what one will with one's own; *(b)* the best title is conquest; *(c)* any method of hurting enemies is lawful.] [48a] In order to deal root and branch with the second principle asserted by the compromisers, we must settle a two-pronged plea advanced in its favor. It is suggested (1) that a title of conquest is valid, since the children of Israel occupying the promised land by this title at first, drove out seven nations (Josh. 1) and when they were violently deprived of that right, they used the force of arms to renew it, as we see in the books of Judges, Samuel, Kings, and Maccabees. Since this could not have happened if the conquest had not conferred a just title, it must be so. (2) All four kingdoms of which Daniel 2 speaks acquired a right to lordship by title of conquest. Had their right been null from the start, it could not have acquired validity by laying the foundation of a right to lordship later. In support of this it is said that the kingdom of England was conquered by Britons, Saxons, and Normans, and that we may not doubt that these conquests had a right, since that right brought forth a succession of mighty saints and canonized kings. The same can be said of other kingdoms.

I reply, as above, that this principle is a nest of heresy for men of arms, inculcating rapacious and predatory attacks against their weaker brethren. No catholic is free to question this, in view of the Scripture: "Woe to you, destroyer! Will you not yourself be destroyed?" (Isa. 33:1); "The violence of the wicked will sweep them away" (Prov. 21:7); and in his denunciation of the Pharisees, the Truth says: "You are full of extortion and rapacity!" (Matt. 23:25).

This is proved: (1) It all too easily happens that conquerors let the garment of charity slip; and if they have no charity, then what they are doing is simply seizing others' goods. So it comes about that conquerors seize others' goods without right, and so for all their conquering, seizing, and spoiling, they acquire absolutely no title in right to their spoil. The premise is demonstrated above in ch. 15, on the sixteen conditions of charity. For charity does not seek to hold property, nor does it contemplate doing harm to a brother from ambition for temporal goods. But the opposite is usually the case with a conqueror.

(2) The fact that one occupies goods which were previously unowned does not give one an absolute right to occupy them. *A fortiori* the fact that one occupies goods to which somebody previously had a right does not give one an absolute right to occupy them. The premise is demonstrated in ch. 5: were it not so, God would have had no right to expel our first parents from Paradise. The conclusion is demonstrated as follows: — Occupying goods which nobody owns without provocation or outrage is less discrepant with justice than seizing a just man's goods. If it were not so, there would be nothing left in this regard to which abuse of goods or injury of the neighbor might refer — a contradictory conclusion. [. . .]

[48d] Granted that conquest alone is not enough to ground a title of possession, we have to see what else is required. And it is clear that what is needed is charity in the conqueror, authorization by the Creator, and unlicensed intrusion on the part of the previous possessor. The first of these is demonstrated from the argument so far: without the title of charity nobody can be lord of anything. The second is demonstrated by the need for ratification, confirmation, and authorization by the Sovereign Lord for any creature to have anything, absolutely speaking. And the third is demonstrated by what was said in ch. 18 above about the transferal of a kingdom from a race on account of wrongs, injurious conduct, outrages, and various perfidy. For although an individual may sometimes be punished in the body as an example of patience, or to acquire merit, or to declare the glory of God, as in the case of Job and the man born blind; nevertheless, for the spoiling of a kingdom or a city to be justified, it must be presumed that the objects of the spoil had been misused. For if their right use had been maintained, the spoilers would have had no right to dispossess those whom they have despoiled. So Augustine writes, "We see that the extent of empire has been much increased by the wickedness of those outside it, whose offenses have licensed the waging of just war and the enlargement of the empire" (*City of God* 4.15).

ch. 27. [62d] It would be the best form of government for a people to be ruled solely through the law of God by judges. Within the constraints of our fallen state, the nearer a form of government comes to the state of innocence, the better and more wholly satisfactory it is. But this "aristocratic" form we have described [i.e., rule by judges] would be more like the state of innocence, and so more satisfactory. In the state of innocence itself there would be no law but natural law, no taxes or civil lordship, which are required by our state of imperfection in a monarchial form of civil government. This is shown from Christ's law, where the apostles are forbidden to be monarchs: "The kings of the Gentiles exercise lordship over them, and those in authority over them are called benefactors. But not so with you" (Luke 22:25f.). [. . .]

[63b] Again: — That was the form of government [i.e., by judges] that God first instituted for his people, criticizing the other form which was practiced by the gentiles. But God cannot be mistaken, and his ordinance should be taken by statesmen as a model. So that form of government is preferable to the gentile form. This premise is demonstrated by reference to the people of Israel from the time the Law was given (i.e., in Exod. 20). They were governed by judges according to God's laws until the time of Samuel, by which point the government of the people of God had passed through the hands of fourteen judges (see the books of Joshua, Judges, Ruth, and 1 Samuel). The second part of the premise is demonstrated from 1 Samuel 8:5-7 where the people address Samuel: "'Now appoint for us a king to govern us like all the nations.' But the thing displeased Samuel, when they said, 'Give us a king to govern us.' And Samuel prayed to the Lord. And the Lord said to Samuel, 'Hearken to the voice of the people in all that they say to you; for they have not rejected you, but they have rejected me from being king over them.'" Here is a straightforward criticism of the monarchical constitution. The reason for it is that a people that acknowledges an earthly lord or monarch is more likely to fix its hope in man; so that forgetting the religious worship in which the judge has instructed it, it becomes irreligious and impious, like the gentiles. That is said more directly in Hosea 13:9-11, where we read: "You cause your own destruction, O Israel. In me alone is your help. Where now is your king? Let him afford you a great deliverance in all your cities! Where are your judges, of whom you said, 'Give me a king and princes!'? I will give you a king in my anger. . . ." So it is shown that the form of government which God instituted is better than the gentile form, which the Jewish people incurred blame for insisting on.

It is an indication of this that in the period of the judges the Jews were very well governed. In the period of the kings they were governed less well, since in the reign of Jeconiah they were made captive for seventy years in Babylonia as a penalty for the sin of idolatry and the other sins which proliferated (see Jer. 52). But in the third period, that of priestly government, which lasted to the advent of Christ, they were governed worst of all. The sins of the chief priests in conspiring to put Christ to death were responsible for the worldwide captivity of the Jews to this very day — which was why Jesus wept (Luke 19:41). The undoubted cause of this was the adulteration of the law of the Lord at that time by Pharisaic tradition and Roman innovations. For at the time of our Savior the office of High Priest was offered by the Roman emperors for purchase, as is mentioned by Bede's gloss on Luke 3:2, "Under the High Priests Annas and Caiaphas the word of the Lord came upon John the son of Zachariah in the desert." [. . .]

From which we may reasonably conclude that the best thing for the catholic church would be to be governed purely and in accordance with Christ's rule by successors to the apostles who were devoid of avarice. A mixture of such a regime with the coercive lordship of secular potentates would be less good. But worst of all is the situation in which the church's prelates on the basis of their own traditions insinuate themselves into the business preoccupations of civil lordship.

[65a] The probable conclusion from the argument is that it is with forms of government as with states of life. Given the time and place, it is more expedient for

the church to concentrate upon the active life and leave off contemplation than to give itself wholly to speculation (see ch. 25). In the same way it is more expedient for the church, given the sinfulness of an unruly people which needs a harsher restraint to curb rebellion against God's law, that it should have kings to administer civil punishments than that there should only be apostolic rulers to handle such a situation, governing the people solely by evangelical law. However, as the active life achieves nothing of moral worth without the contemplative life to animate it, so human law and the king's office are of value only insofar as the evangelical law directs them — especially in restraining the acquisitive greed of kings and magnates from accepting inducements to obstruct the course of justice. It was for this that Saul and his successors were ejected from the throne of Israel (1 Sam. 15:26); and an appetite for such inducements to exonerate the guilty is no less serious a matter in royal counselors and ministers than it is in kings' own persons. Yet I know that it would be better absolutely for the whole church to be governed by the evangelical law alone, as it would be better that the people had no sin which required such an office, but observed the rule of charity entirely. In the same way it would be better absolutely that no one should be subject to a sentence of death; yet with so many cases meriting the extreme penalty, it is more expedient that there should be kings to impose it. From evil, therefore, comes the usefulness that kings of the earth and their laws possess.

ch. 30. [69c] Every contingent reality takes us back to some essential reality; and so from the contingent fact that there may be this or that entitlement to princely rule we must go back to examine the ground of princely rule as such. Aristotle (*Politics* 1288a15f.) expresses the view that the chief cause of civil kingship is conspicuous virtue in the king. That in itself is sufficient for evangelical kingship; and together with the consent of the people it is sufficient for civil kingship. We have said (ch. 21) that legal entitlement is not enough without the additional title of charity; and so, without doubt, neither are hereditary succession and popular election enough by themselves.

The point is demonstrated in the case of hereditary succession as follows. No creature can be a lord without entitlement by charity (ch. 22 above). But since the Fall the succession of generations always involves a breach in charity (as is proved by the fact that original sin obstructs charity). Since the Fall, therefore, no one has succeeded to a continuous lordship. So we must depend upon a different title for possessing lordship. In support of this argument, imagine Peter to be the eldest son of a king, both of whose parents have died; he is not yet baptized, which would entitle him under human law in Christendom to succeed his parents in the kingdom. Clearly, since Peter is an unbeliever in mortal sin, he has no true lordship; but even according to civil laws of doubtful validity, he will gain that lordship when he is baptized. By that act, then, he will acquire a true title; and since no other title that he presently lacks will serve, it must be the title of baptismal grace. This, then, is what he must acquire in addition to the line of natural succession which has been unaffected by his state of mortal sin. Since, then, the Christian church forbids him by civil law to exercise kingly rule within the church, any actual mortal sin must exclude lordship *a fortiori;* for original sin is the least of mortal sins, punished with the greatest mildness.

From this we conclude that every Christian king, knight, or civil lord of any kind owes more to his spiritual Father (his principal Lord by hereditary succession) than to his earthly father; for it is by the kingly rule of God that his right is revived through the grace of baptism. Without the new birth by which he is the adoptive son and heir of God, he cannot enter the Kingdom of Heaven (John 3:5); and so without the grace of baptism, strictly speaking, he cannot rightly enter upon any temporal lordship. Scripture, it seems to me, constantly implies this when it tells of many cases in which the second-born succeeded in place of the firstborn. It was not Adam's firstborn, Cain, but the later child, Seth, who was appointed to inherit the world in himself and his descendants. From his line Noah sprang, and all other lines were drowned in the flood (Gen. 7:23). Nor was Ishmael, the firstborn, bearer of the succession given to Abraham, but his younger son, Isaac (Gen. 17:19ff.); and similarly Jacob, Isaac's younger, displaced Esau (Gen. 27:37). So, too, it was Judah, not Reuben, Jacob's firstborn, from whom the Lord was descended.

From *The King's Office*

ch. 1. [4d] So God must have two representatives *(vicarii)* in his church, the king in temporal matters and the priest in spiritual. The king must restrain the disobedient with severity, as did the divine presence in the age of the Old Testament. The priest, however, acting in the age of grace, must exercise mildness in his ministry of God's command to the humble, as did the human person of Christ, at once both king and priest. So Augustine says that the king bears the image of God, the bishop the image of Christ [actually Ambrosiaster, *Quaestiones cxxvii veteris et novi testamenti* 35], speaking, that is, of their ministry. This is governed by apostolic rule about the grades of honor to be assigned to the members of the church (1 Cor. 11:3): "I want you to understand that the head of every man is Christ, the head of a woman is her husband, and the head of Christ is God." From these considerations it appears that it is right for Christ's representative *as* Christ to be ruled as head by Christ's representative as God.

Objection 1: The implication would seem to be that kingly power and dignity is higher than the priestly, which contradicts many laws and, indeed, my own opinion, often repeated.

Reply: In Christ kingly and priestly attributes, whether assigned to his divinity or to his humanity, have an equal dignity. This apart, the function of kingship is indeed superior to the function of priesthood. This is symbolically expressed in the person of Melchizedek, who, as the apostle says, was a type of Christ in his twofold dignity. But in Genesis 14:18 his royal title is given first, a form of speaking preserved by the apostle at Hebrews 7:1. For the function of kingship in Christ is the more general function, since his rule over his handiwork began first, extended more universally, and historically endured for longer than his blessings of salvation. And so Augustine says that the title of king has a certain priority of origin, or at least has a formal, representative appropriateness to God the Father. [. . .]

[5b] *Objection 2:* This means that we must honor evilly disposed kings. But any kind of honor, it would seem, is by its nature a recognition of virtue, as Aristotle says (*NE* 1123b35). Since evilly disposed unbelievers have no virtue, they deserve no honor, only contempt for their vicious character. Further, it seems that their dignity and power as kings is lost, since they have ceased to be true lords and so can no longer be kings either. How would they have an honorable standing when the only standing such supposed unbelievers can have is the worst and most abominable?

Reply: St. Peter says we must be subject to the evilly disposed (1 Pet. 2:18); there must, then, be some ground for the honor due to them, as St. Augustine says. I accept the first part of the objection, that honor can only be paid on the ground of some virtue. When we pay honor to rational creatures, or to their relics or images, our honor is due first to God, whose virtue it is to have brought all these things into being for the benefit of mankind. To avoid idolatry, the honor we pay to any creature at all, not the sun and moon only, must be solely on the ground that it is God's handiwork. [. . .]

Evilly disposed kings deserve honor in the first place because they are rational creatures in whom not only the traces *(vestigium)* but also the image *(ymago)* of the Trinity is visible, and in the second place because they have the power conferred on them by God to benefit his church and so render God effective service, however damnably they may abuse it. There are many reasons to honor God *in* them, and so to "honor" *them* in a different sense. For there is one kind of honor paid on the ground that it is appropriately deserved; the twofold honor paid to evil kings, however, is of another sort. It is clear how we are to interpret Augustine, Boethius, and other theologians when they say that in honoring someone on grounds that are not personal to him, it is not himself that one honors, but someone else in whom we discover that ground. So in praising someone we need to be clear about the ground of our praise, if we are not to lie. Lying, according to Chrysostom (*Opus imperfectum in Matthaeum,* of doubtful authorship), has no ground nor virtue. The same potentate who is detestable on the ground of his vice may at the same time be loved on the ground of his human nature and his position of responsibility. In the same way God, on different grounds, at one and the same time hates and loves his creatures.

But there is a further conclusion from points we have constantly made: — Such "kings" could remain kings only in a qualified sense; yet they possess the kingly power which they abuse, and so in reality possess the power and dignity consequent on the kingly position, though without deserving it. Tyrants destined to damnation, who are only kings and lords in a purely nominal sense, possess an *unformed power* for kingly and lordly rule, though that power is not actually lordship. They have, then, the standing of kingly power, and so many goods are bestowed through them, which are the grounds for our continuing to pay them honor representatively.

(F) SERVITUDE

From *Civil Lordship*

bk. 1 ch. 32. [75b] In this matter one point derived from the principles of Christ's law must be held beyond question: a Christian may rightly submit to servitude, and so another Christian may rightly demand of him that he do so. Three justifications for this principle can be inferred from Scripture: (i) to do penance for sins past; (ii) to acquire merit; (iii) to take precaution against vice. [. . .] As concerns masters *(domini)*, however, it is beyond question that they are required to act in charity, since otherwise they could not be lords of anything at all. And so they are required, in the second place, to love their slaves as themselves, since without the love of all there is no love for Christ (cf. Rom. 13:9f.). In the third place, then, they must not demand any service from their slaves other than that which will promote their own or some other person's merit; consequently, they must not keep them from due attendance at divine worship. From which we conclude that civil lordship over a brother is like conquest, and can scarcely be maintained without sin. For only a natural slave in need of restraint from his own stupidity, or one whose conduct is disorderly, in need of perfection to attain his reward, should, for this reason, be subjected to servitude by a master who acts in charity in pursuit of these goals. Wherefore Ephesians 6:9 says: "Masters, do the same to them, and forbear threatening, knowing that their Master, who is in heaven, sees, and that there is no partiality with God." From which it is clear that by the law of love masters ought to obey and faithfully serve their own servants — vast though the merriment of civil lawyers at the idea may be! [. . .]

    ch. 34. [79a] But there is a further question: are the civil laws about hereditary slavery consistent with the law of Christ? Apparently not. "The son shall not bear the iniquity of the father" (Ezek. 18:20, i.e., an offense against God), without iniquity on his own account as well. *A fortiori*, then, for an offense against another man he will not inherit liability from his father without some culpability of his own. But it is not universally the case that there is contributory personal guilt or responsibility on the part of slaves' children that makes them liable to civil servitude. So the law of hereditary slavery is tainted with injustice. Again: in line with what we proved in the last chapter, slavery on the ground of parentage could arise only from a legal right of the father to sell his offspring. But no such legal right exists; so hereditary slavery cannot rest on the ground of parentage as such. The minor premise is demonstrated by the argument that nobody has a legal right to sell what he does not possess. But a father who is a slave does not possess his children, whose status is superior to his own. Therefore he has no legal right to sell them, for property in them is denied him for his whole life. Even if we allow that they are still "his," his relation to them is not that of civil ownership, so how can a right of sale derive from it? There is, in fact, no civil ownership or possession of a child by a father. On the contrary, since the human person is of infinite worth, superior to any possible material consideration, it would seem that any sale of the vendor's self or children is disallowed in common law. Human traditions deem an exchange to be unlawful when one is defrauded into paying above the true value as determined by the mean; all the more so, then, when some petty price is given in exchange for a person, for whose redemption Christ did not disdain to give his life! [. . .]

In resolving this question this point is to be observed: it is neither sufficient nor even possible to make an ordinance of the form, "the descendant of a civil slave is himself a slave." Otherwise Christ himself would be a slave, for he descended from the tribe of Judah which as a whole was subjected to slavery in Egypt at the time of Moses, as Exodus 1 shows. And in that case God would have wronged the Egyptians in taking their slaves from them. And consequently God would not have been able to free his servants' own slaves from civil slavery, for if the succession of civil slavery ought to be maintained from generation to generation, he would have to maintain the relation of master and civil slave. Obviously, if children are as servile as their parents in physical constitution or level of civilization, as can often happen, then the civil lord is obliged to enslave a slave's child subject to the three conditions in chapter 21 above [sc. for right of conquest: charity in the conqueror, unworthiness of the conquered, divine authorization]. Otherwise he is not.

So the alleged claims of human ordinance are evidently inadequate in such a matter. There are three formal demonstrations of this: (1) If the temporal lord does not treat his slave as he would wish to be treated in similar circumstance, he lapses from charity, and so from civil lordship; but since "slave" and "master" are correlative terms, the slave *ipso facto* lapses from civil slavery. The purpose for which God introduced civil lordship was that there might be a power to compel rebellious slaves to observe Christ's law (cf. Luke 22:25, "The kings of the gentiles exercise lordship over them . . ."). To fail of this self-justifying purpose is to fail of lordship itself.

(2) Lordship subsists only to the extent that God accepts it as in keeping with divine law. But God accepts the civil lord's treatment of a slave only when it benefits the church, and therefore the slave himself. It is not fitting for a slave's child to be treated as a civil slave, therefore. Imagine that God disposes him to sacrifice to him "three days' journey into the desert," i.e., in formal religious penitence; then anyone who stood in his way would be no less a tyrant than Pharaoh with the children of Israel. Furthermore, the principle was clearly established above, that lords treat slaves with humility, knowing that it is by God's special favor that they have the power to exercise the responsibility over their slaves' lives in love. It follows they would not be conforming to the conditions of their office, which make them responsible to the supreme Lord for the diligent discharge of care. In truth, since this is a burden, they ought to want to be rid of it. [Demonstration (3) omitted.]

To the first objection [in favor of hereditary slavery] we reply: not everything over which one may give directions is subject to civil sale. This is clear in the case of virtues and mental acts. Heavenly and sublunary bodies are another example, with all their spiritual accidents. And the human body itself cannot legally be the object of a civil sale. Nothing is saleable unless the lordship can be transferred from vendor to purchaser for a price. This cannot lawfully happen with the human body, since no one can remain in a state of grace without being lord of his own body. A man may therefore make a sale or binding covenant with regard to the *labor* of his body, but not lawfully with regard to the body itself. Indeed, the irrationality of the attempt would itself incur a loss of lordship of one's body, and so one would end up trying to sell what one did not own! This is the sense in which Scripture describes the sinner as "sold under sin" (Rom. 7:14). But the appearance of lordship or exchange in such a sale is illusory; for the devil and sin have only *unrighteous* lordship over man, and the devil is only *supposititiously* "king" over all the children of pride and "prince" of the world. But in such a transaction the exchange is unjust on either side, and so the purchase or sale is void. There is, however, another kind of natural purchase, in which a creature buys lordship from God without a price, on the basis of his merit; and here the seller does not part with the lordship of the object of the sale, and the giver does not renounce the lordship of the gift. (Cf. Isa. 55:1: "Come buy wine and milk . . . without price.") There is a third kind of sale in which the substance is sold in its accidents, or it is pretended so: and in this sense Joseph and other slaves are said in Scripture to be "sold." [. . .]

It is lust for power *(libido dominandi)*, failure to observe divine law, and the blind credulity induced by civil princedom, that magnates should think it no less natural and right for all their slave's offspring to serve them and their offspring than for fire to burn.

Translation: Editors, from the Wyclif Society editions, ed. R. L. Poole, J. Loserth, F. D. Matthew, A. W. Pollard, and Charles Sayle (London, 1885-1922). The editors acknowledge gratefully the assistance of John Kilcullen in relation to the text and translation of *De civili dominio* 1.1-10.

Antonios IV

(Patriarch 1389-97)

By the end of the fourteenth century, the territory actually ruled by the Byzantine emperor was reduced to little more than the wedge of land at the eastern point of which stood Constantinople. South and east the city looked across the Bosporus to its former possessions in Asia Minor, now ruled by the Turks. The Turks sat on the western shore of the Aegean, too, leaving only two isolated areas of Greece in the emperor's hands. The historically Orthodox kingdoms of Serbia and Bulgaria wavered between a Greek and a Latin alliance. In these fragile circumstances, the wider network of religious influence that the church provided was of cardinal importance in maintaining the semblance of imperial leadership, as is illustrated by the relations between Constantinople and Russia. Politically, Russia was under the dominance of the Mongols, under whose overlordship power was divided between two major rivals, in the east the prince of Moscow, an Orthodox Christian, and in the west the grand duke of Lithuania, a pagan prince who in the fourteenth century accepted baptism from the Latin Church. Religious leadership lay with the metropolitan archbishop of Kiev, who, without changing his title, transferred his seat to Moscow early in the century. But appointment to the metropolitanate lay in the hands of the patriarch of Constantinople, and so, effectively, with the emperor, for whom the loyalty, and especially the financial contributions, of these rival vassals of the Mongol Khans was an urgent matter. In the fourteenth century emperors managed to offend both parties by a vacillating policy over whether there should be a second metropolitanate for western Russia, and which of the two should have the title of Kiev.

Meanwhile, the position of the emperor was understood to be a matter of faith for the Orthodox theological tradition. The famous letter from Patriarch Antonios to Basil I of Moscow (ca. 1394) illustrates the difficulty of this position. Even as he wrote, or shortly after, the Turks began an eight-year siege of Constantinople, which seemed to herald the end of the empire. The precise reason for the prince's formal

514

removal of Emperor Manuel II's name from the diptyches (i.e., the list of those commemorated in prayer at the Eucharist) is not clear, nor does it seem to have been a part of any consistent policy, for we hear no more about it. But in Constantinople it had frightening implications on both political and theological fronts.

Further Reading: J. Meyendorff, *Byzantium and the Rise of Russia* (Cambridge: Cambridge University Press, 1981); D. M. Nicol, *Church and Society in the Last Centuries of Byzantium* (Cambridge: Cambridge University Press, 1979); D. M. Nicol, *The End of the Byzantine Empire* (London: Edward Arnold, 1979).

From *Letter* 447

Furthermore, I hear of words spoken by Your Excellency about my mighty and sacred sovereign and emperor *(basileus)* which cause me grief. They tell me that you prevent the metropolitan from commemorating the holy name of the emperor in the diptyches, something that cannot happen; and that you say, "We have a church, but no emperor; nor do we count on having one," which is quite wrong.

The holy emperor has a great position in the church: he is not as other rulers and local princes are; and this is because the emperors, from the beginning, established and reinforced true religion in all the inhabited world; they convoked the ecumenical councils; and everything declared in the divine and holy canons about true doctrine and the government of Christian people they confirmed and gave legal force to; they struggled hard against heresies; and imperial decrees, together with the councils, defined the metropolitan sees of primates, the division of their provinces and their boundary lines. Which is why the emperors have a most honorable position in the church, even if God has allowed the nations [the Turks] to encircle the emperor's seat of government. Yet still today the emperor receives the same coronation from the church; he occupies the same position and is prayed for in the same terms: he is anointed with the solemn myrrh; he is crowned king *(basileus)* and sovereign of the Romans, i.e., of all Christians; and his name is commemorated by all patriarchs, metropolitans, and bishops in every place where the name of Christian is professed. No other ruler or local prince ever has this privilege. Such is his universal authority that even the Latins, who have no communion with our church, afford him the same honor and reverence as they used to of old when they were united with us. How much more, then, should Orthodox Christians treat him so!

The pagans have encircled the emperor's seat, but that is no reason for Christians to despise him. They should find it a matter of instruction and sober reflection that if the great emperor, the universal lord and ruler, clothed with so much power, has run into such straits, other local princes with limited jurisdiction and fewer subjects are likely to suffer worse. Indeed, Your Excellency and the territories belonging to you suffer frequently from siege and captivity inflicted at the hand of the irreligious — yet it would hardly be fair of us to think less of Your Excellency, but both our Insignificance and the holy emperor himself write to you in the style of ancient tradition, according you the same honor in our letters, documents, and messages that the great kings of Muscovy had before you.

My son, you are wrong to say, "We have a church, but not an emperor." It is not possible for Christians to have a church and not an emperor. Church and empire are entirely one and interwoven, and cannot be separated. The only emperors Christians reject are heretics who have attacked the church and introduced perverted dogmas which depart from apostolic and patristic teaching. My great and holy sovereign by the grace of God is most orthodox and faithful, the champion, defender, and avenger of the church. It is not possible that there should be a primate who does not commemorate his name.

Hear what the prince of the apostles, Peter, says, in the first of his general epistles: "Fear God, honor the king *(basileus)*" (1 Pet. 2:17). He did not say "kings," which might be taken to mean those who are variously called kings among the nations. He said "the king" to indicate that there is but one catholic king. And who is that? At that time it was a pagan, who persecuted Christians; but the holy apostle foresaw that Christians would in the future have one king, and so instructed them to honor the pagan emperor *(basileus)*, that they might learn how to honor the religious and orthodox emperor. And if other Christians have styled themselves "emperor" [i.e., the Western emperor], it is all unnatural and irregular, the result of tyranny and violence. What fathers, councils, or canons had anything to say about those? High and low they proclaim the natural emperor, whose legislation, ordinances, and commands are accepted throughout the inhabited world. He alone, and no one else, is commemorated in prayer by Christians everywhere.

Translation: Editors, from *Acta et Diplomata Graeca Medii Aevi*, ed. Mikolsich and Müller, vol. 2 (Athens: Spanos, 1961).

Jean Gerson

(1363-1429)

Mystical and spiritual theologian, philosopher, statesman, university administrator, and leading conciliarist churchman, Jean Gerson (Charlier) was a dominating figure in the landscape of the early fifteenth century. As with other outstanding late medieval thinkers, his ideas remained a shaping force for several centuries, largely owing to their exposition by the eminent Sorbonist theologians, Jacques Almain (ca. 1480-1515) and John Mair (Major) (ca. 1468-1550). They presented a fruitful blend of nominalist, naturalist, trinitarian, and realist elements, formed under the influences of Ockham and Aristotle mediated by the nominalist Pierre d'Ailly, and of Augustine and Pseudo-Dionysius mediated by Bonaventure and the Victorines. All these elements entered into the ecclesiological and political formulations developed by Gerson in response to the crisis of the Great Schism and the urgency of church reform.

He began his lifelong association with the University of Paris in 1377 as a member of the College of Navarre, coming under the tutelage of d'Ailly, who was to be a lasting friend. While working on his doctorate (1381-94), he enjoyed the distinction of preaching at the royal court and serving as almoner to the duke of Burgundy. In 1395 he succeeded d'Ailly as chancellor of the university, retaining the post *in absentia* after 1415, until his death.

His strategic post obliged him to embark on diplomatic missions to end the papal schism. He traveled to Avignon in 1403-4, to Marseilles and Rome in 1407 for negotiations with the rival popes, Benedict XIII and Gregory XII. The failure of negotiation to bring about the desired abdication of both popes converted him to the conciliar solution of the crisis, which he had previously been reluctant to endorse. In a series of tracts, including *On the Authority of the Council (De auctoritate concilii)* and *On the Unity of the Church (De unitate ecclesiae)*, he strongly defended the convocation of the Council of Pisa in 1409, which deposed the two papal rivals and elected Alexander V. However, the persisting recalcitrance of the "deposed" popes, together with the new pope's deeply incensing the university by promoting mendicant privileges, prompted Gerson to call for a second council. When Alexander's successor, John XXIII, under pressure from the emperor Sigismund, convoked the Council of Constance late in 1414, he attended as representative of the French monarch, the university, and the ecclesiastical province of Sens (Pascoe 1973, 10).

Along with d'Ailly, Gerson played a leading role in the council's two-year pursuit of a resolution. When John fled Constance after the council refused to confirm his title, Gerson preached a celebrated sermon addressing the confusion elicited by the pope's departure, urging the council to press on unwaveringly with the work of unification to which it was called by the Holy Spirit of Christ, the church's one divine head. The ecclesiology of the sermon was reflected in the famous decree *Haec sancta synodus* (1415), which based the jurisdictional supremacy of the general council in matters of faith, reform, and the extirpation of schism on power held "immediately from Christ" by virtue of its representing the "Catholic church." Before the council's successful completion of its mission in the deposition of John and Benedict, the abdication of Gregory, and the election of Martin V, Gerson had produced two further definitive statements of conciliar responsibility and authority: *On the Church's Deposition of the Pope (De auferibilitate Papae ab ecclesia)* and *On Church Power (De potestate ecclesiae)*. The latter work in particular contributed to the emerging view of the universal council, invested with the power of the mystical corporate whole, as not merely a latent potency to be exercised in rare emergencies but as an ongoing regulative, advisory, and disciplinary right. This view was reflected in the demand of the decree *Frequens* (1417) for papal convocation of general councils at regular, stipulated intervals.

Gerson made only a minor contribution to the labors of administrative reform, partly owing to his heavy involvement in the condemnation of heresies — those of Wyclif and Hus, as well as the theory of tyrannicide set forth by the Paris theologian Jean Petit to justify the murder of the duke of Orléans by the duke of Burgundy's assassins in 1407. His protracted attack on Petit's position cost him not only the Burgundian patronage but also his personal safety in Paris. After a short exile, he returned to Lyons, where he spent the remaining decade of his life promoting reform of diocesan synods, writing mystical and spiritual works, and educating youth, including the sons of King Charles VII, for whom he produced several treatises on the education of princes.

The passages below from *On Church Power* exhibit the range of Gerson's theoretical influence, from ecclesiological concepts to formal political principles.

His model of the church is clerical, hierarchical, supernatural, and corporative. His definition and scholastic analysis of "church power" make clear that the acting church (the material cause) is the clergy, not the whole company of believers or its individual members, as in Marsilius, Ockham, and Wyclif; its form is the hierarchy of offices established by Christ, not necessarily wedded to the personal work of sanctifying grace, as in Wyclif; its efficient cause is Christ's bestowal, and its end the corporate good of eternal felicity (ch. 1). In the exercise of its twofold power of order and jurisdiction (ch. 2), the clerical hierarchy perform Christ's own action of purifying, illuminating, and perfecting the saints (Pascoe 1973, 31-32).

Ecclesiastical corruptions such as schism, heresy, clerical immorality, papal usurpation, and other violations of the evangelical law disrupt this descending order of christological action, assaulting the unity and integrity of the church, so that urgent reform is required. When the disturbance is centered on the church's earthly head, as in a papal schism, then the Spirit is especially operative in the universal episcopal council that most fully embodies the church's hierarchical endowment, her power in its "formal," "invariable" aspect, and so "represents the universal church sufficiently and completely," including papal authority within itself (ch. 7).

Gerson and his colleagues must meet the papalist objection that the representative authority of the general council depends on authorization by the church's earthly head, who holds immediately from Christ the plenitude of church power, considered formally and subjectively. In a classic conciliarist distinction, he admits that the pope holds this plenitude *in its height* (as exceeding other authorities), but attributes to the council the plenitude *in its breadth* (as the totality of authorities), so that it can assemble and act representatively *as the church* when the pope reneges on his duty of convening it (ch. 11).

To overcome the further obstacle presented by Roman plenitude to the council's deposition and election of popes, Gerson further distinguishes, following d'Ailly, two aspects of church power: its "assignation" to particular persons and its "exercise or execution" (ch. 6), both of which are characterized as entailing mutability, variability, and human mediation. Although, he argues, Peter received full church power immediately from Christ, his successors receive it by human election and consecration, according to the providential evolution of canon law (ch. 9). Moreover, Christ granted the full power of assignment "not to one, but to a unity" (the whole church), representatively present in the general council, precisely because the church's unity (her *building up*) is the purpose of the power (ch. 11). On the same account, the entire church or council holds the full power to regulate its use, providing the "one ineffaceable and incorruptible rule . . . by reference to which [its] abuse . . . can be repressed, controlled, and moderated" (ch. 11), whether or not there is a ruling pope.

In that the council's exercise of its twofold plenitude in the absence of, or against, the supreme pontiff invariably contravenes canon law, Gerson extensively invokes the principle of *epikeia*, or "flexibility" (see on Perkins below, pp. 771-77), almost a commonplace in earlier conciliarist writing, permitting the letter of the law to be overruled in the light of its true and enduring intention. Since all law aims (but church law more directly) at the common good of communal charity, unity, and peace, the concept of *epikeia* brings into play both natural and divine law, political rationality and theological wisdom in a manner characteristic of other Gersonian and conciliarist principles: those of necessity, the proportionality of means to end, and the subordination of part to whole.

More than others of his conciliarist collaborators, whose thinking had a naturalist or secularizing bent, Gerson resisted the temptation to assimilate ecclesiastical and civil polity, being as occupied with the divergences as with the convergences of the two spheres, and preferring theological to canonist formulations of church power. Nevertheless, his concluding discussion highlights a generic political conceptuality applicable to both polities. In the first place, he derives church power and all other powers from a primary system of divinely willed justice, conceived as *an order of God-given rights* or entitlements, thereby endorsing the universal application of subjective rights theory. In the second place, he subsumes church and civil commonwealth under the *genus* of *political community,* construed in Aristotelian fashion as *perfect* or *self-sufficient* and *sovereign* or *self-governing,* thus emphasizing their proper independence, in a traditionally Parisian manner. Thirdly, he extols the superiority of a mixed constitution in both spheres.

Further Reading: D. C. Brown, *Pastor and Laity in the Theology of Jean Gerson* (Cambridge: Cambridge University Press, 1987); J. Morrall, *Gerson and the Great Schism* (Manchester: Manchester University Press, 1960); F. Oakley, *The Political Thought of Pierre d'Ailly: The Voluntarist Tradition* (New Haven: Yale University Press, 1964); L. B. Pascoe, *Jean Gerson: Principles of Church Reform* (Leiden, Brill, 1973).

From *On Church Power and the Origin of Law and Right*

1. Church power is the power which was supernaturally and specially granted by Christ to his apostles and disciples and to their legitimate successors, to the end of time, for the building up of the church militant, according to the evangelical laws, to attain eternal felicity.

By "power" is meant a proximate faculty to issue in act — the term "proximate" allows that a remote and obediential faculty may issue in act exceptionally, since "with God nothing is impossible" (Luke 1:37). "Church," as used in connection with the phrase "church power," is a shorthand expression for those who have been ordained to the ministry of God by a special rite, from the lowest grade of clergy to the highest dignity, the papacy.

In this definition church power is distinguished from every other power in terms of its four causes, as follows. The chief *efficient cause* is given in the words, "granted by Christ." There follows the *material* or *subjective cause,* "to his apostles . . . etc." The *formal cause* is implied in the expression "according to the evangelical laws," which explain the condition on which power is exercised. Lastly, the *final cause* is determined "for the building up of the church militant to attain eternal felicity." The adverb "specially" distinguishes power from the supernatural gifts which may be conferred upon any Christian pilgrim, such as faith, hope, charity, prophecy, fear, piety, etc.

If I am not mistaken, this definition fits all church power completely and exclusively. All other power is conferred naturally (efficient cause), or is governed by natural or human law (formal cause), or is intended immediately and principally to a natural end (final cause), or belongs to its possessors by virtue of natural gifts apart from supernatural gifts like faith, hope, and charity (subjective cause). Secular power, accordingly, can be held by those who are not baptized Christians, while church power is necessarily based on supernatural gift. In common law it requires baptism, which is a character that incorporates believers into the church militant and makes them competent to exercise church power. Our position, then, allows that charity, or sanctifying grace, though appropriate for those who are to receive or already hold church power, is not required for the conferral of title, as though without it there were no ground for such power to subsist. (This was the old Waldensian error, shared by the Poor Men of Lyons and rightly condemned, though recently revived by Wyclif and his followers.) Why? To avoid the permanent instability and uncertainty in the hierarchical structure of church power, since no one would know whether to look on it with love or hate — quite apart from whether it possessed the grace of predestination, which they say is the necessary source of title and right for any power!

Working from this definition of church power in general, then, we proceed to its specific types. There is a complex set of distinctions to be noticed here, as indicated by the qualifications to the genus, which constitute the species.

2. Church power is first of all divided into the *power of order* and the *power of jurisdiction.*

Then the power of order has two aspects: one exercised on the *true body of Christ* [i.e., the Eucharist] in consecrating it, the other exercised on the *mystical body of Christ* [i.e., the church] or its members. This latter has two functions: the administration of the true body of Christ; and the administration or celebration of any other sacrament, e.g., ordination, confirmation, or penitential absolution.

The power of jurisdiction is of two kinds: public *(in foro exteriori)* and private *(in foro conscientiae interiori)*. The power of public jurisdiction must be considered in two aspects: as it derives immediately from Christ through the Gospel law; and as additional powers derive from human organization or donation by secular princes. (An alternative principle of division will be explained below.) The power of private jurisdiction has two sources: one lies in the voluntary submission of those over whom the power is exercised, as when a penitent submits to a presbyter or an ordinand to a bishop; the other lies in the authority of the superior, subjecting one or another person to this or that whether he likes it or not. We observe that the difference between these two is very considerable. Those who make only a superficial survey may make pronouncements with great facility, but failing to make their pronouncements consistent, they end up in self-contradiction, so that their teaching is either erroneous or unintelligible, or contorted and opaque. But the wise man tells us that "the doctrine of the prudent is easy" (Prov. 14:6 Vulg.) because they explain the distinctions methodically and systematically, separating the precious from the worthless, and taking care that the light of truth should not be obscured by clouds of error, but should blaze like a smokeless flame. [. . .]

6. Church power may and must be considered in three ways: —

(1) *Formally and abstractly in itself* and without respect to any particular person or thing.

(2) *Materially or with respect to its assignation* to particular persons by legitimate right. This is commonly done by consecration and election. As the apostle says, "One does not take the honor upon himself, but he is called by God, just as Aaron was" (Heb. 5:4). In this aspect power is called *ministerial institution,* which refers both to the act of conferral and to the power conferred.

(3) *In respect of its exercise or execution,* since, as Aristotle says, power is frustrated if it is not exercised.

This consideration [i.e., chapter] is useful in distinguishing and resolving the various ways in which theologians and canonists speak of church power, since ignorance or inadvertence about this distinction is a frequent cause of error. As will be shown below, there are different things to be said about church power considered formally and absolutely, materially or in respect of someone, and as exercised, or "executive" power. [. . .]

7. Church power, *formally and abstractly in itself,* is invariable; it remains unchanged from the birth of the church until the end. This must certainly be the case if the church, considered, as we have indicated, in its essential and permanent parts — the papacy, the cardinalate, the patriarchate, the archiepiscopate, the episcopate, and the priesthood — is the integrity of all these parts, so that if one of these powers were completely removed, it would no longer be the church as perfectly instituted, seminally and in germ, as it were, by Christ. Suppose, for instance, the papacy were removed from the other inferior powers: what remains will not be called the church. So to ask whether papal authority is greater than the church or *vice versa* amounts to asking whether the whole is greater than the part, or whether the part is less than the whole. It follows, then, that if a general council represents the universal church sufficiently and completely, it must necessarily include papal authority, whether there actually is a pope or whether there has ceased to be one through natural or civil death. And we may say the same of the power of the Roman church, of the sacred college, of the episcopal power, and of the priesthood, which is the power of the church's lesser prelates entrusted with the cure of souls. [. . .]

8. Church power, *materially* or *with respect to its assignation* to particular subjects, can be called variable and removable in many instances. This is demonstrated daily, when changes are made through new consecrations or new elections or institutions of ministers. Consequently, we can say the same thing in regard to the papal power, which is mutable and removable by natural death, as is obvious, or by civil death, namely, by deposition, at least in regard to the plenitude of jurisdiction. (How and for what reasons the pope may be deposed I have explored more extensively in other short treatises.) So, as the pope can renounce the papacy and give a bill of divorcement to his bride, the church, even without fault on her part though not without a cause, so the church can dismiss her spouse's vicar, and give him a bill of divorcement, without guilt on his part but not without cause. [. . .]

From this Scripture [Jethro's advice to Moses, Exod. 18], written with the finger of God, there are many things to be learned. Particularly, that if Moses, who spoke with God familiarly "as a man speaks to his friend" (Exod. 33:11), attended obediently to the advice of a Gentile in the government of all Jewry, how much more obediently should the Supreme Pontiff attend to the decision of the whole church or of a General Council called in its name. Again, if Moses is criticized for handling minor cases, what are we to say of all those profane and unfitting preoccupations which incessantly absorb the care and attention of the Supreme Pontiff and his Curia? What about the conferral of benefices, even tiny ones, and the documents that need signing by the pope's own hand? What about the exaction of annates and innumerable like matters, carried on to the neglect of all attention, concern, or interest for what is spiritual or divine, or for what touches the faith and practice of Christianity? The conclusion we must reach from the precept and council given to Moses in the law, as well as from Christ's institution in St. Matthew (18:18), is that there never was to this day, and never will be in future, a worse plague in the church — both in itself and in its structure of authority — than the neglect of General and Provincial Councils. There will be no authority in the church if the Supreme Pontiff wishes to usurp all the prerogatives of the lower clergy: their institution, their rights, their estates, their positions and responsibilities. The Supreme Pontiff should recall that God gave him the highest power in the church to build it up, using such judgment as a wise man would use. But a wise man, though himself invariable, varies his use of power, just as a General Council, though functioning only for a fixed period, varies its geographical and other circumstances. Let the use of his own judgment be restrained, then, and let the church's polity remain in that best of all forms of government that it enjoyed under Moses, a mixed polity made of three strands. It was a monarchy in the person of Moses, an aristocracy in the seventy-two elders, and a meritocracy in the selection of rulers to serve under Moses from the people and from each of the tribes. [. . .]

9. Church power *in respect of its exercise or execution* is mutable and variable in many ways. This consideration [chapter], together with the two preceding ones, completely resolves the question whether ecclesiastical power is *given immediately* from God or *mediated* through men.

It should be conceded without a doubt that church power considered in the first way [i.e., formally and abstractly in itself] was and is given immediately from Christ the God-Man in such a way that excludes any other agency in its institution. Not even an assembly of the whole human race, excluding only Christ, could have instituted a power of this sort, though it could institute for itself an imperial power to take supremacy over all regal, ducal, gubernatorial, or baronial power, over any other purely secular power in fact. Moreover, it could not institute for itself a priesthood nor a papacy, such as the church has; and in the same way it could not abolish them, since it could not change the law of Christ. (Change to the law of Christ would be a necessary implication of any such alteration, following the apostle's principle [Heb. 7:12], that "when there is a change in the priesthood, there is necessarily a change in the law as well.")

If, however, church power is considered in the second way [i.e., materially or with respect to its assignation], *at the birth of the church* it was granted *immediately* by God both to Peter and to the apostles and disciples, on whom Christ immediately conferred the priesthood over his true and his mystical body. So the apostle Paul says that he did not receive the Gospel from man (Gal. 1:12), and similarly with the mystery and administration of the body of Christ: "I received from the Lord what I also delivered to you" (1 Cor. 11:23). It is probable as a consequence that, just as Christ conferred this power originally on his apostles and disciples immediately, assigning it to them and not to others, so also he granted its use, act, or exercise immediately, since he who gives the form gives also the consequence of the form.

Yet finally we should say that, notwithstanding all this about the early church, the *successors* of Peter and of the other apostles by canon law were and are (short of a miracle or new revelation) instituted *through the mediation of men,* by consecration, election, or some other kind of institution. Likewise they received and receive the use and exercise of power through the mediation of human ministry or grant.

And perhaps in regard to the use and exercise of church power, too, after the immediate grant of the power and its use made by Christ to the apostles and disciples, as the number of believers increased, a limitation was imposed upon the use of power to avoid schism and to establish an example for the future; and this was done through Peter, as Supreme Pontiff, with the consent of the whole of the primitive church or a General Council; so that anyone could no longer exercise this power upon anyone he wished. In this the primary intention of Christ was respected, that his church should be ruled imperially, under and by one monarch, just as there is one faith, one baptism, and one church by the unity both of its primary head and his vicar; for this is the best kind of rule, particularly in spirituals, to conserve the unity of the faith to which all men are bound. It is quite another matter with civil laws: nations do not have to have conformable or identical laws, since social expectations and conditions differ from territory to territory; the church's sword, moreover, is a spiritual sword, excommunication, which can be extended without difficulty to distant lands, further than the material sword can reach. Precisely for this reason it was not required, nor even appropriate perhaps, that temporal power should be constituted in a single, permanent worldwide monarchy; yet the spiritual power, as we have said, and as theologians and the church have traditionally insisted, was instituted by divine right preeminently in the person of Peter with the words "Feed my sheep" (John 21:18). [. . .]

10. Church power in its plenitude is *formally and subjectively* in the Roman pontiff alone. Two points are supposed in this statement: —

First, though someone not a priest may be elected pope, as also a layman may be elected bishop, he cannot bear the title Supreme Pontiff without first being ordained priest and bishop. Though he could exercise certain powers of jurisdiction on the basis of his election, he could not until his episcopal consecration exercise the plenitude of church power, i.e., both the power of order and the power of jurisdiction. This is evident from the terms themselves. (There is, however, a considerable confusion created by the lawyers, who refer to plenitude of papal power when they mean only the power of jurisdiction — a terminological convention that would seem to have the absurd implication that a mere layman, even a woman, could be pope and have the plenitude of ecclesiastical power!)

Secondly, and following from this, it is of Christ's institution that no one in the church should grant or be granted hierarchical positions, i.e., those of purgation, illumination, and perfection, without the actual or implied authorization of the supreme hierarch and monarch of God's Holy Church; confusion in the church should be avoided, and it should be governed by the best form of government like the Church Triumphant. John in the Apocalypse says that he saw "the city, new Jerusalem, coming down out of heaven" (Rev. 21:2); and Moses was told: "See that you make everything according to the pattern which was shown you on the mountain" (Heb. 8:5). To these suppositions we must add Aristotle's dictum, that *actions belong to suppositions.* From this and preceding discussions, then, we reach this definition: Plenitude of church power is the power of order and of jurisdiction supernaturally given by Christ to Peter, as his vicar and first monarch, for himself and for his successors to the end of time, for the building up of the church militant to attain eternal felicity. [. . .]

11. Church power in its plenitude is in the church *as its end,* which regulates the application and use of this sort of plenitude of church power either directly or through a General Council sufficiently and legitimately representing it. It is clear, at any rate, that the plenitude of church power was given to Peter by Christ for the building up of his church, as our definition has it in conformity with the Apostle Paul's assertion (2 Cor. 10:8). For this reason Augustine says, with certain others, that "the keys of the church were given not to one, but to a unity, and that they were given to the church." And this can fittingly be understood as this consideration puts it, because the keys of the church were given *for* the church and its unity as for an end. Also this plenitude of church power can be said to be in the church or the council not only *formally and abstractly in itself* but also in the two other ways: *in respect of its assignment* to particular persons, and *in respect of the regulation of its use,* if there should be any complaint that it was being abused.

It is certain that the plenitude of church power is in the church in these three ways, and in the General Council as its representative. Concerning the first and second ways, indeed, there is no objection raised. And there would be none concerning the third either, if we bore in mind the definition of the plenitude of church power, which stipulated that it was given for the building up of the church. Since, then, the Supreme Pontiff who possesses it subjectively is liable to sin and may wish to pervert this power to the destruction of the church, and the sacred college, too, given to assist him as a sort of aristocratic council, is not confirmed in grace or faith, there remains one ineffaceable and incorruptible rule from the best legislator, Christ, by reference to which abuse of this sort of power can be repressed, controlled, and moderated. Now this rule is either the church or a General Council. So, then, since the mean of virtue can only be determined in terms of how a wise man shall judge, the final point of reference for this wisdom shall be made to the church, where wisdom is incorruptible, or to a General Council. This is the basis for many things that have been decided and enacted through this sacred council [of Florence]: for instance, the decision that the pope can be judged and deposed by the council. For he is subject to it in the regulation of his power in regard to its use; and it can say to him, "Why do you do so?" (And so on. I have taken the matter further in my Sermon entitled "A Safe Journey. . . .")

To this consideration [i.e., chapter] we may add that the plenitude of church power, considered *in its breadth,* is not as such in the pope alone (except in a special sense "originally," i.e., as the source of it in a certain limited sense). For this breadth of power comprehends in itself the other ecclesiastical powers all together from the highest to the lowest. And the papal plenitude of church power is among them, integrally part of the whole, and so is not greater than, or superior to the power of the whole church, as a part is not greater than the whole. If, on the other hand, the plenitude is considered *in its height,* then beyond doubt the papal plenitude of church power exceeds and towers greater than the rest. But, then, the rest can in no way constitute a General Council. As we said earlier, a General Council, as such, necessarily includes the papal authority whether a pope exists or not; for if there is a pope and he is willing to do his duty in convoking the council, certainly it must be authorized by him. If he refuses, however, stubbornly and destructively to the church, action should be taken as if there were no pope. The church still retains the power of assembling and organizing itself, and of making provisions for the use of papal power in the second and third ways, i.e., in respect of its assignment and its use; the situation corresponds to that of a chapter and a dean, or a university and its rector.

But the principal objection is raised: what, after the pope's death or ejection, is the council empowered to do?

In the first place it has the power to create a single pope for itself, whether in the accustomed way through the election of the lord cardinals, or in another way through compromise; or through the way of the Holy Spirit, if there is a reasonable hope that thus all can be brought to agree upon one candidate; or perhaps even by waiting for miraculous divine guidance, as in the election of Matthias (Acts 1:26). There is no objection to this proposition about the first power of the council, that it is empowered to make one head for the church.

There are many other powers which, if the pope is dead or ejected, the council can exercise, whether directly or through some administrative organ acting on behalf of the whole council, as has often been the practice in this council in handling various decisions and decrees involving the exercise of coercive jurisdiction, such as the summoning and deposition of the pope, or such cases as involve excommunication and interdiction, relaxation and absolution, like the case of Tridentinum and Argentinum; and in all these instances we find the words, "the Holy Synod speaks . . . , decides . . . , defines. . . ." We find in the early councils in the time of the apostles and later, that even when there was a living pope, it was the council and not the pope that spoke. So the apostles and elders, in recording the decisions of the council in Acts 15:28, said "It has seemed good to the Holy Spirit and to us . . ."; and something similar is noted in Acts 6:2 in the summoning of the church by the twelve apostles. In General Councils there are found such modes of expression as, "The holy council decided . . . ," "the council resolves . . . ," "the holy council determines . . . ," "by the authority of the holy council . . . ," "Let the synod's decree take effect . . . ," and so on and so forth. [. . .]

It remains to be asked, in discussing this hypothetical situation, whether there is any power peculiar to the pope by which he can do something of which no other ecclesiastical power is factually or legally capable. And it seems *prima facie* that there is no such power, following the majority opinion of the theologians, who say that the power of order is equal in all priests (the term "priests" being used, as in the New Testament, to include bishops). It does not appear that there is any act of order for which papal authority is competent and episcopal authority *de facto* incompetent. And on any account of the power of jurisdiction, it appears that in default of a pope the council can grant it, for instance in placing certain communities at its own discretion under the power of a given bishop for the purpose of maintaining a lawful and valid sacramental ministry.

12. [. . .] We should add that the Supreme Pontiff and his college should have such disposal of the goods of the church as to maintain a decent and sufficient state, but not so as to cause the other members of the body to collapse by the excessive weight of the head; nor should they wish, belying the nature of a single member, to take over all the functions of the other members, to each of which, the apostle says, is given its proper function; for if all were an eye or a head, where would the foot or the hand be (cf. 1 Cor. 12:14ff.)? This touches the conferral of benefices, the loathsome multiplication of exemptions, which is a source of constant error and confusion in the church hierarchy, something which can be said of the other matters too. The reservation of so many cases, besides, and of so many secret excommunications; the facile summoning to court of cases, profane and religious, by ordinaries; and that such cases of religion, called by particular ordinaries who notoriously scandalize their dioceses in doctrinal matters especially, aim at suppressing the study of letters where it flourishes — what is all this but to open the door wide to error? Church power must finally contain itself within its own bounds, and remember that secular power has its proper rights, dignities, laws, and courts, even among unbelievers, which church power should not infringe nor arrogate to itself unless the abuse of secular power not only clearly wrongs church power but creates a scandal for the faith and blasphemes the Creator. In that case it is appropriate to invoke the concluding element of this twelfth consideration: *in such circumstances* church power has a kind of ruling, directive, regulatory, and organizing supremacy. This, and no more, is proved by the arguments usually adduced to show that papal plenitude of power is superior to all other church and temporal power. In fact the power of the universal church in this respect, or of a General Council legitimately convened, may be said to be greater in its representative standing and inclusiveness, greater in its claim to God's infallible direction, greater in its power to correct established practice both in its head and its members, greater in its power to enforce its judgments, greater in its ability to reach a final resolution of difficult questions of faith, greater in fact because more comprehensive. For it represents — in principle at least — every power and every political regime, papal, imperial, royal, aristocratic, and meritocratic, — as has been proved elsewhere from the definition: A General Council is a gathering of every estate of the hierarchy of the whole catholic church convened by legitimate authority in one place, excluding no Christian person who demands a hearing, for the wholesome deliberation and ordering of those things that concern the proper government of the said church in faith and morals.

13. Church power, like power of any other kind, originates in *primary justice,* upon which all rights, laws, jurisdictions, and dominions rest in a system as complex as it is beautiful.

The definition of *justice* is: a perpetual and constant will to assign everything its proper right. This definition applies first to the justice of God in his ordered relation to his creatures. God, indeed, is the only being that has a perpetual and constant will to assign everything what is proper to it — "proper" not in the strict sense that it is *owed* to it, but within the terms of the Creator's free and generous gift of value to each creature. Of any thing, then, we may say that it has "right" to the extent that it has "being." For everything has the right, or title, to possess whatever it may be that the absolute norm of primary justice prescribes that it possess.

The definition of *right* is: a proximate faculty or power which belongs to some subject as prescribed by primary justice. This prescription is called *law,* since law is a rule in conformity with what right reason prescribes; and in God the prescription of right reason and the prescription of primary justice come to one and the same thing. The term "proximate" is included in the definition in order to distinguish right from the *obediential power* that any creature may possess. We speak of an "obediential" or "logical" power to indicate that the right or law in question is not proper to the creature. So, for example, the damned have no right to eternal blessedness, and a star has no right to the degree of brightness with which the sun shines; yet they are both capable in principle ("obedientially") of these things, and it lies within the absolute power of God to bring them about. [. . .]

Having spoken about justice, right, law, jurisdiction, and dominion, let us say something about *political community (politia),* which may be defined as a community *(communitas)* organized to some perfect end. Organization, or order, is the disposition of equal and unequal elements in which each has its proper place. It was, then, an inspired saying of the prophet, that "the work of justice is peace" (Isa. 32:17 Vulg.). How so? Because peace is simply "the tranquillity of order" (Augustine, *City of God* 19.13 [cf. p. 155 above]), created by justice when it assigns everything its proper right. So "justice and peace have kissed each other" (Ps. 85:11).

Political community is *heavenly,* about which we shall not speak at present, or *human,* i.e., of our pilgrim state. And of this there are two kinds, *churchly* (commonly and appropriately so-called) and *secular.* Three types of secular community are distinguished in Aristotle's *Politics* (1279a32ff.): kingdom, aristocracy, and what he calls by the general term "polity," which we can translate "timocracy." A *kingdom* is a political community under one good man, or more elaborately, a perfect community considered as a whole, governed under one man by his own good laws for the common weal. For the one man is "good," whether king, emperor, or monarch, if for the most part he means to use his power of government not for his own but the common good. An *aristocracy* is a political community under a few good men, or more elaborately, a perfect community considered as a whole, under a few men such as a senate, who for the most part mean good for the common weal by their own laws. A *polity* in this special sense, or *timocracy,* is a political community under the largest number of good men, or more elaborately, a perfect community considered as a whole, governed by the largest number who for the most part intend to benefit the common weal by their own laws.

The term *perfect community* is defined in opposition to *a sphere of economic interaction* which cannot fully provide for itself. The phrase "by their own laws" defines a sovereign government by its power to rule the political community at its own discretion, not under the constraint of laws imposed from outside.

Every church community, then, whether governed by one man or by few or by a majority, is properly called "divine," since it must submit to direction by supernatural laws. It is clear, then, that in the church these three types of political constitution are united, since there is but one divine law. It is quite different from civil community. [. . .]

Following Aristotle's threefold categorization of political community in natural government, we may distinguish papal, collegial, and synodal government (i.e., of a General Council) within the community of the church. The papacy is like a monarchy, the college of cardinals like an aristocracy, the General Council like a timocracy. Or, more accurately, it is like the perfect political community which is a blend of all three.

There are political communities, if they deserve the name, which are opposite to these three, not governed by liberal and, so to speak, paternal regimes, but by despotism and the yoke of slavery. This may come from their own evil deserts, by the permission of God, who, as Job says (34:30), "makes a hypocrite to rule" for the sins of the people; or it may be some other just disposition of God. Aristotle calls the first of these tyranny, the second oligarchy, and the third democracy. In a tyranny one man has control, seeking only his own good, trying to keep his subjects powerless, uninstructed, and divided against each other. In an oligarchy a few with the same disposition have control over the rest. In a democracy a corrupted people rules itself, each individual seeking his own, not the common good.

On this basis the reflective reader may pursue the question whether there are three corresponding corrupt forms to be found in ecclesiastical community. [. . .]

Translation: Editors, from *Oeuvres Complètes,* vol. 6, ed. P. Glorieux (Paris: Desclée, 1965).

John Fortescue

(ca. 1395–ca. 1477)

Sir John Fortescue was a distinguished practitioner and influential theorist of English common law in the tradition of Bracton, who had brought the Roman legal renaissance to bear on the heritage of Germanic and feudal customs and statutes. Fortescue's contribution testified to the profound impact of Thomistic thought across the spectrum of the law schools. His pages are replete with references not only to Thomas Aquinas's treatment of law in the *Summa Theologiae* (1a2ae.90-105) and to the discussion of political rule in that portion of *On the Government of Rulers* widely attributed to Ptolemy of Lucca (see p. 321 above), but also to the later treatise of the same name by Giles of Rome. In comparison with Aquinas, or even with his future countryman Richard Hooker, Fortescue's exposition and application of the natural law tradition is somewhat lacking in theological precision. Such a deficiency, however, may be pardonable in a man who was four times governor of Lincoln's Inn, eight times elected to Parliament, appointed justice of the peace thirty-five times in seventeen counties and boroughs, and chief justice of the King's Bench for more than eighteen years. Naturally, the immense influence of his legal judgments and theories on the course of English law is not detachable from the interest of his thought for us.

It is hardly surprising that his major treatises were composed only after his legal career had been abruptly terminated in 1461 by the deposition of King Henry VI in favor of Edward Duke of York. So joined was Fortescue's fate to the Lancastrian regime that he went into exile with the defeated king and queen. From his initial refuge in Scotland he probably wrote *On the Nature of the Law of Nature (De natura legis naturae)*, which appealed to the law of nature to establish the Lancastrian succession to the English throne; and subsequently, during a longer French sojourn in St. Mihiel in Bar, he supposedly produced *In Commendation of the Laws of England (De laudibus legum Anglie)*, an enthusiastic apology for English government and laws, in the form of a dialogue between Henry VI's son, Prince Edward, and the chancellor. Some time in or after 1471 he composed, under the title *On the Monarchy of England,* a set of proposals for administrative reform intended to strengthen the power of the Crown, possibly in anticipation of Henry VI's restoration, which, however, never transpired. Subsequently, he presented "an updated and revised version" to Edward IV (Lockwood 1997, xix), whose government prudently pardoned him and appointed him to the royal council.

Of importance for political theory are two constitutional contributions of Fortescue's work: his grounding of kingly rule in the law of nature and his distinction between "royal rule" and "royal and political rule."

On the Nature of the Law of Nature appeals to natural law to render authoritative and certain judgment on the right of royal succession in sovereign kingdoms. The judgment is authoritative because natural law bears a superior dignity by virtue of its emanation from original justice, being coeval with the original righteousness of Adam's created government *(dominium)*. The judgment is certain because, unchanged by Adam's sin, natural law never ceases to establish and validate just government in the fallen state of humankind (bk. 1, chs. 5, 36). Employing a feudal conceptuality that may be indebted to Richard FitzRalph or John Wyclif, Fortescue construes regal and proprietary government in Augustinian fashion as divine institutions for postlapsarian society. The same law of equity that once blessed innocent humankind with the fullness of liberty and "a share of all things," subjects guilty humanity to the constraints of kingly rule and private property (1.10, 19, 20). Not the law of *nations* but the law of *nature* is the foundation of rule and property; the common observance of what "natural reason has established" merely bestows a common name on these institutions (1.19).

Concerning the succession to the English throne, the judgment of the law of nature runs against the Yorkist title by prohibiting one of the conditions on which it rests, namely, descent through a woman. In subordinating the woman to the man's authority the law of nature excludes her both from exercising royal government and from bequeathing it to her progeny. Of particular theological interest in this legal solution is the relationship between divine law and the law of nature: on the one hand, God's repromulgation of the law of nature revealed in Scripture increases its clarity and force, rendering the penalties for its violation more severe; on the other, God's repromulgation depends for intelligibility and juridical force on the prior rationality and authority of the law of nature, a point used later by Hooker against the Puritans' ethical positivism (2.28, 29).

Fortescue's distinction of "royal" and "political" rule to render the synthetic "royal and political" rule displays a fertile elusiveness (perhaps confusion) of terms, not characteristic of Thomas Aquinas or of Giles of Rome (who offered an apology for "royal" over "political" rule in his *De regimine principum* 2.2.3; 3.2.3, 6-8, 27, 29), but strikingly reminiscent of Ptolemy of Lucca, who both had difficulty in distinguishing regal and despotic rule (*De regimine principum* 2.8.1, 6, 9; 2.9.1; 4.8.4) and tended to present limited monarchy as "political rule" (2.8; 3.20; 4.1; 4.19.4-5). Putting aside the shifting meanings of the elemental political forms, Fortescue's mixed regime combines the hereditary possession of kingdoms by monarchs with the equitable rule of law, representative consent of subjects, and "the administration of many" (1.17). Desirous of vindicating the "natural" status of all just government, he concedes a theological foundation to royal rule in the sovereign government of God the Creator, and, following Ptolemy (*De regimine principum* 2.9.4), to *political* rule in man's created state of innocence (somewhat departing from 1.5, 36), upholding the *equal theological dignity* of all three regimes as vehicles of divine government. Nevertheless, he gives theological pride of place to his synthetic polity, comparing its law to that eschatological law "by which all the blessed reigning together with Christ are ruled in their native country" (1.22). Moreover, he constantly returns (as does Ptolemy) to the evil propensities of "royal government" and its origin in unjust human ambition, which the law of nature providentially bends to the utility of the human community (1.18).

In Praise of the Laws of England further amplifies the disparity of the two politics by an exposition of their different historical origins. Whereas royal rule, he tells us, originated in the reduction of a people to servitude by military conquest and so usurped the title of kingship for unbroken domination (indistinguishable from tyranny), royal and political rule originated in the free incorporation of a multitude into a single social body of interest and law, into a unified common good that required from its inception a guiding and controlling hand (12, 13).

Fortescue's celebrated organic elaboration of this freely incorporated body politic, echoing John of Salisbury's earlier model, emphasizes the stable, interdependent, and independent functioning of the civil parts made possible by the persisting structure of law. The impression left by his praise of the English constitution, that it indeed approaches the rule of Christ over his saints, illustrates his prevailing inclination toward the hegemony of the law of nature.

Further Reading: J. M. Blythe, translator and author of introduction, *Ptolemy of Lucca, "On the Government of Rulers"* (Philadephia: University of Pennsylvania Press, 1997); J. H. Burns, "Fortescue and the Political Theory of *Dominium*," *Historical Journal* 28 (1985): 777-97; S. B. Chrimes, *English Constitutional Ideas in the Fifteenth Century* (Cambridge: Cambridge University Press, 1936); S. B. Chrimes, ed. and trans., *De laudibus legum Anglie,* with introduction and notes (Cambridge: Cambridge University Press, 1942); A. B. Ferguson, *The Articulate Citizen and the English Renaissance* (Durham, N.C.: Duke University Press, 1965); A. Gross, *The Dissolution of the Lancastrian Kingship: Sir John Fortescue and the Crisis of Monarchy in Fifteenth Century England* (Stamford, England: Paul Watkins, 1996); S. Lockwood, ed., *Sir John Fortescue, "On the Laws and Governance of England"* (Cambridge: Cambridge University Press, 1997); J. Lockwood O'Donovan, *Theology of Law and Authority in the English Reformation* (Atlanta: Scholars Press, 1991).

From *The Nature of the Law of Nature and Its Judgment upon the Succession to Sovereign Kingdoms,* Part 1

16. O Samuel, prophet of the Lord, the Lord did not command thee to proclaim to the people of Israel the law of what king soever they pleased, but he himself, stirred up to that severity by the rash request of the people, said unto thee: "Hear thou their voice, but take them to witness, and tell them beforehand the Law of the King *(ius regis)*, not the law of every king, but the law of the king who is to reign over them" (1 Sam. 8:9). Nor didst thou, the prophet, set before them the rights of a king in general, but following faithfully the command of God, thou didst say to the people: "This is the law of the king who is to reign over you. He shall take your sons and set them in his chariots . . ." (1 Sam. 8:11). St. Thomas, in the book above mentioned (*On Princely Government* — [but this reference, like Fortescue's other references to the second and subsequent books of this work, actually comes from the portion attributed to Ptolemy of Lucca]), which he wrote to the king of Cyprus, mentioning the various kinds of government which the Philosopher [Aristotle] teaches, commends especially for his own part the regal government and the political government *(dominium regale et dominium politicum)* (2.8), which kinds of government Ægidius Romanus (Giles of Rome), describing in his *De regimine principum (On Princely Government)* saith: "That he is the head of a regal government, who is so according to the laws which he himself lays down and according to his own will and pleasure; but he is the head of a political government, who governs the citizens according to the laws which they have established" (2.2.3). But that there is a third kind of government, not inferior to these in dignity and honour, which is called the political and royal *(politicum et regale)*, we are not only taught by experience and ancient history, but we know hath been taught in the doctrine of the said St. Thomas. For in the kingdom of England the kings make not laws, nor impose subsidies on their subjects, without the consent of the three estates of the realm. Nay, even the judges of that kingdom are all bound by their oaths not to render judgment against the laws of the land, although they should have the commands of the sovereign to the contrary. May not, then, this form of government be called *political*, that is to say, regulated by the administration of many? And may it not also deserve to be named a *royal* government, seeing that the subjects themselves cannot make laws without the authority of the sovereign, and the kingdom, being subject to the king's dignity, is possessed by kings and their heirs successively in hereditary right, in such manner as no dominions are possessed which are only *politickly* ruled?

18. Think over again, I pray you, O law of the king, and consider in thy mind how thou didst hear above most truly declared that the kingly power took its origin under and from the *law of nature*, and by it always was and is regulated; to which it is no objection that wicked men began that power. For although the Jews gave Christ to death, God the Father also delivered him to death by their means; but the Jews did it for envy, the Father for pity. And in like manner, although the unjust began the kingly dignity for ambition, the law of nature began it for man's good by means of those unjust — they by sin, the law by a most righteous working; so that in one and the same act not only the virtue of justice but the maliciousness of sin contended in the works of nature's law. Thus, also, the iniquity of Cain first for avarice set up landmarks in the earth, and the pride of Nimrod first usurped dominion over men, and yet nothing better or more convenient that these things could have befallen the human race; inasmuch as, if all things had remained common as before, and there had been no dominion over men upon earth, public affairs after man's sin would have

managed very ill for man, and for want of justice the human race would have torn it-self to pieces in mutual slaughter. For "the gentiles," as the Apostle says in Rom. 2:14, "although they have not the law, do by nature the things which are of the law, and not having such a law, are a law unto themselves, who show the work of the law writ-ten in their hearts." But as to the manner in which the nations began the kingly power by means of the law of nature, or rather in which the law itself began it by means of the nations, St. Thomas, in the first book of his treatise *De regimine principum* [i.e., *On Kingship* 1.1, see p. 330 above] is believed to have truly taught when he said that among things which are co-ordinated into one, something is ever found which is naturally regulative of another. As in the universe of bodies, the earthly bodies are regulated by the first body, that is the heavenly, and the same are governed by the rational creature, and man's body by his soul, and the parts of the soul, as the irascible and the concupiscible, by the reason, and all the members of man's body by the head and the heart (1.9). And as it is the nature of man to be a so-cial and political animal, living in a multitude, (as in the same book is clearly proved), and as everyone naturally provides and contrives for his private and partic-ular interest, the multitude of human society, if it were not ruled by some one who would take charge of it, would waste away and perish, more especially since man's nature has been spoilt by sin, by which it has been made prone to go wrong (1.5-8). [. . .]

19. For we cannot allow the kingly power to have been instituted at the first by any other law than the law of nature, since it hath been shown above that there was no other law at the time of its institution. And although the civil laws say, that na-tions have been divided and kingdoms founded by the law of nations as is expressed in the aforesaid title of the *Digest* (1.1.5), yet that it no way detracts from what hath been said above. For in the same title it is expressly taught that that which natural reason establishes among all men is preserved among all nations, and is called the *law of nations*, as being a law which all nations use. And what is it which natural rea-son has established among all men but that natural equity which is nature's law? What else, then, is the *jus gentium* which our laws so highly extol, but those laws of nature's code which all nations observe? For when the nations adopted for their own purposes certain laws of nature, which were so convenient for them that without them they could not live rightly, those laws so admitted by them obtained the name of the law of nations. For let it not be suspected that the laws of the nations become the laws of the faithful because the nations made use of them. For the gentiles of old time reckoned idolatry among their chiefest laws. Yet what more abominable could be named among believers? But in truth it is only those laws of nature which the na-tions have admitted for their own government, as distinguished from other laws of nature to which all nations do not assent, which the civil law designated by the name of *jus gentium*. For nowhere in the whole series of the Old Testament do we read of any laws being designated "laws of nations," for it was the civil law only which first distinguished laws from laws under that name. For it is known beyond doubt that custom among the gentiles, although of the longest, and although it have passed into a customary law, is not on that account binding under the name of law of nations upon the faithful among whom the custom itself hath not taken root. For although

those sacred civil laws tell us that by the law of nations were established buyings, sellings, hirings, and the like (Dig. 1.1.5; Inst. 1.2.2), it is nevertheless clear and beyond doubt that contracts of this kind existed lawfully thousands of years before nations began to be. For before the Deluge there were no nations, but, as St. Augustine shows in the fifteenth book of the *City of God* (actually 16.11), in the days of Peleg, who was sixth from Noah, and whose name is interpreted *division*, the earth was first divided, and the people was parted into seventy-two nations and as many tongues, whilst the sons of Noah built the Tower of Babel; and before this division it is evident that there were no nations, but in the whole world there was but one nation, one people, and one tongue.

Whence in Gen. 10:32 it is written: "These are the families of Noah after their peoples and nations, and by these were the nations divided in the earth." And in Gen. 11:6 the Lord says: "Behold the people is one, and they have all one language," words which the Saint aforementioned remarking, saith in his book above-mentioned (16.5): "And the Lord God said: 'Behold the people is one, and they all have one language.'" That, therefore, which the laws tell us, namely, that the contracts above-mentioned were instituted by the law of nations, is and can be nothing more than if they had said that such contracts were instituted by that law of nature which nations use in those cases, and thus not primarily or originally, but secondarily and by way of assent were instituted by the law of nations. And in this fashion ought to be understood the words above quoted which say that nations were separated and kingdoms founded by the law of nations, for before the separation of nations a law of nations did not exist. Wherefore nations could not have been put asunder in the first instance by the law of nations, but it is evident that nations when separated created that law. Neither, therefore, were buyings, sellings, and the like begun by the nations, but, having been invented by the law of nature according to right reason, were according to the same reason ratified and admitted by the law of nations.

20. When the Lord had said to Adam: "In the sweat of thy face thou shalt eat thy bread" (Gen. 3:19), was it not lawful for Adam from time to time to sell to another the bread which the Lord had called his own? And when it is written in the fourth chapter of Genesis that Abel offered the firstlings of his flock, were not those things then his own which Holy Scripture speaks of as such? And at that time it is evident that no law of nations existed, seeing that two brothers could not constitute nations. Wherefore it must be of necessity conceded that property in things, especially in things acquired by the sweat of the brow, first accrued to man by the law of nature alone, seeing that there was then no other human law; and consequently buyings, sellings, lettings, hirings, and the like, took their origin from the law of nature, which is a perpetual law, and, as the canons above-mentioned say, began from the beginning of the rational creation, and varies not with time, but subsists unchangeable (D. 5 d.a.c. 1). The state of man, however, was changed by sin, but not the law of nature, concerning which the civil laws say that the natural laws which are observed among all nations, being established by a certain divine providence, abide always firm and immutable. For the very law which now makes us say, "this is mine and that thine," before the sin of man forbade to say so. For that law is the same when it decrees the innocent man to enjoy his liberty, and when it deprives of his lib-

erty and thrusts into fetters the same man conscious of guilt, and for his crime strips him of all his goods. For in these things there is a change of man's condition and deserts, but not of nature's law. It is the same sun which condenses liquid mud into brick, and which dissolves frozen water into liquid; and the breath which kindles the lighted torch into flame is the same which cools the hot porridge; for in these cases the qualities of the objects affected produce the changes which the objects themselves undergo, but the efficient cause continues steadfast and is not changed. And thus the equity of natural justice, which once allotted to man in his innocence a share of all things, is no other than that equity which for his offence deprives man, corrupted by sin, of the blessing of such community. Is the law of nature then not constant and perpetual? And doth it not, itself unchanged, always allot to each and every one that which is his due? O law of kings, how dost thou compare thyself with this law? Thou hast ever been conversant with sinners upon earth, this law once in Paradise had the glory through grace of governing the innocent. Thou wast constituted by man's cunning, this, as the laws say, by divine providence. Thou didst proceed from the nations of the earth, this from God. Thou art changeable with the will of man, this, unchangeable, abides ever one and the same. And since she rule the king under whom thou servest, shall she not govern thee his servant? For, truly, to rule the king is nothing else but to rule his acts, among which thou art conspicuous. Cease then to strive with the law of nature, for she is thy mistress, and the mistress of thy lord. If thou dost well thou wilt be adopted and loved by her as a daughter, but if ill thou wilt be punished as a handmaid.

22. And although thou, O law of the king, hast most rightly considered the prince under whom thou warrest, who at his nod directs everything in his kingdom, to be in this like unto God, who governs the universe as he wills, whence thou didst no less wisely boast thyself, as his decree, to be like unto the law of God, whose will is law. Take heed, nevertheless, with trembling, lest, puffed up with these thoughts, thou rashly exalt thyself above *the laws of a king who governs his people royally and politickly.* For thou art like unto the law of God by which he rules in the whole earth; but *those laws* are like unto that law by which all the blessed reigning together with Christ are ruled in their native country, in that peace which they long for, (of whom some are senators, and sit upon thrones judging men; yea, and some, as saith the Apostle, shall judge angels [1 Cor. 6:3]) where there shall not be wanting the consent of all the citizens in every judgment of the king.

And St. Thomas saith, in the second book of his *De regimine principum,* that the political government is to be preferred to the royal, if the former be referred to that sound state of human nature which is called the state of innocence, in which there was not a royal but a political government (2.9). Nevertheless, since God ruling in heaven and earth is ever of one and the same power and majesty, and the judgments which ye laws both pronounce are not the judgments of man (as Jehoshaphat says in 2 Chron. 19:6), and so neither of the kings to whom ye are subject, but are the judgments of God who is no accepter of persons, nor yet of peoples (for as St. Peter saith in Acts 10:35: "In every nation he who feareth him, and worketh righteousness, is accepted with Him"); wherefore, seeing that the equal likeness of God hath rendered equal the kings under which ye rule His people, and both are monarchs in their kingdoms as God is sole monarch in the world, so reckon ye yourselves as equal laws, without disparity of power or dignity.

From Part 2

28. Whatever the law of nature ordains, if the prince hath also by his edict commanded the same thing, that edict forthwith binds his subjects more stringently than the law of nature had done before; so that, if any one from that time forward shall transgress such edict, he shall not only be punished according to the sentence of the law of nature, but shall pay a greater penalty for contempt of the prince's command. Wherefore, although by the law of nature it be not allowed to kill, still, after that the Lord forbade murder by edict written on the tables of stone, to kill was a much greater crime than it had been before, and subjected the offender to a heavier punishment. Thus Cain, who had committed fratricide at a time when the whole world was ruled under the law of nature, is not ordered to be slain, but is permitted to go forth a wanderer and a fugitive (Gen. 4:12-15); but after that murder had been forbidden in Mount Sinai, every man guilty thereof was ordered to be put to death, as we are more expressly informed in Deuteronomy (probably 19:11-12). Two chains bind also more strongly than one — yea and a triple cord, as the wise man says, is hard to break; wherefore, when the authority of the prince, by definite sentence, shall have judged anyone to be guilty for his crime, the severity of that sentence binds an offender more strongly afterwards than the edict of the prince or the law of nature had done before. Whence, though the divine command had judged him who ate of the forbidden tree to be in danger of eternal death, Christ's passion reduced the elect therefrom; but neither that passion nor any other satisfaction has to this hour mitigated the punishment which, for the same fault, the Lord inflicted on man by his definite sentence. What woman with child ever was delivered without pain? Or what man ever ate his bread without labour? Nor has the seed of the serpent ever yet found peace with the seed of the woman. Therefore, if what the law of nature has laid down concerning the female sex the divine decree shall also have ordained, not only would the sentence of the law of nature be thereby fenced in more firmly, but the woman too, when transgressing it, would be smitten with heavier punishment. Wherefore, since this same thing which the law of nature had prohibited hath been forbidden by the final sentence of the Lord under a heavier penalty, it remains solid and firm; so that it can by no means be weakened, to the injury of its principal part. Have we not then now discovered in this investigation what we suspected we should discover — namely, that the woman is repelled from the kingdom in dispute under hazard of a greater sin by the divine law than by the human? But she is also put away from it much more strongly and firmly by the above-mentioned divine judgment than before. For since to despise the command of the prince, ordering the sentence of the law of nature to be observed, is a matter of greater guilt than to neglect the simple sentence of nature, we discern it to be far more culpable to despise the judicial sentence of the prince, definitely pronounced, since such sentence is proved to bind more strongly than his simple edict. And inasmuch as the Lord has judicially decreed that the woman should always be under the power of the man (which is, not to reign in such a kingdom), the divine law has made it wickedness and sin to ambition the said kingdom, as the law of nature had made it already, and repels the woman more strongly and more firmly than before from entering thereupon. I do not, then, while alleging the divine law in this dispute, appear to retreat from the authority of the law of nature, but to follow it more closely than before, while I confirm its sentence by authority of a higher law. Wherefore, O most Righteous of Judges, prohibit the king's daughter from any more demanding her father's kingdom, since thou knowest its entrance to be shut against her with so many bolts and bars, that henceforth all ingress thereunto is for her impossible.

29. [. . .] We find then that it is not because by the aforesaid sentence of God the woman was commanded to be subject to the man, that she was originally subjected to him; but because, before that sentence was passed, she was enjoined by decree of the law of nature to obey him. And this decree she transgressed by presuming to direct the man. Thereupon there proceeded from the divine counsel, at the prompting of justice, that sentence by which she paid the penalty of her crime, and knew herself more certainly than before to be subjected to the man. So, too, it was not by force of this sentence that the doubts and difficulties of our question were originally and entirely solved; but it was because they were originally cleared up by the judgment of the law of nature that that sentence was afterwards pronounced by the Lord, by which the judgment of the law of nature is endowed with greater strength than it had before. And hence we discern that our question is solved by the decree of the law of nature alone, and not by the ruling of the aforesaid sentence. For not that which confirms, but that which is confirmed, is considered to be the efficient cause. For thus the things which are forbidden by the moral commandments are not on that account sins, as though unless so forbidden they would not have been sins. But because they were before found to be sins by the law of nature, they were also forbidden by divine edict, and thereby became much more grievous sins than they were before; and the guilt of those who commit them is aggravated, and rendered so much the greater, as they are committed, not only against the commands of God, but also against the dictates of the law of nature. And on this account those sins which were committed only against the ceremonial precepts, especially in respect of the same object, were less blameworthy than those which were committed against the moral.

Translation: Chichester Fortescue, in *The Works of John Fortescue, Knight,* collected and arranged by Thomas (Fortescue) Lord Clermont, vol. 1 of *Sir John Fortescue, Knight: his life, works, and family history,* 2 vols. (London, publication for private distribution, 1869).

From *A Treatise in Commendation of the Laws of England*

12. Formerly, men who excelled in power, being ambitious of honour and renown, subdued the nations which were round about them by force of arms; they obliged them to a state of servitude, absolutely to obey their commands, which they established into laws, as the rules of their government. By long continuance and suffering whereof, the people, though under such subjection, finding themselves protected by their governors from the violence and insults of others, submitted quietly to them, thinking it better to be under the protection of some government than to be continually exposed to the ravages of everyone who should take it in their heads to oppress them. From this original and reason, some kingdoms date their commencement; and the persons invested with the power, during such their government, from ruling, *(regendo)*, assumed and usurped to themselves the name of ruler, or king *(rex)*, and their power obtained the name of regal [Augustine, *City of God* 5.12; Isidore, *Etymologies* 9.3; *Sentences* 3.48, see p. 207]. By these methods it was that Nimrod first acquired to himself a kingdom, though he is not called a king in the Scripture, but a mighty hunter before the Lord (Gen. 10:9). For as an hunter behaves towards beasts, which are naturally wild and free, so did he oblige mankind to be in servitude and to obey him. By the same methods Belus reduced the Assyrians (Augustine, *City of God* 16.17); so did Ninus [son of Belus] the greatest part of Asia; thus the Romans arrived at universal empire; in like manner kingdoms began in other parts of the world. Wherefore, when the children of Israel desired to have a king, as all the nations round about them then had, the thing displeased God, and he commanded Samuel to show them the manner of the king who should reign over them, and the nature of his government; that is, mere arbitrary will and pleasure, as is set forth at large, and very pathetically, in 1 Samuel (8:10-18). And thus, if I mistake not, most excellent prince, you have had a true account how those kingdoms first began, where the government is merely regal. I shall now endeavour to trace the original of those kingdoms, where the form of government is political, that so, the first rise and beginning of both being known, you may more easily discern the reason of that wide difference which occasioned your question.

13. St. Augustine, in his book *De civitate Dei*, has it, "That a people is a body of men joined together in society by a consent of right, by an union of interests, and for promoting the common good" [a lengthy rendering of Scipio's definition quoted by Augustine from Cicero's *De republica* 1.25.39 — a definition that Augustine, in fact, rejects on theological grounds (19.21). See above, pp. 161-62]; not that a people so met together in society can properly be called a body as long as they continue without a head; for, as in the body natural, the head being cut off, we no longer call it a body, but a trunk; so a community without a head to govern it, cannot in propriety of speech be called a body politic. Wherefore the Philosopher, in the first of his *Politics*, says, "Whensoever a multitude is formed into one body or society, one part must govern, and the rest be governed" (Aristotle, *Politics* 1254a28). Wherefore it is absolutely necessary where a company of men combine and form themselves into a body politic that some one should preside as the governing principal, who in kingdoms goes usually under the name of king *(rex, a regendo)*. In this order, as out of an

embryo, is formed an human body, with one head to govern and control it; so from a confused multitude is formed a regular kingdom, which is a sort of a mystical body, with one person as the head, to guide and govern. And as in the natural body, according to the Philosopher, the heart is the first thing which lives, having in it the blood which it transmits to all the other members, thereby imparting life, and growth, and vigour (Aristotle, *On the Parts of Animals* 647b4); so in the body politic the first thing which lives and moves is the intention of the people, having in it the blood, that is, the prudential care and provision for the public good, which it transmits and communicates to the head, as the principal part, and to all the rest of the members of the said body politic, whereby it subsists and is invigorated. The law under which the people is incorporated may be compared to the nerves and sinews of the body natural; for, as by these the whole frame is fitly joined together and compacted, so is the law that ligament, to go back to the truest derivation of the word *lex, a ligando,* by which the body politic and all its several members are bound together and united in one entire body. And as the bones and all the other members of the body preserve their functions, and discharge their several offices by the nerves, so do the members of the community by the law. And as the head of the body natural cannot change its nerves or sinews, cannot deny to the several parts their proper energy, their due proportion and aliment of blood, neither can a king, who is the head of the body politic, change the laws thereof, nor take from the people what is theirs by right, against their consents. Thus you have, Sir, the formal institution of every political kingdom, from whence you may guess at the power which a king may exercise with respect to the laws and the subject. For he is appointed to protect his subjects in their lives, properties, and laws: for this very end and purpose he has the delegation of power from the people, and he has no just claim to any power but this. Wherefore, to give a brief answer to that question of yours concerning the different powers which kings claim over their subjects, I am firmly of the opinion that it arises solely from the different natures of their original institution, as you may easily collect from what has been said. [. . .]

Translation: Francis Gregor, in *The Works of John Fortescue, Knight: His Life, Works, and Family History,* 2 vols. (London, publication for private distribution, 1869).

Nicholas of Kues

(1401-64)

Nicholas of Kues (on the Mosel in Germany) was, like his fellow conciliarist Jean Gerson, both a mystical theologian steeped in the Pseudo-Dionysian tradition of Christian Neoplatonism and a political thinker of considerable influence. Even more than in Gerson's case, Nicholas's political formulations were penetrated by his controlling Neoplatonic ideas of harmony, hierarchy, equality, and consent. His portrayal of the structure of governing authority in church and empire in *The Catholic Concordance (De concordantia catholica)* is a complicated balance of descending and ascending themes, a true "coincidence of opposites." A similar reconciliation of paradox was exhibited in his ecclesiastical and intellectual career; his conversion as a cardinal to the extreme papalist standpoint involved no base self-contradiction, but a quite cogent shift of emphasis from the ascending to the descending elements of his system.

The Catholic Concordance was composed in 1443 while Nicholas was a delegate to the Council of Basel, and was submitted to the council in the wake of its loud proclamations of legislative and judicial supremacy over the pope. Although a clear apology for the conciliarist position, the treatise is, nevertheless, a work of moderation. It recognizes that the unity and harmonious order of the church require unambiguous headship and strict hierarchy as well as corporate consent, elective representation, and restraint from below. The more "modern" features of Nicholas's conciliarism stand out against a conservative, traditionalist backdrop.

Unquestionably, the notion of "consent," and its elaboration as "consensus," is the focus of theological and political interest, displaying not only the voluntarist and humanistic character of Nicholas's political ideas but their mystical tendency as well, whether they are in ecclesiastical or secular garb. Both are discernible in the role of consent in supporting such claims as: *(a)* that the church's representation by a universal council is more "certain" and "infallible" than its representation by the pope; and *(b)* that the decrees of a universal council, properly constituted and functioning according to principles of natural law, have a greater infallibility than papal decrees.

a. Certainty of political representation inheres in the bond of mutual consent, analogous to the marital bond, between the community and its representative (e.g., a diocese and its bishop). Whereas the universal council incorporates representatives who are bound in this way to particular communities from every part of the church, the pope lacks that *specific* representative relationship to every part of the church (2.18.158, 164). The community, comprised of men "by nature . . . equal in power and equally free," expresses its consent through the electoral act, which cooperates with divine providence in constituting political authority. Thus the equal will of each and the combined wills of all resemble, and are one with, the divine will (2.14.127; 2.19.168; 3.4.331).

b. Not only the authority of rulers but also the binding force of their law depend on free and public concurrence. The consensus or "mystical agreement" of disparate wills in conciliar decisions testifies to the presence of the Holy Spirit, so that definitions of the council must be considered "infallibly decided by Christ" (2.3.77). In attributing infallible right in matters of faith to such consensual judgments, Nicholas of Kues is attributing a supernatural, pneumatological property to an ecclesiastical body constituted and functioning according to "natural" political principles. It is just this intimate association, even interpenetration, of natural and supernatural principles that makes *The Catholic Concordance* an indispensable aid to grasping an important and neglected relationship in the history of modern political thought: between democratic liberalism and Christian mysticism.

Further Reading: A. Black, *Council and Commune: The Conciliar Movement and the Fifteenth Century Heritage* (London: Burns & Oates; Shepherdstown, W. Va.: Paternoster Press, 1979); J. P. Dolan, *Unity and Reform* (Notre Dame, Ind.: University of Notre Dame Press, 1962); P. Sigmund, *Nicholas of Cusa and Medieval Political Thought* (Cambridge, Mass.: Harvard University Press, 1963); M. Watanabe, *The Political Ideas of Nicholas of Cusa with Special Reference to His "De Concordantia Catholica"* (Geneva: Droz, 1963).

From *The Catholic Concordance,* Book 2

[References to the text of ecumenical councils are given to J. D. Mansi, ed., *Sacrorum conciliorum nova et amplissima collectio* (Paris: H. Welter, 1901-27), abbreviated M.]

3. [75] The acts of the Eighth Council clearly teach that a full universal council is constituted of the five patriarchal sees. For it is said at the end of that Council that Emperor Basil "by divine help and grace" brought together the five patriarchs, "the builders of the tabernacle of the church, from the ends of the earth" (M. 16, 179). [. . .] Hence I do not think that (all the) emphasis should be placed on the (form of the) convocation of the council in determining its validity, provided that at least the fathers are there who represent the universal church. But if neither the fathers who are the heads of the churches are there nor is there a legitimate convocation by the highest power, there is no doubt that the universal church cannot be represented in that council. But where it has already been legitimately called together and the fathers who are the heads (of the churches) have not yet come together, I do not believe that one should proceed immediately, for we read that many councils including those which had been properly called have been in error. Rather it is necessary to wait for the fathers, although not all of them, for it is sufficient for a majority to be there if all have been called. [. . .]

[77] Now this is an essential requirement for a universal council at which general matters are to be discussed that a hearing be given to all in complete freedom, not in secret but publicly. If anything is then defined by general agreement it is considered to be inspired by the Holy Spirit and infallibly decided by Christ who is present among those gathered in his name. This was the way it was at the Council of Nicaea where, we read in the acts of the Council of Chalcedon, the Holy Spirit was clearly present among the fathers. The Council added that the Holy Spirit commands what is commanded in councils of this kind, so that he who violates them rejects the grace of the Holy Spirit. The holy synod said: "We all say this. Anathema be he who rejects it" (M. 6, 627). This is the way it was with all orthodox councils. And therefore at the end of the Eighth Council when the reason was given that it should be obeyed, the Council said: "By the power given to us by the Holy Spirit who is our most high and mighty pontiff." And below: "Who does not know that Christ the Lord, infinite and incomprehensible, who said: 'Where two or three were gathered' etc., was in the midst of the sacred synod?" (M. 16, 199ff.). That the power of the council is most high is evident from what Elpidius, a man of respectable rank, said to the Council of Chalcedon, as it appears in the first action: "Today the God of all, the Word, the Saviour, has given himself to you for judgment. He accepts those who decide, and he honors the authority of their decision" (M. 6, 619). The first and fifth actions of the Eighth Council contain the statement which is the basis of the fathers' power in council when they say: "The most holy representatives of old Rome and we who are representatives of the other sees decide all these things today by the grace of Jesus Christ who granted us the power of the highest priesthood, that of binding and loosing, etc." (M. 16, 86). Hence the power of binding and loosing was given to Peter as the representative of the church. This is the statement on which the decision of the synod bases its force. [. . .]

4. [78] I have said that if a (conciliar) definition is made with (general) agreement we believe that the Holy Spirit who is the author of peace and concord has acted. For it is not human but divine that various men brought together in complete freedom of speech should come to agreement as one. And this should be presumed in all cases. This is the way it appears in the fifth action of the Eighth Council where the fathers, when they speak of the decision of the council, assert that they were prompted by divine inspiration because the decision was promulgated with the unanimous agreement of the holy synod (M. 16, 80). [. . .]

[81] Especially in matters of the faith, which is necessarily one and unchangeable — as it has been and will remain — the holy universal council should always be guided by the rules that the Holy Spirit has now clearly expressed in the canon of the Holy Scripture and in past councils. It should search the Scriptures when in doubt,

as was done in the Sixth Universal Council and in many others, and then from what has been said the (resulting) definition will necessarily be free of error. However if these conditions are not observed, especially a free hearing for all, and if attempts are made in synods to adopt things that are opposed to the faith of the Roman church, it is proper to issue a protest and to appeal to a future council, as is demonstrated above. And this is demonstrated more clearly still in the letter from Pope Leo [the Great, 440-61] and the Roman synod to Empress Pulcheria which says that the legates of the Apostolic See at the Synod of Ephesus [430] protested its invalidity because of the force and intimidation employed, and stated that no physical pressure could cause them to depart from the faith which they had brought from the see of Peter to the holy synod (*Ep.* 45.2). From this it can also be concluded that the faith of the Roman church can be overruled by no universal synod — this being true [...] of the faith of that whole church expressed in its patriarchal synod.

14. [127] [...] All legislation is based on natural law and any law which contradicts it cannot be valid, see D. 9 d.p.c. 11 and D. 10 c. 4. Hence since natural law is naturally based on reason, all law is rooted by nature in the reason of man. The wiser and more outstanding men are chosen as rulers by the others to draw up just laws by the clear reason, wisdom, and prudence given them by nature and to rule the others by these laws and to decide controversies for the maintenance of peace, as is contained in D. 2 c. 5. From this we conclude that those better endowed with reason are the natural lords and masters of the others but not by any coercive law or judgment imposed on someone against his will. For since all are by nature free, every governance, whether it consists in a written law or is living law in the person of a prince — by which subjects are compelled to abstain from evil deeds and their freedom directed towards the good through fear of punishment, can only come from the agreement and consent of the subjects. For if by nature men are equal in power *(potentes)* and equally free, the true properly ordered authority of one common ruler who is their equal in power cannot be naturally established except by the election and consent of the others, and law is also established by consent. See D. 2 c. 1 and D. 8 c. 2 where it says: "An agreement of every race and city among themselves" etc. and "There is a general agreement in human society to obey their kings" etc. Note that for the convenience of human society men wish to make a general agreement to obey their kings. Since in a properly-ordered government an election of the ruler ought to take place by which he is set up as judge of those who elect him, rightly-ordered lords and rulers are established by election, and through election they are established as general judges over those who elect them. [...]

[130] Furthermore the canons are based on natural law. Even the ruler has no power to violate natural law, and therefore he also has no power over a canon based on, or incidentally following from, natural law. And because this is the case, how can we say that it is in the power of a judge to adopt canons and statutes? If this were so, if he himself had the power to make the canons, a judge could not be charged with an unjust decision, since the decision would be the law, and therefore it would always be just. But because law ought always to be reasonable, possible and not against the custom of the country, see D. 4 c. 2, we cannot call something a law which is not accepted by the usage of the users — whether in the civil or canon law, see D. 4 d.p.c. 3

544

and chapters which follow. Hence if approval through use is required of laws as is said in that chapter, it cannot be right to condemn someone as guilty for violating a new law because he could not violate something which did not yet exist. Thus he must have broken a law that has been adopted and accepted in custom and usage. And from this it is clear that the law or canon is a standard for every judge, and that any judge who makes a decision is subject to all the laws and canons.

[131] Furthermore, if it is true that a canon is approved by agreement, usage, and acceptance, then the strength of all legislation comes from acceptance. Hence the canons of the common council are rightly called those of the church. For the church is a congregation. One person cannot properly issue church canons. Thus we see that canons are issued in the councils by harmonious acceptance, consent and subscription, but the decretals of judicial decisions of the Roman pontiffs or those on doubtful points in new situations have been confirmed as just, not out of pure authoritative will (of the pope) but because the canons agree that those decisions should be made, — a point which ought to be noted. [. . .]

15. [132] From the above it is now clear that the binding force of every law consists in concord and tacit or express consent which is given either through usage or by the action of those with others under their authority, because they represent them or rule over them. For just as the bishop and his chapter are said to make up the diocesan church because that gathering potentially contains all the others who belong to the same church so that they are all considered to be represented by them, so also a metropolitan and his suffragan bishops constitute the church of a province, and a patriarch with his metropolitans, the church of a patriarchate. Hence the authority of any gathering extends to all represented in potentiality in that gathering. [. . .]

18. [164] [. . .] For one body to be established in a harmony of subjects and ruler, reason and natural and divine law all require that there be mutual consent in this spiritual marriage which is demonstrated by the election by all and the consent of the one elected, just as a spiritual marriage is rightly established by consent between Christ and his church [. . .]. Hence if right order is to be preserved, the text of the Council of Toledo in D. 51 c. 5 and those in D. 62 c. 1 and D. 23 c. 1 and similar texts should be observed so that parish priests and curates are elected or at least some convenient provision is made for consent to their appointment, as is stated in D. 67 c. 1 and D. 63 c. 20. Then the clergy should elect the bishop with the consent of the laity, see D. 63 c. 11 and 12, and the bishops the metropolitan with the consent of the clergy, see D. 66 d.a.c. 1. The metropolitans of the provinces with the consent of the bishops should elect the representatives of the provinces who assist the pope and are called cardinals and those cardinals should elect the pope, if possible with the consent of the metropolitans. [. . .]

19. [167] [. . .] Not that the power to rule which is in rulers comes in its entirety from the people, but . . . just as the moving and sensible parts of the soul are produced out of the potency of matter but its rational part comes from God, so the priesthood which is the soul of the church militant derives its moving, vegetative, and sensible power to rule from the faithful subjects — a power which comes from the potency of matter of the faithful by way of voluntary subjection — but the power of the rational soul which comes from above, it receives from God through the sacraments. In this way power from on high can flow in sweet harmony to the body of the subjects through the mediation of a power which comes from it and is granted by it in order to bring about a salutary union (of the faithful) with Christ, the head. Hence Pope Hormisdas [514-23] says to the bishops of Spain: "Let not the blessing which we believe comes from God through the laying-on of hands be sold for money. Who would think that something is valuable if he has sold it? Let the election observe proper reverence for the priests to be ordained, keeping in mind that the weighty decision of the people is the judgment of God. For God is present where there is genuine consent without irregularity" (*Ep.* 25.2). And although God has reserved the deposition of the most high priests for himself, he has given their election to the faithful, see D. 79 in the final chapter (c. 11), and divine grace appoints the one who is chosen by common consent, see C. 8 q. 2 c. 2. [. . .] And it is a happy thought that all power, whether spiritual or temporal and corporeal, is potentially in the people, although in order for the power to rule to be activated there must necessarily be the concurrence of that formative radiance from above to establish it in being since it is true that all power is from above — I speak of properly ordered power — just as from the potential of the earth, the lowest of the elements, various vegetable and sensible beings are produced through the mediating influence of heaven. Hence it was not inappropriate for the Abbot Joachim when he discussed the Apocalypse (*In Apocalypsim* [Venice, 1527]) to say that the people represent the Father, the secular clergy the Son, and the religious the Holy Spirit, because as the Son comes from the Father, so the clergy comes from the laity, and as the Holy Spirit comes from both, so the religious proceed from the laity and the clergy.

From Book 3

4. [325] We must discuss further the electors of the empire mentioned in X 1.6.34. The jurists hold that they act as electors in the name of the Roman people. [. . .] As is said in a certain place above, every well-ordered empire or kingdom is based on election, and then the ruler is truly considered to have been appointed by the providence of God. Thus Emperors Valentinian and Marcian when they write to Pope Leo on convening the synod [the Council of Chalcedon], say: "The victorious and august Valentinian and Marcian in glorious triumph, to Leo, most reverend Archbishop of the glorious city of Rome: We have attained this most high rule by the providence of the true God and the election of the most excellent senate and the whole army" (Leo, *Ep.* 73).

[328] Who, I ask, gave the Roman people the right to elect the emperor, if not divine and natural law? For in every kind of government rulers are chosen for their positions in a harmonious, rightful and holy fashion through voluntary subjection and consent. For all violence is opposed to law. There is a general agreement among men to obey kings (see D. 8 c. 2, Cod. 3.13.7).

[331] Summarizing what has been said above, all legitimate authority arises

from elective concordance and free submission. There is in the people a divine seed by virtue of their common equal birth and the equal natural rights of all men so that all authority — which comes from God as does man himself — is recognized as divine when it arises from the common consent of the subjects. One who is established in authority as representative of the will of all may be called a public or common person, the father of all, ruling without haughtiness or pride, in a lawful and legitimately established government. While recognizing himself as the creature, as it were, of all his subjects as a collectivity, let him act as their father as individuals. This is that divinely ordained marital state of spiritual union based on a lasting harmony by which a commonwealth is best guided in the fullness of peace toward the goal of eternal bliss. [. . .]

[338] Since this matter [the imperial election] has been discussed quite eloquently by many writers, it may be sufficient for us to recognize that our imperial electors, when they elect the emperor by virtue of the united common consent of all who are under the empire, do this because all have agreed to transfer their power to them — and that agreement included the Roman pontiff, Gregory V. It follows that the emperor is created by election without confirmation by anyone — just as in electing a pope, the universal authority of the church is rightly transferred to the cardinals by the common consent, tacit or sometimes express, of all, and therefore the pope is elected without confirmation by anyone.

[339] Just as elective authority is given by agreement to certain rulers in the two estates, so, since an equivalent authority should have the right to take away this power, I do not believe that the Roman pontiff alone can withdraw this power from those princes; but when the consent of both the Roman pontiff and of all the others concurs, there is no doubt that this power can be taken away from them. It is the common opinion of all the experts on the subject that the Roman people can take the power to make laws away from the emperor because he derives his power from the people. [The revocability of imperial power by the Roman people was, in fact, a disputed interpretation of Cod. 1.17.] Thus we read that when the Roman people, ruled for a long time by kings, could no longer endure their haughtiness, they created annual rulerships and two consuls, and also dictators and other arrangements that seemed to suit their governmental needs at the time.

Translation: Paul E. Sigmund (Cambridge University Press, 1991). Used with permission.

PART 5

RENAISSANCE, REFORMATION, AND RADICALISM: SCHOLASTIC REVIVAL AND THE CONSOLIDATION OF LEGAL THEORY

Whether the political thought of Christian thinkers in the sixteenth and early seventeenth centuries should be called early modern or premodern is both a fascinating and an exasperating question that holds out considerable theoretical rewards together with a morass of complications and ambiguities. At the most elementary level, one's orientation to it will depend upon which thinkers and which ideas are under consideration. Not only did an unprecedented diversity of schools, theories, and approaches flourish within this span of time, but typically they combined traditional elements and novel developments, or found new uses for well-traversed concepts. In the French, English, and Spanish kingdoms, for example, the long tradition of theocratic kingship could not have been stronger, but this cluster of biblical and imperial motifs was now undergirding an unprecedented movement of centralization, even in ecclesiastical matters. Moreover, it was closely connected, especially in civilian circles, to a distinctively modern concept of political sovereignty. Nevertheless, the import even of this concept varied with its users, and in the work of a theologian such as Calvin could be regarded as essentially premodern. In the jurisprudential sphere, long-standing theories of *ius naturale* and *ius gentium* were undergoing developments and refinements related to expanding international trade and the discovery, conquest, and colonization of hitherto unknown territories. Such developments sometimes stayed firmly within a Thomistic theoretical framework, and sometimes ran along more voluntarist and individualist lines, inspiring later, more unambiguously "modern" formulations. Out of the Renaissance came new and revived forms of political writing such as utopian speculation and sermonic satire, which were used, however, to express both conservative and revolutionary intentions.

Of course, the answer to the question presumes a clear understanding of what constitutes "modern" political theory. There is a set of political principles and ideas broadly accepted as "modern" that were also influential in the sixteenth and early seventeenth centuries. Most notable are those of social and governmental compacts, natural and political subjective-rights, public utility, majority vote, constitutional structures and constraints on political authority, popular representation, communal will, and the rule of law. If, however, by "modern" is meant the elaboration of these principles and ideas apart from or in opposition to the traditional Christian theological framework of divine and natural law, providence and salvation, justice toward God and neighbor, church and commonwealth, public and private righteousness and virtue, then the political thought of thinkers in this period is, hardly surprisingly, not modern. Admittedly, the Italian renaissance (particularly the northern city republics) gave rise to an antique classicism that bypassed the theological tradition with subversive consequences, and in the extreme case of Machiavelli's "reason of state" directly attacked it. But the majority of thinkers anathematized the Machiavellian project, and intended to harmonize classical forms and substance with the biblical and theological inheritance.

Undoubtedly, the most transformative aspect of sixteenth-century political and legal thought was the critical investigation of early and foundational texts which epitomized the humanist project of cultural renewal. Openness to the authority of sources, together with awareness of their distance from the received medieval traditions of thought, was a pervasive and sometimes explosive agent of change. Both theology and jurisprudence underwent significant hermeneutical shifts with some analogous features. While biblical humanists and Reformers sought to liberate the authentic word of God, historically given in the Greek and Hebrew Scriptures, from the corrupting excrescences of ecclesiastical tradition, legal humanists sought to establish the original intention and scope of the Roman law texts (sometimes going behind the Justinianic editors), in order to demonstrate their authentic classical wisdom and enduring normativity. And as closer exegesis of the Old and New Testaments undercut the hermeneutical traditions of the papalist church, so similar attention to Roman law undercut the prevailing constructions of imperial hermeneutics. In both spheres, the result of the novel approaches was similar: greater institutional independence and self-sufficiency at the national level.

Apart from the ascendancy of the national church and national law, sixteenth-century movements, especially theological movements, gave rise to other, possibly more important, developments in ecclesiological, legal, and political theory. To distinguish the contributions from different sources in this period is no easy task, so intertwined are they. It is difficult, for example, to disentangle the contributions of jurists and theologians to the rise of political resistance theory: lawyers working for members of the Schmalkaldic League initially articulated, out of constitutional and civil law arguments, the right of the "inferior magistrates" of the German empire to resist the sovereign power, with which Luther publicly concurred in 1530; similarly, French legists such as Claude de Seyssel and Charles Dumoulin extolled the roles of public bodies (regional *parlements* [courts] and the Estates General) in bridling royal power and protecting the distribution of rights, which roles were radicalized and given theological exposition by Huguenot reformers in the 1570s and 1580s. It is just as well that contemporary scholars are disinclined to exaggerate the politically groundbreaking character of Reformation theologies. Several of the most formative Christian political minds of the period, those of the Paris scholastics John Mair and Jacques Almain and the humanist Thomas More, were active before Luther's programmatic political treatises of the early 1520s.

At the same time, nothing is gained by underestimating the political contributions of Reformation theologies — Lutheran, Zwinglian, Calvinist, or Anabaptist. Their conceptions of ecclesial and civil community and authority, of divine and human freedom and law, contained a good deal of groundbreaking political substance. From their reorientation to the Bible and the church fathers flowed genuinely original theopolitical syntheses with unprecedented effects. Luther's early reconstruction of Christian freedom through the polarity of "the two kingdoms" generated a uniquely complex tension between the Christian conscience and the civil order. On the one hand, it opened to believers a communion of salvation and charity devoid of juridical and political dimensions, while removing involvement in civil society from the controlling dynamic of Christian faith and freedom. On the other, the providential role assigned to temporal government rendered magistracy a high and indispensable earthly office with an independent sphere of divinely ordained action. Drawing on Luther and Zwingli among a myriad of late medieval sources, Anabaptist movements further radicalized this polarity, either by repudiating altogether the benefits and obligations of civil commonwealth or by attempting to absorb political order within a revolutionary communal eschatology. Arguably, both radicalizing moves were less original than Luther's dialectic, and to some extent Zwingli's, in that they recapitulated features of perfectionist traditions of ascetic withdrawal, anarchy, and revolution from the thirteenth century onward: Catharist, Albigensian and Waldensian, Spiritual Franciscan, Beghard and Beguine, Lollard, Hussite and Taborite. Here, too, however, powerful social visions were not lacking, such as that of regenerate temporal lordship in the service of regenerate community elaborated by the author of *On the New Transformation of the Christian Life*, which shares the social imagination of Thomas More's *Utopia* but substitutes apocalyptic expectation for Christian-Platonic irony. Moreover, Calvin's harmonizing of ecclesiastical and secular disciplines sustained a fertile dialectic of spiritual communion and political order, godliness and civility, education and restraint, that was genuinely novel, though heavily indebted to Bucer and foreshadowed by the republicanism of the Dominican reformer of Florence, Savonarola. Finally, the political covenantalism developed by Scottish and French Calvinists in the second half of the century (connected with Bullinger, Tyndale, and Hooper as well as Calvin) constituted a strikingly novel and influential chapter in the history of social and political compact-theory.

To summarize the key developments in Christian political thought from Mair to Grotius, we must resist encyclopedic pretensions and focus on those that have theological and philosophical, as well as historical, prominence. These, in our judgment, are connected with the neo-scholastic revival of Thomistic legal and political theory, northern humanist reflection on Christian society, and Protestant formulations of the church and of civil polity.

① Revival of Thomistic Legal and Political Theory. Much of the most formidable political thought of the sixteenth and early seventeenth centuries issued from expositors and admirers of Thomas Aquinas in France, Spain, Italy, and England. Before 1550 the leading figures of the Thomistic political revival were Italian and Spanish Dominicans: the formidable Cardinal Cajetan; Francisco de Vitoria, founder of the "Salamancan school"; and his disciple, Domingo de Soto, while after 1550 the mantle passed to the Italian and Spanish Jesuits: most notably, to Antonio Possevino and Robert Bellarmine, and their even more celebrated contemporaries, Luis de Molina and Francisco Suárez. Although a more eclectic thinker, indebted to English Reformation theology and the common law tradition, Richard Hooker also benefited from the reinvigoration of Thomistic natural law. From its inception shortly after 1500, the turn to Thomas was a turn away from the nominalist and conciliarist teachings of the dominant Paris masters, John Mair and Jacques Almain, who carried on the Gersonian tradition; but the very incompleteness of that turning away was a source of theoretical originality and power. At critical junctures the Ockhamist-Gersonian influence inserted itself into the Thomistic fabric, giving a distinctive texture to neo-scholastic political thought: the attribution of divinely ordained, natural subjective rights to individuals and corporations; the twofold derivation of political rule from communal will and divine will; the voluntaristic understanding of law in general as obligation, and of the law of nations in particular as positive law; and the conception of papal authority as exclusively spiritual, yet entailing indirect authority over temporalities.

The theoretical accomplishments of the Thomistic revival arose as responses to the momentous religio-political developments of the century: the disintegration of the *old* Christian Roman Empire in western Europe, exacerbated by the advent of Protestant polities, and the Spanish pursuit of a *new* Christian empire through the conquest of non-Christian peoples. Instead of Christendom as a politico-spiritual unity under emperor and pope, the neo-scholastics offered a commonwealth of Christian nations, equal in temporal sovereignty and in spiritual obedience to papal direction. They balanced the natural origin of civil rule with its dual orientation to natural and supernatural ends, arguing that princely authority is held, *not from, but under* Christ's vicar, who is entrusted with earthly oversight of the salvation of souls. Consequently, Catholic governments, in remaining loyal to the papal commonwealth, would suffer no political disadvantage vis-à-vis their heretical counterparts, while Protestant governments would suffer a chronic lack of legitimacy and security vis-à-vis the universal church.

The neo-scholastic response to the moral ambiguities of Spanish empire building in the Americas demonstrated the same theoretical balance. Spanish Thomists defended the natural rights of unevangelized and unconverted barbarians to govern themselves and to remain unmolested in ownership of lands and possessions outside of papal jurisdiction, against all attempts to deny them these rights on account of unbelief, irrationality, or moral turpitude, and to subject them to the coercive judgment of the Roman pontiff as universal spiritual and temporal sovereign. Their discussions of what modes of action were morally and legally available to the Spaniards in their dealings with the Indians, and what were not (exemplified by Vitoria's *De Indis*), constituted an unprecedented application of Thomistic legal theory to international relations, in which the *law of nations (ius gentium)* underwent extensive theoretical elaboration, primarily in the principles of just war. In denying the justice of the subjugation of American natives by Spanish *conquistadores*, they appealed to widely accepted customs concerning the rights and obligations of international intercourse, including the conditions on which and methods by which war may be justly waged. However, their arguments also paid due respect to the imperative of the salvation of souls and to papal prerogatives over evangelization and its temporal requirements (e.g., that the faith of converted populations be protected from the hostility of infidel rulers). Most impressive in the accounts of Vitoria and Suárez of justice in war are the scope and complexity of the considerations, the range of rights and obligations brought to bear on every practical judgment, the delicate balance between considerations of what is legally permitted to the offended party and what serves the common good of all the peoples involved. Suárez's achievement beyond Vitoria lies in the precision and thoroughness of his moral-legal principles, such as the immunity of the innocent (noncombatants) from direct military attack.

Of Protestant political thinkers who significantly borrowed from the *Prot.* Thomistic tradition, Richard Hooker, following in the footsteps of Fortescue, most resembles the Catholic scholastic mainstream in his overarching legal typology and his theory of political society and government, while Hugo Grotius most resembles it in his theory of just war and conception of international law. Hooker's idea of the foundation of civil polity is particularly close to the Salamancan school in its dialectic of rational human sociality and political will: political authority depends on an act of individual and communal consent (compact), and the transfer (as opposed to delegation) of power to the ruler. In constructing his ethics of war, Grotius, like his Spanish predecessors, regarded war as an exercise of governmental authority and subjected it to far-ranging and complex moral-legal principles, giving as much, if not more, weight to considerations of social welfare and the requirements of the gospel law. Although his theory of civil polity gives a more prominent role to individual rights than its Catholic counterparts, these particular claims are derived from, and subject to, a more far-ranging social rationality.

II. The Northern Humanist Ideal of Christian Society. In style, the "transalpine" *Humanist* tradition of Christian humanism, most influentially represented by Desiderius Eras- *trad,* mus and Thomas More, could not have been further removed from Thomistic scholasticism. It elevated rhetoric and satire over logical and metaphysical analysis, *different!* Christian moral instinct over legal formulations, education over restraint, and the spiritual and moral fabric of Christian society over governmental policies. Its controlling theme of renewal was that expressed by Paul's injunction to the Roman Christians: "Do not be conformed to this world but be transformed by the renewal of your mind that you may prove what is the will of God, what is good and acceptable and perfect" (Rom. 12:2). However, Paul's injunction was interpreted by the problematic of education in Plato's *Republic,* book 7: how to liberate men's reason from the cave of illusion and passion into the light of the transcendent Good. For Erasmus and More, only the revelation in the New Testament, as recovered by humanist scholarship, of the divine-human perfection of Christ and the nature of true discipleship could disperse the illusory shadows of corrupt European Christendom and expose its darkness. But humanist pedagogy and arts of persuasion had their auxiliary part to play, as handmaids to revelation, both in cultivating virtue and in criticizing the status quo.

Satire was indispensable to them as a method of unmasking routine vice in contemporary thought and action, disclosing its ludicrous stupidity and, perhaps more importantly, its institutional aspect. Accepting Plato's insight that polities degenerate in spirals of bad education, bad practices, bad laws, and bad leadership, they were especially occupied with the institutionalized deceptions, vices, and injustices sustained by the powerful orders and classes in church and commonwealth. They castigated the self-seeking flattery of courtiers, the warmongering of the military aristocracy, the idle extravagance of the gentry, the abusive agriculture of the landed classes, the insatiable greed of merchants and financiers, the Machiavellian politics of imperial expansion, the legal oppression of the poor, the counterfeit piety and morality of worldly clerics, and the legalism and superstition of ecclesiastical discipline. Traditional scholastic modes of argument they regarded as causes and symptoms rather than medicines, moving too much within the corruptions and deceptions of the present. Their assault on scholasticism in the political sphere was aimed squarely at the late medieval natural law tradition, viewed as an unholy marriage of Aristotelian and civilian theory that had suppressed the teaching of Christ in the Sermon on the Mount by pronouncing the blessing of nature on the repulsion of force with force, individual and collective "rights," the institution of private property and the economic transactions emerging from it. Thus they anticipated (even provided) the central strand of ethical polemic in Luther's early thought and in much Anabaptist writing.

There is a studied ambiguity in the social ethics of Erasmus and More which has excited and perplexed their interpreters: How conformable could political society be to the teachings of Christ? Did they advocate Christ's injunctions of humility, turning the other cheek, possessing all things in common, as the only true Christian *social* ethic? While Erasmus condemned war as the most unchristian and unnatural of human pursuits, he nevertheless admitted its moral justification on rare occasions. Similarly, while More appeared to regard common possession as most in keeping with the deepest rational desires of human nature, he did not, apparently, envisage its wide-scale adoption. The resolution of this ambiguity is surely that, firmly anchored in the Franciscan tradition, they both considered Christ's example and teaching to be the whole normative revelation of human nature, the beginning and the end of human thought and action, and of morality in every sphere. To them the question of the moral necessity of property and of waging war, given the present state of human blindless and self-love, was beside the point. Such institutions could never be self-contained moral goods, belonging to a "nature" independent of Christ and subject to laws that could be analyzed apart from his commands. They condemned the complacency of such analysis, which could never fully bring to light the

554

folly and evil in which these institutions were implicated. It is striking, however, that many of their concrete judgments come close to what the best of scholastic analysis produced, suggesting that their quarrel with the schoolmen was more theological and methodological than ethical.

III. Protestant Conceptions of the Church and of Civil Polity. Luther's early theology of "two realms" and "two governments" deeply offended the humanists' prophetic and pedagogical conviction of the unity of Christian society, not only in its failings but in its hope of regeneration. In Luther's soteriology, the grace of Christ, uniting believers in a bond of freedom and love, hardly dispelled the shadows of the cave; it simply transcended them, for political society remained the unregenerate community of corrupted human nature. The community of "the sword" rather than "the word," civil polity could not be more than the worldly condition of redemption, the arena but not the vehicle of the Spirit's work. As much as Erasmus and More were committed to the renaissance of civil society by the leaven of Christ, so Luther was committed to the eschatological separation of the realms, a separation that attained a social completion in Anabaptism. The gulf was never more unbridgeable for him than in the ethical realm: between the gospel ethic of self-sacrificial love contained in the Sermon on the Mount and the civil law of public judgment and punishment, of "natural" rights setting bounds to individual and collective self-seeking. His humanist contemporaries were as scandalized as we are on occasion by his enthusiastic exaggeration of the remoteness of the magistrate's scourge from Christ's forgiveness and mercy. On many more occasions, however, they must have been impressed, as we are, by the humanity of Luther's ethical advice (e.g., to small traders) that issues from a dialectic of Christ's injunctions and the worldly conditions of life. Here we encounter the gospel as a force of transformation within the secular business of society.

Luther's increasing turn to the civil magistrate to reform and oversee external church order was never as compelling theologically as historically, for it sat ill with his idea of the clergy's entirely spiritual authority. To accommodate it he had to relocate many institutional elements of the church within the "worldly realm," yielding to the distinction, central to Zwingli's reformation, between the invisible church of God's elect and the visible church in which the reprobate and elect are mixed. From Zwingli's perspective, however, the magistrate's involvement in ecclesiastical jurisdiction struck a less discordant note, on account of his closer harmonizing of the ends of civil and ecclesiastical discipline. To such a harmonizing the mature Melanchthon gave an impressive theological systematization in his exposition of the two tables of the Law and the three uses of the law. The Erastian turn was consummated in an Anglican setting by Richard Hooker's full-blown integration of the visible church and the commonwealth into a single body politic with two "regiments" united in the national government of "king in parliament."

Calvin's advance over his remarkable teacher, Martin Bucer, was to anchor the government of the church more transparently in her evangelical mission and God's revealed law, as Catholicism had claimed to do. According to his critics, his corresponding weakness (also Catholic) was the inflexibility with which he extracted ecclesiastical offices and discipline from the New Testament and the soteriological weight he accorded these, despite adhering to the ecumenical concept of *adiaphora.*

555

In the tradition of Zwingli, Melanchthon, and Bucer, he found the key to coordinating the goods of civil and ecclesiastical polities within an Augustinian framework of eschatological separation, in the dialectic of law and promise, from God's work in creation to his work of restoration. The resulting theory hovered between a Gelasian dualism and a more Hildebrandine subjection of temporal authority to spiritual, while Genevan practice, with its legislated austerities in both spheres, its structure of moral supervision, and its zealously active citizenry-cum-congregation, realized many of the aspirations of Christian humanism from Savonarola to More, yet stopping short of the radicalism of some Anabaptist experiments.

Though Calvin's theocratic approach to civil government, like Luther's, discouraged reflection on the best form of government or on its constitutive legal foundations, certain of his followers, religious dissidents for the most part who had taken refuge in Geneva, brought constitutional concerns into the theological foreground. These appeared in the Calvinist camp as early as 1556, with Bishop John Ponet's *A Shorte Treatise of Politike Power*; yet the high watermark of Calvinist constitutional theorizing was reached in the 1570s among the French Protestant intelligentsia, who included the humanist legal scholar François Hotman and the classicist and Genevan theologian Theodore Beza. For the Huguenot thinkers, as for Ponet, the impetus came neither from Calvin's theology nor from their Genevan experience, but from the religious persecution of Protestants by Catholic monarchs. Its theoretical substance came from legal traditions in England and France, earlier renaissance thought, and from Zwinglian and theological sources.

Two themes ran through this theorizing. The first was that the constitutive or "fundamental" law of any Christian polity established true public service of God as required by the first table of the revealed law, and, along with it, the divinely ordained distribution of authority to ensure universal obedience to God's commands. The second theme, developed largely out of the thought of John Knox, was that the fundamental law of any Christian polity originated in a divine-human covenantal agreement, to which both ruler *and* people were parties, on the model of the covenants made by God with Israel. In adapting Knox the Huguenot polemicists cast his thought in an explicitly constitutional and populist form; for where Knox had merely assigned to the nobles in their capacity as lesser magistrates the obligation to ensure that the monarch upheld the terms of the national covenant, the author of the Huguenot tract *Vindiciae, contra tyrannos* construed the nobles, assembled in their councils, as representatives of the people as a whole, whose covenantal (and hence constitutional) standing was superior to that of the ruler. The people not only constituted the ruler by electing or (after God's election) acclaiming him, but were obliged to judge his fulfillment of God's covenantal stipulations.

Huguenot covenantalism posed the problem of Christian division within a single state in an acutely ironic manner, in that it appeared to deny the only alternative to official persecution of dissenters, namely, official toleration of them. As a widely distributed minority in a Catholic commonwealth, the Huguenots could hardly appeal to the territorial solution that had served the Protestant cause elsewhere. Their manifestos placed them even more out on a limb than did those of the English Separatists, who also demanded toleration for themselves alone, as a halfway house to total national reform, but did not, like the Huguenots, embrace the unity of church and commonwealth. Indeed, the subsequent appropriation of Huguenot argument by the French Catholic Leaguers had much more historical credibility. Unhappily, the most efficacious voice for religious toleration in France belonged not to the humanists, from Erasmus to Castellion, but to the secularizing monarchists *(les Politiques)*. However, humanist influence was felt among the Dutch Remonstrants in the next century, as the thought of Grotius illustrates.

With Althusius's *Politics Methodically Set Forth (Politica methodice digesta),* Reformed covenantalism assumed an Aristotelian and natural law form. Althusius construed a variety of covenantal associations as the building blocks of an encompassing political society, attributing to each the political authority to interpret and uphold the foundational law of the Decalogue in their respective spheres, or at their levels of jurisdictional competence. While sovereign authority was vested in the universal political community, which delegated it in two directions, to the ruler and to the people's guardians and representatives, the universal polity itself was a thoroughly federal construction, lending an ideal theological-legal form to the actual constitutions of the German empire and Dutch Provinces.

Bibliography: F. J. Baumgartner, *Radical Reactionaries: The Political Thought of the French Catholic League* (Geneva: Droz, 1975); N. Cohn, *The Pursuit of the Millennium: Revolutionary Millenarians and Mystical Anarchists of the Middle Ages* (London: Temple Smith, 1970); P. Collinson, *The Elizabethan Puritan Movement* (London: Cape, 1967); K. Davis, *Anabaptism and Asceticism: A Study in Intellectual Origins* (Scottdale, Pa.: Herald Press, 1974); J. A. Fernández-Santamaria, *The State, War, and Peace: Spanish Political Thought in the Renaissance, 1516-1559* (Cambridge: Cambridge University Press, 1977); H.-J. Goertz, *The Anabaptists* (English translation) (London and New York: Routledge, 1996); J. W. Gough, *The Social Contract: A Critical Study of Its Development* (Oxford, 1957); B. Hamilton, *Political Thought in Sixteenth Century Spain: A Study of the Political Ideas of Vitoria, De Soto, Suárez, and Molina* (Oxford: Clarendon Press, 1963); J. H. Hexter, *The Vision of Politics on the Eve of the Reformation: More, Machiavelli, Seyssel* (London: Allen Lane, 1973); H. Hillerbrand, ed., *Radical Tendencies in the Reformation: Divergent Perspectives* (Kirksville, Mo., 1988); J. Lecler, *Toleration and the Reformation* (English translation), 2 vols. (New York and London: Association Press and Longmans, 1960); J. Lockwood O'Donovan, *Theology of Law and Authority in the English Restoration* (Atlanta: Scholars Press, 1991); M. Mullett, *Radical Religious Movements in Early Modern Europe* (London: Allen & Unwin, 1980); S. E. Ozment, ed., *The Reformation in Medieval Perspective* (Chicago, 1971); S. E. Ozment, ed., *Mysticism and Dissent* (New Haven: Yale University Press, 1973); A. Pagden, ed., *The Languages of Political Theory in Early-Modern Europe* (Cambridge: Cambridge University Press, 1987); J. G. A. Pocock, *The Ancient Constitution and the Feudal Law: A Study of English Historical Thought in the Seventeenth Century* (Cambridge: Cambridge University Press, 1957); M. Prestwick, *International Calvinism* (Oxford: Clarendon Press, 1985); Q. Skinner, *The Foundations of Modern Political Thought,* vol. 2 (Cambridge: Cambridge University Press, 1978); J. M. Stayer, *Anabaptists and the Sword* (Lawrence, Kans.: Coronado Press, 1973); P. Zagorin, *Rebels and Rulers, 1500-1660* (Cambridge: Cambridge University Press, 1982).

Thomas More

(1478-1535)

Sir Thomas More is probably most remembered for being beheaded by King Henry VIII upon refusing to take the oath of royal supremacy that recognized the monarch as the earthly head of the English church. This Catholic martyr met his death at the pinnacle of public eminence and power, having risen from the legal profession up the ladder of appointments in the royal administration to succeed the disgraced Cardinal Wolsey as lord high chancellor. In the tradition of medieval statesmen, he combined a political career with intensive study and literary production, as classicist, theological controversialist, and philosopher. Steeped in humanist scholarship, an intimate of John Colet and Erasmus, More thoroughly belonged to the lively circle of northern renaissance Christian humanists.

His two books of *Utopia*, completed in 1516 prior to his full-time employment in the king's service, fairly defy interpretation, unless read in the light of the tensions generated in his own life by contemporary intellectual issues. They are a conversation with the foundations of Western Christianity in Greek philosophy and the Gospels from a standpoint of deep disaffection with the status quo — of scholastic preoccupation with logical refinement, of legal positivism and the legalistic spirit set adrift from the weightier concerns of justice, of rival secular and ecclesiastical hierarchies succumbing to ossification and decadence, and of rising mercantile ambition unfettered by piety and morality. Against the defects of his age More sets a Christian rationality at once familiar and alien. This is the rationality of equality in the pursuit of spiritual freedom, of community in material possessions, of disciplined pleasure and willing industry, of humble service and mutual respect, and of natural beauty, health, and simplicity. Supposedly unique to the happy inhabitants of Utopia, it is familiar in part from the ethical injunctions and example of Jesus and his disciples as well as from the communal disciplines and the spiritual intensity of monastic life. Yet it is in some respects alien to the full revelation of Christ in the Gospels, to the complete apostolic order of the church, and to the deeper theological motivations of monastic piety.

Thus, the thorny exegetical puzzle posed by More's Utopian vision concerns its precise meaning for authentic Christian aspirations. Every serious reader of the work is compelled to ponder the extent to which his fictive commonwealth is, on the one hand, a heuristic tool of radical social criticism, and on the other, an effective guide to the renovation and renewal of sixteenth-century Christian civilization. In one way More's second book is dispensable to the apology for social reform, for the first contains Hythloday's entirely convincing diagnosis of the corruptions, vices, injustices, and irrationalities afflicting his own commonweal, followed by his hardhitting but plausible legislative recommendations for removing them, or at least greatly reducing them.

However, Utopia is indispensable to More's assault on the complacency of his contemporaries, focused in his portrayal of the whole order of private property as an institutionalization of human pride. He seeks to draw his readers into his own yearning for a holier and more righteous society, in which all Christians, priests and laymen, strive for a closer approximation to the communion of evangelical law and love which is the fulfillment of human nature. Among the unnatural institutional forms of contemporary Christendom, More assails the civil law (as Fortescue and Wyclif had done before him) for the failure of its myriad, complicated formulations to be ethically transparent, unlike the few and lucid laws of Utopia. In the sphere of international law he follows Erasmus in reproaching the institution of "the League" for undermining the natural bonds knitting distinct nations into one universal human community. In this he anticipates later natural law criticism of the idea that international relations can be conjured out of a moral vacuum through artificial and arbitrary covenants.

Further Reading: J. Dunn and I. Harris, *More* (Cheltenham: Edward Elgar, 1997); J. H. Hexter, *More's Utopia: The Biography of an Idea* (Princeton: Princeton University Press, 1952); J. H. Hexter, *The Vision of Politics on the Eve of the Reformation: More, Machiavelli, and Seyssel* (London: Allen Lane, 1973); G. M. Logan, *The Meaning of More's "Utopia"* (Princeton: Princeton University Press, 1983); C. Starnes, *The New Republic: A Commentary on Book I of More's "Utopia" Showing Its Relation to Plato's "Republic"* (Waterloo, Ont.: Wilfred Laurier University Press, 1990); L. Strauss, *Studies in Platonic Political Philosophy* (Chicago: University of Chicago Press, 1983).

From *Utopia,* Book 1

[Raphael Hythloday, conversing with Peter Giles and Thomas More in Antwerp, recounts a conversation at the home of Cardinal John Morton in England.]
[p. 22] [*The Causes and Punishment of Felony*] [. . .] It chanced on a certain day, when I [Raphael] sat at his table, there was also a certain layman cunning in the laws of your [English] realm. Who, I cannot tell whereof taking occasion, began diligently and earnestly to praise that strait and rigorous justice which at that time was there executed upon felons, who, as he said, were for the most part twenty hanged together

on one gallows. And, seeing so few escaped punishment, he said he could not choose but greatly wonder and marvel how and by what evil luck it should so come to pass that thieves, nevertheless, were in every place so rife and so rank.

Nay, sir, quoth I (for I durst boldly speak my mind before the cardinal), marvel nothing hereat: for this punishment of thieves passeth the limits of justice, and is also very hurtful to the weal-public. For it is too extreme and cruel a punishment for theft, and yet not sufficient to refrain and withhold men from theft. For simple theft is not so great an offence that it ought to be punished with death. Neither there is any punishment so horrible that it can keep them from stealing which have no other craft whereby to get their living. Therefore in this point, not you only but also the most part of the world be like evil schoolmasters, which be readier to beat than to teach their scholars. For great and horrible punishments be appointed for thieves, whereas much rather provision should have been made that there were some means whereby they might get their living, so that no man should be driven to this extreme necessity, first to steal and then to die.

Yes, quoth he, this matter is well enough provided for already. There be handicrafts, there is husbandry to get their living by, if they would not willingly be nought.

Nay, quoth I, you shall not escape so: for, first of all, I will speak nothing of them that come home out of the wars maimed and lame, as not long ago out of Blackheath field and a little before that out of the wars in France; such, I say, as put their lives in jeopardy for the weal-public's or the king's sake, and by reason of weakness and lameness be not able to occupy their old crafts, and be too aged to learn new: of them I will speak nothing, forasmuch as wars have their ordinary recourse. But let us consider those things that chance daily before our eyes.

First there is a great number of gentlemen which cannot be content to live idle themselves, like dors [drones], of that which others have laboured for: their tenants, I mean, whom they poll and shave to the quick by raising their rents (for this only point of frugality do they use, men else, through their lavish and prodigal spending, able to bring themselves to very beggary); these gentlemen, I say, do not only live in idleness themselves, but also carry about with them at their tails a great flock or train of idle and loitering serving-men which never learned any craft whereby to get their livings. These men, as soon as their master is dead, or be sick themselves, be incontinent thrust out of doors. For gentlemen had rather keep idle persons than sick men, and many times the dead man's heir is not able to maintain so great a house and keep so many serving-men as his father did. Then in the mean season they that be thus destitute of service either starve for hunger or manfully play the thieves. For what would you have them to do? When they have wandered abroad so long, until they have worn threadbare their apparel and also appaired [impaired] their health, then gentlemen, because of their pale and sickly faces and patched coats, will not take them into service. And husbandmen dare not set them a-work, knowing well enough that he is nothing meet to do true and faithful service to a poor man with a spade and a mattock for small wages and hard fare, which, being daintily and tenderly pampered up in idleness and pleasure, was wont with a sword and a buckler by his side to jet through the street with a bragging look and to think himself too good to be any man's mate. Nay, by Saint Mary, sir, quoth the lawyer, not so. For this kind of men must be made most of. For in them, as men of stouter stomachs, bolder spirits, and manlier courages than handicraftsmen and plowmen be, doth consist the whole power, strength, and puissance of our army, when we must fight in battle.

Forsooth, sir, as well you might say, quoth I that for war's sake you must cherish thieves; for surely you shall never lack thieves while you have them. No, nor thieves be not the most false and faint-hearted soldiers, nor soldiers be not the cowardliest thieves: so well these two crafts agree together. But this fault, though it be much used among you, yet is it not peculiar to you only, but common also almost to all nations.

[. . .] But yet this is not only the necessary cause of stealing. There is another, which, as I suppose, is proper and peculiar to you Englishmen alone.

What is that? quoth the cardinal.

Forsooth, my lord, quoth I, your sheep that were wont to be so meek and tame and so small eaters, now, as I hear say, be become so great devourers and so wild, that they eat up and swallow down the very men themselves. They consume, destroy, and devour whole fields, houses, and cities. For look in what parts of the realm doth grow the finest and therefore dearest wool, there noblemen and gentlemen, yea and certain abbots, holy men no doubt, not contenting themselves with the yearly revenues and profits that were wont to grow to their forefathers and predecessors of their lands, nor being content that they live in rest and pleasure nothing profiting, yea, much annoying the weal-public, leave no ground for tillage. They enclose all into pastures; they throw down houses; they pluck down towns and leave nothing standing but only the church to be made a sheep-house. And as though you lost no small quantity of ground by forests, chases, lands, and parks, those good holy men turn all dwelling places and all glebeland into desolation and wilderness. Therefore that one covetous and insatiable cormorant and very plague of its native country may compass about and enclose many thousand acres of ground together within one pale or hedge, the husbandmen be thrust out of their own, or else either by covin and fraud or by violent oppression they be put besides it, or by wrongs and injuries they be so wearied, that they be compelled to sell all. By one means, therefore, or by other, either by hook or crook, they must needs depart away, poor, silly, wretched souls, men, women, husbands, wives, fatherless children, widows, woeful mothers with their young babes, and their whole household small in substance and much in number, as husbandry requireth many hands. Away they trudge, I say, out of their known and accustomed houses, finding no place to rest in. All their household stuff, which is very little worth though it might well abide the sale, yet being suddenly thrust out they be constrained to sell it for a thing of nought. And when they have wandered abroad till that be spent, what can they then else do but steal, and then justly pardy be hanged, or else go about a-begging? And yet then also they be cast in prison as vagabonds, because they go about and work not, whom no man will set a-work, though they never so willingly proffer themselves thereto.

For one shepherd or herdman is enough to eat up that ground with cattle, to the occupying whereof about husbandry many hands were requisite. And this is also the cause why victuals be now in many places dearer. Yea, besides this the price of wool is so risen, that poor folks, which were wont to work it and make cloth thereof, be now able to buy none at all. And by this means very many be forced to forsake work and to give themselves to idleness. For after that so much ground was enclosed for pasture an infinite multitude of sheep died of the rot, such vengeance God took of their inordinate and insatiable covetousness, sending among the sheep that pestiferous murrain which much more justly should have fallen on the sheepmasters' own heads. And though the number of sheep increase never so fast, yet the price falleth not one mite, because there be so few sellers; for they be almost come into a few rich men's hands, whom no need forceth to sell before they lust, and they lust not before they may sell as dear as they lust.

Now the same cause bringeth in like dearth of the other kinds of cattle, yea, and that so much the more because that after farms plucked down and husbandry decayed there is no man that passeth for the breeding of young store. For these rich men bring not up the young ones of great cattle as they do lambs. But first they buy them abroad very cheap, and afterward, when they be fatted in their pastures, they sell them again exceedingly dear. And therefore (as I suppose) the whole incommodity hereof is not yet felt; for yet they make dearth only in those places where they sell. But when they shall fetch them away from thence where they be bred faster than they can be brought up, then shall there also be felt great dearth, store beginning there to fail where the ware is bought. Thus the unreasonable covetousness of a few hath turned that thing to the utter undoing of your island, in the which thing the chief felicity of your realm did consist. For this great dearth of victuals causeth men to keep as little houses and as small hospitality as they possibly may, and to put away their servants; whither, I pray you, but a-begging or else (which these gentle bloods and stout stomachs will sooner set their minds unto) a-stealing?

Now to amend the matter, to this wretched beggary and miserable poverty is joined great wantonness, importunate superfluity, and excessive riot. For not only gentlemen's servants, but also handicraftsmen, yea, and almost the plowmen of the country, with all other sorts of people, use much strange and proud newfangleness in their apparel, and too much prodigal riot and sumptuous fare at their table. Now bawds, queans, whores, harlots, strumpets, brothel houses, stews; and yet another stews, winetaverns, ale-houses, and tippling houses, with so many naughty, lewd, and unlawful games, as dice, cards, tables, tennis, bowls, quoits, do not all these send the haunters of them straight a-stealing, when their money is gone? Cast out these pernicious abominations; make a law that they which plucked down farms and towns of husbandry shall re-edify them, or else yield and uprender the possession thereof to such as will go to the cost of building them anew. Suffer not these rich men to buy up all to engross and forestall, and with their monopoly to keep the market alone as please them. Let not so many be brought up in idleness; let husbandry and tillage be restored; let clothworking be renewed, that there may be honest labours for this idle sort to pass their time in profitably, which hitherto either poverty hath caused to be thieves, or else now be either vagabonds or idle serving men, and shortly will be thieves.

Doubtless unless you find a remedy for these enormities you shall in vain advance yourselves of executing justice upon felons. For this justice is more beautiful in appearance and more flourishing to the shew than either just or profitable. For by suffering your youth wantonly and viciously to be brought up, and to be infected, even from their tender age, by little and little with vice, then, a [in] God's name, to be punished when they commit the same faults after being come to man's state, which from their youth they were ever like to do; in this point, I pray you, what other thing do you than make thieves and then punish them?

[. . .] But now, Master Raphael, I would very gladly hear of you, why you think theft not worthy to be punished with death, or what other punishment you can devise more expedient to the weal-public. For I am sure you are not of that mind, that you would have theft escape unpunished. For if now the extreme punishment of death cannot cause them to leave stealing, then, if ruffians and robbers should be sure of their lives, what violence, what fear, were able to hold their hands from robbing which would take the mitigation of the punishment as a very provocation to the mischief?

Surely, my lord, quoth I, I think it not right nor justice that the loss of money should cause the loss of man's life. For mine opinion is, that all the goods in the world are not able to countervail man's life. But if they would thus say, that the breaking of justice and the transgression of the laws is recompensed with this punishment, and not the loss of the money, then why may not this extreme and rigorous justice well be called plain injury? For so cruel governance, so strict rules and unmerciful laws be not allowable, that if a small offence be committed, by and by the sword should be drawn. Nor so stoical ordinances are to be borne withal, as to count all offences of such equality, that the killing of a man or the taking of his money from him were both a matter, and the one no more heinous offence than the other, between the which two, if we have any respect to equity, no similitude or equality consisteth. God commandeth us that we shall not kill. And be we then so hasty to kill a man for taking a little money? And if any man would understand killing by this commandment of God to be forbidden after no larger wise than man's constitutions define killing to be lawful, then why may it not likewise by man's constitutions be determined after what sort whoredom, fornication, and perjury may be lawful? For whereas, by the permission of God, no man hath power to kill neither himself nor yet any other man, then, if a law made by the consent of men concerning slaughter of men ought to be of such strength, force, and virtue, that they which contrary to the commandment of God have killed those whom this constitution of man commanded to be killed, be clean quit and exempt out of the bonds and danger of God's commandment, shall it not then, by this reason follow that the power of God's commandment shall extend no further than man's law doth define and permit? And so shall it come to pass, that in like manner man's constitutions in all things shall determine how far the observation of all God's commandments shall extend. To be short, Moses' law, though it were ungentle and sharp, as a law that was given to bondmen, yea, and them very obstinate, stubborn, and stiff-necked, yet it punished theft by the purse, and not with death. And let us not think that God in the new law of clemency and mercy, under the which he ruleth us with fatherly gentleness, as his dear children, hath given us greater scope and licence to the execution of cruelty one upon another.

Now ye have heard the reasons whereby I am persuaded that this punishment is unlawful. Furthermore, I think there is nobody that knoweth not how unreasonable, yea, how pernicious a thing it is to the weal-public that a thief and an homicide or murderer should suffer equal and like punishment. For the thief, seeing that man that is condemned for theft in no less jeopardy nor judged to no less punishment than him that is convict of manslaughter, through this cogitation only he is strongly and forcibly provoked, and in a manner constrained, to kill him whom else he would have but robbed. For the murder being once done, he is in less fear and in more hope that the deed shall not be betrayed or known, seeing the party is now dead and rid out of the way, which only might have uttered and disclosed it. But if he chance to be taken and descried, yet he is in no more danger and jeopardy than if he had committed but single felony. Therefore while we go about with such cruelty to make thieves afraid, we provoke them to kill good men.

Now as touching this question, what punishment were more commodious and better, that truly in my judgment is easier to be found than what punishment might be worse. For why should we doubt that to be a good and a profitable way for the punishment of offenders, which we know did in times past so long please the Romans, men in the administration of a weal-public most expert, politic, and cunning? Such as among them were convict of great and heinous trespasses, them they condemned into stone quarries, and into mines to dig metal, there to be kept in chains all the days of their life. But as concerning this matter, I allow the ordinance of no nation so well as that which I saw, while I travelled abroad about the world, used in Persia among the people that commonly be called the Polylerites, whose land is both large and ample and also well and wittily governed, and the people in all conditions free and ruled by their own laws, saving that they pay a yearly tribute to the great king of Persia. [. . .]

They that in this land be attainted and convict of felony, make restitution of that which they stole to the right owner, and not (as they do in other lands) to the king, whom they think to have no more right to the thief-stolen thing than the thief himself hath. But if the thing be lost or made away, then the value of it is paid of the goods of such offenders, which else remaineth all whole to their wives and children. And they themselves be condemned to be common labourers; and, unless the theft be very heinous, they be neither locked in prison nor fettered in gyves, but be untied and go at large, labouring in the common works. They that refuse labour, or go slowly and slackly to their work, be not only tied in chains, but also pricked forward with stripes; but being diligent about their work they live without check or rebuke. Every night they be called in by name, and be locked in their chambers. Beside their daily labour, their life is nothing hard or incommodious. Their fare is indifferent good, borne at the charges of the weal-public, because they be common servants to the commonwealth. But their charges in all places of the land are not borne alike, for in some parts that which is bestowed upon them is gathered of alms. And though that way be uncertain, yet the people be so full of mercy and pity, that none is found more profitable or plentiful. In some places certain lands be appointed hereunto, of the revenues whereof they be maintained; and in some places every man giveth a certain tribute for the same use and purpose.

Again, in some parts of the land these serving-men (for so be these damned persons called) do no common work, but as every private man needeth labourers, so he cometh into the market-place and there hireth some of them for meat and drink and a certain limited wages by the day, somewhat cheaper than he should hire a free man. It is also lawful for them to chastise the sloth of these serving-men with stripes. By this means they never lack work, and besides the gaining of their meat and drink, every one of them bringeth daily something into the common treasury. All and every one of them be apparelled in one colour. Their heads be not polled or shaven, but rounded a little above the ears, and the tip of the one ear is cut off. Every one of them may take meat and drink of their friends, and also a coat of their own colour; but to receive money is death, as well to the giver as to the receiver. And no less jeopardy it is for a free man to receive money of a serving-man for any manner of cause, and likewise for serving-men to touch weapons. The serving-men of every several shire be distinct and known from other by their several and distinct badges which to cast away is death, as it is also to be seen out of the precinct of their own shire, or to talk with a serving-man of another shire. And it is no less danger to them for to intend to run away than to do it indeed. Yea, and to conceal such an enterprise in a serving-man it is death, in a free man servitude. Of the contrary part, to him that openeth and uttereth such counsels be decreed large gifts, to a free man a great sum of money, to a serving-man freedom, and, to them both, forgiveness and pardon of that they were of counsel in that pretence. So that it can never be so good for them to go forward in their evil purpose as, by repentance, to turn back.

This is the law and order in this behalf, as I have shewed you. Wherein what humanity is used, how far it is from cruelty, and how commodious it is, you do plainly perceive, forasmuch as the end of their wrath and punishment intendeth nothing else but the destruction of vices and saving of men, with so using and ordering them that they cannot choose but be good, and what harm soever they did before, in the residue of their life to make amends for the same. Moreover it is so little feared that they should turn again to their vicious conditions, that wayfaring men will for their safeguard choose them to their guides before any other, in every shire changing and taking new; for if they would commit robbery they have nothing about them meet for that purpose. They may touch no weapons; money found about them should betray the robbery. They should be no sooner taken with the manner, but forthwith they should be punished. Neither they can have any hope at all to scape away by fleeing. For how should a man that in no part of his apparel is like other men fly privily and unknown, unless he would run away naked? Howbeit, so also fleeing he should be descried by the rounding of his head and his ear mark. But it is a thing to be doubted that they will lay their heads together and conspire against the weal-public. No, no, I warrant you. For the serving-men of one shire alone could never hope to bring to pass such an enterprise without soliciting, enticing, and alluring the serving-men of many other shires to take their parts. Which thing is to them so impossible, that they may not as much as speak or talk together or salute one another. No, it is not to be thought that they would make their own countrymen and companions of their counsel in such a matter, which they know well should be jeopardy to the concealer thereof and great commodity and goodness to the opener and detector of the same. Whereas, on the other part, there is none of them all hopeless or in despair to recover again his former state of freedom by humble obedience, by patient suffering, and by giving good tokens and likelihood of himself, that he will ever after that live like a true and an honest man. For every year divers of them be restored to their freedom through the commendation of their patience.

[The conversation having turned to other matters, Raphael continues to speak.]

[p. 50] [*Private and Common Possessions*] Howbeit, doubtless, Master More (to speak truly as my mind giveth me), where possessions be private, where money beareth all the stroke, it is hard and almost impossible that there the weal-public may justly be governed and prosperously flourish. Unless you think thus: that justice is there executed where all things come into the hands of evil men, or that prosperity there flourisheth where all is divided among a few, which few, nevertheless, do not lead their lives very wealthily, and the residue live miserably, wretchedly, and beggarly. Wherefore when I consider with myself and weigh in my mind the wise and godly ordinances of the Utopians, among whom with very few laws all things be so well and wealthily ordered that virtue is had in price and estimation, and yet, all things being there common, every man hath abundance of everything. Again, on the other part, when I compare with them so many nations ever making new laws, yet none of them all well and sufficiently furnished with laws, where every man calleth that he hath gotten his own proper and private goods, where so many new laws daily made be not sufficient for every man to enjoy, defend, and know from another man's that which he calleth his own; which thing the infinite controversies in the law, daily rising, never to be ended, plainly declare to be true: These things (I say) when I consider with myself, I hold well with Plato, and do nothing marvel that he would make no laws for them that refused those laws whereby all men should have and enjoy equal portions of wealths and commodities.

For the wise man did easily foresee this to be the one and only way to the wealth of a commonality, if equality of all things should be brought in and stablished. Which, I think, is not possible to be observed where every man's good be proper and peculiar to himself. For where every man under certain titles and pretences draweth and plucketh to himself as much as he can, so that a few divide among themselves all the whole riches, be there never so much abundance and store, there to the residue is left lack and poverty. And for the most part it chanceth that this latter sort is more worthy to enjoy that state of wealth than the other be, because the rich men be covetous, crafty, and unprofitable. On the other part the poor be lowly, simple, and by their daily labour more profitable to the commonwealth than to themselves. Thus I do fully persuade myself that no equal and just distribution of things can be made, nor that perfect wealth shall ever be among men, unless this propriety be exiled and banished. But so long as it shall continue, so long shall remain among the most and best part of men the heavy and inevitable burden of poverty and wretchedness. Which, as I grant that it may be somewhat eased, so I utterly deny that it can wholly be taken away. For if there were a statute made that no man should possess above a certain measure of ground, and that no man should have in his stock above a prescript and appointed sum of money, if it were by certain laws decreed that neither the king should be of too great power, neither the people too haut and wealthy, and that offices should not be obtained by inordinate suit, or by bribes and gifts, that they should neither be bought nor sold, nor that it should be needful for the officers to be at any cost or charge in their offices (for so occasion is given to them by fraud and ravin to gather up their money again, and by reason of gifts and bribes the offices be given to rich men, which should rather have been executed of wise men) — by such laws, I say, like as sick bodies that be desperate and past cure be wont with continual good cherishing to be kept and botched up for a time, so these evils also might be lightened and mitigated. But that they may be perfectly cured and brought to a good and upright state, it is not to be hoped for, whiles every man is master of his own to himself. Yea, and whiles you go about to do your cure of one part you shall make bigger the sore of another part, so the help of one causeth another's harm, forasmuch as nothing can be given to any one unless it be taken from another.

But I am of a contrary opinion, quoth I, for methinketh that men shall never there live wealthily where all things be common. For how can there be abundance of goods or of anything where every man withdraweth his hand from labour? Whom the regard of his own gains driveth not to work, but the hope that he hath in other men's travails maketh him slothful. Then when they be pricked with poverty, and yet no man can by any law or right defend that for his own which he hath gotten with the labour of his own hands, shall not there of necessity be continual sedition and bloodshed? Specially the authority and reverence of magistrates being taken away, which, what place it may have with such men among whom is no difference, I cannot devise.

I marvel not, quoth he, that you be of this opinion. For you conceive in your mind either none at all, or else a very false image and similitude of this thing. But if you had been with me in Utopia and had presently seen their fashions and laws, as I did which lived there five years and more, and would never have come thence but only to make that new land known here, then doubtless you would grant that you never saw people well ordered but only there.

From Book 2

[Hythloday describes the commonwealth of Utopia.]

[p. 103] [*Legal Justice*] They [the Utopians] have but few laws, for to people so instruct and institute very few do suffice. Yea, this thing they chiefly reprove among other nations, that innumerable books of laws and expositions upon the same be not sufficient. But they think it against all right and justice that men should be bound to those laws which either be in number more than be able to be read, or else blinder and darker than that any man can well understand them. Furthermore, they utterly exclude and banish all attorneys, proctors, and sergeants at the law, which craftily handle matters, and subtly dispute of the laws. For they think it most meet that every man should plead his own matter, and tell the same tale before the judge that he would tell to his man of law. So shall there be less circumstance of words, and the truth shall sooner come to light, whiles the judge with a discreet judgment doth weigh the words of him whom no lawyer hath instruct with deceit, and whiles he helpeth and beareth out simple wits against the false and malicious circumventions of crafty children. This is hard to be observed in other countries, in so infinite a number of blind and intricate laws. But in Utopia every man is a cunning lawyer; for (as I said) they have very few laws, and the plainer and grosser that any interpretation is, that they allow as most just. For all laws (say they) be made and published only to the intent that by them every man should be put in remembrance of his duty. But the crafty and subtle interpretation of them (forasmuch as few can attain thereto) can put very few in that remembrance, whereas the simple, the plain, and gross meaning of the laws is open to every man. Else as touching the vulgar sort of the people, which be both most in number and have most need to know their duties, were it not as good for them that no law were made at all, as, when it is made, to bring so blind an interpretation upon it, that without great wit and long arguing no man can discuss it? To the finding out whereof neither the gross judgment of the people can attain, neither the whole life of them that be occupied in working for their livings can suffice thereto.

[p. 105] [*International Treaties*] As touching leagues, which in other places between country and country be so oft concluded, broken, and renewed, they never make none with any nation. For to what purpose serve leagues, say they, as though nature had not set sufficient love between man and man? And who so regardeth not nature, think you that he will pass for words? They be brought into this opinion chiefly because that in those parts of the world leagues between princes be wont to be kept and observed very slenderly. For here in Europe, and especially in these parts where the faith and religion of Christ reigneth, the majesty of leagues is everywhere esteemed holy and inviolable, partly through the justice and goodness of princes, and partly at the reverence and motion of the head bishops. Which, like as they make no promise themselves but they do very religiously perform the same, so they exhort all princes in any wise to abide by their promises, and them that refuse or deny so to do, by their pontifical power and authority they compel thereto. And surely they think well that it might seem a very reproachful thing if, in the leagues of them which by a peculiar name be called faithful, faith should have no place. But in that new found part of the world, which is scarcely so far from us beyond the line equinoctial as our life and manners be dissident from theirs, no trust nor confidence is in leagues. But the more and holier ceremonies the league is knit up with, the sooner it is broken by some cavillation found in the words, which many times of purpose be so craftily put in and placed, that the bands can never be so sure nor so strong but they will find some hole open to creep out at, and to break both league and truth. The which crafty dealing, yea, the which fraud and deceit, if they should know it to be practised among private men in their bargains and contracts, they would incontinent cry out at it with an open mouth and a sour countenance, as an offence most detestable, and worthy to be punished with a shameful death, yea, even they that ad-

568

vance themselves authors of like counsel given to princes. Wherefore it may well be thought, either that all justice is but a base and a low virtue and which avaleth [abases] itself far under the high dignity of kings, or, at the least wise, that there be two justices: the one meet for the inferior sort of the people, going afoot and creeping low by the ground, and bound down on every side with many bands because it shall not run at rovers; the other a princely virtue, which like as it is of much higher majesty than the other poor justice, so also it is of much more liberty, as to the which nothing is unlawful that it lusteth after. These manners of princes (as I said) which be there so evil keepers of leagues, cause the Utopians, as I suppose, to make no leagues at all, which perchance would change their mind if they lived here. Howbeit, they think that though leagues be never so faithfully observed and kept, yet the custom of making leagues was very evil begun. For this causeth men (as though nations which be separate asunder by the space of a little hill or a river were coupled together by no society or bond of nature) to think themselves born adversaries and enemies one to another, and that it were lawful for the one to seek the death and destruction of the other if leagues were not. Yea, and that after the leagues be accorded, friendship doth not grow and increase, but the licence of robbing and stealing doth still remain, as far forth as, for lack of foresight and advisement in writing the words of the league, any sentence or clause to the contrary is not therein sufficiently comprehended. But they be of a contrary opinion, that is, that no man ought to be counted an enemy which hath done no injury; and that the fellowship of nature is a strong league, and that men be better and more surely knit together by love and benevolence than by covenants of leagues, by hearty affection of mind than by words.

Text: Everyman's Library (London: J. M. Dent & Sons, 1910).

Desiderius Erasmus
(1466/69–1536)

The most celebrated scholar and man of letters of his day, courted by the most powerful crowned and mitered heads of Europe (Bainton 1969, 13), Erasmus of Rotterdam was and remains the unmatched prodigy of sixteenth-century humanism. His literary influence has been as extensive as his output was varied, and his output included editions and translations of the Greek New Testament and of classical Latin and Greek, pagan and patristic authors, collections of maxims, letters, satires, works of pedagogy, exhortation, controversy, adulation, and advice. Until late in his career, devotion to his scholarly and literary vocation kept him itinerant and impecunious, despite his international repute. In abode, as in spirit, Erasmus was consummately the humanist "citizen of the world."

In his mature work the goals of the brilliant rhetorician and erudite classicist are blended with strong christocentric piety and reforming zeal, dedication to the text of the New Testament, and an intellectual mix of patristic and Florentine Neoplatonism and Roman Stoic moralism. Important among his formative influences were his youthful contact with the *devotio moderna* of the Brethren of the Common Life, his deep friendship with English humanists John Colet (a distinguished New Testament exegete) and Thomas More, and his encounter in 1501 with the Franciscan Jean Vitrier, a passionate monastic reformer and devotee of Origen's theology, whom he would come to revere as a singular embodiment of the *philosophia Christi*. Also crucial for his mature writing were his travels between 1506 and 1509 among Italian humanist scholars and men of letters, who shared their expertise in textual criticism, philology, pedagogical and dialogical method, as well as his firsthand experience of Pope Julius II's incessant military campaigns and oppressive taxation of the populace in reconquered papal territory, and of the debauchery and sycophancy of the Roman curia.

Following a lengthy stay in England (1509-14), in which he wrote and revised his most famous work, the *Praise of Folly* (*Moriae encomium* — alternatively, "praise

570

of More"), Erasmus spent several highly productive years in the Netherlands. During these he published an edition of Jerome's letters (1516), his first edition of the Greek New Testament with a fresh Latin translation (1516), and two political writings, *The Education of a Christian Prince* (*Institutio principis christiani* [1516]) and the *Complaint of Peace* (*Querimonia pacis,* now known as *Querela pacis* [1517]). The latter writings, though different in form, tone, and purpose, share a common perspective that is in some respects continuous with an earlier political piece, the *Panagyric for Archduke Philip of Austria* (*Panegyricus*), published in 1504. All three works extol the classical ideal of a Christian prince as a paragon of virtue and wisdom, whose humanity and dedication to the common good are demonstrated above all by his cultivation of the arts of peace and (here is the Erasmian twist) by his abhorrence of war as an unrivaled evil for his subjects' material and spiritual welfare.

An extravagant Ciceronian oration, the *Panagyric* is less overtly biblical, christocentric, and Platonic than the later productions. The *Education*, being a Renaissance version of the medieval "mirror of princes" genre — Erasmus's first offering to Prince Charles (later Charles V) upon his appointment as royal councillor — presents fewer hermeneutical difficulties than the more satirically opaque *Complaint*, which recalls the shifting rhetorical postures of his *Praise of Folly*. Both works, however, were intended to influence princely policy as well as public sentiment (not to speak of encouraging royal patronage); even the *Complaint* is not lacking in that immediate, practical instruction which floods the *Education*.

Together with an earlier essay, *War Is Sweet to Those Who Have Never Tried It* (*Dulce bellum inexpertis*), published originally in the 1515 edition of his *Adages*, the *Complaint* has earned Erasmus the reputation of a "pacifist." Indeed, he considered his "pacific ethic," expounded most fully here, to be his most original contribution to political reflection (Faludy 1970, 148), and many of his admirers concur. However, the epithet "pacifist" is inaccurate in as much as he explicitly concedes in various places (most notably, under the rubric "On starting war" in his *Education*) that war may be an "unavoidable" last resort required by the obligations of governing, and must be conducted within specifiable ethical guidelines. At the same time the epithet does convey his deep evangelical skepticism about the morality of waging war and his ethical preoccupation with war avoidance. He does not repudiate just-war theory so much as sideline it, out of his conviction that war is infinitely more a disease of humankind to be cured than a remedy to be administered: that both the "insatiable lust" for armed conflict and the evils bred by it threaten to destroy man's natural endowments for society, rationality, and friendship, and their perfecting in his obedience to Christ's example and commands. Erasmus presents Christ as incarnating the divine-human spirit of unanimity, harmony, and reconciliation, to which the lives of Christians are individually and communally ordered; and he dwells on the disparity between Christ's earthly communion, the church, and the "armed camp" that Europe had become, ravaged by incessant, unrestrained warfare among princes and nations, undertaken for discreditable reasons such as the avenging of "trifling" injuries, the pursuit of territorial expansion, and worst of all, the consolidation of "despotic power."

As Erasmus shunned detailed analyses of conflicts and preferred allusions over examples, we are not well equipped to weigh his judgments about contemporary affairs. It seems clear that he was responding along some of the same lines as his mentors, Colet, More, and Vitrier, to widespread political instability and moral anxiety bred by the inflated dynastic and territorial ambitions of the ruling houses in Europe (the Medici, the Valois, and the Hapsburgs). His concrete proposals for reducing occasions for armed conflict had among their aims the dismantling of conventional peaceful mechanisms of empire, through intermarriage, inheritance, and treaties, on the grounds that such international ties were politically alienating and conflict breeding. His alternative was a collection of somewhat insular, territorially static polities, ruled by Christian princes worthy of their high calling and joined together by revitalized bonds of faith, morality, and cultural communication, a Platonic vision of Christendom. In this scenario war had an attenuated use as the means of last resort to defend long-suffering and innocent Christians against heathen aggression and oppression, where conversion was impossible or had failed.

Further Reading: R. H. Bainton, *Erasmus of Christendom* (New York: Collins, 1969); A. G. Dickens and W. R. D. Jones, *Erasmus the Reformer* (London: Methuen, 1994); G. Faludy, *Erasmus of Rotterdam* (London: Eyre & Spottiswoode, 1970); L. Jardine, ed., *Erasmus, "The Education of a Christian Prince"* (Cambridge: Cambridge University Press, 1997); F. José, "Erasmus on the Just War," *Journal of the History of Ideas* 34 (1973): 209-26; J. McConica, *Erasmus* (Oxford: Oxford University Press, 1991); E. E. Reynolds, *Thomas More and Erasmus* (London: Burns & Oates, 1965); R. J. Schoeck and B. Corrigan, eds., *The Collected Works of Erasmus* (Toronto: University of Toronto Press, 1974); J. D. Tracy, *The Politics of Erasmus* (Toronto: University of Toronto Press, 1978).

From *The Complaint of Peace*

[p. 294] Only men, for whom concord was so fitting and who have the greatest need of it, are not reconciled to each other by nature, so powerful and effective in other respects, or united by education; they can be neither bound together by the many advantages of agreement nor persuaded to love each other through their awareness and experience of many powerful evils. All men have the same shape and voice, whereas all other kinds of animal differ very widely in bodily shape; to man alone has been given the power of reason, which is common to all and shared with no other living creature. He is the only animal with the gift of speech, the chief promoter of friendly relationships; the seeds of learning and the virtues alike are implanted in him, along with a mild and gentle disposition which is inclined towards good will between him and his fellows, so that he delights in being loved for himself and takes pleasure in being of service to others — so long as he has not been corrupted by base desires, as if by Circe's potions, and degenerated from man to beast (cf. Homer, *Odyssey* 10.235ff.). Hence it is, I believe, that the word "humane" is generally applied to anything to do with mutual good will. Man has also the capacity for tears, proof of a disposition which is readily persuaded, so that if some difference has arisen and a cloud has overcast the clear sky of friendship, a reconciliation can easily be achieved.

Now take a look at all the reasons nature has provided for concord. She was not satisfied simply with the attractions of mutual good will; she wanted friendship to be not only enjoyable for man but also essential. So she shared out the gifts of mind and body in a way that would ensure that no one should be provided with everything and not need on occasion the assistance of the lowly; she gave men different and unequal capacities, so that their inequality could be evened out by mutual friendships. Different regions provided different products, the very advantage of which taught exchange between them. To all other creatures she assigned their own armour and weapons for self-protection, but man alone she made weak and unarmed and unable to find safety except in treaties and the need of one man for another. Need created cities, need taught the value of alliance between them, so that with combined forces they could repel the attacks of wild beasts or brigands.

Indeed, there is nothing in human affairs which can be self-sufficient. At the very start of life, the human race would have died out at once if it had not been propagated by conjugal harmony; for man would not be born at all, or would die immediately after birth and lose life as he entered it, if the tiny infant were not helped by the kind hand of the midwife and the kind care of his nurse. To meet the same need, nature has implanted the glowing spark of family affection, so that parents can love the child they have not yet seen; and to this she has added the reciprocal love of children for their parents, so that in turn they can relieve the helplessness of the old by their support; and we have what all alike find praiseworthy and the Greeks name so aptly "mutual affection" *(antipelargōsis)*. Then there are the ties of kinship and affinity, and similarity of disposition, interests, and appearance amongst several people which is certain to foster good will; many too possess a mysterious kind of spiritual perceptiveness and a marvellous propensity towards a reciprocal love, something which the Ancients attributed in admiration to a man's godhead.

So nature provided all these arguments for peace and concord, so many lures and inducements to draw us towards peace, so many means of coercion. But then what Fury appeared with such harmful powers, to scatter, demolish, and destroy them all and to sow an insatiable lust for fighting in the human heart? If custom did not blunt first our sense of amazement and then our awareness of evil, who would believe that there are men endowed with human reason who thus fight, brawl, and rage against each other in perpetual discord, strife and war? Finally, they confound everything, sacred and profane, with pillaging, bloodshed, disaster, and destruction; no bond is sufficiently sacred to check them in their frenzy for mutual extinction. Were there nothing else, the common name of "man" should be sufficient to ensure concord amongst men. But granted that nature, who is such a powerful influence even on wild animals, can do nothing for men, has Christ no influence at all on Christians? And granted that nature's teaching may well prove inadequate, although it is highly effective even where there is no perception, since the teaching of Christ is so far superior to nature's, why does it not bring home to those who profess to follow it the importance of what it is especially trying to promote, namely peace and mutual good will? Or at least dissuade men from the wickedness, savagery, and madness of waging war?

[p. 300] Tell me, what induced the Son of God to come to earth if not his wish to reconcile the world with the Father, to bind men together with mutual and inde-structible love, and, finally, to make man his own friend (cf. John 15:12-17)? He was an envoy on my behalf, he did my business. And it was because the name of Solomon means "peace-making" or "man of peace" that he was chosen to prefigure him; for though David was a great king, since he was a warrior and defiled with blood he was not permitted to build the house of the Lord (1 Chron. 22:8) — in this respect he was unworthy to prefigure a peace-making Christ. Now consider this, warrior: if wars undertaken and fought by God's command desecrate the fighter, what will be the effect of wars prompted by ambition, anger, or madness? If the shedding of pa-gan blood pollutes a god-fearing king, what will result from wholesale Christian bloodshed? I implore you, Christian prince, if you are truly a Christian, to look at the example of your Prince, behold the manner of his entry upon his reign on earth, his passage through it, his departure thence, and then you will understand how he wished you to rule in such a manner that peace and concord are the chief of your concerns.

When Christ was born, did the angels sound trumpets of war? The Jews heard the noise of the trumpet, for they were permitted to wage war, and this was the ap-propriate sign for men whose law told them to hate their enemies. But the angels of peace sing a very different song in the ears of a people seeking peace. They do not sound the war-trumpet or promise victories, triumphs, and spoils of war. No, it is peace they proclaim, in accordance with the pronouncements of the prophets, and they proclaim it not to those who breathe war and slaughter, who are filled with fury and longing for arms, but to men of good will whose inclination is towards concord. Men may suggest what reasons they like for their own malady, but if they did not love war they would not engage in perpetual warfare amongst themselves in the way they do.

Then when Christ reached manhood, what else did he teach and expound but peace? He repeatedly greeted his disciples with an assurance of peace, saying, "Peace be with you," and bade them use that form of greeting as the only one worthy of Christians (Matt. 10:12f.). The apostles also remember this command when they start their letters with words of peace, wishing peace to those whom they especially love (e.g., Rom. 1:7; 1 Cor. 1:3). To wish good health for anyone [salve, the classical Roman greeting] is an excellent thing, but a prayer for peace is a prayer for the sum total of happiness. Now see how at the hour of his death Christ is deeply concerned to commend peace to his hearers, as he had so often done throughout his lifetime. "Love one another," he says, "as I have loved you" (John 13:34); and again, "I give you my peace, I leave you my peace" (John 14:27). You hear what he leaves his people? Not horses, bodyguards, empire or riches — none of these. What then? He gives peace, leaves peace — peace with friends, peace with enemies. Now please consider what he begged from his Father at the Last Supper, in his final prayers as the hour of death drew near. He knew he would be granted whatever he asked and so, I think, he sought no ordinary thing. "Holy Father," he said, "keep them through thy name, that they may be one as we are" (John 17:11). Please note that Christ asks for his people a special sort of concord: he said not that they should be of one mind but that they might be one, and not just in any way, but, as he said, we are one who are united in the most perfect and inexpressible way; and incidentally he indicated that there is only one way for men to be preserved — if they unite among themselves to foster peace.

The princes of this world mark their men by distinctive attire so that they can be picked out from the others, especially in time of war; but look at the mark Christ has used to indicate his followers — none other than that of mutual love. "By this sign," he said, "men shall know that you are my disciples," not if you are dressed in a special way or eat special food, not if you spend your time on excessive fasting or exhaustive study of the Psalms, but "if you love one another" — and in no common manner, but "as I have loved you" (John 13:34-35). The precepts of the philosophers are without end, the pronouncements of Moses and the kings are many and various, but Christ said only: "This is my sole commandment: love one another" (John 15:12). And in prescribing a form of prayer for his disciples, does he not give in its opening words a wonderful suggestion of Christian concord? "Our Father," he says (Matt. 6:9). The spoken prayer is one for God, the petition is one which is common to all men, for they are all one household, one family, dependants of one Father; how then is it right for them to contend amongst themselves in continual warfare? How can you call on a common father if you are drawing a sword to thrust in your brother's vitals? And as Christ wished this one concept to be deeply implanted in the minds of his followers, he drove home his concern for concord with so many signs, parables, and commandments.

[p. 303] Every Christian word, whether you read the Old Testament or the New, reiterates one thing: peace with unanimity; while every Christian life is occupied with one thing: war. What is this more than brutal brutality, which in so many instances can be neither controlled nor tamed? Men so minded should surely either cease to pride themselves on the name of Christian or put into practice the teaching of Christ through concord. How long will their way of life continue to conflict with the name they bear? Mark your home or your clothing as much as you please with the sign of the cross, but Christ will not recognise any such mark but the one he himself commanded, that of concord.

The disciples were gathered together when they saw Christ ascend to heaven (Acts 1:9), and together when they were bidden to await the Holy Spirit (Acts 1:5), and he had promised he would always be in their midst when men were gathered together (Matt. 18:20), lest anyone should hope Christ would ever be present at wars. Then there is that fiery spirit [i.e., at Pentecost]: what else can it be but love? Nothing is so beneficial to all as fire, and fire is kindled from fire without diminishment. If you want to see how that spirit is the parent of concord, look at the effect of it. The apostle said that all men were of one heart and one soul (Acts 4:32). Remove the spirit from the body and the whole structure of its components collapses at once. Remove peace and the whole community of Christian life is destroyed. Theologians declare that Christians today have numerous sacraments which infuse them with heavenly spirit. If their claim is true, where is the special effect of that spirit — one heart and one soul? But if the sacraments are mere fictions, why are they held in such high honour? I say this not to belittle the sacraments in any way but to make Christians more ashamed of their conduct.

Does not the very decision to call the Christian people a church imply a common purpose? What is there in common between the church and an armed camp? One signifies bringing together [*ecclesia* means "assembly"], the other tearing apart. If you take pride in being a member of the church, what have you to do with wars? If you are outside the church, what have you to do with Christ? If you all share the same house, serve a common prince, fight for the same cause, have been initiated by the same sacraments, enjoy the same benefits, live on the same pay, and seek a joint reward, why are you always quarrelling amongst yourselves? Even amongst godless soldiers, comrades at arms hired and paid for the task of carrying out slaughter, we see what harmony there can be simply because they fight under the same standard. Yet so many factors fail to unite those who claim to be god-fearing men. Do so many of the sacraments effect nothing? Baptism is common to all; by this we are reborn in Christ, cut off from the world, inserted among the members of Christ. What can be so much a united whole as the members of the same body? Thus through baptism there is neither slave nor free man, neither barbarian nor Greek, neither man nor woman, but all are the same in Christ who brings all into harmony. For the Scythians, a little blood drunk by both from the same cup joins two men so closely that they do not hesitate even to die for a friend (Herodotus, *Historiae* 4.70), and amongst the heathen, friendship is also sacred when a shared meal has brought men together. Yet the heavenly bread and mystical chalice do not unite Christians in the friendship which Christ himself held sacred, and which they renew daily and represent in sacrifice.

If Christ achieved nothing, what is the need of so many ceremonies today? If he achieved something which matters, why is he so neglected today, as if all he did was to stage some foolish farce? Does any man dare to approach that sacred table, the symbol of friendship, the communion sacrament of peace, if he intends to make war on Christians, and prepares to destroy those whom Christ died to save and to drink the blood of men for whom Christ shed his own blood? O hearts harder than adamant, when fellowship can be found in so many circumstances but there is such unaccountable discord in life! The same law governs birth, the same necessity brings all to old age and death. All share the same founder of the human race, the same author of their faith; all are redeemed by the same blood, all are initiated by the same rites and sustained by the same sacraments. Whatever benefits come from these stem from the same source and are shared equally amongst all. There is the same church and the same reward offered to all. Moreover, the heavenly Jerusalem to which Christians aspire takes its name from a vision of peace (cf. Augustine, *City of God* 19:11 [see above, p. 152]), and meanwhile the church on earth is its image. How then does it come to differ so markedly from its exemplar? Has nature, inventive in so many ways, made no progress along the many roads open to her? Has Christ himself accomplished nothing with his many commandments, mysteries, and parables? Evil unites even evil men, as the saying goes, but neither good nor evil unites Christians among themselves.

[p. 310] But I have long been hearing the sort of excuse clever men produce for their own wrongdoing. They protest that they act under compulsion and are dragged unwillingly into war. Pull off your mask, drop your pretences, examine your own heart, and you will find that anger, ambition, and folly brought you to war, not any constraint — unless you define constraint as something not altogether to your liking! Such trappings are for the people; God is not to be fooled by pretence. Yet meanwhile solemn prayers are offered, and peace is sought with noisy clamour and deafening roar of voices: "Grant us peace, we beseech you, hear us!" Surely God could justly answer: "Why do you mock me? You are asking me to remove what you bring on yourselves of your own choice. You pray to be let off what is your own responsibility."

If any sort of affront can start a war — why, who has nothing to complain of? Incidents arise between husband and wife which are best overlooked, unless you want their mutual good will to be destroyed. If something of the same sort arises between princes, why need there be an immediate rush to arms? There are laws, there are learned men, venerable abbots, and reverend bishops whose sound advice could have calmed a stormy situation. Why do the princes not ask them to arbitrate? They could hardly pick out any so partisan that they would not depart with a better solution than they would achieve by arms. Hardly any peace is so unjust that it is not preferable to a war, however just that may be. First count all the separate demands and concomitants of war, and then you will see how much you profit by it!

The supreme authority is that of the pontiff of Rome. But when nations and princes are violently engaged in wicked wars which may go on for years, what has become of papal authority then? Where is the power second only to Christ's? It should surely have been exercised, were its holders not gripped by the same passions as the people. When the pontiff calls for war, he is obeyed. If he calls for peace, why is there not the same obedience to his call? If men prefer peace, why were they so eager to answer the summons of Julius as a war leader, though scarcely anyone responds to Leo's appeal for peace and concord? [The Medici pope, Leo X, who succeeded Julius in 1513, had been active in promoting peace between England and France.] If the authority of the pontiff is truly sacrosanct, it should surely most prevail whenever it appeals for what was the special message of Christ. But when those whom Julius could rouse to engage in a war of deadly destruction cannot be similarly stirred when the most holy pontiff Leo appeals in so many ways of Christian concord, they make it clear that under pretext of serving the church they are the slaves of their own desires, to say nothing harsher than that.

If you are genuinely tired of war, let me give you a word of advice on how you can maintain concord. A sound peace does not rest on alliances and treaties between men, which, as we see, can often lead to wars. The very sources from which the evil springs and the base passions which give rise to your conflicts must be cleansed. And while each individual is the slave of his desires, the state suffers; nor does any individual attain the very end he pursues with his evil designs. The princes must learn wisdom and use it for their subjects, not for themselves, and they should be truly wise, measuring their majesty, happiness, wealth, and magnificence by the factors which make them truly great and glorious. Their intention towards their country should be that of a father towards his family. A king should think himself great if the subjects he rules are of the very best, happy if he makes his people happy, exalted if the men he governs enjoy the greatest measure of freedom, wealthy if they are wealthy, prosperous if his cities prosper in unbroken peace. And the nobles and holders of office should model their attitude on that of their prince, judging everything by the country's interests; by this means they will also have acted properly in their own interests.

If a king is of this intention, will he be easily persuaded to extort money from his subjects in order to pay barbarian mercenaries? Will he reduce his people to famine to enrich some godless army leaders? Will he expose the lives of his people to so many hazards? I think not. He should exercise his power within limits, remembering that he is a human being and a free man ruling over men who are also human and free and, finally, that he is a Christian ruler of Christians. The people in their turn should defer to him only so far as is in the public interest. A good prince should demand no more, and a bad one will in fact have his desires held in check by the combined will of the citizens. Neither side should consider personal interests.

All honour to those who have used their talents or wisdom for the prevention of war and the establishment of concord; in short, to the man who has directed all his efforts, not to procuring the greatest force of fighting men and engines of war, but to ensuring that there shall be no need of them. Yet out of so many Roman emperors, only Diocletian is recorded as having conceived this noblest of designs. But if war is unavoidable, it should be conducted in such a way that the full force of its calamities must fall on the heads of those who gave cause for it. As things are now, princes wage war unscathed and their generals thrive on it, while the main flood of misfortune sweeps over the peasants and humble citizens, who have no interest in war and gave no occasion for it. Where is a prince's wisdom, if he takes no thought of this, or his heart, if he reckons it of small consequence? Some plan must be devised whereby the power to rule shall not change hands so frequently and be forever on the move, because every innovation in affairs creates disturbance, and disturbance creates war. It could easily be achieved if royal children had to marry within the bounds of their own territory, or if, when an alliance between neighbours was desirable, all parties should renounce their expectations of succession. Nor should a prince be permitted to sell or transfer any part of his realm, as if free cities were his personal property: for the cities subject to a king's rule are free, unlike those which are slaves under a tyrant's domination.

In the kind of intermarriage we have today it may happen that a native Irishman suddenly becomes emperor of the Indies, or the previous ruler of Syria unexpectedly finds himself king of Britain. As a result of this, neither country will have a ruler; someone will have abandoned his old country and not be recognised by his new one, as he is wholly unknown and born in a different world. Meanwhile, as he tries to consolidate his position and establish himself by conquest, he drains away and exhausts the resources of one of the countries, and while struggling to retain his hold on two places, though he is hardly fit to administer one, more often than not he loses them both.

There should be agreement between princes once and for all on what each of them should rule, and once territories have been assigned to them, no alliance should extend or diminish these and no treaty tear them apart. Thus each ruler will try to make every improvement he can in his own portion, and by applying all his energies to one territory, he will try to leave it to his children enriched in the best way he can. By this means the future could be one of universal prosperity every-where. It remains for the princes to be bound together not by marriage alliances or artificial associations, but by friendship which is genuine and disinterested, and above all by a like and common desire to be of service to mankind. A prince should be succeeded either by his next of kin or by one judged most suitable by vote of the people; for the others, it should be enough if they rank amongst eminent members of the nobility.

It is royalty's duty to know nothing of personal inclinations and to judge everything by the common good. Accordingly, the prince should avoid distant journeys; indeed, he should never be willing to go beyond the bounds of his own realm, and should keep in mind the saying tested and proved throughout the centuries: "Better master's face than the back of his head" (Cato, *Res rustica* 4.1). He should think himself enriched not if he has robbed others but if he has improved what is his own. When war is under discussion, he should not seek counsel from young men, who like the idea of war simply because they have no experience of the evils it brings, or from those who gain control by general disturbance of the peace, who flourish and fatten on the miseries of the people. He should call on older men of prudence and integrity, whose devotion to their country is proved. Nor should a war be rashly started to suit the whim of one individual or another, for a war once begun is difficult to end. Something so highly dangerous, more so than anything, must not be undertaken except by the consent of the whole people.

The causes of war must be removed immediately. Some things must be overlooked; such courtesy will encourage courtesy. There are times when peace has to be paid for. If you calculate all a war would have cost and the number of citizens you will save from death, peace will seem cheap at the price, however much you paid for it; the cost of war would have been greater, quite apart from the blood lost by your subjects. You must work out how much evil you avoid and how much good you can preserve, and you will not regret the cost. Meanwhile the bishops should carry out their duties, the priests be true priests, the monks be mindful of their profession, and the theologians teach what is worthy of Christ. Let all combine against war, all be watch-dogs and speak out against it. In private and in public they must preach, proclaim, and inculcate one thing: peace. Then if they cannot prevent a conflict to settle the issue, they must certainly not approve or take part, lest they should be responsible for giving a good name to so criminal or at least so questionable a practice.

[p. 316] Are you longing for war? First take a look at what peace and war really are, the gains brought by one and the losses by the other; this will enable you to calculate whether there is anything to be achieved by exchanging peace for war. If it is something for admiration when a kingdom is prosperous throughout, with its cities soundly established, lands well cultivated, excellent laws, the best teaching, and the highest moral standards, consider how you will necessarily destroy all this happiness if you go to war. By contrast, if you have ever seen towns in ruins, villages destroyed, churches burnt, and farmland abandoned and have found it a pitiable spectacle, as indeed it is, reflect that all this is the consequence of war.

It you judge it a serious thing to introduce the criminal dregs of hired mercenaries into your country, to feed them on your people's misery, to submit to them, fawn on them, indeed, to entrust yourself and your safety to their will, you must realise that this is a condition of war. If you abominate robbery, this is what war teaches; if you abhor murder, this is the lesson of war. For who will shrink from killing one man in hot blood when he has been hired for a pittance to slaughter so many? If neglect of the law is the most imminent threat to civil authority, why, "the law says nothing when arms hold sway" (Cicero, *Pro Milone* 4.11). If you believe that fornication, incest, and worse are loathsome evils, war is the school where these are taught. If irreverence for and neglect of religion is the source of every evil, religion is entirely swept away by the storm of war. If you judge the state of your country to be worst when the worst people in it have the most power, in time of war the lowest kinds of criminal are the rulers; war has most need of those whom in time of peace you would nail to the cross. For who will be better at leading troops through hidden tracks than a trained brigand? Who will be bolder at plundering houses and despoiling churches than a housebreaker or tomb-robber? Who will be so eager to strike down and disembowel a foe as a gladiator or murderer? Or so suitable for setting fire to cities and engines of war as an incendiary? Who will defy the waves and hazards at sea like a pirate trained by a lifetime of plundering? If you want to see clearly how immoral a thing is war, you have only got to look at the agents it employs.

If nothing should be so important to the conscientious prince as the welfare of his subjects, it is essential that war should be particularly hateful to him; if his happiness is to rule a happy people, he must cherish peace above all. If the chief desire of a good prince should be that his subjects are as good as they can be, he ought to loathe war as the cesspool of every iniquity. If he would believe that his personal wealth resides in the possessions of the citizens, he must avoid war by every possible means, for it will certainly wear down everyone's resources if it is to have a successful outcome, and what was won by honest skill must be squandered on individuals who are no more than murderers and monsters.

Then too, princes must consider over and over again that every man is won over by his own cause and smiled on by his own expectations, and that what seems perfectly just in the heat of the moment may often prove the opposite; self-deception of this kind is not infrequent. However, imagine a cause which is undoubtedly just and a war which is wholly successful in outcome, and then make sure you weigh up all the disadvantages of actually fighting the war against the advantages won by victory, and see if the victory was worth while. It can scarcely ever be bloodless, so now you have your people defiled by human blood. Then reckon the damage to individual morals and public discipline, for which no gain can compensate. You empty your purse, plunder your people, burden the just, and incite the unjust to further crimes, and even when you have ended the war, its legacy remains with you. Skilled crafts will have fallen into disuse and trade and business interrupted, for you will have been forced to cut yourself off from many places in order to blockade your enemy. Before the war, all neighbouring regions were yours, for peace makes everything common to all through trade. See what you have done: even the country which is especially yours can now hardly be called your own.

Translation: Betty Radice (University of Toronto Press, 1986). Used with permission.

Martin Luther

(1483-1546)

To acclaim or denounce Martin Luther as the father of the Protestant Reformation is platitudinous and possibly overstated. Nevertheless, his pronouncement of God's justification of the sinner through faith in Jesus Christ and not through righteous works contributed to dismantling the edifice of medieval Christendom with a more sweeping stroke than any of his reforming predecessors, Wyclif and Marsilius included, and supported an equally sweeping reintegration of Christian belief and practice.

In less than a decade, from 1515 to 1523, the principal features of Luther's theological innovation were settled. Their vast ecclesiological implications were first perceptible in his attack on papal indulgences, the most extreme development of the juridical commerce of penances. The declaration in the Ninety-five Theses (1517) that the truly contrite "participates in all the blessings of Christ and the church," and so has "full remission of penalty and guilt, even without indulgence letters" (Theses 36f.), cast doubt upon the exercise of calculating juridical-moral equivalents of sin, penalty, and supererogatory merit. It portrayed the *communio sanctorum* in a different light, as the complete sharing in spiritual goods, as well as in sin and suffering, by those united in Christ's spirit. Increasingly Luther grasped the superfluousness, indeed the antagonism, of the church's external constitution, hierarchical, juridical, and sacramental, to her inner spiritual reality and to the eschatological dynamic of revelation, justifying faith, and self-sacrificial love. His major tracts of 1520 unfold a more drastic ecclesiastical reconstruction than Marsilius and Wyclif had imagined, their assault on clerical jurisdiction and Roman primacy paling beside his reduction of the seven sacraments to two (baptism and the Lord's Supper) and his demolition of the sacerdotal priesthood as a superior estate.

As with his predecessors, Luther's spiritualizing of the church was counterbalanced by an extension of civil power; but an extension invigorated and circumscribed by the theological rationale of the "priesthood of all believers." We profit by coming to his fullest celebrated treatment of temporal authority, *Temporal Authority: To What Extent It Should Be Obeyed* (*Von weltlicher Obrigkeit, wie weit man ihr Gehorsam schuldig sei* [1523]), from his earlier writings (1520), *The Address to the German Nobility* (*An den christlichen Adel deutscher Nation*) and *The Freedom of the Christian* (*Von der Freiheit eines Christenmenschen*), where he argues that all Christians participate equally in the kingship and priesthood of Christ by their baptism into one gospel and one faith. Each has, on the one hand, the same freedom from spiritual bondage to temporal powers and vicissitudes, and on the other, the same authority to confess Christ to one another and to intercede in prayer for one another. Differences and inequalities of authority among Christians arise from their diverse temporal offices (*Ämter*) or stations (*Stände*) (e.g., of spouse, parent, servant, merchant, ruler, subject, pastor). Only the pastor of a congregation has the *regular* public prerogative and duty to preach and administer the sacraments; likewise, the secular magistrate alone has the public power to publish and coercively enforce laws. Luther's *Address* leaves us with the impression that the civil ruler, in uniquely combining the evangelical authority of the Christian man with the public power of coercive jurisdiction, occupies a privileged position from which to effect ecclesiastical reform and maintain the church's external discipline. But this impression is belied by his argument in *Temporal Authority*.

The argument here is controlled by his distinction of the two realms or kingdoms (*Reiche*) and their corresponding governments (*Regimente*), variously designated as "temporal" (*das weltliche Reich*) and "spiritual" (*das geistliche Reich*) or as "the kingdom of God" or "of Christ" (*Reich Gottes/Christi*) and "the kingdom of the Devil" or "of the world" (*Teufels Reich/Reich der Welt*). These broadly signify the antithetical communities of fallen, corrupted human nature and of humanity united to Christ: the former a frail, transient network of external human relationships resting on selfish and destructive strivings after worldly goods; the latter a spiritual reciprocity of persons securely resting on shared faith, humility, and love. The governments ordained by God for the two communities consist, on the one hand, of "the sword" and "the civil law," and on the other, of "the word of Christ" and "the Holy Spirit"; the former constrains wills through external demands and sanctions, the latter harmonizes them freely and inwardly. Both regiments serve "the kingdom of Christ" in the struggle for human souls against "the kingdom of the devil," but only in strict separateness. Their confusion, always the devil's work, occurs when any human authority tries to legislate and enforce true Christian faith, thereby usurping the Spirit's work and denying both divine freedom and human conscience.

Thus did Luther simultaneously vindicate civil rule as a Christian work against Anabaptist rejection of it *and* repudiate the direct interference of secular authority with, or on behalf of, Christian freedom. This ran contrary to the political reformation envisaged by Zwingli and the rebellious German knights, to papal and imperial suppression of local reform initiatives, and to the violent, popular implementations of reform incited by Carlstadt, Münzer, and the Zwickau prophets in the Saxon towns and cities.

The key to Luther's independent course was his insight that every Christian exists in both realms and is subject to both regimes, so that his inward dispositions

[margin note: duties in the 2 kingdoms]

and outward actions are structured by this dual membership. As a member of Christ's royal priesthood, the Christian lives out his Lord's commands in the Sermon on the Mount, practicing humility and long-suffering, unbounded forgiveness and generosity to friend and enemy alike. As a member of secular society, overwhelmingly composed of heathens and hypocrites, the Christian willingly submits to the civil law and to the magistrate, upholding their authority and assisting their work of civil justice. But he acts in the temporal order *always* on behalf of others, *never* on his own behalf, for while he himself has (or should have!) no need of the restraint, protection, and vindication effected by "the sword," his weaker neighbor does have need of them. Moreover, unregenerate human society as a whole ("the kingdom of the world") depends on them for its preservation. So, although the Christian never calls upon the magistrate to avenge and redress injury to himself, he accepts civil judgment instigated without his complaint, for the sake of the temporal order.

Scholars are generally agreed that Luther's doctrine of the two realms and governments underwent shifts in the course of successive expositions, with consequences for his political ethics. They have attended especially to his endorsements, from the late 1520s, of the central role of civil magistrates in the evangelical reform and the supervision of churches in their jurisdictions. These endorsements appear to refine the line of thought in the *Address,* in that they justify the magistrate's intervention *as that of a Christian with a special obligation to act,* an obligation that flows from his strategic public position, but not from his coercive jurisdiction. Scholars have also noticed Luther's later tendency to relocate "spiritual" matters (e.g., heresy, ecclesiastical *adiaphora*) within the magistrate's temporal jurisdiction, sometimes with recourse to natural-law political principles. *[margin note: increasing advocacy of temporal rules' involvement in spir. matters]*

A parallel shift has been remarked in his conceptualizing of the way in which every Christian participates in the "two kingdoms": from 1530, involvement in the temporal kingdom becomes an intrinsic necessity. Luther perceives more clearly not only the old Adam's continuing need for coercive restraint, but also the individual's need for the whole range of natural goods embedded within temporal relationships. He increasingly affirms that temporal offices, even as forms of law and power (for the ruler's office remains paradigmatic), serve the divinely created social order as well as the fallen human condition, so that, e.g., parenthood and proprietorship form part of God's original provision for the fulfillment of human physical needs.

Corresponding to his refocusing of the temporal realm is his refocusing of the spiritual realm in the direction of *inwardness and transcendence of the social as such.* In *The Sermon on the Mount,* a published exposition of Jesus' address, based on sermons delivered in Wittenberg between November 1530 and April 1532, he conceives the Christian individual as two persons: a *Christ-person* subject only to Christ's commands and a *Weltperson* caught up in a network of social obligations. While Christ's commands still dictate some lines of external conduct, they chiefly concern the "right relation of the heart to God," the Christian's inner freedom or distance from the requirements of the social world. Thus the *Weltperson* is a proprietor while the *Christ-person* is ready to surrender all property on God's account; the *Weltperson,* when maliciously injured, lodges a complaint before a court, while the *Christ-person* *[margin note: importance of inward disposition while engaging in worldly affairs]* suffers patiently, forgiving the offender. The Christian is no longer, as in *Temporal Authority,* warned against seeking legal redress of injuries, but is chiefly warned against the worldly motivations that infect legal action. In political as in legal and economic conduct, the *Weltperson* is in practical control, judging according to canons of responsible social rationality. >

Luther's deliberations on issues of current business ethics in the treatise *Trade and Usury (Von Kaufshandlung und Wucher)* are, broadly speaking, illuminating applications of the earlier doctrine contained in *Temporal Authority.* The treatise combines two compositions: (1) an attack on the prevailing "sharp" commercial practices, particularly of monopolistic trading companies, written in 1524 in response to the failure of a succession of imperial diets to restrain them effectively; and (2) an attack on usury directed primarily at the most common form of commercial investment contract (the *Zinskauf*). The attack was formulated originally in two sermons of 1519-20 in opposition to, on the one hand, a radical evangelical condemnation of usury that denied the debtor's legal and moral obligation to the usurer, and on the other, the canonist attempt to construe the investment contract as nonusurious. Both compositions give a prominent place to Christ's injunctions in the Sermon on the Mount concerning the "righteous" handling of material possessions, which generally prescribe three modes of "exchanging external goods": namely, openhandedly allowing one's property to be snatched away, freely giving to anyone in need, and lending without charge or assurance of return. To these Luther appends buying and selling as a fourth mode, permitted rather than normative, a concession to the exigencies of fallen community. Despite his approbation of private property, he regards commercial and mercantile transactions with the eye of Franciscan suspicion, as almost inevitably contaminated by avarice, and roundly condemns the maximizing of profit — the "chief maxim" of the merchant class.

However, his grudging admission that trade "can be practiced in a Christian manner" commits him to offering ethical guidelines. He warns against pricing and purchasing practices that use to advantage rather than seek to relieve the neighbor's genuine need, whether he be rival supplier or consumer. He warns, too, against standing surety for loans and investments, condemning this institution for its mistrust and usurpation of God's providential work. In brief, he proposes that only the prevalence of free Christian lending and responsible (preferably regulated) pricing policies, together with the elimination of credit, will restore to trade its relatively benign countenance.

Further Reading: P. Althaus, *The Theology of Martin Luther* (English translation) (Philadelphia: Fortress, 1966); P. Althaus, *The Ethics of Martin Luther* (English translation) (Philadelphia: Fortress, 1972); W. D. J. Cargill Thompson, *The Political Thought of Martin Luther* (Brighton, Sussex: Harvester Press, 1984); F. E. Cranz, *An Essay on the Development of Luther's Thought on Justification, Law, and Society* (Cambridge, Mass.: Harvard University Press, 1959); H. G. Koenigsberger, ed., *Luther: A Profile* (London: Macmillan, 1973); J. Pelikan, *Spirit versus Structure: Luther and the Institutions of the Church* (London: Collins, 1968).

From *Temporal Authority: To What Extent It Should Be Obeyed*

[WA 11 247] First we must provide a sound basis for the civil law and sword so no one will doubt that it is in the world by God's will and ordinance. The passages which do this are the following: Romans 13:1-2: "Let every soul be subject to the governing authority, for there is no authority except from God; the authority which everywhere exists has been ordained by God. He then who resists the governing authority resists the ordinance of God, and he who resists God's ordinance will incur judgment." Again, in 1 Peter 2:13-14: "Be subject to every kind of human ordinance, whether it be to the king as supreme, or to governors, as those who have been sent by him to punish the wicked and to praise the righteous."

The law of this temporal sword has existed from the beginning of the world. For when Cain slew his brother Abel, he was in such great terror of being killed in turn that God even placed a special prohibition on it and suspended the sword for his sake, so that no one was to slay him (Gen. 4:14-15). He would not have had this fear if he had not seen and heard from Adam that murderers are to be slain. Moreover, after the Flood, God reestablished and confirmed this in unmistakable terms when he said in Genesis 9:6, "Whoever sheds the blood of man, by man shall his blood be shed." This cannot be understood as a plague or punishment of God upon murderers, for many murderers who are punished in other ways or pardoned altogether continue to live, and eventually die by means other than the sword. Rather, it is said of the law of the sword, that a murderer is guilty of death and in justice is to be slain by the sword. [. . .]

Hence it is certain and clear enough that it is God's will that the temporal sword and law be used for the punishment of the wicked and the protection of the upright.

[margin, handwritten: role of temporal gov't: punish & protect]

Second. There appear to be powerful arguments to the contrary. Christ says in Matthew 5:38-41: "You have heard that it was said to them of old: An eye for an eye, a tooth for a tooth. But I say to you, Do not resist evil; but if anyone strikes you on the right cheek, turn to him the other also. And if anyone would sue you and take your coat, let him have your cloak as well. And if anyone forces you to go one mile, go with him two miles," etc. Likewise Paul in Romans 12:19: "Beloved, defend not yourselves, but leave it to the wrath of God; for it is written, 'Vengeance is mine; I will repay, says the Lord.'" And in Matthew 5:44: "Love your enemies, do good to them that hate you." And again, in 1 Peter 3:9: "Do not return evil for evil, or reviling for reviling," etc. These and similar passages would certainly make it appear as though in the New Testament Christians were to have no temporal sword.

Hence, the sophists also say that Christ has thereby abolished the law of Moses. Of such commandments they make "counsels" for the perfect. They divide Christian teaching and Christians into two classes. One part they call the perfect, and assign to it such counsels. The other they call the imperfect, and assign to it the commandments. This they do out of sheer wantonness and caprice, without any scriptural basis. They fail to see that in the same passage Christ lays such stress on his teaching that he is unwilling to have the least word of it set aside, and condemns to hell those who do not love their enemies (cf. Matt. 5:17-22). Therefore, we must interpret these passages differently, so that Christ's words may apply to everyone alike, be he perfect or imperfect. For perfection and imperfection do not consist in works, and do not establish any distinct external order among Christians. They exist in the heart, in faith and love, so that those who believe and love the most are the perfect ones, whether they be outwardly male or female, prince or peasant, monk or layman. For love and faith produce no sects or outward differences.

Third. Here we must divide the children of Adam and all mankind into two classes, the first belonging to the kingdom of God, the second to the kingdom of the world. Those who belong to the kingdom of God are all the true believers who are in Christ and under Christ, for Christ is King and Lord in the kingdom of God, as Psalm 2:6 and all of Scripture says. [. . .]

Now observe, these people need no temporal law or sword. If all the world were composed of real Christians, that is, true believers, there would be no need for nor benefits from prince, king, lord, sword, or law. They would serve no purpose, since Christians have in their heart the Holy Spirit, who both teaches and makes them to do injustice to no one, to love everyone, and to suffer injustice and even death willingly and cheerfully at the hands of anyone. Where there is nothing but the unadulterated doing of right and bearing of wrong, there is no need for any suit, litigation, court, judge, penalty, law, or sword. For this reason it is impossible that the temporal sword and law should find any work to do among Christians, since they do of their own accord much more than all laws and teachings can demand, just as Paul says in 1 Timothy 1:9, "The law is not laid down for the just but for the lawless."

Why is this? It is because the righteous man of his own accord does all and more than the law demands. But the unrighteous do nothing that the law demands; therefore, they need the law to instruct, constrain, and compel them to do good. A good tree needs no instruction or law to bear good fruit (cf. Matt. 7:17-18); its nature causes it to bear according to its kind without any law or instruction. I would take to be quite a fool any man who would make a book full of laws and statutes for an apple tree telling it how to bear apples and not thorns, when the tree is able by its own nature to do this better than the man with all his books can describe and demand. Just so, by the Spirit and by faith all Christians are so thoroughly disposed and conditioned in their very nature that they do right and keep the law better than one can teach them with all manner of statutes; so far as they themselves are concerned, no statutes or laws are needed.

You ask: Why, then, did God give so many commandments to all mankind, and why does Christ prescribe in the gospel so many things for us to do? [. . .] To put it here as briefly as possible, Paul says that the law has been laid down for the sake of the lawless (1 Tim. 1:9), that is, so that those who are not Christians may through the law be restrained outwardly from evil deeds, as we shall hear later. Now since no one is by nature Christian or righteous, but altogether sinful and wicked, God through the law puts them all under restraint so they dare not wilfully implement their wickedness in actual deeds. In addition, Paul ascribes to the law another function in Romans 7:7-13 and Galatians 3:19, 24, that of teaching men to recognize sin in order that it may make them humble into grace and unto faith in Christ. Christ does the same thing here in Matthew 5:39, where he teaches that we should not resist evil; by

586

this he is interpreting the law and teaching what ought to be and must be the state and temper of a true Christian, as we shall hear further later on.

Fourth. All who are not Christians belong to the kingdom of the world and are under the law. There are few true believers, and still fewer who live a Christian life, who do not resist evil and indeed themselves do no evil. For this reason God has provided for them a different government beyond the Christian estate and kingdom of God. He has subjected them to the sword so that, even though they would like to, they are unable to practice their wickedness, and if they do practice it they cannot do so without fear or with success and impunity. [. . .]

If anyone attempted to rule the world by the gospel and to abolish all temporal law and sword on the plea that all are baptized and Christian, and that, according to the gospel, there shall be among them no law or sword — or need for either — pray tell me, friend, what would he be doing? He would be loosing the ropes and chains of the savage wild beasts and letting them bite and mangle everyone, meanwhile insisting that they were harmless, tame, and gentle creatures; but I would have the proof in my wounds. Just so would the wicked under the name of the Christian abuse evangelical freedom, carry on their rascality, and insist that they were Christians subject neither to law nor sword, as some are already raving and ranting.

To such a one we must say: Certainly it is true that Christians, so far as they themselves are concerned, are subject neither to law nor sword, and have need of neither. But take heed and first fill the world with real Christians before you attempt to rule it in a Christian and evangelical manner. This you will never accomplish; for the world and the masses are and always will be un-Christian, even if they are all baptized and Christian in name. Christians are few and far between (as the saying is). Therefore, it is out of the question that there should be a common Christian government over the whole world, or indeed over a single country or any considerable body of people, for the wicked always outnumber the good. [. . .]

For this reason one must carefully distinguish between these two governments. Both must be permitted to remain; the one to produce righteousness, the other to bring about external peace and prevent evil deeds. Neither one is sufficient in the world without the other. No one can become righteous in the sight of God by means of the temporal government, without Christ's spiritual government. Christ's government does not extend over all men; rather, Christians are always a minority in the midst of non-Christians. Now where temporal government or law alone prevails, there sheer hypocrisy is inevitable, even though the commandments be God's very own. For without the Holy Spirit in the heart no one becomes truly righteous, no matter how fine the works he does. On the other hand, where the spiritual government alone prevails over land and people, there wickedness is given free rein and the door is open for all manner of rascality, for the world as a whole cannot receive or comprehend it.

Now you see the intent of Christ's words which we quoted above from Matthew 5:39, that Christians should not go to law or use the temporal sword among themselves. Actually, he says this only to his beloved Christians, those who alone accept it and act accordingly, who do not make "counsels" out of it as the sophists do, but in their heart are so disposed and conditioned by the Spirit that they do evil to

587

no one and willingly endure evil at the hands of others. If now the whole world were Christian in this sense, then these words would apply to all, and all would act accordingly. Since the world is un-Christian, however, these words do not apply to all; and all do not act accordingly, but are under another government in which those who are not Christian are kept under external constraint and compelled to keep the peace and do what is good. [. . .]

[253] Fifth. But you say: if Christians then do not need the temporal sword or law, why does Paul say to all Christians in Romans 13:1: "Let all souls be subject to the governing authority," and St. Peter: "Be subject to every human ordinance" (1 Pet. 2:13), as quoted above? Answer: I have just said that Christians, among themselves and by and for themselves, need no law nor sword, since it is neither necessary nor useful for them. Since a true Christian lives and labors on earth not for himself alone but for his neighbor, he does by the very nature of his spirit even what he himself has no need of, but is needful and useful to his neighbor. Because the sword is most beneficial and necessary for the whole world in order to preserve peace, punish sin, and restrain the wicked, the Christian submits most willingly to the rule of the sword, pays his taxes, honors those in authority, serves, helps, and does all he can to assist the governing authority, that it may continue to function and be held in honor and fear. Although he has no need of these things for himself — to him they are not essential — nevertheless, he concerns himself about what is serviceable and of benefit to others, as Paul teaches in Ephesians 5:21–6:9. [. . .]

Thus you observe in the words of Christ quoted above from Matthew 5 that he clearly teaches that Christians among themselves should have no temporal sword or law. He does not, however, forbid one to serve and be subject to those who do have the secular sword and law. Rather, since you do not need it and should not have it, you are to serve all the more those who have not attained to such heights as you and who therefore do still need it. Although you do not need to have your enemy punished, your afflicted neighbor does. You should help him that he may have peace and that his enemy may be curbed, but this is not possible unless the governing authority is honored and feared. [. . .]

Sixth. You ask whether a Christian too may bear the temporal sword and punish the wicked, since Christ's words, "Do not resist evil," are so clear and definite that the sophists have had to make of them a "counsel." Answer: You have now heard two propositions. One is that the sword can have no place among Christians; therefore, you cannot bear it among Christians or hold it over them, for they do not need it. The question, therefore, must be referred to the other group, the non-Christians, whether you may bear it there in a Christian manner. Here the other proposition applies, that you are under obligation to serve and assist the sword by whatever means you can, with body, goods, honor, and soul. For it is something which you do not need, but which is very beneficial and essential for the whole world and for your neighbor. Therefore, if you see that there is a lack of hangmen, constables, judges, lords, or princes, and you find that you are qualified, you should offer your services and seek the position, that the essential governmental authority may not be despised and become enfeebled or perish. The world cannot and dare not dispense with it.

Here is the reason why you should do this: In such a case you would be entering entirely into the service and work of others, which would be of advantage neither to yourself nor your property or honor, but only to your neighbor and to others. You would be doing it not with the purpose of avenging yourself or returning evil for evil, but for the good of your neighbor and for the maintenance of the safety and peace of others. For yourself, you would abide by the gospel and govern yourself according to Christ's word (Matt. 5:39f.), gladly turning the other cheek and letting the cloak go with the coat when the matter concerned you and your cause. In this way the two propositions are brought into harmony with one another: at one and the same time you satisfy God's kingdom inwardly and the kingdom of the world outwardly. You suffer evil and injustice; you do not resist evil, and yet at the same time you do resist it. [. . .]

harmonizes the two: inward/ outward

[257] In short, since Paul says here that the governing authority is God's servant, we must allow it to be exercised not only by the heathen but by all men. What can be the meaning of the phrase, "It is God's servant," except that governing authority is by its very nature such that through it one may serve God? Now it would be quite un-Christian to say that there is any service of God in which a Christian should not or must not take part, when service of God is actually more characteristic of Christians than of anyone else. It would even be fine and fitting if all princes were good, true Christians. For the sword and authority, as a particular service of God, belong more appropriately to Christians than to any other men on earth. Therefore, you should esteem the sword or governmental authority as highly as the estate of marriage, or husbandry, or any other calling which God has instituted. Just as one can serve God in the estate of marriage, or in farming or a trade, for the benefit of others — and must so serve if his neighbor needs it — so one can serve God in government, and should there serve if the needs of his neighbor demand it. For those who punish evil and protect the good are God's servants and workmen. Only, one should also be free not to do it if there is no need for it, just as we are free not to marry or farm where there is no need for them.

You ask: Why did not Christ and the apostles bear the sword? Answer: You tell me, why did Christ not take a wife, or become a cobbler or a tailor. If an office or vocation were to be regarded as disreputable on the ground that Christ did not pursue it himself, what would become of all the offices and vocations other than the ministry, the one occupation he did follow? Christ pursued his own office and vocation, but he did not thereby reject any other. It was not incumbent upon him to bear the sword, for he was to exercise only that function by which his kingdom is governed and which properly serves his kingdom. Now, it is not essential to his kingdom that he be a married man, a cobbler, tailor, farmer, prince, hangman, or constable; neither is the temporal sword or law essential to it, but only God's word and Spirit. It is by these that his people are ruled inwardly. This is the office which he also exercised then and still exercises now, always bestowing God's word and Spirit. And in this office the apostles and all spiritual rulers had to follow him. For in order to do their job right they are so busily occupied with the spiritual sword, the word of God, that they must perforce neglect the temporal sword and leave it to others who do not have to preach, although it is not contrary to their calling to use it, as I have said. For each one must attend to the duties of his own calling. [. . .]

[259] From all this we gain the true meaning of Christ's words in Matthew 5:39, "Do not resist evil," etc. It is this: A Christian should be so disposed that he will suffer every evil and injustice without avenging himself; neither will he seek legal redress in the courts but have utterly no need of temporal authority and law for his own sake. On behalf of others, however, he may and should seek vengeance, justice, protection, and help, and do as much as he can to achieve it. Likewise, the governing authority should, on its own initiative or through the instigation of others, help and protect him too, without any complaint, application, or instigation on his own part. If it fails to do this, he should permit himself to be despoiled and slandered; he should not resist evil, as Christ's words say.

Be certain too that this teaching of Christ is not a counsel for those who would be perfect, as our sophists blasphemously and falsely say, but a universally obligatory command for all Christians. Then you will realize that all those who avenge themselves or go to law and wrangle in the courts over their property and honor are nothing but heathen masquerading under the name of Christians. It cannot be otherwise, I tell you. Do not be dissuaded by the multitude and common practice; for there are few Christians on earth — have no doubt about it — and God's word is something very different from the common practice. [. . .]

[261] You may ask, "Why may I not use the sword for myself and for my own cause, so long as it is my intention not to seek my own advantage but to punish evil?" Answer: Such a miracle is not impossible, but very rare and hazardous. Where the Spirit is so richly present it may well happen. For we read thus of Samson in Judges 15:11, that he said: "As they did to me, so have I done to them," even though Proverbs 24:29 says to the contrary: "Do not say, I will do to him as he has done to me," and Proverbs 20:22 adds: "Do not say, I will repay him his evil." Samson was called of God to harass the Philistines and deliver the children of Israel. Although he used them as an occasion to further his own cause, still he did not do so in order to avenge himself or to seek his own interests, but to serve others and to punish the Philistines (Judges 14:4). No one but a true Christian, filled with the Spirit, will follow this example. Where reason too tries to do likewise, it will probably contend that it is not trying to seek its own, but this will be basically untrue, for it cannot be done without grace. Therefore first become like Samson, and then you can also do as Samson did.

Pt. 2. *How Far Temporal Authority Extends.* [261] We come now to the main part of this treatise. Having learned that there must be temporal authority on earth, and how it is to be exercised in a Christian and salutary manner, we must now learn how far its arm extends and how widely its hand stretches, lest it extend too far and encroach upon God's kingdom and government. It is essential for us to know this, for where it is given too wide a scope, intolerable and terrible injury follows; on the other hand, injury is also inevitable where it is restricted too narrowly. In the former case, the temporal authority punishes too much; in the latter case, it punishes too little. To err in this direction, however, and punish too little is more tolerable, for it is always better to let a scoundrel live than to put a godly man to death. The world has plenty of scoundrels anyway and must continue to have them, but godly men are scarce.

It is to be noted first that the two classes of Adam's children — the one in

590

God's kingdom under Christ and the other in the kingdom of the world under the governing authority, as was said above — have two kinds of law. For every kingdom must have its own laws and statutes; without law no kingdom or government can survive, as everyday experience amply shows. The temporal government has laws which extend no further than to life and property and external affairs on earth, for God cannot and will not permit anyone but himself to rule over the soul. Therefore, where the temporal authority presumes to prescribe laws for the soul, it encroaches upon God's government and only misleads souls and destroys them. We want to make this so clear that everyone will grasp it, and that our fine gentlemen, the princes and bishops, will see what fools they are when they seek to coerce the people with their laws and commandments into believing this or that. [. . .]

Hence, it is the height of folly when they command that one shall believe the Church, the fathers, and the councils, though there be no word of God for it. It is not the church but the devil's apostles who command such things, for the church commands nothing unless it knows for certain that it is God's word. As St. Peter puts it: "Whoever speaks, let him speak as the word of God" (1 Pet. 4:11). It will be a long time, however, before they can ever prove that the decrees of the councils are God's word. Still more foolish is it when they assert that kings, princes, and the mass of mankind believe thus and so. My dear man, we are not baptized into kings, or princes, or even into the mass of mankind, but into Christ and God himself. Neither are we called kings, princes, or common folk, but Christians. No one shall or can command the soul unless he is able to show it the way to heaven; but this no man can do, only God alone. Therefore in matters which concern the salvation of souls nothing but God's word shall be taught and accepted. [. . .]

Besides, we cannot conceive how an authority could or should act in a situation except where it can see, know, judge, condemn, change, and modify. What would I think of a judge who should blindly decide cases which he neither hears nor sees? Tell me then: How can a mere man see, know, judge, condemn, and change hearts? That is reserved for God alone, as Psalm 7:8f. says: "God tries the hearts and reins"; and, "The Lord judges the peoples." And Acts 1:24 says, "God knows the hearts"; and Jeremiah 17:9f.: "Wicked and unsearchable is the human heart; who can understand it? I the Lord, who search the heart and reins." A court should and must be quite certain and clear about everything if it is to render judgment. But the thought and inclinations of the soul can be known to no one but God. Therefore, it is futile and impossible to command or compel anyone by force to believe this or that. The matter must be approached in a different way. Force will not accomplish it. And I am surprised at the big fools, for they themselves all say: *De occultis non iudicat Ecclesia,* the church does not judge secret matters. If the spiritual rule of the church governs only public matters, how dare the mad temporal authority judge and control such a secret, spiritual, hidden matter as faith?

Furthermore, every man runs his own risk in believing as he does, and he must see to it himself that he believes rightly. As nobody else can go to heaven or hell for me, so nobody else can believe or disbelieve for me; as nobody else can open or close heaven or hell to me, so nobody else can drive me to belief or unbelief. How he believes or disbelieves is a matter for the conscience of each individual, and since this

*on
coercing
beliefs*

takes nothing away from the temporal authority the latter should be content to attend to its own affairs and let men believe this or that as they are able and willing, and constrain no one by force. Indeed, it is a work of God in the spirit, not something which outward authority should compel or create. Hence arises the common saying, found also in Augustine, "No one can or ought to be forced to believe."

[. . .] Why do they persist in trying to force people to believe from the heart when they see that it is impossible? In so doing they only compel weak consciences to lie, to disavow, and to utter what is not in their hearts. They thereby load themselves down with dreadful *alien sins,* for all the lies and false confessions which such weak consciences utter fall back upon him who compels them. [The scholastic category of *peccata aliena* included various kinds of personal involvement in another party's sin: by, e.g., counseling, approving, or even failing to criticize.] Even if their subjects were in error, it would be much easier simply to let them err than to compel them to lie and to utter what is not in their hearts. In addition, it is not right to prevent evil by something even worse. [. . .]

[265] But, you say: Paul said in Romans 13:1 that every soul should be subject to the governing authority; and Peter says that we should be subject to every human ordinance (1 Pet. 2:13). Answer: Now you are on the right track, for these passages are in my favor. St. Paul is speaking of the governing authority. Now you have just heard that no one but God can have authority over souls. Hence, St. Paul cannot possibly be speaking of any obedience except where there can be corresponding authority. From this it follows that he is not speaking of faith, to the effect that temporal authority should have the right to command faith. He is speaking rather of external things, that they should be ordered and governed on earth. His words too make this perfectly clear, where he prescribes limits for both authority and obedience, saying, "Pay all of them their dues, taxes to whom taxes are due, revenue to whom revenue is due, honor to whom honor is due, respect to whom respect is due" (Rom. 13:7). Temporal obedience and authority, you see, apply only externally to taxes, revenue, honor, and respect. Again, where he says, "The governing authority is not a terror to good conduct, but to bad" (13:3), he again so limits the governing authority that it is not to have the mastery over faith or the word of God, but over evil works.

This is also what St. Peter means by the phrase, "human ordinance." A human ordinance cannot possibly extend its authority into heaven and over souls; it is limited to the earth, to external dealings men have with one another, where they can see, know, judge, evaluate, punish, and acquit.

Christ himself makes this distinction, and summed it all up very nicely when he said in Matthew 22:21, "Render to Caesar the things that are Caesar's and to God the things that are God's." [. . .]

[268] Again you say: "The temporal power is not forcing men to believe; it is simply seeing to it externally that no one deceives the people by false doctrine; how could heretics otherwise be restrained?" Answer: This the bishops should do; it is a function entrusted to them and not to the princes. Heresy can never be restrained by force. One will have to tackle the problem in some other way, for heresy must be opposed and dealt with otherwise than with the sword. Here God's word must do the fighting. If it does not succeed, certainly the temporal power will not succeed either,

*on
heresy*

even if it were to drench the world in blood. Heresy is a spiritual matter which you cannot hack to pieces with iron, consume with fire, or drown in water. God's word alone avails here, as Paul says in 2 Corinthians 10:4-5: "Our weapons are not carnal, but mighty in God to destroy every argument and proud obstacle that exalts itself against the knowledge of God, and to take every thought captive in the service of Christ." [. . .]

[270] But you might say: "Since there is to be no temporal sword among Christians, how then are they to be ruled outwardly? There certainly must be authority even among Christians." Answer: Among Christians there shall and can be no authority; rather all are alike subject to one another, as Paul says in Romans 12:10: "Each shall consider the other his superior"; and Peter says in 1 Peter 5:5: "All of you be subject to one another." This is also what Christ means in Luke 14:10: "When you are invited to a wedding, go and sit in the lowest place." Among Christians there is no superior but Christ himself, and him alone. What kind of authority can there be where all are equal and have the same right, power, possession, and honor, and where no one desires to be the other's superior, but each the other's subordinate? Where there are such people, one could not establish authority even if he wanted to, since in the nature of things it is impossible to have superiors where no one is able or willing to be a superior. Where there are no such people, however, there are no real Christians either.

What, then, are the priests and bishops? Answer: Their government is not a matter of authority or power, but a service and an office, for they are neither higher nor better than other Christians. Therefore, they should impose no law or decree on others without their will and consent. Their ruling is rather nothing more than the inculcating of God's word, by which they guide Christians and overcome heresy. [. . .]

Pt. 3. [271] Now that we know the limits of temporal authority, it is time to inquire also how a prince should use it. We do this for the sake of those very few who would also like very much to be Christian princes and lords, and who desire to enter into the life in heaven. Christ himself describes the nature of worldly princes in Luke 22:25, where he says: "The princes of this world exercise lordship, and those that are in authority proceed with force." For if they are lords by birth or by election they think it only right that they should be served and should rule by force. He who would be a Christian prince must certainly lay aside any intent to exercise lordship or to proceed with force. For cursed and condemned is every sort of life lived and sought for the benefit and good of self; cursed are all works not done in love. They are done in love, however, when they are directed wholeheartedly toward the benefit, honor, comfort, and salvation of self.

I will say nothing here of the temporal dealings and laws of the governing authority. That is a large subject, and there are too many lawbooks already, although if a prince is himself no wiser than his jurists and knows no more than what is in the lawbooks, he will surely rule according to the saying in Proverbs 28:16 (Vulgate): "A prince who lacks understanding will oppress many with injustice." For no matter how good and equitable the laws are, they all make an exception in the case of necessity, in the face of which they cannot insist upon being strictly enforced. Therefore, a

593

prince must have the law as firmly in hand as the sword, and determine in his own mind when and where the law is to be applied strictly or with moderation, so that law may prevail at all times and in all cases, and reason may be the highest law and the master of all administration of law. To take an analogy, the head of a family fixes both the time and the amount when it comes to matters of work and of food for his servants and children; still, he must reserve the right to modify or suspend these regulations if his servants happen to be ill, imprisoned, detained, deceived, or otherwise hindered; he must not deal as severely with the sick as with the well. I say this in order that men may not think it sufficiently praiseworthy merely to follow the written law or the opinions of jurists. There is more to it than that. [. . .]

First. He must give consideration and attention to his subjects, and really devote himself to it. This he does when he directs his every thought to making himself useful and beneficial to them; when instead of thinking: "The land and people belong to me, I will do what best pleases me," he thinks rather: "I belong to the land and the people, I shall do what is useful and good for them. My concern will be not how to lord it over them and dominate them, but how to protect and maintain them in peace and plenty." He should picture Christ to himself, and say, "Behold, Christ, the supreme ruler, came to serve me; he did not seek to gain power, estate, and honor from me, but considered only my need, and directed all things to the end that I should gain power, estate, and honor from him and through him. I will do likewise, seeking from my subjects not my own advantage but theirs. I will use my office to serve and protect them, listen to their problems and defend them, and govern to the sole end that they, not I, may benefit and profit from my rule." In such manner should a prince in his heart empty himself of his power and authority, and take unto himself the needs of his subjects, dealing with them as though they were his own needs. For this is what Christ did to us [Phil. 2:7]; and these are the proper works of Christian love. [. . .]

Second. He must beware of the high and mighty and of his counselors, and so conduct himself toward them that he despises none, but also trusts none enough to leave everything to him. God cannot tolerate either course. He once spoke through the mouth of an ass (Num. 22:28); therefore, no man is to be despised, however humble he may be. On the other hand, he permitted the highest angel to fall from heaven; therefore, no man is to be trusted, no matter how wise, holy, or great he may be. One should rather give a hearing to all, and wait to see through which one of them God will speak and act. The greatest harm is done at court when the prince gives his mind into the captivity of the high and mighty and of the flatterers, and does not look into things himself. When a prince fails and plays the fool, not just one person is affected, but land and people must bear the result of such foolishness.

Therefore, a prince should trust his officials and allow them to act, but only in such a way that he will still keep the reins of government in his own hands. He must not be overconfident but keep his eyes open and attend to things; and, like Jehoshaphat did (2 Chron. 19:4-7), ride through the land and observe everywhere how the government and the law are being administered. In this way he will learn for himself that one cannot place complete trust in any man. You have no right to assume that somebody else will take as deep an interest in you and your land as you do yourself, unless he be a good Christian filled with the Spirit. The natural man will not. And since you cannot know whether he is a Christian or how long he will remain one, you cannot safely depend on him. [. . .]

[276] Third. He must take care to deal justly with evildoers. Here he must be very wise and prudent, so he can inflict punishment without injury to others. Again, I know of no better example of this than David. He had a commander, Joab by name, who committed two underhanded crimes when he treacherously murdered two upright commanders (2 Sam. 3:27; 20:10), whereby he justly merited death twice over. Yet David, during his own lifetime, did not have him put to death but commanded his son Solomon to do so without fail (1 Kings 2:5f.), doubtless because he himself could not do it without causing even greater damage and tumult. A prince must punish the wicked in such a way that he does not step on the dish while picking up the spoon, and for the sake of one man's head plunge country and people into want and fill the land with widows and orphans. Therefore, he must not follow the advice of those counselors and fire-eaters who would stir and incite him to start a war, saying: "What, must we suffer such insult and injustice?" He is a mighty poor Christian who for the sake of a single castle would put the whole land in jeopardy. [. . .]

[278] Fourth. Here we come to what should really have been placed first, and of which we spoke above. A prince must act in a Christian way toward his God also; that is, he must subject himself to him in entire confidence and pray for wisdom to rule well, as Solomon did (1 Kings 3:9). [. . .] Then the prince's job will be done right, both outwardly and inwardly; it will be pleasing to God and to the people. But he will have to expect much envy and sorrow on account of it; the cross will soon rest on the shoulders of such a prince. [. . .]

Translation: J. J. Schindel, revised by W. I. Brandt, *Luther's Works,* vol. 45 (Philadelphia: Fortress Press, 1962). Used with permission.

From *The Sermon on the Mount*

Matt. 5:5: *Blessed are the meek, for they shall inherit the earth.* [WA 32 316] This statement fits the first one well, when he said: "Blessed are the spiritually poor." For as he promises the kingdom of heaven and an eternal possession there, so here he also adds a promise about this temporal life and about possessions here on earth. But how does being poor harmonize with inheriting the land? It might seem that the preacher has forgotten how he began. Whoever is to inherit land and possessions cannot be poor. By "inheriting the land" here and having all sorts of possessions here on earth, he does not mean that everyone is to inherit a whole country; otherwise God would have to create more worlds. But God confers possessions upon everyone in such a way that he gives a man wife, children, cattle, house, and home, and whatever pertains to these, so that he can stay on the land where he lives and have dominion over his possessions. This is the way Scripture customarily speaks, as Psalm 37:34 says several times: "Those who wait for the Lord will inherit the land"; and again (Ps.

37:22): "His blessed ones inherit the land." Therefore he adds his own gloss here: to be "spiritually poor," as he used the expression before, does not mean to be a beggar or to discard money and possessions. For here he tells them to live and remain in the land and to manage earthly possessions, as we shall hear later.

What does it mean, then, to be meek? From the outset here you must realize that Christ is not speaking at all about the government and its work, whose property it is not to be meek, as we use the word in German, but to bear the sword (Rom. 13:4) for the punishment of those who do wrong (1 Pet. 2:14), and to wreak a vengeance and a wrath that are called the vengeance and wrath of God. He is only talking about how individuals are to live in relation to others, apart from official position and authority — how father and mother are to live, not in relation to their children nor in their official capacity as father and mother, but in relation to those for whom they are not father and mother, like neighbors and other people. I have often said that we must sharply distinguish between these two, the office and the person. The man who is called Hans or Martin is a man quite different from the one who is called elector or doctor or preacher. Here we have two different persons in one man. The one is that in which we are created and born, according to which we are all alike — man or woman or child, young or old. But once we are born, God adorns and dresses you up as another person. He makes you a child and me a father, one a master and another a servant, one a prince and another a citizen. Then this one is called a divine person, one who holds a divine office and goes about clothed in its dignity — not simply Hans or Nick, but the Prince of Saxony, father, or master. He is not talking about this person here, letting it alone in its own office and rule, as he has ordained it. He is talking merely about how each individual, natural person is to behave in relation to others.

Therefore if we have an office or a governmental position, we must be sharp and strict, we must get angry and punish; for here we must do what God puts into our hand and commands us to do for his sake. In other relations, in what is unofficial, let everyone learn for himself to be meek toward everyone else, that is, not to deal with his neighbor unreasonably, hatefully, or vengefully, like the people whom they call "Headlong Hans." They refuse to put up with anything or to yield an inch, but they tear up the world and the hills and want to uproot the trees. They never listen to anyone nor excuse him for anything. They immediately buckle on their armor, thinking of nothing but how to take vengeance and hit back. This does not forbid the government to punish and to wreak vengeance in the name of God. But neither does it grant license to a wicked judge, burgomaster, lord, or prince to confuse these two persons and to reach beyond his official authority through personal malice or envy or hate or hostility, as commonly happens, under the cloak and cover of his office and legal right. This would be as though, in the name of the government, our neighbors wanted to take some action against us which they could not get away with otherwise. [. . .]

So select one of the two, whichever you prefer: either to live in human society with meekness and patience and to hold on to what you have with peace and a good conscience; or boisterously and blusterously to lose what is yours, and to have no peace besides. There stands the decree: "The meek shall inherit the earth." Just take a look for yourself at the queer characters who are always arguing and squabbling about property and other things. They refuse to give in to anybody, but insist on rushing everything through headlong, regardless of whether their quarreling and squabbling costs them more than they could ever gain. Ultimately they lose their land and servants, house and home, and get unrest and a bad conscience thrown in. And God adds His blessing to it, saying: "Do not be meek, then, so that you may not keep your precious land, nor enjoy your morsel in peace."

But if you want to do right and have rest, let your neighbor's malice and viciousness smother and burn itself out. Otherwise you can do nothing more pleasing to the devil or more harmful to yourself than to lose your temper and make a racket. Do you have a government? Then register a complaint, and let it see to it. The government has the charge not to permit the harsh oppression of the innocent. God will also overrule so that his word and ordinance may abide and you may inherit the land according to this promise. [. . .]

Matt. 5:38-40: *You have heard that it was said: "An eye for an eye and a tooth for a tooth." But I say to you: Do not resist one who is evil. But if anyone strikes you on the right cheek, turn to him the other also; and if anyone would sue you and take your coat, let him have your cloak as well.* [. . .] [388] This saying has been the undoing of many people; not only Jews but even Christians have stumbled on it. For it seemed to them that it was too strict and severe to forbid any resistance to evil at all, since we have to have law and punishment in society. Some have cited the contrary example of Christ (John 18:22, 23). When he was struck on one cheek before the priest Annas, he did not offer the other one; instead he declared his innocence and rebuked the high priest's servant. That seems to be a violation of this text.

On that basis they said it was not necessary to turn the other cheek to an assailant, and they gave the text a helping hand by saying that it was enough for a person to be ready in his heart to offer the other cheek. They said the right thing, but they interpreted it the wrong way. They supposed that offering the other cheek to an assailant meant saying to him: "See, take his cheek, too, and hit me again," or throwing your cloak to the man who wants to take your coat. If that were the meaning, we would finally have to surrender everything, house and home, wife and children. We say, therefore, that all it does is to proclaim to every Christian that he should willingly and patiently suffer whatever is his lot, without seeking revenge or hitting back.

But the question and argument still remain. Must a person suffer all sorts of things from everyone, without defending himself at all? Has he no right to plead a case or to lodge a complaint before a court, or to claim and demand what belongs to him? If all these things were forbidden, a strange situation would develop. It would be necessary to put up with everybody's whim and insolence. Personal safety and private property would be impossible, and finally the social order would collapse.

To answer this, you must always pay attention to the main point, which is, that Christ is addressing his sermon only to his Christians and seeking to teach them the kind of people they should be, in contrast to the carnal ideas and thoughts that still clung to the apostles. They imagined that he would institute a new realm and empire and set them up in it to rule as lords and to conquer their enemies and the wicked world. Thus flesh and blood has always expected to find its own dominion, honor, and advantage in the Gospel, and an escape from all suffering. The pope has longed for this, too, and his realm has developed into nothing more than a secular dominion, so dreadful that the world has had to submit to him.

Now, too, we see the whole world seeking its own advantage in the Gospel. This has brought on the rise of so many sects, whose only aim is their own advancement and aggrandizement, together with the extermination of others. So it was with Münzer and his peasants, and more recently with others, too. Even real Christians are sometimes tempted this way. They see that the world at large, and particularly their own government, is being so poorly managed that they feel like jumping in and taking over. But this is wrong. No one should suppose that God wants to have us govern and rule this way with the law and punishment of the world. The Christians' way is altogether different. They neither deal with such things nor care about them. They are perfectly content to leave these things to the care of those who are authorized to distribute property, to do business, to punish, and to protect. As Christ teaches (Matt. 22:21): "Render to Caesar the things that are Caesar's." For we have been transferred to another and higher existence, a divine and an eternal kingdom, where the things that belong to the world are unnecessary and where in Christ everyone is a lord for himself over both the devil and the world, as we have said elsewhere.

It is the duty and obligation of those who participate in this earthly regime to administer law and punishment, to maintain the distinctions that exist among ranks and persons, to manage and distribute property. This way everything will be in good shape, and everyone will know what he is to do and to have; no one will meddle in another man's office or pry into his affairs or take his property. That is what lawyers are for, to teach and manage such matters. But the Gospel does not trouble itself with these matters. It teaches about the right relation of the heart to God, while in all these other questions it should take care to stay pure and not to stumble into a false righteousness. You must grasp and obey this distinction, for it is the basis on which such questions can be easily answered. Then you will see that Christ is talking about a spiritual existence and life and that he is addressing himself to his Christians. He is telling them to live and behave before God and in the world with their heart dependent upon God and uninterested in things like secular rule or government, power or punishment, anger or revenge.

Now, if someone asks whether a Christian may go to court or defend himself, the answer is simply no. A Christian is the kind of person who has nothing to do with this sort of secular existence and law. He belongs to a kingdom or realm where the only regulation should be the prayer (Matt. 6:12): "Forgive us our debts as we forgive our debtors." Here only mutual love and service should prevail, even toward people who do not love us, but who hate us, hurt and harm us. It is to these Christians that he says they should not resist evil, that they should not even seek revenge, but that they should turn the other cheek to an assailant.

A related question is this: May a Christian be a secular official and administer the office and work of a ruler or a judge? This would mean that the two persons or the two types of office are combined in one man. In addition to being a Christian, he would be a prince or a judge or a lord or a servant or a maid — all of which are termed "secular" persons because they are part of the secular realm. To this we say: *affirmation of the secular* Yes, God himself has ordained and established this secular realm and its distinctions, and by his word he has confirmed and commended them. For without them this life could not endure. We are all included in them; indeed, we were born into them even before we became Christians. Therefore we must also remain in them as long as we are on earth, but only according to our outward life and our physical existence.

There is no getting around it, a Christian has to be a secular person of some sort. As regards his own person, according to his life as a Christian, he is in subjection to no one but Christ, without any obligation either to the emperor or to any *dual roles* other man. But at least outwardly, according to his body and property, he is related by subjection and obligation to the emperor, inasmuch as he occupies some office or *relational roles are secular* station in life or has a house and home, a wife and children; for all these are things *✳* that pertain to the emperor. Here he must necessarily do what he is told and what this outward life requires. If he has a house or a wife and children or servants and refuses to support them or, if need be, to protect them, he does wrong. It will not do for him to declare that he is a Christian and therefore has to forsake or relinquish everything. But he must be told: "Now you are under the emperor's control. Here your name is not 'Christian,' but 'father' or 'lord' or 'prince.' According to your own person you are a Christian; but in relation to your servant you are a different person, and you are obliged to protect him."

You see, now we are talking about a Christian-in-relation: not about his being a Christian, but about this life and his obligation in it to some other person, whether under him or over him or even alongside him, like a lord or a lady, a wife or children or neighbors, whom he is obliged, if possible, to defend, guard, and protect. Here it would be a mistake to teach: "Turn the other cheek, and throw your cloak away with your coat." That would be ridiculous, like the case of the crazy saint who let the lice nibble at him and refused to kill any of them on account of this text, maintaining that he had to suffer and could not resist evil.

Do you want to know what your duty is as a prince or a judge or a lord or a *!* lady, with people under you? You do not have to ask Christ about your duty. Ask the imperial or the territorial law. It will soon tell you your duty toward your inferiors as their protector. It gives you both the power and the might to protect and to punish within the limits of your authority and commission, not as a Christian but as an imperial subject. What kind of crazy mother would it be who would refuse to defend and save her child from a dog or a wolf and who would say: "A Christian must not defend himself"? Should we not teach her a lesson with a good whipping and say: "Are you a mother? Then do your duty as a mother, as you are charged to do it. Christ did not abrogate this but rather confirmed it."

This is what is told about many of the holy martyrs. When they were called to *going to war is OK* arms even by infidel emperors and lords, they went to war. In all good conscience they slashed and killed, and in this respect there was no difference between Christians and heathen. Yet they did not sin against this text. For they were not doing this as Christians, for their own persons, but as obedient members and subjects, under obligation to a secular person and authority. But in areas where you are free and *✳*

without any obligation to such a secular authority, you have a different rule, since you are a different person.

Just learn the difference between the two persons that a Christian must carry simultaneously on earth, because he lives in human society and has to make use of secular and imperial things, the same way that heathen do. For until he has been transferred bodily from this life to another one, his flesh and blood is identical with theirs; and what he needs to provide for it does not come from the spiritual realm but from the land and soil, which belongs to the emperor. Now, with this distinction of the boundary between the province of the Christian person and that of the secular person you can neatly classify all these sayings and apply them properly where they belong, not confusing them and throwing them in one pot, the way the teaching and administration of the pope have done.

So much for the person who has obligations toward other persons under the secular law, the law of fathers and mothers, lords and ladies. But what if only your own person is involved and an injury or injustice has been done to you? Is it right to use force in guarding and defending yourself against this? The answer is no. Here even the secular and imperial law teaches: "Striking back makes a quarrel, and the one who strikes back is wrong." By this action you will be interfering in the judge's office and usurping his right for yourself, for it is his duty to punish. So it is in other cases. The fact that someone has stolen or robbed from you gives you no right to steal or rob from him and to take something from him by force. Our natural inclination is to take swift vengeance, before a person has a chance to turn around. This should not be. But if you are unwilling or unable to stand it, you can always take him to court and get what is coming to you there.

It is permissible to use orderly procedure in demanding and obtaining your rights, but be careful not to have a vindictive heart. Thus it is proper for a judge to punish and execute, and yet he is forbidden to have any hatred or vindictiveness in his heart. It is a common circumstance that people abuse their office to gratify their own whims. Now, where this is not the case and you are simply seeking to use the law for your protection and self-preservation against violence and malice, rather than for your vindictiveness or malevolence, you are not doing wrong. When the heart is pure, then everything is right and well done. The danger here is that the wicked world, along with our flesh and blood, always seeks its own advantage and yet puts on a lovely front to hide the scoundrel within. [. . .]

Certainly we are not compelled or obliged to let every insolent person run rampant all over the place and to take it silently without doing anything about it — not if we can follow orderly procedure in defending ourselves. Otherwise, however, all we can do is to suffer if someone treats us unjustly or violently. We must not sanction a wrong, but we must testify to the truth. In opposition to violence and malice, we may certainly appeal to the law. Thus, before the high priest Annas, Christ himself appealed to the law and asked for justice (John 18:23); nevertheless he let himself be struck, offering not only his other cheek but his whole body.

Thus when a Christian goes to war or when he sits on a judge's bench, punishing his neighbor, or when he registers an official complaint, he is not doing this as a Christian, but as a soldier or judge or lawyer. At the same time he keeps a Christian heart. He does not intend to harm anyone, and it grieves him that his neighbor must suffer grief. So he lives simultaneously as a Christian toward everyone, personally suffering all sorts of things in the world, and as a secular person, maintaining, using, and performing all the functions required by the law of his territory or city, by civil law, and by domestic law. [. . .]

A Christian should not resist any evil; but within the limits of his office, a secular person should oppose every evil. The head of a household should not put up with insubordination or bickering among his servants. A Christian should not sue anyone, but should surrender both his coat and cloak when they are taken away from him; but a secular person should go to court if he can to protect and defend himself against some violence or outrage. In short, the rule in the kingdom of Christ is the toleration of everything, forgiveness, and the recompense of evil with good. On the other hand, in the realm of the emperor, there should be no tolerance shown toward any injustice, but rather a defense against wrong and a punishment of it, and an effort to defend and maintain the right, according to what each one's office or station may require. [. . .]

Matt. 5:42: *Give to him who begs from you, and do not refuse him who would* ~~On~~ *possessions* *borrow from you.* [395] He points to three ways that the Christians should suffer with regard to their temporal possessions: they should let them be taken away from them, they should be happy to lend them, and they should give them away. Here the current teaching did not go beyond the secular and imperial law, which does not tell you to give your property away to someone else or to let him take it away from you. It only teaches you how to manage and do business with your property so that you get a good return on it by your buying, selling, and trading. Now, Christ is not preaching about this. He leaves the division of property and business to the teaching of reason. But he points to the three things that a Christian ought to have beyond all this: he should let things be taken away from him, either by force or under the pretext of the law; he should be happy to give them away; and he should be happy to lend them. Here again we must distinguish between secular law and the teaching of Christ. According to secular law you may use your possessions, do business with them, buy them and sell them. Thus we read that the holy patriarchs had business dealings with money and property just as other people do, just as everyone must do if he is to live in human society and support his wife and children. All this belongs to a life where the stomach has its rights, too; and it is just as necessary as eating and drinking.

But Christ teaches you in addition that you should still be willing to let everything be taken away from you, and do so gladly, doing good or contributing or lending where you can, and submitting to violence not only with regard to your property but also with regard to your life, as was said in the preceding text. Especially should you be willing to do so for the sake of the Lord Christ, if you are threatened on account of the Gospel. [. . .]

But here we must be careful not to give rogues and rascals the chance to take advantage of this doctrine and to declare: "The Christians have to stand for anything. Therefore it is all right to lay hands on their property, to take it and steal it. A Christian has the obligation to throw the door open on everything he has, to give or lend as much as any impudent scoundrel may ask for without demanding it back."

That was how that miserable apostate, Emperor Julian [361-63, the last pagan Roman emperor], made fun of this text. He took whatever he wanted from the Christians, saying he wanted to pay them in their own coin. No, my dear fellow, you have it wrong. [. . .]

Christ is not telling me to give what I have to any scoundrel that comes along and to deprive my family of it or others who may need it and whom I am obliged to help, and then to suffer want myself and become a burden to others. He is not saying that we should go and lend to everybody, but "to him who begs from us," that is, to the one who really needs it, not to the one who develops a whim that he would like to take something from us by force; such people are well off enough already, or they want to support themselves at other people's expense, without working. Therefore it is important to be careful here and to ascertain what sort of people there may be in a city, who there is poor and badly off and who is not, rather than to let in any vagrant or tramp who is not in need and who could very well support himself. [. . .]

For this you need to employ your secular person, to be prudent in your contacts with other people, to recognize the poor, and to see the kind of people with whom you are dealing and those to whom you should or should not give. Then if you see that it is a genuine seeker, open your hand and lend it to him if he can pay you back. But if he cannot, then give it to him free, and call the account square. There are pious people who would like to work and to support themselves, with their wife and children, but who can never prosper and must occasionally get into debt and difficulty. For the benefit of such people every city should have its common treasury and alms, and it should have church officials to determine who these people are and how they live, so as not to let any of the lazy bums become a burden to other people.

Translation: Jaroslav Pelikan, *Luther's Works.* vol. 21 (St. Louis: Concordia Publishing House, 1956). Used with permission.

From *Trade and Usury*

[WA 15 294] It is our purpose to speak about the abuses and sins of trade, insofar as they concern the conscience. The matter of their detrimental effect on the purse we leave to the princes and lords, that they may do their duty in this regard.

First. Among themselves the merchants have a common rule which is their chief maxim and the basis of all their sharp practices, where they say: "I may sell my goods as dear as I can." They think this is their right. Thus occasion is given for avarice, and every window and door to hell is opened. What else does it mean but this: I care nothing about my neighbor; so long as I have my profit and satisfy my greed, of what concern is it to me if it injures my neighbor in ten ways at once? There you see how shamelessly this maxim flies squarely in the face not only of Christian love but also of natural law. How can there be anything good then in trade? How can it be without sin when such injustice is the chief maxim and rule of the whole business?

On such a basis trade can be nothing but robbing and stealing the property of others.

When once the rogue's eye and greedy belly of a merchant find that people must have his wares, or that the buyer is poor and needs them, he takes advantage of him and raises the price. He considers not the value of the goods, nor what his own efforts and risk have deserved, but only the other man's want and need. He notes it not that he may relieve it but that he may use it to his own advantage by raising the price of his goods, which he would not have raised if it had not been for his neighbor's need. Because of his avarice, therefore, the goods must be priced as much higher as the greater need of the other fellow will allow, so that the neighbor's need becomes as it were the measure of the goods' worth and value. Tell me, isn't that an un-Christian and inhuman thing to do? Isn't that equivalent to selling a poor man his own need in the same transaction? When he has to buy his wares at a higher price because of his need, that is the same as having to buy his own need; for what is sold to him is not simply the wares as they are, but the wares plus the fact that he must have them. Observe that this and like abominations are the inevitable consequence when the rule is that I may sell my goods as dear as I can. [. . .]

You ask, then, "How dear may I sell? How am I to arrive at what is fair and right so I do not take increase from neighbor or overcharge him?" Answer: That is something that will never be governed either by writing or speaking; nor has anyone ever undertaken to fix the value of every commodity, and to raise or lower prices accordingly. The reason is this: wares are not all alike; one is transported a greater distance than another and one involves greater outlay than another. In this respect, therefore, everything is and must remain uncertain, and no fixed determination can be made, anymore than one can designate a certain city as the place from which all wares are to be brought, or establish a definite cost price for them. It may happen that the same wares, brought from the same city by the same road, cost vastly more in one year than they did the year before because the weather may be worse, or the road, or because something else happens that increases the expense at one time above that at another time. Now it is fair and right that a merchant take as much profit on his wares as will reimburse him for their cost and compensate him for his trouble, his labor, and his risk. Even a farmhand must have food and pay for his labor. Who can serve or labor for nothing? The gospel says: "The laborer deserves his wages" (Luke 10:7).

But in order not to leave the question entirely unanswered, the best and safest *solutions* way would be to have the temporal authorities appoint in this matter wise and honest men to compute the costs of all sorts of wares and accordingly set prices which would enable the merchant to get along and provide for him an adequate living, as is being done at certain places with respect to wine, fish, bread, and the like. But we Germans have too many other things to do; we are too busy drinking and dancing to provide for rules and regulations of this sort. Since this kind of ordinance therefore is not to be expected, the next best thing is to let goods be valued at the price for which they are bought and sold in the common market, or in the land generally. In this matter we can accept the proverb, "Follow the crowd and you won't get lost." Any profit made in this way I consider honest and proper, because here there is always the risk involved of having to suffer loss in wares and outlay, and excessive profits are scarcely possible.

Where the price of goods is not fixed either by law or custom, and you must fix it yourself, here one can truly give you no instructions but only lay it on your conscience to be careful not to overcharge your neighbor, and to seek a modest living, not the goals of greed. Some have wished to place a ceiling on profits, with a limit of one-half on all wares; some say one-third; others something else. None of these measures is certain and safe unless it be so decreed by the temporal authorities and common law. What they determine in these matters would be safe. Therefore, you must make up your mind to seek in your trading only your costs, trouble, labor, and risk, and on that basis raise or lower the prices of your wares so that you set them where you will be repaid for your trouble and labor.

I would not have anyone's conscience be so overly scrupulous or so closely bound in this matter that he feels he must strike exactly the right measure of profit to the very heller. It is impossible for you to arrive at the exact amount that you have earned with your trouble and labor. It is enough that with a good conscience you make the effort to arrive at what is right, though the very nature of trade makes it impossible to determine this exactly. The saying of the Wise Man will hold good in your case too: "A merchant can hardly act without sin, and a tradesman will hardly keep his lips from evil" (Sir. 26:29). If you take a trifle too much profit unwittingly and unintentionally, dismiss the matter in the Lord's Prayer where we pray, "Forgive us our trespasses" (Matt. 6:12). After all, no man's life is without sin; besides, the time will come in turn when you get too little for your trouble. Just throw the excess in the scale to counterbalance the losses you must similarly expect to take. [. . .]

In determining how much profit you ought to take on your business and your labor, there is no better way to reckon it than by computing the amount of time and labor you have put into it, and comparing that with the effort of a day laborer who works at some other occupation and seeing how much he earns in a day. On that basis figure how many days you have spent in getting your wares and bringing them to your place of business, and how much labor and risk was involved; for a great amount of labor and time ought to have a correspondingly greater return. That is the most accurate, the best, and the most definite advice and direction that can be given in this matter. Let him who dislikes it, better it himself. I base my case (as I have said) on the gospel that the laborer deserves his wages (Luke 10:7); and Paul also says in 1 Corinthians 9:7, "He who tends the flock should get some of the milk. Who can go to war at his own expense?" If you have a better ground than that, you are welcome to it.

Second. A common error, which has become a widespread custom not only among the merchants but throughout the world, is the practice of one person becoming surety for another. Although this practice seems to be without sin, and looks like a virtue stemming from love, nevertheless it generally ruins a good many people and does them irreparable harm. King Solomon often forbade it, and condemned it in his proverbs. [. . .]

Standing surety is a work that is too lofty for a man; it is unseemly, for it is a presumptuous encroachment upon the work of God. In the first place, Scripture commands us not to put our trust and reliance in any man, but in God alone. For human nature is false, vain, deceitful, and unreliable, as Scripture says and experience daily teaches. He who becomes surety, however, is putting his trust in a man, and risking life and property on a false and insecure foundation. It serves him right when he fails, falls, and is ruined.

In the second place, the surety is trusting in himself and making himself God (for whatever a man trusts in and relies upon is his god). But his own life and property are never for a single moment any more secure or certain than those of the man for whom he becomes surety. Everything is in the hand of God alone. God will not allow us a hair's breadth of power or right over the future, nor will he let us for a single moment be sure or certain of it. Therefore, he who becomes surety acts in an un-Christian way; he deserves what he gets, because he pledges and promises what is not his and not in his power, but solely in God's hands. [. . .]

[300] Perhaps you will say, "How then are people to trade with one another if surety is improper? That way many would be left behind who might otherwise get ahead." Answer: There are four Christian ways of exchanging external goods with others, as I have said elsewhere. [In his *Short Sermon on Usury* (1519; WA 6, 3-6) and his *Long Sermon on Usury* (1520; WA 6, 36-60), Luther calls "Christian" only the first three of the four modes of exchange.] The first way is to let them rob or steal our property, as Christ says in Matthew 5:40: "If anyone takes away your cloak, let him have your coat as well, and do not ask it of him again." This way of dealing counts for nothing among the merchants; besides, it has not been held or preached as common teaching for all Christians, but merely as a counsel or a good idea for the clergy and the perfect, though they observe it even less than do the merchants. But true Christians observe it, for they know that their Father in heaven has assuredly promised in Matthew 6:11 to give them this day their daily bread. If men were to act accordingly, not only would countless abuses in all kinds of business be avoided, but a great many people would not become merchants, because reason and human nature flee and shun to the uttermost risks and damages of this sort.

The second way is to give freely to anyone who needs it, as Christ also teaches in the same passage (Matt. 5:42; Luke 6:30). This too is a lofty Christian work, which is why it counts for little among the people. There would be fewer merchants and less trade if this were put into practice. For he who does this must truly hold fast to heaven and look always to the hands of God, and not to his own resources or wealth, knowing that God will support him even though every cupboard were bare, because he knows to be true what God said to Joshua: "I will not forsake you or withdraw my hand from you" (Josh. 1:5); as the proverb has it, "God still has more than what he ever gave away." But that takes a true Christian, and he is a rare animal on earth, to whom the world and nature pay no heed.

The third way is lending. That is, I give away my property, and take it back again if it is returned to me; but I must do without it if it is not returned. Christ himself defines this kind of transaction in what he says in Luke 6:35, "Lend, expecting nothing in return." That is, you should lend freely, and take your chances on getting it back or not. If it comes back, take it; if it does not, it is a gift. According to the gospel there is thus only one distinction between giving and lending, namely, a gift is not taken back, while a loan is taken back — if it is returned — but involves the risk that it may become a gift. He who lends expecting to get back something more or something better than he has loaned is nothing but an open and condemned usurer, since even those who in lending demand or expect to get back exactly what they lend, and take no chances on whether they get it back or not, are not acting in a Christian way. This third way too (in my opinion) is a lofty Christian work; and a rare one, judging by the way things are going in the world. If it were to be practiced generally, trade of all sorts would greatly diminish and virtually cease.

These three ways of exchanging goods, then, observe in masterful fashion this matter of not presuming upon the future, and not trusting in any man or in oneself but clinging to God alone. Here all transactions are in cash, and are accompanied by the word which James teaches, "If God wills, so be it" (James 4:15). For here we deal with people as with those who are unreliable and might fail; we give our money freely, or take our chances on losing what we lend.

Now someone will say, "Who can then be saved? And where shall we find these Christians? Why, in this way there would be no trade left in the world; everyone would have his property taken or borrowed away, and the door would be thrown open for the wicked and idle gluttons — of whom the world is full — to take everything with their lying and cheating." Answer: I have already said that Christians are rare people on earth. This is why the world needs a strict, harsh temporal government which will compel and constrain the wicked to refrain from theft and robbery, and to return what they borrow (although a Christian ought neither to demand nor expect it). [. . .]

You still have a grain of comfort too in the fact that you are not obligated to make a loan except out of your surplus and what you can spare from your own needs, as Christ says of alms, "What you have left over, that give in alms, and everything is clean for you" (Luke 11:41 Vulgate). Now if someone wishes to borrow from you an amount so large that you would be ruined if it were not repaid, and you could not spare it from your own needs, then you are not bound to make the loan. Your first and greatest obligation is to provide for the needs of your wife and children and servants; you must not divert from them what you owe them. The best rule to follow is this: If the amount asked as a loan is too great, just go ahead and give something outright, or else lend as much as you would be willing to give, and take the risk of having to lose it. John the Baptist did not say: "He who has one coat, let him give it away"; but, "He who has two coats, let him give one to him who has none; and he who has food, let him do likewise" (Luke 3:11).

The fourth way of exchanging goods is through buying and selling, but for hard cash or payment in kind. He who would use this method must make up his mind to rely not on something in the future but on God alone; also, that he will have to be dealing with men, men who will certainly fail and lie. Therefore, the best advice is this: whoever sells should not give credit or accept any security, but sell only for cash. If he wishes to lend, let him lend only to Christians, or else take the risk of loss, and lend no more than he would be willing to give outright or can spare from his own needs. If the temporal government and regulations will not help him to recover his loan, let him lose it. Let him beware of becoming surety for anyone; let him much rather give what he can. Such a man would be a true Christian merchant; God would not forsake him, because he trusts properly in Him and cheerfully takes a chance in dealing with his untrustworthy neighbors. [. . .]

[307] Another fine bit of sharp practice is for one man to sell to another, on promise of future delivery, wares that the seller does not have. It works this way: A merchant from a distance comes to me and asks me if I have such and such goods for sale. Although I do not have them I say Yes anyway and sell them to him for ten or eleven gulden, when they could otherwise be bought for nine or less, promising delivery in two or three days. Meanwhile, I go out and buy the goods where I knew in advance that I could buy them cheaper than I am selling them to him. I deliver them, and he pays me for them. Thus I deal with his (the other man's) own money and property without any risk, trouble, or labor, and I get rich. That is appropriately called "living off the street" on someone else's money and goods, without having to travel over land or sea.

Another practice called "living off the street" is this: When a merchant has a purseful of money and no longer cares to venture on land and sea with his goods, but to have a safe business, he settles down in a large commercial city. When he hears that some merchant is being pressed by his creditors and lacks the money he must have to satisfy them, but still has good wares, he gets someone to act for him in buying the wares, and offers eight gulden for what is otherwise worth ten. If this offer is turned down, he gets someone else to make an offer of six or seven gulden. The poor man begins to be afraid that his wares are depreciating, and is glad to accept the eight gulden so as to get hard cash and not have to suffer too great a loss and disgrace. It may also happen that needy merchants themselves seek out tyrants and offer their goods for ready cash with which to pay their debts. These tyrants drive hard bargains, and eventually get the wares at a low enough price; afterward they sell them at their own price. Such financiers are known as "cut-throats," but they pass for distinguished and clever people. [. . .]

[312] On the trading companies I ought to say a good deal, but the whole subject is such a bottomless pit of avarice and wrongdoing that there is nothing in it that can be discussed with a good conscience. Who is so stupid that he cannot see that the trading companies are nothing but pure monopolies? Even the temporal laws of the heathen forbid them as openly harmful to the whole world, to say nothing of divine right and Christian law. They control all commodities, deal in them as they please, and practice without concealment all the tricks that have been mentioned. They raise or lower prices at their pleasure. They oppress and ruin all the small businessmen, like the pike the little fish in the water, just as if they were lords over God's creatures and immune from all the laws of faith and love.

So it happens that all over the world spices must be bought at whatever price they choose to set, and they vary it from time to time. This year they raise the price of ginger, next year that of saffron, or vice versa; so that in the end it all comes out the same: they do not have to suffer any loss, injury, or risk. If the ginger spoils or they have to take a loss on it, they make it up on saffron, and vice versa, so that they make sure of their profit. All this is contrary to the nature, not only of merchandise, but of all temporal goods, which God wills should be subject to risk and uncertainty.

But they have found a way to make safe, certain, and continual profit out of unsafe, uncertain, and perishable goods; though because of it all the world must be sucked dry and all the money sink and swim in their gullets.

How could it ever be right and according to God's will that a man in such a short time should grow so rich that he could buy out kings and emperors? They have brought things to such a pass that everybody else has to do business at the risk of loss, winning this year and losing next year, while they themselves can always win, making up their losses by increased profits. It is no wonder that they quickly appropriate the wealth of the whole world, for a pfennig that is permanent and sure is better than a gulden that is temporary and uncertain. But these companies are always dealing with permanent and sure gulden for our temporary and uncertain pfennigs. Is it any wonder that they become kings and we beggars?

Kings and princes ought to look into this matter and forbid them by strict laws. But I hear that they have a finger in it themselves, and the saying of Isaiah (1:23) is fulfilled: "Your princes have become companions of thieves." They hang thieves who have stolen a gulden or half a gulden, but do business with those who rob the whole world and steal more than all the rest, so that the proverb remains true, "Big thieves hang little thieves." [. . .]

This is why no one need ask how he may with a good conscience be a member of a trading company. My only advice is this: Get out; they will not change. If the trading companies are to stay, right and honesty must perish; if right and honesty are to stay, the trading companies must perish. The bed is too narrow, says Isaiah, one must fall out, the covering is too small, it will not cover both (Isa. 28:20). [. . .]

Translation: C. M. Jacobs; revised by W. I. Brandt, *Luther's Works,* vol. 45 (Philadelphia, Fortress Press, 1962). Used with permission.

Francisco de Vitoria

(ca. 1483-1546)

The Spanish Dominican theologian Francisco de Vitoria is the celebrated founder of what came to be known as "the school of Salamanca," the hub of the Thomist revival in the sixteenth and seventeenth centuries. A remarkable teacher, he could boast among his progeny a host of distinguished theologians, philosophers, and jurists, including the Dominican Domingo de Soto (1494-1560) and the Jesuit theologians of a later generation, Luis de Molina (1535-1600) and Francisco Suárez (1548-1617), all of whom made important contributions to political and legal theory. The Spanish master reinvigorated Thomist thought not only by infusing it with humanist elegance of form and expression, but also by fertilizing it with fresh theoretical strands and by applying it with practical imagination to the pressing national and international issues of his day. In Spain his influence supplied a counterfoil to the Erasmian humanism of the University of Alcalá; while beyond Spain, it was formative for Tridentine and post-Tridentine scholasticism and, perhaps most importantly, touched such seminal figures in the sphere of international jurisprudence as the Dutch Protestant Hugo Grotius (1583-1645) and the émigré Italian civil lawyer in Oxford, Alberico Gentili (1552-1608).

Vitoria's intellectual and teaching career was decisively shaped by his youthful study of arts and theology in Paris (1509-22), then under the sway of nominalism, humanism, and religious revival (Doyle 1997, 11). His chief theological mentor at the Dominican College of St. Jacques was Peter Crockaert, who, reacting against the Gersonian nominalism of his own teacher, the renowned Scot, John Mair, promoted Thomistic orthodoxy by organizing his lectures around Aquinas's *Summa Theologiae* instead of Lombard's *Sentences,* an innovation that Vitoria would faithfully adopt. In the course of his doctoral work, Vitoria edited an edition of the *Prima Secundae* of the *Summa* under Crockaert's direction (1512), and contributed to an edition of the *Summa theologiae moralis* of Antoninus of Florence (1389-1459), an earlier Thomist response to Parisian nominalist and conciliarist ideas.

After a brief spell of theological teaching in Valladolid, Vitoria was elected in 1525 to the Prime Chair of Theology at the University of Salamanca, which he occupied until his death. He spent these twenty years delivering the compulsory sets of textbook lectures, bending the rules as much as possible in favor of Aquinas's *Summa* and delivering a series of immensely influential *relectiones* ("rereadings"), that is, longer considerations of textually related issues, frequently of ecclesiological, political, or moral timeliness. While he published nothing, some of his lecture courses have been preserved with exceptional fullness in the notes of his students, owing to his practice of slow dictation. Fortunately, the most authoritative surviving manuscript of thirteen *relectiones* (all of which appeared in print within twenty years of his death) appears to derive from a "copy in Vitoria's own hand or one that circulated on his authority" (Pagden and Lawrance 1991, xxxiii).

Of most import for political theory are the *relectiones* on civil power (1528), on ecclesiastical power (1532, 1533), on the "affair of the Indies," and its continuation, on the law of war, the latter two delivered in 1539. These are masterful developments and applications of Thomistic thought within the early to mid-sixteenth-century Spanish context, where the dominating issues were: the defeated rebellion of Castilian cities against the Castilian Crown in 1520-21; the resurgence of conciliarism at the reforming, "schismatic" Council of Pisa and Milan in 1511-12; the spread of the "Lutheran heresy"; the incessant warring of the French and Hapsburg monarchs complicated by the Turkish menace; and the Spanish wars of colonial conquest in America. Although our readings from the *relectiones* entitled *The American Indians (De Indis)* and *The Law of War (De iure belli)* highlight Vitoria's theoretical contribution in the sphere of international justice and law, his earlier *relectiones* warrant brief comment, not least because his later contribution is interwoven with their political and ecclesiological arguments.

His treatment of civil power, in *Civil Power (De potestate civili)*, combines a naturalist, Thomist account of its purpose (to safeguard the common good) with a more voluntarist and communal account of its formation, invoking both human and divine agency and law. On the one hand, he construes the commonwealth, invested with divinely ordained, natural rights, as the material cause of *civil authority* (i.e., of the jurisdictional structure of offices and powers) by the mechanism of delegation. On the other, he insists, against the populism of the *comunero* movement, that *royal power*, i.e., the executive right or prerogative, comes immediately from God (as efficient cause), being neither conceded nor retained by the community (1.3f.). By divine will the monarch stands above the whole commonwealth as well as its individual members, there being no legal appeal from the king to the commonwealth (2.1). At the same time, the ruler remains a member of the commonwealth, bound in conscience by its laws, as to the terms of a treaty (3.4). His demonstration of the foundation of kingship in natural and divine law repudiates simultaneously the "heretical" protest that kingship contravenes "evangelical freedom" (1.5) and the misguided assertion that it depends on divine grace, and so is not validly instituted among unbelievers (1.6).

His *relectiones* on ecclesiastical power define its sacramental-juridical nature, its Petrine monarchial structure, and its distinction from and superiority to civil power. Firstly, Vitoria asserts the operative character of priestly, sacramental power in its achievement of supernatural effects, and in the case of penance, its truly juridi-cal character, against Lutheran understandings of the sacraments as declarative, nonjuridical, and congregational. In addition, he defends ecclesiastical jurisdiction (in the external forum) against nonjurisdictional, spiritualizing ecclesiology (*Eccle-siastical Power* 1.2.1ff.; 2.2.1). Secondly, he asserts the descending movement of church power from Christ to Peter and his papal successors, and to the apostles and their episcopal successors, repudiating the conciliarist attempt to invest it "immedi-ately in the whole universal Church" on analogy with the natural powers of the civil community (2.1.1; 2.4.1ff.; 2.5.1ff.; 6.1ff.; 1.4.1ff.). Thirdly, he produces an account of spiritual-temporal relations which, though "dualist," is weighted in favor of papal plenitude. On the one hand, he rejects the ascription of *unrestricted,* universal, tem-poral power to the papacy that destroys the self-sufficiency of civil rule (1.5.1ff.). On the other, he concedes that the pope's spiritual plenitude involves temporal pleni-tude in respect of spiritual purposes, so that, when the latter render it necessary, he may exercise the whole spectrum of secular powers, including those of constituting and deposing princes, and dividing empires (1.5.6ff.). Vitoria stands in the Ockhamist-Sorbonist tradition of regarding the papal exercise of such powers as oc-casional and "mediate," but departs from this tradition in denying to the civil sover-eign reciprocal powers of intervention in spiritual matters.

By rejecting papal imperialism, Vitoria had, well before his *relectiones* of the late 1530s, discredited the original, most powerful title of the Castilian Crown to dominion in America: namely, Pope Alexander VI's Bulls of Donation of 1493, granting to Ferdinand and Isabella "possession of all the lands inhabited by non-Christians they might discover in the Atlantic" (Pagden and Lawrance 1991, xxiv). Largely owing to the moral outrage of missionaries, controversy had long surrounded the Spanish methods of implementing their title — through the slaughter, enslavement, and coer-cive evangelization of the native Americans. Far from indifferent to this controversy, King Ferdinand had sought theological and legal advice and, guided by it, promulgated in 1512-13 legislation to regulate the conduct of the *conquistadores* and reduce the abuses of the *encomienda* system of serf labor. His successor, Emperor Charles V, al-though party to the vast conquests in Mexico and Peru that desolated the Aztec and Inca empires, was receptive to more humane colonizing enterprises and to theological direction. Indeed, the comprehensive and drastic reform intentions of his *New Laws of the Indies,* published in 1542, show the direct impact of the arguments of Vitoria and Bartolomé de Las Casas, however sadly ineffectual they proved. Vitoria's death pre-ceded by five years the celebrated Valladolid debate of 1551 on the lawfulness of the war against the Indians, at which the opposing cases were presented by Las Casas and Sepúlveda, the leading Spanish Renaissance scholar.

The American Indians is Vitoria's most complete investigation of the right (*ius*) or titles by which the Spanish had conquered the Americas and subjected their native population to Spanish rule. His investigation is organized in three "ques-tions." The first considers four grounds for denying the "barbarians" true dominion (i.e., political jurisdiction and ownership of property) prior to the arrival of the Spaniards. Finding them wanting, he considers in the second question a further seven "unjust" titles for the Spanish possession of territories legitimately held by local inhabitants, some of which involve the doubtful rights of universal empire. Third, he considers seven possible "just" grounds or titles for the Spanish waging of war against the American peoples.

He disposes of the first two grounds for denying true dominion to the barbarians — that they are sinners and unbelievers — by demonstrating the ground of human lordship to be man's creation as a rational being in the image of God, which neither mortal sin nor unbelief obliterate (1.2). His Thomistic thesis is that all forms of human dominion flow from natural or human law (1.3). Here, as in *Civil Power,* the Lutheran threat makes it tactically expedient for him to direct his assault against the FitzRalph-Wyclif version of the Augustinian thesis of righteous lordship rather than its papalist predecessor (as represented by James of Viterbo and Giles of Rome), although the earlier is more germane to the papal claim of universal sovereignty. The latter two grounds for denying dominion to the barbarians — that they are irrational or mad — test the theological seriousness of Vitoria's conception of rational humanity. While admitting that irrational creatures, e.g., animals who neither *rule* nor *own* their acts and bodies, cannot be victims of an injustice and cannot have legal rights, he admits no class of human beings — neither barbarians, nor children nor madmen — to be irrational in this subhuman sense, and so incapable of suffering injustice and devoid of legal rights (1.4-6). Madmen may not, perhaps, be civil owners, but no men are slaves by nature, lawfully deprived against their will of freedom, lands, possessions, and government — despite the use made of Aristotle's arguments by apologists for the Spanish conquests! Moreover, the barbarians' civilizational attainment is incontrovertible proof of their "judgment" (1.6).

His attack on the imperial title for Spanish conquests entails an exhaustive refutation of arguments for universal civil jurisdiction per se, and for universal Roman, and Roman Christian, jurisdiction (a refutation faithfully repeated by Suárez), which definitively signals the eclipse of world empire by political pluralism (2.1). He confidently seeks to establish, almost entirely from scriptural evidence, that truly universal jurisdiction has never been a de facto or de jure reality. His attack on the papal title for Spanish conquests broadly conforms to the Paris tradition (from John of Paris onward) of limiting papal authority, which asserts that the pope has no temporal authority per se and that his spiritual authority (unlike Christ's) does not extend to unbelievers. Vitoria's denial that refusal to accept the Christian faith justifies war on the barbarians involves him in explaining the grounds of faith and the nature of efficacious evangelization, so as to emphasize rational freedom and to condemn perfunctory and intimidating methods of eliciting consent, in either religious or political matters (2.4, 6).

The possible "just titles" for Spanish rule in the Americas with which Vitoria concludes his investigations depend for the most part on rights of individuals and political communities under the *ius gentium,* the violation of which would justify Spanish measures to defend them and to redress, even to punish, injuries. Such are rights to travel on land and sea, to communicate and trade with foreign neighbors, to share in their common resources, to take up domicile and marry among them, providing that no harm is thereby inflicted (3.1). Although inclined to underestimate the probable harm resulting to native peoples from Spanish exercise of these rights, Vitoria appreciates the *perceived threat* of harm that impels the Indians to re-sist the invaders, and so severely circumscribes the latter's rights of redress and pun-ishment. He also recognizes that the Spanish are entitled to defend the natural rights of Indians, e.g., rights of the innocent to life, or of a political community to change its government, when menaced from within or without (3.5ff.). In that the propaga-tion of the gospel is a divine imperative as well as a natural right, the protection — indeed, facilitation — of preaching and conversion is the most potent title for Span-ish rule over the barbarians, and also the clearest demonstration of the papal prerog-ative of regulating temporal affairs for spiritual ends (3.2, 3, 4). However, even this is hemmed in by moral reservations; and in any case, none of the titles excuses the un-restrained self-interest, brutality, and contempt for native welfare typical of Spanish conduct in the Americas.

His subsequent *relection, The Law of War,* restates many of the natural law and *ius gentium* principles articulated in *De Indis* within a formal discussion of the law-fulness for Christians of waging war, the causes and authorization of just war, and the conduct of just war (and just victory). His treatment was the basis for even more elaborate discussions, such as that of Suárez (see below, pp. 736-42). We must con-tent ourselves with pointing to three central axioms of Vitoria's ethic of war: *(a)* that waging war is an act of political authority with the purpose of safeguarding the com-mon good by avenging and punishing wrongdoing; *(b)* that waging war belongs by natural right to independent commonwealths or sovereign rulers who exercise this power on behalf of the world community; and *(c)* that the juridical purpose of war constrains at every point the means that are deployed.

Further Reading: D. Deckers, *Gerechtigkeit und Recht: eine historisch-kritische Untersuchung der Gerechtigskeitslehre des Francisco de Vitoria (1483-1546)* (Freiburg: Universitätsverlag Freiburg Schweiz, 1991); J. P. Doyle, trans., *Vitoria, "On Homicide" and "Commentary on Summa theologiae IIa-IIae Q. 64"* (Milwaukee: Marquette Univer-sity Press, 1997); J. A. Fernández Santamaria, *The State, War, and Peace: Spanish Political Thought in the Renaissance, 1516-1599* (Cambridge: Cambridge University Press, 1977); B. Hamilton, *Political Thought in Sixteenth-Century Spain: A Study of the Political Ideas of Vitoria, De Soto, Suárez, and Molina* (Oxford: Clarendon Press, 1963); J. Muldoon, *Popes, Lawyers, and Infidels: The Church and the Non-Christian World, 1250-1550* (Liverpool: Liverpool University Press, 1979); A. Pagden, *The Fall of Natural Man: The American In-dian and the Origins of Comparative Ethnology,* 2nd ed. (Cambridge: Cambridge Univer-sity Press, 1986); A. Pagden, ed., *The Languages of Political Theory in Early Modern Europe* (Cambridge: Cambridge University Press, 1987).

From *The American Indians*

q.1 a.3. *Whether unbelievers can be true masters.* We must now discuss of *whether a man can be deprived of dominion by reason of being an unbeliever.*

On the one hand it seems that he can. Heretics can have no dominion *(dominium),* so unbelievers, who are no better than heretics, can have no dominion either. The major premiss is clear from the decretal (VI 5.2.19), which warns that the goods of heretics are to be confiscated *ipso iure.* I reply with the following propositions:

1. *It is no impediment for a man to be a true master, that he is an unbeliever.* This is the conclusion of St. Thomas Aquinas, *ST* 2a-2ae.10.10.

This can be proved first by authority, from Holy Scripture, which often calls unbelievers such as Sennacherib, Pharaoh, and others "kings"; Paul (Rom. 13:1-5) and Peter (1 Pet. 2:13-14, 18) gave orders to obey the rulers, who in their day were all unbelievers, and ordained that servants should obey their masters; Tobit ordered a kid to be returned to the pagans because he thought it was stolen (Tob. 2:11-14), which he would not have done if the pagans had no right of ownership *(dominium).*

We have also a proof based on reason. Aquinas shows that unbelief does not cancel either natural or human law, but all forms of dominion derive from natural or human law; therefore they cannot be annulled by lack of faith.

Hence the objection is a manifest error, like the preceding one, and heretical too. It is clear that it is not lawful to take away the possessions of Saracens, Jews, or other unbelievers on the grounds of their unbelief *per se;* to do so is theft or robbery, no less than it would be in the case of Christians. Joseph made all the land of Egypt pay tribute to Pharaoh, who was an unbeliever (Gen. 47:20). [Vitoria's further propositions, concerning the property of heretics, are omitted.]

q.1 a.4. *Whether irrational men can be true masters.* It remains to discuss whether men who are irrational or mad can be true masters. And first of all it may be debated *whether a man requires the use of reason in order to have dominion.*

Conrad Summenhart concludes that dominion may belong to irrational creatures, both sensate and insensate (*Septipertitum opus de contractibus* 1.6). His proof is that dominion is nothing other than "the right to use a thing for one's own benefit." Yet brute creatures have this sort of use of grasses and plants: "And God said, Behold, I have given you every herb bearing seed which is upon the face of the earth, and every tree in which is the fruit of a tree yielding seed; to you it shall be for meat. And to every beast of the earth, and to every fowl of the air, and to every thing that creepeth upon the earth, wherein there is life, I have given every green herb for meat: and it was so" (Gen. 1:29f.). So, too, the stars have the right to shed their light: "And God set them in the firmament of the heaven to give light upon the earth, and to rule over the day and over the night" (Gen. 1:17f.). The lion has dominion over all the animals that walk upon the earth, whence it is called "king of beasts"; and the eagle is lord of all birds of the air, according to the psalm: "The house of the eagle is their leader" (Ps. 104:17 Vulgate). Silvestro Mazzolini da Priero shares this view, pointing out that the elements exercise dominance over one another (*Summa Syluestrina, s.v. dominium* 1-2).

Let us answer with the following propositions, beginning with this first:

1. *Irrational creatures clearly cannot have any dominion,* for dominion is a legal right, as Conrad Summenhart himself admits. Irrational creatures cannot have legal rights; therefore they cannot have any dominion. The minor premiss is proved by the fact that irrational creatures cannot be victims of an injustice *(iniuria),* and

therefore cannot have legal rights: this assumption is proved in turn by considering the fact that to deprive a wolf or a lion of its prey is no injustice against the beast in question, any more than to shut out the sun's light by drawing the blinds is an injustice to the sun. And this is confirmed by the absurdity of the following argument: that if brutes had dominion, then any person who fenced off grass from deer would be committing a theft, since he would be stealing food without its owner's permission. [. . .]

And again: wild animals have no rights over their own bodies; still less, then, can they have rights over other things. The major premiss is proved by the fact that it is lawful to kill them with impunity, even for sport; as Aristotle says, hunting wild animals is naturally just (*Politics* 1256 9-25).

Finally, these wild beasts and all irrational beings are subject to the power of man, even more than slaves; and therefore, if slaves cannot own anything of their own, still less can irrational beings. This argument is confirmed by Aquinas (*ST* 1a2ae.1.1-2, 6.2; and *Summa contra gentiles* 3.2): only rational creatures have mastery over their own actions, as Aquinas also shows in *ST* 1a.82.1. If, then, brutes have no dominion over their own actions, they can have no dominion over other things.

Although this argument may seem a mere quibble over words, it is quite improper and contrary to normal usage. We do not speak of anyone being "the owner" (*dominum*) of a thing unless that thing lies within his control. We often say, for example: "It is not in my control, it is not in my power," meaning I am not master or owner of it. By this argument brutes, which do not move by their own will but are moved by some other, as Aquinas says, cannot have any dominion.

The objection proposed by Silvestro Mazzolini da Priero, namely that dominion sometimes means not a legal right but merely *de facto* power, such as the dominance of fire over water, is invalid. If this definition of dominion were correct, then a robber would have the right over other men to commit murder simply because he had the power to do so, and a thief would have the right to steal money. Therefore, when he speaks of the stars "ruling" over day and night or calls the lion "king of the beasts," these are mere figures of speech.

q.1 a.5. Whether children can be true masters. On the other hand, what of a different question, raised in connexion with children before the age of reason: can they be legal masters? Children seem in this respect not to be any different from irrational beings. As the Apostle says: "the heir, as long as he is a child, differeth nothing from a slave" (Gal. 4:1). But a slave cannot be a master; *ergo*, etc.

Let us answer with this second proposition:

2. *Children before the age of reason can be masters.* This is self-evident, first because a child can be the victim of an injustice; therefore a child can have legal rights, therefore it can have a right of ownership, which is a legal right. Again, the possessions of an orphan minor in guardianship are not the property of the guardians, and yet they must be the property of one of the two parties; *a fortiori* they are the property of the minor. Again, a child in guardianship may legally inherit property; but an heir is defined in the law as the person who succeeds to the inheritance of the deceased, hence the child is the owner of the inheritance (Dig. 44.3.11; Inst. 2.19.7). Furthermore, we said earlier that the foundation of dominion is the fact that we are

formed in the image of God; and the child is already formed in the image of God. The Apostle goes on to say, in the passage of Galatians quoted, "the heir, as long as he is a child, differeth nothing from a slave, though he be lord of all" (Gal. 4:1). The same does not hold of an irrational creature, since the child does not exist for another's use, like an animal, but for himself.

q.1 a.6. *Whether madmen can be true masters.* But what of madmen (I mean the incurably mad, who can neither have nor expect ever to have the use of reason)? Let us answer with this third proposition:

3. *These madmen too may be true masters.* For a madman too can be the victim of injustice; therefore he can have legal rights. I leave it to the experts on Roman law to decide whether madmen can have civil rights of ownership. Whatever the answer to that, I conclude with this final proposition:

4. *The barbarians are not prevented by this, or by the argument of the previous article, from being true masters.* The proof of this is that they are not in point of fact madmen, but have judgment like other men. This is self-evident, because they have some order in their affairs: they have properly organised cities, proper marriages, magistrates and overlords, laws, industries, and commerce, all of which require the use of reason. They likewise have a form of religion, and they correctly apprehend things which are evident to other men, which indicates the use of reason [*cf.* Aristotle's criteria for civil society, *Politics* 1328 6-22]. Furthermore, "God and nature never fail in the things necessary" for the majority of the species, and the chief attribute of man is reason; but the potential which is incapable of being realised in the act is in vain.

Nor could it be their fault if they were for so many thousands of years outside the state of salvation, since they were born in sin but did not have the use of reason to prompt them to seek baptism or the things necessary for salvation.

Thus if they seem to us insensate and slow-witted, I put it down mainly to their evil and barbarous education. Even amongst ourselves we see many peasants who are little different from brute animals.

q.1 conclusion. The conclusion of all that has been said is that the barbarians undoubtedly possessed as true dominion, both public and private, as any Christians. That is to say, they could not be robbed of their property, either as private citizens or as princes, on the ground that they were not true masters. It would be harsh to deny to them, who have never done us any wrong, the rights we concede to Saracens and Jews, who have been continual enemies of the Christian religion. Yet we do not deny the right of ownership of the latter, unless it be the case of Christian lands which they have conquered.

To the original objection one may therefore say, as concerns the argument that *these barbarians are insufficiently rational to govern themselves* and so on:

1. Aristotle [referring to the passage on "natural slaves," *Politics* 1255a28-34] certainly did not mean to say that such men thereby belong by nature to others and have no rights of ownership over their own bodies and possessions. Such slavery is a civil and legal condition, to which no man can belong by nature.

2. Nor did Aristotle mean that it is lawful to seize the goods and lands, and enslave and sell the persons, of those who are by nature less intelligent. What he meant

to say was that such men have a natural deficiency, because of which they need others to govern and direct them. It is good that such men should be subordinate to others, like children to their parents until they reach adulthood, and like a wife to her husband. That this was Aristotle's true intention is apparent from his parallel statement that some men are "natural masters" by virtue of their superior intelligence. He certainly did not mean by this that such men had a legal right to arrogate power to themselves over others on the grounds of their superior intelligence, but merely that they are fitted by nature to be princes and guides.

Hence, granting that these barbarians are as foolish and slow-witted as people say they are, it is still wrong to use this as grounds to deny their true dominion; nor can they be counted among the slaves. It may be, as I shall show, that these arguments can provide legal grounds for subjecting the Indians, but that is a different matter.

For the moment, the clear conclusion to the first question is therefore *that before arrival of the Spaniards these barbarians possessed true dominion, both in public and private affairs.*

q.2 a.1. *First unjust title, that our most serene Emperor might be master of the whole world.* [Vitoria presents five arguments in support of the emperor's universal mastership.]

But this opinion is without any foundation. I reply as follows:

1. My first proposition is that *the emperor is not master of the whole world.* The proof of this is as follows: dominion *(dominium)* can exist only by natural law, divine law, or human law. But the emperor is not master of the world by any of these. The minor premiss is proved as follows.

First, as regards natural law: St. Thomas rightly says that in natural law all are free other than from the dominion of fathers or husbands, who have dominion over their children and wives in natural law (*ST* 1a 92.1; 1a 96.4); therefore no one can be emperor of the world by natural law. St. Thomas also says that dominion and supremacy *(praelatio)* were introduced by human law, not natural law (*ST* 2a-2ae 10.10). Otherwise there would be no good reason why imperial dominion should belong to the Spaniards rather than to the French. Aristotle puts it this way: power is of two kinds, family power like that of a father over his sons or a husband over his wife, which is natural, and civil power, which may indeed have had its origin in nature and may thus be said to belong to natural law, since as St. Thomas says "man is a civil animal" (*On Kingship* 1.1 [see above, p. 330]), but which was undoubtedly not instituted by nature, but by an enactment *(lex)*.

Second, as regards divine law: we nowhere read of the emperors and masters of the world before the advent of Christ, even though Bartolus of Sassoferrato, in that gloss of his on *Ad reprimendam* (X 1.31.8), adduces Nebuchadnezzar, of whom it was said: "Thou, O king, art a king of kings, for the God of heaven hath given thee a kingdom, power, and strength, and glory, and wheresoever the children of men dwell hath he given into thine hand, and made thee ruler over them all" (Dan. 2:37-38). But it is certain that Nebuchadnezzar did not receive some special gift of imperial power from God; the meaning of the passage is simply that he rules like any other prince, since as Paul says "there is no power but of God" (Rom. 13:1), and "by me kings reign and princes decree justice" (Prov. 8:15). Besides, Nebuchadnezzar's empire did not reach *de iure* over the whole world, as Bartolus thinks, since the Jews were not by right his subjects. And this last fact proves that no one was ever master of the whole world by divine law, because the people of Israel was free of any foreign suzerain — indeed, was expressly forbidden by law from having any foreign master: "thou mayest not set a stranger over thee" (Deut. 17:15). And although St. Thomas Aquinas appears to affirm that God delivered imperial power to the Romans because of their justice and patriotism and excellent laws [actually Ptolemy of Lucca. *De regimine principum* 3.4], and Augustine says the same thing (*City of God* 3.10), we are not to understand that they held their empire by divine institution or livery of seisin *(traditio),* but that divine providence brought it about that they should obtain universal empire by some other right, such as just war or some other way. This was not the sense in which Saul and David received their kingship "from God."

This point can easily be understood by anyone who examines the method of succession by which the empires and dominions of the world have been handed down to our own day. Leaving aside those which passed away before the Flood, it is clear that after Noah the world was divided into various countries and kingdoms. This was either ordered by Noah himself, who lived for three hundred and fifty years after the flood (Gen. 9:28) and sent out expeditions to colonise the various regions of the earth, according to the account of Berosus of Babylon; or, as seems more likely, by mutual consent of the nations, as various families colonised different countries. So Abraham said to Lot: "Is not the whole land before thee? Separate thyself, I pray thee, from me; if thou wilt take the left hand I will go to the right, or if thou depart to the right hand then I will go to the left" (Gen. 13:9). We are told in Gen. 10 how the great grandsons of Noah divided "in their lands and after their nations" (Gen. 10:32), either because in some lands certain men set themselves up as tyrants for the first time (as was the case of Nimrod, of whom it is said that he first "began to be a mighty one in the earth," Gen. 10:8), or because some of them gathered together in one commonwealth and by common consent set up a prince. What is certain, however, is that dominions and empires began on earth in one of these two not dissimilar ways; and they have since been handed down by inheritance or conquest or some other title until our own times, or at least down to the advent of our saviour. So it is obvious that no one before Christ obtained an empire by divine law; and the emperor is not entitled on any such grounds to arrogate to himself the dominion of the whole world, nor, as a consequence, of these barbarians.

Since the advent of our Lord, however, it might be claimed that there has existed a single emperor of the world by livery of seisin from Christ, since he was master of the world by his human nature according to the verse "All power is given unto me in heaven and in earth" (Matt. 28:18). This is to be understood as referring to his humanity according to Augustine and Jerome; and according to the words of the Apostle, "for he hath put all things under his feet" (1 Cor. 15:27), and it is taken to mean that, as he left one vicar on earth in spirituals, so too he left a vicar, namely the emperor, in temporals. St. Thomas says that Christ was the true master and monarch of the world from the moment of his birth, and that Augustus was unwittingly his regent. This obviously means regent in temporal, not spiritual things. And therefore,

618

if Christ's kingdom was temporal, it embraced the whole world; so it follows that Augustus was master of the world, and by this token so are his successors.

But this too is quite invalid as an argument. First, it is by no means certain that Christ was temporal master of the world according to his humanity — more probably not, since the Lord himself seems to have asserted: "My kingdom is not of this world" (John 18:36), from which St. Thomas [Ptolemy of Lucca] deduced in *De regimine principum* 3.13 that Christ's dominion is directly ordained for the salvation of the soul and spiritual goods, though it is not excluded from temporal things insofar as they are ordained for spiritual ends. It is thus clear that St. Thomas did not hold the opinion that Christ's kingdom was of the same type as civil and temporal kingship, although for the purposes of redemption he had complete power even in temporal matters. Apart from this purpose, however, he had no power. Besides, even if he was a temporal lord, it is mere guesswork to deduce that he left this power to the emperor, since there is no mention of such a thing in all Scripture. As for the point that St. Thomas says that Augustus Caesar was Christ's vice-gerent, the first point is that he said this in *De regimine principum*, but elsewhere, when specifically discussing the power of Christ (*ST* 3a.59), he made no mention of this temporal power of Christ; and the second point is that St. Thomas meant that Augustus was "vice-gerent of Christ" in the sense that temporal power is subject and subservient to spiritual power. Indeed, in this sense kings are ministers of bishops, just as the craft of the armourer is subservient to the crafts of knighthood and war; but the knight or the general is not an armourer himself, even though he exercises command over the armourer in the manufacture of arms. So St. Thomas comments expressly on the passage in question (in John 18:36) that Christ's kingdom was not temporal, as Pilate understood it, but spiritual, as the Lord himself declared: "thou sayest that I am king; to this end was I born, and for this cause came I into the world, that I should bear witness unto the truth" (John 18:37). It is evident, therefore, that to say that there is a single emperor and master of the world by livery of seisin from Christ is simple twisting of the evidence.

An obvious confirmation is the following: if the emperor was master by divine law, how did the empire come to be divided into its western and eastern components? The division was first made between the sons of Constantine the Great; later Pope Stephen transferred the western empire to the Germans, as stated in the decretal *Venerabilem* (X 1.6.34). The comment of the *Glossa ordinaria* on this decretal, to the effect that the Greeks ceased to be emperors from this moment, is ignorant and wrong, since the German emperors never claimed that their title made them lords of Greece. Besides, the emperor of Constantinople John VIII Palaeologus was recognised as the legitimate emperor at the Council of Florence (1439).

Furthermore, the patrimony of the church is not subject to the emperor, as even the jurists, among them Bartolus himself, admit. But if everything in the world was subject to the emperor by divine law, no emperor could remove anything from that subjection by a donation or other title, any more than a pope can exempt anyone from the papal power. But the kingdoms of Spain and France are not subject to the emperor, as stated in Innocent III's decretal *Per uenerabilem* (X 4.17.13), even though the author of the *Glossa ordinaria* [the German Johannes Teutonicus] wilfully adds that this is only so *de facto,* but not *de iure.*

Finally, the doctors admit that city republics which were once subject to the empire may gain their independence by invoking custom. This could not be so if their subjection were a matter of divine laws.

Third, as regards human law: it is established that in this case, too, the emperor is not master of the whole world, because if he were it would be solely by authority of some enactment, and there is no such enactment. Even if there were, it would have no force, since an enactment presupposes the necessary jurisdiction; if, therefore, the emperor did not have universal jurisdiction before the enactment of the law, the enactment could not be binding on those who were not his subjects. Nor does the emperor have universal dominion by legitimate succession, gift, exchange, purchase, just war, election, or any other legal title, as is established.

Therefore the emperor has never been master of the whole world.

2. The second conclusion is that even if the emperor were master of the world, he could not on that account occupy the lands of the barbarians, or depose their masters and set up new ones, or impose taxes on them. The proof is as follows. Even those who attribute dominion of the whole world to the emperor do not claim that he has it by property *(per proprietatem)*, but only that he has it by jurisdiction *(per iurisdictionem)*. Such a right does not include the license to turn whole countries to his own use, or dispose at whim of townships or even estates.

q.2 a.4. *Fourth unjust title, that they [the American Indians] refuse to accept the faith of Christ, although they have been told about it and insistently pressed to accept it.* [Vitoria presents three arguments justifying the Spanish occupation of Indian lands on account of their refusal to accept the Christian faith, and then two conclusions in reply.]

2. My second conclusion is that *the barbarians are not bound to believe from the first moment that the Christian faith is announced to them,* in the sense of committing a mortal sin merely by not believing a simple announcement, unaccompanied by miracles or any other kind of proof or persuasion, that the true religion is Christian, and that Christ is the Saviour and Redeemer of the universe. [Vitoria refers here to the *requerimiento* or juridical "summons" that the conquistadors were required to read to the Amerindians before attacking them, which set out the Spanish title to *dominium* in the Americas and demanded that they accept both this title and the "Holy Trinity."]

The proof follows from my discussion of the first proposition. If they were excused before they heard anything about the Christian religion, then again they are not obliged by a simple statement or announcement of this kind. Such an announcement is no argument or reason for believing; indeed, as Cajetan says (in *ST* 2a2ae.1.4), it is foolhardy and imprudent of anyone to believe a thing without being sure it comes from a trustworthy source, especially in matters to do with salvation. But the barbarians could not be sure of this, since they did not know who or what kind of people they were who preached the new religion to them. This is confirmed by St. Thomas, who says that things which are of faith visibly and clearly belong to the realm of the credible; the faithful man would not believe them unless he could see that they were credible, whether by palpable signs or by some other means (*ST* 2a2ae.1.4, 1.5). Therefore where there are no such signs nor any other persuasive factor, the barbarians are not obliged to believe. A further confirmation is that if the Saracens were to preach their own sect in this simple way to the barbarians at the same time as the Christians, it is clear that the barbarians would not be obliged to believe the Saracens. Therefore, since they would not be able or obliged to guess which of these two was the truer religion without some more visible proof of probability on one side or the other, the barbarians are not obliged to believe the Christians either, unless the latter put forward some other motive or persuasion to convince them. To do so would be to believe too readily, like the "light-headed man" (Sir. 19:4). And this is confirmed by the Lord's words: "if I had not done among them the works which none other man did, they had not had sin" (John 15:24). Where there are no miraculous signs or other reasons for belief, there will be no sin.

From this proposition it follows that if the faith is proposed to the barbarians only in this way and they do not accept it, the Spaniards cannot use this pretext to attack them or conduct a just war against them. This is obvious, because the barbarians are innocent on this count, and have not done any wrong to the Spaniards.

The corollary is proved by St. Thomas's teaching that for the just war a just cause is required; namely, that those who are attacked have deserved attack by some culpable action (*ST* 2a2ae.40.1). Hence Augustine says (*Quaestiones in Heptateuchum* 6.10): "The usual definition of just wars is that they are those which avenge injustices *(iniuriae),* when a nation or city is to be scourged for having failed to punish the wrongdoings of its own people or to restore property which has been unjustly stolen." If the barbarians have done no wrong, there is no just cause for war; this is the opinion shared by all the doctors, not only theologians but also jurists such as Hostiensis, Innocent IV, and others; Caejetan expounds it eloquently in his commentary on *ST* 2a2ae.66.8. I know of no author who opposes it. Therefore this would not be a legitimate title for occupying the lands of the barbarians and despoiling their previous owners of them.

3. My third conclusion is that *if the barbarians are asked and advised to listen to peaceful persuasion about religion, but refuse to do so, they incur unpardonable mortal sin.* The proof is that if their own beliefs are gravely mistaken, as we suppose they are, they can have no convincing or probable reasons for them, and are therefore obliged at least to listen and consider what anyone may advise them to hear and meditate concerning religion. Furthermore, belief in Christ and baptism is necessary for their own salvation: "he that believeth and is baptised shall be saved, but he that believeth not shall be damned" (Mark 16:16). But they cannot believe if they have not heard (Rom. 10:14). Hence they are obliged to listen, because if they were not obliged to hear they would be beyond all salvation through no fault of their own.

4. My fourth conclusion is that *if the Christian faith is set before the barbarians in a probable fashion,* that is with probable and rational arguments and accompanied by manners both decent and observant of the law of nature, such as are themselves a great argument for the truth of the faith, and if this is done not once or in a perfunctory way, but diligently and observantly, *then the barbarians are obliged to accept the faith of Christ under pain of mortal sin.* The proof follows from the third proposition: if they are obliged to listen, then they are also obliged to acquiesce with what they hear if it is reasonable. This is clear from the passage: "Go ye into all the world, and

preach the gospel to every creature; he that believeth and is baptised shall be saved, but he that believeth not shall be damned" (Mark 16:15-16). And also from "there is none other name under heaven given among men, whereby we must be saved" (Acts 4:12).

5. My fifth conclusion is that *it is not sufficiently clear to me that the Christian faith has up to now been announced and set before the barbarians in such a way as to oblige them to believe it under pain of fresh sin.* By this I mean that, as explained in my second proposition, they are not bound to believe unless the faith has been set before them with persuasive probability. But I have not heard of any miracles or signs, nor of any exemplary saintliness of life sufficient to convert them. On the contrary, I hear only of provocations, savage crimes, and multitudes of unholy acts. From this, it does not appear that the Christian religion has been preached to them in a sufficiently pious way to oblige their acquiescence; even though it is clear that a number of friars and other churchmen have striven industriously in this cause, by the example of their lives and the diligence of their preaching, and this would have been enough, had they not been thwarted by others with different aims.

6. My sixth conclusion is that, however probably and sufficiently the faith may have been announced to the barbarians and then rejected by them, *this is still no reason to declare war on them and despoil them of their goods.* This conclusion is expressed by St. Thomas in his *ST* 2a2ae.10.8, where he says that unbelievers who have never taken up the faith such as the pagans and the Jews are by no means compelled to believe. And this is the common conclusion of the doctors of both canon and civil law. The proof is that belief is a matter of will, but fear considerably diminishes the freedom of will (Aristotle, *NE* 1110a1-12). To come to the mysteries and sacraments of Christ merely out of servile fear would be sacrilege. A further proof is the passage in Gratian's canon *De Iudaeis* (D. 45. c. 5): "Concerning the Jews, the holy Council laid down that no one should use force to compel belief, since God is merciful to those he wishes, and hardens the hearts of those he wishes." There is no doubt that this opinion of the Council of Toledo means that threats and terror should not be used to bring the Jews to the faith. And St. Gregory the Great expressly says the same in the canon *Qui sincera:* "those who sincerely desire to lead those outside the Christian religion to perfect faith should be careful to use blandishments, not cruelty" (D. 45. c. 3). Those who act otherwise and decide to tear them from their accustomed religious observances and rites under this pretext are serving their own ends, not God's. The proposition is also proved by the use and custom of the church, since no Christian emperor, with the benefit of the advice of the most holy and wise popes, has ever declared war on unbelievers simply because they refused to accept the Christian religion.

Besides, war is no argument for the truth of the Christian faith. Hence the barbarians cannot be moved by war to believe, but only to pretend that they believe and accept the Christian faith; and this is monstrous and sacrilegious. Duns Scotus says that it is a religious act for princes to compel unbelievers with threats and terror (*Comm. in Sent.* 4.4.9); but this can only be understood to refer to unbelievers who are already the subjects of Christian princes. Of such subjects I shall speak later. But the barbarians do not belong to this group, and therefore I do not believe that Scotus would have applied his assertion to these barbarians of ours.

It is therefore clear that this title to the conquest of the lands of the barbarians, too, is neither applicable nor legitimate.

q.2 a.5. *Fifth unjust title, the sins of the barbarians.* This next title is also seriously put forward by those who say that, although the barbarians may not be invaded because of their unbelief or their refusal to accept the Christian faith, war may nevertheless be declared on them for their other mortal sins, which according to the proponents of this argument are manifold, and very serious to boot.

Concerning mortal sins, however, they make a distinction. Some sins, they say, are not against natural law, but only positive divine law; and for these the barbarians cannot be invaded. But others, such as cannibalism, incest with mothers and sisters, or sodomy, are against nature; and for these sins they may be invaded and compelled to give them up. The reasoning behind this is that in the former category of sins against positive law, it cannot be demonstrated by evidence that they are sinful, whereas in the case of sins against the law of nature the barbarians can be shown that they are committing an offence against God, and may consequently be compelled not to offend him further. Again, they can be forced to observe a law which they themselves profess; and this is the case with natural law. This is the opinion of St. Antonino of Florence (*Summa theologica* 322.5.8), following Agostino Trionfo (*De potestate ecclesiastica* 1.23.4); and the same opinion is held by Silvestro Mazzolini da Priero (*Summa Syluestrina, s.v. papa*), and Innocent IV in his commentary on the decretal *Quod super his* (X 3.34.8), where he expressly says: "I believe that if the gentiles break natural law, which is the only law they have, they may be punished by the pope." He adduces to this purpose the fact that the Sodomites were punished by God (Gen. 19:24f.); "since God's judgments are examples to us, I do not see why the pope, who is the vicar of Christ, should not be empowered to do the same." So says Innocent; and by this argument, they might also, on the pope's authority, be punished by Christian princes.

But on the other hand I adduce the following proposition: *Christian princes, even on the authority of the pope, may not compel the barbarians to give up their sins against the law of nature, nor punish them for such sins.*

I reply with the following proofs. First of all, our opponents' presupposition that the pope has jurisdiction over the barbarians is false, as I have said above (2.2).

Second, they either interpret "sins against the law of nature" in a universal sense, as including theft, fornication, and adultery; or in the special sense of "sins against nature" as defined by St. Thomas (*ST* 2a2ae.154.11-12), that is to say, not only "against natural law" but "against the natural order," or what is described by the word "uncleanness" in 2 Cor. 12:21, which the *Glossa ordinaria* explains as pederasty, buggery with animals, or lesbianism, which are referred to also in Rom. 1:24-7. Now if they interpret the expression exclusively in the second of these two ways, one may argue against them that murder is as serious a sin, or more serious; and therefore it is clear that if it is lawful to punish men for these "sins against nature," it must also be lawful to punish them for murder; and similarly, blasphemy is as serious a sin, and so it is obvious that one may punish them for blasphemy too, and so on. But if they extend their interpretation to include the general sense of "any sin against the law of nature," the reply is that it is not lawful to punish them for fornication, and therefore it is not lawful to punish them for the other sins against natural law. The minor premiss is clear from 1 Cor. 5:9-13, which says: "I wrote unto you in an epistle not to company with fornicators . . . and not to keep company, if any man *that is called a brother* be a fornicator or an idolater," and then adds: "For what have we to do to judge them also that are without?" St. Thomas expounds this as meaning that prelates have received power only over those who have subjected themselves to the faith (in 1 Cor. 5:12, lect. 3). It is quite clear, then, that Paul means that the judgment of unbelievers, whether they be fornicators or idolaters, is none of his business.

A further argument is that not all sins against natural law can be demonstrated to be so by evidence, at least to the satisfaction of all men. Furthermore, to make this assertion is tantamount to saying that the barbarians may be conquered because of their unbelief, since they are all idolaters. Besides, the pope may not make war on Christians because they are fornicators or robbers, or even because they are sodomites; nor can he confiscate their lands and give them to other princes; if he could, since every country is full of sinners, kingdoms could be exchanged every day. And a further confirmation is that such sins are more serious in Christians, who know them to be sins, than in the barbarians, who do not. Besides, it would be extraordinary that the pope would be able to pronounce judgments and inflict punishments on unbelievers, and yet prevented from making laws for them.

And there is a further argument, which seems to conclude the matter. Either the barbarians are obliged to suffer the penalties ordained for these sins, or they are not. If they are not, the pope is not empowered to inflict them. If they are, then they are obliged to recognise the pope as their lord and legislator; but if this is the case, then the very fact that they refuse to recognise him as such is a reason for declaring war upon them. But even my opponents deny this conclusion, as I have said above. It would indeed be extraordinary that they should be able to deny the authority and jurisdiction of the pope with impunity, and yet be obliged to suffer his judgments. Again, those who are not Christians cannot accept the judgment of the pope, since the pope cannot condemn or punish them by any right other than that he is the vicar of Christ. But all these opponents, St. Antonino and Silvestro Mazzolini da Priero as well as Agostino Trionfo and even Innocent IV himself, admit that unbelievers cannot be punished on the grounds that they have not accepted Christ. Therefore they cannot be punished because they do not accept the judgment of the pope; the latter presupposes the former.

And a confirmation that neither this nor the preceding title is sufficient is that even in the Old Testament, where affairs were conducted by force of arms, the people of Israel never occupied the lands of the unbelievers either on the grounds that they were infidels and idolaters or because they were otherwise sinners against nature, even though they were sinful in many ways, being idolaters and sinners against nature, for instance by sacrificing their own sons and daughters to demons. They only conquered such peoples by God's special gift, or because they refused to allow them free passage, or because they had wronged them first.

Besides, what do these opponents mean by "professing" the law of nature? If they mean "knowing what it is," the barbarians do not have complete knowledge of it. But if they mean "being willing to observe the law of nature," I counter by pointing out that, in this case, they must also mean "willing to observe the whole of Christ's law," since if they knew that Christian law was divine law, they would be willing to observe it. In this sense, they no more "profess" divine law than Christian law.

And again, we actually have better proofs to show that Christ's law is true and God-given than to show that fornication is evil or that the other things prohibited by natural law are to be avoided. Therefore, if the barbarians can be forced to keep the law of nature because it can be proved, they can also be forced to keep the law of the Gospels; but this is indeed an incredible deduction.

q.2 a.6. *Sixth unjust title, by the voluntary choice of the barbarians.* This is yet another title which can be and is alleged. Whenever the Spaniards first make contact with the barbarians, they notify them that the king of Spain has sent them for their benefit, and advise them to take him and accept him as their lord and king. And the barbarians have replied that they agree to do so. And "nothing is so natural as that the wishes of an owner who wishes to transfer his property to another should be ratified" (Inst. 2.1.40).

But on the other hand I propose that this title, too, is inapplicable. This is clear, first of all, because the choice ought not to have been made in fear and ignorance, factors which vitiate any freedom of election, but which played a leading part in this particular choice and acceptance. The barbarians do not realise what they are doing; perhaps, indeed, they do not even understand what it is the Spaniards are asking of them. Besides which, the request is made by armed men, who surround a fearful and defenceless crowd. Furthermore, since the barbarians already had their own true masters and princes, as explained above, a people cannot without reasonable cause seek new masters, which would be to the detriment of their previous lords. Nor, on the contrary, can the masters themselves elect a new prince without the assent of the whole people. As I have said before, they are not obliged to believe in the Christian religion, nor in the dominion of the pope, and hence not in the dominion of the emperor either.

Since, therefore, in these methods of choice and acceptance some of the requisite conditions for a legitimate choice were lacking, on the whole this title to occupying and conquering these countries is neither relevant nor legitimate.

q.2 a.7. *Seventh unjust title, by special gift from God.* Here is the last title that may be alleged. Some, I know not who, say that the Lord has by his special judgment damned all these barbarians to perdition for their abominations, and delivered them into the hands of the Spaniards just as he once delivered the Canaanites into the hands of the Jews (Num. 21:3).

But I am unwilling to enter into a protracted dispute on this argument, since it is dangerous to give credit to anyone who proclaims a prophecy of this kind contrary to common law and the rules of Scripture unless his teaching is confirmed by some miracle. The proclaimers of this prophecy offer no such miracles.

Besides, even if it were true that the Lord had decided to bring about the destruction of the barbarians, it does not follow that a man who destroyed them would thereby be guiltless. The kings of Babylon who led their armies against Jerusalem and enslaved the children of Israel were not guiltless, even though all this in fact came about by the special providence of God, as had often been foretold (cf. Jer. 25:11f.). [. . .]

q.3 a.1. *First just title, of natural partnership and communication.* (1) My first conclusion on this point will be that *the Spaniards have the right to travel and dwell in* *those countries, so long as they do no harm to the barbarians, and cannot be prevented by them from doing so.*

The first proof comes from the law of nations *(ius gentium)*, which either is or derives from natural law, as defined by the jurist: "What natural reason has established among all nations is called the law of nations" (Inst. 2.1.1-4). Amongst all nations it is considered inhuman to treat strangers and travellers badly without some special cause, humane and dutiful to behave hospitably to strangers. This would not be the case if travellers were doing something evil by visiting foreign nations. Second, in the beginning of the world, when all things were held in common, everyone was allowed to visit and travel through any land he wished. This right was clearly not taken away by the division of property; it was never the intention of nations to prevent men's free mutual intercourse with one another by this division. Certainly it would have been thought inhuman to do so in the time of Noah. Third, all things which are not prohibited or otherwise to the harm and detriment of others are lawful. Since these travels of the Spaniards are (as we may for the moment assume) neither harmful nor detrimental to the barbarians, they are lawful.

Fourth, it would not be lawful for the French to prohibit Spaniards from travelling or even living in France, or vice versa, so long as it caused no sort of harm to themselves; therefore it is not lawful for the barbarians either. Fifth, exile is counted amongst the punishments for capital crimes, and therefore it is not lawful to banish visitors who are innocent of any crime. Sixth, it is an act of war to bar those considered as enemies from entering a city or country, or to expel them if they are already in it. But since the barbarians have no just war against the Spaniards, assuming they are doing no harm, it is not lawful for them to bar them from their homeland.

A seventh proof is provided by Virgil's verses:

What men, what monsters, what inhuman race,
What laws, what barbarous customs of the place,
Shut up a desert shore to drowning men,
And drive us to the cruel sea again!

(*Aeneid* 1.539-40, Dryden's translation)

An eighth proof is given in the words of Scripture: "Every living creature loveth his like" (Sir. 13:15), which show that amity between men is part of natural law, and that it is against nature to shun the company of harmless men. A ninth argument is the passage, "I was a stranger and ye took me not in" (Matt. 25:43), from which it is clear that, since it is a law of nature to welcome strangers, this judgment of Christ is to be decreed amongst all men. And a tenth, the jurist's determination that by natural law running water and the open sea, rivers, and ports are the common property of all, and by the law of nations ships from any country may lawfully put in anywhere (Inst. 2.1.1-4); by this token these things are clearly public property from which no one may lawfully be barred, so that it follows that the barbarians would do wrong to the Spaniards if they were to bar them from their lands. Eleventh, the barbarians themselves admit all sorts of other barbarians from elsewhere, and would therefore do wrong if they did not admit the Spaniards.

Twelfth, if the Spaniards were not allowed to travel amongst them, this would be either by natural, divine, or human law. But they are certainly allowed to do so by divine and natural law. But if there were a human enactment which barred them without any foundation in divine or natural law, it would be inhumane and unreasonable, and therefore without the force of law.

Thirteenth, either the Spaniards are their subjects, or they are not. If they are not their subjects, the barbarians cannot enjoin prohibitions on them; if they are their subjects, then the barbarians ought to treat them fairly. And fourteenth, the Spaniards are the barbarians' neighbours, as shown by the parable of the Samaritan (Luke 10:29-37); and the barbarians are obliged to love their neighbours as themselves (Matt. 22:39), and may not lawfully bar them from their homeland without due cause. As St. Augustine says, "when one says 'Love thy neighbour,' it is clear that every man is your neighbour" (*De doctrina Christiana* 1.30.32).

(2) My second proposition is that *the Spaniards may lawfully trade among the barbarians, so long as they do no harm to their homeland*. In other words, they may import the commodities which they lack, and export the gold, silver, or other things which they have in abundance; and their princes cannot prevent their subjects from trading with the Spaniards, nor can the princes of Spain prohibit commerce with the barbarians.

The proof follows from the first proposition. In the first place, the law of nations is clearly that travellers may carry on trade so long as they do no harm to the citizens; and second, in the same way it can be proved that this is lawful in divine law. Therefore any human enactment which prohibited such trade would indubitably be unreasonable. Third, their princes are obliged by natural law to love the Spaniards, and therefore cannot prohibit them without due cause from furthering their own interests, so long as this can be done without harm to the barbarians. Fourth, to do so would appear to fly in the face of the old proverb, "do as you would be done by."

In sum, it is certain that the barbarians can no more prohibit Spaniards from carrying on trade with them, than Christians can prohibit other Christians from doing the same. It is clear that if the Spaniards were to prohibit the French from trading with the Spanish kingdoms, not for the good of Spain but to prevent the French from sharing in any profits, this would be an unjust enactment, and contrary to Christian charity. But if this prohibition cannot justly be proscribed in law, neither can it be justly carried out in practice, since an unjust law becomes inequitable precisely when it is carried into execution. And "nature has decreed a certain kinship between all men" (Dig. 1.1.3), so that it is against natural law for one man to turn against another without due cause; man is not a "wolf to his fellow man," as Ovid [actually Plautus, *Asinaria* 495] says, but a fellow.

(3) My third proposition is that *if there are any things among the barbarians which are held in common both by their own people and by strangers, it is not lawful for the barbarians to prohibit the Spaniards from sharing and enjoying them*. For example, if travellers are allowed to dig for gold in common land or in rivers or to fish for pearls in the sea or in rivers, the barbarians may not prohibit Spaniards from doing so. But the latter are only allowed to do this kind of thing on the same terms as the former, namely without causing offence to the native inhabitants and citizens.

The proof of this follows from the first and second propositions. If the Spaniards are allowed to travel and trade among the barbarians, they are allowed to make use of the legal privileges and advantages conceded to all travellers.

Secondly, in the law of nations *(ius gentium)* a thing which does not belong to anyone *(res nullius)* becomes the property of the first taker, according to the law *Ferae bestiae* (Inst. 2.1.12); therefore, if gold in the ground or pearls in the sea or anything else in the rivers has not been appropriated, they will belong by the law of nations to the first taker, just like the little fishes of the sea. And there are certainly many things which are clearly to be settled on the basis of the law of nations *(ius gentium)*, whose derivation from natural law is manifestly sufficient to enable it to enforce binding rights. But even on the occasions when it is not derived from natural law, the consent of the greater part of the world is enough to make it binding, especially when it is for the common good of all men. If, after the dawn of creation or after the refashioning of the world following the Flood, the majority of men decided that the safety of ambassadors should everywhere be inviolable, that the sea should be common property, that prisoners of war should be enslaved, and likewise that it would be inexpedient to drive strangers out of one's land, then all these things certainly have the force of law, even if a minority disagree. [. . .]

(5) My fifth proposition is that if the barbarians attempt to deny the Spaniards in these matters which I have described as belonging to the law of nations, that is to say from trading and the rest, the Spaniards ought first to remove any cause of provocation by reasoning and persuasion, and demonstrate with every argument at their disposal that they have not come to do any harm, but wish to dwell in peace and travel without any inconvenience to the barbarians. And they should demonstrate this not merely in words, but with proof. As the saying goes: "in every endeavour, the seemly course for wise men is to try persuasion first" (Terence, *Eunuchus* 789). But if reasoning fails to win the acquiescence of the barbarians, and they insist on replying with violence, the Spaniards may defend themselves, and do everything needful for their own safety. It is lawful to meet force with force [Dig. 1.1.3]. And not only in this eventuality, but also if there is no other means of remaining safe, they may build forts and defences; and if they have suffered an offence, they may on the authority of their prince seek redress for it in war, and exercise the other rights of war. The proof is that the cause of the just war is to redress and avenge an offence, as said above in the passage quoted from St. Thomas (*ST* 2a2ae.40.1). But if the barbarians deny the Spaniards what is theirs by the law of nations, they commit an offence against them. Hence, if war is necessary to obtain their rights, they may lawfully go to war.

But I should remark that these barbarians are by nature cowardly, foolish, and ignorant besides. However much the Spaniards may wish to reassure them and convince them of their peaceful intentions, therefore, the barbarians may still be understandably fearful of men whose customs seem so strange, and who they can see are armed and much stronger than themselves. If this fear moves them to mount an attack to drive the Spaniards away or kill them, it would indeed be lawful for the Spaniards to defend themselves, within the bounds of blameless self-defence; but once victory has been won and safety secured, they may not exercise the other rights of war against the barbarians such as putting them to death or looting and occupying their communities, since in this case what we may suppose were understandable fears made them innocent. So the Spaniards must take care for their own safety, but do so with as little harm to the barbarians as possible since this is a merely defensive war. It is not incompatible with reason, indeed, when there is right on one side and ignorance on the other, that a war may be just on both. [. . .]

q.3 a.2. *Second possible title, for the spreading of the Christian religion.* My first proposition in support of this is that *Christians have the right to preach and announce the Gospel in the lands of the barbarians.* This conclusion is clear from the passage: "Go ye into all the world and preach the gospel to every creature" (Mark 16:15); and "the word of God is not bound" (2 Tim. 2:9). Second, it is clear from the preceding article, since if they have the right to travel and trade among them, then they must be able to teach them the truth if they are willing to listen, especially about matters to do with salvation and beatitude, much more so than about anything to do with any other human subject. Third, if it were not lawful for Christians to visit them to announce the Gospel, the barbarians would exist in a state beyond any salvation. Fourth, brotherly correction is as much part of natural law as brotherly love; and since all those peoples are not merely in a state of sin, but presently in a state beyond salvation, it is the business of Christians to correct and direct them. Indeed, they are clearly obliged to do so. Fifth and finally, they are our neighbours, and I have said above (3.1) "and God gave them commandment, each man concerning his neighbour" (Sir. 17:14). Therefore it is the business of Christians to instruct them in the holy things of which they are ignorant.

(2) My second proposition is that although this right is common and lawful for all, *the pope could nevertheless have entrusted this business to the Spaniards and forbidden it to all others.* The proof is that although the pope is not a temporal lord, as shown above (2.2), he nevertheless has power in temporal things insofar as they concern spiritual things. And since it is the pope's special business to promote the Gospel throughout the world, if the princes of Spain are in the best position to see to the preaching of the Gospel in those provinces, the pope may entrust the task to them, and deny it to all others. He may restrict not only the right to preach, but also the right to trade, if this is convenient for the spreading of the Christian religion, because he has the power to order temporal matters for the convenience of spiritual ones. So if these things are convenient for this purpose, they belong to the authority and power of the supreme pontiff. And it is quite clear that they are convenient, because if there were an indiscriminate rush to the lands of these barbarians from other Christian countries, the Christians might very well get in each other's way and start to quarrel. Peace would be disturbed, and the business of the faith and the conversion of the barbarians upset. Besides, the princes of Spain were the first to undertake the voyages of discovery, at their own expense and under their own banners; and since they were so fortunate as to discover the New World, it is just that this voyage should be denied to others, and that they alone should enjoy the fruits of their discoveries. In the same way, the pope has always had the power to distribute the territories of Saracens among Christian princes for the preservation of peace and the progress of religion, especially in places where there had never before been any Christian princes.

(3) My third proposition is that if the barbarians permit the Spaniards to

preach the Gospel freely and without hindrance, then *whether or not they accept the faith, it will not be lawful to attempt to impose anything on them by war, or otherwise conquer their lands.* This was proved above in my refutation of the fourth unjust title (2.4); and it is obvious, because no war can be just when not preceded by some wrong, as St. Thomas says (*ST* 2a2ae.40.1).

(4) My fourth conclusion is that if the barbarians, either in the person of their masters or as a multitude, obstruct the Spaniards in their free propagation of the Gospel, the Spaniards, after first reasoning with them to remove any cause of provocation, *may preach and work for the conversion of that people even against their will,* and may if necessary take up arms and declare war on them, insofar as this provides the safety and opportunity needed to preach the Gospel. And the same holds true if they permit the Spaniards to preach, but do not allow conversions, either by killing or punishing the converts to Christ, or by deterring them by threats or other means. This is obvious, because such actions would constitute a wrong committed by the barbarians against the Spaniards, as I have explained, and the latter therefore have just cause for war. Second, it would be against the interests of the barbarians themselves which their own princes may not justly harm; so the Spaniards could wage war on behalf of their [the princes'] subjects for the oppression and wrong which they were suffering, especially in such important matters.

From this conclusion it follows that on this count too, if the business of religion cannot otherwise be forwarded, that the Spaniards may lawfully conquer the territories of these people, deposing their old masters and setting up new ones and carrying out all the things which are lawfully permitted in other just wars by the law of war, so long as they always observe reasonable limits and do not go further than necessary. They must always be prepared to forego some part of their rights rather than risk trespassing on some unlawful thing, and always direct all their plans to the benefit of the barbarians rather than their own profit, bearing constantly in mind the saying of St. Paul: "all things are lawful unto me, but all things are not expedient" (1 Cor. 6:12). Everything that has been said so far is to be understood as valid in itself; but it may happen that the resulting war, with its massacres and pillage, obstructs the conversion of the barbarians instead of encouraging it. The most important consideration is to avoid placing obstructions in the way of the Gospel. If such is the result, this method of evangelisation must be abandoned and some other sought. All that I have demonstrated is that this method is lawful *per se.* I myself have no doubt that force and arms were necessary for the Spaniards to continue in those parts; my fear is that the affair may have gone beyond the permissible bounds of justice and religion.

This, then, is the second possible legitimate title by which the barbarians may have fallen under the control of the Spaniards. But we must always keep steadfastly before us what I have just said, lest what is in substance lawful becomes by accident evil. Good comes from a single wholly good cause, whereas evil can come from many circumstances, according to Aristotle (*NE* 110635) and Dionysius the Pseudo-Areopagite (*Divine Names* 4.30).

Translation: Jeremy Lawrance and Anthony Pagden (Cambridge University Press, 1991). Used with permission.

The Schleitheim Articles

(1527)

The Schleitheim Articles are widely regarded as a landmark in the theological consolidation of Anabaptism because their positions, though not predominant among Anabaptist congregations at the time of their composition, were universally accepted among Anabaptists within thirty-five years. Their distinctive formulations of ecclesiological separatism and apolitical pacifism are generally thought to be the work of Michael Sattler, ex-prior of a Benedictine monastery in the Black Forest near Freiburg im Breisgau who had deserted to the Anabaptist ministry, possibly in 1525 under the influence of invading peasants. The gathering of Swiss and South German Brethren in the border hamlet of Schleitheim in February 1527 agreed upon the "articles of brotherly union" in the wake of the Peasants' War; the untimely death of Conrad Grebel and execution of Felix Mantz, the leading lights of the Zürich movement; and mounting persecution from Zwinglians and Catholics alike. Not surprisingly, their profession exhibits a close identification with the persecuted apostolic church, seeking to be faithful amidst the trials and tribulations of the last days, conscious of God's impending judgment.

The letter framing the seven articles, also attributed to Sattler, has left scholars to identify the "false brothers," and more broadly, the constituency or constituencies against whom the articles were composed. Were they "libertines from St. Gall" or the mainstream Strasbourg reformers, Bucer and Capito (with whom Sattler had vainly hoped to make common cause), or the spiritualizing Hans Denck or more Zwinglian-minded Anabaptist leaders such as Balthasar Hubmaier, or local leaders of a "nonseparating" stamp — or, indeed, all of these (Klaassen 1987, 98-99)? The key to an answer is that the articles concern the features of Anabaptist ecclesiology that most sharply distinguish it from Lutheran, Zwinglian, and Bucerian: especially adult baptism (1); complete separation of the regenerate from the unregenerate "world," which includes the unreformed and insufficiently reformed churches and civil society (4); and consequently, rejection of the use of the civil "sword" as divinely ordained only "outside the perfection of Christ" (6), and of the civil oath as well (7). The arguments put forward for separation and apolitical pacifism recall not only Luther's early "two kingdoms" polarity, but the traditional justifications for monastic and clerical disciplines of withdrawal from secular involvements. Sattler's Anabaptism presents an egalitarian exposition of the priesthood of all believers based on a perfectionist, sectarian application of Christ's ethic of the Sermon on the Mount.

Further Reading: W. Klaassen, "The 'Schleitheim Articles' and 'The New Transformation of Christian Living': Two Responses to the Reformation," *Historical Reflections/Réflexions Historiques* 14 (1987): 95-111; W. Packull, "The Origin of Swiss Anabaptism in the Context of the Reformation of the Common Man," *Journal of Mennonite Studies* 3 (1985): 36-59; C. A. Snyder, *The Life and Thought of Michael Sattler* (Scottdale, Pa.: Herald Press, 1984); C. A. Snyder, "The 'Schleitheim Articles' in the Light of the Revolution of the Common Man: Continuation or Departure?" *Sixteenth Century Journal* 16 (1985): 419-30; J. M. Stayer, *Anabaptists and the Sword* (Lawrence, Kans.: Coronado Press, 1972).

The Brotherly Agreement of Some Children of God Concerning Seven Articles

Among all who love God and are children of light may there be joy, peace, and mercy from our father, through Jesus Christ, together with the gifts of the spirit, who is sent by the father to all believers for their strength, consolation, and perseverance through every grief until the end, amen. These children of light are dispersed to all the places which God our Father has ordained for them, and where they are assembled with one mind in one God and father of us all. May grace and peace exist in all your hearts, amen.

Beloved in the Lord, brothers and sisters, our first and paramount concern is always what brings you consolation and a secure conscience, which has been misled previously. We are concerned about this so that you may not be separated from us forever, like foreigners, and almost completely excluded, as is just. We are concerned that you might turn, rather, to the truly implanted members of Christ, who are armed with patience and self-knowledge, and so that you may again be united with us in the power of one divine, Christian spirit and zeal for God.

It is also evident that the devil has slyly separated us through a thousand tricks, so that he might be able to destroy the work of God which has partly begun in us through God's mercy and grace. But the faithful shepherd of our souls, Christ, who has begun this work in us, will direct it until the end, and he will teach us, to his honor and our salvation, amen.

Dear brothers and sisters, we who are assembled together in the Lord at Schleitheim, are making known through a series of articles to all who love God that, as far as we are concerned, we have agreed that we will abide in the Lord as obedient children of God, sons and daughters, and as those who are separated from the world — and who should be separated in all that they do and do not do. And may God be

separation

praised and glorified in unity, without any brother contradicting this, but rather being happy with it. In doing this we have sensed that the unity of the father and our common Christ have been with us in spirit. For the Lord is the lord of peace and not of dissension, as Paul shows (1 Cor. 14:33). You should note this and comprehend it, so that you understand in which articles this unity has been formulated.

Some false brothers among us have nearly introduced a great offense, causing some to turn away from the faith because they suppose they can lead a free life, using the freedom of the spirit and Christ. But such people lack truth and are given over (to their condemnation) to the lasciviousness and freedom of the flesh. They have thought that faith and love may tolerate everything, and that nothing will damn them because they are such believing people.

Observe, you members of God in Christ Jesus, faith in the heavenly father through Jesus Christ does not take this form. It does not result in such things as these false brothers and sisters practice and teach. Protect yourselves and be warned about such people, for they do not serve our father, but their father, the devil.

But you are not this kind of people. For those who belong to Christ have crucified their flesh with all its lusts and desires. You certainly know what I mean and the brothers we are talking about. Separate yourselves from these brothers, for they are perverted. Ask the Lord that they acquire the knowledge to repent, and that we have the steadfastness to proceed along the path we have undertaken, following the honor of God and his son Christ. Amen.

The articles we have discussed and about which we agree are these: baptism, the ban [excommunication], the breaking of bread [Lord's Supper], separating from the abomination [the existing polity], shepherds in the community [ministers], the sword, the oath, etc. [Apparently, no agreement was reached on the issue of whether to pay taxes imposed by secular authorities.]

First, concerning baptism, note this. Baptism should be given to all who have learned repentance, amendment of life, and faith through the truth that their sin has been removed by Christ; to all who want to walk in the resurrection of Jesus Christ and to be buried with him in death so that they can be resurrected with him; and to all who desire baptism in this sense from us and who themselves request it. Accordingly, all infant baptism, the greatest and first abomination of the pope, is excluded. You have the basis for this in the testimony of Scripture and the custom of the apostles: Matthew 28:19; Mark 16:16; Acts 2:38, 8:36, 16:31-33, and 19:4. We wish to maintain this position on baptism simply, yet firmly.

Second. We have agreed as follows concerning the ban. The ban should be used against all who have given themselves to the Lord and agreed to follow his commandments, and who have been baptized into the one body of Christ, letting themselves be called brother or sister, and who nevertheless sometimes slip and fall into error and sin, and have been unknowingly overtaken. These people should be admonished twice privately and the third time should be punished or banned publicly, before the whole community, according to the command of Christ, Matthew 18:15-18. This banning should take place, according to the ordinance of the spirit (Matt. 5:23f.), before the breaking of bread, so that we are all of one mind, and in one love may break from one bread and eat and drink from one cup.

Third. We are agreed and united about the breaking of bread as follows. All who wish to break one bread in memory of the broken body of Christ, and all who wish to drink from one cup in memory of the blood that Christ shed, should previously be united in the one body of Christ — that is, God's community, of which Christ is the head — namely, through baptism. For as Paul shows (1 Cor. 10:21), we cannot simultaneously sit at the Lord's table and the devil's table. We cannot simultaneously drink from the Lord's cup and the devil's cup. That is, all who have fellowship with the dead works of darkness do not partake of the light. Thus, all who follow the devil and the world have nothing in common with those who are called out of the world to God. All who reside in evil have no part of what is good. And it must be thus. He who has not been called by one God to one faith, to one baptism, to one spirit, and to one body in the community of all the children of God, may not be made into one bread with them, as must be the case if one wants to break bread truly according to the command of Christ.

Fourth. Concerning separation we have agreed that a separation should take place from the evil which the devil has planted in the world. We simply will not have fellowship with evil people, nor associate with them, nor participate with them in their abominations. That is, all who have not submitted themselves to the obedience of faith, and have not united themselves to God so that they want to do his will, are a great abomination before God. Since this is so, nothing but abominable things can issue from them. For there has never been anything in the world and among all creatures except good and evil, believing and unbelieving, darkness and light, the world and those who are out of the world, God's temple and idols, Christ and Belial, and neither may have anything to do with the other. And the commandment of the Lord is evident — he tells us to become separated from evil (2 Cor. 6:17). In this way he wants to be our God, and we will be his sons and daughters. Further, he also admonishes us to withdraw from Babylon and worldly Egypt so that we will not participate in the suffering which the Lord will inflict upon them (Rev. 18:4ff.).

From all this we should learn that everything which is not united with our God and Christ is the abomination which we should flee. By this we mean all popish and neo-popish works and divine services, assemblies, ecclesiastical processions, wine shops, the ties and obligations of lack of faith, and other things of this kind, which the world indeed regards highly but which are done in direct opposition to the commandments of God, as is the great injustice in the world. We should leave all these things and have nothing to do with them, for they are vain abominations which make us hated by our Christ Jesus, who has liberated us from the servitude of the flesh and made us suitable for service to God through the spirit, which he has given us.

Thus, the devilish weapons of force will fall from us, too, such as the sword, armor and the like, and all their uses on behalf of friends or against enemies; [such nonviolence is commanded] by the power of the words of Christ, "You should not resist evil" (Matt. 5:39).

Fifth. We have agreed as follows concerning the shepherds in the community of God [i.e. ministers]. According to Paul's prescription (1 Tim. 3:7), the shepherd in God's community should be one who has a completely good reputation among those who are outside the faith. His duties should be to read, to admonish, to teach, to warn and to punish or ban in the community; to lead all sisters and brothers in prayer and in breaking bread; and to make sure that in all matters that concern the body of Christ, the community is built up and improved. He should do this so that the name of God is praised and honored among us, and the mouths of blasphemers are stopped.

Should this pastor be in need, he should be provided for by the community that chose him, so that he who serves the gospel should also live from it, as the Lord has ordained (1 Cor. 9:14). But if a shepherd should do something requiring punishment, he should not be tried except on the testimony of two or three people. If they sin [by testifying falsely], they should be punished in front of everybody so that others are afraid.

But if a shepherd is banished or through the cross [execution] brought to the Lord, another should be ordained in his place immediately so that God's little people are not destroyed, but maintained and consoled by the warning.

Sixth. Concerning the sword we have reached the following agreement. The sword is ordained by God outside the perfection of Christ. It punishes and kills evil people and protects and defends the good. In the law the sword is established to punish and to kill the wicked, and secular authorities are established to use it. But in the perfection of Christ the ban alone will be used to admonish and expel him who has sinned, without putting the flesh to death, and only by using the admonition and the command to sin no more.

Now, many who do not recognize what Christ wills for us will ask whether a Christian may also use the sword against evil people for the sake of protecting the good or for the sake of love. Our unanimous answer is as follows: Christ teaches us to learn from him that we should be mild and of humble heart, and in this way we will find rest for our souls. Now, Christ says to the woman taken in adultery (John 8:11), not that she should be stoned according to the law of his father (yet he says, "As the father has commanded me, this I do" [John 8:28]), but that she should be dealt with in mercy and forgiveness and with a warning to sin no more. And Christ says, "Go and sin no more." We should also hold to this in our laws, according to the rule about the ban.

Secondly, it is asked about the sword, whether a Christian may pass judgment in worldly quarrels and conflicts at law such as unbelievers have with one another. This is the answer: Christ did not want to decide or judge between brother and brother concerning an inheritance, and he refused to do so (Luke 12:14f.). Thus, we should do likewise.

Thirdly, it is asked about the sword, whether a Christian may hold a position of governmental authority if he is chosen for it. This is our reply: Christ should have been made a king, but he rejected this (John 6:15) and did not view it as ordained by his father. We should do likewise and follow him. In this way we will not walk into the snares of darkness. For Christ says: "Whoever wants to follow me should deny himself and take up his cross and follow me" (Matt. 16:24). Also, Christ himself forbids the violence of the sword and says, "Worldly princes rule," etc., "but not you" (Matt. 20:25). Further, Paul says: "Those whom God foresaw, he also ordained that they should be equal to the model of his son," etc. (Rom. 8:30). Also Peter says: "Christ has suffered, not ruled, and he gave us a model, so that you shall follow in his footsteps" (1 Pet. 2:21).

635

Lastly, it should be pointed out that it is not fitting for a Christian to be a magistrate for these reasons: the authorities' governance is according to the flesh, but the Christian's is according to the spirit. Their houses and dwellings remain in this world, but the Christian's is in heaven. Their weapons of conflict and war are carnal and only directed against the fortifications of the devil. Worldly people are armed with spikes and iron, but Christians are armed with the armor of God — with truth, and with justice, with peace, faith, and salvation, and with the word of God. In sum, what Christ, our head, thought, the members of the body of Christ through him should also think, so that no division of the body (of the faithful) may triumph through which it would be destroyed. Now, as Christ is — as is written about him — so too must the members be, so that his body may remain whole and united for its own benefit and edification.

Seventh. We have reached agreement as follows concerning the oath [i.e., swearing oaths]. The oath is a confirmation among those who are quarreling or making promises. And it has been ordained in the [Mosaic] Law that it should take place truthfully and not falsely, in the name of God alone. Christ, who teaches the perfection of the law, forbids his followers all swearing, either truthfully or falsely, either in the name of heaven or of earth or of Jerusalem or by our own head (Matt. 5:34f.). And he does this for the reason which he gives afterward: "For you are not able to make a single hair white or black." Notice this! All swearing has been forbidden because we cannot fulfill what is promised in swearing. For we are not able to alter the slightest thing about ourselves.

Now, there are some who do not believe God's simple command. They speak as follows and ask: "Did God not swear to Abraham on his own godhead when he promised that he wished him well and wanted to be his God, if he would keep his commandments? Why should I not swear also when I promise somebody something?"

Our answer is this. Listen to what Scripture says. Because God wanted to prove conclusively to the heirs of the promise that his counsel does not waver, he sealed it with an oath, so that we could rely on the consolation received through two unwavering things [i.e., the promise and the oath; Heb. 6:17f.] about which it is impossible for God to lie. Note the meaning of this passage of Scripture: "God has the power to do that which he forbids you. For all things are possible for him" (Matt. 19:26, Mark 10:27). God swore an oath to Abraham (Scripture says) in order to prove that his counsel never wavered. That is, no one can resist or hinder his will, and so he was able to keep the oath. But, as has been said above by Christ, we can do nothing to keep or fulfill an oath. Therefore we should not swear at all.

Some now say further: "In the New Testament it is forbidden by God to swear; but it is actually commanded in the Old, and there it is only forbidden to swear by heaven, earth, Jerusalem, and by our head." Our answer is this. Listen to Scripture — "He who swears by the temple of heaven swears by the throne of God and by him who sits on it" (Matt. 23:22). Notice that it is forbidden to swear by heaven, which is a throne of God. How much more is it forbidden to swear by God himself? You fools and blind people, which is greater, the throne or he who sits on it?

Some say further: "Why is it now unjust to use God as a witness to the truth, when the apostles Peter and Paul have sworn?" (cf. Matt. 26:74; Acts 18:18). Our answer is that Peter and Paul testify only to that which God promised Abraham through the oath. And they themselves promised nothing, as the examples clearly show. For testifying and swearing are two different things. When a person swears, in the first place he makes a promise about future things, as Christ — whom we received a long time later — was promised to Abraham. But when a person testifies, he is testifying about the present, whether it is good or evil, as Simon spoke to Mary about Christ and testified to her: "This child is ordained for the fall and resurrection of many in Israel, and as a sign which will be rejected" (Luke 2:34). Christ has also taught us this same thing when he said: "Your speech should be 'yea' or 'nay' for anything else comes from evil" (Matt. 5:37). Christ says, "Your speech or words should be 'yea' or 'nay,'" so that none can understand it in the sense that he has permitted swearing. Christ is simply "yea" and "nay" and all who seek him in simplicity will understand his word. Amen.

Dear brothers and sisters in the Lord, these are the articles about which some brothers have previously been in error and have understood differently from the true understanding. The consciences of many people have been confused through this, as a result of which the name of God has been greatly blasphemed. Therefore it has been necessary for us to reach agreement in the Lord, and this has happened. May God be praised and glorified!

Now, because you have amply understood the will of God, which has now been set forth through us, it will be necessary for you to realize the will of God, which you have recognized, perseveringly and without interruption. For you know well what reward the servant deserves who knowingly sins.

Everything that you have done unknowingly or that you have confessed to having done unjustly is forgiven you through the faithful prayer which is performed by us in our assembly for all our failures and our guilt, through the merciful forgiveness of God and through the blood of Jesus Christ. Amen.

Beware of all who do not walk in the simplicity of the divine truth which is encompassed in this letter from us in our assembly. Do this so that everyone among us may be subject to the rule of the ban, and so that henceforth false brothers and sisters may be prevented from joining us.

Separate yourselves from that which is evil. Then the Lord will be your God, and you will be his sons and daughters.

Dear brothers, keep in mind how Paul admonished Titus. He said this: "The saving grace of God has appeared to all. And it disciplines us so that we shall deny ungodly things and worldly lusts and shall live chastely, justly, and piously in this world. And we shall await our same hope, the appearance of the majesty of the great God and our savior, Jesus Christ, who gave himself to redeem us from all injustice, and to purify a people as his own who would be zealous for good works" (Titus 2:11-14). If you think about this and practice it, the lord of peace will be with you.

May the name of God be eternally blessed and highly praised, Amen. May the Lord give you his peace. Amen.

Translation: Michael G. Baylor (Cambridge University Press, 1991). Used with permission.

Hans Hergot

(d. 1527)

A Nürnberg printer and colporteur, Hans Hergot was executed in May 1527 (on the same day that Michael Sattler was burned at the stake), charged with distributing a seditious tract entitled *The New Transformation of Christian Living*, of which he was the suspected author. The tract demonstrated close acquaintance with the thought of Thomas Münzer, whose work he had printed, and a knowledge of Luther that would have come easily to someone in his trade. The work was divided into two parts, the first of which was a prophetic vision of Christendom radically transformed by the Holy Spirit, and the second was a prophetic diatribe against the existing authorities and an apocalyptic warning to them — a reversal of the order of More's *Utopia*, in which criticism of the status quo preceded imaginative social construction. As with *Utopia*, so this writing has provoked speculations about multiple authorship and a time lag between the parts — the first composed during the peasant uprisings and the second after their brutal suppression — but these do not undermine the work's present theological and editorial unity.

Hergot's vision drew on the Joachite eschatology of three historical ages (of Father, Son, and Spirit) amalgamated with the tradition of royal messianism surrounding the German emperors and the millenarianism of the Bohemian Taborites. This heady cocktail had penetrated into the Rhineland in the last decade of the fifteenth century to inspire the peasant *Bundschuh* movements and much of Münzer's revolutionary apocalyptic as well. The vision is of an egalitarian, agrarian society organized on a parochial basis in which goods are held in common for the use of all, habitation is after the Carthusian pattern, farming and crafts operate harmoniously, and every invidious ground and sign of social distinction has disappeared. Contrary to the tradition of Schleitheim Anabaptism, the baptized here are not separated from civil polity; rather, the civil and ecclesiastical orders are entirely integrated in an ascending hierarchy of government, terminating in a universal Shepherd (priest and king) — an organization that resembles more closely the conciliarist model of the church than the federalism of the empire, but with highly symbolic overarching geopolitical and linguistic divisions. The ministry of divine worship is lay and elective, as generally in Anabaptism, while church practice is broadly Reformed or evangelical, with some conspicuously Catholic elements.

The <u>enemies</u> of Hergot's revelation on whom he pronounces God's imminent <u>wrath are the ruling nobility and the Lutheran "scripture wizards" who theologically</u> <u>collude with them, the unjust acquitting the unjust</u>. In the manner of Joachim and the Free Spirits, Hergot pits the truth-telling Spirit of the untutored against the lying scriptural glosses of the "scribes." Though holding that the revolting peasants *were* the frail agents of divine judgment and martyrs to the Spirit's design, he proposes that the instruments of God's *coming* punishment will be the feuding nobles themselves and the invading Turks, while the tribulation of the prophets will continue until God's wrath is accomplished and his kingdom appears.

It is precisely the eclecticism of Hergot's prophetic voice that underlies its importance. For it suggests how a far-flung outburst of enthusiasm for divine or evangelical law, as opposed to corrupt and compromised human ordinances, was a connecting thread among myriad reforming orientations in the early sixteenth century — humanist, Lutheran, mystical, and apocalyptic — all of which intersected with the German Peasants' War and the development of Anabaptism and other strands of Christian social radicalism. It represents the apocalyptic extreme within a spectrum of theopolitical dialectics in which visions of Adamic, christological, and ideal community (Wycliffite, Franciscan, Augustinian, and Platonic) were brought to bear on current social realities.

Further Reading: Walter Klaassen, "The 'Schleitheim Articles' and 'The New Transformation of Christian Living': Two Responses to the Reformation," *Historical Reflections/ Réflexions Historiques* 14 (1987): 95-111; Walter Klaassen, *Living at the End of the Ages: Apocalyptic Expectation in the Radical Reformation* (New York: University Press of America, 1992); F. Seibt, "Johannes Hergot: The Reformation of the Poor Man," in *Profiles of Radical Reformers* (English translation), ed. H.-J. Goertz (Kitchener, Ont., and Scottdale, Pa.: Herald Press, 1982), 97-106; J. M. Stayer, *The German Peasants' War and Anabaptist Community of Goods* (Montreal and London: McGill-Queen's University Press, 1991); M. Steinmetz, ed., *Hans Hergot und die Flugschrift "Von der newen Wandlung Eynes Christliochen Lebens." Faksimilewiedergabe mit Umschrift* (Leipzig: VEB Fachbuchverlag, 1977); G. Zschaebitz, "'Von der newen wandlung eyenes Christlichen lebens' — eine oft missgedeutete Schrift aus der Zeit nach dem Grossen Deutschen Bauernkrieg," *Zeitschrift für Geschichtswissenschaft* 8 (1960): 908-18.

From *The New Transformation of Christian Living*

Beware, devil! Hell will be destroyed!   *dispensations*

1. There have been three transformations. The first was the way of God the Father in the Old Testament. The second transformation was the way of God the Son

639

with the world in the New Testament. The third transformation will be that of the Holy Spirit. It will be a transformation from the evil in which they [the world] now find themselves.

I, an ordinary man, make known what is about to take place, for the honour of God and the common good ["for the honour . . . good" being a slogan of the peasant movement]. God will humble all estates, the villages, castles, nunneries and monasteries, and establish a new transformation in which no one will say: "That is mine."

The sects [i.e., monastic orders] will be humbled. Their houses will be reduced to rubble and their people and activities will disappear. The villages will increase in goods and inhabitants and will be delivered from all oppression. The hereditary nobility will disappear and the common people will possess their houses. The monasteries will lose their four orders and the beggars' staff [the mendicant orders and others with mendicant privileges], and other rich monasteries will also lose their tithes and rents. All sects will disappear and be made into one. All things, wood, water, pasture, etc., will again exist for the use of the whole parish. *— common ownership*

Each country will have only one ruler. The spiritual and secular powers in whatever form they have today will pass away. Obedience to spiritual and secular authorities will be dissolved. The servants of rulers and lords will abandon their service. It will be futile for anyone to attempt to maintain his social station.

These articles have grown from the understanding I acquired concerning the Christian sheepfold. I recognized the great affliction of the same and said: "O eternal God! how distressing is the condition of your christian sheepfold!" Then I understood that God has dismissed the two shepherds [pope and emperor] who had been put in charge of the christian sheepfold, together with all their company. The great efforts they now make to save themselves are in vain.

Then I understood that God has begun anew and that he has appointed one single shepherd over his sheepfold by giving him the whole earth. This took place as follows. God has given every parish its own Common and assigned to it as many people as it will support. Everything that grows on that Common belongs to the parish and to the people who live on it. Everything is designated for common use; they will eat out of one pot, and drink out of one flask. They will be obedient to one man to the degree required by the honour of God and the common good. This man will be called the Provider of the Parish. The people will all work in common at the tasks to which they are suited and are able to perform. All things will be held in common so that no one will be better off than anyone else. The land will be free, for no one will pay either tithe or taxes. Nevertheless, they will be protected by the authorities. The new life of these people will be better than that of all the monastic orders. They will believe in God and prove it by their actions, by prayer, fasting, contemplation on God's suffering and divine mercy, and in other ways.

splitting up families? When these people have children they will bring them to the church at age three or four and dedicate them to God. The Provider will come, receive them, and commit them to the person among them who is most godly. They will be in a house where this man, as a true father, will bring them up to the glory of God and the common good. The girls will be given into the charge of an honourable, godly woman or virgin in that same house. She will teach the children until they are of marriageable age. They will be taught whatever they are most inclined to learn, all to the honour of God and the common good of the people.

From the ranks of these lay people one of every twelve persons will be chosen for the service of God and the common good. These will be in charge of divine worship to teach the people. The monasteries, both male and female, along with their endowments will no longer have [a special role] in the spiritual care of the people. For all must become part of this new order. The four [mendicant] orders will become part of it, for they will no longer receive alms. The other monasteries and foundations will no longer receive tithes and rents. Even the nobility will be part of the new way. The beggars will come too; they will receive adequate provision along with all others. Thus the human race will be humbled. They will live together in a community of houses in the manner of the Carthusians. [The Carthusians, who lived silent and contemplative lives and had never needed reformation, could still provide a standard of communal piety and virtuous conduct.]

They will always be ready to raise a company of soldiers when it is necessary for the honour of God and the common good. They will have a house in which the aged will be cared for with food and drink and all other physical necessities more adequately than in any hospital.

There will also be a house for those who are ill with leprosy of the body and another for those who have illness in the soul. They will remain in that house until they repent of their sin.

All artisans will be there such as tailors, cobblers, weavers of wool and linen, smiths, millers and bakers, indeed, whatever crafts are required for each Common. All crafts will again be restored to their true usage. The artisans will abandon the striving for their own gain and devote themselves to the common good throughout the whole Common. Then the Lord's Prayer will be fulfilled and they will take to heart the word the Lord uses frequently in that prayer: "our," "our," "our."

Every craftsman will take another and teach him the craft for the sake of the common good and they will prosper. They will call on and worship God, the choice and highest good, and all of God's saints. For God's sake they will forsake their own interests and any mean behaviour.

They will wear one kind of garment which has been produced on the Common in the colours white, grey, black and blue. Their food and drink likewise is what they can produce. Everything on their Common will be theirs such as wood and water; it will all be used for the common good. Whoever produces something on his Common will barter it for other goods. They won't eat meat in Advent and between Ascension Day and Pentecost. [Periods of fasting will now be times of rejoicing.]

Of the seven sacraments they will observe three; the other four will be regarded as good works. They will be absolutely bound to this and whoever does not adhere will be severely punished. This will be the penalty for anyone from the parish: he will be bound hand and foot and people will walk over him to his great shame whenever he does it. The sacrament of unction will be regarded at that time as prayers to the saints. The sacrament of confirmation will be considered a confession of faith when a person becomes thirty years of age [supposedly the age of Jesus at his baptism].

641

The Providers of the parish will choose one head or lord over themselves for the whole country. He will be lord over that same country. They will not be required to pay him tithe or rent. He will travel from one Common to another across the whole land and oversee all the Parish Providers and ensure that the honour of God and the common good be observed in the whole Common. He will eat what they eat and drink and what they can produce on their Common. What ever else he deserves as a recognition of his work he will expect from God.

war When the ruler wages war he will be given every third man from every Common insofar as it concerns the honour of God and the common good. They will follow him obediently on foot and mounted. This ruler will mint a coin on which will appear the name JESUS and the inscription will be the name of the Common in which it is minted and the country of that ruler. The coin will be valid in all the Languages of the world [i.e., in the three sacred languages that define geographical areas: namely, Latin, Hebrew, and Greek]. Although he will receive neither tithe nor rent, this ruler will be able to take care of all the needs of the country. Working through the Parish Providers, he will ensure that each one keeps paths and roads in good repair.

The Ruler will engage men who are wise in agriculture and others who are wise in the Scriptures. Those wise in agriculture will know what and how much the fields will yield. The fields will nourish the body and each Common will have its man. The men wise in Scripture will teach the word of God for the salvation of the soul and thus nourish the soul with Scripture. Again there will be one to each Common. This ruler will rebuild old churches where they will worship God. They will be nourished from the Common.

This ruler will grant each Provider the right to mint coins as needed for the common good. The ruler will live in the centre of that land and everything that is in that land will belong to the people of the Common. Two or three times a year or whenever necessary he will assemble all the Providers and receive reports on any surplus in goods or manpower. He will have special houses built in which to store excess food from the Commons for the benefit of the people of that country or for the help of other countries.

The ruler will support a university in his country where they will instruct men in the honour of God and the common good. All useful books will be found there. He will arrange for divine worship in all the Commons which will be oftener and better than anything now done in the monasteries. The soul will be nourished with the word of God as often as the body is fed. The ruler will be satisfied with one country and will be content with what Common and country will yield. Whatever is in that country will belong to him and the people.

Twelve of these rulers will choose a head or ruler who will travel about and supervise the twelve rulers in order to ensure that they are ruling the twelve countries properly. He will mint a coin which will be worth twelve times that of the coins minted by those under him. It will bear the image of God and the name of the country. He will eat and drink with the Twelve whatever they are able to provide in their houses. He will be called a Quarter Lord of the Latin Language. The twelve rulers will come to him once or twice a year to report to him the surplusses and shortfalls of their countries. He will confirm the popular election of the Twelve and will be the supervisor of the rulers under him to ensure that none will seek his own good and command them that they also so teach their people in order that none seek his own but the common good. He will be wise in Scripture and agriculture and will mint a coin of bronze and gold with the name of Jesus and the name of the Quarter of the Language in which it is minted. There will be four of these Quarter Lords in the Latin Language. These languages will be given to those lands with which they are identified. Four rulers will exercise authority in them.

Each one of these four rulers will mint a coin of gold and bronze with the same value of all the other coins minted by the subject rulers in his Quarter. Again each one has a university in his Quarter in which the three languages Latin, Greek, and Hebrew will be taught. This is necessary for the ultimate installment of the one shepherd. Every Quarter Lord will have no more than one central retail store large enough for the countries which he governs.

⟨According to the same pattern there will be four Quarter Lords in the Hebrew and Greek Languages. There too each one will mint a coin of gold and bronze which will all be of the same pattern as the others with the name JESUS and the name of the Quarter in which it is minted.⟩

These twelve men of the three Languages will visit the rulers under them, each in his Quarter, to ensure that the rule is just according to the honour of God and the common good. They will decree that they should instruct others under them similarly concerning God's honour and the common good.

These Twelve will also elect a Supreme Ruler who will confirm the Twelve when they are elected in their Quarters. He will travel through the three Languages and ensure that they rule justly according to the honour of God and the common good. If the Supreme Ruler is unable to complete his supervision due to his death, the Twelve will elect someone else to his office who will begin his service where his predecessor left off. This man will be confirmed by God. He, too, will mint a coin of gold and bronze which will have the cumulative value of all the Quarter coins. The image will be the name JESUS and the inscription "One Shepherd and One Flock" (cf. John 10:16).

This then, is how the two shepherds of the present will be dismissed, and the one future shepherd established. All their effort and labour will be in vain until the new order comes. Until then there will be no peace.

This gift of the earth and of one shepherd will restore the use of the earth and its fruit for the needs of man in body and soul. Because of this gift the little villages will be able to defend their Common against the large cities and lords. Whatever they will find on the Common will be theirs. The cities will surrender their houses and they will be reduced to rubble for they will no longer need them. The monastery buildings on their Common will be adequate and they will occupy them to the honour of God and the common good. It is important to take care that these houses not be damaged in this rebellion of the people. In the gift of this new order no one will remain in the state he now occupies for all will be changed to a unified order.

The aristocracy of virtue will be the boast of this new order, the big cities of the countries will be their artisans' tools, and the master artisan will be God and the common people. Thus all sects will be forged into a single one.

Through this provision the nobility of birth and the present order [will daily yield] to wise and pious men from the common people who will rule in the new order. These men will be chosen from all estates wherever they can be found. By this gift the villages and cities will be delivered from all oppression. And through it there will be one shepherd and one flock on this earth. This shepherd will truly confess: "I believe in the Holy Spirit," and will prove it by his actions. All monastic foundations will lose their position, rents, and whatever they have. After their dismissal we will no longer be able to put them to shame with this word of God: "Give Caesar what belongs to him" (Matt. 22:21) [alluding to monastic exemptions from civil taxes]. For they have been dismissed by God and will be dismissed by the world as well. Miracles and wonders will prove the reality of this dismissal, as much as is necessary to ensure belief. Because of them the people will be caught up in the fear and love of God; they will begin to put away selfish striving and act for the common good.

2. This book affects all estates in the whole world, spiritual and secular, noble and common, kings and monarchs, burghers and peasants, and concerns the one as well as the other, cities, principalities, and people. Whatever has been proclaimed by God affects everyone equally. Therefore no one should be wrathful. Whether God's wrath goes forth or relents, it is all the same to him. His punishment will nevertheless take its course. But the world and especially the scripture wizards at the courts of the princes and in the large cities [i.e., Luther and scripturally learned Lutheran leaders] imagine that their wisdom and understanding is so great that it surpasses God's wisdom. Indeed, all of God's proclamation which he has spoken through all the prophets is worth nothing. All the miracles which he shows us every day in the heavens [such popular omens of catastrophe as eclipses and comets] are as nothing and called mere fables by the scripture wizards. In this way they seek to overthrow God's power so that nothing is valid except their wisdom. [. . .]

But now things are happening. He [the common man who has the Spirit] is learning things in a way the scripture wizards don't like. He is speaking the whole truth and that the scripture wizards can't tolerate.

Thus it is that they complain loudly to the princes and kings that the printing presses should be suppressed, and that this vilifying of people and exposing of wickedness ought not to be tolerated. For the devil tells them how their shame will be exposed. As long as one spoke and wrote the truth to princes and kings, knights and counts, noble and commoner, about their injustice, printed it and sent it into the world so that everyone could hear what kind of people these were, the scripture wizards loved it and agreed that it was right so to expose the injustice of the nobility.

But now that their own injustice also is to be made public they howl "Murder!," and suppress all printing so that it can't happen [a possible reference to Luther's suppression of Carlstadt's writing]. Nevertheless, all of God's proclamation must be heard in the whole world, not only once, but often, often even as Noah announced often to the world for one hundred years that God would destroy them. Now, however, when one announces to the scripture wizards that God's patience is exhausted, they become furious. They do not consider the great miracles that have taken place in the heavens and on earth.

The nobility and the princes have seen God's power and authority. No house,

644

[Handwritten margin note: peasant uprising = God's work (judgment)]

castle, or city offers security. When God's wrath goes forth none of them can help, and they abandon house and castle and flee. For the fear of God pursued everyone as we have seen. Who is to say? If the Emperor and all the princes had come they would not have scared the nobility as much in a year as God did in ten weeks! [i.e., God working through the peasant uprisings that ran from the beginning of March to mid-May 1525]. But they don't believe it. They say that the peasants did it, to which I say no. Peasants with threshing flails can't break down a stone wall even if they work a long while. To say that the peasants did it is simply robbing God of his honour. And then they encourage the nobility: "Beat the peasants to death because they are mad and break down your castles!" [See Luther's *Against the Murdering Robbing Hordes of Peasants*, 1525]. This is the wisdom of the scripture wizards. Thus one blind man teaches another and both fall into the ditch as God himself said. If they would teach the truth according to the gospel there would not be the disunity and strife on earth which we now have. [. . .]

I have written this booklet not in anger nor to condemn anyone nor to incite the world to wrath, but to promote peace and concord. Strife creates nothing but strife, but wholesome peace creates wholesome peace. This has been clearly visible in all the recent conflict. Had the scripture wizards not been so busy teaching strife, there would have been much less of it. The most one can gain from strife is a bit of grease for the shoes; I can do without that meagre gain. Nor do I desire to share with the peasants the loot they gained from their revolt. They have been amply paid for it.

Is it not true that many scripture wizards and masses of other people on earth acted as unjustly as the peasants? But no one says about them: "Stab them to death! Beat them to death!" But God, who summons to battle as the true commander, marches to meet them and will strike them more powerfully than he struck the peasants. But then they have acted with violence a thousand times greater than that of the peasants. God is not much concerned with houses of stone and wood, be they cities or castles. But the houses in which God lives are the poor folk, the peasants and burghers whom God himself has created. He will not suffer that they be destroyed. However, he suffers and allows them to be abused until his time comes.

All things happen according to design. I believe that God will not again arouse the peasants against their masters in a revolt. His work with the peasants was done for the benefit of the nobility and the scripture wizards. Since in their ingratitude they have not recognized that God did it for them, he is bringing against them, for the blood of the peasants they offered him, the Turk and all the infidels. We see the beginning now of the real conflict. And it is not only the Turk. His supreme holiness, our father, the pope and all the high prelates are at strife with each other and each one thirsts for the blood of the other.

[Handwritten margin note: further judgment to come by the Turk]

God forbid that the conflict also comes to Germany as it has come to Italy, involving all the principalities in antagonism and war. I suspect that it will come to Germany as well. May God have mercy on us, for the rulers and great ones here are as contentious as elsewhere. Anyone pipes a merry tune, and they dance and say: "First rate, do it again!" The scripture wizards love it; they laugh up their sleeves and approve of growing strife and murder. They interpret the Scriptures in a way that produces feuding and quarreling. Trust that God will hear the prayers of the godly

[Handwritten note: Isn't he doing the same?]

and prevent such discord in Germany. The scripture wizards believe that the Gospel should be enforced by the sword. It is not true. I believe that if God wills it, a person will believe. Let others believe as they please. [. . .]

My booklet does not cause rebellion. It merely identifies those who sit in wickedness so that they may repent and pray to God for mercy. For God will not be defeated as the peasants were. God himself will fight against you as the booklet clearly states. No innocent person need have any fear. But whoever knows of his own guilt, let him flee to God and beg for mercy without delay, for God intends to pull up the weeds (Matt. 13:25-30). They will devour those who believe. They don't know that Moses tells us that if we believe the voice of God we will be blessed in our going out and coming in. We believe God's voice; what he has promised will happen (Deut. 28:1-14).

This matter has long eaten away at my conscience. I am a simple man, but could no longer endure it. I thus make it public in the name of God.

I have seen three tables in the world. The first overflowed with too much food. The second was middling, with enough for every need. The third was very needy. Then those who sat at the overflowing table came and attempted to take the little bread from the third table. That is the source of the trouble. But God will overturn the overflowing and needy tables, and confirm the one in the middle.

Translation: Walter Klaassen, from M. Steinmetz, ed., *Hans Hergot und die Flugschrift "Von der newen Wandlung Eynes Christliochen Lebens." Faksimilewiedergabe mit Umschrift* (Leipzig: VEB Fachbuchverlag, 1977).

Stephen Gardiner

(1497-1555)

Stephen Gardiner has the unenviable reputation of being simultaneously the foremost among Henry VIII's traditionalist, antireforming bishops and a key abettor of the king's break with Rome, defender of the royal headship of the English church. An impartial inspection, however, of a career that ended as Queen Mary's lord chancellor does not allow us to dismiss his seemingly contradictory allegiances as the insincere posturing of an ambitious and pragmatic spirit. Rather, they probably reveal the cast of mind of a conscientious Catholic lawyer of a southern humanist stripe. Undoubtedly, a compelling concern of Gardiner's career, typical of his age, appears to have been the benefits of true Christian piety for "this-worldly" social and political discipline. Conversely, his fear and hatred of "evangelical" (Lutheran) doctrine and reform was always bound up with a perceived threat of moral and social disorder.

Gardiner's animosity toward the Lutherans is well concealed in *On True Obedience (De vera obedientia)*, penned in 1535 as propaganda for the king's supreme headship in the wake of a parliamentary act making refusal to acknowledge it treason. Indeed, his grounding of human obedience in the authoritative revelation of Scripture, in the righteousness made possible by Christ's obedience and in the requirement of faith itself, must have done quite as much to invite the Strasbourg republication of the oration, with a preface by Bucer, as his substitution of royal for papal jurisdiction. Beneath the diplomatic gloss, the core doctrine resonates with authenticity: namely, the monarch's divinely ordained supremacy over his entire kingdom, including both lay and clerical orders, and his subjects' virtually unlimited duty of obedience to him. To Gardiner's mind supremacy and obedience were indispensable to the presence of divine truth in civil and ecclesiastical polity. By the time of Mary's accession, he was persuaded of God's ordination of a supreme authority over the universal church, to whom unlimited obedience was necessary if the true deposit of Catholic faith and worship were to be safeguarded — a departure, but not that great a departure, from his earlier position. To his mind, what Rome's supremacy lacked in biblical evidence compared with the royal supremacy, was more than compensated for by its evident historical necessity and the testimony of canon law.

Needless to say, it was not the consistency of Gardiner's mind, but his treacherous backsliding, that impressed the English Protestant exile who, in 1553, published a translation of this tract as part of an organized assault on Mary's Romanist church hierarchy.

Further Reading: P. S. Donaldson, ed., *A Machiavellian Treatise* (Cambridge: Cambridge University Press, 1975); G. R. Elton, *Reform and Reformation* (London: Arnold, 1977); J. A. Muller, *Stephen Gardiner and the Tudor Reaction* (London: SPCK, 1926); J. A. Muller, *The Letters of Stephen Gardiner* (Cambridge: Cambridge University Press, 1933); F. Raab, *The English Face of Machiavelli* (London: Routledge & Kegan Paul, 1964); G. Redworth, *In Defence of the Church Catholic: The Life of Stephen Gardiner* (Oxford: Blackwell, 1990).

From *On True Obedience*

The king (say they) is head of the realm but not of the church. O what an absurd and foolish saying is that? As though, because the people beginneth now to believe in God, it were a just cause why they should be no more in subjection to the king, God's lieutenant, but be exempt quite from his body. But Paul taught not so, which said that the authority of masters over their servants should not be changed or diminished through professing of Christ, but warned them to keep it still in perfect authority, bidding servants to be obedient unto their bodily masters for God's sake (Col. 3:22). The converting of a wife unto faith withdraweth nothing from the authority of her husband, for he is the head of the wife still; and because she, after she had professed the faith, should shew no token of misorder whereby she might pluck the minds of some from religion, St. Peter's mind was that wives, having professed the faith, should leave off the office of preaching which they executed by words and win (without the word) their husbands through their chaste conversation (1 Pet. 3:1f.). Therefore the authority of the master towards the servant and the right of the husband's superiority over the wife is not lost by the mean of religion: and shall it be lost to the king? Who forasmuch as he (yea though he be an infidel) representeth as it were the image of God upon earth so that he is called the head and the guide of the people, shall his state be nipped off because of the Christian profession? And shall he be called no more the head of the people, which is the church, but the nearer he draweth to God by faith (which is the only mean to come to God) shall he so much the further go away from God's image? And shall he begin to be had in so much less reverence with the people for that name's sake that he ought most chiefly to be honoured for? Truly if he be the head of the people, and that by the ordinance of God, as no man sayeth nay, yea even as well when the people as the prince be most far dissevered from God through infidelity, how much more now, seeing they accord through the power of God in one profession of faith and by that means are a church, ought he to retain the name of supreme head? And that he may worthily be taken for the head of the church still, he representeth the office that he occupieth in God's stead, much more honourably now than beforetime when he wandered in the darkness of infidelity. Paul without difference biddeth men obey those princes that bear the sword (Rom. 13:4). Saint Peter speaketh of kings by name (1 Pet. 2:13), Christ himself commandeth tribute to be paid unto Caesar (Matt. 22:21), and checked his disciples for striving who should be greatest: "Kings of the nations" (quoth he) "bear rule over them" (Luke 22:25), declaring plainly in so great variety of degrees and orders which God doth garnish this world withall that the dominion and authority pertaineth to none but to princes.

But here some man will say to me: you travail about that that no man is in doubt of. For who ever denied that the prince ought to be obeyed? It is most certain that he that will not obey the prince is worthy to die for it: as it is comprehended in the old law and also confirmed in the new law. But we must see (will he say) that the king do not pass the limits appointed him, as though there must be an arbiter for the ordering of his limits. For it is certain that obedience is due, but how far the limits of requiring obedience extend, that is all the whole question that can be demanded. What manner of limits are those that ye tell me of seeing the Scripture hath none such? But generally speaking of obedience which the subject is bounden to do unto the prince, the wife unto the husband, or the servant to the master it hath not added so much as one syllable of exception, but only hath preserved the obedience due to God safe and whole, that we should not hearken unto any man's word in all the world against God. Else the sentences that command obedience are indefinite or without exception, but are of indifferent force universally, so that it is but lost labour for you to tell me of limits which can not be proved by any testimony of Scripture. We are commanded doubtless to obey. In that consisteth our office which if we mind to go about with the favour of God and man we must need show humbleness of heart in obeying authority, how grievous so ever it be, for God's sake not questioning nor inquiring what the king, what the master, or what the husband ought or may command other to do. And if they take upon them, either of their own head or when it is offered them, more than right and reason is, they have a lord unto whom they either stand or fall and that shall one day sit in judgment even of them. Yet for all this some man will say: Yea, but ye promised in the beginning to speak of that which you are about now to avoid your hands of, having forgotten your purpose, as it appeareth. No Sir, say I, I avoid not my hands of it, but I say it is sufficiently confirmed by these that we have spoken of before, that princes ought to be obeyed by the commandment of God: yea and to be obeyed without exception, as a thing whereof there is no mention in that law, which if thou put any thing to or take any thing from, thou art a wicked man: what would we have more?

Translation: attributed to John Bale (Rome, 1553), reproduced in Pierre Janelle, *Obedience in Church and State: Three Political Tracts by Stephen Gardiner* (Cambridge: Cambridge University Press, 1930).

Philipp Melanchthon

(1497-1560)

It is difficult to overstate the importance of Philipp Melanchthon (Schwartzerdt) for the course of the Protestant Reformation. Not only was he a leading Lutheran church reformer, theologian, educator, and administrator in electoral Saxony and throughout the German territories, but through his unrivaled participation in major religious colloquies, as well as through his published work, he shaped international Lutheranism and its ecumenical dialogue with Zwinglian and Calvinist reform and with Catholicism. Behind his far-reaching involvements and influence lay the intellectual achievement of a systematic evangelical theology closely integrated with humanist scholarship and classical thought.

A prodigious classicist even before his arrival in Wittenberg in 1518, renowned for his Greek grammar, his translations and editions of ancient authors, Melanchthon's conversion to theology and the scriptural text impeded neither his polymathic ambitions nor his literary productions in rhetoric, dialectics, the physical sciences, history, psychology, and moral philosophy. The key to his enduring intellectual breadth and consistency was the conviction that the end of all scientific experience and reasoning was knowledge of God, which faith in Christ's grace refined and ordered. His harmonizing of the certainties of revelation and natural reason, of scriptural faith and humanist method has inevitably elicited conflicting interpretations and assessments, as have his theological formulations on such subjects as free will, predestination, the relation of justification and sanctification, and his ecumenical rapprochements. To the extent that these controversies touch on his political thought, it is pertinent to observe that he not only structured it according to Luther's law-gospel dialectic, but in the course of his intellectual development revised the dialectical terms in a manner resembling Luther's own political evolution.

Conventionally, scholars map the course of Melanchthon's theological career by comparing successive editions of his most systematic and widely read theological work, the *Loci Communes Theologici*, recognized as groundbreaking in its method of

650

theological exposition by key scriptural themes. In his original (1521) edition, he organized his theological "topics" *(loci)* under the controlling Pauline themes of the power of sin, the work of the law, grace and its fruits. Most important for his political thought was his conviction that the central work of the law (or of God through the law) was to reveal human sin, to mortify the self-love of men and uncover the viciousness and futility of their so-called virtues. He admitted natural moral laws, that is, universal common judgments that men should worship God, harm no one, and make common use of things, the latter two anchored in the impulses and necessities of social life. However, he emphasized the "carnal" nature of unregenerate morality and its idolatrous ignorance of God on the one hand, and on the other, the spiritual intention of God's revealed law (the Ten Commandments); its requirement of true repentance, faith, and spiritual regeneration; and the inward and outward rigor of its demands, in conformity with Christ's Sermon on the Mount.

Melanchthon's 1555 *Loci,* which, like Calvin's 1559 *Institutes,* was much expanded, contained a lengthy and remodeled discussion of law, the heart of which was his detailed exposition of the Ten Commandments. Now, in scholastic fashion, he simply identified the divinely revealed *lex moralis* with God's eternal, unchangeable wisdom and righteousness, the light of which was implanted in all men at their creation but was darkened by human sin. Eclipsing the earlier tension between the natural and divine laws, he made possible, by identifying them, an unproblematic integration of social and political morality into the Christian ethic. In common with Luther's later reconceptualizing of the "two kingdoms" as the realms of inner freedom and outward social obligation, Melanchthon's integration embodied a less rigorous reading of God's worldly demands than earlier. In his 1555 treatment of poverty (included below), the faithful were no longer restrained by the Spirit of Christ from litigating in the courts or urged to boundless sharing of their possessions; property, as a divinely ordained social institution, had shed its former generic association with human avarice. As with Luther, Melanchthon's shift came largely out of his encounter with the religious and civil unrest of the peasant uprisings and Thuringian Anabaptism, which made him appreciate the social and civil stability enshrined in natural law philosophy. He never, however, incorporated Luther's inner-outer dialectic; his dialectic (like Calvin's) was between obedience to the two tables of the Law. Fulfillment of the second table depends absolutely on fulfillment of the first; only those who truly know, honor, and love God through faith by the grace of Christ are capable of social obedience and social virtues.

His well-known schema of the "three uses" of the law — to foster external or civil morality, to pronounce God's wrathful judgment on sin and the sinner, and to educate the faithful in God's will — reinforced the dialectic of law and gospel by the prominence it accorded to the second use, that of preparing the sinner to receive the proclamation of grace. At the same time, he gave to civil morality its theological due by making it a work universally required by and pleasing to God. The third use completed his rebuttal of contemporary antinomian arguments.

His incorporation of political obedience under the fourth command of the Decalogue, that requiring obedience to parents, was a move of immense popularity, taken over from Luther. Melanchthon's employment of it accounted largely for its prevalence among Tudor English reformers educated by the *Loci,* and no doubt fed the patriarchial theory of government.

Further Reading: G. Kisch, *Melanchthons Rechts- und Soziallehre* (Berlin: De Gruyter, 1967); S. Kusukawa, *The Transformation of Natural Philosophy: The Case of Philip Melanchthon* (Cambridge: Cambridge University Press, 1995); C. L. Manschreck, *Melanchthon: The Quiet Reformer* (New York: Abingdon Press, 1958); J. S. Oyer, *Lutheran Reformers against Anabaptists: Luther, Melanchthon, and Menius and the Anabaptists of Central Germany* (The Hague: Nijhoff, 1964); W. Pauck, *Melanchthon and Bucer* (Philadelphia: Westminster, 1969); P. Schwarzenau, *Der Wandel im theologischen Ansatz bei Melanchthon* (Gütersloh, 1956); R. Stupperich, *Melanchthon* (English translation) (Philadelphia: Westminster, 1965).

From *Loci Communes* (1555)

ch. 7. *Of Divine Law:* Let me first set forth the old and customary divisions. The law in Moses has three parts. The first part is called *lex moralis,* that is, laws about virtues; henceforth in this essay I will call this *eternal law,* or the law about the judgment of God against sin. The second part is *lex cerimonialis,* that is, laws about the church, which are concerned with external works, like sacrifices, and prohibited eating of the flesh of swine, all of which were established for a certain time, as in ancient Judaism. The third part is *lex judicialis,* that is, laws about civil government, about justice, inheritance, and peace. There is a great difference between the first part, which pertains to the eternal, and the other two, which pertain to the temporal. All men should know that the laws about ceremonies in the books of Moses, and also the laws about the civil government of Israel, were to remain only until the coming of the Messiah and the true expiatory sacrifice.

God established the government of Israel that there might be a certain people and land in which the Messiah would appear and preach and perform signs, suffer, and rise from the dead; and that there should be a certain school in which God would reveal himself and perform signs, and give, explain, and maintain his promises. God chose a suitable place almost in the middle of the known earth, between the great empires of the Chaldeans, Assyrians, and Egyptians. There he established, in the eyes of all, the successors of Abraham. Along with the promise of a Messiah, he also decreed a temporal government, which does not now bind us, for it ceased with Judaism. This can be gathered from Acts 15 and the entire Letter to the Galatians. This should be remembered in order to avoid falling into the fantastic contention of Thomas Münzer, who says that a Christian in court must render judgments according to the law of Moses; he would destroy the Roman law which is now used. He who does not distinguish between such temporal law and eternal law will suffer many errors.

Eternal law is given the weak name *lex moralis.* We refer to the Ten Commandments as the eternal law because the principal parts of eternal law are included in the

Decalogue. However, when we use the term "Ten Commandments," this should not be childishly understood as referring only to ten sentences but rather to the entire law, which is called *lex moralis;* but we will not here quarrel about words.

First, however, I want to give this definition: The divine law, which is called *lex moralis,* or the law of virtues, or law of the judgment of God, or the Ten Commandments, is the eternal, unchangeable wisdom and principle of righteousness in God himself. A portion of this wisdom was imparted to man in the creation and later God's word was given that we might know the nature of God himself and his demand that we be like him in wisdom and righteousness. He did this that we might not vex him in mind, heart, or works, and that we might know his anger toward all who do not have perfect obedience, and his condemnation of them to eternal punishment.

Of the Fourth Commandment: In Moses it is written that God commanded him to make *two* stone tablets on which God then wrote the Ten Commandments (Deut. 4:13; 10:3f.). This is significant, for the two tablets indicate a distinction among the commandments. The first three commandments speak of the true knowledge of God, how he reveals himself to us through his word, how he imparts to us his wisdom and knowledge, and how we must accept him, first and before all others. These three commandments constitute the first table; the following seven commandments constitute the second. [. . .]

But the first must be included in all the commandments, so that God may be obeyed and honoured as he has decreed. True knowledge of God comes in faith, fear, and trust. We must first know *Jesus Christ,* the Son of God, and receive forgiveness of our sins through him, before we are pleasing to God and become his dwelling place.

After this, obedience in the second table is highly pleasing to God, a divine service, for Christ says in Matthew 22:39: "The second commandment is like the first, you shall love your neighbour as yourself!" Note that Christ deems this social obedience of the second table so highly that he says: "These commandments are equally as high as the first and highest commandment." No angel and no man would dare to speak so if the Son of God had not himself thus spoken; but note that Christ wants the knowledge of God and the virtues embraced in the first table to come first and burn in every heart. The tables are similar in that as God himself is, so are these commandments, beneficent, true, and pure; for he maintains an unalterable distinction between virtue and vice; and he truly wants rational creatures to be like him. The obligation to both tables is equal, for the second table becomes a divine service when done in obedience to the first commandment. [. . .]

This fourth commandment (Exod. 20:12; Deut. 5:16) reminds us that we owe obedience to our parents, of whose bodies and blood we have received our body and blood. But all creatures owe much more obedience to God because they were created by him, and have their being and lives from him. And just as parents have an inexpressibly great natural love toward their children, which has a special name *storgē;* so God has an inexpressibly great love toward his only begotten Son, *Jesus Christ,* and toward *us,* poor creatures, who have refuge in *Christ.*

In this fourth commandment we should be able to see that God earnestly wants order and government instead of the kind of freedom in which everyone may exercise all his wantonness, as a wolf in the forest that runs wild and plunders and eats whatever he can overtake.

Now the corrupted nature in men is such that it would like to live freely, without God, without law, without any fear. One sees godless, wanton people, tyrants, Cyclops, and Centaurs living thus, and they give to this desolate existence the honourable name of freedom. But there is no freedom when there is no order, for then no man is secure from others. A wanton and malicious man might by sheer force deprive his neighbour of life or seize his neighbour's wife, or daughter, or property, as Cain did in murdering his brother, and Tarquinius in shaming Lucretia, and as Ahab did in taking Naboth's inheritance. Such disorder and unbridled living is not human freedom, but wolfish license; to call it "freedom" is to misuse a noble term, for freedom means an orderly use of one's own body and goods, by choice, in accordance with divine law and other true statutes. Note the speech which Cicero received from Crasso, "We are servants of the law so that we can be free." In all of life and in the use we make of all creatures, the Ten Commandments, that is, the divine law, should be our bridle, should bind our hearts, mouths, hands and all our members, as God frequently has commanded: "You shall heed the ordinances that I have commanded, that you may live!" (Deut. 4:1).

Good Works in the Fourth Commandment: The following good works pertain to this commandment:-

First, parents, schoolteachers, sovereign authorities, and all rulers, high or low, in true knowledge of God and of the Lord Jesus Christ, in fear of God and in faith, should love those subject to them, charge and rule them with this table of the Ten Commandments, and punish external disobedience, each one after his calling. They should protect the obedient, and help them to maintain body and life, reputation and profession — all to the end that they may know God, be in his true church, and praise him in eternity. That they may call on God, let each one truly serve in his calling, and grasp not at a foreign vocation, nor make an obstacle for others and a confusion of order. In 1 Thessalonians 4:11, St. Paul charges the brethren "to aspire to live quietly, to mind your own affairs, and to work with your hands."

And children, students, and subjects, of high or low status, in true knowledge, reverence, and faith, should love and esteem their fathers and mothers, schoolteachers, and the persons who provide good government, law, and justice, as if all were by divine wisdom ordained. They should be obedient to them in externally commanded works, each in his order, after his calling and station. They should thank God for good government, and heartily beseech him to be the father of every house and to be present in all government.

Each one should understand his calling and his office, and truly serve therein, and should not grasp after a foreign calling, thereby causing dissensions, tumult, hate, homicide, and destructions.

In general, the gratitude of all is embraced in this commandment. One who helps another in distress acts as a father or mother. But what is gratitude, and why should one who has been helped give thanks?

These are extraordinary questions; for the virtue which one calls "gratitude" is itself extraordinary and not well known.

Gratitude is a virtue which comprises two other important virtues: truth and justice. First, there is the truth that we confess with our hearts and mouths when we speak of whom we have received help, when we are not proud and do not boast that we have ourselves with our own wisdom or our own strength done so and so. Second, there is justice, for in gratitude we behold our special obligations to the benefactor and feel that we must return as we have received. By divine wisdom justice is an ordained equality of exchange. Buyers and sellers should maintain such equality, and others also, for men could not live with one another if one part only took and devoured and the other part only gave and suffered. Rational men know well that justice is of this nature. To preserve the equality of justice, God ordained that truth in rulers be matched with truth, and benefit with benefit. Solomon speaks of ingratitude, saying (Prov. 17:13), "From the house of the ungrateful, misfortune will not depart." The curses in Deuteronomy 27, where the ingratitude of children to parents is mentioned, are also based on this sense of justice.

Of a Threefold Use of the Divine Law: Man does not have forgiveness of sins through the law, or by the merit of his own works; neither is he justified, that is, he does not please God, even though he lives an extremely moral life. No man can fulfil the law; that is, no man can really be conformed to God's will as he in the law has indicated that we should be. No one in this corrupted nature is without sin. So one may ask: For what, then, is the law useful? Answer: There are three principal uses of the law.

The first use is civil; law teaches and with fear and punishments forces one to keep his external members under discipline, according to all the commandments about external works. The tongue is not to speak outrageous words about God; the hands are not to kill and not to steal another's goods; the body is not to practice external immorality; and the tongue is not to speak lies. This civil use is binding on all men, although the works are not holy; and this external obedience is possible for all men on several levels, as previously indicated with regard to free will. God's earnest pleasure is that all men observe external morality *(Zucht);* he punishes external vice with public plagues, with the sword of the authorities, and with illness, poverty, war, dispersion, distress in children, and with various misfortunes. And he who is not converted to God falls into eternal punishment. But remember that although this external morality does not merit forgiveness of sins, and although it does not justify a person before God, it is pleasing to God, even though it is a long way from a fulfilment of the law.

The second use of the law is more important; namely to preach the wrath of God. Through the preaching of the law God accuses the heart, causes it to be alarmed, and drives it to such anguish that, as Hezekiah notes, men say: "Like a lion he has smashed all my bones" (Isa. 38:13). Men feel God's wrath against sin, and if they do not receive comfort through the Christ, they sink into eternal anguish and flight, as did Saul and Judas. Hundreds of thousands of men fall into eternal punishment, even for a small sin, when God glances at us angrily.

St. Paul often speaks of this use. In Romans 4:15 he says: "The law brings wrath," that is, fright, anguish, and flight in the presence of God's judgment *(Gericht)* against sin. Hundreds of thousands of men live in apparent security, but this judgment finally comes to all. Moreover, many men who feel this judgment are comforted, converted, and blessed again through the gospel, but some fall into despair and eternal anguish.

Deuteronomy 4:24 says: "God is a devouring fire."

Psalm 58:11: "Surely there is a God who judges and punishes men."

Psalm 62:12: "Thou dost requite a man according to his work."

Psalm 50:3, 6: "Surely God will come, he will not keep silence; before him will go a devouring fire . . . and the heavens will declare that God is a judge."

Nahum 1:2: "The Lord is avenging and wrathful, and keeps wrath for his enemies."

Zephaniah 1:12: "God will come, and with his light will search out those people who take their ease and say 'God will not do good, nor will he do ill'!"

Job 9:2: "I know that thou dost punish the sinner."

Solomon 8: "Sin does not remain unpunished" (cf. Eccles. 8:12f.). And in the last chapter: "All men shall fear God, and keep his commandments; for God will bring everything that happens, good and evil even though it be secret, into judgment" (Eccles. 12:13f.).

To summarise: God is equally just *(gerecht)* toward all; therefore he punishes sin in all, although it may not happen at the same time. He created knowledge of his law in our nature, that we might know his righteousness *(Gerechtigkeit)*. He proclaimed great miracles, that we might know his nature, what he calls right, what sin and injustice are, and he has from the beginning of the world, especially in his church, maintained knowledge of all the necessary commands. He uses his law to strike down our sinful hearts. As Paul says, in Romans 7:13, "Sin works death through the law." Job 6:4 says the same: "The arrows of the Almighty are in me; the terrors of God are arrayed against me."

Whoever has felt divine judgment and this sorrow of heart well knows that it is the same as death if God does not again grant comfort through our Lord Jesus Christ.

Contemplate the fact that God will judge and that his judgment is very serious, for the law is God's wisdom. We cannot eradicate the light that God planted in men when he created them. And he openly proclaimed the Ten Commandments, to the accompaniment of miracles, so that the light would not be extinguished by the doubts of the human reason in our disorganised nature. God added eternal and temporal punishments to the law, for he wants physical punishments to remind us of his law when human reason disputes it.

God also ordained the office of preaching, that it might take his place in combating sin through the word, and, for the sake of Christ the mediator, proffer grace. Through preaching God produces terror and comfort. The Son of God himself originated the office of preaching in Paradise by saying that he will accept fallen men again, and will rescue them from death. At first he punishes the sin and says: "What have you done?" (Gen. 3:13). It was no jest when Adam and Eve heard the divine Majesty himself speak, for then and there they felt death. But the Son of God himself voiced a wonderful absolution, and said to them: "The seed of the woman shall bruise the head of the serpent" (3:15). From this they understood that they would not die; the woman would have a seed; and they understood that they would again be returned to grace, because the seed of the woman would again overthrow the power of the serpent, and would again give righteousness and life. This comfort the Son of God wrought in the heart of Adam and Eve when he spoke the eternal word.

In the office of preaching in his Church God wants us to proclaim what he is and how he ennobled human nature in creating it in his own image. But against God's will, human nature fell away from God, and is no longer the image of God. Therefore human nature is under God's disfavour; no longer to be like God is to be in sin. In his law he indicates that we are to be as he is and as he wishes. He will maintain this very important doctrine in his Church.

One needs the preaching of law, as St. Paul says, for "Through the law comes knowledge of sin" (Rom. 3:20). Yes, the law is not only a witness to what sin is, but to what God is; one must learn what sin is if one is to know what God is and what is repugnant to his divine wisdom and order.

St. Paul says in Romans 1:18 that sin is to be punished through the word of God in the office of preaching: "The wrath of God is revealed from heaven against all ungodliness and wickedness of men." Christ speaks in the same way when he says that he has not come to destroy the law, but to fulfil it. The highest law, which we call *lex moralis,* is the eternal unchangeable wisdom and righteousness in God himself, which he nevertheless revealed to us. No one can obliterate this wisdom and righteousness in God himself; it is and remains eternal, and at all times it condemns that which is repugnant to it. Because of this wisdom and righteousness in God the awful wrath of God against our sin was poured on Christ the Lord; thus we are accepted for his sake, as will be described more fully later.

Christ the Lord himself preaches and explains the Ten Commandments. He says: "The Holy Spirit will punish the world on account of the sin of not believing in me" (John 16:8f.). Through the office of preaching, God punishes the world's frightful, terrible ignorance, in that men know not the Son of God, nor the promise of the Son of God and the forgiveness of sins and grace; and the heart that does not call on the Son of God in true faith and trust does not receive forgiveness of sins. The Holy Spirit punishes such sins as contempt of God, false security, doubt of God's word, and indolence in the maintaining of divine doctrine. The Holy Spirit also punishes sins against men, such as tumult, hate, envy, murder, adultery, robbery, and lies. Paul frequently says: "Whoever sins will not inherit the kingdom of God" (1 Cor. 6:9f.; Gal. 5:21; Eph. 5:5). In these and similar words the apostles preach and explain the Ten Commandments, and command us to know and always to preach them in the Christian Church, that through such preaching hearts may be freed from blindness and false security, and earnestly consider and feel God's wrath.

Christ himself said: "Preach in my name repentance and forgiveness of sins" (Luke 24:47)! And since we are to feel repentance and terror in our hearts, we must know what sin is in its many forms.

This involves the second use of the divine law, and we should remember it well, so that we may earnestly and firmly maintain and preach the true meaning of the Ten Commandments. For several years the Anabaptists have been clamouring that one should not preach the Ten Commandments, on the grounds that whoever is born anew is led by the Spirit to do good works without the aid of the word, and that such good works supersede the commandments. Such statements of the Anabaptists display empty blindness and entail many errors and blasphemies. In contrast to this, consider that even Christ himself preaches and explains the Ten Commandments, and give thanks to God for his wisdom in revealing his nature and ours, and for the revelation that after the resurrection we shall again be like him.

Also consider that the light of natural law was planted in man when he was created, but in the heathen it has been obscured, and they have allowed terrible sins which are contrary to the natural light in men, that is, contrary to the natural law. They have invented many gods and have imagined all of them to be eternal; they have even invoked dead men. They have allowed adultery and exchange of wives. Such blindness has prevailed among the heathen, but in his church God has maintained the true understanding of his law. It is a devilish blasphemy, therefore, to say that one is not to preach the divine law, for this is to assert that one is not to say what God is like, nor to point out the distinction between God, who is wise, true, good, just, and pure, and other things, which are not. The divine law is God's wisdom imparted to us. And the ingratitude of those who despise this gift of God is enormously great, whether in devils or men. One cannot speak too much of this wisdom of God.

The third use of the preaching of the law is concerned with those saints who now are believers, who have been born again through God's word and the Holy Spirit, of whom this word was said: "I will put my law in your heart" (Jer. 31:33; Heb. 8:10). Although God now dwells in these and gives them light, and causes them to be conformed to him, nevertheless, all such happens through God's word, and the law in this life is necessary, that saints may know and have a testimony of the works which please God. Since all men in this mortal life carry in themselves much weakness and sin, daily penance before God ought to increase, and we ought even more to lament our false security and impurity. Such can come about through the divine word, through a consideration of the punishments on others, or through our own punishment.

ch. 8. *Of the Distinction of Commandment and Counsel:* The Anabaptists flit about and pretend great works of holiness, and in their hypocrisy say they have nothing of their own. They fake great patience and practice no vengeance and no resistance. Just so, a thousand years ago similar devilish hypocrites flitted about. Carpokrates and his companions desired not only to have their money in common, but also their wives. Although this is a frightful example to mention, it is necessary for us to remember that we must consider how terribly the devil fumes and rages when he has an opportunity; and that we must be forearmed, prepared, and strengthened with pure doctrine, and daily cry to the Lord Christ to enlighten and guide us with his gospel and his true Holy Spirit, and drive the lying devils far away. At present the monks have not raged as grossly as the Anabaptists and have not said that it is necessary to make inheritance and money common, but they have said such is a counsel of perfection. In these speeches of the monks there are many great lies; therefore, I will give a brief reminiscence.

A commandment is so called because it speaks of necessary obedience. Everything that is contrary to the commandments is sin, and this brings eternal punishment if man is not converted to God.

A counsel is a doctrine, not a commandment; it does not demand a work, even though it praises the work as blameless and useful.

Now the monks have selected three such works, namely, not to exercise vengeance or resistance; not to have property; and to live chastely without matrimony. The monks say that the gospel has counseled these three works, and they then devise lies, saying that these works merit forgiveness of sins, that they are perfection, and that they are higher than the works of divine commandments. In our times the Anabaptists particularly have written books which are full of frightful errors and lies. Although basic and lengthy instruction on these topics would be very useful, I will here speak briefly. Whoever has learned the other articles in order — what law is, the difference between law and gospel, how before God man is justified through faith, and that God has ordained worldly authority — can from this basis also determine what one is to do about resistance, property, and chastity.

First, it is obvious that our works cannot merit forgiveness of sins; so also are our works not perfection, for in this weak life we are still far from fulfilment of the law, and much sin, doubt and disorder remain in us, as Job 9:2 says, "No man is justified before God" [loosely paraphrased]. Therefore it is empty blindness when men extol their own works as perfection, as if such works were a complete fulfilment of the divine law, and as if such holiness were higher than commanded works.

Of Poverty: "Poverty makes woe." This is a true proverb, and it is necessary to understand it, for the monks say that it is a counsel to be poor. The first distinction to be made is between poverty and not having property, for one can be very poor even though he has property. How many hundreds of thousands of heads of households have for themselves and for their poor children their own cottages, beds, clothes, and food, and nevertheless have not all the necessities of life! These are called poor, and are truly poor, although they have property, and more is to be said later about bearing poverty in patience. These, however, the Anabaptists attack, saying that Christian men should not own property, but should have all goods in common, and they make a command of this. The monks are subtler; they say poverty is a counsel, a special holy work.

These opinions of the Anabaptists and monks are erroneous and false. The seventh commandment, "You shall not steal," shows that it is right, and a divine order, to have property. These grave words of the seventh commandment confirm the right to have property for every one, and they draw a wall about each one's house and trade *(Nahrung)*.

And this should be noted very carefully; the orderly regulations of the human race in authority, courts, punishments, marriage, property, buying, and selling are so decreed and maintained through divine wisdom and power, that the devils which oppose such regulations may not completely destroy them.

And order in the human community is a clear testimony to God; for in the punishments of murderers and the like, one acknowledges that God exists, that he is a just judge, and is present among men. Through his beautiful order God would be known, and through such means and bonds he wants us to be drawn together, and to serve one another, as do the Son of God and angels who are pleasing to God.

Works of such service are divine worship in the faithful, for men acknowledge

God by being obedient to him in his ordained order; and men are not to be torn from God's ordered stations, but should be maintained and honoured in them. The Lord speaks frequently in the prophets, as in Zechariah: "I have not commanded you to fast, but I have commanded you to render true judgments" (cf. Zech. 7:4ff.).

Knowing now that this (characteristic of the) physical order, ownership of property, is pleasing to God, one should further know that abandonment of property is of two kinds: that which is compelled and that which is hypocritically chosen.

Forced abandonment occurs when pious Christians, because of their confession, are exiled and compelled to leave their goods and children. In this abandonment, having patience is to invoke God; it is to worship in one's confession, even though life is taken away. This patience and firmness in confession are commanded and necessary works, not simply counsels. The Lord Christ speaks of this abandonment when he says (Mark 10:29f.): "There is no one who has left house or brothers, or sister or mother or father or children or land, for my sake and for the gospel, who will not receive a hundredfold even in this life, despite persecutions, and in the age to come eternal life."

Poverty can also result from many other misfortunes, such as fire or war, in which house and castle are destroyed. In these and similar misfortunes, those persons who turn to God have patience and do good work and worship.

Hundreds of thousands of God-fearing householders are poor, although they possess property; that is, although they own something, they and their children do not have the proper necessities of life. This is called poverty. In this circumstance patience is a good work, pleasing to God, as the text says: "Blessed are the poor in spirit" (Matt. 5:3), that is, those who for God's sake are patient in their poverty, although they work and maintain property, as much as God permits to them. For it is God's will that all be not equally strong or equally rich. It is virtue and strength from the Holy Spirit, wisely and rightly to bear poverty, and not to design evil, dishonourable things to become rich, as Judas and many others did. Patience is to be further discussed later.

However, the voluntary abandonment of one's own goods in the erroneous opinion that begging is a holy work of divine worship is not only not a counsel but a lie, a mistake. "Vainly they honour me with the commandments of men" (Matt. 15:8f.). Also, whoever obtains bread from another by begging, if he himself has property and has forsaken it without being persecuted, if he does not perform some honourable work such as teaching to obtain bread, if he is able and not prevented from working, he is a thief. The cloisters, therefore, have always been full of thieves, and this is still more sinful in that they have sold the Mass and the dead pageantry.

This also should be noted. When God gives property and a tolerable trade, we should first of all know that having property is pleasing to God; and we should acknowledge it as a gift from God, thank him for it, and ask God to sustain and bless our poor children with the benefits of our trade. And we should ask about the correct usage. With regard to this, everyone should look carefully at the lovely passage in Solomon, "Out of your spring let the little brooks flow . . . however, you alone are to remain master of it, so that it does not become alien to you" (Prov. 5:15, 17). You should preserve the ground and the principal benefit for the virtuous rearing of your children, but as much as possible you should distribute the fruits to others, to the churches, to schools, and to the poor. This passage expressly confirms property, and gives instruction about its use, teaching both how to economise and how to limit liberality. From the spring let the brook flow out to others, but this does not mean that you are to repudiate your house and goods. And an understanding of this lovely passage, which God speaks through the wise king Solomon, discloses much useful doctrine, which should be well known in order to combat the hypocrisy and the lies of the Anabaptists and the monks.

Translation: C. L. Manschreck (New York: Oxford University Press, 1965). Used with permission.

John Calvin

(1509-64)

John Calvin may largely take the credit for conceiving and implementing a reintegration of political order and spiritual community that transformed the historical complexion of Reformation Christianity. By the time of his 1536 *Institutes,* the "two kingdoms" dialectic had issued in, on the one hand, the jettisoning of political order from spiritual community by the Anabaptist separatists, and on the other, the cozy assimilation of spiritual community to political order by Lutheran rulers. Not even the free cities of the empire and states of the Helvetic Confederation were effectively defining the church's evangelical autonomy, despite the theological ministrations of Bucer and Capito at Strasbourg, Zwingli at Zürich, and Oecolampadius at Basel. Against both excessive ecclesiastical dependence on or separation from the civil polity, Calvin, in Bucer's footsteps, renovated an essentially Gelasian model of church-commonwealth relations with reformed evangelical content. His thought of the 1540s and 1550s built up the visible church as an integrated structure of divinely constituted offices and powers — disciplinary, proclamatory, and sacramental. Correspondingly, he constructed civil polity from educated moral sentiment as well as from external law and judgment. Even more than the later Luther, he converted the polarizations of the two-kingdoms model into parallelisms, stressing harmonization of the spiritual and the temporal realms as of two communal realizations of God's will for fallen mankind, one direct and the other indirect.

The wide-ranging inspiration drawn from Calvin's political thought by Protestant thinkers, disproportionate to the literary space that it occupied, was partly owing to its synthetic achievement in blending patristic, scholastic, and Lutheran theological elements with ideas and methods drawn from classical political philosophy, and humanist literary, historical, and legal scholarship. Contributing to his political formation were his studies at Paris, Orléans, and Bourges; the influence of contemporary reformers; and his pastoral experience in the reforming cities of Basel, Strasbourg, and most importantly, Geneva.

662

Concerning his youthful study at the Collège de Montaigu, an interesting (and neglected) question concerns the possible political influence of the Paris master John Mair, with his powerful combination of Scotist, Ockhamist, and Gersonian ideas, including concepts of prepolitical, individual rights; communal sovereignty; conciliar representation; and law as coercive command. Although Calvin's political theology turned out to be vastly more conservative than Mair's, they do share a voluntarist concept of law. Calvin's concept, however, may owe more to his legal studies under celebrated humanist scholars (1528-33), who would also have opened up for him the coherent rationality and cultural meaning of the Roman civil law and its relationship to classical political thought.

Within a year of arriving in Basel as a French evangelical exile, Calvin had completed his original *Institutio Christianae religionis.* Modeled largely on Luther's *Short Catechism* of 1529, this work was a compendious exposition of Christian doctrine with the professed intention of vindicating the French evangelicals from charges of Anabaptist sedition. Its concluding chapter, "On Christian Liberty, Ecclesiastical Power, and Civil Administration," introduced enduring themes of his political reflection: the freedom of the individual's conscience in relation to external ecclesiastical regulations not explicitly contained in Scripture (the *adiaphora*); the unsurpassed dignity and social utility of civil magistracy, along with the restriction of its competence to the spheres of civil justice and external morality; and the obedience owed by Christian subjects to every de facto ruler, regardless of the deficiencies of his title or conduct (excepting his injuries against God) (Höpfl 1982, 35-54).

The theoretical developments discernible in successive editions (French and Latin) of his *Institutes* convey the movement of Calvin's political theology over his career. His second revised (Latin) edition of 1543 showed the impact of five years of reforming ministry, beginning with his turbulent Genevan pastorate where he had failed to establish the Reformed liturgy, doctrine, and government on account of recalcitrant civil authorities; his subsequent ministry within Bucer's advanced reformation at Strasbourg that strengthened his confidence and determination; and his return to Geneva with enhanced authority to devise for the city a set of ecclesiastical ordinances that defined the church's offices, ensured a well-trained company of clergy, and instituted the consistory comprised of clergy and lay elders as the agency of disciplinary practice. Thus the most striking advance of the 1543 *Institutes* was its vastly extended ecclesiology, focusing on a collegial clerical order that bore the authority of Christ's *imperium,* and on a consistory that had the status of an apostolic juridical institution actively applying Christ's law (Höpfl 1982, 104-15). Albeit the consistory structure of church discipline left a supportive role for civil coercion in religious matters, just as the collegial selection of clergy left room for confirmation of appointments by the civil magistrates as well as for popular consent, Calvin's increasingly dogmatic pronouncements about church order were accompanied by a novel tendency to envisage the civil sphere in parallel terms: he modified his earlier cautious indifference to alternative civil polities by endorsing aristocracy with democratic elements as the form of government most approved by experience and Scripture.

While his final revision of 1559 contained no new political departures, it offered the most developed presentation of earlier positions, being the fruit of mature theological reflection over almost two decades of pastoral ministry in Geneva (conducted for the most part in uneasy cooperation with the ruling city council) and gathering up material from sermons, lectures, polemical writings, and biblical commentaries. Moreover, it sealed the growing international influence of Calvin and the Genevan church as the chief vehicle of the rapid dissemination of his theology and reformation throughout Europe and the New World.

The Political Theology of the 1559 "Institutes." Of eighty chapters, political themes occupy only one, entitled "Of Civil Government," which appears as a concluding appendage to Calvin's lengthy discussion of the church that covers the remaining nineteen chapters of his fourth and final book. The preceding books treat the central theological topics of evangelical Christianity: human knowledge of God in himself, of his creation and governance of the world, of human sin and of Christ's person and work in redemption; faith and its effects in repentance, righteousness, justification, liberty, prayer, and assurance of election.

For Calvin the law, in its dialectical relation to divine grace, promise, and freedom, is the constitutive structure of Christian spirituality and morality, binding together the civil and ecclesial realms in a single overarching unity of revelation and salvation. As promulgated in the human heart at creation, as dimly present to the conscience of fallen mankind, as repromulgated in the revealed religion of Moses, as affirmed within the gospel of love, the moral law is always a revelation of Christ's power and promises to the human creature (2.7.1-4). Following Bucer and Melanchthon, he accords to the moral law the three uses of: (1) demonstrating to sinners their unrighteousness and condemnation so that they may flee to Christ's mercy (theological use); (2) restraining the evildoing of the unregenerate for the sake of the commonweal (civil use); and (3) instructing the elect in the path of sanctification (pedagogical use) (2.7.3-12). Thus the juridical positivization of the moral law in civil and church polities integrates their respective common goods into the divine scheme of salvation.

Moreover, the moral law has a threefold involvement in Calvin's concept of Christian liberty, expounded as having three parts: (1) transcendence of the law's condemnation by a conscience seeking assurance of justification (3.19.2-3); (2) free obedience to the law's commands by the conscience liberated from "legal necessity" (3.19.4-6); and (3) unfettered use of things indifferent to salvation by the spiritualized conscience (3.19.7), bound only to human traditions as they edify the Christian community and its members (2.19.14-15). In charity the spiritualized conscience observes the *adiaphora* — the inessential externalities of conduct (in worship, dress, manners, or discipline) — as human and not divine institutions; conversely, the human authority legislates the *adiaphora*, conscious of their limited authority and variability among communities.

Calvin's political discourse proper (in 4.20) begins with an explication of the Lutheran "two kingdoms/two regiments" paradigm, perennial to his thought and vital to his defense of civil government against its Anabaptist detractors. His defense exhibits the tensions of Luther's later reflection on political rule: on the one hand, it is the punitive order of restraint required by unregenerate evildoers, and on the other, the institutionalization of the natural human regard for harmonious and eq-

roles of civil gov't :

uitable order in social relationships. While government prevents and extirpates crimes against God and neighbor such as idolatry, property violation, and civil disturbance, it also "fosters and maintains" public worship, "form[s] our manners to civil justice," and cultivates the social virtues of honesty, modesty, and peaceableness (4.20.1-2). By comparison with even the later Luther, Calvin gives a more unequivocal endorsement of the magistrate's juridical role vis-à-vis ecclesiastical order, along with a more humanistic and classical account of civil community (also 2.2.13, 15).

His discussion of magistrates focuses on the close relation between their office and work and God's particular will. He proposes that *God acts* in their appointment, their authority (official and personal), and every one of their juridical acts, so that they should seek to "exhibit a kind of image of the Divine Providence, guardianship, [. . .] and justice" (4.20.6). Consequently, rulers should be concerned primarily with declaring and vindicating God's honor, and secondarily with vindicating the innocent poor, needy, and oppressed (4.20.9). As "guardians and maintainers of the laws," servants of divine command and natural equity, magistrates may be required to "execute public judgment" by waging war on criminal assaults from outside their territories, but only when "compelled by the strongest necessity" (4.20.12). Calvin repeats his preference for aristocracy (pure or democratically modified) as the form of government most conducive to the magistrates' mutual instruction, assistance, and restraint, and repeats as well his prohibition of private men passing judgment on their de facto regimes (4.20.8).

His consideration of law is primarily concerned to refute the view that Christian polities should be ruled by "the law of Moses" rather than by "the law of nations" (4.20.14). Accordingly, he argues that, of the three parts of the Mosaic Law, only the moral remains universally binding (4.20.15), the ceremonial and judicial laws having been, respectively, abrogated and legitimately passed over as the peculiar forms of piety and justice ordained by God for the Jewish people (4.20.15). In that diversity belongs naturally to civil constitutions, they are bound to conform to no historical polity, but only to equity itself (4.20.16). Calvin's confidence in civil laws *surprisi?* as the "sinews" of the body politic is reflected in his confidence in all forms of judicial proceedings. He is less equivocal than Luther in endorsing litigation, partly because he regards every judicial judgment as a vindication of the commonweal as much as of the directly injured party, and so can more easily imagine the accuser as public-spirited and free from vengeful motives toward the offender (4.20.19-20).

Calvin's treatment of "the people" is largely devoted to showing that the obedience of subjects is due even to the most malevolent tyrant in whom they can discern no vestige of the image of God (nor even of humanity). His Gregorian (Gregory the Great) argument that subjects must meekly and patiently bear the "iniquities" perpetrated by tyrants on account of the "sacred majesty" with which God has invested their office is nuanced by his concluding admissions that: (1) in Old Testament times God raised up "deliverers" from among the people to curb the "unbridled domination" of "insolent" princes, and (2) "popular magistrates," appointed to protect the people's liberty against royal aggression (among which are included the parliamentary estates), are entitled and required to restrain tyranny

(4.20.31). Early on Calvin may have conceived this constitutional remedy with one eye on contemporary Lutheran accounts of the "lesser magistrates" and the other on royal persecution of the French Reformed church. However that may be, it was swept into the current of western European resistance theory, along with his traditional reminder that political authority which acts against God abrogates itself and must not be obeyed (4.20.32).

Calvin on Usury. Calvin's undated "letter of advice" *(consilium)* on usury merits inclusion not only because it bears slightly on the monumental debate about the role of Calvinism in the advent of modern capitalism, but as demonstrating his ethical method. Substantively, it surpasses Luther in removing the religious obstacles to capitalist economics by defending the equitable loan contract, the productivity of money, and the morality of profit making without, however, accepting usury as an economic occupation or denying the vicious baseness of much usurious practice. Methodologically, his argument is as much dependent on philosophical concepts (e.g., prudence, moderation, natural equity, justice, and the public good) as on biblical injunctions.

Further Reading: H. Höpfl, *The Christian Polity of John Calvin* (Cambridge: Cambridge University Press, 1982); G. L. Hunt, ed., *Calvinism and the Political Order* (Philadelphia: Westminster, 1965); J. H. Leith, *Calvin's Doctrine of the Christian Life* (Louisville: Westminster–John Knox, 1989); T. H. L. Parker, *Calvin's Old Testament Commentaries* (Edinburgh: T. & T. Clark, 1986); T. Torrance, *Kingdom and Church: A Study in the Theology of the Reformation* (Edinburgh: Oliver & Boyd, 1956).

From *Institutes of the Christian Religion* (1559), Book 3, Chapter 19

7. The third part of this liberty is, that we are not bound before God to any observance of external things which are in themselves indifferent *(adiaphora)*, but that we are now at full liberty either to use or omit them. The knowledge of this liberty is very necessary to us; where it is wanting our consciences will have no rest, there will be no end of superstition. In the present day many think us absurd in raising a question as to the free eating of flesh, the free use of dress and holidays, and similar frivolous trifles, as they think them; but they are of more importance than is commonly supposed. For when once the conscience is entangled in the net, it enters a long and inextricable labyrinth, from which it is afterwards most difficult to escape. When a man begins to doubt whether it is lawful for him to use linen for sheets, shirts, napkins, and handkerchiefs, he will not long be secure as to hemp, and will at last have doubts as to tow; for he will revolve in his mind whether he cannot sup without napkins, or dispense with handkerchiefs. Should he deem a daintier food unlawful, he will afterwards feel uneasy for using loafbread and common eatables, because he will think that his body might possibly be supported on a still meaner food. If he hesitates as to a more genial wine, he will scarcely drink the worst with a good con-

science; at last he will not dare to touch water if more than usually sweet and pure. In fine, he will come to this, that he will deem it criminal to trample on a straw lying in his way. For it is no trivial dispute that is here commenced, the point in debate being, whether the use of this thing or that is in accordance with the divine will, which ought to take precedence of all our acts and counsels. Here some must by despair be hurried into an abyss, while others, despising God and casting off his fear, will not be able to make a way for themselves without ruin. When men are involved in such doubts, whatever be the direction in which they turn, everything they see must offend their conscience. 8. "I know," says Paul, "that there is nothing unclean of itself" (by unclean meaning unholy); "but to him that esteemeth anything to be unclean, it is unclean" (Rom. 14:14). By these words he makes all external things subject to our liberty, provided the nature of that liberty approves itself to our minds as before God. [. . .]

9. It is, however, to be carefully observed, that Christian liberty is in all its parts a spiritual matter, the whole force of which consists in giving peace to trembling consciences, whether they are anxious and disquieted as to the forgiveness of sins, or as to whether their imperfect works, polluted by the infirmities of the flesh, are pleasing to God, or are perplexed as to the use of things indifferent. It is, therefore, perversely interpreted by those who use it as a cloak for their lusts, and they may licentiously abuse the good gifts of God, or who think there is no liberty unless it is used in the presence of men, and, accordingly, in using it pay no regard to their weak brethren. [. . .]

12. The matter still remains uncertain, unless we understand who are the weak and who are the Pharisees; for if this distinction is destroyed, I see not how, in regard to offences, any liberty at all would remain without being constantly in the greatest danger. But Paul seems to me to have marked out most clearly, as well by example as by doctrine, how far our liberty, in the case of offence, is to be modified or maintained. When he adopts Timothy as his companion, he circumcises him: nothing can induce him to circumcise Titus (Acts 16:3; Gal. 2:3). The acts are different, but there is no difference in the purpose or intention; in circumcising Timothy, as he was free from all men, he made himself the servant of all: "Unto the Jews I became as a Jew, that I might gain the Jews; to them that are under the law, as under the law, that I might gain them that are under the law; to them that are without law, as without law (being not without law to God, but under the law to Christ), that I might gain them that are without law. To the weak became I as weak, that I might gain the weak: I am made all things to all men, that I might by all means save some" (1 Cor. 9:20-22). We have here the proper modification of liberty, when in things indifferent it can be restrained with some advantage. What he had in view in firmly resisting the circumcision of Titus, he himself testifies when he thus writes: "But neither Titus, who was with me, being a Greek, was compelled to be circumcised: and that because of false brethren unawares brought in, who came in privily to spy out our liberty which we have in Christ Jesus, that they might bring us into bondage: to whom we gave place by subjection, no, not for an hour, that the truth of the gospel might continue with you" (Gal. 2:3-5). We here see the necessity of vindicating our liberty when, by the unjust exactions of false apostles, it is brought into danger with weak consciences. In

all cases we must study charity, and look to the edification of our neighbour. "All things are lawful for me, but all things edify not. Let no man seek his own, but every man another's wealth" (1 Cor. 10:23f.). [. . .]

14. Since by means of this privilege of liberty which we have described, believers have derived authority from Christ not to entangle themselves by the observance of things in which he wished them to be free, we conclude that their consciences are exempted from all human authority. For it were unbecoming that the gratitude due to Christ for his liberal gift should perish, or that the consciences of believers should derive no benefit from it. We must not regard it as a trivial matter when we see how much it cost our Saviour, being purchased not with silver or gold, but with his own blood (1 Pet. 1:18, 19); so that Paul hesitates not to say that Christ has died in vain, if we place our souls under subjection to men (Gal. 5:1, 4; 1 Cor. 7:23). Several chapters of the Epistle to the Galatians are wholly occupied with showing that Christ is obscured, or rather extinguished to us, unless our consciences maintain their liberty; from which they have certainly fallen, if they can be bound with the chains of laws and constitutions at the pleasure of men. But as the knowledge of this subject is of the greatest importance, so it demands a longer and clearer exposition. For the moment the abolition of human constitutions is mentioned, the greatest disturbances are excited, partly by the seditious, and partly by calumniators, as if obedience of every kind were at the same time abolished and over-thrown.

15. Therefore, lest this prove a stumbling-block to any, let us observe that in man government is twofold: the one spiritual, by which the conscience is trained to piety and divine worship; the other civil, by which the individual is instructed in those duties which, as men and citizens, we are bound to perform. [. . .] To these two forms are commonly given the not inappropriate names of spiritual and temporal jurisdiction, intimating that the former species has reference to the life of the soul, while the latter relates to matters of the present life, not only to food and clothing, but to the enacting of laws which require a man to live among his fellows purely, honourably, and modestly. The former has its seat within the soul, the latter only regulates the external conduct. We may call the one the spiritual, the other the civil kingdom. Now these two, as we have divided them, are always to be viewed apart from each other. When the one is considered, we should call off our minds, and not allow them to think of the other. For there exists in man a kind of two worlds, over which different kings and different laws can preside. By attending to this distinction, we will not erroneously transfer the doctrine of the gospel concerning spiritual liberty to civil order, as if in regard to external government Christians were less subject to human laws, because their consciences are unbound before God, as if they were exempted from all carnal service, because in regard to the Spirit they are free. [. . .]

From Book 4, Chapter 20

1. Having shown above that there is a twofold government in man, and having fully considered the one which, placed in the soul or inward man, relates to eternal life, we

civil = external
(incl. external
morality)

are here called to say something of the other, which pertains only to civil institutions
and the external regulation of manners. For although this subject seems from its nature to be unconnected with the spiritual doctrine of faith, which I have undertaken
to treat, it will appear as we proceed, that I have properly connected them, nay, that I
am under the necessity of doing so, especially while, on the one hand, frantic and
barbarous men are furiously endeavouring to overturn the order established by God,
and on the other, the flatterers of princes, extolling their power without measure,
hesitate not to oppose it to the government of God. Unless we meet both extremes,
the purity of the faith will perish. We may add that it in no small degree concerns us
to know how kindly God has here consulted for the human race, that pious zeal may
the more strongly urge us to testify our gratitude. And first, before entering on the
subject itself, it is necessary to attend to the distinction which we formerly laid down
(3.19.16; 4.10), lest, as often happens to many, we imprudently confound these two
things, the nature of which is altogether different. For some, on hearing that liberty
is promised in the gospel, a liberty which acknowledges no king and no magistrate
among men, but looks to Christ alone, think that they can receive no benefit from
their liberty so long as they see any power placed over them. Accordingly, they think
that nothing will be safe until the whole world is changed into a new form, when
there will be neither courts, nor laws, nor magistrates, nor anything of the kind to
interfere, as they suppose, with their liberty. But he who knows to distinguish between the body and the soul, between the present fleeting life and that which is future and eternal, will have no difficulty in understanding that the spiritual kingdom
of Christ and civil government are things very widely separated. Seeing, therefore, it
is a Jewish vanity to seek and include the kingdom of Christ under the elements of
this world, let us, considering, as Scripture clearly teaches, that the blessings which
we derive from Christ are spiritual, remember to confine the liberty which is promised and offered to us in him within its proper limits. For why is it that the very same
apostle who bids us "stand fast in the liberty wherewith Christ hath made us free,
and be not again entangled with the yoke of bondage" (Gal. 5:1), in another passage
forbids slaves to be solicitous about their state (1 Cor. 7:21), unless it be that spiritual
liberty is perfectly compatible with civil servitude? In this sense the following passages are to be understood: "There is neither Jew nor Greek, there is neither bond
nor free, there is neither male nor female" (Gal. 3:28). Again, "There is neither Greek
nor Jew, circumcision nor uncircumcision, barbarian, Scythian, bond nor free: but
Christ is all and in all" (Col. 3:11). It is thus intimated that it matters not what your
condition is among men, nor under what laws you live, since in them the kingdom
of Christ does not at all consist.

2. Still the distinction does not go so far as to justify us in supposing that the Anabaptist
whole scheme of civil government is matter of pollution, with which Christian men   gov't is
have nothing to do. Fanatics, indeed, delighting in unbridled license, insist and vo-   good!
ciferate that, after we are dead by Christ to the elements of this world, and, being
translated into the kingdom of God, sit among the celestials, it is unworthy of us,
and far beneath our dignity, to be occupied with those profane and impure cares
which relate to matters alien from a Christian man. To what end, they say, are laws
without courts and tribunals? But what has a Christian man to do with courts? Nay,

if it is unlawful to kill, what have we to do with laws and courts? But as we lately taught that that kind of government is distinct from the spiritual and internal kingdom of Christ, so we ought to know that they are not adverse to each other. The former, in some measure, begins the heavenly kingdom in us, even now upon earth, and in this mortal and evanescent life commences immortal and incorruptible blessedness, while to the latter it is assigned, so long as we live among men, to foster and maintain the external worship of God, to defend sound doctrine and the condition of the church, to adapt our conduct to human society, to form our manners to civil justice, to conciliate us to each other, to cherish common peace and tranquillity. All these I confess to be superfluous, if the kingdom of God, as it now exists within us, extinguishes the present life. But if it is the will of God that while we aspire to true piety we are pilgrims upon the earth, and if such pilgrimage stands in need of such aids, those who take them away from man rob him of his humanity. As to their allegation that there ought to be such perfection in the church of God that her guidance should suffice for law, they stupidly imagine her to be such as she never can be found in the community of men. For while the insolence of the wicked is so great, and their iniquity so stubborn, that it can scarcely be curbed by any severity of laws, what do we expect would be done by those whom force can scarcely repress from doing ill, were they to see perfect impunity for their wickedness? [. . .]

4. With regard to the function of magistrates, the Lord has not only declared that he approves and is pleased with it, but, moreover, has strongly recommended it to us by the very honourable titles which he has conferred upon it. To mention a few. When those who bear the office of magistrate are called gods, let no one suppose that there is little weight in that appellation. It is thereby intimated that they have a commission from God, that they are invested with divine authority, and, in fact, represent the person of God, as whose substitutes they in a manner act. This is not a quibble of mine, but is the interpretation of Christ. "If Scripture," says he, "called them gods, to whom the word of God came" (John 10:35). What is this but that the business was committed to them by God, to serve him in their office, and (as Moses and Jehoshaphat said to the judges whom they were appointing over each of the cities of Judah) to exercise judgment, not for man, but for God? To the same effect Wisdom affirms, by the mouth of Solomon, "By me kings reign, and princes decree justice. By me princes rule, and nobles, even all the judges of the earth" (Prov. 8:15, 16). For it is just as if it had been said that it is not owing to human perverseness that supreme power on earth is lodged in kings and other governors, but by divine providence, and the holy decree of him to whom it has seemed good so to govern the affairs of men; since he is present, and also presides in enacting laws and exercising judicial equity. This Paul also plainly teaches when he enumerates offices of rule among the gifts of God, which, distributed variously, according to the measure of grace, ought to be employed by the servants of Christ for the edification of the church (Rom. 12:8). In that place, however, he is properly speaking of the senate of grave men who were appointed in the primitive church to take charge of public discipline. This office, in the Epistle to the Corinthians, he calls *kuberneseis*, "governments" (1 Cor. 12:28). Still, as we see that civil power has the same end in view, there can be no doubt that he is recommending every kind of just government. He speaks

much more clearly when he comes to a proper discussion of the subject. For he says that "there is no power but of God: the powers that be are ordained of God"; that rulers are the ministers of God, "not a terror to good works, but to the evil" (Rom 13:1, 3). To this we may add the examples of saints, some of whom held the offices of kings, as David, Josiah, and Hezekiah; others of governors, as Joseph and Daniel; others of civil magistrates among a free people, as Moses, Joshua, and the judges. Their functions were expressly approved by the Lord. Wherefore no man can doubt that civil authority is, in the sight of God, not only sacred and lawful, but the most sacred, and by far the most honourable, of all stations in mortal life.

7. [...] Though among magisterial offices themselves there are different forms, there is no difference in this respect, that they are all to be received by us as ordinances of God. For Paul includes all together when he says that "there is no power but of God," and that which was by no means the most pleasing of all, was honoured with the highest testimonial — I mean the power of one. This, as carrying with it the public servitude of all (except the one to whose despotic will all is subject), was anciently disrelished by heroic and more excellent natures. But Scripture, to obviate these unjust judgments, affirms expressly that it is by divine wisdom that "kings reign," and gives special command "to honour the king" (Prov. 8:15; 1 Pet. 2:17).

8. And certainly it were a very idle occupation for private men to discuss what would be the best form of polity in the place where they live, seeing these deliberations cannot have any influence in determining any public matter. Then the thing itself could not be defined absolutely without rashness, since the nature of the discussion depends on circumstances. And if you compare the different states with each other, without regard to circumstances, it is not easy to determine which of these has the advantage in point of utility, so equal are the terms on which they meet. Monarchy is prone to tyranny. In an aristocracy, again, the tendency is not less to the faction of a few, while in popular ascendancy there is the strongest tendency to sedition. When these three forms of government, of which philosophers treat, are considered in themselves, I for my part am far from denying that the form which greatly surpasses the others is aristocracy, either pure or modified by popular government, not indeed in itself, but because it very rarely happens that kings so rule themselves as never to dissent from what is just and right, or are possessed of so much acuteness and prudence as always to see correctly. Owing, therefore, to the vices or defects of men, it is safer and more tolerable when several bear rule, that they may thus mutually assist, instruct, and admonish each other, and should any one be disposed to go too far, the others are censors and masters to curb his excess. This has already been proved by experience, and confirmed also by the authority of the Lord himself, when he established an aristocracy bordering on popular government among the Israelites, keeping them under that as the best form, until he exhibited an image of the Messiah in David. And as I willingly admit that there is no kind of government happier than where liberty is framed with becoming moderation, and duly constituted so as to be durable, so I deem those very happy who are permitted to enjoy that form, and I admit that they do nothing at variance with their duty when they strenuously and constantly labour to preserve and maintain it. Nay, even magistrates ought to do their utmost to prevent the liberty, of which they have been appointed guard-

ians, from being impaired, far less violated. If in this they are sluggish or little careful, they are perfidious traitors to their office and their country. But should those to whom the Lord has assigned one form of government, take it upon them anxiously to long for a change, the wish would not only be foolish and superfluous, but very pernicious. If you fix your eyes not on one state merely, but look around the world, or at least direct your view to regions widely separated from one another, you will perceive that divine providence has, not without good cause, arranged that different countries should be governed by different forms of polity. For as only elements of unequal temperature adhere together, so in different regions a similar inequality in the form of government is best. All this, however, is said unnecessarily to those to whom the will of God is a sufficient reason. For if it has pleased him to appoint kings over kingdoms, and senates or burgomasters over free states, whatever be the form which he has appointed in the places in which we live, our duty is to obey and submit.

9. The duty of magistrates, its nature, as described by the word of God, and the things in which it consists, I will here indicate in passing. That it extends to both tables of the law, did Scripture not teach, we might learn from profane writers; for no man has discoursed of the duty of magistrates, the enacting of laws, and the common weal, without beginning with religion and divine worship. Thus all have confessed that no polity can be successfully established unless piety be its first care, and that those laws are absurd which disregard the rights of God, and consult only for men. Seeing then that among philosophers religion holds the first place and that the same thing has always been observed with the universal consent of nations, Christian princes and magistrates may be ashamed of their heartlessness if they make it not their care. We have already shown that this office is specially assigned them by God, and indeed it is right that they exert themselves in asserting and defending the honour of him whose vicegerents they are, and by whose favour they rule. Hence in Scripture holy kings are especially praised for restoring the worship of God when corrupted or overthrown, or for taking care that religion flourished under them in purity and safety. On the other hand, the sacred history sets down anarchy among the vices, when it states that there was no king in Israel, and, therefore, every one did as he pleased (Judges 21:25). This rebukes the folly of those who would neglect the care of divine things and devote themselves merely to the administration of justice among men; as if God had appointed rulers in his own name to decide the earthly controversies, and omitted what was far greater moment, his own pure worship as prescribed by his law. Such views are adopted by turbulent men who, in their eagerness to make all kinds of innovations with impunity, would fain get rid of all the vindicators of violated piety. In regard to the second table of the law, Jeremiah addresses rulers: "Thus saith the Lord, Execute ye judgment and righteousness, and deliver the spoiled out of the hand of the oppressor: and do no wrong, do no violence to the stranger, the fatherless, nor the widow, neither shed innocent blood" (Jer. 22:3). To the same effect is the exhortation in the Psalm: "Defend the poor and fatherless; do justice to the afflicted and needy. Deliver the poor and needy; rid them out of the hand of the wicked" (Ps. 82:3, 4). Moses also declared to the princes whom he had substituted for himself: "Hear the causes between your brethren, and judge righteously between every man and his brother, and the stranger that is with him. Ye shall not respect persons in judgment; but ye shall hear the small as well as the great: ye shall not be afraid of the face of man, for the judgment is God's" (Deut. 1:16). I say nothing as to such passages as these: "He shall not multiply horses to himself, nor cause the people to return to Egypt"; "neither shall he multiply wives to himself; neither shall he greatly multiply to himself silver and gold"; "he shall write him a copy of this law in a book"; "and it shall be with him, and he shall read therein all the days of his life, that he may learn to fear the Lord his God"; "that his heart be not lifted up above his brethren" (Deut. 17:16-20). In here explaining the duties of magistrates, my exposition is intended not so much for the instruction of magistrates themselves, as to teach others why there are magistrates, and to what end they have been appointed by God. We say, therefore, that they are the ordained guardians and vindicators of public innocence, modesty, honour, and tranquillity, so that it should be their only study to provide for the common peace and safety. [. . .]

10. But here a difficult, and as it seems, a perplexing question arises. If all Christians are forbidden to kill, and the prophet predicts concerning the holy mountain of the Lord, that is, the church, "They shall not hurt or destroy" (Isa. 11:9), how can magistrates be at once pious and yet shedders of blood? But if we understand that the magistrate, in inflicting punishment, acts not of himself, but executes the very judgments of God, we shall be disencumbered of every doubt. The law of the Lord forbids to kill; but that murder may not go unpunished, the Lawgiver himself puts the sword into the hands of his ministers, that they may employ it against all murderers. It belongs not to the pious to afflict and hurt; but to avenge the afflictions of the pious, at the command of God, is neither to afflict nor hurt. I wish it could always be present to our mind that nothing is done here by the rashness of man, but all in obedience to the authority of God. When it is the guide, we never stray from the right path, unless, indeed, divine justice is to be placed under restraint, and not allowed to take punishment on crimes. [. . .] Now, if it is true justice in them to pursue the guilty and impious with drawn sword, to sheathe the sword and keep their hands pure from blood, while nefarious men wade through murder and slaughter, so far from redounding to the praise of their goodness and justice, would be to incur the guilt of the greatest impiety; provided always they eschew reckless and cruel asperity, and that tribunal which may be justly termed a rock on which the accused must founder. For I am not one of those who would either favour an unseasonable severity, or think that any tribunal could be accounted just that is not presided over by mercy, that best and surest counsellor of kings, and, as Solomon declares, "upholder of the throne" (Prov. 20:28). This, as was truly said by one of old, should be the primary endowment of princes. The magistrate must guard against both extremes; he must neither by excessive severity rather wound than cure, nor by a superstitious affection of clemency fall into the most cruel inhumanity, by giving way to soft and dissolute indulgence to the destruction of many. It was well said by one under the empire of Nerva, "It is indeed a bad thing to live under a prince with whom nothing is lawful, but a much worse to live under one with whom all things are lawful."

11. As it is sometimes necessary for kings and states to take up arms in order to execute public vengeance, the reason assigned furnishes us with the means of estimat-

War

ing how far the wars which are thus undertaken are lawful. For if power has been given them to maintain the tranquillity of their subjects, repress the seditious movements of the turbulent, assist those who are violently oppressed, and animadvert on crimes, can they use it more opportunely than in repressing the fury of him who disturbs both the ease of individuals and the common tranquillity of all; who excites seditious tumult, and perpetrates acts of violent oppression and gross wrongs? If it becomes them to be the guardians and maintainers of the laws, they must repress the attempts of all alike by whose criminal conduct the discipline of the laws is impaired. Nay, if they justly punish those robbers whose injuries have been afflicted only on a few, will they allow the whole country to be robbed and devastated with impunity? Since it makes no difference whether it is by a king or by the lowest of the people that a hostile and devastating inroad is made into a district over which they have no authority, all alike are to be regarded and punished as robbers. Natural equity and duty, therefore, demand that princes be armed not only to repress private crimes by judicial inflictions, but to defend the subjects committed to their guardianship whenever they are hostilely assailed. Such even the Holy Spirit, in many passages of the Scripture, declares to be lawful.

defensive

12. [. . .] But all magistrates must here be particularly cautious not to give way, in the slightest degree, to their passions. Or rather, whether punishments are to be inflicted, they must not be borne headlong by anger, nor hurried away by hatred, nor burn with implacable severity; they must, as Augustine says (cf. *Ep.* 153.3 [see above, p. 120]), "even pity a common nature in him in whom they punish an individual fault"; or whether they have to take up arms against an enemy, that is, an armed robber, they must not readily catch at the opportunity, nay, they must not take it when offered, unless compelled by the strongest necessity. For if we are to do far more than that heathen demanded, who wished war to appear as desired peace, assuredly all other means must be tried before having recourse to arms. In fine, in both cases, they must not allow themselves to be carried away by any private feeling but be guided solely by regard for the public. Acting otherwise, they wickedly abuse their power which was given them not for their own advantage, but for the good and service of others. On this right of war depends the right of garrisons, leagues, and other civil munitions. By garrisons I mean those which are stationed in states for defence of the frontiers; by leagues, the alliances which are made by neighbouring princes, on the ground that if any disturbance arise within their territories they will mutually assist each other and combine their forces to repel the common enemies of the human race; under civil munitions I include everything pertaining to the military art.

13. Lastly, we think it proper to add, that taxes and imposts are the legitimate revenues of princes, which they are chiefly to employ in sustaining the public burdens of office. These, however, they may use for the maintenance of their domestic state, which is in a manner combined with the dignity of the authority which they exercise. Thus we see that David, Hezekiah, Josiah, Jehoshaphat, and other holy kings, Joseph also, and Daniel, in proportion to the office which they sustained, without offending piety, expended liberally of the public funds; and we read in Ezekiel that a very large extent of territory was assigned to kings (Ezek. 48:21). In that passage, indeed, he is depicting the spiritual kingdom of Christ, but still he bor-

rows his representation from lawful dominion among men. Princes, however, must remember, in their turn, that their revenues are not so much private chests as treasuries of the whole people (this Paul testifies, Rom. 13:6), which they cannot, without manifest injustice, squander or dilapidate; or rather, that they are almost the blood of the people, which it were the harshest inhumanity not to spare. They should also consider that their levies and contributions and other kinds of taxes are merely subsidies of the public necessity, and that it is tyrannical rapacity to harass the poor people with them without cause. These things do not stimulate princes to profusion and luxurious expenditure (there is certainly no need to inflame the passions, when they are already, of their own accord, inflamed more than enough), but seeing it is of the greatest consequence that whatever they venture to do, they should do with a pure conscience, it is necessary to teach them how far they can lawfully go, lest, by impious confidence, they incur the divine displeasure. Nor is this doctrine superfluous to private individuals, that they may not rashly and petulantly stigmatise the expenditure of princes, though it should exceed the ordinary limits.

[margin: on used # - never for excess!]

14. In states the thing next in importance to the magistrates is laws, the strongest sinews of government, or, as Cicero calls them after Plato, the soul, without which the office of the magistrate cannot exist; just as, on the other hand, laws have no vigour without the magistrate. Hence nothing could be said more truly than that the law is a dumb magistrate, the magistrate a living law. As I have undertaken to describe the laws by which Christian polity is to be governed, there is no reason to expect from me a long discussion on the best kind of laws. The subject is of vast extent, and belongs not to this place. I will only briefly observe, in passing, what the laws are which may be piously used with reference to God, and duly administered among men. This I would rather have passed in silence, were I not aware that many dangerous errors are here committed. For there are some who deny that any commonwealth is rightly framed which neglects the law of Moses, and is ruled by the common law of nations. How perilous and seditious these views are, let others see: for me it is enough to demonstrate that they are stupid and false. We must attend to the well-known division which distributes the whole law of God, as promulgated by Moses, into the moral, the ceremonial, and the judicial law, and we must attend to each of these parts, in order to understand how far they do, or do not, pertain to us. Meanwhile, let no one be moved by the thought that the judicial and ceremonial laws relate to morals. For the ancients who adopted this division, though they were not unaware that the two latter classes had to do with morals, did not give them the name of moral, because they might be changed and abrogated without affecting morals. They give this name specially to the first class, without which true holiness of life and an immutable rule of conduct cannot exist.

[margin: moral law ①]

15. The moral law, then (to begin with it), being contained under two heads, the one of which simply enjoins us to worship God with pure faith and piety, the other to embrace men with sincere affection, is the true and eternal rule of righteousness prescribed to the men of all nations and of all times, who would frame their life agreeably to the will of God. For his eternal and immutable will is that we are all to worship him and mutually love one another. The ceremonial law of the Jews was a tutelage by which the Lord was pleased to exercise, as it were, the childhood of that people, until the fulness of the time should come when he was fully to manifest his wisdom to the world, and exhibit the reality of those things which were then adumbrated by figures (Gal. 3:24; 4:4). The judicial law, given them as a kind of polity, delivered certain forms of equity and justice, by which they might live together innocently and quietly. And as that exercise in ceremonies properly pertained to the doctrine of piety, inasmuch as it kept the Jewish church in the worship and religion of God, yet was still distinguishable from piety itself; so the judicial form, though it looked only to the best method of preserving that charity which is enjoined by the eternal law of God, was still something distinct from the precept of love itself. Therefore, as ceremonies might be abrogated without at all interfering with piety, so, also, when these judicial arrangements are removed, the duties and precepts of charity can still remain perpetual. But if it is true that each nation has been left at liberty to enact the laws which it judges to be beneficial, still these are always to be tested by the rule of charity, so that while they vary in form, they must proceed on the same principle. Those barbarous and savage laws, for instance, which conferred honour on thieves, allowed the promiscuous intercourse of the sexes, and other things even fouler and more absurd, I do not think entitled to be considered as laws, since they are not only altogether abhorrent to justice, but to humanity and civilised life.

16. What I have said will become plain if we attend, as we ought, to two things connected with all laws — viz. the enactment of the law and the equity on which the enactment is founded and rests. Equity, as it is natural, cannot be the same in all, and therefore ought to be proposed by all laws, according to the nature of the thing enacted. As constitutions have some circumstances on which they partly depend, there is nothing to prevent their diversity, provided they all alike aim at equity as their end. Now, as it is evident that the law of God which we call moral is nothing else than the testimony of natural law, and of that conscience which God has engraven on the minds of men, the whole of this equity of which we now speak is prescribed in it. Hence it alone ought to be the aim, the rule, and the end of all laws. Wherever laws are formed after this rule, directed to this aim, and restricted to this end, there is no reason why they should be disapproved by us, however much they may differ from the Jewish law, or from each other. The law of God forbids to steal. The punishment appointed for theft in the civil polity of the Jews may be seen in Exodus 22:1. Very ancient laws of other nations punished theft by exacting the double of what was stolen, while subsequent laws made a distinction between theft manifest and not manifest. Other laws went the length of punishing with exile, or with branding, while others made the punishment capital. Among the Jews the punishment of the false witness was to "do unto him as he had thought to have done with his brother" (Deut. 19:19). In some countries, the punishment is infamy, in others hanging, in others crucifixion. All laws alike avenge murder with blood, but the kinds of death are different. In some countries, adultery was punished more severely, in others more leniently. Yet we see that amidst this diversity they all tend to the same end. For they all with one mouth declare against those crimes which are condemned by the eternal law of God — viz. murder, theft, adultery, and false witness; though they agree not as to the mode of punishment. This is not necessary, nor even expedient. There may be

a country which, if murder were not visited with fearful punishments, would instantly become a prey to robbery and slaughter. There may be an age requiring that the severity of punishments should be increased. If the state is in troubled condition, those things from which disturbances usually arise must be corrected by new edicts. In time of war, civilisation would disappear amid the noise of arms, were not men overawed by an unwonted severity of punishment. In sterility, in pestilence, were not stricter discipline employed, all things would grow worse. One nation might be more prone to a particular vice, were it not most severely repressed. How malignant were it, and invidious of the public good, to be offended at this diversity, which is admirably adapted to retain the observance of divine law. The allegation that insult is offered to the law of God enacted by Moses where it is abrogated, and other new laws are preferred to it, is most absurd. Others are not preferred when they are more approved, not absolutely, but from regard to time and place, and the condition of the people, or when those things are abrogated which were never enacted for us. The Lord did not deliver it by the hand of Moses to be promulgated in all countries, and to be everywhere enforced; but having taken the Jewish nation under his special care, patronage, and guardianship, he was pleased to be specially its legislator, and as became a wise legislator, he had special regard to it in enacting laws. [. . .]

[handwritten margin note: Jewish civil law was not for everyone — the details will vary from time/place]

18. Let such persons [zealous litigants] then understand that judicial proceedings are lawful to him who makes a right use of them; and the right use, both for the pursuer and for the defender, is for the latter to sist [present] himself on the day appointed, and, without bitterness, urge what he can in his defence, but only with the desire of justly maintaining his rights; and for the pursuer, when undeservedly attacked in his life or fortunes, to throw himself upon the protection of the magistrate, state his complaint, and demand what is just and good; while, far from any wish to hurt or take vengeance — far from bitterness or hatred — far from the ardour of strife, he is rather disposed to yield and suffer somewhat than to cherish hostile feelings towards his opponent. On the contrary, when minds are filled with malevolence, corrupted by envy, burning with anger, breathing revenge, or, in fine, so inflamed by the heat of the contest, that they in some measure lay aside charity, the whole pleading, even of the justest cause, cannot but be impious. For it ought to be an axiom among all Christians, that no plea, however equitable, can be rightly conducted by any one who does not feel as kindly towards his opponent as if the matter in dispute were amicably transacted and arranged. Some one, perhaps, may here break in and say, that such moderation in judicial proceedings is so far from being seen, that an instance of it would be a kind of prodigy. I confess that in these times it is rare to meet with an example of an honest litigant; but the thing itself, untainted by the accession of evil, ceases not to be good and pure. When we hear that the assistance of the magistrate is a sacred gift from God, we ought the more carefully to beware of polluting it by our fault.

[handwritten margin note: on litigation (it can be good)]

19. Let those who distinctly condemn all judicial distinction know that they repudiate the holy ordinance of God, and one of those gifts which to the pure are pure, unless, indeed, they would charge Paul with a crime, because he repelled the calumnies of his accusers, exposing their craft and wickedness, and at the tribunal claimed for himself a privilege of a Roman citizen, appealing, when necessary, from

the governor to Caesar's judgment-seat. There is nothing contrary to this in the prohibition which binds all Christians to refrain from revenge, a feeling which we drive far away from all Christian tribunals. For whether the action be of civil nature, he only takes the right course who, with innocuous simplicity, commits his cause to the judge as the public protector, without any thought of returning evil for evil (which is the feeling of revenge); or whether the action is of a graver nature, directed against a capital offence, the accuser required is not one who comes into court, carried away by some feeling of revenge or resentment from some private injury, but one whose only object is to prevent the attempts of some bad men to injure the commonwealth. But if you take away the vindictive mind, you offend in no respect against that command which forbids Christians to indulge revenge. But they are not only forbidden to thirst for revenge, they are also enjoined to wait for the hand of the Lord, who promises that he will be the avenger of the oppressed and afflicted. "But those who call upon the magistrate to give assistance to themselves or others anticipate the vengeance of the heavenly Judge." By no means, for we are to consider that the vengeance of the magistrate is the vengeance not of man but of God, which, as Paul says, he exercises by the ministry of man for our good (Rom. 13:4).

20. No more are we at variance with the words of Christ who forbids us to resist evil, and adds: "Whosoever shall smite thee on thy right cheek, turn to him the other also. And if any man will sue thee at the law, and take away thy coat, let him have thy cloak also" (Matt. 5:39, 40). He would have the minds of his followers to be so abhorrent to everything like retaliation, that they would sooner allow the injury to be doubled than desire to repay it. From this patience we do not dissuade them. For verily Christians were to be a class of men born to endure affronts and injuries, and be exposed to the iniquity, imposture, and derision of abandoned men, and not only so, but were to be tolerant of all these evils; that is, so composed in the whole frame of their minds, that, on receiving one offence, they were to prepare themselves for another, promising themselves nothing during the whole of life but the endurance of a perpetual cross. Meanwhile, they must do good to those who injure them and pray for those who curse them, and (this is their only victory) strive to overcome evil with good (Rom. 12:20, 21). Thus affected, they will not seek eye for eye and tooth for tooth, (as the Pharisees taught their disciples to long for vengeance), but (as we are instructed by Christ), they will allow their body to be mutilated and their goods to be maliciously taken from them, prepared to remit and spontaneously pardon those injuries the moment they have been inflicted. This equity and moderation, however, will not prevent them, with entire friendship for their enemies, from using the aid of the magistrate for the preservation of their goods, or, from zeal for the public interest, to call for the punishment of the wicked and pestilential man, whom they know nothing will reform but death. All these precepts are truly expounded by Augustine, as tending to "prepare the just and pious man patiently to sustain the malice of those whom he desires to become good, that he may thus increase the number of the good, not add himself to the number of the bad by imitating their wickedness. Moreover, it pertains more to the preparation of the heart which is within than to the work which is done openly, that patience and good-will may be retained within the secret of the heart, and that may be done openly which

678

we see may do good to those whom we ought to wish well" (Augustine, *Ep.* 138.12f.).
[. . .]

duties of citizens

22. The first duty of subjects towards their rulers is to entertain the most honourable views of their office, recognising it as a delegated jurisdiction from God, and *1) respect* on that account receiving and reverencing them as the ministers and ambassadors of God. For you will find some who show themselves very obedient to magistrates, and would be unwilling that there should be no magistrates to obey, because they know this is expedient for the public good, and yet the opinion which those persons have of magistrates is that they are a kind of necessary evils. But Peter requires something more of us when he says: "Honour the king" (1 Pet. 2:17); and Solomon, when he says: "My son, fear thou the Lord and the king" (Prov. 24:21). For under the term honour, the former includes a sincere and candid esteem, and the latter, by joining the king with God, shows that he is invested with a kind of sacred veneration and dignity. We have also the remarkable injunction of Paul: "Be subject not only for wrath, but also for conscience sake" (Rom. 13:5). By this he means that subjects, in submitting to princes and governors, are not to be influenced merely by fear (just as those submit to an armed enemy who see vengeance ready to be executed if they resist), but because the obedience which they yield is rendered to God himself, inasmuch as their power is from God. I speak not of the men as if the mask of dignity could cloak folly, or cowardice, or cruelty, or wicked or flagitious manners, and thus acquire for vice the praise of virtue; but I say that the station itself is deserving of honour and reverence, and that those who rule should, in respect of their office, be held by us in esteem and veneration.

23. From this, a second consequence is that we must with ready minds prove *2) obedience* our obedience to them, whether in complying with edicts, or in paying tribute, or in undertaking public offices and burdens which relate to the common defence, or in executing any other orders. [. . .] Under this obedience, I comprehend the restraint which private men ought to impose on themselves in public, not interfering with public business, or rashly encroaching on the province of the magistrate, or attempting anything at all of a public nature. If it is proper that anything in a public ordinance should be corrected, let them not act tumultuously, or put their hands to a work where they ought to feel that their hands are tied, but let them leave it to the cognisance of the magistrate, whose hand alone here is free. My meaning is, let them not dare to do it without being ordered. For when the command of the magistrate is given, they too are invested with public authority. For as, according to the common saying, the eyes and ears of the prince are his counsellors, so one may not improperly say that those who by his command have the charge of managing affairs, are his hands. [. . .]

= don't get involved in their role

25. But if we have respect to the word of God, it will lead us farther and make us subject not only to the authority of those princes who honestly and faithfully perform their duty toward us, but all princes, by whatever means they have so become, although there is nothing they less perform than the duty of princes. For though the Lord declared that a ruler to maintain our safety is the highest gift of his beneficence, and prescribes to rulers themselves their proper sphere, he at the same time declares that of whatever description they may be, they derive their power from none but

Even if they're bad princes

him. Those, indeed, who rule for the public good are true examples and specimens of his beneficence, while those who domineer unjustly and tyrannically are raised up by him to punish the people for their iniquity. Still all alike possess that sacred majesty with which he has invested lawful power. [. . .]

29. [. . .] Since the duty of all is not to look behind them, that is, not to inquire into the duties of one another, but to submit each to his own duty, this ought especially to be exemplified in the case of those who are placed under the power of others. Wherefore, if we are cruelly tormented by a savage, if we are rapaciously pillaged by an avaricious or luxurious, if we are neglected by a sluggish, if, in short, we are persecuted for righteousness' sake by an impious and sacrilegious prince, let us first call up the remembrance of our faults, which doubtless the Lord is chastising by such scourges. In this way humility will curb our impatience. And let us reflect that it belongs not to us to cure these evils, that all that remains for us is to implore the help of the Lord in whose hands are the hearts of kings, and inclinations of kingdoms. "God standeth in the congregation of the mighty; he judgeth among the gods" (Ps. 82:1). Before his face shall fall and be crushed all kings and judges of the earth who have not kissed his anointed, who have enacted unjust laws to oppress the poor in judgment, and do violence to the cause of the humble, to make widows a prey, and plunder the fatherless.

30. Herein is the goodness, power, and providence of God wondrously displayed. At one time he raises up manifest avengers from among his own servants, and gives them his command to punish accursed tyranny, and deliver his people from calamity when they are unjustly oppressed; at another time he employs for this purpose the fury of men who have other thoughts and other aims. Thus he rescued his people Israel from the tyranny of Pharaoh by Moses; from the violence of Chusa, the king of Syria, by Othniel; and from other bondage by other kings or judges. Thus he tamed the pride of Tyre by the Egyptians; the insolence of the Egyptians by the Assyrians; the ferocity of the Assyrians by the Chaldeans; the confidence of Babylon by the Medes and Persians — Cyrus having previously subdued the Medes, while the ingratitude of the kings of Judah and Israel, and their impious contumacy after all his kindness, he subdued and punished — at one time by the Assyrians, at another by the Babylonians. All these things, however, were not done in the same way. The former class of deliverers being brought forward by the lawful call of God to perform such deeds, when they took up arms against kings, did not at all violate that majesty with which kings are invested by divine appointment, but armed from heaven they, by a greater power, curbed a less, just as kings may lawfully punish their own satraps. The latter class, though they were directed by the hand of God, as seemed to him good, and did his work without knowing it, had nought but evil in their thoughts.

31. [. . .] Although the Lord takes vengeance on unbridled domination, let us not therefore suppose that that vengeance is committed to us, to whom no command has been given but to obey and suffer. I speak only of private men. For when popular magistrates have been appointed to curb the tyranny of kings (as the Ephori, who were opposed to kings among the Spartans, or Tribunes of the people to consuls among the Romans, or Demarchs to the senate among the Athenians; and

perhaps there is something similar to this in the power exercised in each kingdom by the three orders, when they hold their primary diets), so far am I from forbidding these officially to check the undue license of kings, that if they connive at kings when they tyrannise and insult over the humbler of the people, I affirm that their dissimulation is not free from nefarious perfidy; because they fraudulently betray the liberty of the people, while knowing that, by the ordinance of God, they are its appointed guardians.

32. But in that obedience which we hold to be due to the commands of rulers, we must always make the exception, nay, must be particularly careful that it is not incompatible with obedience to him to whose will the wishes of all kings should be subject, to whose decrees their commands must yield, to whose majesty their sceptres must bow. And, indeed, how preposterous were it, in pleasing men, to incur the offence of him for whose sake you obey men! The Lord, therefore, is King of kings. When he opens his sacred mouth, he alone is to be heard, instead of all and above all. We are subject to the men who rule over us, but subject only in the Lord. If they command anything against him let us not pay the least regard to it, nor be moved by all the dignity which they possess as magistrates — a dignity to which no injury is done when it is subordinated to the special and truly supreme power of God. On this ground Daniel denies that he had sinned in any respect against the king when he refused to obey his impious decree (Dan. 6:22), because the king had exceeded his limits, and not only been injurious to men, but, by raising his horn against God, had virtually abrogated his own power. On the other hand, the Israelites are condemned for having too readily obeyed the impious edict of the king. For, when Jeroboam made the golden calf, they forsook the temple of God, and, in submissiveness to him, revolted to new superstitions (1 Kings 12:28). With the same facility posterity had bowed before the decrees of their kings. For this they are severely upbraided by the Prophet (Hos. 5:11). So far is the praise of modesty from being due to that pretence by which flattering courtiers cloak themselves, and deceive the simple, when they deny the lawfulness of declining anything imposed by their kings; as if the Lord had resigned his own rights to mortals by appointing them to rule over their fellows, or as if earthly power were diminished when it is subjected to its author, before whom even the principalities of heaven tremble as suppliants. I know the imminent peril to which subjects expose themselves by this firmness, kings being most indignant when they are contemned. As Solomon says, "The wrath of a king is as messengers of death" (Prov. 16:14). But since Peter, one of heaven's heralds, has published the edict "We ought to obey God rather than men" (Acts 5:29), let us console ourselves with the thought that we are rendering the obedience which the Lord requires, when we endure anything rather than turn aside from piety. And that our courage may not fail, Paul stimulates us by the additional consideration (1 Cor. 7:23), that we were redeemed by Christ at the great price which our redemption cost him, in order that we might not yield a slavish obedience to the depraved wishes of men, far less do homage to their impiety.

Translation: Henry Beveridge (Edinburgh, 1845).

Letters of Advice 6.1 (On Usury)

From John Calvin to one of his friends.

I have not personally experienced this, but I have learned from the example of others how perilous it is to respond to the question for which you seek my counsel. For if we should totally prohibit the practice of usury, we would restrain consciences more rigidly than God himself. But if we permit it, then some, under this guise, would be content to act with unbridled license, unable to abide any limits.

If I were writing to you alone, I would have no fear of such a thing, for your prudence and the moderation of your heart are well known to me. But because you seek counsel for another, I fear that if I say anything he might permit himself more than I would prefer. Nonetheless, since I have no doubt that, in the light of human nature and the matter at hand, you will thoughtfully consider the most expedient thing to do, I will share what I think.

First, there is no scriptural passage that totally bans all usury. For Christ's statement, which is commonly esteemed to manifest this, but which has to do with lending (Luke 6:35), has been falsely applied to usury. Furthermore, as elsewhere, when he rebukes the sumptuous guests and the ambitious invitations of the rich, he commands us to call instead the blind, the lame, and the other poor of the streets, who cannot repay. In so doing he corrects the world's vicious custom of lending money [only to those who can repay] and urges us, instead, to lend to those from whom no hope of repayment is possible.

Now we are accustomed to lending money where it will be safe. But we ought to help the poor, where our money will be at risk. For Christ's words far more emphasise our remembering the poor than our remembering the rich. Nonetheless, we need not conclude that all usury is forbidden.

The law of Moses (Deut. 23:19) is quite diplomatic, restraining us to act only within the bounds of equity and human reason. To be certain, it would be desirable if usurers were chased from every country, even if the practice were unknown. But since that is impossible, we ought at least to use it for the common good.

Passages in both the prophets and the Psalms display the Holy Spirit's anger against usurers. There is a reference to a vile evil (Ps. 55:11 Vulgate) that has been translated by the word *usura*. But since the Hebrew word *tok* can generally mean "defraud," it can be translated otherwise than "usury."

Even where the prophet specifically mentions usury, it is hardly a wonder that he mentions it among the other evil practices (Neh. 5:10). The reason is that the more often usury is practised with illicit license, the more often cruelty and other fraudulent activities arise.

What am I to say, except that usury almost always travels with two inseparable companions: tyrannical cruelty and the art of deception. This is why the Holy Spirit elsewhere advises all holy men, who praise and fear God, to abstain from usury, so much so that it is rare to find a good man who also practises usury.

The prophet Ezekiel (22:12) goes still further, for in citing the horrible case in which the vengeance of God has been kindled against the Jews, he uses the two Hebrew words *neshek* and *tarbith* — a form of usury so designated in Hebrew because of the manner in which it eats away at its victims. *Tarbith* means "to increase," or "add to," or "gain," and with good reason. For anyone interested in expanding his personal profit will take, or rather snatch, that gain from someone else. But undoubtedly the prophets only condemned usury as severely as they did because it was expressly prohibited for Jews to do. Hence when they rejected the clear commandment of God, they merited a still sterner rebuke.

Today, a similar objection against usury is raised by some who argue that since the Jews were prohibited from practising it, we too, on the basis of our fraternal union, ought not to practise it. To that I respond that a political union is different. The situation in which God brought the Jews together, combined with other circum- *context?* stances, made commerce without usury apt among them. Our situation is quite different. For that reason, I am unwilling to condemn it, so long as it is practised with equity and charity.

The pretext that both St. Ambrose and Chrysostom cite is too frivolous in my judgment, that is, that money does not engender money. Does the sea or the earth engender it? I receive a fee from renting a house. Is that where money grows? Houses, in turn, are products of the trades, where money is also made. Even the value of a house can be exchanged for money. And what? Is money not more productive than merchandise or any other possession one could mention? It is lawful to make money by renting a piece of ground, yet unlawful to make it from money? What? when you buy a field, is money not making money?

How do merchants increase their wealth? By being industrious, you answer. I readily admit what even children can see, that if you lock your money in a chest, it will not increase. Moreover, no one borrows money from others with the intention of hiding it or not making a profit. Consequently, the gain is not from the money, but from profit.

We may therefore conclude that, although at first such subtleties appear convincing, upon closer examination they evaporate, since there is no substance to them. Hence, I conclude that we ought not to judge usury according to a few passages of Scripture, but in accordance with the principle of equity.

An example ought to clarify the matter. Take a rich man whose wealth lies in possessions and rents but who has no money on hand. A second, whose wealth is somewhat more moderate — though less than the first — soon comes into money. If an opportunity should arise, the second person can easily buy what he wants, while the first will have to ask the latter for a loan. It is in the power of the second, under the rules of bargaining, to impose a fee on the first's goods until he repays, and in this manner the first's condition will be improved, although usury has been practised. *the good of others*

Now, what makes a contract just and honest or unjust and dishonest? Has not the first fared better by means of an agreement involving usury by his neighbour than if the second had compelled him to mortgage or pawn his goods? To deny this is to play with God in a childish manner, preferring words over the truth itself. As if it were in our power, by changing words, to transform virtue into vice or vice into virtue. I certainly have no quarrel here.

I have said enough; you will be able to weigh this more diligently on your own.

Nonetheless, I should hope that you will always keep in mind that what we must bring under judgment are not words but deeds themselves.

Now I come to the exceptions. For, as I said at the beginning, we must proceed with caution, as almost everyone is looking for some word to justify his intention. Hence, I must reiterate that when I approve of some usury, I am not extending my approval to all its forms. Furthermore, I disapprove of anyone engaging in usury as his form of occupation. Finally, I grant nothing without listing these additional exceptions.

The first is that no one should take interest (usury) from the poor, and no one, destitute by virtue or indigence or some affliction or calamity, should be forced into it. The second exception is that whoever lends should not be so preoccupied with gain as to neglect his necessary duties, nor, wishing to protect his money, disdain his poor brothers. The third exception is that no principle be followed that is not in accord with natural equity, for everything should be examined in the light of Christ's precept: Do unto others as you would have them do unto you. This precept is applicable every time. The fourth exception is that whoever borrows should make at least as much, if not more, than the amount borrowed. In the fifth place, we ought not to determine what is lawful by basing it on the common practice or in accordance with the iniquity of the world, but should base it on a principle derived from the word of God. In the sixth place, we ought not to consider only the private advantage of those with whom we deal, but should keep in mind what is best for the common good. For it is quite obvious that the interest a merchant pays is a public fee. Thus we should see that the contract will benefit all rather than hurt. In the seventh place, one ought not to exceed the rate that a country's public laws allow. Although this may not always suffice, for such laws quite often permit what they are able to correct or repress. Therefore one ought to prefer a principle of equity that can curtail abuse.

But rather than valuing my own opinion over yours, I desire only that you act in such a humane way that nothing more need be said on the matter. With that in mind, I have composed these thoughts more out of a desire to please you than out of any confidence of satisfying you. But owing to your kindness toward me, I know you will take to heart what I have offered.

I commit you to God, my most excellent and honoured friend. May he preserve you and your family. Amen.

Translation: Mary Beaty and Benjamin W. Farley (Louisville: Westminster–John Knox Press, 1991). Used with permission.

John Knox

(1505-72)

During the reign of Mary Tudor several eminent Protestant refugees from England sojourning in Reformed cities on the Continent wrote impassioned tracts exhorting all parts of the civil commonwealth to fulfill the duties to which God's law bound them. The Edwardine bishop, John Ponet, exiled in Strasbourg, formulated these duties in terms about equally indebted to Reformed theology, renaissance classicism, late medieval scholasticism, and the English common law tradition (see pp. 695-701 below). By contrast, John Knox and Christopher Goodman, contemporary exiles in Calvin's Geneva, concentrated in a more narrowly scriptural manner on the duties of religious reformation flowing from the first table of God's revealed law. While the labors of Knox and Goodman lacked Ponet's theoretical breadth, they displayed a compensating theological intensity. For enduring interest, Knox's addresses of 1558 surpass Goodman's *How Superior Powers ought to be Obeyed of their Subjects* of the same year, chiefly on account of their recasting of Christian political thought along Old Testament lines.

Penned in the wake of Mary Tudor's re-Catholicizing measures, her persecution of Protestants and marital alliance with the Spanish throne, these fiery pieces are conventionally described as anti-Marian resistance literature of a Calvinist stripe. They all advocate an active civil defense of divine law against the impious and unjust policies of monarchs, a defense led and authorized by the nobility or "lower magistrates" who have the divinely instituted office of restraining, correcting, and in the last resort removing their sovereigns. In the case of the Scottish polity to which Knox principally addresses himself, the meaning of this civil defense was nuanced by the more fluid situation obtaining between the reforming "lairds"; the calculating French regent, Mary of Guise; and the Catholic episcopal establishment. Not surprisingly, these clarion calls remained an embarrassment to Calvin and an annoyance to Queen Elizabeth I.

The prophetic self-consciousness that dominated Knox's communications in exile had continuously defined his vocation from the time of his youthful ministry to the rebellious Scottish lairds besieged in St. Andrews Castle in 1547 for murderously avenging the burning of the Protestant preacher George Wishart, and his subsequent servitude of eighteen months in a French galley. His ministry in the England of Edward VI, although distinguished by a royal chaplaincy and offer of a bishopric (declined), provided him with ample occasions for criticism and exhortation, notably over the popish compromises of national liturgical reform. With the accession of Mary Tudor, the growing Catholic repressiveness of Mary of Guise, and the reforming vacillation of the Scottish nobility, the scope and urgency of Knox's prophetic mission vastly increased, particularly in his native land. His Scottish missionary work of 1555-56 proved so effective among the powerful magnates that the Catholic bishops were forced to wait until his return to the Continent to excommunicate him.

Their sentence was the formal reason for his three admonitory appeals of 1558 — to the regent, the nobility, and the commonality of Scotland. His other notorious political writing of that year, the *First Blast of the Trumpet Against the Monstrous Regiment of Women,* was, by his own account, called forth primarily by the lawless and blasphemous conduct of the English "Jezebel." Albeit his vituperative and hysterical rhetoric and rigid Old Testament hermeneutic do not enhance the theological stature of these communications, nevertheless they offer an original combination of noteworthy political themes that include: *(a)* the permanent political office of the prophet made necessary by the systemic violation of God's law by human law, and *(b)* the universal civil duty of suppressing idolatry, rooted in the Christian commonwealth's covenantal relationship with God and fulfilled in a plurality of divinely authorized civil vocations.

a. Having cast off the priestly vestment of sacramental grace, the minister of God dons the prophet's mantle of saving admonition. The prophet does not *administer* God's law in popish fashion, but *proclaims* it. Above all, he proclaims God's accusing and avenging law that condemns and punishes the sinner. Alike the wayward subject and ruler deserve condemnation, on account of the plainness of God's law, made visible in nature, in history, and in scriptural testimony. Thus the English commonwealth stands convicted of violating the divine prohibition of female rule, by the scriptural text most authoritatively, but also by the clear witness to woman's frailty and her subjection to the male in the animal world, by historical records, Roman law, daily experience, and rational judgment — an argument remarkably reminiscent of John Fortescue's. Even more, the rulers and people of England and Scotland (excepting the faithful Protestant remnant) stand convicted of violating the divine prohibition of idolatry by continuing to adhere to popish religion, in defiance of Scripture's unclouded testimony concerning true belief, worship, and community. There is no appeal to civil or ecclesiastical tradition, custom, or statute that can mitigate these communal offenses against God's revealed will.

Repeatedly Knox discerns God's *present* command, violation, and punishment in God's historical dealings with Israel, reading the Old Testament as a legal casebook, a catalogue of juridical precedents (Kyle 1984, 44, 48), with two striking results. The first is the binding authority for all Christian commonwealths of the Mosaic "judicial" requiring the capital punishment of idolaters — a future English Puritan theme. The second is the scrutability of God's historical providence. For their rebellion against God's law, England and Scotland have (like Israel and Judah) been betrayed "into the hands of strangers"; by the device of royal marriages, their "liberties, laws, commodities, and fruits" have been "translated" to "the power and distribution" of the Spanish king and French dauphin *(First Blast)*.

b. His addresses to the Scottish estates portray the suppression of idolatry as simultaneously a religious and a civil duty. His letter to the commonality emphasizes the equal public obligation of all Christians, on account of their equally standing under God's law, judgment, and elective grace — i.e., their single vocation within Christ's covenant of salvation. His original move, not present in earlier theological uses of covenantal ideas (in, e.g., Bullinger, Tyndale, Hooper, or Calvin), is to conceive every reforming Christian polity on analogy with the Israelite as having entered into a corporate "league" or "covenant" with God, in which God's promise of collective blessing and protection is met by a collective commitment to the purification of common service and worship *(Appellation)*. Such, in Knox's view, were the covenants embraced by Edward VI's government and by the Scottish reformation parliament of 1560, after which both polities were obliged to put to death their incorrigibly popish monarchs *(Appellation;* cf. Mason 1994, xxii-xxiii).

The single covenantal obligation of upholding God's law is articulated in a plurality of reciprocal and complementary tasks appointed to the three estates. So Knox advises the regent of Scotland that God has exalted her *above* the commonwealth, despite her natural unsuitability, for the reformation of religion and administration of God's inflexible justice *(Letter to the Regent)*. He exhorts the Scottish nobles to deliver God's innocent prophets from unjust ecclesiastical sentences and to ensure true Christian instruction to their subjects, forcibly removing and punishing their popish deceivers, and correcting and repressing even the monarch's idolatry — short of capital punishment, as that measure is apparently reserved to their English counterparts. To the commonality he assigns more modest tasks toward the maintenance of true preaching and right sacramental administration.

Further Reading: R. L. Greaves, *Theology and Revolution in the Scottish Reformation: Studies in the Thought of John Knox* (Grand Rapids: Christian University Press, 1980); R. G. Kyle, *The Mind of John Knox* (Lawrence, Kans.: Coronado Press, 1984); R. A. Mason, ed., *John Knox: On Rebellion* (Cambridge: Cambridge University Press, 1994).

From *The First Blast of the Trumpet Against the Monstrous Regiment of Women*

The Kingdom appertains to our God. Wonder it is that amongst so many pregnant wits as the isle of Great Britain hath produced, so many godly and zealous preachers as England did sometime nourish, and amongst so many learned and men of grave judgment as this day by Jezebel are exiled, none is found so stout of courage, so faithful to God, nor loving to their native country, that they dare admonish the inhabitants of that isle how abominable before God is the empire or rule of a wicked woman, yea, of a traitoress and bastard; and what may a people or nation, left destitute of a lawful head, do by the authority of God's word in electing and appointing common rulers and magistrates. That isle, alas, for the contempt and horrible abuse of God's mercies offered, and for the shameful revolting to Satan from Christ Jesus and from his Gospel once professed, doth justly merit to be left in the hands of their own counsel and so to come to confusion and bondage of strangers.

But yet I fear that this universal negligence of such as sometimes were esteemed watchmen shall rather aggravate our former ingratitude than excuse this our universal and ungodly silence in so weighty a matter. We see our country set forth for a prey to foreign nations; we hear the blood of our brethren, the members of Christ Jesus, most cruelly to be shed; and the monstrous empire of a cruel woman (the secret counsel of God excepted) we know to be the only occasion of these miseries; and yet with silence we pass the time as though the matter did nothing appertain to us. But the contrary examples of the ancient prophets move me to doubt of this our fact. For Israel did universally decline from God by embracing idolatry under Jeroboam. In which they did continue even unto the destruction of their commonwealth (1 Kings 12:25–13:10). And Judah with Jerusalem did follow the vile superstition and open iniquity of Samaria (Ezek. 16:46f.); but yet ceased not the prophets of God to admonish the one and the other, yea, even after that God had poured forth his plagues upon them. For Jeremiah did write to the captives in Babylon and did correct their errors, plainly instructing them who did remain in the midst of that idolatrous nation (Jer. 29:1-28). Ezekiel from the midst of his brethren prisoners in Chaldea did write his vision to those that were in Jerusalem, and, sharply rebuking their vices, assured them that they should not escape the vengeance of God by reason of their abominations committed (Ezek. 7–9).

The same prophets, for comfort of the afflicted and chosen saints of God who did lie hid amongst the reprobate of that age (as commonly doth the corn amongst the chaff), did prophesy and before speak the changes of kingdoms, the punishments of tyrants, and the vengeance which God would execute upon the oppressors of his people (Isa. 13, Jer. 46, Ezek. 36). The same did Daniel and the rest of the prophets, every one in their season.

By whose examples and by the plain precept, which is given to Ezekiel, commanding him that he shall say to the wicked: "Thou shalt die the death" (Ezek. 33:8), we in this our miserable age are bound to admonish the world and the tyrants thereof of their sudden destruction, to assure them, and to cry unto them, whether they list to hear or not, that "the blood of the saints, which by them is shed, continually cries and craves vengeance in the presence of the Lord of hosts" (cf. Rev. 6:10). And further, it is our duty to open the truth revealed unto us unto the ignorant and blind world, unless that to our own condemnation we list to wrap up and hide the talent committed to our charge. I am assured that God hath revealed to some in this our age that it is more than a monster in nature that a woman shall reign and have empire above man. And yet with us all there is such silence as if God therewith were nothing offended. [. . .]

688

From *The Appellation of John Knox from the cruel and most unjust sentence pronounced against him by the false bishops and clergy of Scotland to the nobility and estates of Scotland*

[. . .] And thus much for the right of my appellation which, in the bowels of Jesus Christ, I require your Honours not to esteem as a thing superfluous and vain, but that ye admit it and also accept me in your protection and defence, that by you assured I may have access to my native country which I never offended, to the end that freely and openly in the presence of the whole realm I may give my confession of all such points as this day be in controversy. And also that you, by your authority which ye have of God, compel such as of long time have blinded and deceived both yourselves and the people to answer to such things as shall be laid to their charge. But, lest some doubt remain that I require more of you than you of conscience are bound to grant, in few words I hope to prove my petition to be such as without God's heavy displeasure ye cannot deny. My petition is that ye, whom God hath appointed heads in your commonwealth, with single eye do study to promote the glory of God, to provide that your subjects be rightly instructed in his true religion, that they be defended from all oppression and tyranny, that true teachers may be maintained, and such as blind and deceive the people, together also with all idle bellies which do rob and oppress the flock, may be removed and punished as God's law prescribeth. And to the performance of every one of these do your offices and names, the honours and benefits which ye receive, the law of God universally given to all men, and the examples of most godly princes, bind and oblige you.

My purpose is not greatly to labour to prove that your whole study ought to be to promote the glory of God; neither yet will I study to allege all reasons that justly may be brought to prove that ye are not exalted to reign above your brethren as men without care and solicitude. For these be principles so grafted in nature that very ethnics [pagans] have confessed the same. For seeing that God only hath placed you in his chair, hath appointed you to be his lieutenants, and by his own seal hath marked you to be magistrates and to rule above your brethren, to whom nature nevertheless hath made you like in all points (for in conception, birth, life, and death ye differ nothing from the common sort of men, but God only, as said is, hath promoted you and of his especial favour hath given unto you this prerogative to be called gods [cf. Ps. 82:6f.]), how horrible ingratitude were it then that you should be found unfaithful to him that thus hath honoured you. And further, what a monster were it that you should be proved unmerciful to them above whom ye are appointed to reign as fathers above their children.

Because, I say, that very ethnics have granted that the chief and first care of princes and of such as be appointed to rule above others ought to be to promote the glory and honour of their gods and to maintain that religion which they supposed to have been true, and that their second care was to maintain and defend the subjects committed to their charge in all equity and justice, I will not labour to shew unto you what ought to be your study in maintaining God's true honour, lest that in so doing I should seem to make you less careful over God's true religion than were the ethnics over their idolatry. But because other petitions may appear more hard and difficult to be granted, I purpose briefly, but yet freely, to speak what God by his word doth assure me to be true: to wit, first, that in conscience you are bound to punish malefactors and to defend innocents imploring your help; secondarily, that God requireth of you to provide that your subjects be rightly instructed in his true religion and that the same by you be reformed whensoever abuses do creep in by malice of Satan and negligence of men; and last, that ye are bound to remove from honour and to punish with death (if the crime so require) such as deceive the people or defraud them of that food of their souls, I mean God's lively word. [. . .]

It is not enough that you abstain from violent wrong and oppression, which ungodly men exercise against their subjects; but ye are further bound, to wit, that ye rule above them for their wealth, which ye cannot do if that ye either by negligence, not providing true pastors, or yet by your maintenance of such as be ravening wolves, suffer their souls to starve and perish for lack of the true food which is Christ's Evangel sincerely preached. It will not excuse you in his presence, who will require accompt of every talent committed to your charge, to say that ye supposed that the charge of the souls had been committed to your bishops. No, no, my lords, for ye cannot escape God's judgment. For if your bishops be proved to be no bishops but deceivable thieves and ravening wolves, (which I offer myself to prove by God's word, by law and councils, yea, by the judgment of all the godly learned from the primitive church to this day), then shall your permission and defense of them be reputed before God a participation with their theft and murder. For thus accused the prophet Isaiah the princes of Jerusalem: "Thy princes," saith he, "are apostates," that is, obstinate refusers of God, "and they are companions of thieves" (1:23). This grievous accusation was laid against them, albeit that they ruled in that city which sometime was called holy, where then were the temple, rites, and ordinances of God, because that not only they were wicked themselves but chiefly because they maintained wicked men, their priests and false prophets, in honours and authority. If they did not escape this accusation of the Holy Ghost in that age, look ye neither to escape the accusation nor judgment which is pronounced against the maintainers of wicked men: to wit, that the one and the other shall drink the cup of God's wrath and vengeance together. [. . .]

If you do think that the reformation of religion and defence of the afflicted doth not appertain to you because you are no kings but nobles and estates of a realm, in two things you are deceived. Former, in that you do not advert that David requireth as well that the princes and judges of the earth be learned and that they serve and fear God, as that he requireth that the kings repent (Ps. 2:10f.). If you therefore be judges and princes, as no man can deny you to be, then by the plain words of David you are charged to be learned, to serve and fear God, which ye cannot do if you despise the reformation of his religion. And this is your first error. The second is that ye neither know your duty which ye owe to God, neither yet your authority which of him ye have received, if ye for pleasure or fear of any earthly man despise God's true religion and contemn your brethren that in his name call for your support. Your duty is to hear the voice of the eternal, your God, and unfeignedly to study to follow his precepts, who, as is before said, of especial mercy hath promoted you to honours and dignity. His chief and principal precept is that with reverence ye receive and embrace his only beloved son Jesus, that ye promote to the uttermost of your powers his true religion, and that ye defend your brethren and subjects whom he hath put under your charge and care.

Now, if your king be a man ignorant of God, enemy to his true religion, blinded by superstition, and a persecutor of Christ's members, shall ye be excused if with silence ye pass over his iniquity? Be not deceived, my lords, ye are placed in authority for another purpose than to flatter your king in his folly and blind rage: to wit, that as with your bodies, strength, riches, and wisdom ye are bound to assist and defend him in all things which by your advice he shall take in hand for God's glory and for the preservation of his commonwealth and subjects, so by your gravities, counsel, and admonition ye are bound to correct and repress whatsoever ye know him to attempt expressedly repugning to God's word, honour, and glory, or what ye shall espy him to do, be it by ignorance or be it by malice, against his subjects great or small. Of which last part of your obedience if ye defraud your king, ye commit against him no less treason than if ye did extract from him your due and promised support what time by his enemies injustly he were pursued.

But this part of their duty, I fear, do a small number of the nobility of this age rightly consider; neither yet will they understand that for that purpose hath God promoted them. For now the common song of all men is, we must obey our kings, be they good or be they bad, for God hath so commanded. But horrible shall the vengeance be that shall be poured forth upon such blasphemers of God, his holy name and ordinance. For it is no less blasphemy to say that God hath commanded kings to be obeyed when they command impiety than to say that God by his precept is author and maintainer of all iniquity. True it is God hath commanded kings to be obeyed, but like true it is that in things which they commit against his glory, or when cruelly without cause they rage against their brethren, the members of Christ's body, he hath commanded no obedience, but rather he hath approved, yea, and greatly rewarded such as have opposed themselves to their ungodly commandments and blind rage, as in the examples of the three children, of Daniel, and Ebedmelech it is evident. The three children would neither bow nor stoop before the golden image at the commandment of the great King Nebuchadnezzar (Dan. 3:16-18). Daniel did openly pray, his windows being open, against the established law of Darius and of his council (6:10). And Ebedmelech feared not to enter in before the presence of Zedekiah and boldly to defend the cause and innocency of Jeremiah the prophet, whom the king and his council had condemned to death (Jer. 38:7-9).

[. . .] Advert and take heed, my lords, that the men who had condemned the prophet were the king, his princes, and council, and yet did one man accuse them all of iniquity and did boldly speak in the defence of him whose innocence he was persuaded. And the same, I say, is the duty of every man in his vocation, but chiefly of the nobility which is joined with their kings to bridle and repress their folly and blind rage. Which thing, if the nobility do not, neither yet labour to do, as they are traitors to their kings, so do they provoke the wrath of God against themselves and against the realm in which they abuse the authority which they have received of God to maintain virtue and to repress vice. [. . .]

After that Moses had declared what was true religion, to wit, to honour God as he commanded, adding nothing to his word, neither yet diminishing anything from it, after also that vehemently he had exhorted the same law to be observed, he denounceth the punishment against the transgressors in these words: "If thy brother, son, daughter, wife, or neighbour, whom thou lovest as thine own life, solicitate thee secretly, saying, let us go serve other gods whom neither thou nor thy fathers have known, consent not to hear him, hear him not, let not thine eye spare him, shew him no indulgency or favour, hide him not, but utterly kill him; let thy hand be the first upon him that he may be slain, and after the hand of the whole people" (Deut. 13:6-9). Of these words of Moses are two things appertaining to our purpose to be noted. Former, that such as solicitate only to idolatry ought to be punished to death without favour or respect of person. For he that will not suffer man to spare his son, his daughter, nor his wife, but straitly commandeth punishment to be taken upon the idolaters (have they never so nigh conjunction with us) will not wink at the idolatry of others of what estate or condition soever they be. [. . .]

The second is that the punishment of such crimes as are idolatry, blasphemy and others that touch the majesty of God doth not appertain to kings and chief rulers only, but also to the whole body of that people and to every man, and according to that possibility and occasion which God doth minister to revenge the injury done against his glory, what time that impiety is manifestly known. [. . .]

If any think that this my affirmation touching the punishment of idolaters be contrary to the practice of the apostles who, finding the gentiles in idolatry, did call them to repentance, requiring no such punishment, let the same man understand that the gentiles before the preaching of Christ lived, as the Apostle [Paul] speaketh, without God in the world, drowned in idolatry, according to the blindness and ignorance in which then they were holden as a profane nation whom God had never openly avowed to be his people, had never received in his household, neither given unto them laws to be kept in religion nor polity. And therefore did not his Holy Ghost, calling them to repentance, require of them any corporal punishment according to the rigour of the law, unto the which they were never subjects, as they that were strangers from the commonwealth of Israel. But if any think that after that the Gentiles were called from their vain conversation and, by embracing Christ Jesus, were received in the number of Abraham's children and so made one people with the Jews believing; if any think, I say, that then they were not bound to the same obedience which God required of his people Israel what time he confirmed his league and covenant with them, the same man appeareth to make Christ inferior to Moses and contrarious to the law of his heavenly Father. For if the contempt or transgression of Moses' law was worthy of death, what should we judge the contempt of Christ's ordinance to be (I mean after they be once received)? And if Christ be not come to dissolve but to fulfil the law of his heavenly Father (Matt 5:17), shall the liberty of his Gospel be an occasion that the especial glory of his Father be trodden underfoot and regarded of no man? God forbid. [. . .]

And therefore I fear not to affirm that it had been the duty of the nobility, judges, rulers and people of England not only to have resisted and againstanded Mary, that Jezebel whom they call their queen, but also to have punished her to the death, with all the sort of her idolatrous priests, together with all such as should have assisted her what time that she and they openly began to suppress Christ's Evangel, to shed the blood of the saints of God and to erect that most devilish idolatry, the papistical abominations and his usurped tyranny, which once most justly by common oath was banished from that realm.

From *Letter To His Beloved Brethren the Commonalty of Scotland*

[...] Neither would I that ye should esteem the reformation and care of religion less to appertain to you because ye are no kings, rulers, judges, nobles, nor in authority. Beloved brethren, ye are God's creatures, created and formed to his own image and similitude, for whose redemption was shed the most precious blood of the only beloved son of God, to whom he hath commanded his Gospel and glad-tidings to be preached, and for whom he hath prepared the heavenly inheritance, so that ye will not obstinately refuse and disdainfully contemn the means which he hath appointed to obtain the same, to wit, his blessed Evangel, which now he offereth unto you to the end that ye may be saved. For the Gospel and glad-tidings of the kingdom truly preached is the power of God to the salvation of every believer, which to credit and receive, you, the commonalty, are no less addebted than be your rulers and princes.

For albeit God hath put and ordained distinction and difference betwixt king and subjects, betwixt the rulers and the common people in the regiment and administration of civil policies, yet in the hope of the life to come he hath made all equal. For as in Christ Jesus the Jew hath no greater prerogative than hath the Gentile, and man than hath the woman, the learned than the unlearned, the lord than the servant, but all are one in him (cf. Gal. 3:28), so is there but one way and means to attain to the participation of his benefits and spiritual graces, which is a lively faith working by charity. And therefore I say that it doth no less appertain to you, beloved brethren, to be assured that your faith and religion be grounded and established upon the true and undoubted word of God than to your princes or rulers. For as your bodies cannot escape corporal death, if with your princes ye eat or drink deadly poison (although it be by ignorance or negligence), so shall ye not escape the death everlasting, if with them ye profess a corrupt religion. Yea, except in heart ye believe and with mouth ye confess the Lord Jesus to be the only saviour of the world, (which ye cannot do, except ye embrace his Evangel offered), ye cannot escape death and damnation (Hab. 2:4). For as the just liveth by his own faith, so doth the unfaithful perish by his infidelity (Mark 16:16; John 3:18). And as true faith is engendered, nourished, and maintained in the hearts of God's elect by Christ's Evangel truly preached, so is infidelity and unbelief fostered by concealing and repressing the same. And thus, if ye look for the life everlasting, ye must try if ye stand in faith, and if ye would be assured of a true and lively faith, ye must needs have Christ Jesus truly preached unto you.

And this is the cause, dear brethren, that so oft I repeat and so constantly I affirm that to you it doth no less appertain than to your kings or princes to provide that Christ Jesus be truly preached amongst you, seeing that without his true knowledge can neither of you both attain to salvation. And this is the point wherein I say all man is equal: that as all be descended from Adam, by whose sin and inobedience did death enter into the world, so it behoved all that shall obtain life to be ingrafted in one, that is, in the Lord Jesus, who, being the just servant, doth by his knowledge justify many (cf. Rom. 5:12, 18; 11:24; Isa. 53:11): to wit, all that unfeignedly believe in him. [. . .]

Not only I, but with me also divers other godly and learned men, do offer unto you our labours faithfully to instruct you in the ways of the eternal our God and in the sincerity of Christ's Evangel, which this day by the pestilent generation of Antichrist (I mean by the pope and by his most ungodly clergy) are almost hid from the eyes of men. We offer to jeopard our lives for the salvation of your souls, and by manifest Scriptures to prove that religion which amongst you is maintained by fire and sword, to be vain, false, and diabolical. We require nothing of you but that patiently ye will hear our doctrine, which is not ours but is the doctrine of salvation revealed to the world by the only Son of God, and that ye will examine our reasons, by the which we offer to prove the papistical religion to be abominable before God. And last we require that by your powers the tyranny of those cruel beasts (I mean of priests and friars) may be bridled till we have uttered our minds in all matters this day debatable in religion. If these things, in the fear of God, ye grant to me and unto others that unfeignedly for your salvation and for God's glory require the same, I am assured that of God ye shall be blessed, whatsoever Satan shall devise against you. But and if ye contemn or refuse God who thus lovingly offereth unto you salvation and life, ye shall neither escape plagues temporal, which shortly shall apprehend you, neither yet the torment prepared for the devil and for his angels, except by speedy repentance ye return to the Lord, whom now ye refuse, if that ye refuse the messengers of his Word.

But yet I think ye doubt what ye ought and may do in this so weighty a matter. In few words I will declare my conscience in the one and in the other. Ye ought to prefer the glory of God, the promoting of Christ his Evangel, and the salvation of your souls to all things that be in earth; and ye, although ye be but subjects, may lawfully require of your superiors — be it of your king, be it of your lords, rulers, and powers, that they provide for you true preachers and that they expel such as under the names of pastors devour and destroy the flock, not feeding the same, as Christ Jesus hath commanded. And if in this point your superiors be negligent or yet pretend to maintain tyrants in their tyranny, most justly ye may provide true teachers for yourselves, be it in your cities, towns, or villages; them ye may maintain and defend against all that shall persecute them and by that means shall labour to defraud you of that most comfortable food of your souls, Christ's Evangel truly preached. Ye may, moreover, withhold the fruits and profits which your false bishops and clergy most injustly receive of you unto such time as they be compelled faithfully to do their charge and duties which is to preach unto Christ Jesus truly, rightly to minister his sacraments according to his own institution, and so to watch for the salvation of your souls, as is commanded by Christ Jesus himself and by his Apostles Paul and Peter. [. . .]

And if ye think that ye are innocent because ye are not the chief authors of such iniquity, ye are utterly deceived. For God doth not only punish the chief offenders, but with them doth he damn the consenters to iniquity; and all are judged to consent that knowing impiety committed give no testimony that the same displeaseth them.

Text: Geneva, 1558; reprinted in R. A. Mason, ed., *John Knox: On Rebellion* (Cambridge University Press, 1994).

John Ponet

(ca. 1514-56)

The political radicalism of John Ponet's *A Shorte Treatise of Politike Power,* published in 1556, was both a sign of the exceptional times and an exceptional sign of the times. Its advocacy of resistance to blasphemous tyrants in church and commonwealth placed it alongside the anti-Marian tracts of Ponet's fellow exiles, John Knox and Christopher Goodman. While Ponet's political outlook was hardly more extreme than theirs, it was more incongruous, biographically considered — so incongruous that his authorship of this treatise became obscured within decades of its publication. Generations of English readers were little disposed to identify the cryptic initials on the early editions with the Strasbourg exile who had been a promising Henrician scholar, highly placed Edwardine bishop, intimate protégé of Archbishop Thomas Cranmer, and staunch supporter of his ecclesiastical legacy.

Popular incredulity was not so much misled as superficial. While readers correctly surmised that English Protestant dignitaries were not given to extolling the legal subjection of the monarch and the subject's duty of civil rebellion, Ponet's posture was, nonetheless, intelligible against the background of the English common law tradition that included John of Salisbury's legal radicalism as well as Fortescue's conservative constitutionalism, and in the light of the current theological humanism, his acquaintance with Plato, Aristotle, and Cicero, as well as the late medieval schoolmen (among whom Marsilius of Padua in expurgated versions was enjoying English popularity), and Calvin's thought mediated largely by Peter Martyr Vermigli (Lockwood O'Donovan 1991, 97). Drawing on these sources, Ponet stressed the active obligations of ruler and subject alike to sustain a righteous, peaceful polity in accordance with natural and divine laws of justice and equity.

The passages below contain some noteworthy theoretical features.

a. Ponet's opening defense of the principles of private and public morality as divine commandments revealed to human reason rather than inventions of atheistic reason is directed chiefly against the Machiavellian politics imputed to Queen

Mary's "time-serving" prelates and advisers. Only when moral principles are understood as the instruments of divine governance, he argues, can human political authority be understood as God's instrument for promulgating and vindicating his law for the common life.

b. From the origin of political authority in God's postdiluvian institution of capital punishment for the human crime of murder arises its limitation: that it extends *only* over man's "body and life" and, within limits, over those temporal possessions that "breed controversy and discord," and emphatically *not* over the "soul and conscience" — a strikingly narrow circumscription reminiscent of the early Luther.

c. Ponet's radical doctrine of the people's *permanent* sovereign discretion over the form of civil rule (savoring of Ockham, Marsilius, and conciliarist theory) is moderated by his advocacy of the mixed state, i.e., Fortescue's "royal and political rule," as the most stable and just law-polity. Importantly, the principle of men's equal subjection to the restraining force of the law obliges the ruler to obey not only natural and divine laws, but just human customs and statutes.

d. The constitutional and corporatist aspects of Ponet's argument are qualified by his investing of absolute political authority in the individual's conscience. By ascertaining and applying God's will revealed in nature and Scripture, it is the final arbiter of political right and wrong, and the spring of obedience or disobedience to established power. Such is the public authority of the private man's conscience that it may justly dictate tyrannicide as the course of action required by the gravity of the ruler's iniquity and the negligence of the people's duly constituted representatives.

Further Reading: W. S. Hudson, ed., *John Ponet (c. 1513-1572): Advocate of Limited Monarchy* (Chicago: University of Chicago Press, 1942); P. Lake and M. Dowling, *Protestantism and the National Church in Sixteenth Century England* (London: Croom Helm, 1987); J. Lockwood O'Donovan, *The Theology of Law and Authority in the English Reformation* (Atlanta: Scholars Press, 1991); B. Peardon, "The Politics of Polemic: John Ponet's 'Short Treatise of Politic Power' and Contemporary Circumstance, 1553-1556," *Journal of British Studies* 22, no. 1 (1982): 35-49; Q. Skinner, *The Foundations of Modern Political Thought,* vol. 2 (Cambridge: Cambridge University Press, 1978); M. Walzer, *The Revolution of the Saints* (Cambridge, Mass.: Harvard University Press, 1965); D. H. Wollmann, "The Biblical Justification for Resistance to Authority in Ponet's and Goodman's Polemics," *Sixteenth Century Journal* 13, no. 4 (1982): 29-41.

From *A Short Treatise of political power, and of the true Obedience which Subjects owe to Kings and other civil Governors, with an Exhortation to all true natural Englishmen*

Whereof political power groweth, wherefore it was ordained, and the right use and duty of it. [3] As oxen, sheep, goats, and such other unreasonable creatures cannot for lack of reason rule themselves, but must be ruled by a more excellent creature, that is man; so man, albeit he have reason, yet because through the fall of the first man his reason is wonderfully corrupt, and sensuality hath gotten the upper hand, is not able by himself to rule himself, but must have a more excellent governor. The worldlings thought this governor was their own reason. They thought they might by their own reason do what them lusted, not only in private things, but also in public. Reason they thought to be the only cause that men first assembled together in companies, that commonwealths were made, that policies [polities] were well governed and long continued. But men see that such were utterly blinded and deceived in their imaginations, their doings and inventions (seemed they never so wise), were so easily and so soon (contrary to their expectation) overthrown.

[4] Where is the wisdom of the Grecians? Where is the fortitude of the Assyrians? Where is both the wisdom and force of the Romans become? All is vanished away, nothing almost left to testify that they were, but that which well declareth that their reason was not able to govern them. Therefore were such as were desirous to know the perfect and only governor of all constrained to seek further than themselves, and so at length to confess that it was one God that ruled all. By him we live, we have our being, and are moved. He made us, and not we ourselves. We be his people and the sheep of his pasture. He made all things for man, and man he made for himself, to serve and glorify him. He hath taken upon him the order and government of man, his chief creature, and prescribed him a rule, how he should behave himself, what he should do, and what he may not do.

This rule is the law of nature, first planted and graffed only in the mind of man, then after (for that his mind was through sin defiled, filled with darkness, and encumbered with many doubts) set forth in writing in the Decalogue or Ten Commandments; and after reduced by Christ our Saviour to these two words: "Thou shalt love thy Lord God above all things, and thy neighbour as thyself." The latter part whereof he also thus expoundeth: "Whatsoever ye will that men do unto you, do ye even so to them" (Matt 22:37-39; 7:12).

[5] In this law is comprehended all justice, the perfect way to serve and glorify God, and the right mean to rule every man particularly, and all men generally; and the only stay to maintain every commonwealth. This is the touchstone to try every man's doings (be he king or beggar) whether they be good or evil. By this all men's laws be discerned, whether they be just or unjust, godly or wicked. As for an example. Those that have authority to make laws in a commonwealth make this law that no pins shall be made but in their own country. It seemeth but a trifle. Yet if by this means the people may be kept from idleness it is a good and just law and pleaseth God. For idleness is a vice wherewith God is offended; and the way to offend him in breach of these commandments: Thou shalt not steal, thou shalt not kill, thou shalt not be a whoremonger, etc. For all these evils come of idleness. On the other side, if the people be well occupied in other things, and the people of another country live by pin making, and uttering [marketing] them, then if there should be a law made that they might not sell them to their neighbours of the other country, otherwise well occupied, it were a wicked and an unjust law. For taking away the means whereby they live, a means is devised to kill them with famine, and so is not only this commandment broken: "Thou shalt not kill" (Exod. 20:13; Deut. 5:17), but also the general law that sayeth: "Thou shalt [p. 6] love thy neighbour as thyself." And "what-

697

soever ye will that men do unto you, even so do you unto them" (Lev. 19:18; Matt. 7:12). For you yourselves would not be killed with hunger. [. . .]

Again, a prince forceth his subjects (under the name of request) to lend him that they have, which they do unwillingly; and yet for fear of a worse turn they must seem to be content therewith. Afterward he causeth to be assembled in a parliament such as perchance lent nothing, or else such as dare not displease him. They to please him remit this general debt. This is a wicked, ungodly, and unjust law. For they do not, as they would be done unto, but be an occasion that a great number be undone, their children for lack of sustenance perish through famine, and their servants forced to steal, and perchance to commit murder. So that if men will weigh well this order and law that God hath prescribed to man . . . [7] they may soon learn to try good from evil, godliness from ungodliness, right from wrong. And it is so plain and easy to be understood that no ignorance can or will excuse him that therein offendeth.

Against the offenders of this law there was no corporal punishment ordained in this world till after the destruction of the world with the great flood. For albeit Cain and Lamech had committed horrible murders, yet were they not corporally punished, but had a protection of God that none should lawfully hurt them. But after the flood, when God saw his gentleness and patience could not work his creatures to do their duties unforced, but iniquity prevailed and mischief daily increased, and one murdered and destroyed another, then was he constrained to change his leniency into severity, and to add corporal pains to those that would not follow, but transgress his ordinances. And so he made this law, which he declared to Noah: "He that sheddeth the blood of man, his blood shall be shed by man. For man is made after the image of God" (Gen. 9:6f.).

By this ordinance and law he instituteth political power and giveth authority to men to make more laws. [8] For he that giveth man authority over the body and life of man, because he would have man to live quietly with man, that all might serve him quietly in holiness and righteousness all the days of their life, it cannot be denied but he gave him authority over goods, lands, possessions, and all such things as might breed controversies and discords, and so hinder and let that he might not be served and glorified as he requireth. . . . But whether this authority to make laws, or the power to execute the same, shall be and remain in one person alone or in many it is not expressed, but left to the discretion of the people to make so many and so few as they think necessary for the maintenance of the state. Whereupon in some places they have been content to obey such laws as were made by one, as the Israelites were with those that Moses ordained, the Lacedemonians with those that Lycurgus made, the Athenians [9] with those that Solon gave them. And in some places with such as were made by certain outchosen men, as in Rome by the ten men. And in some they received none but such as all the multitude agreed unto. Likewise in some countries they were content to be governed, and the laws executed, by one king or judge, in some places by many of the best sort, in some places by the people of the lowest sort, and in some places also by the king, nobility, and the people altogether. . . . For where that mixed state was exercised, there did the commonwealth longest continue. But yet every kind of these states tended to one end, that is, to the maintenance of justice, to the wealth and benefit of the whole multitude, and not of the superior and governors alone. And when they saw that the governors abused their authority they altered the state. As among the Israelites, for the iniquity of the children of Samuel their judge, from judges to kings; among the Romans, for the tyranny and oppression that [10] Tarquinius used over the people (as the chief occasion) and afterward for his sons' lewdness (as the outward occasion), from kings to consuls, and so from consuls (for their evil demeanour) to *Decemviri* and *Triumviri* . . . ; and so from change to change, till it came to the state imperial, yet always preserving and maintaining the authority, albeit they altered and changed the kind of government. For the ethnics [i.e., pagans] themselves, being led only by the law of nature and their own reason, saw that without political power and authority mankind could not be preserved, nor the world continued.

Whether kings, princes, and other governors be subject to God's laws, and the positive laws of their countries. [42] Neither is that power and authority which kings, princes, and other magistrates of justice exercise only called a power, but also the authority that parents have over their children and masters over their servants is also called a power; and neither be the parents nor masters the power itself, but they be ministers and executors of the power, being given [43] unto them by God. . . . And they [kings], being but executors of God's laws and men's just ordinances, be also not exempted from them, but be bounden to be subject and obedient unto them. For good and just laws of man be God's power and ordinances, and they are but ministers of the laws, and not the law's self. And if they were exempt from the laws, and so it were lawful for them to do what them lusteth, their authority being of God, it might be said that God allowed their tyrannic robbery of their subjects, killing them without law, and so God the author of evil, which were a great blasphemy. Justinian the emperor well considered when he made this saying to be put into the body of the laws. "It is a worthy saying" (saith he) "for the majesty of him that is in authority, to confess that the prince is subject to the laws, the authority of the prince doth so much [44] depend on the authority of the laws." And certainly it is more honour than the honour of the empire to submit the principality unto the laws. For indeed laws be made that the wilful self-will of men should not rule, but that they should have a line to lead them, as they might not go out of the way of justice, and that (if any would say they did them wrong) they might allege the law for their warrant and authority. It is also a principle of all laws grounded on the law of nature that every man should use himself and be obedient to that law that he will others be bounden unto. For otherwise he taketh away that equality (for there is no difference between the head and foot concerning the use and benefit of the laws) whereby commonwealths be maintained and kept up. What equality (I beseech you) should there be where the subject should do to his ruler all the ruler would and the ruler to the subject that the ruler lusted?

In what things, and how far subjects are bound to obey their princes and governors. [50] Thus they [Queen Mary's bishops] go about to blear men's eyes to confirm and increase their devilish kingdom. But popish prelates' practices are no warrant to discharge a Christian man's conscience. He must seek what God will have him do, and not what the subtlety and violence of wicked men will force him to do. He may not rob Peter to clothe Paul, nor take from God his due to give it unto civil power; neither may he make confusion of the powers, but yield unto every one that is his due; nor yet obeying the inferior's commandment leave the commandment of the highest undone. "Yield unto Caesar those things that be Caesar's" (sayeth Christ) "and unto God those things that be God's" (Matt. 22:21). Civil power is a power and ordinance of God appointed to certain things, but no general minister over all things. God hath not given it power over the one and the best part of man, that is, the soul and the conscience of man, but only over the other and the worst part of man, that is, the body and those things that belong unto this temporal life of man.

Whether it be lawful to depose an evil governor, and kill a tyrant. [106] [...] As God hath ordained magistrates to hear and determine private men's matters, and to punish their vices, so also will he that the magistrates' doings be called to account and reckoning, and their vices corrected and punished by the body of the whole congregation or commonwealth.

As it is manifest by the memory of the ancient office of the high Constable of England, unto whose authority it pertained not only to summon the king personally before the parliament or other courts of judgment (to answer and receive according to justice) but also upon just occasion to commit him unto ward.

Kings, princes, and governors have their authority [107] of the people, as all laws, usages, and policies [i.e., polities] do declare and testify. For in some places and countries they have more and greater authority, in some places less. And in some the people have not given this authority to any other, but retain and exercise it themselves. And is any man so unreasonable to deny that the whole may do as much as they have permitted one member to do, or those that have appointed an office upon trust have not authority upon just occasion (as the abuse of it) to take away that they gave? All laws do agree that men may revoke their proxies and letters of attorney when it pleaseth them: much more when they see their proctors and attorneys abuse it.

But now to prove ... that it is lawful to kill a tyrant: there is no man can deny but that the ethnics (albeit they had not the right and perfect true knowledge of God) were endued with the knowledge of the law of nature. For it is no private law to a few or certain people, but common to all: not written in books, but graffed in the hearts of men; not made by man, but ordained of God: which we have not learned, received, or read, but have taken, sucked, and drawn it out of nature. Whereunto we are not taught but made, not instructed but seasoned, and [108] (as St. Paul sayeth) man's conscience bearing witness of it (Rom. 2:15). This law testifieth to every man's conscience that it is natural to cut away an incurable member, which (being suffered) would destroy the whole body.

Kings, princes, and other governors, albeit they are the heads of a political body, yet they are not the whole body. And though they be the chief members, yet they are but members; neither are the people ordained for them, but they are ordained for the people. [...]

[110] Good kings, governors, and states in time past took it to be the greatest honour that could be, not to take cities and realms to their own use (when they were called to aid and relieve the oppressed) as princes do nowadays, but to rescue and de-

liver the people and countries from the tyranny of the governors, and to restore them to their liberty. So did the Romans the Lacedemonians out of the tyranny of Onabis, and all Greece from the bondage that Philippus (Demetrius's son), king of Macedonia, had them in. So did the noble men of the people of God also come to their high estimation and honor, as Gideon, Barak, Jephthah, and Samson, who for the delivery of his country from the power of the idolatrous cruel Philistines pulled upon himself present death. So that this principle that evil and evildoers ought to be punished and rotten members to be cut away was no peculiar law of the ethnics, but it proceedeth of nature, and therefore common to all men, as it is plain by the chronicles and experience of all ages, and purposely exemplified for our sure stay and learning as well in the Book of Judges as in many other histories of Holy Scriptures. ... [111] And albeit some do hold that the manner and mean to punish evil and evildoers is not all one among Christians (which be in deed that they profess in words) and ethnics, which think it lawful for every private man (without respect of order and time) to punish evil; yet the laws of many Christian regions do permit that private men may kill malefactors, yea though they were magistrates in some cases: as when a governor shall suddenly with his sword run upon an innocent, or go about to shoot him through with a gun, or if he should be found in bed with a man's wife, or go about to deflower and ravish a man's daughter; much more if [he] go about to betray and make away his country to foreigners. Nevertheless, forasmuch as all things in every Christian commonwealth ought to be done decently and according to order and charity, I think it cannot be maintained by God's word that any private man may kill, except, (where execution of just punishment upon tyrants, idolaters, and treacherous governors is either by the whole state utterly neglected, or the prince with the nobility and council conspire the subversion or alteration of their country and people), [112] any private man have some special inward commandment or surely proved motion of God: as Moses had to kill the Egyptian, Phineas the lecherers, and Ehud King Eglon, with such like (Exod. 2:11f.; Num. 25:7f.; Judges 3:14-22); or be otherwise commanded or permitted by common authority upon just occasion and common necessity to kill.

Text: 1556 edition, facsimile in Winthrop S. Hudson, ed., *John Ponet (1516?-1556): Advocate of Limited Monarchy* (University of Chicago Press, 1942). Spelling and punctuation updated by Editors.

Thomas Cartwright

(1535-1603)

For three decades of Queen Elizabeth I's reign, Thomas Cartwright gave theological leadership to the Presbyterian platform in English church reform. Like his eminent collaborator, Walter Travers, his theological and ecclesiological horizons were formed initially in the training ground of Edward VI's Cambridge (1550-53) under the sway of Martin Bucer, and later decisively set by a sojourn in Beza's Geneva (1571-72).

His first significant contribution to Presbyterian reform was his sensational lecture series on the book of Acts, given in 1570 as Lady Margaret Professor at Cambridge, in which he laid out the apostolic standard of church organization as an essentially presbyterian polity, comprised of a purely "spiritual" episcopacy, governing "presbyteries" or "congregational sessions," parochially elected ministers, and deacons. While costing him his professorship, his brash proposals achieved the desired impact, helping to foment the Puritan agitation in Parliament that would climax in the *Admonition* of 1572. Composed by his younger protégés, John Field and Thomas Wilcox, *An Admonition to the Parliament* called on the government to institute God's law for his church against the proud and rebellious episcopal regime, bringing the established ministry, worship, and discipline in line with the apostolic model of the best Reformed churches, characterized by the primacy of preaching, simplified administration of the sacraments without superstitious ornamentation, and an effective system of admonition and correction.

As a result of this fiery tract, Cartwright became embroiled in a bitter and protracted literary controversy with the establishment churchman John Whitgift, who had already succeeded in destroying his Cambridge career. Whitgift's publication of his *Answer* to the *Admonition* elicited Cartwright's *A Reply to An Answer made of M Doctor Whitgift Against the Admonition to the Parliament by T. C.*, which in turn elicited Whitgift's *Defence of the Answer,* to which Cartwright issued a rejoinder in two parts, *The Second Reply against Master Whitgift's Second Answer touching the Church*

Discipline and *The Rest of the Second Reply of Thomas Cartwright against Master Doctor Whitgift's Second Answer Touching the Church Discipline*. Subsequently Cartwright took flight, continuing his Presbyterian ministry to English congregations in Antwerp and Middelburg, and enhancing his international reputation. Upon his return to England in 1585 he resumed his strong leadership of an increasingly persecuted and beleaguered movement, translating and promoting Travers's *Book of Discipline*, supporting the underground "conferences," and surviving two years of imprisonment (1590-92) to take part in the Puritan petition to James I in 1603 prior to his first Parliament.

Cartwright's published replies to Whitgift exhibit two prominent themes, which the passages below are arranged to illustrate. These themes are equally prominent in Travers's writings. The first is the primacy in church and commonwealth of God's revealed commands; the second is the conformity of commonwealth to church. While both were common threads of Reformed Protestantism on the Continent, their English Presbyterian development had peculiar features.

a. In their opposition to the external ecclesiastical forms (of liturgy, vestments, offices, and discipline) legislated by Elizabeth's parliament of 1559, Cartwright and Travers repudiated Calvin's notion of "things indifferent" (*adiaphora*), i.e., not regulated by God's express law, which might be variably decided on other grounds by ecclesiastical authorities, including civil sovereigns. Instead they proposed the comprehensive regulation of Christian action by God's revealed commands, either by his "particular" commands or, in the case of apparently free action, by his "general" commands. On the principle that particular commands elicit the more perfect obedience, Cartwright argued that the church's ministries and discipline are, in all important respects, established by Christ's particular directives, given in the speech and practice of the apostles and evangelists, as recorded in Acts and the Epistles; while "unspecified" details of orders and ceremony, etc., are subject to Christ's general directives delivered by St. Paul.

Although he recognized that the divine law allows more latitude in the political constitution of civil commonwealths, Cartwright severely limited the scope of unregenerate "common reason," as is demonstrated by his argument for the permanently binding force of certain Mosaic "judicial" laws. While concurring with Calvin that it is the "perpetual equity" of these laws that binds, he maintains that every revealed command of God remains in force unless Scripture testifies to its revocation or restriction; and that in the case of the judicials which prescribe the death penalty for stubborn idolatry, blasphemy, and other crimes, Scripture vindicates the enduring authority of the commands, revealing the inseparability of positive form and universal content.

b. To Whitgift's repeated admonition that the regime of the church should reinforce that of the commonwealth, as episcopacy does monarchy, and his frequent dwelling on the subversive political effects of Presbyterian "democracy," Cartwright offered a twofold reply. On the one hand, he argued the reverse: that the civil polity should be conformed in its practices and laws, though not necessarily in its constitution, to the "spiritual" polity of the well-ordered church. On the other, he argued that Presbyterian polity, being "mixed," under the monarchy of Christ, the aristocracy of ruling "assemblies of elders," and the democratic principles of congregational election and consent, did in fact reinforce the English civil polity. Particularly striking is the proximity of the eschatological ordering and the spiritual-ethical ordering of commonwealth to church.

Further Reading: P. Collinson, *The Elizabethan Puritan Movement* (London: Jonathan Cape, 1967); P. Collinson, *The Religion of Protestants* (Oxford: Clarendon Press, 1982); P. Lake, *Anglicans and Puritans? Presbyterianism and English Conformist Thought from Whitgift to Hooker* (London: Unwin Hyman, 1988); A. F. S. Pearson, *Thomas Cartwright and Elizabethan Puritanism, 1535-1603* (Cambridge: Cambridge University Press, 1925).

(A) DIVINE LAW

From *A Reply to An Answer*

[1.190] But to the end it may appear that this speech of yours doth something take up and shrink the arms of the Scripture, which otherwise are so long and large, I say that the word of God containeth the direction of all things pertaining to the church, yea, of whatsoever things can fall into any part of a man's life. For so Solomon saith in the second chapter of the Proverbs (2:9): "My son, if thou receive my words, and hide my precepts in thee, etc., then thou shalt understand justice, and judgment, and equity, and every good way." St. Paul saith that: "whether we eat or drink, or whatsoever we do, we must do it to the glory of God" (1 Cor. 10:31). But no man can glorify God in anything but by obedience; and there is no obedience but in respect of the commandment and word of God: therefore it followeth that the word of God directeth a man in all his actions; and that which St. Paul said of meats and drinks, that they are "sanctified unto us by the word of God" (1 Tim. 4:5), the same is to be understanded of all things else whatsoever we have the use of. But the place of St. Paul in Romans (14:23) is of all other most clear, where, speaking of those things which are called indifferent, in the end he concludeth that "whatsoever is not of faith is sin": but faith is not but in respect of the word of God; therefore whatsoever is not done by the word of God is sin. [191] [. . .] Not that we say as you charge us in these words, when you say that we say that "no ceremony, etc., may be in the church, except the same be expressed in the word of God"; but that in making orders and ceremonies of the church it is not lawful to do what men list, but they are bound to follow the general rules of the Scripture, that are given to be the squire [i.e., square] whereby those should be squared out.

[195] Which rules I will here set down, as those which I would have as well all orders and ceremonies of the church framed by, as by the which I will be content that all those orders and ceremonies which are now in question, whether they be good

and convenient or no, should be tried and examined by. And they are those rules which St. Paul gave in such cases as are not particularly mentioned of in the Scripture. The first, that they offend not any, especially the church of God (1 Cor. 10:32). The second is (that which you cite also out of Paul), that all be done in order and comeliness (1 Cor. 14:40). The third, that all be done to edifying (1 Cor. 14:26). The last, that they be done to the glory of God (Rom. 14:6f.).

So that you see that those things which you reckon up of the hour, and time, and day of prayer, etc., albeit they be not specified in the Scripture, yet they are not left to any to order at their pleasure, or so that they be not against the word of God; but even by and according to the word of God they must be established, and those alone to be taken which do agree best and nearest with these rules before recited. And so it is brought to pass (which you think a great absurdity), that all things in the church should be appointed according to the word of God: whereby it likewise appeareth that we deny not but certain things are left to the order of the church, because they are of that nature which are varied by times, places, persons, and other circumstances, and so could not at once be set down and established forever; and yet so left to the order of the church, as that it do nothing against the rules aforesaid. But how doth this follow, that [196] certain things are left to the order of the church, therefore to make a new ministry by making an archbishop, to alter the ministry that is appointed by making a bishop or pastor without a church or flock, to make a deacon without appointing him his church whereof he is deacon, and where he might exercise his charge of providing for the poor, to abrogate clean both the name and office of the elder, with other more? How, I say, do these follow that, because the church hath power to ordain certain things, therefore it hath power to do so of these which God hath ordained and established; of the which there is no time, nor place, nor person, nor any other circumstance, which can cause any alteration or change?

From *The Second Reply against the Second Answer*

[94] To prove that there is a word of God for all things we have to do, I alleged that otherwise our estate should be worse than the estate of the Jews, which the *Answer* confesseth to have had "direction out of law in the least thing they had to do." And when it is the virtue of a good law to leave as little undetermined and without the compass of the law as can be, the *Answer,* in imagining that we have no word for divers things wherein the Jews had particular direction, presupposeth greater perfection in the law given unto the Jews than in that which is left unto us. And that this is a principal virtue of the law may be seen not only by that I have showed: that a conscience well instructed and touched with the fear of God seeketh for the light of the word of God in the smallest actions; but even by common reason, the masters whereof give this rule: "that it greatly behoveth those laws which are well made (as much as can be) to determine of all things and to leave as few things as may be to the discretion of the judges." [. . .]

[95] It is not (as the *Answer* surmiseth untruly) that the magistrate is simply

bound unto the judicial laws of Moses; but that he is bound to the equity which I also called the substance and marrow of them. In regard of which equity I affirmed that there are certain laws amongst the judicials which cannot be changed. And hereof I gave example in the laws which command that a stubborn idolater, blasphemer, murderer, incestuous person, and such like should be put to death. For the first point that the equity of the judicial doth remain and therefore ought to be a rule to direct all laws by, to let pass the authority of Masters Calvin and Beza [Cartwright refers us to Calvin's *Institutes* 4.20.16 and to Beza's "book of putting heretics to death," presumably *De haereticis* (1554), Beza's repudiation of Castellion's book of the same title] [96] and other writers of our time that have written with any judgment of this matter (which do in plain words affirm that there is a perpetual equity in them and that our laws, albeit they differ in form, yet ought to retain the reason or ground of them), I say to let that pass; it is to be considered that all these laws moral, ceremonial, and judicial, being the laws of God and by his revealed will established, must so far forth remain as it appeareth not by his will that they are revoked.

And seeing that the alteration which is come in this behalf is by the coming of our Saviour Christ only, it is to be inquired what those laws are which be put end unto. Which thing may be considered in that division which St. Paul useth where he saith that our Saviour Christ came to make peace first between God and men and then between men and men: that is to say, between the Jews and Gentiles (Eph. 2:11-18). The ceremonial law therefore being a law of enmity (which as a wall held out the Gentiles from joining themselves unto the Jews), was necessary amongst other causes in this respect to be taken away. The curse of the law for the breach of any [of] the laws of God either pertaining to the Jews in times past or unto us now, being that which maketh the wall between the Lord and us, was for our reconciliation with his majesty necessarily to be removed. Whereupon followeth first that the moral law (as that which neither hindereth our reconciliation with the Lord nor our good agreement with men) is in as full strength as ever it was before the coming of our Saviour Christ. [. . .]

[97] Secondly it followeth hereupon that those judicial laws of Moses which are merely politic and without all mixture of ceremonies must remain as those which hinder not the atonement of the Jews and Gentiles with God or of one of them with another. Beside that it being manifest that our Saviour Christ came not to dissolve any good government of commonwealth, he can least of all be thought to have come to dissolve that which himself had established. And of this point the *Answer* hath two contrary sentences, one of Musculus [Lutheran theologian (1514-81)] which saith that the judicial law is abrogated; the other of Beza which is the same with that which I have brought reasons of: that is to say, that the judicial law being given unto the Jews, is not yet abrogated, so that if they had any estate of commonwealth in the Land of Canaan, they should be constrained to use that form of government which was given unto them of Moses. Now albeit those laws given unto the Jews for that land do not bind the gentiles in other lands, for so much as the diversity of the disposition of the people and state of that country gave occasion of some laws there which would not have been in other places and peoples; yet for so much as

there is in those laws a constant and everlasting equity whereupon they were grounded, and the same perfecter and farther from error than the forge of man's reason (which is even in this behalf shrewdly wounded) is able to devise, it followeth that even in making politic laws for the commonwealth Christian magistrates ought to propound unto themselves those laws, and in light of their equity, by a just proportion of circumstances of person, place etc., frame them.

Furthermore, that the equity of the judicial law remaineth not as a counsel which men may follow if they list and leave at their pleasure, but as a law whereunto they be [98] bound, what better proof can we have than the Apostle, which, after he had alleged divers similitudes fetched of the common use of men to prove that a minister of the Gospel ought to be maintained of the church's charge, unto the adversary which might except that those were but human reasons he allegeth as the eternal law of God one of the judicial laws of Moses, which was that a man should not muzzle the mouth of the ox which treadeth out the corn (1 Cor. 9:3-9; cf. Deut. 25:4). Where it is manifest that he doubteth not to bind the conscience of the Corinthians unto the equity of that law which was judicial. Likewise of the finding of the priests in the service of the altar commanded in the Law he concludeth that those which preach the Gospel should live off it. And this maintenance of the priests, albeit in the manner of provision it was ceremonial, yet as it was a reward of their service due by men (as the punishments also, if they had failed in their duties), was mere judicial. Whereupon it is brought to pass that in those judicials, to all the circumstances whereof we are not bound, we are notwithstanding bound to the equity.

It remaineth to show that there are certain judicial laws which cannot be changed, as that a blasphemer, contemptuous and stubborn idolater, etc. ought to be put to death. The doctrine which letteth this at liberty, when they can allege no cause of this looseness but the coming of our Saviour Christ and his passion, faulteth many ways. And first it is a childish error to think that our Saviour Christ came down to exempt men from corporal death which the law casteth upon evil-doers; when as he came not to deliver from death which is the parting of the body from the soul, but from that which is the separation both of body and soul from the gracious presence of the Lord. And if it were so that our Saviour Christ had borne in his own body this civil punishment of public offenders, it must follow thereupon not (which the Doctor [Whitgift] fancieth) that it is in the liberty of the magistrate to put them to death, but that he must willy-nilly (if they repent) keep them alive. For if our Saviour Christ hath answered that justice of God in his law whereby he hath commanded that such malefactors should [99] be put to death, it should be great injustice to require that again in the life of the offender. So that either our Saviour Christ hath answered that justice of God which he requireth in his law concerning the death of such offenders, and then it cannot be asked again in the body of the offender, or else he hath not answered it, and then remaineth of necessity to be answered in the life of the offender. [. . .]

[117] Therefore to close upon this question, I will add this: that the magistrates which punish murder and thefts and treasons, with other transgressions of the

Second Table, severely, and are loose in punishing the breaches of the First Table, begin at the wrong end, and do all one with those which, to dry up many rivers fed continually by one fountain, begin at the channels where it divideth and parteth itself into many arms — which as it is an endless labour, so is this also that they go about. For when as St. Paul teacheth that God for just revenge of the dishonour of his name and staining of his glory giveth men into wicked minds to the committing of all kinds of sins contained in the Second Table, be they never so horrible, and so maketh the breach of the First Table cause of the breach of the Second, it cannot be, (let the magistrate lay as good watch as he can, both multiply and aggravate his punishments as much as he can), I say it cannot be but where either the First Table is broken or the breach not duly revenged, swarms of treasons, thefts, murders, adulteries, perjuries, and such like must needs break out in those governments. And therefore, as the short and easy way to dry up the channels and rivers [118] is to stop the head and fountain of all, so the only remedy of purging the commonwealth of these pestilences is to bend the force of sharp and severe punishments especially against idolaters, blasphemers, contemners of true religion and of the service of God. And therefore I conclude that those which would have the severity of the law against idolaters abated do, all unawares, not only thereby utter the small price which they set either of God's glory or of the salvation of their brethren, but withal declare themselves enemies to commonwealths and of all both civil and godly honesty of life.

(B) CHURCH AND COMMONWEALTH

From *A Reply to An Answer*

[3.189] It is true that we ought to be obedient unto the civil magistrate which governeth the church of God in that office which is committed unto him, and according to that calling. But it must be remembered that civil magistrates must govern it according to the rules of God prescribed in his word, and that as they are nurses so they be servants unto the church, and as they rule in the church so they must remember to subject themselves unto the church, to submit their sceptres, to throw down their crowns, before the church, yea, as the prophet speaketh, to lick the dust of the feet of the church (Isa. 49:23). Wherein I mean not that the church doth either wring the sceptres out of princes' hands, or taketh their crowns from their heads, or that it requireth princes to lick the dust of her feet (as the pope under this pretence hath done), but I mean, as the prophet meaneth, that whatsoever magnificence, or excellency, or pomp, is either in them, or in their estates and commonwealths, which doth not agree with the simplicity and (in the judgment of the world) poor and contemptible estate of the church, that they will be content to lay down.

And here cometh to my mind that wherewith the world is now deceived, and wherewith M. Doctor goeth about both to deceive himself and others too, in that he thinketh that the church must be framed according to the commonwealth, and the church government according to the civil government, which is as much to say, as if a man should fashion his house according to his hangings, when as indeed it is clean contrary, that, as the hangings are made fit for the house, so the commonwealth must be made to agree with the church, and the government thereof with her government. For, as the house is before the hangings, and therefore the hangings which come after must be framed to the house which was before, so the church being before there was any commonwealth, and the commonwealth coming after must be fashioned and made suitable unto the church. Otherwise God is made to give place to men, heaven to earth, and religion is made (as it were) a rule of Lesbia, to be applied unto any estate of commonwealth whatsoever.

Seeing that good men, that is to say, the church, are, as it were, the foundation of the world, it is meet that the commonwealth which is builded upon that foundation should be framed according to the church, and therefore those voices ought not to be heard: "This order will not agree with our commonwealth. That law of God is not for our state. This form of government will not match with the policy of this realm."

From *The Rest of the Second Reply*

[64] To that I alleged "that the commonwealth government must be framed unto the church, and not the church government unto the commonwealth, as the hangings to the house and not the house to the hangings," he [Whitgift] answereth [in his *Second Answer*] as though I had meant that the "form of the government must be changed and made the same with the form of the church government," which is an open wresting of my words, seeing all know "that to be framed according to another thing is not all one as to be made the same with it"; unless he that commandeth his hangings to be framed to his house commandeth that his house and hangings should be made the same, or that the Master which biddeth his servant frame himself to him biddeth him to give commandment for commandment, cheek for cheek, blow for blow.

Therefore, my meaning could not be such; but it was as it is, which I also expounded in the example of the prince, the principal part of the commonwealth: "that if there were any custom, prerogative, or pomp in the commonwealth *before the prince joined himself to the church*, contrary to the order of a church well established, that that should be corrected."

And if I had had any such meaning as he surmiseth, yet our commonwealth could have received no such change by this, considering that I had both declared my liking of it, and showed how the form thereof resembleth the form of the church government. Whereby also appeareth what a shameful slander it is which he surmiseth of me that I "would have princes throw down their crowns before the seniors of the church etc." — which I precisely prevented with plain words, because I knew with whom I had to do. Albeit, that "princes should be excepted from ecclesiastical discipline," and "namely from excommunication," as he here and otherwhere signifieth, I utterly mislike. [. . .]

[66] To that I alleged that the church is "the foundation of the world," and therefore the commonwealth, builded upon it, must be framed unto it, he saith that "it is obscure, etc." But it is for want of light in himself, for otherwise the thing is clear. And to leave Solomon's proverb (Prov. 10:25), which Rabbi Levi Ben Gerson doeth so interpret, and whereof indeed the sense may well be that where the wicked are carried away with the tempest, the just not only stand fast, but be the cause why the world standeth; I say to leave that, St. Peter plainly confirmeth that the cause why this world endureth is for that the full number of the elect is not yet gathered; so that, as soon as they are assembled by the ministry of the church, there shall be forthwith an end of the world (2 Pet. 3:9).

Texts: In *Works of John Whitgift, D.D.,* ed. J. Ayre for the Parker Society, 3 vols. (Cambridge University Press, 1851-53) *(Reply to an Answer)*; Zürich, 1575 *(Second Reply to Second Answer)*; Zürich, 1577 *(Rest of Second Reply to Second Answer).*

Vindiciae, contra Tyrannos

(1579)

The *Vindiciae, contra tyrannos* (*Legal Remedy against Tyrants*, but known always by its Latin title), though first published in Edinburgh, constituted one strand of the French Protestant (Huguenot) response to Henri III's Catholic policy of intolerance and persecution inaugurated by the notorious St. Bartholomew Massacre of 1572. In its radical analysis of the basis, purpose, and limits of royal rule and the lawful resistance to tyranny, the tract reveals the extreme exasperation of Protestant nobility, of regional and civic authorities and their constituencies with the Valois dynasty. The mystery of the authorship behind the pseudonym of Stephanus Junius Brutus the Celt, persisting after centuries of speculation and scholarship in favor of either Hubert Languet or Philippe de Mornay or some combination of the two, is probably the least compelling of the mysteries surrounding the text.

The most perplexing concerns the application of the text's argument to the religious polity of France in the 1570s. For the political-covenantal theology at the heart of the argument appears better suited to the situation of the Scottish reforming lords whom John Knox exhorted, or of the English Presbyterian parliamentarians of the 1630s and 1640s, than to the beleaguered French Calvinist minority of the 1570s whose aspirations ran more along the lines of obtaining official toleration than converting the nation to Reformed Christianity. Moreover, its author's address to all attentive French Christians is as enigmatically nonpartisan as the broad appeal of his claim to be countering the pernicious effects of Machiavelli's doctrine on the royal household, its advisers, and the powerful elites (echoes of Ponet!). However, the central role in his argument played by the "true religion" unavoidably diminishes his common cause with Roman Catholic contemporaries.

The treatise's significance rests chiefly on its ingenious blending of Old Testament covenantal and theocratic themes with natural-law, Roman legal arguments of various stripes — corporational, constitutional, and liberal — furnishing a synthesis of unprecedented scope and complexity. To appraise it requires our attending to

711

both the coherence and the incoherence of the argument's movement through the sequence of political covenants, analogies, and principles, within the context of four foundational political questions.

The first covenantal formulation arises in the treatment of the first question: Are subjects obliged to obey the commands of princes in violation of God's law? To deny such obligation, the author construes royal authority as a merely delegated exercise of divine authority, instituted and permanently structured by the original covenant between God and king, modeled on God's covenants with successive kings of Israel and Judah (1 Sam. 10:1; 2 Sam. 6:21; 2 Kings 20:5; 2 Chron. 1:9). Initially the covenant is described on the feudal analogy of the liege-lord investing a vassal with a fief, to be possessed and ruled according to laws stipulated by the lord, with forfeiture ensuing from the vassal's waywardness. Even here, though, royal rule has more the character of trusteeship of God's property (i.e., the people) than full-fledged feudal tenure. Further along, the covenant, reformulated as tripartite with alternative Old Testament examples (2 Kings 11:17; 23:3; 2 Chron. 23:16), comprises a unilateral compact with God as the stipulating party and the king and people as separate promissory parties, both of whom promise to uphold God's law in ruling and in obeying respectively.

The ascendancy of the people over the king comes into view when the tripartite covenant is presented as continuing the premonarchical Mosaic covenant between God and the people (Deut. 31:26; also Josh. 1:7-8). This ascendancy occupies the foreground in the author's treatment of the second question: Is it lawful to resist a prince who is violating God's law and ruining the church, and by whom, how, and to what extent should he be resisted? Now the tripartite covenant is recast as between a divine creditor and two unreliable human debtors, both of whom owe to God the care of his church. In case either king or people renege on his/their obligation, the other party stands surety, being held responsible for rendering the whole debt. Disregarding somewhat the evidence of Israel's history, the author is convinced that the people are more competent to fulfill the covenantal obligation, which may require the correction, or at least restraint, of the defaulting monarch and the independent reformation of the church.

Consideration of the mechanics of popular resistance takes the author onto the terrain of corporational and conciliarist theory. The people's agency or lawful power to act, he proposes, operates exclusively through their assembled representatives — the magistrates or "officers of the kingdom" (corresponding to Israel's public authorities) in their parliaments, diets, estates, and other councils. Thus they alone and not private individuals are liable to God for the debt of caring for and defending the church (notwithstanding God's freedom to endow private individuals with juridical power extraordinarily). Moreover, even a single magistrate (or league) entrusted with the welfare of the local church (a covenanting part of the whole) may resist the monarch's idolatry to the point of seceding from his "private tyranny," as did certain Huguenot strongholds.

In the context of the third question, whether it is lawful to resist a tyrant who is ruining the commonwealth, etc., the author elaborates a secondary covenant between king and people that dramatically modifies the analogical relations set up in the earlier formulations. In this "compact of government" establishing the legal framework of just rule, the people take over God's role as the stipulating party; and, moreover, they pledge only a conditional obedience, whereas the king, like his Davidic predecessors, pledges to observe unconditionally the laws of the kingdom *(lex regia)*. Now the people are the creditor before whom king and magistrates are co-debtors; it is the lord from whom, in descending order, magistrates and king hold their fiefs (i.e., their subjects' proprietary rights: collectively, to peace, well-being, and liberty; and individually, to private possessions). Alternatively, the people are the ward of whose estate both parties are co-trustees. These revised covenantal relations are evident in the inauguration of royal rule: while God "elects" kings and gives them their kingdoms, the people "constitute" kings, confirming God's appointment by vote and acclamation, so that the royal power (even in hereditary monarchy) is "received from the people after [God]," in accordance with Israelite custom.

It follows that royal tyranny is a felony against the people, treason against its majesty, for which the tyrant is justly deposed or punished. Failure of the co-tutors of the kingdom or *a part of it* to vindicate the property of their ward and lord renders them traitors and tyrants along with the principal tutor (the king). The federalist motif of the earlier tripartite covenant is still apparent: both king and magistrates are pledged not only to the whole people but also to distinct parts of it, depending, in the case of magistrates, on the territorial scope of their responsibilities.

An even more complicated relationship between corporate part and whole emerges from the fourth question: Is a monarch entitled or even obliged to assist popular resistance against religious and civil oppression in a neighboring kingdom? This is directed at the reluctance of sympathetic Protestant allies to intervene in French affairs. The author portrays the church's unity as such that the welfare of the whole is entrusted to individual princes and the welfare of the parts to all princes together, thereby leaving the way clear for unlimited forcible intervention in her defense across territorial boundaries. But the universal religious covenant implied here comes no closer than the national covenant to resolving the issue of confessional disunity within and among political communities. No amount of "vagueness about the content of the covenant" (Garnett 1994, 1) can make the Israelite model of "holy war" congruous with the Huguenot plea for toleration by the French Catholic monarch and polity.

Further Reading: E. Barker, *Church, State, and Study* (London: Methuen, 1930); J. Dennert, ed., *Beza, Brutus, Hotman: calvinistische Monarchomachen* (Cologne: Westdeutscher Verlag, 1968); J. Franklin, *Constitutionalism and Resistance in the Sixteenth Century* (New York: Pegasus, 1969); G. Garnett, ed. and trans., *Vindiciae, contra Tyrannos; or, Concerning the Legitimate Power of a Prince over the People, and of the People over a Prince* (Cambridge: Cambridge University Press, 1994); R. E. Giesey, "The Monarchomach Triumvirs: Hotman, Beza and Mornay," *Bibliothèque d'humanisme et renaissance* 32 (1970): 41-56; R. M. Kingdon, *Myths about the St. Bartholomew's Day Massacres, 1572-76* (Cambridge, Mass.: Harvard University Press, 1988); M. N. Ratière, "Hubert Languet's Authorship of the 'Vindiciae contra Tyrannos,'" *Il pensiero politico* 14 (1986): 395-420; Q. Skinner, *The Foundations of Modern Political Thought*, vol. 2 (Cambridge: Cambridge University Press, 1978).

From *Vindiciae, contra Tyrannos*

1. [5] The question is, if subjects be bound to obey kings, in case they command that which is against the law of God: that is to say, to which of the two (God or king) must we rather obey. When the question shall be resolved concerning the king, to whom is attributed absolute power, that concerning other magistrates shall be likewise determined.

First, the Holy Scripture doth teach, that God reigns by his own proper authority, and kings by derivation, God from himself, kings from God, that God hath a jurisdiction proper, kings are his delegates. It follows then (Sap. 6:4ff., Prov. 8:15, Job 12:18f.) that the jurisdiction of God hath no limits, that of kings bounded, that the power of God is infinite, that of kings confined, that the kingdom of God extends itself to all places, that of kings is restrained within certain countries, determined by certain confines. In like manner, God hath created of nothing both heaven and earth; wherefore by good right he is lord, and true proprietor, both of the one and the other. All the inhabitants of the earth hold of him that which they have, and are but his tenants and farmers; all who have earthly jurisdiction and precedence of others on any account are his stipendiaries and vassals, and are bound to take and acknowledge their investitures from him. [. . .]

[7] By the same reason the people are always called the Lord's people, and the Lord's inheritance, and the king the administrator of this inheritance, and leader of God's people, which is the title given to David, to Solomon, to Hezekiah, and to other good princes; when also the covenant is passed between God and the king, it is upon condition that the people be, and remain always, the people of God, to shew that God will not in any case despoil himself of his property and possession when he gives to kings the government of the people, but that they should rule them, care for them and well use them; no more nor less than he which makes choice of a shepherd to look to his flocks, remains notwithstanding himself still master and owner of them. [. . .]

[11] Now we read of two sorts of covenants at the inaugurating of kings: the first between God, the king and the people, that the people might be the people of God; the second, between the king and the people, that the people shall obey faithfully, and the king command justly. We will treat hereafter of the second, and now speak of the first.

When King Joash was crowned, we read that a covenant was contracted between God, the king, and the people; or, as it is said in another place, between Jehoiada the high priest, all the people, and the king, that it should be God's people (2 Kings 11:17). In like manner we read that Josiah and all the people entered into covenants with the Lord (2 Kings 23:3). We may gather from these testimonies, that in passing these covenants the high priest did demand of the king and the people in express terms in the name of God, whether they would take order that God might be served purely and properly in the kingdom of Judah; whether the king would so reign that the people were suffered to serve God and held in obedience to his law; and finally whether the people would so obey the king as their obedience should have principal relation to God. It appears by this that the king and the people as parties to the promise did oblige themselves by solemn oath to serve God before all things. And indeed presently after they had sworn the covenant Josiah and Joash did ruin the idolatry of Baal and re-established the pure service of God. The principal points of the covenant were chiefly these: —

That the king himself and all the people should severally serve God, and as a whole take care that he be served according as his law prescribed, which, if they performed, God would assist and preserve their commonwealth: as in doing the contrary, he would abandon and exterminate them, which does plainly appear by the conferring of divers passages of holy writ. Moses, somewhat before his death, propounds these conditions of covenant to all the people, and at the same time commands that the law, the very terms of the Lord's agreement, should be *in deposito* kept in the ark of the covenant. After the decease of Moses, Joshua was established captain and conductor of the people of God. Accordingly the Lord himself admonished him, if he would have happy success in his affairs, he should not in any sort estrange himself from the law (Josh. 1:8). Joshua also, for his part, desiring to make the Israelites understand upon what condition God had given them the country of Canaan, as soon as they were entered into it, after due sacrifices performed, he read the law in the presence of all the people, promising unto them all good things if they persisted in obedience; and threatening of all evil if they wilfully connived in disobedience (Josh. 8:30-35). Summarily, he assures them all prosperity if they observed the law; as otherwise he expressly declared that in doing the contrary they should be dispersed and ruined. This he repeated yet more clearly when he was like to die. Howbeit at all such times as they left the service of God, they were delivered into the hands of the Canaanites and reduced into slavery under their tyranny. [. . .]

[17] Now although the form both of the Jewish church and kingdom itself be changed, for that which was before enclosed within the narrow bounds of Judaea could be dilated throughout the whole world; notwithstanding the same things may be said of Christian kings, the gospel having succeeded the law, and Christian princes being in the place of those of Jewry. There is the same covenant, the same conditions, the same punishments, and if they fail in the accomplishing, the same God Almighty, revenger of all perfidious disloyalty; and as the former were bound to keep the law, so the other are obliged to adhere to the doctrine of the Gospel, for the advancement whereof these several kings at their inaugurating do pledge themselves first and foremost. [. . .]

2. [36] We have shewed before to what end God contracted covenants with the king. Let us now consider wherefore also he allies himself with the people. It is a most certain thing, that God has not done this in vain, and if the people had not "authority to promise, and to keep promise" it were vainly lost time to contract or covenant with them. It may seem then that God has done like those creditors, which having to deal with not very sufficient borrowers, take divers jointly bound for one and the same sum, insomuch as two or more being bound one for another and each of them apart for the entire payment of the total sum, he may demand his whole debt of which of them he pleases. There was much danger to commit the custody of the church to one man alone, and therefore God did recommend and put it in trust "to all the people." The king being raised to so slippery a place might easily be corrupted:

for fear lest the church should stumble with him, God would have the people also to be respondents for it. In the covenant of which we speak, God, or in his place the High Priest are stipulators, the king and all the people, to wit, Israel are promissors, jointly and voluntarily bound for one and the same thing. The High Priest demands if they promise that the people shall be the people of God, that God shall always have his temple, his church amongst them, where he shall be purely served. The king pledges and Israel pledges (the whole body of the people bearing the person of one man) not severally but jointly, as the words themselves make clear, "incontinent" and not by intermission or distance of time the one after the other. We see here then two undertakers, the king and Israel, who by consequence are bound one for another and each for the whole. For as when Gaius and Titius have promised jointly to pay to their creditor Seius a certain sum, each of them is bound for himself and his companion, and the creditor may demand the sum of which of them he pleases. In the like manner the king for himself, and Israel for itself are bound with all circumspection to see that the church be not damnified: if either of them be negligent of their covenant, God may justly demand the whole of which of the two he pleases, and the more probably of the people than of the king, and for that many cannot so easily slip away as one, and have better means to discharge the debts than one alone. [. . .]

[41] But for this occasion it was, that when the kings had broken their covenants, the prophets always addressed themselves to the House of Judah and Jacob, and to Samaria, to advertise them of their duties. Furthermore, they required the people that they not only withdraw themselves from sacrificing to Baal, but also that they call down his idol, and destroy his priests and service; yea, even maugre the king himself. For example, Ahab having killed the prophets of God, the prophet Elijah assembles the people, and as it were convented the estates, and does there tax, reprehend, and reprove every one of them; the people at his exhortation take and put to death the priests of Baal. And for so much as the king neglected his duty, it behoved Israel more carefully to discharge theirs without tumult, not rashly but by public authority, the estates being assembled, and the equity of the cause orderly debated. [. . .]

[46] When we speak of all the people, we understand by that, only those who hold their authority from the people, to wit, the magistrates who are inferior to the king, and whom the people have chosen or by some other means established, as it were, consorts in the empire and kings' ephors, to represent the whole body of the people. We understand also the assembly of the estates, which is nothing else but an epitome, or brief collection of the kingdom, to whom all public affairs are referred; such were the seventy ancients in the kingdom of Israel, amongst whom the High Priest was as it were president, and they judged all matters of greatest importance, those seventy being first chosen as six out of each tribe, which went down to Egypt. Then the heads or governors of tribes, one from each; the judges and provosts of towns; the captains of thousands, of hundreds, and others who commanded over so many families; lastly the most valiant, noble and otherwise notable personages, of whom was composed the body of the states, assembled divers times, as it plainly appears by these words of the holy Scripture: "Then all the elders of Israel gathered

716

themselves together, and came . . . unto Ramah" (1 Sam. 8:4), for the election of Saul; "All Israel" or "All Judah and Benjamin came together." Now it is in no way probable, that all the people, one by one, met together. Of this sort there are in every well governed kingdom princes, officers of the crown, peers, the greatest and most notable lords, the deputies of estates; of whom either the ordinary or the extraordinary council is composed, or the parliament, or the diet, or other assemblies, according to the different names used in divers countries of the world; in which assemblies, the principal care is had both for the preventing and reforming either of disorder or detriment in church or commonwealth. [. . .]

[64] Let us conclude, then, to end this discourse, that all the people by the authority of those into whose hands they have committed their power, or divers of them, may and ought to repress a prince who is commanding impious things or forbidding pious. In like manner, that all, or at the least the principals of provinces or towns, under the authority of the chief magistrates, established first by God and secondly by the prince, may justly hinder the entrance of idolatry within the enclosure of their walls, and maintain their true religion; yea further, they may extend the confines of the church, which is but one, and in failing hereof, if they have means to do it, they justly incur the penalty of high treason against the divine majesty.

It remains now that we speak of particulars who are private persons. First, the covenant between God and all the people who promise to be the people of God does not in any sort bind them; for as that which belongs to the whole universal body is in no sort proper to particulars, so in like manner that which the body owes and is bound to perform cannot by any sensible reason be required of particular persons: neither does their duty anything oblige them to it; for every one is bound to serve God in that proper vocation to which he is called. Now private persons, they have no power; they have no public command, nor any calling to unsheathe the sword of authority; and therefore as God has not put the sword into the hands of private men, so does he not require in any sort that they should strike with it. It is said to them, "put up thy sword into the scabbard" (Matt. 26:52). [. . .]

As all the subjects of a good and faithful prince, of what degree soever they be, are bound to obey him, but some of them, notwithstanding, have their particular duty, as magistrates must hold others in obedience; in like manner all men are bound to serve God, but some are placed in a higher rank, have received greater authority, insomuch as they are accountable for the offences of others if they attend not the charges of the commonalty carefully. The kings, the commonalties of the people, the magistrates into whose hands the whole body of the commonwealth has committed the sword of authority, must and ought to take care that the church be maintained and preserved; particulars ought only to look that they render themselves members of this church. Kings and popular estates are bound to hinder the pollution or ruin of the temple of God, and ought to free and defend it from all corruption within and all injury from without. Private men must take order, that their bodies, the temples of God, be pure, that they may be fit receptacles for the Holy Ghost to dwell in them. [. . .]

3. [76] We have shewed before that it is God that does appoint kings, who chooses them, who gives the kingdom to them; now we say that the people establishes kings, puts the sceptre into their hands, and with their suffrages approves the election. God would have it done in this manner, to the end that the kings should acknowledge that after God they hold their power and sovereignty from the people, and that it might the rather induce them to apply and address the utmost of their care and thoughts for the profit of the people, without supposing that they were raised so high above other men as formed of any nature more excellent than theirs, as men commanding flocks of sheep or herds of cattle. But that they remember they are of the same condition as others, raised from the earth by the voice and as it were upon the shoulders of the people unto their thrones, that they might afterwards bear on their own shoulders the greatest burdens of the commonwealth.

Divers ages before that the people of Israel demanded a king, God gave and appointed the law of royal government contained in Deuteronomy (17:14). When, says Moses, "thou art come unto the land which the Lord thy God giveth thee, and shalt possess it, and shalt dwell therein, and shalt say, I will set a king over me like as all the nations that are about me, thou shalt in any wise set him whom the Lord thy God shall choose from amongst thy brethren. . . ." You see here that the election of the king is attributed to God, the establishment to the people; now when the practice of this law came in use, see in what manner they proceeded.

The elders of Israel, who presented the whole body of the people (under this name of elders are comprehended the captains, the centurions, commanders over fifties and tens, judges, provosts, but principally the chiefest of tribes) came to meet Samuel in Ramah, and not being willing longer to endure the government of the sons of Samuel, whose ill carriage had justly drawn on them the people's dislike, and withal persuading themselves that they had found the means to make their wars hereafter with more advantage, they demanded a king of Samuel (1 Sam. 8:4f.), who asking counsel of the Lord, he made known that he had chosen Saul for the governor of his people (9:16). Then Samuel anointed Saul, and performed all those rights which belong to the election of a king required by the people (10:1). Now this might perhaps have seemed sufficient, if Samuel had presented to the people the king who was chosen by God and had admonished them all to become good and obedient subjects. Notwithstanding, to the end that the king might know that he was established by the people, Samuel appointed the estates to meet at Mizpah, where being assembled as if the business were but then to begin and nothing had already been done, to be brief, as if the election of Saul were then only to be treated of, the lot is cast and falls on the tribe of Benjamin, after on the family of Matri, and lastly on Saul, born of that family, who was the same whom God had chosen. Then by the consent of all the people Saul was declared king (10:17-24). Finally, that Saul nor any other might attribute the aforesaid business to chance or lot, after that Saul had made some proof of his valour in raising the siege of the Ammonites in Jabesh-gilead, some of the people pressing the business, he was again confirmed king in a full assembly at Gilgal (11:14f.). Ye see that he whom God had chosen and the lot had separated from all the rest is established king by the suffrages of the people.

What of David? By the commandment of God and in a manner more evident than the former, after the rejection of Saul Samuel anointed for king over Israel David, chosen by the Lord, which being done the Spirit of the Lord presently left Saul and wrought in a special manner in David (1 Sam. 16:13f.). But David notwithstanding reigns not, but was compelled to save himself in deserts and rocks, oftentimes falling upon the very brim of destruction, and never reigned as king until after the death of Saul; for then by the suffrages of all the people of Judah he was first chosen king of Judah and seven years after by the consent of all Israel he was inaugurated king of Israel in Hebron (2 Sam. 2:4; 5:3). So, then, he is anointed first by the prophet at the commandment of God as a token he was chosen, secondly by the commandment of the people when he was established king. And that to the end that kings may always remember that it is from God, but by the people and for the people's sake that they do reign, and that in their glory they say not (as is their custom) they hold their kingdom only of God and their sword, but withal add that it was the people who first girt them with that sword. . . . Wherefore, although that God had promised to his people a perpetual lamp from the line of David, and that the succession of the kings of Israel were approved by the word of God himself; notwithstanding, since that we see that the kings did not reign before the people had ordained and installed them with requisite ceremonies, it may be collected that the kingdom of Israel was hereditary if we consider the lineage, but that it was wholly elective if we regard the particular persons. [. . .]

[82] Briefly, for so much as none were ever born with crowns on their heads and sceptres in their hands, and that no man can be a king by himself, nor reign without people, whereas on the contrary the people may subsist of themselves, and are prior to the king, it must of necessity follow that kings were at the first constituted by the people; and although the sons and dependants of such kings inheriting their fathers' virtues may in a sort seem to have rendered their kingdoms hereditary to their offsprings, and that in some kingdoms and countries the right of free election seems in a sort buried; yet notwithstanding in all well-ordered kingdoms this custom is yet remaining. The sons do not succeed the fathers before the people have first, as it were, anew established them by their new approbation; neither were they born as heirs already to their fathers, but were approved and accounted kings then only, when they were invested with the kingdom by receiving the sceptre and diadem from the hands of those who represent the majesty of the people. One may see most evident marks of this in Christian kingdoms which are at this day esteemed hereditary; for the kings of France and Spain and England and others are commonly inaugurated and, as it were, put into possession of their authority by the estates of the realm, peers, nobles and magnates who represent the body of the people; no more nor less than the emperors of Germany are chosen by the electors and the kings of Polonia by the Yawodes *(wojewodas)* or palatines, where the right of election is whole and undiminished. [. . .]

[104] If it be objected that kings were enthronized and received their authority from the people who lived five hundred years ago and not by those now living, I answer that the commonwealth never dies, although kings be taken out of this life one after another; for as the continual running of the water gives the river a perpetual being, so the alternative revolution of birth and death renders the people immortal. And further, as we have at this day the same Rhine, Seine and Tiber as was a thousand years ago, in like manner also is there the same people of Germany, France and Rome (excepting those transferred to colonies in the meantime); neither can the lapse of time nor changing of individuals alter in any sort the right of those people. . . .

[159] We have shewed already, that in the establishing of the king there were two alliances or covenants contracted, the first between God, the king and the people, of which we have formerly treated, the second between the king and the people, of which we must now say somewhat. After that Saul was established king, the royal law was given him according to which he ought to govern. David made a covenant in Hebron "before the Lord," that is to say, taking God for witness, with all the ancients of Israel, who represented the whole body of the people, and then it was he was anointed king (2 Sam. 5:3). Joash also entered into covenant with the whole people of the land in the house of the Lord, Jehoiadah the high priest dictating (2 Kings 11:17). [. . .]

In this assembly was the creating of the king determined of, for it was the people who made the king, not the king the people. It is certain, then, that the people by way of stipulation require a performance of covenants. The king promises it. Now the condition of a stipulator is in terms of law more worthy than of a promiser. The people ask the king whether he will govern justly and according to the laws. He promises he will. Then the people answer, and not before, that whilst he governs uprightly, they will obey faithfully. The king therefore promises simply and absolutely, the people upon condition, the which failing to be accomplished, the people rest according to equity and reason quit from their promise.

In the first covenant or contract there is only an obligation to piety, in the second to justice. In that the king promises to serve God religiously, in this to rule the people justly. By the one he is obliged with the utmost of his endeavours to procure the glory of God, by the other the profit of the people. In the first there is a condition expressed, "If thou keep my commandments," in the second, "if thou distribute justice equally to every man." God is the proper revenger of deficiency in the former, and the whole people the lawful punisher of delinquency in the latter, or the estates, the representative body thereof, who have assumed to themselves the protection of the people. [. . .]

[162] If we take into our consideration the realms of these our times, there is not any of them worthy of that name where there is not some such covenant between the people and the prince. It is not long since, that in the empire of Germany the king of the Romans being ready to be crowned emperor was bound to do homage and make oath of fealty to the empire, even as the vassal is bound to do to his lord when he is invested with his fee. . . . When the king of France is crowned, the bishops of Laon and Beauvois, ecclesiastical peers, ask all the people there present whether they desire and command that he who is there before them shall be their king. Whereupon in the form of inauguration he is even said to be "chosen by the people"; and when they have given the sign of consenting, then the king swears that he will maintain all the rights, privileges and laws of France universally, that he will not alienate the demesne, and so forth. . . . In England, Scotland, Sweden and Denmark there is almost the same custom as in France; but in no place is the use more evident than in Spain. For in the kingdom of Aragon, after the finishing of many ceremonies which are used between him which represents the Justice of Aragon, which comprehends the majesty of the commonwealth, seated in a higher seat, and the king which is to be crowned, who swears fealty and does his homage; and having

read the laws and conditions to the accomplishment whereof he is sworn; finally the lords of the kingdom use to the king these words in the vulgar language, "We who are as much worth as you" (thus runs the Spanish idiom) "and have more power than you, choose you king upon these and these conditions; and between you and us there is one who commands more than you." [. . .]

[193] Furthermore, we have already proved that all kings receive their royal authority from the people, that the whole people considered in one body is above and greater than the king, and that the king and emperor are only the prime and supreme governors and ministers of the kingdom and empire, but the people the absolute lord and owner thereof. It therefore necessarily follows that a tyrant is in the same manner guilty of rebellion against the majesty of the people as the lord of a fee who feloniously transgresses the conditions of his investitures, and is liable to the same punishment, yea, and certainly deserves much more greater than the equity of those laws inflicts on the delinquents. Therefore as Bartolus says, "He may either be deposed by those who are lords in sovereignty over him, or else justly punished according to the Julian law on public force" (*De tyranno* 9). The body of the people must needs be sovereign, or those who represent it, which in some places are the electors, palatines, peers, in other the assembly of the general estates. And if the tyranny have gotten such sure footing as there is no other means but force to remove him, then it is lawful for them to call the people to arms, to enroll and raise forces, and to employ the utmost of their power, and use against him all advantages and stratagems of war, as against the enemy of the commonwealth and the disturber of the public peace. [. . .]

[198] Those officers must also remember that the king holds truly the first place in the administration of the state, but they the second, and so following according to their ranks; not that they should follow his courses, if he transgress the laws of equity and justice; not that if he oppress the commonwealth they should connive to his wickedness. For the commonwealth was as well committed to their care as to his, so that it is not sufficient for them to discharge their own duty in particular, but it behoves them also to contain the prince within the limits of his duty; briefly, as the king promises to procure the profit of the commonwealth, so do they. Though that he forswore himself, yet may not they imagine that they are quit of their promise, no more than the bishops and patriarchs if they suffer an heretical pope to ruin the church; yea, they should esteem themselves so much the more obliged to the observing their oath, by how much they find him an oathbreaker. But if there be collusion betwixt him and them, they are prevaricators; if they dissemble, they may justly be called forsakers and traitors; if they deliver not the commonwealth from tyranny, they may be truly ranked in the number of tyrants; as on the contrary they are protectors, guardians and in a sort rulers, if by every means they keep and safeguard that which they have undertaken to safeguard. [. . .]

[207] Therefore those who have promised to serve a whole empire and kingdom, as the constables, marshals, peers and others, or those who have particular obligations to some provinces or cities which make a part or portion of the kingdom, as dukes, marquises, earls, sheriffs, mayors and the rest, are bound to succour the whole commonwealth or that part of the commonwealth which they hold of the people next after the king, and to free it from the burden of tyrants. The first ought

to deliver the whole kingdom from tyrannous oppression, if they can; the other, as guardians of the regions, that part of the kingdom whose protection they have undertaken; the duty of the former is to suppress the tyrant, that of the latter to drive him from their confines. [. . .]

[210] Furthermore, the prince is not established by private and particular persons, but by all in general considered in one entire body; whereupon it follows that they are bound to attend the commandment of all those who are the representative body of a kingdom or of a province or of a city, or at the least of some one of them, before they undertake anything against the prince. For as a ward cannot bring an action but being avowed in the name of his guardian, although the ward be the true proprietor of the estate and the guardian only pro-proprietor with reference to provision for the ward; so likewise the people may not enterprise actions of such nature but by the command of those into whose hands they have resigned their power and authority, whether they be ordinary magistrates or extraordinary, created in a public assembly; whom, if I may so say, for that purpose they have girded with their sword and invested with authority both to govern and defend them. [. . .]

[219] As this church is one, so is she recommended and given in charge to all Christian princes in general and to every one of them in particular; for so much as it was dangerous to leave the care to one alone, and the unity of it would not by any means permit that she should be divided into pieces and every portion assigned unto one particular, God has committed it all entire to particulars, and all the parts of it to all in general, not only to preserve and defend it but also to amplify and increase it as much as might be. Insomuch that if a prince who has undertaken the care of a portion of the church, as that of Germany and England, and notwithstanding neglect and forsake another part that is oppressed and which he might succour, he doubtless abandons the church, Christ having but one only spouse, which the prince is so bound to preserve and defend that she be not violated or corrupted in any part, if it be possible. And in the same manner, as every private person is bound to seek the restoring of the church with bended knee, so likewise are the magistrates to procure the same with feet and hands and with the utmost of their powers. For the church of Ephesus is no other than that of Colossae, but these two are portions of the universal church, which is the kingdom of Christ, the subject of all private men's desires, but which it is the duty of all kings, princes and magistrates to amplify and extend, to preserve and defend, in all places and against all men whatsoever.

Translation: Anonymous, 1689, corrected and adapted. Page references follow the 1579 Edinburgh edition of the Latin text.

Francisco Suárez

(1548-1617)

A late flowering of the School of Salamanca, Francisco Suárez has been esteemed as the most formidable of the Spanish scholastics, and even as the greatest schoolman after Aquinas. He resembles Thomas in the scope of his erudition, theoretical achievement and influence in doctrinal, moral, legal, and political theology, and in metaphysics and epistemology. Never the popular and commanding teacher that Vitoria was, his lasting intellectual contribution came from his lifetime of literary labor that produced twenty-three volumes of writings, half of which were published before his death. He brought to all his investigations a fresh penetration, a synthetic and yet independent intelligence. Whatever they may have lacked in rhetorical power and elegance was outweighed by the integrity, clarity, and completeness of his thought.

Uncharacteristically for a thinker of his rank, Suárez demonstrated no precocity; at the age of sixteen he was twice rejected by the Jesuit order before being admitted at an inferior rank, on account of the impression of physical and mental deficiency that he managed to convey. His studies at the University of Salamanca, having progressed from canon law to philosophy, continued to flounder until, quite suddenly, he entered a period of rapid intellectual development, showing startling philosophical and theological capabilities. His first academic appointment at the age of twenty-three was followed by others in quick succession, so that between 1571 and 1580 he held posts in philosophy and in theology at Segovia, Ávila, and Valladolid, then to be promoted to the chair of theology in the Society's distinguished Roman College. Ill health precipitated his transfer to Alcalá (where he was never appreciated), followed by his return in 1593 to Salamanca. Physically frail and desirous only of writing, Suárez resisted for several years his nomination by King Philip II to the Prime Chair of Theology in Coimbra, but succumbed in 1597, remaining there until 1615 when he was finally allowed to retire to prepare the massive folio volumes of his works.

As with certain other notable scholastics, Suárez made his major political contribution late in his career, after more than two decades of prolific writing. Although he wrote widely on doctrinal themes, his most influential theological treatises (1599, 1605) addressed the contemporary controversy between Dominicans and Jesuits over the relationship of divine grace to human freedom, which he resolved in the Molinist manner through concepts of special divine foreknowledge and "congruent grace." His *Metaphysical Disputations (Disputationes metaphysicae)* (1597) developed original positions on such subjects as the theory of distinctions, the principle of individuation, the status of universals, knowledge of singulars, and the analogicity of being. It became received wisdom in both Protestant and Catholic universities, and was much admired by many outstanding thinkers, including Descartes and Leibniz. His political influence burgeoned with the publication in 1612 of his monumental *Laws and God the Lawgiver (De legibus ac Deo legislatore)*, the fruit of his lectures at Coimbra, followed in 1613 by his commissioned refutation of James I's *Apology*, entitled *A Defence of the Catholic and Apostolic Faith (Defensio fidei Catholicae et Apostolicae)*, to which was posthumously added in 1621 his *On Faith, Hope, and Charity (De fide, spe et charitate)*, containing his disputation on war. Undoubtedly, his theoretical accomplishment in nonpolitical spheres heightened the impact of his political writings, helping to make them the chief vehicle for the transmission of scholastic jurisprudence and political thought to late seventeenth-century thinkers looking for an antidote to Hobbes.

His political theory belongs in the Salamancan mold, in that its Thomistic ground-motif is overlaid by more voluntarist, largely Sorbonist overtones. His *Laws* is broadly constructed as a commentary on *Summa Theologiae* 1a2ae.92-98, but manifests striking divergences: in the space given to such topics as the *ius gentium* and customary law more generally, and the origination of civil authority; in its independent positions on, e.g., the primacy of the element of obligation in law, and the status of the *ius gentium* as human positive law; and in its non-Thomistic conceptualizations, e.g., of the subjective meaning of *ius* and the fundamental political role of collective and individual rights. These departures from Thomas reflect his conversation with such contemporaries as Pedro Ribadeneyra and Robert Bellarmine, his erstwhile colleague in Rome, as well as with his Spanish scholastic predecessors — Vitoria, Soto, and Molina. In addition, he resembles the other Thomists in framing his arguments with a view to rebutting the current political and ecclesiastical heresies: the dangerously amoral "reason of state" philosophy of Machiavelli; the theology of "dominion by grace" (excluding the unbaptized from exercising true political rule), used to justify the Spanish policy of conquest and enslavement of the American peoples, but also associated with the Wycliffite and Machiavellian tendencies of the "Lutherans"; and finally, the antipapalist constitutionalism of the conciliarists. Let us look further at the innovative elements of *Laws* before passing on to Suárez's contribution to just-war theory.

In defining *law* along Gersonian lines, Suárez constructs a middle way between rationalist and voluntarist extremes of conceiving law as, on the one hand, rational judgment about good and evil (a Thomistic tendency), and on the other, externally imposed commands (a nominalist tendency), arguing for the inseparability of the elements of reason and will. Most decisively, in regard to the natural law, he insists that God is bound to forbid intrinsically evil acts and to command intrinsically good acts to his rational creature, so that the natural law is *law* both as cohering with rational nature and as expressing a divine command that imposes obligation (bk. 2, ch. 6).

Also in regard to the *ius gentium*, Suárez appears to follow a more voluntarist course than Thomas. For, in terms of the division of human law bequeathed by Isidore, into the two classes of (1) deductive conclusions from the natural law that derive their force from it as well from the human legislative will, and (2) determinations of, or constructions on, the natural law that derive their force entirely from the human legislative will (*S.T.* 1a2ae.95.2), Thomas identifies the *ius gentium* firmly with the first class (1a2ae.95.4), while Suárez associates it with both classes, effectively creating a third class. He proposes that, as universal custom, the *ius gentium* is comprised of general conclusions from the natural law — "probable inferences" rather than "necessary deductions," in close harmony with human nature (appealing to 1a2ae.95.4 ad 1); but that these are positive in the "absolute" sense of being entirely constituted by human "will and opinion," in the manner of the civil law of individual states (bk. 2, ch. 19: 3-4). Thus, international obligations of, e.g., receiving ambassadors under a law of immunity, allowing freedom of commercial intercourse, waging just war and accepting reasonable truces and peace treaties, are not imposed by the natural law (although they are concluded from it), but by universal customary law, by the "habitual conduct of nations" within a global moral-juridical community (bk. 2, ch. 19, 8-9).

For Suárez, as for Vitoria, the international community from whom the *ius gentium* derives is not a universal polity with full jurisdictional powers. Rather, such powers belong only to less-than-universal political communities, each of which is formed as a *corpus mysticum* through a bond of fellowship by the free consent of its members (bk. 3, ch. 2: 4). He accepts the Gersonian conciliarist principle that the unitive will of political community *requires actualization* in the establishment of government (anarchy being a moral impossibility), concluding that the communal will is not the "proximate [i.e., 'true efficient'] cause" of jurisdictional power (bk. 3, ch. 2: 4). Astutely observing the aspects in which political jurisdiction "transcends human authority as it exists in individual men," he concurs with Vitoria and Cajetan that "its primary and principal author" is God (bk. 3, ch. 3: 3-4), who confers it immediately — not, however (as Vitoria thinks), by a special grant to rulers, but as a natural property or faculty possessed by the political *corpus mysticum* (bk. 3, ch. 3: 5-6).

The extreme voluntarist logic of his notion of "faculty" (bequeathed by the Paris masters Almain and Mair) is demonstrated by his argument that the natural, "quasi-moral properties" of communities, as of individuals, are alienable "like titles of ownership"; so that communities, as individuals, may willingly transfer their freedom (i.e., their faculty of self-government) or may unwillingly be deprived of it for just cause (bk. 3, ch. 3: 7). For example, the American Indians might willingly have transferred their jurisdiction to the Spanish or been deprived of it through a just war, although neither was in fact the case. Indeed, all government involves for Suárez a transfer (rather than mere concession) of communal power to the ruler, in which communal consent plays a necessary and constitutive role, though less obvious in the case of hereditary rule or conquest (bk. 3, ch. 4: 2-5). While sharing Vitoria's abhorrence of the radical conciliarist doctrine of communal sovereignty, he finds congenial the more moderate Ockhamist principle (crucial for the early conciliarists) of the polity's natural right to defend itself against destruction by an intolerable tyrant. Such is the heretical James I of England, who has imperiled the spiritual welfare of his subjects by requiring the oath of allegiance, and so justified the resistance of his commonwealth, authorized and abetted by the pope's wide-ranging, "indirect" powers of temporal intervention (*A Defence of the Faith,* bk. 3, ch. 23; bk. 6, ch. 4).

On the *theory of just war,* Suárez follows lines developed in the sixteenth century by Cajetan and Vitoria, often achieving more precision than they did, yet at the price, perhaps, of a manner so coolly analytic that the reader may compare it unfavorably with the flashes of moral fervor that Vitoria could produce. The heart of the theory lies in the notion that war is, and must be conducted as, an extension of the judicial acts of government into a context where no formal jurisdiction prevails. Morally it is never a contest on an equal footing, nor even a contest between a just and an unjust combatant. It is an encounter between an *offender* against the law of nations and an *authority* empowered to restrain or punish him. Of necessity the authority is one and the same as the offender's victim; that is the compromise forced upon juridical practice by the lack of a superior authority. But the just belligerent may not conduct himself *as* an avenging victim, only as the executor of an even-handed justice.

Just war is either defensive or offensive. (The time-honored technical term "aggressive" is unsuitable, as we take it to be morally laden. When Suárez writes of *bellum aggressivum,* he means simply "taking the initiative in opening hostilities.") Offensive war is either to recover damages or to impose punishment. The right to armed self-defense against an injury lies with anybody, but the right of offensive war lies only with a political authority, which, by definition, acts for the common good and is subject to the restraints of just proportion. Notably, Suárez refuses to allow the category of self-defense to expand beyond the strict limits of active or immediate resistance. (On this point the classic just-war theorists contrast strongly with twentieth-century adapters of their thought, who often allow the scope of defense to expand indefinitely while restricting or abolishing the more disciplined rights of recovery and punishment.)

In defining the immunity of the innocent (noncombatants) from direct attack, Suárez makes his greatest advances on his predecessors. Still at a loss for a precise terminology, he declares that the innocent "as such" may not be killed, and then allows that in case of necessity they may be killed "incidentally." These terms are ambiguous enough, but the illustrations he uses, especially the analogy with a pregnant woman taking an incidentally abortifacient drug needed to protect her life, make it clear that he has in view the distinction between "directly" and "indirectly intended" attack developed by later casuists or, in contemporary parlance, between intended effects and foreseen side effects. It is only "necessity" (i.e., the proportionate good, as later casuists will call it) that justifies putting the innocent at risk at all; but necessity is not a sufficient justification, for the distinction between killing per se and *per accidens* must also be maintained — i.e., their death may not be the *object* of the attack, only a foreseen side effect. This humane doctrine, which still resonates powerfully in a world that has had to confront the ideology of "total war," may strike us at first as contrasting oddly with Suárez's relaxed attitude to the fate of the goods, even of the liberty, of parties innocent of military strife, until, perhaps, we reflect on the logic of using economic sanctions against a society where innocent people may have become wealthy on a foundation of oppression.

Further Reading: P. Dumont, *Liberté humaine et concours divin d'après Suarez* (Paris: Beauchesne, 1936); J. H. Fichter, *Man of Spain: Francis Suarez* (New York: Macmillan, 1940); B. Hamilton, *Political Thought in Sixteenth Century Spain: A Study of the Political Ideas of Vitoria, De Soto, Suárez, and Molina* (Oxford: Clarendon Press, 1963); C. Larrainzar, *Una introducción a Francisco Suárez* (Pamplona: Ediciones Universidad de Navarra, 1980); Q. Skinner, *The Foundations of Modern Political Thought*, vol. 2 (Cambridge: Cambridge University Press, 1978); R. Wilenius, *The Social and Political Theory of Francisco Suárez* (Helsinki: Societas Philosophica Fennica, 1963).

From *Laws and God the Lawgiver*, Book 2

ch. 19. *Is the Law of Nations distinct from Natural Law as a Positive Human Law?* [. . .]
The law of nations and the natural law are alike, firstly, in that both are common to all mankind in some sense, so that in a literal sense either may be called a law *of nations*. This is evident in the case of the natural law, which is why we may notice that in the *Digest* (Dig. 1.1.9), as in many other laws, the natural law seems to be called "the law of nations." More strictly, however, this title belongs to law created by the custom of nations (Inst. 1.2.4).

Secondly, they are alike in their subject matter. The law of nations is solely about interhuman relations, and so is the natural law, wholly or for the most part (for a systematic demonstration see ch. 17 above [not included here]). Consequently, many examples which for this reason jurists classify under the law of nations are only nominal instances, strictly speaking, and actually belong to the natural law, e.g., the law of religion, respect for parents, loyalty to one's country, all of which are mentioned in the *Digest* (Dig. 1.1.2 and 3) though they were rightfully omitted by Justinian from the *Institutes*. A precise categorization would find similar cases in Isidore's list (*Etymologies* 5.6 [see above, p. 210]) such as keeping peace-treaties, truces, the immunity of ambassadors, and so on. (We shall discuss the sense Isidore gives to these below.)

Thirdly, the law of nations and the natural law are alike in that both systems include commands, prohibitions, and also concessions or permissions (cf. ch. 18).

On the other hand, the law of nations differs from the natural law primarily and chiefly in that its affirmative commands do not derive their necessity solely from the nature of the case by clear inference from natural principles. As we have shown, whatever is so derived is natural. The necessity of these commands must arise from some other source. The prohibitions of the law of nations, similarly, are not based on the fact that something is evil in itself, which would make them "natural" simply. Viewed rationally, the law of nations is *constitutive*, not *demonstrative* of evil. It does not forbid things because they are evil, but makes things evil by forbidding them. In law such a difference is real and essential; it is enough, therefore, to constitute a difference between the natural law and the law of nations.

It follows from this that they differ, secondly, in that the law of nations cannot be unchanging to the degree that the natural law is. Immutability springs from necessity; what is not equally necessary cannot be equally immutable (as will be explained more fully in the next chapter).

Thirdly, it follows that even where they seem alike, they are not comparable in every respect. With regard to universality and common international acceptance, the natural law is common to all and can only fail to be observed through someone somewhere being wrong; whereas the law of nations is not observed by all nations all the time, but generally, as Isidore says, by "more or less all." In one place something is not observed, but in another it is held to be the law of nations; yet neither need be wrong. Again, though usually concerned with specifically human questions, the natural law may occasionally deal with questions common to men and animals, such as the permissibility of casual sexual intercourse or fornication and of resistance to violence, to the extent that such acts are encouraged or limited by the natural law. [We have corrected the published text at this point, Editors.] The law of nations, then, is quite different from the natural law, especially in respect of the first point.

The conclusion would seem to be that the law of nations is quite strictly human positive law. This proposition may be inferred from St. Thomas (*ST* 1a2ae. 95.4 [see above, pp. 333-34]) where positive law, as such, is divided into law of nations and civil law; both are said to be "human law" derived from natural law. However, a certain ambiguity attaches to these terms, which must be cleared up and St. Thomas's true sense explained.

Law may sometimes be called "human" not because its authorship is human but because it has to do with human affairs; in this sense the natural law itself is human, since it governs the human race and directs its actions. Aristotle (*NE* 1235a4) seems to have understood the term "human law" in this way, calling it "political" or "civil Law," depending on the translation. Civil law he divides into "natural" and "conventional" (*legitimum* [translating Aristotle's *nomikon*]), meaning by the latter term our "positive civil law." St. Thomas (95.2) also seems to have interpreted "human law" in this way, for he divides it into that which has force from natural reasoning and that which has force from human decision; which seem to be simply natural and positive law. Now, St. Thomas calls positive law "human law," and includes in this category all laws made by men. He then subdivides it, with one type of law reached by way of conclusions deriving their force from natural law, which we speak of as declaring rather than making law, the other by way of determinations, introducing new law, which we call "positive law" in a strict sense. So it seems that in the passage previously referred to St. Thomas has the first of these senses in mind in speaking of the law of nations as human positive law, for he says explicitly that it is reached by way of a conclusion which derives its force from the natural law. (Again in 2a2ae.57.3.) This is not to deny that the phrase "positive human law" is meant literally, i.e., of law made by men; but it is said to be made by way of a conclusion, not by way of a determination, since the law of nations does not provide a complete determination in detail but it is introduced in common usage by way of inference, not strictly necessary but so in keeping with nature that the inference is, as it were, prompted by nature. (So it is understood and supported by Soto, *De Iustitia* 1.5.4; more fully, 3.1.3. Similarly Cardinal Bellarmine, *De Clericis* 1.29, and Covarruvias [2.11.4] on VI *reg. iur.* 4.)

This is quite consistent with the jurists' division of the law of nations into "primary" and "secondary," treating the first of these as part of the natural law and the second as positive human law (Albert of Bologna, *De lege, iure et aequitate* 27; du Pineau on Cod. 4.44). Substantially this is the same as our view of the division; the difference is merely terminological. Their "primary" type is essentially natural law, called "law of nations" only because its use is common to many nations. Our use of the term, however, is precise, determined by source and authority, and coincides with the "secondary" type which they accept as positive human law.

The logic of the assertion may be spelled out on the basis of its terms. The division of law into natural and positive (strictly understood), or into divine and human (using the different authorities) is complete, i.e., the two branches are mutually exclusive, as is accepted. But we have shown that a law of nations is not natural law, strictly speaking, and so not divine; therefore it must be positive and human. A supporting argument may be found in Cicero's judgment that the natural law springs not from the exercise of discretion, but from natural self-evidence. So whatever is not from this source is positive human law. But that is the case with the law of nations; it was not self-evidence, but probability and human calculation that determined it.

We have still to explain how the law of nations differs from the civil law. For all positive law established by men purely for the government of political society is what Aristotle calls "conventional" *(legitimum,* Gk. *nomikon);* and this is what seems to be called civil law to judge from Isidore *(loc. cit.,* quoted in D. 1 c. 8), and as St. Thomas thinks *(loc. cit.).* One difference, you may suggest, is that civil law belongs to one state or kingdom, the law of nations to all peoples. But to this there are objections. One is that this difference is merely a matter of larger or smaller scope, purely accidental. A second and more formidable difficulty is that it seems impossible for the law of nations to be common to all peoples and yet have its source in human will and discretion. For in matters which depend on human discretion and decision one does not expect universal agreement; it is the genius of mankind to form as many plans and judgments as there are minds to conceive them. So it would seem either that the law of nations is not human law, or that this cannot be the difference between it and the civil law.

The resolution I propose is as follows: — The commands of the law of nations differ from those of the civil law in that they are not written but conventional, drawn from practices that are not unique to one state or province, but universal or almost so. For according to the legal traditions we have mentioned, and as we shall see further below, human law has two forms, written and unwritten. It is beyond challenge that the law of nations is unwritten, and so this is the key to its distinction from every form of civil law, whether that of the Empire or the Common Law. Now, the unwritten law is made up of customary practices. Yet if it has arisen from the customary practices of one particular nation and is binding upon that nation only, it is still called civil law. If, on the other hand, it has arisen from customary practices common to all nations and is binding upon all nations, then this, we believe, is the law of nations properly so called, distinct from the natural law in being grounded upon custom rather than nature, distinct from the civil law in origin, basis, and universality, as we have explained.

It seems to me that this is Justinian's view (Inst. 1.2.1), where he says: "The law of nations is common to the whole human race, for in view of the necessities of man, practice required the nations of the earth to establish certain laws for themselves." I attach significance to the words "practice required" and "established." The latter indicates a law "established" — i.e., by men, and not by nature. The latter makes it clear that it was not written statute but practice in which it originated. Isidore (*Etymologies* 5.4 [cf. p. 210 above]) apparently holds the same view, for after distinguishing the three kinds of law, he defines the natural law as "common to all nations, and consist(ing) of what is universally held by natural instinct, not by constitution." This supports our own assertion, and effectively maintains that the law of nations is not based upon natural instinct alone. Later on (*ib.* 6), after giving examples of the law of nations, he concludes: "It is called the law of nations since more or less all nations observe it." [. . .]

[In support of his resolution Suárez first adduces an argument from terminology.] A second line of argument is from examples commonly cited. The practice of receiving ambassadors under immunity and security, considered in abstraction, is not required by natural law, under which it is perfectly possible for one human community to have no ambassadors from another, or even refuse to receive any. The expectation of receiving ambassadors is created by the law of nations, by which a refusal to do so becomes an act of enmity in violation, even if there is nothing wrong with it by natural reason. Once ambassadors are received on the usual terms, to deny immunity is an offense against natural law, since it is a breach of faith and natural justice. But the usual terms and treaties for the reception of ambassadors come from the law of nations. The same applies to a contract or commercial transaction. Three separate elements may be distinguished: (1) the specific form for making the contract, which is normally the concern of civil law, and may often be fixed by the contracting parties provided there is no law to the contrary; (2) the observance of the contract once made, which is clearly the business of the natural law; (3) the freedom to make contracts, whether with friendly or hostile parties, which is determined by the law of nations. For natural law imposes no obligations on this score: in principle one civil society might live in isolation and refuse to have commercial relations with another, even with no ground for hostility; but it has been established by the law of nations that commercial relations shall be free, and it would be a violation if they were prohibited without reasonable cause. This is the sense in which one should interpret Inst. 1.2.2: "By this law of nations almost all contracts — purchase, sale, etc. — have been introduced." This pattern applies to other kinds of agreement.

To make the matter clearer, there are two senses, as suggested by Isidore and other legal and literary sources, in which something may be said to be "the law of nations": first, it is law which binds peoples and races in their relations to one another; secondly, it is law which individual states or kingdoms observe, but which is called the law of nations by virtue of a measure of similarity and agreement.

The first sense, in my view, represents the law of nations, as we have explained it, as formally distinct from civil law. The examples we have discussed of ambassadors and commercial agreements belong to this category. The law of war, too, I believe, belongs to the law of nations in that it is based on the power of a sovereign republic or monarchy to punish or recover injuries inflicted on it by another. Natural reason alone would not require this power to be located in an injured state. Other means of punishment could be devised, or some princely third party be entrusted to act as arbiter with power to compel. But custom has adopted the method we now practice as easier and more appropriate to nature, and it commands the claim of justice to the point that one may not resist it. In the same category I place the law of servitude. Peoples and nations practice this law in common, though it was not required by pure natural reason; again, other means of punishment could be provided. As it is, however, the law has such force as to require the guilty to undergo this punishment when inflicted lawfully, while the victors are not permitted, once hostilities have ceased, to impose any heavier punishment upon their conquered enemies without some special ground. Similarly, treaties of peace and truces may be placed under this head: not, to be sure, the duty of observing them once made, which is a matter of natural law; but the principle that one may not refuse to agree to a reasonable request in due form. This principle is highly compatible with natural reason; yet it is custom and the law of nations which has made it a firm and binding rule.

The rational basis of this part of the law is that the human race, though divided into different peoples and kingdoms, always preserves a certain unity, not only of a biological kind, but a moral and political unity, as is enjoined by the natural precept of mutual love and mercy to be extended to all, including strangers of any nation. So although every sovereign state, commonwealth, or kingdom may constitute a perfect community in itself consisting of its members, yet in terms of the human race every one of them is in some sense a member of a whole; for these communities, taken in isolation, are never so self-sufficient that they need no mutual assistance, society, and communication, sometimes to enhance their well-being and interest, sometimes to meet some moral requirement or need, as their actual practice illustrates. This is why they need some law to direct them and determine the shape of upright conduct in their dealings and associations with one another. Natural reason supplies a good part of this, but it is not enough, and does not determine the details completely; so there was room for specific laws to be recognized on the basis of customary practices. Custom creates law in a single state or province, and so it does in the human race as a whole. It was possible to generate a body of laws of nations from the best practice, especially since the contents were not extensive and lay very close to the natural law, making the derivation of the one law from the other very easy. Of such value was it to mankind and so appropriate to human nature, that, even when the derivation was in principle not strictly necessary, it was naturally fitting and universally acceptable as such.

Law of nations in the second sense includes precepts, practices, and modes of living which do not of themselves and directly relate to mankind as a whole, neither is their immediate end the harmonious society and communication of the nations with each other. In each state they are established by that government which is recognized in the courts. These, however, are practices and laws on which almost all nations agree, or at least act similarly, sometimes in general, sometimes in specific detail.

From Book 3

ch. 2. *Who naturally has the direct power to make human laws?* The question is: does it belong (1) to particular individuals, or perhaps to every particular individual? or does it belong (2) to a collectivity of mankind as a whole?

The first of these cannot be maintained. It is impossible that *every* particular person is superior to every other; and there is no reason in nature that *some* particular people have this power rather than others, since there is no objective ground on which these should, rather than those. [. . .]

To declare our position: from a purely natural point of view, this power does not belong to any individual but to a collectivity of mankind as a whole. This view is commonly accepted and certainly true. It is implied by St. Thomas's view that the prince has a power to make laws, which was transferred to him by the community (*ST* 1a2ae.90.3 *ad* 2 and 97.3 *ad* 3), a view both assumed and expressed in civil law (Dig. 1.4.1 and Dig. 1.2.2.11). [. . .]

In order to clarify the point, we must note that a "multitude" can be conceived in two different ways. First, as a disordered aggregate simply, with no principle of unity, whether on the physical or moral plane, forming no kind of physical or moral entity, and so not constituting one political body, properly speaking, in need of one prince or head. Conceiving the multitude of mankind this way, we cannot attribute such power to it strictly and formally, but at most as an implied potentiality. Yet there is another way to conceive it: as by a special act of will or agreement, it comes together to form a single political community, bound by a single tie of association for mutual assistance in the pursuit of one political end. This is to form a "mystical body" *(corpus mysticum)* which can be described, morally speaking, as "one," and so needs a single head. In a community of such a kind, then, this power exists in the very nature of things, so that those who form such a group may not prevent it. If we imagine men wanting to come together on the condition that they should not be subject to any such power, they would be willing a contradiction, and would accomplish nothing. It is impossible to conceive of a unified political body without political government or a disposition to it. For, in the first place, this unity arises in large measure precisely from subjection to a single rule and a common superior power. In the second place, if there were not a government, this body could not be directed to one end and to the common good. It defies natural reason, then, to assume the existence of a group of human beings united in the form of a single political body, without postulating some common power which the individual members of the community are bound to obey; but if this power does not reside in any specific individual, it must necessarily exist in the community as a whole.

An additional observation: it is not intrinsically necessary that this power located in a multitude should be *one single* power for the whole species, located in the total collectivity of mankind throughout the world. The preservation or welfare of human nature does not require that everyone should be gathered into a single political community. That would hardly be possible indeed, let alone beneficial. Aristotle has said that it is hard to govern too large a city well (*Politics* 1326a25ff.). It is correspondingly harder to govern a kingdom that is too extensive; universal government, then, would be much harder again — i.e., *civil* government. I think it probable, then, that power of this type and fashion never arose in the universal human community, or, if it did, only for the briefest space of time. The division of mankind into political communities happened shortly after the Creation, and this power arose in each of them separately. Augustine (*City of God* 15.8) derives from Gen. 4 that Cain was the first to found his own political kingdom before the Flood, and adds (16.4 on Gen. 10) that after the Flood it was Nimrod. Cain was the first, that is, to leave the paternal home and so subdivide the perfect community; later Nimrod did the same in leaving Noah.

This leads us to conclude that the power of making proper and particular human laws ("civil laws," to govern one particular "perfect community") was never a unitary power for the whole human race. It arose with the subdivision of the human community, as each community was founded and separated off. We conclude, too, that this civil power did not reside in any individual universal ruler, before the coming of Christ at least. At no time did all men agree to confer that power upon a world ruler; nor do we learn that God ever did so. The most likely opportunity for his doing so was with Adam; but we have already excluded that theory. [Adam had domestic, not political, primacy, argued in a passage omitted above.] Finally, no one ever acquired such power by war or other means, as is established from historical records. But what we must say about the situation after Christ's coming we shall see in book 3. [. . .]

ch. 3. *Has the power to make human laws been given by God immediately as author of nature?* The question can be put: from what we have said it seems to follow that this power derives *from* the consent of individual members *to* the community as a whole which they comprise. For the power has the same source as the community where it resides; but that community is formed by voluntary consent of its individual members; and so that is where the power must spring from. The major premise is proved as follows: the power arises with the community; but whatever gives the form, gives the consequents of the form; so what gives rise to the community must give rise to the power and confer it. Against this, however: the individuals had no such power, either wholly or partially, before they came together into one political body; nor did it even arise, as we showed in the last chapter, in the "bare assemblage" (if I may be allowed the phrase) or aggregate of the men who made the community; it could never be the case, then, that the power proceeded immediately from them.

The general opinion appears to be that this power is given immediately by God as author of nature. Men, as it were, provide the material, producing a candidate for holding the power; God imparts the form and confers it. (See Cajetan, *De potestate papae* 2.10, Covarruvias, *Practicae quaestiones* 1.6; and more extensively Vitoria, *De potestate civili*, and Soto, *De iustitia et iure* 4.2.1.)

The argument for this is one I have already made: given that men decide to come together in a single state, it is not in their power to prevent there being such a jurisdiction; which is an indication that it does not flow directly from their decision as its efficient cause. It is like marriage: the husband is the head of the wife, we suppose, by grant of the author of nature himself, not by the wife's decision. Their decision to marry may be free; but once they marry, they cannot prevent this order of precedence arising. In support of this view we quote St. Paul (Rom. 13:1f.): "There is no power except from God . . . therefore he who resists the power resists what God has appointed." In that case, this power is from God; and immediately from God, since there is no other more proximate or immediate source.

A second argument is that there are several acts implied by this power which seem to go beyond what human beings, as individuals, can do; and this is an indication that the power derives not from them but from God. First this power may punish offenders, not excluding punishment by death. Since God alone is Lord of life, he alone, it seems, could have granted this power. Augustine says, "No one has power to harm another except from God" (*De natura boni* 32). Secondly, it may determine in relation to some matter what the mean of virtue necessary to right behavior is, and then, thirdly, bind the conscience to observe it. This especially, as we shall see below, is a prerogative of divine power. Fourthly, it may avenge wrongs done to individuals, a right otherwise restricted by the text: "Vengeance is mine; I will repay, says the Lord" (Rom. 12:19). This demonstrates the divine source of this power, since, were it otherwise, men might just as well have taken other means of avenging wrongs, an idea incompatible with natural justice.

One part of this opinion is clear and beyond dispute; the other requires explanation.

The first is that the power comes from God as its primary and principal author. This seems to be Paul's clear opinion and to be proved decisively by the arguments alleged. Furthermore, since this power is natural and so, whether physical or moral, a good thing as such, valuable and necessary for the flourishing of human nature, it must originate with the author of that nature. Finally, since those who exercise this power in the human community are ministers of God, the power they administer must be received from God; God, then, is not only the ultimate author of this power but its proximate author.

It needs explaining, however, in what sense God may be said to confer this power immediately. Briefly: (1) God gives it as a property entailed by nature, just like any other entailment of a God-given form. This is shown, first, by the fact that there is no special act of conferral or grant distinct from creation; for we would know about such a grant from revelation, which in fact we do not. Moreover, if it were otherwise, it would not be a natural power. So, then, it is given as a property entailed by nature, mediated, indeed, by a demand of natural reason, which demonstrates that

734

God has made sufficient provision for mankind in giving it the power necessary for self-preservation and appropriate government.

But (2) this power does not emerge in human nature until men gather in one perfect community and unite politically. The proof is that the power does not exist in individual men taken one by one, nor in a random gathering or disordered mass without unification in one body. Therefore, such a political body must be constituted before this power arises in men, because the power, at least in the order of nature, presupposes a subject of power. Once constituted, this body is at once, and by force of natural reason, the site of this power. The power is correctly understood, then, only as a property entailed by such a mystical body so constituted. Like an individual man, who by the very fact of being created and having the use of his reason possesses power over himself, and so power to use his faculties and limbs, and is naturally free, i.e., not enslaved but lord of his actions; so a political body of men by the very fact of coming into existence possesses the power of self-government, and so a specific power of lordship over its members. To pursue the analogy; as each individual is given liberty by the author of nature, yet not without the engagement of a proximate cause of his coming into being, i.e., a parent, so a community of men is given this power by the author of nature, yet not without the engagement of the decisions and consent of those who assemble to constitute a perfect community. Yet as in the one case the only necessary thing is the parent's decision to perform the act of generation, and there is no need for a special decision to give the child liberty or any other natural faculty, which follow naturally as such, independently of the special intentions of a progenitor; so in this case, the only necessary thing is the decision to form a perfect community; there is no need for a special decision that the community should have this power; it follows naturally by the providence of the author of nature, and in this sense is rightly said to be conferred "immediately."

(3) I add that though this power is like a natural property of a perfect human community as such, it does not cling to it immutably, but may be transferred from that community, by its consent or other just means, to someone else. [. . .]

ch. 4. *The Implications of this Doctrine.* [. . .] We infer, then, that men as individuals naturally possess a partial capacity to establish or bring to existence a perfect community; but by virtue of the very fact that they do establish it, the power in question comes to reside in this community as a whole. Nevertheless, natural law does not require that it should be exercised directly by the whole community or should always continue to be located there. That would in practice be very difficult; there would be infinite confusion and trouble if everyone had to vote in order for laws to be made; so communities immediately regulate this power by one of the forms of government we have mentioned [monarchy, aristocracy, democracy, and mixed forms], since it is impossible to conceive of others, as a little reflection will show.

The second implication is that civil power residing in an ordinary lawful manner in the person of one individual, or prince, has derived from the people as a community, immediately or at a remove, and could not be just on any other terms. This is the general opinion of the legal commentators on the *Digest* (Dig. 1.4.1, Dig. 1.2.2), and is implied in the texts of the laws themselves. It is the view of

Panormitanus and the canonists (on X 4.17.13), of St. Thomas (*ST* 1a2ae.90.3, 97.3), of Cajetan (*De potestate papae* 2.2, 9), and of Vitoria *(De potestate civili)*, as well as of others cited. The argument we have made for this is that this power naturally belongs to the community first; it can only reside in an individual sovereign prince if it is bestowed on him with the community's consent. [. . .]

Our view may be faulted for implying that royal power is a matter of solely human right, contradicting, it would seem, the language of the Scriptures: "By me kings reign" (Prov. 8:15) and, "For he is God's minister" (Rom. 13:4). Again, it might seem to imply that the kingdom, having given the king his power, is superior to the king, and further, that the kingdom may depose or change its king at will, which is altogether false. This was why Vitoria *(loc. cit.)* held that royal power must be said in principle to be from divine law and granted by God, though on the condition of a human decision. (The contrary is argued by Bertrandi, *De origine iuris* 1, Driedo, *De libertate Christiana* 1.15, and Castro, *De potestate legis poenalis* 1.1.) Vitoria is certainly right if we speak of royal power in an abstract sense, as power located as such in a single person. For the power of government, in its essence as a political phenomenon, is certainly from God as I have said; yet I have also shown how the fact that it resides in *this* individual comes from a grant on the part of the state itself; so in this sense this power is part of human right. Moreover, it is a matter of human decision, as I have shown, that a state or a province is a monarchy, so that the princely office is itself a human institution. As an indication of this, the king's power may vary in extent, depending upon the terms of the constitutional bond between him and his kingdom. So, in the simplest manner of speaking, his power is derived from men.

By the expressions in Holy Scripture two things are meant: (1) that this power *viewed as such,* is from God and, incidentally, that it is both just and in conformity with God's will; (2) that once power has been transferred to the king, he is *then* God's representative whom we are bound to obey by natural right. When a person sells himself as slave to another, the master's power is, simply speaking, humanly given; but once the transaction is complete, the slave is obliged by divine and natural right to obey his master. And this provides the answer to the argument brought in objection: once the power is transferred to the king, he becomes superior to the kingdom which gave it him, since the kingdom has accepted subjection and stripped itself of its former liberty, as in the analogous case of the slave. That is why the king cannot be deprived of his power, since it is a true lordship that he has acquired, conditional only on his not slipping into tyranny, which would entitle the kingdom to wage a just war against him. Of which more elsewhere.

The Three Theological Virtues, Faith, Hope, and Charity: On Charity, Disputation 13, War

An open conflict which frustrates public peace is properly called "war" only when conducted between two princes or states. Between a prince and his state, or between citizens and their state, it is called "sedition." Between private persons it is called "strife" or a "duel." But the difference between these seems to be material rather than formal, and we shall discuss them all, as did St. Thomas (2a.2ae.40-2) as well as others to be mentioned below.

1. *Is war intrinsically evil?* The first heresy is to assert that engaging in war is intrinsically evil and inconsistent with charity. Augustine attributes this view to the Manicheans (*Against Faustus* 22.74); Wyclif, according to the testimony of Waldensis (*De sacramentalibus*), followed them [inaccurate: Wyclif actually holds the second of these two positions, that war is forbidden *between* Christians]. The second error is that war is specifically forbidden to Christians, especially war against other Christians. So Eck maintains (*Enchiridion* 22), and other heretics of our own time — yet making a distinction between two kinds of war, defensive and offensive. We shall explain this pair of terms in paragraph 6.

[Suárez then advances three propositions: (1) War as such is not intrinsically evil or forbidden to Christians. (2) Defensive war may sometimes be not merely permitted, but required. (3) Even offensive war is not evil of itself.]

It remains for us to explain the difference between offensive and defensive war. Sometimes an act may appear to be offensive, when it is defensive in fact: e.g., if an attacker has seized a community's dwellings or property, and that community then invades the attacker's territory, it is not offensive but defensive. So civil laws that license me to repel force with force when anyone tries to drive me from my possession are morally sound, too (e.g., Cod. 8.4.1 and Dig. 43.16.1, 3). That is not offense, but defense, which one may undertake on one's own authority. The laws extend to someone deprived of what they call a "natural" possession while away, and prevented from recovering it on his return. They establish the principle that one may take arms on one's own authority when wrongfully dispossessed, since that is not really offensive, but a defense of one's legal possession. (See also X 2.13.12.)

The point to establish is whether the injury is, morally speaking, *actually being done,* or whether it has *already been done,* so that what one then seeks to achieve through war is redress. In the latter case war is offensive. In the former case war has the character of self-defense, provided that its conduct does not exceed the limits of innocent self-protection. Now, the injury is considered as "actually being done" *either* while the unjust action itself, physically speaking, is being performed — when, for instance, the victim has not yet been entirely deprived of his rightful possession; *or* when he has been so deprived, but takes immediate steps — i.e., without noticeable delay — to protect and reestablish himself. The reason for this is that when one is to all intents and purposes, actually offering resistance and striving as best one may to protect one's right, one is not deemed to have actually suffered the wrong or been deprived of the possession in a final sense. This is the common opinion of the Doctors (see Sylvester, s.v. *bellum* 2; also Bartolus and the jurists on Dig. 43.16.3.9).

Our *fourth proposition* is: — For war to be conducted justly, several conditions must be observed, which may be grouped under three heads. (1) It must be waged by a legitimate authority. (2) There must be a just cause and reason alleged. (3) It must be properly and fairly conducted at its inception, in its prosecution, and in victory. All of this will become evident in the following sections; but this summary proposition can be justified as follows: though not evil in itself, war is surrounded by so much destruction that it is the kind of business that it is very often wrong to undertake. For it to be justified, there are many conditions that must be met.

4. *What is a just cause of war, on the basis of natural reason?* [Suárez proposes, *first,* that there must be a legitimate and necessary ground, noting (1) that it must be serious; and (2) that there are various kinds of provocation that might constitute it.]

Note (3) that when the wrong has been done [i.e., when the war would be offensive] two kinds of case for war may be made. The first is that reparation should be made to the injured party for the damage suffered. There is no problem with the legitimacy of declaring war for this purpose, for if war is justified in terms of the wrong done, it is clearly justified when the purpose is to secure a remedy for the wrongful loss. There are many examples in the Scriptures (Gen. 14, etc.). The other case is that the wrongdoer may be properly punished; but this presents a problem which requires separate treatment.

Our second proposition is that it is a just ground for war that the wrongdoer should be justly punished if he refuses otherwise to give adequate satisfaction for the injury. This view is commonly accepted. In this thesis, as with the preceding one, we must insist on the condition, that the opposing party is not ready to make restitution or give satisfaction; for if he were, the offensive war would be unjust, as we shall demonstrate in what follows. The conclusion is proved in the first place from certain scriptural passages (Num. 25; 2 Sam. 10–11), in which at God's command straightforward punishment was executed on wrongdoing. The reason is that, as within a single state some lawful authority to punish crimes is needed to preserve domestic peace, so in the world as a whole, for the various states to live in concord, there must exist some authority to punish injuries inflicted by one state on another. This authority does not reside in a superior, for they have none, we suppose. Therefore it must reside in the sovereign prince of the injured state, to whom the other is subject on account of the wrong he has done. So this kind of war serves in place of a court administering just punishment.

Objection 1: This is contrary to the text in Romans: "Repay no one evil for evil," and "Never avenge yourselves" (12:17, 19). *Reply:* This is interpreted with reference to private authority and the intent to do evil to another for the sake of it. But if it is done by lawful public authority with the intention of holding an enemy to his duty and bringing what was out of order back into line, it is not only not forbidden but is necessary. So Romans continues (13:4): "for he does not bear the sword in vain; he is the servant of God to execute his wrath on the wrongdoer."

Objection 2: It follows that the same party in the same case is both plaintiff and judge, which is contrary to the natural law. It is evident that it does follow, since the same prince who has been wronged assumes the role of judge by initiating hostilities. *In support* of the objection it may be argued: (1) that private individuals are denied the right to avenge themselves because in effect they would overstep the limits of justice, but the same danger arises in the case of a prince who avenges himself; (2) that any private person unable to secure such punishment through a judge might, by the same reasoning, take the law into his own hands and execute it on his own authority, for princes are granted this privilege solely on the ground that there is no other way to secure a just punishment.

Reply: — It cannot be denied that in this instance one and the same person assumes paradoxically the dual role of plaintiff and of judge. Public authority is like God in this respect, of whom the same is true. But the only reason for it is that this act of punitive justice was indispensable to mankind, and that no more fitting means for it was forthcoming within the limits of nature and human action. In addition, we must anticipate that before the war the offending party was unyielding and unwilling to give satisfaction; if he then finds himself subject to his victim, he must lay the blame at his own door. The case is unlike that of a private individual in two respects. (1) Guided by his own deliberations he will easily exceed the limits of punishment; but public authority is bound to attend to public deliberations and be guided by them, so that it is easier to avoid the destructiveness of private emotions. (2) The authority to punish is as such directed not to the private but the public good, so that it is entrusted not to a private but to a public agent. If this is unable or unwilling to punish, the private agent shall endure his loss patiently. The reply to the first supporting argument is clear from this.

In reply to the second supporting argument, some have indeed maintained that in that situation a private person may punish the offender secretly. In the *Codex* (3.27) there is a title: "When it is permitted to avenge oneself without recourse to a judge." But this has come to be understood to refer to recovery of loss; applied to the punishment of crime, it is an unacceptable mistake. Acts of punitive justice are the prerogative of a jurisdiction which private persons do not possess and do not acquire through others' offenses. Were it otherwise, there would be no requirement to resort to public jurisdictional authority; or at least, since jurisdictional authority would be derived from men, any individual person could have refused to concede it to the magistrate and retained it for himself — an outcome contrary to natural law and good government of the human race. So we reject the inference in the second supporting argument. Laws treat of the nature of the case. It is of the nature of the case that private individuals are readily avenged for offenses because public authority exists; the fact that sometimes this is not possible is, as we have said, an accident, which, as such, must be borne as a necessity. But the necessity involved in the relationship between two sovereign powers is itself of the nature of the case. (We should understand in this way the civil-law glosses cited by Covarruvias. See also Vitoria, *De potestate civili* 6ff., and de Soto, *De iustitia* 4.4.)

Our third proposition is that whoever begins a war without a just ground, sins not only against charity but against justice, too, and so is bound to make reparation for all the damage. This is obvious. [. . .]

It should, however, be noted that Cajetan (on *ST* 2a2ae.96.4) concludes from this that for a war to be just, the prince ought to be so certain of the extent of his power that he is morally assured of victory. For in the first place, he would otherwise be exposed to the obvious danger of doing more harm than good to his own state. Cajetan compares him to a judge, who would be wrong to attempt an arrest without a force that he was certain could not be overpowered. In the second place, to initiate war is to assume the active role; and an active party must always be the stronger, to overcome passive resistance. But this condition does not seem to me absolutely necessary. First, from a human standpoint, it is almost impossible to meet. Secondly, it often serves the common good of the state not to wait for such a degree of certainty but to take the risk, even when the ability to overcome the enemy is in doubt. Thirdly, if it were true, it would never be right for a weaker ruler to make war on a stronger, since the certainty which Cajetan demands would be beyond his reach.

So we should conclude that a prince is obliged to make as sure as possible of victory. He should measure the likelihood of victory against the risk of loss, weighing everything up to see whether the calculation is decisively positive. If he cannot reach as strong a certainty as this, he should at least regard the positive outcome as the more likely, or equally likely, if the danger to the common welfare of his state justifies it. But if the positive outcome is less probable and the war is offensive, then it should almost always be avoided. If the war is defensive, it should be attempted; for then it is a matter of necessity, in the other case a matter of choice. All this follows clearly enough from the principles of conscience and justice.

7. *What is the right way to conduct war?* [Suárez proposes: (1) Before going to war, a prince must declare his grounds and demand restitution. (2) All methods necessary to success may be used, provided they include no intrinsic wrong done to innocent people. (3) After victory damages sufficient for restitution and punishment may be imposed.]

But there remains a further question, whether it is permitted to impose such damages equally on all who are counted as belonging to the enemy. In answering we must note that some persons are said to be guilty, others innocent. The innocent include children, women, and all incapable of bearing arms (by natural law), ambassadors (by the law of nations), and religious persons, priests, etc. (by positive law among Christians) (X 1.34.2, Cajetan on C. 24 q. 3 c. 25, holds that this provision of law has been superseded by custom, which should be observed). All others are considered guilty; for human judgment looks on those who are able to take up arms as having actually done so. Now, the hostile state is composed of both classes; all these persons, therefore, are counted as "the enemy" (Dig. 49.15.24). Strangers and foreigners are in another category, since they form no part of the state and therefore are not reckoned among the enemy, unless they are allies in the war.

Assuming this is true, *our fourth proposition* is that if damages inflicted upon the guilty are enough for restitution and satisfaction, they cannot rightly be extended to the innocent. This is an evident implication of what has been said, for one may not demand greater satisfaction than what is just. The only question is whether victorious soldiers are always bound to proceed in this order, taking reprisals upon the guilty and their property first. The short reply is that they are, other things being equal and within each category of property. For the principle of equity clearly imposes this rule, as will be clearer as we proceed.

Our fifth proposition is that it is permitted to deprive the innocent of their goods, even of their liberty, if such a course of action is essential to complete satisfaction. The reason is that the innocent form a portion of one whole and unjust state; and on account of the whole, the part may be punished even though it does not of itself share in the blame. [. . .]

Our sixth proposition is (a) that innocent persons, as such, may absolutely not be killed, even if the punishment inflicted upon their state would otherwise be thought inadequate. *(b)* They may be killed only incidentally *(per accidens)* when such an act is necessary to the pursuit of victory. The logic of the proposition is that the slaying of innocent persons is intrinsically evil. You may say: that is true of killing on private authority and without just ground; but this is different, involving public authority and just ground. But that means nothing if the killing is unnecessary for victory, as we say, and if the innocent can be separated from the guilty.

Arguments in support of (a): (1) Life is not the same as other possessions. They fall under human dominion, and the state as a whole has a higher right over them than particular persons; so they may be deprived of their property for the guilt of the whole. But life does not fall under human dominion, so that no one may be deprived of life other than for his own guilt. Which is why, of course, a son is never killed for the sin of his father (Deut. 24:16, cf. Exod. 23:7, "Do not slay the innocent"). (2) The innocent would be justified in defending themselves if they were able; so to attack them is unjust. (3) Ambrose imposed severe excommunication on Theodosius for just such a slaughter of the innocent (C. 11 q. 3 c. 69). You ask, who are the innocent in this regard? I reply that they include not only those listed above, but also those capable of bearing arms if it is otherwise clear that they had no part in the crime or the unjust war, for natural law demands that no one actually known to be guiltless shall as such be slain. [. . .]

The second part of this proposition *(b)* is also commonly accepted, and is clearly true of certain procedures necessary for victory but which necessarily involve the death of innocent persons, such as the burning of cities and the sacking of fortresses. Whoever has a right to the end of the war has a right to these means, abstractly speaking, and the death of the innocent is not intended as such, but is an incidental consequence; so it is not held to be *willed* but simply *accepted (permissa)* by the one who exerts his right at a time of need. *Arguments in support:* (1) It would otherwise be impossible to end a war. (2) A pregnant woman may use medicine necessary to preserve her own life, even if she knows that such an act will result in the death of her unborn child. (But these arguments both imply that such procedures are not legitimate *except* in a moment of necessity.)

Arguments to the contrary: — (1) In this case one cooperates positively in securing the death of an innocent person, so one cannot be absolved of blame. (2) To kill an innocent person is no less intrinsically evil than to kill oneself; and to kill oneself in this way, even incidentally, is evil; for example, when soldiers demolish a citadel-wall though they know with certainty that they will be crushed. It is significant that Samson is excused for doing this only because he acted at the prompting of the Holy Spirit (Augustine, *City of God* 1.21, 26; Bernard, *De praecepto et dispensatione* 3; Thomas, *ST* 2a2ae.64.5, ad 4). (3) Evil may not be done that good may ensue. (4) It is forbidden to pull up the tares lest the wheat should be pulled up with them (Matt. 13:29). (5) The innocent persons in question would be justified in defending themselves if they could, so the attack upon them must be unjust. (6) The supporting argument may be reversed: the mother is *not* allowed to use the medicine if she knows for certain that it will cause the death of the child, especially after the infusion of the rational soul. This seems to be the more common opinion (Antoninus, *Summa Theologica* 3.7, 2; Sylvester, s.v. *medicus.* 4; Navarrus, *Summa* 25.62). The logic of this is that if help cannot be given to one without injuring another, it is better to help neither. (On which see C. 14 q.5 c. 10.)

Replies to the arguments: (1) Materially speaking, the victor does not actually kill the innocent; he is not the cause of their death as such, but only incidentally. Morally speaking, he is not guilty of homicide, because he is merely exerting his right, and is not bound to incur a very great cost to himself in avoiding any harm that may result to his neighbor.

(2) It is not intrinsically evil for the same reason that the person in question does not really kill himself, but merely accepts his own death. Whether *that* is allowed depends on the order of charity; that is to say, whether there is such a common good at stake that one ought to expose oneself to so great a peril in defense of it. And there are those who think that Samson's deed may be excused in this way. In his case, however, that argument does not entirely serve. Looked at from a human point of view, the good in question, punishing one's enemies, was not so great as to justify him in incurring death, even incidentally.

(3) *Moral* evils may not be done that good may ensue; but the evils of punishment may, though in this case the evils are accepted as a consequence rather than brought about.

(4) Pulling up tares and wheat was not, in the first place, a lawful necessity. There was no authority for it. And, besides, it did not serve the purpose of the head of the household.

(5) There is some support for the reply that the war in this case may, contingently, be just for both sides. But this does not seem to arise apart from ignorance. My reply is that these people may defend themselves, but no more. That is to say, they may try to stop the burning of the city or the sacking of the citadel, since that is merely to defend their lives, which is perfectly proper to do; but they may not adopt an offensive self-defense, i.e., by engaging in combat with the just belligerents, who are in fact doing them no wrong. But these innocent parties may fight those who are to blame for the war, since they are certainly wronging them.

(6) This opinion must be interpreted as applying *either* when the medicine is not strictly necessary to the mother's life, but perhaps simply to improve her health, in which case the life of the child should have preference — this would seem to be the teaching of Ambrose (*Duties of the Clergy* 3.9) — *or* when it is administered with the deliberate intention of killing the fetus. But if there is both necessity and a right intention, there is no doubt that it is permissible. Besides the considerations already adduced, if the mother were allowed to die, usually the child would die as well. It is better to save the mother's life if possible, accepting the death of the child, rather than accept the death of both. There would, however, be significant doubt if the physical life of the mother were weighed against the spiritual life of the child, if, say, baptism were a possibility; but in this we must observe the rules of the order of charity, mentioned above.

Translation: Editors, from Classics of International Law (Oxford University Press, 1944).

Richard Hooker

(1554-1600)

It is hardly surprising that Richard Hooker's theological consolidation of the Elizabethan Church of England should also be a serious political work, given that the controversy it addressed concerned the basis of the church's official ministry, government, and public worship. Both Romanist and Presbyterian dissenters from Elizabeth's church settlement of 1559 had set Christ's law for his church on earth above man's law, and entrusted its binding interpretation to an authority other than the temporal sovereign. Hooker's defense of the established church, entitled *Of the Laws of Ecclesiastical Polity,* primarily addressed the Presbyterians, who founded church polity and practice on the scripturally revealed commands of God, as mediated by the enlightened consciences of preaching clergy and instructed laity. Most of his polemicism was devoted to portraying the Presbyterian position as scripturally unsound, epistemologically naive, and politically irresponsible.

Hooker's public opposition to Presbyterian ecclesiology did not begin with his initial labor on the *Laws* in 1591, but accompanied his entire career, from his youthful fellowship at Corpus Christi College, Oxford (1577-84), through his Mastership of the Temple (1584-91), where he waged a protracted battle with Walter Travers, the leading exponent, along with Thomas Cartwright (see pp. 702-10), of Presbyterian church reform. Only after Travers's peremptory silencing by Archbishop Whitgift of Canterbury (Shirley 1949, 39) and subsequent removal to Dublin did Hooker quit his post for a living in Wiltshire, wearied by partisan quarrels and desirous of examining at length and in writing the principles of the English church establishment. Through assiduous literary labor he succeeded in publishing in 1593 the preface and first four books of the *Laws,* which undoubtedly owed much to his years of debating. Their appearance in the wake of the executions of prominent Separatists may suggest government sponsorship, an impression strengthened by Hooker's presentation by the Crown in 1595 to the living of Bishopsbourne in Kent, where he worked on the remaining four books of his *magnum opus,* seeing his fifth book published in 1597.

The posthumous publication in 1648 of the sixth and eighth books, which defended, respectively, Anglican discipline and the civil sovereign's power of "ecclesiastical dominion," and in 1662 of the seventh, defending the institution of episcopacy, left posterity with grave uncertainties about their arrangement and authenticity. The long interval before their publication, ambiguity about the state of the manuscripts at Hooker's death, and the contentious character of their subject matter have fed suspicions of extensive textual adulteration. Scholarly reservations have especially alighted on the assertion in book 7 of a divinely instituted episcopacy belonging to the church's essence, and on the principles of popular sovereignty, compact, and consent woven into book 8. In recent years, owing in part to the careful scholarship of the Folger edition of the *Laws* (1977-81), there has been renewed appreciation of the subtlety and complexity of Hooker's positions, the consistency of which has sometimes eluded critics. The balanced interpretations of Hooker's intentions, debts, and legacy offered by, e.g., R. K. Faulkner (1981) and A. S. McGrade (1989), have offset less nuanced, discrediting, and anachronistic judgments.

Hooker's primary intention in the *Laws* was twofold: to deprive the ongoing Puritan struggle for church reform of its theoretical justification and to provide the established church with a coherent theoretical self-accounting. As the preface made clear, his immediate, practical task was to persuade the dissenters to accept a *political resolution* of the church quarrel, i.e., a resolution by "some judicial and definitive sentence" given either by regular authorities or a special council. Such acceptance would presuppose a *properly political understanding of church polity* — one that acknowledged its dependence on political rationality grounded in natural law. For Hooker, the theological task of demonstrating the congruence of Prayer Book Anglicanism with God's revealed truth and law of salvation in Christ, although indispensable, was secondary. Throughout his apology for the ecclesiastical status quo, the "visible" or "external" church of largely human devising occupies the foreground, while the "invisible" or "inward" church of Christ's spiritual government occupies the background: an appeal to "equity and reason," the laws of "nature" and "man," consistently takes precedence over an appeal to supernatural truth and command.

Hooker's first book, setting out his typology of law in a manner reminiscent of St. Thomas in *Summa Theologiae* 1a2ae.90-97 (see pp. 342-51 above), constitutes the theoretical core of his ecclesiology and introduces all of his noteworthy political ideas and principles. His thought is obviously indebted to Aristotle, but also to the English natural law tradition of Fortescue, and to those Gersonian and conciliarist ideas that infiltrated Fortescue and so much of sixteenth-century political thought. The most influential portion of this book is undoubtedly chapter 10, which delineates "human" law (in distinction from moral law) through its inseparable relationship to the origin and authority of government. Notable is Hooker's combining of an Aristotelian account of the origin of *society* with an Augustinian account of the origin of *rule*. Thus he complements man's instinctive and rational sociality with mutual deliberation and resolve in establishing an "order of union" or "law of the Commonweal" for the sake of defending the common good. While his original act(s) of political consent, on which the persisting right of government rests, recalls Fortescue's mystical "compact," he places less emphasis than Fortescue on structures of ongoing public consent, though he, too, approves of "parliaments, councils, and the like assemblies." Despite its liberal elements, his corporation theory has a more conservative tenor (as befits a loyal Elizabethan) than would be suggested by John Locke and Algernon Sydney's later appeal to it. The groundwork for international law that concludes the chapter anticipates the best seventeenth-century developments by anchoring the law of nations in natural human desire for universal society and fellowship, by distinguishing laws grounded on "sincere" and on "depraved" human nature, and making the authority of international law over commonwealths tantamount to that of the civil law over private persons. A further division of law into mutable and immutable (ch. 15) completes the theoretical framework for Hooker's ecclesiological analysis.

The passage from book 3, chapter 9 gives only a glimpse of the relations between reason and revelation, natural and supernatural laws, human and divine, immutable and mutable commands uncovered by Hooker's pervasive political rationality in the course of ascertaining the principles of external church order and demonstrating the reasonableness of Anglican Prayer Book worship and discipline, episcopal jurisdiction, and royal dominion.

Further Reading: R. K. Faulkner, *Richard Hooker and the Politics of a Christian England* (Berkeley: University of California Press, 1981); W. Speed Hill, ed., *Studies in Richard Hooker: Essays Preliminary to an Edition of His Works* (Cleveland: Case Western Reserve University Press, 1972); W. J. Torrance Kirby, *Richard Hooker's Doctrine of the Royal Supremacy* (Leiden: Brill, 1990); A. S. McGrade, ed., *Richard Hooker, "Of the Laws of Ecclesiastical Polity"* (Cambridge: Cambridge University Press, 1989); A. S. McGrade, ed., *Richard Hooker and the Construction of Christian Community* (Tempe, Ariz.: Medieval and Renaissance Studies, 1997); F. J. Shirley, *Richard Hooker and Contemporary Political Ideas* (London: SPCK, 1949).

From *Laws of Ecclesiastical Polity,* Preface

ch. 6. [1] What success God may give unto any such kind of conference or disputation, we cannot tell. But of this we are right sure, that nature, Scripture, and experience itself, have all taught the world to seek for the ending of contentions by submitting itself unto some judicial and definitive sentence, whereunto neither part that contendeth may under any pretence or colour refuse to stand. This must needs be effectual and strong. As for other means without this, they seldom prevail. I would therefore know, whether for the ending of these irksome strifes, wherein you and your followers do stand thus formally divided against the authorized guides of this church, and the rest of the people subject unto their charge; whether, I say, ye be content to refer your cause to any other higher judgment than your own, or else intend to persist and proceed as ye have begun, till yourselves can be persuaded to condemn yourselves. If your determination be this, we can be but sorry that ye should deserve to be reckoned with such, of whom God himself pronounceth: "The way of peace they have not known" (Rom. 3:17).

[2] Ways of peaceable conclusion there are, but these two certain: the one, a sentence of judicial decision given by authority thereto appointed within ourselves; the other, the like kind of sentence given by a more universal authority. The former of which two ways God himself in the Law prescribeth, and his Spirit it was which directed the very first Christian churches in the world to use the latter. [. . .]

[3] Ye will perhaps make answer, that being persuaded already as touching the truth of your cause, ye are not to hearken unto any sentence, no not though angels should define otherwise, as the blessed Apostle's own example teacheth (Gal. 1:8): again, that men, yea councils, may err; and that, unless the judgment given do satisfy your minds, unless it be such as ye can by no further argument oppugn; in a word, unless you perceive and acknowledge it yourselves consonant with God's word, to stand unto [submit to] it, not allowing it, were to sin against your own consciences.

But consider I beseech you first as touching the Apostle, how that wherein he was so resolute and peremptory, our Lord Jesus Christ made manifest unto him even by intuitive revelation, wherein there was no possibility of error. That which you are persuaded of, ye have it no otherwise than by your own only probable collection, and therefore such bold asseverations as in him were admirable, should in your mouths but argue rashness. God was not ignorant that the priests and judges, whose sentence in matters of controversy he ordained should stand, both might and oftentimes would be deceived in their judgment. Howbeit, better it was in the eye of his understanding, that sometime an erroneous sentence definitive should prevail, till the same authority perceiving such oversight, might afterwards correct or reverse it, than that strifes should have respite to grow, and not come speedily unto some end.

Neither wish we that men should do any thing which in their hearts they are persuaded they ought not to do, but this persuasion ought (we say) to be fully settled in their hearts; that in litigious and controversed causes of such quality, the will of God is to have them do whatsoever the sentence of judicial and final decision shall determine, yea, though it seem in their private opinion to swerve utterly from that which is right: as no doubt many times the sentence amongst the Jews did seem unto one part or other contending, and yet in this case God did then allow them to do that which in their private judgment it seemed, yea and perhaps truly seemed, that the law did disallow. For if God be not the author of confusion but of peace, then can he not be the author of our refusal, but of our contentment, to stand unto some definitive sentence; without which almost impossible it is that either we should avoid confusion, or ever hope to attain peace. To small purpose had the Council of Jerusalem been assembled, if once their determination being set down, men might afterwards have defended their former opinions. When therefore they had give their definitive sentence, all controversy was at an end. Things were disputed before they came to be determined; men afterwards were not to dispute any longer, but to obey. The sentence of judgment finished their strife, which their disputes before judgment could not do. This was ground sufficient for any reasonable man's conscience to build the duty of obedience upon, whatsoever his own opinion were as touching the matter before in question. So full of wilfulness and self-liking is our nature, that without some definitive sentence, which being given may stand, and a necessity of silence on both sides afterward imposed, small hope there is that strifes thus far prosecuted will in short time quietly end.

[5] [...] As for the orders which are established, sith equity and reason, the law of nature, God and man, do all favour that which is in being, till orderly judgment of decision be given against it; it is but justice to exact of you, and perverseness in you it should be to deny, thereunto your willing obedience.

[6] Not that I judge it a thing allowable for men to observe those laws which in their hearts they are steadfastly persuaded to be against the law of God: but your persuasion in this case ye are all bound for the time to suspend; and in otherwise doing, ye offend against God by troubling his church without any just or necessary cause. Be it that there are some reasons inducing you to think hardly of our laws. Are those reasons demonstrative, are they necessary, or but mere probabilities only? An argument necessary and demonstrative is such, as being proposed unto any man and understood, the mind cannot choose but inwardly assent. Any one such reason dischargeth, I grant, the conscience, and setteth it at full liberty. For the public approbation given by the body of this whole church unto those things which are established doth make it but probable that they are good. And therefore unto a necessary proof that they are not good it must give place. But if the skilfullest amongst you can shew that all the books ye have hitherto written be able to afford any one argument of this nature, let the instance be given. As for probabilities, what thing was there ever set down so agreeable with sound reason, but some probable shew against it might be made? [...]

From Book 1

ch. 10. [1] That which hitherto we have set down is (I hope) sufficient to shew their brutishness, which imagine that religion and virtue are only as men will account of them; that we might make as much account, if we would, of the contrary, without any harm unto ourselves, and that in nature they are as indifferent one as the other. We see then how nature itself teacheth laws and statutes to live by. The laws which have been hitherto mentioned do bind men absolutely even as they are men, although they have never any settled fellowship, never any solemn agreement amongst themselves what to do or not to do. But forasmuch as we are not by ourselves sufficient to furnish ourselves with competent store of things needful for such a life as our nature doth desire, a life fit for the dignity of man; therefore, to supply those defects and imperfection which are in us living single and solely by ourselves, we are naturally induced to seek communion and fellowship with others. This was the cause of men's uniting themselves at the first in politic societies, which societies could not be without government, nor government without a distinct kind of law from that which hath been already declared. Two foundations there are which bear up public societies; the one, a natural inclination, whereby all men desire sociable life and fellowship; the other, an order expressly or secretly agreed upon touching the manner of their union in living together. The latter is that which we call the Law of a Commonweal, the very soul of a politic body, the parts whereof are by law animated, held together, and set on work in such actions, as the common good requireth. Laws politic, ordained for external order and regiment amongst men, are never framed as they should be, unless presuming the will of man to be inwardly obstinate, rebellious, and averse from all obedience unto the sacred laws of his nature; in a word, unless presuming man to be in regard of his depraved mind little better than a wild beast, they do accordingly provide notwithstanding so to frame his outward actions, that they be no hindrance unto the common good for which societies are instituted: unless they do this, they are not perfect. [. . .]

[3] But neither that which we learn of ourselves nor that which others teach us can prevail, where wickedness and malice have taken deep root. If therefore when there was but as yet one only family in the world, no means of instruction human or divine could prevent effusion of blood (Gen. 4.8); how could it be chosen but that when families were multiplied and increased upon earth, after separation each providing for itself, envy, strife, contention and violence must grow amongst them? For hath not Nature furnished man with wit and valour, as it were with armour, which may be used as well unto extreme evil as good? Yea, were they not used by the rest of the world unto evil; unto the contrary only by Seth, Enoch, and those few the rest in that line (Gen. 6:5; Gen. 5:21-24)? We all make complaint of the iniquity of our times: not unjustly, for the days are evil. But compare them with those times wherein there was as yet no manner of public regiment established, with those times wherein there were not above eight persons righteous living upon the face of the earth (2 Pet. 2:5); and we have surely good cause to think that God hath blessed us exceedingly, and hath made us behold most happy days.

[4] To take away all such mutual grievances, injuries, and wrongs, there was no way but only by growing unto composition and agreement amongst themselves, by ordaining some kind of government public, and by yielding themselves subject thereunto; that unto whom they granted authority to rule and govern, by them the peace, tranquillity, and happy estate of the rest might be procured. Men always knew that when force and injury was offered they might be defenders of themselves: they knew that howsoever men may see their own commodity, yet if this were done with injury unto others it was not to be suffered, but by all men and by all good means to be withstood; finally they knew that no man might in reason take upon him to determine his own right, and according to his own determination proceed in maintenance thereof, inasmuch as every man is towards himself and them whom he greatly affecteth partial; and therefore that strifes and troubles would be endless, except they gave their common consent all to be ordered by some whom they should agree upon: without which consent there were no reason that one man should take upon him to be lord or judge over another; because, although there be according to the opinion of some very great and judicious men a kind of natural right in the noble, wise, and virtuous, to govern them which are of servile disposition (cf. Aristotle, *Politics* 1255a1-3), nevertheless for manifestation of this their right, and men's more peaceable contentment on both sides, the assent of them who are to be governed seemeth necessary.

To fathers within their private families nature hath given a supreme power; for which cause we see throughout the world even from the foundation thereof, all men have ever been taken as lords and lawful kings in their own houses. Howbeit over a whole grand multitude having no such dependency upon any one, and consisting of so many families as every politic society in the world doth, impossible it is that any should have complete lawful power, but by consent of men, or immediate appointment of God; because not having the natural superiority of fathers, their power must needs be either usurped, and then unlawful; or, if lawful, then either granted or consented unto by them over whom they exercise the same, or else given extraordinarily from God, unto whom all the world is subject. [. . .]

So that in a word all public regiment of what kind soever seemeth evidently to have risen from deliberate advice, consultation, and composition between men, judging it convenient and behoveful; there being no impossibility in nature considered by itself, but that men might have lived without any public regiment. Howbeit, the corruption of our nature being presupposed, we may not deny but that the law of nature doth now require of necessity some kind of regiment, so that to bring things unto the first course they were in, and utterly to take away all kind of public government in the world, were apparently to overturn the whole world.

[5] The case of man's nature standing therefore as it doth, some kind of regiment the law of nature doth require; yet the kinds thereof being many, Nature tieth not to any one, but leaveth the choice as a thing arbitrary. At the first when some certain kind of regiment was once approved, it may be that nothing was then further thought upon for the manner of governing, but all permitted unto their wisdom and discretion which were to rule (cf. Cicero, *De Officiis*, 2.12) till by experience they found this for all parts very inconvenient, so as the thing which they had devised for a remedy did indeed but increase the sore which it should have cured. They saw that to live by one man's will became the cause of all men's misery. This constrained them to come unto laws, wherein all men might see their duties beforehand, and know the penalties of transgressing them. [. . .]

[7] [. . .] Laws do not only teach what is good, but they enjoin it, they have in them a certain constraining force. And to constrain men unto any thing inconvenient doth seem unreasonable. Most requisite therefore it is that to devise laws which all men shall be forced to obey none but wise men be admitted. Laws are matters of principal consequence; men of common capacity and but ordinary judgment are not able (for how should they?) to discern what things are fittest for each kind and state of regiment. We cannot be ignorant how much our obedience unto laws dependeth upon this point. Let a man though never so justly oppose himself unto them that are disordered in their ways, and what one amongst them commonly doth not stomach at such contradiction, storm at reproof, and hate such as would reform them? Notwithstanding even they which brook it worst that men should tell them of their duties, when they are told the same by a law, think very well and reasonably of it. For why? They presume that the law doth speak with all indifferency; that the law hath no side-respect to their persons; that the law is, as it were, an oracle proceeded from wisdom and understanding.

[8] Howbeit laws do not take their constraining force from the quality of such as devise them, but from that power which doth give them the strength of laws. That

which we spake before concerning the power of government must here be applied unto the power of making laws whereby to govern, which power God hath over all; and by the natural law, whereunto he hath made all subject, the lawful power of making laws to command whole politic societies of men belongeth so properly unto the same entire societies, that for any prince or potentate of what kind soever upon earth to exercise the same of himself, and not either by express commission immediately and personally received from God, or else by authority derived at the first from their consent upon whose persons they impose laws, it is no better than tyranny.

Laws they are not therefore which public approbation hath not made so. But approbation not only they give who personally declare their assent by voice sign or act, but also when others do it in their names by right originally at the least derived from them. As in parliaments, councils, and the like assemblies, although we be not personally ourselves present, notwithstanding our assent is by reason of others, agents there in our behalf. And what we do by others, no reason but that it should stand as our deed, no less effectually to bind us than if ourselves had done it in person. In many things assent is given, they that give it not imagining they do so, because the manner of their assenting is not apparent. As for example, when an absolute monarch commandeth his subjects that which seemeth good in his own discretion, hath not his edict the force of a law whether they approve or dislike it? Again, that which hath been received long sithence and is by custom now established, we keep as a law which we may not transgress; yet what consent was ever thereunto sought or required at our hands?

Of this point therefore we are to note that sith men naturally have no full and perfect power to command whole politic multitudes of men, therefore utterly without our consent we could in such sort be at no man's commandment living. And to be commanded we do consent, when that society whereof we are part hath at any time before consented, without revoking the same after by the like universal agreement. Wherefore as any man's deed past is good as long as himself continueth; so the act of a public society of men done five hundred years sithence standeth as theirs who presently are of the same societies, because corporations are immortal; we were then alive in our predecessors, and they in their successors do live still. Laws therefore human, of what kind soever, are available by consent.

[10] Now as the learned in the laws of this land observe, that our statutes sometimes are only the affirmation or ratification of that which by common law was held before; so here it is not to be omitted that generally all laws human, which are made for the ordering of politic societies, be either such as establish some duty whereunto all men by the law of reason did before stand bound; or else such as make that a duty now which before was none. The one sort we may for distinction's sake call "mixedly," and the other "merely" human. That which plain or necessary reason bindeth men unto may be in sundry considerations expedient to be ratified by human law. For example, if confusion of blood in marriage, the liberty of having many wives at once, or any other the like corrupt and unreasonable custom doth happen to have prevailed far, and to have gotten the upper hand of right reason with the greatest part, so that no way is left to rectify such foul disorder without prescribing by law the same things which reason necessarily *doth* enforce but is not *perceived* that

so it doth; or if many be grown unto that which the Apostle did lament in some, concerning whom he writeth, saying, that "even what things they naturally know, in those very things as beasts void of reason they corrupted themselves" (Jude 10); or if there be no such special accident, yet forasmuch as the common sort are led by the sway of their sensual desires, and therefore do more shun sin for the sensible evils which follow it amongst men, than for any kind of sentence which reason doth pronounce against it: this very thing is cause sufficient why duties belonging unto each kind of virtue, albeit the law of reason teach them, should notwithstanding be prescribed even by human law. Which law in this case we term *mixed*, because the matter whereunto it bindeth is the same which reason necessarily doth require at our hands, and from the law of reason it differeth in the manner of binding only. For whereas men before stood bound in conscience to do as the law of reason teacheth, they are now by virtue of human law become constrainable, and if they outwardly transgress, punishable. As for laws which are *merely* human, the matter of them is any thing which reason doth but probably teach to be fit and convenient; so that till such time as law hath passed amongst men about it, of itself it bindeth no man. One example whereof may be this. Lands are by human law in some places after the owner's decease divided unto all his children, in some all descendeth to the eldest son. If the law of reason did necessarily require but the one of these two to be done, they which by law have received the other should be subject to that heavy sentence, which denounceth against all that decree wicked, unjust, and unreasonable things, *woe* (Isa. 10:1). Whereas now which soever be received there is no law of reason transgressed; because there is probable reason why either of them may be expedient, and for either of them more than probable reason there is not to be found.

[12] Now besides that law which simply concerneth men as men, and that which belongeth unto them as they are men linked with others in some form of politic society, there is a third kind of law which toucheth all such several bodies politic, so far forth as one of them hath public commerce with another. And this third is the law of nations. Between men and beasts there is no possibility of sociable communion, because the well-spring of that communion is a natural delight which man hath to transfuse from himself into others, and to receive from others into himself especially those things wherein the excellency of his kind doth most consist. The chiefest instrument of human communion therefore is speech, because thereby we impart mutually one to another the conceits of our reasonable understanding (Aristotle, *Politics* 1253a9-18); and for that cause seeing beasts are not hereof capable, forasmuch as with them we can use no such conference — they being in degree, although above other creatures on earth to whom nature hath denied sense, yet lower than to be sociable companions of man to whom nature hath given reason — it is of Adam said that amongst the beasts "he found not for himself any meet companion" (Gen. 2:20). Civil society doth more content the nature of man than any private kind of solitary living, because in society this good of mutual participation is so much larger than otherwise. Herewith notwithstanding we are not satisfied, but we covet (if it might be) to have a kind of society and fellowship even with all mankind. Which thing Socrates intending to signify professed himself a citizen, not of this or that commonwealth, but of the world (Cicero, *Tusculan Disputations* 5.37, *De legibus*

1.12). And an effect of that very natural desire in us (a manifest token that we wish after a sort an universal fellowship with all men) appeareth by the wonderful delight men have, some to visit foreign countries, some to discover nations not heard of in former ages, we all to know the affairs and dealings of other people, yea to be in league of amity with them: and this not only for traffic's sake, or to the end that when many are confederated each may make other the more strong, but for such cause also as moved the Queen of Sheba to visit Solomon (1 Kings 10:1; 2 Chron. 9:1; Matt. 12:42; Luke 11:31); and in a word, because nature doth presume that how many men there are in the world, so many gods as it were there are, or at leastwise such they should be towards men.

[13] Touching laws which are to serve men in this behalf, even as those laws of reason which (man retaining his original integrity) had been sufficient to direct each particular person in all his affairs and duties, are not sufficient but require the access of other laws, now that man and his offspring are grown thus corrupt and sinful; again, as those laws of polity and regiment, which would have served men living in public society together with that harmless disposition which then they should have had, are not able now to serve, when men's iniquity is so hardly restrained within any tolerable bounds: in like manner, the national laws of mutual commerce between societies of that former and better quality might have been other than now, when nations are so prone to offer violence, injury, and wrong. Hereupon hath grown in every of these three kinds that distinction between *primary* and *secondary* laws; the one grounded upon sincere, the other built upon depraved nature. *Primary laws* of nations are such as concern embassage, such as belong to the courteous entertainment of foreigners and strangers, such as serve for commodious traffic, and the like. *Secondary laws* in the same kind are such as this present unquiet world is most familiarly acquainted with; I mean laws of arms, which yet are much better known than kept. But what matter the law of nations doth contain I omit to search.

The strength and virtue of that law is such that no particular nation can lawfully prejudice the same by any their several laws and ordinances, more than a man by his private resolutions the law of the whole commonwealth or state wherein he liveth. For as civil law, being the act of a whole body politic, doth therefore overrule each several part of the same body, so there is no reason that any one commonwealth of itself should to the prejudice of another annihilate that whereupon the whole world hath agreed. For which cause, the Lacedemonians forbidding all access of strangers into their coasts are in that respect both by Josephus and Theodoret deservedly blamed (Josephus, *Contra Apionem* 2.36; Theodoret, *Graecarum affectionum curatio* 9), as being enemies to that hospitality which for common humanity's sake all the nations on earth should embrace.

[14] Now as there is great cause of communion, and consequently of laws for the maintenance of communion, amongst nations; so amongst nations Christian the like in regard even of Christianity hath been always judged needful.

And in this kind of correspondence amongst nations the force of general councils doth stand. For as one and the same law divine, whereof in the next place we are to speak, is unto all Christian churches a rule for the chiefest things; by means whereof they all in that respect make one church, as having all but "one Lord, one faith, and one baptism" (Eph. 4.5): so the urgent necessity of mutual communion for preservation of our unity in these things, as also for order in some other things convenient to be every where uniformly kept, maketh it requisite that the church of God here on earth have her laws of spiritual commerce between Christian nations — laws by virtue whereof all churches may enjoy freely the use of those reverend, religious, and sacred consultations, which are termed Councils General. A thing whereof God's own blessed Spirit was the author (Acts 15:28); a thing practised by the holy Apostles themselves; a thing always afterwards kept and observed throughout the world; a thing never otherwise than most highly esteemed of, till pride, ambition, and tyranny began by factious and vile endeavours to abuse that divine invention unto the furtherance of wicked purposes. [. . .]

ch. 15. [1] Laws being imposed either by each man upon himself, or by a public society upon the particulars thereof, or by all the nations of men upon every several society, or by the Lord himself upon any or every of these, there is not amongst these four kinds any one but containeth sundry both natural and positive laws. Impossible it is but that they should fall into a number of gross errors who only take such laws for positive as have been made or invented of men, and holding this position, hold also that all positive and none but positive laws are mutable. Laws natural do always bind; laws positive not so, but only after they have been expressly and wittingly imposed. Laws positive there are in every of those kinds before mentioned. As in the first kind the promises which we have passed unto men, and the vows we have made unto God; for these are laws which we tie ourselves unto, and till we have so tied ourselves they bind us not. Laws positive in the second kind are such as the civil constitutions peculiar unto each particular commonweal. In the third kind the law of heraldry in war is positive, and in the last all the judicials which God gave unto the people of Israel to observe. And although no laws but positive be mutable, yet all are not mutable which be positive. Positive laws are either permanent or else changeable, according as the matter itself is concerning which they were first made. Whether God or man be the maker of them, alteration they so far forth admit, as the matter doth exact.

[2] Laws that concern supernatural duties are all positive, and either concern men supernaturally as men, or else as parts of a supernatural society, which society we call the church. To concern men as men supernaturally is to concern them as duties which belong of necessity to all, and yet could not have been known by any to belong unto them, unless God had opened them himself, inasmuch as they do not depend upon any natural ground at all out of which they may be deduced, but are appointed of God to supply the defect of those natural ways of salvation by which we are not now able to attain thereunto. The church, being a supernatural society, doth differ from natural societies in this: that the persons unto whom we associate ourselves in the one are men simply considered as men, but they to whom we be joined in the other are God, angels and holy men. Again the church, being both a society and a society supernatural, although as it is a society it have the selfsame original grounds which other politic societies have, namely, the natural inclination which all men have unto sociable life, and consent to some certain bond of association, which bond is the law that appointeth what kind of order they shall be associated in; yet

unto the church as it is a society supernatural this is peculiar, that part of the bond of their association which belong to the church of God must be a law supernatural, which God himself hath revealed concerning that kind of worship which his people shall do unto him. [. . .]

[3] Wherefore to end with a general rule concerning all the laws which God hath tied men unto: those laws divine that belong, whether naturally or supernaturally, either to men as men, or to men as they live in politic society, or to men as they are of that politic society which is the church, without any further respect had unto any such variable accident as the state of men and of societies of men and of the church itself in this world is subject unto — all laws that so belong unto men, they belong for ever, yea although they be positive laws, unless being positive God himself which made them alter them. The reason is, because the subject or matter of laws in general is thus far forth constant: which matter is that for the ordering whereof laws were instituted, and being instituted, are not changeable without cause, neither can they have cause of change, when that which gave them their first institution remaineth for ever one and the same. On the other side, laws that were made for men or societies or churches, in regard of their being such as they do not always continue, but may perhaps be clean otherwise a while after, and so may require to be otherwise ordered than before: the laws of God himself which are of this nature, no man endued with common sense will ever deny to be of a different constitution from the former, in respect of the one's constancy and the mutability of the other. And this doth seem to have been the very cause why St. John doth so peculiarly term the doctrine that teacheth salvation by Jesus Christ, *evangelium æternum,* "an eternal Gospel" (Rev. 14:6), because there can be no reason wherefore the publishing thereof should be taken away, and any other instead of it proclaimed, as long as the world doth continue; whereas the whole law of rites and ceremonies, although delivered with so great solemnity, is notwithstanding clean abrogated, inasmuch as it had but temporary cause of God's ordaining it.

From Book 3

ch. 9. [1] Laws for the church are not made as they should be, unless the makers follow such direction as they ought to be guided by: wherein that Scripture standeth not the church of God in any stead, or serveth nothing at all to direct, but may be let pass as needless to be consulted with, we judge it profane, impious, and irreligious to think. For although it were in vain to make laws which the Scripture hath already made, because what we are already there commanded to do, on our parts there resteth nothing but only that it be executed; yet because *both* in that which we are commanded, it concerneth the duty of the church by law to provide, that the looseness and slackness of men may not cause the commandments of God to be unexecuted, *and* a number of things there are for which the Scripture hath not provided by any law, but left them unto the careful discretion of the church, we are to search how the church in these cases may be well directed to make that provision by laws which is most convenient and fit. And what is so in these cases, partly Scripture and partly reason must teach to discern. Scripture comprehending examples and laws, laws some natural and some positive, examples there neither are for all cases which require laws to be made, and when there are, they can but direct as precedents only. Natural laws direct in such sort, that in all things we must forever do according unto them; positive so, that against them in no case we may do any thing, as long as the will of God is that they should remain in force. Howbeit when Scripture doth yield us precedents, how far forth they are to be followed; when it giveth natural laws, what particular order is thereunto most agreeable; when positive, which way to make laws unrepugnant unto them; yea though all these should want, yet what kind of ordinances would be most for that good of the church which is aimed at, all this must be by reason found out. And therefore, "to refuse the conduct of the light of nature," saith St. Augustine, is not folly alone "but accompanied with impiety" [untraced].

[2] [. . .] And the truth is that all our controversy in this cause concerning the orders of the church is, what particulars the church may appoint. That which doth find them out is the force of man's reason. That which doth guide and direct his reason is first the general law of nature, which law of nature and the moral law of Scripture are in the substance of law all one. But because there are also in Scripture a number of laws particular and positive, which being in force may not by any law of man be violated; we are in making laws to have thereunto an especial eye. As for example, it might perhaps seem reasonable unto the church of God, following the general laws concerning the nature of marriage, to ordain in particular that cousin-germans shall not marry. Which law notwithstanding ought not to be received in the church, if there should be in Scripture a law particular to the contrary, forbidding utterly the bonds of marriage to be so far forth abridged. The same Thomas therefore, whose definition of human laws we mentioned before, doth add thereunto this caution concerning the rule and canon whereby to make them: "human laws are measures" in respect of men whose actions they must direct; howbeit such measures they are as have also their higher rules to be measured by, "which rules are two, the law of God, and the law of nature" (*ST* 1a2ae.95.3). So that laws human must be made according to the general laws of nature, and without contradiction unto any positive law in Scripture. Otherwise they are made ill.

[3] [. . .] It is a loose and licentious opinion which the Anabaptists have embraced, holding that a Christian man's liberty is lost, and the soul which Christ hath redeemed unto himself injuriously drawn into servitude under the yoke of human power, if any law be now imposed besides the Gospel of Jesus Christ, in obedience whereunto the Spirit of God and not the constraint of man is to lead us, according to that of the blessed Apostle: "Such as are led by the Spirit of God, they are the sons of God" (Rom. 8:14), and not such as live in thraldom unto men. Their judgment is therefore that the church of Christ should admit no law-makers but the Evangelists. The author of that which causeth another thing to be is author of that thing also which thereby is caused. The light of natural understanding, wit, and reason, is from God: he it is which thereby doth illuminate every man entering into the world (John 1:9). If there proceed from us anything afterwards corrupt and naught, the mother

thereof is our own darkness, neither doth it proceed from any such cause whereof God is the author. He is the author of all that we think or do by virtue of that light, which himself hath given. And therefore the laws which the very heathens did gather to direct their actions by, so far forth as they proceeded from the light of nature, God himself doth acknowledge to have proceeded even from himself, and that he was the writer of them in the tables of their hearts (Rom. 1:19; 2:15). How much more then he the author of those laws which have been made by his saints, endued further with the heavenly grace of his Spirit, and directed as much as might be with such instructions as his sacred word doth yield! Surely if we have unto those laws that dutiful regard which their dignity doth require, it will not greatly need that we should be exhorted to live in obedience unto them. If they have God himself for their author, contempt which is offered unto them cannot choose but redound unto him. The safest and unto God the most acceptable way of framing our lives therefore is, with all humility, lowliness, and singleness of heart, to study which way our willing obedience both unto God and man may be yielded even to the utmost of that which is due.

Text: ed. J. Keble; 7th ed., revised R. W. Church and F. Paget (1887).

Johannes Althusius

(1557-1638)

Since the late nineteenth century, the political thought of Johannes Althusius has attracted scholarly interest on account of its original blend of organic, covenantal, constitutional, and pluralist features. Drawing on the political organizations of the German empire and the Dutch Provinces, and on a host of contemporary theoretical sources, Calvinist and post-Tridentine Catholic, scholastic and humanist, theological and civilian, Althusius appears to be the transitional figure *par excellence,* straddling late medieval and early modern developments. While his exact relation to these has been debated, particularly as regards the foundations of modern federalism, his achievement of rethinking the medieval heritage in the light of contemporary positions is agreed by all.

As the juridical tenor of his political thought suggests, Althusius pursued studies in the law at the Universities of Köln, Basel, and Geneva from 1581 to 1586, obtaining his doctorate in both civil and ecclesiastical branches, and publishing his first book, *Jurisprudentia Romana,* in 1586. During this period he came under the influence of two French Huguenot humanists: the famous "monarchomach" François Hotman and the Roman legal scholar Denis Godefroy, both of whom combined Calvinist and classicizing orientations. Subsequently he rose to the posts of law professor and, after a period of theological study, rector at the Reformed Academy of Herborn, recently founded as a bastion of Calvinist learning by Count Johan of Nassau, younger brother of William of Orange, who had been active in the Dutch Revolt.

The publication in 1603 of his *Politica methodice digesta (Politics Methodically Set Forth),* following a volume on ethics in 1601, was partly responsible for his appointment in 1604 as syndic of the city of Emden, a port in the German county of East Frisia bordering on the Dutch Provinces, reputed to be the "alma mater" of the Dutch Reformed Church on account of its hospitality to Calvinist refugees and its Reformed Synod of 1571. During his thirty-four years of service to Emden as syndic and (from 1617) church elder, Althusius published two enlarged editions of the *Politics* (1610,

1614) and completed his *Dicaeologica* (1617), which attempted a comprehensive legal synthesis of biblical law, Roman law, and various customary laws (Carney 1964, xvi; 1995, xii). If Emden was the "Geneva of the North," observes Frederick Carney, then Althusius was its Calvin, who uninterruptedly guided and coordinated the city's civil and ecclesiastical affairs until his death (Carney 1964, xvi; 1995, xii).

The *Politics* presents simultaneously an architectonic political conception and a more detailed organizational and administrative blueprint. It attempts to system-atize aspects of contemporary polities by applying rigorous scientific (Ramist) method, with the object of establishing the normative and institutional fabric of po-litical society, leading to further concrete applications. In the wake of its publication, the councillors of Emden probably viewed him as the statesman who would place the city's affairs on a sound scriptural and scientific footing. Once appointed, he proved not at all reluctant to apply his principles and ideas. For example, he trans-formed the city's relationship to its territorial overlord, the count of East Frisia, from one of unilateral homage to one of mutual covenanting, in which the count guaran-teed the city's privileges in exchange for its oath of loyalty (Heuglin 1979, 9-10). The city's newfound status reflected its syndic's axiomatic principle that all political un-ion is federal, based on a covenant, compact, or contract *(foedus, pactum, contractus),* in which the relevant authorities give their mutual consent to binding laws of justice or right.

More precisely, Althusius's distinctive principle is that all *social* union, as well as political union, is federal or covenantal. In an original move, he blends society and polity in a single pluralistic order of intersecting covenantal associations, rein-terpreting the Aristotelian building blocks of the *polis.* The very fabric of society is political in that its constitutive associations are self-governing: this is equally true of the "simple" and "private" associations (family and collegium) as of the "mixed" and "public" associations (city, province, and commonwealth) with their civil and eccle-siastical administrations (2.1). Conversely, the fabric of the commonwealth is thor-oughly social or "symbiotic," its constitutive associations being forms of "communi-cation" or "sharing": of material and spiritual goods *(things),* of diverse labors and occupations *(services),* and of the discipline of just and pious laws *(common rights)* (1.6-10). While conceptually distinguishing the covenantal moments of *(a)* political association and *(b)* subjection to rule, he does not render them as separate cove-nants, but rather as separate phases in single unitive acts undertaken by individuals and communities. In the spirit of the Spanish scholastics, he conceives every associa-tion as displaying a particular balance of natural necessity and human volition, de-pending on its proper purpose — the "natural" family and the "civil" collegium fall-ing at opposite ends of the spectrum (2, 3).

His sociopolitical federalism resembles the earlier French Calvinist model de-veloped in the *Vindiciae, contra tyrannos* in its adroit combining of Old Testament theological motifs with liberal, corporational, and constitutional elements of Ro-man legal theory. His central theological motif is the grounding of all human cove-nants in those of God with Israel recorded in the Hebrew Scriptures, which were ex-plicitly constituted by God's promulgation of laws of piety and justice (summarized in the two tables of the Decalogue). Thus, the communication of right *(ius)* in each sphere and at each level of human association must concretely express the covenantal commands of natural and revealed law.

Althusius concurs with his Huguenot forerunners that at the level of the commonwealth (the most comprehensive public association), the communication of right should rest on explicit ceremonial recapitulations of two Israelite covenants: the theopolitical or *ecclesiastical covenant*, between God, king, and people, in which the king and the people's representatives (the *ephors* and general councils) jointly promise to establish and maintain the true knowledge and worship of God in response to his promise to bless and protect the commonwealth (27.15-23); and the *civil covenant* between the king and the people's representatives (the *ephors*), in which the people, as the mandator, require the elected magistrate to promise under oath to abide by the stipulated conditions of his rule and, in return, swear obedience to him (19.5-30). There is in his theopolitical conception of church-commonwealth relations an Erastian tendency to suppress tensions between the ecclesiastical and civil orders and to invest their coordinated political existence with salvific value.

Despite his emphasis on the rights and freedoms of the corporational units constituting the commonwealth, Althusius retains the concept of universal and indivisible sovereignty *(imperium)*, investing it, however, in the commonwealth rather than the ruler, in opposition to Bodin. In line with corporation theory, he regards the ruler's power as delegated rather than owned, and consequently, as limited and lawful (administrative or executive) rather than absolute, subject to the plenitude of the collectivity *(universitas)*. Central to the administrative system of checks and balances are the *ephors*, the elected guardians of the covenantal "rights" of the commonwealth, as exemplified by the electors of the German empire, whose office is to constitute, advise, and restrain the supreme magistrate within the bounds of law.

Further Reading: F. S. Carney, intro., trans., *The "Politics" of Johannes Althusius* (Boston: Beacon Press, 1964; Indianapolis: Liberty Fund, 1995); G. Duso, *Konsens und Konsoziation in der politischen Theorie des frühen Föderalismus* (Berlin: Drucker & Humblot, 1997); C. J. Friedrich, *Johannes Althusius und sein Werk im Rahmen der Entwicklung der Theorie von der Politik* (Berlin: Drucker & Humblot, 1975); O. von Gierke, *The Development of Political Theory* (English translation) (New York: Fertig, 1966); T. O. Hueglin, "Johannes Althusius: Medieval Constitutionalist or Modern Federalist?" *Publius* 9, no. 4 (1979): 9-41; C. S. McCoy and J. W. Baker, *Fountainhead of Federalism: Heinrich Bullinger and the Covenantal Tradition* (Louisville: Westminster–John Knox, 1991); P. Riley, "Three Seventeenth-Century German Theorists of Federalism: Althusius, Hugo and Leibniz," *Publius* 6, no. 3 (1976): 7-41; J. H. M. Salmon, *The French Religious Wars in English Political Thought* (Oxford: Clarendon Press, 1959).

From *Politica Methodice Digesta*

ch. 1. [1] Politics is the art of associating *(consociandi)* men for the purpose of establishing, cultivating, and conserving social life among them. Whence it is called "symbiotics." [2] The subject matter of politics is therefore association *(consociatio)*, in which the symbiotes pledge themselves each to the other, by explicit or tacit agreement, to mutual communication of whatever is useful and necessary for the harmonious exercise of social life.

[3] The end of political "symbiotic" man is holy, just, comfortable, and happy symbiosis, a life lacking nothing either necessary or useful. Truly, in living this life no man is self-sufficient *(autarkēs)*, or adequately endowed by nature. [4] For when he is born, destitute of all help, naked and defenceless, as if having lost all his goods in a shipwreck, he is cast forth into the hardships of this life, not able by his own efforts to reach a maternal breast, nor to endure the harshness of his condition, nor to move himself from the place where he was cast forth. By his weeping and tears, he can initiate nothing except the most miserable life, a very certain sign of pressing and immediate misfortune. [This sentence and the previous one are taken without acknowledgment from the influential work of Spanish Jesuit Juan de Mariana (1536-1624), *De rege et regis institutione* 1.1. Bereft of all counsel and aid, for which nevertheless he is then in greatest need, he is unable to help himself without the intervention and assistance of another. Even if he is well-nourished in body, he cannot show forth the light of reason. Nor in his adulthood is he able to obtain in and by himself those outward goods he needs for a comfortable and holy life, or to provide by his own energies all the requirements of life. The energies and industry of many men are expended to procure and supply these things. Therefore, as long as he remains isolated and does not mingle in the society of men, he cannot live at all comfortably and well while lacking so many necessary and useful things. As an aid and remedy for this state of affairs is offered him in symbiotic life, he is led, and almost impelled, to embrace it if he wants to live comfortably and well, even if he merely wants to live (cf. Aristotle, *Politics* 1252b29). Therein he is called upon to exercise and perform those virtues that are necessarily inactive except in this symbiosis. And so he begins to think by what means such symbiosis, from which he expects so many useful and enjoyable things, can be instituted, cultivated, and conserved. Concerning these matters we shall, by God's grace, speak in the following pages.

[5] The word "polity" has three principal connotations, as noted by Plutarch (*Moralia* 826c). First it indicates the communication of right *(ius)* in the commonwealth, which the Apostle calls citizenship (Phil. 3:20). Then, it signifies the manner of administering and regulating the commonwealth. Finally, it notes the form and constitution of the commonwealth by which all actions of the citizens are guided. Aristotle understands by polity this last meaning.

[6] The symbiotes are co-workers who, by the bond of an associating and uniting agreement, communicate among themselves whatever is appropriate for a comfortable life of soul and body. In other words, they are participants or partners in a common life.

[7] This mutual communication, or common enterprise, involves (1) things, (2) services, and (3) common rights *(iura)* by which the numerous and various needs of each and every symbiote are supplied, the self-sufficiency and mutuality of life and human society are achieved, and social life is established and conserved. Whence Cicero said: "a political community is a gathering of men associated by a consensus as to the

right and a sharing of what is useful" (*De republica* 1.25.39). By this communication, advantages and responsibilities are assumed and maintained according to the nature of each particular association. [8] (1) The communication of things *(res)* is the bringing of useful and necessary goods to the social life by the symbiotes for the common advantage of the symbiotes individually and collectively. [9] (2) The community of services *(operae)* is the contributing by the symbiotes of their labours and occupations for the sake of social life. [10] (3) The communion of right *(ius)* is the process by which the symbiotes live and are ruled by just laws in a common life among themselves.

This communion of right is called the law of association and symbiosis *(lex consociationis et symbiosis)*, or the symbiotic right *(ius symbioticum)*, and consists especially of self-sufficiency *(autarkeia)*, good order *(eunomia)*, and proper discipline *(eutaxia)*. It includes two aspects, one functioning to direct and govern social life, the other prescribing a plan and manner for communicating things and services among the symbiotes.

The law of association in its first aspect is, in turn, either common or proper. [11] Common law *(lex communis)*, which is unchanging, indicates that in every association and type of symbiosis some persons are rulers (heads, overseers, prefects) or superiors, others are subjects or inferiors. [12] For all government is held together by imperium and subjection; in fact, the human race started straightway from the beginning with imperium and subjection. God made Adam master and monarch of his wife, and of all creatures born or descendant from her (Gen. 1:26f.; 3:16). Therefore all power and government is said to be from God (Rom. 13:1). And nothing, as Cicero affirms, "is as suited to the natural law *(ius naturae)* and its requirements as imperium, without which neither household nor city nor nation nor the entire race of men can endure, nor the whole nature of things nor the world itself" (*De legibus* 3.1.3). If the consensus and will of rulers and subjects is the same, how happy and blessed is their life! "Be subject to one another in fear of the Lord" (Eph. 5:21). [...]

ch. 2. [1] Thus far we have discussed the general elements of politics. We turn now to types of association or of symbiotic life. Every association is either simple and private [e.g., family and collegium] or mixed and public [e.g., city, province, and commonwealth].

[2] The simple and private association is a society and symbiosis initiated by a special covenant *(pactum)* among the members for the purpose of bringing together and holding in common a particular interest *(quid peculiare)*. This is done according to their agreement and way of life, that is, according to what is necessary and useful for organized private symbiotic life. Such an association can rightly be called primary, and all others derivative from it. For without this primary association others are able neither to arise nor to endure.

[3] The efficient causes of this simple and private association and symbiosis are individual men covenanting among themselves to communicate whatever is necessary and useful for organizing and living in private life. Whence arises the particular and private union and society among the covenanters, whose bond *(vinculum)* is trust granted and accepted in their communication of mutual aid, counsel, and right *(ius)*. And such an association, because it is smaller than a public and universal one, also requires less extended communication, support, and assistance.

[4] The members of the private association are individuals harmoniously united under one head and spirit, as members of the same body. For, as Peter Gregory says: "Just as there is one end for the sake of which nature made the thumb, another the hand or foot, still another the whole man; so there is one end to which nature directs the individual man, another the family, and another the city and realm. But that end is most to be esteemed for which nature made the whole man. Accordingly, it is not to be thought that since there is a definite end for each type of assemblage there is none for the whole, nor that since there is order in the parts of human life there is only confusion in the more inclusive kind of life, nor lastly that since the parts are united among themselves by reason of their intending one end the whole itself is disunited" (*De republica* 5.5.13).

[5] The particular interest that is communicated among the symbiotes by a special covenant of this kind, and through which they are united as by a certain bond, consists in symbiotic right *(ius symbioticum)*, together with structure and good order for communicating it with consensus, mutual service, and common advantage. [6] Symbiotic right is what the private symbiote fulfils on behalf of his fellow symbiote in the private association, which varies according to the nature of the association. [. . .] [12] Because of this symbiotic right, the private association often performs as one person, and is acknowledged to be one person. [. . .]

[13] There are two types of simple and private association. The first is natural, and the second is civil. [14] The private and natural symbiotic association is one in which married persons, blood relatives, and in-laws, in response to a natural affection and necessity, agree to a definite communication among themselves. Whence this individual, natural, necessary, economic, and domestic society is said to be contracted permanently among these symbiotic allies of life, with the same boundaries as life itself. Therefore it is rightly called the most intense society, friendship, relationship, and union, the seedbed of every other symbiotic association. Whence these symbiotic allies are called relatives, kinsmen, and friends. [. . .]

ch. 4. [1] This completes the discussion of the natural association. We turn now to the civil association, which is a body organized by assembled persons according to their own pleasure and will to serve a common utility and necessity in human life. That is to say, they agree among themselves by common consent on a manner of ruling and obeying for the utility both of the whole body and of its individuals.

[2] This society by its nature is transitory and can be discontinued. It need not last as long as the lifetime of a man, but can be disbanded honourably and in good faith by the mutual agreement of those who have come together, however much it may have been necessary and useful for social life on another occasion. [3] For this reason it is called a spontaneous and merely voluntary society, granted that a certain necessity can be said to have brought it into existence. For in the early times of the world, when the human race was increasing and, though one family, yet dispersing itself — since all persons could no longer be expected to live together in one place and family — necessity drove diverse and separate dwellings, hamlets, and villages to stand together, and at length to erect towns and cities in different places. Accordingly: "When the head of the family goes out of his house, in which he exercises domestic imperium, and joins the heads of other families to pursue business matters,

he then loses the name of head and master of the family, and becomes an ally and citizen. In a sense, he leaves the family in order that he may enter the city and attend therein to public instead of domestic concerns" (Bodin, *Six Books of the Commonwealth* 1.6).

[4] This is therefore a civil association. In it three or more men of the same trade, training, or profession are united for the purpose of holding in common such things they jointly profess as duty, way of life, or craft. Such an association is called a collegium, or as it were, a gathering, society, federation, sodality, synagogue, convention, or synod. [Althusius includes under collegia the Jewish synagogues and early Christian fellowships.] It is said to be a private association by contrast with the public association. [5] The persons who unite in order to constitute a collegium are called colleagues, associates, or even brothers. A minimum of three persons is required to organize a collegium, because among two persons there is no third person to overcome dissension. This is so even though two persons may be called colleagues so far as the power and equality of office is concerned. Fewer than three, however, are not able to conserve a collegium.

[6] Whoever among the colleagues is superior and set over the others is called the leader of the collegium, the rector or director of the common property and functions. He is elected by common consent of the colleagues, and is provided with administrative power over property and functions pertaining to the collegium. For this reason he exercises coercive power over the colleagues individually, but not over the group itself. [7] Therefore the president of a collegium is superior to the individual colleague but inferior to the united colleagues, or to the collegium over which he presides and whose pleasure he must serve. [. . .]

[8] We will consider first the communication of the colleagues, and their symbiotic right *(ius symbioticum)* in this private and civil association, then the various types of the collegium. Communication among the colleagues is the activity by which an individual helps his colleague, and so upholds the plan of social life set forth in covenanted agreements. These covenants and laws *(pacta et leges)* of the colleagues are described in their corporate books, which we call *Zunftbücher*. Such communication pertains to (1) things, (2) services, (3) right, and (4) mutual benevolence. [. . .]

ch. 5. [1] With this discussion of the civil and private association, we turn now to the public association. For human society develops from private to public association by the definite steps and progressions of small societies. The public association exists when many private associations are linked together for the purpose of establishing an inclusive political order *(politeuma)*. It can be called a community *(universitas)*, an associated body, or the pre-eminent political association. [Here *universitas* is a generic name for political association, though more usually it refers to a municipal association as distinguished from a province or commonwealth.] [2] It is permitted and approved by the law of nations *(ius gentium)*. [3] It is not considered dead as long as one person is left. Nor is it altered by the change of individual persons, for it is perpetuated by the substitution of others. [4] Men assembled without symbiotic right *(ius symbioticum)* are a crowd, gathering, multitude, assemblage, throng, or people. The larger this association, and the more types of association contained within it, the more need it has of resources and aids to maintain self-sufficiency as much in soul as in body and life, and the greater does it require good order, proper discipline, and communication of things and services.

[5] Political order in general is the right and power of communicating and participating in useful and necessary matters that are brought to the life of the organized body by its associated members. It can be called the public symbiotic right. [6] This public symbiotic association is either particular or universal. The particular association is encompassed by fixed and definite localities within which its rights are communicated. [7] In turn, it is either a community (*universitas*) or a province.

[8] The community is an association formed by fixed laws and composed of many families and collegia living in the same place. It is elsewhere called a city (*civitas*) in the broadest sense, or a body of many and diverse associations. Nicolaus Losaeus defines it as "a coming together under one special name of many bodies each distinct from the other" (*De iure universitatum* I.1.2). [9] It is called a representational person and represents men collectively, not individually. Strictly speaking, however, the community is not known by the designation of person, but it takes the place of a person when legitimately convoked and congregated (Dig. 46.1.22).

[10] The members of a community are private and diverse associations of families and collegia, not the individual members of private associations. These persons, by their coming together, now become not spouses, kinsmen, and colleagues, but citizens of the same community. Thus passing from the private symbiotic relationship, they unite in the one body of a community. [11] Differing from citizens, however, are foreigners, outsiders, aliens, and strangers whose duty it is to mind their own business, make no strange inquiries, not even to be curious in a foreign commonwealth, but to adapt themselves, as far as good conscience permits, to the customs of the place and city where they live in order that they may not be a scandal to others. [. . .]

[22] The superior is the prefect of the community appointed by the consent of the citizens. He directs the business of the community, and governs on behalf of its welfare and advantage, exercising authority (*ius*) over the individuals but not over the citizens collectively. [23] An oath of fidelity to certain articles in which the functions of his office are contained stands as a surety to the appointing community. From the individual citizens, in turn, is required an oath of fidelity and obedience setting forth in certain articles the functions of the office of a good citizen.

[24] Such a superior is either one or more persons who have received the prescribed power of governing by the consent of the community. [. . .] [25] And so these general administrators of the community are appointed by the city out of its general and free power, and can even be removed from office by the city. They are therefore temporal, while the community or city may be continuous and almost immortal. [. . .]

ch. 7. [1] We have completed the discussion of the community. We turn now to the province, which contains within its territory many villages, towns, outposts, and cities united under the communion and administration of one right (*ius*). It is also called a region, district, diocese, or community. [2] I identify the territory of a province as whatever is encompassed by the limits or boundaries within which its rights *(iura)* are exercised. [. . .] [3] Two matters are to be discussed. The first is the communion of provincial right, and the second is the administration of it. These two matters contain the entire political doctrine of the province.

The communion of right is the process whereby everything that nourishes and conserves a pious and just life among the provincial symbiotes is procured by individuals and province alike for the need and use of the province. This is done through the offering and communication of functions and goods. [. . .]

[4] The functions of the provincial symbiotes are either holy or civil. Holy functions concern those that are necessary for living and cultivating a pious life in the provincial association and symbiosis. [5] A pious life requires a correct understanding of God and a sincere worship of him. [6] A correct understanding of God is obtained from Sacred Scripture and from articles of faith. "This is eternal life, that they know thee the only true God, and Jesus Christ whom thou has sent" (John 17:3). A correct worship of God is derived from those rules and examples of the divine word that declare and illustrate love toward God and charity toward men.

[7] True and correct worship of God is either private or public. Private and internal worship consists of the expression of confidence, adoration, and thankfulness, the first precept of the Decalogue. Private and external worship consists of rites and actions that revere God, the second precept, or of words that do the same, the third precept. Public worship of God consists of holy observance of the Sabbath by corporate public celebration, the fourth precept.

[8] Civil functions are those that maintain a just life in the provincial association and symbiosis. Whence they include everything that pertains to the exercise of social life. The symbiote is expected to perform those duties of love by which he renders to each his due, and does not do to his fellow symbiote what he does not wish done to himself. Rather he loves him as himself, and abstains from evil.

[9] The duties of justice to the neighbour are either special or general. Special duties are those that bind superiors and inferiors together, so that the symbiote truly attributes honour and eminence by word and deed to whomever they are due, and abstains from all mean opinion of such persons, the fifth precept of the Decalogue. [10] General duties are those every symbiote is obligated to perform toward every other symbiote. They consist of defending and preserving from all injury the lives of one's neighbour and oneself, the sixth precept; of guarding by thought, word, and deed one's own chastity and that of the fellow symbiote, without any lewdness or fornication, the seventh precept; of defending and preserving the resources and goods of the fellow symbiote, and of not stealing, injuring, or reducing them, the eighth precept; of defending and preserving one's own reputation and that of one's neighbour, and of not neglecting them in any manner, the ninth precept; and of avoiding a concupiscent disposition toward those things that belong to our neighbour, and of seeking instead satisfaction and pleasure in those things that are ours and tend to the glory of God, the tenth precept.

[11] The practice of provincial political justice is twofold. First, individual symbiotes manifest and communicate the duties of love reciprocally among themselves, according to special means, person, place, and other circumstances. Second, the provincials as a group and as individual inhabitants of the province uphold and

communicate the duties of both tables of the Decalogue for the sake of the welfare of the provincial association. The former are the private and special practice among the provincials, and the latter are the public and general practice.

[12] These latter general duties are performed by the common consent of the provincial symbiotes. They are (1) the executive functions and occupations necessary and useful to the provincial association; (2) the distribution of punishments and rewards by which discipline is preserved in the province; (3) the provision for provincial security; (4) the mutual defence of the provincials against force and violence, the avoidance of inconveniences, and the provision for support, help, and counsel; (5) the collection and distribution of monies for public needs and uses of the province; (6) the support of commercial activity; (7) the use of the same language and money; and (8) the care of public goods of the province. [. . .]

ch. 8. [1] The administration of provincial right is the process by which the employment and practice of provincial right, both general and special, is appropriately directed to the welfare of the province. Whence this right relates entirely to good ordering and arranging, and has in mind a structure of proper practice and discipline. The administration of this right involves two parts. One part pertains to the members of the province, and the other to its head or president.

[2] The members of the province are its orders and estates, as they are called, or larger collegia. The provincials have been distributed in these orders and estates according to the class and diversity of life they have organized in keeping with their profession, vocation, and activity. Therefore, when ecclesiastical and civil functions of the province are under consideration, each estate or order can centre its attention upon the operation of the provincial right and business among men of its own class, provided it does not usurp and exercise the ordinary jurisdiction. In Germany they are called *die Stende der Landschaft*.

[3] The reason for these estates is that they are necessary and useful to the province, as Jethro, the father-in-law of Moses, declares (Exod. 18:17-25). For no one can be sufficient and equal to the task of administering such various, diverse, and extensive public business of a province unless in part of the burden he avails himself of skilled, wise, and brave persons from each class of men. [. . .] Indeed, by this arrangement certain traces of liberty are retained by the provincials, for each and all see themselves admitted to the administration of public matters. Whence love, benevolence, and common concern are fostered among the provincials when all know that a precise care is exercised for individuals and groups in each class of life, and that their requests for the procurement of necessary and useful things for social life, and for the avoidance of inconvenience and harm, will be heard, and remedies will be sought, even to the extent of aid against those who are more powerful or who disturb the public peace.

[4] The provincial order or estate may be either sacred and ecclesiastical, or secular and civil. In Germany they are known as *der Geistliche und Weltliche Stand* (see 2 Chron. 19:5-11). [5] These orders, together with the provincial head, represent the entire province. All weightier matters are guided by their counsel, and the welfare of the commonwealth is entrusted to them. They admonish the head of the province when he errs, correct the abuse of his power, and punish his seducers and base flatterers.

[6] A collegium of pious, learned, and most weighty men from the collegia of provincial clergymen, elected and commissioned by common consent, represents the sacred and ecclesiastical order. Entrusted to this collegium is the examination and care of doctrine, of public reverence and divine worship, of schools, of ecclesiastical goods, and of the poor. Indeed, the care of all ecclesiastical business and of the holy life in the entire province is entrusted to it in order that all the saints may unite for a common ministry, and constitute one mystical body. [. . .] Whence these ecclesiastical colleagues are called bishops, inspectors, rectors, and leaders of provincial ecclesiastical matters. [. . .]

[7] The care of religion and divine worship obligates these inspectors to inquire and discover whether the doctrine of God and of our salvation is rightly and publicly taught in the entire province and the parts thereof, and whether God is truly, sincerely, freely, and publicly worshipped according to his Word by everyone in the entire province. At opportune times, they are obligated to remove corruptions, idolatries, superstitions, atheisms, heresies, and seeds of schism, that nothing in any way detrimental to pure religion may be undertaken, and that the life of the church and the functions of religion may be administered well. [. . .]

ch. 9. [1] Now that we have discussed particular and minor public associations, we turn now to the universal and major public association. In this association many cities and provinces obligate themselves to hold, organize, use, and defend, through their common energies and expenditures, the right of the realm (*ius regni*) in the mutual communication of things and services. [2] For without these supports, and the right of communication, a pious and just life cannot be established, fostered, and preserved in universal social life.

[3] Whence this mixed society, constituted partly from private, natural, necessary, and voluntary societies, is called a universal association. It is a polity in the fullest sense, an imperium, realm, commonwealth, and people united in one body by the agreement of many symbiotic associations and particular bodies, and brought together under one right. For families, cities, and provinces existed by nature prior to realms, and gave birth to them.

Many writers distinguish between a realm (*regnum*) and a commonwealth (*respublica*), relating the former to a monarchical king and the latter to polyarchical optimates. But in my judgment this distinction is not a good one. [4] For ownership of a realm belongs to the people, and administration of it to the king. Thus Cicero, as cited by Augustine, says: "a commonwealth is the weal of the people," although it may be well and justly ruled either by a king, by a few optimates, or by the whole people (*De republica* 1.25.39; cf. Augustine, *City of God* 19.21, p. 161 above). Indeed, any polity whatever, including a city, can be called a commonwealth, such as the Athenian, Spartan, Hebrew, and Roman commonwealths, of which many have not been without their kings. [. . .]

[5] We will discuss, first, the members of a realm and, then, its right. The members of a realm, or of this universal symbiotic association, are not, I say, individual men, families, or collegia, as in a private or a particular public association. Instead, members are many cities, provinces, and regions agreeing among themselves on a single body constituted by mutual union and communication. Individual per-

sons from these group members are called natives, inhabitants of the realm, and sons and daughters of the realm. They are to be distinguished from foreigners and strangers, who have no claim upon the right or the realm. It can be said that individual citizens, families, and collegia are not members of a realm, just as boards, nails, and pegs are not considered parts of a ship, nor rocks, beams, and cement parts of a house. On the other hand, cities, urban communities, and provinces are members of a realm, just as prow, stern, and keel are members of a ship, and roof, walls, and floor are essential parts of a house. [. . .]

[7] The bond of this body and association is consensus, together with trust extended and accepted among the members of the commonwealth. The bond is, in other words, a tacit or expressed promise to communicate things, mutual services, aid, counsel, and the same common laws (iura) to the extent that the utility and necessity of universal social life in a realm shall require. Even the reluctant are compelled to comply with this communication. However, this does not prevent separate provinces of the same realm from using different special laws. Plato rightly said that this trust is the foundation of human society, while lack of trust is its plague, and that trust is the bond of concord among the different members of a commonwealth. For the promise of so many different men and orders has as its purpose that the diverse actions of the individual parts be referred to the utility and communion of one commonwealth, and that inferiors be held together with superiors by a certain fairness in the law (ius). [. . .]

[12] Such are the members of the realm. Its right is the means by which the members, in order to establish good order and the supplying of provisions throughout the territory of the realm, are associated and bound to each other as one people in one body and under one head (1 Sam. 10:25). [13] This right of the realm (ius regni) is also called the right of sovereignty (ius maiestatis). It is, in other words, the right of a major state or power as contrasted with the right that is attributed to a city or a province. [. . .]

[15] What we call this right of the realm has as its purpose good order, proper discipline, and the supplying of provisions in the universal association. Towards these purposes it directs the actions of each and all of its members, and prescribes appropriate duties for them. Therefore, the universal power of ruling (potestas imperandi universalis) is called that which recognizes no ally, nor any superior or equal to itself. And this supreme right of universal jurisdiction is the form and substantial essence of sovereignty (maiestas) or, as we have called it, of a major state. When this right is taken away, sovereignty perishes. [. . .]

[16] The people, or the associated members of the realm, have the power (potestas) of establishing this right of the realm and of binding themselves to it. So Vasquez demonstrates from Bartolus and other authorities (Illustrium controversiarum, 1.47; Bartolus, Commentarii on Dig. 1.1.9; 1.4.1; 1.1.5; 12.6.64). And in this power of disposing, prescribing, ordaining, administering, and constituting everything necessary and useful for the universal association is contained the bond, soul, and vital spirit of the realm, and its autonomy, greatness, size, and authority. Without this power no realm or universal symbiotic life can exist. [17] Therefore, as long as this right thrives in the realm and rules the political body, so long does the realm

live and prosper. But if this right is taken away, the entire symbiotic life perishes, or becomes a band of robbers and a gang of evil men, or disintegrates into many different realms or provinces.

[18] This right of the realm, or right of sovereignty, does not belong to individual members, but to all members joined together and to the entire associated body of the realm. For as universal association can be constituted not by one member, but by all the members together, so the right is said to be the property not of individual members, but of the members jointly. Therefore, "what is owed to the whole *(universitas)* is not owed to individuals, and what the whole owes individuals do not owe" (Dig. 3.4.7.1). Whence it follows that the use and ownership of this right belong neither to one person nor to individual members, but to the members of the realm jointly. By their common consent, they are able to establish and set in order matters pertaining to it. And what they have once set in order is to be maintained and followed, unless something else pleases the common will. For as the whole body is related to the individual citizens, and can rule, restrain, and direct each member, so the people rules each citizen.

[19] This power of the realm *(potestas regni)*, or of the associated bodies, is always one power and never many, just as one soul and not many rules in the physical body. The administrators of this power can be many, so that individuals can each take on a share of the function of governing, but not the plenitude of power. And these individuals are not themselves in control of the supreme power. Instead they all jointly acknowledge such a power in the consent and concord of the associated bodies. Whence jurists have declared the rights of sovereignty and of the realm *(iura maiestatis et regni)* to be indivisible, incommunicable, and interconnected, so that whoever holds one holds them all. Otherwise two superior entities would be established in one imperium. But a superior entity can have no equal or greater superior. And imperium and obedience cannot be mingled. These rights can, however, be lawfully delegated, so that in their administration someone other than their owner may perform the duties of a supreme magistrate.

[22] [...] Therefore, the king, prince, and optimates recognize this associated body as their superior, by which they are constituted, removed, exiled, and deprived of authority. [...] For however great is the power that is conceded to another, it is always less than the power of the one who makes the concession, and in it the pre-eminence and superiority of the conceder is understood to be reserved. Whence it is shown that the king does not have a supreme and perpetual power above the law, and consequently neither are the rights of sovereignty his own property, although he may have the administration and exercise of them by concession from the associated body. And only so far are the rights of sovereignty ceded and handed over to another that they never become his own property.

ch. 18. [48] Administrators of this universal association are of two kinds: the ephors and the supreme magistrate. Ephors are the representatives of the commonwealth or universal association to whom, by the consent of the people associated in a political body, the supreme responsibility has been entrusted for employing its power and right in constituting the supreme magistrate and in assisting him with aid and counsel in the activities of the associated body. They also employ its power and right in restraining and impeding his freedom in undertakings that are wicked and ruinous to the commonwealth, in containing him within the limits of his office, and finally in fully providing and caring for the commonwealth that it not suffer anything detrimental by the supreme magistrate's private attachments, hatreds, deeds, negligence, or inactivity.

[49] These ephors, by reason of their excellence and the office entrusted to them, are called by others patricians, elders, princes, estates, first citizens of the realm, officials of the realm, protectors of the covenant entered into between the supreme magistrate and the people, custodians and defenders of justice and law (ius) to which they subject the supreme magistrate and compel him to obey, censors of the supreme magistrate, inspectors, counsellors of the realm, censors of royal honour, and brothers of the supreme magistrate.

[50] From these things it is apparent that ephors, as the feet and foundations of the universal society or realm, are the means by which it is sustained and conserved during times of interregnum and peril, or when the magistrate is incapable of exercising imperium, or when he abuses his power, as Botero says (De politia, 4.3). They do this in order that the commonwealth may not become exposed to dangers, revolutions, tumults, seditions, and treacheries, or occupied by enemies. [51] For the ephors establish the head of the political body, and subject the king or supreme magistrate to law (lex) and justice. They establish the law, or God, as lord and emperor when the king rejects and throws off the yoke and imperium of law and of God, and ceasing as a minister of God, makes himself an instrument of the devil. These ephors, together with the supreme magistrate, are said to carry the weight and burden of the people (cf. Num. 11:16f.).

Translation: F. S. Carney (Indianapolis: Liberty Fund, 1995). Used with permission.

William Perkins

(1558-1602)

Perkins achieved distinction as a preaching theologian in Cambridge in the last decade of the sixteenth century. Here he encountered controversy, especially as an early advocate of a predestinarian account of salvation and faith deriving from Beza and the Reformed theologians of Heidelberg, in which role he would be widely influential on seventeenth-century Puritanism. Despite an unenviable reputation for pronouncing the word "damn" with such an emphasis "as left," according to Samuel Clarke, "a doleful echo in his auditors ears a good while after," the spirit of his thinking was pastoral rather than dogmatic. His concern in *A Golden Chaine* and *The Cases of Conscience* lay with the question of how a proper ease of conscience may be recognized and justified; and many of his other writings illustrate that intensely Puritan interest in the practical forms and details of daily social life. *Christian Oeconomie* is perhaps the most important Puritan document on their conception of marriage and the household. *A Treatise of the Vocations or Callings of Men* is of importance for the newly emerging Protestant concept of work. Perkins belonged to that strand of sixteenth-century Puritanism which, while thoroughly Calvinist in doctrinal matters, avoided the ecclesiastical controversies that were to force the division between Puritan and Anglican (represented in this collection by Thomas Cartwright, pp. 702-10 above), and was content with the liberties of practice afforded by the Church of England and established by law.

In undertaking a discussion of justice from the point of view of equity, Perkins was exploiting a theme characteristic of his century, though rather insufficiently commented on in contemporary writing. The term "equity" had come into Western medieval thought from a double source: in Roman law it was recognized as a canon of interpretation; in Aristotelian scholasticism *aequitas* was used as a synonym for the term *epikeia*, a contraction of Aristotle's *epieikeia*, representing a justice that is not strictly according to law (*NE* 1137a31-1138a2). "Halfway between legal and natural justice," as Robert Grosseteste had characterized it in 1250, *epikeia* stood for the capacity to inform decisions under law with a reasonable sense of natural justice, and where necessary, to dispense altogether with law. In both canon law and English legal history, the concept of equity pointed in the direction of dispensations from law, allowing legal requirements to be overridden in the interests of natural justice. The English development in the fifteenth century of courts of equity under the supervision of the Lord Chancellor gave institutional expression to this idea, and equity continued to imply powers of dispensation from law.

In the literary traditions of the Renaissance, however, there was a shift of emphasis from reasonableness to mercy. Equity-*epikeia* became identified with the clemency described by Seneca's *De clementia,* a favorite text of the period, as "an inclination of the mind to mildness." In Perkins we can discern all these influences at work, together with a theologizing move characteristic of the Reformation emphasis on forgiveness and the universality of sin. Equity appears as a humble moderation in passing judgment, such as befits those who know their own sinfulness and dependence on the mercy of God. His contemporary, William Shakespeare, explored this theme extensively in *Measure for Measure* and *The Merchant of Venice*. Perkins also brings the subject back to the diction of the New Testament with the appeal to the occurrence of the word *epieikeia,* a term which had had a looser but by no means incompatible sense when St. Paul used it. His discussion of equity assumes something axiomatic to the Puritan sensibility: that what has been discussed as the virtue of a judge is, in fact, every Christian's business. Equity must be exercised both in public and in private; but every Christian's business lies in the realm of public as well as private equity, since that moderation with which it would behoove a judge to decide, were a matter brought to court, it already behooves a Christian to observe outside the court, "in suing bonds and taking forfeitures."

Further Reading: P. G. Caron, *"Aequitas" romana, "Misericordia" patristica et "Epikeia" aristotelica nella dottrina dell' "Aequitas" Canonica* (Milan: Giuffrè, 1971); J. D. Cox, *Shakespeare and the Dramaturgy of Power* (Princeton: Princeton University Press, 1989); F. d'Agostino, *La tradizione dell' epikeia nel Medioevo latino* (Milan: Giuffrè, 1976); R. T. Kendall, *Calvin and English Calvinism to 1649* (Oxford: Oxford University Press, 1979); G. L. Mosse, *The Holy Pretence* (Oxford: Blackwell, 1957).

From *A Treatise of Christian Equitie*

Phil. 4:5: *Let your moderation of mind be known to all men: the Lord is at hand.*

[501] [. . .] For the first: *Christian equity is a rare and excellent virtue, whereby men use a true mean and an equal moderation in all their affairs and dealings with men, for the maintaining of justice and preservation of peace.* This I take to be the true description of the general nature of this virtue: and herein, first, I say it is a virtue which is conversant about practising of a moderation in all our courses and dealings *with men.* For we men can use no mean nor moderation with God, but if we do evil it is all too much, and if we do good, it is all too little. Again, equity and moderation

is to be performed of God towards men, and not of men towards God. For if men deal not equally towards God, the fault is theirs and not his — God is not worse for it; but if God dealt not moderately with men, the world would not last one hour. And lastly, where there are no faults, there is no forgiveness; where no infirmities, there needs no moderation: but in God there is no want, no error, no imperfection; but his love, his mercy, and his works of love and mercy towards mankind, and to his church especially, are most perfect. Therefore, there needs no moderation, nor forbearance towards God, but towards men, who, being flesh and blood, and full of infirmities (from which regeneration itself doth not fully free us), do therefore stand in need of this virtue to be practised amongst them, else their society and fellowship cannot endure. And further, all men in this case are alike, and therefore one hath good cause to bear with another. The prince is flesh and blood as well as his subjects; the husband is flesh and blood as well as the wife is; the pastor is a man as his people and hearers are. Hence it followeth that therefore one is subject to infirmities as well as another: and therefore I conclude that in all our courses and dealings of man with man in this world, there must be practised *a Christian moderation.*

Secondly, I say in the description that the end of this virtue is *to maintain justice and to preserve peace,* which two are the very sinews and strength of a Christian kingdom: for where we do not to other men as we would others should do to us, there is no justice; and where we will not pass by small faults and forbear infirmities, there can be no peace. Such is the excellency of this virtue, as it serves to maintain two other such great and principal virtues, as are even the heart and the brain of the commonwealth — namely, justice and peace.

But for the more exact and particular knowledge of the nature of this necessary virtue, let us descend to the particular branches and kinds of it. Christian equity, therefore, is either public or private.

Public equity is that which is practised in public meetings and assemblies of men, as in courts of justice, assizes, sessions, councils, parliaments, and such like. The matter whereabout this public equity is conversant is the right and convenient, and the moderate and discreet *execution of the laws of men.* [...] In the laws of commonwealths two things are to be considered, the sight whereof will give great light, to know more perfectly what this public equity is. These are: (1) the extremity of the law and (2) the mitigation of the law. Both these are put into the hand of the magistrate by God himself, to be ordered according to his discretion and as the circumstance requireth; and of them in order.

The *extremity of law* is when any law of man is urged and executed straightly and precisely, according to the literal sense and strict form of the words, and the exact meaning that can be made out of the words without any manner of relaxation, at that time when there is good and convenient cause of mitigation in regard of the person offending. (The point cannot well be expressed in fewer words.) The principal and most material clause in this description of extremity is in those words: "at that time when there is just cause of mitigation in regard of the person offending." For if there be no good cause of mitigation, then it is not called extremity, but justice of the law. But when there is good cause why, in a Christian consideration of some circumstances, this justice should be mitigated, and yet is not, but contrariwise is extremely urged, and pressed to the furthest, then it is extremity. Now this extremity of the law is in this case so far from justice as indeed it is flat injustice. And herein is the proverb true, *Summum ius, summa iniuria:* that is, the extremity of the law is extreme injury. And of this doth the Holy Ghost mean (Eccles. 7:7), "be not over just": that is, press not justice too far, nor urge it too extremely in all cases, lest sometimes you make the name of justice a cover for cruelty.

Now beside this, there is a second thing in the hand of the magistrate, namely, the *moderation, relaxation, or mitigation of this extremity.* And that is when the proper form of the words and the strictest meaning of the law is not urged, and the punishment prescribed in the law is moderated or lessened or deferred, or (it may be) remitted, upon good and sufficient reason, and in such cases as whereof the law speaks not directly, nor the law-maker did purposely aim at. The ground of this mitigation is because no law-makers, being men, can foresee or set down all cases that may fall out. Therefore, when the case altereth, then must the discretion of the law-maker show itself, and do that which the law cannot do. This mitigation is in the hand of the magistrate, as well as the extremity: nay, it is a part of his duty as well as the former; and he offends as well that neglects to mitigate the extremity when just occasion is, as he that neglects to execute the extremity when there is need. As, therefore, he is in no way fit to be a judge, who hath no knowledge or care to execute the law, so he is but half a judge, who can do nothing but urge the law, and is not able also to mitigate the rigour of the law when need so requireth. Therefore every magistrate is to practise this with the other, and not to separate those things which God hath joined.

But now, lest this moderation and mitigation of man's laws (which is the practise of public equity) should turn to the maintenance of malefactors, the abolishing of laws, the despising or weakening of authority, (which in these days little needeth), we must, therefore, now remember this caution: *that there must be no mitigation but honest, profitable, and convenient.* If any man ask: When is it so? I answer: in three cases. First, when the mitigation stands with the law of nature. Secondly, when it agreeth with the moral law or any part of the written word [of Scripture]. Thirdly, when an inferior law is overruled or countermanded by a higher law. In these three cases the moderation of men's laws, and the mitigation of the punishment due by the extremity of these laws, is honest and good, and may and ought to be practised. But if it be contrary, and not warranted by some of these, then that mitigation is flat injustice and a manifest wrong unto the law.

That the difference of these two, the extremity and mitigation, may better be discerned, let us consider it in some examples.

It is the law of England and many other countries that the thief shall die. Now, though the word of God hath not the same punishment in plain terms, yet is the law good and warrantable, as shall appear in the sequel, and I think is doubted of by none. The drift of this law is to repress that common and general sin of thievery, a prevailing sin as any other, and so far prevailing as the rigour of good law is necessarily required for the repressing of it; so that this law was made for the cutting off of such rotten members as do but corrupt others, and of whose amendment there is no hope. Now suppose a young boy, pinched with hunger, cold, and poverty, steals meat, apparel, and other things for relief, being pressed to it by want, and not having knowledge or grace to use better means. To put this person to death for this fact is the extremity of the law, in respect of the circumstances of the person who did it, being a child, and of the end for which he did it, to relieve his wants. Now the moderation of this case is, when upon these considerations — that first, he is not an old nor practised thief, but young and corrigible, one that, being reformed, may live long and prove a good member in the commonwealth; and secondly, that his theft was not heinous, but the things he stole were of small value; and thirdly, that he did it not upon a malicious, cruel and injurious intent, but to relieve his hunger and want — the equity or moderation, I say, in this case, is not to inflict death, (for that were extremity), but to determine a punishment less than death, yet such a one as shall be sufficient to reform the party from his sin, to punish the fault, to terrify others, and to satisfy the law. [. . .]

[505] To proceed further. As this public equity principally stands in the moderation of the laws of men, so it descends more specially even to all the public actions of a man's life, so that by the rule and direction of this equity, thus described, men may know how to guide themselves in suing bonds and taking forfeitures; and how men may with good conscience carry themselves in suretyships, in taking of fines, in letting of leases, and in all manner of mutual bargains betwixt man and man. By virtue of this, a man may see how to frame all these and such like actions in such sort as himself shall reap credit and gain enough, and his neighbour help and succour by him. For in forfeitures of bonds, forfeitures of lands, or leases, in suretyships, in rents, in fines and all other dealings of men together, there are these two things. First, the extremity — that is, that which the law will afford a man in that case; and there is secondly the moderation of the extremity upon good and convenient reasons. Let us consider of them in some few examples.

A man is bound to another in an hundredth pound, to pay fifty at a day. The same man, not by negligence, but by some necessity, breaks this day and afterwards brings the principal debt. Now to take the forfeiture is in this case extremity, though the law doth yield it. And if a man stand upon this extremity, he deals not honestly and equally, but hardly and extremely, with his neighbour; and the law cannot free him in this case from manifest injustice. What is then the moderation in this case? Even this: to take thine own, and remit the forfeiture. The reason is because the cause and ground of appointing a forfeiture was not for advantage, but only for the better security of the principal, which, seeing thou hast, thou has that which the law did intend thee. [. . .]

[506] Now in these and all other public dealings betwixt men in the world, a man observes public equity when he dealeth not with his neighbour according to that extremity which the strict words of the law will bear, but according to that moderation which good conscience requireth, and which the law itself in some cases doth admit. By the knowledge of these two, a man that hath any conscience may see how to carry himself in all these civil affairs in an even, upright, and equal course, and warrantable not only by the law of the land, but even by the law and word of God. And I make this distinction of the law of the land and the word of God because we are to know this for a rule: *that every extremity which a law in the strictest acception*

doth afford is not warrantable to be urged by the word of God; and yet notwithstanding, it is good, convenient, and requisite that the extremity be warranted by the law, because in some cases it must needs be executed. The laws of men may ordain and appoint extremity, but the law of God must tell us when to urge them and when to moderate them. [. . .]

To return then to the matter and to end this point of public equity: if any man shall object that this moderation is wrong to the law, I answer: it is not; for it is neither against the law nor altogether beside the law, but only beside the strictest meaning of the law. Nay it is included in the law as well as the extremity is, though not in the same manner: for the extremity is warranted by the law, mitigation is but tolerated; the law alloweth extremity, but it only admitteth a mitigation. So then, both extremity and mitigation are within the law, but it is the hand principally of the magistrate, and in some cases of other men also, to discern the several circumstances when the one is to be executed and when the other. And according as these two are justly and wisely executed or neglected, so is the justice of the law executed or neglected.

The want of this equity in men's public actions is the cause of much cruelty, oppression, and inequality in dealings betwixt man and man, because extremity is for the most part only regarded, and mitigation is banished out of all bargains. And it is impossible to keep good conscience in forfeitures of bonds, and in forfeiture of lands, suretyships, fines, rents, and such kind of actions, unless there be due regard had to the practice of this public equity. Men therefore must consider that they are Christians and live in a Christian commonwealth; and they must not stand only upon the law, and the advantage that the law gives. As they are men they have a law of the country which may allow extremity; but as they are Christians they live under a law of God, the eternal law, which must judge them at the last day: the righteous law, which no creature shall ever be able to blame of injustice or of extremity. And men must know that God himself commands this equity of one man to another.

But if men, for the fear of God, will not deal equally and moderately with them that are in their power, but stand strictly upon forfeiture and other extremity, then must the godly magistrate exercise his power, and by the force of his authority cause them to mitigate their extremity and to put in practice that equity which becometh Christians. And let every judge and magistrate know that, by the law of the everlasting God, he not only may but is bound thus to do to them who will not do it of themselves. It may be, therefore, good counsel to all men, rather to practise this Christian equity of themselves than to be compelled to it by authority; for every virtue and good work, the more free and voluntary it is, the more acceptable is it to God, and more commendable before men. And let all men remember that, whereas the strict words of men's laws seem to give them leave to urge the extremity, yet cannot that excuse them, nor free them from the danger of God's law which commands them to practise Christian equity and moderation. [. . .]

[507] Now in regard of this that hath been delivered touching public equity, lawyers must not think that I have gone beyond the compass of my calling and encroached upon their liberties. For they are to know that the laws of men are polity, but equity is Christianity. Now Christianity was before there were any laws of men, and therefore they must be ordered according to the rules of Christianity. Again, di-

vines must take lawyers' advice concerning extremity and the letter of the law — a good reason then that lawyers take the divines' advice touching equity, which is the intent of the law. Moreover, their law is but the minister of equity, but our law, the word of God, is the fountain of equity. Therefore the principal rules of equity must they fetch from our law, considering that law without equity is plain tyranny. Lastly, in the first Christian commonwealth that ever was — namely, the Jews, the divines — that is, the priests of those days, were the only lawyers; for their positive laws were the judicial laws given by God himself, whose interpreters were the priests and Levites. If therefore, once the divines had so much to do with positive laws, it may not now be thought amiss if they give advice out of the word of God touching the equal execution of the laws of men.

And so much touching the doctrine of public equity grounded upon the word of God.

Now followeth the second kind of equity, called *private*, namely that which is to be exercised betwixt man and man in their private actions. But ere we go further, some may demand the difference betwixt public and [p. 508] private actions. Private actions of men are such as are practised amongst men without any help of the law, as, contrariwise, public actions are such as cannot be performed but by the help of the law and the hand of the magistrate. [. . .]

[508] Now let us come to search more nearly into the nature of this virtue. *Private equity is a moderate, even, and equal carriage of man's self in all his private words and deeds towards all other men, and all their words and deeds.* First, I say, it is "of man's self," that is, betwixt both extremes, neither bearing all things, nor revenging everything. Secondly, I say "towards all other men," wherein I comprehend all men and all sorts of men: husbands, wives; magistrates, subjects; teachers, hearers; masters, servants; parents, children; men, women; neighbours in towns, fellows in societies; in service, in labour. In a word, none are excepted who any way do live or converse together, but of them all it is true that if there be not a moderation and a forbearance, one of another, there can be no peace amongst them, but their lives shall be all (as it were) a hell upon the earth. Seeing, therefore, the necessity and excellency of this virtue is such that the due practice of it is the ornament of families and societies, and the comfort of a man's life in this world, let us enter into a more particular consideration thereof. Private equity hath four degrees or principal duties. First, to bear with natural infirmities. Secondly, to interpret doubtful things in the better part. Thirdly, to depart from our own right sometimes. Fourthly, to forgive private and personal wrongs.

Text: (Cambridge: Legat, 1609).

The *Convocation Book* (1606)

At the Elizabethan Reformation the Church of England laid claim to a moderately Erastian form of church polity, which assigned to the secular ruler, de facto a monarch, "the cheefe gouernment of all estates of this Realm, whether they be Ecclesiasticall or Ciuile." In response to the objection that this left government of the church in lay hands, Article 37 insisted that only jurisdictional power was meant — not "the ministring either of God's word, or of Sacraments" — and appealed for support to the testimony of Holy Scripture to the role of kings in the history of Israel and Judah. Further than that official definitions did not seek to go.

At the beginning of James I's reign (1603), however, the Houses of Convocation undertook to produce an extensively developed doctrine of civil and ecclesiastical government and a series of canons that would define Anglican orthodoxy on the subject. The background to this enterprise was, in Reformed circles, the steady radicalization of the constitutionalist tradition and the beginnings of a doctrine of popular sovereignty, while in Roman Catholic circles there was a polemical reassertion of older papalist doctrines about the right of popes to depose recalcitrant kings, culminating in the frightening work directed by Suárez "against the heresies of the Anglican sect" (*Defence of the Catholic and Apostolic Faith* [1613]), which James undertook to rebut with his own pen. In response to these hostile developments, an Anglican political theology began to emerge that was at once more romantic and more defiant than that bequeathed by the Reformation. Deeply authoritarian, monarchist by conviction rather than default, it associated royal power with the *patria potestas* that belonged to Adam as a gift of creation, and linked it as the senior partner in a collaboration with priestly authority that had descended unbroken since the first moments after the fall. This high-political Anglicanism, which was to stoke the fires of conflict that led finally to the Civil War, is captured for us at an early moment, in the *Convocation Book*.

That this valuation of monarchy gained a purchase on the Anglican mind without being promoted by government (at least, not for very long), is suggested by the fact that it came to be considered problematic in government circles. To the ex-

778

tent that the king's initial disposition was conciliatory toward Roman Catholics, he was even less inclined than Elizabeth's church had been to parley with Puritan dissidents aligned with European Reformed churches. Yet the public alarm excited by the Gunpowder Plot (1605) soon made it important for the throne to assert its Reformed credentials and make friends of the European opponents of papacy. At this point, energetic action was taken by James himself to put a stop to the Convocation's speculations. He made his reason quite clear: "in saying that even tyranny is God's authority, and should be reverenced as such," it queered the pitch of the "Hollanders" against the throne of Spain, a cause which England had espoused militarily in Elizabeth's reign and which James, though by a more peaceable path, was not inclined to throw over. Even more alarming: "If the king of Spain should return to claim his old pontifical right to my kingdom, you leave me to seek for others to fight for it; for you tell us upon the matter beforehand, his authority is God's authority, if he prevail." Convocation was told that it had "dipped too deep into what all kings reserve among the *arcana imperii*," and ordered to stop work. Its "book" remained unpublished until a copy appeared in 1689, written in the hand of the Prolocutor of Convocation, the later bishop John Overall, who is as likely as not the effective author. The purpose of its publication at that point was to vindicate the Anglican establishment's view of government after the Glorious Revolution, an event that had, of course, seemed to others, not least John Locke, to give fuel to theories of popular sovereignty.

The opening chapters and canons, reproduced below, set the tone for the whole work. While clearly engaging popular sovereignty as the major threat, they offer no conciliatory gestures to papal claims. An Erastian seniority of secular rule is unflinchingly maintained against a background of a primeval history that finds monarchy in Adam from creation, but priesthood consequent upon the fall. The resulting identification of political and parental authority *(patria potesta)*, perhaps derived from Peter Gregory of Toulouse, on whom Althusius also drew, became a distinctive element in Anglican political apologetics. As maintained by Robert Filmer's *Patriarcha* during Charles I's reign, it had to combat the mainstream view on the Catholic side represented by Suárez, that Adam's authority before the fall was purely domestic, and it fell victim on the Protestant side, in turn, to the scornful polemics of Locke.

The return to primeval history (reminiscent of some high medieval conflicts over priesthood and kingship) is significant from a number of points of view. It was apparently prompted by George Buchanan's *Rerum Scoticarum Historia* (1582), which combined Renaissance and Reformed influences to justify an aggressively populist antimonarchism. When in canon 2 we have a first, hostile sighting of a presocial state of nature, an idea which would have such powerful influence upon Hobbes, Locke, and Rousseau, it is owing to Buchanan. But while the whole *Convocation Book* is written as history, and displays at many points the pedantry of Renaissance antiquarianism, the form can scarcely disguise its underlying message: nothing has ever happened to change anything. It is from nature, rather than history, that it derives the Erastian partnership of civil and ecclesiastical authority, which, once instituted, continues throughout sacred history, with variation but without alteration. The Jewish exiles owed Babylon, and the postexilic community owed Persia, precisely the same allegiance that their ancestors had owed Moses and David, even in "ecclesiastical" causes. The incarnation itself makes no difference. The second person of the Trinity, having himself instituted this very order, is hardly likely to disturb it. Not only the existing civil structures, but even the ecclesiastical ones, were treated with great deference by the incarnate Christ. He modeled the threefold ministry of priests, bishops, and archbishops (!) upon the forms already established in the "national church" of Jewry (2.6).

Here we can take the measure of the work's antipapal interest. On earth Christ's kingly rule was a property only of his divine and not of his human nature. And after the ascension, when the human nature came to share the kingship proper to the divine, there were no implications for the church's authority and structure. The customary genteel anathema is pronounced against the idea that "he did make (the apostles) . . . partakers of his regal authority whereof his human nature was then actually possessed" (2.8). In a self-betraying moment, the Convocation declares that Christ was "content" to be "only" a spiritual king to rule men's hearts. This was something neither papal nor Reformed apologists could accept, and shows what a surprising breadth of ground could be common to the enemies of Anglicanism.

Further Reading: K. Fincham, *Prelate as Pastor: The Episcopate of James I* (Oxford: Clarendon Press, 1990); K. Fincham, *The Early Stuart Church, 1603-42* (Basingstoke, Hampshire: Macmillan, 1993); W. M. Lamont, *Godly Rule, 1603-1660* (London and New York: Macmillan, 1969).

From *Concerning the Government of God's Catholic Church and the Kingdoms of the Whole World*, Book 1

1. Amongst the rest of the titles and attributes of God in the Scriptures, which are common to the blessed Trinity, these following are three, viz. Creator, Lord of lords and King of kings; which be there applied as well to the Son of God, or Lord Jesus Christ, the second Person in the said blessed Trinity, as to God the Father, and to God the Holy Ghost. Agreeably whereunto, and not otherwise, our chief purpose being to imitate the Scriptures, in setting out and describing the deity and dignity of our Saviour Christ, by his Almighty power, and universal government of all the world, as heir of all things, and head of his Church; we hold it fit to begin with his divine power of creation: and thereupon in the sense aforesaid do affirm that he in the beginning did create both heaven and earth; and that amongst the rest of the creatures which he then made, he created our first parents, Adam and Eve, from whose loins mankind is descended.

If any man therefore shall affirm with any pagan, heretic, atheist, or any other profane persons, which know not, or believe not the Scriptures, either that heaven and earth had no beginning or that the world was made by angels, or the devil; that the world was not otherwise made by Christ than as he was an instrument of God the Fa-

ther for the making of it; or that he did not, as God, create our said parents, Adam and Eve, he doth greatly err.

2. To him that shall duly read the Scriptures, it will be plain and evident that the Son of God, having created our first parents, and purposing to multiply their seed into many generations, for the replenishing of the world with their posterity, did give to Adam for his time, and to the rest of the patriarchs and chief fathers successively before the flood, authority, power and dominion over their children and offspring, to rule and govern them; ordaining by the law of nature, that their said children and offspring (begotten and brought up by them) should fear, reverence, honour and obey them. Which power and authority before the flood, resting in the patriarchs and in the chief fathers, because it had a very large extent, not only for the education of their said children and offspring, whilst they were young, but likewise for the ordering, ruling and governing of them afterwards, when they came to man's estate. And for that also it had no superior authority, or power, over, or above it on earth, appearing in the Scriptures, although it be called either patriarchal, regal and imperial, and that we only term it *potestas patria;* yet being well considered how far it did reach, we may truly say that it was in a sort *potestas regia,* as now, in a right and true construction, *potestas regia* may justly be called *potestas patria.*

If any man shall therefore affirm that men at the first, without all good education, or civility, ran up and down in woods and fields, as wild creatures, resting themselves in caves, and dens, and acknowledging no superiority one over another, until they were taught by experience the necessity of government; and that thereupon they chose some amongst themselves to order and rule the rest, giving them power and authority so to do; and that consequently all civil power, jurisdiction, and authority, was first derived from the people, and disordered multitude; or either is originally still in them, or else is deduced by their consents naturally from them; and is not God's ordinance originally descending from him, and depending upon him, he doth greatly err.

3. By the sin of our first parents, Adam and Eve, both they and in them all their posterity, being so fallen from God as that they were not able by any natural powers or faculties in them to discharge their duties towards him, or rightly in any sort to know him as they ought unto salvation, or serve his divine majesty, it pleased Almighty God in mercy (besides the law of nature left in them) to propound unto them another kind of doctrine than nature could ever have taught them, viz. the mystery of salvation through our Lord and Saviour Jesus Christ; how the Son of God, who created them when they were not, should in fulness of time take upon him their nature, and reconcile to God again as many as should believe in him; the ground of which doctrine God himself did lay down as the foundation of the church of Christ, when he said that "the seed of the woman should break the serpent's head" (Gen. 3:15).

If any man therefore shall affirm either that our first parents after their fall, or consequently any of their posterity, could serve or please God truly by any natural powers or faculties that were left in them after the said fall; or that the mystery of salvation through Jesus Christ was not a secret whereunto our corrupt nature could not attain; or that our Saviour Christ is not the promised seed that should break the serpent's head; or that any can possibly be partakers of everlasting life without faith in him, he doth greatly err.

4. As the Son of God, having created mankind, did ordain by the law of nature and light of reason that there should be some amongst them furnished with lawful power and civil authority to rule and govern the rest in things belonging to this natural life and civil society, according to the true rules both of nature and reason: so did he also, according to the supernatural doctrine of the Gospel, not only ordain that there should be some likewise in his church to rule and govern it, but also gave them another kind of power, superiority and authority, which is termed Ecclesiastical, both for the teaching and instructing of his people in the mysteries hid from nature concerning their salvation through the seed of the woman, and for the better direction and government of them in the service of God touching their duties to God and their neighbours. The institution of which ecclesiastical calling and authority, as also the manner of the worship of God through the blessed seed from the fall of our first parents till the flood, although besides their sacrifices, prayers and preaching they be not expressly set down in the Scriptures; yet it is not to be doubted, but that, first, Adam for his time and afterwards the heads of every family of the faithful were not only civil governors over their kindred, but likewise had the power and execution of the priest's office; and that they were themselves instructed and taught from God, as they afterward did instruct and teach such as were under them, in the said mysteries of man's restitution through the promised seed by faith and in the right worship and service of the true God.

If any man shall therefore affirm that the Son of God, having from the beginning a church upon earth, did leave them till the flood without priests and priestly authority to govern and instruct them in those ways of their salvation and in the right manner of the worship and service of God, or that they might teach them any other doctrine in that behalf than that which they had received from God himself, he doth greatly err.

5. As all mankind from the creation of the world till the flood descended from the loins of Adam; so after the flood have they all descended from the three sons of Noah: Sem, Cham, and Japhet (Gen. 9:18f.).

And therefore if any man will affirm with any pagan or profane atheist either that there was not any such general deluge or that there is any nation or people in the world that doth not descend from one of the said three sons of Noah, he doth greatly err.

6. Noah lived after the flood three hundred and fifty years and saw his children's children wonderfully multiplied; during which term of years he was the patriarch or chief governor over them, ruling and ordering of them by virtue of that superiority, power and authority which was given unto him by Almighty God and was also warranted by the laws of nature and reason. Touching this patriarchal, or in effect regal, government of Noah there is more expressed in the Scriptures than there was before the flood of the power and authority of Adam or any of the chief fathers and rulers that were descended from him. For now there is mention made by God himself of punishing blood by blood, which was done by the sword of justice, being the chief ensign and warrant of supreme and regal authority. Also the extent of this right and authority was so large as that he lawfully distributed the whole world unto his said three sons and their posterity. So that his said three sons after him were by the ordinance of God (the chief author of the said distribution) made three great princes; and also the sons of those three great princes (of whom about seventy are named) were the heads and governors of the families and nations that descended from them, according to their tongues, in their several countries.

If any man shall therefore affirm either that the civil power and authority which Noah had before the flood was by the deluge determined; or that it was given unto him again by his sons and nephews; or that he received from them the sword of his sovereignty; or that the said distribution did depend upon their consents, or received from them any such authority as without the same it could not lawfully have been made; or that this power, superiority and authority and all the parts thereof which Noah's three sons and their children had (as is before declared) did not proceed originally from God or were not properly his ordinances, but that they had the same from the people, their offspring, he doth greatly err.

7. It is also certain that as the civil magistrates, and their authority, continued after the flood for the government of mankind according to the laws of God and nature, that thereby they might be kept in order, touching their duties both towards God and their neighbours, agreeably to the said laws, written afterwards more fully, by God himself in Two Tables: so did the priesthood and authority ecclesiastical also by the like ordinance of God continue especially amongst the offspring of Sem, both to govern them ecclesiastically and to instruct them in the mysteries of their salvation through the blessed seed of the woman, according to the doctrine of the Gospel, which was from time to time in divers manners delivered by the Son of God unto them. This priestly office and ecclesiastical authority was yet joined (as before the flood) with the office of the chief fathers and civil governors. Noah himself was both a prince and a priest; he built altars, offered sacrifices, and taught the church, after the flood, three hundred and fifty three years, all that which he had learnt from his fathers concerning the creation of the world, the fall of man, and of his restitution by Christ, and generally all that did concern necessarily either civil societies and government or ecclesiastical assemblies and authority, not omitting the very ceremonies. After Noah the chief fathers, Sem, Abraham, Isaac and Jacob did execute that office, God himself renewing unto them this promise of salvation through the blessed seed; and not only confirming the same to Abraham and his posterity by the sacrament of circumcision, but likewise teaching and instructing them in that heavenly mystery, sometimes by his own voice, and sometimes by visions, and divers other ways, whereof the Scriptures make more plain mention than they do of the delivery of the same evangelical doctrine before the flood.

If any man shall therefore affirm either that the priestly office, and authority ecclesiastical, which Noah had before the flood, was by that deluge determined, or that it was by the election of his offspring conferred again upon him; or that Sem, Abraham, Isaac and Jacob, were neither priests, nor had any ecclesiastical authority, until they were chosen thereunto by their children and nephews; or that the priesthood and ecclesiastical authority were not the ordinances of God, for the governing and instructing of the church, according to the will and directions of God himself delivered and revealed unto them, as is aforesaid, he doth greatly err.

8. As before the flood Cain and his posterity were opposite to the posterity of

Seth, and might therefore generally have been called the Church Malignant; so fell it out after the flood in the generations of Japhet, but especially of Cham, against the posterity of Sem, in whose lineage the true worship of God through the blessed seed was especially continued; and not that only, but in like manner as the children of Seth in process of time provoked against them the wrath of God by corrupting their ways and following in their conversation the generations of Cain, and were in that respect, all of them, with the rest of Cain's offspring justly punished and drowned by the flood, saving eight persons (Noah and his wife, Sem, Cham and Japhet, and their three wives), so did the posterity not only of Cham and Japhet, as well before as after the confusion of tongues and the death of Noah, but likewise the offspring of Sem (who were called more effectually to the knowledge of the mysteries of Christ and right service of the true God) leave the ways of Noah and Sem, and gave just occasion to Almighty God (had he not bound himself by his covenant to the contrary) to have drowned them all again. Nimrod, descended of Cham, not contenting himself with the patriarchal or regal mild government ordained of God by the laws of reason and nature, became a tyrant and lord of confusion (Gen. 10:8-12); and by histories it is apparent that within few ages after the death of Noah his sons great barbarism and confusion fell among their generations through their pride and dissoluteness, in that they thought scorn to be governed either civilly or ecclesiastically as God himself by Noah had ordained, or to be ruled otherwise than as they list themselves: and touching the service of God and the ecclesiastical authority they mingled with true religion many false worships, and chose priests among themselves to serve God after their own fashions; or rather they devised to themselves many gods and found out priests accordingly, such as were content to train them up in those kinds of impiety. In Chaldea itself and the places adjacent the children of Sem were all of them almost grown to be idolaters; insomuch as God himself, to keep a remnant more carefully that should through the public profession of his name be partakers of his mercies in Christ, called Abraham with his family from the habitation of his fathers, to become a stranger in the land of Canaan (Gen. 12:1-3).

If therefore any man shall affirm that the said posterity of Noah his children did well in altering either the manner or form of civil government which God had appointed, by bringing in of tyranny or factious popularity; or of the ecclesiastical, by framing unto themselves a new kind of priesthood and worship after their own humours; or that it was lawful for such as then served God upon any pretence to have imitated their examples in either of those courses, he doth greatly err.

9. It is apparent in the Scriptures, that although God was not pleased that the issue of Jacob's children should, by the example of the sons of Noah, grow up to become the heads of so many several nations, but continuing together, should make one people and nation to be ruled and governed by the same laws and magistrates; yet it seemed good to his heavenly wisdom, that in so great a people as he foresaw should descend from Jacob's children no one tribe or family should continue charged both with the regal and ecclesiastical functions; and therefore Jacob making way to the fulfilling of the will of God herein, did take just occasion, moved thereunto by the Spirit of God, to deprive his eldest son Reuben of his interest by birthright in both those prerogatives, to be disposed afterward by God upon other of his brethren. Now after Jacob's death, the former thereof, viz. the sceptre, in process of time fell to Judah, as Jacob before had prophesied (Gen. 49:3f., 10); and the other also, viz. the priesthood, was afterwards given to Levi by God's ordinance.

10. After Jacob's death, till Moses was sent to deliver the children of Israel out of Egypt, there is little in the Scriptures touching either the civil or ecclesiastical government. It appeareth that Joseph, being a great prince in Egypt by the king's authority, whilst he lived was chief amongst his brethren, but after his death, through the tyranny of the kings of Egypt which God suffered to lie heavily upon them for many years, the civil authority which any of the tribes had was very small; there was such jealousy of their number (which daily increased above all ordinary expectation) as it is not likely that the kings successively would suffer any great authority to rest in them; howbeit, we think they had some, either the chief heads of the tribes generally, or of the tribe of Ephraim and Reuben (for it may be Jacob's prophecy of Reuben's losing the prerogatives of his birthright was not presently executed) which did in their civil affairs appertaining to themselves bear some chief sway amongst them. And touching the priesthood, although the people were then generally much polluted with idolatry, yet therein also they had some, most likely the firstborn, who, although they durst not there offer sacrifices to God as they should in that servitude, yet some of them (we doubt not) instructed the people in matters concerning the promises of the blessed Seed, and performed as they might the other offices of their priesthood, although many of the people and of the priests, as it seemeth, were then greatly polluted with idolatry.

If any man therefore shall affirm either that the uniting of the children of Jacob into one nation, or the severing of the civil and ecclesiastical functions (the prerogatives of birthright) from Reuben the first-born and dividing of them from one person, was made by themselves; or that their servitude in Egypt was unjustly suffered to lie upon them so long by Almighty God; or that they being his church, he left them destitute of such comforts of direction and instruction as were necessary, those times considered, for their civil or ecclesiastical estate; or that the people took then upon them the appointing of the heads of their tribes and families or the choice of their civil superiors or of the priests; or that the example of those wicked kings may be any lawful warrant for any other king so to oppress the people and church of God, he doth greatly err.

11. When the time came that God in mercy was pleased to deliver the children of Israel out of Egypt, and to place them in the land which he had promised them, he raised up his servants, Moses and Joshua, to take that charge upon them; and accordingly Moses being made their prince, or (as the Scripture speaks) their king, did not only by God's appointment and assistance lead them out of Egypt, but governed them (being six hundred thousand men on foot, besides women and children) forty years by his authority in the wilderness; and Joshua likewise succeeding Moses in the same princely power and authority, did after many difficulties bring them into the land of Canaan, and gave them lawful possession thereof. So that, although formerly the children of Israel were kept in such great servitude and bondage, whilst they were in Egypt as notwithstanding their number they were no way able like a free people to lift up their heads; yet now they are knit together in one body and settled as a particular state and free nation in their own country, being ruled and governed

successively after a mild and temperate manner first by Moses in the wilderness (as is aforesaid) and then by Joshua in Canaan whilst he lived.

If any man therefore shall affirm either that the children of Israel were delivered out of Egypt by their own strength and not by God's especial direction and mighty power; or that it had been lawful for them (not warranted by God) to have departed thence as they did without licence first obtained of king Pharaoh; or that Moses and Joshua were not called to that high authority by God himself, but received the same from the people, as depending upon their choice; or that Dathan and Abiram (descended from Reuben) can be justified in challenging of Moses, that he took too much upon him in executing only that authority which God had given him (cf. Num. 16:1-3), he doth greatly err.

12. As Almighty God took order for the settling of his people in the land of Canaan, and established a princely authority to rule and govern them civilly, so was he no less careful of his church. For howsoever the priesthood was disposed of before this time, yet now it is apparent in the Scriptures that the same was after settled in the tribe of Levi; and Aaron was made by God's appointment (for the better government of the church) the Chief and High Priest (Exod. 28:1); the whole priesthood being assigned to his children and their offspring, as well to succeed him in the said highest place as also to execute the other inferior functions belonging to priests; and the rest of the tribe of Levi were to attend other ecclesiastical services.

If any man therefore shall affirm either that the tribe of Levi was assigned by the people to undertake the said ecclesiastical offices; or that Aaron and his posterity were chosen by the people to be their priests; or that they were not chosen directly by God himself; or that the people had any lawful interest at any time afterwards either to choose their priests or (being appointed of God, as is aforesaid) to deprive them of their places; or that Corah, of the tribe of Levi, can be justified in saying that Aaron took too much upon him, thereby repining either that Aaron was rather made High Priest than he himself, or that the priesthood was annexed to Aaron's posterity whereas the rest of the Levites were to serve in inferior places, he doth greatly err.

Text: *The Convocation Book of MDCVI*, Library of Anglo-Catholic Theology (Oxford, 1844).

Hugo Grotius

(1583-1646)

To conclude our selection of readings with Hugo Grotius is to make a statement at once about the shape of the tradition and about Grotius himself. In the early modern era there emerged from the theopolitical tradition a new and distinctive approach to political thought, effectively independent of theological premises. *That* such a change took place is hardly to be doubted, but when, and by what stages is a matter for debate. An excellent case can be made for putting the threshold some seventy-five years after Grotius's *Right of War and Peace (De iure belli ac pacis)* (1625). This has the advantage of taking Locke, and even Hobbes, seriously as Christian thinkers, and counting Cromwellian liberalism (as voiced by Milton) as part of the Christian theopolitical tradition. Compelling arguments can also be marshaled for putting the threshold earlier, as the impulses that led to the change belong to the sixteenth-century Renaissance; Machiavelli, perhaps, may be singled out as a dramatic point of departure. Then Grotius becomes a significant figure in the public inauguration of the rationalist era, dressing its iconoclastic principles in an overcoat of piety and organizing them in a systematic science of natural law.

In our opinion, however, there is much to be said for the old view that something dramatically new came to pass in the mid–seventeenth century, something of which Hobbes is a symbol, and which, for all its undeniable antecedents, marks a decisive break between the theological and the rationalist traditions. The key to this interpretation lies in the reading of Hobbes and Grotius side by side. Grotius, for all his embrace of the program of a humanist science, was a true heir of the theological tradition; Hobbes, for all his wealth of theological opinions, broke with the structure of Christian political thought.

To read Grotius comprehensively is far from easy. He is the last great figure in whose thought a unity of theology, law, philology, and history is effective. He was the epitome of late Renaissance man, a polymath who ranged across the boundaries of our modern disciplines, and there are few modern readers, even among the ranks of professional scholars, who can claim the competence to read the whole of his output with understanding. Furthermore, his style of writing sets many traps for the incautious. The page is crowded with quotations — classical, biblical, patristic, occasionally contemporary — spilled extravagantly across its surface. Only on closer examination do we find that they are quite careless, and often do not support the case that Grotius himself intends to make, but merely illustrate the vast range of commonplace and philosophical opinion through which an encyclopedic discussion has to pick its way. To discover his own views we must isolate the terse dialectical argument, which develops a complex position so economically that crucial moves can very easily be overlooked. Grotius is a dangerous person to quote, at least for those whose taste in quotations, like his own, is confined to single sentences or less. (To assist the reader to follow the structure of his argument, we have resorted below to placing some sections of illustrative quotation in smaller typeface.)

Yet stylistic economy alone cannot take all the blame for making him one of the most startlingly misunderstood figures in early modern thought. There is a persistent misreading of his intentions which constitutes a sobering object lesson in the history of scholarship. Five Latin words isolated from the "Prolegomena" of *The Right of War and Peace* are still found — as they have been found for generations — quoted in every encyclopedia article: *etiamsi daremus Deum non esse*, "even were we to accept that God did not exist"; and on the basis of these five words Grotius is marked out as a pioneer of "secular" natural law theory. Only a small proportion of those who quote them have read the sentence in which they occur, let alone the context of the discussion, or anything further that the author wrote. And this lopsided characterization has a history as long as the name of Grotius itself. For at the time of their first publication, the Vatican took offense at them (though they had a good pedigree in scholastic theology), and placed the book on the Index. That was the cue for Grotius to be claimed by younger figures who really did aspire to found a moral science that would be valid independently of God. But such a thing was not Grotius's purpose, and we hope that the selections which follow may persuade readers that to understand Grotius as a legal and political theorist implies understanding him also as a lay theologian.

Not only his mind, but his biography, too, was decisively shaped by theology. Hugo Grotius (de Groot) laid the beginnings of a reputation in his native Holland, while scarcely more than a schoolboy, by his contributions to the study of classical texts and by his original poetry in Latin. Later, a lawyer by training and a politician by practice, he became deeply and learnedly embroiled in the great theological controversy which shook the Netherlands in the second decade of the seventeenth century, between a doctrinally freer Erastian Reformed tradition, which he believed to be the authentic mind of the Dutch laity, and the superlapsarian Calvinism prevailing among the Reformed clergy. Attempting unconvincingly to walk a middle path between the two camps ("Remonstrant" and "Counter-Remonstrant," respectively), he badly offended the latter, and when, for reasons of state, the Counter-Remonstrants secured the support of the prince of Orange at the Synod of Dort (1619), Grotius came close to losing his head, a fate which befell his friend and leader Oldenbarnevelt. He was condemned to prison for life.

This traumatic climax to his early career, though borne at the time with a widely admired generosity, left a deep scar. It is difficult to read the paragraphs on capital punishment (2.20.12-16 below) without being struck at once by their (all too) studied objectivity and the deep current of hostility to those who had "thought it quite appropriate for (themselves) to have the power of life and death over their fellow-citizens." The austere high-mindedness that made him famous was never free of a thread of self-pity. After a famous escape in a trunk, organized by his wife, he spent the rest of his days in exile, including two lengthy periods in France, the latter in the curious role of Swedish ambassador. It was during his first French period that he wrote *On the Right of War and Peace*, which cemented his worldwide renown as a humanist and intellectual. The later years were spent, apart from diplomatic duties, in composing a detailed commentary on the New Testament which in many ways pioneers historical and philological approaches, as well as in engaging in deeply frustrating endeavors to foster ecumenical understanding among the separated churches of Christendom.

To his contemporaries his ecclesiological opinions seemed elusive and uncertain. In some quarters he was believed to be effectively a Roman Catholic, in others effectively a Socinian (Unitarian). His interest in the English church earned him Anglican admirers who claimed him noisily for their interest. Yet the confusion reflects more on his failure to conform to the main currents of his time than on any secretiveness or obscurity in his thought. He believed there was a primitive, authentic Christianity, which could be established on the basis of the Scriptures and the fathers of the undivided church. It was incumbent upon all Christians to seek the unity of the church on the basis of this ancient doctrine and practice. The Roman Catholic Church he thought of simply as "unreformed," a repository of faith and superstition, a confusion of true doctrine and heretical deviations; supralapsarian Calvinism of the Dortian type he regarded as having fallen into a pagan fatalism; its Remonstrant opposition he considered not free of leanings toward Pelagianism. The chief corruption of Christianity in his time, however, was not so much heresy as polemicism, in whatever cause it might be enlisted.

Behind these ecclesiological positions lie two substantive theological theses which give shape to his political work, too. These are the teleological significance of all existence and the universal competence of divine law. In these two theses Grotius stood with his predecessors, especially with the Salamanca school, with whom, while keeping his distance, he often had a common mind, and among the Reformers with Melanchthon. The importance of the first thesis has been underlined by the recent discovery of his early *Meletius* (1611), which opposes the division between the dogmatic and the practical impulses within theology. The role of Christian doctrine is to lay before us God as our supreme good, and to evoke our worship and service; and by this criterion important doctrinal issues may be distinguished from trivial speculative quibbles. For any thing to exist is for it to have a mode of being *for God*, i.e., a law of its being. And here is the basis of the second thesis; law is metaphysics, and metaphysics law. "What God has shown to be his will, that is law" was the opening sentence of his first legal work, *De iure praedae* (1604). The great "Prolegomena" of his major work, two decades later, was written to develop it. Far from replacing divine law with an autonomous rational politics, this essay, summarizing the whole approach of the massive *Right of War and Peace,* aims to demonstrate the comprehensive claim of divine law (in the form of natural Right) upon every variety of human relation, not least those which lie *outside* the scope of human legal constitutions — war itself affording many examples, though it was also governed by a customary law of nations. Grotius was famous as an apologist for natural religion. The universal evidence of natural law was, for him, a proof that God was active, not that God was dispensable.

The second thesis may be summed up by the simple statement: there was no "state of nature," no unnormed, presocial human existence, before which norms of human society must be brought to justify themselves. This point of view Grotius undertook to argue by engagement with two cardinal texts from the humanist canon: the speech of Carneades in Cicero's *De republica* (known through Lactantius's use of it) and Horace's third *Satire.* Even the state of humanity "prior to" civil society, a state which was daily given substance by new reports of uncivilized tribes in newly discovered lands, was, in Grotius's view, subject to the same divine law that underlay the developed political constitutions of the Christian world. The relation that he traces between "pure nature" and civil society is conceived on familiar classical lines, as the relation between the fundamental *principles* of human society and the *determinations* of those principles that each society makes. Natural Right thus serves as a basis on which all human law, including international law, is developed. But human law is answerable to divine law not only in the form of natural Right, but in the form of revelation, both in the Old and New Covenants. The "evangelical law," then, constitutes the highest point of legal disclosure, and the legal practices of Christian civilization, which themselves form a higher layer of customary international law, reflect the advances in human law made possible by the gospel.

In all the passages below, Grotius touches on a distinction made by Aristotle (*NE* 1130b31ff.) between two kinds of justice, "justice in transactions" and "justice in distributions." He is both fascinated and dissatisfied with this distinction, and dissatisfied, moreover, with its treatment in St. Thomas (cf. pp. 343-45 above) and his more recent disciples, where it appears in the terms "commutative justice" and "distributive justice." Grotius's reconstruction of it is one of his most valuable theoretical contributions. The ways in which Aristotle and the scholastics attempted to distinguish the two types will not serve. The truth is simple: the one kind of Right attends to a "faculty," the other to a "fitness." That is to say, "expletive" justice is simply a matter of "implementing" *(explere)* rights that already obtain; "attributive" justice is a much more creative matter of recognizing and responding to some potential, which has no claim of subjective right but has a rightness. So Grotius incorporates the traditional feudal responsibility of the ruler to exercise *beneficia* into his other responsibility, that of exercising justice, with the result that the concept of justice is broadened and, of course, by no means confined to rulers.

This was important to the wider program of his book. Throughout *The Right of War and Peace* we meet his recurrent insistence that "merely expletive justice" is not enough to account for duties of restraint in war. Yet what lies beyond expletive justice is still justice, and therefore *ius,* "Right," and consequently "law." Grotius is often credited with an influence in the development of the concept of subjective rights. Though the definitions given in 1.1 hardly advance beyond what we have read in Gerson (see above, p. 528), to the extent that subjective right now plays a theoretical role in defining expletive justice, we have reached a new stage in the entrenching of the idea. Yet here, once again, it is important to notice the context in which the idea of a subjective right has arisen for Grotius, the problematic about the dual character of justice. In using the idea of a subjective right to pinpoint the idea of "merely" expletive justice, he has eloquently indicated its limitations. There is an extensive and more important role for the idea of Right, he tells us, than can ever be conveyed by the idea of "rights." (In translating, we have had to face the usual impossibility of rendering the word *ius* into English so as to retain its legal sense on the one hand and to indicate its connection with *iustitia*, "justice," on the other. Here we follow the practice of translating *ius* as Right throughout, following precisely [unlike some other English translations] Grotius's use of singular and plural, and using an initial capital where it is equivalent to "law" or "justice," retaining the lowercase when we take the sense to be a concrete right, whether objective, "a right to something," or subjective, "somebody's right.")

The thrust of Grotius's doctrine of Right is well exemplified by the long chapter on punishment (*Right of War and Peace* 2.20), the opening segment of which has been chosen both for the interest of the subject matter, of which there is rather little extended discussion in Christian writing, and as a fine example of the baroque Grotian style which hides a nuanced doctrine behind a welter of misleading quotation. It has proved possible to read it as a "retributivist" account of punishment, anticipating Kant; it has proved equally possible to read it as a "consequentialist" account, anticipating Bentham; but neither reading does justice to the subtlety of the author's balance. The reader will need to bear in mind that this book is about the Right *of war*, and that the goal of this discussion is to understand the conditions of *penal war*. This gives particular point to the distinction between the *justice of the punishment as such*, residing simply in the expletive justice of a penalty that fits the crime and is sufficient for the justice of divine punishment, and the *justice of our punishing*, which requires further rational purposes lying within the scope of prudence. In this way Grotius establishes a basis for saying that the bare "right to punish" is not a sufficient ground for war. Punishment, especially in war, must be integrated into a policy that takes responsibility for social welfare. To this distinction he adds another characteristic one, between natural Right and gospel law. Both demand that punishing be accommodated to rational social projects, but Christ's teaching radicalizes the thrust toward self-renunciation and self-control, yet always in a way that recognizably makes explicit *as law* the anticipations of the wisest pagan and Jewish philosophers. In this way Grotius can ground a demand for higher standards of humanity and moderation among the Christian nations than are found at large, yet without denying that there is such a thing as universally recognized natural Right. Christ's teaching does not, however, overthrow the conditions of social rationality; it does not countenance idealistic projects to abolish punishment entirely, or even to abolish the death penalty.

The link between Grotius's theology and theory of punishment can be ex-

plored from the theological side in one of his most influential books, *The Satisfaction of Christ (De satisfactione Christi)* (1617), written to defend the penal-substitu-
tion doctrine of Christ's death against the Reformed churches' most notorious
heretic, Socinus (Fausto Sozzini, 1539-1604). Grotius believed that Socinus misunderstood the orthodox doctrine by conceiving of the relation of God to sinners as
that between creditor and debtor, a relation able to be dissolved by unilateral remission from the creditor's side. (He cannot have been displeased that the Socinians
shared this mistake with many of his orthodox Calvinist opponents!) Rather, the intelligibility of the doctrine turned on the understanding that God acted as the ruler
of the universe, and the atonement was an "act of jurisdiction." A ruler, like a creditor, is free to forgive, unlike a judge entrusted with the administration of a law. But a
ruler, unlike a creditor, cannot simply waive the right, but has responsibility for upholding justice for the whole community. This passage reflects importantly not only
upon Grotius's theory of punishment, but upon his polemic against the notion of an
unnormed state of nature. The distinctive feature of punishment, he believes, is that
it is necessarily administered by "a superior" (a doctrine still maintained in *Right of
War and Peace* 2.20.3, though with greater flexibility). A universe in which the idea
of vindicating Right can have a meaning is not a universe of primitive equals, whose
fundamental form of relating is the contract, but a universe in which the primal government of God has generated a range of governmental forms, from purely moral
authority at one extreme to political structures at the other.

Further Reading: L. Besselink, "The Impious Hypothesis Revisited," *Grotiana* 14-15
(1993-94): 3-63; J. Dunn, *Grotius* (Cheltenham: Edward Elgar, 1997); L. Foisneau,
Politique, Droit et Théologie chez Bodin, Grotius et Hobbes (Paris: Kimé, 1997); P.
Haggenmacher, *Grotius et la doctrine de la Guerre Juste* (Paris: Presses Universitaires de
France, 1983); H. J. M. Nellen and E. Rabbie, eds., *Hugo Grotius: Theologian* (Leiden:
Brill, 1994); Richard Tuck, *Natural Rights Theories: Their Origin and Development* (Cam-
bridge: Cambridge University Press, 1979).

From *The Right of War and Peace,* Prolegomena

[5] It would be pointless to engage in a discussion of "Right," if there were in fact no
such thing. So it will serve both to introduce our undertaking and to defend it
against future critics, if at this point we can dispose briefly of that misguided view.
But so as not to engage in argument with a crowd, let us give it a spokesman — and
who better than Carneades, who acquired what the Academy (to which he belonged)
saw as the highest skill, to employ his powers of advocacy as readily in the cause of
falsehood as of truth? In his attack on justice, especially that justice which concerns
us now, the strongest argument he found to deploy was this: Rights sanctioned by
men for their own advantage were very various, and changed with the social expectations and the times; natural Right there was none, since human beings and other
animals were inclined by nature to the pursuit of their own interests; in sum, either

there was no such thing as justice, or such justice as existed was pure folly, for concern for others' welfare damaged one's own.

[6] But this philosophical doctrine, echoed also in the poets —

Nature cannot distinguish between right and wrong

(Horace, *Satires* 1.3.113)

— simply must not be conceded. Though man is an animal, he is an extraordinary one, much more differentiated from all other species than they from each other, as is shown by the many activities peculiar to the human race. Among these distinctive features of human behavior is *desire for society* — by which is meant not any kind of herding together, but peaceable society with members of the same species, organized appropriately to human rational capacities. This desire is what the Stoics meant by *oikeiōsis* ("identification"). So, then, the generalization that every animal is solely inclined to pursue its individual interest, cannot bear scrutiny. [7] Actually, some other animal species, too, combine self-interest with concern for others, for their own young, on the one hand, and for members of the same pack, on the other. In their case we suppose that sociable behavior arises from an objective principle of rational order, since they do not display a comparable intelligence in tackling other, apparently no more formidable tasks. The same may be said about children, who, independently of education, evince benevolent tendencies toward others (sharply observed by Plutarch [*Moralia* 608d]), as, for instance, when at that age compassion manifests itself spontaneously. But in the adult human being, who has mastered the principle of matching like actions to like circumstances, there is another factor. Together with a highly developed need for society — alone among animals man employs speech in the service of this need — it is equally clear that there is a capacity for grasping and acting on general precepts, the equipment for which does not belong to the constitution of animal species in general, but only to humans.

[8] This social instinct characteristic of the human intelligence, which we have sketchily described, is the source of *a right in the technical sense of the term* [i.e., a subjective right, see 1.1.5 below]. Here we include: not touching others' property; restoring others' property, if we have it, as well as any gain we may have made from it; the obligation to keep promises; making good damage for which we are to blame; and deserving punishment (as it applies to human relations) [i.e., the duties of "exchange justice"].

[9] From this sense of Right there flows *a second, wider sense*. It is not only the capacity for society, which we have discussed, that distinguishes human beings from other animals, but the capacity to exercise judgment, not least in calculating future as well as present joys and harms and the courses of action likely to lead to either. To use one's human intelligence in such matters, to act upon a well-formed judgment, without the distorting influence of fear or some immediately attractive pleasure and without being swept away by sudden impulse, is considered appropriate to human nature. Correspondingly, action inconsistent with such judgment is considered "contrary to natural Right" — which means, the Right of human nature. [10] To this belongs the prudent allocation of resources in *adding* to what individuals and collec-

tives own; so that sometimes a wiser person is favored over someone less wise, sometimes a neighbor receives preferential treatment over a foreigner, sometimes a poor man is treated more generously than a rich man, depending on what is being done in each case and what the business in hand requires. There is a long tradition of treating this [i.e., what is commonly called "distributive justice"] as an aspect of Right in the technical and strict sense of the term. But Right technically so called is actually quite different, since it consists in letting someone keep, or have, what is already his.

[11] These observations [i.e., on the narrower and wider senses of Right] would have a place even were we to accept the infamous premise that God did not exist or did not concern himself with human affairs. As it is, however, rational reflection and unbroken tradition combine to inculcate the opposite presumption, which is then confirmed by a range of arguments and by miracles attested in every period of history. From this there follows *a further principle:* that we must obey God without qualification, as our creator to whom we owe ourselves and all that we possess. Especially must we do so since he has shown himself by many means to be both Supreme Good and Supreme Power. To those who obey him he is able to give the highest rewards, eternal rewards, indeed, since he is himself eternal; that he is willing to, is something we should anyway believe, but all the more so if he has promised it explicitly. And that, as we Christians believe with an assurance based on proofs of unquestionable reliability, is precisely what he has done.

[12] This consequently affords a *second source of Right* to complement natural Right, a Right which originates in the free will of God, to which our very reason itself categorically demands that we defer. But, of course, the natural Right we have discussed, both in its "social" and its wider sense, though deriving from principles intrinsic to man, can also be appropriately attributed to God, by whose will these principles have come to be operative in human nature. (This was what Chrysippus and the Stoics meant by their saying that the source of Right is Jove. The Latin *ius* may quite probably derive from the name Jove.) [13] But God gave new prominence to these principles, too, in publishing his laws, aiding those especially whose intellectual powers were less adept at reasoning. Our contradictory impulses, meanwhile, both self-interested and altruistic, he forbade to go astray, using the law to curb the more powerful of them more effectively, imposing restraint both on their ends and on their means. [14] Sacred history, moreover, besides the commands it contains, offers considerable reinforcement to our social affections by teaching us that all mankind has sprung from common first parents. This throws new light upon the old dictum of Florentinus (in Dig. 1.1.3), that there is a natural affinity among us which makes it wicked for one man to plot the destruction of another. Human tradition regards parents as like gods; they are owed obedience — not infinite obedience, but obedience of a special kind.

[15] A final step: — It is a principle of natural Right to observe agreements. It was necessary for human society for there to be some means by which one might bind oneself, and no other natural means can be imagined. And this principle is *the source from which civil Rights derived;* for in the formation of a civil society or in its subjection to a ruler or rulers, a promise is made, or deemed to have been made implicitly by the very nature of the undertaking, to abide by whatever the majority, or those entrusted with power, should decide.

[16] The view attributed to Carneades, then, as well as to others:

Expediency, the virtual mother of justice and fairness

(Horace, *Satires* 1.3.98)

is, if we measure words carefully, untrue. The mother of natural Right is human nature, which would incline us to one another's society even if we had no needs at all. The mother of civil Right, on the other hand, is obligation created by agreement, and since this derives its force from natural Right, nature may be said to be its grandmother. But natural Right is helped out by the fact of interest *(utilitas)*, for the author of our nature made us one-by-one and weak, with many things wanting for a proper life, to induce us the more to cultivate society. And interest provided the occasion for civil Right, since that act of civil association or subjection was devised at the prompting of certain interests. Interest plays a part, finally, in the framing of positive law, which always has, or should have, some social interest in view. [17] But just as the Rights of any civil society have that society's interest in view, so it was possible for Rights to arise by consent among all or most civil societies, Rights which served the interest not of particular societies but of the whole international community; and, indeed, it is clear that they did arise. This is what is called the Right of nations *(ius gentium)*, when we distinguish it from natural Right *(ius naturae)*.

This branch of Right was overlooked by Carneades when he divided the whole subject into natural Right and the civil Right of particular peoples. He ought undoubtedly to have mentioned it, since he proposed to speak about Right between peoples in the speech that he subjoined on war and its acquisitions. [18] He then made a further mistake in dismissing justice as "folly." He admits that a citizen is not foolish to conform to civil Right in civil society, even if his respect for Right implies the loss of certain personal advantages. But, then, neither is a people foolish to uphold the common Rights of peoples rather than its own advantages. The logic in the two cases is the same. If a citizen who breaches civil Right for his own immediate interest destroys the fabric which protects the enduring interests of himself and his posterity, so a people that violates natural Rights and the Rights of nations, undermines the supports of its own future tranquillity. But then, even were there no advantage to be gained from observing Right, it would be wisdom rather than folly to follow a policy to which we sense our nature inclining us.

[19] So, then, it is not the whole truth to say: "You will have to admit that justice arose from fear of its opposite" (Horace, *Satires* 1.3.111); or as one of the characters [Thrasymachus] in Plato's *Republic* explains it (359b): laws were devised from fear of being wronged, and men were led to practice justice by a kind of compulsion. The force of this applies only to institutions and laws devised to *enable the execution of Right*, i.e., when the weak, to avoid oppression by the strong, combine in numbers to institute courts and uphold them by their common efforts, so that together they may prevail over those whom they could not stand up to one by one. In this restricted sense we may acceptably allow the saying that Right is what the stronger decided. It reminds us that without the support of power, Right cannot achieve its goal

in the external world. So Solon used to boast that he had made great efforts to "yoke together force and Right" (Plutarch, *Life of Solon* 86c).

[20] Yet even entirely without the support of force, Right has effect. Justice makes the conscience confident, injustice afflicts it with tortures and miseries, such as Plato (*Gorgias* 524-25) imagines taking place in the bosoms of tyrants. Justice secures the approval of most honest minds, injustice the condemnation. And, most of all, justice has the support of God and injustice his opposition. Though he reserves his judgments for after this life, nevertheless he often gives representative warnings of them in this life, as many historical examples teach us.

[21] The primary reason that so many people imagine justice, while demanded of citizens, to be superfluous in a nation or its ruler, is that they see no reason for Right save the advantage that it yields; and that advantage is obvious in the case of a civil society whose individual members lack the strength to protect themselves. Large states, on the other hand, which seem to contain all that they need to preserve their life, have no apparent need of a virtue which has reference to others, the virtue of justice. [22] But — to leave aside the point I have made already, that Right is not only for advantage — there is no state so strong that it does not sometimes need the help of others from outside it, either to support its trade or to repel the force of foreign peoples marshaled against it. Which is why even the most powerful nations and kings desire to make treaties — which are denied all force by those who suppose that justice can apply only within the confines of a state. The saying is very true: let go of Right, and nothing is certain.

[23] If there is no community which can be preserved without Right, as Aristotle demonstrated by his memorable example of the brigands [actually, Plato, *Republic* 351c], there is certainly a need for Right in the community which unites either the whole human race or a number of peoples. That was evident to whoever said, "treachery is not allowed, even for one's country's sake." And Aristotle (*Politics* 1324b35f.) sharply criticizes those who want only the justest of rulers among themselves, but never give a thought to what is right and wrong in dealing with foreign peoples.

[24] The saying of a king of Sparta, "Happy the state whose boundaries are fixed by spear and sword!" was amended by Pompey (whom I quoted just now on the opposing side): "Happy the state with justice for its boundary line!" For this he could have invoked the authority of another king of Sparta, who preferred justice to bravery in war, arguing that bravery ought to be governed by a kind of justice, but that if all men were just they would have no need for bravery (Plutarch, *Moralia* 213c). Bravery itself the Stoics defined as "virtue fighting on behalf of equity" (Cicero, *De Officiis* 1.19). Themistius in his address to Valens (*Oration* 10.132bc) argues impressively that kings who meet the criterion of wisdom think not only of the nation for which they are responsible but of the whole human race, so that they are allies, as he puts it, not of the Macedonians or Romans, but of mankind. The name of Minos was odious to future generations simply because he restricted his sense of justice to within the boundaries of his realm.

[25] Far from admitting the doctrine which some promote, that all rights disappear in war, we should never undertake a war except for the prosecution of Right,

nor should we wage it except within the limits of Right and good faith. Demosthenes observed appropriately that wars are waged against those who cannot be compelled by courts. Courts prevail over those who think themselves too weak to resist them; those who make, or think, themselves the equal of the courts, are dealt with by war. But for wars to be just, they must be conducted as scrupulously as courts. [26] So, then, if "laws are silent among arms," it is the *civil* laws that are so, laws governing courts, the laws of peacetime, not those other laws that are perpetually in force and appropriate for each and every season. [. . .]

From Book 1

ch. 1. *The meaning of "war" and "right."* [3] The title of this work, *On the Right of War and Peace*, should be understood in the first place in terms of the questions I have begun by raising: Is there such a thing as a just war? and What is just conduct in war? "Right" in this context means simply, *what is just* — "just" being understood in a negative rather than a positive sense, to mean "what is not unjust." "Unjust," in turn, means what is inconsistent with the nature of a society of rational beings.

To defame someone for one's own advantage, Cicero says, is "against nature" (*De Officiis* 3.5.21); and supports this with the argument that such behavior must tend to undermine human society and confidence. Florentinus says it is wicked for one man to plot the destruction of another, because there is a kind of affinity established among us by nature (Dig. 1.1.3). And Seneca: "Just as all the members of the body agree that the preservation of each is for the good of the whole, so we men protect one another because we are born to community. There can be no security for society without affection and care for its participants" (*De ira* 2.31).

However, "society" can be of two kinds: a society of equals, e.g., brothers, citizens, friends, allies; and a society of unequals, Aristotle's *kath' huperochēn*, as of father and children, master and servant, king and subjects, God and men (*NE* 1158b12). So there are two kinds of justice, the justice of those who live together as equals, and the justice of those who rule and are ruled, in whatever respect that relation is relevant. The technical terms *rectorial Right* and *equatorial Right* refer, I believe, to these two.

[4] There is a second distinct sense of "right" deriving from the first, which is attributed to a subject ["subject" in the grammatical, not the political, sense]. A right is a *moral quality attaching to a subject enabling the subject to have something or do something justly*. A right, in this sense, attaches to the subject even though it is sometimes associated with a thing. An example: the ownership of an estate carries with it the right to certain services. These are called "real rights" in contrast to "purely personal rights." It is not that real rights do not also attach to persons; they simply attach to the person who has the thing. A moral quality may be said to be "perfect," in which case it is called a "faculty," or it may be less than perfect, in which case it is

called a "fitness." These two categories correspond to the categories of *act* and *potency* in metaphysics.

[5] The lawyers call a faculty a *suum*, i.e., "one's own"; we shall call it simply "a right in the strict sense." Within this category belong: (i) a "power," which may be a power over oneself, which is called a "liberty," or over others, e.g., the powers of fathers and of lords; (ii) a "domain," which may be either total or less than total like a right of usufruct or pledge; (iii) a "credit," which corresponds to a debt. [6] But a faculty, again, is of two kinds [corresponding to the two kinds of justice in §3 above]: "vulgar" and "eminent." A vulgar right is acquired for some private purpose; an eminent right takes priority over it, as, for example, when the community claims a right over its members and their property for the sake of the common good. So (i) the power of rulers is superior to the powers of fathers and lords; (ii) royal domain has a prior claim on property in service of the common good to that of the individual owners; (iii) debts owed the commonwealth for public uses take priority over debts to private creditors.

[7] A fitness (*axia* in Aristotle, i.e., "dignity," *NE* 1131a24ff.) is interpreted by Michael of Ephesus as *to prosarmozon* or *to prepon*, i.e., that which is suitable, which in this context amounts to the same thing.

[8] To a faculty corresponds *expletive justice*, i.e., justice in the strict sense of the term. This is what Aristotle calls *sunallaktikē dikaiosunē*, the justice of transactions, but that name is too restrictive. When somebody who holds some property of mine returns it to me, that is not a *sunallagma* or "transaction"; yet the kind of justice that governs it is the same. His other name for it, *epanorthōtikē* or "corrective" justice, is happier. To a fitness corresponds *attributive justice*, which Aristotle calls *dianemētikē*, "distributive" justice (*NE* 1130b-1132b). This is associated with those virtues which serve the interest of other people, such as liberality, compassion, prudent government.

Aristotle's assertion that expletive justice attends to "simple" or "arithmetic proportion," attributive justice to "compound" or "geometric proportion" (though mathematicians use the term "proportion" only for the latter kind of relation) is one of those doctrines that may often hold true, but not always. The essential difference between expletive and attributive justice does not lie in these different types of proportion, but, as we have said, in the different types of right to which they attend. So a contract of partnership is discharged (*expletur* — [i.e., with expletive justice]) by observing geometrical proportion; on the other hand, a solitary qualified candidate may be appointed to a public office, an act of attributive justice but using simple commensuration.

No more persuasive is the popular doctrine that attributive justice has to do with public affairs, expletive justice with private. Disposing of one's property by will is an act of attributive justice; and when the state reimburses expenses that citizens have incurred on public business, that is an act of expletive justice. This distinction was correctly remarked by Cyrus's tutor (Xenophon, *Cyropaedia* 1.3.17). Cyrus had proposed to give the smaller boy the smaller tunic, though it was not his own, and the larger boy the larger tunic; but his tutor told him: "That is the way to proceed when you are commissioned to decide what would be suitable. But

798

when you have to judge whose tunic it is, then you compare the rival claims to ownership: ought the person who stole it to have it? or the person who made it or bought it?"

[9] There is a third sense of the term "Right," which means the same as "law," understanding "law" in a broad sense as *a rule of moral action obliging us to do what is correct*. It implies obligation; for counsels are not called "law" or "Right" even if they take the form of nonbinding precepts. Permission, too, is strictly not an act of law; rather, it is the negation of an act, except in so far as it obliges someone else not to interfere. Our definition contained the words "obliging us to do what is correct" *(rectum)* not "what is just"; for Right in this sense is not only concerned with matters of justice, such as we have explained it, but of other virtues too. However, from this sense of Right *(ius)* the word "just" comes to have a looser sense equivalent to "correct" *(rectum)*.

The best analysis of Right in this sense is Aristotle's: there is natural Right, on the one hand; on the other, there is voluntary Right (which he calls legal Right, using the word "law" in a narrower sense than ours, or sometimes *to en taxei*, positive Right). The same distinction can be traced in Hebrew, which, when it uses words carefully, calls natural Right *mitzvôth* (*dikaiōmata* in the Greek of the Septuagint), and positive Right *heiqîm* (Gk. *entolai*).

[10] Natural Right is what correct reasoning prescribes when it identifies moral turpitude or moral necessity in a given act by virtue of its compatibility or incompatibility with our rational and social nature, with the inference that acts of that kind have been forbidden, or commanded, by the author of nature, God. Acts which are the object of such prescription are obligatory or illicit *in themselves,* from which we infer that they are necessarily required or forbidden by God. This is what distinguishes them not only from human Right but from divine voluntary Right; for that does not require or forbid things obligatory or illicit in themselves, but makes them illicit by forbidding them, or obligatory by commanding them.

We should note that there is a looser sense (what the scholastics like to call a "reductive" sense) in which some things are said to be of natural Right because they are not inconsistent with it; as we have now defined as "just" those things that are not unjust. Sometimes, too, the phrase is used in a secondary sense of actions which reason identifies as virtuous, or superior to the alternative, though not obligatory. We should also notice that natural Right is not only to do with acting in situations that arise independently of human will, but with many situations which arise as a consequence of human actions. Ownership of property, as we know it now, is a human institution. But given that institution, natural Right is enough to forbid me to take your property without your permission.

So Paul the Jurist says that theft is prohibited by natural Right; Ulpian says it is condemned by nature (Dig. 47.2.1, 50.16.42). Euripides says that it displeases God:

> God hates violence. He has ordained that all men
> fairly possess their property, not seize it. So
> the rich man who is wicked must be left in peace.
> There is the sky, which is all men's together, there

is the world to live in, fill with houses of our own
nor hold another's, nor tear it from his hands by force.

(*Helen* 903-9)

Yet natural Right is not susceptible of change, even by God. For though God's power is immeasurable, yet there are things to which it does not reach; things which may be spoken of, but no more, since the words have no sense in reality, but contain internal contradiction. So God could not make twice two anything other than four, nor something evil in itself other than evil. This is the meaning of Aristotle's saying: "Some things are understood to be evil the moment they are named" (*NE* 1107a9f.). For as the essence of any thing, once it exists in a certain manner, depends on that thing alone, so does any property necessarily implied by that essence. But the evil of some acts in comparison to rational nature is such a property. This, then, is a standard by which even God himself allows himself to be judged (as is plain from Gen. 18:25, Jer. 2:9, Mic. 6:2, Rom. 2:6, 3:6).

There is, however, sometimes a misleading appearance of change in matters which are the subject of natural Right, where it is not natural Right which changes (since it cannot) but the matter on which it prescribes. For example: when my creditor receives what I owe him, I no longer have to pay, not because natural Right has ceased to require that debts be paid, but because the debt I owed is no longer outstanding. So Arrian argues in his *Epictetus* (1.7.16): "For there to be a debt it is not sufficient that there was a loan; the loan must remain undischarged." Similarly, if God commands that someone be killed or his goods confiscated, that does not make murder or theft allowable. "Murder" and "theft" are terms which imply moral fault; and it will not be murder or theft when it happens at the instigation of the supreme lord of life and property.

Some things are prescribed by natural Right not directly, but conditionally upon a certain state of affairs. Thus community of goods was prescribed by nature before the introduction of property, and the pursuit of one's own right by force before the introduction of civil laws. . . .

[12] There are two ways of demonstrating that something is of natural Right, one *a priori*, the other *a posteriori*. The former needs more *finesse*, so the latter is more often encountered. The *a priori* proof is to show that there is a necessary compatibility or incompatibility of some thing with our rational and social nature. The *a posteriori* proof, which does not admit of absolute certainty but of a reasonable degree of probability, infers that something is of natural Right from the fact that it is accepted by all nations, or at least by the more civilized. For a universal effect must follow from a universal cause; but what cause could there be for such a generally held evaluation other than what is called the "common sense" of mankind?

Hesiod's line is a favorite: "A story that everybody tells cannot fail" (*Works & Days* 763 [idiosyncratically interpreted]). And Heraclitus, who thought "common reason" was the best "criterion of truth," used to say: "What generally seems to be the case deserves our credit" (Diels, *Fragmenta Veterum Stoicorum* DK22. A16). Aristotle: "The best thing is when everyone agrees on what is said" (*Eudemian Ethics* 1216b28); and Cicero: "The agreement of all nations on a matter is reckoned as natural Right" (*Tusculan Disputations* 1.13.30). Seneca: "It is an argument for the truth of something that everybody thinks it so" (*Epistulae morales* 117.6). Quintilian (*Institutio* 5.10.12): "We count as certain what secures the agreement of common opinion."

Still, the qualification "or at least by the more civilized" is not without its point.

As Porphyry (*De abstinentia* 4.21) rightly says: "Some nations have become savage and inhuman, and a fair-minded judge would not condemn human nature from such examples." Andronicus of Rhodes (*Aristotle's Ethics Paraphrased* 5.10): "Among men of right and healthy mind there is a fixed standard of justice, which we call 'natural.' It makes no difference if it does not seem just to those whose minds are sick and perverted. It is not wrong to say that honey tastes sweet just because some sick people do not find it so." Plutarch does not disagree: "By nature man was not made, nor is, a cruel or unsociable animal; but he becomes so when he adopts unnatural evil ways. By training, however, and change of place and style of life he may be tamed again" (*Life of Pompey* 633d). Aristotle presents this description of man's peculiar characteristics: "Man is an animal of natural mildness" (*Topia* 130a28). And elsewhere (*Politics* 1254a36f.) he says: "We must look for what is natural in things that are naturally arranged, not in corrupted specimens."

From Book 2

ch. 20. *Punishment.* [1] We began our discussion of the causes of war by distinguishing *injury threatened* from *injury inflicted;* and within the latter category we made a further distinction between *reparation* and *punishment.* We have now disposed of reparation; it remains to discuss punishment, which demands especially careful treatment since confusion about the source and nature of punishment has been the source of many mistakes.

The most general definition of punishment is *suffering harm imposed for doing harm.* One may, of course, be prescribed tasks to perform as a punishment; but the tasks are chosen for their burdensomeness, and so count as suffering. Sufferings and inconveniences, such as exclusion from assemblies or public offices, which arise as a consequence of contagious illness, physical disability, or impurity of various kinds, of which the Hebrew law is full, are not punishments strictly speaking, though, with a measure of rhetorical extravagance, they may be called so because of their resemblance to punishments.

The principle that one who has done harm may suffer harm, the "ancient law of Rhadamanthus" as philosophers described it, is, as we have said, among those things which nature itself declares to be allowable, not unjust. This is the force of Plutarch's remark in his essay *On Exile:* "Justice accompanies God as avenger against those who offend against the divine law. All humankind observes it as the basis of relations among citizens" (*Moralia* 601b). Plato said: "Nobody, God or man, would dare to say that the offender should not be punished" (*Euthyphro* 8d). The noblest element of justice, in Hierax's definition, was "to exact punishment of those who have done injury" (Stobaeus, *Anthologies* 3.9.55), and Hierocles called it the "medicine of wickedness." It was Lactantius who said: "It is no light mistake to characterize chastisement, whether by man or God, as vengefulness and ill will, supposing it an offense to punish an offender" (*De ira Dei* 17). The very term "punishment," if properly used, implies retribution for offense, as Augustine observed: "Every punishment that is just is a punishment for sin" (*On Free Choice* 3.18.51). This applies as much to punishments inflicted by God, though through human ignorance, as the same author noted, it may happen that "the punishment is evident, the guilt not so."

[2] But it is controversial whether justice in punishment belongs to the attributive or expletive type [see above, 1.1.8]. Some argue that it is attributive justice on the grounds that graver punishments are given for graver offenses, lighter for lighter, and that punishment is handed down by the community as a whole to its members. But behind this lies a fallacious assumption, that attributive justice is in question wherever proportionate equality has to be achieved among more than two terms. In the opening section of this work we have shown this not to be so. Furthermore, the fact that graver punishments are given for graver offenses, lighter for lighter, is a consequence, not a goal of penal practice. The immediate goal is that the punishment should fit the crime:

> Why doesn't reason employ weights and measures of her own
> and curb offences with the type of punishment suited to each?

> Let's have a fair penalty-scale for offences, or else
> you may flay with the terrible cat something which merits the strap.
> (Horace, *Satires* 1.3.78f., 117f.)

Divine law follows the same principle (Deuteronomy 25:2f. and *Novella* 105 of Leo).

No less mistaken, as will appear, is the other assumption, that punishments are handed down by the community to its members. We have already shown that the essential principle of attributive justice is neither, on the one hand, this kind of proportionate equality nor, on the other, the activity of the community toward its members; it is the respect due to that kind of "fitness" which does not amount to a "right" in the strict sense, but gives an occasion for Right. Certainly the person punished must be "fit" or "meet" for punishment, but the point of punishment is not to *award* something, which is what attributive justice requires.

Yet those who maintain that punishment belongs to expletive justice (or "commutative," to use the common term) hardly make a better case. They often describe the business as though something has to be returned to the offender, as in a contract. The common, and evidently loose, expression, that some punishment is "due" to an offender, has misled them. When something is due to someone in the strict sense, that person may claim it as a right against someone else. But to call a punishment "due" is simply to say that it is fair.

It is, however, true that the primary and essential exercise of justice in punishment is expletive. For punishment to be correctly executed, the punisher must have a right to punish, a right which originates in the offense. It is something else that makes punishment like contract: namely, that like a vendor who is deemed to have accepted all the natural obligations of a sale without explicit statement to the effect, the offender is deemed to have freely accepted punishment. Since no serious crime can go unpunished, one who directly wills the crime, wills to deserve the punishment.

So the emperors would say to this or that offender: "You have subjected yourself to this punishment"; and those who adopt criminal courses are said to be "punished already in their own intention"; that is to say, they have freely accepted the liability for punishment. In Tacitus a woman who had intercourse with a slave is said to have consented to her own enslavement, since that was the punishment for such offenses [Grotius has apparently misremembered *Annals* 12.53]. Michael of Ephesus, in his commentary on Aristotle's *NE* bk. 5, wrote: "There is a kind of give and take, which constitutes a transaction. The thief takes money or something else, and gives his punishment in return." And later: "Transactions, in ancient usage, were held to include not only voluntary contracts but legal prohibitions."

[3] But who is the subject of this right? To whom is it owed? The matter is not settled by simple appeal to human nature. Natural reason prescribes no more than that an offense may be punished; it says nothing of who may punish it, except that it is clearly very suitable that punishment be administered by a superior. This is not absolutely necessary, unless we take "superior" in a wide sense, as proposed by some theologians, to include a moral superiority which may be attributed to any law-abiding person relative to the offender, who has forsaken the status of a man for the inferior status of a beast.

Cf. Democritus (in Stobaeus, *Anthology* 4.6[47].19): "Rule belongs by nature to the superior." And Aristotle (*Politics* 1332b12ff.) says that both in natural and conventional relations, the lower serve the higher.

It follows at least that one should not be punished by someone as guilty as oneself.

This is the point of Christ's judgment, "Let him among you without sin cast the first stone" (John 8:7) — that is, without a *comparable* sin. The corruption of Jewish morals in the period was such that those who affected the appearance of great saintliness wallowed in adulteries and similar outrageous crimes (cf. Rom. 2:22). Christ's judgment is repeated by the apostle: "Therefore you have no excuse, O man, whoever you are, when you judge another; for in passing judgment upon him you condemn yourself, because you, the judge, are doing the very same things" (Rom. 2:1). And there is something in Seneca that is relevant: "There is no authority in the judgment of someone who deserves to be judged himself" (pseudo-Seneca, *De remediis* 7.1). Elsewhere he writes, "We shall become more tolerant from self-inspection if we cause ourselves to consider: 'Have we ourselves never been guilty of such an act?'" (*De ira* 2.28). And Ambrose, in his *Apology for David* (2.2.5): "Anyone who will judge another must first judge himself, lest he condemn in others faults of less weight than his own."

[4] The second question concerns the end *(finis)* which punishment serves. So far we have established simply that no wrong is done offenders who are punished; but it does not follow that they absolutely must be punished. Indeed, that would be

untrue. Many offenders are forgiven; for both God and men forgive, and both God and men are commonly praised for doing so.

Plato famously said: "Judgment by sentence of law is never inflicted for harm's sake" (*Laws* 854d); and again: "The point of the penalty is not the crime that has been, for what is done will never be undone, but the crime that will be next time" (934a); which Seneca paraphrases: "A sensible person does not punish a person because he has sinned, but in order to keep him from sin; for while the past cannot be recalled, the future may be forestalled" (*De ira* 1.19). The same author says somewhere else: "Neither shall we injure a man because he has done wrong, but in order to keep him from doing wrong, and his punishment shall never look to the past, but always to the future; for that is not anger, but precaution" (2.31). In Thucydides, too, Diodotos addresses the Athenians in the Mytilene debate: "Whatever wrong I may prove against them, I shall not propose their execution unless it is expedient" (*Histories* 3.44).

But this is true of human punishments because one man is so tied to another by consanguinity that he ought to do him no harm save in pursuit of some good end. With God it is quite another matter. Plato is mistaken to extend his view to include God; for his acts rest simply upon the right of supreme dominion, especially when they correspond in some special way to human desert. They do not need the justification afforded by pursuit of an extrinsic end.

In this sense Jewish commentators explain the text of Solomon that bears on this point: "The Lord has made everything for its purpose, even the wicked for the day of trouble" (Prov. 16:4). That is to say, when God punishes the wicked, he does so for no other purpose than to punish. Yet even if we prefer the more general interpretation, it amounts to the same: God made everything for himself, that is, by right of his supreme liberty and perfection, with no ulterior end or purpose. For God is described as *autophuēs*, i.e., not sprung from any other thing. Holy Scripture, at any rate, confirms that there is no further purpose in the punishment of some whom God punishes justly, when it says that he "take(s) delight in bringing ruin upon (them)" (Deut. 28:63), and that he mocks them (Prov. 1:26) and laughs them to scorn (Ps. 2:4). Then there is the Last Judgment, which puts an end to hope of improvement; and even in this life there are some indiscernible punishments, such as "hardening," which substantiate the point we are making against Plato.

But when a man punishes a fellow man, his natural equal, there must be some further point to it.

And this is the force of the scholastic doctrine that the mind of the avenger must not "rest in" doing someone harm. But it was anticipated by Plato in the *Gorgias* (468c), where he says that those who punish someone with death, exile, or fine, ought not to "will that simply," but only "for some good." And by Seneca, who says that one should approach the task of punishment "not with the plea that revenge is sweet, but that it is expedient" (*De ira* 2.33). Aristotle, too, says in the *Politics* (1332a10ff.) that some things are creditable in themselves, others of necessity; and punishment is his example of the latter kind.

[5] What, then, of the satirist's maxim, "the enemy's suffering soothes the wound" (Publius Syrus, 294)? Or Cicero's dictum, "Punishment assuages grief" (*Pro Caecina* 12.35)? Or Plutarch's quotation from Simonides, "A sweet and simple

matter to supply the service of satisfaction to a sore and inflamed spirit" (*Life of Aratus* 1048e)? [So Grotius's text. Probably Simonides and Plutarch wrote, "Even cruelty is sweet, supplying the service of satisfaction to a sore and inflamed spirit."] This reaction belongs to those elements of nature which men share with the beasts; for in beasts, as in men, there occurs anger, a "seething of the heart's blood with desire to inflict revenge" as Eustratius well describes it (*Commentary on Aristotle's Ethics* 6.1). But in itself this longing is so irrational that it often turns against objects that have done no harm, against the young for example, of the beast that has done the injury, or against insensate objects, as when a dog turns on the stone that has been thrown at him. Considered in itself this longing is inconsistent with the function of reason, which is to rule the affections; and so it is inconsistent with natural Right, since that is the dictate of nature only to the extent that it is rational and social. Reason prescribes that one man shall do nothing to harm another except for some good purpose. In the enemy's suffering, taken abstractly and in isolation, there is only an illusory and imaginary good to be had (as in excess of riches and many other such things).

This is what is meant when vengeance *(ultio)* is disapproved of not only by Christian writers but by philosophers in general. Seneca writes: "'Revenge' is an inhuman word, and yet one accepted as legitimate, however just it may be held to be, and differs only in degree from insult" [but Grotius's text is defective and hardly makes good sense; what Seneca wrote was: "and 'retaliation' *(talio)* is not much different except in rank"]. "The man who returns a smart commits merely the more pardonable sin" (*De ira* 2.32). Indeed, according to Maximus of Tyre (*Dissertations* 18.9), "He who takes vengeance is more wicked than he who first injured him"; while Musonius says, "It is bestial, not human, to brood on how to bite the biter and to hurt the hurter" (in Stobaeus, *Anthologies* 3.19.16). In Plutarch Dion, who developed Platonism into a public philosophy, says: "In the eyes of the law vengeance is more justifiable than unprovoked offense; but in nature they arise out of one and the same failing" (*Life of Dion* 979a).

It is inconsistent, then, with the nature of human interaction to take satisfaction in another's pain *qua* pain. The less successfully anyone uses reason, the more inclined to revenge.

So Juvenal writes:

"But revenge is an excellent thing, sweeter than life itself."
That is what non-philosophers say. You sometimes see them
blazing inside for a trivial reason, or none at all.
Any occasion, however small, is an excuse for anger.
Chrysippus would not agree, nor the gentle-hearted Thales,
nor the great old man who used to live near sweet Hymettus.
He would never have given his accuser a drop of the hemlock
which he had to drink in his cruel cell.
Benign philosophy gradually takes off most of our vices and all of our errors;
she is the first to teach us what is right.
It is always a small
and mean and feeble mind that takes a delight in vengeance.

805

You can see the proof in the following fact: no one exults in revenge
more keenly than a woman.

(*Satires* 13.180-92
[with the inauthentic lines included in
Grotius's quotation indicated by italics])

Lactantius writes to the same effect: "The unseasoned and unwise respond to injury
with blind and irrational rage, and try to give those who hurt them as good as they get" (*Divine Institutes* 6.18).

What emerges from this is that one man cannot punish another simply for the
sake of punishing; but we will see what advantages may follow to justify a punishment.

[6] Here it is relevant to introduce that analysis of punishments which is
found in Plato's *Gorgias* and in the philosopher Taurus (as cited by Aulus Gellius, *Attic Nights* 7.14). They both analyzed punishment on the basis of its ends; but Plato
supposed there were two ends, amendment and example, while Taurus added a
third. He called it vengeance *(timōria)*, but in the sense that Clement of Alexandria
defined as "returning evil for evil for the avenger's benefit" (*Pedagogue* 1.8).

Aristotle omits exemplary punishment and has only amendment and vengeance,
which, he says "is performed for the satisfaction of the avenger" (*Rhetoric* 1369b12ff.). Plutarch, too, included vengeance, when he said, "When vengeance catches up with offenders
speedily it is not only a restraint on future wrongdoers, but a strong consolation to their victims" (*Moralia* 548e). It is this kind of punishment, strictly speaking, which Aristotle assigns
to "transactional justice" (as he calls it).

But the matter needs to be looked at more closely. Let us propose, then, that
the benefit envisaged in punishment will be either (i) that of the offender, or (ii) of
the person whose interests were damaged by the crime, or (iii) of people in general.

[7] To the first of these three is assigned that kind of punishment referred to
variously by philosophers as *nouthesia*, "correction," *kolasis*, "chastisement," or
parainesis, "reproof." Paulus the Jurist calls it "punishment designed for amendment" (Dig. 48.19.20), Plato "for wisdom" (*Laws* 933e), and Plutarch "medicine for
the soul," which proceeds with the aim of improving the offender using the medical
principle of applying contrary influence (*Moralia* 550a, 559f). For since every action, and especially deliberate and repeated action, creates a certain proclivity which,
when it is established, we call a "habit," one must remove the attractiveness from
vices at the earliest moment, and there is no surer way than by some painful consequence to rob them of their charm.

Apuleius cites the Platonists (*Plato* 2.7) as saying that no punishment can be so gravely
damaging to an offender as impunity and freedom from the reprehension of his fellow men.
And in Tacitus we read: "a sick and obsessive mind, corrupt and a source of corruption, needs
remedies to suppress the blaze no less intense than the lusts which fuel it" (*Annals* 3.54).

A punishment that serves this end may be imposed in nature by anyone who
has competent judgment and is not himself subject to similar or comparable faults.

This is evident from the case of verbal castigation: "To chide a friend as he has deserved is ungrateful labor but useful in its season" (Plautus, *Trinummus* 23f.). When it is a matter of corporal punishment, though, or of any other form which implies physical coercion, a distinction is made between those who may and may not impose it — not a distinction in nature, which would be incapable of making it (save in the case of children where reason imposes the exercise of this right especially upon their parents, by virtue of the close emotional bond), but a distinction made in those laws which, to avoid quarrels, restrict the common exercise of neighborly prerogative within the human race to near relations.

Evidence of this is plentiful, but see Cod. 9.15. Xenophon's boast to his soldiers is relevant here: "If I have chastised anyone for his good, I judge that I am accountable as parents are to their children and teachers to their pupils. Doctors, too, cut and cauterize for their patients' good" (*Anabasis* 5.8.18). And Lactantius: "God commands us always to have our hands poised over the young, to smack them conscientiously when they offend, lest our misguided and indulgent love bring them up to bad ways and encourage them in vice" (*Divine Institutes* 6.19).

The only argument by which this category of punishment could be extended to the death penalty depends on the so-called "reductive sense," which allows that a negative may stand for the opposite positive. So, just as Christ said that it would have been *better* (i.e., *not so bad*) for some that they had never been born, so it is *better* (i.e., *not so bad*) for incurable characters that they should die rather than live on, when it is certain that the longer they live the worse they will turn out.

Seneca says of such as these that execution may sometimes be an advantage to the executed (*De ira* 1.6), and Iamblichus, "As it is better for a gangrene to be cauterized, so it is better for a reprobate to be hanged" (*Protrepticus* 2). Plutarch calls them "a danger to everyone, but especially to themselves" (*Moralia* 551e), and Galen, accounting for the death penalty first as a prevention of further crime, second as a deterrence to others, adds: "Thirdly, it is better for themselves that they should die, since their soul is so corrupt as to be uncurably evil."

Some people hold that these are those who, according to the Apostle John, "sin unto death" (1 John 5:16). But since evidence for such a judgment is treacherous, charity forbids us to jump to the conclusion that anyone is lost. The implication is that only in exceptional circumstances could chastisement be taken to this limit.

[8] The advantage which the victim may derive consists in being protected from the repetition of the crime, either at the same offender's hands or others'. Gellius quotes Taurus's description of this kind of punishment, as follows: "The dignity or authority of the victim must be protected against contempt or loss of honor that may follow from a failure to respond" (*Attic Nights* 7.14). The reference to injured authority implicitly includes an injury to freedom or to any other of the victim's rights. In Tacitus we find the expression, "guaranteeing security by just retribution" (*Annals* 14.61 [misleadingly quoted]). The victim's protection from the same offender may be secured in three ways: by removing the offender, by depriving him of power to do harm, and by teaching him through suffering of his own not to offend, (which coincides with punishing for the offender's advantage, which we have

just discussed). Protection from other offenders requires an open and exemplary punishment.

By bare natural Right — i.e., abstracting from all laws, divine and human, and from any feature which is not necessarily implied in the case — even private retribution directed to these ends is not excluded, though always within the limits of what is fair. This may be carried out either by the victim or by someone else on his behalf, since it is naturally fitting for one man to help another.

This is the sense in which we may accept Cicero's inclusion, in a list of instances of natural Right, of "vindication" as contrasted with "gratitude." Natural Right he describes as that which "innate force, rather than opinion, commends to us"; and to avoid misapprehension about the scope of the word, he defines vindication as "that by which we repel violence or indignity from ourselves and those relations whom we must cherish, and by which we punish crimes" (*De Inventione* 2.22.65). In the speech of Mithridates from Trogus (in Justinus's epitome) men are said "to draw the sword against a robber, if not in defense, at any rate in vengeance" (*Histories* 38.4.2). And Plutarch in his *Life of Aratus* (1048d) speaks of the "law of reprisal." This kind of natural-Right defense supports Samson's profession that he would be innocent if he maltreated the Philistines who had maltreated him (Judges 15:3); and after taking vengeance he uses the same argument to justify himself, saying that he had only done to them what they had done to him (11). And the Plataeans in Thucydides argue that they punished their enemies according to the universally established law, that an enemy in course of attack may be repelled without impiety (*Histories* 3.56). Demosthenes, speaking against Aristocrates (*Orations* 23.61), says that there is a common law among mankind that we may repel one who uses violence to seize our goods. In Sallust Jugurtha asserts that Adherbal conspired against his life, and adds that the Romans would fail to do what was good and right if they prevented him "from the right of nations," i.e., from vengeance (*Jugurtha* 22). Aristides the Orator [= P. Aelius Aristides] adduces poets, law codes, proverbs, orators, sources of every kind in fact, to support the view that one may make reprisals on aggressors (*Orations* 3.138). Ambrose commends the Maccabeans for avenging the slaughter of their innocent brethren, even on the sabbath (*Duties of Clergy* 1.40). The same author, speaking in response to Jewish complaints about the burning of a synagogue by Christians, says: "If I were to proceed by the right of nations I could mention all the churches Jews burned down in the time of the Emperor Julian," using "right of nations" to mean equal retaliation (*Ep. extra collectionem* 1a [= *Ep.* 40].15). Similarly, in Tacitus (*Histories* 4.32) Civilis says: "A fine reward I have received for my labor: my brother's death, imprisonment, this savage outcry from the army demanding my execution. All of which I insist should be punished by the right of nations."

But because of the distortion which our judgment suffers when our own affairs and emotions are engaged, families formed settlements and appointed judges; and to these alone was given the power to repay injury, while others were denied the freedom which had been theirs by nature.

Lucretius (*De rerum natura* 5.1147ff.) writes: "The steps that each took to avenge his anger, Fierce beyond all that our mild laws permit us now, Have made this age weary of men of arms." Demosthenes (*Orations* 54.19): "It was preferable that the penalty for each offense should be in the laws, and that they should not be judged by inclination or arbitrary resolve of whoever." Quintilian (*Major Declamations* 13.11): "Avenging wrongs is inimical not only to law but to peace. There are laws, political institutions, and courts available for those who are not ashamed to seek the vindication of the law." The Emperors Honorius and Theodosius (Cod. 1.9.13): "The purpose of empowering courts and protecting public law in the community is that no one should be entitled to allow himself the right of vengeance." King Theodoric (in Cassiodorus, *Epistles* 4.10): "Hence the reverence in which laws came to be held, so that nothing might be done with high hand or on private impulse."

The old natural liberty remains, however, primarily in locations where there are no courts, such as at sea. Here we might mention the action of Julius Caesar, who, when still a private citizen, gave chase in a hastily gathered fleet to some pirates who had held him captive, scattered or sunk their ships, and when the proconsul failed to proceed against his prisoners, set sail again and crucified them at sea. The same principle will hold in desert places, or where nomadic life is followed.

Nicholas of Damascus (in Stobaeus, *Anthologies* 3.10.69) reports that personal vengeance was the custom of the Umbrici, and to this day the practice is accepted without punishment among the Moschi when a certain period has elapsed after appeal to a judge. The practice of single combat which prevailed among German tribes before Christianity (and in some places has hardly died out) has the same origin. Velleius Paterculus (*Histories* 2.118) tells us that the Germans were amazed when they were acquainted with the pattern of Roman rule, because "justice puts an end to injuries; and what is customarily settled by arms, is resolved by law." Hebrew law (Num. 35:19) allows a relative to kill a murderer outside the place of asylum; and Jewish commentators note correctly that retaliation in the cause of a slain victim may be carried out with a high hand, whereas in the case of injury such as bodily harm to the plaintiff himself it requires a judge, since it is more difficult to maintain moderation where one is more closely affected. The same custom of private punishment of murder is attested in the most ancient stratum of Greek civilization by Theoclymenes' words in Homer's *Odyssey* (15.272ff.). The most frequent examples, however, arise in situations where there is no common judge between the parties. "The just war is defined," Augustine tells us, "as that which avenges an injury" (*Questions on the Heptateuch* 6.10); and Plato (*Republic* 471b) approves contest by war "until the guilty party is compelled by their innocent victims to render justice."

[9] The advantage of everyone else, the third end of punishment, is subject to the same distinctions as the advantage of the injured party. Punishment serves either to prevent the offender from hurting others as he has hurt his victim, which involves removing him, incapacitating him, depriving him of the power to do harm, or amending his ways; or it is to prevent anyone else from being led on by seeing him go scot-free to molest others, and this is achieved by exemplary punishments (*paradeigmata* as they are called in Greek, *exempla* in Latin). The purpose of these is to inspire fear in the many by punishing the one: "that others may be deterred by the class of punishment," as the legal phrase has it; "that others may be prudently diffident," says Demosthenes (*Orations* 59.77).

In nature the power to exercise this punishment may rest with anyone.

So Plutarch (*Moralia* 817de) says that a good man is nature's appointed magistrate — and for life; for within the terms of simple natural Right government belongs to whoever promotes justice. Cicero demonstrates the doctrine that "the wise man is never a private citizen" from the example of Scipio Nasica (*Tusculan Disputations* 4.23.51). Horace describes Lollius

809

as "consul for many a year" (*Odes* 4.9.39); and in Euripides' *Iphigenia in Aulis* (375) it is said: "Whoever is preeminent in wisdom is ruler."

Within the state, however, such things must be interpreted within the terms set by its laws.

On this form of natural Right Democritus's memorable observations deserve quotation (Stobaeus, *Anthology* 4.2[44].15ff.). First, on the right to kill animals: "On killing animals or abstaining from killing them, the situation is as follows: those which do harm or intend harm may be killed without guilt; indeed, there is a presumption in favor of killing them. . . . Things which do unwarranted harm must on every occasion be killed." It is not improbable that this custom was operative among virtuous men before the Flood, before, that is, God made known his will about the use by human beings of other animals for food. The next excerpt reads: "What I have written about foxes and poisonous snakes must be applied also, I imagine, to human beings," and then: "To kill a robber or a thief, whoever he be, involves no guilt, whether one does it with one's own hand, by issuing the order, or by casting one's vote on a jury." Seneca seems to have had this passage in mind when he wrote: "When I command a criminal to be beheaded . . . I shall look and feel as I might if I were killing a snake or any poisonous creature"; and in another passage: "We would not crush even a viper or a water-snake or any other creature that harms by bite or sting if we could make them kindly in future, or keep them from being a source of danger to ourselves and others. Neither, therefore, shall we injure a man because he has done wrong, but in order to keep him from doing wrong" (*De ira* 1.16; 2.31).

But since it frequently demands great care to establish facts and great prudence and equity to fix a penalty, those human communities with organized systems of justice have resolved, in order to avoid disputes caused by people without public credibility taking too much on themselves, to delegate the task to those whom they have judged most reliable and prudent, or have hoped might prove so. Democritus again (in Stobaeus, *Anthology* 3.38.53): "The laws would not have forbidden us to live under private authority, were it not for the mutual abuse that would result. Personal resentments were ever the source of civil strife." But as with vengeance [i.e., punishment for the second end, §8 above], so now with exemplary punishment there remain traces of the primitive order of Right in places and among persons not subject to a defined jurisdiction. Besides which there are occasional exceptional cases.

In the customary law of the Jews, when a Jewish man apostatized from God and the law, setting himself up as a pioneer of false cultic practices, he could be killed by anybody. Jewish commentators call it "the judgment of zeal" and say that the custom arose from Phineas, the first to exercise it (Num. 25:7ff.). Mattathias killed a Jew who was polluting himself with Hellenistic religious rites (1 Macc. 2:24). Thirty other Jews were killed by their fellow countrymen, as we read in the book called 3 Maccabees (7:15). This was the ground on which the crowd rushed to stone Stephen, and the oath taken against Paul (Acts 7:58, 23:12f.). Many other examples can be found in Philo and Josephus. But then many peoples have preserved a full right of punishment, even by death, for masters over servants and parents over children. In Sparta the ephors could kill a citizen without due process.

810

This will suffice as an exposition of natural Right in punishment, and an indication of how far it remains in place.

[10] Our next task is to see whether the Gospel law has imposed further restrictions upon our freedom. There is nothing surprising, after all, as we have already said, in the idea that divine law prohibits certain things allowed in nature and in civil laws; and that is especially true of the Gospel law, law in its most perfected form — attached, moreover, to the promise of a supernatural state, which, we could reasonably suppose, demands virtues beyond the scope of natural precepts to achieve.

Such forms of *chastisement* (cf. 7 above) as leave neither infamy nor permanent harm behind them, and are required appropriately by the age or condition of the offender, when carried out by those to whom human law allows it, i.e., parents, guardians, masters, teachers, are in no way inconsistent with evangelical precepts. This can be appreciated from their very nature. They are medicines of the soul, as harmless as distasteful healing drugs.

With *vengeance* (cf. 8 above) it is another matter. To the extent that it is simply the satisfaction of resentment, it is forbidden even on natural principles; its incompatibility with the Gospel we have shown above (cf. 6 above). Hebrew law not only forbids the cherishing of hatred against a neighbor (i.e., a fellow countryman), but requires that certain common services should be rendered to enemies of this kind (Lev. 19:17, Exod. 23:4f.). Since in the Gospel "neighbor" comes to include all men, it is evident that we are required not only not to hurt our enemies but to render them kindnesses, which is what Matt. 5:44 explicitly demands. However, the law permitted the Jews to avenge more serious injuries, not taking the law into their own hand but only through the courts. This is not permitted us by Christ, as is made quite clear by the contrast: "You have heard that it was said 'An eye for an eye and a tooth for a tooth'. But I say to you . . ." (Matt. 5:38f.). Although the words which follow have to do strictly with self-defense, a liberty which is also somewhat restricted, they imply *a fortiori* a condemnation of vengeance, since they repudiate the ancient permission as suitable only to a less perfect age. "It is not that just defense is not just; it is simply that patient suffering is better" (*Apostolic Constitutions* 6.23).

[There follows a long quotation from Tertullian, *Against Marcion* 4.16, the text of which may be found above, pp. 28-29.]

We see that Tertullian thinks that demanding retaliation is not only forbidden to Christians, but that it is allowed to Jews not as a blameless course but only for the sake of avoiding greater evil. There is no doubt that this is true of demands that spring from hatred, as we have shown above. It was disapproved of by the wisest Jewish sages, who studied the sense and not merely the letter of the law, as we may see in Philo, where we find the Alexandrian Jews at the time of Flaccus's Jewish persecution declaring: "We take no pleasure, my lord, in taking revenge upon our enemies, for we are taught by the sacred laws to have compassion on men" (*Against Flaccus* 14). This is the point of Christ's demand that we should forgive all who have sinned against us without qualification (Matt. 6:14f.), that is, we are not to be moved by our ill treatment to plan, or hope for, ill to befall them.

Someone who does so is, to borrow Claudian's words, "savagely seeking to make the law's vengeance his own" (*Carmina* 17.224f.). Lactantius, recalling Cicero's saying that "the first duty of justice is to do no harm to another unless provoked by injury," comments that a straight and true sentiment has been corrupted by two words ([i.e., *lacessitus iniuria*] *Divine Institutes* 6.18, quoting *De Officiis* 1.7.20). Ambrose says that this saying of Cicero lacks the authority of the Gospel (*Duties of the Clergy* 1.28 [see above, p. 84]).

But what shall we say of that form of vengeance which does not brood on the past but simply takes precautions for the future? This, too, Christ would have us forgo, above all if the one who has hurt us shows credible signs of penitence (Luke 17:3, Eph. 4:32, Col. 3:13). These texts are all in fact concerned with a more generous measure of forgiveness, including the restoration of the offender to the privileges of his former friendship, and so they rule out *a fortiori* anything in the way of punishment. Furthermore, even should signs of penitence be lacking, the command about giving away the cloak instructs us to put up with additional injury within reasonable limits.

Even Plato said that wrong should not be returned "though we should have to endure worse" (*Crito* 49b). Maximus of Tyre has the same opinion (*Oration* 12). Musonius said that he would neither initiate nor be an agent for someone's initiating an action for insult (the sort of thing Christ indicated by someone smiting us on the cheek), since it is much better that such things should be let pass (in Stobaeus, *Anthology* 3.19.16).

But if letting the matter pass involves great danger, we should be content with such precautions as will do as little harm as may be. Not even the Jews practiced retaliation regularly, as Josephus (*Antiquities* 4.8.35) and other Jewish teachers record, but the injured party would customarily settle, in addition to the compensation required by Exod. 21:19, which is simple, not penal, damages, for a further pecuniary imposition in lieu of retaliation. Favorinus tells us that the same was done in Rome (Gellius, *Attic Nights* 20.1.38). So Joseph, the stepfather of our Lord Jesus, believing his wife guilty of adultery, preferred to separate from her than to prosecute her and disgrace her. This he is said to have done because he was "a just man," that is, a man of integrity and flexibility (Matt. 1:19).

Ambrose comments on this passage that the character of a just man is remote not only from the harshness of revenge but from the censoriousness of laying charges (*Exposition of the 118th Psalm* 7.24). Lactantius, before him, said that it would never be right for a just man to accuse anyone on a capital charge (*Divine Institutes* 6.20). Justin (*Apology* 1.7), speaking of those who accused the Christians, says: "We seek no punishment for their libels against us. Their degeneracy, their ignorance of everything good is punishment enough."

It remains to discuss punishments which serve not one individual's good but that of the public (cf. 9 above), either by removing or restraining the offender or by deterring others by a severe example. Elsewhere [in bk. 1, ch. 2, not included here, discussing the moral status of war in Christ's teaching] we have decisively established that Christ did not abolish these punishments, since in giving his own commands he made it plain that nothing in the law was canceled. Moreover, the law of Moses, which was to be valid for as long as the Jewish state survived, strictly ordered magistrates to punish homicide and other crimes (Exod. 21:14, Num. 35:31-34, Deut. 19:13). But if Christ's commands were compatible with the requirement of the death penalty in the Mosaic law, they can also be compatible with human laws that imitate divine law in this respect.

[11] The contrary point of view is defended by pointing to the boundless forbearance of God in the New Covenant, which is a model for mankind to imitate, and not least God's representatives, the magistrates. In this argument there is a measure of truth, but its implications are not as extensive as is claimed. For the revelation of the extent of God's mercy in the New Covenant has to do specifically with sins against the Adamic law or against the law of Moses, committed before men had knowledge of the Gospel (Acts 17:30, Rom. 2:25, Acts 13:38f., Heb. 9:15). Sins committed subsequently, especially in a spirit of resistance, confront a threat of judgment far more severe than that prescribed by Moses (Heb. 2:2f., 10:29, Matt. 5:21f., 28). Not only in the next life but in this life, too, God often punishes such guilty deeds (1 Cor. 11:30). And pardon is not usually granted for such offenses except to those who impose punishment on themselves, so to speak, through deep regret (1 Cor. 11:31, 2 Cor. 2:7). The opposing argument is then pressed to the conclusion that there should be no punishment for those who are affected by remorse. But — not to labor the point that human beings could hardly agree on an objective measure for genuine repentance, and that if it were enough to make some kind of profession of it, no one would ever be punished — God himself does not always grant a full reprieve to those affected by remorse, as the example of David illustrates. In that case the sinner was spared the lawful punishment of violent and early death, but still was made to bear severe afflictions. So today God may reprieve a sinner from the penalty of eternal death, yet inflict early death as a temporal punishment, directly or through a magistrate.

[12] This conclusion encounters the further objection that when life is taken, time to repent is cut short. The objectors must be aware, however, that conscientious magistrates take serious account of this, and never allow anyone to be hustled off to execution without the time to confess their sins and to experience remorse. A repentance of this kind, which death prevents from issuing in good works, may for all that be accepted by God, as is shown by the case of the thief who was crucified with Christ. But if it is argued that a longer span of life could have produced a more serious self-examination, it must be said in reply that there are cases to which Seneca's epigram is applicable: "We shall grant you the only boon still left for you, death!," as well as his other: "Let them cease to be evil in the only way possible!" (*De ira* 1.16, 15). Or, as Eusebius the philosopher put it: "This is their way, since they have no other, to slip the chain of evil here and make good their escape" (Stobaeus, *Anthology* 4.5[46].41).

Taken together with what we said at the outset, this will serve as an answer to those who think that Christians are forbidden categorically either to punish at all or to impose the death penalty. The opposite is implied by the apostle's teaching, which not only mentions the use of the sword enacting divine vengeance as part of the function of kings (Rom. 13:4), but then urges us elsewhere to pray that kings may become Christians and use their office to protect the innocent (1 Tim. 2:2-4 [imaginatively construed!]). Such is the wickedness of a great part of humankind even in this age of Gospel proclamation, that this cannot be done unless the death of some serves to restrain the outrageousness of others. Even so, with all these gallows and executions for the guilty, the innocent are still not afforded sufficient protection.

Still, it will not be beside the point for Christian rulers to model themselves in some respects upon Sabaco king of Egypt, famous for his conscientiousness, who according to Diodorus Siculus (*History* 1.65), commuted capital penalties into sentences of hard labor with excellent results. Strabo, too, says that some clans in the Caucasus region "put no one to death even for the worst offenses" (*Geography* 11.11.8). And Quintilian's observation (*Institutio* 12.1.42) should not be underestimated: "No one will doubt that if the guilty can be reformed somehow, as everyone agrees may sometimes happen, it is of more advantage to the state to save them than to punish them." Balsamon (*On Photius's 'Nomocanon'* 16.5) notes that several Roman laws which once carried the death penalty were altered by later Christian emperors to prescribe other sanctions instead, that the condemned might be affected by a more intense remorse and the public be warned by a more protracted penalty.

[13] In identifying the three ends of punishment, which have been our subject, certain important points were apparently missed by Taurus the philosopher, who is quoted by Gellius (*Attic Nights* 7.14) as follows: "Whenever there is good ground for hope that the offender will reform himself anyway without being punished, or, on the contrary, no ground for hope that he could be reformed or improved at all; whenever there is no ground for fear that the victim's dignity will suffer from the offense to it; whenever the crime does not create a precedent which needs to be met by deterrence; then whatever the crime may have been, it does not seem worth the effort to impose a punishment." He implies that punishment is ruled out when one of the ends is inapplicable. On the contrary, they must all be inapplicable if the punishment is to be out of place. Furthermore, he omits the end of removing an incorrigible offender to prevent him from re-offending even more seriously. And the mention of offended dignity must be expanded to include the other forms of loss that we fear from crime. Seneca was more accurate: "In the punishment of injuries these three aims, which the law has had in view, should be kept in view also by the prince: either to reform the man that is punished, or by punishing him to make the rest better, or by removing bad men to let the rest live in greater security" (*De clementia* 1.22). If by "the rest" we understand the past victims of crime as well as the potential victims, we have a complete account, except that we must add "restraining" to "removing." For it includes imprisonment and any other means of sapping their energies. The summary which Seneca makes elsewhere is less complete: "Always in every case of punishment he will keep before him the knowledge that one form is designed to make the wicked better, the other to remove them" (*De ira* 1.19). Less adequate still is Quintilian's observation, "All punishment is directed not to crime but to example" (*Declamations* 274).

[14] The conclusion that emerges from our discussion so far is that it is perilous for a Christian in a private capacity to assume responsibility, in his own or in the public interest, for the punishment, especially capital punishment, of a criminal; and that de-

spite the fact, as we have noted, that this may sometimes be permitted by the law of nations. It is, then, a commendable practice on the part of some nations to issue warrants to private fleets authorizing them to act against any pirates they encounter on the high seas; so that when the occasion arises, they may take advantage of them to proceed as public agents and not on their own responsibility. [15] A similar principle underlies the widely accepted practice by which it is not open to anyone to initiate criminal prosecutions, but confined to public officials entrusted with this task. The point of this is that no one should do anything leading to the shedding of another person's blood except under the constraints of office. This meets the intention of the canon of the Synod of Seville (73): "If a believer comes forward to inform, and as a result of his information someone is proscribed or executed, he is banned from communion even at the point of death." [16] A further conclusion follows from this argument: a true Christian is most unwise, acting improperly in fact, to nominate himself as candidate for any public office that involves decisions about shedding blood; suggesting that he thought it quite appropriate for himself to have the power of life and death over his fellow citizens, as though he stood head and shoulders above the rest, a sort of god among men. For to this point, surely, Christ's warning of the danger of judging others, since with the judgment we pronounce on others we must expect in similar cases to be judged by God (Matt. 7:2), is entirely pertinent.

Translation: Editors, from the edition of B. J. A. de Kanter-Van Hettinga Tromp (Leiden, 1939; Aalen, 1993), based on the 1631 edition. Quotations from Horace and Juvenal in the versions by Niall Rudd (Harmondsworth: Penguin Books, 1973; Oxford University Press, 1991); quotations from Euripides in the version by Richmond Lattimore (University of Chicago Press, 1956); and quotations from Seneca are in the version by John W. Basore (Cambridge, Mass.: Harvard University Press; London: Heinemann, 1928).

From *The Satisfaction of Christ*

ch. 2. *How God is to be considered in this connection: it is shown that God is to be considered as ruler.* [1] Armed with our understanding of the state of the controversy and with Scriptural support for the view which undergirds the faith of the church, to dispel the objections which Socinus finds impressed upon him by his "reason" — or to tell the truth, by his misuse of it — we must first of all be quite clear about the part God plays, the office he fills, in the business under consideration. *Setting free from punishment:* that is the nature of the business, as Socinus acknowledges. To which we add that it is also *imposing punishment.* From either point of view the implication is that God must be conceived in the matter *as a ruler.* To impose punishment or to set someone whom you might have punished free — in Scriptural terms "to justify" — is primarily and essentially the prerogative of a ruler as such: a father in the family, a king in the state, God in the universe.

[2] Though generally self-evident, this may be proved quite simply by the argument that punishment is the ultimate form of coercion, and coercion is the pre-

rogative of a superior or "higher power" (Rom. 13:1). Seneca has defined clemency as "the leniency of a superior towards an inferior in fixing punishment" (*On Clemency* 2.3). This is not disproved by the fact that vengeance sometimes seems to be assigned to private individuals invested with no higher power. For this vengeance is either *de facto,* and not *de iure,* and so simply contrary to natural equity; or it represents some right which does not primarily or essentially belong to the person, but has been granted to him by someone else. (In this way a father may kill his daughter's rapist, and anyone may kill an outlaw.) Or else, finally, it is not the act of punishment itself that is allowed, but only the right to sue for punishment either by God or some other ruler. To these various forms of vengeance there correspond as many forms of pardon or forgiveness of offense, which both Scripture and common parlance often assign to private persons. But the proof of this thesis needs no laboring, since Socinus himself states somewhere (*Jesus Christ the Saviour* 3.1) that in punishing and absolving mankind God must have the standing of a prince, a statement which he could hardly have improved on. This was James's point, when he said that there is "one lawgiver . . . who is able to save and to destroy" (James 4:12).

[3] This, then, is God's true role in the business; and with this point established, it is easy to dismiss the alternatives. In the first place we grant Socinus his insistence that God must not be viewed in this case as a *judge under the law;* for such a judge could not set a guilty person free from punishment, not even by transferring the punishment to someone else; it is not that this would be unjust in itself, but it would not conform to the law which he had been appointed to administer.

Lactantius put the point as follows: "A judge cannot grant pardon for offenses, since he is the servant of another's will. God can do so, because he is the interpreter and judge of his own law. It is not to be supposed that in making the law he deprived himself of all his power. He has the freedom to forgive" (*De ira Dei* 19.9). And Seneca says correctly: "Mercy (*clementia*) has freedom in decision; it sentences not by the letter of the law, but in accordance with what is fair and good" (*De clementia* 2.7). *Equity* lies within the competence of a judge whose powers are tied to statute, also a characteristic of the judge who is bound to the letter of the law, but *mercy* in its strict sense is the prerogative of the sovereign ruler in a community. Seneca also encourages a prince to reflect: "anyone can violate the law to kill, none but I, to save" (1.5). Augustine acknowledged this distinction: "Judges are prohibited by statute from revoking a sentence duly pronounced on one found guilty. But will the emperor be bound by this law? Certainly not! He has sole right to revoke a sentence, to reprieve a prisoner awaiting execution, and to pardon him" [actually "Ambrosiaster," *Questions on the Old and New Testaments* 115.45]. Symmachus says: "Magistrates are thought to sentence badly if they are milder than the laws prescribe; it is a different matter with the imperial authority, which acts fittingly in mitigating the severe rigors of the law" (*Relatio* 49.4, *Epistle* 10.63). Cicero had this in view in his address to Caesar in the defense of Ligarius (*Pro Ligario* 30): "'I did not do it! It never entered my mind!' That is how one usually speaks to a judge; but I am speaking to a father: 'I was wrong, unthinking, I am sorry. I throw myself on your mercy, beg pardon for offending, implore you to overlook it.'"

[4] Yet although in the passage just referred to Socinus treats God as the sovereign prince, throughout the whole controversy he assigns him a very different role:

that of the injured party, in fact. He claims that an injured party is in every case a *creditor of punishment,* and has the same kind of right in punishment as other creditors have in what they are owed, a right which he even describes from time to time as "ownership" *(dominium).* And so he insists repeatedly that God must be viewed in this context as "injured party," "creditor," "owner," deploying these three terms as though they amounted to the same thing. Since this mistake is in evidence on every page of Socinus's treatise, and could almost be called his "primary error" on this subject, it demands a precise rebuttal.

[5] To accomplish this, we propose as our first thesis: *punishing is not an act within the competence of the injured party as such.* The proof: otherwise, every injured party should automatically have the right to inflict punishment, which is obviously false. We have shown that punishment is an act of "the higher power," which Socinus himself admits when he says that God must here be viewed as a prince. This concession provides the premise for another, quite conclusive argument: if God punishes as a prince, as a prince he revokes punishment, not as injured party. We cannot ascribe the same function to two different roles. This is not to deny that God, who punishes or pardons offenses, is rightly called an injured party; but it does deny that he may be said to punish or pardon *as* injured party. It is an accepted principle that a predicate may be ascribed to a subject which does not belong to it as such; e.g., "the lawyer sings" — not, that is, *as* lawyer, but as a musician. Lactantius observed correctly: "We rise to vengeance not because we have been injured, but to safeguard order, to correct public practice and to suppress anarchy. This is righteous anger, as necessary in God as in man, in that God sets man the example" (*De ira Dei* 17).

[6] It is a standard rule that no one is fit to judge in his own cause, but this rule does not belong to natural, but to positive Right, and is therefore not universal. It evidently does not apply to sovereign rulers, in which term I include parents in their responsibility for their families. Commentators on Dig. 28.5.42 observe that emperors judge in their own cause. This can even happen in criminal cases, as in lèse-majesté, and in wars declared by one king on another on the ground of actual harm; there is a clear instance in 2 Sam. 10:2ff. So princes punish or pardon crimes of which they are the victims, but not *as* the victims. For if it were as victims that they acted, other victims would have the same right, whereas in fact they can neither punish nor pardon their assailants. Equally, if it were as victims that princes punished or pardoned, they would not have the right to punish crimes if they were not the victims, which is contrary to reason and experience. And in case we are tempted to think that the reason a prince punishes wrongdoers is that they injure the state over which he presides, we observe that it is within his right, and good policy, to punish subjects who commit major offenses beyond the territorial limits and against foreigners. The conclusion is evident: a victim has no right of punishment as such, since you can have a victim without the right, and the right without the victim; on the contrary, this right belongs as such to the superior. For as soon as you have "higher power," you have the right to punish, and if you do not have the one, you do not have the other.

[7] But whatever we say of the right to command punishment must be understood to apply to the right to grant impunity. For these are naturally connected.

Socinus was misled, perhaps, because sometimes in the sacred writings, in the Lord's Prayer for instance, God's forgiveness of sins is set before us as an example, that we may pardon others their sins against us. But he should have realized that examples are drawn not only from things of the same proximate kind, but from things which have some resemblance, especially things which are synonymous on account of the resemblance, though of different immediate kinds. So Christ forbids us to pass judgment (i.e., without mercy) lest we be judged ourselves; and he adds that the measure we give will be the measure we get (Matt. 7:1f.). In this case the "judging" we may do is quite different in kind from the "judging" done to us. The one is a judgment of liberty, the other a judgment of authority. Similarly, it is one thing for God and other rulers to "forgive" offenses, quite another for private persons to "forgive" when someone has harmed them. For the opposite of the one is to punish, the opposite of the other is to sue for punishment, to desire it, or even to "have a complaint" (Col. 3:13). Substantially they are different; accidentally they are somewhat alike. Both are prompted by benevolence or *philanthrōpia;* both have effect of freeing the offender from some liability, either entirely or as much as lies with the one who forgives. This comparability is enough to give the example point.

[8] The second thesis is: *the injured party as such has no right in punishment by nature.* This is somewhat more than the first thesis claimed. There it was said that it did not lie with the injured party to inflict the punishment; here he is denied the right not only to perform the act himself but to oblige someone else to perform it. That is to say, in punishment the injured party is not really a creditor; yet Socinus thinks of him as such, and often goes back to the point as though it were beyond question. The term "creditor" is meant here not in the philologically exact sense of someone who reposes trust in another, but more loosely, in keeping with the legal definition: "creditors are those who are owed something for any reason."

[9] The proof of this thesis is as follows: —

We assume the well-known division of Right *(ius)* into two branches, natural and positive. A debt must in every case have its source in one or the other. Natural Right consists in the equalization of things with each other, and so this is the case with natural debt as well. Positive Right is Right created by definite decision, and here, too, there are two branches, contract and law *(lex).* Contract is the effect of a power which one has over oneself and one's possessions; law is the effect of a power which one has over others and their possessions. Positive debt does not concern us here, which is why we have added the phrase "by nature"; we shall give reasons for this below.

"By nature" an act of yours does not, and in fact cannot, create a debt to me other than that of *material equality,* i.e., you should restore precisely the amount you have deprived me of. In one word this is called "indemnification" or "restitution." Which is why Aristotle referred to the creditor, perfectly correctly, as "he who has less" (*NE* 1131b14). But this holds good, as Aristotle also notes (25f.), not only for voluntary transferals but for involuntary. Just as you are bound to return a loan or pledge, so you are bound to return a stolen object. In this way we can become creditors in natural Right as the result of crime. And this is not only true of crimes which involve the alienation of material property, but of other acts that do harm; so that someone who inflicts a wound is liable for the ensuing doctor's fees, for the expenses of treatment and for loss of labor. Some have found it surprising that Aristotle included homicide among the "transactions" *(sunallagmata)* which fall under "regulative" *(diorthōtikon)* justice. But Eustathius [actually Michael of Ephesus, commenting on 1130b33] has observed correctly that this is because some compensation for damage is usually awarded to the wife, children, or relatives of a slain man (on which see Dig. 48.8.4.1). In the same way, anyone who damages another person's good name with a lie, must make good the damage done to his position by stating the truth.

[10] The conclusion of this argument is clear: the debt which naturally ensues from crime is something other than punishment. For the primary and essential cause of that debt-in-nature is not the wrongness of what was done but the deprivation that I suffer from it. For even where no one is to blame for my deprivation, as in the case of a pledge, restitution is owed to me all the same. But the cause of punishment is simply the *wrongness of what was done*, not *the deprivation I suffer*. An action may be punished appropriately even if nobody has suffered deprivation, as in the case of unsuccessful attempts at serious crime. [11] And there is another way in which they differ, no less important. What and how much restitution must be made is determined by the nature of the situation. The terms of a punishment, on the other hand, though, as we shall argue, there will be a certain natural equivalence between them and the event which gave rise to them, have to be settled by free decision. There is yet a further consideration, that a punishment, i.e., the actual giving or performing of this or that, is not required to be given effect until the guilty party is actually condemned; but restitution is already required in every sense. And a debt of restitution descends to an heir, punishment does not.

I mention these points only to avoid the careless confusion of punishment with what is, strictly speaking, "owed" to an injured party. [12] It is true, meanwhile, that positive law, like contract, may *create* some kind of right for a creditor to prosecute for punishment, clearly distinguished in statute from a prosecution for restitution or damages (Dig. 47.2.55.3). But this provision is usually made in relation to pecuniary fines which not only penalize the offender but compensate the victim. The provision hardly occurs in relation to corporal punishments, where there is no material gain to the victim. [13] So we see kings and other sovereign rulers pardoning the guilty and demanding only compensation for the damage. No one considers this unjust. Yet if punishment were owed the victim, it would be unjust, especially if there were no interest of the state in granting pardon (Cod. 2.2.2). The fact that lower magistrates cannot remit corporal punishments has nothing to do with any supposed right of the victim in punishment, for they would still not be able to do so even if the victim agreed; it is simply that the law of the superior has not devolved this power upon them — has explicitly ruled it out, in fact. A parallel situation must be supposed in the relation of kings to God, in respect of those crimes which they are absolutely required by divine law to punish.

[14] This leads to the conclusion that God, too, is not strictly a creditor in punishment for the wrong we do him. The alternative position would have to rely either on natural Right, derived from the nature of the case, or on statutory Right. We

have shown convincingly, I think, that natural Right does not make the victim a creditor in punishment. But a statute creating such a creditor's right to punishment (as distinct from a punishment as such) has never been produced; and if it were to be, we would be bound to think it a bad one, since no reason could be given for such a piece of legislation.

[15] The objection may occur that in remitting punishment for sins God is occasionally compared, as at Matt. 18:35, to a creditor who waives his right. But as we have shown, a comparison does not require the two things be of the same proximate kind; any resemblance will suffice. Christ, in washing the disciples' feet, gave his disciples an example that they should do as he had done, that is, serve one another. But God forgiving sins resembles a creditor waiving his right more closely than he does a victim forgiving the offense, which is what we have been discussing. For God and the creditor not only have a similar motive, benevolence, and a similar effect, to free another from misery or harm; they are alike, too, in having a preceding *right*: God to punish, the creditor to exact the debt. In both cases the result is to terminate an existing obligation. The obligations, like the modes of terminating them, are different; but since this does not touch the point of the comparison, it does not destroy the resemblance, or "parable."

[16] Here, then, is our third thesis: *the right of punishment in the ruler is neither the right of absolute ownership nor a right of credit.* This is proved in the first place from the final cause, which is usually the best way of distinguishing "faculties" [i.e., rights; cf. *The Right of War and Peace* 1.1.5 above, pp. 797-98]. Rights of absolute ownership and credit are constituted for the benefit of the one who has them, but the right of punishment is not for the sake of the one who punishes, but for the sake of some community. For all punishment aims at the common good, and particularly at the preservation of order and deterrence. Apart from this there would be no reason to want the right to punish, whereas rights of ownership and of credit are intrinsically desirable. In line with this God himself says that he takes no pleasure in the punishment of those who are punished (Ezek. 18:23). Again, it is never inconsistent with justice to waive a right of ownership or credit, since it is the nature of property that one may use it or not as one chooses. But there are offenses (of the impenitent, for instance) which it would be wrong for a ruler, even God, to leave unpunished, as Socinus admits (1.1). The right of punishment, therefore, is not the same as a right of ownership or credit. No one, after all, is admired for being "just" because he uses his right of property or calls in a debt. But any ruler, God included, may be commended for his "justice" when he punishes severely rather than pardon. "Just art thou, O Lord, in these thy judgments" (Rev. 16:5). (This has been argued at several points above.) Again, virtues are distinguished by their objects. But the virtue displayed in waiving a right of ownership or credit is called "liberality"; and it is different from the virtue exercised in remitting punishment, which is "clemency."

Translation: Editors, from *De satisfactione Christi,* ed. E. Rabbie (Assen, 1990).

Subject Index

active and contemplative lives, 34-35, 193, 203, 261, 316, 491, 508

Adam, Adamic community (common use of earth's resources), 76-78, 84-85, 91, 102-3, 205, 260, 311, 322-23, 363, 468, 474, 484-85, 491, 496, 506, 531, 536, 626, 639-44, 761

almsgiving, 69, 74-79, 87-88, 101-3, 359-60, 446, 485-86, 497, 504-5, 584, 602, 605-6

angels, 61, 134, 143, 151, 197-98, 268, 415, 419

anointing (consecration)
  of bishops (priests), 252-57, 372, 383-84, 521, 524
  of kings, emperors, 174-75, 251-59, 263, 267, 366, 372, 386, 718-19
  See also image of Christ

apocalyptic. *See* eschatology

Aristotelian ideas/influence, 234, 238, 278, 309, 320-62, 390-91, 397-98, 413-52, 517-20, 613-30, 695, 723-56, 758-60, 790, 797-820
  Latin translations of Aristotle's works, 237, 321
  Western reception of Aristotle's political philosophy, 237-38

Augustinian ideas/influence, 104, 195, 241, 245-46, 256, 277, 280, 298, 309-11, 322, 362-86, 391, 424-25, 482-98, 555-69, 581-608, 668-70, 733, 809

Averroism, Latin, 321, 394, 413

barbarian invasions/kingdoms, 169-76, 204-6
  church in, 171-72, 204, 208
  law codes, 171

beatitude (blessedness), 134, 141, 147, 151-52, 160, 338-40, 430, 520

Bible, Holy Scripture
  authority of (against ecclesiastical tradition), 426-27, 437, 455, 457-60, 464, 470, 484, 503, 704-5, 746, 774, 780-81
  interpretation of, 449-50, 458-59
  scholarship of, 550, 570, 789
  translation of, 484, 570-71

Cain and Abel, 110, 143, 146-47, 260, 262, 273, 509, 533, 535, 537, 585, 654, 698, 733, 783-84

canon law, 205, 297-98, 300, 303-4, 395, 501, 501-19
  ecclesiology of, 228, 233, 389
  Decretum of Gratian, 205, 237, 278, 297-305, 458-59
  Decretists and Decretalists, 234, 297-305

Christendom. *See* Christian Roman Empire; jurisdiction(s); pope (papacy); spiritual and temporal powers

church
  councils, 67, 170-71, 177, 212, 216, 225, 246, 284, 411, 458, 517-29, 541-47, 746, 752-53
  discipline, 200, 394, 407-12, 556, 663, 702, 767
    correction, 454-55, 457-60, 486, 499, 593, 633
    excommunication (banning) 242, 245-46, 398, 408, 427, 451, 524, 633-35, 637, 741
    suspension, 128, 398, 408, 427, 451
  doctrine, 411, 427, 484, 543-43

821

estates of, 311, 485-86, 687, 689
intercession with civil judges, 95-97, 107, 119-31
reform of, 231-35, 240-41, 392-94, 517-29, 540-47, 549-51, 555-57, 580-84, 631-36, 662-66, 685-94, 702-10, 743-47, 754-56
theory of (ecclesiology)
  body of Christ (*corpus mysticum*, corporation), 217, 235, 362, 389-90, 401-2, 518, 522-27, 636, 753-54, 767
  hierarchy, 363-81, 389, 393, 518-29, 541-47
  soul of society, 9, 13, 40, 266, 278, 289
  "spiritual," 398, 427, 551, 581-82, 611, 631-37, 702-3
    nonclerical, 631-37
    nonjurisdictional, 389, 393-94, 426, 436-39, 507, 593, 631-46
    nonproprietary, 389, 394, 439-47, 504-5
  universal *(regnum)*, 379-81, 463-64, 490, 552, 752-53
  visible ("mixed") and invisible, 555, 587, 744
  the whole (company) of the faithful, 252, 394, 424, 426, 455, 461-64
See also Christian Roman Empire; communication; community of goods; conciliarism; jurisdiction, ecclesiastical; property, corporate; spiritual and temporal powers
Ciceronian ideas/influence, 278, 343, 570-71, 675, 695, 729, 751, 760-61, 790, 797, 808-9
See also Stoicism
citizenship *(civilitas)*, 170, 195, 420, 670, 751
Christian, 13, 40, 45, 670
city, 148-49, 331, 393, 416, 578, 643, 662-64, 733, 757-58, 761, 767-64
heavenly/"two cities," 45, 109-11, 143-63
Jerusalem, 65, 144-45, 152, 235, 312, 576
clergy (clerical order, priesthood)
  apostolic authority (powers) of, 233, 240, 244-47, 250-67, 338, 362-63, 398, 405-7, 430, 438, 447, 520-27, 611, 663
    primacy of preaching, 438, 656-58, 702
  bishop(s), 174-75, 192-93, 246, 252, 298-99, 316, 744
    collegiality of, 450-52, 526, 543, 767
    lay investiture of, 232, 240, 250-51, 256
    ministerial rule, 195-203, 470-71, 593
    powers (of order and jurisdiction), 385, 398, 401, 405, 407, 447-51, 457-60, 520, 524, 747
  dispossession of, 426, 477, 484, 486, 502-5
  Israelite priesthood (priesthood of law),

99, 252, 256, 264, 273, 286-88, 315, 363-64, 380, 383-85, 472, 507, 521, 714, 716, 720, 777, 785-86
  natural and Christian ("spiritual") priesthood, 339, 380-85, 423, 428-29, 782-86
  priesthood of the faithful, 384, 581-82, 631-37
See also church; jurisdiction, ecclesiastical; pope (papacy); spiritual and temporal powers
coercion of belief. *See* evangelization, coercive; heretics, coercion of
commerce/trade
  international, 580, 627-28
  justice in, 358-61, 511-13, 584, 603-8, 655
  profit, 360-61, 584, 602-8, 644, 666, 683
See also lending
common good
  and individual (private) good, 280, 321, 326, 330, 341, 345, 470-71, 477, 566, 678, 684, 739
  civil/natural, 94-95, 238, 323, 338-39, 342, 414, 427-29, 528, 540, 566-67, 579, 640-44, 740, 820
  final/supernatural, 338-40, 381, 528
See also justice; law
commonwealth
  organic analogy, 278, 289-90, 293, 532
  public welfare (utility), 277-79, 282-84, 461-62, 472, 474, 672-74, 678-79, 721-22, 766, 795
  res publica, 110, 161-63, 279, 760, 767
See also church; political society
communication, communion (fellowship sharing), 47, 49-51, 147, 149-50, 317, 331, 485, 487-88, 495, 551, 559, 569, 625-26, 732, 747, 751-53, 758-68
community, 85-86, 110, 342-43
  of goods, 309, 311-18, 554, 638-44, 659, 800
    in early church, 100-101, 313, 315
conciliarism, conciliar theory, 392-93, 398, 425-27, 517-29, 552, 610-11, 724, 726
  General Church Council
    infallibility/inspiration of, 392-93, 455, 462-64, 517-18, 525-27, 541-43, 746, 753
    representativeness of, 393, 522, 527, 541-43
    supremacy (doctrinal and jurisdictional) of, 393, 449-51, 518-27, 541
conscience, 391, 591-92, 597, 604, 607-8, 632, 637, 646, 663, 666-68, 679, 682, 689-90, 696, 699-700, 705, 707, 734, 740, 746, 771, 775-76, 796

consent, communal and individual, 185, 425, 433, 508, 531, 533, 536, 540-47, 579, 625, 718-19, 726, 733, 744-45, 748-50, 764, 766, 769
consensus, 161, 393, 421-22, 425, 541-43, 618, 632-33, 761, 768
coronation, 251-59, 515
See also anointing
counsel, 224, 579
versus flattery, 184-85, 187, 279, 594
"mirror of princes" literature, 180-95, 217-27, 268-96, 321, 518, 571
covenants/compacts
international (treaties), 364-65, 374, 559, 568-69, 578-79, 796
political (civil/ecclesiastical), 334, 551, 556-57, 686, 711-22, 744, 758-70, 794-95
biblical models of, 143, 556, 687, 711-13, 714-20, 758-59
See also commerce; lending
crime(s), 126, 292, 373-74, 398, 562, 626, 706-8, 741, 774, 800, 803, 812, 814, 819
murder, 17, 26, 44, 62, 113, 115, 117, 142, 167, 226, 245, 280, 284, 325, 347, 431, 518, 537, 564, 580, 585, 595, 615, 623, 644-45, 657, 659, 673-74, 676, 677, 690, 696, 698, 706, 708, 740-42, 800
See also heresy; idolatry; sin(s)

daemons, 44, 141, 151, 246, 265
the Devil (Satan), 18-19, 21, 58, 151, 196, 232, 247, 273, 278, 293, 299, 513, 582, 597-98, 632-34, 636, 658-59, 688, 690, 694
See also eschatology
dominion, lordship
civil, 311-12, 369, 440-43, 454, 473-75, 485-86, 489-98, 508-13, 611-17
divine, 487-98, 697, 734, 804, 815-20
evangelical (by grace), 391, 394-95, 484-86, 488-98, 513, 521, 610, 612, 724
just and unjust, 235, 364, 366, 369-72, 380, 387, 494, 503
natural, Adamic, 84-85, 157, 197, 326, 395-96, 454, 474-75, 484-86, 491, 493, 495, 531-32, 536, 612, 614-15, 617, 627, 741, 778-79, 781
See also clergy (priesthood); Jesus Christ; jurisdiction(s); property
Donation of Constantine, 228-30, 233-34, 241, 260-61, 265-66, 409-10

empire(s), 164, 265, 413-22, 612, 618, 642-43
Christian (Holy) Roman, 58, 110, 137-38, 195, 452, 464-66, 546-47, 550, 552, 720

emperor (powers, rights), 57, 62, 75, 140-42, 170-71, 233, 266, 467-70, 617-20
Justinian's restoration of, 169, 171-72, 189
Gregory VII's reformation of, 231-35, 240-49
monotheism 2, 58, 167-68
translation(s) of, 363, 365, 409-10, 619
law of (*Corpus juris civilis*), 171, 189-94, 233, 269, 278, 727, 730
Christian Roman—Byzantine, 169, 306, 476-77, 514-16
church in, 172, 189-94, 212-15, 476-81, 514-16
emperor, 3-5, 172, 180-95, 212-15, 306, 477-78, 514-16, 542, 619
Christian Roman—Carolingian, 173-75, 216-27, 394, 410
Roman (pre-Christian), 16-22, 110, 139-40, 150, 164-65, 262, 339-40, 390, 413-14, 464-66
emperor (powers, rights of), 14, 280, 467-70, 618-19
Pax Romana, 58-59, 166-68, 414, 422
Roman civil law, 209-10, 302, 414, 799
Spanish, 552-53, 610-30
universalism, 57-59, 413-22, 524
equality, 47-54, 52-54, 59, 76, 183, 191, 492, 495, 542, 544, 547, 558, 566, 593, 596, 693, 732, 797
of "the common man," 638-46
of ruler and ruled, 181-82, 184, 196-99, 205, 249, 696, 699, 718
See also commerce/trade; community; justice
equity, 206, 209, 283-84, 289, 519, 536, 665, 674, 676, 678, 682, 684, 703, 706-8, 740, 747, 771-77, 796, 810, 816
eschatology, 111, 178, 205, 231, 313, 551, 709-10
Antichrist, 201, 491, 694
apocalyptic, 15-22, 111, 195, 240, 641-49
evangelization, spread of gospel, 57-65, 170-73, 274, 276, 613, 629-30
coercive, 190-91, 611-12, 613, 620-22

faith, faithfulness, 72, 112, 158-63, 381, 386, 439, 455, 543-44, 568, 581, 595
fall of mankind, 299, 474, 491, 495-96, 508, 531, 696, 748, 781
forgiveness, 97, 107, 116, 124-25, 187, 406-7, 635, 653, 655-59, 772-73, 777, 803, 811-12, 816-18, 820
See also sacrament, penance; penitence

freedom(s), 281, 330, 419-20, 426, 633, 653-54
civil, 470-72, 477-81, 536, 663, 671-72, 766
natural, 300-301, 346, 441, 445, 457, 472, 536, 544, 617, 725, 735, 808
spiritual, in Christ (evangelical), 70, 79, 328-29, 457, 470-73, 551, 582, 587-91, 610, 664, 666-70, 724
See also conscience
friendship, 150-51, 334-35, 571-72, 576, 579, 762, 812

Gersonian ideas/influence, 453, 552, 609, 663, 724-25, 744
good, goodness
and being, 155-56, 485, 489, 492
order of goods (highest good), 147, 151-52, 155-63, 485, 488-90, 554, 794
See also virtue(s), prudence
government. See jurisdiction(s); king(s); political authority; political society; rulers

heresy, heresies, 28-29, 67-68, 72, 190-91, 274, 276, 399-400, 411, 457-60, 503, 518, 767, 778
Gnostic, 16-22
Iconoclast, 212-15
Joachite, 309-19, 638
Manichean, 106, 115-17, 737
papal, 444, 450, 453-55, 470
heretics, coercion (punishment) of, 108, 131-33, 190-91, 590-93, 613-14, 648-49
hierarchy
cosmic, 155-56, 363-64, 367-68, 371-78
social, of ends and functions, 238, 323, 337-40, 400
See also church, theory of; order; subjection
history, 164-68, 178, 639, 780-86
Holy Spirit, 589-90, 631-37, 657-58, 746, 753, 774
of judgment (condemnation), 639, 644-46, 682, 690, 692
of love (righteousness), 575, 586-87, 631-37
of truth, 462-64, 488-89, 518-19, 526, 647, 755

idolatry, 64, 263, 384, 507, 534, 624, 686-92, 703, 706-8, 715-16, 767, 785
polytheism, 58-59, 63-64, 784
See also heresy, schism(s)
image of God (Christ), 61, 74, 184, 187, 214, 236, 250-51, 253-56, 282, 292, 294, 307, 509-10, 612, 615-16, 657, 665, 670, 693

individual, individualism, 394-96, 724, 732-33, 735
inequality, 341-42, 415, 582, 797
injustice (injury), 69, 288, 357, 478, 559-67, 584, 602-3, 607-8, 612, 615, 627, 678, 682, 697-98, 738, 748, 796, 801, 817-20
Naboth's vineyard, 75-77, 654
persecution, 10-12, 25-26, 172, 263, 283, 556, 631, 644-46, 660, 666, 680, 685-86, 703, 711
investiture controversy. See bishops, lay investiture of

Jesus Christ:
communicable powers, 382, 436-37, 520-25, 573, 577
counsels/commands and example, 75, 310-19, 437, 444-47, 486, 554, 558, 583-86, 588-89, 595-602, 605, 632-37, 658-61, 678
kingship and priesthood of, 178, 236, 250-65, 285, 338, 382-85, 509
nonjurisdictional authority of, 437, 780
poverty, 310-19, 329, 394, 426, 444-47, 484-85, 490
subjection of (to temporal ruler), 437-38
as Truth, 485, 487-89
universal lordship of, 238, 273-74, 316, 381, 394, 402, 780
See also law, gospel; perfection, evangelical
Jews, 58, 73, 190, 212, 262-63, 274, 351, 507, 614, 616, 618, 677, 683, 705, 715, 811
See also clergy, Israelite priesthood; kingship in Old Testament; law, divine; political society, best polity
judgment, 419, 772, 774, 776, 793, 808
by court judges, 122-28, 149, 193, 208-9, 493-94, 497-98, 568, 588, 591, 600, 776, 816
by God (Christ), 16, 96-97, 121, 188, 193, 208, 243, 248, 425-26, 429, 437-39, 493, 495, 537-38, 591, 623, 655-58, 680, 693-94, 739, 776, 792, 803, 817-18
by the multitude (people), 433-34, 700
by rulers, 9, 17, 199, 225, 241, 271, 274-75, 283, 385, 404, 405, 425, 428, 435, 508, 537, 544-45, 585-90, 596, 664-65, 673, 690, 726, 738-39, 776, 816
by the saints, 72, 244, 270, 275, 536, 635
See also church, discipline; Holy Spirit; rulers, correction of
judicial process, 678-79
advocacy and prosecution, 122-23, 130, 193-94, 271, 568
litigation, 209, 274-75, 318, 444, 486, 498,

503-4, 566, 583-84, 587, 590, 598, 600-
601, 665, 677
jurisdiction(s)
combining of, 190, 192, 195, 225-26, 231,
638
comparisons of, 398, 390-92, 519, 523-24,
663, 703-4, 708-9
conflict of, 67-74, 232, 240, 250-51, 256,
397
ecclesiastical, 170, 228-49, 260-76, 284-86,
339-40, 387, 398, 405-9, 450, 457-64,
517-29, 555, 610, 663, 704-5, 744-47,
753-56, 766-67
"regular" and "casual" (direct and indirect), 375, 402, 456, 589-93
secular, 236-37, 250-59, 266, 329-37, 339-
41, 392, 404, 407-9, 477-81, 591, 620,
670, 766-70
secularizing of, 394, 398, 425-27, 447-52,
486, 555, 690-91, 778-80
See also empire(s); kings, kingship; pope
(papacy)
justice, 108, 208-9, 224, 288-89, 305, 326,
355-61, 370, 417-19, 527, 531, 536, 672-73,
771-72, 791-820
divisions of, 355-57, 765, 790-91, 793-94,
797-98
in economic exchange, 358-61
restitution, 127-31, 564, 738, 740, 801,
818-19
and righteousness, 47-49, 161-63
and piety, 51, 161-63, 368-70, 383, 398,
409, 429, 697, 720
honour of God, 249, 643-46, 665-66,
672, 689, 707-8
satisfaction, 537, 738-40, 804-6
See also commerce; law; punishment; right

kingdom(s), 139, 417, 539-40, 618
of God (heaven), 119, 251, 257-59, 487,
509, 532, 693
transference of, 288-89, 291, 578, 687
"two kingdoms," 119, 551, 555, 582-602,
662, 664-65, 669-70
king(s), kingship, 330
advice to. *See* counsel
as brigands, 214, 245, 333, 539
christological models of, 250-59
mediatorial, 180-88, 236
ministerial, 172-73, 195-200, 205-7
patriarchal, 778-86
divine appointment of, 216, 218-19, 221,
404, 508, 610, 618, 717-19
by the church's institution, 234, 261-67,
365-67, 372, 380, 385-87

by civil (natural) institution, 385-86,
391, 404-5, 456, 467-68, 539-40, 617,
717-19, 736
divine commission/delegation (as
vicegerent of God, Christ), 222, 227,
236, 256-59, 282-83, 335, 404, 585, 714,
736, 779
divine removal of, 265, 411, 718
hereditary succession of, 290, 434, 508,
530, 537-38, 719, 726
and law, 236-37, 286
lawgiving, legislating, 171, 206, 209, 420
above law *(imperium, plenitudo
potestatis)*, 184-85, 237, 349-50, 363
under law, 184, 208, 237, 238, 283, 286-
88, 349-50, 569, 610, 699, 769-70
lay person (office), 267, 582
in Old Testament, 69, 75-77, 98, 131, 214,
264-65, 287, 290, 294-95, 353, 614, 617,
688, 691
David, 110, 173-74, 207, 222, 248, 255,
257-58, 284, 295, 574, 595, 618, 671,
674, 718-20, 780
Josiah, 287, 295, 674
Melchizedek, 174, 178, 252, 255, 262,
273, 285, 383-84, 509
Saul, 248-49, 253-54, 285, 290, 508, 618,
655, 717-20
Solomon, 174, 222-24, 264, 290, 295,
574
protector of the church, 217-18, 225, 227,
248, 253, 259, 722
as providers, 181, 183, 185, 307-8, 335-37,
340
and reason, virtue, 33-34, 61-62, 187, 195,
207, 217, 222-23, 279, 287, 307, 330,
336, 508, 510
rewards of, 140, 218, 219, 226, 335
See also counsel; image of God; judgment;
providence; rulers; virtue(s), prudence;
wisdom

law, divine/revealed, 324-26, 343-44, 407, 425,
429, 438, 456, 528, 531, 537-38, 618-19,
703, 753-54, 789
of Christ (gospel law, New Law), 115-17,
238, 299, 314, 325, 344, 430-31, 438-39,
457, 470-73, 486, 497-508, 523, 553-55,
590, 624-25, 753-55, 782, 790-91, 810-13
and gospel/grace/promise, 115-18, 344,
556, 586-87, 650-51, 664, 706, 715
Mosaic (Old Law), 206, 286, 326, 344, 351,
357-58, 429, 431, 470-73, 537, 574-75,
585, 618, 636, 682, 692, 715, 812-13

Ten Commandments, 299-300, 352-53, 537-38, 653-58, 697, 697-98
  "Two Tables" of, 556, 653-55, 672-73, 675-76, 685, 707-8, 765-66
  typology of (moral, sacramental, judicial), 106, 115, 352-53, 652, 665, 675-76, 703, 705-8, 777
  uses of, 35, 106, 586, 655-58, 664
  versus human law, 219, 440, 442, 501-2, 511, 555, 563, 641
  written in the heart, 286-88, 299, 534, 658
law, human (positive), 324-25, 347-54, 486, 496, 498-501, 537, 753-55
  civil, 210, 238, 301-3, 347, 407-8, 496, 501, 508, 524, 536, 559, 599-602, 665, 675-77, 707, 729, 733, 750-52, 797
  constitutional ("fundamental"), 556-57, 714-17
  customary (custom) 132-33, 210, 302-3, 325, 343, 350-51, 431, 452, 473, 475, 604, 620, 664, 684, 725, 729-31, 750
  law of nations (ius gentium)/international, 205-6, 210, 238, 299-303, 324-25, 347, 355-56, 465, 534-35, 552-53, 609-10, 612-13, 626-30, 724-27, 745, 751-53, 790, 794, 814
law of nature (natural law), 205, 210, 237-38, 300-304, 342-43, 345-46, 350-52, 355-56, 383, 465, 496, 530-38, 544, 602, 612-30, 652-58, 696-97, 699-700, 712, 747-56, 774, 781-82, 790, 799-801
  change of (secondary precepts), 346, 456, 729, 752
  divisions of, 298, 300-301, 727
law, theory of, 205, 209-11, 237-38, 278, 283-84, 298-303, 324-26, 430, 744, 749, 794, 799
  as coercive command, 431, 439, 496, 537, 724-25, 749, 752
  and common good, 342-43, 347, 431-34
  interpretation of, 349-50, 352-53, 432, 514, 568, 594, 771, 773-77
  just and unjust, 113-14, 345, 346, 431, 496, 627, 676, 697
  "living law," 99, 237, 544, 675
  and necessity, 349-50, 461-62, 472, 474-75, 519, 594, 728
  and righteousness (virtue), 72, 343-45, 348, 360-61, 586-87
  rule of, 195, 325, 430, 434-35, 480, 530-40, 696, 770
  as universal reason (Word, Logos), 5, 30, 36, 40, 43, 421, 528
  See also equity; king(s) and law; pope, supremacy of

law-making (legislating), 342, 351
  See also king(s) and law; people as legislators
legal positivism. See law, human/positive
legists (civilians, jurists), 209-10, 237, 297, 302, 390-91, 399, 414, 499, 530-40, 549-50, 593-94, 734, 737, 757, 769, 777, 799
lending, 357, 361, 366, 487-88, 584, 601-7, 775
  usury, 130, 361, 409, 584, 606, 666, 682-84
liberty, liberties. See freedom(s)
love (charity)
  of God and neighbour, 112, 125, 127, 134, 145, 409-10, 508, 574, 595-602, 627, 653, 765
  love of self, 145
  ordered (disordered), 157-63, 249, 310, 418-19, 485-88, 497, 511
  See also law, divine; sin, pride

marriage, 92-93, 252, 292, 302, 771
martyrs, martyrdom, 23, 25-26, 61, 106, 118-19, 471, 558, 599
military service, 2-3, 5-6, 24, 27-28, 134-35, 600-601
monarchy, 413-22
  absolute (potesta absoluta/ordinata), 234, 374-78
  divine (cosmic) model of, 58-62, 323, 330, 335-38, 340-41, 363-68, 532, 536-37, 792, 815-20
monasticism, monks, 6, 190, 195, 235, 268, 313, 315, 391, 476-81, 518, 558-59, 638-44
  monastic vows, 315, 351, 472
  See also poverty, Franciscan
Moses, 260, 264, 290, 295, 363, 384, 421, 522, 692, 715, 780, 785-86

Noah, 157, 197, 260, 262, 273, 363, 618, 626, 698, 733, 782-84

oaths, 44, 193-94, 243, 246, 295, 323, 374, 533, 632, 636, 764
  See also covenant(s)
obedience
  of Christ, 75
  to God (Christ), 556, 583, 599, 653-55, 659-60, 681, 704, 714-16, 794
  See also perfection, evangelical; subjection
Ockhamist ideas/influence (nominalism), 394-96, 453, 517, 552, 609, 663, 696
office(s), public/social, 45, 98, 251, 255-56, 291, 510, 551, 582-83, 654, 662, 670-71, 764, 814-15
  vs. person, 596-602, 679

order
  political/social, 106, 155, 528, 654, 659-60,
    662, 747-49, 754, 764
  universal, of all beings, 155-56
  See also hierarchy; jurisdiction(s); peace;
    spiritual and temporal powers

patriarchs (of Israel), 69-79, 97, 145, 158,
  260, 263, 273, 383, 509, 618, 636, 781-85
Paul, St., 90, 92-94, 127, 406, 411, 637, 677-
  78, 694, 708, 734, 746
peace (tranquillity), 58-59, 94-95, 111-12,
  118, 135, 146, 148, 151-63, 374, 413-22,
  424, 429, 436, 528, 544, 572-80, 587-89,
  596-97, 629, 674, 746, 772-73, 795
  pacifism, 40, 57, 571-80, 631-37
people (multitude, citizen body)
  as corporation, 391, 539-40, 700, 712-14,
    719-22, 750, 768-69
  as legislators, 342, 351, 392, 425, 432-34,
    533, 750
  as sovereign, 423, 425, 556, 696, 698, 700,
    713, 719-22, 767-69, 778-79, 781, 783,
    786
  See also political authority; political soci-
    ety; rulers
penitence, 107, 120-21, 127, 248, 295, 512,
  658, 812-13
perfection, 147, 493, 804
  evangelical, 310-19, 444-47, 471-73, 490-
    91, 551, 585-86, 631-37, 658-61
  of rational soul, 157, 160, 280, 414-16
  See also good, goodness; Jesus Christ; po-
    litical society, perfect; poverty, Francis-
    can
Peter, St., 406, 411, 470, 519, 523, 524, 637,
  694
  See also pope, successor to St. Peter
philosophers, philosophy, 9-11, 30-38, 307,
  429, 453, 483, 570, 724
  See also Aristotelian, Augustinian,
    Ciceronian, Gersonian, Ockhamist, Pla-
    tonic, Thomist ideas/influence; wisdom
Platonic ideas/influence
  Greek (Byzantine), 30-38, 180-88, 306,
  Latin (Augustinian, pseudo-Dionysian),
    105-6, 260, 362-78, 393, 482-98, 517,
    541-47, 675
  Renaissance, 413, 421, 553-54, 570, 695,
    768, 795, 796, 801, 803-6, 809, 812
political authority
  creativity of, 238, 323, 336-38, 425
  distinction from epistemological authority,
    454-55, 457-60

divine commission/delegation of, 665, 670,
  673, 679, 681, 689, 712, 734
divine ordination/appointment of, 90, 92-
  94, 127, 157, 206, 238, 665, 670, 689,
  696, 698, 725, 733-34, 749, 781
lawfulness/limits, 304, 590-93, 620-25, 663,
  665, 674, 696, 700, 759
  of infidel rule, 323, 457, 473-75, 552-53,
    610, 612-17
ministerial, 172-73, 195-200, 205-7, 269-
  76, 420, 593-95
naturalness of, 322, 331, 342-43, 416, 520,
  523, 534, 552, 664-65, 734, 747-49, 761,
  781
from people
  as delegation of power (a trust), 425,
    610, 700, 720-22, 759
  as transfer of power, 553, 725-26, 732,
    735-36
"two authorities," 177-79, 194, 212-17, 231,
  236, 252, 382, 456, 527, 662, 668-70,
  778-86
See also dominion; judgment; jurisdic-
  tion(s); king(s), kingship; office; pope
  (papacy); virtue(s)
political society (polity)
  best polity (regime), 353-54, 393, 486, 506-
    7, 523, 528-29, 531-33, 536, 663, 665,
    671, 696, 698, 704
  as corporation (*corpus mysticum*), 282,
    285, 389-90, 425, 520, 539-41, 725, 732,
    735, 750, 758-70
  federal polity, federalism, 557, 713, 717,
    722, 758-70
  forms of, 332, 528, 532, 671-72, 767
  international, 552, 572
  participation in, 322-23, 324, 391, 751
  perfect (self-sufficient), 238, 321, 332, 340-
    41, 393, 427-28, 520, 528-29, 735, 760,
    764
  powers, rights of, 390-93, 455, 460-61
  rejection of ("separatism"), 551, 555, 631-
    37, 662, 669
  universal, 413-22, 424, 725, 731, 752, 795
  See also Adamic community; conciliarism;
    common good; consent; people; repre-
    sentation; rulers
political theory
  development of, 277, 390, 519-20, 542,
    549-51, 758-70, 787-88
  imperialist-royalist, 56-65, 180-94, 250-59,
    381-475, 482-513
  papalist, 228-30, 240-49, 260-76, 362-87
pope, papacy

divine commission, as Vicar of Christ, 339, 364, 524, 409
divine institution, 455-56, 466-67, 524
inerrancy of, 233, 391
ministerial authority of, 249, 271-76, 399, 401-3, 455, 470-71, 523
Roman primacy, 172, 177, 179, 242, 250, 450-52
successor to St. Peter, 244, 249, 265, 406, 452, 611
supremacy (sovereignty, plenitude of power) of
  in church, 268, 273, 519, 524-25, 611
    juridical, 242, 244, 273-75, 364, 372-78, 387, 404, 469
    legislative, 242, 375
  in church and civil polity (spiritual and temporal), 229-35, 241-49, 273, 275, 363-78, 400, 402, 403, 411, 436, 450, 470-73, 524-25, 527, 611, 613, 623-24, 629
    "power of the keys," 232-33, 242-44, 270
    direct and indirect powers, 375, 402, 611, 726
  See also monarchy, absolute
poverty
  Franciscan/evangelical (controversy over), 236, 309-19, 394-95, 423, 442-47, 453-54, 484-85, 496, 658-61
  "spiritual," 595-96, 642, 660
  See also almsgiving
property (ownership), 256, 326, 356, 368-70, 408, 442, 474-75, 531, 535, 598-602, 741, 797-800, 818-20
  communal character of, 47-49, 91, 317, 359, 404, 497
  corporate 313, 566-67
    of church, 69, 235-36, 316-18, 373, 399, 401-3, 449, 477-81
    of civil community, 307, 566-67, 627-28, 674-75
  possession, righteous and unrighteous, 101-3, 108, 130, 133, 156, 235, 311, 317, 364, 368-70, 484-86, 493
  private, 91, 101-3, 238, 298, 301-3, 310, 313, 317, 346, 358-59, 395, 403, 442, 446-47, 477-81, 487, 496, 511-13, 559, 566-67, 597, 601-8, 659-61
  use of, 319, 370, 399, 401, 442-47, 492-98, 660-61
  See also almsgiving; dominion; virtue, liberality
prophet(s), 69, 214, 219, 227, 264, 271, 288, 463, 647-49, 686, 716

Daniel, 462, 671, 681, 688, 691
Jeremiah, 365, 688
Samuel, 264, 273, 284-85, 294, 366, 507, 532, 699, 718
Protestant Reformation
  Anabaptism/radicalism, 551, 555, 582, 598, 631-37, 657-61, 669, 755
  Anglicanism, 743-56, 778-86
  Calvinism (Puritanism), 551, 555, 662-722, 743, 757-77
  Lutheranism, 551, 555, 581-608, 647-49, 724
  precursors of, 426-27, 482
  Zwinglianism, 555, 556, 582, 662
Providence, 42, 196, 203, 219, 290, 294, 324, 331, 335-38, 342, 413-41, 473-74, 494, 519, 535-36, 542, 546, 551, 584, 604-7, 665, 672, 680, 686-87, 697, 790
public/private, 679, 680-81, 717, 722, 738-39, 752, 758, 761-67, 772, 777, 810, 814
  See also common good; commonwealth; property
punishment, 36-37, 43, 94, 108, 288, 292, 357-58, 537-38, 564-66, 590, 626, 654, 674, 676, 678, 726, 731, 738, 774, 791-92
  capital, 68, 82-84, 94-95, 107, 119-31, 352, 499, 508, 559-64, 585, 673, 676, 678, 687-92, 696, 698, 703, 706-8, 734, 774-75, 782, 789, 807-8, 810-16
  God's (earthly and final), 156, 429, 439, 647-49, 653, 655-58, 678, 734, 804, 813, 815-20
  theory of, 801-20
  See also judgment; justice

reason and revelation, 383, 392, 424, 426, 454, 456-59, 462-64, 554, 601, 754-56, 787
renaissance classicism/humanism, 277-96, 413-22, 541, 549-50, 553-55, 570, 609, 663, 685, 695, 757, 779, 787-90, 787-820
  pedagogy, 553-54, 558-80
  satire/social criticism, 554-55, 558-80
representation, political, 393, 425, 432, 541-47, 712, 716-18, 750, 759, 764, 769
  See also conciliarism
right(s), 84-86, 210-11, 237-8, 301-2, 311, 314, 677, 737, 777, 792-820
  civil, 399, 601-2, 615-16, 758-69, 795, 797-98, 815, 817-20
  divine, 348-49, 456, 520, 527, 613, 629, 700, 816-20
  natural
    objective, 317, 326, 790-91, 793-820
    subjective (individual and communal), 391, 395-96, 399, 406-7, 426, 439-47,

456, 495, 520, 527, 612-16, 625-29, 724, 726, 748, 790-91, 797-801, 818

See also dominion; justice; law

rulers (magistrates)

correction of, 202, 408-12, 556, 700, 717, 720, 769-70

corruption of, 200-202, 354

deposition of, 242, 244-45, 387, 403, 408, 411-12, 518, 521-22, 525, 530, 546, 721, 778

election of, 261, 266, 354, 405, 432, 434, 519, 524, 544, 547, 625, 643, 688, 717-21

See also king(s); people; political authority

sacraments, 581, 611, 641

baptism, 369, 371, 508-9, 520-21, 576, 621, 633-34

Eucharist, 389, 405, 521, 576, 634

penance, 226-27, 285, 369, 371, 394, 398, 405, 407-8, 426-27, 511, 581

schism(s), 177, 189-90, 212, 449, 484, 517-18, 767, 788-89

See also heresy, heresies

sin(s)

avarice, 51, 75-79, 209, 312, 314, 418, 422, 474, 497, 561-62, 602-3

blasphemy, 21, 494, 499, 501, 527, 623, 635, 637, 658, 686, 691, 695, 703, 706-8

idleness, 560, 567, 602, 697

mortal, 364, 369, 371, 373-74, 398, 407, 465, 508, 620-25

pride, 154, 197-99, 247-49, 547, 559

in society, 137-38, 560-67

venial, 486, 490-91, 500, 604

See also counsel vs. flattery; crime; fall of man; heresy; idolatry; tyranny, tyrants; vengeance

slavery, 80-82, 136-37, 157-58, 206, 301-2, 331, 341, 347, 356-57, 428, 486-87, 511-13, 564-65, 611, 616-17, 731, 740, 803

spiritual, 62, 80-82, 139, 158, 269-70

society

household (paternal rule), 112, 148, 153, 157, 332, 360, 416, 478, 595, 599, 601, 654-55, 748-49, 761-62, 771, 779, 781-84

sociality, 54-55, 153-54, 328, 329, 384, 534, 553, 572-73, 626, 744, 747, 753, 758-60, 790, 793-95, 800-801

renewal (reform) of, 553-55, 558-59

revolutionary, 638-46

universal, 149-50, 569, 745, 751-52

voluntary, 391, 761-63, 767

See also church; common good; community; friendship; political society; vice

sovereignty (divine, imperial, papal, popular,

regal). *See* dominion; empire; king(s); monarchy; people; pope (papacy)

spiritual and temporal powers, 98-100, 170, 174-75, 177-79, 212-15, 252-53, 323, 362-78, 385-87, 509, 778-86

"two swords," 234, 258-59, 269, 276, 284, 363, 368, 371, 409, 524

See also jurisdiction(s); political authority, "two authorities"; subjection

Stoicism, 4-5, 8, 30, 43, 46-47, 70, 84-85, 91, 149, 205, 284, 288, 320, 474, 794, 796

subjection

to civil authority, 92-95, 174, 266-67, 320, 327-28, 578, 583, 588, 599, 663, 665, 669, 679, 691, 748

to domestic authority, 92-93, 157

of kings to priests, 178-79, 240-49, 261-67, 284-89, 321, 339-40, 363-87, 400, 709-10

of priests to kings, 178-79, 251-59, 264, 400, 438

See also clergy (priesthood); pope, supremacy of; spiritual and temporal powers; tyranny, obedience/nonresistance to

taxation, taxes (tribute), 94, 307-8, 438, 476-81, 482-83, 588, 592, 633, 643-45, 674-75

theologians, authority of, 455, 458, 501, 777

Thomistic ideas/influence, 322, 394, 397-98, 530-40, 552-53, 609-30, 723-56

toleration, religious, 556-57, 711, 713

tyranny, tyrants, 247, 279, 292-96, 324, 327, 332-35, 349, 480-81, 492, 510, 513, 518, 529, 537, 654, 779, 785

disobedience to, 267, 329, 666, 681

by divine permission 219, 304, 370, 492, 494, 529, 699

as divine punishment for sins of the ruled, 202, 279, 294-96, 324, 680

Nimrod as first tyrant, 263, 303, 533, 539, 618, 784

obedience/nonresistance to, 196, 202, 261, 324, 333-34, 665, 680, 779

prevention of, 332-33, 435, 460-61

by public authority, 334, 665, 681, 685, 712-13, 717, 721

resistance to, 279, 295-96, 324, 329, 333, 411, 550-51, 680, 689-96, 700-701, 711, 717, 726, 736

See also counsel vs. flattery; idolatry; injustice

usury. *See* lending

vengeance, 115-16, 122, 298, 302, 585, 589-90, 596, 598, 600, 621, 628, 673, 678, 680, 738-39, 805-14, 815
vice(s). *See* sin(s)
virtue, virtues, 49, 110, 151-52, 162, 280, 289, 338-40, 386, 398, 409, 414, 424, 429, 646, 653-54, 734
   clemency (mercy), 95-96, 107, 119-32, 563, 673, 772-75, 812, 815-16
   gratitude, 654-55
   humility, 644, 772
      of rulers, 173, 176-79, 196-99, 206-7, 226, 247-49, 547
      of subjects, 202-3, 671, 679
   liberality, 87-88, 357
   patience, 313-16, 587-88, 590, 597, 601, 604, 659-60, 678, 739, 812
   piety, 44-45, 58-59, 223-24, 653, 765
   prudence, 184, 187, 223-27, 415, 594-95, 810
   See also equity; justice; love; wisdom
vocation, 589, 654, 691, 717, 766, 771
voluntarism, 394-96, 541, 552, 610, 663

war
   conquest, 165-66, 505-6, 532, 578
   evils of, 117, 150, 248, 554, 560-61, 573, 575-80
   morality of ("just war"), 106, 108, 305, 327, 354-5, 505-6, 553, 571, 595, 599, 612-13, 613-30, 673-74, 726-27, 737-42, 791, 796-97
      self-defense, 210, 301-2, 554, 599-600, 613, 628, 713, 722, 726, 731, 737, 748, 807-8
   peace as aim of, 152-54, 674, 738
wealth, 53, 75-79, 101-3, 181-83, 490-91, 566-67
wisdom, 30, 79-82, 88, 183, 221, 223, 462-64, 489, 544, 577-78, 657-58, 749, 796, 809

Scripture Index

Genesis

1:1-31	337
1:17f.	614
1:20	468
1:26	74, 84, 157
1:26f.	761
1:29f.	614
2:18	85
2:20	85, 751
3:13	656
3:15	781
3:16	761
3:19	535
4	733
4:8	748
4:12-15	537
4:14-15	585
4:17	144, 733
5:21-24	748
6:4	262
6:5	748
7:23	509
9:1	197
9:6	585
9:6f.	698
9:18f.	782
9:23	203
9:25	80
9:27	262
9:28	618
10	733
10:8	618
10:8-12	366, 784
10:9	539
10:32	535, 618

11:6	535
12:1-3	784
13:2	441
13:9	618
14	738
14:14	102
14:18	178, 366, 509
17:8	441
17:19-21	509
18:25	800
19:24f.	623
21:10	145
25:23	263
27:29	263
27:37	263, 509
27:40	80
47:20	614
47:20-21	81
47:22	81
49:3f.	785
49:10	785

Exodus

2:11f.	701
3:14	35
12:35f.	503
14:14	42
18	522
18:17-25	353, 766
20:1-17	115, 507
20:12	653
20:17	502
21:14	813
21:19	812
21:23	357

22:1	357, 676
23:4f.	811
23:7	741
28:1	786
28:1f.	383
33:11	522

Leviticus

13:1-59	385, 405
19:17	811
19:18	698

Numbers

11:16f.	770
16:1-3	786
16:31-35	99
21:3	625
22:28	594
24:18	273
25:4	738
25:7f.	701
25:7ff.	810
27:18-20	290
31:17	85f.
35:19	809
35:31-34	813

Deuteronomy

1:13	353
1:15	353
1:16	672f.
2:29	468
2:37	468
4:1	654
4:13	653

4:24	656	4:1	86	**1 Chronicles**		
5:16	653	4:17f.	199	22:8	214, 574	
5:17	698	8:4	716f.	29:11	257	
5:19	658	8:4f.	718			
5:21	502	8:5-7	507	**2 Chronicles**		
6:4	115	8:7	354	1:9	712	
8:2f.	36	8:9	533	9:1	752	
8:5	36	8:10-18	539	19:4-7	594	
8:11	36	8:11	533	19:6	536	
10:3f.	653	9:16	718	23:16	712	
13:6-9	692	10:1	712, 718	26:18	99	
15:6	81	10:6	253	26:19	99	
17:8	375	10:17-24	718			
17:9	363	10:25	768	**Nehemiah**		
17:14	718	11:14f.	718	5:10	682	
17:14-20	340	13:14	333			
17:15	618	15:11	590	**Job**		
17:15-19	363	15:17	198, 201, 249	1:1	101f.	
17:16-20	673	15:26	508	6:4	656	
17:18f.	286f.	16:13f.	718f.	7:1	136, 151	
18:13	351			9:2	656, 659	
19:11f.	537			12:6	494	
19:13	813	**2 Samuel**		12:18f.	714	
19:19	676	2:4	719	28:18f.	82	
21:10-14	82	3:27	595	34:30	200, 219	
21:14	82	5:3	719, 720	41:34	197	
21:23	72	6:21	712			
23:19	682	6:22	207	**Psalms**		
24:16	741	10–11	738	2:1f.	131	
25:2f.	802	11:2-27	201	2:4	804	
25:4	707	20:10	595	2:8	274	
26:3	351	24:1-17	202	2:10f.	131, 690	
27:15-26	655			2:12	122	
28:1-14	646	**1 Kings**		3:3	143	
28:63	804	2:5f.	595	3:5	79	
30:14	82	3:5	223	4:5f.	342	
31:26	712	3:9	595	4:8	421	
32:35f.	28	3:10-14	223f.	7:8f.	591	
		8:28f.	222	8:2	78	
Joshua		10:1	752	8:6f.	84	
1:5	605	12:25–13:10	688	9:9	335	
1:7f.	712	12:28	681	17:2	283	
1:8	715	21:2	77	18:1	143	
8:30-35	715	22:38	214	19:7	299, 343	
9:21	86			23:4	200, 284	
		2 Kings		24:1	102, 256, 316	
Judges		6:15-19	86	25:17	149	
3:14-22	333, 411, 701	6:22f.	86	28:8	257	
14:4	590	11:17	267, 712, 714, 720	30:25	122	
15:3	808	14:5f.	334	36:1	37	
15:11	590	20:5	712	37:22	595f.	
21:25	672	22:14	463	37:34	595	
		23:3	712, 714	45:6	257	
1 Samuel		25:6f.	295	45:6f.	259	
2:29	199			45:7	257	

45:9	251
45:10	317
50:3	656
50:6	656
50:12	273
50:21	481
51:4	349
53:8	124
55:11	682
58:11	656
62:12	656
63:8	75
68:18	308
72:7	59
72:8	59
72:9	403
72:11	119
76:5	79
82:1	45, 680
82:3f.	354, 672
82:6f.	45, 689
82:7	45
85:11	528
87:1	312
95:2	226
104:17	614
105:17-18	80
105:18	80
105:19	80
110:4	252
111:10	79
112:9	17
118:18	36
118:22	265
119:85	270
126:5	227
132:1	422
144:15	163
147:12-14	152

Proverbs

1:26	804
2:9	704
3:3	37
3:13	37, 223
3:16a	37
3:28	78
5:15	82
5:17	660
8:14-16	218f.
8:15	16, 348, 617f., 714
8:15f.	670
9:9	132
9:10	37
10:25	710

11:14	224, 331
13:22	133
14:6	521
15:22	224
16:4	804
16:14	681
17:2	81
17:6	130
17:13	655
19:14	92
19:17	74
20:22	590
20:26	334
20:28	673
21:1	16, 335
21:7	505
22:3f.	37
22:7	81, 82
22:28	214, 270
24:21	679
24:21f.	14
24:29	590
28:5	37
28:16	593
29:19	132

Ecclesiastes

4:9	331
5:9	332
7:7	774
8:12f.	656
10:16	217
12:13f.	656

Song of Solomon (Cant.)

2:15	500
6:9	273

Isaiah

1:20	289
1:23	293, 608, 690
2:4	59
5:8	77
6:1	90
9:6	500
9:7	255
10:1	499, 751
11:9	673
13	688
13:2-3	294
14:13	197
22:22	257, 259
28:16	86
28:20	608
32:17	528

33:1	505
33:15f.	209
38:13	655
40:9	252
42:7	257, 259
49:23	708
51:7	73
53:8	124
53:11	693f.
54:1	144
55:1	81, 513
59:7f.	37
66:5	28

Jeremiah

1:10	271, 293, 365
2:9	800
11:20	498
12:1	494
17:9f.	591
22:3	672
22:29f.	83
23:5f.	252
25:11f.	625
27:4f.	219
29:7	163
31:33	658
38:7-9	691
46:1-26	688
52:28-30	507

Ezekiel

3:18	275f.
7:1-27	688
8:1–9:10	688
16:46f.	688
18:20	511
18:23	820
20:25	215
22:12	682
29:18f.	294
33:8	688
34:2	331f.
34:4	200
36:5-7	688
37:24	332
43:12f.	431
48:21	674

Daniel

2:21	41, 265
2:23	462
2:33f.	20
2:34f.	265
2:37f.	617

2:41-45	20f.	**Ben Sirach**		6:26	504
3:16-18	691	3:30	78	6:31	504
3:29	131	4:8	78f.	6:33	32, 488
4:17	219	10:2	291	7:1f.	818
5:21	219	10:4	41	7:2	815
6:10	691	10:8	288	7:7	125
6:22	681	13:15	626	7:8	125
7:14	339	17:14	629	7:11	125
7:15-18	164	19:4	621	7:12	697f.
7:20-22	18	26:29	604	7:17f.	586
7:23ff.	19	27:11	79	8:8-10	134
8:12	19	32:1	199	8:9-10	117
8:23f.	19			8:20	314
9:27	19	**Wisdom (Sap.)**		9:6	270
12:3	223	3:6	135	9:37	272
		3:7	223	10:5	405
Hosea		6:4f.	714	10:7	406
5:11	681	6:6	248, 287	10:8-10	406f.
8:4	219, 492, 494	7:7-11	489	10:9f.	313
10:12	78			10:12	416
13:9-11	507	**1 Maccabees**		10:12f.	574
13:11	201, 219	2:24	810	10:16	119
				10:19	462
Micah		**St. Matthew**		10:28	119
6:2	800	1:19f.	123	10:29f.	42
		4:9	16, 245	10:30	119
Nahum		4:17	344	10:35	21
1:2	656	5:3	312, 660	10:36	148
		5:5	595-97	10:37	497
Habakkuk		5:9	135	10:39	72
2:4	693	5:13	42	10:42	315
		5:17	83, 115, 498, 692	11:11	135
Zephaniah		5:17-22	585	11:25	463
1:12	656	5:18	499	11:28-30	71, 220
3:7-13	43f.	5:20	344	11:29	249
		5:21f.	692, 813	12:25	20, 416
Zechariah		5:23f.	633	12:35	124
7:4ff.	660	5:33-37	636f.	12:42	752
7:10	28	5:38	115	12:50	490
8:17	28	5:38-41	597-601	13:25-30	646
9:9	252	5:38f.	811	13:29	741
		5:39	118, 634, 678	13:30	22
Malachi		5:40	444, 605	13:43	79f.
2:7	340, 463	5:40f.	348	14:16	447
3:2	14	5:41	411	15:8f.	660
4:2	79f.	5:42	601-2, 605	16:18	229
		5:44	120, 585, 811	16:18f.	170, 232, 241, 243,
Tobit		5:45	22		265
2:11-14	614	6:9	124, 575	16:19	98, 229, 258, 369,
		6:12	124, 125, 136, 163,		385, 405, 448
1 Esdras			598, 604	16:24	310, 635
4:29-31	81	6:14	97, 124	17:27	16
		6:14f.	812	18:6	499
2 Esdras		6:20	78	18:7	151
15:1	28	6:21	136	18:9	292

18:15-17	373
18:15-18	406, 633
18:18	385, 405, 523
18:19	42
18:20	575
18:35	820
19:4f.	93
19:12	310
19:18	444
19:21	310, 312, 491
19:23	497
19:26	636
19:27	312
19:29	444, 445
20:6	272
20:25	635
20:28	199
21:12	202
21:13	316
22:15-21	214
22:17	73, 438
22:18-19	74
22:20	74
22:20f.	438
22:21	74, 117, 468, 592, 598, 644, 700
22:39	653
23:4	349
23:12	53
23:22	636
23:25	505
23:35	119
24:12	151
24:15	20
24:15-17	18
24:21	18
24:48-51	199
25:28	494
25:33f.	22
25:41	22
25:43	626
26:4	293
26:52	717
26:52f.	119
26:56	471
26:74	637
27:31	447
28:18	618
28:19	406, 449, 633

St. Mark

2:15f.	447
6:8	314
10:18	124
10:19	444

10:27	636
10:29f.	489, 660
10:30	315
10:44	249
16:15	629
16:15f.	621f.
16:16	621, 633, 693

St. Luke

1:2	215
1:32	255
1:37	520
1:79	257, 259
2:1	422
2:14	416
2:34	22, 637
3:2	507
3:11	446, 606
3:14	117, 135
5:31	438
6:20	445
6:27	446
6:27f.	28
6:29	444
6:30	605
6:35	605, 682
6:37f.	125
6:45	124
9:1	382
10:1	405
10:7	314, 603, 604
10:12	22
10:19	17f.
10:29-37	627
10:34	200
10:38-42	316
11:4	125
11:9	125
11:10	125
11:13	125
11:17	253
11:31	752
11:41	606
12:4	270
12:13f.	437
12:14f.	635
12:19	77
14:10	593
14:12f.	497
14:26	497
16:9	77, 101
16:24	78
17:3	812
17:34f.	21
18:2f.	19

18:19	124
18:20	444
18:30	490
19:8	129f.
19:31	71f.
19:41	507
20:4	75
22:19	405
22:25	272
22:25f.	506, 512, 593
22:38	234, 259, 276
22:49-51	234
22:51	119
23:34	97
24:47	657

St. John

1:3	492
1:9	755
1:12	124
1:17	115
3:5	509
3:18	693
3:18-21	22
4:24	373
5:43	19, 201
6:15	635
7:51	225f.
8:2-11	107f., 635
8:3-7	122
8:7	125
8:7-9	83
8:9-11	84
8:11	635
8:28	635
8:34	158, 201
8:44	156
8:50	249
10:1f.	293
10:16	643
10:30	74
10:35	670
12:6	235, 447
13:29	447
13:34	117, 574
13:34f.	575
14:9	74
14:27	574
15:12	575
15:12-17	574
15:14f.	214
15:24	621
16:8f.	657
16:14	74
16:15	74

16:33	42	1:14	285	13:4	16, 83, 264, 354,	
17:3	765	1:18	657		409, 736, 738,	
17:11	574	1:19	756		814	
18:10f.	234	1:21-25	143	13:4-6	404	
18:11	276	1:21-27	623	13:5	328	
18:22f.	597	1:22	37	13:6	16	
18:23	600	2:1	803	13:7	214, 275	
18:36	437, 619	2:3-6	120f., 800	13:8	117, 127	
19:23	422	2:4	122	13:9f.	502, 511	
19:32f.	457f.	2:14f.	82	13:10	134	
20:21	416	2:15	700, 756	14:6f.	705	
20:21-23	406	2:17-20	37	14:14	667	
20:22	405, 407	2:22	803	14:23	704	
21:15	276	2:25	813			
21:15-17	232	3:6	800	**1 Corinthians**		
21:17	273, 406	3:16-18	37	1:2	426	
21:18	524	3:17	745	1:3	574	
		3:20	657	1:28f.	206	
Acts of the Apostles		4:15	655	3:19	53	
1:5	575	5:5	134	3:22	317	
1:9	575	5:12	693f.	4:7	366	
1:24	591	5:13	300	4:12	13	
1:26	526	5:18	693f.	4:21	198	
2:38	633	5:19	75	5:9-13	624	
2:44f.	235	6:22	152	6:1f.	73	
3:6	272	6:23	339	6:2	271	
4	446	7:7	502	6:3	244, 536	
4:12	622	7:7-13	586	6:4f.	270	
4:32	145, 313, 441, 447,	7:12	352	6:5	73	
	575	7:14	513	6:7	444	
4:33	100	8:14	755	6:9f.	657	
5:1-11	198	8:17	214, 373	6:12	630	
5:29	349, 681	8:30	635	6:17	257	
6:2	526	8:31f.	489	6:19	253	
7:51	500	9:21	144	7:7	135	
7:58	810	9:22f.	145	7:21	669	
8:36	633	10:8	82	7:23	79, 269, 668, 681	
9:6	270	10:14	621		604, 707	
10:4	134f.	11:24	693f.	9:3-9	317	
10:26	198	12:1	254	9:13	635	
10:35	536	12:2	553	9:14	14	
13:38f.	813	12:8	670	9:17	269	
15	652	12:10	593	9:19	667	
15:10	470	12:17	738	9:20-22	451	
15:28	526, 753	12:19	28, 585, 734, 738	10:4	389	
16:3	667	12:20f.	678	10:17	634	
16:31-33	633	13:1	16, 19, 222, 370,	10:21	668	
17:30	813		588, 592, 596,	10:23f.	704	
19:4	633		617, 671, 678,	10:31	705	
20:28	426		761, 816	10:32	509	
23:12f.	810	13:1f.	585, 734	11:3	523	
		13:1-5	614	11:23	813	
Romans		13:1-7	92-94, 195	11:30f.	36	
1:3	119	13:1-8	127	11:32	392	
1:7	574	13:3	671	12:12-27	527	
				12:14ff.		

12:28	213, 670
12:31	341
14:26	705
14:33	633
14:40	705
15:24	381
15:27	618
15:28	143
15:46	143

2 Corinthians

1:19	490
1:23f.	439
1:24	198
2:7	813
3:3	73
4:5	198
5:6	338
5:21	72
6:10	13, 496
6:16	253
6:17	634
8:9	504
8:12	445
10:3	13
10:4f.	593
10:8	402, 525
12:21	623
13:10	402, 470

Galatians

1:8	746
1:12	523
2:3-5	667
2:9	449
2:11	411
2:16	72
2:19	72
3:11	72
3:13	72
3:19	35, 586
3:23f.	35
3:24	32, 586, 676
3:28	669, 693
4:1	615f.
4:4	72, 118, 422, 676
4:7	272
4:21–5:1	144f.
5:1	668, 669
5:4	668
5:6	117, 134
5:17	147
5:21	657

Ephesians

1:21	254
2:2	17
2:11-18	706
2:19-22	253
3:17	79
4:5	75, 752f.
4:11-16	392, 451
4:12	213
4:14	79
4:32	812
5:2	254
5:5	657
5:21	761
5:21–6:9	588
5:23f.	451
5:27	367
6:9	511
6:12	71
6:16	81

Philippians

1:23f.	72
2:7	594
2:8	75
2:9-11	119
2:10f.	31, 33
3:12	6
3:20	13, 760
4:5	772
4:13	42

Colossians

1:16	492
1:18	451
3:11	669
3:13	812, 818
3:25	206

1 Thesssalonians

2:6f.	206
2:7	198
4:11	654

2 Thessalonians

2:3f.	18
2:4	201
2:8-12	19
2:10f.	201
2:15	215

1 Timothy

1:5	37f.
1:7	37f.
1:8	37f.

1:9	82, 586
1:17	144
2:1-2	44
2:2	95, 163
2:2-4	814
3:7	634
4:5	704
5:8	157
5:16	87
6:1f.	469
6:8	312
6:10	310
6:17f.	358

2 Timothy

2:4	179, 270
2:9	629
3:16	439

Titus

2:11-14	637

Hebrews

1:3	74
1:9	257
2:2f.	813
2:7	415
2:7-9	254
5:4	521
6:17f.	636
7:1	509
7:7	366
7:12	431, 523
7:17	252
8:1	383
8:5	524
8:10	658
9:4	200
10:29	813
10:30	28
13:7	213f.
13:17	213

James

1:17	136, 492
1:25	431, 470
3:2	500
4:12	438, 816
4:15	606
5:16	123

1 Peter

1:18f.	81, 668
2:4	265
2:9	195, 252

2:13	588, 592	5:5	593	Jude	
2:13f.	585	5:8	71	10	751
2:14	596				
2:15	14	**2 Peter**		**Revelation**	
2:17	14, 41, 516, 671,	2:5	748	1:6	339, 384
	679	2:19	139, 158	3:7	257, 259
2:18	510, 614	3:9	710	5:10	339
2:18f.	333			6:10	688
2:21	635	**1 John**		14:6	754
3:9	585	1:8	122, 500	16:5	820
4:8	122	2:17	312	17:12-14	20
4:10	342	3:2	134	18:4ff.	634
4:11	591	3:8	312	20:6	339
5:3	199, 272	5:16	807	21:2	312, 524